Poetry
Criticism

Guide to Thomson Gale Literary Criticism Series

For criticism on	Consult these Thomson Gale series
Authors now living or who died after December 31, 1999	*CONTEMPORARY LITERARY CRITICISM (CLC)*
Authors who died between 1900 and 1999	*TWENTIETH-CENTURY LITERARY CRITICISM (TCLC)*
Authors who died between 1800 and 1899	*NINETEENTH-CENTURY LITERATURE CRITICISM (NCLC)*
Authors who died between 1400 and 1799	*LITERATURE CRITICISM FROM 1400 TO 1800 (LC)* *SHAKESPEAREAN CRITICISM (SC)*
Authors who died before 1400	*CLASSICAL AND MEDIEVAL LITERATURE CRITICISM (CMLC)*
Authors of books for children and young adults	*CHILDREN'S LITERATURE REVIEW (CLR)*
Dramatists	*DRAMA CRITICISM (DC)*
Poets	*POETRY CRITICISM (PC)*
Short story writers	*SHORT STORY CRITICISM (SSC)*
Literary topics and movements	*HARLEM RENAISSANCE: A GALE CRITICAL COMPANION (HR)* *THE BEAT GENERATION: A GALE CRITICAL COMPANION (BG)* *FEMINISM IN LITERATURE: A GALE CRITICAL COMPANION (FL)* *GOTHIC LITERATURE: A GALE CRITICAL COMPANION (GL)*
Asian American writers of the last two hundred years	*ASIAN AMERICAN LITERATURE (AAL)*
Black writers of the past two hundred years	*BLACK LITERATURE CRITICISM (BLC)* *BLACK LITERATURE CRITICISM SUPPLEMENT (BLCS)*
Hispanic writers of the late nineteenth and twentieth centuries	*HISPANIC LITERATURE CRITICISM (HLC)* *HISPANIC LITERATURE CRITICISM SUPPLEMENT (HLCS)*
Native North American writers and orators of the eighteenth, nineteenth, and twentieth centuries	*NATIVE NORTH AMERICAN LITERATURE (NNAL)*
Major authors from the Renaissance to the present	*WORLD LITERATURE CRITICISM, 1500 TO THE PRESENT (WLC)* *WORLD LITERATURE CRITICISM SUPPLEMENT (WLCS)*

ISSN 1052-4851

Poetry Criticism

*Excerpts from Criticism of the Works
of the Most Significant and Widely
Studied Poets of World Literature*

Volume 79

Michelle Lee
Project Editor

THOMSON

GALE

Detroit • New York • San Francisco • New Haven, Conn. • Waterville, Maine • London

Poetry Criticism, Vol. 79

Project Editor
Michelle Lee

Editorial
Dana Barnes, Thomas Burns, Elizabeth Cranston, Kathy D. Darrow, Kristen Dorsch, Jeffrey W. Hunter, Jelena O. Krstović, Thomas J. Schoenberg, Noah Schusterbauer, Lawrence J. Trudeau, Russel Whitaker

Data Capture
Frances Monroe, Gwen Tucker

Indexing Services
Factiva, Inc.

Rights and Acquisitions
Margaret Abendroth, Aja Perales, and Timothy Sisler

Composition and Electronic Capture
Gary Oudersluys

Manufacturing
Rhonda Dover

Associate Product Manager
Marc Cormier

LIBRARY OF CONGRESS CATALOG CARD NUMBER 91-118494

ISBN-13: 978-0-7876-9876-8
ISBN-10: 0-7876-9876-8
ISSN 1052-4851

Printed in the United States of America
10 9 8 7 6 5 4 3 2 1

Contents

Preface vii

Acknowledgments ix

Literary Criticism Series Advisory Board xi

Preface

*P*oetry Criticism (*PC*) presents significant criticism of the world's greatest poets and provides supplementary biographical and bibliographical material to guide the interested reader to a greater understanding of the genre and its creators. Although major poets and literary movements are covered in such Thomson Gale Literary Criticism series as *Contemporary Literary Criticism* (*CLC*), *Twentieth-Century Literary Criticism* (*TCLC*), *Nineteenth-Century Literature Criticism* (*NCLC*), *Literature Criticism from 1400 to 1800* (*LC*), and *Classical and Medieval Literature Criticism* (*CMLC*), *PC* offers more focused attention on poetry than is possible in the broader, survey-oriented entries on writers in these Thomson Gale series. Students, teachers, librarians, and researchers will find that the generous excerpts and supplementary material provided by *PC* supply them with the vital information needed to write a term paper on poetic technique, to examine a poet's most prominent themes, or to lead a poetry discussion group.

Scope of the Series

PC is designed to serve as an introduction to major poets of all eras and nationalities. Since these authors have inspired a great deal of relevant critical material, *PC* is necessarily selective, and the editors have chosen the most important published criticism to aid readers and students in their research. Each author entry presents a historical survey of the critical response to that author's work. The length of an entry is intended to reflect the amount of critical attention the author has received from critics writing in English and from foreign critics in translation. Every attempt has been made to identify and include the most significant essays on each author's work. In order to provide these important critical pieces, the editors sometimes reprint essays that have appeared elsewhere in Thomson Gale's Literary Criticism Series. Such duplication, however, never exceeds twenty percent of a *PC* volume.

Organization of the Book

Each *PC* entry consists of the following elements:

- The **Author Heading** cites the name under which the author most commonly wrote, followed by birth and death dates. Also located here are any name variations under which an author wrote, including transliterated forms for authors whose native languages use nonroman alphabets. If the author wrote consistently under a pseudonym, the pseudonym will be listed in the author heading and the author's actual name given in parenthesis on the first line of the biographical and critical introduction. Uncertain birth or death dates are indicated by question marks. Single-work entries are preceded by the title of the work and its date of publication.

- The **Introduction** contains background information that introduces the reader to the author and the critical debates surrounding his or her work.

- The list of **Principal Works** is ordered chronologically by date of first publication and lists the most important works by the author. The first section comprises poetry collections and book-length poems. The second section gives information on other major works by the author. For foreign authors, the editors have provided original foreign-language publication information and have selected what are considered the best and most complete English-language editions of their works.

- Reprinted **Criticism** is arranged chronologically in each entry to provide a useful perspective on changes in critical evaluation over time. All individual titles of poems and poetry collections by the author featured in the entry are printed in boldface type. The critic's name and the date of composition or publication of the critical work are given at the beginning of each piece of criticism. Unsigned criticism is preceded by the title of the source in which it appeared. Footnotes are reprinted at the end of each essay or excerpt. In the case of excerpted criticism, only those footnotes that pertain to the excerpted texts are included.

- Critical essays are prefaced by brief **Annotations** explicating each piece.

- A complete **Bibliographical Citation** of the original essay or book precedes each piece of criticism.

- An annotated bibliography of **Further Reading** appears at the end of each entry and suggests resources for additional study. In some cases, significant essays for which the editors could not obtain reprint rights are included here. Boxed material following the further reading list provides references to other biographical and critical sources on the author in series published by Thomson Gale.

Cumulative Indexes

A **Cumulative Author Index** lists all of the authors that appear in a wide variety of reference sources published by Thomson Gale, including *PC*. A complete list of these sources is found facing the first page of the Author Index. The index also includes birth and death dates and cross references between pseudonyms and actual names.

A **Cumulative Nationality Index** lists all authors featured in *PC* by nationality, followed by the number of the *PC* volume in which their entry appears.

A **Cumulative Title Index** lists in alphabetical order all individual poems, book-length poems, and collection titles contained in the *PC* series. Titles of poetry collections and separately published poems are printed in italics, while titles of individual poems are printed in roman type with quotation marks. Each title is followed by the author's last name and corresponding volume and page numbers where commentary on the work is located. English-language translations of original foreign-language titles are cross-referenced to the foreign titles so that all references to discussion of a work are combined in one listing.

Citing *Poetry Criticism*

When citing criticism reprinted in the Literary Criticism Series, students should provide complete bibliographic information so that the cited essay can be located in the original print or electronic source. Students who quote directly from reprinted criticism may use any accepted bibliographic format, such as University of Chicago Press style or Modern Language Association (MLA) style. Both the MLA and the University of Chicago formats are acceptable and recognized as being the current standards for citations. It is important, however, to choose one format for all citations; do not mix the two formats within a list of citations.

The examples below follow recommendations for preparing a bibliography set forth in *The Chicago Manual of Style,* 14th ed. (Chicago: The University of Chicago Press, 1993); the first example pertains to material drawn from periodicals, the second to material reprinted from books:

Linkin, Harriet Kramer. "The Language of Speakers in *Songs of Innocence and of Experience.*" *Romanticism Past and Present* 10, no. 2 (summer 1986): 5-24. Reprinted in *Poetry Criticism.* Vol. 63, edited by Michelle Lee, 79-88. Detroit: Thomson Gale, 2005.

Glen, Heather. "Blake's Criticism of Moral Thinking in *Songs of Innocence and of Experience.*" In *Interpreting Blake,* edited by Michael Phillips, 32-69. Cambridge: Cambridge University Press, 1978. Reprinted in *Poetry Criticism.* Vol. 63, edited by Michelle Lee, 34-51. Detroit: Thomson Gale, 2005.

Suggestions are Welcome

Readers who wish to suggest new features, topics, or authors to appear in future volumes, or who have other suggestions or comments are cordially invited to call, write, or fax the Associate Product Manager:

Associate Product Manager, Literary Criticism Series
Thomson Gale
27500 Drake Road
Farmington Hills, MI 48331-3535
1-800-347-4253 (GALE)
Fax: 248-699-8054

Acknowledgments

The editors wish to thank the copyright holders of the criticism included in this volume and the permissions managers of many book and magazine publishing companies for assisting us in securing reproduction rights. Following is a list of the copyright holders who have granted us permission to reproduce material in this volume of *PC*. Every effort has been made to trace copyright, but if omissions have been made, please let us know.

COPYRIGHTED MATERIAL IN *PC*, VOLUME 79, WAS REPRODUCED FROM THE FOLLOWING PERIODICALS:

American Poetry Review, v. 32, January-February, 2003 for "Dead Man Talking, an interview with Marvin Bell" by Thom Tammaro and Kristin Garaas-Johnson. Reproduced by permission of the authors.—*Antioch Review,* v. 48, summer, 1990. Copyright © 1990 by the Antioch Review, Inc. Reproduced by permission of the Editors.—*Book Collector,* special number for the 150th anniversary of Bernard Quaritch, 1997 for "Bernard Quaritch and 'My Omar': The Struggle for Fitzgerald's *Rubáiyát,*" by Arthur Freeman. Reproduced by permission of the author.—*College Literature,* v. 32, fall, 2005. Copyright © 2005 by West Chester University. Reproduced by permission.—*Comparative Literature Studies,* v. 23, summer, 1986. Copyright © 1986 by the Pennsylvania State University. Reproduced by permission of the publisher.—*ELH,* v. 34, December, 1967. Copyright © 1967 by the Johns Hopkins University Press. Reproduced by permission.—*Essays in Literature,* v. 5, spring, 1978. Copyright © 1978 by Western Illinois University. Reproduced by permission.—*Explicator,* v. 51, summer, 1993. Copyright © 1993 by the Helen Dwight Reid Educational Foundation. Reproduced with permission of the Helen Dwight Reid Educational Foundation, published by Heldref Publications, 1319 18th Street, NW, Washington, DC 20036-1802.—*Feminist Review,* v. 78, 2004. Copyright © 2004 by Feminist Review, Ltd. Reproduced with permission of Palgrave Macmillan.—*Free Inquiry,* v. 23, winter, 2002-2003. Copyright © 2002-2003 by the Council for Democratic and Secular Humanism, Inc. Reproduced by permission.—*Iowa Review,* v. 12, winter, 1981 for "Interview with Marvin Bell" by Ed Folsom, David Groff, David Hamilton, Dee Morris, and Fred Woodard. Copyright © 1981 by the University of Iowa. All rights reserved. Reproduced by permission of the *Iowa Review.*—*Journal of Modern Literature,* v. 27, fall, 2003. Copyright © by the Indiana University Press. Reproduced by permission.—*Literary Imagination: The Review of the Association of Literary Scholars and Critics,* v. 6, spring, 2004 for "Edward Fitzgerald and Other Men's Flowers: Allusion in the *Rubáiyát* of Omar Khayyám" by Christopher Decker. Copyright © 2004 by Oxford University Press. Reproduced by permission of the publisher.—*North American Review,* v. 280, January-February, 1995. Copyright © 1995 by the University of Northern Iowa. Reproduced by permission from the *North American Review.*—*Notes and Queries,* v. 49, March, 2002. Copyright © 2002 by Oxford University Press. Republished with permission of Oxford University Press, conveyed through Copyright Clearance Center, Inc.—*Ohio Review,* v. 17, spring-summer, 1976. Copyright © 1976 by the Editors of the *Ohio Review.* Reproduced by permission.—*Papers of the Bibliographical Society of America,* v. 69, 1975 for "Edward FitzGerald's Revisions" by Gerald D. Browne. Reproduced by permission of the publisher and author.—*Parnassus: Poetry in Review,* v. 4, fall-winter, 1975 for "Less Pose than Prose" by David Leviten. Copyright © 1975 by the Poetry in Review Foundation, NY. Reproduced by permission of the publisher.—*Raritan,* v. 19, winter, 2000. Copyright © 2000 by *Raritan: A Quarterly Review.* Reproduced by permission.—*Review of National Literatures,* v. II, spring, 1971. Copyright © 1971 by St. John's University. Reproduced by permission.—*Twentieth Century Literature,* v. 50, spring, 2004. Copyright 2004 by Hofstra University Press. Reproduced by permission.—*University of Hartford Studies in Literature,* v. 18, 1986. Copyright © 1986 by the University of Hartford. Reproduced by permission.—*Victorian Newsletter,* spring, 1960 for "The *Rubáiyát's* Neglected Reviewer: A Centennial Recovery" by Michael Wolff; fall, 1969 for "Abandon the Day: FitzGerald's *Rubáiyát* of Omar Khayyám" by David Sonstroem. Copyright © 1969 by New York University. Reproduced by permission of *The Victorian Newsletter* and the respective authors.—*Victorian Poetry,* v. 14, autumn, 1976 for "FitzGerald and Minor Mid-Victorian Poets" by Michael S. Helfand; v. 19, spring, 1981 for "Fugitive Articulation: An Introduction to *The Rubáiyát of Omar Khayyám*" by Daniel Schenker; v. 20, summer, 1982 for "FitzGerald and Other Minor Mid-Victorian Poets" by Michael S. Helfand. Copyright © 1976, 1981, 1982 by West Virginia University. Reproduced by permission of the authors.—*Women's Studies,* v. 12, 1986. Reproduced by permission of Taylor & Francis Group, LLC, http://www.taylorandfrancis.com.

COPYRIGHTED MATERIAL IN *PC*, VOLUME 79, WAS REPRODUCED FROM THE FOLLOWING BOOKS:

Bixler, Frances. From "Journey into the Sun: The Religious Pilgrimage of Anne Sexton," in *Original Essays on the Poetry of Anne Sexton.* Edited by Francis Bixler. University of Central Arkansas Press, 1988. Copyright © 1988 by the University

Thomson Gale Literature Product Advisory Board

The members of the Thomson Gale Literature Product Advisory Board—reference librarians from public and academic library systems—represent a cross-section of our customer base and offer a variety of informed perspectives on both the presentation and content of our literature products. Advisory board members assess and define such quality issues as the relevance, currency, and usefulness of the author coverage, critical content, and literary topics included in our series; evaluate the layout, presentation, and general quality of our printed volumes; provide feedback on the criteria used for selecting authors and topics covered in our series; provide suggestions for potential enhancements to our series; identify any gaps in our coverage of authors or literary topics, recommending authors or topics for inclusion; analyze the appropriateness of our content and presentation for various user audiences, such as high school students, undergraduates, graduate students, librarians, and educators; and offer feedback on any proposed changes/enhancements to our series. We wish to thank the following advisors for their advice throughout the year.

Marvin Bell
1937-

American poet and essayist.

INTRODUCTION

A renowned poet and educator long associated with the University of Iowa Writers' Workshop, Bell has produced more than seventeen volumes of poetry and currently serves as Poet Laureate of the state of Iowa. Critics have cited numerous poets whose work has influenced Bell, including John Donne, Wallace Stevens, and William Carlos Williams.

BIOGRAPHICAL INFORMATION

Bell was born in New York City on August 3, 1937; his parents were Saul Bell, a Jewish immigrant from the Ukraine who ran a five-and-dime store, and Belle Spector Bell. He grew up in Center Moriches, a rural area of Long Island, and attended Alfred University in Alfred, New York, where he earned a B.A. in 1958. In 1961 Bell received an M.A. from the University of Chicago and in 1963 he earned an M.F.A. from the University of Iowa. In 1963 Bell joined the army and served for two years as a Foreign Military Training Officer, holding the rank of lieutenant. After his discharge from the service, Bell began teaching at the University of Iowa Writers' Workshop, first as a visiting lecturer, then as assistant professor, associate professor, and finally professor of English; he is currently the Flannery O'Connor Professor of Letters at Iowa. He has also served as a visiting professor at a number of other colleges and universities, among them Oregon State University, Goddard College, the University of Hawaii, the University of Washington, the University of the Redlands, and Illinois College. Bell has been married twice—in 1958 to Mary Mammosser, and in 1961 to Dorothy Murphy; he has two sons, Nathan Saul and Jason Aaron.

Bell has received numerous awards for his poetry. His 1969 collection *A Probable Volume of Dreams* was a Lamont Poetry Selection of The Academy of American Poets. That same year he was awarded the Bess Hokin Award from *Poetry* magazine and in 1970 the Emily Clark Balch Prize from the *Virginia Quarterly Review.* Bell's volume *Stars Which See, Stars Which Do Not See* was a finalist for the National Book Award in 1977. In 1994 Bell was awarded the American Academy of Arts and Letters Award in Literature. He has also been the recipient of a Guggenheim fellowship (1976), two National Endowment for the Arts fellowships (1978 and 1984), and two Senior Fulbright Scholar awards, the first to Yugoslavia in 1983, and the second to Australia in 1986. In 2000 he became the first Poet Laureate of the state of Iowa. Referring to himself as "tri-coastal," Bell currently divides his time between the East Coast, Iowa, and the Pacific Northwest.

MAJOR WORKS

Bell's first important volume of poetry was *Things We Dreamt We Died For,* published in 1966, which was followed three years later by the award-winning *A Probable Volume of Dreams.* His major volumes from the 1970s are *The Escape into You: A Sequence* (1971), *Residue of Song* (1974), and the highly-acclaimed *Stars Which See, Stars Which Do Not See* (1977). The latter volume marked a change in Bell's poetry in terms of both form and content: his work became less experimental stylistically and he began to deal with nature, an element that was missing in his earlier work—surprisingly so, as critics point out, since as a child he was surrounded by woods and water. In 1981 Bell published *These Green-Going-to-Yellow: Poems* and in 1987 he issued a volume of *New and Selected Poems. The Book of the Dead Man* (1994) and *Ardor: The Book of the Dead Man, Volume 2* (1997) contain sequences of poems, each consisting of lines that form complete sentences, listing the attributes and attitudes of "the dead man." Bell's most recent volumes include *Rampant* (2004) and *Mars Being Red* (2007), a volume of highly political poems responding to what Bell considers his country's policies of military aggression. Bell's poetry has also appeared in a wide variety of anthologies including *Contemporary American Poets* (1969), *New Voices in American Poetry* (1973), *Fifty Years of American Poetry* (1984), *The Vintage Book of Contemporary American Poetry* (1990), and *Contemporary American Poetry* (1985, 1991, 1996, and 2000). In addition, Bell wrote "Homage to the Runner," a column about poetry, for the *American Poetry Review* from 1975 to 1978 and from 1990 to 1992. He served as editor and publisher of the journal *Statements* from 1959 to 1964 and as the poetry editor of the *North American Review* (1964-69) and the *Iowa Review* (1969-71).

CRITICAL RECEPTION

Critical appraisals of Bell's poetry have been mixed, occasionally colored by prejudice against his affiliation with the University of Iowa—"that apprentices' academy," as David Leviten calls it. Daniel McGuiness suggests that the rather lukewarm reception of *New and Selected Poems* may have been due to the fact that "workshop bashing became the dominant mode of book reviewing in America" around the time that Bell's volume came out. According to McGuiness, Bell's book deserved a Pulitzer Prize, but failed to get one because many critics disparaged what they considered the sameness of the poetry emerging from the Iowa Writers' Workshop. Thus their message to those associated with Iowa, claims McGuiness, was: "get a real job, lead a real life, write real poems that end the way poems, lives, and jobs are supposed to end—with a bang, not a whimper."

Although Bell's later work tends to be more accessible to readers, his early poetry has often been regarded as obscure and difficult. In an interview with Wayne Dodd and Stanley Plumly, Bell admitted that the poems of *The Escape into You* and *Residue of Song* are "convoluted in syntax, complicated in metaphor (and sometimes in tense) sometimes, perhaps, near-hysterical in their movements." Leviten sees progress even within individual poems, contending that Bell's poetry is often "clumsy," but that it tends to improve as it goes along. He offers as an example the poem "Father," directing the reader to notice "how it begins with clanking syllables that, as the stanza develops, become less clogged and almost melt on the tongue." McGuiness notes changes from Bell's early work in *New and Selected Poems* to the poetry of the 1990s, beginning with *Iris of Creation: Poems* (1990): "tone from wisecracking to wisdom, diction from gnarled to planed, and a look toward the reader that is still insistent but far gentler." Richard Jackson comments that, beginning with the "dead man" poems of the 1990s, Bell's work exhibits a duality encompassing joy and sadness. "Reading Bell's poems," according to Jackson, "always reminds us of the joy of living, though certainly not pure joy," since there is more than a hint of melancholy in most of his pieces. For Jackson, *The Book of the Dead Man* is "one of the most complex, most original books in a long time."

PRINCIPAL WORKS

Poetry

Two Poems 1965
Poems for Nathan and Saul 1966
Things We Dreamt We Died For 1966

A Probable Volume of Dreams 1969
The Escape into You: A Sequence 1971
Residue of Song 1974
Stars Which See, Stars Which Do Not See 1977
These Green-Going-to-Yellow: Poems 1981
Segues: A Correspondence in Poetry [with William Stafford] 1983
Drawn by Stones, by Earth, by Things That Have Been in Fire: Poems 1984
New and Selected Poems 1987
Annie-Over [with William Stafford] 1988
Iris of Creation: Poems 1990
The Book of the Dead Man 1994
A Marvin Bell Reader: Selected Poetry and Prose (poetry, essays) 1994
Ardor: The Book of the Dead Man, Volume 2 1997
Poetry for a Midsummer's Night 1997
Wednesday: Selected Poems, 1966-1997 1998
Nightworks: Poems 1962-2000 2000
Rampant 2004
Mars Being Red 2007

Other Major Works

Old Snow Just Melting: Essays and Interviews 1983

CRITICISM

David Leviten (essay date fall/winter 1975)

SOURCE: Leviten, David. "Less Pose than Prose." *Parnassus: Poetry in Review* 4, no. 1 (fall/winter 1975): 206-10.

[*In the following review of* The Residue of Song, *Leviten finds Bell's poetry "clumsy," but at the same time "moving."*]

> The intellect does not sing; that is not its function.
>
> ANTONIO MACHADO

Reading and rereading Marvin Bell's latest volume has been puzzling, sobering, and, finally, unsettling. This middle-aging poet who has published several volumes—one going back to the Fifties—and who teaches poetry writing at that apprentices' academy, Iowa, still puts his sounds together at times as clumsily as Dreiser did his chunks of prose. And occasionally, as with Dreiser, the clumsiness is moving. And, contrarily, like a good prose writer, his skills increase with the larger units of stanza, poem, sequence, and extend even to unify the entire volume by thematic word repetition, image-repetitions, puns and near-puns, and, in the sequence about his dead father, by occasional near rhymes joining the endings of several poems. So here he suggests a sonnet sequence chiming poem with poem:

> . . . its roots sucking life from the dead. That's
> a thought you can follow, inside, where you do.
>
> I just want to be happy again. That's
> what I was, happy, maybe am, you would know.

Unfortunately this otherwise rather dogged poet does not sustain his formalism; or, perhaps fortunately, since formalism—that unamerican vice—takes off from a zest for pattern that might offend the scruples of the Puritan engineer, for whom a poem is a (free verse) machine breathing words. And no spare parts. Anyway, here's a stanza from his **"Father"** series. Notice the overkill: how it begins with clanking syllables that, as the stanza develops, become less clogged and almost melt on the tongue, like the memory of the dead he is evoking. And notice in the first few lines how Bell labors his imagery (he is a conscious, an all-too-often self-conscious, laborer whose self-criticism often keeps him from taking off):

> Out from muted bee-sounds and musketry
> (the hard works of our ears, dissembling),
> under steeply-held birds (in that air
> the mind draws of our laid breathing),
> out from light dust and the retinal gray,
> your face as in your forties appears
> as if to be pictured, and will not go away.

This passage seems typical: line by line uncertainties of sound and of suggestion—"laid" being an ambiguity suggesting sex *and* death—the "t," "s," etc., as if the poet breathed his meaning too heavily. Finally, a kind of half-hearted form, a failure to exploit the resonance of rhyme. "Away" ends the stanza neatly by chiming with "gray," but why not parallel it with "ear(s)" or "hear(s)" rhyming with "appears" and so further amplify sound and sense? Here the word-machine operates, but not on many cylinders. This is not a petty point, as the poet, at his rhyme's end at mid-line, seems to sense: "O anything will do / to sink a song to you." Note the self-consciously jingling self-deprecation and, for the son of a Russian-Jewish immigrant, the I hope unconscious Yiddishism of "k" for "g" in "sink." Once again the sounds are goin*k* ba*t*; more crucially, the poet too rarely hears his own voice or anyone else's with precision. Ole Ez, thou shouldst be teaching at this hour!

However, in an essay in *American Poetry Review,* Bell states he has shifted his faith in poetry as word play, as surrealist-image-mystery-mongering,—they tend to negate meaning,—to a poetry of content, of thought, of "indications of mentality," which suggests Frost's definition of poetry as the emotion of having a thought and, beyond that, as metaphor—or, more broadly, as

analogy, since without analogy the mind is reduced to monistic monotony, to the dead level of 1 + 1 or despairingly to 0 + 0, identity as non-being. Similarly the ideologues and their pop disciples unmask all ideality—which implies form, whether it's Platonic-mathematical, musical, visual, or poetic—and reduce it to chaos or a few Freudian, Marxist, or romantic-primitive counters so that the naively accepting layman-poet accepts their doctrines and lets it deaden his poems.

Unfortunately, Bell has been infected, like the rest of us, by *the* authority, though it's old hat by now: scientific materialism. As a result, he calls his poem on consciousness **"Shit,"** though he is nostalgic for it as being sweet shit, a honeycomb; i.e., he reduces "mind" to "brain" and tragedy (in "Aristotle") to the pathetic "a fall from a high place by a weak / sister"—as if Oedipus were a traveling salesman and not a passionate tyrant, one of whose last acts was to curse his own sons. Willy Loman he wasn't! And "love"—here it's a belated example of art imitating life—suffers a seaweed change into something banal and grotesquely estranged from itself, which feels true to some facts of American life, but seems pointless poetically and humanly speaking without the genius of a Baudelaire to express its sterile horror. So Bell, in **"Impotence,"** presents an adulterous situation in which the cheating husband is so exhausted and bored by the cheating wife who comically(?), guiltily, murmurs "my husband" that his offending member can't even rise to the occasion. And of course, take note, feminists: this female is faceless—and, male chauvinists: bares no roller-coaster curves, only an abstractly metaphorical orifice. Which may be the weary point of the poem. So eroticism fails; even pornography is not achieved. Only the caution: "You wanted orgasm and repose. / You wanted love without memory."

There's something disconcertingly neoclassical about this poet. "He stooped to truth and moralized his song"—as if Dr. Johnson succumbed to the white breasts of an actress backstage and then decided it was irrational. But as a Jewish family man, indeed, the self-confessed "last poet of the family," Bell's heart has its reasons of which the penis is only limply aware. And, fortunately, in the best poems of the book—**"Residue of Song," "Death of a Critic,"** and **"The Hurt Trees"**—Bell transcends or at least puts to good use the self-conscious cleverness of what are probably the earlier poems and the generic, "classical" imagery of his "thoughtful" pose. **"A Residue of Song"** has an especially beautiful fusion of sight and touch imagery, so that this poem, with its long elegiac lines, is tenderly precise, not coldly so. The strange shifting of persons, places, and times, the wife being seen as the abandoned past now addressing the poet, is subtly moving:

> "One appointment leads to another in these soft days.
> A photograph of flowers the skin remembers,

a bowl of leaves before the kitchen screen,
is to this life as you are to mine. Your cries,
for ecstatic madness, are not sadder than some things.
From the residue of song, I have barely said my love
    again,
as if for the last time, believing that you will leave
    me."

"Death of a Critic," with the sure, spare vision of an
ex-photographer evokes person, place, and aura in a
way that the "father" sequence, with its elaborate link-
ages, rarely did:

I look up into the death of my father
as I have always done, and the landscape
he passes—a few trees, white winter bark,

the cool green streets ending in fog,
several short coastal steeples, lighthouse,
and that farther knowledge which locates

as objects he must leave: buoy and flag,
channel, inlet and harbor, horns
of salvage and unfriendly witness.

Finally, **"The Hurt Trees,"** Bell's "Ode to Dejection,"
beautifully sums up the whole volume in its five-part
structure, which repeats the five-part division of the
book, although the imagery of stone, trees, stars is balanced somewhat by "mid-country" particulars, distilling
a cold clarity and brilliance in this Winter landscape:

Heaven has come down to earth
like rain to dry crackers,
in fact as sleet to these branches,

Like: chance, functioning with elegance.
The dead leaf and the globe
and our elastic yearnings

wind in the mind around limbs
which we call "fingers,"
or "heaven," that goal for cows.

More vitally, however, in these lines, by his very denial
of a literal heaven, "that goal for cows," the poem at-
tains it through a flight of imaginative wit rooted in
perception, therefore earning its generalization: "chance,
functioning with elegance." Here, for once in Bell, a
dead-level identity is transcended: for the moment of
perception, that Blakeian eternity, the non-human world
is held lovingly up to the eye and the mind's eye in a
way that Wordsworth and Stevens would have applauded. Of course, the poem sinks back—but movingly—to the "still lives of stones," those obsessive
counters of "dead" nature, atoms solid as Newton's. As
if matter hadn't been exploded and converted into
energy, which is the traditional attribute of spirit, "pure
act!" No! American poets have reason enough for
depression in The Great American Desert, but even
isolation is a socially conditioned fact and not a
metaphysical one, at least not to the self-forgetting

contemplative eye. *Esse Percipi!* With our Berkeley
which art in heaven, seeing is believing!

Marvin Bell, Wayne Dodd, and Stanley Plumly (interview date November 14, 1975)

SOURCE: Bell, Marvin, Wayne Dodd, and Stanley
Plumly. "A Conversation with Marvin Bell." *Ohio Review* 17, no. 3 (spring/summer 1976): 40-62.

[*In the following interview, conducted on November 14,
1975, Bell discusses his literary influences and his
evolving poetic voice.*]

[*Interviewer*]: *I am interested in your new role as poetry
commentator, but I want to start out talking about your
poems. You have a poem which you read last night that
speaks of Donne as your first influence, and I guess you
have moved through, as we all have, several models of
poets—Wallace Stevens might be an intermediate
figure—and certainly in your new work William Carlos
Williams is the model. I'd like to know how you
perceived this as happening through, now, three books
of poetry—and into a fourth.*

[Bell]: It's always been difficult for me to answer the
question, "What are your influences?" because they've
been so many and various that the list doesn't mean
much to anyone who might hear it. But it is true that a
good number of the poems I wrote and published are
metaphysical by nature and perhaps metaphysical by
method in the terms in which literary critics and
scholars use that word *metaphysical*: to refer to certain
ways of approaching material. And so I am perfectly
willing to try to categorize the changes that have come
about in my writing recently as being those of someone
who has slept happily with Donne and now sleeps with
Williams. It's not that simple, obviously. At the same
time, I do feel as if the book that I am going to publish
next will be, in a very real sense, my first book. I always
figured—I used to tell my students, and I think some of
them will remember this—that I felt I'd be a beginner
until about the age of 40. Well, I'm 38 now and I'm
getting closer to what might be a beginning. I think
without having known it I was right and that it was
necessary for me, as it might not have been for many
others, to try a great many different things in writing
before I could feel that I'd found whatever it is that
would be my own language: you know, a language that
embodies deep feeling and meaningful experience. So
it's taken a long time. There were times when reviewers held it against me that I was willing to try various
things, but that's their problem, not mine.

*Let's talk about what you think your metaphysics were
and about how you think what you're doing now is different from that approach to a poem.*

As you know, a good number of the poems that appeared in my last two books are convoluted in syntax, complicated in metaphor (and sometimes in tense) sometimes, perhaps, near-hysterical in their movements, and I in no way regret or disown these. I don't find attractive that way of doing things that requires poets to say "I'm finished with all that," or "I'll never write like that again." I'm happy to have become what I am now by having been what I was then. But I always envied those poets who I knew had made aesthetic decisions that had enabled them to write very accessible poems. My poems were difficult for some readers. Now, *I* think the difficulty in them is earned and valuable. But that's what *I* think. That isn't what *they* all thought. In any case, it required real exertion on the part of some readers to read and understand some of those poems, and I always envied friends of mine, poets I knew, who had decided, somehow, maybe without really deciding, that they could write in a style that was very accessible to other people and at the same time be as profound and as intelligent as anyone. And I've come finally to realize that that, of course, is true: that there isn't anything one can't do simply. Like designers we all strive for a profound simplicity, right? And we're always specially interested in the kind of teaching, too, that derives from profound simplicity: hence, the Western interest in Zen teaching, and so forth. Well, I'm naturally interested in the same thing, and finally I think I've come to a point where I *can* write poetry in a way that is accessible to anyone who wishes to read it. And I'm really happy about it.

And you note as the chief difference now the accessibility of the word on the page?

That's one of the chief symptoms, I think.

How do you feel about the difference? How do you feel as a poet, as a man writing, dealing with language and experience? How is that different for you?

Well, I tried hard to be an experimental poet when I started, as I guess all of us did. But *real* developments, *real* changes in art come about, it seems to me, after many years of hard work and hard thought and perhaps some luck—not from deciding at an early age that one is going to be experimental. That just makes for junk. Neither of you has ever seen the first poems I wrote, but they were examples of word play, and that's really all they were. I did write many kinds of verse that I thought were experimental in some sense. But I think that being interested in metaphor for its own sake, being that interested in convoluted syntax, sometimes for its own sake, and so forth, made poetry a kind of barrier between the poet and experience, between the poet and emotion. Sometimes, of course, that led to discovery. As I say, I don't in any way disown my earlier poems. I think there were kinds of experience and other

kinds of discoveries that, in the poetry I wrote in earlier books, I could only approach that way then. But it's just taken me years to . . . well, once I said in print that I wanted my poems to be both surprising and inevitable at every turn. But now it seems to me that that's a false distinction. I think there's a kind of inevitability which includes, which subsumes surprises, and that's really what one strives for. There's a passage that appeals to me greatly in the *ABC of Reading,* where Pound is trying to decide how to go about specifying the nature of poetry. And he says, "Well, we could begin with a statement by Dante, 'A canzone is a composition of words set to music.' Or we could begin with a statement by Coleridge or DeQuincey which says, 'The quality of a great poet is everywhere present, and nowhere visible as a distinct excitement.'" What that second statement suggests is that fireworks in a poem get in the way of the poem as a whole. They draw attention to themselves in a way that injures the poem as a whole. That makes emotional sense to me, and maybe I can say, very quickly, something that makes sense in terms of all of this by simply saying that I think Williams' later poems are just wonderful. I think *Asphodel, That Greeny Flower* is—well, even Auden, who probably was not partial to Williams' work, thought it was one of the great love poems in the English language. I think it's just a marvelous poem. I think Book V of *Paterson* is a marvelous lyric poem all by itself. So it's the late Williams, or the old Williams, if you will, whose work I feel very close to now.

As you said, your more recent poems are clearly more accessible and inviting: they invite the reader in. And you say you now feel that is the way to go, and that you can do it. Do you think this is at all because you feel you've reached the stage where you have, in quotation marks, "something to say"? Do you think in part you are saying that you feel more?

Well, to some extent that's true. I think what happens—I'm guessing, of course—but I think what might happen for some of us is that what one has to say, in a sense, becomes at some point congruent with the way in which one would say it, so that there's no longer any distinction, if ever there was, between what it is one's poems are about or deal with and the way in which one writes things on the page. So in that sense, what it is one has to say becomes natural subject matter for poetry. Before that—I don't know. It's always dangerous to talk about what one has to say, because you and I both know that poems don't get written by thinking of something to say; but I know what you mean and to some extent it is true.

Do you think that the greater accessibility of your new poems in any way comes from this new interest you have in—to use a phrase from one of your APR [American Poetry Review] *columns—"an attention to the materials of the poem?"*

I think in that column I was talking about how the aesthetic process works *in general,* and it seems to me the aesthetic process, whatever medium one's involved with, or whatever art form one's involved with, works more or less the same way at all times: and that is that one distracts the conscious mind so that the subconscious and one's deep feelings and so forth can make themselves known—as they always will. And so I wouldn't want to say that I paid more attention to the materials of the poem before than I do now, or now than I did before. I think I tried to pay as severe attention to the materials then as I do now, and now as I did then.

Okay, but there is something you're paying more attention to now than you did then, and I think that that's the difference you're after. I don't know quite what the vocabulary for that difference would be.

I don't want to be deceptive about this, so I should admit that there are changes in attitude that go along with these changes in method—change, growth, I don't know which it is. I hope it's growth rather than just change, obviously. But there are changes in attitude. I think American poetry is often very tiresome. That is, contemporary American poetry has been tiresome in its discovery of the individual self, over and over and over, and its discovery of emotions that, indeed, we all have: loneliness, fear, despair, ennui, etcetera. I think it can get tiresome when the discovery of such emotions is more or less all the content there is to a poem. We know those things. I think people who don't read or write poetry know those things, after all. So I sort of write poetry nowadays from some other attitudes, I think, that came upon me without my ever really thinking about them. I think, for example, that it's ultimately pleasanter and healthier and better for everyone if one thinks of the self as being very small and very unimportant. And one of my new poems that I know you've seen, a poem called **"Trinket,"** more or less says that very thing right out. The poem actually says, "I love watching the water / ooze from the crack in the fern pot," and goes on talking about what effect it has on the person watching this and concludes by saying that it's things like this which give the self the notion of the self one is always losing until, the poem says, "these *tiny* embodiments / small enough to contain it." And I believe that. And I think, as I may not always have thought, that the only way out from the self is to concentrate on others and on things outside the self.

Would you talk a bit about the idea of modesty in poetry and maybe even of the role of modesty in your *work?*

I did use the word *modesty* in one of those articles for the *American Poetry Review* and I tried to define it in a special way. I think I spoke of poetic modesty with regard to the materials of the poem. I can't quite sum up what I said at the time, but I guess what I meant was that there is a kind of physical reality that we all share a sense of. I mean, we might argue about what reality is, but we all know how to walk across a bridge—instead of walking across the water, for instance. And it seems to me that one definition of modesty in poetry would be a refusal to compromise the physical facts of what it is that is showing up in one's poems.

What else is involved in the changes in yourself?

There's much more from nature in my poetry now than there was before, too, and I can say something that might be telling about this. There are poets in America who brag about living on farms: some brag about living on farms and farming; some brag about living on farms and not farming; some brag about living in nature, but not necessarily on farms. Well, I grew up in the country, in the *real* country, where I was surrounded by duck farmers and potato farmers and fisherman, and I never thought it was anything to brag about. It seemed a nice place to grow up, but it didn't seem to me it was better or worse than any other kind of life. As a result, when I started writing poetry, I really wasn't interested in putting nature in my poems at all. I think my earlier poems would have been better had I been more interested in putting nature into them somehow, but I wasn't. I was interested in the discoveries that language could make all by itself. That doesn't quite make sense, but I know you know what I mean. And I was interested in relationships between people. I wrote one whole book of poems-in-series about the relationships between a couple of people, or among several people. But now, for whatever good reasons, I *am* interested in allowing nature to have the place in my poems that it always had in my life.

Do you think that suggests, in some paradoxical way maybe, that you have, nonetheless, gone more into the self? There seems to be more easy access to you and to your life, to a kind of rhythm there.

I agree.

You're talking about how you upheave *the personal. More personal and, perhaps, less private?*

Yes. I remember once reading at San Francisco State College, reading from the book of poems-in-series called **The Escape Into You,** and I remember a girl who was in the audience coming up afterwards and saying to me, "These poems are like an eye, evading and evading, and then there comes a moment near the end of each poem when the eye sees what it didn't want to see, what it held back from seeing before, and the poem bursts through to its real subject." And I thought she was right. That's what those poems are like.

* * *

Okay, now for an impossible, even outrageous, question: What do you believe in?

What do I believe in? Well, I believe in accepting physical reality for what it appears to be, which is not a very profound belief. I believe as did Hardy and Frost, and as I think Stafford does, in the indifference of nature to man. I don't see that as bad, but merely as a fact. I believe in what I think is still called utilitarianism, the greatest good for the greatest number. You know, my principles are ordinary humanitarian principles, I think and I hope.

What I want to know is: whatever it is you believe in, at what point does that, in its variety and in its intensity or relaxation—whatever the temperament of it happens to be—at what point does it intersect with what you write?

Well, I believe that acceptance of the facts is not only healthy but necessary to what one might call happiness, and that acceptance of death—not merely one's own death but the death of others and the deaths of loved ones and even the death of the planet, death of the culture, certainly, perhaps even the death of the universe—is not to be avoided but to be approached and embraced. There are many kinds of uses for poetry. There's a kind of poetry which tries to promote useful illusions. I think of that as being a kind of Romantic poetry (with a large R). There's a kind of poetry, which one sees a lot of in our century, which is a kind of debunking poetry, which tries to rub our faces in the nitty-gritty of the truth and insist that things are much worse than we ever thought. Neither of these kinds of poetry satisfies me very much. I would like to write poetry which finds salvation in the physical world and the here and now and which redefines the soul, if you will, in terms of emotional depth, and that emotional depth in terms of the physical world and the world of human relationships. I think I told you before, off the tape, that I had agreed to try to provide a book to fit the special format of a particular poetry series, and I am going to try to do it. And though it may sound silly to say it right out this way, what I'm trying to do is to write about forty poems about the soul. Now, these poems contain a lot of the physical world.

This seems to be counter *to William's notion of "no ideas but in things." What is an idea for you?*

Well, it's very complicated, and let me say some things you've heard me say or seen me say in print before. Williams does say, early in *Paterson*, "Say it! No ideas but in things." And a little later he says, "No ideas but in the facts." But his own practice belies a narrow interpretation of that line. In fact, he was a master of

abstractions. His poetry is very intellectual, most of his best poetry extremely intellectual. A poem that is anthologized over and over, "The Descent," is a poem composed almost entirely of abstract language and abstract thought. I don't mean to be endorsing abstract language, but merely to be pointing out that Williams was not simply a descriptive poet. And when Pound defined an image he didn't define it in terms of an object or the presence of images in the mind or anything like that. He said an image was "an intellectual and emotional complex in an instant of time." Now, that means that one has in an image both the physical world and the subjective self. And if anything interesting has been happening in terms of methods in twentieth-century poetry, it probably is in those terms that it has been happening. That is, that the physical world and the subjective self have come together in poetry in a new way.

Lately, you wrote about the recent attempt by some poets to woo *the unconscious, in what you saw as an illegitimate or too-direct way. I wonder . . . what do you think is, in fact, the function of the unconscious in poetry?*

It seems to me there's been a lot of loose talk about the subconscious in poetry. I think the subconscious is the subconscious because it's the *sub*conscious. That is, it remains below conscious apprehension.

As Jung says, it must always *remain below.*

Right. Of course. By definition. And what the loose talk about the subconscious in poetry has produced is a poetry of strange effects and interesting fireworks, so that one gets a poem of interesting free association which really doesn't reveal any more of the subconscious than a straightforward, descriptive poem about a rose would, and perhaps much less. The trouble with surrealism is, as Wallace Stevens said, that anyone can make a clam play an accordion. Actually, it might be pretty interesting to hear a clam playing "Lady of Spain" on an accordion, but only for a while, unless, of course, he had a very good voice. So, strangeness in poetry has, in the recent past, passed for a kind of special interest in the subconscious when, in fact, it was nothing of the sort. Instead, what one saw in the poems which imitated this fashionable method was more and more reference to jewels and to wings and to other items—that is, to things which really came from conscious notions that the poet had about himself or herself. In other words, the poets were turning to jewels because they wanted to be valuable, or the poets were sprouting wings from their shoulder bones because they wanted to transcend the material world. Now that's a bit of an oversimplification on my part, and indeed these jewels and wings turn up, in some cases, in some excellent poems by excellent poets—for example, in wonderful poems by James Wright. But jewels and wings of that sort also began to turn up in the second-rate followers of such poets. What was really going on was that the conscious mind was giving itself away by its very conscious selection of which strange thing would be used in the poem. One rarely found such poets likening their bones to trash, for example. They likened them to jewels and diamonds. They were anxious to grow wings, but they rarely grew matted hair, for example, in their poems. And it seems to me that the poets were, in such cases, consciously giving *themselves* more and more value, and that the poems had very little to do with the subconscious, or at least no more to do with the subconscious than any other poem.

Do you think that's in part because of the lack of a guiding and unifying emotional content for those poems? Depth psychologists tell us that the "language" of the unconscious is images, the only language it has, archetypal and otherwise. And this is in large part the language of emotion. So I wonder whether what you're suggesting might not also be talking about the absence of a controlling emotion, which would have been a way, maybe, into legitimate touchings of the unconscious through imagery.

Sure. But language works by connecting things up, so that if a poet provides five lines in which each line is stranger than the preceding line, how is one to know whether or not the emotion is genuine? It might well have been so for the poet, it might well not be so for the reader.

Well, it does seem to me that one of the ways of getting embodied in the poem the authentic emotion that the writer is remembering and is trying to find a local habitation and a home for is by allowing those images which most intimately attach to or connect with that emotion in his own psyche to find themselves into the poem.

Sure. But you see, right away I want to ask how do we know, in fact, that those are the images? Which dream, for example, is the poet remembering, if any? Which parts of which dreams is the poet remembering, if any? Is the poet in fact remembering the dreams accurately or does the conscious mind change the images that were seen? It seems to me that our experience in these matters is very incomplete, and that most of the explanations of the subconscious are nifty but convincing only at times, or only partially convincing. There are many ways of talking about certain mysterious aspects of human experience, but I don't, myself, think of them as anything but ways of talking about those unknowns. Even the notion that the only language the subconscious has is images is, I think, too limited a view.

In conclusion about this, though, what are you saying? Not just that all that happens in a poem is, of course,

very conscious, in the best sense of the word contrived, *but that the* sources *are all conscious?*

No, I'm saying that the subconscious will be present in a poem no matter what, that one's values will give themselves away in one's poems no matter what. What it really comes down to is that I'm also shaped by my experience. I'm a small-town boy. I grew up thinking that many things were fairly simple. I grew up in a house that was a very nice house for children to be growing up in, but which, in fact, did not contain art work or many books, and I felt no lack because of it. I played with a concert band more often than I played with an orchestra; that may say something about one's background. Now, I was educated to many other kinds of tastes and interests, but I think . . . it's hard to explain. I never read fiction when I was in high school, and I don't read very much fiction now, but I did read a lot of philosophy. And it seemed to me that the conclusions philosophers would come to after complex and convoluted thought processes would invariably, would inevitably, be the same conclusions that the butcher on the corner would also have come to, but intuitively. It really seemed to me that language was an imperfect medium which was easily misused. And I still believe that that's true.

To what end? A kind of witch-doctoring in poetry? People trying to claim magical properties for things that are quite natural events?

Well, I think, yes, one has to distinguish between mystery and mystification.

Do you believe in mystery?

Oh, absolutely. If by "mystery" you mean that there are things we don't know the causes of or the effects of.

How do you get that into your work?

Get it into my work?

How does it affect your work? How does it come into one's poems? If it exists, and you're being honest about your experience, and some of your experience, ergo, is mysterious, then how do you get that into your poems? You don't get it in, is that what you're saying? It just happens?

I would tend to say, "in mysterious ways." I think that if we were to talk, for example, about something that sounds much smaller, that is, poetic voice instead of, say, mystery, we would have to admit immediately that the voice of a poet is the result of a great many aspects of the person's language and methods of perception, all kinds of things. It would be difficult to explain it. And that's why each poet sounds like himself or herself and not like anyone else. At least that's true after having written for many years. There are so many aspects to it. It seems to me that mystery in poetry also comes about, or apprehension of mystery comes, arrives in a poem, for many reasons and in many ways. For so many reasons and in so many ways that we can't possibly describe them all.

Do you think your poems have mystery? There are certain poets who thrive on being mysterious—not obscure, but mysterious.

Some poets are spooky. Or some poems, I should say, by some poets, are spooky.

One clichéd version of the classical reasons for writing a poem is this: to forge order out of chaos.

Well, there are some people who forge chaos out of order, I think, and I'm not much interested in their poetry, or that way of doing things.

Are you clarifying certain things in your work? Or merely representing certain things?

Well . . . the reason I'm stuck is because I'm not able to make that kind of distinction, which approaches a distinction between form and content, that, as you well know, all poets are unable to make when they're writing up to their abilities. So that the way in which something is becoming clear in a poem is identical to and simultaneous with the something that is becoming clear.

But the result of your poem, the poem that results is, in fact, a clarifying?

Well, I think *real* mysteries can't be answered. Real mysteries remain mysteries. One doesn't clarify them. One can ask questions about them more and more clearly and/or more and more interestingly. I think there are some poets who specialize in mystification, which is a different thing. That's a deliberate or perhaps unintentional attempt to confuse, but to confuse in arty ways.

To create the effect of profundity?

Right. Now, why they do it or whether they do it intentionally I can't say. But I do make a distinction in my mind—and, again, I think this is the habit of a small-town boy—between what is merely arty and what is artful. And it seems to me that a great deal of poetry at any given time is arty and not artful. That is, it is filled with clutter, albeit so-called "creative" clutter, and filled with b.s. But it's natural to me to make such distinctions, and it might not be natural to others to make such distinctions.

Do you ever feel a desire or need or impulse to write a poem that you think of as an attempt to recreate a sense of the mystery of an event or a moment or a situation?

Well, I mentioned before that I'm going to try to write—and in fact I am writing—a number of poems that I say are about the soul, and I think that the use of the term *soul* in these poems is a way to create a metaphor for what remains a mysterious dimension of experience.

How about an example from the poems you read last night?

Well, perhaps this one will serve. You know, most poems are written about moments of intensity, mental and/or physical, moments of ecstasy perhaps, moments of keen perception and heightened feeling and heightened awareness and so forth, but in fact, of course, a good part of our waking hours are spent in a state that is not nearly that intense and not nearly that alert, but a state of torpor. That's what the poem **"Unable to Wake in the Heat"** is about. I don't want to try to make the poem bigger than it is (it's not a very long poem), but it's about that state of not-waking—you know, with a hyphen, *not-waking*—that we often find ourselves in. But it's put in terms of a very common event, and if, in fact, I hadn't been half awake and half asleep one day in a hot Iowa summer, I might not have written such a poem.

The extraordinary of the ordinary?

Sure.

What about content in poems? I have heard people say that Eliot was a poet of content, *as opposed, say, to Wallace Stevens, a master of music.*

It's certainly a matter of emphasis and not a clear-cut distinction that's being made when someone says that Eliot is a poet of content in a way that Stevens is not. But I think I see what such a remark means. Stevens in many of his poems invents the terms of the poems. And then employs them in such a way that a kind of poetic equation is created . . . an equation which is then solved, in a sense, in the poem. And other examples: It seems to me that Donne is a poet who often sets up the terms in his poems, creates the terms of the poems within the poems, whereas Williams takes the terms as they are in the outer world and then employs them. And it's not a matter, so much, of how long a poem is as of the intensity of attention with which the poet uses those things that are brought into the poem from the outside world, and how many times and in what ways, and to what length. I mentioned earlier Williams' long poem *Asphodel, That Greeny Flower,* which is a marvelous example of a poem in which *all kinds* of things are welcomed into the poem from out there, and then picked up over and over again, and employed in such a way that they make a whole greater than the sum of the parts. Although I've written few, if any, poems which sound like William Stafford's poems, nonetheless his practice seems attractive to me, and it seems to me that in his poetry and also in the poetry of John Ashbery, to choose a very different example, all kinds of things are welcomed into the poems at all times and in all ways, and indeed, that was true, of course, for Wordsworth's poetry. And it seems true in general of poetry. That is, the history of poetry seems, in part, to be the history of finding ways to employ in poetry that which was formerly thought not to be fit for poetry.

Ashbery would have to admit a great deal into those poems, or he wouldn't get all that language. But your newer poems, vis-a-vis the model of Williams, or that kind of ghost, are much narrower on the page and generally shorter and more economical and in a more relaxed diction than anything you've done before. Now, at what point do you select and not admit?

Well, I hope what you say is true about my new poems. I feel they're more economical and more relaxed, and yet in some way more attentive, perhaps, than the poems I wrote earlier. But surely that's not to disclaim a continuing process of selection during the writing. It's difficult for me to explain it. I think that my sense of line has changed partly in reaction to what seems to be the clutter one sees in so much poetry now. That is, the imagination machine has long since been set free to walk and talk and think all on its own.

But don't you think that it's been done because people want to be significant?

I think they want to be individual even more than significant—not that they don't wish to be significant also.

False models of power?

Right. Also, it's a kind of simple notion of *Show and Tell,* or rather, *Show, Don't Tell.* The importance of specificity in art is so overwhelming a principle sometimes that one forgets that the quality of the art may really depend on other things. And it seems to me that if one were just to arbitrarily read through a dozen magazines of poetry today, one would be struck by how many words there are in the magazines and in the poems. So many would-be images, so many objects, so much furniture in the poetry. One wearies of even the good stuff. And, so, partly, I'm sure, my practice is a reaction to what I see around me. I also believe that if there are three things in a line, each of them will get, say, a third as much attention as if there were one. Now, that doesn't mean that I can only put one thing in one line, but it is a sort of general principle that I

believe in. Also, I'm always after a sense of measure. As you know, I used to be a musician, and the notion of music in poetry is very important to me, and the use of the line is very important to me, and rhythm in poetry is very important to me. I'm always searching for the right sense of measure in terms of my own language. And all of that in terms of my own memory and experience, and it now seems right to me to write in the way I'm writing, and I guess that's why I do it.

In a book, oddly enough, about fiction—Wayne Booth's The Rhetoric of Fiction, *one of the finest books on fiction I've ever read—there's a chapter called "Telling and Showing." And that's always seemed to me to kind of summarize one of the chief impulses of . . .*

Actually, the greater possibility, it seems to me, is to both show *and* tell—but not to simply tell what one can show, and not to simply show what needs to be told. One of the things that the great modern poets did was to talk profoundly about life in their poems, instead of simply showing us circumstances and attitudes. And for a while we lost that.

Was it through incompetence, or was it because some things simply can't be at that moment in the poem translated, or analogized?

I think it was the mid-twentieth-century environment. I think it was all that which McLuhan discusses, for better or worse. I think it was just the technological and material bent of American sensibilities, and the dependence on the image, the dependence on television if you will. And someone (or many people) has to restore discourse to poetry. Not discourse by itself, but discourse as a part of it. One of the things I like about William Stafford and, as I said, one of the things I like about William Carlos Williams' work so much, is that in both one finds a hand out to welcome anything that might come into the poem. Now whatever comes into the poem has to be imbedded in the texture of the poem, obviously. It can't just be an item that's thrown in for what it's worth. In the work of people whom we sometimes describe as surreal, one finds little firecrackers in the lines, and they're wonderful by themselves, but that's as far as it goes. In the work of a Williams or a Stafford one finds all kinds of things welcomed into the poem, including ways of writing that other people are afraid to use—ways which other people rule out because they feel such ways are sentimental, or because they think such ways are rhetorical, or whatever. And in some cases that might be right and in some cases it might not be.

Or the intensity is such that they can't afford to relax for a single moment.

If one doesn't insist that poetry be intense, then there are some things one can say that one couldn't say otherwise in the poem. It just seems to me every deci-

sion implies a counter-decision. If one elects to do this or that, one by implication elects not to do something else. It would be possible to think of discourse in poetry as a requirement that makes poetry difficult. And that might be thought of as a plus, that is, requiring discourse and many other possibilities of poetry might be seen as a way of insisting that poetry be something more than casual observation and random inventions. But I don't really think of it quite that way. I'm thinking in fact, right now, of something very different. I am more interested in ways in which poetry is shown to be *easy,* both to read and to write. Not easy because slack or flat or prosaic or pedestrian, but easy because little is put between what the writer, and then the reader, knows and sees and feels and experiences, and the language itself. It seems to me there's a profound ease possible to both the writing and the reading of poetry. On a somewhat tangential note perhaps, I remember an interview with James Wright—I think it appeared in the *Paris Review*—in which he said that he seemed to have no talent for happiness. Well, I feel differently—at least at this moment—about my own life. I feel that I do have a capacity to be happy, even at moments of stress and pain. And it is important to me now, more so than it once was perhaps, to reaffirm that in the very methods by which I write.

A technical question. This is an old-fashioned kind of question. As a matter of fact, I think it was the kind of question that was asked in the late forties or early fifties. It may even sound like a workshop question. But what, for you, determines a line? You know: if twenty-five years ago I'd asked Williams that, I would have gotten one answer; or if I had asked Lowell when he was writing Lord Weary's Castle, *I would have gotten one answer; or Ginsberg when he was doing* Howl, *I bet I would have gotten one more answer.*

Well, I can make, I think, a very elaborate analysis of free verse lines, and of my own practice, which of course has changed over the years. And I even have a somewhat elaborate theory about what is really going on in the handling of the line by most free verse poets. But that's much too elaborate and much too theoretical to discuss at length here. But I think that . . . when Williams uses the words "variable foot," we're talking about something that could *sort of* be described, but which isn't very helpful as a term. On the other hand, when he uses a term that seems even more vague—that is, the word "measure"—*that* seems to me infinitely more helpful. It seems to me that one does have to have a sense of measure, a sense that the music and the "timing" of the poem matters to the person who is speaking. That is—not so much that it matters, but that it is part and parcel of what he or she is saying. My handling of lines has changed over the years. I think that as a younger poet I was, like many young poets, placing too much importance on the ends of lines. So that I was do-

ing things that were too clever. I was enjambing lines in a way that was very clever and sometimes deliberately misleading for a moment. I think that was wrong. In a sense, that's putting too much emphasis on the ends of the lines. Content is related to this, but music is more to the point, and one does want to continually vary the reader's expectations. Or play off of them. One wants to reward them—perhaps only seem to reward them.

Having set the reader up to a certain extent?

Right. Surprise him. It seems to me that the first line, and then the first two lines, of any poem, set up certain expectations and dismiss other possibilities. And that you identify the line as a unit—whatever kind of unit it's going to be—in the beginning of a poem, and that then, having made that identity clear, you can change it, or play off of it. If one never sets up an identity, perhaps that's another way of setting up a line—a line is a line because it never sets up that kind of identity—but it seems to me in general not as profitable a way of doing things. You know, almost every poet seems to begin a poem with a line or a phrase or perhaps several lines that have come into his or her head, and which carry with them not merely a proposal of content but a deep emotional sense which is tied to the music which he or she hears buzzing inside, which may or may not be attached to *particular* words sometimes. I think that's important to us all. We do hear the language. On the other hand, I think it's a mistake to go so far as to say, as some poets do, that poetry is meant simply to be read aloud.

* * *

I want to ask you now how you feel about the columns you're doing for the American Poetry Review? *You surely have an intention behind them, and an audience in mind.*

Well, I resisted agreeing to write those columns for some time. I have no message to proclaim, though I think my columns must indicate certain values that I hold as opposed to other values someone else might hold. I would like to direct attention *toward* poems rather than away from poems. I would like to suggest by example that one can talk fairly easily about poetry without resorting to the supernatural and hokum. I think there's been a lot of hokum around in the last ten or fifteen years. I think that I would like to indicate through my columns that most times what people think in general is not true in the specific; that, for example, whatever is said about poetry of the fifties in general will not necessarily be true of any particular poem written in the fifties. Likewise, whatever anyone says in general about poetry of the sixties or of the seventies, say, will not necessarily be true of any particular poem written in either of those periods. I think that the literary world tends to produce cliché thinking and to pass on received opinion, and I'd like to legislate against that by example in those columns. I'd like to suggest, too, that poetry, like water, seeks its own level, and that while there's no good or evil about it, it is possible to read or write poetry of great excellence. You know, there has been for a long time a continuing movement in America toward what is thought of as "creativity," and the results of that creativity occur at all levels and in all ways and in all forms, and I think it might be helpful to keep reminding people that some poems are better than others.

You have for a long time been associated with a poetry workshop, and there are many, many workshops, poetry workshops and fiction workshops, around the country. I suppose Iowa is the most famous, and it's the oldest. How do you feel about large numbers of students getting together in a kind of congregation to exploit the muse, as it were?

The muse is resistant to exploitation, I think, and no one who doesn't need to write will keep writing for very long. But naturally I think the program I teach in is pretty good or I wouldn't teach in it. It may surprise you to learn, however, that I think a good many writing programs around the country are not very helpful for the people who enroll in them and, in fact, may even be harmful. Again, I think any notion of what a writing program is or of whether such a program is good or bad has to be put in terms of an individual program. I think some programs are lousy, I think some programs are neither here nor there, and I think some programs may be good. I know of one program that's good; it's the one I teach in. I think it's good because it exists primarily as an excuse for a community for writers. It doesn't pretend to teach talent to anyone. *I* certainly don't pretend to teach anyone to be talented.

Can creative writing be taught? I don't know. I think it can be *learned.* Can the writing of poetry be taught? I don't know. I think it can be learned, because every good poem is an example of someone who learned how. It gives young poets, or older poets, for that matter, a chance to talk poetry if and when they want to. It gives them a chance to receive some talk about their own poems if and when they want to. It allows them to demand of themselves that they test their commitment to writing by writing. It forces them to pay attention to their own poems and to other people's poems. I can conceive of the possibility that for some people this might be bad. Generally, however, it seems to be good. But it all remains mysterious. I remember talking to John Logan about this many years ago, and he said at that time that he didn't know of any good poet who hadn't at one time or another been a member of some kind of literary community, whether it was at a college or in the cafés of Paris or elsewhere. And, you know, I

think it's been true for a very long time now that the academy is hardly an insulated world, it's hardly an ivory tower.

What brought you to Iowa?

I was living in Chicago, and I had an old ROTC commission, which I had accepted in the days when it was wise to accept one, and I knew that I would have to go into the Army sooner or later. I'd made many unsuccessful attempts to resign my commission, and it seemed to me that I was just then testing my commitment to writing and to poetry. That is, it was the first time I had had any chance to write much poetry—there had been too much going on, too many responsibilities taking my time before that. I had been part of a class that John Logan was teaching at the downtown center of The University of Chicago. Later, I was part of another group that Logan led, a group that had no academic affiliation but was called "the poetry seminar," which met in the offices of the Midwest Clipping Association in downtown Chicago. That was the group that also contained Dennis Schmitz, Bill Knott, and Naomi Lazard. And Charlie Simic was there for a time, he says. And Roger Aplon, and William Hunt, and some other people. So, I asked Logan, "What can I do to delay my going into the Army so I can write a great many poems between now and then?" See, I had the idea that I had to write a lot to learn how to write because I hadn't been brought up in a home where literature was important, and the only way I knew how to write—or to learn to write—was to try everything I could think of. So I asked John Logan what to do about it, and he said, "Well, there's this thing called "The Writers' Workshop" at the University of Iowa, and there's a poet there whom I know and respect named Donald Justice—why don't you see about going there?" And one thing led to another and I did. That was a way of pretending for awhile that I was a Ph.D. candidate and thus delaying the Army—delaying my entrance into active duty anyway. Then I went away, and I did indeed have to go into the Army. I went in for almost two years and had a very strange and humanitarian job, and then was asked to come back to Iowa City to teach at the University, which is what I did.

Did you ever learn anything about writing poems by being in a workshop?

Oh, I learned a lot about writing poetry by writing, and being at the workshop gave me a chance to do it. I also learned a lot about writing poetry by hearing people who knew something about it talk about it. Even when they weren't being very articulate I could often tell what they meant, or what the emphasis was, so that I've learned—I think I've learned things about poetry and literature, and even about life, from all kinds of people. In fact, I don't think I ever had a teacher—no matter how bad that teacher might have seemed to most people—from whom *I* didn't learn something because, for better or worse, I've always tried to take the teacher's position in my mind while I listened. So, no matter what the teacher was saying, whether I disagreed finally or not, I would try to see what the terms were within which what the teacher was saying could be true. I learned a great deal from John Logan, and I think I learned a great deal from Donald Justice, and I learned a lot from friends who taught me indirectly, either by talking about poetry or simply by showing me their poetry.

Do you ever miss those days . . . I mean the days in which you could just sit down and talk about poems with your peers?

Sure, it was a lot easier being a student than being a teacher.

What convergence of forces—or whatever phrase you want to come up with—causes the particular poet (in this case you, of course) to be what you are, that brings about the kind of poem you're writing, the kind of commitment you've made, for better or worse—as in marriage.

Well, in answering that I want to separate the time when one *can,* if one chooses to, be part of a workshop or poetry seminar or whatever, and the time that comes later. One of the good things about being part of a group of young poets for me was that at the time no one felt any pressure to publish. There wasn't, for example, the pressure that some people feel now to publish in order to get a teaching job. In those days if one had decent academic credentials—which I did, you see: I had already taken a Masters degree at The University of Chicago, for example—one could count on a teaching job. So there was no pressure to publish, and as I recall my friends and I were not in any hurry to. That's all changed now. Graduate students who write poetry are anxious to publish, perhaps too anxious. Well, in that atmosphere it was possible to think of oneself as simply trying to *learn* to write—trying *all* kinds of different things. In fact, there was a period when if a poet's first book showed an ability to write, the critics were very pleased. Unfortunately, I published my first book just after that period, and my ability to write was held against me openly by several critics who believed the ability to write was somehow contradictory to perception and emotion. In any case I didn't mind, because I do think that it takes ten or twenty years of writing before one has a sense of one's language. I'm not sure that's true of everyone, but it was true for me because, again, I didn't grow up in a house where literature or art were important. No one actively hated them—they simply weren't part of the scene. The south shore of Long Island, out where I grew up, at the time I lived

there, was, as I said, an area inhabited by potato farmers, fishermen, duck farmers, cauliflower farmers, small business men, and commuters—those who rode the trains a long way to New York City for jobs. There was little industry then on Long Island, and that's still true. It was very rural. The ocean, the bay, and the sound all came together in the little town where I grew up, and I think of mine as a happy childhood. But art was no part of it. My notion of music, as I said, was to play a trumpet in the band, and I only played in the orchestra under duress. I felt, I think, very sophisticated to be seriously interested in jazz, but it never occurred to me that there would be another kind of sophistication out of which one might be interested in, say, ballet, or string quartets maybe. Now, I've been lucky and I've discovered things like string quartets and ballet, but as *you* know, having written so many poems about the place where *you* grew up and the kind of life *you* led there, one doesn't suddenly become a different person. One doesn't go away to college and become a different person.

How important is your background as a source? How do those things converge?

My father was an immigrant from the Ukraine and he was a man of great common sense, as so many of our fathers were. And he wouldn't accept criticism of other people very often. He would refuse it by saying, "Well, he has to make a living too." Which is a kind, a very sophisticated kind, of common sense, it seems to me. It's not so much a justification of sin and evil as it is an acceptance of an impure world in which we do the best we can. I think, you know . . . I wasn't writing any poetry to speak of while my father was still alive. There was a time at which I thought maybe my poetry was an attempt to make conversation with him after he had died, and to some extent I tried to do that. I set out at one point to write a book's worth of poems to and about my father. It turned out I only saved thirteen of them and made them into a little section in one of my books. That was a way of trying to be done with what I thought was an ongoing conversation. But you know, in looking back it's not just a question of looking back to familial matters and what my father was like and my mother is like and my sister is like and what my childhood was like, so much as it's a way of accepting attitudes that I can see in a better light by looking back. For example, you know that I recently wrote a couple of poems that have to do with the killing of animals. One is about something I had to do when I did some work on a duck farm—when, after picking up the eggs, I would have to pick up the ducklings that had contracted an extremely contagious disease and kill them by smashing their heads against a tree. A very brutal act, but nonetheless not an act which I thought ugly at the time, though it's terribly ugly to report. Again, many years later in Iowa, having caught a rather large catfish, I was instructed to kill it by hitting it over the head with a hammer. And apparently I couldn't hit it hard enough, because the more I hit it the more it came to life, until finally I managed to kill it. Well, I wrote a poem about the duck-killing episode—or those duck-killing episodes—a poem called **"After the Ducks Went In."** And I wrote a poem about the catfish episode called **"A Fish: On Beauty,"** because it seemed to me that, you know, the more I hit that fish, trying to kill it, the uglier it got. Which is a way of saying that maybe our notions of beauty are notions that are static and dead, and that we think, finally, that life is ugly. Though in fact we shouldn't, and the implication is obviously that what we think is ugly is beautiful, and what we think is beautiful may in fact be in some sense quite ugly. You see, those both came out of reports of experience in which I tried to see what my attitude *really* was, not what my attitude *should* have been.

Any last remarks—about form and content, about your writing from here on? What do you look for in a poem?

Well, I *am* a believer in poetry as content. Now I don't mean content as opposed to form. But I do believe that poetry has content. I don't believe that it's just a form. It's not in my nature to believe that. And I'm partial to discourse and the special wisdom and intelligence that can show up in poetry, but not to the exclusion of other things. When I stopped writing the childishly experimental poetry with which I began, I secretly still thought of myself as being experimental—in content. I still do, though I wouldn't want to announce this too loudly. I'd like to write a poetry which has little if any insistence about it, as little as possible. I would like to write a poetry which doesn't seem either to button-hole the reader, or demand too much allegiance, or demand that too much of the world be given up for the special world of the poem. At the same time, I have never lost my interest in experimental methods. But now I'd like to employ methods which are experimental without necessarily appearing to be.

You know that I was a potter for a while, and I was a photographer for quite some time, and I was a musician for a very long time, and I felt that one of the delightful things about musicians, potters and photographers was that they continually talked to themselves in terms of their craft, and not of their art. In fact, many of the great photographers in this country insist on calling their photographs "pictures." And very often talented jazz musicians will talk about their "songs," which is a pretty low-key word for their compositions. I really believe that the self is very small, very unimportant, and only receives its definition, its value, in terms of things outside the self and people outside the self. I think I *know* now that I really believe it, whereas once I

believed it without knowing I believed it. The next book may be telling. As for plans, I intend to proceed as always on the basis of what I am and what I don't know.

Marvin Bell, Ed Folsom, David Groff, David Hamilton, Dee Morris, and Fred Woodard (interview dates June 12 and 19, 1981)

SOURCE: Bell, Marvin, Ed Folsom, David Groff, David Hamilton, Dee Morris, and Fred Woodard. "Interview with Marvin Bell." *Iowa Review* 12, no. 1 (winter 1981): 2-36.

[*In the following interview, conducted on June 12 and June 19, 1981, Bell explains the theories behind his poetry and discusses some of the work of other poets he admires.*]

PART ONE

[*The Iowa Review*]: *Though one often finds small birds and trees in your poems, not many people, I suppose, have called you a nature poet. Might it be possible to say, that if you are not a nature poet exactly, you are a nature poet inexactly?*

[Bell]: You know, that sounds pretty precise. I grew up in the country. Most people think I'm from New York City because my biography always says that I was born there. I was, but only because that was the nearest hospital. I grew up in a little town called Center Moriches, which might have had as many as 2500 people. I doubt that it has more than 3000 now. It's on the southern shore of eastern Long Island. There were woods across the street, and there was water at the end of every street that went south; and the bay was there, the Great South Bay. The Sound, the ocean, the canals, the creeks—there was one creek that came right up in the middle of town. I used to go down to steal boats for the day.

What did you do out on the Sound that led to your becoming a poet?

Well, my father ran a five-and-ten. And my relationship to the water was the same as that of other people. We either owned boats or borrowed them; and we went out with people who were clammers. We crabbed a lot and fished a lot. By and large, fishermen don't swim, at least not where I come from. They don't think of the water as a place to swim in; they think of it as something to farm. So I grew up without swimming at all; I swim like a stone. When I was little it never dawned on me that it might be foolish to be running around on the muddy deck of a clamming boat with the old guy we called Uncle John, if I couldn't swim. Now I know better.

I never thought of writing poetry, if that's what you're asking. In fact, I never wrote any poetry in high school and I didn't write any poetry to speak of in college. I never thought of being a poet. That wouldn't have been something one would have thought about where I grew up. In fact, there were very few books in the house. There were some condensed versions of *Reader's Digest* novels, as I recall; and there were some encyclopedias which were for the betterment of the children.

Were there hobbies you had with an aesthetic bent to them?

I did a great many things that put me in touch with odd people. For example—this seems as if it might have nothing to do with literature, but I think it does have something to do with it in my case—I became an amateur radio operator. My sister's father-in-law was an amateur radio operator. His call sign was W2EBT. He called himself Two Eggs Bacon and Toast. Sometimes he called himself Elderly, Bald and Toothless. He was a life insurance salesman. Probably to get rid of me after dinner one Thanksgiving at his house, he showed me up to his shack in the attic and gave me earphones and showed me how to work the receiver. Well, one thing led to another and I became an amateur radio operator. I used to handle messages a lot, what they called "traffic."

In code?

In code. It's a lot faster in code. I know that doesn't sound right but actually it is. It's much faster, much surer when there is the possibility of interference. I did a lot of that. Well, in those days, people who were amateur radio operators were almost always odd ducks. Just by virtue of being one, having gotten my license and built my first transmitter and power supply (which was a kind of necessity or otherwise one was looked down upon), just by virtue of those things, I could ride my bicycle to nearby towns and knock on the door of someone whose address I'd taken out of The American Radio Relay League Directory of Hams, and this odd duck would come waddling to the door and he would take me to his odd duck shack and he'd talk odd duck to me for hours.

I also started playing trumpet when I was in the fourth grade and played with all kinds of groups for years and years. I played with a dixieland group on the radio when I was in college. I played with what we used to call combos, with marching bands, and summer bands and orchestras. I was part of a travelling trumpet trio for a while and did solos and played with brass quintets and sextets. Just all kinds of things. Then, later on, I gave a lot of attention to photography, what used to be called "creative photography." I was a potter too.

When did you begin writing poetry?

I started writing seriously after college. That would have been about 1959. I started writing it more seriously when I got to Chicago, which would have been about 1960.

Can you remember when you began reading poetry?

Oh, I started reading in college. I can remember reading a poem in an issue of *New World Writing* which interested me because the author was identified as an ex-paratrooper, I think—or something like that. Anyway, it was something macho and it reassured me that I would not be in trouble for reading this poem. The first line of it was "Fuzz clings to the huddle"; and the last was, "We rise and leave with Please." It wasn't about football as far as I could tell. I had no idea what it was about. So I went to Dr. Finch, who was our creative writing teacher at Alfred University and a cellist in the orchestra in which I played, and asked him what the poem meant. He said, "I don't know much about modern poetry; ask Miss Tupper." So I went to Miss Tupper, who was my history of English literature teacher, and she said, "Oh, I don't know much about modern poetry. Have you asked Dr. Finch?" So I never got an answer; but, of course, I was foolish to think there was one.

What was your experience like in the Workshop here at Iowa?

It was fun. Many of the students in the Workshop now are older than other students; but then all of the students in the Workshop were older than other students. It was a somewhat disreputable thing to do. If it wasn't the only graduate writing program or the only community of its kind in the country, it was certainly the only one that anyone knew about. And the people here had all been out of school a while. They had been in the Army or had been bumming around or had held a job here or there. And they were all odd ducks, too, or they wouldn't have ended up in such a place.

This was in the early sixties?

Yes, I came here in February of '61. Then you still had people on the GI bill you see, from the Korean War. Don Justice was the poet. Paul Engle ran the Workshop and also helped teach. His way of teaching was to leave the room a lot. We met him in the temporary building known as UTA, University Temporary A, which was behind the Union which now of course is a parking lot. It had a hot water flushing toilet. There was a back room which was the office. The phone would ring in the back room and Paul would jump up, run to the back room and answer the phone, and then he would come back and announce something new, such as the Iowa Natural Gas Fellowship.

But Paul was amazing, not only for his ability to raise money but for his ability to join in a discussion, after having missed most of it, and say something absolutely right. Don will confirm this for you. His instincts and his spontaneous responses were very good.

So Don was the teacher, when you were here.

That's right, I had one serious teacher of poetry writing before Don—that was John Logan in Chicago. At the downtown center of the University of Chicago first, and then in a group that was called "the poetry seminar" but which was not, in fact, a course. It was just a bunch of poets around Chicago—led by Logan—who got together periodically. In fact, we just had a reunion in Chicago, a bunch of us: Dennis Schmitz was part of that and Charlie Simic, Bill Knott, Naomi Lazard, Barbara Harr, Bill Hunt, Roger Aplon, a whole bunch of people.

Who else was teaching on a visiting basis that you remember?

Here in the Workshop? Oh, nobody. The Workshop was much smaller; it was one section. There weren't any sections; there was just us. There were enough people in the Workshop by the end of my three year stay so that it was hoped a few would cut each class. Indeed, one could count on it. Nobody wanted everyone to come to class; that would make a few too many.

When I was invited back here to teach in the fall of 1965, Paul had apparently been accepting people out of his hotel suite in New York City. We had ninety poets in the Workshop. I'm not making this up—ninety poets and three teachers. I had a Form of Poetry class which met in a chemistry amphitheater. I remember standing before them in my Army crew-cut and saying, "Well, I have two more weeks to put in in the Army. So, I'll see you in two weeks." I really did. I had to go back to the Army for two weeks.

What kind of poetry were you writing when you were here as a student?

Obscure poetry. I fancied myself an experimental poet; I was pretty sure I was an experimental poet because my poems didn't make sense. Of course, I thought they made sense; but I don't think now that they made sense in the way that poems ought to make sense. I could write poems that made sense; but those weren't the poems that interested me. I haven't the foggiest notion why they accepted me. I think again that things were so different in those days that anyone who had been writing for a while and, indeed, publishing, as I had—not in good magazines, but somewhat widely; I had been writing reviews and had even started a little magazine in Rochester called *Statements*—anybody who'd been doing things like that was odd enough and committed enough to be let in, I think. That's all I can guess.

So between the time you were an undergraduate at Alfred, professing to know nothing at all or caring hardly anything about poetry and the time you spent a year at Syracuse as a graduate student in journalism you had somehow gotten into it.

Oh, I was always interested in language. I mean, I edited the school newspaper and I wrote all kinds of things. Again, you have to realize how stupid I was, coming from that little town where people, by and large, didn't go to college and not having come from a home full of books. I did get books from the town library. But you have to remember how stupid I was. I went to college thinking the people who majored in English studied grammar. I actually thought that, until my junior year. I knew that people read books but I didn't know they studied them.

While in high school, you discovered the town library?

Oh, yes. There was a little house which was opened for a couple of hours a few nights a week and was manned by a volunteer from Brookhaven National Lab. I would go and take books out, mostly philosophy. And then I'd bring them back late and he would cut my fines.

I used to read things—you'll laugh—used to read things like books by John Dewey. I was more interested in things like that. I never read much fiction and I still don't. Except for graduate school, I have never read much fiction. My wife reads everything and she tells me about it. But I like books of ideas. I think it may come from being that smalltown boy who had a vague sense—and I want to emphasize "vague"—that there might be another kind of world somewhere. Therefore, one had to instruct oneself, so that one would have opportunities. I liked literature which had an instructional side to it, and I still do.

Occasionally, you come to passages like that in much older poetry. A passage in Sir Gawain and the Green Knight *will tell you how to skin a deer.*

Now that's really useful. But I like instruction about thinking, how to think about things, or instructions about morals and ethics—ethics in particular. My poetry is probably full of that stuff.

A lot of your nature poetry will say such things as here's a way you can think about a tree . . . and, here's another way you can think about a tree.

That's right. I like that. I find that fascinating and I can remember, even as a kid, working in the five-and-ten, someone would say something to me—I mean the most innocuous thing, something about where something could be found in the store or what I should do next or what I should go find in the basement. There would be something odd to my mind about the way he or she had said it; and as I carried out the chore, I would think to myself, if he had used this word instead of that word, the tone would have been entirely different. And, of course, I just ascribed that to my own neurosis. I didn't realize that there were all kinds of people who did that and they were called poets.

This has to do with what you said earlier, that the poems you wrote when you were in the Workshop seem now to you to make sense but not to make the kind of sense you think a poem should make. That is an interesting statement because, for me, your poems make a kind of sense. I mean, that's one way of describing them. I would say your poems make a kind of sense before I'd say your poems make sense. It's always been my suspicion, that, as I read one of your poems and have to work so hard to make the jumps and connections, that those connections that I work for to make the poem open for me are connections that for you make perfect sense.

Yeah. There was a wonderful poet, who died fairly recently, named Ed Mayo. Lived over in Des Moines. He used to create an annual event, a poetry day at Drake University. He would get a bunch of us to come, poets from around Iowa, and we would bring a few students with us. We'd all read to an auditorium which would be sparsely filled. Sparsely filled? Which would be fairly empty. Mostly we'd be reading to ourselves. We'd play jokes on each other and so forth. He always liked my poems; and at the end of the evening, after we'd had pizza at his house or something, as we were going out to our cars, he would always come out on the lawn with me and put his arm around me, and, as he'd walk me to the car, he would praise my poetry. Then he would suggest that if I could only put in the connections, if I could slow down and not think so fast, it would be even better. I would always promise to try. But I must confess that the connections do seem absolutely obvious to me.

I wouldn't want you to slow down and work all the connections out because, obviously, what makes the poem work for your reader is the involvement that's necessary to make those connections, to work for the connections. But my sense has always been that your motivation was not to make the reader work. I've always sensed a kind of surprise on your part when people say, "But there's a jump here that I just can't see." Do you think there is, on your part, an increasing attempt to make those connections somewhat clearer? I find, for example, your poems are becoming longer and more leisurely in pace, in this latest collection particularly.

I hope you're right. Again, though, it's hard for me to know because, if something seems unclear in my poems, I always try to make it clear: So the jumps that remain in the poem seem to me easy steps rather than jumps.

My idea of how things are written now—I wouldn't have put it this way ten years ago—is something like this: one writes something down, then one writes the next thing. That's my theory of composition, I think. Now, the trick there is that the next thing that one writes must be something that interests one in sequence. It's less a jump than an extension. I mean, you can't put down just anything; you must put down something you're genuinely interested in, involved in. But how can you trust it merely to be the next thing? Well, it must occur to you for some reason. Now if the poem pays attention to itself, then that means the poet is paying attention to these things and making the connections. If not now, later. It's what Bill Stafford refers to in an essay as "the coherence of the self." You write down one thing and then write the next thing. The rhetoric teachers are going to be furious.

As a rhetoric teacher, I have often said much the same thing, except I will add that the one rule of composition is that the next thing you say has to make sense in terms of the last thing you have said.

Right. If not then, later.

Mostly "right then," in rhetoric. But what is the unit of a poem for you? Is it a statement, like a sentence?

Oh. I don't know that I can answer exactly because I don't think in terms of units. I can talk of poetry in terms of units. I can talk about metrical units, or syntactical units, or the line or the stanza; but I don't exactly think about it that way myself. I think it's more a matter of voice. Voice in poetry depends on phrases, not on words, and phrases make up sentences. So, if one is writing in lines, the line and the sentence and the way in which they hold hands makes a difference, obviously. Everything makes a difference; the rhythms make a difference, even if one is writing in so-called free verse. Auden, you know, published a list of what he thought a person should do to become a poet: and the poet was not only to read certain books and write certain kinds of poems but was also supposed to have a garden and a pet. I can't remember whether he includes this in his list, but it always seemed to me to be an advantage to play a musical instrument.

Because of the phrasing?

Yeah. I think it helps one's ear. Reading poetry helps one's ear, especially reading formal poetry at first. But it does become intuitive after a while. I mean, when Miles Davis plays a trumpet solo, he's not counting.

You mentioned poetry making the kind of sense that for you a poem should *make. I'm wondering what that is for you. What is the way a poem should make sense?*

Well, this is hard to say. Poetry is probably mostly about what life feels like. But, in order to create in poems this precise emotion, something else has to be precise first. What has to be precise first is the plot of the poem. I *think* people still call it a plot. The words have to correspond in the first place to their denotations, even though they may have been picked as much for their connotations. What is suggested can't be clear unless what is actually said is clear first. That obscure poetry I was writing way-back-when offered a vague content; it was word play. I haven't gotten over word play and hope not to, but it wasn't much more than word play. It was pretty good in the way it sounded. I mean, it sounded and looked on the page rather interesting; but it didn't make much sense. This is hard to explain; maybe if I come at it obliquely. I think when young poets are obscure, they're usually obscure out of fear. Anytime you say anything directly to someone, you can be hated for it. You can at least be argued with. You can be made fun of—that especially. So it's much safer, in a way, to find a technique that sneers at clarity and appears to be superior *because* of that sneering. But really it's just fear, the fear of saying something straight. But that doesn't mean saying a flat thing that has about it no depth and which leads to nothing else.

I want to back up a bit. I'm thinking about the implied analogy between music and your writing. Your obscure poetry reminds me of learning the scales, so to speak. Then as you take yourself more seriously, trying to make poetry make sense, you began to play with those scales to develop a melodic line. All this brings me to the question of your early training in music and your performance of various types of music: were you conscious of moving from one type to the next, from dixieland jazz, to marching band music, combo jazz, et cetera?

Oh, I was very aware of the differences. The reason I gave up music . . . I started giving it up in high school. I was going to go to the Oberlin Conservatory and decided not to. In effect, I gave up music then, though I kept playing for years and years. I gave it up because I knew I wouldn't be good enough. I was pretty good, to be honest. I had been trained in so-called serious music and I also played jazz, which is what I wanted to do because who wants to be a trumpeter in an orchestra. It's like being the male in ballet of twenty years ago; you're just a leaning post, you know. So I would have wanted to play jazz, but I knew that I would never be good enough. For a number of reasons. But the most important of which was that, when I took solos, I saw notes; and that's a terrible limitation. You can't play that way; it has to be more intuitive than that. My solos weren't any good. My solos on the piano were much better than my solos on the trumpet and I couldn't play the piano. I never had a piano lesson in my life. I only played the piano late at night when the pianist wanted to dance.

As the years have gone by and my poetry has changed, I've tried to find what my content is, what my forms are. When I came to the Workshop in 1961, there was not that much free verse being written. It didn't appear on the worksheets that often. In order to justify my writing free verse, I had to be able to defend it in the terms used by formalists. So I learned everything I could about meter; and someone would arch an eyebrow and say, "This appears to be in free verse," talking about a poem of mine that appeared on the worksheet. And I'd say, "Oh, no. It's in sprung accentuals with variant lines." I can remember that I was admired for breaking the rules but getting away with it. That's the way they put it. Now, it's gone whole hog the other way; one is grateful for a metrical poem to put on the worksheet, occasionally.

Were you reading Williams at that time?

I sort of read everybody. Williams was always an interest of mine, but I read widely. I read everything but not in any order.

My question about Williams has to do with things you've been saying: the sequencing of the poem or making sure that the next image follows from the other though not necessarily in logical progression. One of my favorite poems of yours—I think it was in The Iowa Review—*"Someone's got to say Williams . . ."*

Oh, yeah.

You remember it? It ends something like, "While you, Jersey, you just tapped your foot and kept your head." And there's that wonderful sense of "tapping the foot" and not "using the head" but "keeping" the head. It's always struck me as a description, not only of Williams' poetry, which I think it is, but a description of your inheritance from Williams' poetry.

Well, maybe so. I'm glad you remembered that poem. I didn't put it in a book and I'd forgotten about it.

Do you think that Williams gains in clarity as he gets older?

Oh, yeah. Williams is a great example of one of the reasons I was glad to become a poet. It's an art that one can get better at. To go back to music, I remember Cat Anderson, the trumpet player who was the scourge of the high registers. I went to see Basie in Birdland or Basin Street one time; Cat Anderson had no lip left. He couldn't get above the staff. He would sort of put up his horn to play solos, but the second man would cover for him. There are a lot of fields in which that is true; there's a peak and after that it's downhill. Well, it's not that way with poetry or, at least, it doesn't have to be. Williams is one of the great examples; he's not even that good until he gets old. I mean, he's pretty good; but, hell, you know . . .

We've been tracing your growth toward being a poet and toward taking poetry seriously, as something one might do. Was there any time in your development when you began to get a sense of an American poetic tradition behind you, a tradition that you tapped into?

I was always aware of it. I mean, you know, I'd read everybody as I say. I admire so many poets that the list doesn't mean anything in terms of influences. I admire Emily Dickinson tremendously; I think I know her poetry pretty well. But I can't say that I can show any results in my own writing from having admired her work. I guess I need to go back a bit and say that the contemporary poets who I read with great pleasure when I was first starting to write more and more seriously, in Syracuse and then in Rochester and then in Chicago, were the Beat poets. That probably would be surprising to many people; but my first wife, or the woman who would become my first wife, and a friend of mine named Al Sampson—who was also a graduate student in journalism at Syracuse and who also quit to go take an English degree at Chicago—and I would frequent a bad Italian restaurant. We'd go there early in the day, and have an antipasto for lunch and a pizza for supper. And we'd just sit there in front of this terrible mural of Venice and read *Howl* to one another or poems by Corso or Ferlinghetti.

I have to mention again that I always liked odd ducks among people—and strange people among ducks—and when I went to college, Alfred University turned out to be a lucky choice. I know I sound like I'm getting off the subject but I'll circle around. At Alfred University, which is a private university, there is also a State College of Ceramics actually contained within the private university. The State College of Ceramics has a design department; and the design department was, and pretty much still is, the freakiest thing you ever saw. When Moholy-Nagy created a likeness to the *Bauhaus* in Chicago, he refused to have grades or degrees; one just showed one's work and at the end of the year you were told whether or not you could stay. Well, when Moholy died, his Chicago version of the *Bauhaus* was in financial jeopardy and so they linked up with the Illinois Institute of Technology and became what's now known as the Institute of Design. A number of the teachers, being idealistic about the old system, rebelled against the notion of degrees and grades and fled. Some of them, for no reason that anyone could ever explain to me, ended up in the design department at the State College of Ceramics of Alfred University. Well, these kids on the streets of New York are no fools; they realized that if they went to the State College of Ceramics they wouldn't have to pay tuition. In those days there was no tuition at a state school in New York. So these wonderful artists from New York, who were all absolutely off-the-wall, showed up in the design department of the College of Ceramics of Alfred University. I

wasn't worthy of their company, but I knew enough to know that these were special people and that they had their eye on something; it wasn't the same thing that most people had their eye on. So I watched them from a distance. Gradually, I became friends with them. I learned a lot just by watching them. They were very strange people.

Did they introduce you to the Beats?

They were strange people at a time when there were fewer strange people. At least it seemed so, certainly in colleges. I had been in and out of the Village—I was a Long Islander. I had a sense of the music world there. In those days, a person might be called a Bohemian. The Beats were picked up by the newspapers and made famous because they were "Bohemian." Their poetry interested me because it was defiant. You may not remember this, but when Paul Carroll founded *Big Table* magazine in Chicago, the title was provided by Jack Kerouac who got up one morning and saw a note he'd written to himself. He'd just moved into a new apartment—the note said, "Buy a big table." So he sent a telegram to Paul Carroll: "Call it Big Table." The first issue of *Big Table* was the censored issue of *The Chicago Review,* which Paul Carroll had been editing and which was to contain works by Ginsberg, Kerouac, Corso, Whalen, Orlofsky, John Rechy, perhaps John Ashbery and so forth. In one of the darker days of the University of Chicago, they banned the issue. Anyway, as I recall, there were benefit readings in San Francisco, Chicago and New York by Ginsberg, Corso and others to raise money for *Big Table.* And the newspapers made this front page news. Corso came out on the stage in one of these cities, walked to the microphone to begin the evening and said, "Fried shoes." The people went crazy. That was the strangest thing they'd ever heard, the wildest event of their lives. You have to remember what we looked like then, you know.

Did you ever go back from the Beat poets to Whitman?

Oh, sure, yeah. I always thought of Whitman and Dickinson as being polarities somehow. But that's really inhibiting. I mean, if you start thinking of Whitman and Dickinson as being polarities, then you feel you have to join up and there's no way to join up. They're so much what they are that it's better not to think about them as antitheses.

One of the things I think I see you admiring in Dickinson is her rebellious attitude, a kind of insistence on herself that Whitman has and that the Beats have too.

Oh, absolutely. I've said it elsewhere: I would love to have been born in Defiance, Ohio. Wouldn't that be great! "I'm from Defiance and I ought to know."

And yet that doesn't seem to be the stance of your poetry, which moves away from a simple defiant mood to a more steady or stable attitude.

Corrective, I think. I think I'm often corrective; in fact, I think my poems often begin in the middle of something, as if I had just thought something and now I'm refuting it or as if I'm hearing someone else's statement and am refuting it.

That's often how the lines work, isn't it? You get from one line to another by refuting something that . . .

Yes, that's right.

I'm thinking, too, about how often your lines occur to me as linear, as in linear improvisation in jazz. That is, I often pick a tonal quality of a word or phrase and find myself going back and forth through the poem in search of the tonal logic as I do with music, in search of resonance.

That's true, that is the way music works. I wouldn't say it's deliberate; it is intuitive, I guess. But I think it's there. One needs that sort of thing, the more so if one writes so-called free verse because that's what rhyme and meter do for the poem. They create effects that harmonize with or play off of other effects.

Might it not also do something else? In formal poetry, you always know why the line ends where it does. With the free verse line, you're always invited to ask the question. Doesn't the end of any free verse line suggest that it might have ended elsewhere?

Absolutely. And the answer, I think, is yes, it could have ended elsewhere. But there is a further answer: that is, because it is the way it is, it creates this effect and not the other effect.

But as you read it, do you find yourself reading the lines differently from time to time, like a jazz musician, improvising within a form?

I think, yes. There is a way of using a line to create momentum; and what it does is to create momentum first for the poet and later for the reader. Some of my poems are, in that sense, jazzy; others are not. It takes a short line to create an effect which seems jazz-like. Once you write long lines, it doesn't work out that way, I don't think. But I'm guessing.

Like Williams jazzing up Whitman by breaking those lines up into short lines.

Oh, see now, Williams is a genius. I mean, he realized that his so-called triadic stanza isn't a stanza at all; it's just three margins. It's brilliant and I envy it. I would like to use it. I think I understand it and know how to do it; but one doesn't dare. Some people have dared, but perhaps not wisely because Williams owns it. It's going to be another two hundred years before he won't

own it. Maybe I can overcome that sense of his prepossessing it. The trick to his three-line stanza is that his syntax is continually various; the length of the phrase varies a great deal and the syntax contains great variety. So you're always being surprised by where a line ends and very often by where a line begins. It's just that he never lets up for a moment. The trick to that three-line stanza is that it can make prose into poetry. You can do it yourself: take any piece of prose and put it in three-line stanzas but make sure that the lines are not equal, that you sometimes have longer phrases and sometimes shorter phrases, that you stop one line and start another in the middle of a phrase, occasionally, so that you interrupt yourself a lot, and you'll turn it into poetry. Figure it this way: if the end of a line is special by virtue of being the end of the line, and if the beginning of a line is special by virtue of being the beginning of a line, and if the first line of a stanza is special by virtue of its being the first line of the stanza, if the last line of a stanza is special by virtue of its being the last line of the stanza, and if the only middle line of a stanza is special by virtue of its being the only line between two others—then how many effects are taking place in what period of time in a poem written in short lines in three-line stanzas? It's astonishing!

Then to complicate things further, think of each of those lines in the triadic stanza containing a variable foot.

So-called, yeah. It's fun to set a metronome going while Williams reads those poems on records. It's not possible to read all the phrases in "The Descent," say, in the same amount of time. But it almost comes out. That is, sometimes a phrase takes what you might call two measures and sometimes a phrase takes a half a measure, so you could think of it as being equivalent to changes in time in a piece of music. The music, say, is in four-four time and suddenly you have a six-eight measure. Happens all the time. The real problem, of course, is that Williams' terminology was just a hoax. He was forced to defend his practice of free verse by using the terms of metricians, and so he had to continue to speak about feet.

Where does a poem start for you? With a thought, a sound, an argument, a rhythm?

Well, it's changing, I'm glad to say, but for years I would have had to say it begins with some words that make some sense but seem to want to make more sense—not just words out of syntax but some words that make a piece of syntax. It might be a phrase, it might be most of a sentence, it might be a whole sentence, it might be one line or two lines. These words have about them an emotional resonance. They also seem to be *located* somehow, but the circumstances of their location are yet to be discovered.

This is very difficult to explain, but after running this morning I was sitting in the bathtub reading the poetry of D. H. Lawrence. The bathtub is perfect, if the water's warm, for Lawrence. He's so florid, but I was liking a lot of it. The word coming out at me was *vain*—not about Lawrence, but it's a word that he uses a lot, I think maybe with more meaning than he intends it to have. There was something about his use of *vain* that I wanted to put in a location. As it happens I don't have any more ideas about that, no more words about it. It might not come to anything at all.

I would love to get more people into my poetry. You asked in the very beginning of this conversation about how much of a nature poet I am. All poets are nature poets I guess. If a poet were to write only about machines we could probably make an argument that he or she was a nature poet. But it's hard to put people into poems, except for oneself or an imagined self. It's very difficult to put them in the poems and not just use them, to put them in the poems and make them any more than stick figures.

Your new volume seems much more aware of people, generally, and to care more for expressing our "human condition." So let me ask whether you see yourself as a political poet, inexactly.

Well, to this extent: even when I stopped writing obscurely way back when, I secretly considered myself an experimental poet. I figured that I was a poet of content, in a way that I thought was experimental. I still think I'm a poet of content. That isn't the way poetry is talked about, alas. When we think about poetry in the academy, we kind of assume that it is talked about in terms of content. But except for rare occasions, poems are *not* talked about in terms of content. Think of what reviews and critical articles are like; they generalize the particulars of a poet's book into broad statements about style and theme. But the real liveliness of poetry, and the meaning in poems, is in the individual poem, in the particulars of a poem. Even the notion of talking about a book may be harmful. We should probably confine ourselves to speaking poem by poem, but we want to learn about people and so we try to look at all the poems to see what the person is like.

Well, I still secretly—and I guess it's not so secret anymore if I say it—think of myself as an experimental poet, and the experimentation resides in what I do with content. In the poem, **"These Green-Going-to-Yellow,"** for example, what interests me is an argument that's being made about our conception of God. Not that I had that argument to begin the poem. If I were to summarize some of the argumentative aspects of that poem, I'd start by saying that it's trying to suggest a greater involvement with people. Even in the middle of New York City someone has planted a gingko, why? The poem supposes it's because when those leaves fall on the sidewalk they look like hands that are treating us

more gently than any person ever would. Later on, I say "we have no experience to make us see the gingko or any other tree," which sounds to me like a very odd thing to say. On the other hand it sounds to me like an inevitable thing to say because whatever our experience of the gingko or other trees *is*, it's experience from a distance.

We have no experience to see the gingko as gingko, rather than as something that relates to ourselves. We see the gingko as ourselves in the gingko. It's an insight that goes all through your work. I think back to "I wanted to see the self, so I looked at the mulberry." Much of your "nature poetry" is a very interesting argument with the pathetic fallacy, back and forth: that we do see ourselves in nature and that we know we can't see ourselves in nature. The poems work on that tension, often playing with it, saying yeah I see this and this, and I also see this and this, and therefore we really don't see anything, do we, except ourselves. What we say about it is what we see.

That sounds right to me.

Your poems are filled with leisurely moments in which, say, you listen to a tree, with all the ironies on the surface: "I know I'm not listening to this tree because trees don't laugh, do they?" And the next stanza begins, "In spring, when the trees laugh . . ." There's a wonderful give and take where you extend out into the trees and then look back and say, "of course we don't extend out into trees."

There was a point early in my writing when I would have thought of myself as a metaphysical poet. Maybe I should still, but in any case at that time I would have thought of metaphysical poets partly in terms of a balancing of opposites. That can be just a trick; again, I don't hold that out as an advantage necessarily.

The way I see **"Stars Which See, Stars Which Do Not See"** *is in exactly the terms we've been using, that there is a way of personifying stars and there's a way of seeing them as cold, isolated bodies that may even be dead. The scientific way of looking at them, and also the personifying and emotive way of looking at them.*

Oh sure, that is the way they work. That's how the title works for that particular poem which is a God's-in-his-heaven-all's-right-with-the-world scene down by the river on a Sunday morning. But, as the poem suggests, there are undercurrents. My big son Nathan wrote a make-believe review for his school newspaper once of what was supposed to be a record album by himself, since he's a musician, and he called the title, with unerring accuracy an archer might envy, "Stars in the Skies, Stars in My Eyes." He always had the ability to see through me.

"These Green-Going-to-Yellow" balances similar opposites.

Yeah, that's true. Michael Anania, the poet and fiction writer from Chicago, told me about something he had seen at the Edward Hopper show in New York City. I've been to the Hopper show, but I guess I haven't looked at these sketches. Michael says there are some sketches for paintings in which Hopper wrote in the colors; he thinks that Hopper wrote in, in one area of one drawing, "green going to yellow." I suspect he wrote something more like "green to yellow."

When you were putting this book together, when did you decide that that would be the title poem?

I'm afraid I have to admit that I thought it would be the title when I wrote the poem. I thought, "This has got to be the title of the book."

Why is that?

It sounds relevant for its content, but really I was in love with it as a phrase. It's an odd phrase. I've always liked titles that are odd.

And it seems appropriate, because in this book you appear to be more content to be in the middle of things. So many of these poems begin and stay in the middle of a situation. They're kind of green-going-to-yellow poems, in a number of ways. And it's a middle life book.

I hope you're right. That is, I hope it turns out to have been only the middle of my life.

The poems in the middle section go back to something you used to do a lot but didn't do at all, I think, in **Stars Which See**—*titles that move directly into the first line.*

I like titles which offer a little surprise in the space between the title and the first line. One of the surprises can turn out to be that the poem has already begun. Another thing you asked before was how a poem begins for me and, as is the case with most poets, most poems begin from a phrase. Sometimes that phrase is the title.

"These Green-Going-to-Yellow" . . .

No, no. There the phrase comes out of the middle of the poem.

One of the most surprising titles for me is **"A Motor."**

I also like off-handed titles, when the poem weighs a lot, somehow. This is a poem that is very serious and goes on for some ways. It begins with the sound of a plane in the air—a motor. Of course, it must have more emotional resonance than that or one wouldn't keep it; and you can come up with as many connotations for it as I can. We all contain a kind of biological motor that can give out. I found a title for an old poem this morning which I would have put in this book if I could have finished it. I changed two or three words and redid the last sentence; and I found a title in the middle of the poem after I had changed one word. I changed "water" to "winter." Then I had the title; it comes over parts of two lines: **"Feet in Winter, Head in the Sun."** It's a poem in which I'm standing out in the backyard thinking about something that happened when I was a kid. I used to go to Yankee Stadium for double-headers, thanks to an old lady I knew named Jessie Quince who had been a rabid New York Yankee fan. She had once lived in an apartment building with Bill Dickey and Frank Crosetti and a lot of the great Yankees from that time. She worked for my father—she was another odd duck. She was divorced, which was almost unheard of; no one knew a divorced person where I came from. Her house had burned down and so she had put a tar roof over her basement, and she lived in the basement. She had no intention of rebuilding her house; the basement was all the room she needed. She had a coin collection at the time her house burned down. Every once in a while she'd give me some coins, some of which would have been melted from the fire—wonderful. Every year for my birthday, she'd take me to a double-header at Yankee Stadium. And, sometimes, I would stand outside by the clubhouse afterwards hoping DiMaggio or, at least, Snuffy Stirnweiss would come out and I could get an autograph. One day there was a swarming and a worried-looking policeman but it was only—and you must remember that I was a young boy—it was only Humphrey Bogart and Lauren Bacall. But, in the poem, as I stand out back, listening to the gutters rumble with thawing snow, Bogart's face comes back, with all its ugliness, rather than the heroes' faces. So, I'm standing there in the water; it's a three-day-old snow, just melting. So, I changed the word "water" to "winter." Instead of standing in water; I'm now standing in winter. It's mythic.

But in finding that word, in finding "winter," you were controlled by the dimensions of the first word, rhythmically and in sound.

Oh, yeah; one of the tricks is to forget that damn first word. You're right. It's hard to substitute for a word a word that contains more syllables. Unless you've made a rhythmic mistake in the first place. Sometimes all it takes is a word or two words or three words to fix up a poem or one word here and two words there. A great portion of the process of revision, for me, is letting enough time elapse so that I arrive at the point at which the poem has already arrived, so that I can see it and accept it for what it is. Before that, my revision tends to be a strain; it tends to be a violent changing of the poem, which won't work. I have to let poems lay around. Do poems lay around or lie around? I should have been an English major.

They lay around, naturally.

Most poems lay around. You guys don't know it, but I published a poem in Kim Merker's limited edition, ***Things We Dreamt We Died For*** which is called **"What I Did in Paris in the Twenties"** and the first line is "I lay around."

That may be saying more than you meant to say.

Or I may have meant everything it says. Paris in the twenties was very exciting.

The most muted aspect of your poetry for me is its music, as opposed to the modulation of a speaking voice. You seem to cultivate an odd duck's way of talking about whatever is around.

I'm trying to use a voice that *is* a voice, not of the page but of the vocal chords, a voice one can hear.

I find that particularly evident in this book. I mean, this book seems to be held together by that voice. In every poem, I can hear that same voice telling me the poem, whereas, in **Stars Which See,** *I heard very different voices. Even when the pace picks up here, I hear the same voice tell the poems.*

I hope you're right.

And it has a certain social validity to it; that is, it's not anybody else's voice.

If that's true, then I'm lucky. ***Stars Which See, Stars Which Do Not See*** is a pretty book even when it's quarreling with the reader, or with the self, or with concepts. Its poems are beautiful, even elegant. And I knew that. I'm pleased with its being like that. But the poems I have written since are not pretty in that sense. They have to be authenticated by means of the voice and by means of the physical evidence of the world that each poem offers. If they are not, they'll fall on their faces.

Was there a period you went through after **Stars** *when you were not writing much?*

It's happened after every book. Boy, how I wish it wouldn't. But it happened after this book, too; an involuntary silence.

Are you waiting for that voice to clear away?

I think that must be part of it. It's hard not to write a poem that sounds like what you've been writing. I am beginning to write again.

Do you have steady habits of writing, times of day?

I wish I did. I think it's good for people to have such habits. I don't. I tend to boil over on my own schedule, an erratic schedule. All I can be sure of is that I love to write when I'm writing. It just plain feels good; I enjoy it. That is, if poems worth saving are coming out. I want the mind to be doing things, somehow, things it can only do in poems. Whatever they are.

What are they?

I was trying to escape. You know, Williams says in the beginning of "Asphodel"; he says, "It is difficult to get the news from poems yet men die miserably every day for lack of what is found there." And, of course, those are ironic lines because the man who's going to die if news can't be found in poems is Williams, in this case, because he's trying to confess something. And he wants it understood and he wants it accepted. In fact, he wants to be patted on the head and told, "That's alright, dear, I love you anyway." But I should add that somewhere else Williams says something about finding truth only in poems. I believe that there's some area of truth that *can* only be found in poems. I really believe that. Again, maybe it's just in my nature to believe that. Remember, I always like things which are instructional, even corrective. I always like things which constitute a moral engagement with the world or, at least, an interest in ethics. So, it may just be in my nature.

Here we go back to content again.

It's the crust of the poem, I mean, if a poem is only music, what chance does it have? Music is better music. That the poem aspires to the condition of music is, to me—forgive me—a limited notion of poetry. I think it aspires to something else.

Off and on, in casual conversation, you have made remarks like, "That's poetry." "That's not poetry." "You can tell that's a line of poetry." "That's prose." I wonder when you're making judgments like that . . .

Poetry has something to do with a quality of imagination, I think. Now, it can be bad poetry. But, when I say, "That's poetry." "That's not poetry," I'm making a distinction of genre. Okay? It can be slight poetry. It can be useless poetry. For example—and I know this is heresy—but I think many of the ideas in the poetry of Wallace Stevens, who was considered a poet of ideas, to be essentially useless ideas. That's a whole category of ideas in my thinking: *useless ideas,* ideas which aren't ideas at all, unless you wear special glasses. I think that Williams is a much smarter poet than Stevens. I'll get a lot of letters about that. But I think one of the tests of the intelligence is its ability to extend its labors. And where does one extend one's labors? Into the theoretical world that depends on words or into the world of physical evidence? It seems to me far more difficult and profound to extend them into the world of physical evidence.

That's what you mean by useful, that the ideas connect with what one calls the world?

Even as I say it, I realize that the word, "useful," isn't quite accurate; but, yes, ideas which are at least engaged, somehow, with the physical world.

Williams is always talking about things being grounded, whereas Stevens is always working up toward or into the blue.

But Stevens is well organized, as a good executive would have to be. One has the feeling that, if Stevens had given some of his actuarial tables to Williams, Williams would have messed them all up, in some interesting way, and he would have charged everybody the wrong premiums.

Or he would have incorporated them into a poem.

That's right. You know the famous interview with Mike Wallace—of all people—he reads a passage from *Paterson* and says, "That sounds like a shopping list." And Williams says, "It is."

Then there's the report of the well-digging: "two feet of shale and . . ."

But Williams knew when to stop. In my opinion, Charles Olson didn't know when to stop. Williams always did something with the facts but Olson's facts took over his mind, I think.

A poet I admire very much among contemporary poets—and it seems difficult, somehow, to mention his name because he died recently—is James Wright. Everybody will be mentioning his name, with good reason. But long before he died I had become terribly involved with poems of his, in several books, particularly *Two Citizens* and *To A Blossoming Pear Tree*. His whole sense of what poetry is appeals to me a great deal.

Ethical reasons, there too, right?

Well, yeah, though he isn't beset by as much thinking about things as I am. He feels his way through things more than I usually do.

But there's a moral edge.

Oh, absolutely, that's right, yeah; indeed, he even says things in poems which pay homage to his readings in the classics and his readings in moralistic texts.

He disavowed Two Citizens *in an interview in* APR.

Yeah, well, two of his friends convinced him it was a bad book; but they were wrong. For one thing, that book contains one of the best poems I know, a poem called "The Old WPA Swimming Pool in Martins Ferry, Ohio," which begins, "I am almost afraid to write down / This thing." It's an incredible poem and it's in *Two Citizens*. And there are others, the ars poetica that begins the book is pretty interesting, I think. He says something very telling in it. He's talking at one point about his Aunt Agnes who is a sloppy woman, a woman one would not be attracted to ordinarily; and he talks about his uncle who's married to her. "He's one of the heroes of love," he says, "because I know he lay down with Agnes at least twice." He goes on like that; and, of course, he's setting you up because, as it turns out, a bunch of boys chased a goat one day, and threw stones at it. The goat goes up into an alley and here's Agnes. Agnes gathers the goat up into her arms and protects it. Well, of course, Agnes was terrific. In the same poem, he says at one point, "Reader we had a lovely language. We would not listen."

PART TWO

Marvin, you talked about the influence of Dewey; and I've wondered how seriously to take that. I mean, we've talked about the ethical aspect of your poetry. My memory of Dewey and ethics is that Dewey was a pragmatist. After the First World War, most of Dewey's followers thought that ethical element reflected a permutation of New England puritanism; and yet most could agree that his ethics were those of a practical man, as he moved through various ethical considerations, in education, in aesthetics and so on. So when I come back to the business of ethics in your poetry, having your remarks about Dewey to think back on, I want to know what you took from Dewey.

I'll tell you why I ask the question: I find a kind of polarity in a lot of your poetry. That is, you'll take a position and then, very soon afterwards, you introduce the opposite of that position. Later you'll attempt to make a synthesis in which more questions are asked than are answered. The moral forces governing your work never seem to add up to an absolute position. Rather, your work offers possibilities, let loose with their opposites, in a game of wit and irresolution, leaving to the reader such conclusions as he chooses to make from a dense and tonally reflexive language. While one can take seriously an influence from Dewey, ethics seems to me to be more rigid than all that, seems to me to be a kind of order, the manipulation of which adds up to specific judgments as to belief or behavior. If, then, making judgments in the world really adds up to question marks, how can it be said of your poetry that you, as poet, have worked within ethical parameters? Or are you satisfied that any poem is in itself an ethical statement?

Okay, well, that description of some of my poems seems a fair description. What carries over for me from Dewey is that sense of being practical. They used to call him "the practical philosopher." On the one hand, he may have been in part a puritan; he certainly wanted everything to be useful and to produce a desired result. On the other hand, he would recommend that the chairs in classrooms not be bolted, which seems mildly liberating. So, what I think I carry over—not just from Dewey but from other people who interested me—was a sense of the usefulness of ideas. In fact, I came to believe—I think I came to believe—that ideas which are not useful ideas are not actually ideas. That sounds terrible because we all know that there is theoretical mathematics as well as applied mathematics; and, in fact, as a mathematics student, I was always interested in the theoretical even to the point of trying to disprove theorems—all those things that kids do. But it seems to me still that there is such a thing as a useless idea. I think I was saying something like this last time. And there has been in my poetry, whether there still is or not I'm not positive, but there has been in my poetry a strong argumentative or correctional element; and I've accepted that. That's something many poets would think a liability. Perhaps I should too; but it's just part of my nature: I like things to be useful. I like wisdom in poems; I really do. I continue to like Stafford's poems for the wisdom in them. I continue to like Williams' poems for the wisdom in them. And yet I don't feel that poetry depends on wisdom. There are a few of my poems in which, I think, I make statements having directly to do with ethics; the best example may be a poem called, **"After the Ducks Went In."**

If I look at poems from *These Green-Going-to-Yellow* and look for ethical edges, if you will, or the edges of ethics, perhaps—I am not sure how to articulate it—and yet . . .

There are quite a few passages in which you seem to have something you want to say; but I am not sure whether you'd think of this as ethical or not. For example, the second poem in the manuscript, "Hale-akala Crater, Maui," where you say "It wasn't perfection I wanted, / with its need for form, hollow / unbroken shell, for all we know." That seems to be making a judgment, more likely about poetry and art than about society and social problems, but that kind of definitive statement appears once in a while in your poems. "I know what poetry is" is another one—remember that?

Oh, yes. That's in **"You Can Keep the Sun out of Your Eyes with Just One Hand."** "I know by now that art / is a part of life, and I know what part / it is"

and then there was, in an earlier version of the poem, a colon instead of a period and it said, "The arty part." I swear—I swear it was in there. Somebody told me to take it out, and he was right.

And then you make, in I think a related line, an attractive statement, "I would hope to hell / not to cover my tracks with elegies."

Right. Some of the statements that I would regard as having an ethical basis have to do with our acts in literature as writers, even as readers.

I was going to ask, when you mentioned useless ideas, whether you had a sense of the ends toward which your ideas intended to be useful, some selection of ends that interested you more than others.

Well, my notion of that is too ideal, I think. You know, one way to change society is to cut off the heads of all the people who are in positions of power; but then, inevitably, the people who take their positions grow heads that are strikingly similar. The other way, though it often seems so theoretical, the other way is to change individual consciousness. If artists, writers, teachers of any kind have anything to do with changing the world, that's the way they do it, it seems to me. Now, you know, we're always talking about how little influence serious literature has; on the other hand, someone arguing with me said, "Well, now, there are some books in the libraries of all people who are in positions of power." I hesitate to think what books those might be nowadays, but . . .

You were on a good investigative track when you asked how much involvement with ethics these statements have, which is sometimes not much, but here's another example. At the end of a poem which begins, "He said to / crawl *toward* the machine guns," the poem says, "I made a man / to survive the Army, which means / that I made a man to survive / being a man." Well, that's a position. Is that a useful idea? I suppose it might be to someone who was, say, eighteen, who was thinking of joining the army and thought he would be more manly for it.

It's fairly common for poets to devalue the literal statement of what's in their poems. Creeley talks in an interview about the literal statement of a poem not being what's principally of value in the poem, although it may matter. That's such a truism about modern poetry, that you're surprising me, somewhat, with the interest you take in having things to say. Even unto aphorisms. Some of your statements have an aphoristic ring to them.

Well, I've always been interested in statements. In fact I published and edited a literary magazine years ago which was called *Statements*. I chose that title deliberately. It lasted for five issues over five years, and each issue was a different size.

Do you like aphorisms for their own sake?

I like aphorisms which are metaphysical. I used some in books you know. "If you can't get up, get down; if you can't get across, get across"—that's a Yiddish proverb, although it sounds like Zen. Or in an early book, one of the two Yiddish proverbs I used was "Dumplings in a dream are not dumplings but a dream." I mean, that seems to me a hard-nosed distinction that is useful. But I like those kinds of things. My favorite little tale, I don't know what it is—fable I guess—is supposed to be a story they tell in the Mideast. It's about the scorpion and the frog. The scorpion comes to the frog and says, "Give me a ride on your back across the river." The frog says, "Do I look stupid? If I put you on my back, you'll sting me to death." But the scorpion says, "Why would I do that? If I stung you to death, I'd drown." The frog says, "You've got a point there. Hop on," and starts across the river. Halfway across, the scorpion stings the frog. The frog is going into paralysis and says, "What'd you do that for?" And the scorpion sort of shrugs and says, "I don't know. It's the Mideast."

I heard a story recently that reminds me of the way your poems work. It must be an old joke because I think I remember hearing it before, but you know, coming in the middle of the interview, I was thinking, "Well, that works just like a Marvin Bell poem works." I heard it as a Texas Aggie joke, it could be anything. There were a Frenchman, an Italian, and a Texas Aggie who had been on a large luxury cruiser and the cruiser had sunk and everything had gone down except for one lifeboat, with these three guys in it. And they'd been rowing for days and they were dehydrated and they had no water and no food and they were tired and they were rowing and rowing in the middle of the ocean. Eventually a little bottle floats up to the boat and they look over and the Frenchman leans over and picks the bottle up, pulls the cork out of the bottle and a genie comes out. He says, "I will grant you any wish that you want. Each of you has one wish, any wish." And the Frenchman says, "Mon Dieu, this is marvelous, what luck, what good fortune." He says, "I wish that I were on the Left Bank at a sidewalk cafe drinking the best French wine." Poof, he's there. The Italian says, "I wish I were in St. Peter's listening to the Pope celebrating Mass." And he's there. The genie looks at the Aggie and says, "And what is your wish?" The Aggie looks around and he says, "I wish to hell those two guys were back here helping me row!"

That does put the dilemma all right.

"I wish to hell those two guys were back here helping me row!" There we are. He may be a little dumb, but my god he's going to have somebody in there helping him row. That Aggie knows damn well he's not a god.

That is terrific.

You said that you like wisdom in poetry.

I confess that I do.

And yet you said that you don't think poetry depends upon that.

No. Wisdom by itself is not enough.

What is most necessary?

Maybe I could say two things at once. Poetry is a kind of reporting. Stafford has a poem called "Reporting Back" and that's what poetry is. Now if a poet is like me, he has to report back ideas as well as other things because he can't stop having them. Some poets are able to report back without ever stating ideas directly, without statements of any sort in their poetry. It's not part of their normal way of thinking. So, why are those pieces of wisdom—if that's what they are—in the poem? Well, because that's part of the poet's experience, having those ideas and trying to find a place for them or opposing them to other evidence. So . . . poetry depends on reporting something: you're reporting your feelings, you're reporting the place and the plot, you're reporting your ideas.

But lots of writing can be reporting, so is there something without which poetry cannot be? Don Justice's phrase for it, his phrase for what just had to be there, was "technical virtue." Then he sort of apologized for using the term but came back to it and said "yeah, I really believe that; without that you don't have poetry. At least not very good poetry." I wondered whether there was something, maybe not calling it that. Maybe something quite different . . .

Well, that seems like a good phrase. I mean there has to be some . . . poetry has to protect its language as it goes along, I think. "Technical virtue," Don's phrase, seems a good phrase for it. There has to be—I mean, maybe that phrase of his takes in not only questions about what is formal, which we might propose, but also questions about what is moral or ethical. "Technical virtue" seems like a wonderful phrase. If he's not using it today I'd like to employ it. Sure, the poem seems to pay attention to itself, if one is technically virtuous, if one's virtue can be seen in one's technique, that is, and if one's technique can be seen in the virtue that is expressed in the poem—that seems a little more difficult to pin down.

Your poems seem to listen to themselves intently as they go along. I want to ask about the closure of a poem, where you come to rest. "The Hedgeapple," for instance, ends so perfectly—"So: here."

I hope you're right. I've been worried about that ending ever since I wrote it.

Oh, I really like that. I keep coming back to it. As against "So there."

Right. I guess that sums up a number of the ideas swirling about in the poem. One is that "the language we spoke seemed to make light everywhere / because we stopped to look," so we were lucky—the poem actually says, "We were lucky," the three of us, look: here we had this social interchange going around about this hedgeapple. The good thing that emerges from this has to do with the three of us sharing the experience and even talking about it. The hedgeapple is perfect by itself and doesn't require us. In the end there's another idea and that is about who owns this hedgeapple. "We thought we didn't take her hedgeapple," the poem says, and then right away it says, "We should have given it back." We didn't take it but in a sense we did. We used it, and we didn't include the woman in that act of possession. So I can't give her the hedgeapple back, it's her hedgeapple, how can I give it back to her? And furthermore, I'm no longer there. But I can give her (and you) this that we made out of the hedgeapple, which is now another form of the hedgeapple. "So: here."

It's a wonderful opening to the book. Because that's what every poem does, right?

Exactly. That's why I put it first.

There's a very interesting way in which in that poem the word "light" becomes radiant itself. You begin to collect all the possibilities. Radiance, I mean, it's almost as if the poem is itself a gesture making light of that situation but the light is also reflective of an inner knowledge that the poem allows for the three involved in that experience. "Light" becomes one of your most repeated words in the volume.

There's a lot of light there, yeah. I don't know if that's because light is everywhere or if it's because I grew up on fairly flat land and now live again on fairly flat land.

There's also lightness, deftness. That wisdom that we keep talking about could come across as heavy, heavy-footed—but it never does because there's a kind of "making light" in the poetry. Let's return to your talk last time about writing experimentally. I'd like to get you to say more about the nature of your experimentalism and where it's led you.

Well, I don't want to claim too much and it's hard to put one's finger on it for sure, I guess, but for me it has mostly to do with content and what is acceptable in a poem and how a poem can think, how it can stop and

start up again, what directions—along the periphery of whatever is central to it—it can accept new things from, and so forth. Experiments are tests, right? And so the poem is, for me at least, a kind of test. It's a test of whatever began the poem, whether an image, a piece of language, a phrase, or a sentence or even a statement. By writing the poem I'm testing what I came with.

Testing it to see how it can connect with something else?

To see if it really was something. To see what it connects to. What the context of it was. It's as if a new—I'm not trying to make up metaphors for it now—but it's as if you found a piece of something and were not able to identify it. So now you try to put it in different contexts and run experiments on it to see what it is, to find out what it is.

Just to tie this for a minute with the ends of the poems, it seems to me that a lot of times at the end of the poem you've taken the piece and put it in a certain puzzle. Now you've found some sort of coherence. The end will often be taking that puzzle piece and putting it in place where it works in one or two contexts at once.

That makes sense to me, yeah. To find the place where something belongs; as I say, that doesn't correspond to any established meaning of "experimental" but . . .

*One of the questions you must always be asking, then, is how will this poem extend itself? One of the poems I am very fond of is the one called **"The Canal at Rye."** It begins and makes a change that raises that question.*

I almost didn't put this poem in the book because it becomes so full of statements, so rhetorical and so bald, in a sense, at the end. I do like it—it's not that I didn't like it—but I began to feel scared. . . . But it feels right. The poem says, "Don't let them tell you—/ the women or the men—/ they knew me. / *You* knew me. / Don't let them tell you / I didn't love your mother. / I loved her. / Or let them tell you." Well, now, that's not a poem, that much, so what comes next? I don't think more such statements can follow.

It's the two opening gambits, though, of a lot of the poems: Statement X, elaborate a little, Statement Y, elaborate a little, and where the poems "make light," is in a third move.

That's right. Either way would not mean much: let them tell you, don't let them tell you . . . so what? What does all that matter? But I knew that when I wrote the line, "Do you remember Rye," and began to describe this wonderful canal that's so thin because the water has receded and the sailboats have to go out single-file in the morning . . . when I said "Do you remember

Rye," I didn't know what was going to come next; maybe nothing. But I do implicitly . . . I do believe, in fact, that anything can be connected, and I don't even mean it *can* be connected, I mean that it *is* connected: all things are connected if one can just find the path from one thing to another without going all the way around the world, as it were, without including every possible thing. So I went on with the description for awhile; I mean things do progress out that canal.

So you take the scenic route between two points, not necessarily the shortest.

Well, not the shortest, but the one that will let you arrive at the right place, or at a place worth arriving at, but not until you're ready to arrive there. Imagine someone being told to "go out and become a man" or "go out and become a woman" and you have to end up in this other town, but you can't get there until four years have passed. It's an old story, of course. But this poem begins to talk about a great novelist who lived in Rye, and of course at the end of the poem, if one doesn't know, one will find out that it was Henry James. Henry James wrote books that are not widely read anymore, at least outside of the university. One of the reasons they're thought difficult, and by some people no doubt unworthy, is that the sentences are so long; and as you know as James got older and began to dictate his books his sentences got even longer, because it was so much easier to just walk around the room dictating longer and longer sentences. After a while there was no need for the sentence ever to stop. Okay, so "Not many will be reading / his long sentences." And there's kind of an implication, I guess, whoever's being addressed in this poem is being told, "Well, don't let them tell you," or "Let them tell you"—none of that matters; here's another way to think about me.

"Sentence" can cut two ways here. Of course, syntax is logic—that's part of what that means. "There are reasons / not to, reasons too / to believe or not to. But / reasons do not complete an argument. / The natural end and extension / of language is nonsense." It's true; if language is pushed sufficiently far it turns into nonsense, no matter how sensible it was in the beginning. We see that in certain schools of criticism, we might add. "Yet there is safety / only there," the poem goes on to say; "That is why Mr. Henry James / wrote that way—/ out with the tide"—like those sailboats that went out the canal in Rye—"but further." In language one can go further in some directions than one can ever go in one's physical life. I feel as if maybe I'm squashing it by summarizing it.

So many of your poems seem to begin in impatience, or a sort of rebellion.

Yeah . . .

. . . and end with a kind of ambiguity that you can accept.

Absolutely.

The gesture is "No, not that" and "No, not this"— BUT—and then a long suspension. They end often in gentleness, with an acceptance of ambiguity. It's as if you work what seems to be a dichotomy into an acceptable blur, one you feel you can live with. It's as if there's been a softening of the mood; from abruptness to calmness, at the end of the poems. That's not the way they all work, but many of them do.

I think that's a wise remark. I have been thinking lately that maybe I write as if there's a little crisis at the beginning of every poem, and maybe therefore within the poet, I'm not sure. That may be changing.

The setting of **These Green-Going-to-Yellow** *is a much more populous world, a warmer world; the poems are all making connections with other people, and coming to understandings with others rather than the often solitary understandings of* **Stars Which See.**

There is almost a whole section of this book which contains stories, and for a while I had decided that I would write poems mostly by telling about things that happened. For better or worse, a lot of interesting little things have happened to me, strange little things, like going to Cuba at what proved to be the wrong time, things like that. And I decided to try to put those in poems. After all, one of the secrets of literature every writer knows is that any life will do. It's not necessary to go bathe one's feet in the Ganges and travel around the world and work on a steamer to be a poet, nor is it prohibitive. . . . Meaning is in the small things. That's true, even of architecture.

One thing I see happening in these new poems that I don't think has happened before in your work, at least not frequently, is that part of the warmth here comes from the way you are continually at play with the reader—"What's the matter? / You don't believe the rain in Paris is red?" "If it happened to you, / maybe you wouldn't know what to say." "I never told you. / There was a woman . . ." or "Don't let them tell you . . . they knew me." There's that "you" that comes so often at the beginning of these poems and is always addressed in a playful way, as if to say that there's something here I'm not about to tell you, but there's something else I am *about to tell you.*

Or again that place where you say, in **"Things I Took,"** *"Look at stanza one / compared to stanza two . . ." You step back and say, okay reader, let's take a look at this poem, and let's do a little analysis here; it's kind of interesting, isn't it, the difference between stanza one and stanza two, and what I could have put in one and couldn't put in the other.*

Well, I like intimacy in poems, and I think poems also gain from being addressed to someone, even if the reader doesn't know who that someone is. I think the tone of the poem is helped too, to speak about a smaller thing, perhaps. I like those things; again, to think of the beginning of the James Wright poem that we've already mentioned, "The Old WPA Swimming Pool in Martins Ferry, Ohio," he begins "I am almost afraid to write down / This thing." One can imagine any good teacher saying, "Oh, just cut that stuff out, Jim, and get to it." But enormous intimacy is provided by those lines and, then, you *have* to read on. One of the tests of a first line in a poem is probably, simply, "do you want to read on, or do you want to go out for popcorn?"

There's a kind of trick in these poems that makes you lean into them; it's like The Secret Sharer *where they have to whisper to each other. The poem starts in a kind of low tone, and you have to lean in to have any relationship with it. One of your more intimate poems, called* **"The Last Thing I Say,"** *is interesting for several reasons; one is the intimacy of the occasion and the tenderness of the tone. Another, the way it sits playfully, after* **"The Canal at Rye,"** *where you've said so much about sentences, and then this one turns out to be one long sentence.*

One *hopelessly* long sentence.

How in the world did you get into that; did you say "I'm going to write a poem all in one sentence"?

No, there just didn't seem to be any place to stop until the end of the poem. Again, it's just an intuitive sense of things, but once it got going . . . of course some of it's a decision; there are places where there could have been a period, but instead there's a comma. I wanted it all to run together; I wanted many things to happen at once during the moment in which a father closes—in which I, in fact, close my son's bedroom door and say "sweet dreams." Obviously, in any situation in which your emotions are involved you feel many things at once. The sentence is a little complicated.

You speak in the former poem, **"The Canal at Rye,"** *about long sentences, and avoiding long sentences, and then turning back to the sentence, and then you have this sentence poem.*

That's why it's there, sure; also it's "the last thing I say" in section two.

But not the last thing you say; it's fine having **"The Last Thing I Say"** *not be the last thing you say in the book.*

It was last in the book for a while, but I moved it. That would have been too clever, wouldn't it, if it were last in the book?

After our first discussion, we were talking and you said that as you were thinking more about where the origins of your poems were, you noted that one thing you hadn't said which you think is true is that the origin of many of your poems is in letters you write to friends.

Well, to this extent: when I'm writing, I feel like writing. The opposite of that is true, too, unfortunately. And if I'm writing letters to friends—I tend to write fast; I type with two fingers which allows me to type as fast as I can, and so if I'm writing a letter to someone, I tend to just invent as I go. I mean, once I've answered the three questions that were in the other person's letter, whatever is required, then there's the rest of the letter to be written, and that's an occasion for having fun. So I start having fun with whatever there is to report, or whatever jokes I can make that the other person might like, or whatever. It's the same kind of invention that one is easily seduced by in writing poetry, I think. Sometimes a phrase will come out of it that seems serious, more serious than I meant, or maybe no more serious than I meant, but worth being . . . there's a bigger location for it than that letter, and I want to find that location. That happens sometimes. I'll take phrases right out of essays, and vice-versa; I'll put into essays phrases which are lying there on paper that I hoped would hold a poem. The boundaries between genres don't seem any more fixed to me than they must seem to anyone else.

Speaking of the relationship between poems and letters, this is a good point to move to the book of poems you and William Stafford are doing together, poems written back and forth to each other. Will you talk a little about how that book is constructed?

Oh, in a very loose way, although sometimes the connections that result are not loose. I had thought about doing this, and not just with anybody but in fact with Bill, for years, but I never had the nerve to suggest it. Finally we were both at the First Annual Midnight Sun Writers' Conference in Fairbanks, Alaska, in June of 1979. Maybe that yellowish light that lasts all night at that time of the year there got my nerve up, or maybe I just hadn't had enough sleep, but we were walking along one day midway through the conference and I sort of mentioned this as something I had once thought about, not quite suggesting it, and he right away took up the idea and said, "Great," so I got home and I tried to write a poem to him to start the series; and I was trying to, I felt somehow required to, use material from there in Alaska. In fact, I may have felt required without realizing it to use the pronoun "we," because I kept saying "we, we, we" but the material I wanted to put into the poem didn't have anything to do with Bill; it happened at Mt. McKinley where I went afterward. So I was having a problem with truth; why couldn't I have said "we" even though I was the one on the raft and he wasn't? I couldn't do it. And I still have that darn poem; I've tried to put it in the series over and over, and each time truth rears its ugly head and I can't do it. Well, before I could get anything better written, a poem arrived from him with a note saying, "I wasn't sure who was to begin, so here goes." Now theoretically each poem answers the other in some way, or responds to it, and indeed sometimes the connections are quite clear—there's a little quarrel about attitude or something, how to take something, or there's a parallel plot: my memory stirs his memory, or his memory stirs mine. He has an idea about something; I have a somewhat similar but different idea about something similar. Or a situation that's similar. But sometimes the connections are looser than that, and you have to read into the first poem to see a phrase that triggered the second poem.

My publisher told me that Bill Merwin once suggested something similar to James Merrill, but it never came to be, I think. One has to be able to feel that a project like this is not going to deplete the poems one would otherwise write, deplete the energies. And I feel that I can do both things. Because I feel as if I'm sometimes more than one person. I *know* Bill Stafford can do both. . . . Bill could take on *ten* correspondents like this, and still manage his own work.

Like a chess master, with ten games going on at once.

Absolutely. His attitude toward writing is marvelous. His sense of the forgivable is just wonderful.

The correspondence sounds very sustaining.

I admire his poetry, I admire his lifestyle, I admire everything about him. I always have. It's in my nature to want to make people into fathers, I think. I have to fight against that, and I certainly don't want to do that to him. But I do admire him greatly; he's a genuinely admirable man, with a life made out of whole cloth.

He's the person who says in a poem somewhere, "you feel oppressed? Get up at five a.m."

He's a very interesting man with an extraordinarily unusual mind. I think that, as famous as he is, his work is one of the secrets of American poetry. I think he's famous for a lot of easy reasons, and he's much better than that. His work is experimental—we were talking before about what is experimental—it's experimental in its notion of composition, and it's experimental in its ideas toward the world and how it applies them in the poems.

It may have been Don Justice who said this, but whoever said it, I agree: work that seems very experimental in style often masks a very conventional mind. Work that seems conventional and off-handed in style often masks an unconventional mind. It's not a rule, but . . .

How many poems are going to be in the book with Stafford?

Well, as many as we have when the deadline draws near. The series will continue; the book will just put covers around a section of it.

You're not working toward a conclusion?

Not exactly, but I must confess that when I asked Godine to delay the publication one season I was aware that the series could use another turn in order to be a book. We did have enough poems, but there had been a kind of change after the first eighteen poems or so and now the next change in direction was slow in making itself known. It has worked out very well so far, I think.

And what direction do you see yourself continuing on your own, aside from the poems to Stafford?

I have an idea of the kind of poem I'd like to write. I have some sense of what my language is now. There's a line between being fluent and being facile. In any case, I don't have to make as many choices now as I once had to make about style, for example. I know what my language is; I might push it in this direction or that, but I know where it's located within me. I would like to increase my range, and of course everyone would like to extend his emotional depth. And everyone has in mind poems by other people they would have liked to have written.

Like "The Old WPA Swimming Pool . . ."

Right. I would like to write a poem like "Asphodel, That Greeny Flower." That seems to be one of the great poems—about as long a poem as I would ever want to write. I don't have any burning desire to write an epic. The only good that comes out of it is critical attention, as far as I can tell. I would rather have written "Asphodel, That Greeny Flower" than *Paterson*. I recognize *Paterson* as a marvelous poem, and Book V of *Paterson* as a lyric poem all by itself. But I still would rather have written "Asphodel, That Greeny Flower."

And you don't seem to be looking for all-encompassing metaphors, like the city of Paterson.

No. That, to me, always rings hollow. I would like very much to have written a book like Williams' *Spring and All* which actually he wrote in 1923 and which is prose and poetry, the poetry partly illustrating the radical aesthetic idea of the prose.

When I went to Spain for most of a year I took two books: I took a dictionary and I took *Spring and All.* I had a notion of keeping a journal that would result in a book similar in form to *Spring and All,* but I never did it, although I probably have the pieces, not just in a journal but in miscellaneous pages gathered over the years. I could probably put together a book that would be similar to *Spring and All.* Maybe I will.

Daniel McGuiness (essay date summer 1990)

SOURCE: McGuiness, Daniel. "Exile and Cunning: The Recent Poetry of Marvin Bell." *Antioch Review* 48, no. 3 (summer 1990): 353-61.

[*In the following essay, McGuiness examines Bell's recent work and speculates on how the poet's experience at the University of Iowa has informed his poetry while at the same time limiting critical appreciation of his work.*]

Here's a poem from Marvin Bell's next book:

"A Man May Change"

As simply as a self-effacing bar of soap
escaping by indiscernible degrees in the wash water
is how a man may change
and still hour by hour continue in his job.
There in the mirror he appears to be on fire
but here at the office he is dust.
So long as there remains a little moisture in the stains,
he stands easily on the pavement
and moves fluidly through the corridors. If only one
cloud can be seen, it is enough to know of others,
and life stands on the brink. It rains
or it doesn't rain, or it rains and it rains again.
But let it go on raining for forty days and nights
or let the sun bake the ground for as long,
and it isn't life, just life, anymore, it's living.
In the meantime, in the regular weather of ordinary
    days,
it sometimes happens that a man has changed
so slowly that he slips away
before anyone notices
and lives and dies before anyone can find out.

And here is Jacques Moran writing at the end of Samuel Beckett's *Molloy:*

But in the end I understand this language. I understood it, I understood it, all wrong perhaps. That is not what matters. It told me to write the report. Does this mean I am freer now than I was? I do not know. I shall learn. Then I went back into the house and wrote. It is midnight. The rain is beating on the windows. It was not midnight. It was not raining.

Beckett and Bell are odd bedfellows, but tucking them in together for a moment might help us reflect on the situation. Odd journeys for dark and unnamed purposes make fiction dramatic and life hell. Beckett's life seemed all drama: exile, cunning, war, a quick knife on an empty street. Bell's life has centered on one small Iowa town for most of it: scrubbed undergraduates, backyard trees, drives in the country. Yet he is also an exile: from Long Island, from Chicago, from the center of things. That life, that career, is at a provocative moment. Marvin Bell's next book will be the one that comes after his *New and Selected Poems* (Atheneum, 1987). This is an awkward and telling point in any poet's c.v. (a Beckettian moment, perhaps: "I can't go on, I'll go on") since it's an opening after a closure. Or as Beckett's Moran puts it: "If there is one question I dread, to which I have never been able to invent a satisfactory reply, it is the question what am I doing."

Though most of the assessments were positive for Bell's *New and Selected Poems,* there was no tumult and little traducing. There were no major awards. Donald Justice, Bell's partner in harness at Iowa all those years, grabbed a Pulitzer for his *Selected Poems* (Atheneum, 1979). He deserved it. So did Bell. Bell didn't get it. How come? Well, you can give it to a formalist any day of the week, these days, and the letters column of the dreaded NY-TBR stays silent. You can give it to a guy (or gal) whose humility is writ large in every little poem, *à la* Larkin. But can you give it to a guy unbuffeted by the winds of a snow-white drove of faddists? Or a guy perceived to be, in some bizarre sense, powerful even in the importance of his place of exile? That's probably not the issue, or maybe it is. Justice stepped out before workshop bashing became the dominant mode of book reviewing in America, before your affiliations made a difference, before the lines were drawn in this strange battle. Justice's move to Florida must have been motivated, in part at least, by weariness brought on at the cornhusk barricades against this year's disparagers. Now, the new formalists and the neo-narrators are out there, boys, with blood in their eyes, iambs in their teeth, and stories to tell, and their message is clear: get a real job, lead a real life, write real poems that end the way poems, lives, and jobs are supposed to end—with a bang, not a whimper.

In the poem above, for example, there's this man, perhaps he's read Roethke about the sorrow of paper clips, perhaps he's read Beckett, perhaps not, perhaps he's only listened to Springsteen, but he's waiting for the extraordinary: an ark that needs building or devils to put behind him. Attention must be paid, Uncle Charley said. Living is better than life but somebody's got to take note, write it down, make it part of Molloy's and the public's record. "On the brink" is testimony to the power of the precipice where a wet bar of soap can turn your end into headline material. I'm not suggesting this poem is autobiography; it seems very far from it. What I'm saying is that Marvin Bell's next book will expand and continue one of the most remarkable and important poetic lives in America.

Here's another poem, **"Not Joining the Wars,"** from Marvin Bell's next book:

Sometimes there isn't any light when
that flash comes. All day, all night,

you went looking for a spark to
bring daytime to your words, that look
of freshness when things go up fast
and the siren volunteers the town
into the blaze, though nothing can be saved.

Lots of things sound like applause:
the dead hands of leaves in October,
or the slapping of tank treads in parade.
Some people can ripple pages in a book
or pause at length till cheered.
It's hard, waiting it out underneath
others' victories and the crackling leaves.

You are possibly one of the lost ones
by choice. You take no maps, blunder
casually from the path, till deep in woods
(the light is slanted, the footing funereal)
that scent gathers, slowly wrapping each
pore with the smell of scrubbed air,—
and you have gotten clean away.

In an age when poetics are drawn up by William Bennett and Jimmy Stewart, it must be weird out there in the heartland watching pathology slouch toward you from the east like Andrew Marvell astride a somewhat rougher beast than MacLeish's. Our changing, Beckettian man waiting for rain (but surely not Eliot's rain), having heard the distant artillery and for one stanza sought it and for one stanza fled it, knew for all three stanzas that history laughs at choice and leaves you where it wants to—unless you choose to be lost. "I'm for the woods," didn't somebody say? That first stanza's sequence of visual images (light, flash, spark, blaze), the second stanza's sequence of noises (applause, leaves, tank treads, rippling pages) seem like algebraic factors in an equation or premises in an enthymeme: given those sights, given those sounds, is it any wonder you seek the smell (third stanza) of solitude where the light slants like Emily's did during the funeral in her brain. Good senses make good neighbors.

For Marvin Bell it has always seemed so. My book tells me that those seven-line groupings were called Troilus stanzas until James I borrowed them from Chaucer and they became known as rhyme royal. And we have seen similar stanzas from Bell before: the *New and Selected Poems* show us that three six-lined stanzas, looking very much like Berryman's dream song stanzas, were the form of Bell's book-length autobiographical sequence, *The Escape into You* in 1971. We also know, from the *New and Selected Poems,* interesting things, like his omission of so much of *Residue of Song* (1974) except (most notably) for the sequence **"You Would Know,"** which is also in that characteristic three-stanza form, but this time with seven lines. But having found a comfortable form like that one, Bell is not content, nor formless. In **"The Bow,"** another new poem, again in three seven-line stanzas, archery is the image and the message is similarly about missing marks, but achieving a kind of consolation:

Now, when I can make a line from any
three things, and see my ignorance
coming before what could have been
hasn't missed its time and not happened yet,
I find an old bow and cheat the string
tight somehow, and let fly. Even without
a target it will find straw, if I let it fly.

Beckett could never find such consolations, but Bell's persistence in accepting the world is every bit as fierce as Beckett's rejection of it. Bell has taken the time to assemble his best for us, paused, and then come ahead. Most of all, this new work reminds us of constant and subtle changes: tone from wisecracking to wisdom, diction from gnarled to planed, and a look toward the reader that is still insistent but far gentler. The most intriguing things to trace from the *New and Selected Poems* into the next book will be: his attitude toward narrative, his increasing interest in prose, and, in one case at least, a new expansiveness. The earlier books eschew narrative for the most part, just as the later books embrace it. The breakthrough book remains his best—*Stars Which See, Stars Which Do Not See*—in which the comfort of plot runs along just beneath the lines. In his recent poems Bell might be calling back the mysteries of those first books without losing the relaxation gained in the later. The new poems are more meditations in the early sense but prosier now, less opaque, susceptible to the working out of metaphor very near to meaning, but never discursive. In **"Pages: Port Townsend,"** a sequence of prose poems, Bell explains the difference between the truth of narrative and the lyric's lie of love:

> Now, it is necessary to note that many have travelled the line to reach the paragraph, but it is rare that anyone successfully travels the paragraph to reach the line. The novelist who ends up a poet began as a poet. It is at least as necessary now to establish the difference between loving and believing in. In the middle of a busy street, against the traffic, a young woman stopped to say that she was unable to decide which she wanted most: to be loved or to know the truth. For the moment, she wanted only orgasm and repose. As for the truth . . . as another woman said to me during a walk in the woods, "There are people who get it, and there are people who don't."

It is instructive to note how that distinction (and a key phrase) is retained and reworked for another recent poem called **"Sevens (Version 3): In the Closed Iris of Creation."** The controlling image is scissors, beginning things, cutting permanence into plot, slicing truth into beauty and whatever's on the other side of the empty gash time makes through things:

To choose between knowing the truth
or, on the other hand, orgasm and repose,
always with the patience of a cricket on guard
in case Spring should arrive in disguise,
hiding its muscular body under rags,
its footsteps muffled by the mating of vines—
to choose at all, we have to crawl

on bare knees down alleys of pumice
and plead among the red columns of silos,
in the dust of exploding grains,
with shaking hands and trembling lips
plead for a severing of knives.

Perhaps that is why the format of these poems seems less important than ever—and more. Few poets are as aware of their environment as Marvin Bell, and he once more has found his own distinctive path. We have all noted how much of Bell's recent work has been in prose. As a small example, note that the **"Three Implements"** in *Drawn by Stones, by Earth, by Things That Have Been in the Fire* (1984) have become **"Two Implements"** in the *New and Selected Poems,* perhaps because the poems about the sugar hammer and the pasta shears are prose paragraphs and the one about the tortilla press is lineated and left out. Elsewhere in **"Pages: Port Townsend,"** another "explanation" might be found:

> The essence of the poetic sentence is the phrase as it holds hands with the line. And the secret that contains the poem made of sentences composed of phrases distributed in lines is just this: prose was always poetry. Today, prose has the greater freedom to be poetry, because poetry is the victim of its own conventions. Most poems today are written to sound like poems; hence, written according to vaguely understood, ill-defined conventions of theme, development, what constitutes a beginning of a poem, what constitutes an ending, how does a poem sound and proceed, etc. It would be a happier and more productive circumstance if poets tried to write bad poems, without being silly or nonsensical. For then every move made by a poet to make the poem less like other poems would only make the poem more and more interesting. One must constantly understand the hidden rules of poetry so as to better violate them.

Beckett's Moran said about rules: "And if I submit to this paltry scrivening which is not of my province, it is for reasons very different from those that might be supposed. I am still obeying orders, if you like, but no longer out of fear. No, I am still afraid, but simply from force of habit." Furthermore, Bell's confidence with form is matched at least once in his recent work by something relatively new: extension.

Bell's new long poem, entitled **"Initial Conditions,"** consists of twenty stanzas of eighteen (long) lines each, an extended, self-reflexive meditation on craft—Pope with a heart, Keats with a head. The plot tells the story of a man sitting in a café reading the poems of two women, Emily Dickinson and Marianne Moore, and writing a poem about a man in a café writing a poem about what he has learned lately about poetry. The story and the lessons are elemental. "Water is foremost," Pindar says. Poems are about being aware of the body, how it's organized around a central spine where the meaning starts and where the meaning hides at once—which is just the first of his paradoxes. From that spine

things spread out—like bones or books or bees after flowers that will make both honey and the comb to hold it. It's the interval—the point just beyond whatever's spreading, waiting to be filled, that is the poem, that is life:

> If it were not for words, poor words,
> I would never have known the wish that things
>   continue.

Water is foremost, we have read, and feeds the vegetable (*pace* Marvell), but it's the animal oil in us that feeds fire, consuming all our afterthoughts in passion. Thank the lord for sex, he says, but neither flora nor fauna can account for poems or Beethoven quartets. What art is after is to "spot what disturbs the air with heavy laughter." Here's where the poem, so redolent of Whitman, makes the bardic palatable for our postmodern condition. The preposterous necessity of death makes it "miraculous to be alive in a tungsten universe" that will inevitably burn out—but with Pater's hard, gem-like flame. Isn't this a high form of irony we're talking about here, that missing leaf that Whitman always seemed to need? Like Whitman, Bell has been accused of being a poet of self-absorption, and he is in this *cellular* sense: he is permeable but intact, taking in and giving out, and he's a poet, not of the grass, but of the sturdier trees. Writing is vegetative, but sterner, threshing the wheat from the chaff with a flail (to mix up a metaphor, which may be the point). He has learned to be stoic from the women he's been reading. There's sustenance, he says, in the "blows of a pencil against the grain of a page":

> At impact a purity
> is born from the attraction
> and repulsion of an instant.

Finally it is love of the world's particulars and attention to the imagination's tender possibilities that make even ironic affirmation credible. It's a great poem. Among other things, you realize, with a start, that each of these stanzas could be a smushed "Escape" song, eighteen lines, and you even start searching for the volta until you get control of yourself. Remember when you read this poem that Beckett's Moran has sketched the blacker version:

> All I know is what the words know, and the dead things, and that makes a handsome little sum, with a beginning, a middle and an end as in the well-built phrase and the long sonata of the dead. And truly it little matters what I say, this or that or any other thing. Saying is inventing. Wrong, very rightly wrong. You invent nothing, you think you are inventing, you think you are escaping, and all you do is stammer out your lesson, the remnants of a pensum one day got by heart and long forgotten, life without tears, as it is wept. To hell with it anyway.

Even though one of Bell's recent poems, called **"The Retaliatarians,"** acknowledges contemporary abuse of the particular, especially through technology, we see no lessening of enthusiasm for it in these poems. After all, what are the alternatives? Narrative? He's done it. Discursive? Read *Old Snow Just Melting*. He's done it. In a response (in the *Georgia Review*) to Christopher Clausen's notorious essay "Poetry in a Discouraging Time," Bell goes as far as he may have ever gone in defending his poetic:

> But one of the truths we have discovered over many civilizations, painfully, at great cost, is that generalizations are wrong. Moreover, totalitarianism feeds on generalizations, as does prejudice, sentimentality, and injustice. Charity, analysis, and fairness attend the specific. Every generalization is defeated by every instance. The English language is precise, analytical, almost surgical. The American version of it may be more so (let's argue). Politics is the devious art of the general. Telling the truth is the art of the specific.

That's what Marvin Bell does as a poet and what he does as a teacher. Finally, in a year in which we mourn Beckett's passing, we can turn to another of Bell's recent poems, a variation on Drummond de Andrade called **"Poem after Carlos Drummond de Andrade,"** and find consolation and celebrations enough as the poem ends:

> It's life that will consume you in the end, but in
>   the meantime . . .
> It's life that will eat you alive, but for now . . .
> It's life that calls you to the street where the
>   wood smoke hangs, and the bare hint of a
>   whisper of your name, but before you go . . .
>
> Too late: Life got its tentacles around you, its
>   hooks into your heart, and suddenly you come
>   awake as if for the first time, and you are
>   standing in a part of the town where the air
>   is sweet—your face is flushed, your chest
>   thumping, your stomach a planet, your heart
>   a planet your every organ a separate
>   planet, all of it of a piece though the pieces
>   turn separately, O silent indications of the
>   inevitable, as among the natural restraints
>   of winter and good sense, life blows you
>   apart in her arms.

Richard Jackson (essay date January/February 1995)

SOURCE: Jackson, Richard. "Containing the Other—Marvin Bell's Recent Poetry." *North American Review* 280, no. 1 (January/February 1995): 45-8.

[*In the following essay, Jackson praises* The Book of the Dead Man *for its originality and mastery of poetic form.*]

In the "Author's Preface" to *A Marvin Bell Reader*,[1] a book which collects most of the essential writings from one of America's few indispensable poets, Bell writes:

"I don't want to get fancy about epiphanies, enlightenment, the higher good and the greater good, belief, ecstasy, transformation, transcendence, evolution, or entropy. Rather, I want to get rabid about dirt and shoelaces, sex and sorrow. The one contains the other." Certainly this reader, blending a poetic prose and, in Bell's special sense of the word, a prose-like poetry ("prose was always poetry") enacts this Whitmanesque sense of inclusiveness: one contains the other. The reader itself collects a number of Bell's major poems, "pages" of diary entries and notes, three memoirs (one including a few important new poems), three of his enormously influential essays from *American Poetry Review,* and a sampling from his most recent book, ***The Book of the Dead Man***[2], published at about the same time. The reader, in addition, provides an enriching way to read ***The Book of The Dead Man,*** which is one of the most original and masterful books of poetry in a while.

The originality stems from Bell's unique poetic. Here, for example, is a passage from a diary entry: "Most poems today are written to sound like poems; hence, written according to vaguely understood, ill-defined conventions of theme, development, what constitutes a beginning of a poem, what constitutes an ending, how does a poem sound and proceed, etc. It would be a happier and more productive circumstance if poets tried to write bad poems, without being silly or nonsensical. For then every move made by the poet to be less like other poems would only make the poem more and more interesting" (21 Dec 86). What Bell calls for again and again is an honesty and commitment to the art, which means, in Pound's terms, to "make it new." Bell's poems, founded in a very colloquial rhetoric, make stunning leaps and turns with the seeming ease of someone out for a walk (Bell's metaphor) and yet the care and pacing of a sophisticated art. The result, as he says in one poem, is to raise "the emotional ante." All of a sudden there is a lot at stake, and the possibility for failure looms large for the poet who would be an original.

Bell says, in "Three Propositions," that the essence of this stance is a sense of "helplessness." By that he means, as he suggests in the diary entry, a reliance on the self, on chance and the imagination rather than on teachers and what others say is a good poem. This is the only way discoveries can be made, as he suggests in another essay, "The Technique of Re-Reading"—the poet has to listen to his or her own poem, to what it is trying to say to the poet, to the ghost poem behind the words on the page, to possibility. In "Three Propositions" he cites his favorite quote from Machado to explain this predicament of the poet: "people possess four things / that are no good at sea: / anchor, rudder, oars, and / the fear of going down." Poetry, he says, is "abandonment" of four things: stability, predetermined direction, worry about what propels the poem, and the fear of failure.

One does not hold onto the version of Keats's "negative capability" without a sense of self effacement and irony, the very tone that informs the essays. Of course, one could point to the sequence of poems, **"Ecstasy,"** **"Short Version of Ecstasy,"** and **"Cryptic Version of Ecstasy"** to quickly see this. Part 2 of **"Who & Where"** begins "Who I am is a short person with small feet / and fingers." A few lines later: "I see writers grow huge / in their writings. I get smaller yet." The poem then ends with an ironic gesture that is also a sincere embrace: "I take a step. The wind takes a step. / I take a drink of water. The earth swallows. / I just live here— like you, like you, like you." Reading Bell's poems always reminds us of the joy of living, though certainly not a pure joy. In some poems there is a melancholic ring, as in **"Sevens (Version 3): In the Closed Iris of Creation,"** which begins "A pair of heavy scissors lay across the sky / waiting for an affirmation," then moves through a number of instances of sadness before ending with "the shapes to come when love / began to sever us." Typically, the bulk of the poem undercuts that simplistic view, as, for example, when he says "we laugh so hard we lose our bodies momentarily, / we are also, at the same time, absorbing / the shivering of the cities." And more, the language itself, filled with inventive and imaginative metaphors such as that "heavy scissors," affirms a joy in language, in vision, that counterpoints any sadness.

This duality forms the basis for the counterpointing in Bell's **"Ending With a Line By Lear,"** one of the most powerful recent elegies, buried here in an essay, "What Became of What: An Autobiography" (there are several other very fine poems in the essay). The tension derives from a struggle to remember, and indeed the poem begins: "I will try to remember." A number of short, clipped sentences follows, filled with oppositions: the father is there in body at the funeral but of course not there, there are images that suggest that the speaker is making present some of the father's past, the speaker feels left behind but also is sinking into the earth with the father. The cumulating effect of these sentences is incredible and keeps underscoring the fact and the resistance to the fact: "I don't want him to go." The poem ends with a resistance to life and yet an affirmation of it, a reference to the poet's own situation and to the condition of an art (a whole tradition of poetry since Shakespeare) we have seen as both joyful and sad at once: "My father's grave. I will never again. / Never. Never. Never. Never. Never."

This duality appears in another form in **"Poem After Carlos Drummond de Andrade."** The poem ends with a long paragraph/line (breaking expectations again):

"Too late. Life got its tentacles around you, its hooks into your heart, and suddenly you come awake as if for the first time, and you are standing in a part of town where the air is sweet—your face flushed, your chest thumping, your stomach a planet, your heart a planet, your every organ a planet . . . as among the natural restraints of winter and good sense, life blows you apart in her arms." The complexity here is rich: the tentacles are both a danger and an embrace, there is a rising consciousness of being alive and a corresponding sense of the closeness of death, there is a sense of the self as scattered and a sense, through the repetition, of the intensification and gathering of the parts—planets into the solar system that is the poem. Even the last phrase makes use of this counterpointing to leave us nearly out of breath with wonder: if there is a poetry accountant's bottom line, it is simply an amazing joy at being alive, at feeling the good and the bad, the self and the world— "the one contains the other."

This duality and counterpointing is crucial for understanding *The Book of the Dead Man.* In fact one can see in *A Marvin Bell Reader,* itself a fine and independent book, some of the background for the Dead Man poems (three are included at the end of that book), yet still be surprised at the originality of the poems themselves as they unfold as a separate book. In one of the diary passages in the ***Reader*** (21 Dec 86) Bell writes: "The question of what I am up to. I am carving my own face. I am taking responsibility for the furrows on the hillsides and the wheel marks in the grass. . . . I am in the distance and at home, hurrying to move and hurrying not to move." This kind of inclusiveness is apparent in poems like **"Unless It Was Courage,"** where Bell, looking up into the "nothing" that is the opening at the bottom of a hot air balloon, nonetheless concludes that the vision "was enough, it seemed, as it ran skyward and away. / There I was, unable to say what I'd seen. / But I was happy, and my happiness made others happy." Besides this inclusiveness, besides the way the poet makes a vision out of the lack of vision in the tradition of great Romantic poets like Wordsworth and Keats, there is a "small" but essential principle for Bell's poetics operating in this diary entry, and which forms the rhythmic basis for *The Book of the Dead Man,* that is, a sort of chiasmic reversal—"hurrying to move and hurrying not to move." It is a rhetorical extension of the idea of being happy and making others happy, being at a distance and at home, looking at the shoelaces as we saw earlier but also at the stars, and in fact is what allows the poet such an easeful, freewheeling romp from a grain of sand to infinity.

What, then, is the Dead Man? For one, he is that same character who looked up into the nothingness of the balloon and saw an ample vision. "But do not think one can know nothing so easily," Bell says in his "Preface" to the book. The Dead Man bases his poetic logic upon extensions of Bell's earlier principles of inclusiveness and counterpointing: here the Dead Man's desire to "accept all and everything" is manifest as paradox, the Dead Man as "material mystic," "perfected fallibility," satisfied dissatisfaction, and the like. The logic extends to the level of the line where "under the rule of the Dead Man the sentence once more invigorates the line." Of course, this skeletal description does little to flesh out the rich texture and uniqueness of the sequence of 33 poems in two parts, the second half often ironically extending the material from the first or introducing a totally other context for it. These are poems that begin with a sort of chiasmic gambit: the opening two lines (one line is always a sentence even when they run over) repeat one element that is then developed by association, opposition, synonym, pun (verbal and visual), tautology, zeugma (pure and impure), shifts in language level from the colloquial to scientific, etc., anaphoras, parallel construction, aphorism, and a host of other strategies. And the speaker himself, described in the "Preface" as wearing Bell's characteristic "watch cap" is both the poet and various projections of the poet.

What we have in **The Book of the Dead Man,** then, is one of the most complex, most original books in a long time. The book as a whole follows the general pattern of a life as in, say, a biography, a loose pattern that allows for surprises along the way. Generally, the poems cover a number of topics, and the whole book moves from beginnings in poems that explore what it is to be, to feel, to sense, to other issues. So, for example, the book begins to explore the external world from baseball and games, to government, the social life. Then we move in an inner way toward dreams, the psychic life, questions about happiness, ethics. The book ends with two poems about our relation to the cosmos. However, even in sketching out such a description it must be noted that the counterpointed vision also means that to talk about the cosmos is to talk about the self and its tiniest sensations, to talk about government is also to talk about the self's needs—one thing is always seen in contrast to several other things, and the mode is often one that allows the speaker to call himself the "resident tautologist."

The best way to understand the richness of the book as a whole, and of each individual poem, is to see how the first half of the first poem progresses line by line:

> The dead man thinks he is alive
>   when he sees blood in his stool.
> Seeing blood in his stool, the dead
>   man thinks he is alive.
> He thinks himself alive because he
>   has no future.
> Isn't that the way it always was, the
>   way of life?

> Now, as in life, he can call to people
>   who will not answer.
> Life looks like a white desert, a blaze
>   of today in which nothing distinct
>   can be made out, seen.
> To the dead man, guilt and fear are
>   indistinguishable.
> The dead man cannot make out the
>   spider at the center of its web.
> He cannot see the eyelets in his
>   shoes and so wears them unlaced.
> He reads the large type and skips the
>   fine print.
> His vision surrounds a single tree,
>   lost as he is in a forest.
> From his porcelain living quarters, he
>   looks out at a fiery plain.
> His face is pressed against a frameless
>   window.
> Unable to look inside, unwilling to
>   look outside, the man who is dead
>   is like a useless gift in a box wait-
>   ing.
> It will have its yearly anniversary, but
>   it would be wrong to call it a holi-
>   day.

The poem begins with a chiasmus (this opening gambit changes as the series proceeds but remains as base of reference), a structure that tends to negate the distinction between cause and effect and thus sets us up for a shift in traditional logical connections. We get to the third line by the repetition, with a difference, of the idea of thinking himself alive, and then add the notion of a loss of future based upon the possible ramifications of blood in the stool. That is reinforced by the "was" in the next line, and then the paradox emerges with full force: for the dead man death is also life—"the way of life." Life is again what links the next line, but the death motif now becomes a sense of loneliness—no one answers. This is metamorphosed into the idea of the "white desert" (pun on "white noise"?) in the next line and also an emphasis on the present that has been lurking in the observation of the first line and the "Now" of the previous line. At this point, all tenses are in operation, linked, so that not only can "nothing distinct . . . be made out," but as he says in the next line, upping "the emotional ante," "guilt and fear are indistinguishable." Of course, these larger issues have been lurking all along despite the emphasis on the sense impressions—but now they come to the forefront (the poems constantly shift foregrounds and backgrounds).

From this point, the notion of not being able to make out anything distinctly is transferred to the spider image: is the dead man caught in the web, alone, facing death, facing the void? The next line undercuts such notions and brings us back to the mundane, the shoes ("eyelets" here being a pun to recall lightly the notion of vision)—the unlaced suggests a kind of casualness, an idea reinforced by the cavalier way he reads contracts in the next line. The dead man saves himself from the despair of some of the bigger issues by focusing, as he says in the "Preface," on the fragment over the whole and, here, the tree for the forest. The forest then is metamorphosed, by opposition, into the fiery plain—recalling the isolated "white desert" from earlier. This movement through space—from the bathroom to a desert, forest, plain, counterpointed against the shoes and the spider, suggests a world where large and small coincide, where the usual visual boundaries dissolve, where, as in the next line, he sees through "a frameless window." Paradoxically, while he looks and sees some things he doesn't see others: he is unable to see inside or outside because these distinctions are no longer descriptive of his world—he waits, like a "gift in its box," a vision waiting to be seen. This brings us to the anniversary image of the last line, and the notion of time again, which we have been looking at in terms of space. The whole section has explored the problem of vision, its psychology and ambiguities, in the context of mortality, and it has done so through a series of surprising images and statements that don't seem at first to be linked but which actually follow a distinct poetic logic of their own.

The vocabulary of the second part of the poem, with words like *diagnosis* and *autopsy,* certainly extends this notion of mortality, but the second part also adds a sense of delight. After all, as he says, everything is its opposite: "up is down." The notion of speech, talking to other people, the future are also developed so that by the end the dead man seems both content and ready to explore. The next poem begins, "The dead man thinks he is alive when he hears his bones rattle," and then associates the bones with the body, pottery, a chandelier, pixels on a screen and several other things as now the focus turns more from worries over mortality to exploring the dead man's mode of living. The sequence keeps interlocking such images so that, by the end of the book, a rich texture of images, many repeated with differences to suggest modes of development, reveals a complex joy in the fragile and confused life we live in a nearly impenetrable universe.

In such a world, the Dead Man redefines everything, especially given his tautological perspective, his play of oppositions. In **#25, "About the Dead Man and Sin,"** an ethical system emerges that is coincident with the flux of history, and with whatever presents itself—"The dead man takes his direction from the placement of his feet, convinced that a pair of anything is no accident." In **#31** Love is redefined in unromantic and ironic terms: "The dead man and his wife bump their skeletons together like keys in a pocket." And in **#32** the apocalypse becomes not a metaphor for endings but for beginnings: "When the dead man reaches the Void, he

may throw an empty eyeball into space to start the whole thing up again." Ultimately, what *The Book of the Dead Man* does, by all its verbal pyrotechnics, is redefine sensibility, and this is the most essential thing any poetry can do. *The Book of the Dead Man* redefines our sensibilities, the way we look at the world, and redefines our poetry and the possibilities for future poetry. This is an astounding feat. There's not a greater gift any poet or poetry can bring.

Notes

1. New England University Press, 1994

2. Copper Canyon Press, 1994

Marvin Bell, Thom Tammaro, and Kristin Garaas (interview date April 26, 2001)

SOURCE: Bell, Marvin, Thom Tammaro, and Kristin Garaas. "Dead Man Talking." *American Poetry Review* 32, no. 1 (January/February 2003): 25-31.

[*In the following interview, conducted on April 26, 2001, Bell explains his method of selecting individual poems for inclusion in the collection* Nightworks: Poems 1962-2000 *and discusses the composition of his "dead man" poems, particularly "Sounds of the Resurrected Dead Man's Footsteps."*]

"Sounds of the Resurrected Dead Man's Footsteps (Abandonment of Distinctions)"

When there is no good or bad, no useful or useless, no up, no down, no right way, no perfection, then okay it's not necessary that there be direction: up is down.

When there is no pain, no welcoming, no hospitality, no disdain, there's no need to be stoical, the opportunity itself becomes disingenuous, emotion embodied in all things earth air fire and water.

When there is no adversity, no rise and fall, no ascension, no decline, no frost too early, no season too soon, then there's no planet too unstable, no ship in the sky better than another for the journey of a lifetime.

When there is no attachment, no necessity, no need, no outcome, no consequence of importance, then naturally sick is well, and the end leads to a green beginning.

When there is no one face, no two faces, no fragility of disposition, no anticipation, no revelation at midnight, then naturally years pass without anyone guessing the identity of the dead man.

When there is no balance, no even or uneven, no regulation, no permissible range, no parallax, no one sunrise, then naturally the dead man from a little salt on his tongue may concoct a new perspective.

When there is no more luck, no far side to a hard edge, no final rain, no fatal dehydration, no unwelcome visitation, no lingering suspicion, no terminal judgment, then the dead man is all black cats and rabbit paws.

When there is nowhere to go to find him, no circumstance, no situation, no jewel in the crown, no gem of the ocean, no pearl of the Antilles, no map, no buried treasure, only woods and more woods, then suddenly he will appear to you with a cortege of wolves or foxes in the midst of your blues.

When there is no measure of candlepower sufficient to enlighten, no temperature, no tolerance, no voltage, no current, no draw, no output, then it's historical lunacy to throw off a moon.

When there is no beginning, no end in sight, no perspective, no proportion, no discrete color, no golden triangle, no light at tunnel's end, no subjective complexion, then okay it's not a matter of where.

When there is no sin, no vice, no turning back, no other way, no help, no consolation, no punishment, no reward, then okay there's no good reason, and the ragamuffin arrives with the royalty.

When there is no more accidental, no inadvertence, no anthropological terrain sufficiently confined, no chaos unlinked to further chaos, no anarchy within anarchy, no thing of discrete substance, then nothing may come between thought and feeling.

When there is no birthday, no anniversary, no jubilee, no spree, no holiday, no one mass, meeting or service, then naturally it is up to each person whether to go ahead or turn back.

When there is no more wrinkling and weeping, no physiognomy of pleasure, no anticipation, no abundance, nothing extra, then okay it's the way it is, not the way we remember.

When there is no more regularity, no bottle of seeds, no injection of pollen, no gauze to map the outpouring, no tourniquet to staunch the expression, no crutch, no illness or health, then okay why not truth and beauty, why not blameless, helpless truth and beauty?

When there is no end result, no picaresque interval, no immediate or impending, nothing imminent that is not also the past, then why not roses and rubles, peace and prosperity, and okay it's not inconsequential to have come and gone.

When there is no more appetite, no inhalation, no absorption, no osmosis, no digestion, then okay let the reverie commence in the ether.

When there is no one body, no two bodies, no bird that was not a fish, no fish that will not hover, no snake that cannot learn to walk, no man or woman who did not crawl, then the possible and the probable conjoin to grant the blue heron a step.

When there is no more approbation, no license, no all-time immunity, no obedience or disregard, no loyalty that is not also the pick of the litter, no luck but dumb luck, then okay it's not a show, and spunk is what it takes.

When there is nothing but the client's good suit, the jury's self-doubt, the time since the crime, the charts and photos, the measurements and samples, then what knowledge is on trial, what rote redundancy passes for fact, what past lingers?

Where there is no more overriding impulse, no search for the truth that is not a battle to the death, no word left to meaning, no uncontested jurisdiction, no unacceptable flimflam, how then is a spinoff, a byproduct, an effect less significant than its cause?

When there is no more this way and that, hither and yon, north and south, no front-and-back, no side-to-side, no kitty-corner, no abreast, no opposite then suffice it to say that something happened.

When there is no more sacred or heretical, no promise, no guarantee, no warrant that places the millennium, no voltage too high or current too strong, then naturally there can be no one side, no one alone, no other and no otherwise.

When there is no more beseeching or gratitude, no seats remaining on the metaphysical seesaw, no zero-sum activity, no acquisition that is not also a loss, no finitude, then of course the dead man smiles as he blows a kiss through the wispy curtain of closure.

* * *

[*Tammaro*]: *So, Marvin, **Nightworks: Poems 1962-2000** is out. Thirty-eight years of poems. I'm curious about how this book defines you. When you look back, there are more than just poems there.*

[Bell]: Probably so. It's a lifetime. It's also a life. Well, *Nightworks* is thick enough to hold open a small door, but it's also a small selection from previous books. I did a selected with Atheneum in 1987 and had the same questions. How much of each book does one include? Do you excerpt sequences? *The Escape into You* is a sequence. So are *The Book of the Dead Man* and *Ardor*. There are long poems commissioned for books about the photography of Robert Heinecken and the paintings of Georgia O'Keeffe. What about uncollected poems from magazines and specialized anthologies? How about poems not published because time went by with other projects in view? How does one select? Rightly or wrongly, I decided to excerpt every series because otherwise the book would be, I felt, too thick. I took a dozen poems apiece from *The Book of the Dead Man* and *Ardor,* seventeen from the fifty-three in *The Escape into You* and twenty-one from the newest poems called **"Sounds of the Resurrected Dead Man's Footsteps."** Some poets simply publish a collected. They let the future decide. I can't say I know the right way to do it. I'm one of those who had to write a lot, and leave a lot unfinished, and throw away a lot.

[*Tammaro*]: *Did you bring anyone in, any friends, when you were putting the book together?*

Only my wife, Dorothy. I've never sent my manuscripts to others for advice. I did show the manuscript of *Stars Which See, Stars Which Do Not See* to a friend who happened to be in town, and he confirmed something I already sensed: that two of the poems didn't fit the book. Generally, however I do the work myself.

[*Tammaro*]: *When you look at a book of four decades of poems, what do you see in that arc from the early sixties to now?*

Each book was markedly different from the one before it. But time, and the limits of a selected, have blurred the distinctions. What do I see? In *Nightworks,* first I see someone learning to write and needing to write. Then I see an attitude, or philosophy, or vision— whatever you want to call it—that found many modes of expression and a range of circumstance. Of course now I see things about myself that I didn't know when I was writing the poems. The earlier poems look to me as if they were written by someone I used to know well. The other side of that, however, is that *he* didn't know *me* [laughing].

[*Tammaro*]: *Were you tempted to revise any of the work?*

Not now.

[*Tammaro*]: *By revising, I mean revising work already published in books.*

Only a couple of poems were altered from book to book. It's difficult to go back, especially if you feel experimental, which I always have. It's hard to go back to that person you used to be. It would be like rewriting letters you wrote when you were, twenty. How could you re-enter that sensibility?

[*Tammaro*]: *I've been reading Galway Kinnell's* New and Selected Poems. *He mentions in his foreword to the book that he can't leave a poem alone, and he talks about revising poems that he knows have already been in book form.*

Galway values the "mouth feel" of words, and he writes and reads aloud in a way that shows it. I wonder if he feels his verbal music has changed down the years and, if it has, is it now a better music or just a different music? These judgments are subjective.

[*Tammaro*]: *You bring such a different consciousness to a poem ten years later. It's hard to re-enter the original consciousness of that poem.*

That's right.

[*Garaas*]: *What assumptions do you make when you revise?*

I don't assume anything consciously. I just jump back in. Assumptions made outside the poem for the sake of the poem aren't my cup of tea. In any case, the poem, if it's any good, tests your assumptions. Revising free verse is somewhat different from revising formalist poetry. Rhyme and especially meter suggest an ideal form, a possibility of perfection that comes with loyalty to a codified form. But free verse finds its form inside the poet. It may be just as sublime but it's not in league with an ideal.

I've developed over the years a way of writing that doesn't involve as much ordinary revision as it once did. Now it's dangerous for me to say that, because someone may assume that I just said I don't revise. I do revise, of course, but now I try to do more of it in the white heat of composition. I try to get it right as I go, and if the energy flags I walk away from the poem. Sometimes it happens that I can't get back into that poem and I have to abandon it. To revise or extend a poem, I have to get back into the energy of the piece. I have to get into the feeling of it. I have to get my head located once again among the things of the poem, among the circumstances of the poem. I have to be again the poet who wrote that poem, which I can't always succeed in doing. And some poems don't want to come to life and breathe, and all the labor in the world will not make them do it. They may be improved in some classroom way by revision, but they will never get up and dance. I leave those poems behind. I have found that the amount and character of revision is directly related to where I started, and it is possible, it turns out, to start further down the road.

[*Garaas*]: *Which collection of poems do you feel contains your best work?*

Are you asking me to choose among my children? At any time, I'm probably going to say it's the book of the moment. I was the poet of *Things We Dreamt We Died For,* my first book, a limited edition which stuck close to home. I was that same poet plus a few years when *A Probable Volume of Dreams* appeared, the book of a young man still learning to write who had been in the Army and was now a teacher. Then *The Escape into You,* a young man's tortured sequence about love, marriage, divorce, sex and politics. It's quite different, but again it's who I was. The title of the fourth book, *Residue of Song,* suggests that which remains and the grit beneath song, and it contains a baker's dozen from an ongoing conversation with my father. He was an immigrant from Ukraine and passed away before I began to write. So there is a dark residue at the base of that book, and perhaps an anti-poetic bent.

The poems in **Stars Which See, Stars Which Do Not See** were written in what is sometimes called the "plain style." I needed to clarify. And things went on from there. If you ask me what portion of my writing best represents me now, I have to say it's the poems called **"Sounds of the Resurrected Dead Man's Footsteps,"** an outgrowth of *The Book of the Dead Man.* The reason it represents me now is that over the years I've come to realize that most of the time I am thinking many things at once. That's how my brain works. There are different ways in which brains work. This was explained to me one time by a polymath who knew the science. Mine works in a way that I believe she referred to as "explosive." The signals . . . what do you call those things?

[*Tammaro*]: *Synapses?*

Synapses, yes, they fire from different locations and . . . I can't fully explain it. Where signals intersect, there's a mini-explosion, if you will, and apparently that accounts for the way my brain works. I have a tendency to constantly be amalgamating several things at once arriving from divers angles. The Dead Man poems allowed me to license that manner of thinking. As do the poems that followed.

[*Tammaro*]: *If I remember correctly, every line in the Dead Man poems is a sentence. It's a grammatical sentence. In some ways, it's a kind of litany.*

Yes, in a Dead Man poem the sentence is the line, and the line is the sentence. There are one or two early exceptions. You see, I had come to feel through the years that the sentence is the secret, not just to prose but to poetry too. I saw that syntax provides all the opportunities, and that, for the free verse poet, the line by itself means nothing except insofar as it holds hands with syntax.

I don't think of free verse simply as an absence of meter. I don't think of it as a form or an absence of form. I think of it as a method for finding new forms. The line, of course, is important to all poets, but for free verse poets how to charge the line is a special issue because free verse doesn't normally employ a pattern of rhyme or rhythm, which can be powerful allies. The line apart from syntax carries no significance for me. Thus, the elastic sentence of the Dead Man poems offers plenty of variety even though every line is end-stopped. It's not unlike Whitman, of course. It's not unlike Christopher Smart. I experimented—I mean, I had

suffered line disease for so long [laughter] that in a way this was my recovery. What was the next step in terms of enjambments: not to use them at all.

[*Tammaro*]: *Go the other way?*

And to vary and compile the sentences. You know, it's seductive—having written a number of poems now in which the elasticity (or compression) of the sentence is paramount, as opposed to the usual blend of enjambments and end-stops. I wouldn't say that others should write that way. But for me it became irresistible. The sentences pile up, they layer perception in a way that matches my experience of the world. They modify the usual lyric possibility, especially with regard to organization and what some people call "closure." By the way, people send me "Dead Man" and "Dead Woman" poems. It's a form for anyone who can use it, though naturally the character of a true Dead Man poem depends on more than style. I'm a little sorry I didn't include in *Nightworks* the prefaces from *The Book of the Dead Man* and *Ardor.* They describe the terrain.

[*Tammaro*]: *You've sandwiched your work in* **Nightworks** *with Dead Man poems. It appears that looking for something new and experimental has been invigorating for you.*

It's the only way I know. As we speak, I'm between books and I'm not sure what I'll write next, if in fact I write at all. I found with the Dead Man poems that I could include anything if I could build a matrix for it. I found that it allowed me to touch on philosophical matters both within that matrix and outside it, which is the way I prefer to do it. I've said many times that I like ideas to have some dirt on their shoes and, you know, the Dead Man's shoes have a lot of dirt on them! The Dead Man poetic allows me to express what most matters to me in poetry: a philosophic stance embedded in what we take to be the material world. Then, also, it allows me to override distinctions, indeed as death erases them and as a particular viewpoint in life may undo them. So the Dead Man is alive and dead at the same time. He is not me but someone who knows a lot about me. The poetics gives me a good deal of flexibility. In the beginning, it also gave me a chance to, you know, to include jokes. There may not be jokes in the Dead Man Resurrected poems, but there are definitely jokes in the Dead Man poems. Kierkegaard said that laughter is a kind of prayer. Dead Man jokes are jokes of the Absurd, and absurdity is part of the scheme.

[*Tammaro*]: *When did you first meet the Dead Man? When did he introduce himself to you?*

It was winter. I was living in Port Townsend, Washington, on the Quimper Peninsula. The wind was trying to rip to shreds the American flag above the post office. I had recently put together a *New and Selected Poems* that was to be issued by Atheneum in 1987. I was reading Max Frisch's *Sketch-Books*. Our sons now lived far away. I was nearing fifty. There were many things on my mind. Life and death things. Love and loneliness things. Seeing and believing things. I was writing what I called "Pages"—pages mixing poetry with paragraphs whose character was something in between that of prose-poetry and the personal journal. Then I wrote a poem out of nowhere. That is, it seemed to come from elsewhere. I don't want to say that a voice was speaking through me. I'm not that mystical.

[*Tammaro*]: *You're not channeling, right! When did this happen?*

December of 1986. It felt as if it came from a book lost to antiquity, perhaps a "wisdom" book such as *The Egyptian Book of the Dead* or *The Tibetan Book of the Dead.* I called the poem **"From: *The Book of Dead Man"*** and included it in **Iris of Creation,** which appeared in 1990: I had no intention of writing another Dead Man-poem, let alone *The Book of the Dead Man.* At the time, it seemed like—excuse the joke—a dead end, although it turned out to be an open road.

[*Tammaro*]: *Would you read that poem?*

Sure. This is the original version of that first Dead Man poem. Before it reappeared in **The Book of the Dead Man,** I made a few changes.

From: The Book of the Dead Man

1. *About the Dead Man*:
The dead man thinks he is alive when he sees
   blood in his stool.
Seeing blood in his stool, the dead man thinks
   he is alive.
He thinks himself alive because he has no
   future:
Isn't that the way it always was, the way of life?
Now, as in life, he can call to people who will
   not answer.
Life looks like a white desert, a blaze of today
   in which nothing distinct can be made out,
   seen.
To the dead man, guilt and fear are
   indistinguishable.
The dead man cannot make out the spider at
   the center of its web.
He cannot see the eyelets in his shoes and so
   wears them unlaced.
He reads the large type and skips the fine print.
His vision surrounds a single tree, lost as he is
   in a forest.
From his porcelain living quarters, he looks out
   at a fiery plain.
His face is pressed against a frameless window.
Unable to look inside, unwilling to look outside,
   the man who is dead is like a useless gift in its
   box waiting:

it will have its yearly anniversary, but it would
   be wrong to call it a holiday.

2. *More about the Dead Man*:
The dead man can balance a glass of water on
   his head without trembling.
He awaits the autopsy on the body discovered
   on the beach beneath the cliff.
Whatever passes through the dead man's
   mouth is expressed;
everything that enters his mouth comes out
   of it.
He is willing to be diagnosed, as long as it
   won't disturb his future.
Stretched out, he snaps back like elastic.
Rolled over, he is still right-side-up.
When there is no good or bad, no useful or
   useless, no up, no down, no right way, no
   perfection, then ok it's not necessary that
   there be direction: up is down.
The dead man has the rest of his life to wait for
   color.
He finally has a bird's-eye view of the white hot
   sun.
He finally has a complete sentence, from his
   head to his feet.
He is, say, America, but he will soon be, say,
   Europe.
It will be necessary merely to cross the ocean
   and pop up
in the new land, and the dead man doesn't
   need to swim.
It's the next best thing to talking to people in
   person.

As you can see on the page, the original is not always one sentence to a line.

[*Tammaro*]: *Time to revise!*

I didn't know, when I wrote it, that later I would make it all one sentence per line. It was moving that way, but I didn't yet see it. In fact, I didn't write another Dead Man poem for four years. After four years I wrote a second one, and the next thing I knew I wrote another and another, and I was hooked. The strategy hooked me, the inclusiveness hooked me, the new way of thinking about syntax and line hooked me. The possibility of making a sentence that integral and elastic hooked me. The sheer metabolics of the thing hooked me. And of course the content had hooked me years before.

[*Tammaro*]:*While you were writing those, were you writing other kinds of poems too, or were you totally occupied by the Dead Man poems?*

Once I wrote the second Dead Man poem, it was pretty much all Dead Man.

[*Tammaro*]: *He had you in his grip!*

I didn't resist. It seemed to me a richer trail than any other I might have followed at the time. I had been fallow, awaiting a new form. However, I did write a poem now and then outside the Dead Man series, usually for a special anthology or an event.

[*Tammaro*]: *But the Dead Man was occupying your writing life.*

He was.

[*Tammaro*]: *The Dead Man was in charge.*

Yes. You know, I have a rule that whenever I give students a writing assignment, Teacher has to do the assignment too. During that time, whenever my students and I had assigned writing to do, whatever the assignment, I would turn it into a Dead Man poem. I wrote many more Dead Man poems than appeared in *The Book of the Dead Man* and *Ardor*. And the same is true of **"Sounds of the Resurrected Dead Man's Footsteps."** There are many more than appear in *Nightworks*. Is it wasteful? Perhaps. We work as we have to. And I happen to think it's useful, and a sign of respect to students, when the teacher gets down in the trenches with them.

William Carlos Williams made a remark in *Paterson* I find compelling. He wrote, "Only one solution," then there is a colon, "Only one solution: to write carelessly so that nothing that is not green will survive." Now he probably *had* to think that way because he was a doctor when they made house calls. He was terribly busy. And his metabolism was on fire. Well, I am somewhat the same. My metabolism and my lifestyle have never lent themselves to a writing schedule. I've always been more or less willing to jump into the middle of anything.

Along that line, if I had known how to become the cornet player I needed to be to play the best, most challenging jazz, I might have stayed with it. I was a pretty fair country cornet player, and I played with all kinds of groups, but I knew I would never be good enough as a jazz musician. Even though I played jazz, I didn't know how, and I came from a small town where we didn't know where to go to learn how. We didn't know you *could* go. Long before I stopped playing, I knew I would quit. Well, one of the things I love about jazz is that you jump into the middle of it, and you sink or swim, you improvise, you know the chord structure and you use it or you don't use it, and you have to think on your feet. I like the feeling of thinking on your feet, and I would like to incorporate it into writing. Not, obviously, to superficial ends. So the attitude I prefer is a mixture of being aware and unaware at the same time. Does that make sense?

[*Tammaro*]: *Last night during your reading, and then again just a little while ago, you made an interesting comment about your sense of free verse, that it is a way of learning new forms. Is there someone out there you feel is using free verse the way you conceive of it?*

I can't name just one or two because there are dozens writing in dozens of ways. And that's the point: free verse is an opportunity for new looks, sounds and structures. As far as I know, no one else is doing what I'm doing in the Dead Man and Dead Man Resurrected poems. Obviously, I have my own poetics. I'm not a joiner. As for free verse poets to admire, there are dozens, maybe hundreds. Of course, among the big mommies and daddies, one still begins with Whitman and Williams.

[*Tammaro*]: *Right.*

And Marianne Moore, even when she was writing syllabics. You know, Williams wasn't nervous about Stevens as a competitor. He had a tricky relationship with Stevens, who condescended to him. But he was impressed by Marianne Moore. He felt that she always wrote poetry. Whether it was her best or her worst, the essential quality of poetry was present in every poem. Williams sensed that she understood, and I think it's true, that the seeds for the new poetry were in prose. She sometimes used syllabic counts, which of course one cannot hear and which do not eliminate stresses, to create a poetry not unlike free verse.

Williams himself was busy trying to express the American idiom and eventually employing what he called "the variable foot," which is a cagey notion, perhaps intended to impress metricians. He was trying to modulate free verse and also to write in the American idiom, by which he meant American rhythms and phrases. It was his achievement and his misfortune that his small idiomatic poems are more widely known than his more substantial work.

As you come forward, closer to my generation—I'm skipping well ahead now—the generation of American poets ahead of mine was a fabulous generation for exploding into individual voices. It includes accomplished formalists, and it also includes a great number of poets who started as formalists and moved into free verse. It's impossible to name just a few, but we could start with Robert Creeley. His stance toward writing comes out of Charles Olson, but his sense of language seems to me to come from Williams. There were other clear descendants of Williams, such as Denise Levertov. And there was Olson and his idea of "projective verse," and the poets who, like Creeley, were associated with Black Mountain College, and there were the Beats, above all Ginsberg, who was Whitmanian. There was John Logan writing rhyming free verse. There were formalists, such as Donald Justice, who turned to free verse with a memory of meters—which is one common sound of free verse. There are a trainload of distinctive free verse voices in that generation: Kinnell, Bly, Sexton, Plath, Merwin, Snyder, Stafford, Mezey, Corso, O'Hara, Koch, Ashbery, Oppen, Zukofsky, Rich, Hugo, Dugan, Ignatow, McGrath, Carruth, James Wright. I have just begun. That generation goes on and on.

[*Tammaro*]: *One reason I'm after this is that my students want to understand the conversation between formalism and informalism.*

Look, I think I have fallen in love with the way of the Dead Man poems, which dispenses with the argument. I don't know for certain, but the experiment of free verse may be over. And I think that's what I felt when I—what?—abandoned?—enjambments entirely. I felt the experiment was over, that the battle had been won. It was won by the generation ahead of mine, and, if I may say it, mine. And maybe one generation after me, maybe two. I don't know how old I am now [laughing]. It depends on how many hundreds of years old I am. The battle is over. And it is important to acknowledge that there are also, still, as always, accomplished formalist poets among us. Formalism is just like free verse in that one has to be engaged by the materials. Eliot said it: No verse is free for the man who would do a good job. Man or woman.

[*Garaas*]: *So where do you see poetry going?*

Other things are happening besides the long dialogue between formalists and free verse writers. One of them, going on for a long time now, is the influence of other cultures and their writing. In other words, our poetry has become worldlier. Also, literary theory has had a big influence in the past decade. One can debate whether or not theory has been useful. Some of it seems to me to be baby knowledge, constantly rediscovering the extent to which language is relative and subjective. That's baby knowledge. The world is impure, so is language, get on with it! Poems concerned mainly with the impossibility of total communication, or the distance between the word and the thing, are sophomoric, no matter how lively. They're reductive and conceptually backward. There is a whole school of American brainiac poets who constitute an avant garde that has shrunk poetic content. They are very good at delineating the microscopic. But the great experimentalists expanded content.

On the other hand, some poems are verbally exciting— that much, anyway—precisely because they are acting out a theory. And much of that poetry is now written in paragraphs or even whole pages. And it's all interesting to me as lively surface work. I suspect that, for some poets, intense self-consciousness is confirmation of their intelligence. Well, there are all kinds of poetries out there. Some gain force from the ethnicity of the poet, some from drawing on other cultures, some from theory, some from verbal magic and some from a poet's vision.

[*Garaas*]: *Who's doing that?*

Oh, don't make me name names. I would be embarrassed to have forgotten some. In any case, there are a thousand poets out there, and more than a few of these little-known poets are the equals of poets known to many.

[*Tammaro*]: *I want to be able to tell my students about new, younger writers. It's like bibliotherapy: you read someone's work and then you want to say to a student, "Why don't you read this and then come back in a week."*

Sometimes they read it.

[*Tammaro*]: *Right, right.*

It can be beneficial to read recent books. But it's often more useful to read work that is too old to be part of the poetry wars, or at least work not caught up in fashionable opinion. I tend not to read a book that has just become big news. I prefer to wait two years.

[*Tammaro*]: *Earlier you mentioned "a thousand poets." It sounds as if the poetic life in this country is very healthy. Sometimes I hear people complaining, "There are too many poets in America," and I wonder about the other arts: do painters complain of too many painters? Do photographers complain of too many photographers? Are there too many guitar players? Too many dancers? Too many sculptors? There's a sense of people wanting to close the gates.*

There's nothing wrong with playing a game, or even practicing an art, as well as one can.

[*Tammaro*]: *Right!*

We can't create more good poems by preventing bad poems. And even the weakest poems are valid as self-expression. Poetry, like water, seeks its own level. Everyone starts from somewhere and, if they go on with it, they get better. The notion that we should limit the number of poetic licenses seems miserly. I mean, we have plenty of highways.

[*Garaas*]:*So what do you think it takes to be a successful writer, knowing there are all kinds of poets out there? What would be a success story for you?*

There are good poets and there are better poets. What do you mean by successful?

[*Garaas*]:*I have my own ideas about that, but I'm interested in yours.*

Well, I think poets feel successful when they write a poem that seems to them fully realized. But then there's worldly success, recognition for being a poet or, even better, recognition for a poem. And that is a rubbery thing. Suppose you start out thinking it would be wonderful to be published in a good magazine. And maybe it happens. Then you decide it would be really wonderful if they would run two of your poems at the same time. And maybe that happens. Then you think, well, it would be even more wonderful if they would print my name on the cover. And that happens. So then you say, I would never want anything else in life if someone would just publish a book of mine. And maybe that happens too. And then you think, why wasn't I nominated for the big prize?

Muhammad Ali had the definitive word about this. He was being interviewed by Howard Cosell. Cosell interviewed him for a long time. Finally, Cosell said, Tell me, Muhammad, what is the most important thing in your life? Ali said something like, It's my religion and my charity work. And Cosell said, Wait a minute! You may be the most famous man in the world, you have been heavy-weight champion, you've dined with presidents, with kings and queens, and you're telling me the most important thing in your life is your work for charity? And Ali said, You know, Howard, a man wants a car and he gets one, and then he wants a better car. He wants a house and he gets a house, and then he wants a bigger house. Ali said, We're never satisfied, and you know why? Because the objects of our desire are finite—and "finite" is my word because I don't recall the word he used—he said, The objects of our desire are finite, but our desire is infinite.

The response of others is a bonus I cherish. And I'm like anyone, sometimes thinking, well gee, this book should have been noticed here or there. But one doesn't have any control over that, especially if one is not an active networker. I just don't want to live that way, so I don't. And I think I've been lucky. There are good poets out there struggling to find publishers for their first or second books, and there are many others who have published books throughout their careers yet have had to look periodically for another publisher. I have been very fortunate, thanks to the late Harry Ford, who published seven of my books at Atheneum, to Sam Hamill, who has published four books at Copper Canyon, and to others for particular books that appeared from other publishers.

Do I think *Nightworks* should have been on the list of Pulitzer Prize nominees? Absolutely. To me it's an indication of the limitations of the committee, or perhaps of the process, that it was not, but of course it wasn't for me to decide, and it shouldn't be given importance. I know many writers who have had enormous literary success and who have not been made happy or contented by it. They wanted something from art that art could never give them. You know, often we work hard at something because we have it in our heads that it will lead to something else. And we don't really appreciate it for what it is. Well, that attitude courts disappointment. Poetry, like all art, is a manifestation of other, deeper things. It can be too highly prized by the poet. It can never be too highly prized at the moment of a poet's or reader's engagement with it, but it can be crucially overestimated in a larger context.

If I could draw cartoons, I would draw an ambitious poet scaling Parnassus, the mountain that the great poets ascend. Picture our poet climbing Parnassus and destroying everything in his path. He cuts down whatever is in his way, uses everyone, maneuvers to his advantage, and makes it. He—or she—arrives at the top, having wrecked everything in the name of art, and when he looks up he sees that all around him are much higher peaks labeled Grief, Love, War, Peace, Poverty, Illness, Family, Ecstasy—you know, big things. And it turns out that Parnassus is not the highest place around after all.

So, I think you know that "success" is a tricky word. Someone asked Picasso which of his paintings was his favorite, and he said, famously, "The next one." I think every writer feels that way because, when you're writing, you escape time. When you're totally engaged by the materials, you escape time. And then, if you can also make a poem that says more than words can say, well, then you're really onto something. If you're lucky enough, it happens once in a while. That is success of an important kind, the only kind that sustains you, though "success" seems too limited a word for it. Has all this made sense?

[*Garaas*]:*Sure, sure, definitely it does. So what would you say you have gained as a writer?*

Good question. Poetry has given me a way to locate and embed my sense of what meaning is, my sense of life and death, and my sense of much else. It's given me a method by which to track and understand vision and emotion. A lot of language is always going through me. Poetry has helped me to confirm that everything goes together, that things can enter my consciousness from all different angles, and, if I'm alert enough, I can spot how they fit together. And if I'm lucky and receptive, the pieces suggest a bigger whole, and with a few red threads I can sew them together. But look at the differences from book to book. I feel as if I have been more than one poet. It's a stream, it's a continuing process, and there aren't any watersheds at which points one can say, This is it, this is what I wanted, because it's not about wanting.

[*Tammaro*]: *In one of your autobiographical pieces, you mention that earlier in your life you were interested in music, photography, pottery, and then eventually poetry. I'm wondering how poetry emerged from that cluster. When did you know that it gave your life coherence and meaning, that it nourished you and would eventually push those other arts into the background?*

A lot of it was dumb luck and what was available. In the small town where I grew up on the south shore of eastern Long Island, music was available. I started cornet in fourth grade. As I mentioned earlier, I eventually gave it up because I wasn't going to be good enough as a jazz musician. I'm pretty sure now that I would not have been good enough, even if I had found a way to pursue it. So I gradually let it slip. Creative photography was another matter. By the way, we called it "creative photography" to distinguish it from photojournalism.

[*Tammaro*]: *Like using the term "creative nonfiction" to distinguish it from journalism?*

Exactly. That was a very exciting time. The great photographers were unusual people. I had always been interested in odd ducks. Before photography, before pottery and poetry, there was amateur radio. My call sign was W2IDK. One of the things I liked about being a ham radio operator was that it was filled with odd grownups—not kids, but grownups. They were odd ducks, and they were nice to me. I would pedal my bike up back roads to visit them, and they would teach me radio. They were a community within the community.

Now, creative photography, when I began to make photographs, was not yet widely taught in universities. I felt like an outsider among outsiders, involved in something new and experimental. I stumbled onto this person and that person, beginning with Nathan Lyons, whose name serious photographers will know, and one thing led to another. But eventually I quit photographing. One reason was that it was going to be difficult to maintain a darkroom. I was headed into the Army and who-knows-where afterward. Another was that I had the feeling that I had learned what I needed from photography. I had learned a way of seeing. Also, I had theoretical questions with the medium itself. I didn't think that creative photography could continue to distinguish itself amidst the proliferation of images everywhere. Moreover, I felt that an image had a fatally tenuous, and potentially misleading, connection with its content and with the intention of the photographer. Yet to add words to it to direct the viewer, as some people did, vulgarized it. Clarence John Laughlin, for example, the photographer who helped save the Watts Towers with his color slides in *Life* magazine, was a wonderful photographer who had a happy habit of talking his photos to death. Talking about deeper meanings, you know, and giving his pictures symbolic titles. He was a better photographer than that. He didn't need that stuff.

An image lives on its own as an image. Photography is a print-making medium. So I had some theoretical problems with its place in society, and it was difficult to keep a darkroom, and I felt I had learned what I could. I gave it up gradually. First I started taking out my 4 × 5 camera without film. I would set it up, put the black hood over my head and adjust the tilts, swings, bellows and lens, compose the image, and then move on.

Eventually I stood the camera in my apartment in Hyde Park in Chicago and pointed it at objects on a table lit by a single lamp. I would look at the ground glass and compose the image, but I wouldn't shoot the picture. Later, in Iowa City, I returned to taking pictures for a time, but I had already begun to quit. This may sound strange, but after a while I felt that I didn't need the camera either.

Pottery. I knew I wouldn't continue, because I couldn't work that hard, physically. And I struggled awkwardly to make pots. Let me tell you a story. As a graduate student bum at the University of Iowa, I had the key to the pot shop when my friend Frank DiGangi and his wife Carole Worthington came to visit. Frank was not a potter, but he had been required to take a pottery course as a sculpture major at Alfred University. I said to him, I've got the key, let's throw some pots, and off we went. I sat at the wheel struggling with bottle shapes, the only form I was throwing at the time, and I looked over at Frank. He's a big guy. And he was throwing effortlessly. Now, he was not throwing a great pot, but his relationship to the clay was natural, and mine, I realized then and there, was not. I remember thinking, Yes, that's the way it should be, and so a few days later I turned in the key. Before I turned in the key I lined up all my bisqued pots, gathered stones and broke them. Dorothy made me keep a couple of the finished pots, but I never threw another one. The years went by, and Frank DiGangi and Carole Worthington became fabulous production potters.

[*Tammaro*]: *So with words and poetry, I'm going to guess, you felt more of a natural affinity.*

Yes.

[*Tammaro*]: *It was natural, and you could do it easily, the way your friend threw pots. Your relationship with words felt right.*

Yes. Though "easily" isn't quite right. "Naturally" is and so is "helplessly." I'm naturally a verbal sort, and the language as it comes and goes within me leans toward combinations and transformations.

[*Tammaro*]: *Obviously, you were a young man working your way through these things called "the arts," and you were trying them out, like trying on clothes. Something fits really well and the rest of the stuff you leave behind and you walk out feeling great!*

In the beginning, my interest in the arts was mainly in the unusual wiring of some people. People can be wired differently, one from another, and it's in the arts where you see it clearly. I was fascinated by the eccentricity of individual expression and also by the possibility that the arts could say more than words can say. That even poetry could use words to get beyond words. Of course, once you become interested in an art, you become interested also in people who are involved in that art. Theater people get interested in a community of actors. It can move in either direction. You like theater people, say, and the next thing you know you are absorbed by theater. You are intrigued by poets, and the next thing you know you are involved with poetry. Maybe it's also because they're having the best parties.

[*Tammaro*]: *Bill Stafford has a wonderful thought about the community of readers and writers: "The literary world is a community in that one interchanges with others naturally and becomes an insider, not by deals or stealth, but by a natural engagement with the ongoing work of other writers, editors, and publishers."*

Bill felt that writing was a natural human activity, and he had a humorous way of talking about poetry editors. He would say, Well, there are many magazines out there and many editors, and they *need* our poems. Bill had a special maneuver he would sometimes perform during readings. He'd be reading along, and of course he was a beloved reader and a beloved poet, and sometimes after he read a poem, you'd hear little "oohs" or murmurs from the audience because people liked it. And he would say, "This poem appeared in . . . ," and he would name some little magazine, and if you had never heard him do this, you'd think, Is he going to brag about his publishing? And then he would say, "But before the heroes at such-and-such a magazine took this poem, it went to some other magazines where the editors were not so heroic." And he would turn over the page on which he had typed or pasted his poem—because that's how he carried his poems to a reading—and he would start to read the list of magazines that had rejected the poem. The list would contain both well-known magazines and magazines one had never heard of, and it would go on and on and on and on. He might read twenty or thirty names, and it was a lesson for the whole audience: that it only takes one editor to say yes.

[*Tammaro*]: *I saw him do this on several occasions.*

The lesson is also that rejection is not personal, that others are getting their poems back the same day you get yours. So it's the writing that matters, and one should let the chips fall where they may.

[*Tammaro*]: *I always loved it when he would give readings. He would come to the podium and never have any books. Most writers want to read from their books. Bill would reach into his pocket like he was looking for a scrap of paper and he'd pull out a wad of paper and unfold it. And there would be a dozen or so poems that he had put together for the reading that night. He would read from scraps of paper—not from his new and selected poems or any of his sixty books.*

Occasionally the version he was carrying was not identical to the version in the book. Several times I heard him read a poem that I recognized as being different from the book version. It had been changed a little in typing a copy to carry—accidentally, I felt. But it didn't matter to him. The quality that made that particular piece a poem was still there, he felt, even if some of the words had been changed—which is almost heretical, you know.

[*Tammaro*]: *You collaborated on a couple of books with him,* Segues *and* Annie-Over. *You had a special relationship with him, and you taught with him at Port Townsend. Have you had that sense with other writers?*

I have good friends, but no one else with whom I have written poems back-and-forth. Bill and I did it without intending to publish the poems as a series. Then Steven Cramer, who was working at Godine, offered to do a collection, so we cut it off at a point that made a book. It was good to do. It made the mail more interesting. Bill would sometimes send more than one poem. One would be for the series, and the others would be poems he had written the same day. He was prolific!

[*Tammaro*]: *It might be a good exercise for young writers to engage in things like that to keep the juices going.*

That's a point we made in the introductions to *Segues* and *Annie-Over*. That any two or three or four can do this. It's a back-and-forth thing. I have been told that a poet in the generation ahead of mine suggested to a friend that they try this, years ago. But the second poet wouldn't do it, and I can imagine many poets would not, because you have to submerge your ego to the whole, you have to be willing to pick up a thread from the other person's poem and react. I felt that I tried to adopt Bill's manner in writing back. I wasn't all that successful, but it stands as an example of the writing life and the possibility of community. And Bill told me he felt the best poems he had written that year were for what became *Segues*.

[*Tammaro*]: *Reading some of your autobiographical pieces, I noticed that you talked about a child's sense of playfulness that you remember from when you were growing up. I see some of that in your work—certainly in the Dead Man poems, there's a lot of playfulness—and I'm thinking of all the different mediums in which you've worked. I'm wondering if playfulness has sustained you over the years.*

It has helped. Playfulness is just an interest in the materials. Someone hands you blocks when you're little, and it turns out they can be used to make designs or spell words, and maybe the shapes and words lead onward, but always there's an interest in the materials themselves, and it never goes away for a writer. Even when one's subject is dramatic, horrific, or profound, there's still that pleasure in the writing.

[*Tammaro*]: *There must be something nourishing about it because, if there were no nourishment, you wouldn't be doing it. It must nourish something in the soul.*

Yes, certainly it's something like that. Writers are people who are helpless not to write. Is it endorphins? Is it the feeling of escaping time? Is it linked to vision and expression? Is it the playfulness, the materials handled like toys? Is it needing to say more than words can say? Or is it simply, finally, that the imagination—and I would add philosophy—are survival skills?

[*Tammaro*]: *It's interesting to hear you say all of those things, how much more important they are than success.*

They are, but we're all human, and we can't help but be affected by what goes on. Robinson Jeffers remarked that a poet doesn't need protection from his enemies, but from his friends, the implication being that flattery doesn't help, either. Jeffers was fierce. I once visited his tower. I was living in San Francisco. I called Carmel. I'm usually too shy to do this sort of thing, but I wanted very much to see it.

[*Tammaro*]: *Hawk Tower.*

Hawk Tower. I found a phone number for his son, who lived there, not in the tower but in the larger, adjacent Tor House. I said to him, I've been living in San Francisco, and I'm about to leave, and I may not be back. Is there any chance that I can come see it, and he said okay. It turned out he had a nephew visiting who took me through the tower. There is a staircase inside the wall, up to the roof.

[*Tammaro*]: *When you were an undergraduate at Alfred University in the 1950s, hanging around the ceramic shop, was that workshop/studio environment interesting to you? And I'm wondering if you carried some of that with you to Iowa. Or was it already there in Iowa?*

A workshop community already existed in Iowa City. Artist communities have meant a lot to me. The first was at Alfred. It was dumb luck that I went there. Generally, people from my home town didn't attend college, and Alfred was a random choice on my part. Well, the Design Department of the College of Ceramics, which is a state college but is housed in the private university, attracted wonderful, freaky young artists, many of them from New York City. Being a state college inside a private university, the Alfred Design Department was probably the cheapest art school they could find. Yet the faculty was outrageously good. Well,

I had never before seen young people who, because they had work to do, didn't care what other people thought of them.

In the 50s, we cared too much about what other people thought. It was easy to offend people then. Omigoodness, it was so easy to offend people. It wasn't a bad time. I don't want to endorse stereotypes about the period. Nonetheless, I had not yet seen young people who had work to do, a passion for work that defined their sense of themselves. I used to take late walks, in any weather, and I would usually stop at the Design Department because there were always students there making lithographs, potting and painting, and they'd have food, they'd have music. They were having a lot more fun than most of the other students. And I, I wanted to be one of them, although I didn't know how to, so I just watched. By the way, I didn't try potting at Alfred. I threw my first pot years later. But I did begin photographing while there. And I was still playing my horn.

After Alfred, I did a semester of graduate journalism in Syracuse. And from there I moved to Rochester and then to Chicago. In Chicago I fell in with the young photographers who were studying with Aaron Siskind and Harry Callahan at the Institute of Design. And I also took up with a group of poets who made up what was known as "The Poetry Seminar," though it wasn't connected to a college. First I took a registered class from John Logan, who was teaching at Notre Dame and riding the bus to Chicago one night a week to teach in the downtown center of the University of Chicago. Then Logan invited me to join The Poetry Seminar, poets who met informally with Logan. It included some very talented poets. Dennis Schmitz and Bill Knott were in it, Charles Simic passed through, as did Naomi Lazard, William Hunt and Roger Aplon. So here was another special community, and it made a difference to me.

It was Logan who suggested I go to Iowa City to the Writers' Workshop. Chicago was the farthest west I had been. I was nervous about Iowa, so I took the bus. I thought, that's the wilds! And there again, in Iowa City, I ran into a community of young, energetic writers. It's good luck when you run into other people, especially of your own age, who are interested in what drives you. You feed off each other.

[*Tammaro*]: *So when you got there as a teacher, did you want the workshop to be a version of what you found at Alfred? Is that something you tried to create?*

I suppose so—not so much to create as to maintain. Really, Iowa City was already a very lively community of artists. So when I was asked back to teach in the fall of 1965, one of the attractions was being among other writers. You know, I had not published a book yet. It was different then. People made decisions about you without looking first at a bibliography to prove what they thought. They had confidence in their judgments. Or maybe it was only the people at the Workshop who had confidence. In any case, when I was hired to teach the young poets, I felt myself to be one of them, and that's how I taught. Those early students were close friends of mine, and we were all just in it together. To me, the idea of a workshop is that we're all in it together. But of course I got older and I published books.

[*Tammaro*]: *And the students got younger.*

And the students got younger, of course, so I can't just be one of them anymore.

[*Tammaro*]: *Sure, but you felt—and helped to foster—a sense of community there.*

I hope so. I'm more alone now than I was then. Of course, you can't help that, and as you go on working in your art, you carve your own path, which diverges from everyone else's path. You start together in some anteroom. Then each of you goes off into your own tunnel, as it were, from where each of you can hear your friends' tools clanking against the pipes as they work. But ever afterward, you see the result, not the method. You have become a specialist of your own way of writing.

[*Garaas*]: *Do you think that's where the basis of the idea of "workshop poetry" comes from?*

What is that, what is workshop poetry?

[*Garaas*]: *Something manufactured, homogenized?*

[*Tammaro*]: *Formulaic?*

The workshop has taken the blame for there being a style of the age. But there is always a style of the age. Second-best poetry is always second-best poetry. It has nothing to do with workshops. I was asked about this during a forum at the Des Moines National Poetry Festival: Someone asked about the controversy over workshops, and I said what I believe: people who don't like workshops hate young people. That's it. After all, no one pretends to teach genius. Can poetry writing be taught? Nobody knows, but we know it can be learned. And a lot of learning seems to go on in the presence of other poets, even of teachers.

Beginners are beginners, young people are young people, and art is a great big yes! People come to writing programs as they come to art classes and to writing classes at the undergraduate level. These are the last places where they are giving their teachers a chance to

say yes. All their lives people have been saying, Don't do this, do that, and Don't do it this way, do it that way. In art you get a chance to hear Yes. Yes, try it, make something where before there was nothing.

But the literary world contains a lot of paranoia. You're a writer; maybe you're a poet. All around you, a devastatingly commercial society seems to be saying, Why bother? That creates a kind of paranoia which, in turn, turns into blame. People used to go to Paris and hang around the café tables. That was their workshop. Greenwich Village was another. Iowa City and other writing programs are places where writers gather now.

People who blame Iowa City will talk about the sameness of workshop poetry. And my response is simple. I just start naming poets whose books they probably know and who attended the Iowa poetry workshop. I just start naming them. I ask: does Michael Burkard write like Rita Dove? Does Rita Dove write like James Tate? Does James Tate write like Tess Gallagher? Does Tess Gallagher write like Sandra Cisneros? Does Sandra Cisneros write like Juan Felipe Herrera? Does Juan Felipe Herrera write like David Schloss? Does David Schloss write like Larry Levis? Did Larry Levis write like William Stafford? Did William Stafford write like Donald Justice? Does Donald Justice write like Barrett Watten? Does Barrett Watten write like Norman Dubie? Does Norman Dubie write like Robert Grenier? Does Robert Grenier write like W. D. Snodgrass? Does W. D. Snodgrass write like Mona Van Duyn? Does Mona Van Duyn write like Joy Harjo? Does Joy Harjo write like Peter Klappert? Does Peter Klappert write like Marcos McPeek Villatoro? Does Marcos McPeek Villatoro write like Michael Harper? Does Michael Harper write like Debora Greger? Does Debora Greger write like David St. John? I mean, hello! The cats are talking! I could go on like this for two hundred names. I wonder if people blame art departments for mediocre art. I suppose the ignorant do.

[*Tammaro*]: *Again, the analogy; are there too many musicians? Is the music department responsible for bad music, or photography departments responsible for bad photography?*

No. It's just that, when a great number of people practice an art, not everyone is going to be the best.

[*Tammaro*]: *Exactly.*

Earlier you asked what kind of age this is for poetry. It's a rich time for poetry all over the world and in this country too. Three hundred years from now, readers will look back and think the poetry of this time equivalent to that of one of the great Chinese dynasties when poetry thrived. That's a problem for editors of anthologies. It's hard to see through the fog created by the politics of poetry, which I think are awful right now, never worse perhaps, but that's a social function, not an aesthetic one.

[*Tammaro*]: *So how does a young writer who is involved in all that, who is in the swirl of things, keep his or her bearings? How does a young poet stay the course? You've been a witness for forty years, you've seen what happens.*

Well, most young writers eventually quit. They quit because they need to make a living. They quit because they no longer can find the time, energy, or mental space for it. Others quit because they didn't receive public success early and needed it. Some quit because they have long term emergencies. Then there are those who don't quit art but change art forms.

In the end, as I said earlier, writers are people who are helpless not to write. They go on writing no matter what. Think of Ray Carver, who was struggling to make a living for so many years. At one time he took two jobs at once. He was teaching at the University of Iowa for the Writer's Workshop and he also had a job in California, and he was flying between the two campuses. The story goes that he told United Airlines that if they'd give him a pass to fly free, he would mention them in his short stories. Reportedly they gave him the pass but took it back once they saw how much he was using it. At one time, Ray wrote in his parked car. People who need to write will write.

But there's another kind of writer. The one who writes as one more aesthetic event in his or her life. The kind of writer who leads a rational, reasonable existence, and art is simply a civilized function of it. Those writers write a poem now and then, or a story now and then, and more power to them. But the other kind of writer, of course, is the one who doesn't just write now and then but is writing all the time, even when he or she is not recording it.

[*Tammaro*]: *I think about a class of twenty-five undergraduates, and I wonder how many of them are going to write seriously for the rest of their lives. So maybe what we're doing is building an audience.*

Well, poetry has an importance to a culture all out of proportion to its sales. Poetry doesn't have to be defined by books; it doesn't have to sell widely for poetry to matter. The same is true for good prose. Did you know that Phil Jackson, the basketball coach, gives each of his players a book before each road trip? Generally, of course, they don't read them. When asked about it he said, Well, that book will sit on a shelf in the player's house, and maybe someday he'll take it down and read it. It's a nice idea. Mark Twain said that the man who does not read has no advantage over the one who can-

not read. Look, as I said earlier, the imagination, and philosophy too, are not just college electives or personal pleasures. They are survival skills.

[*Tammaro*]: *So you get to Iowa in 1965, and forty years later you're the Poet Laureate of Iowa. What does the Poet Laureate of Iowa do? I mean this kid from Long Island finds himself in Iowa in 1965 and forty years later he's the Poet Laureate. The first one, not the second, third or tenth!*

As I understand it, someone phoned the governor's office and asked who the Poet Laureate was and found out there wasn't one. So the next thing you know there was a movement, and then a committee. There are no official duties. It's mainly honorific. I prefer to think that these poet laureate positions should not be about the poets who hold them. I like to think that the appointment is an acknowledgment that there are writers among us including poets, and that it matters. As for the consequences of serving in the position—I've always tried to be accessible, so that's no different. I do receive a few extra e-mails and phone calls, and requests to do this and that. By the way, I own a cap that carries the words, "Poultry Lariat."

[*Tammaro*]: *So it's been fun?*

It's been an opportunity to talk turkey about poetry. Earlier, we were talking about whether poetry matters. Poets have various ideas about who they write and read aloud for. Some people write and read for the Faithful Thirteen—the experts, those with clout. I prefer to read for those who came because their girlfriend or boyfriend or spouse came, or their teacher told them to and they're not sure what they're in for. I hope they will leave feeling that, even in its eccentricity, poetry is a natural thing. I would like to interest them enough so they return for the next reader. It's not about me, it's about poetry. And I find that people are interested in poetry if you talk turkey to them. One can. One can speak informally by the light of a high standard. That was my aim when I wrote essays for *The American Poetry Review* under the title "Homage to the Runner."

[*Tammaro*]: *Sometimes it's nice to preach to the converted. It feels good. You feel like a success when everyone is "amen-ing" along with you, but sometimes it's nice not to have the converted out there.*

I think most literary conversions turn out to be temporary. That's okay. True believers are not ideal either. Speaking of preaching, I have been twice asked to deliver summer sermons to the largest Unitarian fellowship in Seattle, and I'm not a Unitarian. I didn't know what to expect. Well, it was okay. The first time, there was quite a bit of applause afterwards. And the fellow leading me off the stage said, "I've been coming to this fellowship for five years, and I've never before heard a sermon applauded." I was wearing an eye patch that summer, and I think I got the sympathy vote.

[*Tammaro*]: *The Dead Man gives a sermon from the pulpit. So are you retired or retiring at this point from teaching?*

I'm in "phased retirement," during which I teach one semester a year for five years. The prerequisite to phased retirement is geezerhood.

[*Tammaro*]: *How long have you been doing that?*

I began teaching but one term a year for Iowa in the fall of 2000. However, I've been taking brief residencies elsewhere, and I'll continue to do that.

[*Tammaro*]: *So the pace is going to continue.*

I've always liked the students, and I've always liked teaching. Of course, there are also corporate aspects to teaching. So Dorothy and I like the feeling of being free to go. And we do go. We have become tri-coastal. I had better explain. Our permanent address is Iowa City. We're there for the first semester, usually second semester too, but we also go to eastern Long Island for two months a year. One of our sons lives in New York City, and we go east to lure him out to the Island. Our other son lives in Signal Mountain, Tennessee, with our daughter-in-law and their two children. We visit them periodically. We also go to Florida to visit my mother. And finally, we spend long summers in Port Townsend, Washington, and sometimes in Seattle before that. So most years, we're on the East Coast, we're in the Northwest, and we're in Iowa, and I call it "tri-coastal."

[*Tammaro*]: *The Third Coast.*

Iowa's the third. You know, Iowa used to be tropical sea coast [laughter].

[*Tammaro*]: *Obviously, you like to teach. You wouldn't do it for forty years if you didn't like it. And I'm just wondering, how do you approach poems in a workshop?*

I try for a dynamic by which everyone speaks up. You know, not everyone will, and not everyone can. I prefer not to be the first person to talk, but very often students wait for the teacher to speak. I also play the dummy. If something can be misunderstood, I'm the one who doesn't understand it, because every poet needs to realize that a reader doesn't know everything the poet knows about a poem. There isn't any one way. It depends on the poem. I think most workshops run about the same, which is to have the poet read the poem and then have the class discuss it and from there expand into more general notions about writing.

But you know it isn't about poems as much as it's about writing. Time, reading, and hormones take care of a lot. I've been asked to write a book about writing poetry, and I think I have not done it because, to my mind, there's very little to say and it's all obvious. So I attempt to create a situation, a matrix, in which the writing life can flourish. I disdain theory and prefer expansive experimentation to reductive experimentation. But I will defend the right of any student to write as he or she chooses.

[*Tammaro*]: *What you're saying dovetails with the way you worked last night.*

As a teacher, I would like to create permission for all kinds of writing, for lots of writing, lots of talk, lots of energy. I prefer a discussion that doesn't define a poet by one poem, and that allows the good stuff and the bad stuff to mingle. That keeps our eyes on the future. A future in which people are willing to try anything. Then of course it's important for a teacher to know when to get out of the way, especially with graduate students. In the end, the students should feel that they did it themselves.

[*Tammaro*]: *Okay, that was the question I was going to ask you. What's the best thing a teacher can do for a student?*

To set him or her free from assumption, prejudice and convention, free even from the teacher. And to give the student, especially young students, a sense of verbal and imaginative audacity. Young poets try not to fall on their faces in public, but to become a better and better poet you have to be willing to fall on your face in public. You know, trying to write a good poem is like running off a cliff to see if you can fly. Most of the time you can't, but every once in a while something happens. Randall Jarrell wrote that a poet is someone who walks around in a thunderstorm, hoping to be hit by lightning, and then Jarrell went on to say a good poet is someone who has been hit three or four times, while a great poet is one who has been hit seven or eight times. I may not have remembered the numbers quite right. Years ago, a friend and I used to walk in the countryside talking about such matters, and we would ask ourselves how many poems in a book have to be good for that book to be thought good? We'd say twelve, no, seven, make it five, then three, and of course we eventually decided that sometimes one is enough.

[*Tammaro*]: *Just one good poem. Like buying a CD for one song and the rest are all bad. But you keep playing it.*

Yes, I guess that could happen.

[*Garaas*]: *I hate when that happens! I feel like I'm being ripped off!*

Understandably. You heard the one great song and expected more. But it's still a great song. You can put it in your anthology!

[*Garaas*]: *I was just wondering if there was anything you'd like to leave us with. If you could say one thing to sum up your sentiments toward your readers or other writers, anything we should really keep in mind, any lasting words.*

I tend to think in terms of being useful to young poets. Okay. Here are three things I believed from the start. First, there is no one way to write and no right way to write. That goes for what you write and also for how you get it written. Second, we're all in this together. And third, art is a way of life, not a career. You know, for me it's never been just about the books.

FURTHER READING

Criticism

McGuiness, Daniel. Review of *The Book of the Dead,* by Marvin Bell. *Antioch Review* 53, no. 2 (spring 1995): 246.

Brief review of *The Book of the Dead,* suggesting that the volume represents a turn—apparently a traumatic one—in the poet's life.

Parker, James. "The Ocean in the Head." *New York Times Book Review* (April 18, 2004): 28.

Review of Bell's *Rampant,* which the critic praises as an excellent collection.

Schneider, Rebecca Dinan. "Bringing Poetry to the People: Six State Poets Proclaim Virtues of Verse." *Writer* 114, no. 4 (April 2001): 34-9.

Brief discussion of Bell's literary career and his understanding of his role as Poet Laureate of Iowa.

Taylor, John. Review of *Nightworks: Poems 1962-2000,* by Marvin Bell. *Poetry* 179, no. 2 (November 2001): 112-14.

Discusses the innovative and unpredictable quality of Bell's poetry.

Yezzi, David. Review of *Ardor: The Book of the Dead Man, Volume 2,* by Marvin Bell. *Poetry* 172, no. 5 (August 1998): 288-89.

Considers Bell's 1998 volume of poetry "modest and homey" despite its appeal to the heart rather than the head.

Thomas Deloney
1543?-1600

English poet and fiction writer.

INTRODUCTION

Deloney is best known for his popular ballads and for his prose fiction featuring the lives of merchants and artisans.

BIOGRAPHICAL INFORMATION

Very little is known about Deloney's life. He was born around 1543, although some scholars place the date as late as 1560. He was possibly from Norwich, a center of Flemish and French Protestant immigrants working in the silk trade, but that is conjecture based on his occupation, his French surname, and the fact that the earliest ballad attributed to Deloney was published there. He was by trade a silk-weaver who traveled around the English countryside looking for work. Information about his education is virtually nonexistent; however, his writings and translations demonstrate his familiarity with several works of English literature and a working knowledge of Latin. Deloney gave up traveling and took up residence in London sometime around 1586. He began writing and circulating political ballads that were typically anti-Catholic, pro-Protestant, and strongly patriotic. His primary cause, however, was the condition and reputation of tradesmen and artisans. He was jailed for a short time for publishing a ballad railing against foreign competition in the cloth trades. Another ballad, protesting grain shortages, led to a warrant for his arrest, but he eluded capture. In his last years, he began writing fictional prose narratives about the lives of skilled workers like himself. Deloney died in 1600.

MAJOR WORKS

Deloney's poetry was almost completely devoted to the popular ballad, a form through which he could reach a broad audience and convey his social and political messages. The subjects of most of his ballads came from current social problems or from the chronicles, and his rhymes were set to common tunes familiar to the majority of the populace. The primary exception was the rather lengthy *Canaans Calamitie, or the Dolefull*

Destruction of faire Jerusalem (1618), Deloney's single attempt at a more sophisticated metrical arrangement and a more complicated treatment of historical subject matter—the destruction of Jerusalem.

The number of ballads composed by Deloney is not known with any certainty. Most were originally published as broadsides and a good many of them were lost. Those that are still extant appear in two collections: *The Garland of Good Will* (1593), consisting of twenty-seven ballads, and *Strange Histories, of Kings, Princes, Dukes, Earles, Lords, Ladies, Knights, and Gentlemen* (date unknown), consisting of eleven ballads and a prose dialogue.

In addition to his poetry, Deloney wrote a number of works of prose fiction, a genre considered by many literary historians to be the precursor of the English novel. His characters were members of the merchant class or artisans like himself—weavers and shoemakers—always favorably represented as valuable members of their communities. His fictional works include *The Gentle Craft. A Discourse Containing Many Matters of Delight* (1597), *The Pleasant History of John Winchcomb, in his younger years called Jack of Newberie* (1597), and *Thomas of Reading* (1598-99).

CRITICAL RECEPTION

Deloney's ballads were enormously popular during his lifetime and long after his death; along with his other works, they were widely reprinted and circulated throughout the seventeenth century and even into the eighteenth century. They were designed to appeal to a mass audience and often carried a strong political message. According to Francis Oscar Mann, Deloney was "completely representative of the sixteenth-century ballad-writers" and had mastered the form so thoroughly that he was often referred to as "the great Ballad-maker T. D." Nonetheless, Mann contends, despite several works that exhibited "delicacy of diction and a rare simplicity of feeling," Deloney's verse "was often merely a mechanical process."

Like all good balladeers, Deloney was intent upon pleasing his audience. Robert A. Schwegler notes that Deloney's adaptation of a moral tale from Sir Thomas Malory's *Le Morte d'Arthur*, involving the fight between Lancelot and Tarquin, "clearly show[s] that he felt that the appeal of romance materials for his audience lay in their potential for exciting, even violent action uncomplicated by moral issues or depth of characterization." Deloney was apparently correct in his assumptions about the taste of his contemporaries since several playwrights, including William Shakespeare, quoted from the poem, which Deloney titled "The Noble Acts of Arthur of the Round Table." Eugene P. Wright (see Further Reading), however, cautions against assuming that Deloney's ballads "play merely upon simple people's base interests in sensationalism or sentimentality," although he acknowledges that the poet's subjects were generally chosen for their popular appeal. Nonetheless, according to Wright, "the best of Deloney's ballads possess many of the same qualities that were later to make his prose works successful: a vitality in the telling of an heroic tale, an effective use of dialogue, and a familiar portrayal of the common man."

PRINCIPAL WORKS

Poetry

Strange Histories, of Kings, Princes, Dukes, Earles, Lords, Ladies, Knights, and Gentlemen date unknown
The Garland of Good Will 1593
Canaans Calamitie, or the Dolefull Destruction of faire Jerusalem 1618

Other Major Works

The Gentle Craft. A Discourse Containing Many Matters of Delight (prose fiction) 1597
The Pleasant History of John Winchcomb, in His Younger Years Called Jack of Newberie (prose fiction) 1597
The Second Part of the Gentle Craft [fragment] (prose fiction) c. 1600
Thomas of Reading. Or, The Sixe Worthy Yeomen of the West. Now the Fourth Time Corrected and Enlarged (prose fiction) 1598-99

CRITICISM

Francis Oscar Mann (essay date 1912)

SOURCE: Mann, Francis Oscar. "The Poetry of Deloney." In *The Works of Thomas Deloney,* pp. 31-43. Oxford: Clarendon, 1912.

[*In the following excerpt, Mann discusses Deloney's mastery of the ballad form, which was perfectly suited for conveying his social and political messages to a mass audience.*]

Deloney's novels seem to have been, more or less, experiments, entered upon in the last three years of his life. With the exception of the tracts relating to the Archbishop of Cologne, his earlier extant work is entirely in verse, and in contemporary opinion he stands forth, not so much as a novelist but as the 'great Balladmaker T. D.' Deloney was an artisan, seeking originally no doubt to increase a scanty wage by literary work, and to such a one the medium of the ballad was the easiest for reaching a wide and popular audience. Thus, with the exception of *Canaans Calamitie* (a more ambitious piece of work), his poetic faculty exercised itself entirely in the ballad style and metre, and his work is completely representative of the ballad activity of the later sixteenth century.

The term 'ballad' in modern literature seems to be used loosely for nearly every kind of lyric, but more scientifically for those traditional poems which retain in part the conventions and spirit of an earlier poetic age, when literary composition was more communal than individual, and the emotional atmosphere more simple and epic. The true ballad, whether taken down from a twentieth-century tradition or found in a fifteenth-century manuscript, has distinguishing features of its own which mark it off from the poetry of more complex and sophisticated ages, and these peculiar features are fully explained by the circumstances of primitive composition. The poet of modern civilization is a lonely Heine or prophetic Blake pouring forth bitterness or celestial intoxication from the height of his own egoism. Primitive poetry was the voice of the people, more the rhythm of an elemental civilization than the expression of individual desires and convictions. The source of modern poetry is the individual soul brooding on 'things past, present, and to come', the source of ancient poetry was the gathering of the people for work or play, who lightened communal labour at the oar or reinforced communal pleasure in the dance by rhythmic music and rhymes. Now a Byron or Shelley sings to a merely receptive audience; then the people were audience and performer too and bore the burden

> *Binnorie, O Binnorie,*

or took up the alternate lines:

> She sat down below a thorn,
> *Fine flowers in the valley;*
> And there she has her sweet babe born,
> *And the green leaues they grow rarely.*

With the metres of Provence, the French *ballata* or round dance conquered Teutonic Europe, and the 'glad animal movements' of the 'carols' demanded a tune to dance to, and a kind of poetry in which all could take part. Hence doubtless the form of both ballads and nursery rhymes. The formal peculiarities of the genuine folk-ballad can be catalogued with some preciseness, and among these may be noted the almost verbatim repetition of speeches and messages, the tendency to accentuate the last and weak syllable of a metrical line, the use of assonance, the spirited openings *in medias res,* the delight in bright elemental colours, and the use of magic numbers such as seven and three.

But while the folk-ballad flourished in mediaeval England and owed so much of its dramatic intensity and lyrical spontaneity to the circumstances of its communal composition, the individual minstrel whose songs were his own property and who only sang them in return for some gratuity to an audience entirely passive must have existed from the earliest times.

> Men speke of romances of prys,
> Of Horn child and of Ypotys,
>   Of Bevis and sir Gy,

wrote Chaucer in his *Sir Thopas,* his own delicate parody of the popular poesy of his age, and the minstrel, leaving aside the tragic themes of contemporary life which made the very stuff of the communal ballad, hawked round the country from alehouse to alehouse decrepit versions of sentimental French romance, striking up in the usual medicant key,

> Lythe and listen, gentlemen,
> A story I yow bitelle,

and demanding perhaps a gratuity in pence or ale. Less often his wares would consist of love-lyrics such as *Bytuene Mershe and Aueril,* or of political songs such as those of Laurence Minot (c. 1350). Wherever men and women came together, for work or play, at the fairs and markets, or travelling the great roads on business or on pilgrimage, the professional minstrel was sure to make one of the company to help while away the leisure hour or tedious journey. Chaucer's pilgrims amused themselves with their own stories, but the ordinary devotees of St. Thomas of Canterbury or Our Lady of Walsingham were not so self-sufficing. 'When divers men and women will go thus,' William Thorpe told his examiners, 'they will ordain before to have with them both men and women that can well sing wanton songs.'[1] Laurence Minot stands out as the first definite figure of the professional minstrel in mediaeval England, one who strikes a clear individual note, and, half poet, half journalist, clothes political feeling and contemporary events in the garb of popular metres.

> How Edward þe King came to Braband
> And tok homage of all þe land
>
> How Edward at Hogges vnto land wan,
> And rade thurgh France or euer he blan.

Intinerant minstrelsy was no less popular in Tudor than in mediaeval times, and with the invention of printing the oral ballad, whether of traditional or individual composition, began to be thrown into type and circulated in broadsides. But the sixteenth-century broadside versions of the older and true ballads are unfortunately by no means mere transcripts from tradition, but have usually passed through the hands of an editor with a literary method of his own, appealing to a different kind of audience. The folk-ballad, governed by the conditions of its composition, told the story in lyrical glimpses and tense dialogue, originally no doubt eked out by action and dancing, but the Elizabethan editor, with his eye on passive and not too intelligent listeners, aimed at a remorseless recounting of the whole story from beginning to end. Hence, instead of the opening *in medias res* of

> Hie upon Hielands,
>   And low upon Tay,
> Bonnie George Campbell
>   Rode out on a day,

the Elizabethan ballad type begins with a long explanatory introduction.

> Both gentlemen, or yeomen bould,
>   Or whatsoeuer you are,
> To haue a stately story tould
>   Attention now prepare.
>
> It is a tale of Robin Hood,
>   Which I to you will tell,
> Which being rightly vnderstood,
>   I know will please you well.
>
> This Robbin (so much talked on)
>   Was once a man of fame,
> Instiled earle of Huntingdon,
>   Lord Robert Hood by name.

Similarly the old lyric narrative, such as,

> O ye've had a cruel mither, Willie,
>   And I have had anither,
> But we shall sleep in Clyde's water
>   Like sister and like brither,

is replaced by prosaic explanation:

> And to his little daughter Iane
>   Fiue hundred pounds in gold,
> To be paid down on marriage-day,
>   Which might not be controlled.
> But if the children chance to die
>   Ere they to age should come,
> Their vncle should possess their wealth;
>   For so the will did run.

Yet in spite of this change from an intense method of poetry to another, dangerously prosaic, a fair amount of genuine folk-poetry was often enclosed in the shapeless padding of the later editor. The *Robin Hood Ballads* as they appear in the broadsides of the sixteenth and seventeenth centuries are excellent examples of the way in which the ancient habits of traditional poetry cling on in an age of professional balladists. Endless dilutions and accretions have reduced this popular epic to an average level of pedestrianism, but here and there the old literary methods strike out the old vigour from a page of dull narrative.

> Come thou hither to mee, thou lovely page,
>   Come thou hither to mee;
> For thou must post to Nottingham,
>   As fast as thou can dree.

In many cases, no doubt, the traditional ballad was only lightly touched and modernized, and where the editor was a versifier of some skill it is difficult to distinguish between the original and the later additions. While the history of the *Robin Hood Ballads* can be fairly well made out, from Langland's reference to them in the fourteenth century until their appearance in the various *Garlands* of the seventeenth, the question of the originals of *Come over the Borne, Bessie,* of *Walsingham,* and of many another popular Elizabethan poem remains entirely obscure. We can only surmise that the printed ballads of the sixteenth century represent a small and edited portion of a large oral tradition, most of which has now perished unrecorded.

The broad question of the relation of traditional poetry to the work of the individual ballad-writer suggests itself at once in connexion with the poems of Deloney. There can be no doubt that in many of his poems, and especially in those which seem most successful to the modern reader, he has either merely written down or closely imitated folk tradition. In *Iacke of Newberie* he plainly indicates the communal origin of the song of Flodden Field: 'Wherefore in disgrace of the Scots, and in remembrance of the famous atchieued victory, the Commons of *England* made this Song: which to this day is not forgotten of many'[2]; and the two other traditional versions of the same song given in Child's *Ballads* conclusively prove that in this case at least Deloney was merely printing a traditional ballad. Similarly *The Faire Flower of Northumberland* (*Iacke of Newberie,* p. 33) in *motif* and treatment alike might be purely traditional, and *Walsingham*[3] (p. 365) is almost certainly built up on a traditional foundation. But lacking further evidence we can only draw strong inferences from style and matter, without reaching any absolutely definite conclusion.

The great bulk of sixteenth-century ballad literature, however, is the lineal descendant, not of the communal ballad, but rather of the minstrel's songs of the Middle Ages, and plainly the individual work of the professional entertainer, catering for the amusement of the general public with matter drawn from all sources. While the communal ballad was the folk expression of large simple emotions, the ordinary Elizabethan ballad is journalism pure and simple, and Autolycus the ballad-hawker, eternally alive in the *Winter's Tale,* hawks round, not the *Douglas Tragedy* or the *Death of the Earl of Murray,* but *How a usurer's wife was brought to bed of twenty money-bags at a burden,* and 'another ballad *Of a fish that appeared upon the coast on Wednesday the fourscore of April, forty thousand fathom aboue water, and sung this ballad against the hard hearts of maids*'. A glance at the *Roxburghe Ballads,* the *Shirburn Collection,* or the *Registers of the Stationers' Company,* will show that Shakespeare has scarcely done more than 'hold the mirror up to nature'. The following are representative titles of ballads registered with the Stationers' Company:

> *A true relacon of the birth of Three Monsters in the Citty of Namen in Flaunders.*
>
> *The wofull complaynt of Ffraunce for the deathe of the late kinge* Henry *the Ffourth.*
>
> *A lamentacon of a Yonge man for the deathe of his Mother.*
>
> *How Maydes shulde penne the Dore &c.*
>
> *A ballet intituled taken out of Ye XIII Chapter of Saynt Luke.*
>
> *Tydinges of a Huge and Ougly childe borne at Arneheim in Gelderland.*
>
> *A ballet against Swerynge.*

Thus it may be gathered the Elizabethan ballad was the vehicle for popular edification, instruction, and amusement, and supplied the vulgar with sermons, history, politics, sentiment, and the latest news. Of this multifarious activity Deloney is almost completely representative, combining in his work all the different functions of the sixteenth-century ballad-maker. As a modern newspaper reporter hurries his exclusive news into print, so Deloney registered **"A ioyfull songe of the Roiall Receauing of the queenes maiestie into her camp at Tilbery: the 8 and 9 of August 1588,"** the very day after the event; and as modern newspapers send broadcast over the land accounts of criminals, trials, inquests, and accidents, so Deloney circulated the **"Lamentation of Pages Wife of Plymouth, the Death and Execution of Fourteen most wicked Traitors,"** the **"Lamentation of Beccles,"** and probably many another news sheet of which no trace remains. The Elizabethan appetite for history he satisfied with paraphrases from the Chronicles of Holinshed and Grafton; he touched on social questions of the day in his ballad on the **"Scarcity of Corn"**; dealt with the religious and political question in **"Truth and Ignorance"** and **"Judith and Holofernes,"** and served up moral exhortations and advice in **"Repent, England, Repent"** and **"Salomons good housewife."** Nor did he forget the business of mere amusement, but in the **"Kings daughter of France, Patient Grissel,"** and

"King Edward the third, and the faire Countesse of Salisbury," set forth the pretty sentimental stories as dear to the Elizabethan heart as to the mediaeval.

While Deloney is so completely representative of the sixteenth-century ballad-writers, from the very conditions which called forth his work, it was impossible for him to maintain any constant level of excellence. The public was his master, and to please it he ransacked all the sources at his command—the chroniclers, the stage, tradition, and contemporary history, but he could not handle all these topics with the same degree of facility. Such lyrics as the **"Weauers Song"** in *Iacke of Newberie,* or Cutbert's **"Countrey Iigge"** in *Thomas of Reading,* flowed easily and delightfully from his pen, but in his narrative ballads he seems often to have flagged, and perhaps more especially in the *Strange Histories,* which may have been a volume hastily 'yarked up' for the printer, to supply immediate necessity. The great fault of the average Elizabethan ballad is lack of imagination, and in the ballads 'taken from the chronicles' Deloney has seldom assimilated the story completely enough to reproduce it in an artistic or dramatic form. Hence his poems are too often little more than a metrical paraphrase of the prose, and refractory rhymes deliver him over to all sorts of temptations. Thus where Holinshed writes: 'Thomas Gurney . . . flieng vnto Marcels, three years after being knowne, taken and brought toward England was beheaded on the sea', Deloney renders the passage:

> Commandement was sent by one called Lea
> he should be beheaded forth with on the sea,[4]

inventing a fictitious name to solve the difficulty of rhyming, and where he describes the imprisonment of Edward II by his Queen, an epithet contradictory to the sense is his only escape from the same *impasse*:

> Our comely King, her husband *deere,*
> Subdued by strength as did appeare,
> By her was sent to prison stronge.[5]

Ballad-making to him was often merely a mechanical process; he used words and metre not to body forth a dramatic story, hot and incandescent in his mind, but to worry a narrative into the compass of a catch, and thus he does not escape at times a woful pedestrianism of style.

> The Saylers and the shipmen all,
>   through foule excesse of wine,
> Were so disguisde that at the sea,
>   they shewd themselues like swine.[6]
>
>   . . . . .
>
> Three score and ten were dround in all,
>   and none escaped death,
> But one poore Butcher which had swome
>   himself quite out of breath.[7]

Nor is this pedestrianism entirely limited to the narrative ballads.

In **"The Widdowes Solace"** a beautiful verse:—

> 'Twas neither *Cressus* treasure,
>   nor Alexanders fame,
> Nor Solomon by wisdome,
>   that could deaths fury tame.
> No Physicke might preserue them
>   when Nature did decay:
> What man can hold for ever,
>   the thing that will away?

is followed by this bathetic advice:—

> If he were true and faithfull,
>   and louing unto thee,
> Doubt not but ther's in *England,*
>   enough as good as he.
> But if that such affection,
>   within his heart was none:
> Then giue God praise and glory,
>   that he is dead and gone.[8]

Such alternations seem to show a certain unsureness of taste and feeling that was shared by other and much greater writers of the Elizabethan age, but there is an individual strain of bourgeois materialism in Deloney's work which recalls the same weakness in the powerful Hogarth. 'O faulce and foule disloyall men!' cries Deloney of the Babington conspirators:

> what person would suppose,
> That clothes of veluet and of silke
>   should hide such mortall foes?[9]

and Hogarth brings the Industrious Apprentice safely to the arms of his master's daughter and the Mayoral seat in the Guildhall.

But Deloney must not be judged by his worst poems. His ballads on the stirring events of his time are comparable with those of Laurence Minot for a vigour and force that marks them for contemporary documents. As Minot wrote from the exultation of a fierce English heart:

> Whare er ȝe, Skottes of Saint Johnes toun?
> þe boste of ȝowre baner es betin all doune,

so Deloney in a truer, greater cause could write even while the wrack of the great Armada was still strewing the northern seas:

> O Noble *England,*
>   fall doune vpon thy knee:
> And praise thy God with thankfull hart
>   which still maintaineth thee
> The forraine forces,
>   that seekes thy vtter spoil:
> Shall then through his especiall grace

be brought to shamefull foile.
With mightie power
   they come vnto our coast:
To ouer runne our country quite,
   they make their brags and boast.
In strength of men
   they set their only stay:
But we, vpon the Lord our God,
   will put our trust alway.[10]

The patriotism that saved Elizabeth's England lends a boldness and vigour to the **"Winning of Cales"** and his three **"Armada Ballads,"** and where he touches religion sincerity infuses his verse with the energy of poetry, as in **"Truth and Ignorance"**:

But many Kings and Prophets
   as I may say to thee:
Haue wisht the light that you haue,
   and neuer could it see,

or in **"Holofernes"**:

Lo here behold how God prouides
   for them that in him trust:
When earthly hope is all in vain,
   he takes vs from the dust.

He writes with real sympathy of the emotions and troubles of domestic life, so that his paraphrase of *Salomons good houswife, in the* 31 *of his Proverbes* is completely delivered from the monotony of mere hackwork, and the **"Lamentation of Mr. Pages Wife"** becomes informed with a touching indignation. Where he deals with the topics of common artisan life, in the poems scattered through his novels, he writes with a singular freshness in that happily careless vein that is lacking in modern poetry. His more slender lyrics, such as **"Walsingham," "The Spanish Ladies Love,"** and **"Age and Youth,"** are distinguished by a delicacy of diction and a rare simplicity of feeling that has made them remembered in later times when their author's name was forgotten or ignored.

Perhaps the chief literary influence moulding the ballad of the sixteenth century was exercised by the *Mirrour for Magistrates*. The tragic encyclopaedia of the *Fall of Princes* had eternal attractions for mediaeval readers, and the literary tradition merely took new form with the same popularity in the Elizabethan collection of doleful tragedies, related in the first person and clothed in long-drawn leisurely verse. Its influence is seen chiefly in the 'Lamentation' type of ballad, exemplified in Deloney's work by the **"Lamentation of Shores Wife"** and the **"Lamentation of Beccles,"** and in the lugubrious choice of historical topics illustrated by ballads such as **"The lamentable death of King Iohn; Of Edward the second, being poysoned"**; and the **"Imprisonment of Queene Elenor."** The *Mirrour for Magistrates* (1587) had previously treated many of the subjects of De-

loney's ballads,[11] and *Strange Histories* may perhaps be regarded as a bourgeois imitation of the more aristocratic prototype, even in its inclusion of the prose passage amongst the verse.[12] But while the balladist of necessity squeezed 'strange and lamentable' histories into the compass of a common rhythm and bore in mind always that his audience wanted rhymes 'to the tune of *Fortune'* or *'Prince Arthur died at Ludlow',* authors like Daniel and Drayton could treat the same subject in much the same spirit in the larger and statelier stanzas of ten-syllabled verse. While Deloney scribbled his verses to the thin quavering of a street tune running through his head, Drayton and Daniel unfolded their tragic themes in the long march and rich cadences of the literary metres that had developed with the school of Spenser. *Canaans Calamitie* is the evidence that Deloney, writing up history into ballads for the marketplace and tavern-door, did not nevertheless escape altogether the literary ambitions of his age, and, not merely content with the metrical paraphrasing of dolorous passages from the chronicles, really aimed, once at least, at a poem of some size and construction, where the treatment of tragic history and the metrical arrangement should be definitely nobler in tradition. The stanza he chose was that of Shakespeare's popular *Venus and Adonis,* and the subject, epic; in the choice of the one he reflects the Renaissance desire for dignified form, in the choice of the other its desire for dignified matter. The 'little epic' was a favourite variety of Elizabethan poetry, which lent scope for the skilful handling of metre, for description, action, and narrative, giving many of the opportunities of the epic without its difficulties of construction,—a variety which is exemplified in Shakespeare's *Venus and Adonis* and *The Rape of Lucrece,* in Marlowe's *Hero and Leander,* and profusely in the works of Drayton and Daniel.

In *Canaans Calamitie* Deloney leaves the simpler opportunities of the ballad metre and manages to attain in some degree to the dignity which marks the smaller epic, his first stanza recalling in the determination of its melancholy the opening verse of Milton's immature and mannered poem on *The Passion*:

Like to a Mourner clad in dolefull black,
   That sadly sits to heare a heauie tale:
So must my pen proceed to shew the wrack,
   That did with terror *Syon* hill assaile.
What time *Ierusalem* that Cittie faire,
Was sieg'd and sackt by great *Vespatians* heire.

                                     Canaans Calamitie

For now to sorrow must I tune my song,
And set my harp to notes of saddest woe,
Which on our dearest Lord did seize ere long,
Dangers, and snares and wrongs, and worse than so,
Which he for us did freely undergo:

Most perfect Hero, tried in heaviest plight
Of labours huge and hard, too hard for human wight.

"The Passion"

But Deloney's muse, though not only of the ale-house
to which Nash relegated it, was not capable of filling a
canvas with such a large historical piece as the destruction of Jerusalem. His stanzas are never entirely secure
from the pedestrianism that marks his inferior ballads,
and his diction lacks the strength to support an epic
story. Hence he endeavours to escape from the larger
tragic issues of his subject by sliding into the
'Lamentation' point of view—

God grant we may our hatefull sins forsake,
And by the Jewes a Christian warning take

—by dropping easily into the narrative method of the
poetical chronicler, and weakening the tragedy of a
catastrophe by overemphasis of the pathetic elements.
In common with many of the Elizabethan dramatists
Deloney had the power of creating pathetic situations
from the simplest and barest elements of life, and probably the episode of Miriam and her son, in spite of its
extravagant subject and grotesque exaggeration of
circumstance and feeling, is the best part of his ambitious poem. In its fantastic setting of discordant and
unpleasing detail there is a simple directness of feeling
in the entreaty of Miriam's son for food, which recalls
the vivid dialogue of the murderous father and his son
in *The Yorkshire Tragedy*—'O what will you do, father?
I am your white boie.'—'Thou shalt be my red boie.'[13]
Deloney from much the same situation creates the same
kind of pathos:

I am (deere Mother) hungry at the heart,
And scalding thirst, makes me I cannot speake,
I feele my strength decay in euery part,
One bit of bread, for me good Mother breake,
My lesson I haue learnd, where you did lay it,
Then giue me some-what: you shall heere
me say it.[14]

But this measure of success is an indication of his
limitations. A story dealing with the more simple and
elemental emotions he could throw into verse with success, and embody a fancy in a pleasant lyric. But probably the complex and graver emotions never came home
to his heart nor hence the adequate means of their
expression home to his mind, and he remains, when all
is said and done, not so much the author of **Canaans
Calamitie** as 'the great Ballad-maker T. D.'

Notes

1. *The Examination of William Thorpe* (1407), in Arber's *Garner.*

2. p. 25, ll. 34-6, and note.

3. See note thereon, *infra,* pp. 579-80.

4. p. 410, ll. 77-8.

5. p. 402, ll. 3-5.

6. p. 387, ll. 46-9.

7. p. 389, ll. 117-20.

8. p. 331.

9. p. 467, ll. 102-5.

10. p. 468.

11. e. g. King John's Death, Locrine, Albanact and
Humber, Edward II.

12. p. 415.

13. sc. iv.

14. p. 434, ll. 505-10.

Robert A. Schwegler (essay date spring 1978)

SOURCE: Schwegler, Robert A. "The Arthur Ballad:
From Malory to Deloney to Shakespeare." *Essays in
Literature* 5, no. 1 (spring 1978): 3-13.

[*In the following essay, Schwegler traces the development of Deloney's poem "The Noble Acts of Arthur of
the Round Table," based on the works of Thomas
Malory and later used by Shakespeare who quoted the
poem in* Henry IV, Part 2.]

Thomas Deloney's poem, **"The Noble Acts of Arthur
of the Round Table,"**[1] a ballad version of the fight
between Lancelot and Sir Tarquin from Sir Thomas
Malory's *Le Morte Darthur,* is an Elizabethan broadside
ballad (often mistakenly cited as a Middle English
ballad) that was popular enough to be quoted in several
Renaissance plays, including Shakespeare's *2 Henry IV.*
The history of the poem, from its roots in Malory,
through Deloney's transformation of the story, to
Shakespeare's use of it as a comment on Falstaff's
character, should be interesting to students of both
Middle English and Renaissance literature because it
provides a good illustration of the changes romance
materials were likely to undergo in the hands of an
Elizabethan popular writer. The transformation from
medieval romance to Elizabethan ballad is particularly
clear in this case because Deloney took most of his
poem directly from Malory, generally preserving the
exact wording of his source, while at the same time
omitting large portions of the story and altering its
structure radically.

A comparison of the ballad with its source reveals the
kind of changes Deloney made to please his audience,
and it provides a good index to the taste of the audience
for popular literature in the late sixteenth and early

seventeenth centuries. That the poem succeeded in pleasing its audience is evident from its appearance in many printed editions throughout the period and from the use of quotes from it in several plays as examples of broadside balladry and as devices for commenting on the taste and attitudes of a character.

Though **"The Noble Acts of Arthur of the Round Table"** is a Renaissance poem, it has been cited in reference works and in discussions of Arthurian literature as a medieval ballad.[2] The latest edition of *A Manual of the Writings in Middle English* follows earlier editions of the *Manual* in listing the poem as a Middle English ballad.[3] The source of this confusion over the poem's status is probably the fragmentary text preserved, without attribution, among many genuine medieval ballads and romances in Bishop Percy's Folio Manuscript.[4] It is this text, and not the numerous Renaissance prints, that is usually cited as a Middle English ballad even though the manuscript's editors correctly indicate that the poem "was written towards the end of Queen Elizabeth's reign, probably by Thomas Deloney."[5] The poem is, however, an Elizabethan production, and references to it as a Middle English work should be corrected. There is no evidence of its existence before the 1590's, but there are many surviving texts and references to the poem dating from the last years of the sixteenth century and the first half of the seventeenth. It appears in all the numerous editions of Thomas Deloney's **The Garland of Good Will** (c. 1596; first surviving edition, 1628), and in many broadsides from the first part of the seventeenth century.[6] Shakespeare quotes from it in *2 Henry IV*:

FAL[STAFF].

'When Arthur first in court'—Empty the jordan. . . .
'And was a worthy king'—How now, Mistress Doll?[7]

In *The Little French Lawyer* (1623), Fletcher introduces two lines from the middle of the ballad, "He strook so hard, the Bason broke, / and *Tarquin* heard the sound,"[8] and Marston quotes the opening line in *The Malcontent* (1604), "'When Arthur first in court began'. . . ."[9] Though the poem was well known after the 1590's, there is no trace of it in ballad form before this period. While the poem's Arthurian subject matter and the many medieval ballads and romances surrounding it in the Percy Folio could easily cause the Folio text to be mistakenly identified as medieval, it actually differs very little from the text in the prints and was probably copied from one of them.[10]

Though one critic dates the ballad between 1586 and 1596 on the grounds of its narrative technique and style,[11] any venture of this sort is probably doomed to failure because most of the ballad is copied directly from its source, Sir Thomas Malory's *Le Morte Darthur*. The editor of the "Malory" section of *A Manual of the Writings in Middle English* is correct when he says that Malory provided "most of the content"[12] of the poem, but he understates the case.

"The Noble Acts of Arthur of the Round Table" is little more than a rimed version of parts of Malory's text; many lines in the poem are almost direct quotations from the "Tale of Sir Lancelot Du Lake" in Caxton's version of Malory.[13] The ballad omits parts of Malory's text in order to produce a briefer and simpler account of the events and alters other parts to meet the demands of rime, meter, and line length; beyond this the texts correspond closely. Malory's text reads:

> Thou arte saide sir Turquine e/y [the] biggest man that euer I meete withall, the best breathed, and lyke one a knight that I hate aboue al other knights, and t/y [that] thou be not he, I wyll lightly accorde with thee, and for thy loue I wyl deliuer all the prysoners that I haue, that is three score & foure, so that thou wylte tell mee thy name, and thou and I wee be felowes togyther, and wyll neuer fayle thee whyle I lyue.[14]

The corresponding section of the ballad reads:

> Thou art (quoth *Tarquin*) the best Knight,
>   that euer I did know;
> And like a Knight that I did hate,
>   so that thou be not he,
> I will deliuer all the rest,
>   and eke accord with thee.[15]

The numerous printed editions of this ballad and the appearance of quotations from it in plays bear witness to its popularity and show that Deloney correctly judged the tastes of a late sixteenth- and early seventeenth-century audience. The poem's subject is one which this audience would be likely to find appealing. The story of the fight between Lancelot and Tarquin is a good representative of one particularly popular kind of broadside ballad, the verse treatment of a well-known story from history, legend, or literature. These renditions are usually hack productions which tell the story briefly, emphasizing elements of love and adventure, and occasionally concentrating on a particularly pathetic or dramatic episode. Included in this category are ballads such as "Leander's Love to Loyal Hero," "The Wandering Prince of Troy," "The Judgment of Solomon," "Patient Grissel," and "The Battle of Agincourt."[16]

Deloney's attempts to please his audience went far beyond choice of subject matter. The changes he made in the material he received from Malory clearly show that he felt that the appeal of romance materials for his audience lay in their potential for exciting, even violent action uncomplicated by moral issues or depth of characterization. He altered the emphasis and structure of Malory's tale radically, turning the moral drama of his source into a tale of pure action with little, if any, moral import. In Malory's "Tale of Sir Lancelot Du Lake," Lancelot demonstrates his perfection as a knight and vindicates the moral ideals and code of Arthur's kingdom by overcoming, in a series of episodes, opponents whose actions run counter to the ideals of Arthur's court and threaten to undermine the order of the kingdom. Instead of telling a single story, the "Tale of Sir Lancelot Du Lake" utilizes the cumulative effect of separate but roughly parallel episodes to present its thematic content. The ballad concentrates on Lancelot's fight with Sir Tarquin, a single episode from the "Tale of Sir Lancelot Du Lake." By omitting most of the episodes found in its source, the ballad loses the cumulative effect which demonstrates "by repetition of one victory after another, how Lancelot is without doubt the noblest and most perfect of all men on earth,"[17] and portrays "the ideal political structure triumphing over those elements which would threaten peace and justice."[18]

While the ballad does demonstrate that Lancelot is morally superior to Tarquin and is the better warrior, it does so in a way which eliminates the moral complexity of Malory's version of the episode. In the "Tale of Sir Lancelot Du Lake," Tarquin appears twice before he meets Lancelot. In each appearance he defeats one of Lancelot's fellow knights of the Round Table, beats him "with sharpe thornes all naked" and throws him into "a deepe dongeon, where he knewe many of his felowes."[19] Before he meets Tarquin, Lancelot aids King Bademagus in his fight against three treacherous knights of the Round Table. When Lancelot finally encounters Tarquin, he does so while searching for his companion Sir Lionel, who, unknown to Lancelot, has been captured by Tarquin. Thus in Malory's version, the fight between Lancelot and Tarquin is a conflict between the representatives of two different moral codes, Tarquin representing treachery, revenge, and disorder, and Lancelot representing loyalty, kindness, and order. Lancelot's fight with Tarquin is also, like his fight against the treacherous knights, a battle against the forces which threaten the order of Arthur's kingdom. The moral drama inherent in Malory's version becomes explicit in an interchange at the height of the struggle when Tarquin explains that he has mistreated many knights because he has been searching for Lancelot in order to avenge his brother, slain by Lancelot:

> And for sir Launcelots sake I haue slaine an hundred good knightes, and as manye I haue vtterly mayned, that neuer after they myght helpe themselfe, and many haue dyed in my pryson and yet I haue three score and foure, and all shall be delyuered, so that thou wylt tell me thy name, and, so it be that thou bee not syr Launce-lot. Now see I well sayd sir Launcelot that such a man

I myght bee there shoulde bee betwene vs two mortall warre, and nowe syr knyght at thy request I will that thou wyte and knowe that I am syr Launcelot du lake. . . .[20]

The ballad, however, omits a number of significant details. It does not characterize Lancelot by telling of his aid to King Bademagus, nor does it indicate his loyalty to fellow knights by telling of his search for Sir Lionel. The only indication of Lancelot's character comes in the lines,

> But one Sir *Lancelot du Lake,*
>   who was approued well,
> He in his fights and deeds of arms,
>   all other did excell.
>
> (ll. 13-16)

The only motivation given for his quest is a desire to "go proue himselfe, / in some aduenturous sort" (ll. 10-20). Besides the knight who lies bound on Tarquin's horse when Lancelot meets him, the ballad gives little evidence of Tarquin's misdeeds beyond the lines,

> And as I vnderstand thou hast,
>   so farre as thou art able,
> Done great despight and shame vnto
>   the Knights of the round Table.
>
> (ll. 53-56)

Since the ballad provides no depth of characterization, Lancelot and Tarquin appear only as good and bad characters in the simplest sense. They do not represent differing moral codes, nor does their conflict represent a clash between moral systems. The bulk of the ballad is simply a detailed account of their fight, which concentrates on action and physical detail and eliminates any mention of the moral aspect of the conflict. In Malory's version, the long interchange between Tarquin and Lancelot makes explicit the moral concerns of the story; the ballad removes all moral ramifications from the passage:

> His name is Sir *Lancelot du Lake,*
>   he slew my brother deare;
> Him I suspect of all the rest,
>   I would I had him here.
> Thy wish thou hast but now vnknowne,
>   I am *Lancelot du Lake.*
>
> (ll. 93-98)

The ballad does not even preserve the structure of its source. Malory presents a series of parallel episodes, but the ballad concentrates on a single event, the fight with Sir Tarquin; all other incidents in the ballad stand in direct causal relationship to the central event and are developed, with minimal detail, only to the extent necessary to prepare for the central event. In *Le Morte Darthur,* Sir Tarquin's mistreatment of defeated knights is a subject of major concern which receives the same extended treatment as the fight; the ballad refers only briefly to his imprisonment of "threescore Knights, / and foure" (l. 37) and to the "great despight and shame" (l. 55) he perpetrated upon knights of the Round Table. Though the ballad has been called "an epitome in ballad stanza of the Tarquin episode in Sir Thomas Malory's *Morte Darthur*,"[21] this is only partly true because the ballad does not actually summarize its source. It borrows part of the story, suppresses the rest of it, and alters the structure to turn it into a tale of uncomplicated, exciting action.

The change from moral drama to pure action is not an accidental one resulting from Deloney's lack of ability as a writer, for *Jack of Newbury* and Deloney's other prose tales show that he could write with a measure of skill and seriousness when he wanted to. Deloney probably transformed Malory's tale to please the tastes of his Elizabethan audience; the descent to pure action reflects considerable differences between the audiences for the Middle English *Le Morte Darthur* and the Elizabethan ballad. While chivalric romances remained popular throughout the sixteenth century, their audience gradually changed from a sophisticated elite to an unsophisticated mass: "Published in such cheap editions that anyone could buy them, these knightly romances provided the populace with a literature of escape analogous to that now [c. 1935] supplied by a deluge of short stories and novels."[22] We need not suppose that all Elizabethans failed to perceive and enjoy the more serious aspects of the romances, but many Elizabethan readers looked only to their surface qualities, and it was to this audience that **"The Noble Acts of Arthur of the Round Table"** addressed itself. This audience craved tales of incredible adventures in exotic settings and stories of faithful couples overcoming extreme hardships for the sake of love;[23] the ballad provided an uncomplicated, exciting action in simple style with an archaic setting to satisfy the taste for "histories of knight errantry in strange and wonderful opera lands."[24]

It might be argued that the changes Deloney made in the Lancelot story were attempts to give it the kind of brevity and immediate impact demanded by the broadside ballad form and not responses to his audience's taste for sensational action. But to argue this way is to miss the point. The broadside form could have arisen and prospered only if it met the needs of its audience, and the requirements it imposed are to a great extent a reflection of its audience's taste. While there are broadside ballads that do not stress action at the expense of character and theme, most do,[25] and the transformations that Malory's story underwent at Deloney's hands illustrate the kind of artistic choices that accompanied the creation of many other pieces of Elizabethan popular literature.

Shakespeare's use of the ballad in *2 Henry IV* is a recognition of the changes Deloney made in the story,

substituting violent action divorced from serious concerns for a portrayal of combat as a test of moral character and as a means of resolving political conflicts. Falstaff quotes the opening lines of the ballad as he comes on stage near the beginning of the Boar's Head Tavern scene, interrupting them with a reference to a chamber pot ("jordan") and following them by some bawdy jesting with Doll Tearsheet and Hostess Quickly:

FAL[STAFF].

> 'When Arthur first in court'—Empty the jordan. . . .
> 'And was a worthy king'—How now, Mistress Doll?

HOST[ESS].

> Sick of a calm, yea, good faith.

FAL.

> So is all her sect; and they be once in a calm they are sick.

> (II.iv.33-38)

Falstaff's lines are not simply an indication of his less-than-lofty taste in literature and his boorish manners; they also touch on some of the play's major concerns: the proper behavior for a king, the nature of true heroism, and the problem of political instability. Shakespeare uses the ballad in two ways to comment on these matters. The quoted lines stand by themselves, and they serve as an allusion to the whole ballad.

Falstaff actually misquotes the ballad. The opening lines of Deloney's text set the scene for Lancelot's adventure:

> When *Arthur* first in court began,
>   and was approved king:
> By force of armes great victories won,
>   and conquest home did bring.
> Then into *Britaine* straight he came,
>   where fiftie good and able
> Knights then repaired unto him,
>   which were of the round Table.

> (ll. 1-8)

Falstaff alters "and was approved King" to "And was a worthy King," thus raising, by implication, the question of what constitutes worthiness in a ruler. The rebellion and anarchy plaguing England through most of *2 Henry IV* (and in *1 Henry IV*) is the product of Bolingbroke's unworthiness, the result of his murdering Richard II, his usurping the throne, and his political maneuvering to maintain his reign. The restoration of order at the end of *2 Henry IV* and Hal's emergence as a model king in *Henry V* is possible precisely because Hal is worthy—he is free from the sin of his father's usurpation, and he is willing to abjure his riotous habits and companions in favor of public duty:[26]

. . . The tide of blood in me
Hath proudly flow'd in vanity till now.
Now it doth turn, and ebb back to the sea,
Where it shall mingle with the state of floods,
And flow henceforth in formal majesty.

(V.ii.129-33)

The mention of Arthur in this context is appropriate because to Shakespeare's audience, Arthur (often claimed as the ancestor of the Tudor line) was a model of kingly behavior who ruled over an English empire and a nobility unified by the institution of the Round Table. Yet though Arthur was generally regarded as a heroic figure and was included among the Nine Worthies, the Elizabethan audience was also probably aware of him as an example of a ruler whose person and kingdom were undone by lust and treachery.[27] That Shakespeare intended the reference to have this second meaning as well is clear from the numerous other references in the play to legendary figures who were admirable in many ways but were destroyed either by their own excesses or the treachery of those about them. Most of these references involve distortion, parody, or crude humor. Doll Tearsheet, for example, compares Falstaff to a number of heroes, many of whose ends were less than glorious: "Thou art as valorous as Hector of Troy, worth five of Agamemnon, and ten times better than the Nine Worthies" (II.iv.216-18). Pistol's ravings cover similar grounds, ". . . Compare with Caesars and with Cannibals, / and Troyant Greeks" (II.iv.163-164), and he describes Doll to Falstaff as the "Helen of thy noble thoughts" (V.v.33). The effect of these references is not simply to echo Henry IV's worries about the dangerous potential of Hal's association with Falstaff (IV.iv.58-66), but also to call into question the standard models of heroic behavior and to indicate their potential for encouraging foolish or vicious as well as noble behavior.

One of the functions of the scenes involving Falstaff, Pistol, Shallow, and their companions is, as James Black points out, to present parodies of heroism as contrasts to the valiant and magnanimous behavior of Hotspur and Hal at the end of *1 Henry IV* (recalled at the beginning of *2 Henry IV* by the eulogies of Hotspur: I.i.105-18; I.iii.18-45). As he says, "The rejection of Falstaff, then, is a rejection not only of false justice or of the world, the flesh, and the devil, it also is a rejection of false heroics, of counterfeit honor."[28] The situation is somewhat more complex, however, because Shakespeare criticizes as well as praises Hotspur's heroic, chivalric, yet headstrong behavior,[29] and because the behavior of Falstaff and the others is in itself an illustration of how easily chivalric idealism can be debased. Shallow's boast about having played the part of Sir Dagonet (King Arthur's fool) in "Arthur's Show" (III.ii.273-76), an annual archery contest where participants took the names of Knights of the Round

Table,[30] indicates how readily the forms and attitudes of chivalry lent themselves to travesty and devaluation. Shakespeare's allusion to Deloney's ballad helps set the terms for the treatment of false heroism in the scenes that follow it (II.iv; III.ii), and it also helps show how the materials for chivalric idealism and heroism could be debased into models for violent behavior lacking any honorable moral or political purpose.

Though Falstaff quotes only the first two lines of the ballad and makes no mention of Lancelot, Shakespeare, as we will see, probably intended his audience to recognize the lines as an allusion to the whole ballad and to see that Falstaff's attitudes towards heroism and combat are similar to those displayed in the ballad. Ballads were often referred to by first lines alone—entries in the Stationers' Register were often made in this manner.[31] In *The Little French Lawyer,* moreover, Fletcher quotes from the middle of the ballad, confident that his audience will recognize the lines as an allusion to the entire story.[32]

The dominant effect of the ballad, and the one that might reasonably be expected to be apparent to the play's audience, is its emphasis on exciting action, particularly feats of arms, accompanied by heroic posturing and boasts:

> Ha, ha (quoth *Tarquin* tho):
> One of vs two shall end our liues,
>   before that we do go. . . .
> They buckled then together so,
>   like two wilde Boares, so rushing:
> And with their swords and shields they ran
>   at one another lashing,
> The ground besprinkled with bloud.
>   *Tarquin* began to faint. . . .

(ll. 102-04, 109-14)

This reduction of heroism in combat to boasting and swordplay characterizes also the comic scenes in *2 Henry IV.*

Pistol, Shallow, and Falstaff portray many of their exploits—in war, in love, in their various adventures—in heroic terms and as armed conflicts. For them, however, combat is not a way of resolving political and moral conflicts or the result of a clash between two strong personalities. It is instead a game, preferably a verbal game (actual combat is often avoided unless the opponent is clearly inferior or can be hoodwinked), designed soley to enhance the fortune or reputation of one person at the expense of another. In the various combats—real, remembered, verbal, or sexual[33]—scattered throughout the comic scenes, slapstick action and empty boasting, "swaggering," take the place of serious fighting and the expression of heroic, chivalric ideals:

Pist [ol]

    . . . . [*Snatches up his sword.*] Then death rock me
    asleep, abridge my doleful days! Why then let griev-

ous, ghastly, gaping wounds Untwind the Sisters Three!
Come, Atropos, I say!

HOST[ESS].

Here's goodly stuff toward!

FAL[STAFF].

Give me my rapier, boy.

. . . . .

HOST.

Here's a goodly tumult! I'll forswear keeping house
afore I'll be in these tirrits and frights! [*Falstaff thrusts
at Pistol.*] So! Murder, I warrant now! Alas, alas, put
up your naked weapons, put up your naked weapons.
[*Exit Bardolph, driving Pistol out.*]

. . . . .

FAL.

Have you turned him out a-doors?

BARD.

Yea, sir, the rascal's drunk. You have hurt him, sir, i'
th' shoulder.

(II.iv.192-97, 200-04, 209-11)

The arbitrariness of Pistol's actions and, in the following quote, Shallow's evident enjoyment (in retrospect)
of violence for its own sake illustrate what can become
of chivalric heroism once the moral impetus behind
combat has been lost:

SHAL[LOW].

The same Sir John, the very same. I see him break
Scoggin's head at the court gate, when a was a crack,
not thus high; and the very same day did I fight with
one Samson Stockfish a fruiterer, behind Gray's Inn.
Jesu, Jesu, the mad days that I have spent! And to see
how many of my old acquaintance are dead!

(III.ii.28-34)

It should be noted that Falstaff's quotation of the ballad
comes just before Pistol's arrival at the Boar's Head
Tavern and the senseless, fustian-filled battle between
the two. Thus it is not inappropriate to view Falstaff's
behavior in this scene and others in the light of
broadside models. That Falstaff, with some humor of
course, views himself as a broadside hero, is clear from
his reaction after he has tricked Sir John Coleville into
surrendering: ". . . and I beseech your Grace, let it be
booked with the rest of this day's deeds, or by the Lord
I will have it in a particular ballad else, with mine own
picture on the top on't, Coleville kissing my foot . . ."
(IV.iii.44-48).

All this is in sharp contrast to the noble, chivalrous
combat between Hal and Hotspur that resolves the
conflicts in *1 Henry IV* and to the magnanimity of Hal's
eulogy over the fallen Hotspur:

Ill-weav'd ambition, how much art thou shrunk!
When that this body did contain a spirit,
A kingdom for it was too small a bound;
But now two paces of the vilest earth
Is room enough. This earth that bears thee dead
Bears not alive so stout a gentleman.

. . . . .

Adieu, and take thy praise with thee to heaven!
Thy ignominy sleep with thee in the grave,
But not remember'd in thy epitaph.[34]

The scenes involving Falstaff and his companions are a
good example of how chivalric idealism can be debased
when only the forms are preserved and the political and
moral impetus behind it is lost. Thus, Shakespeare's use
of the ballad is not merely a recognition of the changes
Malory's story underwent in Deloney's hands, but also
a criticism of the cultural context that encouraged such
transformations. The history of this story, from Malory,
to Deloney, to Shakespeare, is in a small way a history
of the decline and debasement of a cultural ideal.

Notes

1. This title appears in Thomas Deloney's *The
Garland of Good Will* (London, 1628). The earli-
est broadside edition has the title, "The Noble
Acts Newly Found, of Arthur of the Table Round"
(London, c. 1615), and the version preserved in
Bishop Percy's Folio Manuscript has the title, "Sir
Lancelot of Du Lake" (*Bishop Percy's Folio
Manuscript,* ed. John W. Hales and Frederick J.
Furnivall (London: Trübner, 1868), I, 84-87. The
poem is often referred to by the title from the
manuscript. The version from *The Garland of
Good Will* (1631) is printed in *The Works of
Thomas Deloney,* ed. Francis Oscar Mann (Oxford:
Oxford Univ. Press, 1912), pp. 323-26.

2. See, for example, R. W. Barber, *Arthur of Albion*
(New York: Barnes and Noble, 1961), pp. 120-21,
and George Watson, et al., *The New Cambridge
Bibliography of English Literature,* I (Cambridge:
Cambridge Univ. Press, 1974), 400.

3. J. Burke Severs, ed., *A Manual of the Writings in
Middle English: 1050-1500,* I (New Haven: Con-
necticut Academy of Arts and Sciences, 1967), 51,
gives this entry among its descriptions of Middle
English works: "SIR LANCELOT DU LAKE . . .
This is a ballad in 124 verses in the Percy Folio
MS, relating Lancelot's victory over Sir Tarquin
in single combat." This is only a minor revision of
the entry in John Edwin Wells, *A Manual of the
Writings in Middle English: 1050-1500* (New
Haven: Connecticut Academy of Arts and Sci-
ences, 1916), p. 48.

4. *Bishop Percy's Folio Manuscript,* ed. Hales and
Furnivall, I, 84-87. Part of the poem is missing
due to damage in the manuscript.

5. Ibid., I, 84

6. *The Garland of Good Will* was probably issued for the first time in 1596 (*The Novels of Thomas Deloney,* ed. Merritt E. Lawlis [Bloomington, Indiana: Indiana Univ. Press, 1961], p. xxvi, n. 10). No early editions of *The Garland* have survived, however, and the earliest known edition dates from 1628 (*STC* 6553.5). The poem was first entered in the Stationer's Register as a broadside by Edward Alde on June 8, 1603 under the title, "The noble Actes nowe newly found of ARTHURE of the round table" (Edward Arber, *A Transcript of the Registers of the Company of Stationers of London: 1554-1640 A.D.,* [London and Birmingham: Privately Printed, 1875-1894], III, 236). There is no evidence that the poem appeared on broadsides before the date of the entry. The earliest surviving broadside dates from c. 1615 (*STC* 6558.5).

7. William Shakespeare, *The Second Part of King Henry IV,* ed. A. R. Humphreys (London: Methuen, 1966), pp. 64-65. All quotes are taken from this edition.

8. John Fletcher, *The Little French Lawyer,* in *The Works of Francis Beaumont and John Fletcher,* ed. A. R. Waller (Cambridge: Cambridge Univ. Press, 1906), III, 398.

9. John Marston, *The Malcontent,* ed. Bernard Harris (London: Benn, 1967), p. 41.

10. The manuscript was probably copied from an early edition of *The Garland of Good Will* (c. 1600). See my "Sources of the Ballads in *Bishop Percy's Folio Manuscript,*" Diss. Univ. of Chicago, 1976, pp. 327-38.

11. Merritt E. Lawlis, "Shakespeare, Deloney, and the Earliest Text of the Arthur Ballad," *Harvard Library Bulletin,* 10 (1956), 131.

12. Robert H. Wilson in *A Manual of the Writings in Middle English: 1050-1500,* ed. Albert E. Hartung, III (New Haven: Connecticut Academy of Arts and Sciences, 1973), 768.

13. Mann. *Deloney,* pp. 570-72, calls the ballad a paraphrase of Malory, but though he prints the section of *Le Morte Darthur,* he does not note that much of the ballad is copied directly, not paraphrased, from its source.

14. *The Story of Kynge Arthur, and also of his Knyghtes of the Rounde Table* (London: Thomas East, [1585]), sig. H2. This edition of Malory is closest in time to the ballad.

15. Mann, *Deloney,* p. 325, ll. 83-88. The ballad is printed on pp. 323-26; all quotations are taken from this edition and are followed by line references.

16. "Leander's Love to Loyal Hero" and "The Judgment of Solomon" are printed in *A Pepysian Garland,* ed. Hyder E. Rollins (Cambridge: Cambridge Univ. Press, 1922), pp. 49-53, 350-55. "Patient Grissel" and "The Wandering Prince of Troy" appear in *The Euing Collection of English Broadside Ballads* (Glasgow: Univ. of Glasgow Pub., 1971), pp. 123-24, 127-28. "The Battle of Agincourt" is printed in *The Pepys Ballads,* ed. Hyder E. Rollins, I (Cambridge, Mass.: Harvard Univ. Press, 1929), 12-15.

17. Edmund Reiss, *Sir Thomas Malory* (New York: Twayne, 1966), p. 92.

18. Elizabeth T. Pochoda, *Arthurian Propaganda:* Le Morte Darthur *as an Historical Ideal of Life* (Chapel Hill: Univ. of North Carolina Press, 1971), p. 93.

19. *The Story of Kynge Arthur,* sig. 17.

20. Ibid., sig. H2.

21. David C. Fowler, *A Literary History of the Popular Ballad* (Durham, N.C.: Duke Univ. Press, 1968), p. 133.

22. Louis B. Wright, *Middle-Class Culture in Elizabethan England* (Chapel Hill: Univ. of North Carolina Press, 1935), p. 376.

23. Wright, pp. 375-417, surveys the Elizabethan taste in fiction.

24. Ibid., pp. 377-78.

25. See. for example, the various kinds of ballads printed by Hyder E. Rollins, ed., *A Pepysian Garland* (Cambridge: Cambridge Univ. Press, 1922).

26. Derek Traversi is a major exponent of this view of the play. See *Shakespeare from* Richard II *to* Henry IV (Stanford, Calif.: Stanford Univ. Press, 1957), pp. 1-11.

27. Charles Bowie Millican, in *Spenser and the Table Round* (Cambridge, Mass.: Harvard Univ. Press, 1932), gives an excellent summary of Arthur's Elizabethan reputation as a hero, a model ruler, and a supposed ancestor of the Tudor line. Yet Shakespeare's audience was undoubtedly also aware, through Malory or some other source, of the tragic ending of the Arthurian story. Richard Lloyd's *A Briefe Discourse of the Most Renowned Actes and Right Valiant Conquests of those Puisant Princes, Called the Nine Worthies* (London, 1584) provides an interesting view of Arthur and the rest of the Nine Worthies because in re-telling their stores it treats each one as a hero, yet uses four of them (Arthur, Hector, Alex-

ander, Julius Caesar) as examples of sinners whose behavior should be a warning to the reader and five of them (Joshua, David, Judas Maccabeus, Charlemagne, Guy of Warwick) as examples of righteous men whose behavior ought to be imitated.

28. James Black, "Counterfeits of Soldiership in *Henry IV*," *Shakespeare Quarterly*, 24 (1973), 382.

29. Cf Traversi, *Shakespeare,* p. 93: "He appears as a man who has failed to mature, whose 'honour'—overtaken by the changing times—is in the last analysis an empty rhetorical device, and who will shortly be eliminated from a world in which he has resolved to play a part without, like Coriolanus after him though on a simpler level, understanding the true nature of the issues in which his fate, and the manoeuvres of the politicians around him, have involved him."

30. Millican, *Spenser,* pp. 64; 103-05; 175-76; n. 99.

31. Rollins, *Analytical Index,* passim.

32. *Works,* ed. Waller, II, 398.

33. Sexuality and chivalric combat are yoked together in Falstaff's comment, ". . . for to serve bravely is to come halting off, you know; to come off the breach, with his pike bent bravely; and to surgery bravely; to venture upon the charged chambers bravely . . ." (II.iv.48-52).

34. *The First Part of Henry IV,* ed. A. R. Humphreys (London: Methuen, 1960), p. 159 (II.iv.87-92, 98-100).

FURTHER READING

Criticism

Dahl, Torsten. "Deloney the Elizabethan." In *Linguistic Studies in Some Elizabethan Writings,* Vol. 1, pp. 13-33. Copenhagen, Denmark: Universitetsforlaget, 1951.
    Examination of the language and stylistic features of Deloney's writing.

Reuter, O. R. *Proverbs, Proverbial Sentences and Phrases in Thomas Deloney's Works.* Helsinki, Finland: Societas Scientiarum Fennica, 1986, 146 p.
    Examination of Deloney's frequent use of proverbs popular among the Elizabethan working class.

Wright, Eugene P. "The Poetry." In *Thomas Deloney,* pp. 20-50. Boston: Twayne, 1981.
    Survey of Deloney's entire poetic output—the extant ballads collected in *The Garland of Good Will* and *Strange Histories,* as well as the poet's most ambitious work, *Canaans Calamitie.*

Additional coverage of Deloney's life and career is contained in the following sources published by Thomson Gale: *Dictionary of Literary Biography,* **Vol. 167;** *Literature Criticism from 1400 to 1800,* **Vol. 41;** *Literature Resource Center;* **and** *Reference Guide to English Literature,* **Ed. 2.**

Edward FitzGerald
1809-1883

English poet, translator, essayist, and letter writer.

INTRODUCTION

Best known for his translation of the *Rubáiyát of Omar Khayyám, Astronomer Poet of Persia* (1859), FitzGerald also composed original poetry, although it is considered far less successful than his translations. He considered himself a true artist rather than a literal translator and is credited with making the *Rubáiyát* accessible to English audiences.

BIOGRAPHICAL INFORMATION

FitzGerald was born Edward Purcell on March 31, 1809, in Bredfield House in Suffolk, England, the sixth of eight children. His parents, John Purcell and Mary Frances FitzGerald Purcell, were both descendents of Irish aristocrats, and since FitzGerald's mother's family was the more prominent, John Purcell took his wife's name in 1818 after the death of his father-in-law. Young Edward was educated at King Edward VI Grammar School in Bury St. Edmunds and at Trinity College, Cambridge, earning his degree in 1830. While at Cambridge, FitzGerald made the acquaintance of Alfred, Lord Tennyson, Thomas Carlyle, and William Makepeace Thackeray; he carried on an extensive correspondence with all three throughout his life. FitzGerald traveled briefly to Paris after graduation, but soon returned to Suffolk, where he took up residence in a modest cottage on his parents' estate, becoming very nearly reclusive although he was still quite young. During this period he wrote a number of poems, few of which were published, and then began translating the verse dramas of Spanish playwright Pedro Calderón de la Barca. He was persuaded by the scholar Edward Byles Cowell, who was himself fluent in a number of languages, to study Persian, which introduced him to the poem whose translation would become his most famous work.

The 1850s were unhappy years for FitzGerald. His father, who had lost a great deal of money in mining speculation, declared personal bankruptcy and left FitzGerald's mother; he died in 1852. Three years later, FitzGerald's mother also died, but with her personal fortune intact. She left FitzGerald an inheritance that guaranteed his financial security for the remainder of his life. In 1856 FitzGerald's closest friends, Cowell and his wife, left England for an academic position in India, and FitzGerald was devastated by the loss. That same year, he married Lucy Barton, the daughter of his friend Bernard Barton, the Quaker poet. The marriage proved disastrous for the completely mismatched couple and they separated within months of their wedding, after which FitzGerald became even more reclusive. He abandoned his home in Suffolk and lived in a succession of rented rooms. Beginning in 1863, he spent his summers aboard a yacht he had constructed to meet his own specifications. In 1864 he bought a cottage, which he named Little Grange, near Woodbridge; he renovated it over the next ten years. He continued to live in rented rooms until 1874, when he finally moved into Little Grange. FitzGerald died on June 14, 1883.

MAJOR WORKS

Although FitzGerald wrote a number of original poems, few were ever published. Of those that were, the best-received was "The Meadows in Spring," composed when he was only twenty-two years old and published anonymously in April of 1831 in Hone's *Year Book* and in July of that same year in the *Athenaeum,* whose editors apparently thought the poem was the work of Charles Lamb. In 1832 FitzGerald wrote "To a Lady Singing" and in 1834 another periodical, *The Keepsake,* accepted "The Old Beau" for publication. In 1839 FitzGerald wrote "Bredfield Hall," a tribute to his birthplace in Suffolk; also published anonymously, this poem was often erroneously attributed to Tennyson.

FitzGerald anonymously published his blank verse translation of *Salamán and Absál,* an allegorical poem by the Persian poet Jāmī (1414-1492), in 1856. His masterpiece, the very liberal translation of Omar Khayyám's *Rubáiyát,* was first published in 1859 at FitzGerald's own expense, the work having been rejected by *Fraser's Magazine.* It originally consisted of seventy-five quatrains, but was expanded to one hundred and ten in FitzGerald's revision of 1868, and then reduced to one hundred and one in the revisions of 1872 and 1879.

In addition to his poetry, FitzGerald published *Euphranor: A Dialogue on Youth* (1851), a set of discussions featuring four Cambridge students, one of them modeled on FitzGerald's friend W. K. Brown, and narrated by their mentor, an elderly Cambridge physician. A year later, FitzGerald published a book of aphorisms and quotations titled *Polonius, a Collection of Wise Saws and Modern Instances.* He also translated a number of plays, among them *Six Dramas of Calderón* (1853) and Aeschylus's *Agamemnon* (1865). FitzGerald was also a prolific letter writer and he carried on a regular correspondence with such contemporaries as Tennyson, Thackeray, and Carlyle. His letters were collected in *Letters and Literary Remains of Edward FitzGerald* (1889) and in *Letters of Edward FitzGerald* (1980).

CRITICAL RECEPTION

Critics seem to agree that FitzGerald's original work, with the possible exception of "The Meadows in Spring," is mediocre at best, but they generally offer high praise for his translation of the *Rubáiyát,* crediting him with introducing the work to readers in England and America. Biographer Morley Adams, writing in 1911, believes that Khayyám's poem would have "remained in oblivion" were it not for FitzGerald. Michael Wolff reports that the translation was generally ignored when first published, and, in fact, it too had a "narrow escape from oblivion." However, nearly a decade later, the poem was revised by FitzGerald and reviewed in the *North American Review,* and its popularity soon grew. It had become "a literary fad" even during FitzGerald's lifetime and by the end of the nineteenth century its admirers had become a cult (which then spawned an anticult), according to John D. Yohannan. Although Khayyám's original text dated back to the twelfth century, its "philosophy of despair" apparently matched the prevailing mood of *fin de siècle* England and America; however, as Yohannan points out, the work had as many opponents as proponents. The critic claims that the *Rubáiyát* "was the shibboleth for such various and often conflicting dogmas as theosophy, aestheticism, eroticism, determinism, socialism, materialism, and numerous types of occultism." Its centennial in 1959 was that year's "second most celebrated literary centenary," eclipsed only by Charles Darwin's *Origin of Species.* More recently, however, the *Rubáiyát* has again become neglected, at least among literary scholars. Stressing the poem's continued popularity with readers, Daniel Schenker notes that "few poems are so widely circulated . . . and yet so rarely talked about."

Critics still debate the degree of originality present in FitzGerald's version of the *Rubáiyát.* Adams acknowledges that FitzGerald's most famous work was not original, but contends nonetheless that his translation exhibits pure genius. Michael S. Helfand notes that there is "growing scholarly and critical consensus that

[FitzGerald's] work should be studied not as translation but as his own creation." Frederick A. De Armas regards the *Rubáiyát* as a combination of "the richness of Persian literature" and "the Victorian translator's own poetic abilities." Gary Sloan offers high praise for FitzGerald's efforts: "By culling, combining, omitting, patching, and tinkering, FitzGerald conferred order on a welter of variegated musings." FitzGerald himself referred to his art as a "poetic transfusion" rather than a literal translation. In an often-quoted line from FitzGerald's correspondence, he explained his aversion to literal translations, contending that the work must "live." "Better a live Sparrow than a stuffed Eagle," FitzGerald wrote to his mentor and publisher Edward Byles Cowell. However Cowell, like a number of his contemporary critics, disapproved of FitzGerald's liberal reworkings of the original text.

William Cadbury, who refers to the poem's "failure to transcend" the limitations of human life, is one of many critics who have commented on the work's relentlessly gloomy tone. David Sonstroem, too, remarks on the *Rubáiyát*'s "helpless, sodden pessimism and richly melancholic despair," despite the frequently-quoted lines involving "a jug of wine, a loaf of bread, and thou" that seem to offer some consolation. For Sonstroem, who compares the work to the typical *carpe diem* poem from the same time period, the *Rubáiyát*'s principal sentiment might involve abandoning the day rather than seizing it. The poem's ultimate irony, however, is that the poet/narrator fails to do even that. Schenker notes that "the Victorian era saw the development of all kinds of self-help books for the benefit of the masses, and perhaps this is the genre to which the *Rubáiyát* ultimately belongs: 'infinite resignation made simple.'"

PRINCIPAL WORKS

Poetry

"The Meadows in Spring" 1831

Salamán and Absál [translator; from *Sáláman and Absál* by Jāmī] 1856

Rubáiyát of Omar Khayyám, Astronomer Poet of Persia [translator; from *The Rubáiyát* by Omar Khayyám] 1859

Other Major Works

Euphranor: A Dialogue on Youth (dialogues) 1851

Polonius, a Collection of Wise Saws and Modern Instances [editor] (aphorisms and quotations) 1852

Six Dramas of Calderón, Freely Translated [translator] (dramas) 1853

Agamemnon [translator; from *Agamemnon* by Aeschylus] (drama) 1865

The Downfall and Death of King Oedipus. 2 vols. [translator; from *Oedipus Rex* and *Oedipus at Colonus* by Sophocles] (dramas) 1880-81

Works of Edward FitzGerald (poetry, dramas, essays, and aphorisms) 1887

Letters and Literary Remains of Edward FitzGerald. 7 vols. (letters, poetry, and dialogues) 1889

Letters of Edward FitzGerald. 4 vols. (letters) 1980

CRITICISM

Morley Adams (essay date 1909)

SOURCE: Adams, Morley. "Works." In *Omar's Interpreter: A New Life of Edward FitzGerald,* pp. 111-28. London: The Priory Press Hampstead, 1911.

[*In the following excerpt from his biography of FitzGerald, originally published in 1909, Adams offers a brief overview of the author's translations and original poetry.*]

The literary output of Edward FitzGerald was not prodigious, and probably in his bibliography there is little that has in it the stuff of immortality. **Omar** [*The Rubáyát of Omar Khayyám*], of course, will live. It has taken its place in the literary firmament as one of the brightest stars, and by its genius has placed Edward FitzGerald among the prophets. But it may be urged that **Omar** is not an original work, and this is correct, but **Omar** without FitzGerald, it is safe to assert, would ever have remained in oblivion, or at most, would have had an exceedingly limited number of readers and less admirers. Of the original works of FitzGerald, his letters and one or two poems, with here and there a fine passage of prose, display the genius of the translator of **Omar,** but the remainder of his works are mediocre.

His bibliography, in chronological order, is as follows:

1831	*The Meadows in Spring.*
	Will Thackeray.
1832	"Canst Thou, My Clora?"
1833	"On Annie Allen."
	"'The Old Beau.'"
1839	"Bredfield Hall."
1841	"Chronomoros."
1847	*Notes to the "Table Talk of John Selden."*
1849	*Memoir to Bernard Barton.*

1851	*Euphranor.*
1852	*Polonius.*
1853	*Six Dramas from Calderon.*
1855	*Euphranor (Second Edition).*
1856	*Salaman and Absal.*
	Attar's "Bird Parliament."
1859	*Omar Khayyam.*
1860 & 1861	"F." Articles to *East Anglian Daily Times.*
	"Parathina" contributions to *Notes and Queries.*
1862	*Virgil's Garden*
	Omar Khayyam (reprint)
1865	*Magico and Such Stuff as Dreams are made of.*
	Agamemnon
1868	*Two Generals.*
	Omar Khayyam (2nd Edition).
1868 to 1870	"E. F. G." Articles to *East Anglian Daily Times.*
1871	*Salaman and Absal* (2nd Edition).
1872	*Omar Khayyam* (3rd Edition).
1876	*Agamemnon* (2nd Edition).
1877 & 1878	"Effigy" Articles to *East Anglian Daily Times.*
	Notes on Charles Lamb.
1879	*Salaman and Absal* (3rd Edition).
	Omar Khayyam (4th Edition).
	Readings in Crabbe.
1880	Articles in *Temple Bar.*
1880 & 1881	*Œdipus*
1882	*Virgil's Garden.*
	Euphranor (3rd Edition)

In addition to the above FitzGerald wrote some notes to *Wesley's Journal* which have been lost, but may some day be re-discovered, in which event their publication would be of much interest. FitzGerald often quoted Wesley and his *Journal* was among his favourite books.

His first poem, published in Hone's *Year Book* in 1831, was the charming **"Meadows in Spring,"** a lyric, beautiful in sentiment and admirable in construction.

"The Meadows in Spring."

'Tis a dull sight
　　To see the year dying,
When winter winds
　　Set the yellow wood sighing:
　　Sighing, oh! sighing.

When such a time cometh,
　　I do retire
Into an old room

Beside a bright fire:
Oh, pile a bright fire!

And there I sit
Reading old things,
Of knights and lorn damsels
While the wind sings—
Oh, drearily sings!

I never look out
Nor attend to the blast;
For all to be seen
Is the leaves falling fast:
Falling, falling!

But close at the hearth,
Like a cricket, sit I,
Reading of summer
And chivalry—
Gallant chivalry!

Then with an old friend
I talk of our youth—
How 'twas gladsome, but often
Foolish, forsooth:
But gladsome, gladsome!

Or to get merry
We sing some old rhyme,
That made the wood ring again
In summer time—
Sweet summer time!

Then go we to smoking,
Silent and snug:
Nought passes between us,
Save a brown jug—
Sometimes!

And sometimes a tear
Will rise in each eye
Seeing the two old friends
So merrily—so merrily!

And ere to bed
Go we, go we,
Down on the ashes,
We kneel on the knee,
Praying together!

Thus, then, live I,
Till 'mid all the gloom,
By Heaven! the bold sun
Is with me in the room
Shining, shining!

Then the clouds part,
Swallows soaring between,
The Spring is alive,
And the meadows are green!

I jump up like mad,
Break the old pipe in twain,
And away to the Meadows,
The Meadows again!

This lyric, so sweetly tender, with its lights and shades and its quiet easy-flowing rhythm, was written when FitzGerald was only twenty-two, and it bears evidences of that retrospective sadness which even in those early days had tinged his life. The last line of each stanza, with its haunting refrain, is wistful in the extreme. In the eighth stanza he approaches the humorous with "Nought passes between us save a brown jug"—and its sly one-word last line "Sometimes!" but he at once smothers it and gets back to pathos in the next verse. Suddenly, in the midst of his musings of dark winter, he realises the sun has come back, that the Spring is alive, the meadows green, and:

I jump up like mad,
Break the old pipe in twain,
And away to the Meadows,
The Meadows again.

The world would have been thankful for more of this sylvan, lyric song, and when we consider FitzGerald's love of simple country scenes and nature generally it is perhaps strange that he wrote so little in a similar strain.

The next year he wrote those beautiful verses **"To a Lady Singing."** Many think that he had Annie Allen in mind when writing them.

"To a Lady Singing."

Can'st thou, my Clora, declare,
After thy sweet song dieth
Into the wild summer air,
Whither it falleth or flieth?
Soon would my answer be noted
Wert thou but sage as sweet-throated.

Melody, dying away,
Into the dark sky closes,
Like the good soul from her clay,
Like the fair odour of roses;
Therefore thou now art behind it,
But thou shalt follow, and find it.

Nothing can utterly die:
Music aloft up-springing
Turns to pure atoms of sky
Each golden note of thy singing:
And that to which morning did listen
At eve in a rainbow may glisten.

Beauty when laid in the grave
Feedeth the lily beside her,
Therefore the soul cannot have
Station or honour denied her;
She will not better her essence,
But wear a crown in God's presence.

The last two verses were added at a later date. The poem is one of singular beauty, especially the first three verses, and it is cause for wonder that no composer has—so far as I know—ever set them to music. The fanciful idea in the third verse of the golden notes of the singer ascending to the heavens in the morning to scintillate in the evening rainbow, is as charming as it is original. The last verse certainly does not improve the poem, the ideal ending is the last line of the third verse.

"The Old Beau" appeared in *The Keepsake* in 1834. It is in many respects a fine poem reminiscent of the old English ballads, written in a jaunty style, the kind of thing one would go a-hunting to. An old Beau reviews his life and laments modern decadence:

> The days we used to laugh, Tom,
>   At tales of love, and tears of passion;
> The bowls we used to quaff, Tom,
>   In toasting all the toasts in fashion;
> The heaths and hills we ranged, Tom,
>   When limb ne'er fail'd, when step ne'er falter'd;
> Alas! how things are changed, Tom,
>   How we—and all the world—are alter'd.

The complete poem contains ten eight-lined verses, in which the Beau describes his College days, how now even the climate has grown several degrees colder and the world is fast hastening towards dissolution.

> The world, I oft suspect, Tom,
>   Draws near its close; and isn't it better
> To die, when no respect, Tom,
>   Is shown from creditor to debtor?
> When tradesfolk make a row, Tom,
>   A year or two if you delay them,
> And often ask you now, Tom,
>   With perfect *nonchalance,* to pay them?

"Bredfield Hall" was written in 1839, and is, but for one or two slight metrical faults, a very fine poem in the Tennyson style. It is a kind of panorama of events, the scene being laid at his birthplace, Bredfield Hall (now called "Bredfield House" and at the time of his birth the "White House").

On several occasions I have visited Bredfield House, which stands on high ground about a mile and a half outside Woodbridge. From the highest point may be seen the waters of Hollesley (called Hosely) Bay where, as mentioned in the poem, Nelson's fleet anchored after its return from Trafalgar, and a delightful view of the surrounding country may be obtained.

The poem is so good, and so little known, that I give it in full:

"Bredfield Hall."

> Lo, an English mansion founded
>   In the elder James's reign,
> Quaint and stately, and surrounded
>   With a pastoral domain.

> With well-timber'd lawn and gardens
>   And with many a pleasant mead,
> Skirted by the lofty coverts
>   Where the hare and pheasant feed.

> Flank'd it is with goodly stables,
>   Shelter'd by coeval trees:
> So it lifts its honest gables
>   Toward the distant German Seas;

> Where it once discern'd the smoke
>   Of old sea-battles far away:
> Saw victorious Nelson's topmasts
>   Anchoring in Hollesley Bay.

> But whatever storm might riot,
>   Cannon roar, and trumpet ring,
> Still amid these meadows quiet
>   Did the yearly violet spring:

> Still Heaven's starry hand suspended
>   That light balance of the dew,
> That each night on earth descended,
>   And each morning rose anew:

> And the ancient house stood rearing
>   Undisturb'd her chimneys high,
> And her gilded vanes still veering
>   Toward each quarter of the sky:

> While like wave to wave succeeding
>   Through the world of joy and strife,
> Household after household speeding,
>   Handed on the torch of life:

> First, Sir Knight in ruff and doublet,
>   Arm in arm with stately dame;
> Then the Cavaliers indignant
>   For their monarch brought to shame:

> Languid beauties limn'd by Lely;
>   Full-wigg'd Justice of Queen Anne:
> Tory squires who tippled freely;
>   And the modern Gentleman:

> Here they lived, and here they greeted,
>   Maids and matrons, sons and sires,
> Wandering in its walks, or seated
>   Round its hospitable fires:

> Oft their silken dresses floated
>   Gleaming through the pleasure ground:
> Oft dash'd by the scarlet-coated
>   Hunter, horse, and dappled hound.

> Till the Bell that not in vain
>   Had summon'd them to weekly prayer,
> Call'd them one by one again
>   To the church—and left them there!

> They with all their loves and passions,
>   Compliment, and song, and jest,
> Politics, and sports, and fashions,
>   Merged in everlasting rest!

So they pass—while thou, old Mansion,
    Markest with unalter'd face
How like the foliage of thy summers
    Race of man succeeds to race.

To most thou stand'st a record sad,
    But all the sunshine of the year
Could not make thine aspect glad
    To one whose youth is buried here.

In thine ancient rooms and gardens
    Buried—and his own no more
Than the youth of those old owners,
    Dead two centuries before.

Unto him the fields around thee
    Darken with the days gone by:
O'er the solemn woods that bound thee
    Ancient sunsets seem to die.

Sighs the self-same breeze of morning
    Through the cypress as of old;
Ever at the Spring's returning
    One same crocus breaks the mould.

Still though 'scaping Time's more savage
    Handywork this pile appears,
It has not escaped the ravage
    Of the undermining years.

And though each succeeding master,
    Grumbling at the cost to pay,
Did with coat of paint and plaster
    Hide the wrinkles of decay;

Yet the secret worm ne'er ceases,
    Nor the mouse behind the wall;
Heart of oak will come to pieces,
    And farewell to Bredfield Hall!

In 1851 appeared the first edition of *Euphranor* which FitzGerald, not thinking a great deal of, called "a pretty specimen of a chiselled cherry-stone," though this does not give a particularly lucid idea of *Euphranor*, a "chiselled cherry-stone" being a mystery understood by few. What he probably wished to convey was that it was a small work delicately executed. The *Euphranor* is a beautiful piece of Plato-like writing in fine but simple English. Four Cambridge undergraduates, Euphranor, the hero, an impulsive, enthusiastic, hot-headed youth; Lycion, a generous, indolent fop; Phidippus, a warm and simple-hearted Esau (drawn from FitzGerald's friend W. K. Brown), and Lexilogus, of giant intellect, but humble and ingenuous. The narrator, a Cambridge physician, is an elderly, sobered kind of guardian of the youths.

Euphranor consists largely of the discussions of the quintette; they talk of chivalry, education, literature, sport, etc., and in these talks are some charming passages, especially in the references to Tennyson. The little work is full of a sweet poetical spirit, permeated with the FitzGerald pathetic wail of the ever-passing happiness.

One of the finest parts is the description of the Boat-race:

The Boat-Race, from Euphranor.

"Shortly after this, the rest of us agreed it was time to be gone. We walked along the fields by the Church (purposely to ask about the sick Lady by the way), cross'd the Ferry, and mingled with the crowd upon the opposite shore; Townsmen and Gownsmen, with the tassell'd Fellow-commoner sprinkled here and there—Reading men and Sporting men—Fellows, and even Masters of Colleges, not indifferent to the prowess of their respective Crews—all these, conversing on all sorts of topics, from the slang in *Bell's Life* to the last new German Revelation, and moving in ever-changing groups down the shore of the river, at whose farther bend was a little knot of ladies gathered up on a green knoll faced and illuminated by the beams of the setting sun. Beyond which point was at length heard some indistinct shouting, which gradually increased, until 'They are off—they are coming!' suspended our conversation among ourselves; and suddenly the head of the first boat turn'd the corner: and then another close upon it; and then a third; the crews pulling with all their might compacted into perfect rhythm; and the crowd on shore turning round to follow along with them, waving hats and caps, and cheering, 'Bravo, St. John's! Go it, Trinity!'—the high crest and blowing forelock of Phidippus's mare, and he himself shouting encouragement to his crew, conspicuous over all—until, the boats reaching us, we also were caught up in the returning tide of spectators, and hurried back towards the goal; where we arrived just in time to see the Ensign of Trinity lowered from its pride of place, and the eagle of St. John's soaring there instead. Then, waiting a little while to hear how the winner had won and the loser lost, and watching Phidippus engaged in eager conversation with his defeated brethren, I took Euphranor and Lexilogus under either arm (Lycion having got into better company elsewhere), and walked home with them across the meadow leading to the town, whither the dusky troops of Gownsmen with all their confused voices seem'd, as it were, evaporating in the twilight, while a nightingale began to be heard among the flowering chestnuts of Jesus."

Polonius, a Collection of Wise Saws and Modern Instances, appeared in 1852. It consists, as the title suggests, of a number of aphorisms and selections, many of them of some considerable length, from the works of Carlyle, Bacon, Selden, Milton, Scott, Goethe, etc., Carlyle largely predominating. The preface contains some delightful passages:

When Sir Walter Scott lay dying, he called for his son-in-law, and while the Tweed murmured through the woods, and a September sun lit up the towers, whose growth he had watched so eagerly, said to him, "Be a good man; only that can comfort you when you come to lie here!" *"Be a good man!"*

To that threadbare truism shrunk all that gorgeous tapestry of written and real romance!

"You knew all this," wrote Johnson to Mrs. Thrale, rallying for a little while from his final attack—"You knew all this, and I thought I knew it too; but I know it now with a new conviction."

Perhaps, next to realising all this in our own lives (when just too late), we become most sensible of it in reading the lives and deaths of others, such as Scott's and Johnson's; when we see all the years of life, with all their ambitions, loves, animosities, schemes of action—all the *"curas supervacuas, spes inanes, et inexspectatos exitus hujus fugacissimae vitae"*—summed up in a volume or two; and what seemed so long a history to them, but a Winter's Tale to us.

Death itself was no truism to Adam and Eve, nor to many of their successors, I suppose: nay, some of their very latest descendants, it is said, have doubted if it be an inevitable necessity of life: others, with more probability, whether a man can fully comprehend its inevitableness till life itself be half over; beginning to believe he must die about the same time he begins to believe he is a fool.

> As are the leaves on the trees, even so are man's
>   generations;
> This is the truest verse ever a poet has sung:
> Nevertheless few hearing it hear; Hope, flattering
>   alway,
>   Lives in the bosom of all—reigns in the blood of
>   the Young.

The following also is very fine:

> "And why," says the note-book of one *nel mezzo del cammin di nostra vita,* "does one day linger in my memory? I had started one fine October morning on a ramble through the villages that lie beside the Ouse. In high health and cloudless spirits, one regret perhaps hanging upon the horizon of the heart, I walked through Sharnbrook up the hill, and paused by the church on the summit to look about me. The sun shone, the clouds flew, the yellow trees shook in the wind, the river rippled in breadths of light and dark; rooks and daws wheeled and cawed aloft in the changing spaces of blue above the spire; the churchyard all still in the sunshine below."

Polonius was followed, in 1853, by the *Six Dramas from Calderon,* consisting of a translation or adaptation of six Spanish plays by Calderon. In 1855 came a second edition of *Euphranor,* followed in 1856 by *Salaman and Absal.*

Jami, the author of *Salaman and Absal,* was a Persian poet who was born in 1414 and died in 1492. He attended the great Samarcand School, but went back to Herat, called hither, he said, by a dream. He joined the strange Sufi sect and lived a solitary philosophical life, but the Muse compelled him to write poetry, and in addition he wrote a great number of volumes on theology, grammar, etc.

Salaman and Absal is an allegory and FitzGerald translated the poem into blank verse, and the incidents into a sparkling unrhymed metre.

Briefly the story is this: The Shah of Yunan invokes heaven for a son, and in answer to his prayers a beautiful and gifted child, Salaman, is given him. Absal, a young and beautiful girl, becomes the foster-mother of the divine Salaman, and as the child grows to manhood he falls in love with her, and devotes all his time at her shrine.

Being rebuked by the Shah, he flies with Absal to the desert and from thence on a boat with magic properties to a fair isle of Paradise. For a time they dwell here, until Salaman, awaking from his dream and full of contrition, returns to his father. But his old passion returns and not being able to decide 'twixt love and duty, he decides to die with Absal. Together they fling themselves in a fire and Absal perishes, but Salaman being protected by magical arts is preserved.

As in many of his other translations, the work of FitzGerald in this poem is good in parts. Taken as a whole the story is wearisome, but such passages as the following, which is a description of the sea upon which Salaman and Absal sail to the beautiful island, rescue it from mediocrity:

> He halted on the Seashore; on the shore
> Of a great Sea that reaching like a floor
> Of rolling firmament below the Skies
> From Kaf to Kaf, to Gau and Mahi down
> Descended, and its Stars were living eyes.
> The Face of it was as it were a range
> Of moving Mountains; or a countless host
> Of Camels trooping tumultuously up,
> Host over host, and foaming at the lip.
> Within, innumerable glittering things
> Sharp as cut Jewels, to the sharpest eye
> Scarce visible, hither and hither slipping,
> As silver scissors slice a blue brocade.

Attar's *Bird Parliament* came in the next year, 1856, and like *Salaman and Absal* is an adaptation. Its author, Farid-Uddin Attar, was also a Persian poet, born in 1119.

The Birds meet together to select a King and each states his claim to sovereignty. The Tajidar is finally chosen and after his oration on the search for the author of life a band of birds set out on a pilgrimage to discover the mystery of life and many, under the lead of Tajidar, ultimately gaze on the vision of God.

FitzGerald's translation bears the marks of infinite care, but it savours so strongly of the Oriental, that to the average reader it is confusing.

FitzGerald's next work was his masterpiece, the immortal *Rubaiyat,* the first edition of which he published at his own expense in 1859.

Viewed in the light of its present-day popularity, when it is selling in its thousands, it appears well-nigh inconceivable that the *Rubaiyat* suffered the fate of many of the world's masterpieces and was practically a rejected MS.

If it was not actually returned to FitzGerald accompanied by the polite little rejection note: "The Editor presents his compliments to the writer of the enclosed MS., the *Rubaiyat of Omar Khayyam,* and regrets that he is unable to avail himself of the use of it," the fact remains that FitzGerald sent it to *Fraser's Magazine* and twelve months later, as it had not been used, he wrote for its return.

FitzGerald had two hundred and fifty copies printed and he sent a few to his various friends, and as the others failed to sell, he gave them to Mr. Quaritch, who put them in his "twopenny box," indeed, many of them were sold for I*d.*—to-day they are worth £30. . . .

Michael Wolff (lecture date spring 1960)

SOURCE: Wolff, Michael. "The *Rubáiyát*'s Neglected Reviewer: A Centennial Recovery." *Victorian Newsletter,* no. 17 (spring 1960): 4-6.

[*In the following essay, originally delivered as a lecture, Wolff recounts the critical reception of the* Rubáiyát *when it first appeared in 1859, noting that one hundred years later, critical response to the work had changed considerably.*]

Edward FitzGerald's *Rubáiyát of Omar Khayyám* has been 1959's second most celebrated literary centenary (second that is to Darwin's *Origin of Species*). There have been two attractive reprints of the first edition of the *Rubáiyát,* one by Professor A. J. Arberry of Cambridge, the other by Professor Carl J. Weber of Colby or, if I may say so, of the Victorian Group of the Modern Language Association. But, of the books which survived, the *Rubáiyát* was the least celebrated in 1859. Of twenty-five influential book-reviewing journals of the day, twenty-three reviewed Darwin's book and twenty-two Tennyson's first four *Idylls of the King;* twenty reviewed *Adam Bede;* there were sixteen reviews of Mill's *On Liberty,* eleven of Ruskin's *Two Paths,* nine of *The Ordeal of Richard Feverel,* and eight of Smiles's *Self-Help* (Wolff, "Victorian Reviewers and Cultural Responsibility," *1859,* p. 283). Even Arnold's little pamphlet, *England and the Italian Question,* had

four notices, and comments on the various part-issues of *A Tale of Two Cities* and *The Virginians* appeared regularly among the miscellaneous items in the literary gossip columns.

How was FitzGerald's poem received? According to Professor Weber it "dropped into the world of 1859 with no more sound than that of a feather falling into the Grand Canyon" (p. 12). According to Professor Arberry it was "freezingly disregarded" (p. 28). The story of the poem and its narrow escape from oblivion can be easily summarized. FitzGerald had been interested in Omar's verses since 1857. In early 1858 he had sent thirty-five quatrains to *Fraser's Magazine* in answer to a request for a contribution. Not hearing from *Fraser's,* he retrieved them about a year later, added more stanzas, and asked Quaritch, the bookseller, to get them privately printed. Most of the 250 copies were put on sale in spring 1859. About two years later, after the price had been reduced, one copy was bought and that chain of interest soon to become world-wide was started. Whitley Stokes, Rossetti, Swinburne, Burne-Jones were links in that chain. So was Charles Eliot Norton, who reviewed FitzGerald's second version of his poem for the *North American Review* in October 1869. This review has hitherto been considered the first public recognition of the poem (Arberry, p. 17), and it led in turn to a review in the June 1870 *Fraser's,* thought of as the first English review. Ten years has always seemed to literary historians a long time for a poem like the *Rubáiyát* to have had to wait for acknowledgment, and we might briefly state what has been recorded of the circumstances immediately surrounding the poem's publication.

On the last day of March 1859 FitzGerald asked Quaritch to advertise the *Rubáiyát* in "the *Athenaeum* & any other Paper you think good: sending Copies of course to the *Spectator* & c." A few days later he sent money to pay for advertisements in "the *Saturday Review,* the *Athenaeum,* & any other Weekly Paper you like." Quaritch had already sent a copy to the British Museum under the provisions of the Copyright Act, and advertisements duly appeared on 9 April 1859 in all the papers mentioned by FitzGerald. These have been thought to be, as Professor Arberry puts it, "the only Press notices that the *Rubáiyát* enjoyed for many years" (pp. 13, 23-24).

But more happened to the *Rubáiyát* in 1859 than has been previously recorded. In the first place, Quaritch placed advertisements not only in the *Athenaeum* and the *Saturday Review* but also in the *Examiner* and the *Spectator.* Moreover, there are some additional facts which show that, despite its apparent neglect, the book was afforded the routine treatment of a new publication. Both important trade journals, the *Publishers' Circular* and the *Bookseller,* listed the **Rubáiyát** in their April numbers. That Quaritch actually distributed copies is indicated by the claim of the editor of *Publishers' Circular* that his records were accurate because "the books themselves passed through our hands" (1 March 1859). However, the first evidence that review copies were sent out is the appearance of the hitherto unrecorded notice, under the heading "Our Library Table," in the 11 June *Athenaeum,* where the **Rubáiyát** was briefly credited with "an abundance of gorgeous imagery" and "an excellent biographical introduction." But most important of all, and the topic of this paper, is an almost three-column review in the *Library Gazette* for 1 October 1859. So, although notices in the *Athenaeum* and the *Literary Gazette* were late in coming, it seems clear that all the major reviewing organs were probably given an opportunity to notice the poem. Nevertheless, only one magazine actually reviewed the **Rubáiyát** and that was the *Literary Gazette.*

What was the standing of the *Literary Gazette* in 1859? It had only three years to run, having long since lost the eminence it had attained under William Jerdan in the 1830's; its circulation seems to have been only one-third that of the *Spectator,* one-tenth that of the *Athenaeum,* and one-fifteenth that of the *Saturday Review* (Ellegärd, *Readership of the Periodical Press in Mid-Victorian Britain,* p. 22). On the other hand, it still carried more advertising than any of the other papers except the *Athenaeum,* and it was, according to an official list published in 1859, along with the *Athenaeum* and the *Saturday Review,* one of the only three weeklies taken in the Reading Room of the British Museum. Also in 1859, the *Bookseller* devoted the first two of a series of articles called "Our Literary Journals" to the *Literary Gazette,* so we can hardly call a review even in the pages of its latest volumes obscure. The *Bookseller's* article for 1 March mentioned the efforts of its new proprietors, Bradbury and Evans (also publishers of *Punch*), and its new editor, Shirley Brooks (later editor of *Punch*), to revive its flagging circulation. Brooks gave up in May 1859 and was succeeded by, to quote the *Bookseller* for 25 May, "the Rev. Professor [Henry] Christmas, F.S.A., F.R.S., F.R.S.A., & c., a gentleman of cyclopaedic information." When we couple this change in personnel with the *Literary Gazette's* announcement in December that it had again changed owners (though not editors) and that after the end of the year a new feature would be the publication of "important ecclesiastical intelligence," we may conjecture that the *Literary Gazette* under Christmas's editorship would not attempt to build circulation but rather intellectual prestige. Perhaps a recondite pamphlet like the **Rubáiyát** did not appeal to an editor of Brooks' rather light-hearted inclinations, but was later taken down from some shelf by the new editor or by one of his new staff-members.

The critique of the **Rubáiyát** in the *Literary Gazette* is worthy of resurrection, not only as, to date, the first critical treatment of the **Rubáiyát** (and probably the only one of the first edition) but for the insight shown by the reviewer. Internal evidence gives us no clue as to his identity, but he deserves his niche in literary history for the tolerance and taste which enabled him, while contemptuous of the creed of the **Rubáiyát,** to praise the beauty of the poetry unreservedly. That he was no Orientalist is indicated by one of his first remarks that "if the astronomer-poet of Persia appears as well in his native garb as he appears in English, it was certainly high time that he should be brought out of his obscurity." He may possibly have been familiar with other Persian poetry but all the details in the review about the life and beliefs of Omar, as well as some descriptive criticism, are taken from FitzGerald's preface, nor is there any realization of FitzGerald's role in manipulating his original. In the light of this relative ignorance, the reviewer's perceptive admiration is quite remarkable, especially since the fatalism of the poem meets, as we might expect, with his thoroughly confident disapproval. It was perhaps easy enough for "advanced" circles such as Rossetti's to appreciate the wonder of FitzGerald's verses. Sympathy with the thought, personal recognition of the mood of sophisticated and quiet cynicism, would naturally lead them to cherish the plangent harmonies of the poetry. The reviewer had no such sympathies: he talks of "crushing fatalism," of "the Gospel of Despair," of "repulsive theories." But his honesty even permits him to praise the poem's sceptical tone, leading him to say that "few poets, ancient or modern, have given fuller utterance to the subtlest speculations with which the human intellect can be occupied." How easily these words could have been applied in 1859 to FitzGerald's friend, the Tennyson of *In Memoriam*; how narrow the dividing line at this time between the respectable poetry of questioning faith and the suspect poetry of speculative doubt!

The reviewer willingly acknowledges that, among the Persian poets of whom he has heard, none has written "so earnestly, or with so much poignancy, and richness and depth of feeling," communicating so effectively "expressions of life-long habitudes of thought," and the reviewer's careful balance of praise and blame shows itself clearly in his comments that "nothing can be more dreary than the merriment in which he seeks to drown his despair, and nothing more beautiful than the manner in which he discourses of both. What could be better expressed than the following?" he continues, citing the four stanzas beginning

> Think, in this batter'd Caravanserai
> Whose Doorways are alternate Night and Day,
>   How Sultan after Sultan with his Pomp
> Abode his Hour or two, and went his way.

His longest extract is the famous eight-stanza section called by FitzGerald, though only in the first edition, "Kuza-Nama" or "The Epistle of the Pots," of which perhaps the best-remembered is the following:

> And, strange to tell, among the Earthen Lot
> Some could articulate, while others not:
>   And suddenly one more impatient cried—
>   "Who *is* the Potter, pray, and who the Pot?"

Aptly he summarizes the thought of the poem: "Everywhere the same crushing fatalism presents itself. The poet maintains that man must be unaccountable, because he has not the choice of his actions; his volitions are but the subordinate pulsations of an invisible Destiny; . . ."

> And that inverted Bowl we call the Sky,
> Whereunder crawling coop't we live and die,
>   Lift not thy hands to *It* for help—for It
> Rolls impotently on as Thou and I.

In the light of what we now know of FitzGerald's role in organizing and adapting his original material, it is intriguing to read as the conclusion of this review that "Never was the Gospel of Despair preached more fervently than it is in the pages of Khayyam, and few of our modern fatalists could express their convictions with so much terse vigour, or deck their repulsive theories with so many quaint beauties as this Eastern poet and sage." For FitzGerald himself the reviewer had a word of gratitude: "We must thank the modest translator of this powerful and original poet for the valuable contribution . . . which he has made to our current literature." We can surely be excused for finding in this review an instinctive awareness that (had the full story been known) FitzGerald, though himself a *modern* fatalist, was in fact a powerful and original poet.

Perhaps this review does not really alter the history of the *Rubáiyát*'s reception, but its existence is a testimony to the alertness of at least one member of the reviewing fraternity. The *Rubáiyát* was not entirely ignored; and the notice it received was not entirely unworthy of it.

I hope that my contribution to a centennial program lies not alone in my ostensible topic, but in the implication of my paper that, for 1859, in literary studies, the gap between the significance of the documents and the productive research of scholars is greatest in the field of journalism, for if my instance has been at all representative, it will reinforce the emerging view that Victorian periodicals are neglected far out of proportion to their importance. We have perhaps a sound sense, as we have considerable knowledge, of the writers of that year whom we still read. The poets, the novelists, the essayists, the scientists, the theologians, of 1859; Tennyson and FitzGerald; Dickens, Eliot, Meredith, Reade, Thackeray, and Trollope; Arnold, Mill, Ruskin; Darwin and Huxley; F. D. Maurice and J. H. Newman receive their approximate due. But the journalists are relatively ignored; so today I have introduced the anonymous reviewer of the *Rubáiyát,* the first to discuss in print a masterpiece which had to wait for ten years—and a new version in a new edition—for its next public recognition.

William Cadbury (essay date December 1967)

SOURCE: Cadbury, William. "FitzGerald's *Rubáiyát* as a Poem." *ELH* 34, no. 4 (December 1967): 541-63.

[*In the following essay, Cadbury contends that applying the conventional rules of analysis of lyric poetry to the* Rubáiyát *yields an unsatisfactory reading of the work.*]

It seems at first, and it has seemed to most, that we should look to FitzGerald's Omar for the rewards appropriate to lyric structures. Despite its fragmentation into rubáiyát the poem seems to be presented to us as lyric poems always are, as an utterance by the poet which we in effect overhear, and which lets us take on, for the duration of the literary experience, the poet's single and unified attitude to what he says. To take in a fully rendered attitude towards specific issues, an attitude which will expand our models of the attitudes we may take in real life, is to garner the reward of lyric.[1] Though the elements of the attitude of a long poem like the *Rubáiyát* might be many, and might be complexly interrelated, there would be nothing wrong with that. Intricate as the attitude may be, our role as readers of lyric requires that we look to and take from the poem as complex and rich an attitude as we can create from our interaction with it. That is what lyric is all about.

Yet with the *Rubáiyát* the process doesn't quite work— the reward is not forthcoming. There seem to be gross inconsistencies in the attitude rendered which we simply cannot force into a unified response. Even if we dull our analytic response to put these aside, the philosophic stance we then take on seems to do injustice to the poem—we are reduced to an attitude pleasant but slight, thematically acned as it were. Yet we know that the poem has pleased many and pleased long, and not just adolescents; and I think that the reason may be that know it or not we have looked for and in some sense found a reward different from that we get from lyric. If, then, we treat the poem as belonging to a different genre from lyric we may have a way of explaining our nagging satisfaction without embarrassment at regression to adolescent pleasures. We need not be young again to like it.

Let us try out the proposition that we read the *Rubáiyát* not as lyric, but as what I have called anti-lyric.[2] Let us assume that the reward we garner is not of a fully rendered attitude to experience, but of a comprehension and internalization of a rendered character who may have a variety of attitudes which have in common only that he can hold them. The poem is not, I think, in any profitable sense FitzGerald's utterance as "Sohrab and Rustum" is Arnold's, or "Fern Hill" Thomas's. No part of the poem can be made to square with any other, no part presents an attitude by which the poet or the poem can be made to stick, but each part leads on to the next for modification. We cannot see the poet, as we might see Arnold or Thomas, as "the kind of man who could take this attitude to write this poem," but must see him as very close to a dramatic character, someone affected by the world he presents to us as much as he effects its presentation.

Yet unlike dramatic characters the presentor has no character by which we can know him except in what he says. He is not defined by circumstances like a Browning monologist, nor does what he says lead him to any action in the surface of the poem except the continuation of the surface of the poem. He is both creator of and a part of the internal fiction, and so we have a form which splits the difference between lyric and drama. As in Pound's *Cantos,* say, or *In Memoriam,* the different voices which the rubáiyát make up imply a changeable character behind them, a character who can be put through something by what he says.

If this "character" exists only as we must make him up as an abstraction which is a modelled explanation of the poem's ostensible statements, that is only to say that he exists on the same level as the "attitude" of lyric. The attitude of lyric is a wholeness with regard to disparate issues; but so is this character. The only difference is that this character's wholeness is with regard to issues which are themselves attitudes; and these attitudes are themselves each a wholeness with regard to disparate issues. Complex, granted. But it was not complexity which troubled us, but gross inconsistency, a different matter.

This character by whom we make sense of the bewildering array of attitudes can only be called a narrator, since he has no existence in the surface of the poem, but only as an inferred and abstracted presentor. Nonetheless he is different from the narrator of lyric, since in reading lyric we always try to feel that it is not a "man" who enriches and expands our models of potential attitudes, but the interplay of the issues themselves which thus presents an expanding, not a changing attitude. For all the changes in tone of *Wichita Vortex Sutra,* for instance, we get no sense of a narrator as changing in the course of the poem—he is best read as expanding *his* attitude in light of the different issues which arise from his attempt to "Face the Nation / Through Hickman's rolling earth hills . . . South to

Wichita."[3] There is no sense of Ginsberg's character at the end as different from the beginning, though there is a sense that his character could expand its attitudes to cope with the interplay between his motives and the possibilities for their fulfillment which emerged. A character like Ginsberg's is a ground from which emerges the figure of the expanding attitude caused by the interplay of issues. The narrator of the *Rubáiyát,* on the other hand, *is* different at his end from what he was at his beginning. The issues, for all their shiftiness, are the ground from which emerges the figure of the changing character caused by the interplay of attitudes. We take the poem as "a man being changed," rather than as "a complex attitude being manifested."

To forestall the charge of subjectivism, we might reduce this point to rule: If the interplay of issues in a poem allows us to focus on their own internal logic without the necessity for recourse to a narrator, then we may treat the poem as lyric. If on the other hand the pattern and progression of the issues are not moved by their own internal logic, but provide discontinuities, false starts, seeming rests which are not, paradoxes, and the like, then we must postulate an external logic in the attitudes which move the issues. And these attitudes require the retroduction of a narrator, a character whose interposition moves the issues in ways which they cannot move themselves. And this is to say we find anti-lyric only when we must.[4] Even when (as in Ginsberg's poem) style and tone imply a character for the presentor, we need not focus on him for explanation of the poem if the issues move themselves along, if, that is, the logic of the poem's argument is completely built into the possibilities of the world being presented. By a basic rule of critical economy, then, the explanation through anti-lyric may be unnecessary even in cases where a full description will have to recognize a narrative presence. But where this economy cannot be satisfied, we must find the next simplest explanatory device, and this is, in those cases I call anti-lyric, the device of the abstracted narrator, who thus figures in an explanation because he must, not in a description because he may.

Cases are useful, especially (as Robert Lane points out) cases which lie near boundaries: Despite the clear and nasty narrative presence in "Locksley Hall," who is so much in the poem as to be situationally located, the logic of the poem is entirely internal; it works out in clear progression, from possibilities present in the described situation, an advancing series of commitments which can solve the problem of love which is supposed to be "love for ever more" but turns out not to be. The issues raised by this problem are self-developing, since all the answers are to be found in the possibilities of the issues as they move themselves through temporary resting-places. Because the poem makes perfect sense without him, we see the clearly existent narrator as a smoke-screen, a superimposed defensive device which reduces the poem from statement to metaphor.[5] The poem is thus lyric, because its explanation can dispense with the narrator's character, though its description would include it.

In Memoriam, on the other hand, has no situationally defined narrator distinct from the "poet," yet the poem cannot be explained without constant reference to a narrator's character. The poem is a series of fully rendered but wrong attitudes leading eventually to right ones, but the wrong attitudes cannot move beyond themselves without outside help. There is nothing in section 47, for instance, which makes its attitude internally invalid. Yet it is reversed entirely by section 95. The reversal must come from a latent attitude not in the poem but in the narrator—where else could it come from? The poem's economy requires a character to explain shifts not internally necessary, even though that character is not so apparent in the surface of the poem as in "Locksley Hall." For adequate explanation, economy requires that we see in the poem's transaction with us a special relationship between the internal logic and our own apprehension of what moves it. And this is to say that we see a special relationship between the poem and ourselves, a categorization in terms of genre.

The rewards of our transaction with the **Rubáiyát,** I argue, might well be taken in coin similar to that we garner from *In Memoriam.* The poems share the special relationship to us which requires for explanation that we retroduce a narrative presence whose character moves the internal logic beyond the ways in which it can move itself. This special relationship, moreover, is shared by other such diverse works as *The House of Life,* "Sea Surface Full of Clouds," and the *Cantos* of Pound. And while the structure of criticism exists independently of authorial intention, it is at least interesting that FitzGerald seems to ask criticism of just this sort. He writes of his "*Paraphrase of a Syllabus* of the poem."[6] He calls his product "most ingeniously tesselated into a sort of Epicurean Eclogue in a Persian Garden."[7] He compares his Omar to Hamlet (surely a dramatic character first and poet second), and though he does "not wish to show Hamlet at his maddest . . . mad he must be shown, or he is no Hamlet at all."[8] He writes, again to Cowell, that "My translation will interest you from its *Form,*"[9] and in a later letter to Bernard Quaritch he describes that form in terms of a narrator who undergoes the experience of which the poem is record: "He begins with Dawn pretty sober and contemplative: then as he thinks and drinks, grows savage, blasphemous, etc., and then again sobers down into melancholy at nightfall."[10] In the preface to his first edition he claims that his "old Tentmaker, who, after vainly endeavouring to unshackle his steps from Destiny, and to catch some authentic Glimpse of TO-MORROW, fell back upon TO-DAY (which has outlasted so many To-

morrows!) as the only Ground he had got to stand upon, however momentarily slipping from under his Feet."[11] Though no one reading the letters could miss FitzGerald's sense of kinship with Omar, who to what he predicts as Cowell's amazed repugnance "breathes a sort of Consolation to me!,"[12] and with whose accurate though unliteral rendering FitzGerald is clearly first concerned, we must see that he suggests for his audience a rather different reward from the recovery of the quatrains as Omar wrote them. As he puts it in the preface to his second edition, "whereas with [other Persian poets] the Poet is lost in his Song, the Man in Allegory and Abstraction; we seem to have the Man— the *Bonhomme*—Omar himself, with all his Humours and Passions, as frankly before us as if we were really at table with him, after the Wine had gone round."[13] He wishes us to recover this man, thinking, drinking, and all.

The scholiast has not followed this lead, but has emphasized either the explicative relationship between the translator and his original or the lyric relationship between the poet and his thought.[14] There is no full reading of the poem as a developing and unified structure, since modern accounts have been satisfied with proof of unity of mood or of thought, the unities appropriate to analysis of lyric.[15] Yet FitzGerald's description of form speaks of thinking as well as of thought, of experience as well as of mood. As our analysis of genre implies, we should be concerned with the relationship between the narrator and his thought as he thinks it, not solely with the thought of that narrator's original in Náishapúr or his creator in Suffolk. We should, both by FitzGerald's suggestions and by the practices of modern criticism, be spurred to analysis primarily of what the poem does, not of what its poet says.

Analysis of the poem's form may specify the shifting attitudes to shifting issues which at every stage are whole but which in the aggregate prove by their variety and course a character, a man who can go through such changes in attitude. But at the same time we must be conscious of the extensive but not infinite range of the issues to which he takes his different attitudes. He has a sequence of feelings, but it is in regard to a world which is schematized as a set of issues. Since his motives are for thinking through his place in the world, it is not so much a single structure which he creates, as a set of parallel structures, of which the constituents are differently valued but patterned in the same relationships to each other. What we have mentioned as modifications of his view in response to the pressure of his motives appear on the surface of the poem (in what it is saying at any point) as indications through imagery that he is in fact in one or another of these parallel structures. The attitude taken to the issues of that structure, or the part of it which implies the whole, can then be inferred from tone and from the way in which he moves to another structure or aspect of one to solve the imbalances of the responsive attitude.

For the structure of issues, then. We find that the narrator of the **Rubáiyát** has a neatly differentiated, though interlocking set of three ways of structuring the world, three contexts for his attitudes. These cover, by differing emphasis and valuations of the parts of a picture, the issues of the poem. The three are united by the relationship described in quatrain 11, of handily absolute syntax:

> With me along the strip of Herbage strown
> That just divides the desert from the sown,
>   Where name of Slave and Sultán is forgot—
> And Peace to Mahmúd on his golden Throne![16]

The world is three things: a sown field; a strip of herbage, usually described as a garden; a desert.[17] The orders of fertility and sterility are at the extremes, in the sown field which is associated with the things of the Sultan (especially, as we shall see, knowledge and power), and in the empty desert which is associated with the things of the Slave (especially sin and its defense in piety). The difference is split by the strip of herbage, which is neither uniformly full of naturally recurring natural objects like the field, nor uniformly empty like the desert, but is pleasingly disordered as it is "scattered" or "strown" with human beings, who are guests on the grass, like stars in an otherwise empty sky (1, 101).

The attitude which views the world as a strip of herbage or garden rejects the idea of control of the environment through "wit" (71), as it is attempted by the dramatis personae of the sown field, the Sultan and Doctor (27) of power and knowledge. But it also rejects the idea of the other kind of control of human destiny, control through the submission of "piety" (71) as it is attempted by the Slave and Saint (27) who characteristically inhabit the desert. In the garden, therefore, we are not concerned with the Sultanly "Glories of this World" (13), and so we do not bother to fling "the Golden Grain" (15) in the concern with "Worldly Hope" (16) which would be appropriate if we viewed the world as a field. Nor, on the other hand, are we concerned with an unworldly hope of a future reward in the Slavish "Prophet's Paradise" (13), and so we do not "heed the rumble of a distant Drum" by taking "Credit" rather than "Cash" (13) and retiring as "thoughtful Soul[s] to Solitude" (4), as is appropriate for those who fully accept the desert view. Rather in the garden, concerned with neither worldly nor unworldly hope for the future, we "Look to the blowing Rose about us" (14), and with what security the present offers we "make the most of what we yet may spend" (24).

Characteristic actions of various kinds are linked to the three views of the world. In the field where growth is natural, "the seed of Wisdom did I sow" (28), but since

men are not plants the wisdom turns to dust, to "no such aureate Earth . . . / As, buried once, Men want dug up again" (15).[18] In the desert where nothing grows, but where all things are viewed as created by God as pots are made by a potter, men as pots discuss theology. In the garden, finally, where neither nature nor God is appealed to for human validation, men as men drink and pour wine to the roses.

Though drinking is characteristic of the garden, it takes place in all three worlds, in appropriately differing ways and means. In the field, wine belongs in the tavern and is brought by "an Angel Shape" (58) who signifies by this designation the blessings of the gods on men who view themselves as parts of a growing and recurring nature and who use nature's gifts as they come. In the desert wine is brought to the potter's shop (since the whole world is the shop of this potter, where else could it be brought?) by the porter with the creaking shoulder-knot (90), who like every created one else does God's bidding (what else could he do?) and creaks and anguishes as he does so. In the garden Sákí brings the wine for men to drink under the stars, in fellowship.

The drinking of wine from a cup or bowl is likewise linked to appropriately differing forms and implications of the bowl of life itself. In the field of natural forms the cup is the "inverted Bowl" of a hostile and incomprehensible sky "Whereunder crawling cooped we live and die" (72) like everything else, inside the nature which contains us. In the desert the cup appears as the broken or breakable bowl which is image for a pious humanity (62, 85) which is not contained by nature beyond it, but is that nature itself, at the mercy of the random gods like all else. In the garden, however, since nature is neither beyond man nor coterminous with him but is contained by man, the cup is for man's use and pleasure—neither imprisoning nor characteristically fragile, the cup which man holds holds in its turn the wine which he uses, and, inverted, its wine may "quench the fire of anguish in some Eye / There hidden" (39) in the ground. To be entirely and solely human, to drink with one's fellows in the garden of this world, is to be able to see the human relationship not with plants or gods, but with men living and dead. To invert the cup is to feed one's forebears, to find a continuity between living and dead through shared acceptance of this life and through rejection of the knowledge and piety which belong to field and desert.

Man's transience is emphasized, though in different ways, by the views of reality centering on both field and desert, since the field shows man's inferiority to the eternally recurring natural grain while the desert shows his inferiority to eternally existent gods. But the garden view provides a more hopeful idea, the idea of a continuity in human life itself, a continuous progression in which each drinker feeds a dead one, and feeling is validated by being shared among generations. In the garden where man and his cultivated flowers are one, a sense of continuity is possible, because the knowledge of each man's passing (so much more disturbing than the passing of individual plants) is relieved by the feeling of contact between generations. But in the field and desert that spurious consolation is denied, and in these views we must see that although grain and gods are eternal, individual man simply passes, is necessarily discontinuous in all meaningful senses with the others of his kind.

The basic motive of the poem is clear: If we can view the world as garden—if we can, in effect, feel like the roses we create and enjoy, and so ignore knowledge, piety, and the sense of sin—then the lower and middle worlds, the worlds of forebears and fellows, will be quite compatible. "Oh, Wilderness were Paradise enow" (12) under this dispensation.[19] But the enemy of this view is clear enough too: Since we can, unlike the roses, know enough to know we might know more, and since we are in fact afflicted with a sense of sin and with awareness of the God who creates it and ourselves, then from the point of view of the discontinuities among us the compatibility seems frivolous. If the enemy view, the view of field or desert, wins out, then we will be forced to find that what really counts is not the compatability between lower and middle worlds, but the conflict between middle and upper, between mankind and heaven.

The structures of horizontal and vertical topography which we have abstracted are a spatialized picture of the issues of the poem inferred from the interrelations of its images. Yet the poem's structure comes to us not spatially but temporally, from the presentation of the narrator's shifting attitudes to these issues. The poem as we experience it is the progression of the narrator's feeling as he is led from one to another of the issues by the pressure of his own thought. And our explanation must do justice to the abstract pattern of this progression of attitudes, as well as to the pattern of issues.

In each of what seem to me four similarly patterned sections of the *Rubáiyát,* a sequence of feeling is carried through, though with a variety of backing and filling, twists and turns, which localize the pattern of feeling involved but do not finally obscure it. Each section opens with what the narrator tries to maintain as a stable attitude which will cope with the issues he intends to analyze; but as the section moves along flaws and inadequacies in the attitude emerge; each section then ends with a new and different attitude which at least avoids the flaws of the old, and which is reinspected and stabilized in the opening attitude of the following section. The attempt at rest is continually subverted by flaws in the state in which rest is attempted, and these flaws push the poem along as they impel modifications in attitude by the narrator.

In the first section (1-24) the doomed attitude is comfortable nostalgia at the passing of Eastern worthies, David and Jamshyd and Bahrám and the rest.

> Iram indeed is gone with all his Rose,
> And Jamshyd's Sev'n-ringed Cup where no one knows;
>   But still a Ruby kindles in the Vine,
> And many a Garden by the Water blows.
>
>   (5)

Throughout the section there is a sense of continuity, even of contract, between the present inhabitants of the garden and those who went before, as the rose shows "where some buried Caesar bled" and as we learn that the "Hyacinth the Garden wears / Dropped in her Lap from some once lovely Head" (19).[20] Because it is possible for us to make contact with the past, we must take tender care of the very herb of the garden—"Ah, lean upon it lightly! for who knows / From what once lovely Lip it springs unseen?" (20). And as the past is available to us, we will be available to our future, when we in our turn "Descend—ourselves to make a Couch—for whom?" (23). We are then kin with those who died before us, and with those who will come after.

But the tenuousness of this attitude, its base in fantasy, makes rest in it impossible. Pleasure in contemplation of the theme of "ubi sunt," the narrator finds, is a manufactured tranquility, for "What have we to do / With Kaikobád the Great, or Kaikhosrú?" (10). Impatience with the sentiment he detects in himself undercuts the softer with a tougher attitude than contemplation of change, and as "ubi sunt" gives way to "carpe diem" the narrator decides that we must orient ourselves to the present, not to the past or future, and therefore "make the most of what we yet may spend" (24). The images of cash and credit (13), of the not so "aureate earth" (15), of "Ashes" and "Snow upon the Desert's dusty Face" (16), imply a kind of self-irony which works against the delights of Persianism and fantasy. The garden, inspected, is merely a decorated desert, and the notion of man's self-sufficiency to be linked with his past is self-delusion.

The narrator is concerned in this first section with the relationship between lower and middle worlds, the topographical concern which we have specified as characteristic of the garden view. When he finds by the end of the section that they have no meaningful relationship, it points up for him the lack of a meaningful relationship in the other topographical possibility, the contact between middle and upper worlds. So with the beginning of the second section (25-54), he adopts the security of an attitude of laughter at his vain attempts, in his own past, to search for knowledge, to see life as a field for man's sowing. Though with the Doctors and Sages and even Saints who "discussed / Of the Two

Worlds so wisely" (26) he "heard great argument / About it and about" (27), so that he can say of himself, appropriately for a toiler in the field, "With them the seed of Wisdom did I sow" (28), he found that "this was all the Harvest that I reaped—/ 'I came like Water, and like Wind I Go'" (28).

But precisely because, in wittily deriding his own philosophy and the thoughts of the "foolish Prophets" (26) he listened to, he is arguing from the safety of his cynicism, the feelings of incompleteness in the attitude of cynicism can break through, and they disturb the balance of tones which he tries to maintain. Laughter at the hopelessness of looking for truth gives way to anger that it can't be found, that the desert which gives back dust for grain is not the field that he hoped. With the middle and upper worlds unconnected by the natural reason which should give them coherence, the question of heaven which makes them so becomes important. Despite the irony directed at Tennyson's respectful awe in the imitated phrase "behind / The Veil" (34; cf. *In Memoriam,* 56), the narrator finds that although the attempt to find "THE SECRET" (49) is hopeless, it is not necessarily silly.

The ostensible answer which the section gives to the question of knowledge is like the answer of the first section to its question of human continuity—be like the flowers, and moreover find warrant for the likeness in the necessity for submission to the will of heaven:

> As then the Tulip, for her morning sup
> Of Heav'nly Vintage, from the soil looks up,
>   Do you devoutly do the like, till Heav'n
> To Earth invert you—like an empty Cup.
>
> (40)

If we were like the flowers, we might and should avoid "the vain pursuit / Of This and That" (54), and so, comfortably, we might be "Perplexed no more with Human or Divine" (41). But throughout this section a more intense feeling intrudes, as the narrator recognizes that we *might* be more than subhuman. Instead of a consolation, wine becomes vengeance for the "insolence" of heaven (30);[21] the "clod of saturated Earth" (38) who is man seems hardly submissive as he explains the hopelessness of things "with fugitive / Articulation" (36). The insolent "Maker" who creates darkness and drama "for the Pastime of Eternity" (52) begins to receive some merited questioning. The garden view, whether of cash or Jamshyd, falls apart under the pressure of awareness that things perhaps did not *have* to be this way, that we are *forced* "in this clay carcass crippled to abide" (44).

With the loss of compatibility between the lower and middle worlds, then, the narrator is able to learn a new attitude which impels him to a more severe questioning

than the unthinking devotion of the tulip, as he sees the middle world in terms of the upper world which it implies. As the questioning is more severe, the Persianisms which were a sign of sentimentality drop out, and the language of the whole section becomes more intense, and more abstract. In the second section as in the first, the security of an initial attitude seems to have brought on its own decay, to have led to feeling rather than to the intended safe recapitulation of something over and done with.

With the decision not to "endeavor and dispute" (54), then, the search for knowledge is rejected, and the third part (55-84) begins. Knowledge now seems impossible, and so the field, like the garden before it, is seen as no better than the desert for man. Yet knowledge is only part of man's conceivable achievement, only one way of coming to grips with and controlling the human lot. So to select the grape as refuge from the impossibility of significant knowledge, as the narrator now does in order to "Divorce . . . old barren Reason from my Bed" (55), is to limit himself to an unnecessarily sentimental condition of elegant bravado, much like that of the first section with its sentimental Persianism. But the narrator has been brought to a more serious frame of mind by the experience of the pressure of thought which moved the first two sections. The trivially posturing dependence on wine with which he attempts a stable attitude at the beginning of the third section brings on much more easily than before an undercutting reaction against the very hedonism to which he has been reduced.

What Paul Goodman would call a "hidden plot" rising from the latent seriousness of the narrator's character begins in the third section to dominate the "apparent plot" in which the narrator has sought to resolve life's problems by manifesting his pose of hedonistic acceptance.[22] In the first two sections the hidden plot was strong enough only to subvert the superficial attitude achieved—now it dominates the surface of the poem. The narrator is forced by his thought itself, as he has gone through it, to put his money on his sense of justice rather than on his sense of style. The obvious injustice of man's condition, the trick of heaven by which a silly rebelliousness is made necessary, leads him here from the strategy of ironic self-deprecation of the second part to the open avowing of a just rage in the third.

The opening of the section with a mildly ironic claim of a "brave Carouse" (55) leads to more fully ironic praise of the wine which can "The Two-and-Twenty jarring Sects confute" (59). The wine becomes, bitterly, a more true religion than any other we can know, a "sovereign Alchemist" (59), "The mighty Mahmúd" himself (60). Wine is, in fact, the only thing which can provide what God should provide. And yet the narrator knows that it is second best, and a poor second. If it confutes the sects, it shouldn't. Life's lead should be gold, and it isn't. We should need no tawdry anodynes, but they are all we have. And it is hardly our fault! If the grape is interdicted and a curse, "Why, then, Who set it there?" (61). The only thing which can console us we know to be no good—and in this double awareness the narrator is carried beyond the problem of knowledge to the problem of piety, which, faced head on, can lead in turn only to rage at heaven.

He is brought to face the human ability to conceive of immortality but to know that it is "Lies" (63), just as he had been brought to face the human ability to conceive of knowledge but to know that we are imprisoned in our clay. He is now aware that religious values are only projections of ourselves—"Heav'n but the Vision of fulfilled Desire, / And Hell the Shadow from a Soul on fire" (67). And rage at this state of things fills this part of the poem. Our slavish state in the desert is again seen as necessarily subhuman, but this time to be subhuman is an outrage where before it was a strategy. Our servitude is presented in a striking series of images which tumble all over each other. We are shadows (68), checkers (69), the balls in a game (70). "Piety and wit" have nothing to do with universal justice (71), and even the imprisoning sky "As impotently moves as you or I" (72).

We have never had freedom, and the narrator knows that our piety is only the slavish submission to knowledge of the bondage of predestination. The poem moves here to tragic recognition, before moving away again. For despite knowledge of bondage, the narrator asserts freedom with all the tragic hero's grand refusal to accept the facts he knows: "let the Dervish flout; / Of my Base metal may be filed a Key / That shall unlock the Door he howls without" (76). We know, from what he has claimed before, that the claim is false—wine gets us no salvation. But as a tragic action it is "true" just because the narrator can say it. And again, climactically:

> O Thou, who didst with pitfall and with gin
> Beset the Road I was to wander in,
>   Thou wilt not with Predestined Evil round
> Enmesh, and then impute my Fall to Sin!
>
> (80)

This too is untrue. "Thou wilt not" denies all that the poem has claimed, because "Thou wilt," precisely. And yet the action is grand, the emotional fervor convinces. Through understanding as much as he does, the narrator comes to rejection of the understanding, and so defeats the system. We make *value,* he demonstrates, from "the Darkness into which Ourselves, / So late emerged from, shall so soon expire" (67). Where affirmation of truth means submission, denial of the facts becomes the affirmation of the self, hopeless and false but better than nothing, which is the only alternative.

The easy Persianism of the first part has been long left behind. Yet it was a more adequate, a more logical response to the poem's issues, its organization of reality, than this, in its acceptance of wilderness as "Paradise enow." Still, looking at the narrator's character as he is brought through the sequence of his attitudes, if we have to choose between that tinsel paradise and this beleaguered desert, we will not hesitate to choose the rebellion against logic and acquiescence before we choose the garden. Knowledge of ignorance and the piety of blasphemy have come to seem more important than release through wine, since the narrator is so much the better man in rage than in hedonistic satisfaction.

The narrator has gained stature enough to learn the limitations of hedonistic escape and to prove his virtue through resistance to things as they are. With that done, he can simmer down. As between each of the first three sections a completed attitude allowed leisure to inspect the consequences of statement, but the inspection impelled a new feeling, so between third and fourth sections the completed feeling again allows freedom to inspect, to work out the consequences of the rebellious vision in a series of ironic allegories which will impel their final feeling, their changing attitude, too.

The last long section (92-101) like the others moves from stable detachment to a progressive involvement, from ironic allegory of the human condition as now known to a more proper feeling for the condition than detachment. But this time the feeling is a close, a return to the position of the poem's opening, now more fully comprehended. As the section opens, the narrator tells us that religious observations are over, that he has been left in the condition he had tried to reject:

> As under cover of departing Day
> Slunk hunger-stricken Ramazán away,
>   Once more within the Potter's house alone
> I stood, surrounded by the Shapes of Clay.
>
> (82)

This is a return to reality, to isolation, to an accurate image of man without the false consolations of knowledge and piety, which have been "hunger-stricken." It is, in short, for the first time a direct presentation of man's lot as imaged in the desert which had always been implied, but not before shown.

This organization of the issues, like the others which open sections, is an attempt at a stable attitude which will be an effective pose for the narrator's security. Like those of the second and third sections, this initial attitude turns back upon the narrator in ironic self-deprecation the very seriousness of the attitude with which the previous section closed. The narrator creates a parody of himself and us in the talking pots who argue the necessity for a benevolent world from their sense of justice.[23] And as he does so he in effect laughs at how silly he looked in the last section, trying, pot that from the view of the desert he thinks he is, to find a reasonable belief that the universe will take care of him or that he may reject its disdain. "Surely not in vain" (84), says one of the pots, is the effort of creation. "He's a Good Fellow, and 'twill all be well" (88), says another, again parodying Tennyson. They argue the necessity for a loving God as *In Memoriam* does, and yet they're only talking pots. Like Chanticleer on dreams, they are funny because they talk like people. And if people are in fact pots, as in the desert they seem to be, why then the narrator, a tragically posturing pot, is funny indeed.

Yet Chanticleer is not a man, and the pots are people. Though God has no more responsibility to do right by us than any potter has to do right by his pots, and though the pots are funny because presumptuous, the desert view implied by the potter's shop is not funny at all. The pots are people imaged as manufactured, subhuman; and, as in the second and third sections, acceptance of the subhuman as image of man impels anger at the scheme of things which can both let us be low and imagine the high. So again wine becomes more serious for the narrator. It leads again to blasphemy, as he perceives what we ought to have in its place. By now forced to comprehend man's desert state, he looks at the garden from the desert, and parodies the sacramental wine in a set of biblical echoes:

> Ah, with the Grape my fading Life provide,
> And wash the Body whence the Life has died,
>   And lay me, shrouded in the living Leaf,
> By some not unfrequented Garden-side.
>
> (91)

Since there is no prospect of immortality, and no trust in a benevolent God, we must make our own substitute. Now rather than the earlier image of Jesus suspiring from the ground (4), it is the wine-soaked corpse who "such a snare / Of Vintage shall fling up into the Air / As not a True-believer passing by / But shall be overtaken unaware" (92). Like Saul on the road to Damascus, the true-believer will be overtaken by a greater truth.

But all this blasphemy is finally unsatisfying, like the ironic and blasphemous attitudes of previous sections. Again here, since he feels what might be in what he says, the narrator is led by the demands of the "hidden plot" within his character to dissatisfaction with the complacency of the parody. No matter how many times he takes the pose of hedonistic satisfaction to praise wine, he is always aware that it is a feeble substitute. He knows two things: the wine is all he has—"I wonder often what the Vintners buy, / One-half so precious as the stuff they sell" (95)—and it does no good—"Yet Ah, that Spring should vanish with the Rose" (96). All his posturings, all attempts to make the desert into a garden, make no difference to the essential human fact of transience. And he feels this now seriously and soberly indeed, having been brought through so many subterfuges to awareness of it; and so he spells out openly, from the unconcealed heart of his character and his imagery, what has been only implied, the real anguish that there is no possibility of finding the truth which would make the posturings unnecessary:

> Would but the Desert of the Fountain yield
> One glimpse—if dimly, yet indeed, revealed,
>   To which the fainting Traveler might spring,
> As springs the trampled herbage of the field!
>
> (97)

The fountain which would make sense of it all must exist, for the rest of nature, with its eternal return, its continuity between parts, proves it. Yet field and fountain are not for us, who are of the desert. God is not with us but against us, and so we cannot "with Him conspire" or "remold" "this sorry Scheme of Things" "nearer to the Heart's Desire" (99).

The meaning of the *Rubáiyát,* then, when we consider the sequence of the narrator's attitudes as they work through the issues which the imagery presents, can only be said to lie in the narrator's character, in the emergence of its hidden plot of serious thought through its apparent plot of ironic, hedonistic, blasphemous posturing. The meaning, in short, is the narrator's transformation through acceptance of himself as a serious man. Though his philosophical position at the end is not much different from what it was at the beginning, the man who holds that position is different, a better man than he was at first because of what he has gone through. He is more aware, resigned for better reasons. The sequence of his attitudes has been from Persian posturing to tragic rebellion to knowledge of limitations. And his final acceptance is therefore of both truths, that we humans are good enough to conceive a benevolent world, and that no such conception will disturb the actual world's malevolence to us. The tragic vision of the third section is in the fourth undercut and put in its place by the final realization that tragic visions are posturings like others, that rage is no better anodyne than wine.

So in the last two quatrains the narrator can only inspect the new-found position from the only point of view left, that of a helpless trust in what we at least have. The gesture called for in the garden which we make for ourselves is entirely in keeping with the poem's final attitude with regard to its various issues—Sákí is to "turn down an empty glass" for the narrator, among the "star-scattered," predestined "Guests" (101). There is no longer any fanciful suggestion that we might feed our dead ancestors with our ritually spilled wine and so prove continuity and meaningful kinship. The poem is, by its end, entirely too serious to be satisfied with any lesser extravagance than the extravagance of truth. We are alone in the garden we make up—there are no ancestors here. But if we are alone, still we are here, and we still may act. And the gesture of overturning the empty cup asserts our existence as well as our passing. Social fellowship in the middle world, alien alike from nature and from God, for what little it's worth, is still possible. It must, of necessity, be enough.

The pregeneric form of the *Rubáiyát,* then, in light of the relationship between issues and attitudes which we have analyzed, must, when we back off and look at it all at once, be called ironic rather than tragic.[24] Like all ironies, the *Rubáiyát* moves from illusion to reality in a binding, not a loosing way. There is no joy in Mudville by the poem's close, but as in Casey's case there is pleasure, for this is the way things are and sluggers and sages alike must learn their limitations. Tragedies, like ironies, move from the illusions of human power which would, if proved non-illusory, eventuate in the form of romance, to the realities of the punishments of a world of experience in which things do not go as humans will them. But the movement of tragedy is different from that of irony, in that with the end of tragedy a greater freedom emerges to transcend the bondage of the natural world.

In tragedies a worthy hero loses a bad world which he would deserve to keep if it were a good one and if he had comprehended or could comprehend it—if, that is, wishes were horses and we had our 'druthers. In poems like "Dover Beach," "Empedocles on Etna," and "Howl," a narrator's thought presents a maleficent world, but his sequence of attitudes shows him earning virtue through the act of refusing to capitulate to it. The world is bad, yet the fact that human valor deserves to win makes insignificant the fact that it doesn't. Unlike irony, tragedy gives us a narrator or hero who doesn't quite know what's happening, so that we can see him as better than he thinks he is. The sense he makes of things is not quite our sense.

The *Rubáiyát* cannot reasonably be called tragic, because the narrator accepts limitations which perfectly match what he presents as his universe's law, whereas in tragic forms the process of acceptance transcends that law, proves a virtue greater than the law allows. When Childe Roland blows his horn, he beats the system which should have meant he couldn't blow it. But when the narrator of the *Rubáiyát* finally turns down the convivial glass in vinous resignation, and thus imitates in his poor human way the gods who have inverted the bowl of the sky, he does so only in the way that humans can, and so accepts his limitations as Ro-

land did not. It is to gods, to things as they are, that he proves fealty, and not to transcending man.

The failure to transcend, let me emphasize, is in no sense a failure of the poem. Literary forms have their own virtues, and we must not ask them to covet their neighbors' patterns and points. The *Rubáiyát*'s narrator, much like the woman of Stevens' "Sunday Morning," comes to find an accurate, nontrivial, unposturing mode of action which perfectly matches what he has learned of his world, and so we find him no better than he should be, but no worse. His transformation is the only one possible for a poem which denies transcendence—from trivial to nontrivial hedonism, from elegant but silly Persianism to full and nonethnic humanity. The narrator realizes that he has no out, that the world he accurately describes leaves him no room for meaningful action of even the tragic hero's rebellious kind. All he can do is return to his start, pretend that the garden is true vision of this world while knowing all the time that the world is really a desert and the garden an illusion. He accepts his bondage as the tragic hero never does.

The narrator gains virtue in our eyes through his ability to follow his thought where it leads him. But the virtue will avail nothing, and so we find his position to be ours, to be in keeping with the conclusions which the sequences of feeling and thought in the poem have compelled. And the poem's complexity and excellence lie precisely in its structure and the way the structure works itself out within the anti-lyric genre—for through the narrator's sequence of provisional attitudes, the ongoing relationship of attitudes to issues, we find that the hedonism which at first seemed so adolescently trivial is not so trivial after all. When there is nothing else, the human desert can only be made to be a garden through willed acceptance. And no matter what we may think of this as philosophy, it has the only truth which we can ask of poetry, the truth of fully realized virtual life.

Notes

1. See Paul Goodman's analysis of Catullus' lyric "Iam ver egelidos" for analysis and theoretical explanation of the purely lyrical poem. *The Structure of Literature* (Chicago, 1962), pp. 184-92. For the explanation of lyric as an "internal mimesis of sound and imagery" in which we overhear the poet's controlled associations (a formulation not in conflict with Goodman's) see Northrop Frye, *Anatomy of Criticism* (Princeton, 1957), p. 250 (for the quoted phrase) and pp. 270-81, esp. p. 272. For the relationship between the genre of pure lyric and its modification in anti-lyric, used and elaborated on in this paper, see my "Lyric and Anti-Lyric Forms: A Method for Judging Browning," *UTQ* [*University of Toronto Quar-*

terly], XXXIV (1964), 49-67. The emphasis in the present paper on genre as defined through the rewards offered the reader in his transaction with the poem is new, and is in response to the proof that the literary experience is socially learned behavior in Morse Peckham, *Man's Rage for Chaos* (Philadelphia, 1965), as well as to Robert E. Lane's convincing demonstration that to talk about "the work itself," without reference to a reader of it, is nonsense, what Lane calls "Original Error." *The Liberties of Wit,* (New Haven, 1961), esp. ch. II.

I am indebted to the University of Oregon Office of Scientific and Scholarly Research for financial support of this study. An earlier version of this paper was presented to English Section II of the Philological Association of the Pacific Coast on November 28, 1964, at Palo Alto.

2. Noam Chomsky argues a "tacit knowledge" which "may very well not be available to the user of the language" as the way around the final appeal to "linguistic intuition" which might not structure a grammar his way but which there is "no way to avoid" as a court of last appeal. The argument gives me heart, and I think theoretical justification, for claiming that experiencers of literature have the same kind of tacit knowledge despite the evidence of published readings with which I disagree. *Aspects of the Theory of Syntax* (Cambridge, Mass., 1965), p. 21 (for the quoted phrases), and esp. pp. 21-24.

3. Allen Ginsberg, *Wichita Vortex Sutra* (n. p.: Coyote Books, 1966, distributed by City Lights Press), ll. 1-2, 5. City Lights Press will in the near future bring out a collection of Ginsberg's recent poetry which will include this poem, I am told.

4. "What is it to supply a theory? It is to offer an intelligible, systematic, conceptual pattern for the observed data. The value of this pattern lies in its capacity to unite phenomena which, without the theory, are either surprising, anomalous, or wholly unnoticed." N. R. Hanson, *Patterns of Discovery: An Inquiry into the Conceptual Foundations of Science* (Cambridge, 1961), p. 121. See Chapter IV ("Theories") and Ch. VI ("Elementary Particle Physics") for explanation and demonstration of the retroductive inference on which I base my argument.

5. For close analysis of this kind of lyric, see my "The Utility of the Poetic Mask in Tennyson's 'Supposed Confessions,'" *MLQ* [*Modern Language Quarterly*], XXIV (1963), 374-85.

6. Letter of December 8, 1857 to Edward Byles Cowell, quoted in A. J. Arberry, *The Romance of the Rubáiyát* (New York, 1959), p. 85.

7. Letter to Cowell of November 2, 1858, quoted in Arberry, p. 95.

8. The letter of December 8, 1857.

9. Letter of September 3, 1859, quoted in Arberry, p. 94.

10. Quoted in Alfred McKinley Terhune, *The Life of Edward FitzGerald* (New Haven, 1947), p. 227.

11. Quoted in Joanna Richardson, ed., *FitzGerald: Selected Works* (Cambridge, Mass., 1963), p. 233.

12. Letter of May 7, 1857, quoted in Arberry, p. 57.

13. Quoted in Richardson, p. 235.

14. Of those whose principal interest has been in FitzGerald's transmutation of his sources, we may single out Arberry, *Romance,* who traces the "patient scholarly labour that went into the writing of the poem" (p. 6), and John W. Draper, "FitzGerald's Persian Local Color," West Virginia University *Philological Papers,* XIV (1963), 26-56, who shows the accuracy of the rendering to Persian custom and style. Though Arthur C. Benson, *Edward FitzGerald,* English Men of Letters (New York, 1905), and A. M. Terhune, *Life,* intend critical biographies and so deal with all these matters, the approach of each to the *Rubáiyát* is to emphasize fidelity to (Benson) or divergence from (Terhune) the sources. Terhune traces briefly the broad outlines of the structure as it is suggested in the letter to Quaritch (see above, n. 10), but does not investigate the way in which the thought moves the narrator (pp. 227-30, of which some 20 lines are Mr. Terhune's commentary and the rest quotation or analysis of the fidelity of quatrain 81).

Those who are concerned with the *Rubáiyát's* philosophic thought, who take it to have what A. Y. Campbell calls "the true lyrical *cry*" ("Edward FitzGerald," in H. J. Massingham and Hugh Massingham, edd., *The Great Victorians* [London, 1932], pp. 199-209; p. 205), may be divided into a group which sees the poem as essentially Omarian, an expression of Persian hedonism, and a group which takes it as what Campbell calls the "exquisitely melodious testament of a Victorian pagan" (p. 199). The first tradition is the older. H. Schütz Wilson, in "The Rubáiyát of Omar Khayyám, The Astronomer-Poet of Persia," *Contemporary Review,* XXVII (1876), 559-70, argued that Omar "'denied divinely the divine'" (p. 562), and was rebutted by [Richard Holt Hutton], who in "A Great Poet of Denial and Revolt," *Spectator,* XL (1876), 334-6, denied that there is in the poem any "nobleness in the moral sense" (p. 334), but rather the "bitterness of a defiant heart" (p. 334).

John Hay, in *In Praise of Omar, An Address Before the Omar Khayyám Club* (Portland, Maine, 1905), follows Wilson's approval of what Hay calls a "faith too wide for doctrine and a benevolence untrammeled by creed" (p. 10) given forth both by Omar and by FitzGerald, "a reincarnation of Omar" (p. 4).

E. G. Parrinder, splitting the Wilson-Hutton difference, would assign the poem's implicit mysticism to Omar, its agnosticism to FitzGerald, thus reducing FitzGerald to simplifier of Oriental complexity ("Omar Khayyám—Cynic or Mystic," *London Quarterly and Holborn Review,* CLXXXVII, Sixth Series, XXXI [1962], 222-26). Frank Kermode, reducing in another way, sees FitzGerald's "good mid-Victorian talent under Persian stimulus" as creating an "approved burgher escape-myth" out of "the finesse of so foreign a poet as Omar" ("Allusions to Omar," *New Statesman,* LXIV [1962], 146-7). Both arguments seem to me entirely wrong, as shown by Arberry, Draper, and Terhune.

In the critics who, finally (and rightly), view the poem as what Hugh Walker calls "a 'criticism of life,' not in some far-off country and among unfamiliar men, but here and now" (*The Literature of the Victorian Era* [London, 1921], pp. 480-90; p. 489), two main lines of argument may be detected, essentially those of Hutton and Wilson though now applied not to Omar but FitzGerald. On Hutton's side, not surprisingly, is G. K. Chesterton, who despite his approval of the "indescribably manly, firm . . . way of phrasing the pessimism" calls pessimism "a thing unfit for a white man" (*The Victorian Age in Literature* [New York, 1913], pp. 192-95; p. 195). Less racist, John Drinkwater detects in FitzGerald's poem an "accidental quality" which keeps it from among "the very greatest moral poems in the language" (*Victorian Poetry* [New York, 1924], pp. 215-20; p. 216). William O. Raymond also sees a fatal flaw in "the passivity of FitzGerald's philosophic pessimism" ("The Mind's Internal Heaven in Poetry," *UTQ,* XX [1951], 215-32; p. 221).

Though Hutton and his tradition seem often led to rejection of the *Rubáiyát* on religious grounds, Edward Mortimer Chapman, whose religious interest is plain, sees the poem as meeting the needs of Victorian doubters assailed by too hardy an optimism: "It is when they are told that the instincts of their hearts are nonsense [that] . . . Omar's jovial cynicism seems like a gospel" (*English Literature in Account with Religion* [Boston, 1910], pp. 445-59; p. 457). His sympathetic treatment is like Wilson's, and is echoed in Campbell and in Benson, who sees the poem as showing "the spirit, at once timourous and indomitable . . . in its utter nakedness" (*Edward FitzGerald,* p. 108). Benson thus contrasts again with Terhune, who emphasizes the contrast between FitzGerald's religion and the religious implications of his translation.

15. It is interesting to note that where Hugh Walker claims of the poem that "the parts are bound together as intimately as those of *In Memoriam,* though by a less palpable bond" (*Literature,* p. 486), and treats the poem accordingly, as whole in its thought, Oliver Elton, who notes too the poem's interweaving, comes from his observation to claim that "all attempts to methodize are vain and destructive" since emotional unity precludes unity of thought (*Survey of English Literature 1780-1880* [New York, 1920], IV, 119).

16. I follow the 1879 or fourth edition, reprinted in George B. Woods and Jerome H. Buckley, *Poetry of the Victorian Period* (Chicago, 1965), pp. 425-31. The parenthetical references are to the rubáiyát or quatrains as numbered in that edition.

    In the first edition the first line had "along some strip"—the change to "the" seems to heighten the topographical emphasis as much as it "lightens the weight" of the line (Benson, p. 103).

17. Arberry notes that the "romantic setting of a garden, which is wanting in the original of Omar" was planned by FitzGerald as early as his letter of July 26, 1856 to Tennyson. He notes too that the "Strip of Herbage" comes from the phrase *lab-i kisht* which "FitzGerald found 'constant in his quatrains'" (*Romance,* pp. 47, 199). Draper, making the same point, specified that the Persian phrase is merely "margin of the sown," not quite a garden ("Local Color," p. 29). As this and a few other changes make clear, the topographical organization of the poem is largely FitzGerald's addition to his sources (see below, nn. 18-20).

18. Arberry points out that "FitzGerald invented the conceit of 'sowing'" which does not appear in the original, and that the conceit, invented, led to the "reaping" of a "harvest." While Arberry's claim is that the motive was the allusive ring of FitzGerald's own early Latin translation of Omar, mine is of course that the whole image complex is essential to the world-view of the sown field (*Romance,* p. 125).

19. Parrinder points out that in the original "Paradise . . . should be rendered 'A Sultan's dominion'" ("Cynic or Mystic," p. 224; supported by Arberry, *Romance,* p. 121). In my terms, if the phrase had been literally translated it would have drawn the desert to the field (to which pertains the Sultan) rather than to the garden—again, then, a change from the sources supporting my reading.

20. Draper points out that the conceit is not in any of FitzGerald's sources, and that in it he "extends" both Persian and western "literary convention" ("Local Color," pp. 35-36).

21. Again the originals to which the quatrain may be traced show no sense of anger at a maker's "insolence" (Terhune, *Life,* p. 225; Arberry, *Romance,* pp. 22, 129).

22. The concept is here extended from Goodman's use with regard to dramatic structures. *Structure,* ch. II, esp. pp. 33-35.

23. Hutton puts it well—"The . . . wonderful conversation among the clay images of a potter's shop . . . is intended to take off the speculative imbecility of man in dealing with these large problems" (*Spectator,* p. 336).

24. As was the case with genre, I work within the formulation of Northrop Frye in *Anatomy of Criticism* in analyzing pregenre, accepting his specification of four possible forms and reworking the logical rules by which I think we should come to them (see *Anatomy,* Third Essay). I take pregenre to be the explanatory abstraction by which criticism assigns meaningful categories to the shapes of internal fictions, as I take genre to be the explanatory abstraction by which criticism assigns categories to the potential rewards for audiences in their transactions with literary works. The two abstractions I take to be both inclusive and exhaustive as explanatory devices, though of course there is much more that can and should be said in the process of description (including, I might add, Mr. Frye's concepts of mode and symbol). But proof of this contention must be reserved for fuller treatment.

David Sonstroem (essay date fall 1969)

SOURCE: Sonstroem, David. "Abandon the Day: FitzGerald's *Rubáiyát of Omar Khayyám." Victorian Newsletter,* no. 36 (fall 1969): 10-13.

[*In the following essay, Sonstroem compares the overwhelmingly pessimistic tone of the* Rubáiyát *with the "limited optimism" expressed in carpe diem poetry.*]

Edward FitzGerald's **Rubáiyát of Omar Khayyám** bravely offers its famous remedy, "A Book of Verses . . . / A Jug of Wine, a Loaf of Bread—and Thou" (st. 12),[1] as triumphant insulation against the thought of eternal extinction. But this quatrain, like some other passages expressing optimism or satisfaction, is rather out of keeping with the rest of the poem, whose overall impression is of helpless, sodden pessimism and richly melancholic despair. The poem as a whole offers a suggestive departure from the carpe diem sentiments found in this quatrain, introducing the traditional motif only to belie it. By this means the poem achieves an especially poignant—and peculiarly Victorian[2]—pathos.

The typical carpe diem poem expresses limited optimism. It holds that experiencing and enjoying every moment of life to the utmost, usually in pursuit of love, serves to counterbalance the prospect of a short life followed by interminable death. According to the economics of *Catullus V,* for example, the one large debit of death is liquidated by countless kisses. Impending death lends an additional exciting urgency to the poet's amatory pleasure. And that pleasure makes possible a certain insensitivity toward the prospect of death, as despair is erased in a burst of obfuscating enthusiasm. Horace's *Ode I, 11* does not exhibit the same enthusiasm or insensitivity in the face of death as does Catullus' poem, but it, too, presents a purposeful program. More judicious and reasoned than *Catullus V,* it counsels sensibleness rather than ecstasy. Again life and death are viewed partly as an economic matter, a matter of profit and loss (see the verbs *dederint, tribuit, carpe*). Here the reader does not find the suggestion of victory that he does in *Catullus V* but instead the prudent advice to make a partial recovery of future losses—to take what one can get from a losing proposition. Even dreggy wine is potable when clarified. Whereas Catullus' poem is a surprise attack upon death, Horace's is a tenacious holding operation. But, for all their differences, both poems find life and love all the more dear for being under the shadow of death.

Three familiar English poems that employ the motif are Herrick's "To the Virgins, to Make Much of Time," Jonson's "Come, My Celia," and Marvell's "To His Coy Mistress." The first two are marked by a blunted sense of death. In the poem by Herrick, especially, death is still evoked as the reason "to make much of time," but only *pro forma,* to remind the lady of the hoary argument being proffered, mention alone apparently being considered enough to provoke the appropriate response. The familiarity and informality implied in the line, "Old time is still a-flying," show that the *argumentum ad mortem* has become stylized, formulaic, incantatory. And Jonson makes dramatic capital of a similar failure to appreciate death duly. The evil Volpone (who sings "Come, My Celia" in his attempt to seduce the grasping Corvino's wife) cannot successfully contemplate the significance of death but dwells instead upon the meaner consideration of "household spies" and detection. His sense of sin is much stronger than his sense of death, as his words "delude," "beguile," "wile," "sin," "steal," "thefts," and "crimes" reveal. Volpone feels merely lustful and guilty, with no larger view of death to justify his lust, in spite of his pretensions.

The distinctiveness of "To His Coy Mistress" lies in its wit in calling attention to the disparity between problem and answer—the disparity between eternal extinction and light-handed seduction. Marvell has the wit to see and present the act of love as something trivial, playful, something to be treated lightly, even as he sees it as man's most effective retort to death. But for all its distinctiveness, the poem is like those of Catullus and Horace in its vivid appreciation of the fact of death: of "Time's wingèd chariot" and the "Deserts of vast eternity." And in its response—making the best of a bad future by seizing upon life with might and main—it shares with all the poems, Latin and English, what might be called the common denominator of the motif.

II

FitzGerald himself sees his **Rubáiyát** as expressing, at least in part, carpe diem sentiments. In a letter of 12 March 1857, continued 20 March, to E. B. Cowell, he remarks that "Hafiz and old Omar Khayyám ring like true Metal. The Philosophy of the Latter is, alas!, one that never fails in the World. 'To-day is ours, etc.'"[3] In another letter to the same correspondent he does not differentiate between Omar's posture toward life and Anacreon's: "Omar breathes a sort of Consolation to me! Poor Fellow; I think of him, and Olivier Basselin, and Anacreon; lighter Shadows among the Shades, perhaps, over which Lucretius presides so grimly."[4] In his Introduction to the **Rubáiyát** he says that "the old Tent-maker . . . fell back upon TO-DAY . . . as the only Ground he had to stand upon. . . ." Earlier in the Introduction he remarks of the speaker of his poem, "Having failed (however mistakenly) of finding any Providence but Destiny, and any World but This, he set about making the most of it. . . ."

Indeed the **Rubáiyát** does present many of the same elements of the other poems: the young lady, who is being instructed in the grim lot of mankind; time fleeting (st. 7: "The Bird of Time has but a little way / To flutter—and the Bird is on the Wing"); flowers withering on the bough; the denial of an afterlife (st. 35: "'once dead you never shall return'"); the appeal to cosmic economics (st. 13: "Ah, take the Cash, and let the Credit go"; st. 24: "Ah, make the most of what we yet may spend, / Before we too into the Dust descend"); and the request to "fill the Cup." But, even allowing for variations within the traditional attitude, we find that these typical elements do not fall into the typical pattern. They do not make the same sense.

The **Rubáiyát** differs drastically from all the other poems in its crucial gesture—abandoning the day rather than seizing upon it. The gesture of the poem is embedded in the poet's advice to "lose your fingers in the tresses of / The Cypress-slender Minister of Wine" (st. 41. I take the lady here to be largely a metaphor for the wine itself). The symbol for the attitude of the poem is a languid hand rather than a grasping one. A sign of the difference is the poet's turning to wine rather than women for his solace. (Of course, wine and women are together present here as in the other poems, but here the woman's primary function is to bring wine to the poet, whereas in the typical carpe diem poem the wine brings the woman to the poet.)[5] Omar—really a solitary—is not trying to "roll all our strength and all / Our sweetness up into one ball," but rather to drink himself into a forgetful stupor. His aim, to put the matter plainly, is to achieve insensibility, not sexual climax. He is trying to dull and destroy, not sharpen his awarenesses:

> Oh, many a Cup of this forbidden Wine
> Must drown the memory of that insolence!
> Then to the Lip of this poor earthen Urn
> I leaned, the Secret of my Life to learn;
>   And Lip to Lip it murmured—"While you live,
> Drink!—for, once dead, you never shall return."

(st. 35)

Drink, not to enjoy life, or to answer back to impending death, but to drown out the unbearable thought of eternal death.

The poet is quite explicit about the function of wine. In stanza 59 he praises "the Grape" for its power to "confute" the "Two-and-Seventy jarring Sects" and to transmute "Life's leaden metal into Gold." Drunkenness has the power, that is, to erase distinctions, to make all one. Drink enough, and even death and life will seem to become one (st. 42). Yet, as we have seen, the carpe diem poem lives upon the difference between life and death.

The imagery of the poem gives a good sense of the bleary state that the poet is partly experiencing and partly seeking. The same images swirl through the poem—the Sun, the Stars, the Tavern, the Temple, the Rose, the Cup, the Vine, the Wine, the Wilderness or Desert, Paradise, Dust, the Door, the Lip, the Vessel—capitalization calling our attention to these familiar but wandering buoys in a lower-case sea. Reiteration produces a winey, vertiginous effect; after a while we find ourselves reading the **Rubáiyát** as "poetry," in the worst sense of the word, conscious of the rhetorical ride but caring little where we are or where we are being taken.

The effect is furthered by the elaborate way in which images flow in and out of one another, constantly changing their meaning. For example, in stanza 41, "Tomorrow's tangle" is quickly transmuted into the tangles of a girl's hair, only to become the tangle-headedness produced by alcohol. In stanza 20, a human lip turns into a river's lip. The clay for the vessel of stanzas 35 and 36 could have been dug from this same river's lip;

at least the poet thinks that the clay "once did live." The lips of this vessel speak and murmur, and they take and give kisses. Thus life becomes death becomes life; the train of imagery returns to its starting point. But the most spectacular imagistic odyssey is that connected with the cup shape. Man's whole world is seen as being beneath a bowl—"that inverted Bowl they call the Sky" (st. 72). The larger image meets with many reflections: in the wine cup, the burial urn, and especially in man himself, seen as potter's vessel, as (cup-shaped) rose, as tulip, as momentary, superficial bubble of life on the wine of existence. The net effect of this extravagant interrelationship is precisely a "tangle," all things coming to mean all things. And who would seek to comprehend such a state of affairs or strive against it? The drunken vision justifies the drunken state.

The great irony of the **Rubáiyát,** which removes it even further from the typical carpe diem poem, is that the poet fails in his attempt to abandon the day. In fact, he is a failure in a number of respects. For good dramatic reasons, we are not entirely won over to his point of view, in the sense that a reader provisionally accepts, while he reads, views that he ultimately need not espouse. We sympathize deeply, but we do not forget that the poem is launched in the ironic light of false morning.

A sign of the poet's failure (I speak of the dramatic character, of course, and not FitzGerald) is the meandering quality of the poem and its length. Whereas the speaker of the typical carpe diem poem glances once at death and exits toward the love bed, this poet goes on and on, dwelling upon and returning to the considerations he seeks to escape. He drinks to forget, only to find that drinking has turned his painful concern into an obsession. He is a would-be Anacreon who does not rejoice in wine because he sees only the bottom of the cup. He attempts to escape from the ultimate questions by denying their importance (see, for example, sts. 44, 46, and 48); yet the questions keep reappearing. The very stanzaic form (*a a b a*) serves nicely as a metric metaphor for the poem's overall movement: a pessimistic pattern is established (*a a*), the poet attempts to break away from it (*b*), but he ends by reiterating the original predicament (*a*). The poem's most pathetic effect is the speaker's failure to realize that he has failed, to realize that he is incapable of true diversion.

Another sign of the poet's failure is his dramatically appropriate inconsistencies. Sometimes death is seen as the end of individual existence (sts. 24, 25, 35, 46, 48, 62); elsewhere it is seen as offering the possibility of further existence (sts. 39, 44); and elsewhere the future is simply seen to be unknown, a "tangle" (sts. 29, 32, 33, 41, 74). By contrast the typical carpe diem poem is very sure of its metaphysics. The poet says, of man (st. 74), "you know not whence you came, nor why; / . . .

you know not why you go, nor where"; yet he confidently asserts in the previous and following stanzas that all things are predetermined. He urges man to "Waste not your Hour" (st. 54), yet he prays to death to "make haste" (st. 48). Furthermore, he is inconsistent in where he levels his scorn: at "this sorry Scheme of Things" (sts. 99, 81); at philosophy, which calls attention to it (sts. 27-30, 49-56); and at religion, which seeks to soften man's sense of its enormity (sts. 59, 62-63, 82-88). He says that he has "divorced old barren Reason" (st. 55), even as he philosophizes. Such inconsistencies, suggestive of semidrunkenness, indicate the unapprehended failure of his argument.

It is in this context that we must read the poet's carpe diem sentiments. They are just one more of the poses that his deep despair will not permit him to uphold. Almost all of these passages come early in the poem, by stanza 25, and all are effectively contradicted or soon forgotten. We do find the vision of "Paradise enow" (st. 12), and the exhortations to "take the Cash" (st. 13) and to "make the most of what we yet may spend, / Before we too into the Dust descend." (st. 24) But this position is too optimistic to be sustained, for, as the next stanza declares in apparently unconscious contradiction, there is no Cash, there is no present pleasure, to throw into the face of death:

> Alike for those who for TODAY prepare,
> And those that after some TOMORROW stare,
>   A Muezzín from the Tower of Darkness cries,
> "Fools, your Reward is neither Here nor There."

"Here" is just as empty and valueless as "There." Earlier we find the same pattern of carpe diem sentiment followed by a stanza showing that sentiment to be hollow:

> Look to the blowing Rose about us—"Lo,
> Laughing," she says, "into the world I blow,
>   At once the silken tassel of my Purse
> Tear, and its Treasure on the Garden throw."
>
> And those who husbanded the Golden Grain,
> And those who flung it to the winds like Rain,
>   Alike to no such aureate Earth are turned
> As, buried once, Men want dug up again.
>
>   (sts. 14, 15)

Under the cover of death (the latter stanza declares), the difference between having seized the day and having hoarded one's being for the sake of an afterlife is felt to be negligible.

What causes the carpe diem sentiment to collapse is basically the poet's sense of the bankruptcy of life. For all his talk about making merry (st. 23) and being "jocund with the fruitful Grape" (st. 54), he is obviously not enjoying himself. For him there is no real joy in the grape, just as there is no real forgetfulness. As a hedonist, the poet is a failure, a living refutation of the advice that he offers in these passages. He fails because he has answered the carpe diem attitude toward death with the attitude toward life of Ecclesiastes: "vanity of vanities, all is vanity." And therefore he has no "Cash" of life to put up against death's toll. Marvell's witty, complicating, balancing sense of the triviality of life's activity has grown to such dominance in the *Rubáiyát* that life is felt to be valueless, and therefore powerless to offset death. Whereas "Come, My Celia" and "To the Virgins, to Make Much of Time" weaken the carpe diem sentiment with their blunted sense of death, the *Rubáiyát,* with its blunted sense of life, destroys it.

In the light of his confusion and his failure to find a vital counterforce to direct against death, it is not surprising that the final irony of the poem shows Omar, in his effort to flee the problems of life and the thought of death, to be seeking them unawares. He drinks to insulate himself from his vision of the future as a "tangle," but the drunken state only exaggerates his sense of the unbearable and impossible confusion that he is trying to escape. "Tomorrow's tangle" is actually mirrored and endorsed in wine's confusion. Again, an "Angel Shape" appears to him, bearing the Grape as the answer to his metaphysical fears—the Grape that

> all the misbelieving and black Horde
> Of Fears and Sorrows that infest the Soul
> Scatters before him with his whirlwind Sword
>
> (st. 60)

But death itself will come to the poet in exactly the same form, brought by the same angelic Sákí:

> that Angel of the darker Drink
> At last shall find you by the river brink,
>   And offering his Cup, invite your Soul
> Forth to your Lips to quaff. . . .
>
> (st. 43)

Our realization that a drunken stupor can be seen as a type of death reinforces the metaphorical expression of the vicious cycle. Elsewhere we see again Omar abetting his own failure: the world that distresses the poet is seen in terms of

> that inverted Bowl they call the Sky,
> Whereunder crawling cooped we live and die,
>   Lift not your hands to *It* for help. . . .
>
> (st. 72)

Yet he proposes precisely the same predicament for himself after death, carrying the same terms with him into the grave: death, too, is an inverted cup (st. 40), and the poet asks his Sákí to "turn down an empty Glass" upon his grave. Thus the inverted bowl is reiterated. Fleeing the prospect of death, the poet runs into the arms of death; fleeing life's predicament, he bears it with him into the grave.

The poem's betrayal of the carpe diem attitude proves a very effective way of setting forth poignantly and precisely a Victorian state of mind and feeling. Wandering between two worlds, one death, the other powerless to be life, Omar dramatizes one more version of a pervasive Victorian predicament.[6] In its languid hand; its emphasis on wine rather than women; its search for stupor or giddiness; its meandering inconclusiveness; its philosophical and psychological inconsistency, with attitudes foundering upon one another; its sense of a valueless, shadowy life; its troubled perplexity; and (to borrow again from Arnold) its suffering that finds no effective vent in meaningful action, a state "in which there is everything to be endured, nothing to be done," the *Rubáiyát* shows how thoroughly FitzGerald wove his translation into the fabric of Victorian thought and feeling. To the extent that the poem is a reflection of the Victorian period, I venture to say that the age itself found difficulty in sustaining a genuine carpe diem sentiment. Such feelings were doomed to be frustrated; for, although the age was in no danger of adopting Herrick's sanguine view toward death, it, like Omar (and, I might add, FitzGerald himself[7]) often possessed a too blunted view of the stuff of life, or a too distant perspective of it, to appreciate immediately life's substance, value, and power.[8]

Notes

1. All quotations are from the fifth, posthumous version of 1889, although my reading of the poem applies to the earlier versions as well.

2. I treat the English poem as intimately FitzGerald's. The question of how faithfully FitzGerald rendered the spirit of the original Omar Khayyám is beside the point of this essay.

3. *Letters and Literary Remains of Edward FitzGerald,* ed. William Aldis Wright (London, 1903), II, 62.

4. Letter of 7 May 1857, cont. 5 June. In *Letters and Literary Remains,* II, 75.

5. The distinction that I make here does not apply to the poems of Anacreon and his followers—poems that express carelessness as to whether enjoyment comes from wine or women.

6. My own impromptu list of Victorian poems expressing a version of this state of mind includes (in addition to "Stanzas from the Grande Chartreuse") "The Lady of Shalott," "The Lotos-Eaters," *"Perche Pensa? Pensando S'Invecchia," The House of Life, The City of Dreadful Night,* and "An Apology" from *The Earthly Paradise.* Every reader could easily lengthen the list.

7. Although no recluse, he led a very retired existence, preferring village to city, independence to marriage, and letter to face-to-face confrontation.

His flirtation with hedonism—but at one re-move—is a sign of the distance that he required between himself and the active life.

8. The reader may wish to compare with the present study William Cadbury's articulate, well-considered treatment of the personality of FitzGerald's fictitious Omar in "FitzGerald's *Rubáiyát* as a Poem," *ELH,* XXXIV (1967), 541-63—a study that I had not seen when I formulated my own ideas. It, too, notes that "the trivially posturing dependence on wine with which [Omar] attempts a stable attitude . . . brings on . . . an undercutting reaction against the very hedonism to which he has been reduced" (556). But whereas Cadbury sees in the poem an exquisitely just series of conflicting postures, which make a logical progression as well as a psychological maturation, my own sense of the poem is that the narrator's sequence of attitudes is genuinely meandering and confused, and that much of Cadbury's attempt to order the attitudes is as meaningful and thankless as tracing patterns in cloud formations. The patterns are there, to be sure, but they are neither substantial nor significant.

John D. Yohannan (essay date spring 1971)

SOURCE: Yohannan, John D. "The Fin de Siècle Cult of FitzGerald's *Rubaiyat of Omar Khayyám.*" *Review of National Literatures* II, no. 1 (spring 1971): 74-91.

[*In the following essay, Yohannan comments on the popularity of FitzGerald's translation at the end of the nineteenth century.*]

A translated Persian poem, which was Edward FitzGerald's consolation against a melancholy life, became—even in his own lifetime—a literary fad in both England and America. After FitzGerald's death in 1883, it was to become a cult and indeed to produce its own anticult.

Some critics remained content to explain the extraordinary success of the poem in purely aesthetic terms: John Ruskin, for instance, thought it "glorious" to read;[1] Holbrook Jackson saw it as part of the maturing "Renaissance" of English poetry that had begun with Blake and passed through Keats to arrive at Dante Gabriel Rossetti;[2] Theodore Watts-Dutton judged it generically—with the entire *fin de siècle* preoccupation with Persian poetry, in Justin McCarthy, John Payne, and Richard LeGallienne—as merely another species of Romanticism.[3]

But such a view could hardly explain the excessively strong feelings the *Rubaiyat* engendered in both proponents and opponents—feelings which lay at the levels of psychological bent or philosophical bias considerably below the level of a purely aesthetic need. More to the point was the explanation of Elizabeth Alden Curtis, herself a translator of the *Rubaiyat.* For her, Omar was the "stern materialist from mystic skies," who, by combining Horatian hedonism with Old Testament fatalistic pessimism, had produced a "fundamental human cry [that] had no nationality."[4] For Richard Le-Gallienne, too, there was more to the poem than its poetry, which he had successfully adapted as he had that of Hafiz. To be sure, the Khayyam-FitzGerald *Rubaiyat* was "one of the finest pieces of literary art in the English language"; but, he added, "this small handful of strangely scented rose-leaves have been dynamic as a disintegrating spiritual force in England and America during the last 25 years."[5] A few years later, LeGallienne wrote *Omar Repentant,* a book of original verses in the rubaiyat stanza in which he advised the young:

> Boy, do you know that since the world began
> No man hath writ a deadlier book for man?
> The grape!—the vine! oh what an evil wit
> Have words to gild the blackness of the pit!
> Said so, how fair it sounds—The Vine! The Grape!
> Oh call it Whiskey—and be done with it![6]

Whether the *Rubaiyat* was a "disintegrating" force would depend on one's spiritual view—whether of religion or temperance: but at any rate, the poem seemed to have much more relevance to the age than most native contemporary poetry. A. C. Benson, looking back at that time, later wrote:

> It heightened the charm to readers, living in a season of outworn faith and restless dissatisfaction, to find that eight hundred years before, far across the centuries, in the dim and remote East, the same problem had pressed sadly on the mind of an ancient and accomplished sage.[7]

The question, of course, was: Precisely what in the contemporary intellectual climate corresponded to precisely what in the philosophical quatrains of Omar Khayyam? Alfred North Whitehead has somewhere spoken of the inability of the nineteenth century to make up its mind as to what sort of cosmogony it wished to believe in. This is certainly demonstrated in the variety of coteries that either adored or despised the *Rubaiyat.* It was the shibboleth for such various and often conflicting dogmas as theosophy, aestheticism, eroticism, determinism, socialism, materialism, and numerous types of occultism. It would not be unfair to classify some of these in the lunatic fringe.

In light of the subsequent furor over the profound implications of the poem, there is a charming innocence in James Thomson's interest in it as an excuse for a good smoke. As early as 1877 Thomson, who wrote under the initials "B. V." (for Bysshe Vanolis, an allusion to his two favorite poets, Shelley and Novalis), contributed an article on Omar Khayyam to a trade journal called *Tobacco Plant.* Despite his admiration for the poet's intellectual fearlessness and daring love of wine, it is obvious that what chiefly interested Thomson was tobacco. Believing that "in default of the weed, [Omar] celebrates the rose," Thomson imagined "What a smoker our bard would have made had the weed flourished in the Orient in his time! Hear him address his Beloved in the very mood of the *narghile* [water-pipe]. . . ." There followed the familiar quatrain beginning "A Book of Verses underneath the Bough."[8] (Twenty years later, Edwin Arlington Robinson, discovering the same poem, was to have the same fantasy!)

More serious challenges in the poem were sensed by translators, editors, reviewers, and readers—both in England and America—to whom it increasingly appealed in the last years of the nineteenth century. John Leslie Garner of Milwaukee, who made his own translation of the *Rubaiyat* in 1888, refused (as had FitzGerald) to accept the Sufistic or mystical interpretation of Omar Khayyam. For him, Omar was a pantheist-fatalist (and a precursor of Schopenhauer), whom the Sufis had taken over after his death, as Huxley had said theologicans craftily are apt to do.[9] That was one view.

Talcott Williams, editing FitzGerald's translation ten years later, was impressed with the power of race rather than religion. Omar's Aryanism as a Persian was more important than the Semitic Islamic faith which he had to accept:

> Watered by his desires, rather than his convictions, the dry branch of semitic monotheism puts forth the white flower of mysticism and sets in that strange fruitage which is perpetually reminding us that under all skies and for both sexes religious fervor and sensuous passion may be legal tender for the same emotions.[10]

If pantheism and fatalism can be bedfellows, why not sex and religion? It was perhaps good Pre-Raphaelite doctrine.

A dominant note in the interpretation of the *Rubaiyat* was struck by a Harvard undergraduate who, along with George Santayana, edited the *Harvard Monthly.* A. B. Houghton announced with surprising urbanity in the mid-eighties that the philosophy of despair Omar passed on to the present generation was equally a refutation of those who believed in a "far off divine event towards which the whole creation moves" and of those who would rebel against "Him." The "He" was not God, but the force of the universe—a pantheistic-materialist force. If this did not make perfect sense, there was little ambiguity about the decadent accents that rang out of the following:

Omar's thought is thoroughly in accord with the essence of the thought of this century. We are no longer a younger race . . . our faces are no longer turned towards the sunrise: they look towards the sunset . . . today we are given over to introspection. We have lost our healthy out of door life . . . our religious faith is disappearing.[11]

At a later date, confessing his love of the *Rubaiyat,* the Hon. John Hay, Ambassador to the Court of St. James, reechoed these sentiments. He marveled at the "jocund despair" which the twelfth century Persian had felt in the face of life's bafflements. "Was this Weltschmerz," he asked, "which we thought a malady of our day, endemic in Persia in 1100?"[12]

The initial impact of the *Rubaiyat* had been as a statement of religious skepticism. It appeared, after all, in 1859, the same year as *The Origin of Species,* a book which Bernard Shaw said abolished not only God but also the Thirty-nine Articles of the Anglican faith. There had been a natural hesitancy on the part of the translator in offering it to a mid-Victorian public, especially as he had had the benefit of a pious clergyman's help in discovering it. After the death of FitzGerald in 1883, however, the poem spoke to a generation who were the products, not of the milieu which had produced the translation, but of the milieu which the translation had helped produce. Its advocates were a bit more aggressive. To these younger devotees (whom perhaps Shaw had in mind when he spoke of "Anacreontic writers [who] put vine leaves in their hair and drank or drugged themselves to death"),[13] the epicureanism of Omar Khayyam was of equal importance with his skepticism. Moreover, the translator was of equal importance with the Persian poet. Out of these two ingredients came the Omar Khayyam Clubs of England and America.

Veneration of the translator tended to surpass worship of the poet. FitzGerald came to be thought of as the author of a poem called *The Rubaiyat of Omar Khayyam* rather than as the man who rendered into English Omar Khayyam's *Rubaiyat.* Theodore Watts-Dunton recalls his excitement in the presence of a man who, as a child of eight, had actually talked with FitzGerald and "been patted on the head by him." In an obituary notice of F. H. Groome, he wrote:

> We, a handful of Omarians of those ante-deluvian days, were perhaps all the more intense in our cult because we believed it to be esoteric. And here was a guest who had been brought into actual personal contact with the wonderful old "Fitz."[14]

One of these early "Omarians" actually depicted himself and his group in the words that Shaw had applied to the unidentified "Anacreontic writers." Sharply distinguishing between two possible interpretations of the *Rubaiyat,* Justin H. McCarthy said that "to some, the head of Omar is circled with the halo of mysticism, while others see only the vine-leaves in his hair."[15] The phrase was repeated in a *Blackwoods* article that described members of the Omar Khayyam Club with vine leaves in their hair drinking cheap Chianti wine and fixing a keen eye on posterity.[16]

The British, or parent, organization of the Omar Khayyam Club came into being in 1892 with Edmund Gosse as President. He was playfully referred to by the members as "Firdausi," in part no doubt in allusion to that poet's preeminence among Persian authors, but probably also because Gosse had written a lengthy poem about Firdausi's legendary exile at the hands of the conqueror Mahmound.[17] There are differing accounts of the number of founding members, who included McCarthy, Clement Shorter (a later president), and Edward Clodd, whose *Memories* in 1916 embalmed some of the Club's earlier activities.[18] It was apparently agreed that membership should never exceed fifty-nine, the year of the appearance of FitzGerald's first edition. The Club's purpose was primarily social, not literary. Its quarterly dinners began at Pagani's Restaurant, then moved to the Florence, and on to Frascati's; still later, when omnibuses showed up on Oxford Street, they returned to Pagani's. The official table cloth bore the insignia of a flagon, the sun, and a total of fifty-nine apples; five apples, denoting the original founders, were always to the right of the cloth.

In 1895, Meredith, Hardy, and Gissing attended one of the dinners; at another were J. M. Barrie, Andrew Lang, Augustine Birrell, and, from the United States, Charles Scribner. An occasional visitor was Henry James. It was humorously reported that the Shah of Persia, during one of his trips to England, was asked to dine at the Omar Khayyam Club, to which he supposedly replied, "Who is Omar Khayyam?"[19] At the March 25, 1897, dinner, Austin Dobson read some verses challenging the supremacy of Horace as the poet of good fellows:

> *Persicos odi*—Horace said
> And therefore is no longer read.
> Since when, for every youth or miss
> That knows *Quis multa gracilis,*
> There are a hundred who can tell
> What Omar thought of Heaven or Hell . . .
> In short, without a break can quote
> Most of what Omar ever wrote.[20]

In the following year, without prejudice to Horace, a fellow at Magdalen College, Oxford, rendered FitzGerald's quatrains into Latin verse "as a breviary for those who make a sort of cult of the *Rubaiyat*"[21] There is an amusing account of the cultists in a satirical skit of the time in which a bright child asks his elder some pointed questions.

Q. Who is this Omar, anyhow?

A. Omar was a Persian.

Q. And these Omarians, as the members of the Omar Khayyam Club call themselves, I suppose they go in for love and paganism, and roses and wine, too?

A. A little; as much as their wives will let them.

Q. But they know Persian, of course?

A. No; they use translations.

Q. Are there many translations?

A. Heaps. A new one every day.[22]

True, there were numerous new translations of the *Rubaiyat,* and some by Club members. But it was common knowledge that "the Club recognizes one and only one translation of Omar Khayyam—that it is concerned with FitzGerald's poem and none other."[23] The figure of the Squire of Sussex was easier for Englishmen to identify with than that of the distant poet of Nishapur.

When John Hay addressed the English Club in 1897, he was able to report that a similar movement was afoot in America, where "in the Eastern states [Omar's] adepts have formed an esoteric sect. . . ." (He had himself heard a Western frontiersman reciting "'Tis but a tent," etc.)[24] In fact, the American Club was formed in 1900, on the ninety-first anniversary of FitzGerald's birth. No doubt the idea had been given encouragement by Moncure Daniel Conway's detailed account, in the *Nation,* of the activities of the English organization—how the British had tried in vain to persuade the Persian Shah to repair the tomb of Omar Khayyam in Nishapur, how the artist William Simpson, visiting the site with the Afghan Boundary Commission in 1884, had brought back seeds of the roses growing at the old tomb, and how he had had them grafted to the roses in Kew Garden.[25]

Thus, what started as a barely audible voice of dissent in 1859 had become by the end of the century, and on both sides of the Atlantic, an articulate caucus of dissidence that threatened to win majority support. Inevitably, the opposition was galvanized into action. Scholars, amateur philosophers, and poetasters took part in an interesting game. The new culture hero, Omar-Fitz, was made to confront some worthy antagonist, who might be a rival philosophy or a large figure in human thought—ancient or modern—designed to serve as foil. But since even the opposition seemed to have a soft spot in its heart for the *Rubaiyat,* the foil often turned out to be a fellow.

An anonymous reply to Khayyam came out in 1899 as *An Old Philosophy.* The rebuttal to the Islamic hedonism of the *Rubaiyat* took the form of one-hundred one quatrains inspired by a sort of liberal Christianity much in the spirit of Tennyson. Altering the typography of FitzGerald's quatrains so that the third line, instead of being indented, was extended, the author rather weakly argued:

The Moslem still expects an earthly bliss,
The Huri's winning smile, the martyr's kiss,
And with fair Ganymedes dispensing wine,
No future lot, thinks he, can vie with this.

There shall no Huris be to please the eye;
No happy hunting grounds shall round thee
lie.
Of sensual pleasures there shall be no need:
Shall not the Great Eternal be thee nigh?[26]

It was not likely that such doggerel would persuade many to shed the vine leaves from their hair.

There was more challenge in a confrontation arranged by Paul Elmer More, the American humanist. For More, the chief intellectual struggle of the time was symbolized in the persons of its two most popular poets: Omar Khayyam and Rudyard Kipling. Kipling advocated the energetic, forward-looking life (perhaps the out-of-door life earlier mentioned by A. B. Houghton?); Omar stood for defeatism and ennui. More observed that for many people, the "virility and out-of-door freedom" of Kipling was a much-needed tonic to the *fin de siècle* mood and entertained the thought that the rising star of Kipling's imperialism—which extolled the "restless energy impelling the race, by fair means or foul, to overrun and subdue the globe"—might signal the decline of the dilletantish and effeminate Omar worship.[27]

For W. H. Mallock, the polarity was between Christianity and the philosophy of Omar Khayyam and Lucretius.

> In Christ, originated that great spiritual and intellectual movement which succeeded, for so many ages, in rendering the Lucretian philosophy at once useless and incredible to the progressive races of mankind; but now, after a lapse of nearly two thousand years, the conditions which evoked that philosophy are once more reappearing.

Those conditions were not indicated exactly, but obviously the new representative of the Lucretian view was Omar Khayyam in his contemporary vogue. Not that he and Lucretius were of identical mind, but a strong enough resemblance existed to warrant offering the ideas of the classical poet in the meter of the *Rubaiyat.* And so the famous opening passage of *De Rerum Natura* comes hobbling out thus:

> When storms blow loud, 'tis sweet to watch at ease,
> From shore, the sailor labouring with the seas:
>   Because the sense, not that such pains are his,
>   But that they are not ours, must always please.[28]

Mallock found Lucretius more relevant to the science of the time than Omar Khayyam; and, though he did not believe that Christianity was still the superstition Lucretius attacked, he urged a second look at the great materialist.

In the opinion of John F. Genung,[29] a rhetorician who wrote and lectured on religious subjects, the proper pendant for the *Rubaiyat* was Ecclesiastes. He did not view Omar with particular alarm. Indeed, he found in him no pessimism, but rather a gaiety that boded well for the future. People were less morose (in 1904) than in the time of Clough and Arnold. Genung could cite no less an activist than Robert L. Stevenson to the effect that

> . . . old Omar Khayyam is living anew, not so much from his agnosticism and his disposition to say audacious things to God, as from his truce to theological subtleties and his hearty acceptance of the present life and its good cheer.[30]

But for all that, Ecclesiastes offered the better alternative.

> We think again of the Epicurean man, the loafer of Omar Khayyam's rose-garden, and our Koheleth ideal looks no more paltry but strong and comely. There is not enough of Omar's man to build a structure of grace and truth upon.[31]

It has been asserted that Robert Browning wrote "Rabbi ben Ezra" as a retort to the "fool's philosophy" of the *Rubaiyat.* It remained for Frederick L. Sargent to stage the debate formally. With a fairness that betrays a real ambivalence in the author's thinking, Sargent matches the seductive pessimism of Omar with the bracing optimism of the Rabbi, giving the polemical advantage to the latter, but gladly permitting the former to continue with his pagan revels—to the satisfaction, no doubt, of an equally ambivalent reader.[32]

So potent was the appeal of the lovely quatrains that some were determined to save Omar Khayyam from the perdition to which his blasphemous ideas assigned him. A way out was provided in the legend that the poet had indeed made a deathbed retraction. Thus there appeared in 1907 a so-called *Testament of Omar Khayyam,* whose author, Louis C. Alexander, announced in his prefatory "Note":

> To those who conceive of Omar Khayyam only as a sot and Agnostic—if not the despairing Materialist and Infidel—of the *Rubaiyat,* these poems will come as a surprise and a revelation . . . For Omar Khayyam was a man of lofty yet humble piety . . . and the majestic figure of the *real* Omar Khayyam—the Astronomer, Poet, Philosopher, and Saint—stands revealed.

The *Wassiyat,* or Testament, consisted of eighty-five quatrains in a Job-like dialogue with God, who justifies himself in rather Browningesque terms:

> For God is the end for which the universe
> Travails by Knowledge and Love and Pain entwined;
> And Joy is its music, and Death, ah! no curse—
> For the enlarged Soul, through it, itself doth find.

The book added as a bonus some odes, presumably composed by the disciples of Omar Khayyam, lauding his piety in stanzas reminiscent of Arnold's "Empedocles." One disciple points out that the Master did teach "in sense / of metaphor and parable" and "feign discontent and doubt," and that one day "lands thou never knewest will proclaim thy fame." Another disciple pleads:

> Hast thou a word, Oh, Master,
> For thy faithful band,
> Who knew thy face unmasked, thy tears beneath thy
>   laugh,
> And the devotion
> Of thy soul's most secret strand,
> And that the wine ne'er flowed thou didst pretend to
>   quaff.[33]

This was, of course, a return to the persistent idea that the sensuous imagery of the *Rubaiyat* is but a cloak to cover the mystical Sufi thought beneath.

H. Justus Williams would not allow this backsliding from the old paganism. His sixty-three quatrains purported to be *The Last Rubaiyat of Omar Khayyam.* These, he maintained, gave proof that the story of the poet's repentance had been exaggerated. Omar was never converted; he only temporarily changed his ways, as is apparent from the following:

> At last! At last! freed from the cowl and hood,
> I stand again where once before I stood,
> And view the world unblinded by a Creed
> That caught me in a short repentant mood.[34]

Obviously, the best, the most effective opposition to Omar Khayyam would have to come from one of his compatriots—a sort of homeopathic treatment for what so many called the sickly *Rubaiyat* malaise. The Reverend William Hastie, a Scottish student of Hegelian idealism, thought he had the cure:

> We confess . . . that we have hated this new-patched
> Omar Khayyam of Mr. FitzGerald, and have at times
> been tempted to scorn the miserable self-deluded,
> unhealthy fanatics of his Cult. But when we have
> looked again into the shining face and glad eyes of
> Jelalleddin, "the glory of religion," our hate has passed
> into pity and our scorn into compassion.

These words were part of an *obiter dictum* on Omar that Hastie permitted himself in a book of adaptations (from the German of Rückert) of some mystical poems of Jelalleddin Rumi.[35] If Christian orthodoxy could not fight off the virus of the *Rubaiyat,* perhaps Islamic mysticism, in the work of a great Sufi poet of Persia, could.

The leading Persian scholar in England, Edward G. Browne, showed sympathy for the spiritual legacy Persia had passed to the world. In *Religious Systems of the World: A Contribution to the Study of Comparative Religion,* he dealt specifically with Sufism and with Bahaism, a new offshoot of Islam, both of which he regarded as pantheistic systems of thought occupying a middle ground between religion and philosophy, and therefore as applicable in England as in Persia.[36] Another scholar in this area, Claud Field, prophesied that the Bahais would improve the quality of both Islam and Christianity. In an article for *The Expository Times* (an Edinburgh religious publication emphasizing the higher criticism), he asserted that, with so much mysticism in the air of late, it behoved Englishmen to know the Master Mystic, Jelalleddin Rumi. It was a pity, he thought, that Rumi did not have his FitzGerald.[37]

That was the difficulty. FitzGerald himself, in deference to the Reverend E. B. Cowell, Omar's true begetter, had expressed the wish that Cowell would translate Rumi, who would constitute a more potent polar force to Omar than did Jami, whose *Salaman and Absal* was FitzGerald's first translation from Persian (published anonymously, 1856). But Cowell never brought himself to deal any more fully with Rumi than with the other Persian poets. When Rumi found a soulmate in the superb Arabic and Persian scholar Reynold A. Nicholson, things looked promising for the anti-Omarians.

Nicholson had begun as a student of classical literature, and some of his early attempts at rendering the Persian poets show that orientation. In a poem on "The Rose and Her Lovers," he was clearly dealing with the familiar Persian theme of the *gul* and the *bulbul,* the rose and the nightingale, but he chose to call the bird Philomel. Very much in the spirit of the late nineteenth century, he allowed himself a parody of the *Rubaiyat* called "Omar's Philosophy of Golf." He experimented with the Persian verse form, the ghazal or lyrical ode, and made the usual translations from Hafiz and the other classical poets of Persia. In an original poem addressed to Hafiz, he both imitated and paraphrased the poet:

> Nightingale of old Iran,
> Haunt'st thou yet Ruknabad's vale,
> Dumbly marveling that man
> Now unqueens the nightingale?
> Zuhra, mid the starry quire,
> Hangs her head and breaks her lyre.[38]

But he came into his element with the translation of some of Rumi's passionate but mystical love poems. Convinced that Rumi was "the greatest mystical poet of any age," he devoted the remainder of his life as scholar and popularizer to the translation, publication, and elucidation of that poet's work.

His absorption with Sufism led him to the belief that many of the popular stories of Islamic literature—the romance of Yusuf and Zulaikha (Joseph and Potiphar's

Wife), the legend of the moth and the flame, of the *gul* and the *bulbul,* were but "shadow pictures of the soul's passionate longing to be reunited with God."[39] But he would not join those who wished to make Omar a Sufi. He contented himself with asking "What should they know of Persia who only Omar know?" It was his belief that

> to find the soul of Persia, we must say good-bye to her skeptics and hedonists—charming people, though sometimes (like the world) they are too much with us—and join the company of mystics led by three great poets, Jelalledin Rumi, Sadi and Hafiz, who represent the deepest aspirations of the race.[40]

Not all students of religion and mysticism in England, however, were prepared to accept the aid of Jelalleddin Rumi and the Sufis. The gloomy Dean Inge, a serious student of the subject, in a course of lectures in the late nineteenth century, spoke with some acerbity of the loose (as he conceived it) mysticism of the Persian Sufis. He held that, in regarding God as both immanent and transcendent, they denied the existence of evil and threw the door open to immorality, lack of purpose, and pessimism. The tendency to self-deification he found in both the Sufis and Ralph Waldo Emerson; where a predecessor of his had accepted both, he now rejected both. "The Sufis or Mohammedan mystics," he said, "use erotic language freely, and appear, like true Asiatics, to have attempted to give a sacramental or symbolical character to the indulgence of their passions."[41] At the High Church level, at any rate, ecumenism was a dubious possibility.

The sum of it was that, whether cultivated as flower or attacked as weed, the **Rubaiyat** continued to thrive. Especially after 1909, when the fiftieth anniversary of the first edition of FitzGerald was celebrated (and the copyright lifted), editions multiplied. Even Nicholson, in that memorable year, edited a reissue of FitzGerald's translation.[42] The explanation of the extraordinary appeal of the poem to readers of all sorts may be found in an area bounded on one side by high art, on another by pop culture, but on the other two sides trailing off into a no-man's-land of unsolved anthropological problems. Andrew Lang found the diagnosis for "Omaritis" (in America, at least) in a condition of middle-browism. "Omar is the business man's poet. . . . To quote Omar is to be cultured." There was so little of him, you could take him everywhere and read him hurriedly as you rushed about your business. The Americans were throwing out Browning and Rossetti and reading Omar along with *David Harum* and *The Virginian.*[43] For the Reverend John Kelman, Omar was not an influenza, but a kind of plague. Calling for a quarantine, he warned that "if you naturalize him, he will become deadly in the West." It would be wiser, he advised, to take the poem as simply a fascinating example of exotic Eastern fatalism.[44] But by 1912 it was probably already too late.

Even more sober commentators, attempting to answer the question, tended to leave it in ambiguity or to raise new and more difficult questions. It helped little for Arnold Smith to tell readers of his book on Victorian poetry in 1907 that the **Rubaiyat** appealed to doubters, atheists, and Christians alike, and that it counseled Epicurean asceticism.[45] Equally unsatisfactory was the commentary of Edward M. Chapman, a historian of religious ideas. It seemed to him that Omar's translator mixed the zest and the satiety of the third quarter of the century. The new discoveries in science, he said, had left the heart clamant, but the deeper feelings did not find utterance; "their burden, therefore, [was] increased by a school of thinkers who would, if they could, have denied them utterance at all." When the new science told people to deny these feelings, when they thought about religion but weren't sure they had a right to, they fell into Omar's mood of jovial cynicism. The "humorous perversity" of the poem, Chapman believed, led directly to the *reductio ad absurdum* of W. E. Henley's verses:

> Let us be drunk, and for a while forget,
> Forget, and ceasing even from regret,
> Live without reason and in spite of rhyme.[46]

Warren B. Blake turned his attention, with more interesting results, to the translator. FitzGerald, after all, was both a symptom of the condition that had produced his poem and a cause of the malady that came out of it. Fascinated by the valetudinarian habits of FitzGerald, Blake said darkly that "the curse of the nineteenth century lay upon him," as it did upon Flaubert, who was also an incomplete man wanting to be either an atheist or a mystic.

> We are waiting to be told what it was that doomed these men, these Flauberts and FitzGeralds, to an incompleteness that seems almost failure. Does the expression "atrophy of the will" help explain the riddle?[47]

The answer is of course not given, but the implied premises of the question say much about the age that made a cult of the **Rubaiyat.** What constitutes success? Are success in art and in life identical? Whatever FitzGerald might have given to life, would it have been more or better than he gave to art?

Notes

1. Quoted in Alfred M. Terhune, *The Life of Edward FitzGerald, Translator of the Rubaiyat of Omar Khayyam* (New Haven, Conn.: Yale University Press, 1947), p. 212.

2. Holbrook Jackson, *Edward FitzGerald and Omar Khayyam, an Essay* (London: David Nutt, 1899), section IV.

3. Theodore Watts-Dutton, *Poetry and the Renascence of Wonder* (London: Herbert Jenkins, 1916), "Poetry."

4. Elizabeth Alden Curtis, *One Hundred Quatrains from the Rubaiyat of Omar Khayyam* (New York: Brothers of the Book, 1899), p. 11.

5. Richard LeGalienne, "The Eternal Omar," in *The Book of Omar and Rubaiyat* (New York: Riverside Press, 1900), pp. 16, 21.

6. Idem., *Omar Repentant* (New York: Mitchell Kennerley, 1908), unpaged.

7. Quoted by John T. Winterich in *Books and the Man* (New York: Greenberg, 1929), p. 332.

8. "B. V.," *Selections from Original Contributions by James Thomson to Cope's Tobacco Plant* (Liverpool, 1889), p. 60 ff.

9. John Leslie Garner, *The Strophes of Omar Khayyam* (Milwaukee: The Corbett and Skidmore Co., 1888).

10. Edward FitzGerald, *The Rubaiyat of Omar Khayyam,* ed. Talcott Williams (Philadelphia: Henry T. Coates & Co., 1898), "Foreword."

11. A. B. Houghton, "A Study in Despair," *Harvard Monthly,* I (Oct. 1885-Feb. 1886), p. 102 ff.

12. John Hay, *In Praise of Omar Khayyam, an Address before the Omar Khayyam Club* (Portland, Maine: Mosher, 1898).

13. Bernard Shaw, "Preface," in Richard Wilson, *The Miraculous Birth of Language* (New York: Philosophical Library, 1948).

14. James Douglas, *Theodore Watts-Dunton, Poet, Novelist, Critic* (New York: John Lane, 1907), p. 79.

15. Justin H. McCarthy, *The Quatrains of Omar Khayyam in English Prose* (New York: Brentano's 1898), "Note on Omar."

16. Cited in *The Book of Omar and Rubaiyat,* p. 47.

17. Edmund Gosse, "Firdausi in Exile," in Helen Zimmern, *Epic of Kings, Stories Retold from Firdausi* (London: T. Fischer Unwin, 1883).

18. Edward Clodd, *Memories* (London: Chapman and Hall, 1916), esp. pp. 89, 98, 161.

19. John Morgan, *Omar Khayyam, an Essay* (Aberdeen: Aberdeen University Press, 1901), "Introduction."

20. Austin Dobson, *Verses Read at a Dinner of the Omar Khayyam Club* (London: Chiswick Press, 1897). "Persian garlands I detest" is William Cowper's rendering of "Persicos odi" from Horace's Odes, I, 38. John Milton's version of "Quis multa gracilis" (Odes, I, 5) is "What slender youth,

bedew'd with liquid odors, / courts thee on roses in some pleasant cave, / Pyrrha?" The two odes are among Horace's best known.

21. Herbert W. Greene, *Rubaiyat of Omar Khayyam rendered into English Verse by Edward FitzGerald and into Latin by . . .* (Boston: Privately printed, 1898).

22. *The Book of Omar and Rubaiyat,* p. 47 ff.

23. *Ibid.,* 37.

24. Hay, *In Praise of Omar Khayyam.*

25. Moncure Daniel Conway, "The Omar Khayyam Cult in England," *Nation,* Vol. LVII, No. 1478 (Oct. 26, 1893), 304.

26. *An Old Philosophy in 101 Quatrains, by the Modern Umar Kayam* (Ormskirk: T. Hutton, 1899).

27. "Kipling and FitzGerald," *Shelburne Essays,* 2d ser. (Boston: Houghton Mifflin, 1905), pp. 106, 117.

28. W. H. Mallock, *Lucretius on Life and Death, in the Metre of Omar Khayyam* (London: Adam and Charles Black, 1900), p. xix and stanza 1.

29. John F. Genung, *Ecclesiastes, Words of Koheleth, Son of David, King of Jerusalem* (Boston: Houghton Mifflin, 1904), p. 167.

30. John F. Genung, *Stevenson's Attitude to Life* (New York: Thomas Y. Crowell, 1901), pp. 16-17.

31. Genung, *Ecclesiastes,* p. 156.

32. Frederick L. Sargent, *Omar and the Rabbi* (Cambridge: Harvard Cooperative Society, 1909).

33. Louis C. Alexander, *The Testament of Omar Khayyam [the Wassiyat] Comprising His Testament (or Last Words), a Song, Hymn of Prayer, The Word in the Desert, Hymn of Praise, also the Marathi or Odes of the Disciples* (London: John Long, 1907), "Note," stanza LXXVI, and "The Marathi."

34. H. Justus Williams, *The Last Rubaiyat of Omar Khayyam* (London: Sisley's Ltd., n.d.), stanza I.

35. William Hastie, *Festival of Spring, from the Divan of Jelalleddin* (Glasgow: James MacLehose & Sons, 1903), p. xxxiii.

36. Edward G. Browne, "Sufism" and "Babism" in *Religious Systems of the World* (London: Swan Sonenschein & Co., 1902), pp. 314 ff., 333 ff.

37. Claud Field, "The Master Mystic," *The Expository Times,* XVII (Oct. 1905-Sept. 1906), 452 ff. Field also wrote *Mystics and Saints of Islam* (London: F. Griffiths, 1910).

38. R. A. Nicholson, *The Don and the Dervish, a Book of Verses Original and Translated* (London: J. M. Dent, 1911), pp. 62, 70 ff.

39. Nicholson, *Mystics of Islam* (London: G. Bell, 1914), pp. 116-17.

40. Nicholson, *Persian Lyrics* (London: Ernest Benn, 1931, "Preface."

41. William Ralph Inge, *Christian Mysticism* (New York: Scribner's, 1899), pp. 118, 321, 371.

42. *Rubaiyat of Omar Khayyam,* translated by Edward FitzGerald, edited with an Introduction and Notes by R. A. Nicholson (London: A. & C. Black, 1909).

43. Andrew Lang, "At the Sign of the Ship," *Longman's Magazine,* July 1904, p. 264.

44. John Kelman, *Among Famous Books* (London: Hodder and Stoughton, 1912), p. 89 ff.

45. Arnold Smith, *The Main Tendencies of Victorian Poetry* (Cournville, Birmingham: St. George Press, 1907), pp. xii, 135 ff.

46. Edward M. Chapman, *English Literature in Account with Religion, 1800-1900* (Boston: Houghton Mifflin, 1910), pp. 457-59.

47. Warren B. Blake, "Poetry, Time and Edward FitzGerald," *The Dial* (Chicago: 1909), XLVI, 177-80.

Gerald D. Browne (essay date 1975)

SOURCE: Browne, Gerald D. "Edward FitzGerald's Revisions." *Papers of the Bibliographical Society of America* 69 (1975): 94-112.

[In the following essay, Browne considers the nature of the revisions FitzGerald made in the second, third, and fourth editions of the Rubáiyát.*]*

It is well known that Edward FitzGerald made extensive revisions among the first four English editions of ***The Rubáiyát of Omar Khayyám.*** The seventy-five quatrains of the 1859 edition, for example, were expanded to 110 in the edition of 1868, but the number was subsequently cut to 101 in the third (1872) and fourth (1879) edition. Moreover, the order of some of the quatrains was changed, and further changes were made within the quatrains themselves. Whether the changes are invariably improvements is arguable, and some editions print more than one version, usually those of 1859 and 1879, in parallel form, thereby allowing the reader to exercise his own critical judgment.

The extent to which FitzGerald revised his other works is much less well known. Indeed, few people have even read the other works. This is ironic since FitzGerald felt that whatever claim he might make on posterity would not be through ***The Rubáiyát,*** but through such works as *The Downfall and Death of King Oedipus* and *Agamemnon.* A study of revisions he made in these provides further evidence of what is apparent among the first four English editions of ***The Rubáiyát,*** namely, that FitzGerald was a most conscientious artist, continually seeking to improve his work and meticulous in details of phrasing and punctuation, although at the same time he was not above deferring to the advice of others. Such a study also reveals how FitzGerald's habits of revision make the text of his work rather less fixed than existing editions suggest. Typically, he made holograph corrections and revisions in copies of an only or a final edition printed during his life. And, typically, the corrections and revisions are not identical in all copies of a given work. As a result, editors of the posthumous editions of the collected works have incorporated some, but not all, of these changes, and they do not agree with one another on the changes they do include.

While the problem in FitzGerald's text may not be one of "infinite variation," a phrase by which Bernard Weinberg describes the text of Balzac,[1] it is nonetheless a perhaps insuperable one of what E. A. J. Honigmann calls textual "instability," in which indifferent variants make like claims on authority.[2] In this respect FitzGerald is not really unusual. Honigmann argues that Shakespeare's is an unstable text, and he marshals evidence drawn from such writers as Milton, Keats, Middleton, Burns, and Hardy—one might add T. S. Eliot as a notable example from our own century[3]—to illustrate how unstable texts are created.

Of course, the term "unstable text" is a general one in the sense that the specific nature of a textual problem will vary from writer to writer. Honigmann imagines Shakespeare to be a writer "so fluent that little verbal changes . . . ran quite freely from his pen when the process of copying refired his mind" (Honigmann, p. 3). FitzGerald, on the other hand, revised more haltingly, sometimes weighing several possibilities, sometimes adopting the suggestions of others. Essentially, the problem in his text lies in the fact that he made revisions in works after they had been printed but in many cases did not see those revisions become part of subsequent printings. In general, we think of a particular edition of a book as a terminus. It represents, however imperfectly, the completion of an effort that began, if it is a first edition, with a manuscript version or versions and continued through possibly several proof stages to the final printing, which is then offered for sale or otherwise distributed. While the author may subsequently revise his work, the revisions usually turn up in a later edition, which is a new and distinct effort.

That FitzGerald should make revisions in printed copies of his works is due at least partly to the fact that as he grew older he experienced trouble with his eyesight. It was simply easier for him to read and correct his work when it was in print. Several letters bear this out. To W. F. Pollock he wrote in 1873, regarding the first edition of *Agamemnon*: "I think you have seen, or had, all the things but the last, which is the most impudent of all. It was, however, not meant for Scholars: mainly for Mrs. Kemble: but as I can't read myself, nor expect others of my age to read a long MS. I had it printed by a cheap friend."[4] In a letter to Fanny Kemble he again expressed his feeling that he wished to spare others the difficulty he had in dealing with manuscript: "I will, by and by, send you a little introductory letter to Mr. Norton, explaining to him, a Greek Scholar, why I have departed from so much of the original: 'little' I call the Letter, but yet so long that I did not wish him, or you, to have as much trouble in reading, as I, with my bad Eyes, had in writing it: so, as I tell him—and you—it must go to the Printers along with the Play which it prates about."[5] In 1875 he remarked in a letter to Thomas Sergeant Perry, regarding his "handy work": "That consists chiefly of things taken—I must not say, translated—from foreign sources; and printed partly to give to Friends, & partly because (as I suppose is the case with others) I can only alter for my best when reflected in Type."[6]

Assuming that an editor of FitzGerald could locate all annotated copies of a given work—an assumption that cannot realistically be made—how would he choose among alternative readings? A dated inscription on the cover will not help in establishing the chronology of variants since the inscription may have been written years after the annotations within the text. In some cases an editor may be directed by a kind of majority rule: a holograph variant that appears in several, although not all, copies examined. In yet other cases he will almost certainly have to rely solely on his judgment. He will then have to "screw his courage to the sticking place and choose between . . . variants."[7] The resulting text may not in all respects be an improvement over the texts of existing editions. But the edition thus produced will, as a whole, be a superior one if the editor has laid all his cards on the table by describing the nature and number of variants he has discovered, as well as his treatment of them. An important failing in existing editions of FitzGerald's works is that they leave the reader largely in the dark concerning their handling of variants. Very often, even, the reader has no way of knowing, short of making his own comparison, that the text of a posthumous edition differs from its purported base text.

We must reckon with three editions of FitzGerald's collected works. These are: *Works of Edward FitzGerald* (two volumes, 1887), edited by Michael Kerney and published by Bernard Quaritch, London, and Houghton, Mifflin and Company, New York and Boston; *Letters and Literary Remains of Edward FitzGerald* (seven volumes, 1902-03), edited by William Aldis Wright and published by Macmillan and Company (an earlier edition, with fewer letters, had been published in three volumes in 1889); and *The Variorum and Definitive Edition of the Poetical and Prose Writings of Edward FitzGerald* (seven volumes, 1902-03), edited by George Bentham and published by Doubleday, Page and Company.

William Aldis Wright was FitzGerald's literary executor, and despite the variorum's titular claim to definitiveness, that distinction has generally been accorded to Wright's edition. Joanna Richardson's *FitzGerald: Selected Works* (1962) reprints portions of Wright, except for a few letters. J. M. Cohen does the same in his *Letters of Edward FitzGerald* (1960). W. F. Prideaux's bibliography of FitzGerald (1901) lists as posthumous material only that edited by Wright. In the section on FitzGerald in *Victorian Poets: A Guide to Research,* Michael Timko says that Wright's is "the definitive edition of the works," and that Bentham's is "the only other edition that bears comparison with the Wright."[8]

Since there are no known manuscripts for FitzGerald's principal works, Wright, Bentham, and Kerney all base their editions on printed copies of FitzGerald's works containing holograph corrections and revisions. Of the three, Wright provides the clearest statement of the nature of his text. He relates how, following FitzGerald's death, "a small tin box . . . containing among other things corrected copies of his [FitzGerald's] printed works" was sent to him by FitzGerald's executors (Wright, I, v). This was accompanied by a letter from FitzGerald to Wright. It reads in part: "I do not suppose it likely that any of my works should be reprinted after my Death. Possibly the three Plays from the Greek [*Agamemnon* and the two-part *Downfall and Death of King Oedipus*], and Calderon's Magico [that is, *The Mighty Magician*]: which have a certain merit in the Form they are cast into, and also in the Versification.

"However this may be, I venture to commit to you this Box containing Copies of all that I have corrected in the way that I would have them appear, if any of them ever should be resuscitated" (Wright, I, v).

Taking the letter at face value, then, Wright's edition is the authorized one. It is well, however, to recall Greg's dictum "authority is never absolute, but only relative."[9] Such nominal authorization as is contained in FitzGerald's letter does not necessarily make Wright's edition authoritative in the deepest sense of faithfully representing the substance of FitzGerald's writings. Wright goes no further than the letter to explain the manner in which he has followed his exemplars of the text. He does not, for example, explain whether he has silently emended at any point, whether he has printed all of FitzGerald's autograph corrections, or whether he has changed any spellings or punctuation. Nor is Wright clear about how much of the material he includes in his edition was contained in the box FitzGerald sent him. It is possible, for instance, that a copy of *Six Dramas of Calderon* was not among the contents of the box. Shortly after FitzGerald's death, Wright wrote to Edmund Gosse, saying: "I asked one of his executors in case any copies of the suppressed translations from Calderon were found to secure me two. One of these was intended for you. The copies were found and I now have the pleasure of sending one for your acceptance."[10] Wright may have kept the other copy for himself and used it as the text for his edition. Support for this conjecture comes from the Wright edition's position with respect to substantive variants in the six Calderon plays; specifically, the Kerney and Bentham editions contain a number of such variants that do not appear in Wright's edition, which follows more closely the 1853 edition. Of course it is possible that in his final revision FitzGerald reverted to earlier ideas. It is more likely, however, that Wright possessed an uncorrected, or relatively uncorrected, copy.

George Bentham gives no explicit statement concerning the nature of his authorities. In general, it may be said that the Bentham edition reprints the several editions of those works that existed in more than one edition in FitzGerald's lifetime and over which the author had direct control. Bentham's practice here is rather perplexing, however. For he does not print the fourth edition of *The Rubáiyát* (1879), the third edition of *Salámán and Absál* (1879), or the second edition of *Agamemnon* (1876), each being the last edition published during FitzGerald's life. Instead he prints what he refers to as the fifth, fourth, and third edition of these, respectively. In other words, Bentham seems to refer to a posthumous edition of each of these works, rather than to an edition printed in FitzGerald's lifetime and annotated by him, and that posthumous edition appears to be Wright's edition of 1889, although Kerney's edition precedes Wright's by two years. It will be seen below how closely Bentham follows Wright in a number of particulars.

The text Bentham prints purports to be a quasi facsimile of one containing FitzGerald's corrections. That is, when showing that a change has been made, the Bentham edition prints the original version, then lines out the affected portion while printing any substitution above it in reduced type, a procedure we may represent

in this way: "Host [upon] *over* host, and foaming from the lip." The bracketed word is that which was originally printed, and the italicized word is the interlinear substitution. Again, however, Bentham's edition can mislead. On occasion the original version of a line is presented inaccurately, and in some instances the revision alone is printed.

Michael Kerney's edition states on the title page that it is "reprinted from the original impressions, with some corrections derived from his [FitzGerald's] own annotated copies." Although Kerney was not as close to FitzGerald as Wright was, he did have a part in the second edition of *Agamemnon*, as well as the fourth edition of **The Rubáiyát** and the third edition of **Salámán and Absál**, all of which were published by Bernard Quaritch. According to the *DNB* [*Dictionary of National Biography*] (XXII, 1162), Kerney served as Quaritch's chief cataloguer and also as his "trusted literary adviser." The phrase is intriguingly vague, but of one interpretation we can be sure: Kerney worked for a time as a publisher's reader, and as such he had something to say about a variety of details, including punctuation, accuracy, and even wording. Several of FitzGerald's letters to Quaritch, discussing among other things the preparation of the second edition of *Agamemnon*, reveal some of the give-and-take between the author and his publisher over such matters as a proposed book's appearance and content.[11] The letters also tell something of the relationship between author and publisher's reader, showing FitzGerald willing to defer to Kerney's judgment in some points and holding fast to his own in others. The Kerney edition is noteworthy in being the first edition of FitzGerald's collected works. It lacks, however, *The Mighty Magician, Such Stuff as Dreams Are Made Of,* and *The Downfall and Death of King Oedipus,* since Kerney was unable to obtain copies of these.

For the purpose of examining more closely some of the variants in the FitzGerald text, I have chosen those works that he singled out as possibly worthy of publication: *Agamemnon, The Downfall and Death of King Oedipus,* and *The Mighty Magician.* In addition I have included *Such Stuff as Dreams Are Made Of,* since it and *The Mighty Magician* were intended to be bound together as a single volume. Besides using the posthumous editions, I have drawn upon the Huntington Library, Harvard University's Houghton Library, and Colby College Library for copies of editions of the separate works published in FitzGerald's lifetime.[12]

AGAMEMNON

FitzGerald's translation of Aeschylus' *Agamemnon* was printed twice in his life. The first edition was not offered for public sale. Instead, copies were privately distributed to some of his friends and a number of other interested persons. The date of the first printing is usually given as 1865; however, A. M. Terhune offers evidence that it should properly be dated 1869.[13] FitzGerald made numerous revisions for the second edition, and it was published by Bernard Quaritch in 1876. Shortly after he furnished Quaritch with the copy for the second edition, FitzGerald remarked in a letter, as an afterthought: "I suppose I may as well see the proof: I can engage that there will be little—if anything to alter *anew*" (Wrentmore, p. 39). This is a curious statement, because in fact most of the alterations were made at the proof stage.[14]

Judging from FitzGerald's letters to Quaritch, as well as from the physical evidence of the book itself, there was an irregularity in the printing of the '76 edition, and it is a moot point whether even annotated copies contain all the revisions FitzGerald intended. In his statement of the book's collation, Prideaux does not include the signatures, and he erroneously gives the pagination as "pp. viii + 80."[15] A more detailed account would read: π^4 1^4 1^{*4} $2\text{-}10^4$, 48 leaves, pp. *i-iii* iv-vi *vii-viii 1* 2-16 9-79 *80* [=88]. It is apparent from this statement that signature 1*, comprising four leaves, was inserted after the rest of the book had been printed, with the result that pagination for eight pages was duplicated. One of FitzGerald's letters (Wrentmore, pp. 46-47) provides additional commentary that something was amiss:

> Yesterday I got home and found the Copy of *Agamemnon*—I must complain that *no* Revises were sent to me after the first Sheet, in spite of my repeatedly asking for them, having some slight alterations to make, which are now impossible, I suppose. And I mark at least *three mis*prints (pp. 66-67-82) in the copy sent.
>
> But there is yet worse. Between pp. 8-9 there is, I suppose, as much as *half a sheet* of Copy (printed, & revised by me) *left out*, as you will see by the Enclosed. All which Mr. Kernee [Kerney] will remember, if the Printer does not: and you will see for yourself at a glance, if you have time to bestow so much upon it.

Bentham's variorum is the only posthumous edition to print the first edition of *Agamemnon*. Bentham notes (II, 322), "The alterations in the text are found in FitzGerald's autograph in all copies of this edition known to me." These correspond with the eleven autograph corrections in the Huntington Library copy of the first edition, with one exception. While the word "fatal" is left unchanged on page 25 of the Huntington copy, it is lined out in Bentham. The word is also left standing in the Harvard and Colby copies. In addition, a comma after "Immortals" is left on page 25 of the Harvard and Colby copies, although it is struck out in the Huntington and silently deleted in Bentham. Here it is interesting to note that when FitzGerald revised a copy of the first edition that he sent to Quaritch to be used as copy in the printing of the second edition, he deleted neither the

comma nor "fatal." He remarked to Quaritch: "Herewith goes up *Agamemnon* whom (for one reason or another) I did not take up to revise until two days ago. I had not looked into it since it was printed" (Wrentmore, p. 43). The Harvard *Agamemnon* also differs from the others in not having the revisions "Dividing" for "That divides the" (11.4) and "of" for "and" (12.16). And at the bottom of page 54 of the Harvard, FitzGerald wrote as a substitute for line 13: "Aye, in a deadlier web than of *that* loom," whereas other copies read "*the* loom" (my italics). Besides silently correcting an occasional printer's error, Bentham is at variance with the first edition, either intentionally or otherwise, in several other instances, such as these examples: "I have" becomes "have I" (II.245.5), "Atreus" becomes "Athens" (247.21), "Chace" becomes "Chase" (251.7), "Drew" becomes "Draws" (251.22), "night" becomes "right" (278.3), "his" becomes "its" (278.7), and "civic" becomes "civil" (288.21).

Bentham contains many more alternations of the second edition of *Agamemnon,* but mostly in accidentals. In this respect Bentham is closer to Wright's edition of 1889 than to the '76 edition, and it will be remembered that Bentham refers to the text he prints as the "third edition." It is the practice of Wright's edition to print such contractions as "coucht," "look't," "slipt," and "launcht" as "couch'd," "look'd," "slipp'd," and "launch'd," respectively. Bentham follows Wright in this. Moreover, where Wright alters the '76 forms of "loos'd," "summoned," "bowed," "escap'd," and "unaveng'd" to "loosed," "summon'd," "bow'd," "escaped," and "unavenged," Bentham does the same. Wright evidently used for his base text an annotated copy of the second edition. Besides the accidentals just mentioned, his edition differs from the printed form of the second edition at a number of points, illustrated in the following full sampling:

> "ravin" for "raven" (VI.303.9)
>
> "Atreidae" for "Princes" (278.16)
>
> "Into the nostril of revolted Heav'n" for "Into the face of the revolted heavens" (306.21)
>
> "hath drest" for "has drest" (331.25)
>
> "Is slain?" for "Is slain;" (334.4)
>
> "Who, wrought by false suspicion to fix'd Hate, / From Argos out his younger brother drove" for "Who, when the question came of Whose the throne? / From Argos out his younger brother drove" (336.19-20).

In a footnote to the last, Wright has these lines as an alternate: "Who, first suspecting falsely, and anon / Detesting him his false suspicion wrong'd, & c." In all these, including the footnote, Bentham follows Wright. Bentham's edition does differ from Wright's and the second edition in printing "unfalter'd" for "unalter'd"

(III.222.10), and in repeating these variants we noted with respect to the first edition: "have I" for "I have," "Chase" for "Chace," and "Draws" for "Drew."

Little can be said of Kerney's edition of *Agamemnon*. Of the posthumous editions his is most faithful to the printed text of the '76 edition, differing only in a handful of accidentals. He must, therefore, have used an unannotated copy of the second edition.

The Downfall and Death of King Oedipus

Although not printed until 1880-81, FitzGerald's translation of Sophocles' two Oedipus plays is an expression of his long-time interest in the Greek dramatist. In a letter to E. B. Cowell, dated 27 August 1867, he tells of rereading the *Oedipus Coloneus* and "com[ing] to doat on the Play even more than I did before" (Wright, II, 234). It cannot have been long after this that he wrote a loose translation of the plays, for in a letter to W. W. Goodwin, written in 1878, he says: "I have had the Choephori, and Sophocles' two Oedi*puses* (!) lying by me these ten years, I believe, wrought into such shape as Agamemnon. They would do, I think, after some polishing, for some Magazine: but no Magazine would entertain them here, and I can have no more to do with Quaritch's separate publications, monstered by him in his Catalogues so as [to] make me ashamed. All these things have really to be done by the Right Man one day" (Wright, IV, 31).

Charles Eliot Norton evidently felt that FitzGerald himself was in fact the "Right Man," for he urged him on in the project, and in 1880 FitzGerald privately printed and sent to Norton part one, *Oedipus in Thebes*; in 1881 he completed, printed, and sent Norton part two, *Oedipus at Athens*. FitzGerald solicited Norton for suggestions, and in 1882 he sent him another corrected copy of both volumes. In one of his letters to Norton he included a twenty-seven line addition to the second part of the translation: "I herewith enclose you a sort of Choral Epilogue for the second Part, which you can stick in or not as you will. I cannot say much for it: but it came together in my head after last writing to you" (Wright, IV, 234).

Those copies of parts one and two, which FitzGerald sent Norton in 1880 and 1881, respectively, are in the Huntington Library. They contain pen and pencil revisions. In fact, revisions are in two hands, apparently FitzGerald's and Norton's. Norton made changes in pencil in both parts. In part one these involve punctuation, word order, an obvious omission of a word in the text, and an alternate form of three lines, which FitzGerald had suggested in a letter. In part two question marks are written in the margin beside several passages. Also, Norton made a number of changes involving substantives. FitzGerald's own annotations are in red ink in part one, and in pencil in part two. For part one he indicated changes in punctuation and substantives; he also included a note concerning Oedipus' self-conviction of the murder of Laius. Part two is more heavily annotated than part one, and here FitzGerald's revisions deal mostly with substantives.

Of the revisions made in these two copies, we may note three points concerning their relation to the text in Wright's edition: (1) In some cases, where both Wright and the first copies sent to North show revision at a common point, the substance of the revision may differ from one to the other. For example, the words "When his mad passion overpast" are substituted for four lines that have been lined out in the copy sent to Norton (*Oed. in Thebes,* 19.20-23), while the words "When his mad Passion having pass'd—" appear in Wright (VI.373.15). The lines "To live while yet I live, & after death / To lie entom'd beside their City gates" are substituted for a line in the copy sent to Norton (*Oed. at Athens,* 13.10), but Wright reads "To live what Life they leave me, and when dead, / Lie tomb'd outside—*outside,* I say—their Gates" (421.21-22). (2) In a number of instances Wright contains substantive variants with respect to the printed text of the first edition, whereas no change is indicated in the first two Norton copies. The first edition reading, "Through street and market-place, or by the tomb / Which shrouds Ismenus' sacred ashes—why" (*Oed. in Thebes,* 5.5-6), becomes in Wright:

> Through street and market, by the Temples twain
> Of Pallas, and before the Tomb that shrouds
> Ismenus' his prophetic ashes—why
>
> (355.5-7)

The line that was first printed "And life with all of us so much for-spent" (*Oed. in Thebes,* 24.14) becomes in Wright "And life with him at least so much for-spent" (379.14). (3) At several points the first copies FitzGerald sent Norton show revisions not found in Wright. The words "For" and "to" are lined out of the phrase "For Oedipus to ask," and "That" and "shd" are written in the margin (*Oed. at Athens,* 12.3). Wright does not alter the original printing. The word "back" is offered in place of the lined-out "home" (*Oed. at Athens,* 13.8), whereas Wright makes no change.

Bentham's edition follows the first edition more closely than does Wright's in the matter of accidentals. His treatment of substantive variants follows Wright, however. There are a few points at which Bentham is at variance with both Wright and the first edition. Most of these are in accidentals, but there are some substantive variants.

The following is a substantial sampling of variants found among Wright's and Bentham's editions of *Oedipus in Thebes,* and that copy which FitzGerald sent

Norton in March 1880. For each example I give first the printed version of the 1880 edition, together with the page and line number, and then any variants. The printed version of the first edition is designated "A"; annotations are designated either "N," for those in Norton's hand, or "F," for those in FitzGerald's hand; Wright and Bentham are "W" and "B," respectively. While B normally gives the original reading in A lined out, with the corrected reading above, my collation notes only the corrected form in B.

> (Key: Restlessly pacing up and down all day, (A.6.37)
>   Restlessly all day pacing up and down, (W, B)

signifies no annotation in the copy sent to Norton, while Wright and Bentham print the same variant.

> Invoking all the Gods withhold from him (A.15.5)
> The Gods invoking to withhold from him (F, W, B)

signifies an annotation in FitzGerald's hand, concurring with the readings in Wright and Bentham.

> Then leaving him to languish for the son
>   (A.33.23, W)
> Then leaving him to languish for his son (B)

signifies a variant in Bentham only.)

1. Restlessly pacing up and down all day, (A.6.37)
    Restlessly all day pacing up and down, (W, B)

2. Invoking all the Gods withhold from him (A.15.5)
    The Gods invoking to withhold from him (F, W, B)

3. And whose live presence is the death of all.
    (A.16.11, W)
    And whose live presence is the death to all. (B)

4. Before the single word—word which you alone
    (A.16.18)
    Before the single word—which you alone (W, B)

5. Have claimed it for himself before you came,
    (A.24.9)
    Have seized it for his own before you came, (W, B)

6. Unjust, of little moment to us all! (A.24.16)
    Unjust, of little moment unto all! (W, B)

7. Within; and she that by that altar stands
    (A.32.19, W)
    Within; and she that by the altar stands (B)

8. Than leaving him to languish for the son
    (A.33.23, W)
    Than leaving him to languish for his son (B)

9. As tenderly as any mother might,
    With those rough hands of his he laid in mine
    (A.36.8-9)

    With those rough hands of his he laid in mine
    As tenderly as any mother might, (W, B)

10. Of Laius ere he left them. (A.37.17)

Of Laius then our Ruler. (F)
Of Laius then our Master. (W, B)

11. From him the craggy height, (A.39.9, B)
    For him the craggy height, (F, W)

12. Has somewhat dimm'd both eyes and memory.
    (A.40.15, W)
    Has somewhat dimm'd my eyes and memory. (B)

13. Sees with his eyes, and well remembers you.
    (A.40.18)
    Sees, and recalls in you the man of yore. (W, B)

14. What shall you now not hear, what not behold,
    Of horror in the palace of your Kings,
    (A.44.10-11)

    What shall you hear—what not behold—of such
    Pollution in the Palace of your Kings, (W, B)

15. Which having seen such things, he cried,
    henceforth
    Should in the night of Hades look on those
    He loath'd to look on, and behold no more
    Those who in life were dearest to his eyes.
    (A.45.17-20)

    Which having seen such things, henceforth,
    he said,
    Should never by the light of day behold
    Those whom he loved, nor in the after dark
    Of Hades, those he loathed to look upon. (N)

    Which having seen such things, henceforth,
    he said,
    Should in the light of day behold no more
    Those whom he loved, nor, in the after-dark
    Of Hades, those he loathed, to look upon. (W, B)

16. To such a pitch of power and glory rose,
    As not a King but envied his estate.
    Now to that depth of degradation sunk
    As not a wretch but may commiserate.
    (A.46.5-8)

    So greatly ruled, and rose to such Renown
    As not a King but envied: now by Fate
    To such a Depth precipitated down
    As not a Wretch but may commiserate. (W, B)

Three of the foregoing require brief comment. Example 11: For his choruses FitzGerald relied heavily, though not wholly, on a translation by Robert Potter. Potter's translation was first published in 1788, and two more editions appeared after his death: one in 1808, the other in 1813. I have examined the first two editions, but not the third, which is the edition FitzGerald evidently used. Sense demands, and at least the first two editions of Potter print, "For." Example 15: FitzGerald suggested a revised form of lines 18-20, in a letter to Norton. The latter copied the revision in his copy and added in parentheses, "Letter of August 5, 1881." Example 16: FitzGerald wrote the version of the final chorus that was printed in the first edition. But when he sent *Oedipus in Thebes* to Norton, he wrote, in a letter dated 4 March 1880: "The Choruses which I believe are thought fine by Scholars, I have left to old Potter to supply, as I was hopeless of making anything of them; pasting, you see, his 'Finale' over that which I had tried" (Bentham, VI, xi). The clipping from Potter is indeed to be found in that Norton copy of the play now in the Huntington Library. Wright and Bentham revert to the version FitzGerald originally had printed, except for the revision of lines 5-8.

THE MIGHTY MAGICIAN AND SUCH STUFF AS DREAMS ARE MADE OF

FitzGerald's translations of these two plays by Calderson were first printed in 1865. The two seem intended as parts of a single project, for the collation is continuous from one to the other. The plays were bound together in only a few copies, however, a point on which Prideaux is worth quoting: "It is stated in the 'Catalogue of the Library of Mr. Edmund Gosse' that the plays were printed separately, and more copies were distributed of the former than the latter. As the collation begins with signature B, it seems probable it was intended that a general title-page should be prefixed, but no copy is known with one. . . . FitzGerald kept the copies of these plays in his own hands, and . . . bound up several copies of them . . . for presentation to his friends. In a letter to Mrs. Kemble . . . he wrote that he had about a hundred copies of the Calderon plays printed" (pp.24-25). That he also distributed each play separately is confirmed by a letter to R. C. Trench: "I took up three sketched out Dramas, two of Calderon, and have licked the two Calderons into some sort of shape of my own, without referring to the Original. One of them goes by this Post to your Grace; and when I tell you the other is no other than your own 'Life's a Dream' you won't wonder at my sending the present one on Trial, both done as they are in the same lawless, perhaps impudent, way" (Wright, II, 190).

The four annotated copies of these Calderon plays that I have seen—one each at Colby College and Harvard, two at the Huntington Library—display a range in number of annotations. The Harvard copy contains the least, with two. The Colby copy and one of the Huntington copies are identical in number (seven) and nature of annotations. The other Huntington copy is more extensively annotated, and it represents a later state in FitzGerald's corrections of the plays. The annotations, especially those in this last copy, show that he went through the plays with some care, even to the extent of deleting a dash or substituting another form of punctuation for it. He was obviously sensible of how such differences in punctuation would produce a shift in nuances, the substitution of a colon for a dash, for instance, tightening a line, making it more decisive. In

some other cases his annotations reflect a lack of decisiveness; and at one point he reached a decision to omit a line only after two forms of the line—one of them his own, the other taken from Nicholas Rowe's play *Jane Shore*—had been tried.

But while FitzGerald is attentive to small details, his attention seems directed at certain kinds of details. Most of his revisions affect style, and occasionally he corrects a printer's error. He did not notice all such errors, though, and in general he seems not to pick up the occasional grammatical lapse. This is consistent with an admission he made in a letter to Wright (IV, 182), in connection with *The Downfall and Death of King Oedipus*: "I want you to be so good as to look it [the proof] over, not to correct printers' Blunders, but mine, as regards obscurity, or bad grammar, which I am apt to fall into by close packing." While possibly FitzGerald made all the corrections in the copy Wright used as his base text, it is at least equally likely that Wright himself made a few changes.

One class of variants in Wright may be attributed to house style. We find "perish'd" (W) / "perisht" ('65), "stopp'd" (W) / "stopt" ('65), and "vanish'd" (W) / "vanisht" ('65), among others. One can be less certain about punctuation. In general Wright punctuates more closely in the use of commas; more often than not he substitutes question marks for the exclamation marks that appear in the '65 text. Bentham sometimes follows Wright in accidentals, sometimes the '65 text.

Below is a table of variants that occur among four copies of the first edition of *The Mighty Magician* and *Such Stuff as Dreams Are Made Of,* and Wright and Bentham. I include all of the substantive variants that I found, but I exclude accidental variants peculiar to Wright and Bentham. As in the table for *The Downfall and Death of King Oedipus,* "A" signifies the first edition as printed, and "W" and "B" = Wright and Bentham, respectively. In addition, "C" = Colby, "D" = Harvard, "E" = Huntington copy with fewer annotations, and "F" = more heavily annotated Huntington copy.

1. and mortal Leda laid; (A.11.31)
   and mortal Leda lay; (W, B)

2. Which time and fond tradition consecrates; (A.12.10)
   Which time and fond tradition consecrate; (W, B)

3. their fathers', (A.23.4, B)
   their father's, (W)

4. to let you in, (A.30.37, W, B)
   to let you in; (F)

5. But lord of nature's secret, (A.31.1, W, B)
   But lord of yet coyer, (F)

6. the very power of him (A.31.3, W, B)
   the very power of Him (F)

7. into the foaming plain; (A.31.39, W, B)
   into one foaming plain; (F)

8. Like a thin cobweb spun 'twixt sea and sky;
   (A.33.6, W, B)
   Like a thin cobweb spun Arachne-web-like; (F)

9. the jewel hid inside. (A.33.15, W, B)
   the treasure hid inside. (F)

10. Obedient to my moon-like magic flow: (A.35.15)
    Obsequious of my moon-like magic flow:
    (C, E, F, W, B)

11. At her dreaming supply (A.37.33)
    At her dreaming ear supply (C, D, E, F, W, B)

12. With the dark hair that was so white upon
    (A.40.2, W, B)
    His once white hair now flowing dark adown (F)

13. Up and about him creeps, as one has seen
    (A.40.5, W, B)
    About him creeps and creeps, as one has seen (F)

14. Round whom her deadly-deathless arms once
    close. (A.40.20)
    Round whom her deadly-deathless arms enclose.
    (C, E, W)
    Whom once her deadly-deathless arms enclose.
    (F, B)

15. Lived eyes that but re-doubled vain desire.
    (A.52.26, W, B)
    Burn'd eyes that but re-doubled vain desire. (F)

16. But not as then?—
                I understand you not—(A.56.7, W, B)
    But not as then?
                I understand you not. (F)

17. No—(A.56.9, W, B)
    No: (F)

18. I know not—(A.56.15, W, B)
    I know not. (F)

19. Why you yourself, Justina.—Oh my God!
    It flashes all across me!—
    What, all your life long giving God his due,
    (A.56.16-18)
    Why you yourself, Justina.—Oh my God!
    What, all your life long giving God his due,
    (C, E, F, W, B)

20. Aye, Cipriano—(A.56.19, W, B)
    Aye, Cipriano; (F)

21. Shepherd and Saviour—(A.56.24, W, B)
    Shepherd and Saviour! (F)

22. Amen! Amen!—(A.57.1, W, B)
    Amen! Amen! (F)

23. and yet no shame—(A.57.2, W, B)
    and yet no shame to fear—(F)

24. Unless with your forgiveness in my hand—
    But say you forgive me!—(F)
        Just.   I forgive! (A.58.16-17)

    Unless with your forgiveness in my hand—
    Forgive me!—But forgive me!
        Just.   I forgive! (C, E)

    Unless with your forgiveness—
        Just.   I forgive! (F, W, B)

25. nor the stars (A.59.7)
    nor the star[16] (F, W, B)

26. The other only suffer'd (A.59.23)
    Which the other only suffer'd (C, E, F, W, B)

27. and kick me oft behind, (A.68.13)
    and kick me off behind, (W, B)

28. twirling through the mask (A.75.4)
    twiring through the mask (C, D, E, F, W, B)

29. But surely, surely—(A.77.5, W, B)
    twiring through the mask (C, D, E, F, W, B)
    But surely, surely—[*A low, long, note of a Trumpet
    within*] (F)

30. that that wept (A.83.36, B)
    that which wept (W)

31. handed him upon their knees (A.91.30, W, B)
    handed me upon their knees (F)

32. Not knowing what she listens or repeats.
    (A.93.11, W, B)
    Unconscious what she listens or repeats. (F)

33. as much your Highness', (A.94.32, B)
    as much as your Highness', (W)

34. Waits but a word (A.96.32)
    Wait but a word (W, B)

35. *Enter* ROSAURA *suddenly* (A.99.sd, W, B)
    Enter suddenly ROSAURA, *drest as a Court Page*
    (F)

36. that dream must be.—(A.113.27, W, B)
    which dream must be.—(F)

37. in that eternal life (A.113.31, W, B)
    To some back platform—(W)

38. With sentinels, that pacing up and down,
    (A.115.23)
    With sentinels a-pacing up and down, (W, B)

39. To some black platform—(A.115.31, B)
    the savage he fore-read (E, F, W, B)

40. Which the first air of waking consciousness
    (A.122.6, W, B)
    Which First air of full selfconsciousness (F)

41. drive the Dream, (A.125.11, W, B)
    if Dream drive, (F)

42. upon the other side (A.127.8)
    on the other side (W, B)

43. the savage he fore-read, (A.128.21)
    the savage he fore-read (E, F, W, B)

44. When Dreaming with the Night shall pass away.
    (A.131.24, W, B)
    When with Night the Dream shall pass away. (F)

At best it is unlikely that FitzGerald finally changed his mind about those revisions that are peculiar to F, say, and that he restored those original readings that are kept in Wright and Bentham. Of the material surveyed here, F shows the most signs of being "corrected in the way that [he] would have [these Calderon plays] appear." Therefore, barring the discovery of evidence to the contrary, such as yet other revisions that suggest an even later reworking, F should be the exemplar for a critical text of the plays.

A more extensive treatment of variants in FitzGerald's works would be within the purview of a critical edition. In the meantime there is still something to be gained from even a partial account of the variants. They show us FitzGerald at work revising. Some revisions are of course a comment on what the poet has suffered at the hands of the printer. But others constitute a broader access to the poet's mind and back in turn to his art. By studying variants such as those present in the translations of Aeschylus, Sophocles, and Calderon, we may not, perhaps, be able to demonstrate FitzGerald's final intentions. But even to extend our knowledge of his uncertainty is to gain some further insight into his achievement.

Notes

1. Bernard Weinberg, "Editing Balzac: A Problem in Infinite Variation," in *Editing Nineteenth-Century Texts,* ed. John Robson (Toronto: Univ. of Toronto Press, 1967), pp. 60-70.

2. E. A. J. Honigmann, *The Stability of Shakespeare's Text* (London: Edward Arnold, 1965).

3. See Robert L. Beare, "Notes on the Text of T. S. Eliot: Variants from Russell Square," *SB* [*Studies in Bibliography*], 9 (1957), 21-49, and William H. Marshall, "The Text of T. S. Eliot's 'Gerontion,'" *SB,* 4 (1951-52), 213-17.

4. George Bentham, ed., *The Variorum and Definitive Edition of the Poetical and Prose Writings of Edward FitzGerald* (New York: Doubleday, Page and Company, 1902), II, xvi.

5. William Aldis Wright, ed., *Letters and Literary Remains of Edward FitzGerald* (London: Macmillan and Company, 1902), IV, 189.

6. I am indebted to Mr. William W. Hill, curator of rare books and manuscripts at Colby College Library, for furnishing me with a copy of this letter.

7. Honigmann, p.168.

8. Frederic E. Faverty, ed., *The Victorian Poets: A Guide to Research* (Cambridge, Mass.: Harvard Univ. Press, 1968), pp. 139-40.

9. W. W. Greg, "The Rationale of Copy-Text," *SB,* 3 (1950-51), 19.

10. E. H. M. Cox, ed., *The Library of Edmund Gosse: Being a Descriptive and Bibliographical Catalogue of a Portion of His Collection* (London: Dulau and Company, 1924), p. 124.

11. C. Quaritch Wrentmore, ed., *Letters from Edward FitzGerald to Bernard Quaritch: 1853 to 1883* (London: Bernard Quaritch, 1926).

12. I have relied on microfilm of the Harvard material, excerpts from which are published here by permission of the Harvard College Library, and I have used xeroxed pages of the Colby material.

13. Alfred M. Terhune, *The Life of Edward FitzGerald* (New Haven: Yale Univ. Press, 1947), p. 323.

14. The proofs now at Harvard's Houghton Library show this.

15. W. F. Prideaux, *Notes for a Bibliography of Edward FitzGerald* (London: Frank Hollings, 1901), p. 36.

16. Someone has erased the final "s" in "stars" in F. The letter is barely discernible at the spot where the paper has been rubbed. The same thing has occurred with a comma after "fore-read" in E (see below, example 43). I cannot be certain of the status of D in these two instances or of C in the latter, since the pages on which the erasures occur are not among the materials sent me. Even if they were, the erasures might not show up on a xeroxed or microfilmed copy.

Michael S. Helfand (essay date autumn 1976)

SOURCE: Helfand, Michael S. "FitzGerald and Minor Mid-Victorian Poets." *Victorian Poetry* 14, no. 3 (autumn 1976): 221-23.

[*In the following excerpt, Helfand contends that because of the erratic manner in which FitzGerald handled revisions to the* Rubáiyát, *the work is textually unstable.*]

Gerald D. Browne has written the most interesting study of Edward FitzGerald's work this year. "Edward FitzGerald's Revisions" (*PBSA* [*Papers of the Bibliographical Society of America*] 69: 94-112) ignores the *Rubaiyat* and instead discusses the changes FitzGerald made in the translations he hoped he would be remembered for, *Agamemnon, The Downfall and Death of King Oedipus* (two parts), *The Mighty Magician* and *Such Stuff as Dreams Are Made Of.* Browne says that these revisions reveal what was also apparent from changes made in the first four editions of the *Rubaiyat,* that "FitzGerald was a most conscientious artist continually seeking to improve his work and meticulous in details of phrasing and punctuation." The poet's changes were almost entirely stylistic. Yet meticulous attention to artistry gave way to carelessness when FitzGerald incorporated these revisions into a new edition. Partially because of failing eyesight, FitzGerald usually postponed revisions until his works were in print. Sometimes the corrections or revisions are not the same in all copies of a specific work and sometimes the revisions did not become part of later printings at all. As a result FitzGerald's work suffers from "textual instability" because "editors of the collected works have incorporated some, but not all, of these changes, and they do not agree with one another in the changes they do include." Browne concludes that future editors of the poet should inform the reader how the problem of variants has been handled. None of the existing editions do this. We clearly need a critical edition which would provide an extensive treatment of variants. . . .

Daniel Schenker (essay date spring 1981)

SOURCE: Schenker, Daniel. "Fugitive Articulation: An Introduction to *The Rubáiyát of Omar Khayyám.*" *Victorian Poetry* 19, no. 1 (spring 1981): 49-64.

[*In the following essay, Schenker recaps the critical history of the* Rubáiyát.]

Over a half century ago Ezra Pound remarked that FitzGerald's re-creation of Omar Khayyám was one of the finest works bequeathed by a generation of Victorian poets.[1] Today, the *Rubáiyát* receives little attention from critics, although the poem is frequently reprinted in sumptuously designed and illustrated trade editions. Probably few poems are so widely circulated (whether read I do not know) and yet so rarely talked about. The situation, of course, was very different in 1861 when Dante Gabriel Rossetti purchased his first copy from London publisher and bookseller Bernard Quaritch. The changing critical fortune of the *Rubáiyát* is one of its more interesting features, and in the first part of this essay I want to make a few brief remarks on the history of the poem. I begin with a hypothetical comparison that will outline some of the difficulties we have reading the *Rubáiyát.*

Let us imagine two hours of classroom discussion, one for the *Rubáiyát* and one for an unimpeachable contemporary masterpiece, T. S. Eliot's "The Love Song of J. Alfred Prufrock." One can easily guess which poem will yield the more fruitful hour of instruction. Even naive readers in our day have some idea where to begin with an Eliot poem: his work signals its own incomprehensibility and quickly shifts the reader into the interrogative mood. Consider, for example, "In the room the women come and go / Talking of Michelangelo." Someone will notice that the doggerel meter and foolishly simple vocabulary are inappropriate for such an oracularly composed line—oracular because the words appear out of the unexplained gap that twice punctuates the verse. Nor is this empty space without significance. The hiatus gives an audience time ("There will be time, there will be time") to cast about: how can this peculiar intrusion follow from the preceding monologue? Is this still Prufrock's voice (if it ever was)? Does "Michelangelo" fit the sense, or is it just a seductively fitting rhyme? And *what* room? The novice's initiation into the mysteries of the poem is well under way.

Our class members will be baffled—disconcertingly baffled into silence—by the seeming clichés and trivialities that are the substance of the *Rubáiyát.* Time is also a central motif in this poem, but it slips away at a leisurely pace, without the hint of life or death imperative in Prufrock's "'Do I dare?' and 'do I dare?'" The measured repetitions of quatrain and white space in the *Rubáiyát* are the soothing music of a complacent universe. As we linger through these lines near the end of the poem,

> Would but the Desert of the Fountain yield
> One glimpse—if dimly, yet indeed, reveal'd,
>   To which the fainting Traveller might spring,
>   As springs the trampled herbage of the field![2]

> (XCVII)

fainting Travellers that *we* are after ninety-six quatrains of enervation, the verse does not impress us as unusual in meter or expression nor otherwise deserving of scrutiny. Nothing in its tone alerts us to a conundrum here, the cryptic "Desert of the Fountain." No unorthodox gesture interrupts the accretion of verses, nor does the harmonious assemblage of words in the quatrain encourage an investigation of this anomaly. *Some* meaning is easily enough reconstructed: fainting travellers *do* have mirages in the desert, so why not a verbal mirage? And the key word "spring" not only evokes all the life sustaining fountains that bubble up through the parched earth, but recalls the desideratum for rebirth that underlies the sentiment and sentimentality of the *Rubáiyát.* If all else fails, the inversion can be blamed on a conjectural peculiarity in the original Persian. Nothing to be alarmed about.

I will pursue at a later time this question of why we fail to respond to the **Rubáiyát** as a work of serious literary art. For now we will satisfy ourselves with an empirical glance at the critical history of the poem. I think that we can identify three approximate stages in the public reception of the **Rubáiyát** that mark its progress from exotic Prophecy to Victorian gimcrack.

Anyone who has spent some time with the poem probably knows the story of how copies of FitzGerald's translation sat many months in Quaritch's pennybox, "having proved hopelessly unsaleable at the published price of a shilling,"[3] until they were brought to the attention of Rossetti and of others through him. The still youthful Pre-Raphaelites and their allies were searching for alternatives to the pieties of mid-century English cultural life, and a note of quiet desperation became progressively more evident in their work throughout this period. By the time of the discovery of the **Rubáiyát,** Rossetti had long abandoned the naturalistic first principles of the original Brotherhood for the sake of his fancy. In the early 1850s, he began painting a scene reminiscent of the brighter moments in a Keatsian ode (*The Bower Meadow*, 1850-72) when all that lay before him were the rotting leaves of a Kentish autumn. Explaining this phenomenon he wrote to a friend: "The fact is, between you and me, that the leaves on the trees I have to paint here appear red, yellow etc. to my eyes; and as of course I know them on that account to be really of a vivid green, it seems rather annoying that I cannot do them so: my subject shrieking aloud for Spring."[4] Algernon Swinburne, a later member of Rossetti's circle, had become by 1861 a disciple of the Marquis de Sade, seeking transcendence in the morally perverse. As he was primarily interested in the **Rubáiyát** as a work of frustrated iconoclasm, Swinburne chose to highlight the angrier (and somewhat unrepresentative) quatrains of the poem, such as number LXXXI, his personal favorite:

O Thou, who Man of baser Earth didst make
And ev'n with Paradise devise the Snake:
    For all the Sin wherewith the Face of Man
    Is blacken'd—Man's forgiveness give—and take!

A mellower Swinburne still had transcendence in mind when he praised the **Rubáiyát** near the end of his career, speaking now in a more traditionally religious idiom: "Every quatrain, though it is something so much more than graceful or distinguished or elegant, is also, one may say, the sublimation of elegance, the apotheosis of distinction, the transfiguration of grace."[5] Perhaps more telling of the impression the poem made than any critical appreciation was Swinburne's borrowing of the verse form FitzGerald adapted from the Persian for his reworking of the bizarre and erotic Tannhäuser legend, his "Laus Veneris":

There is a feverish famine in my veins;
Below her bosom where a crushed grape stains
    The white and blue, there my lips caught and clove
An hour since, and what mark of me remains?

O dare not touch her, lest the kiss
Leave my lips charred. Yea, Lord, a little bliss,
    Brief bitter bliss, one hath for a great sin;
Nathless thou knowest how sweet a thing it is.

                                                        (ll. 165-172)

The transition to social respectability is discernible in the first review of the poem written in America (appearing fully a decade after the initial publication of the **Rubáiyát,**) by Charles Eliot Norton. Ironically, the exoticism of the work impressed him with the homeliness of its sentiments: Omar's message had universal application regardless of its origin. Norton proclaimed that "in its English dress it reads like the latest and freshest expression of the perplexity and of the doubt of the generation to which we ourselves belong."[6] The meaning was so plain that the critic's own voice trailed off after a few initial remarks and the review concluded with a selection of quatrains from FitzGerald's text without further commentary or elucidation.

But neither perplexity nor perversity seems to have been responsible for the wide appeal of the **Rubáiyát** as it went through third and fourth editions. Such phenomena as the Omar Khayyám societies that sprang up in England and America during this period sought rather to institutionalize a cult of spiritual resignation. Their intuition was not unsound, for certainly withdrawal from the world was a dominant theme in FitzGerald's own life. In a letter to Edward Cowell, his close friend and Persian teacher, FitzGerald wrote that his translation of Omar's rubaiyat had been "most ingeniously tesselated into a sort of Epicurean Eclogue in a Persian Garden" (November 2, 1858; Richardson, p. 606). The garden, in fact, is the preferred locale in many of FitzGerald's literary productions, both originals and translations. In this setting, the man who seems to have felt the onset of old age by his middle twenties because he could not escape the banal awareness that all things must pass indulged his predeliction for melancholy. In 1857, he wrote to Cowell: *"July 1st*—June over! A thing I think of with Omar-like sorrow. And the Roses here are blowing—and going—as abundantly as even in Persia" (Richardson, p. 600). The popular audience of the day must have responded to the domestic possibilities of these Epicurean sentiments. Although we never hear FitzGerald muse upon the simple pleasures of home life, his garden eclogue was nonetheless easily assimilated to the beleaguered institutions of home and family. Walter Houghton, examining Victorian attitudes on this subject, has written:

[The home] was much more than a house where one stopped at night for temporary rest and recreation—or procreation—in the midst of a busy career. It was a place apart, a walled garden, in which certain virtues too easily crushed by modern life could be preserved, and certain desires of the heart too much thwarted be fulfilled.[7]

Under this aegis, the poem that was ignored in the pennybox by all but the young Turks in the world of letters became fit for inclusion on the bookshelves of millions of burgher households. People longed for the repose and security of a "walled garden," and FitzGerald, who knew his gardens as only an English country gentleman could, almost by accident provided them with a mental close in faraway Persia that they might retreat to again and again. However, the poem never eliminates all temptation to the more subversive counter-readings, and this I think is another reason for its success: for when the stresses of the day are so great that the *Rubáiyát* cannot be accepted as an emblem of domestic stability, the besieged master or mistress of the house may guiltlessly indulge himself or herself in a momentary escape into its amoral world without husbands or wives or fathers or children or even Englishmen (and yet how English!). FitzGerald's achievement is noteworthy: neither Rossetti nor Swinburne nor Tennyson ever constructed a garden that all at once answered so many pressing needs.

The majority of FitzGerald's published works are translations. This reclusive squire had catholic interests, ranging through classical, Romance, and oriental literatures; now Islamic allegory, now the repartee of the Spanish gracioso might occupy his talents. Refined promiscuity of taste is perhaps endemic to the genius of any great translator. The man or woman who adopts the role of creative artist with regard to his or her peculiar art may take up a polemical stance to reform if necessary prevailing standards of judgment. A translator, however, is bound Odysseus-like to furnish suitable blood for the shades of the departed dead so that they may be readily comprehended by the living. While poets are free to seek after absolutes, translators must look to a golden mean: their work must be both original *and* typical:

> Translations—exactly because of the peculiar conditions of their manufacture—are of special interest to a critic of poetry; for they show him in the baldest form the assumptions about poetry shared by readers and poets. To paraphrase Collingwood, every poem is an unconscious answer to the question: "What is a poem?" But the question is never the same question, any more than the question "What is a man?" is the same question when asked in 1200 or 1600 or 1900. . . . The study of translations, especially from a literature produced by a civilization very different from our own, [is] one of the simplest ways of showing what is expected at various times in answer to the question of "What is poetry?"[8]

In the last third of the nineteenth century, FitzGerald provided a nearly perfect response to the final query, demonstrating his uncanny knack in the *Rubáiyát* for drawing level with his age without exceeding it. An epitome of contemporary writing, the poem is also a convenient benchmark for surveying neighboring precincts of art and expression: the *Rubáiyát* appeared midway between the death of Byron and the advent of Modernism, and is correctly interpreted as a document both of retrospection and of some prophetic power.

FitzGerald could be as successful in maintaining a status quo in literature as he was in preserving an archaic policy of land management on his estates in Victorian Suffolk. Just whose status quo was often hard to discern, though it had a familiar ring whatever it was. The editor of the *Athenaeum* apparently believed that an early FitzGerald composition, **"The Meadows in Spring,"** came from the hand of Charles Lamb. Writing to a correspondent sometime later, Lamb himself pointed to the mistake, but confessed that he envied the writer "because I feel I could have done something like [him].'"[9] Many years after he had written **"Bredfield Hall,"** another original lyric, FitzGerald cleared up a mystery for an old friend, who running across the poem had thought it to be Tennyson's. In a letter, he admitted its authorship

> only to prevent you wasting any more trouble looking through Tennyson for those verses. . . . No; I wrote them along with many others about my old home more than forty years ago, and they recur to me also as I wander the Garden or the Lawn. Therefore, I suppose there is something native in them, though your referring to A. T. proves that I was echoing him.
>
> (Cited in Groome, p. 109).

These brief remarks on the status quo in literature point to a distinction between the translating methods of FitzGerald and his chief inheritor in the next century, Ezra Pound. Both did their best work with the aid of a second language, but in the end Pound strove to escape the voices of past and present. Though committed to tradition, he took risks and asked his audience to do the same: the reassuring Canto I lay at the edge of a familiar horizon beyond which the reader is expected to journey. FitzGerald, when he gave an English life to a play or poem, was more careful to speak in the recognizable cadences of an accustomed language. Thus was he drawn to little projects like the cataloguing of the seacoast dialect of his native Suffolk (which in reality was much derived from the speech of "Posh," a seafaring buddy of his). Yet he did foreshadow Pound in his understanding that the translator should not so much fulfill a role as occupy an office—that of an impromptu shaman before the ell-square pitkin. FitzGerald wrote to Cowell: "At all cost, a thing must live, with a transfusion of one's own worse life if one can't retain the originals better."[10] He did not want to produce imitations of the originals, and although he decided to remain conservative in his choice of idiom, his finished products are incontestably English. If his work suffered at the hands of some nineteenth-century reviewers it was because, ironically, his eye was on the living Englishman and not the dead foreigner. "As for Poetry," he commented in the "Prefatory Letter" to his *The Downfall and Death of King Oedipus,* "I pretend to very little more than representing the old Greek in sufficiently readable English verse: and whatever I have omitted, added, or altered, has been done with a view to the English reader of Today, without questioning what was fittest for an Athenian theatre more than two thousand years ago."[11] Of course, this statement of purpose was wholly out of step with a Victorian literary establishment that believed the translator should make the reader aware of the abyss separating his language and culture from that of his predecessors: thus Browning's jawbreaker of an *Agamemnon.* FitzGerald's motto, "Better a live sparrow than a stuffed eagle," leaves us with the amusing paradox of a private man, publishing anonymously and indifferent to a vulgar audience, who became the most renowned popularizer of an exotic literature in nineteenth-century England.

Collections and "editions" rank second in importance among FitzGerald's works, although he usually performed the functions of redactor and translator simultaneously. He felt obliged to do whatever was necessary to keep something he valued alive. Sometimes just publishing a version of an overlooked work was sufficient, as when he brought out his translations of Calderon's more obscure plays. But even here there was tinkering of the kind best exemplified in his *King Oedipus,* for just as the Victorians had no qualms about making architectural "improvements" in old cathedrals to render them more medieval looking, so FitzGerald saw nothing wrong in tightening up the tragic economy of a Greek drama. He honed Sophocles' plays with a mind to leave "the terrible story to develop itself no further than needs it must to be intelligible, without being descanted, dwelt, and dilated on, after the fashion of Greek Tragedy" (Wright, III, 165). George Crabbe's *Tales of the Hall* was edited with the hope of achieving a similar reduction, and contains prose summaries of sections FitzGerald thought unduly prolix. FitzGerald, rural aristocrat, was unwittingly laboring for the same cybernetic man his contemporary Herbert Spencer had in mind when he formulated the theory that "a reader or listener has at each moment but a limited amount of mental power available."[12] Condensation was as much the key to success in literature as in business in a culture founded upon the cardinal sin of impatience. A biographer tells us that in his later years FitzGerald took an especial delight in planning abbreviations "of big books like *Clarissa Harlowe* and Wesley's *Journal.*"[13]

"How truly language must be regarded as a hindrance to thought," said Spencer (p. 3). FitzGerald, too, had proceeded in his redactions as if each word meant a further enervation of psychic energy. Omar Khayyám, whose impeccable sense of decorum had struck a chord in FitzGerald's soul, was thus an attractive figure for a more pragmatic reason: noted Professor Cowell, "He [Omar] has left us fewer lines than Gray" (cited in Heron-Allen, p. viii).

Before turning to the text itself, a comment on the first and final editions of the *Rubáiyát.*

Meditating over the infant Hartley Coleridge, Wordsworth inadvertently charted the next hundred years of English poetry. Wordsworth's typical inheritor in the nineteenth century would proceed "As if his whole vocation / Were endless imitation" ("Ode: Intimations of Immortality," ll. 107-108). Romantic mellowed into Victorian art. In the process, Tennyson and Browning turned the ambition of the poet from gaining distinction in philosophy toward achieving excellence in "conning a part." By 1909, the appearance of a volume unabashedly entitled *Personae* was anticlimactic. Edward FitzGerald, translator, and as such barometer of mid-century poetic decorum, was not immune to the impulse. His first *Rubáiyát,* the one that sat in Quaritch's penny-box, was as much soliloquy as eclogue, and was not ashamed to say so. The speaker in the poem had a name: the directive "come with old Khayyám" occurs twice in the original version. But with recognition, FitzGerald seems to have consciously decided to remove all traces of intimacy. In the final text, the name Khayyám is mentioned nowhere except in the title. This pattern of revision is the key to all the changes FitzGerald made through five editions. The avant-garde admirers of the poem, Swinburne most notably among them, regretted these alterations which blurred the dramatic immediacy of the original for the sake of an impression of timeless utterance. As the nineteenth century wore on, the poem became more and more a reactionary document, insuring its place in popular literary imagination. I should add that with retrenchment, this work seems to have completed the project Wordsworth had left unfinished: the *Rubáiyát* became the long-awaited great philosophical poem for many like Professor Norton, who, suffering the disorientations of their era, looked to this walled garden of soothing aphorism for reassurance, if not indeed vindication.

The aphoristic quality of the *Rubáiyát* is at the heart of our inability—or disinclination—to say anything about the poem. Speech here is robbed of its potential for innovation just as the New Word of the prophets is continually reduced to an old tale or proverb:

> The Revelations of Devout and Learn'd
> Who rose before us, and as Prophets burn'd
>   Are all but Stories, which, awoke from Sleep
> They told their comrades, and to Sleep return'd.
>
> (LXV)

"Waste not your Hour, nor in the vain pursuit / Of This and That endeavor and dispute," Omar has counselled in a preceding quatrain (LIV). But proverbial wisdom, even when not directly averse to speech, is by nature the enemy of articulation: the wise saw is an instance of discourse divorced from the face-to-face encounters during which people actually speak to one another. As FitzGerald himself noted in his Preface to *Polonius,* the proverb is nothing more than the ossified remains of a collapsed narrative or fable (Richardson, p. 102). Like the bowls and other empty signs throughout the *Rubáiyát,* proverbs are created sufficiently void of meaning to be recyclable in any number of contexts. While this has meant nearly universal acceptance for the poem, it is also worth our remembering that an earlier teacher of wisdom, Ecclesiastes, used the strategy of citing one reasonable proverb against another in his proof of the vanity of all things.

This approach to the *Rubáiyát* emphasizes an underlying nihilism which unfortunately further deflects us from attempting the more serious reading the poem deserves. The poem is not without its more starkly tragic elements. It introduces, for example, various tangible forms, bearing little resemblance to Christian or Platonic genii which reside beyond the world of the senses. The most perfect form in the *Rubáiyát* would be the human body. I say "would be" because the body is something hopelessly mutable, which like "The Flower that once has blown for ever dies" (LXIII). Since the attempt to assemble a complete human form in the poem can never succeed, the *Rubáiyát* remains a veritable butcher shop of dismembered flesh: eyes in the earth, runaway moving fingers, and organs of speech all over the place. Nor is there much impetus to complete any such project: dissolution would overtake the human form the moment it was reassembled because every moment in time is itself a kind of emptiness.

Clay pots and bowls are signs for the body in Omar's world, but like ciphers are always vacant and desiring to be filled with "the old familiar Juice." Naturally, the clay pot is no less subject to decomposition than the human body. Omar toys with the metaphor when, in a more speculative moment, he tries to conceive a world elsewhere:

> I must adjure the Balm of Life, I must,
> Scared by some After-reckoning ta'en on trust,
> > Or lured with Hope of some Diviner Drink,
> To fill the Cup—when crumbled into Dust!

> (LXII)

The reader may easily envision the wine mixing with the pulverized cup to make more clay for new vessels which will again crumble to dust and so on ad infinitum.

More frightening is the prospect that wherever one looks, he will see nothing but a repetition of these bowl-shaped forms:

> And that inverted Bowl they call the Sky,
> Whereunder crawling coop'd we live and die,
> > Lift not your hands to *It* for help—for It
> As impotently moves as you or I.

> (LXXII)

The Bowl, round-rimmed like the *sifr* (or cipher, keystone of Omar's Arabic mathematics),[14] and invoked here through the empty pronoun "It," turns up in natural forms which themselves are emblems of the human body:

> As then the Tulip for her morning sup
> Of Heav'nly Vintage for the soil looks up,
> > Do you devoutly do the like, till Heav'n
> To Earth invert you—like an empty Cup.

> (XL)

Here is the same "empty Glass" turned down by the wine-pourer Saki at the end of the poem as a place-holder for the departed Omar; and when the serving boy is making his rounds among them, "the Guests Star-scatter'd on the Grass" will mirror once again the bowl-shaped starry heavens up above.

FitzGerald had become acquainted with such devices in his previous studies of Persian literature. In Jami's *Salaman and Absal,* which he had also translated, a Shah searched for his dissolute son. FitzGerald's text reads:

> Then bade he bring a Mirror that he had,
> A Mirror, like the Bosom of the Wise,
> Reflecting all the World.[15]

Far more interesting than the text at this point is the footnote he appends, glossing the "Mirror":

> Mythically attributed by the East—and in some wild Western Avatar—to this Shah's Predecessor, Alexander the Great. Perhaps . . . the Concave Mirror upon the Alexandrian Pharos, which by Night projected such a fiery Eye over the Deep as not only was fabled to exchange Glances with that on the Rhodian Colossus, and in Oriental Imagination and Language to penetrate "The WORLD," but by Day to Reflect it to him who looked therein with Eyes to see. The Cup of their own JAMSHID had, whether Full or Empty, the same Property. And that Silver Cup found in Benjamin's Sack—"Is not this it in which my Lord drinketh, and whereby indeed he *Divineth*?"—Gen. xliv. 5. Our Reflecting Telescope is going some way to realize the Alexandrian Fable.

> (pp. 81-82)

Perhaps; but the great concave mirrors are just as likely to expand the empire of cosmic solipsism as to overthrow it. For if the guests be "Star-scatter'd on the

Grass," is it not probable that the stars will be guest-scatter'd in the sky? That the sky is nothing more than an "inverted Bowl," whose worldly reflections should make us tremble as we stare up into its hollowness, was not a theme confined to the *Rubáiyát.* Charles Baudelaire addressed the question of what is above us in "Le Couvercle." In this last poem of the *Nouvelles Fleurs du Mal* sequence, "heaven becomes (by an inversion more serious than blasphemy, an inversion which has contaminated even the limping versification) the lid of a pot or coffin—something which clamps a ceiling on man's aspirations and renders them actually vulgar."[16] In a contemporary English poem on a related artifact, Dante Rossetti's "Troy Town," an empty cup molded in the shape of Helen's breast and given by her as an offering to Venus reflects a future of meaningless destruction on the Plains of Ilion. Actually, definitive annihilation would be a welcome end in each poem, for what terrified these men was not death, but the never ending dying into never ending dying, and the attendant knowledge of everlasting loss. Such was the fear that reigned in FitzGerald's daily existence. In a letter to Frederick Tennyson describing the summer of his thirty-fifth year he wrote:

> A little Bedfordshire—a little Northamptonshire—a little more folding of the hands—the same faces—the same fields—the same thoughts occurring at the same turns of the road—this is all I have to tell of; nothing at all added—but the summer gone.
>
> (October 10, 1844; Richardson, p. 522)

FitzGerald's Omar laments that after he expires and turns to dust he will still somehow be aware of an unabated monotony of enervation:

> Ah, make the most of what we yet may spend,
> Before we too into the Dust descend;
>   Dust into Dust, and under Dust to lie,
> Sans Wine, sans Song, sans Singer, and—sans End!
>
> (XXIV)

The modern reader can hear an echo in Beckett's Unnamable's gasping, "I can't go on, I'll go on"; FitzGerald heard in Omar a voice "as savage against Destiny &c as Manfred," but one disillusioned of Romantic passions, and with dulled sentiments, "mostly of Epicurean Pathos."[17]

I mentioned that organs of speech appear in a number of places throughout the *Rubáiyát,* especially the lips, which also resemble the zero or the circular edge rimming a cup or bowl. The lips encompass Omar:

> And this reviving Herb whose tender Green
> Fledges the River-Lip on which we lean—
>   Ah, lean upon it lightly! for who knows
> From what once lovely Lip it springs unseen!
>
> (XX)

This is a fine example of the claustrophobic sensibility of the poem, which complements in space Omar's awareness of temporal circularity. The form of dismembered lips moves from the blade of grass through the riverbank, only to close in again on a human subject. "Revives" offers no more hope of release into something different than the "reviving" of the new year back in the fourth quatrain which had brought with it unwanted "old Desires." All these lips never say much of consequence: speech rarely has a direction in the poem, and occasionally is unwilling or unable to progress from a phonological square one. One can hear the verbal claustrophobia in this well-known rubai:

> Into this Universe, and *Why* not knowing
> Nor *Whence,* like Water willy-nilly flowing;
>   And out of it, as Wind along the Waste,
> I know not *Whither,* willy-nilly blowing.
>
> (XXIX)

Or the human lips are deprived of speech altogether. David, the archetypal Biblical potentate, stands with locked lips in the sixth quatrain while a nightingale pipes on about wine in the ancient literary language of Persia, a language that was dead even to the ears of Omar's contemporaries. The "Pehlevi" of both Omar and FitzGerald poses as a distinctly apolitical speech which has no force between persons in everyday life. We cannot therefore hold either of them to account for failing to deal with social and ethical problems because it is precisely their claim that language has no power to do so. Politics are merely a "whirlwind Sword" wielded by a "mighty Mahmúed" who stands in apposition to the great dissolver of force and form, "the Grape" (LIX-LX), or wine—which returns us to the nightingale's Pehlevi song and the speech of impotence.

Speech is the placeholder of the sign of desire for a more intimate kind of touch between dissoluble forms:

> Then to the Lip of the poor earthen Urn
> I lean'd, the Secret of my Life to learn:
>   And Lip to Lip it murmur'd—"While you live,
> "Drink!—for, once dead, you never shall return."
>
> I think the Vessel, that with fugitive
> Articulation answer'd, once did live,
>   And drink; and Ah! the passive Lip I kiss'd,
> How many Kisses might it take—and give!
>
> For I remember stopping by the way
> To watch a Potter thumping his wet Clay:
>   And with its all-obliterated Tongue
> It murmur'd—"Gently, Brother, gently, pray!"
>
> (XXXV-XXXVII)

The human presence Omar longs for escapes from lip to lip and all through this lip-sprouting world. Only at times of metamorphosis do we hear speech, for only as one form dies into the next, leaving behind a memory of what is now irretrievably lost, do we learn the differences between forms. Difference and distinction are at the root of "articulation," and are the sine qua non of intelligibility, as Saussure has demonstrated. But articulation in the *Rubáiyát* is always fugitive because visible forms are emblems of mutability; and the meaning of articulation is fugitive from itself when we consider the possibility of making genuine distinctions among these ever-changing shapes. In the lines above, Omar hears a murmur, the word (already repeating its one syllable) that stands for a vocalization on the verge of a linguistic utterance. Several quatrains later, Omar will compress all shapes in the universe between "Máh" (the moon, natural symbol of metamorphosis) and "Máhi" (fish in the sea) (LI). Speech is barely able to distinguish between these two words (with the implication that there is little distinction among all they represent), words which closely resemble the first word from the mouth of every Indo-European infant, the one who is *infans,* literally "without speech." FitzGerald's Omar had a Wordsworthian longing for childhood, but his melancholy, historically and biographically speaking, takes us further back than this. Ecclesiastes' wisdom might be appropriate here:

> If a man beget an hundred children, and live many years, so that the days of his years be many, and his soul be not filled with good, and also that he have no burial; I say, that an untimely birth is better than he. For he cometh in with vanity, and departeth in darkness, and his name shall be covered with darkness. Moreover he hath not seen the sun, nor known any thing: this hath more rest than the other.
>
> (Ecclesiastes 6. 3-5)

Both Omar and the Preacher would agree that the mouth is better used to drink in the obliterating wine, or to give that last parting kiss.

The charge has been made that the *Rubáiyát* is a "period piece,"[18] and thus the question arises: Is it worth anyone's trouble to teach, talk, or write about the poem as if it were as much a living document as "Prufrock"? Or is an occasional reference to the poem necessary only to remind us that it lies mercifully buried in the archive?

The *Rubáiyát* is obviously not the best poem of its age. The various works by Rossetti and Swinburne I have referred to in this essay are more artistically accomplished. But the *Rubáiyát* is perhaps the archetypal Victorian poem. Those 101 quatrains have a little bit of everything from the nineteenth century: dramatic speech, mysticism, Weltschmerz, sentimentality, Manfred, Epicureanism, the palette of Rossetti and Burne-Jones, the "melancholy, long, withdrawing roar" of the sea in "Dover Beach." We see also that FitzGerald, who began with a very modern-looking poem, proceeded as the years went forward to bring his work in line with a more conservative ideal, with a diffidence and an anxiety about the future we now think so characteristic of the period. Yet even the "exotic injections" into Victorian art from Greece and Italy, for which Pound lauded Rossetti and Swinburne, are implied and encompassed in this poem that was itself a paraphrase of an alien culture.

There remains a word or two to be said about the supposed value of the poem as a piece of wisdom literature. Actually, FitzGerald wanted his readers to take an elegantly simple-minded view of Omar's message:

> [Omar's] Worldly Pleasures are what they profess to be without any Pretense at Divine Allegory: his Wine is the veritable Juice of the Grape: his Tavern, where it was to be had: his Saki, the Flesh and Blood that poured it out for him: all which, and where the Roses were in Bloom, was all he profess'd to want of this World or to expect of Paradise.[19]

Only the most scandalized among his audience took him at his word. Everyone else went ahead and read it as an orthodox theological document. The appraisal by Groome around the turn of the century is representative: "It seems to me beyond question that his version of the *'Rubáiyát'* is an utterance of his soul's deepest doubts, and that hereafter it will come to be recognized as the highest expression of Agnosticism" (p. 37). This, however, says little either for the depth of FitzGerald's soul or for agnosticism. Why should we be taken in by these easy pieties tailor-made for a middle-class clientele that couldn't be bothered thinking up its own solutions to metaphysical and moral questions? FitzGerald, perpetrator of these philosophical offenses, was himself never quite satisfied with the fallback position set forth in his *Rubáiyát,* and in much of the work of his friend Tennyson. In *Euphranor, a dialogue on youth* (1851) and in his letters, although one would never guess it from reading the *Rubáiyát,* he was unequivocal in his conviction that the great thinker and artist is fundamentally a man of action—a Dante, a Shakespeare, even a Byron.[20] Once, after reading of blockade and battle in the Fourth Book of Thucydides, he exclaimed in a letter to Cowell:

> This was the way to write well; and this was the way to make literature respectable. Oh, Alfred Tennyson, could you but have the luck to be put to such employment! No man would do it better; a more heroic figure to head the defenders of his country could not be.
>
> (January 25, 1848; Richardson, p. 546)

The Victorian era saw the development of all kinds of self-help books for the benefit of the masses, and perhaps this is the genre to which the *Rubáiyát* ultimately belongs: "infinite resignation made simple." But FitzGerald's skepticism in other writings about the attitudes expressed in his own poem is surely essential to a complete understanding of his work.

With what, then, are we left? A Victorian attic cluttered with antiques? Yes; but we should not find that a deterrent. Some of the finest productions of our own century are nothing but tatters and bric-a-brac in their constituent parts. Perhaps our past inability to salvage the *Rubáiyát* stems from our having forgotten how to read a Victorian poem—or not having forgotten quite enough.

The Russian critic Victor Shklovsky wrote:

> The purpose of art is to impart the sensation of things as they are perceived and not as they are known. The technique of art is to make objects "unfamiliar," to make forms difficult, to increase the difficulty and length of perception because the process of perception is an aesthetic end in itself and must be prolonged. *Art is a way of experiencing the artfulness of an object; the object is not important.*[21]

Nature is important to *us,* but not to art, whose purpose it is to make us forget what we "know" of nature, so that we may learn to see nature all over again, just as a nerve cell, having transmitted a sense impression, has to turn itself off for an instant before transmitting information anew. I am saying, in part, that the universal acceptance gained by FitzGerald's poem as a kind of timely wisdom has rendered the poem overly familiar, less than a true object of art, and therefore an uninteresting subject of inquiry for most modern readers. "Habitualization devours works, clothes, furniture, one's wife, and the fear of war" (Shklovsky, p. 12). This was obviously not the case in 1861, for the *Rubáiyát* captured the imaginations of Swinburne, Norton, and others of their generation precisely on account of its unfamiliar exoticism. Omar's Persian accent was the result of careful and premeditated contrivance. In flat contradiction to some of his other remarks on translation, FitzGerald maintained in a letter to Cowell that the oriental flavor of Eastern works should be preserved in English: "I am more and more convinced of the Necessity of keeping as much as possible of the oriental *Forms* and carefully avoiding anything that brings back Europe and the nineteenth century. It is better to be orientally obscure than Europeanly clear" (Arberry, p. 46). Or again to Cowell: "I like the Hafiz Ode you send me translated, though *that* should be weeded of some idioms not only European, *but Drawing room-European*" (Arberry, p. 46). I suspect that the *Rubáiyát* contained more *"Drawing room-European"* than its author realized: so the transposition of FitzGerald's "Some little talk awhile of ME and THEE" (XXXII) into Eliot's sardonic "Among the porcelain, among some talk of you and me" might well suggest. One can easily visualize the bookshelves of Prufrock's drawing room lined with richly bound editions of the *Rubáiyát.*

Another problem has been that the relative exoticism of the poem too effectively established its status as merely a literary artifact. "Art exists that one may recover the sensation of life; it exists to make one feel things, to make the stone *stony*" (Shklovsky, p. 12). But the Philistine wanted his art soft and fluffy, and the *Rubáiyát* came to look, sound, and act like a poem that knew its place in the world. When, for example, it struck an oracular pose by invoking a tradition of wisdom literature going back to Ecclesiastes, the poem was also signalling that its meaning need not in any disturbing way impinge upon the business of ordinary discourse. Little more than Drawing room-Exotic, it was reckoned fundamentally irrelevant to life, as all art was meant to be. Eventually the language of the *Rubáiyát,* like that of much late Victorian work, became so conventionally ethereal that it had etherized itself for many ears (ours today still included) and required exactly that word in the third line of "Prufrock," along with a whole series of ironic reversals, to electrify us back into unfamiliarity. The opening gesture toward the drawing room in Eliot's poem unexpectedly restored for his contemporaries the "experience of the artfulness": the new awareness that comes through the discovery of what we are through confrontation with what we are not. Perhaps now, after more than half a century, Prufrock and his peers have worn thin enough to allow the strangeness of Omar Khayyám to peep through once again.

Notes

1. "How to Read," in *Literary Essays,* ed. T. S. Eliot (New York, 1968), p. 34.

2. Edward FitzGerald, *The Rubáiyát of Omar Khayyám,* 4th ed., in *FitzGerald: Selected Works,* ed. Joanna Richardson (Harvard Univ. Press, 1963); hereafter cited as Richardson. Unless otherwise noted, all citations are from this text of the fourth edition, the last to appear in FitzGerald's lifetime. (A fifth posthumous edition is virtually identical). In Richardson's selection, the text of the first edition has been conveniently printed on the facing page.

3. Algernon Charles Swinburne, letter to Clement King Shorter, in *The Swinburne Letters,* ed. Cecil Y. Lang (Yale Univ. Press, 1962), VI, 96.

4. John Nicoll, *Dante Gabriel Rossetti* (New York, 1975), p. 58.

5. "Social Verse," in *Works,* ed. Sir Edmund Gosse and Thomas James Wise (London, 1926), XV, 284-285.

6. "Nicholas' Quatrains de Kheyam," in *North American Review,* 109 (October, 1869), 576.

7. *The Victorian Frame of Mind: 1830-1870* (Yale Univ. Press, 1957), p. 343.

8. Reuben Brower, *Mirror on Mirror: Translation, Imitation, Parody* (Harvard Univ. Press, 1974), p. 161.

9. Charles Lamb to Edward Moxon, August, 1831, cited in *Edward FitzGerald: An Aftermath by Francie Groome with Miscellanies in Verse and Prose* (1902; rpt. Freeport, New York, 1972), p. 95; hereafter cited as Groome.

10. April 27, 1859, in Edward Heron-Allen, *The Rubáiyát of Omar Khayyám* [manuscript facsimile with translation] (London, 1898), p. xxvi; hereafter cited as Heron-Allen.

11. *Letters and Literary Remains of Edward FitzGerald,* ed. William Aldis Wright (London, 1889), III, 165; hereafter cited as Wright.

12. *The Philosophy of Style,* ed. Fred N. Scott (Boston, 1892), p. 3.

13. A. C. Benson, *Edward FitzGerald* (London, 1905), p. 51.

14. The historical Omar Khayyám was also famous as a mathematician, and this aspect of his career is touched upon in FitzGerald's quatrains LVI-LVII. The word "sifr" is the Arabic root of our "cipher" and "zero." The Arabic innovation of an empty placeholder was, of course, a momentous occasion in the history of mathematics.

15. A. J. Arberry, *FitzGerald's Salaman and Absal: A Study* (Cambridge Univ. Press, 1956), p. 81.

16. Robert Martin Adams, *Nil* (Oxford Univ. Press, 1966), p. 121.

17. FitzGerald to Alfred Tennyson, July 26, 1856, cited in Iran B. Hassani Jewett, *Edward FitzGerald* (Boston, 1977), p. 73.

18. Walter E. Houghton and G. Robert Stange, "Edward FitzGerald," in *Victorian Poetry and Poetics,* 2nd ed. (Boston, 1968), p. 341.

19. [Edward FitzGerald], *Rubáiyát of Omar Khayyám* (London, 1859), p. ix.

20. FitzGerald to Fanny Kemble, October 24, 1876, in Richardson, p. 713.

21. "Art as Technique," in *Russian Formalist Criticism: Four Essays,* ed. Lee T. Lemon and Marion J. Reis (Univ. of Nebraska Press, 1965), p. 12.

Michael S. Helfand (essay date summer 1982)

SOURCE: Helfand, Michael S. "FitzGerald and Other Minor Mid-Victorian Poets." *Victorian Poetry* 20, no. 2 (summer 1982): 158-62.

[*In the following essay, Helfand discusses recent scholarly contributions on FitzGerald's life and work.*]

There have been two important publications, in recent years, on the life and works of Edward FitzGerald. The first of these, chronologically, is Iran B. Hassani Jewett's *Edward FitzGerald* (1977), one of the best of the seemingly endless volumes of the Twayne series on English authors. After that *The Letters of Edward FitzGerald* (1980) appeared in four volumes meticulously edited by Alfred and Annabelle Terhune. In different ways both studies make significant contributions to our understanding of the literary career of this eccentric, reclusive, and talented writer.

Jewett's primary task in her book is synthetic: she provides a general introduction to the life, the works, and the scholarly and critical issues which have developed in FitzGerald studies over the years. The book is sensitively designed to emphasize FitzGerald's personality (but not his eccentricity) and his various accomplishments, and it is written with tact and grace. She wisely uses the extended space to quote generously from FitzGerald's lesser-known works and to study with care, again with quotations supplied, his seemingly constant revisions of *The Rubáiyát of Omar Khayyám.* She chooses this form to give readers the materials to make their own judgments about the literary interest of the more obscure works and the successes and failures of the revisions.

The longest section of the book is devoted to the *Rubáiyát.* Like the other literary discussions on the book, it does not offer a new interpretation but rather provides in one place the biographical background of the *Rubáiyát,* the history of the translation's "discovery" and fame, which surprised no one more than FitzGerald, and a consensus about the philosophy in the poem, that it advocates a kind of anti-Sufist hedonism. But Jewett's work goes beyond synthesis in certain respects. Her Iranian origins and extensive knowledge of Persian literature and culture (she's the Persian editor of the Twayne World Authors Series) add a special dimension to her analyses of the *Rubáiyát* and FitzGerald's other Persian work. Her conclusions about FitzGerald as an Orientalist strengthen the growing scholarly and critical consensus that his work should be studied not as translation but as his own creation. In fact, the success of the *Rubáiyát* as poetry, Jewett explains (not without irony), comes because "The superficiality of his knowledge of Persian and his confidence in his [inherent English] superiority over Persian poets enabled FitzGerald to compose his masterpiece in his own way, unhampered by bothersome doubts." While FitzGerald undoubtedly shared the Victorian racialist's sense of superiority to orientals, it is also true that he freely adapted and altered texts by writers from other nations and times including his favorite English authors George Crabbe and Charles Lamb. His translating credo, "Better a live Sparrow than a stuffed Eagle," suggests that he felt he had a license to revise, adapt, and enhance the works he translated and edited no matter who wrote them.

Readers should also appreciate Jewett's study and comparison of FitzGerald's lesser-known works with the *Rubáiyát.* This, too, gives a special quality and insight to her work. While she accepts the general judgment that most of these works are inferior to the *Rubáiyát,* she greatly admires *The Downfall and Death of King Oedipus,* claiming that it "approaches Lear in its tragic stature." Furthermore, because she studies all of FitzGerald's work and not just the *Rubáiyát,* her interpretation of FitzGerald's view of life is quite complex. She sees both a mystical and a skeptical side to his character and speculates that FitzGerald's desire to publish the *Rubáiyát* together with the frankly religious and mystical *Salámán and Absál* was partially an attempt to suggest a distance between his own beliefs and those of the epicurean Omar: "FitzGerald knew Omar spoke for him and for all mankind, but he may not have wished to leave Omar as his only spokesman. When the reader judged him, the mystic was to be there with the skeptic." Whatever the truth is about FitzGerald's world view, it is certainly true that had Jewett seen the new edition of his letters she would have avoided this particular speculation about the joint edition. For in the letters it is clear that FitzGerald insisted upon the joint publication only because his religious friend and tutor Edward Cowell specifically asked that the mystical *Salámán* be included to offset the pernicious influence of the irreverent Omar. FitzGerald's own attitude is clear from his remark that in the dual edition Omar "is accompanied by another Persian Poem which, I believe, hangs upon it rather as a dead weight. But the man who taught me both wished to have 'Solomon and Absolom' (as the Printers called it) revived."

So the letters have, in this case, helped us to realize one of the few erroneous judgments in this study. One of the far more numerous correct ones is Jewett's praise of FitzGerald's letters. They "must be regarded as his most delightful literary output," she says, and few who have read the previously published editions would disagree. This new, definitive and more complete edition should be welcomed by those who savor FitzGerald. The editorial policy, all that's new of Fitz we print, however, alarmingly dilutes the quality and interest of the letters in the last volumes. My doubts about the edition have nothing to do with the quality of the scholarship which has gone into it. On the contrary, there is evidence everywhere of the enormous pains taken first by Alfred Terhune, who obviously worked on this project for many years, and later by his wife Annabelle, who finished it after her husband's death. Every sort of editorial aid is available here. There are annotations and explanatory notes galore. No matter appears to have been too obscure or tangential for editorial attention.

There are narratives interspersed among the letters to clarify context whenever necessary. There are seventy-nine pages of biographical profiles which describe the people who figure prominently in the letters. The Terhunes have also included letters to FitzGerald from his famous friends Alfred Tennyson, W. M. Thackeray, and Thomas Carlyle. But these letters are clearly cameo roles which serve to set off FitzGerald's superiority as a letter writer. The editors also correct many errors in the manuscripts and the historical record.

Obviously, the editing is a labor of love and readers will learn much from the immense scholarly undertaking it represents. But the letters themselves are the central attraction, and, for two and a half volumes at least (and occasionally thereafter) we can see why Jewett praises the letters. There are humorous and serious comments about every aspect of life from the quality of food or soil in his garden to the literary, political, and metaphysical controversies of the day. There is gossip about the great and the humble. Tennyson's dissipations, financial speculations, his lust for fame and pandering to popular tastes are discussed with the same concern as Posh Fletcher's peccadilloes. Thackeray's vanity fares just as badly, in FitzGerald's view, as Posh's drinking. No reader will fail to be touched by this fisherman he described as one of nature's gentlemen nor fail to be amused by his ineffectual, paternalistic efforts to make him one of culture's gentlemen as well. It is hard (but fun just the same) to imagine how Carlyle might have reacted to FitzGerald's suggestion that Posh be included among the heroes Carlyle was then writing about. Perhaps he thought FitzGerald was slightly touched?

Then there is the FitzGerald-Carlyle relationship. They became acquainted when Carlyle wrote to have some historical information about the Battle of Naseby researched. Since the battle was fought on FitzGerald's estate the two men became correspondents and then, in a loose way, friends. FitzGerald admired Carlyle, who was already famous when they met, for his independence, his criticism of the age, and his prose style. He often differed with Carlyle, however, on the political issues of the day and on his social style. Here, for instance, is one of FitzGerald's descriptions of an evening with the sage of Chelsea: "I went one evening to Carlyle's: he lectured on without intermission for three hours: was very eloquent, looked very handsome: and I was very glad to get away." As Carlyle became more and more radical towards the end of his life, FitzGerald became more and more disenchanted, but after Carlyle's death and the publication of his controversial *Reminiscences* he had renewed admiration for the intelligence and humanity hidden behind the bombast.

But there are also startling gaps in the gossip. If you hope to find new information about FitzGerald's ill-fated marriage to Lucy Barton, save your money. However candid he might be about his own faults and those of his friends and enemies, about his deep loneliness and emotional loss when the Cowells left for India, he remained the proper, which is to say mute, gentleman when it came to discussing his marriage.

Along with these descriptions and analyses of people, the letters contain in abundance descriptions of natural beauty, discussions of philology, and an enormous amount of literary, art, and music criticism which is shrewd and discerning. Critical reputation or friendship made no difference at all to FitzGerald when he became engaged with any work of art or literature. I'm sure his candid criticism of Tennyson's and Thackeray's later works must have played some part in the slow cooling of their friendships with him. As he grew older and more of a recluse his reading became his life, his one link with the world outside. His great favorites—Dryden, Lamb, Crabbe, Dickens, Scott, Trollope, John Wesley's *Journal,* and Madame de Sevigne's *Letters*—he talks of again and again. He seldom spends much time in dismissing a writer he does not like—except for Robert Browning. FitzGerald simply could not keep quiet about the "gurgoyle style" of Browning's poetry or the pomposity of his personality. Then for serious scholars there is the extended correspondence with Edward Cowell about Persian manuscripts (including the *Rubáiyát*) and literature which shows us, at least partially, the translator in action. In short, the first two and a half volumes are excellent reading on all counts.

The rest of the letters are not nearly so interesting. As his health and eyes failed, FitzGerald could do less and less of the sailing, reading, writing, and travelling which had provided the stimulus for his best letters. After the young man he had hired to read to him had left I found myself hoping that FitzGerald would quickly get glasses or another reader so that he would have something interesting to write about. It is possible that some of his friends stopped corresponding simply because they were bored by his letters. But this is not entirely fair to the contents of the third and fourth volumes. We learn about FitzGerald's reactions to the "Omar craze," follow his correspondence with new American friends like James Russell Lowell and Charles Eliot Norton, and watch with interest the growing eccentricity of his literary projects, the cut and paste jobs on Lamb and Crabbe, and the cutting out of pictures from travel books on Spain to use in an illustrated edition of *Don Quixote.* There is psychological interest here, if nothing else. Nowadays it is heresy to suggest that it might be appropriate to do less than a complete edition of anything when it is possible to do it completely. Yet many scholars have noted that there was little that was really new in the letters which Aldis Wright left unpublished. If the Terhunes had exercised a different editorial policy, omitting trivia and the large numbers of repetitive let-

ters, they might have saved their readers interest, time, and money. But, finally, we have this edition and it is, from a scholarly standpoint, a great success, a monument to the intelligence, leisure, and isolation of a Victorian man of letters and to the perseverance and historical knowledge of his twentieth-century editors.

Frederick A. De Armas (essay date summer 1986)

SOURCE: De Armas, Frederick A. "The Apocalyptic Vision of *La Vida es Sueño*: Calderón and Edward FitzGerald." *Comparative Literature Studies* 23, no. 2 (summer 1986): 119-40.

[*In the following essay, De Armas examines FitzGerald's approach to the art of translation, citing his mastery of Persian in rendering the* Rubáiyát *into English as well as his knowledge of Spanish in translating the verse dramas of Pedro Calderón de la Barca.*]

I

On April 27, 1859, Edward FitzGerald expressed his views on translation in a letter to Edward Byles Cowell, the orientalist who had inspired him to learn Persian: "I suppose very few People have ever taken such Pains in Translation as I have: though certainly not to be literal. But at all Cost, a Thing must *live*: with a transfusion of one's worse Life if one can't retain the Original's better. Better a live Sparrow than a stuffed Eagle" (*Letters,* vol. 2, p. 335).[1] The *Rubáiyát of Omar Khayyám* certainly did live, bringing to the attention of FitzGerald's contemporaries not only the richness of Persian literature, but also the Victorian translator's own poetic abilities. Joanna Richardson comments: "Edward FitzGerald translated the *Rubáiyát of Omar Khayyám.* That, in one brief sentence, is all that most people know of him."[2] And yet, FitzGerald's interest in Spanish language and literature was as intense as his concern with Persian. Edward Byles Cowell, who was instrumental in inspiring and instructing FitzGerald in Persian, first led him to Spanish. They would often meet and read from the seventeenth-century playwright Pedro Calderón de la Barca. Before working on the *Rubáiyát,* FitzGerald turned to this dramatist, translating six dramas (1853). After completing his version of the Persian poem, he again turned to Calderón, this time rendering into English *El mágico prodigioso* and *La vida es sueño.* Both were printed in 1865. Although little attention has been paid to this endeavor by critics of FitzGerald's works,[3] he has found a modest place in the history of Hispanism in English-speaking countries. Edwin Honig asserts: "For the past century the most respectable versions of Calderón in English were Edward FitzGerald's prose and blank-verse translations of *Eight Dramas.* FitzGerald used a stock but modified

Elizabethan diction, cutting long speeches, altering and adding lines as he saw fit, and generally polishing crude surfaces with his own debonair intelligence."[4] Beginning with the reviews of FitzGerald's first volume on Calderón of 1853 and continuing up to the present, critics have tended to deplore the many alterations found in these texts. In one of the most recent (1980) translations of Calderón into English, this view still prevails. Kenneth Muir explains: "Not everyone has approved of Calderón's style." He then cites a passage from FitzGerald and links his approach to Calderón to outmoded Victorian attitudes: "Victorian critics complained of the same things in Shakespeare's early plays, or blamed the groundlings, as FitzGerald blamed Calderón's 'not very accurate audience.'"[5] Is FitzGerald careless with Calderón? This essay will focus on the Victorian writer's translation of *La vida es sueño* in order to suggest some new ways of looking at this old problem. This *comedia* has been chosen from the eight adapted by FitzGerald not only because it is considered Calderón's masterpiece, but also because together with *El mágico prodigioso,* it represents the culmination of FitzGerald's efforts to interpret the Spanish theater.

FitzGerald's pride in his Calderón is evinced in the fact that he reworked the image he had used to describe his translation of the **Rubáiyát** (the live sparrow vs. the stuffed eagle) to refer to his Spanish translation. In a letter to James Russell Lowell, he says of his Calderón: "I am persuaded that, to keep *Life* in the work (as Drama must) the Translator (however inferior to his original) must re-cast that original into his own Likeness: the less like his original, so much the worse: but still, the live Dog better than the dead Lion—in Drama, I say" (*Letters,* vol. 4, pp. 167-68). To prove his point, FitzGerald then asks: "Whose Homer still holds its own? The elaborately exact, or the "teacup-time Parody?" (*Letters,* vol. 4, p. 168). His answer is that Alexander Pope's Homer is the one that still holds its own even though it is far from exact. Contemporary criticism tends to agree with FitzGerald's assessment. Reuben Brower asserts: "Alexander Pope's *Iliad* is a triumph. . . . Since its appearance in the early eighteenth century (1715-20), scholars have kept saying with Richard Bentley that it is 'not Homer,' but readers have happily gone on reading. . . . It has been the most readable and most read of all English translations of Homer."[6] Brower details how Pope was able, as a great poet, to impose his own interpretation of the *Iliad,* one that captured the reader's imagination, making available at least "one level of meaning in the total Homeric vision" (p. 75).

FitzGerald's "dangerous experiment" (*Letters,* vol. 2, p. 85), as he was fond of calling his Calderón, is in many ways similar to Pope's *Iliad.* In both cases the translators turn to a culture and an epoch that is particularly foreign to them and to their readers. Brower comments:

"Part of the excitement in doing a translation is the feeling of foreignness even of the obscurity, of the haunting original" (p. 14). He adds that the greater the distance between poet and translator, the more the latter can rely on his own creativity: "It might be claimed that the more ghostly-mysterious the text seems, the nearer the translator's process approaches free poetic creation" (p. 14). At the same time, it might be added that the translator hopes to unravel the mystery, to interpret the work to his own satisfaction. In this, he resembles those literary critics who believe that interpretation is their main task.

Although the mystery of the original is a spur to free poetic creation and to perceptive interpretation, the translator's own critical bias, the literary tastes of his public, or both lead to other textual alterations that are more predictable and restrictive. The translator thus reads and misreads the original text for his readers[7] in at least two ways: first by reveling in and attempting to unravel the mystery of the original, and second by adding a certain familiarity in the form or in the content. In Edward FitzGerald's alteration of *La vida es sueño,* both the expansive and the constrictive manners are encountered. The first part of the discussion will center on the latter since it is the most easily documented.

II

In 1881, at the bicentennial of Calderón's death, FitzGerald was presented a medal from the Spanish Royal Academy in recognition of his Calderón translations (*Letters,* vol. 4, pp. 461-62). This was also the year in which Marcelino Menéndez Pelayo gave a series of lectures at the *Círulo de la Unión Católica,* which were collected into a book entitled *Calderón y su teatro.* Studying this youthful effort, Bruce W. Wardropper concludes that Menéndez Pelayo "is, *malgré lui,* a Neo-classic critic. However much he might dispute Luzán's claim to speak in absolute terms about literature, Menéndez Pelayo was attracted to the Neoclassic school of aesthetics because its dogmatism and its doctrines of order and unity appealed to his conservative and Catholic mind. He espoused the Neo-classic precepts in spite of the fact that they threatened much of Spanish Catholic Art."[8] Much of the negative criticism that has been applied to Calderón is based on this neoclassical bias, a situation that has led Henry W. Sullivan to proclaim Calderón as a "victim of neoclassicism."[9]

These notions can be traced back to seventeenth-century France, a period that saw continuous adaptations of Spanish *comedias.*[10] Although utilizing the varied plots found in these Spanish plays, the French authors found them to be rough works that needed polishing in order to become true works of art: "Comment enfin achever et polir les formes qu'elle n'avait su qu'ébaucher . . .

?"[11] These *comedias* were the *prima materia* that had to be refashioned into gold by the alchemists or artists who were aware of dramatic precepts derived from the Italian Renaissance commentators of Aristotle.[12] With the eighteenth century, these attitudes became commonplace. In France, they are most clearly expressed by Voltaire.[13] Even Spain absorbed these French attitudes and produced treatises that were critical of Baroque literature. Ignacio Luzán's *Poética* (1737) was to become a model for Menéndez Pelayo's condemnation of Calderón, but the most severe objections to Golden Age drama during the eighteenth century came from Blas Nasarre who "branded Lope de Vega as the 'first corrupter' and Calderón as the 'second corrupter' of the Spanish stage."[14]

Edward FitzGerald's opinions regarding Calderón's dramaturgy are not merely a reflection of Victorian attitudes, as Muir has argued. In his theory and practice FitzGerald often reflects the tenets of the neoclassical or French school. In his reductive and constrictive manner, this Victorian translator attempts to tame much of what he sees as "wild" (*Letters,* vol. 2, p. 547; *Works,* vol. 5, p. 99)[15] in Calderón's drama. He revises the original text so as to bring it closer to neoclassical ideals such as clarity of style, accuracy in geographical and historical data, verisimilitude, decorum, and unity of action.

In his letters, FitzGerald often evinces the concern that his translation of *La vida es sueño* may reflect too accurately Calderón's style: "I was really fearful of its being bombastic" (vol. 2, p. 554). He does not wish his version to smack of the "false heroic" (vol. 2, p. 551). The Victorian translator had expressed similar fears when he published *Six Dramas of Calderón,* adding that many conceits as well as repetitive thoughts and images had to be eliminated (vol. 4, p. 5). This stated preference on the part of FitzGerald is typical of neoclassic criticism. When Ernest Martinenche discusses the difficulty French seventeenth-century playwrights have in adapting *comedias,* he asks: "Comment ramener la négligence passionée et metaphorique de sa poésie au ton d'une savante simplicite?"[16] To achieve clarity of style in *La vida es sueño* FitzGerald eliminates much that the neoclassics would have considered excessive adornment. Puns, especially when uttered by noble characters, are often deleted. Not only are they excessive, but they also cloud the "otherwise distinct outlines of character" (*Works,* vol. 5, p. 5). Furthermore, they infringe upon decorum since characters ought to speak a language suited to their station in life. Rosaura's exclamation, "y apenas llega, cuando llegas a penas" (v. 20),[17] which as served as a point of departure for Bruce Wardropper's penetrating analysis of the initial scenes of the *comedia,*[18] is absent from FitzGerald's version. At the same time, the Victorian poet wishes to convey a sense of the original. In order to preserve both decorum and the original texture, puns are often relegated to the *gracioso.* Indeed, some of the humor is FitzGerald's own, such as: "Like some scared water bird, / As we say in my country, dōve below" (p. 105).

The Victorian translator also shows his propensity for simplifying the style through his elimination of image clusters. E. M. Wilson has pointed out that the four elements are central to Calderón's dramaturgy.[19] As the Spanish play opens, the hipogryph is described thusly:

> . . . rayo sin llama,
> pájaro sin matiz, pez sin escama
> y bruto sin instinto.
>
> (vv. 3-5)

That Rosaura's horse, described in terms of a mythical creature and related to the four elements, unseats Rosaura and literally drops her into Poland has given rise to several interpretations. Angel Cilveti summarizes: "La identificación de hipogrifo con los cuatro elementos, dando de lado a Rosaura, conduce a la caracterización del primero como pasión sexual de proporciones cósmicas, o al símbolo de Segismundo representante del oscuro mundo de los sentidos."[20] The reader would search in vain for this image cluster in FitzGerald's version. This is unfortunate since Calderón clearly links the description of this mythical monster with the lament of a second "monster," that is, Segismundo, who considers himself as a "monstruo humano" (v. 209). In his first soliloquy, the imprisoned prince constructs his lament around the four elements. Describing and desiring the freedom of the *pez, bruto,* and *ave,* inhabitants of the elements water, earth, and air, Segismundo rages against his incarceration, utilizing the element of fire to characterize his own response: "un volcán, un Etna hecho" (v. 164). The volcano, according to Javier Herrero, is an image that partakes in itself of two of the elements, earth and fire. It is a symbolic representation of the "caos cósmico"[21] and is thus central to Calderón's iconic system. That FitzGerald chooses to eliminate this important image cluster is not so much a sign of carelessness or debonaire intelligence, but an indication of his neoclassical perceptions and a desire to update the original so as to make it more acceptable to his audience. The Victorian poet expresses his creativity by replacing the four elements, an "outdated" concept and a reiterative pattern, with other examples from the natural world. Segismundo rages because freedom is granted not only to "guiltless life" but also to "that which lives on blood and rapine" (p. 190), giving as examples the lion, the wolf, the bear, and the panther. Whereas Calderon emphasizes the majesty of nature, a text presented by God to man, FitzGerald focuses on the violence and rapine in nature which Segismundo comes to learn. This substitution allows him not only to move away from outdated and reiterative imagery, but also allows him to establish Segismundo's violent nature as an attempt to emulate the environment in which he is raised.

Although FitzGerald eliminates or substitutes a number of images, he preserves those he believes are central to the understanding of the *comedia*. In a letter to Cowell dated April 3, 1865, the English poet records his pleasure in capturing one such image: "By the bye, I think I have hit off the *Vida's* Almond-tree very well." (vol. 2, p. 547). Curiously the almond tree is an image that is condemned by one of FitzGerald's contemporaries. The usually positive critic Richard Chenevix Trench comments: "His almond-trees, his phoenixes, his 'flowers which are the stars of earth,' and 'stars which are the flowers of heaven,' recur somewhat too often. He squanders . . . seeing that what he has once used, he will not therefore feel the slightest scruple in using a second time or a hundreth."[22] Although FitzGerald must have realized that the almond tree was a commonplace in the theater of the time, he preserves it as a key to Segismundo's transformation. When the rebellious soldiers come to rescue the prince from the tower to which he has been returned after the "dream" or palace experience,[23] Segismundo has second thoughts about embarking on this new adventure since it may turn out to be one more dream that leaves him with nothing. FitzGerald mirrors Calderón in emphasizing the lessons that can be learned from the book of nature. The prince in both the original and the translation no longer holds on to concepts in his obsessive manner of thinking. Instead, as Christopher Soufas affirms, he discovers that: "The more one reads within that world text, the more one grows in wisdom."[24] Up to now, Clotaldo has attempted to teach him through natural examples. At this point, the prince grasps the manner in which this dialogue ought to be unfolded and posits the example of the almond tree to refrain his obsessive nature. FitzGerald has captured and condensed this image in his version, utilizing *almander* for almond-tree, a term he takes from Chaucer:

> Dressing me up in visionary glories,
> Which the first air of waking consciousness
> Scatters as fast as from the almander—
> That, waking one fine morning in full flower,
> One rougher insurrection of the breeze
> Of all her sudden honour disadornes
> To the last blossom, and she stands again
> The winter-naked scare-crow that she was!

> (p. 182)

The almond tree which loses its flowers during a winter storm is a symbol of the impermanency of any temporal state and of the rule of fortune.[25] By speaking of the "insurrection of the breeze," FitzGerald adds immediacy to Calderón's conceptual approach. This phrase points to Segismundo's awareness that the breeze that destroys the flowers can be linked to the insurrection that the soldiers want him to lead. The prince has not only learned the hermeneutics of similitude, which according to Michel Foucault typifies the classical way of thinking,[26] but he is also aware that his violent actions can have a devastating effect in the harmony and beauty of the cosmos.

Segismundo's transformation is here grounded to a central image in Calderón's text. Thus, FitzGerald does not always eliminate images in an attempt to stop that "lluvia de metáforas" which according to Menéndez Pelayo serves to drown Calderón's audience.[27] In the case of the almond tree the image is expanded to show how the violence that the prince had perceived in the blood and rapine of his first soliloquy has now given way to a more sensitive vision of the tragic possibilities of rebellion. With these images from the natural world, FitzGerald attempts to preserve the essential Calderón. They also serve to buttress Segismundo's transformation against the criticism of neoclassic scholars such as Mendéndez Pelayo, who deplores "la violencia que hay en el cambio de carácter de Segismundo."[28] In FitzGerald, the prince's initial violence stems from a misreading of the book of nature. His tutor, Clotaldo, tries to show him how to read the world as text. But, it is not until Segismundo actually lives through the metaphor that life is a dream in the false dream of the palace that he begins to emulate his teacher. Only then does he engage in a positive dialogue with natural forces and adopts the almond tree as an example.

The French school often criticizes the Spanish *comedia* for weak characterization. To resolve this problem, FitzGerald overemphasizes the pupil-teacher relationship between Segismundo and Clotaldo. The latter, a representative of the status quo in the kingdom, is ambiguously portrayed by Calderón, as C. A. Merrick has demonstrated.[29] He had, after all, abandoned Rosaura's mother. FitzGerald replaces this shameful episode with a heroic one, granting further authority to Clotaldo. Indeed, Segismundo's famous second soliloquy is spoken by Clotaldo in FitzGerald's version, once the prince has been returned to the tower in the third act. The Victorian poet refashions the *comedia* into a *speculum principum* where Clotaldo becomes an idealized figure and the mirror to the prince. Segismundo's transformation is partially achieved by listening to his tutor, who understands the meaning of life and expounds upon it through the typical baroque metaphors that life is a dream and a stage:

> And all this stage of earth on which we seem
> Such busy actors, and the parts we play'd,

Substantial as the shadow of a shade,
And Dreaming but a dream within a dream!

(p. 170)

The tone of the soliloquy elevates Clotaldo from a weak character lacking moral courage in Calderón to a heroic status as guide and preceptor to a rebellious youth. FitzGerald interprets and defines the central conflict in the play, leaving little room for the ambiguity that makes of Calderón's masterpiece a most engaging text.

This emphasis on characterization as the presentation of clearly defined traits can be seen as part of the neoclassical desire for verisimilitude. Events in a drama must be probable and likely. Thus the motivation of a character ought to be clearly defined. On the question of verisimilitude FitzGerald wavers between the neoclassical approach and his desire to preserve the mystery and foreignness of the text. In his letters, FitzGerald wonders if he ought to leave *La vida es sueño* "wild" or if he should argue "more probability" into the drama (vol. 2, p. 547). In a note to his translation he warns that he had not eliminated all improbable events from the *comedia*: "The bad watch kept by the sentinels who guarded their state-prisoner, together with much else (not all!) that defies sober sense in this wild drama, I must leave Calderón to answer for" (p. 99).

One clear way to increase verisimilitude in a work is to pay attention to geographical and historical detail. Ignacio Luzán's *Poética,* the most important neoclassical Spanish treatise of the eighteenth century, had criticized Calderón's dramas as "un conunto de absurdos, de anacronismos, de faltas de historia y geografía."[30] FitzGerald's desire to preserve historical accuracy is evinced in his letters when he speaks of his translation of *Guárdate del agua mansa* (vol. 2, p. 91). Here, all he must do is to preserve Caderón's historical details. However, when it comes to *La vida es sueño,* the task of a neoclassic translator is more complex. Menéndez Pelayo considers that: "La geografía y la historia del drama es de todo punto fantástica."[31] FitzGerald does little to increase historical accuracy since the play is not set during a specific historical period, although according to Ervin Brody, it does reflect the turbulent Russian Time of Troubles.[32] What the Victorian writer sets out to do is to increase geographic accuracy and detail. The data provided in *La vida es sueño* are minimal. The reader or audience only knows that the *comedia* takes place in Poland, in a tower close to the border and at Court. There is one more geographical clue. When Segismundo throws a servant from the balcony, he states: "Cayó del balcón al mar" (v. 1430). Neoclassical artists and critics saw in this statement an error since neither Warsaw nor Cracow, the two possible locations for the Polish Court, is by the ocean.[33] FitzGerald first tries to

achieve geographical precision. The stage directions read: "The Palace at Warsaw" (p. 119). Cracow may have been a more accurate setting. One recent critic, Ervin Brody, sees in Segismundo's astonishment on waking at the palace the awe of a foreigner on experiencing the splendor of the beautiful Castle of Wawel in Cracow. Indeed, the seventeenth-century French adaptation of Calderón's masterpiece by the Abbé de Boisrobert has Cracow as the setting.[34] Aware of the inland location of Warsaw, FitzGerald also deletes the scene where Segismundo tosses a servant from a balcony into the sea. In this he is not only avoiding what he thought to be a geographic inaccuracy, but is also eliminating what he may have considered as a "wild" or impossible element in the plot.

Part of the wildness of the plot in FitzGerald's view consists of the excessive importance accorded to the subplot. The Victorian writer expresses his concern over the length of the Rosaura episode in Calderón's *comedia* in a letter of September 1858, where he wishes to "subdue" the Rosaura story "so as to assist and not compete with the Main interest" (vol. 2, p. 319). This negative attitude toward the subplot parallels the neoclassic stance which views the Rosaura episode as "una intriga extrana, completamente pegadiza y exotica que se enreda a todo el drama como una planta parasita."[35] In order to "tame" this "wild" element, FitzGerald deletes most of Rosaura's lines in the second act.

III

FitzGerald's many alterations of the Spanish original do not substantially transform the essential nature of Calderón's play. The work moves from one surprising event to another: From a prince imprisoned by his own father in a tower, to a woman dressed as a man and seeking revenge in a foreign land; from the lament of a monstrous being to the rationalizations of an astrologer-king. One neoclassic critic comments: "Con la inmensa fantasía de que pródigamente le doto la naturaleza, amontonó tantos lances en sus comedias, que hay alguna que cada acto o jornada se pudiera componer otra muy buena; y el vulgo, embelesado en aquel laberinto de enredos, se está con la boca abierta, hasta que al fin de la comedia salen absortos sin poder repetir la substancia de ellos."[36] This is part of the mystery and excitement of Calderón's plays which FitzGerald wishes to capture and yet hold in check.

One way to tame this 'wild'[37] drama is to render it more familiar to his readers or audience. FitzGerald points to Shakespeare in his translation of Calderón so as to make the situations more familiar to the English public. In a letter dated April 10, 1865, FitzGerald claims that his translation is in "Ercles vein" (vol. 2, pp. 548-49). In *A Midsummer Night's Dream,* Bottom, one of the characters who is involved in the play within the play, boasts that he "could play Ercles rarely." Bottom's attempt at playing Ercles or Hercules turns heroic grandeur into comedy. Indeed, these rustic actors' play within the play, *Pyramus and Thisbe,* can serve "to satirize . . . the crude mingling of tragedy and comedy."[38] By referring to Ercles' vein, FitzGerald is not so much adopting the neoclassic critical stance opposed to Calderón's mixture of the serious and the comic in *La vida es sueño,* but is pointing to one of the techniques he uses in his translation to make the text more familiar to an English audience. Considering that it may be difficult for his reader to accept the wild nature of the play's commencement, FitzGerald renders tame the fantastic elements of the first scene through the heightened role of the *gracioso* Clarín, now called Fife. But the mystery, danger, and romance of Calderón's initial evening scene is not lost. In FitzGerald we encounter a touching and comical exchange where Fife and Rosaura pledge to stay together "In a strange country—among savages—" (p. 104) where "bears, lions, wolves" (p. 105)[39] may abide. In their playful conversation they reveal apprehension about what they may find in this foreign land. It is the same apprehension that FitzGerald expects his reader to feel in entering Calderón's fiction. Indeed, Fife and Rosaura heighten the "marvelous" nature of their situation by alluding to *A Midsummer Night's Dream.* Rosaura and her *gracioso* are like the "fairy elves" (p. 104) of Shakespeare, and Fife is another Puck, "following darkness like a dream" (*Works,* p. 104; Shakespeare V, p. 393).[40] What the play has gained in lightness and familiarity it has not lost in mystery. By following a dream Fife and the audience will be delving into the very mystery of life which Segismundo comes to see as a dream.

It is fitting that FitzGerald allude to *A Midsummer Night's Dream* in his translation of Calderón; this play was one of Shakespeare's least popular until the nineteenth century, being considered by some as insipid and ridiculous. Its fantastic elements were a barrier to its acceptance until the German translation by Ludwig Tieck was performed in Berlin in 1827. Tieck not only revived Shakespeare, but also played a crucial role in the restoration of Calderón's place in literature. Indeed, Tieck's enthusiasm for the Spanish playwright led A. W. Schlegel to turn away from his translations of Shakespeare to those of Calderón.[41] In FitzGerald as in the German Romantics, Calderón and Shakespeare are seen as parallel figures.

The parallel between Shakespeare and Calderón is particularly striking when comparing *La vida es sueño* with *The Tempest.* The link between Prospero and Basilio is an obvious one on the surface; both are "wise" men who spend much time in esoteric studies, neglecting or erring in their duties as rulers. While Calderón

portrays Basilio as delving into the secrets of the natural world, particularly astrology, in FitzGerald's version Segismundo views his father more as a magician:

> And you
> With that white wand of yours—
> Why, now I think on't, I have read of such
> A silver-haired magician with a wand,
> Who in a moment, with a wave of it,
> Turn'd rags to jewels, clowns to emperors.

(p. 140)

This is the magic of Prospero whose books and wand can transform the fate of kingdoms. Indeed, Segismundo considers the power that transports him from the tower to the palace and makes him a prince, "some benigner magic than the stars" (p. 140). While the stars, he believes, were the cause of his imprisonment, this magician-father, a figure akin to Prospero, has saved him. He soon discovers that astrologer and magician are one and the same figure. The link between *La vida es sueño* and *The Tempest* is shattered by Segismundo's realization. Whereas Basilio himself is the cause of the injustice by having imprisoned his son, Prospero is the object of treachery by a brother who deposes him. Prospero wants to regain his rightful position; Basilio places obstacles in his son's rightful claim to the throne. And yet, both Basilio and Prospero, through their attempts at control, are in danger of "playing God." Studying certain plays of Shakespeare and Calderón from the perspective of romance, William R. Blue concludes: "The power of art, of magic, of manipulation is something that must be mistrusted and finally abjured by Prospero here and by Basilio in a play by Calderón."[42]

Both *The Tempest* and *La vida es sueño* focus on the play within the play created by the magician-artist, leading Lionel Abel to devote a number of pages in his elucidation of metatheater[43] to a comparison of the plays. Speaking of Shakespeare's work, he comments: "Some dreams are antithetical to thought; the particular dream actualized in *The Tempest* is not. For a perfect revolution is not theoretically impossible."[44] The threat of violence in both works subsides with the dream, the fantastic elements becoming a tool for the achievement of harmony and justice. Prospero's bloodless revolution to regain power as Duke of Milan takes place in the dream-like ambience of the magical island. Segismundo's rebellion, on the other hand, loses its destructiveness when he learns from the "magical" palace dream and ponders on the metaphor that life is a dream. In both works, the realization of the insubstantiality of this life goes hand in hand with the restoration of precisely those earthly glories to the dispossessed. Following the play within the play, which is performed by spirits summoned by the magician, Prospero utters those well-known lines in *The Tempest*:

And, like the baseless fabric of this vision,
The cloud-capp'd towers, the gorgeous palaces,
The solemn temples, the great globe itself,
Yea, all which it inherit, shall dissolve
And, like this insubstantial pageant faded,
Leave not a rack behind. We are such stuff
As dreams are made on, and our little life
Is rounded with a sleep.

                              (IV, vv. 151-58)

Pointing to the kinship in ambience and vision in Calderón and Shakespeare, Edward FitzGerald transforms Calderón's title from *La vida es sueño* to *Such Stuff as Dreams Are Made of.*

IV

Mystery through contextual reinforcement is not dependent solely on Shakespeare. Edward FitzGerald adds among others a Christian mystery, the unfolding of the Last Days, derived in part from the apocalyptic concerns of the Victorian era. In a discussion of the fantastic in literature, Eric S. Rabkin focuses on the Victorian period in order to argue that the notion of history as proceeding "inexorably towards a civilizing goal"[45] is confining to authors such as William Morris, who create "a history in a fairy land so that we can escape into a history that is demonstrably not progressive because it is not connected with our own times."[46] The concept of progress has shattered for some the notions of idyllic or paradisical beginnings. Northrop Frye notes that Charles Darwin was the Copernicus of the Victorian age: "The doctrine of evolution made time as huge and frightening as space: The past, after Darwin, was no more emotionally reassuring than the skies had come to be."[47] In FitzGerald's version, when Segismundo is taken to the palace, he believes that he has awakened in "Fairyland" (p. 140). The weight of his primitive and bestial past seems momentarily suspended. But Segismundo's escape is only illusory and temporary. The palace does not lie outside of time, but is an essential part of the historical process. Northrop Frye comments that a possible response to the fear of history is the elaboration of apocalyptic symbolism.[48] It provides not only a comprehensible beginning and end, but also it goes beyond escape and toward a personal or historical revelation that restores meaning to an increasingly alien and mechanistic process.

A recent essay by Mary Wilson Carpenter and George P. Landow has shown that Victorian authors such as Carlyle, Ruskin, Tennyson, and particularly George Eliot, use heavy allusions to the Book of Revelation as imagistic, thematic, and structuring devices.[49] To these writers must be added the name of Edward FitzGerald. He probably perused a few of the numerous treatises on the subject of apocalypse, popular during the Victorian era. The *Westminster Review,* a periodical that had been most critical of his *Six Dramas of Calderón* in 1853,

would write favorably of Sara Hennell's pamphlet dealing with New Testament prophecy in 1861. The periodical also published that same year an essay on the apocalypse as literature, written by M. W. Call.[50] Furthermore, E. B. Elliott, in his four-volume commentary on Revelation entitled *Horae Apocalypticae,* singled out the year 1866 as the beginning of the millennium.[51] Thus, the apocalyptic references included in FitzGerald's version of *La vida es sueño* are most timely since the book was printed in 1865, the year before the supposed arrival of the millennium.

FitzGerald refashions Calderón by stressing the notion of judgment in the second act of *La vida es sueño.* Segismundo realizes that he has not escaped to Fairyland. The palace is not Prospero's island governed by a benevolent magician. Instead it is ruled by a stern father who chose to incarcerate his own son and raise him as a savage. The prince rebels against "lying prophecies and prophet kings" (p. 163). The weight of a bestial past and of an ominous future is on his shoulders as he fashions apocalypse from his father's fears:

> After a revelation such as this,
> The Last Day shall have little left to show
> Of righted wrong and villany requited!
> Nay, Judgment now beginning upon earth,
> Myself, methinks, in right of all my wrongs,
> Appointed heav'n's avenging minister,
> Accuser, judge, and executioner,
> Sword in hand, cite the guilty. . . .

                              (p. 162)

Revelation to Segismundo is not a vision granted to him by God, but a realization of the injustice to which he has been subjected. This personal revelation will precipitate events that echo those foretold in the Book of Revelation. Segismundo appears to usurp the role of Christ as final judge and uses apocalyptic language to seek personal retribution. By setting himself up as Christ, Segismundo becomes Antichrist, since many believed that he would be a figure that imitates and yet reverses the actions of Christ. Segismundo assumes the role of final judge, but his justice is certainly not divine. Instead of mercy, he is driven by a desire for revenge. Segismundo also sets himself up as king and becomes a tyrant. It was believed that "the last king to rule over the whole earth"[52] would be Antichrist. He would be a tyrant who would bring about a final age of "terror and dread."[53] Segismundo may embody this historical terror.

Although derived in part from the apocalyptic concerns of the Victorian era, the element of Christian mystery may not be of FitzGerald's own making. Instead, he may be assuming the role of interpreter of Calderón, pointing out to his readers an important yet hidden aspect of *La vida es sueño.* Edwin Honig, a recent translator of Calderón's masterpiece into English, has also written a monographic analysis of Calderón's *co-*

medias. In the preface to this study we read: "These chapters grew out of two books of my own translation. The practical problems of translating the plays touched off speculations about their meaning and intention. . . ."[54] A translator often acts as critic, and FitzGerald's emphasis on the topic of Revelation may be viewed as a contribution to Calderonian criticism. Having pointed out the theme, it becomes easier to pinpoint its presence in the original.[55]

When Segismundo sets himself up as a final judge and thus as an Antichrist, he is mirroring his father's apocalyptic fears, which can be gleaned from both the Spanish text and FitzGerald's version. The omens describing Segismundo's birth as described by Basilio can be interpreted as signs of the end. Such signs are necessary since: "The Medieval tradition holds that a number of terrible events or 'signs' will precede Antichrist's rise to power."[56] The writer is free to choose among many such events because "the tradition never developed a standard sequence of specific signs."[57] In *La vida es sueño,* when Segismundo is born, the world is plunged into darkness. FitzGerald renders Calderón's passage as:

> He coming into light, if light it were
> That darken'd at his very horoscope,
> When heaven's two champions—sun and moon I
>   mean—
> Suffused in blood upon each other fell
> In such a raging duel of eclipse
> As hath not terrified the universe
> Since that that wept in blood the death of Christ
>
> (p. 124)

If Antichrist must parallel and yet reverse the figure and actions of Christ, what clearer sign than a birth marked by an eclipse as ominous as the one that occurred at Christ's death? The magnitude of the eclipse sets up the parallel between the two figures. As Antichrist, Segismundo's birth reverses events in Christ's life, since the eclipse occurs at the prince's birth and not at his death. The celestial portent thus augurs the coming of a destructive force. Images of light and darkness also point to the coming conflict between good and evil. Many other portents that can be equated with the coming of Antichrist are evoked by Basilio in both Calderón's and FitzGerald's text. They are of such import that:

> Earth and her cities totter'd, and the world
> Seem'd shaken to its last paralysis.
>
> (p. 124)

FitzGerald is here echoing Calderón's "último parasismo" (v. 695). Both writers emphasize that the signs appear to foretell the end of the world. Furthermore, Segismundo's birth brings about the death of his mother Clorilene:

> The man-child breaking from that living womb
> That makes our birth the antitype of death,
> Man-grateful, for the life she gave him paid
> By killing her. . . .
>
> (p. 123)

Birth ought to be the antitype of death, but Segismundo kills his mother at birth. The word *antitype,* added by FitzGerald,[58] emphasizes the *anti* nature of Segismundo: He is anti-life and Antichrist. As the first, he later becomes an image of death itself. Basilio calls him the "pale horseman of the Apocalypse" (p. 189). As Antichrist he kills his own mother. In FitzGerald's version, Clorilene, before giving birth, dreams that: "A serpent tore her entrail" (p. 123). The serpent is her own son and as the dream foretells, she dies giving birth. The dream reinforces Segismundo's potentially evil nature, since the serpent is commonly associated with Satan and with Antichrist.[59] The notion that Antichrist will be the slayer of his mother is probably derived from the fusion of the deeds of Nero with those of Antichrist. Emerson explains: "Early in the tradition this typological identification of Nero and Antichrist fused with the *Nero redivivus* legend, the belief that Nero himself would return as a great tyrant."[60] The fears expressed that Segismundo will be a great tyrant can be seen as further evidence that he is Antichrist. Although there is no direct reference to Nero in Basilio's speech, Calderón does refer to Nero in act 3 (v. 3050). FitzGerald, on the other hand, leaves out that reference to Nero, but includes the following in Basilio's speech concerning the portents at Segismundo's birth:

> I swear, had his foretold atrocities
> Touch'd me alone, I had not saved myself
> At such a cost to him; but as a king,—
> A Christian king,—I say, advisedly,
> Who would devote his people to a tyrant
> Worse than Caligula fore-chronicled?
>
> (p. 125)

The shift from Nero to Caligula heightens apocalyptic allusiveness. Caligula was reputedly as great a tyrant as his predecessor. Northrop Frye reminds us that his wish to place his own statue for worship in the Temple of Jerusalem linked him to Antiochus Epiphanes, who was the first to desecrate it by dedicating it to Zeus.[61] Indeed Emmerson notes that "Antiochus Epiphanes is the most widely discussed type of Antichrist during the Middle Ages."[62] If Segismundo is to be a tyrant worse than Caligula, then he will be either a type of Antichrist as Epiphanes or Antichrist himself, whose rule will be characterized by desecration and persecution. As a "Christian King," and prophet who foresees and foretells these events, Basilio must not allow this to happen. This is his justification for his imprisonment of his son.

When the king tests Segismundo in act 2, he cannot see that the savage in front of him is of his own making.

The "trumpet sounds" (p. 162) that are heard throughout this act are a reminder to Basilio that the Last Day (p. 161) is at hand if he fails to contain his son, a possible Antichrist. The civil war that ensues in act 3 does little to change Basilio's views. Father and son are each following his own revelation. Basilio sees history in terms of apocalyptic fear, whereas Segismundo, yearning to escape to a land beyond the weight of history, is confronted with a prophecy that labels him as a potential tyrant. His own personal revelation of the injustices of the world make him into a character out of the Book of Revelation since, by setting himself up as final judge, he usurps the role of Christ and becomes Antichrist.

The guidance of Clotaldo, who teaches Segismundo how to read the marvelous book of nature, is the key element in the prince's transformation in FitzGerald's verses. Segismundo ponders on the "visionary glories" of the world through the image of the almond tree that loses its flowers. The transformation from Antichrist to Christian ruler is caused by the reversal of the "most frequently depicted marvel[63] performed by Antichrist. While the figure of the end of time could make trees flower, Segismundo sees how easily these flowers are lost.

As Segismundo pardons the father in FitzGerald's version, he points to Clotaldo as his teacher, calling him "this ancient prophet" (p. 194). The fears of the false prophet Basilio and the vengefulness of a prince who has been caught in a nightmare of injustice vanish as a new vision pervades the work. The whole world has been transformed in Segismundo's eyes into a magical spectacle akin to the play presented by Prospero's spirits in *The Tempest*. The events that surround the prince are perceived as insubstantial a pageant as that presented in Shakespeare's marvelous island.

When Segismundo labels the place of this incarceration as an "enchanted tower" (p. 149) in act 3, we know that the weight of the past has been removed and that the prince no longer regards it as a constrictive edifice, but as one of the contrasting extremes in a life that is no more than a play of light and shadow. Indeed, as he dispenses justice he admits that he may be doing so to "shadows / Who make believe they listen" (p. 195). Holding to this Platonic vision,[64] the prince is ready to face apocalypse. In his final lines, Segismundo merges the magic of this shadow-life with a vision of the Last Days. If the individual can subdue the passions through meditation on the "dream-wise" quality of "human glories" (p. 196), Segismundo argues that then there will be nothing to fear:

> Whether To-morrow's dawn shall break the spell,
> Or the Last Trumpet of the eternal Day,
> When Dreaming with the Night shall pass away.
>
> (p. 196)

In Matthew (24:35) we read after a description of the tribulation of the Last Days the well-known prophecy: "Heaven and Earth shall pass away, but my words shall not pass away." Segismundo's anguish over a savage past, a present of nightmarish injustice, and a future veiled in dark prophecy, has given way to a compassion and equilibrium based on the power of the word of God, on transcendental authority. He forgives the earthly father because he believes in and does not fear the heavenly counterpart.

While Calderón's play emphasizes that the apocalyptic events have brought about a new golden age in human history,[65] FitzGerald prefers to question the possibility of a future in time in order to stress Segismundo's ultimate revelation. In the Victorian translation, Basilio's constrictive view of heavenly signs makes of him a false prophet whose fears shape a dark vision of the future. His son actually becomes a figure akin to Antichrist when the revelation of injustice perpetrated by his own father impels him to usurp the role of final judge. Both Basilio and Segismundo have attempted to impose a restrictive and personal vision on the world. In the end, nature's mysteries save Segismundo, who goes beyond the confines of a history with a savage beginning and a frightening end to a vision of wonderment at the magic play of light and darkness wherein each must discover and perform a prescribed role. Northrop Frye concludes: "Apocalypse is the way the world looks after the ego has disappeared."[66] By surrendering to the mystery of creation, Segismundo paradoxically gains the freedom to act within and beyond time.[67] FitzGerald's prince explains that it matters not if apocalypse is now, if the magic spell is broken, because he resides within the mystery of eternity.

Just as Basilio misreads the heavenly signs, so FitzGerald approaches his translation as a "dangerous experiment" (*Letters,* vol. 2, p. 85), as a deliberate misreading of Calderón's text. His constrictive neoclassicism has sought to tame Calderón's masterpiece just as Basilio, within the text, wishes to subdue Segismundo through incarceration. FitzGerald curtails Rosaura's role, adds poetic probability and verisimilitude, and seeks accuracy of detail. But it is the mystery of the work that has attracted him to it, its mythical qualities and not its historical or geographical accuracy. As the Victorian writer struggles to solve Segismundo's puzzle along with the hero, and as he attempts to fashion the mystery in a way so as to make it more familiar, he begins to move away from the neoclassical frame and searches for a voice in the context of equally compelling visions such as Shakespeare's *A Midsummer Night's Dream* and *The Tempest*. In these texts, the magical qualities of nature and art break the bonds of historicity and probability so as to expand human awareness. The fantastic qualities of the parallel texts lead FitzGerald and Segismundo one step beyond. They seek to comprehend and express the mystery of the text—be it a text about the illusoriness of life (*La vida es sueño*) or the text of life itself, that "sapphire volume of the skies . . . / writ by God's own finger" (p. 191). In this final attempt to render Calderón, FitzGerald takes heed of Segismundo's warning against "misinterpretation" (p. 191). The English version leads us from the constrictive constructs of Basilio and the neoclassic critics to Segismundo's and FitzGerald's new-found awareness. Revelation of the poetic inspiration of the Platonists is now allowed free expression. Calderón and FitzGerald coalesce in the presentation of mystery through an apocalyptic vision.

Notes

1. Alfred McKinley Terhune and Annabelle Burdick Terhune, eds., *The Letters of Edward FitzGerald* (Princeton: Princeton University Press, 1980), 4 vols. All textual references to the letters are from this edition.

2. Joanna Richardson, ed., *FitzGerald: Selected Works* (Cambridge, Mass.: Harvard University Press, 1963), p. 7.

3. Alfred McKinley Terhune, FitzGerald's foremost biographer, presents a detailed history of the Victorian writer's translations of Calderón. He notes, for example, that as early as 1849 FitzGerald and Cowell were already discussing the Spanish playwright. *The Life of Edward FitzGerald Translator of the Rubáiyát of Omar Khayyám* (New Haven: Yale University Press, 1947), p. 162. Terhune also briefly analyzes the alterations made by FitzGerald to the original. In *Edward FitzGerald* (Boston: Twayne Publishers, 1977), Iran Hassani Jewett includes these translations as part of FitzGerald's "minor works" and also gives a brief account of some of the changes effected by the Victorian writer.

4. Edwin Honig, ed., Pedro Calderón de la Barca, *Four Plays* (New York: Hill and Wang, 1961), p. xxiv.

5. Kenneth Muir, *Four Comedies by Pedro Calderón de la Barca* (Lexington: University of Kentucky Press, 1980), p. 5.

6. Reuben Brower, *Mirror on Mirror* (Cambridge, Mass.: Harvard University Press, 1974), p. 56.

7. Misreading has been defined by Harold Bloom as "an act of creative correction." This is indeed what FitzGerald is attempting to accomplish in his translations. However, it would be difficult to see in this Victorian writer a "strong poet" who is intent on "perverse, wilful revisionism." *The Anxiety of Influence: A Theory of Poetry* (Oxford:

Oxford University Press, 1973), p. 30. Bloom establishes a relationship between poetry and criticism since both are "acts of reading." *Poetry and Repression: Revisionism from Blake to Stevens* (New Haven, Conn.: Yale University Press, 1976), p. 26. This essay will point to a similar relationship: Both translator and critic are engaged in acts of reading. For other contemporary theories on the relationship between text and reader, see Jane P. Tompkins, ed., *Reader-Response Criticism from Formalism to Post-Structuralism* (Baltimore: Johns Hopkins University Press, 1980).

8. Bruce W. Wardropper, "Menéndez y Pelayo on Calderón," *Criticism* 7 (1965), 366.

9. Henry W. Sullivan, *Calderón in the German Lands and the Low Countries* (Cambridge: Cambridge University Press, 1983), pp. 101-25.

10. On seventeenth-century adaptations of the *comedia,* see Roger Guichemerre, *La Comédie avant Molière. 1640-1660* (Paris: Armand Colin, 1972); and Alexandre Cioranescu, *Le Masque et le visage* (Geneva: Droz, 1983).

11. Ernest Martinenche, *La Comedia espagnole en France de Hardy a Racine* (Geneva: Slatkine Reprints, 1970; reprint of 1900 edition), p. 137.

12. Debating whether Calderón's *En esta vida todo es verdad y todo mentira* influenced Corneille's *Heraclius,* or whether the reverse was the case, Voltaire concluded that the French dramatist is like the alchemist who can transmute the chaotic *materia prima* found in the Spanish original into artistic gold. For a discussion of this concept, see Frederick A. de Armas, "The Dragon's Gold: Calderón and Boisrobert *La vie n'est qu'un songe,*" *Kentucky Romance Quarterly,* 30 (1983), 335-48.

13. On Voltaire's attitude toward the Spanish *comedia* see Alfonso de Salvio, "Voltaire and Spain," *Hispania,* 7 (1927), 69-110, 157-64; and Donald Schier, "Voltaire's Criticism of Calderón," *Comparative Literature,* 11 (1959), 340-46.

14. Henry W. Sullivan, *Calderón in the German Lands,* p. 114.

15. All page and volume references to Edward FitzGerald's works are to *The Variorum and Definitive Edition of the Poetical and Prose Writings of Edward FitzGerald,* ed., George Bentham (New York: Phaeton Press, 1967; reprint of 1902 ed.), vols. 4 and 5. Subsequent revisions of the text have also been taken into account as detailed by Gerald D. Brown, "Edward FitzGerald's Revision," *Papers of the Bibliographical Society of America,* 69 (1975), 94-112.

16. Ernest Martinenche, *La Comedia espagnole,* p. 137.

17. All verse references to *La vida es sueño* are from Pedro Calderón de la Barca, *La vida es sueño* (*comedia, auto y loa*), ed., Enrique Rull (Madrid: Alhambra, 1980).

18. Bruce W. Wardropper, "Apenas llega cuando llega a penas," *Modern Philology*, 57 (1960), 24-44.

19. E. M. Wilson, "The Four Elements in the Imagery of Calderón," *Modern Language Review*, 31 (1936), 34-47.

20. Angel L. Cilveti, *El significado de "La vida es sueño"* (Valencia: Albatrós Ediciones, 1971), pp. 164-65.

21. Javier Herrero, "El volcán en el paraíso. El sistema icónico del teatro de Calderón," *Co-textes*, 3 (1982), 106.

22. Richard Chenevix Trengh, *Calderón. His Life and Genius* (New York: Redfield, 1856), p. 54.

23. On the palace experience as dream, see Julian Palley, *The Ambiguous Mirror: Dreams in Spanish Literature* (Chapel Hill: Albatrós-Hispanófila, 1983), p. 127.

24. C. Christopher Soufas, "Thinking in *La vida es sueño*," *PMLA*, 100 (1985), 288.

25. On the significance of the almond tree in Golden Age Spanish drama, see Frederick A. de Armas, "The Flowering Almond Tree: Examples of Tragic Foreshadowing in Golden Age Drama," *Revista de Estudios Hispánicos*, 14 (1980), 117-34; and "Los 'naturales secretos' del almendro en el teatro de Calderón," *Actas del VIII Congreso Internacional de Hispanistas* (forthcoming).

26. Michel Foucault, *The Order of Things* (New York: Vintage Books, 1973).

27. Marcelino Menéndez Pelayo, *Calderón y su teatro* (Madrid: A. Pérez Dubrull, 1910), p. 18.

28. Ibid., p. 278.

29. C. A. Merrick, "Clotaldo's Role in *La vida es sueño*," *Bulletin of Hispanic Studies*, 50 (1973), 256-69.

30. Marcelino Menéndez Pelayo, *Calderón y su teatro*, p. 18.

31. Ibid., p. 272.

32. Ervin Brody, "Poland in Calderón's *Life is a Dream*," *Polish Review*, 14 (1969), 47.

33. For other possible interpretations of the word *mar* in *La vida es sueño*, see Enrique Rull's edition of the play cited above, pp. 186-88.

34. Frederick A. de Armas, "The Dragon's Gold," pp. 341-42.

35. Marcelino Menéndez Pelayo, *Calderón y su teatro*, p. 278.

36. This citation from the prologue to Nicolás Fernández de Moratín's *La Petimetra* (1762) is included in the discussion of neoclassic critics of Calderón by Manuel Durán and Roberto González Echevarría, *Calderón y la crítica: historia y antología* (Madrid: Gredos, 1976), vol. 1, p. 21. For another discussion of Calderón and the neoclassics, see Ralph Merritt Cox, "Calderón and the Spanish Neoclassicists," *Romance Notes*, 24 (1983), 43-48.

37. FitzGerald's view of Calderón's drama as "wild" may derive from his mentor, Edward Byles Cowell, who, in his article "Spanish Literature" in the *Westminster Review* 54 (1851), 281-323, repeatedly uses this adjective in his analysis of Calderón's *comedias*. Cowell discusses, for example, the "wild profusion of imagery" in these plays; he complains of "Calderón's wild mistakes"; and stresses that a "wild and grand tone of fiction pervades his poetry" (p. 292). For Cowell's views on Calderón see Frederick A. de Armas, "Rosaura Subdued: Victorian Readings of Calderón's *La vida es sueño*," *South Central Review* (in press).

38. Kenneth Muir, *The Sources of Shakespeare's Plays* (New Haven, Conn.: Yale University Press, 1978), p. 77.

39. Bears, lions, and wolves are again encountered in Segismundo's first soliloquy. Thus FitzGerald, like Calderón, seems fond of reiterative imagery, although the Victorian writer replaces the "outdated" concept of the four elements with images he believes are more pertinent to the situation.

40. All references to *A Midsummer Night's Dream* and *The Tempest* are from *The Complete Works of Shakespeare*, eds., Hardin Craig and David Bevington (Glenview, Il.: Scott, Foresman, 1973).

41. Henry W. Sullivan, *Calderón in the German Lands*, pp. 170-74.

42. William R. Blue, "Calderón and Shakespeare: The Romances." In *Calderón de la Barca at the Tercentenary: Comparative Views*, eds., Wendell Aycock and Sydney P. Cravens (Lubbock: Texas Tech Press, 1982), p. 93.

43. "Una moda superficial y passagera fue creada por el libro de Lionel Abel . . . el cual le dedica varias páginas a *La vida es sueño* considerándola como obra metateatral." Frank P. Casa, José M. Ruano, and Henry W. Sullivan, "Cincuenta años de investigación sobre el teatro español del Siglo de Oro en Norteamérica, 1933-1983," *Arbor* 116 (1983), 82.

44. Lionel Abel, *Metatheater. A New View of Dramatic Form* (New York: Hill and Wang, 1963), p. 68.

45. Eric S. Rabkin, *The Fantastic in Literature* (Princeton, N.J.: Princeton University Press, 1976), p. 82.

46. Ibid., p. 93.

47. Northrop Frye, *Spiritus Mundi* (Bloomington: Indiana University Press, 1976), p. 88.

48. Ibid.

49. Mary Wilson Carpenter and George Landow, "The Apocalypse in Victorian Literature." In *The Apocalypse in English Renaissance Thought and Literature,* eds., C. A. Patrides and Joseph Wittreich (Ithaca, N.Y.: Cornell University Press, 1984), pp. 299-322.

50. Ibid., p. 309.

51. Ibid., pp. 307-8.

52. Marjorie Reeves, "The Development of Apocalyptic Thought: Medieval Attitudes," In *The Apocalypse in English Renaissance Thought and Literature,* p. 44.

53. Bernard McGinn, *Visions of the End* (New York: Columbia University Press, 1979), p. 1.

54. Edwin Honig, *Calderón and the Seizures of Honor* (Cambridge, Mass.: Harvard University Press, 1972), p. vii.

55. Little criticism has been directed to apocalyptic images in *La vida es sueño.* See Frederick A. de Armas, "The Return of Astraea: An Astral-Imperial Myth in *La vida es sueño.*" In *Calderón de la Barca at the Tercentenary: Comparative Views,* eds., Wendell Aycock and Sydney P. Cravens (Lubbock: Texas Tech Press, 1982), pp. 135-59; and "The Serpent Star: Dream and Horoscope in *La vida es sueño,*" *Forum for Modern Language Studies,* 19 (1983), 208-23.

56. Richard Kenneth Emmerson, *Antichrist in the Middle Ages* (Seattle: University of Washington Press, 1981), p. 83.

57. Ibid., p. 84.

58. Calderón's passage has a different emphasis. In the Spanish masterpiece the child by his actions is saying: "Hombre soy, pues ya empiezo / a pagar mal beneficios" (vv. 276-77).

59. Emmerson, *Antichrist in the Middle Ages,* p. 80.

60. Ibid., p. 28.

61. Northrop Frye, *The Great Code* (New York: Harcourt, Brace, Jovanovich, 1982), p. 94.

62. Emmerson, *Antichrist in the Middle Ages,* p. 28.

63. Ibid., p. 134.

64. On *La vida es sueño*'s Platonic vision, see, for example, Michele Federico Sciacca, "Verdad y sueño en *La vida es sueño* de Calderón de la Barca," *Clavileño,* 1 (1950), 1-9; and Harlan G. Sturm, "From Plato's Cave to Segismundo's Prison," *MLN* [*Modern Language Notes*] 89 (1974), 280-89.

65. On the motif of the Golden Age in *La vida es sueño,* see Frederick A. de Armas, "The Return of Astraea."

66. Northrop Frye, *The Great Code,* p. 138.

67. "Faith . . . means absolute emancipation from any kind of natural 'law' and hence the highest freedom man can imagine: freedom to intervene in the ontological constitution of the universe." Mircea Eliade, *The Myth of the Eternal Return,* trans., Willard R. Trask (Princeton, N.J.: Princeton University Press, 1971), pp. 160-61.

Arthur Freeman (essay date 1997)

SOURCE: Freeman, Arthur. "Bernard Quaritch and 'My Omar': The Struggle for FitzGerald's *Rubáiyát.*" *Book Collector* (1997): 60-75.

[*In the following essay, Freeman explores the relationship between publisher Bernard Quaritch and FitzGerald, focusing on the publishing history of the* Rubáiyát.]

As a publisher, Bernard Quaritch's principal claim to memory lies in his association with Edward FitzGerald. Quaritch's imprint appears on the first four editions of **The Rubáiyát of Omar Khayyám** (1859, 1868, 1872, and 1879), as well as on the 1876 'public' *Agamemnon* and the deathbed *Readings in Crabbe* (1883), and his instrumentality in popularizing **The Rubáiyát** was well recognized in its time. 'I am delighted at the glory E. F. G. has gained by his translation', wrote FitzGerald's old friend W. B. Donne in 1876, 'and Bernard Quaritch deserves a piece of plate or a statue for the way he has thrust the Rubáiyát to the front';[1] for his own part Quaritch treasured the relationship, increasingly as time passed and FitzGerald's reputation took wing, and far more for its reflected 'glory' than its cash value.

But profit and proprietorship were never matters of indifference to the great bookseller, as the ensuing narrative will indicate. The tale of the first printing of FitzGerald's slender classic, its initial obscurity, its 'discovery' by various readers—including Swinburne and D. G. Rossetti—in Quaritch's penny-box in 1861, and its subsequent career as an international 'craze' (FitzGerald's own term) is too well-known to repeat in detail,[2] but the beginnings were simple enough. In 1858

FitzGerald had offered thirty-five quatrains to J. W. Parker at *Fraser's Magazine,* but after some six months of silence he reclaimed his manuscript, added forty more quatrains 'which I kept out for fear of being too strong' (EFG to E. B. Cowell, 2 November 1858), and resolved to 'print fifty copies and give [them] away'. In the event he commissioned about 250 wrappered copies from G. Norman, a Covent Garden printer, chose anonymity, and arranged for Quaritch—with whom he had corresponded over book purchases since 1853, and whom 'no wickedness can hurt' (EFG to W. H. Thompson, 9 December 1861)—to put his firm's name and address to the booklet, advertise it, and stock it. FitzGerald himself paid for the printing, the few advertisements, 'and other incidental Expenses regarding Omar', as 'I wish to do you'—he wrote to Quaritch on 5 April 1859—'as little *harm* as possible'. The British Museum stamped their deposit copy on 30 March, a day before FitzGerald's fiftieth birthday, but only two of the review copies that Quaritch sent out bore fruit,[3] and FitzGerald's personal supply of forty copies (requested 5 April, 'by Eastern Rail') might well have lasted him out the decade, given his diffidence in presenting them.[4]

How many Quaritch actually sold at a shilling we do not know, although in 1899 he, or the shop's cataloguer, maintained that it fell 'absolutely dead at the published price', and by July 1861 a number were consigned to the penny-box outside Quaritch's old Castle Street premises—his new shop at 15 Piccadilly having just opened. There they attracted the attention of two literary passers-by, Whitley Stokes and John Ormsby, and through them reached Rossetti and Swinburne, and latterly (when the price had risen, as Swinburne whimsically complained, 'to the sinfully extravagant sum of twopence') a host of new readers, including William Morris, Edward Burne-Jones, George Meredith, and John Ruskin. Perhaps this flutter of activity returned the title to Quaritch's Piccadilly shelves, for an old friend of FitzGerald's found a copy there in December (*Letters,* ii:417), and while part of the press-run may have been 'sold as waste-paper' or 'as much lost as sold' in the bookseller's move, 'some ten copies' turned up in January 1866 (*Letters,* ii:417-18 and iii:81) and temporarily satisfied retail demand. By October 1867 Quaritch was asking 3s. 6d. apiece for these relics ('I blush to see it!' FitzGerald twitted him), which encouraged the prospect of a second edition, with 'some 20 or 30 more Stanzas' (EFG to BQ, 14 October 1867). There is no indication that Quaritch credited FitzGerald's bookbuying account with any part of these late sales, however, as he regarded the remaining stock as his own, and FitzGerald clearly agreed.[5] For the enlarged second edition of 1868 FitzGerald again paid the printer, and left it to Quaritch to 'fix the most saleable price he can; take his own proper profit out of it; and when 50 copies are sold give me mine'. 'It seems absurd to make terms about such a pamphlet, likely to be so slow of sale', he told

Donne (14 February 1868), adding that 'I should be inclined to make the whole Edition over to him except such copies as I want to give away . . . but one only looks more of a Fool by doing so'.

No contracts survive for the 1859 or 1868 editions of *The Rubáiyát,* nor any formal agreements between FitzGerald and Quaritch over future sales, accountability, or—what became significant only in the 1870s, with its blossoming popularity—the copyright of FitzGerald's text. The rights and privileges of the poet and his nominal publisher, never clarified in the first decade of their association, were rendered murkier by the idiosyncrasies of both parties—FitzGerald's unbusinesslike attitude toward his own literary property, and his practice of forever tinkering with his text,[6] set against Quaritch's seigneurial attitude toward his own never-bestselling 'authors', and his personal disinclination to obey copyright deposit requirements, even copyright registry instructions. And the anarchic situation of international copyright law, which led even in FitzGerald's lifetime to dozens of American piracies of *The Rubáiyát* (and one printed at Madras, India, in 1862),[7] complicated the picture by its challenge to any practical control by a *bona fide* trustee. While Quaritch may genuinely have wished to serve his client-friend's best publishing interests, and (less certainly) those of his executors after 1883, the later history of Quaritch's struggle for proprietorship of 'my Omar' is not always edifying. Misunderstanding and misdirection cloud his forgiveable pride in having 'thrust the *Rubáiyát* to the top', while the attitude of his steely-eyed opponent W. A. Wright, bent on curtailing an amicable thirty-year franchise, inspires little more sympathy. But the episode rounds out a celebrated publishing 'romance', and a chronology of the extant letters and drafts of letters between Quaritch, FitzGerald, and FitzGerald's executors—many unpublished—may help to defictionalize it.

* * *

No attitude toward ongoing 'rights' is expressed in the extant letters from FitzGerald to Quaritch of 1859 (*Letters,* ii:331-2) and 1867 (*Letters,* iii:39-40: 'You must tell me, Busy and Great Man as you now are, whether you care to take charge of such a shrimp of a Book if I am silly enough to reprint it'; and iii:50). Regarding the third version of 1872, FitzGerald wrote '*"In re"* The Profits of Omar the Second [*sic*] . . . I write to you from a recollection of our agreeing to share them, as we shared in the publishing: you taking all the trouble etc., I the expense of Printing etc.' He suggests that Quaritch, who apparently had offered him £5, should pay whatever his share might be to the Persian Relief Fund, adding 'I should think your £5 more than covers [it]' (27 August 1872, endorsed by Quaritch indicating that £5 was sent on 3 September).

Now Quaritch was accustomed to 'owning' the rights to books he published, or even of which he held all the stock, and frequently made a fuss about it, as when a provincial newspaper unwittingly reproduced illustrations from Owen Jones's *Grammar of Ornament,* or when a British bookseller advertised for sale an American piracy of another text published in England by Quaritch. But in this instance he cannot have thought matters worth regularizing, and when in 1878 he approached FitzGerald again over a fourth edition, he may have been a little surprised at FitzGerald's rather more precise reaction.

'Do let me reprint the *Rubáiyát*!' he pleaded (18 November 1878). Many in 'a small but choice circle' of admirers want to buy it; 'insatiable' American pirates (the adjective, present in the letter book, is eliminated in the letter as sent) reprint and *misprint* it *'ad libitum'*: 'Allow me to publish another edition, and pay you twenty five guineas as the honorarium.'[8] But FitzGerald had previously (19 August) indicated that he did not want the *Rubáiyát* to be printed separately any more, as Quaritch preferred (having shrewdly perceived that this was its most saleable form), and had diffidently suggested a combination of Omar and Jámí (*Salámán and Absál*), which Quaritch could after all divide up again and sell individually if he chose;[9] and now (23 November) FitzGerald stood by his and his friend E. B. Cowell's preference for the pairing. On 9 December he asked 'whether you wish to undertake the Book: for an Edition of how many Copies; and on what terms', a letter which Quaritch endorsed 'offered £25 for privilege to print 1,000'. FitzGerald objected to quarto format (17 December: 'I have a dislike to see my minor things swelled out into 4to margin as if they were precious'), and thought 1000 copies excessive; on 16 January 1879 he reiterated his preference for 500 copies, which 'will see *me* out', and made three uncharacteristically firm 'stipulations', viz.: (1) 'That Omar, who is to stand *first,* be never reprinted separate from Jámí; (2) FitzGerald is to have proofs and revises and they are to be 'strictly' followed; and (3) FitzGerald's name is not to appear in the book or in advertisements, unless quoted 'from some independent Review'. But the key condition for permitting 1000 copies rather than 500 is 'some understanding as to the Copyright reverting to my Heirs, Executors or Assigns, in some stipulated time after my Decease . . . if you do not care for all such Bother, you have but to drop the thing, and no harm done on either side.'

This is apparently the first mention, on FitzGerald's part, of legal title to his own literary work, and it may well have reflected the advice of his friend and future executor William Aldis Wright, of Trinity College, Cambridge, a formidable Shakespeare and biblical scholar. For to Wright he had reported, a month earlier, Quaritch's repeated applications to reprint **The**

Rubáiyát, culminating in 'a humbugging Letter of his about "his Customers"—"twenty years connection", etc.'. Only for Cowell's sake, who favoured a reprint of *Salámán and Absál,* and 'who has more faith in Quaritch than I', did FitzGerald capitulate (he explained), although he resisted Quaritch's plan for large-paper copies, and mocked 'what he calls an "honorarium" of £25' (EFG to Wright, 17 December 1878). No doubt Quaritch, whose brusqueness belied a painfully sentimental streak, especially concerning his more luminous acquaintances, would have been doubly mortified—had he known—at FitzGerald's condescension, and Wright's sharing it. To FitzGerald's demands, however, he responded unambiguously and at once, 'as I am very anxious not to sever the bond which has connected us for above 20 years'. 'I agree to all the stipulations of your letter of yesterday', he wrote, viz., (1) small format; (2) Omar 'to stand first and never to be reprinted separate from Jámí; (3) proofs and revises to be supplied; (4) anonymity to be respected; (5) Quaritch to pay FitzGerald £25 on completion of printing (FitzGerald had not actually stipulated this); (6) 1000 copies to be printed (Quaritch explained that he would only 'recoup' on the second 500); and (7), later the nub of it all, 'The copyright to remain yours; of course no new edition to be brought out by you or your representatives whilst I have a stock of say fifty unsold copies' (17 January 1879, Letter Book I, p. 222; *Letters,* iv:175-6, from a transcript by Wright).

To this FitzGerald replied on 21 January, 'Well then—take Omar and Jámí on the terms proposed in your letter of Jan. 17. It is not worth more fuss on either side', and requested twenty free copies. The ensuing correspondence never returns to the matter of 'rights'. In May 1880 FitzGerald wrote 'I am glad that Omar has, as I suppose, pretty well cleared his Expenses. I was afraid that Jámí might hang about him: but Cowell wished for him [i.e., the united format]'—not quite the version of the matter he had vouchsafed to Wright.[10] In October 1882 FitzGerald again sought Quaritch's agency for his *Readings in Crabbe,* an edition of fifty copies, 'of which fifty copies you may perhaps sell about twenty-five if you will bestow on them the usual Publisher's care, at the usual Publisher's remuneration' (*Letters,* iv:533-4). As in early days FitzGerald would pay for the printing himself, and 'if you agree to undertake this very lucrative [*sic*] business' would place Quaritch's name on the title-page. This time there were no stipulations.

* * *

FitzGerald died in June 1883, with the Crabbe booklet still in uncirculated sheets. He left a box of corrected copies of most of his writings, with a letter to William Aldis Wright, whom he designated his literary executor. Wright took his duties seriously, and immediately set out to collect and reprint FitzGerald's far-strewn *opuscula,* according to his own firm editorial notions, together with a selection of letters and a biographical memoir of his own. How Quaritch would figure in his plans, if at all, was unclear at the outset, but two more temperamentally incompatible partners could hardly be imagined—Wright cool, precise, patient and donnish, intent on an academically respectable tribute, Quaritch demonstrative, impetuous, market-minded, and—yes—something of a vulgarian. Although common cause, in honouring FitzGerald, might once have united them, manners alone would have set them at odds; and once Quaritch backed down in a bluffing game over prior arrangements, Wright held all the cards. The traditional impression that Wright behaved coldly toward a vulnerably sentimental old man is not altogether unwarranted, but perhaps owes in part to the selectiveness exercised by Quaritch's daughter, in the appendix to her 1926 *Letters from FitzGerald to Quaritch.*

On 22 June 1883, a week after FitzGerald's death, Wright asked Quaritch to replace part of the preface to the Crabbe booklet with revised sheets, 'if there are any copies . . . yet unbound', and hinted that he had embarked on his own edition of FitzGerald—for he mentioned 'the letter of instructions which [FitzGerald] has left for me', and corrected copies of various books by FitzGerald which he possessed, and those which he sought. The executors had found about thirty copies of FitzGerald's Calderón translations (1853), theoretically suppressed, and 'would no doubt be willing to negotiate with you for them' (*Letters to Quaritch,* p. 89).

Quaritch replied promptly (23 June 1883, TCC Add. MS a.283[79]), but rather at cross-purposes, offering to buy 'any books, whether written by Mr. Fitzgerald or owned by him',[11] and to publish a 'Memorial Volume' of FitzGerald's works 'at my expense, giving to you a number of copies in lieu of an honorarium. I do not think there would be sale enough to make the posthumous works a commercial success,—but I gladly risk a loss because I should look upon the last work as a Monument to be erected to E. F.'s memory.' 'I am very proud', he added—as if Wright might forget—'of the fact, that I contributed to make the fame of Omar Khayam.' Wright evidently did not respond, and Quaritch returned to the matter on 19 November 1883, offering to reprint the 1853 Calderón 'uniformly with my last edition [of] Omar' and subsequently 'your volume of Biographical Memoirs the *same size,* so as to form a uniform series.' He offered the services of Michael Kerney, his polymath chief assistant, 'who used to assist Mr. Fitzgerald in bringing out his Omar' (TCC Add. MS a.283[80]).

Wright may well have regarded Quaritch's approach as presumptuous, and answered sharply on 25 November: 'my plan has grown and . . . in the event of my being

able to command sufficient material for carrying out this larger work I shall naturally place it in the hands of my own publishers Messrs Macmillan & Co. With this design on my part Mr. Crabbe one of the executors fully agrees, as do other of Mr. FitzGerald's friends.' He will not allow Quaritch to reprint Calderón, for the present (*Letters to Quaritch,* p. 90).

Quaritch was 'very much astonished and grieved' by this letter, protesting on 27 November that 'it was understood between you and me, that I was to be the publisher of your Memoir', reminding Wright again of his part in FitzGerald's fame ('I consider that it was due to my commercial agency, in distributing at a mere nominal price, the *first* edition of "Omar Khayam", that Fitzgerald obtained his subsequent celebrity'), adding smugly that 'the books Mr. Fitzgerald published elsewhere never had any circulation', and offering to pay for an engraved portrait (£25) as well as £25 more 'for the Manuscript [of "your Memoir"] . . . A *mere* publisher would simply look upon the venture as a commercial one, and as such, I think, it will not be remunerative. I am anxious that my name should remain associated with that of Fitzgerald, regardless of profit. Please reflect again on the subject' (*Letters to Quaritch,* p. 91; original in TCC, Add. MS a.282[81]). To this letter Wright replied sharply again (2 December 1883, *Letters to Quaritch,* p. 92), pointing out that no understanding about publishing had ever been reached, nor even mentioned: 'You must allow me to be the best judge of what I shall ultimately do with my own work. I do not undertake it for profit and therefore should not in any case accept your offer.'

Here the published *Letters to Quaritch* leave Quaritch and Wright, but they continued to correspond and to bicker. On 19 March 1884 (TCC Add. MS a.283[82]) Quaritch pressed Wright 'about Mr. Fitzgerald's unpublished works, letters, etc.', concerning which 'I had some grounds for expecting to hear from you'. There were further exchanges in 1886, 1889, and 1897-9, as we shall see.

But in the meantime Quaritch had become involved in what he professed to abominate, the American *Rubáiyát* industry. Houghton Mifflin & Co., the Massachusetts publishers, distributed through Quaritch a fancy edition (pirated, as always), illustrated by Elihu Vedder: letters to Quaritch of 17 and 24 November 1884 discuss forwarded proofs, 'electros', and positive reviews. Frustrated by Wright in his ambition to publish, distribute, or attach his name to FitzGerald's works, Quaritch took the surprising step of commissioning his own 'Collected Edition', produced in America. He engaged Theodore De Vinne, the distinguished New York printer, to set and print it in large and small paper, a two-volume work including every text known to him, plus an unsigned introduction by Michael Kerney

(Quaritch Letter Book I, pp. 321 (15 October 1886) and 329 (18 November 1886)). He offered Houghton Mifflin the opportunity to be 'the American publisher of Fitzgerald's Works, edited by Michael Kerney—if so, your name shall as such appear on the title pages'. His terms were enticing: 'I do not wish you to "speculate" on the book—you can have copies "on sale" on the same terms as I have your illustrated edition of Omar by Vedder.' Five hundred small-paper and fifty large-paper copies were planned, the cost yet unknown, but 'you could publish the work at whatever price you like'.

I do not think that Quaritch ever admitted responsibility for this project, nor acknowledged that Kerney oversaw it, but a proof of the engraved portrait and signature of FitzGerald (taken from a letter supplied by Quaritch) were sent to Quaritch by H. Costello, a commercial engraver, in March 1886; these appear as the frontispiece to the New York 1887 *Works,* published with the imprint 'New-York and Boston, Houghton, Mifflin & Co. / London, Bernard Quaritch'.[12] Quaritch sent a print of the finished engraving to E. B. Cowell, who thanked him on 3 April 1886, and to Wright, who apparently disliked it: for Quaritch was 'like you, much disappointed with Mr. Costello's etching of Mr. Fitzgerald's photographic portrait [for which] I paid £26/5/—. I hoped for a success and I have had an artistic failure' (5 April 1886, TCC Add. MS a.283[83]). Had Wright known at once of Quaritch's involvement with the unauthorized 1887 collection it is hard to imagine that he would not have protested directly—his own 'standard' collection being well on the way towards publication in 1889. Quaritch sent copies of the 'American' edition to William Simpson, Oliver Wendell Holmes, and E. B. Cowell; Cowell acknowledged Quaritch's 'long regard & esteem' for FitzGerald, but declined to write 'any notice of this Edition and Memoir' because of 'my friendship for Mr. Aldis Wright' (*Letters to Quaritch,* p. 101). Quaritch advertised the collection in his retail catalogues, but as if he were only its English distributor; he also offered Costello's etching separately, for 10s. 6d., with a no-doubt unsanctioned quotation from Cowell's letter of acknowledgement (*Letters to Quaritch,* p. 99).

But Wright was proceeding with his own authorized *Letters and Literary Remains,* and it may not be coincidental that a new correspondence began in November 1887. George Moor, a solicitor of Woodbridge, Suffolk (FitzGerald's home), wrote to Quaritch on behalf of the FitzGerald estate—disingenuously?—asking professional advice about 'the value of the published works and of those unpublished' (28 November 1887, original in Quaritch Letter Book II, p. 11; all the ensuing correspondence is in Letter Book II, between pp. 11 and 23). Quaritch sprang for the bait, and on 29 November declared that 'the copy-right value . . . involves no large pecuniary interest for his estate; since it does not comprise his chief book, the Omar

Khayyám, which has been my property since the issue of the first edition in 1858 [*sic*] . . . as for the other books which he printed, I should consider their copyright value as slender, to be measured, in fact, rather by sentimental than by commercial appreciation'. Quaritch followed this misleading letter with another one, offering £100 for the copyright of everything published and unpublished apart from Omar (which 'I already possess'), as a matter of convenience and sentiment, 'as the author was a dear personal friend of mine'. Or he would make it £150, if manuscript memoranda, etc., were thrown in.

Did Quaritch really imagine that the estate would regard him as the copyright holder for 'Omar' without further demonstration? Or had he simply forgotten the 1878 exchange with FitzGerald on the subject, as he was later to claim? The affair soon got out of hand, as far as Quaritch was concerned. Moor wrote civilly (1 December) that 'if we can get 100£ that sum ought to be acceptable', and Quaritch must have been mentally setting type, and composing his final rebuff to Wright. But on 5 December Moor requested, politely, 'sufficient evidence to satisfy the executors' that Quaritch 'had purchased the copyright of "the Omar Khayyám"'—the executors having been 'not aware' of that circumstance.

Quaritch continued to bluster, but more cautiously. On 6 December he was

> slightly surprised by your letter . . . which is not quite an answer to mine [about selling the other rights]. You have evidently misunderstood [!] my statement with regard to the Omar Khayyám copyright. I am the owner of it not 'by purchase', but by the free gift of the late Mr Edward Fitzgerald, at the time when I <produced *deleted*> published the first edition of the book in 1858.

> He was not, as you must be aware, a man of businesslike habits, from whom legal documents could have been expected—which indeed were hardly required under the circumstances. But he gave very valid confirmation of his gift, by a still further extension of his friendly liberality in conducting through the press, gratis, the successive editions which I produced, in 1868, and 1872, and 1879. All of them were sold entirely as my property and for my sole benefit [!].

To these extraordinary claims—considering that FitzGerald himself paid for the printing of the first three editions and that Quaritch divided the profits for the third and paid for the right to print a specified quantity of the fourth—Quaritch added the odd argument that although his largesse in offering £150 was mainly 'sentimental', it might also forestall American piracies. 'An edition of Mr. Fitzgerald's works in two octavo volumes has recently been produced at Boston', he solemnly informed Moor, so that 'interest and sentiment alike combine to make me more desirous of having Mr. Fitzgerald's remaining copyrights.' The draft of this devilish letter (Letter Book II, p. 13) is almost entirely in Michael Kerney's hand (see below).

Before Moor could reply, Quaritch had second thoughts, or, as he put it,

> made a discovery, which must modify the terms of that letter [of two days ago]. The late Mr. Fitzgerald was in the habit of writing and speaking to me continually for many years of the **Rubáiyát of Omar Khayyám** as 'your book' and 'your Omar', and that created an impression in my mind that the entire copyright of that book was mine in absolute ownership.
>
> I made a search yesterday amongst my old papers and letters, and I find that he so far altered his intention, on the occasion of producing the <fourth edition *deleted*> first edition of the Omar-Jámi (a single book, usually styled the fourth edition of *Omar*) as to reserve for his representatives a right of royalty on any republication, after the exhaustion of my *Omar-Jámí*. He has thus left it questionable whether he <had revoked *deleted*> then cancelled his original <purpose *deleted*> presentation of the *Omar* to me, or whether he reserved to his estate merely the copyright of the *Omar-Jámí*.
>
> In either case, it matters but little at present, as I have still a stock of about 200 copies of the book, and no one has the right to reprint it in England, or to bring out a book which shall comprise it.

Owing to his 'altered view of my position, above stated', Quaritch now offered £250 for all FitzGerald's copyrights (8 December 1887).

On the same day Quaritch wrote to E. B. Cowell, under the impression that Cowell was 'one of the parties in whose name Mr. Moor is acting', sending a copy of the new letter to Moor, explaining the earlier contradictory claim, and asking for help in swaying Wright to let Quaritch publish 'his projected *Life & Letters of Mr FitzGerald*'. Cowell replied on 9 December that he had 'nothing to do' with Wright's project, though they had discussed it at length: the disposition of it 'rests entirely with Mr Wright and the executors'. Quaritch underlined 'and the Executors' in blue pencil, as if planning a flank campaign.

On 11 December Aldis Wright sent Moor a transcript of Quaritch's concessionary letter of 17 January 1879 (*Letters,* iv:176n.), from the archives of the deceased. On 13 December Moor wrote to Quaritch, briefly as ever, 'I am sorry to say you cannot have the refusal of the Copyright of the late Mr Edwd Fitz-Geralds literary works'. Quaritch replied on 14 December, regretting this decision, finding it incomprehensible in terms of the interests of the estate, and wondering 'if there be any private influence which is 'hostile *deleted*' against me', which would thereby 'be greatly 'hostile *deleted*' adverse to the family which you represent, and to the due continuance of the growth of Mr. Fitzgerald's literary reputation'. Not surprisingly, Moor never answered, and his correspondence with Quaritch ceases here: all these painstakingly-worded letters from Quaritch are in

the handwriting of Michael Kerney, the *éminence grise* of the firm, to whom Quaritch habitually deferred in matters of social or legal delicacy.

On the very same day, however (14 December), Kerney also prepared a letter from Quaritch to Theodore De Vinne in New York. No copyright, no scruples: this was publishing hardball. 'I desire to bring out a *cheap* duo-decimo edition [of] Omar Khayyám's Rubáiyát as contained in the two-volume edition of Fitzgerald's Works which you have printed for me'. It was to contain Kerney's biographical preface and his editorial notes from the 1887 *Works,* and the text of both the first and fourth versions, i.e., 1859 and 1879. One thousand copies were desired, and 'the book is to be a very cheap one'. So much for Quaritch's 1879 undertaking to FitzGerald that 'Omar . . . [was] never to be reprinted separate from Jámí,' and so much for his candour as publisher: the title-page Kerney designed for De Vinne (Letter Book II, p. 17) ends with the imprint 'New York /J. W. Bouton /1888'. De Vinne's staff acknowledged Quaritch's letter of 27 December (De Vinne was now in London, and would visit Quaritch personally). Specimen proofs of the 'very cheap' separate *Omar* were sent Quaritch on 3 January 1888 and passed by Quaritch shortly afterward (Letter Book II, pp. 23-4).

Returning to the copyright home front, Quaritch received a letter on 15 December from Colonel Kerrich, on behalf of FitzGerald's executors, requesting details of the publication of **The Rubáiyát** in 1859 and *Agamemnon* in 1876, for the purpose of registering their own copyright. Quaritch replied that

> I never registered any of the books of Mr. Fitzgerald which I published, either at the time of their publication or afterwards, except the fourth edition of the **Rubáiyát of Omar Khayyám,** and even that was done a long time after the publication [in fact in 1884, after Quaritch's impasse with Wright], in deference to the suggestion of some friend. I have always regarded such registration as a mere useless formality. Indeed the whole of the copyright law is in an unsettled, or rather chaotic state, so that nearly every question arising under it seems capable of contradictory decisions by different judges.

Quaritch (or Kerney again) topped off this casual opinion with a reiteration of his offer to buy the copyrights for £250, but three further letters to and from Kerrich (17-19-21 December) made no headway whatever. For purposes of keeping his name 'linked' with FitzGerald's, Quaritch at last must come back to the cold shoulders of W. Aldis Wright.

Three days before Christmas Quaritch tried that unlikely correspondent again, brazenly offering Wright one hundred guineas for 'unpublished copies of four pieces by the late Mr. Fitzgerald—two translations from

Sophocles and one from Calderon'. Wright must by now have been fed up to the teeth, for his Christmas Eve answer is testy and final: no sale, and please note that

> Mr. FitzGerald . . . never parted with the copyrights of his published works although you in 1884 after his death registered the fourth edition of Omar Khayyám as your own. . . .
>
> I have now arranged with his Executors for the transfer to me of the copyright in all his work, published and unpublished, and I have therefore to call your attention to the unauthorized American reprint circulated by you which is an infringement of that copyright. If after this notice you continue to advertise and sell copies of this reprint in this country you will do so at your own risk.

Wright concluded by demanding 'a printer's certificate' of the number of copies of Omar-Jámí produced in 1879.

Quaritch's reply to this chilly dismissal is almost touching. On 27 December 1887 he pulled out all stops ('25 years most friendly relations . . . a question not of business, but of sentiment . . . would gladly pay you double what you can obtain from any other publisher') along with the litany of tradition ('In 1859 Mr. F made me a present of the first edition . . . it was through my exertions that the reputation of the book was established . . . claimed no royalty'). He offered his one trump, however: as long as he possessed fifty copies—and he had now 'little more than a hundred'—no new edition might appear save his own. Therefore he pleaded for the right to print 1000 more copies of a fifth edition, 'for which I would pay any fair price you choose to fix'. He transmitted the printer's certificate, and took 'due notice of what you say about the American "Works"'. Finally, a conciliatory appeal, man-to-man: 'Will you allow me to call on you?'

Wright gave not an inch. On 1 January 1888 he pressed Quaritch for 'more explicit assurance' that he would cease distributing the American *Works*. He declined to allow Quaritch to reprint Omar alone, as

> it was Mr. FitzGerald's express wish that it should never again be published separately, and he made this a condition with you when he gave you permission to print it with *Salámán and Absál*. I cannot therefore violate his distinct orders. Nor can I now make any change in my arrangement for the publication of his Letters and Remains. As I told you when you tried to tempt me with the offer of £25 for my part of the work when ready for press, my object is not gain,

Wright concluded with a devastating thrust, *'and you must not claim a monopoly in the sentiment'*. As an afterthought he offered to buy out Quaritch's stock of the 1879 Omar-Jámí, which of course would remove the impediment to republishing.

What chance of the last? Quaritch had already written to Moor (14 December 1887) that 'under the circumstances, I shall naturally feel no eagerness to divest myself of such [a] possession', although he deleted from the letter as sent the veiled threat which followed, *'unless the public is desirous of buying up my copies at an advanced price'*. In other words, Quaritch knew that he could block a new edition of *The Rubáiyát* as long as he chose to hold more than fifty copies in stock— unless, of course, the copyright holders or their agents systematically ordered them at the published price until they fell below the prescribed level. Quaritch decided not to play that game, however, and on 2 January he appeared to capitulate: the American *Works* would be 'withdrawn from sale by me, and the copies now in my <possession *deleted*> hands shall be sent out of the country'. The remaining copies of Omar-Jámí 'I prefer to keep', but—and this seems curiously magnanimous— 'since you do not intend to reprint the Omar *separately* from the "Remains" . . . I am willing to waive any objection to your collective edition, arising from the stipulation in my agreement with Mr. Fitzgerald that no reprint should be made while I held at least fifty copies'. Wright must have been startled into civility: he replied 'exceedingly obliged by your letter' on 3 January, adding that 'nothing could be more satisfactory, and I accept your assurances with full confidence'.

On the very same day (3 January 1888) De Vinne wrote to Quaritch with 'proof showing the type we propose to use in the new edition of Omar Khayyám'. Do we remember that small exercise in publishing spite? Its resolution borders on the comic: Houghton Mifflin again took up the slack. On 8 May (Quaritch Letter Book II, p. 31) they 'have received from Mr. De Vinne a dummy showing the style of binding . . . for the new edition of the "Rubáiyát", and also a set of proofs . . .'. They submitted details of costing and terms, asking Quaritch how to proceed. Quaritch, now at peace with Wright, washed his hands of the whole affair, but not without profit, for on 23 May he proposed 'that you pay De Vinne's bill (to be ascertained), and £50 to me, and that I transfer to you all the present stock and the stereos'. All that seems to have happened.

The last echoes of these copyright campaigns come in letters preserved in the Wright MSS at Trinity College Cambridge. Wright sent Quaritch the three-volume *Letters* and *Literary Remains of Edward FitzGerald* as a gift, and Quaritch acknowledged 'your extremely beautiful and excellent edition' on 29 June 1889, adding wistfully, 'I wish I had had the honor of being the publisher of these volumes'. On 12 August 1897 Quaritch warned Wright about American piracies circulating freely in England, from which the estate receives nothing, and asked

> Will you grant me the privilege of importing American editions of the book now? I am 78 years of age and

cannot hope to be alive in 1901 when the copy-right expires. You see I am still anxious to connect my name with the memory of Fitzgerald. . . . If you demanded it I should still be willing to pay a moderate premium for the right of importing American editions.

Wright refused yet again, but Quaritch persisted, 'extremely sorry that my letter . . . has given you so much offence', and offering £50 for the permission to import. Nothing, expectably, came of his appeal, but he repeated it on 26 November, and again on 24 February 1898: his point was (as always) that the public favoured the first version text, not the 'authorized' fourth, and that was just what the piracies provided. 'In April I shall be 79 years of age, it is therefore not likely I shall remain alive much longer to trouble about Omar', he reflected, concluding with a rare bookseller's observation, appropriate from the firm which remaindered the book for a penny: 'You have no doubt heard I bought at Sotheby's the first edition of Omar 2 weeks ago for £21.' Three months earlier he had offered just £5 to Cowell for a 'spare copy' of the book, if he had one (Arberry, p. 97), but this sale-room purchase made headlines. Lest anyone should doubt Quaritch's conviction, frowned on by FitzGerald himself, that the 1859 text would retain its ascendancy, 'the 2nd, 3rd & 4th editions [still] sell at low prices'. Once more Wright did not see fit to reply. *'The Worldly Hope men set their Hearts upon'*, their unsentimental friend might have reminded the applicant, *'Turns Ashes—or it prospers: and anon, / Like Snow upon the Desert's dusty Face / Lightning a little Hour or two—is gone'* (first—and in this instance the final—version).

Notes

1. *The Letters of Edward FitzGerald,* ed. A. M. Terhune and A. B. Terhune (Princeton, 1980), i:57; hereafter cited as *Letters.* The letters from FitzGerald to Quaritch are quoted by the Terhunes from C. Quaritch Wrentmore, ed., *Letters from Edward FitzGerald to Bernard Quaritch* (1926, hereafter cited as *Letters to Quaritch*), the originals apparently having not been consulted by them: see below, notes 9 and 10.

2. A summary appears in A. J. Arberry, *The Romance of the Rubáiyát* (1959), pp. 25-30, but the best account of the celebrated 'remaindering' is by Terhune and Terhune (*Letters,* ii:417-18).

3. Arberry (p. 24) and others are wrong in saying that no reviews appeared before Charles Eliot Norton's famous notice of 1869: see Terhune and Terhune, ii:336-7.

4. On 6 December 1861 EFG declared that he had given away only three copies: to E. B. Cowell, George Borrow, and 'old [W. B.] Donne' (*Letters,* ii:419).

5. Terhune and Terhune (ii:332) cast reasonable doubt on one of Quaritch's later anecdotes, describing a visit by FitzGerald to the shop with 'a heavy parcel' of 200 copies, of which he 'made me a present'; but FitzGerald himself told Cowell in December 1861 that 'I gave Quaritch what Copies I did not want for myself' (*Letters,* ii:416).

6. The four lifetime editions of *The Rubáiyát* (1859, 1868, 1872, and 1879) are substantially different, and even the 'final' text is subject to posthumously-recorded variants, bequeathed by FitzGerald to his executors.

7. FitzGerald was rather proud of the unlicensed activity, at first: 'I have not lived in vain, if I have lived to be *Pirated*!', he told Quaritch (31 March 1872), with specific reference to the Indian reprint.

8. Quaritch Letter Book I, p. 219; original in the Wright papers at Trinity College Cambridge (Add. MS a.7^{67}).

9. *Letters to Quaritch,* p. 56; inexplicably omitted from *Letters,* ed. Terhune and Terhune. Quaritch endorsed the original 'Permission to reprint Omar & Salámán'.

10. The passage quoted (a postscript) is printed in *Letters to Quaritch,* p. 79, but is omitted without explanation by Terhune and Terhune, *Letters,* iv:330.

11. On 10 August he sent one of the executors, the Rev. George Crabbe, £20 for 'Mr. FitzGerald's books', noting that '26 Euphranors in sheets'—i.e., copies of FitzGerald's *Euphranor,* 1851—were still outstanding (letter in private collection).

12. The copy itself was provided by Quaritch from London, which may explain the odd-looking 'New-York' in the imprint. See a description in the Bernard Quaritch list 'Seventy-five New Acquisitions, English Literature' (Autumn 1996), item 30.

Christopher Decker (essay date 1997)

SOURCE: Decker, Christopher. Introduction to Rubáiyát of Omar Khayyám: *A Critical Edition,* edited by Christopher Decker, pp. xiii-xlviii. Charlottesville, Va.: University Press of Virginia, 1997.

[*In the following introduction, Decker discusses the composition of the* Rubáiyát, *its early obscurity (due in part to FitzGerald's aversion to publicity), and its eventual "discovery" by the Pre-Raphaelites.*]

Since the turn of the century, reprints of Edward FitzGerald's **Rubáiyát of Omar Khayyám** have abounded on booksellers' shelves. No other book of poetry has appeared in so many guises, from the edition de luxe to the penny pamphlet. It has been issued in illustrated editions, in pocket-size wartime editions for servicemen in combat, in variorum editions, in limited editions, and in cheap paperbacks—FitzGerald's poem is the Proteus of modern book production. This diversity of dress is more than mere adornment. It reflects the poem's uncertain substance. Every reader of the *Rubáiyát* soon discovers that it exists in many textual versions, the fruit of FitzGerald's tenacious revising. Unfortunately, the good intentions of most reprints are undermined by careless editing. Their texts contain inaccuracies, and a complete account of the different versions is hard to come by: the editors of reprints offer one text or another but are often reluctant to explain the reasons for their choice. More often than not the editor's taste has been his guide. One editor likes the first version of the *Rubáiyát,* another prefers the last, and a third clings to the second version as his favorite text. Scholarly editors play the same game, behind the screen of "original intentions," "authoritative text," and more loosely, "what FitzGerald wrote." It is almost the rule that FitzGerald's editors adapt the evidence to suit their editorial theories or to cater to their own preferences. FitzGerald's motivations for revising, for creating a variously beautiful work in verse, are disregarded. It might seem harsh to censure the enthusiasm with which the *Rubáiyát* has been edited and published, when it has yielded such abundance to generations of readers. But enthusiasts are not always the best defenders of the text. The fact remains that reprints and other "editions" misrepresent FitzGerald's work by reproducing the same textual errors, the same oversights, and the same false assumptions. A reliable text of the *Rubáiyát of Omar Khayyám* is needed.

This edition of FitzGerald's *Rubáiyát* is the first critical text of the poem. All four texts of the poem published during FitzGerald's lifetime are presented here, with their original prefaces and notes. The texts have been edited from the earliest editions, and emendations correct original errors in printing and transcription. All the extant versions of the poem, as written by FitzGerald, are supplied in an appendix. Three further appendixes include the poet's Latin translation of *rubáiyát* by Omar Khayyám, a guide to Persian pronunciation, and a select glossary. I explain my editorial procedure in the textual note and append a list of emendations made in the critical text.

The introduction offers a brief sketch of the lives of Omar Khayyám and Edward FitzGerald, lives that press in upon the *Rubáiyát of Omar Khayyám.* From these biographies I turn to a composition history of the four published versions of the poem.

KHAYYÁM AND FITZGERALD

"Omar Khayyám was born at Naishápúr in Khorassán in the latter half of our Eleventh, and died within the First Quarter of our Twelfth, Century." Reading these words, one can scarcely believe that they introduced the most popular verse translation into English ever made. The tone is so matter-of-fact, so unassuming, and except for the closing paragraphs, so self-indifferent. The *Rubáiyát of Omar Khayyám* begins not with an argument or a statement of purpose, but with a biographical preface: the life and beliefs of the mathematician Khayyám. In the long time since this preface was written, little has been added to our knowledge or our understanding of Omar Khayyám. The few facts that survive eight centuries are enmeshed in anecdotes written by persons who could not have known him and who often gathered their information many years after his death. If we add to these stories the oblique reflection of his personality in his treatises on mathematics and natural philosophy, along with the loosely articulated self-portrait in his verse, we have the sum biography of FitzGerald's "astronomer-poet."

Omar Khayyám was born at Nishapur, a city in the northeast province of Persia called Khorassan, in A.D. 1048 and died there in 1131. During his lifetime he became famous for his contributions to mathematics and astronomy, a reputation that still partially eclipsed his Persian verses before FitzGerald's translation rediscovered them. The best brief summary of Khayyám's scientific work is E. S. Kennedy's article "The Exact Sciences in Iran under the Saljuqs and Mongols."[1] Kennedy casts doubt on the traditional view that Khayyám was directly involved with the reformation of the calendar under the Sultan Malik-Shah, a story credited by other writers including FitzGerald. Established evidence of Khayyám's work includes problems in euclidean geometry, geometric solutions to all possible types of cubic equations (by means of intersecting conic sections), and observational astronomy.

Khayyám completed his early education in Nishapur and in Balkh, another city of Khorassan, to the east of Nishapur. His treatise on algebra was written at Samarqand, where he also began his steady rise in the service of the Saljuq sultanate. The Saljuq Turks had invaded the province of Khorassan in the 1030s, and the city of Nishapur surrendered to them voluntarily in 1038. Thus Omar Khayyám grew to maturity during the first of the several alien dynasties that would rule Iran until the twentieth century. Under Saljuq rule, an intolerance of heterodox views prevailed. Many of Khayyám's quatrains in favor of retirement from the heat of public life are merely pragmatic. Why risk your neck (or worse) in the pursuit of civil appointments when you could keep your own counsel and spend your time on cubic equations, watching the stars, and writing poetry? He studiously avoided the dangerous rituals of court life, and when his patron Malik-Shah died in 1092, Khayyám fell from favor. Before returning to permanent retirement in Nishapur, he made the pilgrimage to Mecca required of the faithful. Once in Nishapur, he kept to himself and took few pupils. By an outward show of faith and by carefully restricting his acquaintance, he managed to avoid too much scrutiny of his unorthodox views.

Khayyám's philosophical opinions survive in epistolary and in quasidialogical form. His writings are concerned with many topics, among them ontology; concepts of free will, predestination, and moral obligation; the motivations and responsibility of the Creator; and the problem of universals. The Islamic intellectual tradition borrows extensively from Greek discoveries and advances in the exact sciences, but philosophy was a more problematic subject. The translation and extensive use by Islamic thinkers of scientific works, particularly those of Aristotle, are not matched by an untrammeled enthusiasm for more speculative or abstract philosophy. By its more strident critics, Greek philosophy was seen at best as inapplicable to Muslim life, and at worst as blasphemous. To some radicals, Khayyám was a perfect example of a scientist gone astray, tempted by Greek learning into a rejection of Islam. For an undercurrent of skepticism runs through his writings, and it was this private doubt that got Khayyám into trouble. "Though the Sultan 'shower'd Favours upon him,' Omar's Epicurean Audacity of Thought and Speech caused him to be regarded askance in his own Time and Country." Flouting convention was bound to appeal to FitzGerald, for whom Omar Khayyám seemed a Persian amalgam of Lucretius and Anacreon—atomist and hedonist in one. He suggests in the *Rubáiyát* that Khayyám's religious doubt stemmed from the skepticism inherent in his natural philosophy. The various stories about Khayyám agree with this explanation, insofar as they blame the influence of foreign thinking for his apostasy.

In his preface to the 1859 edition of the *Rubáiyát,* FitzGerald also claims that the relative unpopularity of Khayyám's poetry in Persia stemmed from its religious and prosodical heterodoxy, a reflection of Khayyám's mathematical turn of mind.

> The Mathematic Faculty, too, which regulated his Fansy, and condensed his Verse to a Quality and Quantity unknown in Persian, perhaps in Oriental, Poetry, help'd by its very virtue perhaps to render him less popular with his countrymen. If the Greeks were Children in Gossip, what does Persian Literature imply but a *Second Childishness* of Garrulity? And certainly if no *ungeometric* Greek was to enter Plato's School of Philosophy, no so unchastised a Persian should enter on the Race of Persian Verse, with its "fatal Facility" of running on long after Thought is winded!

FitzGerald's criticism here is, like all criticism, partially autobiographical. For this captious opinion of Persian poetry closely resembles his shortsighted outlook on poems and novels written by his own contemporaries. His letters often complain of the "fatal Facility" of much Victorian writing, its tendency to protract whatever line of thought it was engaged upon, with often a fine ear for profusive sound but really nothing to add in sense. A disapproval of texts both massy and mass-produced led FitzGerald to one extreme of literary criticism—in his spare time he amused himself with abridging literary works by the direct application of scissors and paste.

The passage above also reveals FitzGerald's anxiety about the reception of his own works. Reviewers had disparaged his translations of Calderón for their economy with the literal meaning of the plays. A translation from the Persian would be less likely to encounter much informed criticism, thus evading the capacity of critics to charge him with infidelity to his originals. But how would the English reading public receive such a strange new voice, proposed in an unfamiliar form and couched in exotic apothegms? A prolix era like Omar Khayyám's, or his own, might not appreciate the *Rubáiyát*'s terse concinnity.

FitzGerald's fears lead him to understate Omar Khayyám's early unpopularity. The truth is more complicated. None of Khayyám's contemporaries, who knew the mathematician in person or by his works, refer to his poetry. This may not in itself establish that he wrote no poems at all, but it is clearly unusual that the later, popular conception of the learned scientist relaxing in poetic numbers would not have developed in his lifetime if his authorship was public knowledge. One thing at least is certain: Khayyám's quatrains were not written down in manuscript collections until well after his death. The Iranian writer, scholar, and politician Ali Dashti has studied the process whereby Khayyám's verses achieved their modest reputation in the canon of Persian literature.[2] According to Dashti, the earliest reference to his poetry is in the *Kharidat al Qasr* of Emadoddin Kateb Qazvini, an account of the lives of poets in the Islamic world written about fifty-five years after the death of Khayyám. In the chapter on poets of Khorassan, the author pays tribute to Khayyám's excellence in mathematics and astronomy, adding that in Isfahan a certain Arabic verse of his was often heard. The first quotation of a *ruba'i,* the Persian tetrastich form favored by Khayyám, is in an essay by Fakhroddin Razi (1149-1209), the Persian philosopher and author of works on history, jurisprudence, and astronomy. The occasional attribution to Khayyám crops up in works written from the mid-thirteenth century until the beginning of the fifteenth. The earliest important collections appeared in the first half of the fourteenth century, but even these are based on relatively small groups of quatrains, or *rub'iyat*: thirty-one in the *Nozhat al-Majales* (1330-31), a mere thirteen in the *Mo'nes al-Ahrar* (1339-40). The Ouseley manuscript (1460) in the Bodleian Library at Oxford has 158 quatrains. This manuscript and the so-called Calcutta manuscript, which has 516 quatrains, were the working texts from which FitzGerald composed his *Rubáiyát.* There are many other manuscripts in which quatrains by Omar Khayyám subside or swell in number. All in all, the estimated number of quatrains attributed to Khayyám is an extraordinary 2,213.[3]

Why were Khayyám's verses, if authentic, neglected for so long after his death? And when they began to appear in manuscript collections, why did they burgeon in such absurd proportions? The second question is more easily answered. Just as anonymous writings in the Hippocratic corpus were ascribed to Hippocrates, it was common for poetry written in the style or manner of Khayyám to be attributed to him. His name became a byword for the kind of poetry it inspired. The *ruba'i* is not an intricate form and could be more readily imitated than longer forms like the ode. His imitators allowed themselves considerable freedom. The Khayyám manuscripts contain quatrains expressing such diverse opinions that multiple authorship becomes obvious. Some "wandering quatrains" supposedly by Khayyám are attested in manuscripts of Attár, Rumi, and other Persian poets. Various scholars have tried to pare away the spurious verses, and still the number of "genuine" quatrians varies from 121 to 255 to 143 to 178.

The early neglect of Khayyám's poetry may have been due to his "Epicurean Audacity of Thought and Speech," in FitzGerald's phrase. Dashti believes that Khayyám did not circulate manuscript copies of his poems. After his death, the poems found among his working papers may have been suppressed by his friends. Or perhaps his friends memorized the poems he read to them and later wrote them down, a transmission history that would account for variants in the manuscript texts. Either way, it would have taken some time for his poetry to come to light. The popularity of any poet's work is bound up with the publicity it receives. This not only implies the favor of the reading public or the author's talent for self-promotion, but includes the ways that a poet's work is published. The number of copies produced, the sections of the reading public to which various editions are directed, and marketing strategy in general all influence the reception of a literary work. In this sense, FitzGerald's *ruba'iyat* had a fate remarkably similar to Khayyám's, as will be seen.

Until the popularity of FitzGerald's translation awakened a universal interest in the quatrains of Khayyám, the reputation of the medieval Persian skeptic was supported on the historical importance of his scientific achievements. Scholars of Near Eastern culture still insist that, although they consider Khayyám's quatrains negligible beside his treatise on algebra, they have the greatest admiration for FitzGerald's poem. The caviling about FitzGerald's "free translation" has died down, and most agree that a remarkable transfusion occurred when Khayyám's quatrains were newly enfleshed in the *Rubáiyát of Omar Khayyám.* Readers of several generations have likewise seen FitzGerald and Omar Khayyám as twin souls, or as one soul shared between their verses. This neat biographical twist repeats (too hyperbolically) FitzGerald's own appraisal of his relationship with Khayyám. In fact, the two men were not much alike. To begin with, Khayyám was a great mathematician, so highly respected that he was addressed with the honorifics "Sage of the World," "Philosopher of the Universe," and "Successor to Avicenna."[4] As for FitzGerald, his most recent biographer has shown that his interest in mathematics amounted to less than indifference:

> The course of study, or tripos, that FitzGerald and most undergraduates read was divided into natural philosophy, which was primarily mathematical; theology and moral philosophy, which was largely concerned with the proofs of Christianity; and Greek and Latin literature. And of these burdens mathematics was the greatest, for the majority of undergraduates the most common reason for their needing private crammers, and the usual direct cause of their leaving Cambridge without a degree. . . . FitzGerald and his friends used to have long joint study sessions in the vain hope of coming to grips with the subject. One of Thackeray's delightful drawings of Trinity undergraduates shows a group of his puzzled friends grappling with "Conic Sections," which gave him the title for the sketch. Among the others sits FitzGerald, his down-turned mouth indicating that he is no happier than his fellows, but his rapt, far-away expression suggesting that he has long since given up thinking of ellipses and parabolas.[5]

No doubt some supervisions from Khayyám would have helped the bored undergraduate. FitzGerald did not have the power of sustained mental activity, the *motus animi continuus* of great poets or great mathematicians. He possessed "what Goethe calls the 'Barber's talent' of easy narrative of easy things—can tell of Barton, and Chesterton Inn, but not of Atreus, and the Alps," and he frankly admitted that this talent was not properly suited to literary composition. Writing to Bernard Barton in 1842, he expressed disdain for hack writing: "I know that I could write volume after volume as well as others of the mob of gentlemen who write with ease: but I think unless a man can do better, he had best not do at all; I have not the strong inward call, nor cruel-sweet pangs of parturition, that prove the birth of anything bigger than a mouse."[6] Both he and Khayyám chose the self-contained tetrastich for its epigrammatic conciseness. FitzGerald believed that Khayyám was led by his "Mathematic Faculty" to write in brief and formulaic stanzas, and he himself discovered that the compact stanzas could be "tesselated into a sort of Epicurean

Eclogue in a Persian Garden," thus solving his problem of giving poetical birth to anything "bigger than a mouse."

Khayyám's rejection of court life and praise of retirement are a response to life under Saljuq rule, where death was the likely outcome of political ambition. FitzGerald's situation could not present a starker contrast. Far from risking his life, his only danger was the abysm of ennui. His disgust with the showiness of high society is not Omar Khayyám's fearful preoccupation with the average life span of the Persian elite. Yet somehow the differences between the two poets become blurred in the *Rubáiyát of Omar Khayyám.* To FitzGerald, he and Khayyám were so much alike in the sentiments they expressed that the Persian mathematician seemed the ideal persona for a long lyric of discrete stanzas on friendship, conviviality, retirement, the speciousness of religious comfort, and the pleasure of living because death is so near. His perception of their shared concerns was enough to convince him that at last he had found the poetic influence he had always needed in order to write. The art of the *Rubáiyát* is FitzGerald's, but he needed Omar Khayyám to unearth his buried talent.

Edward FitzGerald and the *Rubáiyát*

The *Rubáiyát of Omar Khayyám* can be read as one of the best poems ever written about the condition of not being a great poet, and not wanting to be. The poem is affined, and affiliated, with Gray's "Elegy Written in a Country Churchyard," that great meditation on the condition of ungreatness. But unlike the Elegy, it surmounts an analysis of modest means with a prescription for the good life. It praises humility not merely because it is Christian to do so, but because the humble life is one in which disappointment is so reduced as to assume the features of contentment. For FitzGerald, rhyme's vexation was less a dull narcotic, numbing pain than a way of taming the fierceness of boredom and loss.

In many ways the *Rubáiyát of Omar Khayyám* is the epitome of FitzGerald's life, a memorious summary of his desires, values, and writing habits. He composed the poem during the most difficult period of his life, when he badly needed the consolation of poetry and Khayyám's philosophy. Only a month before he was introduced to the Persian language, FitzGerald wrote to W. M. Thackeray:

> Meanwhile, I truly believe there is no Man alive loves you (in his own way of love) more than I do. Now you are gone out England, [*sic*] I can feel something of what I should feel if you were dead: I sit in this seedy place and read over Bouillabaisse till I cry again. This really is so: and is poor work: were you back again, I should see no more of you than before. But this is not

from want of love on my part: it is because we live in such different worlds: and it is almost painful to me to tease anybody with my seedy dullness, which is just bearable by myself. Life every day seems a more total failure and mess to me: but it is yet bearable: and I am become a sad Epicurean—just desirous to keep on the windy side of bother and pain.[7]

A "sad Epicurean" was how he had come to see himself in 1852, at the age of forty-three. The letter, choked with colons and repetitions, also shows how deeply FitzGerald felt about his friendships. Friendships were life to him, a life enacted elsewhere by more committed souls. The letter to Thackeray reveals that he saw the slow disembodiment of these friendships, sustained only by letters and intermittent reacquaintance, as a kind of dying. His own life seemed uninteresting compared with those of his friends.

Born in 1809 to wealthy English and Anglo-Irish parents, Edward Purcell (the family name he was first given) knew the securities and discomforts of growing up in a large family belonging to the landed gentry of Suffolk. Seven brothers and sisters made up his childhood companionship, unenlivened by much contact with their parents. Their father, John Purcell, did not leave a great impression on his children, to judge by the spare account of him in his son's letters. He seems to have been kindhearted but largely indifferent to his family. He invested his money in business ventures that failed and spent his time in country sports. Although not dependent on his wife's considerably larger personal fortune, he was plainly unequal to her status and grandiose manner.[8] On the death of Mrs. Purcell's grandfather in 1818, she received an inheritance (in liquid assets and property) of such magnitude that the family name was changed to hers, FitzGerald, as a reflection of the financial imbalance. Only Edward's brother John would later replace the FitzGerald name with the double-barreled Purcell-FitzGerald. Throughout his life, Edward FitzGerald had a strained and unloving relationship with his mother. He resented the duty of attending on her at public functions, and he was embarrassed by her love of finery and social ostentation. Elaborate dinners, impossibly crinolined concerts, church, and London were too much for him. They nurtured in him a life-long aversion to pomp and conventional hypocrisy.

The first breathing space he found outside the close confinement of his family was at school and later at university. FitzGerald matriculated at Trinity College, Cambridge, in 1826. It was here that he formed his ideas of what his life should be. He was a middling scholar in subjects that did not interest him, and since he read only the classical and modern literatures with pleasure, he had just one leg of the tripos to stand on. He sat his final examinations in 1830 and was ranked 106th in the pass degrees.[9] The most valuable thing he had learned as an undergraduate was the importance of friendship. At Cambridge he made the friends, and the kind of friends, that he would always have: scholars, parsons, poets, and public functionaries. Friendships with Tennyson and Thackeray, both of whom he met at Cambridge, persuaded him that he could be a writer, and from time to time he wrote original verses. Once the fever of creation had subsided, however, he had to admit how inadequate his talents for invention really were. He felt more sure of himself in rearranging the work of others. He arranged musical compositions while in the musical society Camus, and later in life he would buy paintings so he could retouch them or cut them to fit frames he already owned. He kept several commonplace books, collecting in them his favorite lines of verse and observations on many other subjects. One of his earliest publications, *Polonius: A Collection of Old Saws and Modern Instances* (London, 1852), was a compilation of aphorisms and witty sayings culled from his restless reading.

In art as in friendship, FitzGerald was most comfortable at a distance. Closeness made him too aware of his insufficiencies, his clumsiness, but living or writing at one remove came more easily. He enjoyed his friends' successes, even if he was slightly envious of them. Tennyson and Thackeray achieved their literary fame before FitzGerald's middle age, and his letters to them are always gently disrespectful, as if afraid that too much congratulation would estrange them. If he shocked or overwhelmed his correspondents (Carlyle once had to admonish him to "send no more bones" from an excavation at Naseby), it was usually because he tried too hard to project his personality, his goodwill, across the physical divide. FitzGerald was well aware of how he threw himself into his letters. He often apologized for writing so copiously and for revealing so much, and he begged his correspondents not to feel compelled to reply or to be disappointed when a meeting between old acquaintances was less satisfying than their epistolary exchange. By losing thoughts of himself in thinking of others, he found life bearable. This habitual transference prepared him for his most important literary friendship, with the "Epicurean Infidel" Omar Khayyám.

It was another friendship, with Edward Byles Cowell, that introduced him to the study of Persian. The poet met Cowell in 1844, when Cowell was eighteen and FitzGerald thirty-five. FitzGerald soon formed a high opinion of Cowell's ability to memorize a vast amount of information and of his "delicacy of discrimination." The son of an Ipswich merchant, Cowell had absorbed a detailed knowledge of Latin, Greek, and French while a pupil at Ipswich Grammar School. His enthusiasm extended to oriental languages, in which he was a precocious autodidact. He taught himself Persian and even attempted to teach himself Sanskrit, though apparently without much initial success. (He persevered, however.

In 1867 he became the first Professor of Sanskrit at Cambridge University.) Soon after their first meeting Cowell was suggesting new authors to FitzGerald, and the two friends would read together when they could, a habit that was not broken until Cowell left for India in 1856.

But that time was still almost ten years away when Cowell translated some of the odes of Háfiz for FitzGerald in the summer of 1846. "Your Háfiz is fine," said the latter,

> and his tavern world is a sad and just idea. I did not send that vine leaf to A. T. but I have not forgotten it. It sticks in my mind.

> In Time's fleeting river
> The image of that little vine-leaf lay,
>   Immovably unquiet—and for ever
> It trembles—but it cannot pass away.

He adds, "It would be a good work to give us some of the good things of Háfiz and the Persians, of bulbuls and ghuls we have had enough."[10] The editors of FitzGerald's correspondence note that this whimsical verse is an altered quotation of Shelley's "Evening, Ponte al Mare, Pisa."[11] FitzGerald's misquotation is made in jest, but it shows how quickly his mind adapted another poet's lines to new purposes. At the time he expressed an eagerness for more translations of Persian literature, but Cowell would not publish his versions of Háfiz's odes until 1854.

FitzGerald's first translation for Cowell was from Lucretius, a poet for whom he felt a certain philosophical kinship, as he would for Omar Khayyám. A letter of early May 1848 contained a "free translation of a fine bit" of *De rerum natura,* accompanied by FitzGerald's exclamation: "I am astonished at the diversity of guesses by divers annotators in the notes to my edition. What is the history of the MSS? They must be as corrupt as those of Aeschylus."[12] These remarks were no doubt intended to draw Cowell out of his inveterate shyness, to prompt him to some learned pronouncement or scholarly labor. But this indirect flattery shows how FitzGerald was alert to complications in transmission history, a sensitivity that would influence his translations of the Khayyám manuscripts and help him defend his opinions about Omar Khayyám.

In 1850 Cowell began tutoring FitzGerald in Spanish, and the older pupil proved so adept that from October 1852 to the summer of 1853 he rendered *Six Dramas of Calderon* into English (published in July 1853). His letters to Cowell's wife worried over his principle of free translation. FitzGerald anticipated unfavorable reviews of the *Six Dramas* well before the harsh criticisms indeed appeared. "What I doubt about in the Book's success is this: that so few read Spanish (though so easy) that the Newspaper Critics either won't notice at all, or condemn as a free Translation (which it is and will profess to be) so as to keep their own ignorance of the matter safe anyhow."[13] His decision to translate freely arose from several causes. Word-for-word prose translations were not to his liking, for they were no more than academic exercises or cribs. Then too, he believed he could "hardly make Calderon interesting to English Readers unless with a large latitude of interpretation." His redrafting of Calderón's dramatic language would make the plays more accessible to an audience unfamiliar with the types and conceits of Spanish drama. But the main reason is that his enthusiasm may have outraced his learning. FitzGerald's command of Spanish was less than fluent, and he depended on Cowell to elucidate the meaning of difficult passages in the original. A free translation might be less open to attack on the grounds of misrepresentation. By translating freely he hoped to protect himself from one kind of adverse criticism, though exposing himself to another.

The reviews were extremely cutting, and as FitzGerald had expected, his critics did not show any knowledge of Spanish themselves, but only criticized him in theory for presenting an adaptation rather than a literal version. The experience was disheartening, and he did not think of publishing another translation for several years. Completing the work on Calderón left him free to indulge his newfound interest in Persian, but it was not clear from the first that FitzGerald and Persian would take to one another.

When FitzGerald visited the Cowells in late December 1852, Cowell suggested that he begin the study of Persian. In a letter to Mrs. Cowell written a few days after Christmas, FitzGerald's name is signed in Persian characters, a mark of gratitude for his friends' hospitality. However, the business of publishing Calderón meant that his Persian studies would hang fire for several months. In September 1853 he wrote to Mrs. Cowell, "I have scarce looked at Persian since I saw you: and believe my knowledge of it will end with the Alphabet if it ever accomplish that."[14] Less than a month after he uttered this gloomy prognosis, he wrote to the Cowells again, still evincing only a casual interest in Persian. He had leafed through Sir William Jones's *Grammar of the Persian Language* (4th ed., 1797) but was uncertain about taking up the language in earnest. Reading his letter, it is not difficult to see that what he expressed as disinclination was really indolence. "In your rambles about Town," he directed Cowell,

> pray ask about that copy of Ferdusí you told me of (an imperfect one, I mean) and also about that common Cheap Persian Dictionary. Do not buy them, however: but let me know what they will cost. I am not sure of even *wanting* either: for I am not *greatly* impressed with the desire to poke out even a smatter of Persian: and, even if I were, I must pause again before entrust-

ing you to buy books for me when you won't let me repay you. I got to the end of *looking at* Sir W. Jones' Grammar yesterday: and was pleased with that bit of Ferdusí which the gallant Sultan Togrul (which so nearly rhymes with "Doggrel") sung out while going into the Battle where he fell. I don't quite understand why the *Horse* should be compared to a furious Elephant, however: and why any Native should call that Elephant Pýl strikes me as odd. I expect it is the story of Togrul that Jones so deftly introduces that gives colour to the Verses.[15]

In the following weeks he acquired a Persian dictionary and Persian texts, staying close to shore and relying on Cowell to steer him through difficult passages. But for one reason or another, he could not give Persian his undivided attention. Letters mention that he was reading *Don Quixote* and Frederick Tennyson's new book of poems, among other things, and that he was greatly distracted by moving out of Boulge Cottage, where he had lived for more than fifteen years.

Despite the subsequent inconvenience of moving into temporary residences only to move out again after a week or so, FitzGerald managed to find the time to translate selections from Jones's *Grammar,* and these he sent to Cowell for correction. By the end of January 1854, he was confident enough in his progress to complain about the translations against which he checked his own renderings: "Certainly Eastwick is *wretched* in the Verse: and both he and Ross (I have both Versions) seem to me on a wrong tack wholly in their *Style* of rendering the Prose. Because it is elegant Persian they try to render it into *Elegant* English; but I think it should be translated *something* as the Bible is translated, preserving the Oriental Idiom. It should be kept as Oriental as possible, only using the most idiomatic Saxon *words* to convey the Eastern Metaphor."[16] Already FitzGerald had developed strong opinions about translating from Persian. He continued to translate from the works of several poets, including Sa'dí, Firdusí, and Háfiz. By early May he had also begun translating **Salámán and Absál**, a Sufi allegory by Jámí.

This sort of work cemented his friendship with Cowell. Cowell's letters to FitzGerald, helpfully attending to every query, are a measure of his devotion to the older man. For many of them were written in the midst of a very busy life. Cowell's learning was largely the result of independent study, but his wife had finally convinced him to enroll in an Oxford college. Cowell matriculated at Magdalen College in 1850, reading for the B.A. he would need if his academic career was to progress. After exams in the autumn of 1854, he was awarded a first class degree. It was during his time as a mature undergraduate that Cowell spent so much time helping FitzGerald with his Persian.

Their correspondence often indicates how far FitzGerald trusted to his more learned friend's judgments on points of translation. In January 1855 he proposed to Cowell that they collaborate on a translation of ***Salámán and Absál***: "In looking over my Salámán I think I see how *that* could be compressed into a very readable form: and should like to manage it with you. You have brought all the Scholarship, and really the Intellect: perhaps I may have the tact to dish up the poem neatly: I mean *in shape*: for believe me your English will be wanted here quite as much as I think mine is wanted in other matters. But don't you or Wife talk of any such intention of ours, or mine; for what I propose is a very little affair, and I hate any of my dabblings to make me seem to set up Author."[17] "Other matters" meant versification, and FitzGerald very quickly composed a "metrical Abstract" of an abridgment of the poem. This he sent to Cowell and asked him to "read and correct" it, adding deferentially: "I have always used the English rendering I found pencilled after your dictation, as the best—the best in English as well as the safest in regard to accurate Translation."[18] At this time FitzGerald was shaken by the sudden death of his mother, and by having "to plague, and to be plagued by, Lawyers, Trustees, and Chancery" over the execution of her estate. At first he stayed in a hotel, but he soon moved into lodgings he had first occupied in 1841. During this lonely and trying period, Cowell and he worked away at the translation of ***Salámán.*** In April, FitzGerald sent *Fraser's Magazine* the final revised copy of their efforts. The editor rejected it, afraid that "it was too long" and not "of a nature to suit his Magazine."[19]

This disappointment lingered until the following January, when FitzGerald had ***Salámán and Absál*** printed privately by the firm of John Childs and Son of Bungay. The circulation of the poem was in this way limited to those friends the poet desired to please. The text was considerably revised from the state in which FitzGerald had offered it to *Fraser's*: "I cut away even more than when you saw it: lightened the Stories, as you desired; cut out *all* the descriptions of Beauty etc. which are tedious, and are often implied; and I think advantageously condensed and retrenched the Love-making."[20]

When FitzGerald received proof for ***Salámán and Absál,*** he requested that the printers also send proof to Cowell. Later the corrected proof was returned to the printer, who then sent back two revises in different layouts. FitzGerald labored over misplaced accidentals in the revise:

> I always knew there might be some obscurity in that passage about the Censor, and from the first pointed it illegitimately in order to conduct the Reader better to the meaning: having it printed thus:
>
> > "and through the Eyes
> > Of Man, the subtle Censor scrutinize"
>
> to show that "Thou" and not "Man" was the Censor. This illegitimate Comma was not put into the proof, but was restored by me in sending it back to Childs.[21]

The poet supervised each stage of the printing to ensure that all features of the text, including punctuation, would appear as he intended them. His fear was that the poem might be misread when the pointing he supplied was altered by careless editing. He might agree to refinements of the translation suggested by Cowell, but he definitely preferred his own punctuation to the printer's house style. At this relatively early stage of FitzGerald's career as a poet and translator, all his qualities as a meticulous author are matured. He uses the proof and revise stages of the printing to make improvements or other alterations to the text. He is scrupulously exact about the accidentals of the text. He is conscious of his readership (limited though it was) and adapts the text where he thinks it will suit both his audience and himself.

When the printer had sent him copies of the final version, he sent a packet of them to Cowell, bidding him to distribute the translation to members of his family. In the letter enclosed with this packet, FitzGerald adds a postscript: "I am very glad to hear of the MS. Transcripts."[22] These were the Ouseley manuscripts in the Bodleian Library. Cowell had been making a survey of them when he came across the manuscript of quatrains attributed to Omar Khayyám.

"Thanks for Omar" is the polite opening of a letter from the third week in July 1856. There follows a long list of FitzGerald's queries about unfamiliar vocabulary in the copy of the Ouseley manuscript Cowell had made for him. This was the last letter he wrote to the Cowells before they sailed for India, where Cowell had been appointed Professor of Modern History and Political Economy at Presidency College, Calcutta. The awareness that Cowell and his wife would soon be leaving had loomed over the publication of ***Salámán and Absál*** and had left FitzGerald melancholic. It was perhaps as a kind of consolation that Cowell wrote as often as he did, reading proof for ***Salámán,*** and finally copying out the Ouseley manuscript for FitzGerald before leaving for India. The Cowells sailed on 1 August 1856.

The later 1850s were the most difficult period of FitzGerald's life. In November 1856 he married Lucy Barton, the daughter of his old friend Bernard Barton, the Quaker poet. By all accounts the arrangement was unsatisfactory to him, and no convincing explanation has ever been offered for why he married at all. His own account of the business is pained and deeply regretful. He wrote to Cowell in India of his surprise that

> You have been told of my Marriage! I said nothing of it to anybody till within a Month of the time: until which Time indeed it was hardly *certain,* long proposed as it had been; and, had Good Sense and Experience prevailed instead of Blind Regard on one side it never would have been completed! You know my opinion of a "Man of Taste"—never so dangerous as when tied

down to daily Life Companionhood—and with one very differently complexioned and educated, and who might have been far far happier and usefuller untied to me. She wants a large Field to work on, and to bestow her Labour on a Field that will *answer* to Tillage—and I have only a little Garden of Tastes and Ideals, and a Heart very dead to better Regards![23]

He was soon harried by all the duties attendant on his newly wedded life. Letter after letter complains of his being in "a total Quandary about a Place of Abode" and having to rein in the new Mrs. FitzGerald, whom he greatly feared was "given to Profusion, and her Hand is out of practice, of course." Both partners were middle-aged and set in their ways, each disinclined to compromise or to accommodate the other. Furthermore, there is every indication that FitzGerald's sentimental and possibly sexual feelings were directed toward younger men rather than his wife (whom he rather coldly referred to as his "Contemporary"). Both soon found their married state intolerable. After eight months, the "couple" separated.

For some weeks early in the new year he retreated to his old rooms at 31 Great Portland Street, and his letters from this period mention Mrs. FitzGerald as being away a good deal of the time. The new year evidently did not revive any old desires other than his fascination with Persian. His studies seem to have helped him bear up under the alternate pressures of loneliness and domesticity. "I have scarce seen any one here: but put my Eyes quite out over a silly Persian Manuscript by Day, and look into the Pit of a Theatre for an Hour at night when I can see no longer. What a waste of Life—if my Life ever could be worth living. I am rather weary of it."[24] During this time the pain of solitariness was lessened at his writing table in long letters to the Cowells about his Persian works and days. Cowell's responses included selected quatrains from an Omar Khayyám manuscript he had discovered in the library of the Asiatic Society. FitzGerald compared these with the Ouseley manuscript and made his slow-winding way through Khayyám's verses.

He was struck by the curious organization of the manuscript and included a note about it in his preface to the 1859 *Rubáiyát*. "As usual with such kind of Oriental Verse, the Rubáiyát follow one another according to Alphabetic Rhyme—a strange Farrago of Grave and Gay. Those here selected are strung into something of an Eclogue, with perhaps a less than equal proportion of the 'Drink and make-merry,' which (genuine or not) recurs over-frequently in the Original." Arbitrary arrangement or cultivated disarray did not suit FitzGerald. He once remarked to Frederick Tennyson, "I am quite-sure gardens should be formal, and unlike general Nature. I much prefer the old French and Dutch gardens to what are called the English." To this he added: "Pray do send me your Poems, one and all: I should like very

much to talk them over with you, however much you might resent me, who am no Poet, presuming to advise you who as certainly are one."[25] (FitzGerald's criticism was that Tennyson had not made the best selection of his poems, that he had included too much.) To FitzGerald it was natural to proceed from general reflections on horticulture—one kind of anthology—to the parterre of a book of poems.

In late February 1857 FitzGerald had written to Garcin de Tassy, the French orientalist and translator of Attár's *Mantic Uttair*,[26] hoping to collate the Ouseley quatrains with "any Copy of Omar Khayyám in all the Paris Libraries."[27] In addition, FitzGerald transcribed quatrains from the Ouseley and forwarded them to France. The outcome of an exchange of letters was Garcin de Tassy's proposition of submitting a collaborative article on Omar Khayyám to the *Journal Asiatique*. However, FitzGerald insisted that the French scholar alone should take credit for the brief introductory study if he wished. Garcin de Tassy's "Note sur les rubâ'iyât de'Omar Khaïyâm" appeared in May 1857.[28] The seven-page text included ten Persian quatrains with French prose translations. As agreed, the article did not mention either FitzGerald or Cowell. By now anonymity had become a habit in FitzGerald's publications. The usual reason for this reticence was the understandable fear of being caught in error. Anonymity might not secure his work from censure, but at least it would ward off the crusty kind of personal attack that Tennyson had suffered from the reviewer "Christopher North."

In June 1857 FitzGerald received from Cowell a transcript of the "Calcutta manuscript." This manuscript consisted of 516 quatrains, which provided FitzGerald with much new material to consider. The parcel arrived on 14 June while FitzGerald was staying in Bedford at the home of a close friend, William Kenworthy Browne. Also in the parcel was a fragrant box, sent as a gift for Mrs. FitzGerald. The gift box had imbued the manuscript with its perfume, so much to FitzGerald's delight that he was moved to melancholy reflections on the absence of his friends, whom the scent and texture of the manuscript had recalled to him.

> It is very pleasant to see the MS. and skim over a few Tetrastichs. . . . And the human Interest which all MSS have beyond Printed Books—written by a living hand at the end of which was a living Soul like my own—under a darker skin—some "dark Indian face with white Turban wreathed" and under an Indian Sun. And you spoke to him those thousands of miles away, and he spoke to you, and this MS. was put into your hands when done; and then deposited in that little box, made also by some dark hand, along with its aromatic Companion: you and your dear Wife saw them after they were nailed down; and directed the Box; and so they have crossed the Atlantic, and after some durance in London have reached my hands at last. I drank your healths in Brandy and Water as I sat alone last night; it is now *almost* a Year since we last met at Rushmere.[29]

A fragrance transformed palpable absence into a kind of presence. It was an event that left its traces on the *Rubáiyát*. There the flowers blooming recall the dead to living memory, and the buried ashes of a bibulous sinner send up a "snare of Perfume" (FitzGerald's wild hyperbole for the reek of a departed alcoholic—even in death the lingering smell of liquor!). As he lay in the paddock next to Browne's house, afloat on summer flowers, he began to translate Omar Khayyám: first into Latin quatrains, then into English. Readers have wondered how an unambitious dilettante could compose a poem so touching and so good as the *Rubáiyát* only to lose the touch himself. The *Rubáiyát* is indeed the "cry of its occasion." All the elements of the poem were mixed and marinated in that summer month: the companionship of Browne (to whom FitzGerald was attracted), conviviality, books of verse and drifts of flowers, but also the pain of a mismanaged life, the absence of the Cowells, an urge to escape, and a "sweet-scented Manuscript."

THE FIRST EDITION

FitzGerald's first rendering of the *Rubáiyát* was a series of Latin quatrains (see appendix 2 below). Not long after, he began to try his hand at English versions, beginning with "a poor Sir W. Jones sort of Parody":

> I long for Wine! oh Saki of my Soul
> Prepare thy Song & fill the morning Bowl;
> For this first Summer Month that brings the Rose
> Takes many a Sultan with it as it goes.

The rhyme scheme he finally chose for the poem derives from his Persian originals, where it varies between *aaba* and monorhyme.[30] In working through the Persian manuscripts he exchanged almost a volume of letters with Cowell from that summer through to January 1858. Their correspondence contains very little in the way of personal narrative, consisting almost entirely of notes and queries about Khayyám's Persian. Soon FitzGerald had prepared a sizable number of quatrains, and he began to think again of publication. He said to Cowell:

> And now about old Omar. You talked of sending a Paper about him to Fraser and I told you, if you did, I would stop it till I had made my Comments. I suppose you have not had time to do what you proposed, or are you overcome with the Flood of bad Latin I poured upon you? Well: don't be surprised (*vext,* you won't be) if *I* solicit Fraser for room for a few Quatrains in English Verse, however—with only such an Introduction as you and Sprenger give me—very short—so as to leave you to say all that is Scholarly if you will. I hope this is not very Cavalier of me. But in truth I take old Omar rather more as my property than yours: he and I are more akin, are we not? You see all Beauty, but you can't feel *with* him in some respects as I do.[31]

Despite his claims to deeper empathy, FitzGerald still sought Cowell's approval before he submitted thirty-five English quatrains to *Fraser's Magazine* in January

1858. This was not to be the *Rubáiyát*'s first publication, however. Despite *Fraser*'s apparent willingness to print the submission, FitzGerald's verses never appeared. He waited a considerable time for the quatrains to be published, finally remarking with astonishment in September 1858:

> As to *my* Omar: I gave it to Parker in January, I think: he saying Fraser was agreeable to take it. Since then I have heard no more; so as, I suppose, they don't care about it: and may be quite right. Had I thought they would be so long however I would have copied it out and sent it to you: and I will still do so from a rough and imperfect Copy I have (though not now at hand) in case they show no signs of printing me. My Translation will interest you from its *Form*, and also in many respects in its *Detail*: very unliteral as it is. Many Quatrains are mashed together: and something lost, I doubt, of such as it is. I purposely said in the very short notice I prefixed to the Poem that it is so short because better Information might be furnished in another Paper, which I though *you* might undertake.[32]

Fraser's delay in printing the thirty-five quatrains had given FitzGerald the idea of further revisions. "As to Omar, I hear and see nothing of it in Fraser yet: and so I suppose they don't want it. I told Parker he might find it rather dangerous among the Divines: he took it however, and keeps it. I really think I shall take it back; add some stanzas which I kept out for fear of being too strong: print fifty copies and give away; one to you, who won't like it neither. Yet it is most ingeniously tesselated into a sort of Epicurean Eclogue in a Persian Garden."[33] The "Yet" of the last sentence is an unexpected conjunction that shows FitzGerald's demure self-confidence about the *Rubáiyát*. Its most likely sympathizer "won't like it neither" (the deliberate solecism, as so often, plays on mingled feelings of egoism and uncertainty), "yet" FitzGerald has to *concede* that his "Epicurean Eclogue" might interest an audience larger than his circle of friends. In mid-January 1859 he again decided to pay the costs of a private printing. "I took my Omar from Fraser, as I saw he didn't care for it; and also I want to enlarge it to near as much as again, of such Matter as he would not dare to put in Fraser."[34]

FitzGerald indeed "enlarged" the version he had originally offered to *Fraser*'s by forty quatrains before again giving it to the printers. The first edition of the *Rubáiyát of Omar Khayyám* consists of a ten-page preface ("Omar Khayyám—The Astronomer-Poet of Persia"), a sixteen-page verse text, and five pages of notes. The verse text of the first edition comprises seventy-five quatrains of which those numbered LIX-LXVI constitute an apologue subtitled "Kúza-Náma" ("the book of the pot"). The poem's bare outline is that of a day in the life of Omar Khayyám, beginning with the call to awaken and ending with the rising moon. Within the linear arrangement of the entire poem most of the quatrains maintain their own integrity. The exceptions are the enjambed stanzas LIV-LV, and the apologue. Any of the other quatrains could be removed from the poem, or altered internally, without interrupting the poem's continuity. Thus the structure of the *Rubáiyát* does not inherently resist revision by the knitting of stanza to stanza. The arrangement of the quatrains is flexible and recombinant in its design.

The first edition of the *Rubáiyát of Omar Khayyám* was published anonymously by the antiquarian bookseller Bernard Quaritch. Quaritch, referred to in later years as the "Napoleon of booksellers" had been active in the London book trade since 1842, when he emigrated from Berlin and found work with Henry George Bohn. By 1847 he had decided to venture into business on his own, aspiring to be "the first bookseller in Europe." He began to issue his "Catalogue of Foreign and English Books" in 1848, and during the Crimean War he became recognized as a dealer in European and oriental linguistics as well as incunabula, manuscripts, Bibles (notably Mazarine Bibles; he obtained six copies over forty years), liturgies, Shakespeareana, early English literature, Americana, cartography, natural history, travel literature, and so on. Over the years Quaritch became notorious for his tactics at auctions and sales of private libraries, as an obituary notice in *Notes and Queries* testified: "The French booksellers found their Waterloo at the famous Didot sale, when he met and beat them. And if he could give nearly 5,000*l.* for one volume, he in 1882 expended 32,000*l.* when the Sunderland Library was sold, and about the same time was the largest purchaser at the Hamilton and Beckford sales. At the recent Ashburnham sale his bill amounted to nearly 40,000*l.*"[35]

Quaritch put out a number of publications of his own. These included Arabic and Turkish dictionaries as well as grammars of Arabic, Persian, and Turkish. But he was really only "a little bit of a new bookseller and a little bit of a publisher."[36] The *Rubáiyát* was an unusual venture for him. His first large catalog appeared in 1858, and in 1860 this catalog offered about seven thousand works to collectors. His catalogs also appeared in monthly numbers, which alternately announced the availability of books for specialists and for bibliophiles. It was in this upsurge of Quaritch's own volumes that the *Rubáiyát* was launched on its maiden voyage. FitzGerald's relationship with the bookseller began in the early 1850s, when the poet began acquiring items from the Quaritch catalogs. Having become acquainted with Quaritch through a correspondence of several years, FitzGerald no doubt found him a congenial and convenient prospect for a publisher.[37]

The poem was entirely printed (250 copies in pamphlet form with paper covers, price 1s.) by G. Norman, Printers, of Covent Garden, by 15 January 1859.[38] FitzGerald himself undertook the costs of printing the slim pamphlet, which Quaritch then distributed, ostensibly to obtain for the translation a wider circulation than any of FitzGerald's earlier works had received.[39] FitzGerald never gave his reasons for choosing an antiquarian bookseller to publish the *Rubáiyát*. *Fraser*'s refusal to print the poem may have seemed to him an indication that it would not be well received by a mass readership. Quaritch's catalogs and circulars, on the other hand, were sent to men who shared FitzGerald's interests, a fit audience though few for poetry of oriental extraction. To show that he had not entirely abandoned his desire to be read by the nonspecialist, FitzGerald paid for other advertisements in the April numbers of the *Athenaeum* and the *Saturday Review.*[40]

But on the whole FitzGerald wished his poem not to attract too much attention, especially to the identity of its author. Among the causes of the *Rubáiyát*'s early obscurity, the foremost is FitzGerald's modest resistance to advertising. Victorian authors and publishers alike understood that the dissemination of literary works had become a competitive enterprise. Advertisements were in some instances essential to the success of a work: they attempted to instruct uncertain public tastes and suggested the direction the fashion in literature was turning. They encouraged the mass audience for literature "to read and to ask for a given title when they entered a circulating library or a bookshop."[41] Unlike most Victorian authors, FitzGerald obstinately opposed the puffing of his work and insisted on his anonymity. In spite of the few simple advertisements he prepared, he had no interest in mounting the carousel of fashion and checked the contagious desire to reach "the Public" whom most authors now (if they intended to make authorship their profession) had in mind when they wrote and revised.

FitzGerald had never anticipated a commercial success for the poem, and indeed it turned out to be spectacularly unsuccessful. He distributed copies to a few friends and took no more trouble about it. But only two years later its "discovery" by the Pre-Raphaelites would launch the turnaround that made the *Rubáiyát* one of the most widely known poems in the English language.

THE SECOND EDITION

According to the account given by Swinburne many years later,[42] the Celtic scholar Whitley Stokes found copies of the *Rubáiyát* in the penny box outside Quaritch's old shop on Castle Street (expansion had since moved the firm's offices to the more upmarket Piccadilly). This was in early July 1861. Stokes gave a copy to Dante Gabriel Rossetti, who went with Swinburne to the shop and bought more copies of the poem at a penny each. Soon the poem was read by William Morris, Edward Burne-Jones, and George Meredith. Beyond the Pre-Raphaelite circle, demand for the poem began to grow. When Quaritch reported in 1866 that he had only ten copies left, FitzGerald pretended indifference. He quietly insisted that ten copies should be "quite enough for the present. I was looking over the old Fellow a few weeks ago, and saw where some things might be transposed, and some added; but one might not improve it after all."[43] Saying that Quaritch's stock was "quite enough" sounds like an outright refusal. But as though in an afterthought, he hints that a new edition might be possible—a revised edition. This mere murmur (and its ulterior assent to Quaritch's plans) complicates the taxonomy of FitzGerald's textual intentions. Though he resisted the idea of publishing only a reprint of the 1859 version, he was attracted by the prospect of revising the poem. Transpositions and new quatrains might not improve the work (and this is only a tic of modesty in the mental ramble of FitzGerald's letter), but nevertheless they would make it new.

The implicit distinction between "new" and "improved" is crucial. Many of the revisions to the second edition (and later to the third and fourth) are indeed improvements on the art of the 1859 *Rubáiyát*. But each version was conceived as an individual intention, a new version that incorporated local improvements to the earlier text.

Despite FitzGerald's protestations, when demand for the *Rubáiyát* exceeded his last ten copies, Quaritch again asked whether FitzGerald would be willing to print a second edition. A halfhearted reply came in early August 1867:

> One Catalogue you sent me some weeks ago recalled to me what Edward Cowell had told me a year ago; viz., that you had partly sold, partly lost, the copies of Omar Khayyám; and thought a small Edition would sell.
>
> Well—I have done with such things; and I suppose you find that such *livraisons,* even if they do sell, are not worth the trouble of keeping, etc.
>
> But as poor Omar is one I have great fellow feeling with, I would rather vamp him up again with a few Alterations and Additions than anything else.
>
> You must tell me, Busy and Great Man as you now are, whether you care to take charge of such a shrimp of a Book if I am silly enough to reprint it.[44]

There is mild annoyance in FitzGerald's hyperactive paragraphing and hints that Quaritch would have been able to supply renewed demand more easily if he (or his shop manager) had not thrown out most of the copies of the 1859 edition. At this Quaritch let the matter drop.

Then, in mid-October of the same year, as FitzGerald was leafing through Quaritch's new catalog, two items caught his eye. He sent off a hastily written note to the bookseller:

> Dear Sir,
>
> Please to post me *9244 Nicolas' Omar Khayyám*: for which I enclose 19s for postage, etc.
>
> This book, and No. 9245 (with my Name too!) remind me of what Cowell has told me more than once; viz, that you thought a small Edition of my Omar would sell in time.
>
> I had always wished to add some twenty or thirty more Stanzas to it and some additional matter: but it seemed absurd to reprint a thing for that alone; and I have no other object. I might also have added to it the translation of Jámí's Salámán and Absál—printed in the same form—of which I have several copies left. . . .
>
> These two would make a Pamphlet more 2/6 than the present Omar (I blush to see it!) at 3/6.[45]

FitzGerald's embarrassment was due to the following entry in *The Catalogue of Oriental Literature (Including Manuscripts, Printed Books, Translations)* for 1867 (no. 239, p. 633): "Item 9245: **The Rubáiyát of Omar Khayyám.** Translated by Edward FitzGerald. sq.8vo.sd. RARE, 3s6d." On 24 October FitzGerald received the "French Omar." It contained 464 quatrains reprinted from an 1857 lithograph of a manuscript in Tehran and translated into French by J. B. Nicolas.[46]

As if to dispute the legitimacy of FitzGerald's recasting of the Persian original, the translator of this "French Omar" (as FitzGerald called it) maintained that the wine so often mentioned by Omar Khayyám was not a symbol for the near-alcoholic Epicureanism implied in FitzGerald's English *Rubáiyát* but was instead a Sufi code for the state of mystical enlightenment. This speculation seemed absurd to FitzGerald, as did the superabundance of Persian quatrains that Nicolas had accepted as authentic. Yet the French edition had a battery of scholarly glosses on the quatrains and argued its case forcefully. Its dubious bulk nevertheless made FitzGerald's selection look arbitrary and amateurish.

Refashioning a second version of the *Rubáiyát of Omar Khayyám* was FitzGerald's disquieted reaction to the French edition. In his prose translation, Nicolas tended toward a more literal rendering of the Persian—just what FitzGerald had avoided. Had he wanted to alter his method of translation, FitzGerald might have responded to Nicolas's version with a yet more extensive text of his own. There were over five hundred quatrains in his copy of the Calcutta manuscript. Yet FitzGerald had never intended to make a scholarly edition and translation, a job more suited to Cowell's philological talents. So rather than change course to compete, he redefined his authority in matters of "old Omar."

Hearing from Mrs. Tennyson that the Poet Laureate had a high opinion of the *Rubáiyát* gave FitzGerald a "spurt," as he put it, "to look what I can do further with

Omar; adding some Quatrains; which may do more harm than good. But a few more will, at any rate, allow for the Idea of *Time passing* while the Poet talks, and while his Humour changes."[47] The additions that would "allow for the Idea of Time passing" would strengthen the narrative frame of the *Rubáiyát*. It is interesting to note that this creative justification of a new textual intention is not expressed until after FitzGerald read Nicolas's edition. FitzGerald's poem would piece together a story latent in thematic affinities among the Persian verses, a poetic purpose absent from Nicolas's translation.

On 2 December 1867 FitzGerald again invited Cowell to oversee his nervous composition of the new *Rubáiyát*: "You may before very long have to exercise on me the Word-picking I have bestowed on you. Yesterday I sent my new Version of Omar to Mr. Childs to be printed: only the Verse part; which I shall send to you in order that you may tell me not only of any *vernacular* faults, but (what I most want to know) if there is now too much of it. . . . I know that one is very apt to go wrong in recastings, additions, etc."[48] More specific queries followed, worries about layout among them. "Was I wrong in printing Kúza Náma—the Persian (as I understand) and not the Arabic Form? It looks so much pleasanter. Somehow I couldn't care to use the Arabic: there is no need to use either. I only did it for fun." He then promised Cowell: "I will write out and send to you what sort of thing I think of adding in the Preface about it. Oh, if you were not so busy, I should try and get *you* to do it. But I won't ask that: and will say very little. After all, people can please themselves as to understanding literally or mystically."[49] FitzGerald had decided to locate his refutation of Nicolas in the preface of the second edition but to reserve the interpretation and enjoyment of the verse for his readers. Cowell suggested reassuringly that FitzGerald might cite him as an authority for the argument against Khayyám's Sufism. FitzGerald drew strength from this: "I am very glad you approve of my alluding to you: with your leave I shall *name* you: but not till have seen the Additional Quatrains. . . . I have desired Mr. Childs to send you a Proof direct. . . . I *know* some of the Stanzas must come out, or change place; but I stuffed all in to see how they would look in print; and we shall see how far you and I agree about them. . . . As to my making Omar worse than he is in that Stanza about Forgiveness [88 in the second edition, 81 subsequently]—you know I have translated none literally, and have generally mashed up two—or more—into one."[50]

In January 1868 FitzGerald was still correcting proof for the second edition, with the printing delayed by problems in the Childs family. (The printers for the second edition were no longer G. Norman, but they would later take over the printing of the 1872 and 1879 editions.) He was acutely fretful about orthography, phrasing, and layout:

> I see I have Jelal*e*ddin which should be Jelal*u*ddin? These Vowels seem to me very fanciful. . . .
>
> "Scatters before him with his Whirlwind Sword." *Conquering, victorious, triumphant,* etc. are weak, because implied. But this Whirlwind which has just struck me may be Bombastes Furioso. . . .
>
> I think of *dele*-ing *Kuza Nama*: first because it looks gawky in the page (and I love my "pretty Page") and secondly because it seems to be the heading of another Poem; as I found from the Printers by their Proof.[51]

By 14 February the edition had still not emerged, though he had corrected and sent in the revises. He wrote to William Bodham Donne:

> The enclosed explains that a new Edition of my old Omar is about to come forth—with a good deal added in verse and prose. The former Edition was as much lost as sold, when B. Quaritch changed houses; he has told Cowell these two years that a few more would sell: A French version has revived my old Flame: and now Mr. Childs will soon send some 200 copies to B. Quaritch.
>
> It seems absurd to make terms about such a pamphlet, likely to be so slow of sale, so I have written to Q. in answer; that he must fix the most saleable price he can; take his own proper profit out of it; and when 50 copies are sold give me mine.[52]

Cowell continued to be concerned about his friend's new venture. He offered to write up an article on the *Rubáiyát,* endorsing FitzGerald's translation. The poet responded that Cowell ought not to spill scholarly ink over "such word pictures as my Omar, etc.," yet he might contribute "an anonymous article in a Paper, or a letter to me. You should just let yourself run wild, for you will never go astray, neither in morals, Taste, nor erudition."[53] Cowell's apology for the *Rubáiyát* did not appear, nor was one really needed. On 25 February the author received his copy of the *Rubáiyát of Omar Khayyám, the Astronomer-Poet of Persia. Rendered into English Verse. Second Edition.* Bound in paper, it was priced at 1s. 6d.

The second edition of the *Rubáiyát* comprises an extensive set of alterations to the text of the first edition. A small number of spelling and punctuation changes standardize internal variations of the earlier edition, such as inconsistent transliterations from the Persian in the preface. (See appendix 3.) Added to the preface are new footnotes and a new five-page conclusion in which FitzGerald vigorously refutes Nicolas's position on Omar's mysticism. To the verse text FitzGerald added not "twenty or thirty" but thirty-five quatrains, so that the *Rubáiyát* of 1868 has 110 stanzas.

Besides the substantial additions to the verse text of the earlier *Rubáiyát,* many of the stanzas printed in 1868 differ significantly in both substantives and accidentals from those of the first edition.

It is also interesting that the price of the poem was raised only from the original first edition price of 1s. to 1s. 6d. The number of copies printed decreased from 250 to 200. Fifty copies were sold in the second edition's first week of publication. Quaritch's 1867 catalog, which had so upset FitzGerald, reveals that Quaritch was advertising his remaining copies of the first edition as *rare* volumes, at what seemed to FitzGerald the astonishing price of 3s. 6d. Quaritch's methods in distributing the *Rubáiyát* in this manner must have stemmed from a number of causes. The original arrangement with FitzGerald was undertaken with no anticipation of popularity or large sales. Correspondingly, the printed stock was limited to a number that might be absorbed by the author's friends and by those interested in translations from the Persian. That FitzGerald paid for the printing of the first edition guaranteed that Quaritch would certainly not suffer any financial loss for his part in publishing the poem. On the contrary, that he marketed the poem in the way familiar to him as a rare book dealer (limited supply, immodest price) may have been at least partly responsible for increasing demand, a claim Quaritch would later make when struggles for the copyright threatened to disinherit him of the *Rubáiyát*'s legacy.[54]

The Third Edition

In 1870 FitzGerald remarked to Quaritch that he hardly expected a third edition of the *Rubáiyát* to appear in his lifetime, but this prediction was only half in earnest. When Quaritch ran out of copies of the second edition, FitzGerald began to assess the prospects for a new version. Remaining in some doubt, he consulted Tennyson in hopes of resolving the editorial dilemma of which *Rubáiyát* to reprint.

> The reason of my asking you is that Quaritch has found admirers in America who have almost bought up the whole of his last enormous Edition—amounting to 200 copies, I think—so he wishes to embark in 200 more, I suppose: and he says that he, and his Readers, like the First Edition best: so he would reprint that.
>
> Of course *I* thought the Second best; and I think so still: partly (I fear) because the greater number of Verses gave more time for the Day to pass, from Morning till Night.[55]

From this letter we see again how an edition of the *Rubáiyát* was produced in response to its social conditions, how it was made to satisfy the taste of persons other than FitzGerald. Quaritch's desire to distribute the *Rubáiyát* in the United States is the clear raison d'être of the third edition. The result of export to America has

a certain irony nevertheless. Among those requesting copies of the poem were publishers who used the texts they received as printer's copy for pirated editions of the *Rubáiyát.*

The letter to Tennyson also reveals FitzGerald's shifting conceptualization of the *Rubáiyát*'s generic status. Intimations of FitzGerald's mixed understanding of the *Rubáiyát* as both translation and poem had already appeared in the form of his response to the French Omar of Nicolas. While raising a scholarly objection to Nicolas's blindness to the internal contradictions of the French edition (in particular, the "anti-Sufi" quatrains in the Tehran manuscript), he still chose to concentrate his attention on altering the *Rubáiyát* for poetic purposes. Once he had extracted Tennyson's praise, he began to revise the *Rubáiyát* as though it were not a translation but an original work of English poetry. A reflection of FitzGerald's inability to decide between versions purely on the grounds of literary judgment appears in a letter of 31 March 1872 to Bernard Quaritch, a letter (here quoted at length) that complicates many controversial issues of editorial theory and method.

> You must think that I have followed Omar underground, not to have answered yours sooner—But I have been looking over him in consequence of your letter, to see what I could make of him. I wonder that, with all your great Business, you care to be troubled again with this little one: but if you really wish to set off old Omar once more to America, I would do what I could for his outfit.
>
> I daresay Edition 1 is better in some respects than 2, but I think not altogether. Surely, several good things were added—perhaps too much of them which also gave Omar's thoughts room to turn in, as also the Day which the Poem occupies. He begins with Dawn pretty sober and contemplative: then as he thinks and drinks, grows savage, blasphemous, etc., and then again sobers down into melancholy at nightfall. All which wanted rather more expansion than the first edition gave. I dare say Edition 1 best pleased those who read it first: as first Impressions are apt to be strongest.
>
> By the same rule might not those who read the 2nd Ed^n first go the other way? The Gentleman in Fraser & some others seemed well satisfied.[56]
>
> As to the relative fidelity of the two Versions, there isn't a Pin to choose—not in the opening Stanzas you send.
>
> All this seems making too much fuss about a small thing. But the truth is, that on looking over the Two Versions, and ready to adopt your plan of reconciling two in one, I considered that such a scheme, with brackets, etc., *would be* making too much of the thing: and you and I might both be laughed at for treating my Omar as if it were some precious fragment of Antiquity.
>
> Besides I doubt if the two Versions could now—as altered—*separately* dove-tail into one another without some fresh alteration—which I have lost heart and even Eyes for.

I doubt therefore that, if Omar be republished, he must go forth in one Shape or another—in his first, or second, suit. And I certainly vote for Version 2, with some whole Stanzas which may be "de trop" cut out, & some of the old readings replaced.

On all which I would ask advice of you & of such as you rely on, who would take the trouble of advising.

I said that I have looked over the two Versions and therefore I can report about them now. My Eyes have been so bad these last two years that I have read scarce anything: and feel a little reluctant to revert even to my little Omar for any purpose of revision.

If, however, you still wish it, I will send you the Poem curtailed, & altered back, as I have proposed.

. . . By the by, Cowell wrote me some months ago that Ed[n] 1 had been reprinted by someone in India. So I have not lived in vain, if I have lived to be *pirated!*[57]

At first FitzGerald expresses the opinion that many subsequent editors would take as justification for editing only one text of the *Rubáiyát.* He says that the first edition was "better in some respects" than the other versions. He then counters this view by citing his reasons for making changes in the second, reasons that accrued only with a rereading of the poem and did not originally reside in his intentions for the work. His wry disparagement of the eclectic text *Rubáiyát* with critical apparatus proposed by Quaritch is instructive. FitzGerald would rather revise the second edition into a new version than conflate the first two versions. His preference is judicious, for he recognized that the two versions could not—owing to their substantial difference— be conflated by selecting one as copy text and emending it with corrections from the other version. Instead, he affirms the integrity of each text.

The revisions he does propose (cutting out "some whole Stanzas" and reinstating "some of the old readings") almost belie this impression. There is no contradiction, however, given the recombinant nature of the *Rubáiyát.* Each text is structurally integral as a poem, and FitzGerald believed that it would be deceptive merely to intermingle the two texts, since this would imply that the two poems were not separate endeavors but stages in a course of trial and error. The quatrains of each text might be deployed in various combinations to constitute different versions. The issue may seem purely theoretical, yet FitzGerald clearly did think of each version as an individual poem, and the forms of his revisions are the result of his interpretation of his own compositional process. The practical difficulty of conflating the 1859 and 1868 texts was not his only consideration. He never wished to suggest to his readers that there was some abstract urtext from which the versions of the poem were derived (other than perhaps the Persian original) or some "final" text toward which both poet and poem had been struggling. Each completed series of revisions would be a renascence of the *Rubáiyát.*

A bound copy of the third edition, received by FitzGerald on 23 August 1872,[58] contained 101 quatrains. Alterations and omissions had been made on the direct advice of Cowell, who had also received proof sheets. Since Cowell's proof copies for the third edition have survived, it is possible to see how completely FitzGerald could alter individual stanzas even at the final stages of his poem's printing. . . . In final form, the first stanza clearly announces that the edition is not a reprinting of an earlier text but a new version. Curiously, FitzGerald gave final authority for omissions to Quaritch, leaving it "to him to settle the Business, and bear the blame" for the little volume now priced at 7s. 6d.[59] Of course Quaritch did not wish to tamper with the text. The omissions had been suggested by Cowell, and Quaritch had asked FitzGerald to let them stand, which they did.

That FitzGerald was willing to relax his control over the form his text would take, granting authority over the *Rubáiyát* to the publishing institution and to a critical public of his immediate acquaintance, suggests that authorial intention in determining the shape of a critical edition is only one element to be considered in the larger social context of the work's transmission. Although he was eager to revise in detail and in design, FitzGerald did not want to trouble the reading public with too much Omar. His intentions are always composite, influenced by his perception of public opinion, shaped by Cowell and by Quaritch.

The Fourth Edition

Reprintings of the third edition in inexpensive "popular editions" by the American firm of James R. Osgood prompted Quaritch to consider in 1877 yet a fourth edition of his own, in larger supply, so as to stand his ground as the authorized publisher of the *Rubáiyát.*[60] Yet when FitzGerald proposed "that Salámán . . . might go along with Omar, if printed at all," Quaritch resisted. The refusal irked FitzGerald, and he complained to Cowell's wife that he had "declined having old Omar reprinted by Quaritch. I think that there has been enough of him, unless he one day come in more reputable Company: but Quaritch would not have Salámán by way of Chaperon: nor would I advise him so to do so far as Profit went. So I must leave Omar to the Americans if they want him."[61]

A letter to Quaritch of 25 January 1878 indicates that FitzGerald had received a copy of one of the American printings. The poet was much impressed by the handsome appearance of this volume and unconcerned that profit from a cheap American edition might not be shared with Quaritch. His only regret was that Osgood had not informed him in advance so that he might oversee the printing. "I wish that, at any rate, they would have let me know of their intention, as I have a few alterations, and an additional note," he lamented. So as not to seem disloyal to Quaritch, FitzGerald confided to him: "Of course *I* should not sanction any Reprint, if ever contemplated, while *your* Edition remains on hand."[62]

But there is something mischievous in this reassurance, with its mock virtuous emphases. The bookseller's manner had nettled FitzGerald, and he rebuffed Quaritch's repeated pleas to reprint the **Rubáiyát** on its own. "I think I will, as I said, leave Omar for the present; there has been Enough of him here, & now will be more in America."[63] Again he needled Quaritch about the bothersome American editions. At the same time, he suggested the reissue of **Salámán and Absál** with a new version of the **Rubáiyát**. Evidently FitzGerald wished to remind Quaritch of American editions until the bookseller capitulated to this demand. But Quaritch persisted obtusely, and FitzGerald returned coy refusals, saying, "I will bide a 'wee' in case of any other Reprint asking his Company." Eventually, FitzGerald proved that he could be pushed to state the reasons for his restraint more elaborately.

> I never even *wished* for a "popular Ed^n" of Omar: but only for one of a price proportionable to his size & value. Even as to market value, the Americans . . . reprinted him for 2s.6d.—which seems to me enough; a very nice 4to wh. I will send you if I can find what they sent me.
>
> Besides this, I fancied that Salámán (which you proposed to print separately) might go along with Omar, if printed at all. Salámán however would be much longer, & not half so welcome: & that is why I did not think he w^d do alone. Besides, I really could not bear another of my things to be separately published, & recommended by Advertisement, so close upon the other two: whereas, *along with* Omar for Trumpeter, Salámán might come modestly forth: *both,* at a moderate price.

At this, Quaritch tried more urgent flattery:

> Do let me reprint the **Rubáiyát**! I have so many inquiries for copies that it is painful to be unable to supply a want felt by that part of the public with which I desire to be in connexion, and which you, as the poet idolized by a small but choice circle, ought to be anxious to gratify personally, rather than throw into the hands of American pirates the opportunity of reprinting and *misprinting ad libitum.*
>
> Allow me to publish another edition, and pay you twenty five guineas as the honorarium. You know it would be well done, and creditable to us both.[64]

FitzGerald levered Quaritch into a republication of both the **Rubáiyát** and **Salámán and Absál.** He issued a series of very specific demands regarding bibliographical details of the new edition, all of them accepted by the bookseller, who wrote:

> As I am very anxious not to sever the bond which has connected us for above 20 years I agree to all the stipulations of your letter of yesterday, and I here briefly recapitulate them:
>
> 1. The smaller page specimen to be adopted.
>
> 2. Omar to stand first and never to be reprinted separate from Jámi.
>
> 3. You to receive proof and revise before going to press.
>
> 4. Your name not to appear in any advertisement of *mine,* and no note of *mine* to be added to my advertisement of your book.
>
> 5. I to pay you £25 on the completion of the printing.
>
> 6. The impression to be limited to a thousand.
>
> 7. The copyright to remain yours; of course no new edition to be brought out by you or your representatives whilst I have a stock of say fifty unsold copies.
>
> If I printed only 500 copies I should not see my money back for printing etc. it is the second 500 which would ultimately recoup me. The frontispiece to Salámán shall be reproduced as you wish it.[65]

These terms constituted the most formal contract yet between FitzGerald and Quaritch, though by the standards of the day it was scarcely more than a gentlemen's agreement. One should remember that Bernard Quaritch Ltd. was an entirely different sort of institution from Chapman and Hall, Richard Bentley, John Murray, Macmillan, Longman, Blackwood's, Edward Moxon, or Smith, Elder. Quaritch was primarily a bookseller, a term that by the early nineteenth century had accrued derogatory connotations when used of a publisher. Not having much trade with poets or men of letters, Quaritch conducted business the way he knew how. In any event, his written promises satisfied FitzGerald.

The agreement also provides the only evidence that Quaritch and FitzGerald had changed the terms of liability and profit sharing for the edition. Previously Quaritch had undertaken the publication on commission.[66] FitzGerald had paid all expenses for printing, binding, and advertising and had left the sales receipts to Quaritch. There is nothing in their correspondence to suggest that this original arrangement altered subsequently or that either party was unhappy with the terms. In 1879, perhaps because of the substantial increase in the number of copies to be printed, Quaritch had assumed financial responsibility for production and advertising costs while paying the author a minor honorarium. Extreme informality characterized the relationship. There was no suggestion that Quaritch wanted to buy the copyright from FitzGerald (and there was no real reason he should do so). FitzGerald did not feel that he was being cheated by Quaritch or that he ever relinquished control over the **Rubáiyát**'s publication to the book dealer.

FitzGerald again carefully reviewed proof and revise for the edition. The text of the 1879 edition is very close to that of the third edition. (Revisions are noted in appendix 1; see, for example, stanza XXXVIII and its precursors.) In August 1879 he received his copy. A letter to Mrs. Cowell wearily exults, "I have now done with it—for Ever!"[67] Edward FitzGerald died in the summer of 1883, in a friend's house.

Postscript

In fact, he had not quite "done with it," as one might have expected from his revisionary habits. The preceding history of FitzGerald's revisions shows that he could never resist making minor alterations or "corrections" to the texts of the *Rubáiyát.* Certain revisions he made in a copy of the fourth edition (discovered after his death) resulted in the only "new" text of the *Rubáiyát of Omar Khayyám* to succeed the original four versions published under FitzGerald's supervision. This "fifth" edition, often presented misleadingly as giving the text of the fourth edition authorized by the poet, has been one of the two most frequently reprinted versions of the *Rubáiyát.* It seems to represent the author's "final intentions" for the poem, and it is often reprinted jointly with the text of the first edition (which of course seems to figure the author's "original intentions"). Yet this "fifth edition" text contains alterations to the poem not made by FitzGerald. I have separated the two textual strata in appendix 1.

Attár's *Conference of the Birds,* another poem FitzGerald translated, offers a parable for the changing, multiplicitous nature of the *Rubáiyát of Omar Khayyám.* In Attár's mystical poem, the birds of the world set off on a pilgrimage to look for their king, the Simorgh. When finally they meet him face to face, he shows them through a looking glass that they and he are one, that he is each one of them and every one of them. Just so, the *Rubáiyát of Omar Khayyám* is each one of its texts and all of the texts together. In this edition, readers will find the fullest account to date of FitzGerald's *Rubáiyát,* a work that found an audience for its every incarnation.

Notes

1. J. A. Boyle, ed., *The Cambridge History of Iran,* 7 vols. (Cambridge: Cambridge Univ. Press, 1968-91), 5:659-79.

2. In this part of the introduction I am greatly indebted to Ali Dashti's *In Search of Omar Khayyám,* trans. L. P. Elwell-Sutton (London: George Allen and Unwin, 1971).

3. Dashti, 33-41.

4. Dashti, 42.

5. Martin, 48.

6. *Letters,* 2:3, 1:308.

7. *Letters,* 2:75-78.

8. The couple separated in 1849, and FitzGerald's father died in 1852, three years before his wife.

9. Martin, 59.

10. *Letters,* 1:538.

11. "Within the surface of the fleeting river / The wrinkled image of the city lay, / Immovably unquiet, and forever / It trembles, but it never fades away." Shelley himself was recollecting Wordsworth's "Elegiac Stanzas, Suggested by a Picture of Peele Castle, in a Storm, Painted by Sir George Beaumont," lines 7-8. I am indebted to Jerome McGann for this reference.

12. *Letters,* 2:601.

13. *Letters,* 2:90.

14. *Letters,* 2:102-3.

15. *Letters,* 2:110.

16. *Letters,* 2:119.

17. *Letters,* 2:153-54.

18. *Letters,* 2:154.

19. *Letters,* 2:161.

20. *Letters,* 2:192.

21. *Letters,* 2:201.

22. *Letters,* 2:222.

23. *Letters,* 2:245.

24. *Letters,* 2:243.

25. *Letters,* 2:56.

26. The Persian poet Farid ud-Din Attár (ca. 1145/6-1221) of Nishapur. In addition to being one of three major Persian poets to write long mystical allegories (a genre of which the *Mantic Uttair,* or *Conference of the Birds,* is the most famous example), Attár was also one of the earliest collectors of Sufi hagiographies.

27. Joseph Eliodore Sagesse Vertu Garcin de Tassy (1794-1878); the second given name sometimes appears as "Héliodore." Garcin de Tassy was one of the most prolific of nineteenth-century scholars of Near Eastern languages and literatures. He compiled grammars and other scholarly books, and articles with his name frequently appear in the *Journal Asiatique* in the latter half of the century. Garcin de Tassy was perhaps most distinguished in his work on Persian and on Hindustani (or Urdu, an Indian language containing

many elements of Arabic, Persian, and other Near Eastern languages). For a biographical profile of Garcin de Tassy, see Sayida Surriya Husain, *Garcin de Tassy: Biographie et étude critique de ses oeuvres* (Pondicherry: Institut Français d'Indologie, 1962).

28. Garcin de Tassy, "Note sur les rubâ'iyât de'Omar Khaïyâm," *Journal Asiatique,* ser. 5, 9 (1857): 548-54. For FitzGerald's account of their correspondence, see *Letters,* 2:192-271.

29. *Letters,* 2:274.

30. ULC Add. 7753/174. Printed in *Letters,* 2:289. For a brief discussion of the poetic models for FitzGerald's rhyme scheme, see Dick Davis's introduction in *Rubáiyát of Omar Khayyám: Translated by Edward FitzGerald* (Harmondsworth: Penguin, 1989), 36-37.

31. *Letters,* 2:305.

32. *Letters,* 2:318.

33. *Letters,* 2:322.

34. *Letters,* 2:325.

35. J. B. McGovern, Obituary, *Notes and Queries,* 3 February 1900, 83.

36. Interview, "Booksellers of To-day: Mr Bernard Quaritch," *Publishers' Circular,* 15 April 1890, 444-45.

37. Though Quaritch's officious and often brusque manner irritated many of his clients, his letters to FitzGerald are for the most part polite and generally deferential.

38. This is the date recorded at Stationers' Hall by Quaritch himself in 1884, as found by Macmillan's solicitors when they investigated Quaritch's copyright claims (Trinity Add. MS a.2838). However, in a letter (now in the British Library volume of W. Aldis Wright's correspondence with the Macmillans, Add. MS 55015) from Quaritch to Edmund Kerrich, Quaritch states that copies of the *Rubáiyát* were "already on sale towards the end of February" and that advertisements for the poem first appeared in a Quaritch catalog of 15 March 1859. The British Museum received its copy on 30 March.

39. This is Quaritch's account in a letter of 27 November 1883 to W. Aldis Wright: "I consider that it was due to my commercial agency, in distributing at a mere nominal price the *first* edition of 'Omar Khayam' [*sic*], that Fitzgerald obtained his subsequent celebrity. The books Mr. Fitzgerald published elsewhere never had any circulation" (Trinity Add. MS a.28381). Quaritch

overstates the case. Almost all of FitzGerald's other works were privately printed and distributed by the author only to his friends. Details of the arrangement between FitzGerald and Quaritch became clearer during the struggle for copyright to the poem after FitzGerald's death. Quaritch gives his commercial agency rather too much credit for the *Rubáiyát*'s success. More influential agents were the Pre-Raphaelite enthusiasm, the popularity of the poem in the United States, and (most important to the poem's circulation in England) the change of publishers after FitzGerald's death to Macmillan and Company.

40. *Athenaeum,* 9 April 1859, 473; the advertisement for the *Rubáiyát* appears at the bottom of the left-hand column, to the left of ads for *The Religion of the Heart* and *The Principles of Hydropathy. Saturday Review,* 9 April 1859, 447; this ad is the fifth item from the top of the center column, above a commentary on the Psalms, below *Ishmael: A Natural History of Islamism,* and sharing the page with *The Gourmet's Guide to Rabbit-Cooking: or, How to Cook a Rabbit in 124 Different Ways. By an Old Epicure.*

41. R. A. Gettmann, *A Victorian Publisher* (Cambridge: Cambridge Univ. Press, 1960), 60.

42. Cecil Y. Lang, ed., *The Swinburne Letters,* 6 vols. (New Haven: Yale Univ. Press, 1959-62), 6:96, 187. The first letter, of 4 March 1896, answered an inquiry from a member of the Omar Khayyám Club of London; the second, of 5 October 1904, was to A. C. Benson, one of FitzGerald's biographers.

43. *Letters,* 2:572.

44. *Letters,* 3:40.

45. *Letters,* 3:50.

46. J. B. Nicolas, *Les quatrains de Khèyam traduits du Persan* (Paris: Imprimerie Impériale, 1867).

47. *Letters,* 3:60.

48. *Letters,* 3:64-65.

49. *Letters,* 3:66-67.

50. *Letters,* 3:68-69. Toward the end of his life, Cowell changed his opinion and reasserted that Khayyám had been a Sufi.

51. *Letters,* 3:78-79.

52. *Letters,* 3:60-82, 81.

53. *Letters,* 3:82.

54. Quaritch's marketing strategy was the staple of modernist book publishing. The limited edition, often obtained by subscription, was the most lucra-

tive way to introduce the latest production of the literary avant-garde. Considering the influence of the *Rubáiyát* on both T. S. Eliot and Ezra Pound, and perhaps on Yeats (who was an occasional guest of the Omar Khayyám Club in London), it is not surprising to find all three poets deeply committed to the production of their books in limited editions or editions de luxe, in addition to the popular trade edition that was the hallmark of literary success (from the publisher's point of view, at least, and often the poet's). As noted earlier, the *Rubáiyát* appeared in these three kinds of editions.

55. *Letters,* 3:336.

56. The "Gentleman in Fraser" refers to an anonymous review of the *Rubáiyát* appearing in *Fraser's Magazine,* June 1870, 777-84. The article was written by Thomas W. Hinchliff, who identified himself in an inquiry to Quaritch in 1876. See Charlotte Quaritch Wrentmore, *Letters from Edward FitzGerald to Bernard Quaritch* (London: Bernard Quaritch, 1926), 13, 42, 43.

57. *Letters,* 3:320-21, 338-39. The Indian piracy mentioned was the version published in Madras in 1862. According to W. F. Prideaux, a bibliographer of FitzGerald's works, the piracy included reprints of the 1859 Quaritch edition and of an article by Cowell that had appeared in the *Calcutta Review* in 1856. It also supplied the translation of Garcin de Tassy along with additional quatrains rendered by Whitley Stokes (the latter was apparently the editor of the volume).

58. *Letters,* 3:371, 372.

59. *Letters,* 3:363. Regarding the number of copies printed: since the Quaritch Papers in the British Library do not date as far back as the nineteenth century, and since other papers maintained by the firm have as yet not been cataloged, one can only rely on FitzGerald's supposition that Quaritch wished to publish two hundred copies of the third edition. This tallies with the number estimated for the other editions. Since FitzGerald (by Quaritch's account) kept fifty copies of the first edition, one may safely hazard that Quaritch chose, until the fourth edition, to have two hundred copies of each edition printed. How many Quaritch actually made available for sale, or in fact sold, is unfortunately indeterminable.

60. Osgood's firm was later subsumed by the publishers Houghton Mifflin. Their sales figures from this period are unavailable, but the Houghton Mifflin archive (conserved in the Houghton Library, Harvard University) shows that from 1880 to 1923 Houghton Mifflin sold 43,112 copies of the *Rubáiyát of Omar Khayyám* in six different editions.

61. *Letters,* 4:68-69, 95, 159-60.

62. Wrentmore, 53-54.

63. Wrentmore, 54.

64. 16 January 1879, Trinity Add. MS a.767. See also *Letters,* 4:102ff.

65. 17 January 1879, Trinity Add. MS b.3118(9).

66. Highly informative definitions and discussions of the types of contract agreements between authors and publishers can be found in Simon Nowell-Smith, *International Copyright Law and the Publisher in the Reign of Queen Victoria* (Oxford: Clarendon Press, 1968); John Sutherland, *Victorian Novelists and Publishers* (London: Athlone Press, 1976); R. A. Gettmann, *A Victorian Publisher* (Cambridge: Cambridge Univ. Press, 1960); and June Steffensen Hagen, *Tennyson and His Publishers* (University Park: Pennsylvania State Univ. Press, 1979).

67. *Letters,* 4:241.

Abbreviations

1859: *Rubáiyát of Omar Khayyám.* London: Bernard Quaritch, 1859.

1868: *Rubáiyát of Omar Khayyám.* London: Bernard Quaritch, 1868.

1872: *Rubáiyát of Omar Khayyám.* London: Bernard Quaritch, 1872.

1872p: Unmarked proof sheets for the 1872 edition. Trinity College Library, Cambridge.

1872r1: Unmarked revise for the 1872 edition. University Library, Cambridge.

1872r2: Second revise for the 1872 edition. Trinity College Library, Cambridge.

1879: *Rubáiyát of Omar Khayyám.* London: Bernard Quaritch, 1879.

ALS: Autograph letter signed.

IELM: *Index of English Literary Manuscripts, 1800-1900: Arnold to Gissing.* Ed. Barbara Rosenbaum and Pamela White. London: Mansell, 1982.

Letters: The Letters of Edward FitzGerald. Ed. A. McK. Terhune and A. B. Terhune. Princeton: Princeton Univ. Press, 1980.

Martin: Martin, Robert Bernard. *With Friends Possessed: A Life of Edward FitzGerald.* New York: Atheneum, 1985.

Trinity: Trinity College Library, Cambridge.

ULC: University Library, Cambridge.

Select Bibliography

PREVIOUS EDITIONS OF FITZGERALD'S RUBÁIYÁT

FitzGerald, Edward. *Rubáiyát of Omar Khayyám, the Astronomer-Poet of Persia, Translated into English Verse.* 1st ed. London: Bernard Quaritch, Castle Street, Leicester Square, 1859. Printed by G. Norman, Printer, Maiden Lane, Covent Garden, London.

———. *Rubáiyát of Omar Khayyám, the Astronomer-Poet of Persia, Rendered into English Verse.* 2d ed. London: Bernard Quaritch, Piccadilly, 1868. Printed by John Childs and Son, Printers.

———. *Rubáiyát of Omar Khayyám, the Astronomer-Poet of Persia, Rendered into English Verse.* 3d ed. London: Bernard Quaritch, Piccadilly, 1872. Printed by G. Norman and Son, Printers, Maiden Lane, Covent Garden.

———. *Rubáiyát of Omar Khayyám, the Astronomer-Poet of Persia, Rendered into English Verse.* 4th ed. London: Bernard Quaritch, 15 Piccadilly, 1879. Printed by G. Norman and Son, Printers, Maiden Lane, Covent Garden.

———. *Works of Edward FitzGerald.* Ed. Michael Kerney. London: Bernard Quaritch, 1887.

———. *Letters and Literary Remains of Edward FitzGerald.* Ed. W. A. Wright. London: Macmillan, 1889.

———. *Edward FitzGerald's Rubâ'iyât of Omar Khayyâm with Their Original Persian Sources, Collated from His Own MSS., and Literally Translated.* Ed. and Trans. Edward Heron-Allen. London: Bernard Quaritch, 1899.

———. *Letters and Literary Remains of Edward FitzGerald.* Ed. W. A. Wright. London: Macmillan, 1902-3.

———. *The Golden Cockerel Rubáiyát.* Ed. Sir Edward Denison Ross. London: Golden Cockerel Press, 1938.

WORKS RELATING TO EDWARD FITZGERALD AND HIS PERSIAN STUDIES

Arberry, A. J. *FitzGerald's Salámán and Absál: A Study.* Cambridge: Cambridge Univ. Press, 1956.

———. *Omar Khayyám.* London: John Murray, 1952.

———. *The Romance of the Rubáiyát.* London: George Allen & Unwin, 1959.

Cowell, Edward Byles. "Hafiz, the Persian Poet." *Fraser's Magazine for Town and Country* 50 (1854): 288-95.

———. "Omar Khayyám, the Astronomer-Poet of Persia." *Calcutta Review* 30, 59 (1858): 149-62.

Cowell, George. *Life and Letters of Edward Byles Cowell.* London: Macmillan, 1904.

Dashti, Ali. *In Search of Omar Khayyam.* Trans. L. P. Elwell-Sutton. London: George Allen & Unwin, 1971.

Davis, Dick. Introduction to *Rubáiyát of Omar Khayyám: Translated by Edward FitzGerald.* Harmondsworth: Penguin, 1989.

Eastwick, E. B. *The Gulistán (Rose-Garden) of Shekh Sâdí of Shíráz. A New Edition, Carefully Collated with Original MSS.* Hertford: Stephen Austin, 1850.

———. *The Gulistan; or Rose-Garden, of Shekh Muslihu'd-din Sadi of Shiraz, Translated for the First Time into Prose and Verse, with an Introductory Preface, and a Life of the Author, from the Atish Kadah.* Hertford: Stephen Austin, 1852.

Elwell-Sutton, L. P. *The Persian Metres.* Cambridge: Cambridge Univ. Press, 1976.

FitzGerald, Edward. *The Letters of Edward FitzGerald.* Ed. A. M. Terhune and A. B. Terhune. Princeton: Princeton Univ. Press, 1980.

———. *Letters of Edward FitzGerald.* Ed. W. A. Wright. London: Macmillan, 1894.

———. *Letters and Literary Remains.* Ed. W. A. Wright. London: Macmillan, 1902-3.

———. *More Letters of Edward FitzGerald.* Ed. W. A. Wright. London: Macmillan, 1901.

Garcin de Tassy, J. E. S. V. "Note sur les rubâ'iyât de'Omar Khaïyâm." *Journal Asiatique,* ser. 5, 9 (1857): 548-54.

———. Review of FitzGerald's *Salámán and Absál* (1856). *Journal Asiatique,* ser. 5, 9 (1857): 290-91.

D'Herbelot, Barthélemy. *Bibliotheque orientale, ou Dictionaire universel.* Paris: Compagnie des Libraires, 1697.

Heron-Allen, Edward. *The Rubâ'iyât of Omar Khayyām: Being a Facsimile of the Manuscript in the Bodleian Library at Oxford, with a Transcript into Modern Persian Characters.* London: Bernard Quaritch, 1898.

———. *Some Side-lights upon Edward FitzGerald's Poem "The Rubâ'iyât of Omar Khayyām."* London: H. S. Nichols, 1898.

Johnson, Francis. *A Dictionary, Persian, Arabic, and English.* London: W. H. Allen, 1852.

Jones, Sir William. *A Grammar of the Persian Language.* 4th ed. London: John Murray, S. Highley, and J. Sewell, 1797.

———. *Poeseos asiaticae commentariorum libri sex, cum appendice.* London: Richardson, 1774.

Jowett, I. B. H. *Edward FitzGerald.* Boston: Twayne, 1977.

Martin, Robert Bernard. *With Friends Possessed: A Life of Edward FitzGerald.* New York: Atheneum, 1985.

Nicolas, J. B. *Les quatrains de Khèyam traduits du Persan.* Paris: Imprimerie Impériale, 1867.

Richardson, John. *A Dictionary of Persian, Arabic, and English.* London: Various publishers, 1806-10.

————. *A Dictionary, Persian, Arabic, and English; with a Dissertation on the Languages, Literature, and Manners of Eastern Nations. . . . A New Ed., Considerably Enlarged, by F. Johnson.* London: Various publishers, 1829.

Ross, James. *The Gulistan, or Flower-Garden of Shaikh Sadi of Shiraz: Translated into English.* London: Richardson, 1823.

Steingass, Francis J. *A Comprehensive Persian-English Dictionary. . . . Being Johnson and Richardson's . . . Dictionary revised. . . .* London: Routledge and Kegan Paul, 1892.

Terhune, A. M. *The Life of Edward FitzGerald: Translator of The Rubáiyát of Omar Khayyám.* London: Oxford Univ. Press, 1947.

Thiesen, Finn. *A Manual of Classical Persian Prosody.* Wiesbaden: Harrassowitz, 1982.

Tutin, J. R. *A Concordance to FitzGerald's Translation of the Rubáiyát of Omar Khayyám.* London: Macmillan, 1900.

Wrentmore, Charlotte Quaritch, ed. *Letters from Edward FitzGerald to Bernard Quaritch.* London: Bernard Quaritch, 1926.

Wright, Thomas. *The Life of Edward FitzGerald.* London: Grant Richards, 1904.

Publishing and Printing

Brown, P. A. H. *London Publishers and Printers, c. 1800-1870.* London: British Library, 1982.

————. *Modern British and American Private Presses, 1850-1965; Holdings of the British Library.* London: British Library, 1976.

Cohen, M. N., and A. Gandolfo, eds. *Lewis Carroll and the House of Macmillan.* Cambridge: Cambridge Univ. Press, 1987.

Dooley, Allan C. *Author and Printer in Victorian England.* Charlottesville: Univ. Press of Virginia, 1992.

Gettmann, R. A. *A Victorian Publisher: A Study of the Bentley Papers.* Cambridge: Cambridge Univ. Press, 1960.

Hagen, June Steffensen. *Tennyson and His Publishers.* University Park: Pennsylvania State Univ. Press, 1979.

Merriam, H. G. *Edward Moxon, Publisher of Poets.* New York: Columbia Univ. Press, 1939.

Moran, James. *Clays of Bungay.* Bungay: Clays, 1978.

Morgan, C. L. *The House of Macmillan, 1843-1943.* London: Macmillan, 1943.

Nowell-Smith, Simon. *International Copyright Law and the Publisher in the Reign of Queen Victoria.* Oxford: Clarendon Press, 1968.

Patten, Robert Lowry. *Charles Dickens and His Publishers.* Oxford: Clarendon Press, 1978.

Savage, William. *A Dictionary of the Art of Printing.* London: Longman, 1841.

Southward, John. *Practical Printing.* London: Powell, 1882.

Sutherland, John. *Victorian Novelists and Publishers.* London: Athlone Press, 1976.

Tanselle, G. Thomas. "The Bibliographical Description of Paper." *Studies in Bibliography* 24 (1971): 27-67.

Todd, W. B. *A Directory of Printers and Others in Allied Trades, London and Vicinity, 1800-1840.* London: Printing Historical Society, 1972.

Textual Criticism

Classical

Maas, Paul. *Textual Criticism.* Trans. Barbara Flowers. Oxford: Clarendon Press, 1958.

Pasquali, Giorgio. *Storia della tradizione e critica del testo.* 2d ed. Florence: Le Monnier, 1952.

Timpanaro, Sebastiano. *La genesi del metodo del Lachmann.* Florence: Le Monnier, 1963.

West, M. L. *Textual Criticism.* Stuttgart: Teubner, 1973.

Modern

Bowers, Fredson. *Bibliography and Textual Criticism.* Oxford: Clarendon Press, 1964.

————. *Essays in Bibliography, Text, and Editing.* Ed. I. B. Cauthen Jr. Charlottesville: Univ. Press of Virginia, 1975.

————. *Textual and Literary Criticism.* Cambridge: Cambridge Univ. Press, 1959.

Brack, O. M., and W. Barnes, eds. *Bibliography and Textual Criticism.* Chicago: Univ. of Chicago Press, 1969.

Gaskell, Philip. *A New Introduction to Bibliography.* Corr. ed. Oxford: Clarendon Press, 1985.

Greg, W. W. "The Rationale of Copy-Text." *Studies in Bibliography* 3 (1950): 19-36; reprinted and revised in W. W. Greg, *Collected Papers,* ed. J. C. Maxwell (Oxford: Clarendon Press, 1966), 374-91.

McGann, Jerome J. *A Critique of Modern Textual Criticism.* Chicago: Univ. of Chicago Press, 1983.

———. *The Textual Condition.* Princeton: Princeton Univ. Press, 1991.

———. ed. *Textual Criticism and Literary Interpretation.* Chicago: Univ. of Chicago Press, 1985.

McKenzie, D. F. *Bibliography and the Sociology of Texts.* London: British Library, 1986.

———. "Printers of the Mind: Some Notes on Bibliographical Theories and Printing-House Practices." *Studies in Bibliography* 22 (1969): 1-75.

Martens, G., and H. Zeller, eds. *Texte und Varianten: Probleme ihrer Edition und Interpretation.* Munich: C. H. Beck, 1971.

Tanselle, G. Thomas. *A Rationale of Textual Criticism.* Philadelphia: Univ. of Pennsylvania Press, 1989.

———. *Selected Studies in Bibliography.* Charlottesville: Univ. Press of Virginia, 1979.

———. *Textual Criticism since Greg: A Chronicle, 1950-1985.* Charlottesville: Univ. Press of Virginia, 1987.

TEXT: Transactions of the Society for Textual Scholarship. New York: AMS Press, 1981-.

Thorpe, James. *Principles of Textual Criticism.* San Marino, Calif.: Huntington Library, 1972.

Zeller, Hans. "A New Approach to the Critical Constitution of Literary Texts." *Studies in Bibliography* 28 (1975): 231-64.

Christopher Decker (essay date March 2002)

SOURCE: Decker, Christopher. "Echoes and Parallels in FitzGerald's *Rubaiyat.*" *Notes and Queries* 49, no. 1 (March 2002): 65-8.

[*In the following essay, Decker offers a list of the parallels between elements of FitzGerald's translation of the* Rubáiyát *and the works of other authors.*]

In the introduction to my edition of Edward FitzGerald's *Rubáiyát of Omar Khayyám* (1997), I discuss FitzGerald's views and practice of 'sympathetic' translation. One aspect of his inventiveness as a translator which deserves further attention is his use of allusion. The following conscious or unconscious verbal parallels

appear in FitzGerald's *Rubáiyát* (references are to the page and stanza numbers of the 1859 text in my edition, except when indicated):

1. *Rubáiyát,* p. 10, IV: 'The thoughtful Soul to Solitude retires'. Cf. Pope, *The Rape of the Lock,* I. 57-8: 'For when the Fair in all their Pride expire, / To their first Elements their Souls retire'.

2. *Rubáiyát,* p. 10, VI: 'the Nightingale cries to the Rose / That yellow Cheek of her's to'incarnadine.' Cf. Shakespeare, *Macbeth,* II. ii. 61-3: 'this my hand will rather / The multitudinous seas incarnadine, / Making the green one red.' In revising 'yellow' to 'sallow' in the 1868 *Rubáiyát* (p. 37, VI), FitzGerald introduced a secondary Shakespearian echo, of *Romeo and Juliet,* II. ii. 69-70: 'Jesu Maria, what a deal of brine / Hath washed thy sallow cheeks for Rosaline!' The erasure of 'yellow' also eliminates an associated echo of the by-then familiar commonplace in *Macbeth,* V. iii. 22-3, 'my way of life / Is fall'n into the sere, the yellow leaf'.

3. *Rubáiyát,* p. 11, XI: 'Here with a Loaf of Bread beneath the Bough, / A Flask of Wine, a Book of Verse—and Thou / Beside me singing in the Wilderness—/ And Wilderness is Paradise enow.' Cf. Shakespeare, *2 Henry VI,* III. ii. 357-64 (Suffolk to Queen Margaret): 'Thus is poor Suffolk ten times banishèd—/ Once by the King, and three times thrice by thee. / 'Tis not the land I care for, wert thou thence, / A wilderness is populous enough, / So Suffolk had they heavenly company. / For where thou art, there is the world itself, / With every several pleasures in the world; / And where thou art not, desolation.'

4. *Rubáiyát,* p. 12, XVII: 'They say the Lion and the Lizard keep / The Courts where Jamshyd gloried and drank deep'. Cf. Sir John Denham, *Coopers Hill* (1668 version), line 235: 'There *Faunus* and *Sylvanus* keep their Courts'. There is a similar interinvolvement of the prospect of death with a play on the words 'life' and 'leaf' in both *Rubáiyát* (1868), p. 51, XCVIII—'Ah, with the Grape my fading Life provide, / And wash my Body whence the Life has died, / And lay me, shrouded in the living Leaf, / By some not unfrequented Garden-side.'—and *Coopers Hill* (1668), lines 285-8—'Yet faintly now declines the fatal strife; / So much his love was dearer than his life. / Now every leaf, and every moving breath / Presents a foe, and every foe a death.' Again, compare also *Macbeth,* V. iii. 22-3, 'my way of life / Is fall'n into the sere, the yellow leaf'.

5. *Rubáiyát,* p. 12, XIX: 'And this delightful Herb whose tender Green / Fledges the River's Lip on which we lean—/ Ah, lean upon it lightly! for who knows / From what once lovely Lip it springs unseen!' Cf. Milton, *Paradise Lost,* IV. 253: 'Grasing the tender herb,

were interpos'd' (in the description of Eden). In translating this stanza, which compares the new grass on a river-bank with an adolescent's fledging moustaches, FitzGerald may also have been mindful of, though not alluding to, lines 65-7 of *Il Penseroso*: 'And missing thee, I walk unseen / On the dry smooth-shaven Green, / To behold the wandring Moon'.

6. *Rubáiyát,* p. 12, XX: 'Ah, my Belovéd, fill the Cup that clears / TO-DAY of past Regrets and future Fears'. Cf. Cowper, *The Task,* Book IV ('The Winter-Evening'), lines 38-41: 'And, while the bubbling and loud-hissing urn / Throws up a steamy column, and the cups, / That cheer but not inebriate, wait on each, / So let us welcome peaceful ev'ning in.' FitzGerald alludes to the same lines by Cowper in a letter written in November 1844 to the Quaker poet Bernard Barton, regarding Harriet Martineau's being cured of a tumour by mesmerism: 'She is the only one I have read of who describes the sensation of *the trance,* which, seeming a painful one to the wide-awake looker-on, is in fact a state of tranquil glorification to the patient. It cheers but not inebriates! She felt her disease oozing away out at her feet, and as it were streams of warm fresh vitality coming in its place. And when she woke, lo, this was no dream!' (*Letters,* ed. Terhune and Terhune, I, 463 and 463 n. 3).

7. *Rubáiyát,* p. 13, XXIII: 'Dust into Dust, and under Dust, to lie, / Sans Wine, sans Song, sans Singer, and— sans End'. Cf. *The Book of Common Prayer,* 'The Burial of the Dead': 'earth to earth, ashes to ashes, dust to dust' and the last line of Jaques's famous speech on the Seven Ages of Man in *As You Like It,* II. vii. 139-66: 'Sans teeth, sans eyes, sans taste, sans everything.' The subtitle of FitzGerald's *Polonius* (1852) is 'A Collection of Wise Saws and Modern Instances'.

8. *Rubáiyát,* p. 13, XXVII: 'Myself when young did eagerly frequent / Doctor and Saint, and heard great Argument / About it and about: but evermore / Came out by the same Door as in I went.' Cf. Dryden, *Virgil's Pastorals,* I. 46-7: 'Yet all the little that I got, I spent, / And still return'd as empty as I went.'

9. *Rubáiyát,* p. 13, XXVII: 'About it and about'. Cf. Pope, *The Dunciad,* IV. 251-2: 'For thee explain a thing till all men doubt it, / And write about it, Goddess, and about it.'

10. *Rubáiyát,* p. 14, XXXI: 'I rose, and on the Throne of Saturn sate'. Cf. Spenser, *The Faerie Queene,* II. ix. 52: 'When oblique *Saturne* sate in the house of agonyes'. The preceding portrait of 'Phantastes' bears a striking, coincidental resemblance to the young Alfred Tennyson, which may be why FitzGerald would have remembered the last line of it.

11. *Rubáiyát,* p. 14, XXXII: 'There was a Door to which I found no Key: / There was a Veil past which I could not see: / Some little Talk awhile of ME and THEE / There seemed—and then no more of THEE and ME.' Here the echoes are faint, but FitzGerald is imitating the manner of Pope. Cf. Pope, *An Essay on Man,* i. 289-90: 'All Nature is but Art, unknown to thee; / All Chance, Direction, which thou canst not see'; and *The Dunciad* (B), IV. 216-22: 'While tow'ring o'er your Alphabet, like Saul, / Stands our Digamma, and o'ertops them all. / 'Tis true, on Words is still our whole debate, / Disputes of *Me* or *Te,* of *aut* or *at,* / To sound or sink in *cano,* O or A, / Or give up Cicero to C or K.'

12. *Rubáiyát,* p. 14, XXXII: 'There was a Veil past which I could not see'; also *Rubáiyát* (1868), p. 42, XXXVII: 'Then of the THEE IN ME who works behind / The Veil of Universe I cried to find'; and *Rubáiyát* (1868), p. 43, XLVIII: 'When You and I behind the Veil are past'. Cf. Tennyson, *In Memoriam A. H. H.,* LVI, 25-8: 'O life as futile, then, as frail / O for thy voice to soothe and bless! / What hope of answer, or redress? / Behind the veil, behind the veil.' As Christopher Ricks notes in his edition of Tennyson's poems (1987), II. 374, 'The "veil" has attracted much commentary' and speculation about Tennyson's source for the word. If Tennyson and FitzGerald had a common source, it is not obvious what this might be. It may seem a slight debt. Yet Tennyson, sensitive to questions of indebtedness whether literary or not, was quick to think himself FitzGerald's creditor for *Rubáiyát,* p. 15, XXXVIII: 'The Stars are setting and the Caravan / Starts for the Dawn of Nothing'—cf. Tennyson, 'The Gardener's Daughter', lines 16-17: 'The summer pilot of an empty heart / Unto the shores of nothing!' (Tennyson's lines themselves owe something to Lord Byron's 'Epistle to Augusta', lines 23-4: 'I have been cunning in mine overthrow, / The careful pilot of my proper woe.')

13. *Rubáiyát,* p. 15, XLI: 'for "Is" and "Is-NOT" though *with* Rule and Line'. Cf. Pope, *An Essay on Man,* III. 103-4: 'Who made the spider parallels design, / Sure as De-moivre, without rule or line?' As Pope's note reports, Abraham de Moivre was accounted, like Omar Khayyám, an eminent mathematician.

14. *Rubáiyát,* p. 16, XLVI: 'For in and out, above, about, below'. Cf. Donne, *Elegy XIX,* 'On His Mistress Going to Bed', lines 25-6: 'License my roving hands, and let them go / Before, behind, between, above, below.' FitzGerald revised his line to the demurely unambiguous 'We are no other than a moving row' in 1868, p. 47, LXXIII.

15. *Rubáiyát,* p. 17, XLIX: ''Tis all a Chequerboard of Nights and Days / Where Destiny with Men for Pieces plays: / Hither and thither moves, and mates, and slays, / And one by one back in the Closet lays.' Cf. a similar

thought in Tennyson, *Maud,* I. iv. 127-8: 'Do we move ourselves, or are moved by an unseen hand at a game / That pushes us off from the board, and others ever succeed?' FitzGerald was, however, translating a distich from the original Persian in which the same image appears; for a comparison with the original of this and other stanzas, see Edward Heron-Allen (ed.), *Edward FitzGerald's Rubâiyât of Omar Khayyâm with Their Original Persian Sources* (London: Bernard Quaritch, 1899).

16. *Rubáiyát,* p. 17, LI: 'nor all thy Piety nor Wit'. Cf. Dryden, 'Ode to Mrs. Anne Killigrew', line 153: 'Not wit nor piety could fate prevent' (see also lines 181 and 191 cited below, no. 21).

17. *Rubáiyát,* p. 18, LXI: 'Then said another—"Surely not in vain / My Substance from the common Earth was ta'en, / That He who subtly wrought me into Shape / Should stamp me back to common Earth again."' Cf. Tennyson, 'To—. With the Following Poem [The Palace of Art], lines 16-19: 'Not for this / Was common clay ta'en from the common earth / Moulded by God, and temper'd with the tears / Of angels to the perfect shape of man.'

18. *Rubáiyát* (1868), p. 42, XXXVII: '"An Understanding blind."' (Altered from 1859, p. 14, XXXIII: '"A blind Understanding!"') Cf. Marvell, 'On Mr. Milton's *Paradise Lost*', line 14: 'O'er which lame faith leads understanding blind'.

19. *Rubáiyát* (1868), p. 51, XCIX: 'Whither resorting from the vernal Heat / Shall Old Acquaintance Old Acquaintance greet'. Cf. Burns, *Tam o'Shanter. A Tale,* lines 1-2: 'When chapman billies leave the street, / And drouthy neebors, neebors meet'; and 'Auld Lang Syne', 1-2: 'Should auld acquaintance be forgot / And never brought to mind'. Both the rhetorical device and the term 'old acquaintance' are to be found elsewhere: see, for example, Dryden's *Aeneid,* VIII. 915-18, or Pope, *The Rape of the Lock,* I. 101-2 (where the device is used twice); and Shakespeare, *Sonnet* 89 or *1 Henry IV,* V. iv. 101. Yet once again the coincidence of these two passages in Burns—a poet admired by FitzGerald as well as by Tennyson—is strongly suggestive of conscious recollection. 'Vernal heat' may be a recollection of Wordsworth, *The Prelude,* IV. ('Summer Vacation'), lines 103-4: 'the vernal heat / Of poesy'.

20. *Rubáiyát* (1868), p. 51, XCIX: 'Under the branch that leans above the Wall / To shed his Blossom over head and feet.' Cf. Ariel's song 'Where the bee sucks, there suck I' in *The Tempest,* V. i. 93: 'Under the blossom, that hangs on the bough.'

21. *Rubáiyát* (1868), p. 52, CVI: 'That we might catch ere closed the Book of Fate.' Cf. Pope, *An Essay on Man,* I. 77-80: 'Heav'n from all creatures hides the book of Fate.' Compare also Dryden, 'Ode to Mrs. Anne Killigrew', line 181: 'The judging God shall close the book of fate'; and note that line 191 of the same poem—'and straight, with inborn vigor, on the wing'—may be incidentally echoed in *Rubáiyát,* p. 11, VII: 'Lo! the Bird is on the Wing.' 'On the wing', however, is a not uncommon phrase. (For a third echo of Dryden's poem, see above, no. 16.)

22. *Rubáiyát* (1872), p. 80, LXXXVII: 'Whereat some one of the loquacious Lot—/ I think a Súfi pipkin—waxing hot—/ "All this of Pot and Potter—Tell me then, / Who makes—Who sells—Who buys—Who *is* the Pot?"' Cf. Pope, *The Rape of the Lock,* IV. 51-4: 'A Pipkin there like *Homer*'s *Tripod* walks; / Here sighs a Jar, and there a Goose-pye talks; / Men prove with Child, as pow'rful Fancy works, / And Maids turn'd Bottels, call aloud for Corks.' The resemblance may only be coincidental, though the aptness of Pope's phantasmagoric Cave of Spleen inhabited by sighing jars and talking 'Maids turn'd Bottels' to FitzGerald's apologue of talking pots is suggestive.

23. The style of FitzGerald's *Rubáiyát* is markedly influenced by Byron's *Childe Harold's Pilgrimage,* whose particular sentiments and language the *Rubáiyát* appears in several places to echo. The clearest examples of this are in *Rubáiyát* (1868), p. 46, LXVI: 'Oh threats of Hell and Hopes of Paradise! / One thing at least is certain—*This* Life flies: / One thing is certain and the rest is Lies; / The Flower that once is blown for ever dies.'—cf. *Childe Harold's Pilgrimage,* II. iv. 36-8: 'On earth no more, but mingled with the skies? / Still wilt though dream on future joy and woe? / Regard and weigh yon dust before it flies: / That little urn saith more than thousand homilies'; and in *Rubáiyát* p. 13, XXV: 'Why, all the Saints and Sages who discuss'd / Of the Two Worlds so learnedly, are thrust / Like foolish Prophets forth; their Words to Scorn / Are scatter'd, and their Mouths are stopt with Dust'—cf. *Childe Harold's Pilgrimage,* II. vi. 51-4: 'The gay recess of Wisdom and of Wit / And Passion's host, that never brook'd control: / Can all, saint, sage, or sophist ever writ, / People this lonely tower, this tenement refit?'

Gary Sloan (essay date winter 2002/2003)

SOURCE: Sloan, Gary. "The *Rubáiyát* of Edward FitzOmar." *Free Inquiry* 23, no. 1 (winter 2002/2003): 59-60.

[*In the following essay, Sloan contends that FitzGerald's translation of the* Rubáiyát *is an improvement on the original Persian text.*]

Long ago in the Protestant hinterlands of northeast Texas, four young infidels consecrated their bibulous souls to an eleventh-century Persian astronomer-poet.

Each Saturday night, in an old Studebaker, we made a pilgrimage to Hugo, Oklahoma, the nearest wet town, to procure libations of Thunderbird wine. As we meandered homeward on isolated back roads, we swilled the "old familiar juice." Between swigs, we recited quatrains from *The Rubáiyát of Omar Khayyám,* the bible for apostate tipplers. The mellifluous verse sweetened our incertitude, alienation, and yearning. It also lent a romantic aura to inebriation.

Existential mysteries pricked us:

> Into this Universe, and *Why* not knowing
> Nor *whence,* like Water willy-nilly flowing;
> And out of it, as Wind along the Waste,
> I know not *Whither,* willy-nilly blowing.

Theological patter availed naught:

> Why, all the Saints and Sages who discussed
> Of the Two Worlds so wisely—they are thrust
> Like foolish Prophets forth; their Words to Scorn
> Are scattered, and their Mouths are stopt with Dust.

In our salad days (the year before), we sought but did not find:

> Myself when young did eagerly frequent
> Doctor and Saint, and heard great argument
> About it and about; but evermore
>
> Came out by the same door where in I went.

How ephemeral and insignificant our lives!

> When you and I behind the Veil are past
> Oh, but the long, long while the World shall last,
> Which of our Coming and Departure heeds
> As the Sea's self should heed a pebble-cast.

Had *we* omnipotence, we would do things right:

> Ah Love! could you and I with Him conspire
> To grasp this sorry Scheme of Things entire,
> Would not we shatter it to bits—and then
> Re-mold it nearer to the Heart's Desire!

Ah, well: "Better be jocund with the fruitful Grape / Than sadden after none, or bitter, Fruit." *Carpe diem,* lads!

Long after the vinous lads had irrevocably scattered, I realized we had exalted the wrong poet. We should have offered oblations to the translator of *The Rubáiyát,* Edward FitzGerald (1809-1883).

FitzGerald brought the artistry of a demiurge to raw material supplied by Omar. In the Persian manuscripts FitzGerald consulted (called the Ouseley and the Calcutta), Omar's rubáiyát (quatrains) are arranged alphabetically, the sequence determined by the last letter of rhyme words. The quatrains have no thematic center or progression. Each is a self-contained unit. By culling, combining, omitting, patching, and tinkering, FitzGerald conferred order on a welter of variegated musings. "He used Omar's detached thoughts," said anthologist Louis Untermeyer, "and wove them into a design. Imposing continuity on the fragments, he achieved a unity the original never possessed." For his publisher, FitzGerald described the narrative structure he concocted: "Omar begins with dawn pretty sober and contemplative; then as he thinks and drinks, he grows savage, blasphemous, etc., and then again sobers down into melancholy at nightfall."

FitzGerald wisely eschewed a literal translation. He imaginatively rendered Omar's thoughts into the idioms of English, at times creating his own metaphors, imagery, and allusions. Charles Eliot Norton, who introduced FitzGerald to American readers, said: "*The Rubáiyát* is the work of a poet inspired by the work of a poet; not a copy, but a reproduction, not a translation, but the redelivery of a poetic inspiration." An early reader correctly surmised "that the beauties of Omar are largely due to the genius of the translator." While many have translated Omar's verse (even Clarence Darrow gave it a whirl), all seem poetasters beside FitzGerald. George Roe paid homage to his gifted predecessor:

> FitzGerald has, with the magic touch of genius, infused into the quatrains he has given us more of the spirit of Omar than all the other English translators combined. His work is full of music; he grasps the poet's meaning with marvelous intuition. With a magnificent disdain of the letter, he presents us with the kernel of the thought; and over the whole he throws the magic mantle of his own personality and talks to us in words that flow from the living depths of a poet's soul.

Intermittently, FitzGerald worked on the poem for twenty-five years. Five editions, none exactly the same, were published—the first in 1859, the last posthumously in 1890. Few poems have been as often reprinted or as widely esteemed by both literati and ordinary readers. "No other poem," said Alfred Terhune, FitzGerald's biographer, "is seen so frequently in the meager libraries of those who make no claim to being either lovers of books or of literature." Some lines are famous: "A Jug of Wine, a Loaf of Bread—and Thou"; "The Moving Finger writes; and, having writ, / Moves on"; "The Flower that once has blown for ever dies"; "Take the Cash, and let the Credit go"; "The Bird of Time has but a little way / To flutter—and the Bird is on the Wing."

While conceding FitzGerald's brilliance, some scholars allege he misrepresented Omar. They believe Omar was a Sufi mystic, not the impious hedonist limned by FitzGerald. Omar scorned the hollow ritual, observances, anthropomorphism, and eschatological literalism of Muslim orthodoxy, they say, not the "true" Islam. According to Sufi belief, the soul was originally absorbed in God. Salvation lay in re-absorption. To achieve the reunion, one had to quell terrestrial desires and constraints. To conceal their heterodoxy from repressive caliphs, Sufi poets adopted an esoteric symbolism wherein a beloved person represented God; wine, the love of God; and drunkenness, spiritual ecstasy. Omar, the argument runs, cloaked his mysticism in the occult symbols deployed by Háfiz, Attár, Jámi, and other Sufi poets.

The truth may never be known. Two intractable difficulties arise.

First, no one has been able to establish a reliable corpus of Omar's verse. The known manuscripts, transcribed centuries after his death, are saturated with interpolations, excisions, and accretions. Of the 1,300 or so quatrains attributed to Omar, no one knows how many are actually his. Estimates range from 12 to 250. In *A Literary History of Persia,* E. G. Browne concluded: "While it is certain that Omar Khayyám wrote many quatrains, it is hardly possible, save in a few exceptional cases, to assert positively that he wrote any particular one of those ascribed to him."

Second, no one really knows whether references to wine and love are symbolic. Many sound literal. In evaluating a 1967 translation of *The Rubáiyát* by Robert Graves and Omar Ali-Shah, who pronounced the poet a devout Sufi, a reviewer for the *Times Literary Supplement* observed: "To prove Khayyám a Sufi involves the dangerous assertion that the poet does not mean what he says."

FitzGerald was certain Omar despised Sufism. In a preface to his translation, FitzGerald cited ancient reports that to his Muslim contemporaries Omar was a bugbear: "His Epicurean audacity of thought and speech caused him to be regarded askance in his own time and country. He is said to have been especially hated and dreaded by the Sufis, whose practice he ridiculed, and whose faith amounts to little more than his own when stript of its mysticism."

FitzGerald twinned Omar with Lucretius, the Roman poet of Epicureanism: "Both were men of subtle, strong, and cultivated intellect, fine imagination, and hearts passionate for truth and justice; who justly revolted from their country's false religion and foolish devotion to it." Omar's search for transcendent meanings led to an epistemological cul-de-sac. Finding no Legislator to ratify values, Omar pursued "sensual pleasure as the serious purpose of life, and *diverted* himself with speculative problems of Deity, Destiny, Matter and Spirit, Good and other such questions." "Not that the Persian has anything at all new," FitzGerald told bibliophile William Donne, "but he has dared to say it, as Lucretius did."

FitzGerald may have suited Omar to his own persuasion. Though a nominal Anglican, this freethinking scion of nobility kept his own counsel. He preferred Lucretius, Montaigne, Voltaire, Diderot, and Hume to Augustine, Aquinas, and Luther. His Holy Communion comprised offertories of wit and ample stoups of port with boon companions like Alfred Lord Tennyson and William Makepeace Thackeray. Visited by a rector determined to edify the wayward parishioner, FitzGerald was peremptory: "Sir, you might have conceived that a man does not come to my years of life without thinking much of these things. I believe I may say that I have reflected on them fully as much as yourself. You need not repeat this visit."

Versed in science (including Darwinism), philosophy, and theology, as well as the arts, FitzGerald was less unwilling than unable to believe. "FitzGerald is best classified as an agnostic," wrote Alfred Terhune. "Although he could not personally find satisfactory answers to the problems of the soul and man's relation to the Creator, he respected others' solutions to these enigmas."

In Omar Kháyyám, FitzGerald found a soul mate. "I take old Omar rather more as my property than yours," he told Edward Cowell, a Persian scholar. "He and I are more akin. You see all his beauty, but you don't feel *with* him the way I do." In a letter to his publisher, FitzGerald echoed the affinity: "Omar is one I have great fellow feeling with." FitzGerald signed himself "Edward FitzOmar."

One of FitzOmar's rubáiyát reads:

> Ah, make the most of what we yet may spend,
> Before we too into the Dust descend;
> Dust into Dust, and under Dust to lie,
> Sans wine, sans Song, sans Singer, and—sans End!

In 1959, the advice sounded good to four kids headed to Hugo. Still does.

Christopher Decker (essay date spring 2004)

SOURCE: Decker, Christopher. "Edward FitzGerald and Other Men's Flowers: Allusion in the *Rubáiyát of Omar Khayyám.*" *Literary Imagination: The Review of the Association of Literary Scholars and Critics* 6, no. 2 (spring 2004): 213-39.

[*In the following essay, Decker discusses FitzGerald's use of literary allusions in his translation of the* Rubáiyát.]

One of the most arresting images called to mind in Edward FitzGerald's **Rubáiyát of Omar Khayyám** is that of the *corpus redivivum,* the buried corpse that turns to flowers gently in the grave. The body's separate members suffer a metamorphosis into other objects that recompose and recollect their bygone looks. Khayyám reflects:

> I sometimes think that never blows so red
> The Rose as where some buried Cæsar bled;
>   That every Hyacinth the Garden wears
> Dropt in its Lap from some once lovely Head.

(XVIII)[1]

Such flowers are an apt metaphor for poetic allusion, since allusion involves the like transformation of a verbal corpus into flowers of new verse. As a poem in which scattered allusions turn outward their local colors, the *Rubáiyát* can be read in part as an anthology of other men's flowers. Yet if this trope comprehends FitzGerald's many acts of allusion in the *Rubáiyát*, it does not use its strength tyrannously to trump other ways of conceiving literary influence. Even within a single poem more than one kind of allusive word-game can be played.

Taken together as a body themselves, allusions in the *Rubáiyát* reflect on FitzGerald's double act: his adding a new poem to English literature, and his making that poem as a translation from a foreign literature in another language. As records of his responses to other poets, FitzGerald's allusions can also be understood as acts of sympathy. Some allusions echo earlier poems in order to affirm what they echo. They body forth sentiments felt through others' words as though glad to have discovered unsuspected correspondences. Picking up admired turns of phrase is a common link in friendly bonds between any two people, and allusion in poetry can likewise be a gesture or token of friendship between any two poets. Yet friendships consist in contrariness as well as affirmation, and disagreements can bring differences to light without disturbing the fundamental affinity for which friends continue to be grateful. FitzGerald's allusions grapple with earlier texts in fond contestation and strive at times for loving mastery. The works of earlier poets can be qualified, line by line, without at last being called into question: lessons to, but always still of, the masters. The *Rubáiyát* prevails upon other poems for memorable speech without necessarily seeking to prevail over them.

Those instances in which FitzGerald's allusiveness exercises its strengths discover metaphors for what, broadly and particularly, alluding can mean as a commemoration or preservation in which fragments of other texts continue to resound and enjoy some persistence of the properties they had possessed (and continue to possess, texts being always both past and present) as part of another verbal body. For allusion occurs under the sign of Orpheus, the head and limbs continuing to sing in spite of their forcible separation, each part endowed

with some vestige of its master's voice. I begin with two instances in which the give and take of allusive echo play upon the give and take of FitzGerald's friendships, before turning to the ways that allusions in the *Rubáiyát* reflect on their sources through metaphors of friendship and also of the remoulding of earth or dust, metempsychosis, reinscription, meetings and greetings, desired and desiring bodies, flowering corpses, and loneliness.

I

Interred in a box in Trinity College Library, Cambridge, is a letter of Edward FitzGerald's not published by the Terhunes in their edition of the poet's correspondence.[2] There may have been some confusion about whether to consider it a letter at all, since it consists of a single poem and appears never to have been sent to its addressee, the Reverend George Crabbe of Bredfield. The letter reaches out for companionship in a community of good spirits:

> Dear Crabbe,
>   When from your walk you're rested,
> And your dinner's half digested,
> Prithee, then set off again
> Through the dirty roads & rain,
> And win your way with courage here
> To smoke cigars & drink small Beer.
> Churchyard I expect & Barton;
> But should they fail—here's I for sartain;
> Who, as ev'n my foes do boast,
> Am always in myself "a Host"—
> And so expecting you to see
> I'm your obedient

E. F. G.

These words beckon hospitably towards both persons and poems. To begin with, the poem invites comparison with its forebears—Horace's *Epistle* 1.5 and its most famous English imitation, Ben Jonson's "Inviting a Friend to Supper." FitzGerald's rewriting of the Horatian occasion reflects on being a *Nachkömmling,* an "aftercomer," in two senses. The poem is written as an invitation to a guest who will arrive after both he and his host have dined, and, by alluding to its own antecedents, the poem announces itself as being also a late arrival. The intertwining of personal and literary associations is extended through its mention of Bernard Barton, the Quaker poet, and Thomas Churchyard (Churchyard's name being felicitously opportune in a poem that alludes—since churchyards, like allusions, are where the living and the dead continue to meet and where the bodies of the dead keep one another company, side by side and row on row).

Enlivening this already companionable forum, FitzGerald punningly alludes in professing to be "always in myself 'a Host.'" This line plays host to the shades of Alexander Pope and Homer:

The King then ask'd (as yet the Camp he view'd)
What Chief is that with Giant Strength endu'd,
Whose brawny Shoulders, and whose swelling Chest,
And lofty Stature far exceed the rest?
Ajax the great (the beauteous Queen reply'd)
Himself a Host: the *Grecian* Strength and Pride.

(*Homer's Iliad* 3.289-94)

To whom the King. With Justice hast thou shown
A Prince's Faults, and I with Reason own.
That happy Man whom *Jove* still honours most,
Is more than Armies, and himself an Host.

(*Homer's Iliad* 9.147-50)[3]

Pope himself—and FitzGerald, too—may have recalled the expression from John Oldham's "David's Lamentation for the Death of Saul and Jonathan, Paraphras'd," in which Jonathan is said to be one

whom loud-tongu'd Fame
Amongst her chiefest Heroes joys to name,
E're since the wond'rous Deeds at Seneh done,
Where he, himself an Host, o'recame a War alone."

(ll. 106-109)[4]

As often happens with verbal echoes, the number of possible antecedents joining the party begins to swell into a veritable host.[5]

Applied to FitzGerald himself, and at the same time looking back to Pope's great translation, the punning allusion seizes on Ajax's manful compactness so as to convert it to a wry self-compliment. On the welcoming face of it, "host" implies not a burly-armed combatant of an hundred-fold strength but a gentleman who has invited his friends over for a drink—if not the proverbial Homeric feasting. Yet there is a fretfulness in and behind the face of this "host." For, as his letters attest so painedly, FitzGerald often worried that the physical profusion of his affection—his letters, invitations, visits, walks, and talks—risked overwhelming the friends on whom he lavished them; his friendship might make him seem, in a wincing irony, "more than Armies, and himself an Host."

And "Host" has its perils when applied to allusion. For does a richly allusive poet assume the "Grecian strength and pride" in borrowing from Homer through Pope? Or does he awaken the suspicion that the plundered armor of mightier original talents only conceals the spindliness of his own verbal invention? FitzGerald was all too aware that his poetical imagination required the help of others' poetry if it were ever to achieve its potential depths and heights, let alone its own Parnassian. Yet here, too, friendship provides an apt metaphor for originality discovered in collaboration. FitzGerald's double allusion does not betray an anxious *agon* with poetical forefathers: it organizes a gathering of literary

friends to celebrate the translation of Omar Khayyám into English. The ***Rubáiyát*** proves itself "a host" in both senses, by marshalling the words of other poems and by hospitably accommodating them to concerted purposes.

It would, however, be a roseate notion of friendship that did not admit the likelihood that, at some time or other, friends will have a falling-out. When the Poet Laureate discovered that a line in the ***Rubáiyát*** strongly reminded him of a line he himself had written, he didn't hesitate to think so—or to say so: "You stole a bit in it from the Gardener's Daughter, I think," he wrote to FitzGerald, quickly conceding, "perhaps not, but it would be quaint if the old poet had the same expression."[6] In the last line of this stanza:

One Moment in Annihilation's Waste,
One Moment, of the Well of Life to taste—
    The Stars are setting and the Caravan
Starts for the Dawn of Nothing—Oh, make haste!

(XXXVIII)

Tennyson's ear had detected a resemblance to:

The summer pilot of an empty heart
Unto the shores of nothing!

(Tennyson, "The Gardener's Daughter," ll. 16-17)[7]

Like Tennyson himself, FitzGerald could not stomach accusations of theft, and he complained dyspeptically to Mrs. Tennyson, "[M]y bile is inwardly on fire. I—I—crib from the Gardener, which the paltry Poet charges me with!" Of course this was meant to be funny, but still, FitzGerald was stung. After hunting gamely through his Persian manuscripts for the other-than-Tennysonian source of his line—in vain—he grumbled to Tennyson, "you may set it down as an Echo of yourself if you will."[8] No sooner had he conceded this than Tennyson, having checked his recollection of the echo against his own copy of the ***Rubáiyát,*** wrote to try to shore up their friendship: "I see—rather to my confusion—that your words or Omar's are not 'bound to the shores of nothing' but 'Starts for the dawn of nothing' wherefore I repent that I made the least-little allusion to the passage.'"[9] The "least-little allusion": this playful batting back of FitzGerald's concession suggests that Tennyson still may have considered himself more sinned against than sinning, despite his stated repentance ("Repentance oft before I swore, *but*. . . ."). Tennyson no longer prefers a charge of petty theft but implies a lesser one of allusion. The reconciliatory gesture shows that making allusions, however least-little, and detecting them can prove a lesson in literature and the matter of tact. Especially between friends, allusions are acts of intimacy, like private jokes, though this intimacy, like any other, can insinuate envy and ill-feeling, much ado about "Nothing." FitzGerald was probably outraged not because Tennyson was wrong. His friend's ear was indeed acute. But an echo of Tennyson's poetry might have implied that FitzGerald secretly coveted what he so often criticised. It admitted Tennyson's priority and confessed his own inadequacy.[10]

Though scorched by the heat of indignation over accusations of literary theft, FitzGerald on other occasions felt quite a different warmth, that of tears shed at his friend's poetry being at once so memorable and so evocative of memory. Nostalgia imbues FitzGerald's recollections of Tennyson's early poems which, he said, "bring back my own youth as well as that which must be perennial in themselves. They make me cry like a fool, some of them."[11] About *The Holy Grail and Other Poems* (1869) FitzGerald confessed that, although only "Northern Farmer, New Style" drew tears to his eyes, yet of the rest of the book "whole phrases, lines, and sentences of it will abide with me, and, I am sure, with men after me."[12] Tears shed in thinking of days that were no more were the touchstones of FitzGerald's criticism of his friend's greatness, but his memoriousness could pain him less pleasurably, too. Though skirting the issue with Tennyson himself, FitzGerald owned up to others that echoes of Tennyson reminded him of his own weakness:

> I do not care about my own verses . . . They are not *original*—which is saying, they are not worth anything. They may possess sense, fancy etc.—but they always recall other and better poems. You see all *moulded* rather by Tennyson etc. than *growing* spontaneously from my own mind. No doubt there is original feeling, too; but it is not strong enough to grow up alone and whole of itself.[13]

There is no truer judgment on all FitzGerald's poetry than this, yet in the *Rubáiyát* he realized his genius in transfusing another's genius, whether in translating a kindred co-author like Omar Khayyám or in alluding.

II

Tennyson's moulding left its imprint on the *Rubáiyát*:

> Then said another—"Surely not in vain
> "My Substance from the common Earth was ta'en,
>   "That He who subtly wrought me into Shape
> "Should stamp me back to common Earth again."
>
> (LXI)

This stanza's common earth is the "common earth . . . ta'en" from Tennyson:

>   Not for this
> Was common clay ta'en from the common earth
> Moulded by God, and temper'd with the tears
> Of angels to the perfect shape of man.
>
> (Tennyson, "To———. With the Following
> Poem ["The Palace of Art"]," ll. 16-19)[14]

As is typical of many echoes in the *Rubáiyát*, this one delivers a contrarian reproof to its source. For it is not "the perfect shape of man" that the pots in the "Kúza-Náma" apologue of the 1859 *Rubáiyát* are discussing but the parlously imperfect:

>   after Silence spake
> A Vessel of a more ungainly Make:
>   "They sneer at me for leaning all awry;
> "What! did the Hand then of the Potter shake?"
>
> (LXIII)

More importantly, this borrowing—again, like others in the *Rubáiyát*—displays all the mimetic force of allusion or echo. "The Sound must seem an Echo to the Sense," Pope had urged. Here the sense of the passage is "echoed" or imitated not by the sounds of English speech but by the act of allusion. A metaphorical relation springs up between the notion of moulding earth or clay and the actual reworking of verbal substance, so that momentarily we are persuaded to think of FitzGerald's appropriation of "common earth" and "ta'en" in this stanza as itself a "remoulding," FitzGerald's common clay is not only the English language more generally but also the "matter-moulded forms of speech" which he appropriates from Tennyson and holds in common with him. And it is the tradition of English poetry that he and all his English-speaking contemporaries had inherited.

The opening of FitzGerald's *Rubáiyát* looks forward and back:

> Awake! for Morning in the Bowl of Night
> Has flung the Stone that puts the Stars to Flight:
>   And Lo! the Hunter of the East has caught
> The Sultán's Turret in a Noose of Light.
>
> (I)

It looks forward to having another drink in the next stanza:

> Dreaming when Dawn's Left Hand was in the Sky
> I heard a Voice within the Tavern cry,
>   "Awake, my Little ones, and fill the Cup
> "Before Life's Liquor in its Cup be dry."
>
> (II)

(Opening time for public houses in the *Rubáiyát* is gratifyingly early, though the speaker, after all, is only dreaming.) It looks back to the opening of *An Essay on Man*:

> "Awake, my St. John! leave all meaner things
> To low ambition, and the pride of Kings.
> Let us (since Life can little more supply
> Than just to look about us and to die)
> Expatiate free o'er all this scene of Man . . ."
>
> (Pope, *An Essay on Man*, i.1-5)[15]

But sleepers can be difficult to wake, and they often require more than a single calling, or recalling. Pope's "Awake" may already represent a prior recollection:

> Awake up, my glory; awake, psaltery and harp: I myself will awake early.
>
> (Psalm 57:8)

> Awake, ye drunkards, and weep; and howl, all ye drinkers of wine, because of the
> new wine; for it is cut off from your mouth.
>
> (Joel 1:5)

> Awake to righteousness, and sin not; for some have not the knowledge of God: I speak this to your shame. But some man will say, How are the dead raised up? and with what body do they come? Thou fool, that which thou sowest is not quickened, except it die: And that which thou sowest, thou sowest not that body that shall be, but bare grain, it may chance of wheat, or of some other grain: But God giveth it a body as it hath pleased him, and to every seed his own body.
>
> (1 Corinthians 15:34-38)

> Awake thou that sleepest, and arise from the dead, and Christ shall give thee light.
> See then that ye walk circumspectly, not as fools, but as wise,
> Redeeming the time, because the days are evil.
> Wherefore be ye not unwise, but understanding what the will of the Lord is.
> And be not drunk with wine, wherein is excess; but be filled with the Spirit . . .
>
> (Ephesians 5:14-18)[16]

Where Pope characteristically employs lexis as efficient ornament, FitzGerald's evocation of these biblical passages in the *Rubáiyát* is aggressively revisionary. That is, he calls biblical idiom into play not to affirm its sources but to be at vexed cross-purposes with them, striking an undercurrent of readerly memory so as to channel it into the *Rubáiyát*'s contrarian, irreverent hedonism. The texts from Psalms and 1 Corinthians celebrate a poetry of divine inspiration, spiritual awakening, and the new life of the body after death: all far removed from the *Rubáiyát*'s purely physical awakening which adumbrates the dawning realization that this world is the only world we can wake up to. (Khayyám's sleepers in particular are in need of being awakened early, since, if they have been following his advice in ebrious overindulgence, they will risk missing, instead of seizing, the best part of the day.) As for the possibility of life after death, the *Rubáiyát*'s version of the body's new life is unmisgivingly unmetaphorical. The body lives on, not *like* a seed that germinates and grows into a stalk, but *as* and *in* it:

> I sometimes think that never blows so red
> The Rose as where some buried Cæsar bled;

> That every Hyacinth the Garden wears
> Dropt in its Lap from some once lovely Head.
>
> (XVIII)

> And this delightful Herb whose tender Green
> Fledges the River's Lip on which we lean—
>   Ah, lean upon it lightly! for who knows
> From what once lovely Lip it springs unseen!
>
> (XIX)

Or, again overturning the Evangelist, bodies are turned to earth again, enriching an unenriching soil:

> And those who husbanded the Golden Grain,
> And those who flung it to the Winds like Rain,
>   Alike to no such aureate Earth are turn'd
> As buried once, Men want dug up again.
>
> (XV)

The texts from Joel and Ephesians come in for pointed controversion by their echoes, like memories of staunch resolutions overwhelmed by the compulsive pleasure of being "drunk with wine, wherein is excess" and filled with spirits. For if Khayyám also chides the unwisdom of not redeeming the time, his wisdom's circumspection leaves no hope of redemption in following the wise:

> Oh, come with old Khayyám, and leave the Wise
> To talk; one thing is certain, that Life flies;
>   One thing is certain, and the Rest is Lies;
> The Flower that once has blown for ever dies.
>
> (XXVI)

"The Rest is Lies," which may be true of even the idea of an Eternal Rest in the prophet's paradise. That FitzGerald was fond of quoting irreverently from the Bible is made plain by the epitaph he chose for his own gravestone: "It is he that hath made us, and not we ourselves" (Psalm 100), which recalls (on the stone where it is inscribed) and is recalled by (FitzGerald may have been thinking of it when translating Khayyám) the lines already cited from the *Rubáiyát*: "'They sneer at me for leaning all awry; / 'What! did the Hand then of the Potter shake?'"

A similar impiety insinuates itself into the echo of Pope, an echo fashioned by several elements: the introductory "awake," the exhortation to acknowledge the vanity of human wishes, and rhythmical cadence.[17] Though the *Rubáiyát* also acknowledges the limits of scientific enquiry in answering questions about the universe and man's place in it, it does not "vindicate the ways of God to man" but proposes instead that divine intentions are unknowable simply because they do not exist, nor have ever existed at any time. It is not clear that FitzGerald's dig at Pope is meant also to comprehend the latter's Catholicism (as against the former's being nominally Irish and denominationally not Catholic), though there are stanzas in the *Rubáiyát* which might have given pause, if not offence, to members of the English Catholic Church, who, by 1859, had been enjoying for some years what Newman scented in the air as "the coming in of a Second Spring . . . a restoration in the moral world."[18] Omar Khayyám's *rosarium* is decidedly not their rosary, and in three stanzas in the 1868 edition (revised from two in 1859) Khayyám's grave assumes the properties attributed to the graves of saints:

> Ah, with the Grape my fading Life provide,
> And wash my Body whence the Life has died,
>   And lay me, shrouded in the living Leaf,
> By some not unfrequented Garden-side.
>
> (XCVIII)

> Whither resorting from the vernal Heat
> Shall Old Acquaintance Old Acquaintance greet,
>   Under the Branch that leans above the Wall
> To shed his Blossom over head and feet.
>
> (XCIX)

> Then ev'n my buried Ashes such a snare
> Of Vintage shall fling up into the Air,
>   As not a True-believer passing by
> But shall be overtaken unaware.
>
> (C)

"Vintage" in stanza C had originally been "Perfume," recalling not only the tradition of trees and flowers blooming yearly on the graves of the saints but also the sweet smell of their corpses; Khayyám exchanges the odor of sanctity for a drunkard's boozy effusions.[19]

FitzGerald left few comments about Pope in his correspondence. Although he could admit that "Pope I admire more and more for his sense," it was only with the proviso that, "As to his poetry, I don't know of much. But still it is prose more beautifully and tastefully dressed than any one has ever made it."[20] These comments, mingling praise with denigration, are characteristic of the nineteenth-century view of English Augustan verse, though when applied to Pope's *Essay*, FitzGerald's criticism harmonizes with Pope's own statement that "I might have done [*An Essay on Man*] in Prose; but I chose Verse, and even Rhyme, for two reasons. The one will appear obvious; that Principles, maxims, or precepts so written, both strike the reader more strongly at first, and are more easily retain'd by him afterwards."[21] Pope's aiming for memorability strikes home again and again in FitzGerald's *Rubáiyát*. Adroit echoes of Pope in the *Rubáiyát* display the familiarity with Pope largely unrevealed in FitzGerald's letters.

FitzGerald takes up the problem of unknowability by again resorting to Pope's *Essay* with mingled echoes of *The Dunciad*:

> There was a Door to which I found no Key:
> There was a Veil past which I could not see:
>   Some little Talk awhile of ME and THEE
> There seemed—and then no more of THEE and ME.
>
> (XXXII)

> All Nature is but Art, unknown to thee;
> All Chance, Direction, which thou canst not see
>
> (*An Essay on Man*, i.289-90)[22]

> While tow'ring o'er your Alphabet, like Saul,
> Stands our Digamma, and o'er-tops them all.
> 'Tis true, on Words is still our whole debate,
> Disputes of *Me* or *Te*, of *aut* or *at*,
> To sound or sink in *cano*, O or A,
> Or give up Cicero to C or K."
>
> (*The Dunciad* (B), iv.217-22)[23]

The echo of *The Dunciad*'s "*Me* or *Te*" directs the memorious reader to the local satire on pedants dissecting verbal minutiae (Richard Bentley, in particular, comes in for rough handling). Pope's satire chimes with the ***Rubáiyát***'s own dismissal of the vanity of learning (stanzas XXV-XVIII, XXXIX, XLIII, and XLV in the 1859 text, and in 1868: "A Hair, they say, divides the False and True; / Yes; and a single alif were the clue" [LI]). This chiming might cause one momentarily to overlook the opposite direction in which FitzGerald's Khayyám is headed: not towards the belief that "All Nature is but Art . . . All Chance, Direction," but towards the certainty of unbelief. The blurring of voices only serves to sharpen the doctrinal differences between the two poems.

FitzGerald's Khayyám fences with Pope's *Essay* elsewhere:

> Who made the spider parallels design,
> Sure as De-moivre, without rule or line?
>
> (*An Essay on Man*, iii.103-104)[24]

> For "Is" and "Is-NOT" though *with* Rule and Line
> And "UP-AND-DOWN" *without*, I could define,
>   I yet in all I only cared to know,
> Was never deep in anything but—Wine.
>
> (XLI)

FitzGerald's insouciant allusion waves away Pope's natural theology, which compares the spider's divinely given feel for geometry with the talent of an Abraham de Moivre (an eminent mathematician, like Omar Khayyám). Idly swaying from "*with*" to "*without*," FitzGerald's Khayyám objects that, no, Man is the measure of all things (swerving momentarily from Lucretius to Protagoras)—an assertion whose force dissipates in the stumbling syntax of "I yet in all I only cared to know," which keeps to its own line on profundity with all a drunkard's clumsy straining after precision.

The *Rubáiyát* gets much from other English poems, but it gives as good as it gets. FitzGerald often bears down upon the texts he alludes to, meaning agreeably to disagree. Yet his perverse revisions are never so overbearing as to diminish our pleasure in his ear's deftness, the way he has of silently procuring the right words to turn on their ear. His allusion to an idyllic tea-time vignette by Cowper finds matter for transformation in its cups:

> And, while the bubbling and loud-hissing urn
> Throws up a steamy column, and the cups,
> That cheer but not inebriate, wait on each,
> So let us welcome peaceful ev'ning in.
>
> (Cowper, *The Task,* "The Winter-Evening," ll. 38-41)[25]

> Ah, my Belovéd, fill the Cup that clears
> To-DAY of past Regrets and future Fears
>
> (XX)

The "Cup that clears" the mind of regrets and fears in the *Rubáiyát*'s springtime does more than freshen its remembrance of "The Winter-Evening." Khayyám's draft of Lethe draws on Cowper but clears its account by cheerfully spiking its purer source. (Allusion pays its tab in kind.) Cheerfully, but not irresponsibly, for, as Khayyám would argue, red wine is not only more stimulating than tea, it is the better anaesthetic for the pain of life and the painful uncertainty of what, if anything, comes after life.

This uncertainty shapes Khayyám's advice elsewhere that solitary tippling is virtue, not vice. Allusive echo again serves to contrast the *Rubáiyát*'s velleities with those of its precursors:

> Now the New Year reviving old Desires,
> The thoughtful Soul to Solitude retires
>
> (IV)

These lines revive Pope's description of the afterlife of English coquettes in *The Rape of the Lock,* an afterlife imagined as a drastic slimming regime in which each lady is reduced to her essential humor:

> Think not, when Woman's transient breath is fled,
> That all her Vanities at once are dead:
> Succeeding Vanities she still regards,
> And tho' she plays no more, o'erlooks the Cards.
>   . . . . .
>
> For when the Fair in all their Pride expire,
> To their first Elements their Souls retire
>   . . . . .
>
> Soft yielding minds to Water glide away,
> And sip, with *Nymphs,* their elemental Tea.
>
> (Pope, *The Rape of the Lock,* i.51-62)[26]

The *Rubáiyát* makes over the first elements of Pope's lines—his words—in a transmigration of "Souls," and Pope's ladies enjoy a second afterlife in the afterlife of Pope's lines in the *Rubáiyát.* Yet whereas Pope's coquettes sip "their elemental Tea"—"elemental" being the word into which "Elements" from the earlier line has glided—FitzGerald's "Soul" retires into "Solitude" where it can be alone with its "old Desires" ("revived" just as Pope's lines are revived and have new life breathed into them)—those inveterate cravings for drafts of vintage, not satisfied even in the grave:

> Ah, with the Grape my fading Life provide,
> And wash my Body whence the Life has died,
>   And in a Windingsheet of Vine—Leaf wrapt,
> So bury me by some sweet Garden—side.
>
> (LXVII)

> And not a drop that from our Cups we throw
> On the parcht herbage but may steal below
>   To quench the fire of Anguish in some Eye
> There hidden—far beneath, and long ago.
>
> (1868, XLII)

In FitzGerald's appropriation of Pope, vine leaves again supplant tea leaves, implying that the oblivion-inducing drink of bibulous sinners prognosticates the future life more reliably than spilt religion or the bottoms of teacups. One thing on which the two poems agree, however, is in admonishing their readers to retreat from worldly vanities which are no earthly use.

Another sort of metempsychosis occurs in the Kúza-Náma apologue, a dream-like episode in which Khayyám hears voices speaking all around him in a potter's shop. The pots and jars speculate on the circumstances of their making and the likely aftermath of their own unmaking. But these pondered imponderables leave them baffled, open-mouthed:

> Whereat some one of the loquacious Lot—
> I think a Súfi pipkin—waxing hot—
>   "All this of Pot and Potter—Tell me then,
> "Who makes—Who sells—Who buys—Who is the Pot?"
>
> (1872, LXXXVII)

The questions die on the air without reply, but at least one possible origin for the animated "pipkin" again lies in *The Rape of the Lock,* this time in Pope's phantasmagorical Cave of Spleen:

> A Pipkin there like *Homer's Tripod* walks;
> Here sighs a Jar, and there a Goose-pye talks;
> Men prove with Child, as pow'rful Fancy works,
> And Maids turn'd Bottels, call aloud for Corks.
>
> (Pope, *The Rape of the Lock,* iv.51-54)[27]

The verbal coincidence is slight—merely a "pipkin"—though the single word is corroborated by context: the sighing jar and the transformation of maids into complaining bottles. Pope's own explicit allusion to Homer in line 51 (instructing his readers to "See Hom. Iliad 18. of Vulcan's walking Tripods") offers a precedent for seizing antiques from elder poets as heirlooms, whether pots or tripods, which would been handy to FitzGerald in lending an English accent to Khayyám's jarring voices.

At times FitzGerald shares Pope's own discontent by sharing his speech:

> Myself when young did eagerly frequent
> Doctor and Saint, and heard great Argument
>   About it and about: but evermore
> Came out by the same Door as in I went.
>
> (XXVII)

> For thee explain a thing till all men doubt it,
> And write about it, Goddess, and about it.
>
> (*The Dunciad,* iv.251-52)[28]

The *Rubáiyát* doubly lashes learned pomposity by laying on Pope's chastisement along with its own. The doubling back of allusion chimes with the lines' other doublings and doublings-back—"doctor and saint," "about it and about," "came out by the same Door as in I went," with the schematic reinforcement of the end-rhyme's return in the fourth line after its suspension in the third. The phrase "about it and about" swells with accumulated exasperation, as a reiteration called out by reiteration.[29] The act of allusion here enacts in itself the realization that the passage of a century or more makes no difference in the appearance of fools or foolish pedants. "Fools change in England, and new fools arise; / For, though the immortal species never dies, / Yet every year new maggots make new flies,"[30] just as "The Eternal Sáki from that Bowl has pour'd / Millions of Bubbles like us, and will pour." The job of exposing the peculiar madness of those wise dogs chained in the pale of words endlessly recurs.

If mindless reiteration is what good allusion responsibly avoids, original reinscription is what it longs to achieve.

> Oh if the World were but to re-create,
> That we might catch ere closed the Book of Fate,
> And make The Writer on a fairer leaf
> Inscribe our names, or quite obliterate.
>
> (1868, CVI)

Khayyám would have "The Writer" compose better lives for his beloved and himself or—the bracing alternative—see to it that they never should exist or have existed (punning on the etymology of "obliterate" to mean "dissolve into its component letters" as well as "to atomize"). Yet in alluding, FitzGerald chooses the former alternative spelled out by Khayyám. For "the Book of Fate" passes into FitzGerald's hands from two of its previous owners:

> The judging God shall close the book of fate
>
> (Dryden, "To . . . Mrs. Anne Killigrew," l. 181)[31]

> Heav'n from all creatures hides the book of Fate
>
> (Pope, *An Essay on Man,* i. 77)[32]

It is also "the Book of Fate" which FitzGerald (himself a writer, though not "The Writer") re-creates and inscribes anew. Allusion here movingly attempts to fulfill the desires it speaks of—re-creating the poetry of Dryden and Pope, re-inscribing Persian speech in an English verse translation—even as the verse acknowledges ruefully how far desire falls short of fulfillment.

The trope of reinscription, and its impossibility, brings Dryden elsewhere into the *Rubáiyát:*[33]

> The Moving Finger writes; and, having writ,
> Moves on: nor all thy Piety nor Wit
>   Shall lure it back to cancel half a Line,
> Nor all thy Tears wash out a Word of it.
>
> (LI)

> Not wit nor piety could fate prevent
>
> (Dryden, "To . . . Mrs. Anne Killigrew," l. 153)[34]

In praising Anne Killigrew, the earlier poem by Dryden resorts to familiar tropes in seventeenth-century theories of translation. Her accomplishments are described as latent in "an early, rich, and inexhausted vein," her father having been "transfused" into her blood and her intelligence innate in her as "if by traduction" (ll. 23-28), the one word "traduction" meaning for Dryden both "translation into another language" and "transmission by generation to offspring or posterity" (*OED*). Dryden joins together these notions of generation and familial inheritance on the one hand, and literary regeneration and inheritance on the other:

> But if thy pre-existing soul
>   Was formed, at first, with myriads more,
> It did through all the mighty poets roll,
>   Who Greek or Latin laurels wore,
> And was that Sappho last, which once it was before.
>
> (ll. 29-33)[35]

Dryden's poem anticipates two kinds of afterlife for the soul: the transmigration set out in these lines and the awakening of the dead to the Last Judgment described in the ode's concluding stanza. The *Rubáiyát* parts company with Dryden in that it anticipates only one Last Thing, not four. But like Dryden's poem, it also wants to have its afterlife both ways. Though it elsewhere takes an atomistic view of the afterlife as merely physical recomposition, the *Rubáiyát* affirms the idea of metempsychosis simply by being a translation which FitzGerald described as a transfusion of

Khayyám's essential spirit into English. Here again, what cannot be accomplished by human beings—the recasting of inevitable lots in life and in death, the rerobing of destinies—is enacted metaphorically by FitzGerald in rewriting Dryden and even in rewriting his own *Rubáiyát* in later versions.

FitzGerald's allusive echoes are not always marked by such gravity, though certain echoes may exert a pull on others, calling them into play. These lines, for example,

> Whither resorting from the vernal Heat
> Shall Old Acquaintance Old Acquaintance greet
>   Under the Branch that leans above the Wall
> To shed his Blossom over head and feet.

> (1868, XCIX)

cannot forget their old acquaintance with Robert Burns:

> Should auld acquaintance be forgot
>   And never brought to mind?
> Should auld acquaintance be forgot,
>   And auld lang syne!

> ("Auld Lang Syne")[36]

FitzGerald's allusion gives the answer home, that neither old acquaintance nor "auld acquaintance" shall be forgot. FitzGerald lived by his friends and his literary friendships with Khayyám, Calderón, and others, and he died by them (he passed away suddenly while visiting his friend George Crabbe of Merton). They were his meat and drink, something "Auld Lang Syne" brings to mind in a confusion of person and drinking vessel reminiscent of those in the *Rubáiyát*:

> And surely ye'll be your pint-stowp,
>   And surely I'll be mine,
> And we'll tak a cup o' kindness yet
>   For auld lang syne!

FitzGerald's lines take more than one cup of human-kindness from Burns:

> When chapman billies leave the street,
> And drouthy neebors, neebors meet.

> (*Tam o' Shanter. A Tale*, ll. 1-2)[37]

Just as neighbors or old acquaintances might meet, so the words that refer to them meet on the printed page. "Old Acquaintance" runs into "Old Acquaintance" in FitzGerald's line, and only a comma stands between "neebors" and "neebors" in Burns. Burns was not the first to use this rhetorical figure in which words stand next to each other as do the ideal bodies they refer to. FitzGerald might again have been mindful of Dryden:

> It seems, as if the Cyclades again
> Were rooted up, and justled in the Main:
> Or floating Mountains, floating Mountains meet:
> Such is the fierce Encounter of the Fleet.

> (*Virgil's Aeneis*, viii. 915-18)[38]

or Pope:

> Where Wigs with Wigs, with Sword-knots Sword-
>   knots strive,
> Beaus banish beaus, and Coaches Coaches drive.

> (Pope, *The Rape of the Lock*, i. 101)[39]

Such collisions do not necessarily clash with FitzGerald's own use of this turn. The meeting of old acquaintances, as FitzGerald knew, was sometimes as fraught a business as the meeting of drouthy neighbors. To make use of a rhetorical figure is not necessarily to allude, yet the coincidence of the two passages in Burns strongly suggests conscious recollection. Moreover, the choice of Burns is felicitously right in that the 1868 *Rubáiyát* arranges the meeting of two sets of old acquaintances: two echoes of Burns and two "old Acquaintance"'s on the printed page.

Burns was a great favorite of one of FitzGerald's oldest acquaintances, Tennyson, who said glowingly to Aubrey de Vere, "Read the exquisite songs of Burns. In shape, each of them has the perfection of the berry; in light the radiance of the dewdrop: you forget for its sake those stupid things, his serious pieces!"[40] So FitzGerald's allusion would have been appreciated by the audience that mattered most to him, even if his recollection of one of Burns's exquisite lyrics did not prevent him from remembering "Tam O' Shanter." Burns is also right for another reason. Tennyson admired "the skill with which Burns . . . immortalised so many of the old songs of Scotland and incorporated great parts of them in his own poetry."[41] Immortalization through incorporation does not need to be an embalming or an entombment but can be a reinvigoration of the living stock of literature. But even without knowing that Burns drew on native traditions north and south of the Scottish border, any reader will notice how Burns's poetry passes back and forth across the border between two poetic dialects, one English and one Scottish. This border-crossing happens within a single poem like "A Red, Red Rose" from one line to the next, with the reader passing that checkpoint of the line-ending (invisible, like many geographical borders):

> And I will love thee still, my Dear,
> Till a' the seas gang dry.

> (ll. 7-8)

The crossing can occur even within a single line of verse, as in line 5: "As fair art thou, my bonie lass." Allusions to Burns, then, are more than apt in a poem which itself incorporates "old songs" such as Burns's (proof of their perdurability) and which negotiates the passage of Khayyám's Persian verses into the English language.

Tennyson thought Burns possessed something of Shakespeare's genius, innovatory because it was reno-vatory: "Burns did for the old songs of Scotland almost what Shakespeare had done for the English drama that preceded him."[42] FitzGerald, in turn, added something to the renovation of English poetry by re-turning lines by Burns and Shakespeare in the *Rubáiyát*. In the stanza just quoted (*Rubáiyát*, 1868, XCIX), the last two lines—"Under the Branch that leans above the Wall / To shed his Blossom over head and feet."—are haunted by Ariel's song, "Where the bee sucks": "Under the blossom, that hangs on the bough" (*The Tempest*, V.i.96).[43] (This blossom of song was soon shed from FitzGerald's poem, for the stanza did not re-appear in 1872 or 1879.) Here again FitzGerald gathers other men's flowers, as he does openly in his notes to the 1859 *Rubáiyát*, where he includes a long passage from Robert Binning's account of the first days of Spring in Persia. The sight of trees in blossom and flowers spring-ing from the soil between patches of still lingering snow moved Binning to compare lines in Shakespeare which might have been written for the scenery:

> And on old Hyems' Chin and icy Crown
> An odorous Chaplet of sweet Summer buds
> Is, as in mockery, set.
>
> (*A Midsummer Night's Dream*, II.i.109-11)[44]

The *Rubáiyát*'s flowers are elsewhere streaked with recollections of Shakespeare:

> And David's Lips are lock't; but in divine
> High piping Péhlevi, with "Wine! Wine! Wine!
>   "Red Wine!"—the Nightingale cries to the Rose
> That yellow Cheek of her's to'incarnadine.
>
> (VI)

The word "incarnadine" inescapably calls to mind its unique appearance in Shakespeare, in *Macbeth*, in Mac-beth's mouth:

>   this my hand will rather
> The multitudinous seas incarnadine,
> Making the green one red.
>
> (*Macbeth*, II.ii.61-63)

FitzGerald's appropriation of "incarnadine" could hardly be said to allude either simply or straightfor-wardly to this moment in the play, when Macbeth's murder of Duncan fulfills the witches' prophecy with shrinking but implacable violence. Macbeth's guilty hand, whose stain he imagines will infect whatever might seek to cleanse it, seems a thing quite apart from the flush of pleasure that FitzGerald's nightingale brings to the rose's cheek. Apart from, and yet also a part of: like "the White Hand of Moses" two stanzas before it, Macbeth's hand lies beneath the surface of the poem and flowers to new life. Just as "never blows so red /

The Rose as where some buried Cæsar bled" (stanza XVIII), it is Duncan's blood and Macbeth's bloody and invisible hand that the *Rubáiyát*'s rose is flush with and incarnates.

Such flowers as this are a melancholy sight, and their streaks may also be from tears. In revising "yellow Cheek" to "sallow Cheek" in the 1868 *Rubáiyát*, FitzGerald introduced a second echo of Shakespeare:

> Jesu Maria, what a deal of brine
> Hath washed thy sallow cheeks for Rosaline!
>
> (*Romeo and Juliet*, II.ii.69-70)

Friar Lawrence expresses his chaste surprise at the instantaneity with which lovers' affections can sway from one object to another. Romeo easily forgets Rosa-line ("I have forgot that name and that name's woe") in forgetting himself over Juliet. In remembering this forgetfulness, FitzGerald sets Macbeth's hand against Romeo's cheek, while shedding another echo of Mac-beth's lugubrious pondering: "my way of life / Is fall'n into the sere, the yellow leaf."[45]

Unseen hands FitzGerald was anxious to exhume from the *Rubáiyát* had been originally bodied forth in this stanza:

> For in and out, above, about, below,
> 'Tis nothing but a Magic Shadow-show,
>   Play'd in a Box whose Candle is the Sun,
> Round which we Phantom Figures come and go.
>
> (XLVI)

The phantom figure who came and went was Donne:

> Licence my roaving hands, and let them go,
> Before, behind, between, above, below
> O, my America! my new-found-land,
> My kingdome safeliest when with one man mann'd.
>
> (Elegy XIX, "To His Mistress Going to Bed," ll. 25-26)[46]

This was perhaps too full-bodied for some of FitzGer-ald's readers, this evocation of an impatient lover or young man carbuncular, who comes and then goes. The second edition of the *Rubáiyát* stiffly forbids any pruri-ent inferences from the echo:

> We are no other than a moving row
> Of visionary Shapes that come and go
>   Round with this Sun-illumin'd Lantern held
> In Midnight by the Master of the Show.
>
> (1868, LXXIII)

The angel shape of Donne's dream-mistress is ef-fectively dispelled from the moving row of FitzGerald's revised line, and gone are Donne's expeditionary look, his Columbian hands, her cartographic body.

Revision can attenuate an undesirable echo, but it can also amplify a desired one.

> And this delightful Herb whose tender Green
> Fledges the River's Lip on which we lean—
>   Ah, lean upon it lightly! for who knows
> From what once lovely Lip it springs unseen!
>
>   (XIX)

For FitzGerald, a river bank one could lie on and feel as though one were lying down with a lover was something akin to an Eden:

> Betwixt them Lawns, or level Downs, and Flocks
> Grasing the tender herb, were interpos'd,
> Or palmie hilloc, or the flourie lap
> Of som irriguous Valley spred her store,
> Flours of all hue, and without Thorn the Rose:
>
>   (*Paradise Lost,* iv.252-56)

In subsequent revisions, FitzGerald altered the first line of his stanza to "And this delightful Herb whose living Green" (1868) and finally to "And this reviving Herb whose tender Green" (1872, 1879)—"reviving" quickening the sense of revival of the past, of the words' past, in the line.

FitzGerald occasionally twitted himself over his own faulty memory, as in the fragment of a memorandum (or possibly an unsent letter) in which he corrected himself:

> I spoilt it. I remember how it is
>   Read rascal in the motions of his back
>   And scoundrel in the *supple* sliding knee.[47]

Yet sometimes he positively wished for forgetfulness, when reading Shakespeare, for example. He remarked to Thackeray in 1831, "I have not read Shakespeare for a long time. I will tell you why. I found that *his manner* stuck so in my head that I was always trying to think in his way; I mean with his quaint words, etc.—this I don't wish."[48] Yet Shakespeare's words would come, whether or not he wished them to. Other voices might drown out his own thoughts, but sometimes he could drown his sorrows in them. They could be a welcome relief from the burden of being alone with himself. Many years later, when looking through the volumes of the new Cambridge Shakespeare, he experienced a visitation: "Hamlet, Macbeth, Tempest, and Shylock—I heard them talking in my room—all alive about me."[49] (This, in a letter to Fanny Kemble, who would have appreciated the remark more pointedly than most.) When melancholy wants company, it can look to the consolations of philosophy: "I should like to see Lucretius: who is a gloomy friend of mine."[50] Or it looks, or listens, for an example of loneliness braving it out. To Thackeray again, in 1852, he confessed, "I am become a sad Epicurean—just desirous to keep on the windy

side of bother and pain."[51] Because words, like people, need someone to turn to, these words turn to Thackeray for understanding by returning to Shakespeare's Beatrice:

> DON PEDRO
>
>   In faith, lady, you have a merry heart.
>
> BEATRICE
>
>   Yea, my lord, I thank it. Poor fool, it keeps on the
>   windy side of care.
>
>   (*Much Ado About Nothing,* II.i.293-95)

FitzGerald's loneliness also found company in Omar Khayyám, himself in need of someone to pass the time with in desolation:

> Here with a Loaf of Bread beneath the Bough,
> A Flask of Wine, a Book of Verse—and Thou
>   Beside me singing in the Wilderness—
> And Wilderness is Paradise enow.
>
>   (XI)

There is more than one singer here amid the ruins of Persepolis: Khayyám, FitzGerald, the readers who might intone these lines, and Shakespeare's Suffolk, speaking his last words to Queen Margaret before going into exile:

> Thus is poor Suffolk ten times banishèd—
> Once by the King, and three times thrice by thee.
> 'Tis not the land I care for, wert thou thence,
> A wilderness is populous enough,
> So Suffolk had thy heavenly company.
> For where thou art, there is the world itself,
> With every several pleasures in the world;
> And where thou art not, desolation.
>
>   (*2 Henry VI,* III.ii.361-68)

A heavenly company meets in the making of allusion, dissolving the loneliness of the writer's solitude in the act of writing by making other writers party to it. Hearing that a friend of his had recently published was a spur to prick the sides of FitzGerald's intent:

> Do you mean it is *your* 'Historical Reveries' is
>   reprinted? Is the *Gazelle Boat*
> *Song* once more afloat?
>   "And I not sing etc."
> I rage with jealousy, and like Mrs. Jarley think of
>   turning Atheist.[52]

The trailing quotation is from *English Bards and Scotch Reviewers:*

> Still must I hear?—shall hoarse Fitzgerald bawl
> His creaking couplets in a tavern hall,
> And I not sing?[53]

There can be no question about what moved FitzGerald to remember these lines to begin with and to have them ready for later use, though it is characteristic of him to push himself forward by alluding to lines that only deprecate his namesake. Every verbal echo in the poem seems to ask, "Shall hoarse FitzGerald bawl . . . and I not sing?"

Literary echoes blend voices in harmonious confusion, sharing songs and cups of remembrance with the past. FitzGerald knew, however, that remembrance can be a cup of kindness yet, or it can be a cup of gall:

> Whether at Naishápúr or Babylon,
> Whether the Cup with sweet or bitter run,
>   The Wine of Life keeps oozing drop by drop,
> The Leaves of Life keep falling one by one.
>
> (1868, VIII)

"The Wine of Life" is drawn from Macbeth:

> Had I but died an hour before this chance,
> I had liv'd a blessed time; for, from this instant,
> There's nothing serious in mortality;
> All is but toys: renown, and grace, is dead;
> The wine of life is drawn, and the mere lees
> Is left this vault to brag of.
>
> (*Macbeth*, II.iii.90-95)

"Old wine in new bottles" is one way to think of translation or allusion, and the *Rubáiyát* takes very seriously the reflection that "There's nothing serious in mortality; / All is but toys." Translation had a quickening influence on FitzGerald's life during one of its darkest passages (his new life as an unhappily married man, the loss of William Kenworthy Brown). The *Rubáiyát*'s life is similarly quickened by the vital influence of other poems both Persian and English transfused into its verbal substance. And the poem urges quickness upon its readers, an urgent vitality in seizing the moment:

> "Awake, my Little ones, and fill the Cup
> "Before Life's Liquor in its Cup be dry."
>
> (II)

> "You know how little while we have to stay,
> "And, once departed, may return no more."
>
> (III)

> The Bird of Time has but a little way
> To fly—and Lo! the Bird is on the Wing.
>
> (VII)

> Ah, Fill the Cup:—what boots it to repeat
> How Time is slipping underneath our Feet
>
> (XXXVII)

> Would you that spangle of Existence spend
> About THE SECRET—quick about it, Friend!
>
> (1868, L)

For what waits in the grave is the counterpart to the dissolute Epicureanism enjoined by Khayyám—the dissolution of consciousness and the body that framed it:

> Ah, make the most of what we yet may spend,
> Before we too into the Dust descend;
>   Dust into Dust, and under Dust, to lie,
> Sans Wine, sans Song, sans Singer, and—sans End!
>
> (XXIII)

Our common humanity inevitably lies in our common death, our reduction to a common dust. The common dust of this stanza is its pinching of "dust" and "sans" from the Book of Common Prayer—"earth to earth, ashes to ashes, dust to dust"—and from the finish line of Jaques's famous speech on the Seven Ages of Man—"Sans teeth, sans eyes, sans taste, sans everything."[54] This allusive remoulding of the Bible and Shakespeare reflects the awareness that acts of remembering—whether in the recomposition of the stuff of bodies or texts—are partial and fragmentary. The sounds made by "all-obliterated" tongues, however, can tend to discordancy, reflecting FitzGerald's own partiality. For the words which follow "dust to dust" in the Book of Common Prayer are "in sure and certain hope of the Resurrection to eternal life, through our Lord Jesus Christ." There is no way the allusion can be recognized without remembering the way its source text is tending, and consequently no way of hearing the allusion as doing anything but failing to harmonize with Christian belief. This untuning of the echo from its source is an impiety nicely turned in the mouth of an author whom FitzGerald described as "an old Epicurean so desperately impious in his recommendations to live only for *Today* that the good Mahometans have scarce dared to multiply MSS of him."[55]

The allusion's being out of tune with its source not only suits the *Rubáiyát*'s heterodox tenor but chimes also with Jaques's complaint. The banished Duke observes that if Jaques, "compact of jars, grow musical, / We shall have shortly discord in the spheres."[56] Khayyám, as FitzGerald understood him, was similarly out of harmony with his own society and its *mores* (being also compact of jars of quite another, vinous sort), not to mention idling in a wilderness. FitzGerald's linking of Jaques to Khayyám is an act of interpretation that sends the *Rubáiyát*'s readers, including its mid-Victorian ones, back to Shakespeare retempered to an impatience with the heavenly harmony of the spheres and a taste for *fêtes champetres*.[57] In the matter of the allusion itself, FitzGerald's "Sans Wine, sans Song, sans Singer, and—sans End!" remembers those parts of the body ("tongue" is, in a sense, already obliterated by being reduced merely to the sense of taste) named by Jaques but transmutes them to those things celebrated by his own poem—wine, song, and singer—while Jaques's deal of infinite nothing or *néant* in "sans everything" becomes the **Rubáiyát**'s loamy paradox of an end without end, death everlasting.

There are other echoes in the **Rubáiyát** so attenuated that one could argue they show only a coincidental resemblance in tone or style, and Tennyson's defensive *caveat* cannot be passed over: "No man can write a single passage to which a parallel one may not be found somewhere in the literature of the world." Yet looking no further in the literature of the world than that worldly self-exploitation in verse, *Childe Harold's Pilgrimage*, turns up a number of passages from which Byron's melancholy ambience seems to have passed to the **Rubáiyát**:

> On earth no more, but mingled with the skies?
> Still wilt thou dream on future joy and woe?
> Regard and weigh yon dust before it flies:
> That little urn saith more than thousand homilies.
> (Byron, *CHP* [*Childe Harold's Pilgrimage*], II.iv.33-36)

> The gay recess of Wisdom and of Wit
> And Passion's host, that never brook'd control:
> Can all, saint, sage, or sophist ever writ,
> People this lonely tower, this tenement refit?
> (Byron, *CHP*, II.vi.51-54)

> Pursue what Chance or Fate proclaimeth best;
> Peace waits on us on the shores of Acheron:
> There no forc'd banquet claims the sated guest,
> But Silence spreads the couch of ever welcome rest.
> (Byron, *CHP*, II.vii.60-63)

> Oh! that the Desart were my dwelling place,
> With one fair Spirit for my minister,
> That I might all forget the human race,
> And, hating no one, love but only her!
> Ye Elements!—in whose ennobling stir
> I feel myself exalted—Can ye not
> Accord me such a being? Do I err
> In deeming such inhabit many a spot?
> Though with them to converse can rarely be our lot.
> (Byron, *CHP*, IV.clxxvii.1585-93)

> Another Voice, when I am sleeping, cries,
> "The Flower should open with the Morning skies."
> And a retreating Whisper, as I wake—
> "The Flower that once has blown for ever dies."
> (**Rubáiyát**, 1868, XXVIII)

> Why, all the Saints and Sages who discuss'd
> Of the Two Worlds so learnedly, are thrust
> Like foolish Prophets forth; their Words to Scorn
> Are scatter'd, and their Mouths are stopt with Dust.
> (**Rubáiyát**, 1859, XXV)

> The Moving Finger writes; and, having writ,
> Moves on: nor all thy Piety nor Wit
> Shall lure it back to cancel half a Line,
> Nor all thy Tears wash out a Word of it.
> (**Rubáiyát**, 1859, LI)

> 'Tis but a Tent where takes his one-day's rest
> A Sultan to the realm of Death addrest;
> The Sultan rises, and the dark Ferrásh
> Strikes, and prepares it for another guest.
> (**Rubáiyát**, 1872, XLV)

> Oh, plagued no more with Human or Divine,
> To-morrow's tangle to itself resign,
> And lose your fingers in the tresses of
> The Cypress-slender Minister of Wine.
> (**Rubáiyát**, 1868, LV)

> With me along some Strip of Herbage strown
> That just divides the desert from the sown,
> Where name of Slave and Sultán scarce is known,
> And pity Sultán Máhmúd on his Throne.
> (**Rubáiyát**, 1859, X)

The echoes of Byron in the **Rubáiyát** suggest that FitzGerald still felt the pull of the Byronic temperament: expansive to the point of self-indulgence, but also sensible, skeptical, heterodox, and Epicurean. These were the qualities of Khayyám's verses that had also "struck a fibre," and FitzGerald elsewhere acknowledged Byron's affinity with those "curious Infidel and Epicurean Tetrastichs . . . as savage against Destiny, etc., as Manfred."[58]

Allusion in FitzGerald's **Rubáiyát** unites different kinds of recognition. In bringing one writer's words quickeningly into play with another's, allusion depends on recognition to bring the reader fully into play as well. Finding points of contact between Khayyám and English poetry, FitzGerald's choice of words and his sensitivity to what his readers might also hear and remember play on a sense of familiarity so as to clasp reader and writer together in sympathetic bonds. The recognition of allusions invites and echoes the recognition of unexpected sympathy which both FitzGerald and many of his readers could feel for the writings of a poet so utterly removed in time, place, culture, and language from their own. Over and over again in the letters written while he was translating Omar Khayyám, FitzGerald remarks on his astonishment at the sympathy between himself and his Persian precursor. Though he generally deferred to his friend and language teacher W. B. Cowell in matters of scholarship, FitzGerald claimed priority in intimacy, for Khayyám and he were "more akin, are we not? You see all Beauty, but you can't feel *with* him in some respects as I do."[59] Leafing through the Khayyám manuscripts, FitzGerald found turns of thought and turns of phrase that sounded both fresh and familiar, giving the impression that what he had long thought was newly expressed in an older tongue. To translate Khayyám was to feel a liberating influence, an inspiration.

Another kind of recognition which the ***Rubáiyát***'s allusions invite is that of esteem, an esteem produced by reader and writer recognizing a shared literary culture. Instead of struggling to displace an already existing tradition of English poetry, FitzGerald writes the ***Rubáiyát*** into that tradition by writing the tradition into the ***Rubáiyát***. The poet's acts of allusion in this way echo the larger re-inscription: the translation of Khayyám's Persian verses into an English poem. And it is in this bid for recognition that FitzGerald's recollections of the speech patterns and poetic devices of the Bible, Shakespeare, Pope, Tennyson, and others are fostering influences over the text, even when their disagreements run deep or refuse to be smoothed over. The course of FitzGerald's echoes maps out a personal version of English literary history: like all kinds of allusiveness, these echoes both discover and invent a tradition, a literature. More importantly for the ***Rubáiyát***. sounding and hearing these echoes bring elements of the English poetical corpus into the process of remembrance and regeneration that FitzGerald's verse relates in imaginations of the body's afterlife. The easy transformation of cadence and diction implies a welcoming reception of poetic influence, tinged with anxiety but not incapacitated by it. Of course FitzGerald might have been troubled by imagining what the dead would think of the uses we find for their legacies and remembrances. But, as he also shows through his allusions, it is in our recollections that we recall the dead to life with words, and with words we minister to our longing for those we respect or love.

Notes

1. Unless otherwise noted, all citations from FitzGerald's *Rubáiyát* are from the 1859 text of the poem as printed in Edward FitzGerald, *Rubáiyát of Omar Khayyám: A Critical Edition,* ed. Christopher Decker (Charlottesville and London, 1997).

2. Trinity College Library, Cambridge, Add. MS. a.7(7), formerly Box 3.7.

3. *The Twickenham Edition of the Poems of Alexander Pope,* 11 vols. (New Haven and London, 1939-1969), 7:207, 439; hereafter cited as TE.

4. *The Poems of John Oldham,* ed. Harold F. Brooks, with the collaboration of Raman Selden (Oxford, 1987), p. 188.

5. Thomas Gray also quotes this phrase in a letter, recognizing something distinctly mock-heroic about the struggle for the Mastership of St. John's College—*Correspondence of Thomas Gray,* ed. Paget Toynbee and Leonard Whibley, corr. and add. H. W. Starr, 3 vols. (Oxford, 1971), 2:861.

6. Edward FitzGerald, *The Letters of Edward FitzGerald,* ed. Alfred McKinley Terhune and Annabelle Burdick Terhune, 4 vols. (Princeton, 1980), 3:337; hereafter cited as *Letters.*

7. *The Poems of Tennyson,* ed. Christopher Ricks, 3 vols. (Harlow, 1987), 1:555; hereafter cited as R.

8. *Letters,* 3:342.

9. *Letters,* 3:345.

10. One wonders whether FitzGerald had overheard the echo of Byron in Tennyson's lines. "The summer pilot of an empty heart" falls on the ear very like "The careful pilot of my proper woe" from Byron's famous and also fitfully echoing "Epistle to Augusta": "I have been cunning in mine overthrow / The careful pilot of my proper woe" (ll. 23-24). See George Gordon, Lord Byron, *The Complete Poetical Works,* ed. Jerome J. McGann, 7 vols. (Oxford, 1980-1993), 4:36. Verbal borrowings often turn out to be heirlooms, passed down from poet to poet; FitzGerald's taking of "in himself a Host" is another example of this.

11. *Letters,* 2:31.

12. *Letters,* 3:183.

13. *Letters,* 2:14. Many of Tennyson's contemporaries found it difficult to get the sound of his poetry out of their heads, and they often labored to purge him from their own poems. Compare Matthew Arnold's comments on his own Oriental poem, *Sohrab and Rustum*: "it is certainly true about the Miltonic air of parts of it—but Milton is a sufficiently great master to imitate . . . Tennyson is another thing—but one has him so in one's head one cannot help imitating him sometimes: but except in the last 2 lines I thought I had kept him out of Sohrab and Rustum. Mark any other places you notice—for I should wish to alter such." See *The Letters of Matthew Arnold,* ed. Cecil Y. Lang, 6 vols. (Charlottesville, 1996-2001), 1:279.

14. R 1:436. The poem first appeared in *Poems,* 1832. John Addington Symonds described Tennyson's hands as "huge, unwieldy, fit for moulding clay or dough." See *The Letters of Alfred Lord Tennyson,* ed. Cecil Y. Lang and Edgar F. Shannon, Jr., 3 vols. (Oxford, 1981-1990), 2:417.

15. TE 3.2:11.

16. All citations are from the Authorized Version.

17. I am grateful to John Hollander for having pointed out to me long ago the *Rubáiyát*'s distinctively recurrent rhythms, in particular the five-foot pattern x / x / x x x / x / shared by line 2 of Pope's *Essay*.

18. Newman was preaching in 1852; cited in Edward Norman, *The English Catholic Church in the Nineteenth Century* (Oxford, 1984), p. 201. On English anti-Catholicism at mid-century, see Norman, pp. 203-205 and 216-19 (where he comments on the struggles of the English clergy with intemperance amongst Irish immigrant worshipers); Norman's earlier *Anti-Catholicism in Victorian England* (London, 1968), esp. pp. 52-79; and D. G. Paz, *Popular Anti-Catholicism in Mid-Victorian England* (Stanford, 1992).

19. "Flourishing vegetation rendered palpable the vigor of a blessed soul: at the tomb of Severus, dried-out lilies spring to life every year, as an image of how the man within 'flourishes like a palm tree in paradise.' . . . When Gregory [of Tours] visited the tomb of a martyr, 'everyone of our party filled our nostrils with the scent of lilies and roses.'"—Peter Brown, *The Cult of the Saints: Its Rise and Function in Latin Christianity* (Chicago, 1981), p. 76. On rosaries and the *rosarium,* see Eithne Wilkins, *The Rose-Garden Game: The Symbolic Background to the European Prayer-beads* (London, 1969), whose opening epigraph is taken from the Persian poet Rumi.

20. *Letters,* 1:104. FitzGerald's comments were made in 1831 in a letter to Thackeray. Arnold's later, famous criticism in "The Study of Poetry" (1880) was that "Though they may write in verse, though they may in a certain sense be masters of the art of versification, Dryden and Pope are not classics of our poetry, they are classics of our prose." See *The Complete Prose Works of Matthew Arnold,* ed. R. H. Super, 11 vols. (Ann Arbor, 1960-1977), 9:181 (Vol. 9: *English Literature and Irish Politics*). Merely by asking "Are Dryden and Pope poetical classics?", Arnold was reacting to what he saw as "many signs to show the eighteenth century and its judgments are coming into favour again" (p. 178). He also may have been echoing Hazlitt's objection in 1818 that "The question whether Pope was a poet, has hardly yet been settled, and is hardly worth settling; for if he was not a great poet, he must have been a great prose-writer." See "On Dryden and Pope," in *The Complete Works of William Hazlitt,* ed. P. P. Howe, 21 vols. (London, 1930-1934), 5:69. Indeed, the echoes of this question seem to have rolled from one great English critic to the next, beginning

with Johnson, who, however, had not thought it fit for further discussion, it being clear to him that it was "surely superfluous to answer the question that has once been asked, Whether Pope was a poet? otherwise than by asking in return, If Pope be not a poet, where is poetry to be found?" See his *Lives of the English Poets,* ed. George Birkbeck Hill, 3 vols. (Oxford, 1905), 3:251.

21. In "The Design," prefixed to *An Essay on Man,* TE 3.1:7.

22. TE 3.1:50.

23. TE 5:363-64.

24. TE 3.2:102.

25. *The Poems of William Cowper,* ed. John D. Baird and Charles Ryskamp, 3 vols. (Oxford, 1980-1995), 2:188. FitzGerald alludes to the same lines by Cowper in a letter of 27 November 1844 to Bernard Barton, regarding Harriet Martineau's being cured of a painful tumour by mesmerism: "She is the only one I have read of who describes the sensations of *the trance,* which, seeming a painful one to the wide-awake looker-on, is in fact a state of tranquil glorification to the patient. It cheers but not inebriates! She felt her disease oozing away out at her feet, and as it were streams of warm fresh vitality coming in its place. And when she woke, lo, this was no dream!" (*Letters,* 1:463 and 463 n. 3).

26. TE 2:149-50.

27. TE 2:188.

28. TE 5:369.

29. Leigh Hunt tested the edge of Pope's line on Tennyson, in a review of the two volumes of his *Poems* (1842):

> Everything even said well is not said fitly. The real feeling is apt to become smothered in the false; thought takes its place, and that alone is perilous; genuine powers prematurely exhibit themselves, taking pains to shew they have come to their full growth, with airs of universality, and profundity, and final judgments; till at last they are in danger of meeting with a very awkward "extreme," and, instead of hitting the real points of their subject, whirl their giddy heads round towards the gentle outer-pole of the heroes of the *Dunciad,*

> Who wrote *about* it, goddess, and *about* it.

Reprinted in John D. Jump, ed. *Tennyson: The Critical Heritage* (London, 1967), pp. 126-36 (p. 135).

30. John Dryden, "Epilogue to The Husband His Own Cuckold," ll. 35-37, in *The Poems of John Dryden,* ed. James Kinsley, 4 vols. (Oxford, 1958), 2:866; hereafter cited as KD.

31. "To the Pious Memory of the Accomplisht Young Lady Mrs. Anne Killigrew, Excellent in the two Sister-Arts of Poësie and Painting. An Ode," KD 1:459-65 (this citation, 1:465). There is a possible reminiscence of line 191 of the same poem—"And straight, with inborn vigor, on the wing"—in *Rubáiyát*, 1859, VII: "Lo! the Bird is on the Wing" (1868, VII: "and the Bird is on the Wing").

32. TE 3.2:23.

33. FitzGerald's allusions to Pope may suggest that public toeing of the commonplace critical line on Dryden and Pope did not prevent Victorian poets from showing their appreciation for Pope by echoing him. One of the best known appearances of Pope's *Iliad* in Victorian poetry is in Browning's recollections of his childhood reading in "Development," and Tennyson told his son Hallam that at the age of "About ten or eleven Pope's *Homer's Iliad* became a favourite of mine and I wrote hundreds and hundreds of lines in the regular Popeian metre, nay even could improvise them, so could my two elder brothers. . . ." See Hallam Tennyson, *Alfred Lord Tennyson: A Memoir by His Son,* 2 vols. (London, 1897), 1:11; hereafter cited as *Memoir.*

34. KD 1:464.

35. KD 1:460.

36. *The Poems and Songs of Robert Burns,* ed. James Kinsley, 3 vols. (Oxford, 1968), 1:443, and 1:444 below; hereafter cited as KB. Kinsley (3:1291) cites John Jamieson, *An Etymological Dictionary of the Scottish Language* (W. Creech, 1808) on "syne": "To a native of this country it is very expressive, and conveys a soothing idea to the mind, as recalling the memory of joys that are past."

37. KB 2:557.

38. KD 3:1286.

39. TE 2:153.

40. *Memoir,* 1:211. DeVere observes that Wordsworth's response was to praise Burns "even more vehemently than Tennyson had done, as the great genius who had brought Poetry back to Nature; but ended 'Of course I refer to his serious efforts, such as the "Cotter's Saturday Night"; those foolish little amatory songs of his one has to forget.'"

41. "Reminiscences by the Right Honorable W. E. H. Lecky," in *Memoir,* 1:202.

42. *Memoir,* 1:202.

43. Unless otherwise noted, all quotations from Shakespeare are taken from William Shakespeare,

The Complete Works, ed. Stanley Wells, Gary Taylor, John Jowett, and William Montgomery (Oxford, 1986).

44. The lines (as printed here) are quoted in Robert B. M. Binning, *A Journal of Two Years' Travel in Persia, Ceylon, etc.* (London, 1857), and reappear in the first of two long passages from Binning quoted in notes 3 and 11 in the 1859 *Rubáiyát.* The sentence which follows the lines from Shakespeare begins, "Among the Plants newly appear'd I recognized some old Acquaintances I had not seen for many a year." Binning reads simply "some acquaintances," a reading FitzGerald restored in his 1872 and 1879 notes, though not before having made his unconscious substitution of Burns again in 1868.

45. *Macbeth,* V.iii.22-23. Macbeth's reflection follows on his fury at the appearance of a servant, pale with fear: "The devil damn thee black, thou cream-fac'd loon! . . . Go, prick thy face, and over-red thy fear / Thou lily-liver'd boy . . . those linen cheeks of thine / Are counsellors to fear. What soldiers, whey-face?" (V.iii.11, 14-15, 16-17).

46. John Donne, *The Elegies; and, The Songs and Sonnets,* ed. Helen Gardner (Oxford, 1965), p. 15.

47. Trinity College Library, Cambridge, Add. MS. a.7(20), formerly Box 3(0). Quoting Tennyson, "Sea Dreams," ll. 163-64; R 2:593.

48. *Letters,* 1:105.

49. *Letters,* 3:575; W. G. Clark and J. Glover, eds. *The Works of William Shakespeare* (Vols. 2-9 edited by W. G. Clark and W. A. Wright), 9 vols. (Cambridge and London, 1863-1866).

50. *Letters,* 2:615. FitzGerald had heard that Tennyson was writing a poem on the Roman poet.

51. *Letters,* 2:75.

52. *Letters,* 2:108 and n. 1.

53. Lord Byron, *The Complete Poetical Works,* ed. Jerome J. McGann, 7 vols. (Oxford, 1980-1993), 1:229.

54. *As You Like It,* II.vii.166.

55. *Letters,* 2:291.

56. *As You Like It,* II.vii.5-6.

57. In FitzGerald's collection of adages, *Polonius* (1852), Shakespeare's absence is as noticeable as his presence in the *Rubáiyát*: only one entry surfaces from the last act of *All's Well That Ends Well.*

58. *Letters,* 2:234.

59. *Letters,* 2:305.

David G. Riede (essay date 2005)

SOURCE: Riede, David G. "Edward Fitzgerald: Melancholy, Orientalism, Aestheticism." In *Allegories of One's Own Mind: Melancholy in Victorian Poetry,* pp. 188-201. Columbus: Ohio State University Press, 2005.

[*In the following excerpt, Riede examines FitzGerald's writings as emblematic of the interest in Orientalism and of the prevailing mood of melancholy—both of which characterized the Victorian Age.*]

Edward Fitzgerald was an exact contemporary of Tennyson and the Brownings, as well as a close friend of Thackeray and Carlyle, and he was probably the most melancholy member of this set of marked melancholiacs. Unlike Tennyson and the Brownings, however, Fitzgerald was an agnostic, and consequently he lacked the strong sense of conscience and duty that might have disciplined and given shape to his anomic imagination. As a result, Fitzgerald saw himself as effeminate, as less a potential "masculine" poet than a mere "feminine" man of taste. As a result, his life and poetic career strikingly reflect the gradual transition of Victorian England from a culture of production to a commodity culture: a major element in his melancholy is his own personal abandonment of original poetry and his sad resignation to a life of passive connoisseurship of aesthetic commodities. Fittingly, his greatest poetic production, *The Rubaiyat of Omar Khayyam,* became not only one of the great poems of the age, but in its various manifestations in giftbook editions, one of its greatest aesthetic commodities. With absurd appropriateness, my voice-recognition software recognizes "Omar Khayyam" as "Hallmark I am."[1]

Fitzgerald's own scant original poetry, lacking the striving and moral earnestness of his contemporaries, settled into a distinctly minor key of melancholy in insignificant reveries of passive melancholia such as **"The Meadows in Spring"**:

> 'Tis a sad sight
>> To see the year dying;
> When Autumn's last wind
> Sets the yellow wood sighing
>> Sighing, ah sighing.

(*Letters,* 1: 98)

The poem seems to epitomize Fitzgerald's life, as described by A. C. Benson: "a melancholy life it was. 'His life,' said one of his friends, 'is a succession of sighs, each stifled ere half-uttered; for the uselessness of sighing is as evident to him as the reason for it'" (177). Fitzgerald stifled his poetic sighing because, like Arnold, he believed that the melancholy of his age and his own temperament were unpoetic.

Fitzgerald would probably not have diverted his melancholy into more significant works than **"The Meadows in Spring"** if he had not found himself in sympathy with the Persian texts introduced to him by E. B. Cowell. It was seemingly inevitable that Fitzgerald would be introduced to Orientalism in one form or another: not only Tennyson but also Fitzgerald's other Cambridge contemporaries were all finding relief from the rigor of Victorian masculine earnestness in detours through the supposedly effeminate and lushly sensual East. In a letter to Frederick Tennyson, Fitzgerald noted that the vigorous conservatism of Disraeli's "Young England" was being pushed aside by a glut of Orientalism: Kinglake's *Eothen,* Milnes's *Palm Leaves,* Warburton's *Crescent and the Cross,* and Henry Herbert's *Marmaduke Wyvil.* As Fitzgerald sardonically put it, "Ye Gods! In Shakespeare's day the nuisance was the Monsieur Travellers who had 'swum in a gundello'; but now the bores are those who have smoked *tschibouques* with a *Peshaw*! Deuce take it: I say 'tis better to stick to muddy Suffolk" (*Letters,* 1: 480). Fitzgerald did stick to muddy Suffolk, but touched perhaps with the traditional scholar's melancholy, he could not resist being drawn into the study of Persia by Cowell, and, in particular, into the study of a Persian allegory by Jámí that might almost have been a model for such melancholy allegories as Shelley's *Alastor* and Keats's *Endymion.* According to Fitzgerald, Jámí's **Salámán and Absál** was an allegory of "Persian Mysticism—perhaps the grand Mystery of all Religions" (*Letters,* 2: 219). Like *Alastor* and *Endymion,* Jámí's poem, or at least Fitzgerald's translation of it, is an allegory of the growth of the protagonist's mind spurred by erotic desire and pursuit of a lost ego-ideal (Lacan's phallus) in the form of a female beauty who seems an image of his own soul. Inevitably, erotic love "infected all his soul with melancholy" (Arberry, 71). Like Endymion, Salámán finds erotic satisfaction with his beloved, Absál, but unlike Endymion's beloved, Absál is not a goddess, and sexual gratification, as in courtly love, can only short-circuit any quest for full self-realization in wisdom. The meaning of Salámán's plight is provided by a Sage in language suggestive of Shelley's *Alastor* and of Ficino's neo-Platonic model of desire for a phantasmic erotic ideal that is degrading and bestial if the lover settles for a material embodiment, but leads to the highest wisdom if not short-circuited by sexual gratification:

> The Mighty Hand that mix'd thy Dust inscribed
> The Character of Wisdom on thy Heart;
> Oh Cleanse thy Bosom of Material Form,
> And turn the Mirror of the Soul to SPIRIT,
> Until it be with SPIRIT all possest,
> Drown'd in the Light of Intellectual Truth.
> Oh veil thine Eyes from Mortal Paramour,
> And follow not her Step!

(76)

Salámán's SPIRIT is willing, but his flesh is weak, and he flees the dictates of conscience as represented by his father "in the Name of God" (75). The resultant conflict between his conscience and his desire is inevitably a will-destroying melancholy:

> Unto the Soul that is confused by Love
> Comes Sorrow after Sorrow—most of all
> To Love whose only Friendship is Reproof,
> And overmuch of Counsel—whereby Love
> Grows stubborn, and increases the Disease.
> Love unreproved is a delicious food;
> Reproved, is Feeding on one's own Heart's Blood.
>
> (77-78)

Like Keats's Endymion, Salámán weds himself to Sorrow, flees the dictates of conscience, and once again finds blissful repletion, this time on a paradisial isle. This sensual idyll, of course, is precisely the temptation that lures a prince from his duty or tempts a Victorian poet to "some paradisal isle" as in "Locksley Hall," or a reclusive, melancholy scholar-poet like Fitzgerald to sensual but emasculating Eastern idylls. The temptation is so great that it can be ended only by magic, in this case a supreme act of the father's will:

> To Gracelessness Ungracious he became,
> And, quite to shatter his rebellious Lust,
> Upon Salámán all his WILL discharged.
> And LO! SALÁMÁN to his Mistress turn'd,
> But could not reach her—look'd and look'd again,
> And palpitated tow'rd her—but in Vain!
> Oh Misery! what to the Bankrupt worse
> Than Gold he cannot reach! To one Athirst
> Than Fountain to the Eye and Lip forbid!—
> Or than Heaven opened to the Eyes in Hell!
>
> (83)

In the Persian original this telepathy is merely magic, but for the Victorian Fitzgerald, as he explains in a note, it is the newest science: "He Mesmerizes Him!" (83n). The result, in either case, is that Salámán becomes Shelley's Poet seeking his vision of the soul within his soul, or an Endymion seeking the unattainable Cynthia, or more literally the prince seeking the character of Wisdom on his heart, turning the mirror of the soul to SPIRIT. In short, *Salámán and Absál,* in Fitzgerald's translation, turns out to be a remarkable reenactment of melancholy Romantic allegories of desire turned to the purposes of Wisdom and, further, of the Victorian exercise of manly self-control, enslaving sensuality to the stern control of "WILL."

Salámán and Absál, however, does not end with Shelleyan longing for an ideal that cannot be reached because it is already internalized, but rather with a final allegorical movement that, like *Endymion,* allows a magical happiness by wedding the protagonist to an erotic object that is both a beautiful woman and the

highest ideal. An allegory of ideology itself, it represents the imaginary solution of an insoluble problem.[2] *Salámán* builds a magic fire and enters it with Absál, but the flame

> passing him, consumed ABSÁL like Straw,
> Died his Divided Self, and there survived
> His Individual; and, like a Body
> From which the Soul is parted, all alone.
>
> (86)

Actually, as the poem later makes clear when expounding the allegory, what dies in the flame is not the soul but the body's sensuality; the fire is

> Ascetic Discipline
> That burns away the Animal Alloy,
> Till all the Dross of MATTER be consumed,
> And the Essential Soul, its raiment clean
> Of Mortal Taint, be left.
>
> (94-95)

Not surprisingly, the consummation of Absál is a torment to Salámán, who is a wiser but a sadder man. Still, in a deft pre-Freudian turn, this newer melancholy is not only *like* mourning but *is* mourning, so the pathological condition of melancholy without an apparent cause and therefore without limit is replaced by the "normal" condition of grief. Salámán goes from illness to health. Further, the Sage, assuming the role of therapist, is able by an act of will to engender a mourning like melancholia that will lead beyond the phantasm of sensual, erotic love to the better and higher libidinal object of the highest beauty and Wisdom. The Sage repeatedly raises a "Fantom Image" of Absál to pacify Salámán's grief, but then annihilates it and replaces Absál with "a Celestial love; / ZUHRAH . . . the Lustre of the Stars" (89). The allegory hardly needs the explication that Jámí, and Fitzgerald, provide:

> what is ZUHRAH?—that Divine Perfection,
> Wherewith the Soul inspir'd and all array'd
> In Intellectual Light is Royal blest,
> And mounts THE THRONE, and wears THE
>   CROWN, and reigns
> Lord of the Empire of Humanity.
>
> (95)

Fitzgerald's *Salámán and Absál* is not a great poem, and it certainly cannot compete with his *Rubaiyat,* but it is nevertheless a remarkable documentation of the intersection of late Romantic, early Victorian melancholy with a languorous desire for sensual pleasure and beauty best explored by an Oriental detour that subjects both effeminate longing and the East to the mastery of conscience. In an overtly allegorical form it represents both the erotic quests of *Alastor* and *Endymion* and also the major concerns of *Pauline, Paracelsus, Maud,* and *Sonnets from the Portuguese*: brooding on erotic desire that is ultimately a yearning for wholeness of being and that, barring magic or divine intervention, is sustainable only as the melancholy of "Infinite passion, and the pain / of finite hearts that yearn."

Fitzgerald was one of Tennyson's few friends who disagreed with Trench's dictum "Tennyson, we cannot live in art!" Rather, like Tennyson's soul in "The Palace of Art," he attempted to remove himself from the demands of Victorian life and live in a quiet aesthetic reverie—if not in a palace of art, at least in a suburban grange akin to Tennyson's "cottage in the vale" ("Palace of Art," 291). He was, however, troubled in conscience by this withdrawal from an active to a contemplative life, viewing it at times as effeminate self-indulgence and casting himself into a chaste and ascetically disciplined life of melancholy contemplation. He was troubled even that his poetic and scholarly Orientalism was mere sensual self-indulgence since he saw "effeminate Persian" as antithetical to vigorously English "masculine thought" (*Letters*, 2: 190), and he even had reservations about appropriating the exotic East as a kind of aesthetic courtesan: "there's all Turkey, Greece, and the East to be prostituted . . . ; and I fear we shan't hear the end of it in our lifetimes. Suffolk turnips seem to be so classical compared to all that sort of thing" (*Letters*, 1: 550). Consequently, it is entirely appropriate that he was attracted to Jámí's allegory with its magical cure for melancholy and surprising kinship with the Keatsian, Shelleyan poetry of sensation celebrated by Hallam.

Fitzgerald's poetry of sensation provides a clear link between the Victorianism of Hallam and Tennyson and the later Victorian aestheticism and decadence primarily through the publication and reception of *The Rubaiyat of Omar Khayyam*, but both Tennyson and Fitzgerald saw art for art's sake as a kind of unmanly hedonism, and Fitzgerald worried that the *Rubaiyat* might be self-indulgent in this way. His sense of the moral value of *Salámán and Absál* and of the possibly corrupting effect of the *Rubaiyat* are both implied in his agreement to publish a fourth edition only on condition that it be bound with *Salámán and Absál,* perhaps as an allegorical corrective pointing from sensual pleasure to Wisdom—or at least, in a Keatsian way, to a beauty that is not valued for its own sake, but because, in the vision of Zuhrah, beauty is truth. To the extent that he could control publication of the *Rubaiyat,* Fitzgerald eventually stipulated that it not be published except "in more reputable Company," with "Salámán by way of Chaperon" (*Letters*, 4: 73).

Salámán and Absál may be seen as an allegorical justification of strenuous melancholy as a path to Wisdom, but Fitzgerald wrote the *Rubaiyat* in what he called a mood of "self-contented indolence" (*Letters*, 2: 50), more like sloth than like the heroic action that he believed necessary to the poet who would write a great poem. His advice to Tennyson had been to overcome the hypochondriacal melancholy indolence of an exhausted civilization, to "fly from England and go among savages" (*Letters*, 1: 623). Only in that way could he reinvigorate the poetic tradition with fresh blood—just what Lady Ellerton had told the poet to do in Kingsley's *Alton Locke*,[3] but he himself turned rather guiltily to the exhausted vein of a great civilization that he believed had been in decline for many centuries. Thinking himself incapable of writing a great original poem, he tried to assuage his melancholy by immersing himself in the languorous, sensual mood of poetic melancholia, dealing in his own susceptibilities by reading and translating the works of kindred spirits. His first exercise in translation, in fact, was with Lucretius, and he found solace for his sadness in other melancholy Epicureans as well, particularly Omar Khayyam: "Omar breathes a sort of Consolation to me! Poor Fellow; I think of him, and Olivier Basselin, and Anacreon; lighter Shadows among the Shades, perhaps, over which Lucretius presides so grimly" (*Letters*, 2: 273).

Fitzgerald was at the most melancholy period in his life when he began to read Omar Khayyam. As a letter to Thackeray indicates, his indolence was anything but self-contented: "Life every day seems a more total failure and mess to me: but it is yet bearable: and I am become a sad Epicurean—just desirous to keep on the windy side of bother and pain" (*Letters*, 2: 75). The tradition of melancholy as a self-indulgently indolent luxury was consolation, but like Arnold, Fitzgerald saw it as unpoetic.

Just as Arnold said of "The Scholar Gypsy" that "Homer *animates*—Shakespeare *animates*—the Gipsy Scholar at best awakens a pleasing melancholy," Fitzgerald also believed that poetry should animate, or should at the very least be vigorous. As he frequently repeated, in poetry "all is got if '*go*' is got" (*Letters*, 2: 74), and he had lost what little "go" he had ever had. Unlike Arnold, who blamed the unpoetic age for his inability to write animating poetry, Fitzgerald blamed himself—he could have gone among savages or at least struggled on in the "vigorous North," but he chose instead to "go on puddling away faintly at Persian" and luxuriating in "the Sweetmeat, Childish Oriental World" (*Letters*, 2: 184). For this reason the resultant poem, the *Rubaiyat,* is, as Christopher Decker has said,

> one of the best poems ever written about the condition of not being a great poet. . . . It praises humility not because it is Christian to do so, but because the humble life is one in which disappointment is so reduced as to assume the features of contentment. For Fitzgerald, rhyme's vexation was less a dull narcotic, numbing pain than a way of taming the fierceness of boredom and loss.

(*Rubaiyat*, xx)

Unlike Browning, Fitzgerald seemed content with being a failure like Andrea del Sarto, but ironically, his retreat into melancholy produced a great poem after all. He had given up the idea of writing a great original poem, but his translation of Omar Khayyam is itself an original poem, inspired by Khayyam but recreating the Persian in his own image and producing a single unified English poem out of Khayyam's disconnected Persian quatrains. Scholars have disagreed about the extent to which Omar Khayyam was a religious poet or was indeed the sad Epicurean that Fitzgerald thought him, but Fitzgerald himself was sure that, as Iago said of Desdemona, the wine he drank was made of grapes, that he wrote "without any Pretense at divine Allegory: his wine is the veritable juice of the grape" (*Rubaiyat,* 6). In any case, Fitzgerald was not concerned to make an accurate translation but to "tesselate" the "scattered" Persian quatrains into a "very pretty *Eclogue*," though one with an un-Christian and un-Victorian moral (*Letters,* 2: 294), and "As to my making Omar worse than he is in that Stanza about Forgiveness—you [Cowell] know I have translated none [of the quatrains] literally, and have generally mashed up two—or more—into one" (*Letters,* 3: 68). What Fitzgerald saw in Omar Khayyam was his own nineteenth-century skepticism, melancholia, and Epicureanism, and he therefore appropriated it as not only a kindred spirit but even as an intellectual property; writing to Cowell, he asserted that "in truth I take old Omar rather more as my property than yours: he and I are more akin, are we not? You see all [his] Beauty, but you can't feel *with* him in some respects as I do" (*Letters,* 2: 305). Strikingly, in a letter to Cowell, Fitzgerald, the Victorian "Hamlet of literature" (Benson, 188), expressed his own immoral skepticism not only behind the mask of Omar Khayyam but also behind the mask of Hamlet's melancholy madness: "I think you would almost feel obliged to leave out the part of Hamlet in representing him to your Audience: for fear of Mischief. Now I do not wish to show Hamlet at his maddest but mad he must be shown, or he is no Hamlet at all" (*Letters,* 2: 305).

The reference to Hamlet is especially important because it indicates how Fitzgerald was not, as he thought, disabled by unpoetic melancholy but empowered by the "imagination penetrative" of melancholy, epitomized by Hamlet's apostrophe to Yorick's skull. That Fitzgerald had precisely this apostrophe in mind is evident when he alludes to it in describing his "Epicurean Infidel" as a "poor little Persian Epicurean, who sings the old standing Religion of the World. 'Let us make the best of To-day,—who can answer for To-morrow!' To this complexion does one come at last?" (*Letters,* 2: 277).

The dominant theme of Fitzgerald's *Rubaiyat* is not Omar Khayyam's but is the theme of Hamlet's grave-yard musings—that human life is returned to dust for any base use: "Imperious Caesar, dead and turned to

clay / Might stop a hole to keep the wind away" (V.i.213-14). The *Rubaiyat* finds a better use for Caesar's clay, though life's insignificance and transience is no less sharply felt:

> I sometimes think that never blows so red
> The Rose as where some buried Caesar bled;
>   That every Hyacinth the Garden wears
> Dropt in its Lap from some once lovely Head.

>   (xviii)

Like Ruskin, Fitzgerald broods most particularly on a Hamlet-like consideration of the lips that once had kissed:

> And this delightful Herb whose tender Green
> Fledges the River's Lip on which we lean—
>   Ah, lean upon it lightly! For who knows
> From what once lovely Lip it springs unseen!

>   (xix)

The most insistent image of the *Rubaiyat* ineluctably summons Yorick's lips in tracing the clay lips of the wine cup to clay lips that once had laughed and kissed in life:

> Then to this earthen Bowl did I adjourn
> My Lip the secret Well of Life to learn:
>   And Lip to Lip it murmur'd—"While you live
> Drink!—for once dead you never shall return."

> I think the Vessel, that with fugitive
> Articulation answer'd, once did live,
>   And merry-make; and the cold Lip I kiss'd
> How many Kisses might it take—and give!

> For in the Market-place, one Dusk of Day,
> I watch'd the Potter thumping his wet Clay
>   And with its all obliterated Tongue
> It murmur'd—"Gently, Brother, gently, pray!"

>   (xxxiv-xxxvi)

The melancholy lesson taught by the lip of the wine cup is entirely orthodox, merely that the body is dust and will to dust return, but Fitzgerald's agnosticism is suggested in a nihilism that also seems to doubt the immortality of the soul: "Thou art but what / Thou Shalt be—Nothing" (xlvii). Also, the still more subversive moral is that God wickedly made life in order to damn it. The stanza in which Fitzgerald may have made Omar "worse than he is" expresses this conviction:

> Oh, Thou, who Man of baser Earth didst make,
> And who with Eden didst devise the snake;
>   For all the Sins wherewith the Face of Man
> Is blackened, Man's Forgiveness give—and take!

>   (lviii)

The close ties of the *Rubaiyat* to Hamlet enable us to see it as an example of melancholic allegory. Seeing the clay lips of the wine bowl as signs of living lips and their dissolution into dust, Omar Khayyam sees as the Benjaminian allegorist to whom nature appears "not in bud and bloom but in the overripeness and decay of its creation . . . As eternal transience."[4] The ultimate melancholy emblem is Yorick's skull or, in Benjamin's term, a "death's head . . . The figure of man's most extreme subjection to nature" (*Origin,* 166). Further, regarded as a translation, Fitzgerald's poem is implicitly allegorical in the sense that it uses language in which the words are at a double remove, at least, from the things signified. Fitzgerald's comments on his mode of translation emphasize the removal of signifier from signified in a striking way; other translators, he remarked, "try to render [elegant Persian] into *Elegant* English; but I think it should be translated *something* as the Bible is translated, preserving the Oriental Idiom. It should be kept as Oriental as possible, only using the most idiomatic Saxon *words* to convey the Eastern metaphor" (*Letters,* 2: 119). The reference to the Bible is to the most authoritative of English texts, but it subverts the authority of even the Bible with the reminder that the vigorous English words are already at a remove from the Oriental idiom, let alone the signified Truth. Further, it undermines the authority of Fitzgerald's English appropriation of Persian thought by stressing, first, the metaphoric character of the Eastern text and thus the originary separation of signifier from signified in the substitutions of emblem for identification, and second, the separation of Saxon words from Oriental idiom. All in all Fitzgerald's theory of translation emphasizes the Benjaminian or deManian sense of the ghostly emptiness of all language in which the sign can only be "*repetition* . . . of a previous sign with which it can never coincide, since it is the essence of this previous sign to be pure anteriority" (de Man, *Blindness,* 207).

Clearly the *Rubaiyat* epitomizes many of the various implications of poetic melancholy in the Victorian age. In the first place, it is bred in the Victorian sense of identification with the melancholy Hamlet, and it represents the "imagination penetrative" identified with Hamlet. Beyond this, it seeks poetic authority through an Oriental detour that will imitate the Bible's cultural authority as it subverts the Bible and even the logos underpinning Western thought by its anticipation, like Browning's, of the poststructuralist theory of language as an allegorical chain of signifiers forever removing itself further from lost and unrecoverable origins.

The great cultural importance of Fitzgerald's *Rubaiyat* is not merely in its exemplification of the Victorian age's melancholy agnosticism but in its exemplary severing of poetic beauty from any kind of Christian duty: it demonstrates that skepticism and pessimism were not poetically disabling but could be the very stuff of poetic beauty. The story of the Victorian reception of the *Rubaiyat* has been often told, but a brief review of

it here will help to establish the transition from Tennysonian melancholy to the art-for-art's-sake aestheticism of Swinburne and the Pre-Raphaelites and finally to the "New Hedonism" of Pater's aestheticism and Wilde's decadence. Not expecting much, if anything, in the way of sales, Fitzgerald anonymously printed 250 copies of the *Rubaiyat* at his own expense with the antiquarian bookseller Bernard Quaritch, and after taking a few copies for distribution to friends he left the bulk of the edition with Quaritch.[5] The demand was nil, and the pamphlets languished in Quaritch's shop until the poem was "discovered" by the Pre-Raphaelites. Swinburne's account of this discovery cannot be regarded as gospel truth, but it will do to summon the spirit of the Pre-Raphaelite enthusiasm:

> Two friends of Rossetti's—Mr. Whitley Stokes and Mr. Ormsby—told him (he told me) of this wonderful little pamphlet for sale on a stall . . . to which Mr. Quaritch, finding that the British public unanimously declined to give a shilling for it, had relegated it to be disposed of for a penny. Having read it, Rossetti and I invested upwards of sixpence apiece—or possibly threepence—I would not wish to exaggerate our extravagance—in copies at that not exorbitant price. Next day we thought we might get some more for presents among friends—but the man at the stall asked twopence! Rossetti expostulated with him in terms of such humorously indignant remonstrance as none but he could ever have commanded. We took a few, and left him. In a week or two, if I'm not mistaken, the remaining copies were sold at a guinea; I have since—as I dare say you have—seen copies offered for a still more extravagant price.
>
> (*Letters,* 6: 188)

Swinburne, Rossetti, and others paid tribute to the *Rubaiyat* by raising its commodity value but more significantly by raising its cultural value. Swinburne paid the even greater compliment of imitation, using the stanza form of the *Rubaiyat* for one of his most important poems, "Laus Veneris," the title poem of the first edition of *Poems and Ballads,*[6] the book that outraged Victorian morality and contributed importantly to the aestheticist and decadent late Victorian reevaluation of the relation of the arts to morality and to the social order. Like the *Rubaiyat,* "Laus Veneris" represents an embrace of languorous beauty at the expense of moral striving. "Laus Veneris" is Swinburne's version of the Tannhäuser legend and recounts the knight's deliberate choice of the pagan Venus and sensual mortality over the Christian religion, asceticism, and the empty promise of immortal, if ethereal, life. Swinburne's poem, with its explicitly sensual refusal of Christ, is far more shocking than Fitzgerald's "sad Epicureanism":

> Alas, Lord, surely thou art great and fair.
> But, lo, her wonderfully woven hair!

And thou didst heal us with thy piteous kiss;
But see now, Lord, her mouth is lovelier.

(ll.17-20)

The moral difference between Fitzgerald's and Swinburne's poems may be most clearly seen in the moral
connotations of the technically synonymous terms
Epicureanism and hedonism. Walter Pater famously
remarked that the word "hedonism" should be avoided
around those who do not know Greek because its connotations are so emphatically of immoral sensuality as
opposed to the Greek ideal of calm and avoidance of
pain. Fitzgerald's poem is sensual with the melancholy
dignity of Epicurean Stoicism; Swinburne's poem, on
the other hand, courts the moral notoriety of hedonism,
and because it vigorously pits the strictures of conscience against sensual indulgence, its sadomasochism
represents a far more intense, pathological melancholy:

Alas thy beauty! for thy mouth's sweet sake
My soul is bitter to me, my limbs quake
As water, as the flesh of men that weep
As their heart's vein whose heart goes nigh to break.

(ll.145-48)

A full discussion of Pre-Raphaelitism and aestheticism
is beyond the scope of the present study, but it is very
much to the point to note that Fitzgerald, far from being
the end of a line of melancholy poetics, clearly connects Tennyson's early Victorian poetry of sensation to
the sensualism of late Victorian poetry and poetics.
Fitzgerald's and Tennyson's commitment to early and
mid-Victorian ideals of masculine vigor made them
ambivalent about indulgence in the lassitude of
melancholia, but for the Pre-Raphaelites and aestheti-
cists, the commitment to art, and particularly to sensual
beauty as an aesthetic ideal, led to a positive celebration of melancholy even as a pathological condition, a
disease. "Laus Veneris," like William Morris's "The
Defence of Guenevere," very specifically represents
what Pater described as the defining characteristic of
aesthetic poetry: "the deliberate choice between Christ
and a rival lover" (191). In his much quieter, more
decorous way, Fitzgerald made the same choice through
Omar Khayyam's call for "a Flask of Wine, a Book of
Verse—and thou" rather than the promise of Paradise
(xi). It is no wonder that the aesthetic school admired
Fitzgerald, whose life and poetry seem defined in Pater's definition of aesthetic poetry as melancholy: "it is
that inversion of homesickness known to some, that
incurable thirst for the sense of escape, which no actual
form of life satisfies" (190). Oddly, and no doubt
coincidentally, Pater's language echoes Paracelsus's
longing for a "form of life unknown." In lines that seem
to sum up the *Rubaiyat,* Pater further characterized
aesthetic poetry as the "continual suggestion, pensive or
passionate, of the shortness of life. This is contrasted
with the bloom of the world, and gives new seduction

to it—the sense of death and the desire of beauty: the
desire of beauty quickened by the sense of death" (198).
Pater's most notorious exposition of aesthetic Epicureanism brings us full circle back to melancholy as "the
emotion of the trapped," the emotion of Mariana or of
the Soul in "The Palace of Art." Unlike the melancholy
of high Victorianism, however, the late-century melancholy of "art for art's sake," intimated in Fitzgerald's
translations and explicit in the work of Pater, Swinburne, Rossetti, and Wilde, has more or less resolved
the dialectic of social conscience and Romantic self by
adopting a late Romanticism that sets aside conscience,
as it sets aside social purpose, as irrelevant to the
purposes of art. Pater's prescription for the aesthetic
life, for "success in life," entirely sets aside all that lies
outside the "abysmal deeps of personality" as it
prescribes hedonistic immersion in solipsistic reverie:
"to burn always" with a hard, gemlike flame in the
ecstatic reception of the "impressions, images, sensations" that constitute all experience:

[E]xperience, already reduced to a swarm of impressions, is ringed round for each of us by that thick wall
of personality through which no real voice has ever
pierced on its way to us, or from us to that which we
can only conjecture to be without. Every one of those
impressions is the impression of the individual in his
isolation, each mind keeping as a solitary prisoner its
own dream of a world.

(160)

The emotion of the trapped carried to its utmost pitch
of intensity, a kind of acute melancholia, is an exaggerated version of sad Epicureanism: it is what Dorian
Gray called the "new hedonism," and it is a condition
explicitly characterized elsewhere in Pater's work as a
disease, the "malady of reverie." By century's end the
Wordsworthian, Coleridgean paradigm of a healthy
imagination has been transformed through various
stages of melancholia to the notion of poetic imagination as morbidly diseased.

Pater's definition of aesthetic poetry, in fact, is a fair
definition of melancholy itself as the emotion of the
trapped: "a passion of which the outlets are sealed, be-
gets a tension of nerve, in which the sensible world
comes to one with a reinforced brilliancy and relief—"
(193). This passion, a strong narcotic, like a poison in
the blood, obviously heightens Fitzgerald's melancholy
reverie, or even Mariana's, to a pitch approaching insanity, like a "beautiful disease or disorder of the senses"
(192), but it originates in a Keatsian as well as Fitzgeral-
dian and profoundly Swinburnean sense that awareness
of the finality of death intensifies the sense of beauty. In
Wallace Stevens's phrase, "Death is the mother of
beauty" ("Sunday Morning") or in Fitzgerald's, "never
blows so red / the rose as where some buried Caesar
bled" (xviii).

Finally, seeing the nineteenth-century poetic tradition as it passes from Tennyson's generation through Fitzgerald and into the aestheticism of Pater and Wilde clarifies the often-noted gender transgressiveness in late-century aestheticism. From Tennyson's association of melancholy sensibility with women and Hallam's sense of the transgressive nature of indulgence in melancholy, poetic sensibility had been figured as potentially unmanly, a loss of vigor and self-control in exchange for appropriating a female or even Oriental erotic reverie. As Fitzgerald saw it, such effeminate melancholy was disabling to masculine, poetic creativity and led him to a resigned acceptance of the devolution of the poet to the mere aesthete, the womanly man of taste: "I pretend to no Genius, but to Taste: which, according to my aphorism, is the feminine of Genius" (*Letters,* 1: 669). The resolution of the gender ambiguities attending melancholy and genius may, perhaps, be glimpsed in the deliberate assumption by the homoerotic Pater, Wilde, and others, of the highest aesthetic sensibility in a disease, a disorder of the senses, as late-century science constructed the discourse of homosexuality, and of a homosexual identity. This is not the place to discuss the late Victorian imbrication of the discourse of melancholia and sexology, but only to note that the disengagement of poetry from the severe moralism of the Victorian age in "art for art's sake" and decadence results in a lassitude commonly regarded as melancholy, but much diminished from the fierce dialectic of conscience and mutinous feeling that I have been exploring. The disengagement, moreover, is also a disengagement from the central moral, ethical, and ideological values of the age, and it marks the marginalization of poetry from public discourse that remains with us over a century later.

Notes

1. A proof of artificial intelligence seems to be the mean-spirited critic in the software who also, ludicrously, calls the wine-bibbing "Rubaiyat" the "liver biopsy" and hears "Keatsian" as "cutesy."

2. See Jameson's definition of ideology as "the function of inventing imaginary or formal 'resolutions' to unresolvable social contradictions" [Jameson, Frederic. *The Political Unconscious: Narrative as Socially Symbolic Act.* Ithaca, N.Y.: Cornell University Press, 1981.] (79). The unresolvable contradiction in this case is the impossibility of reconciling the erotic poetic imagination with the requirements of chaste, manly self-control.

3. See James Eli Adams [*Dandies and Desert Saints: Styles of Victorian Manhood.* Ithaca, N.Y.: Cornell University Press, 1995], 120-21.

4. See chapter 1, 29.

5. See Decker [FitzGerald, Edward. The Rubaiyat of Omar Khayyam: *A Critical Edition,* ed. Christo-

pher Dekker. Charlottesville: University Press of Virginia, 1997.] for the full printing and publishing history, 30-45.

6. Due to his difficulty getting the volume published in England, the first edition was published in America under the title *Laus Veneris and Other Poems and Ballads.* The English edition was more simply called *Poems and Ballads.*

Works Cited

Adams, James Eli. *Dandies and Desert Saints: Styles of Victorian Manhood.* Ithaca, N.Y.: Cornell University Press, 1995.

Arberry, A. J. *Fitzgerald's Salaman and Absal: A Study.* Cambridge: Cambridge University Press, 1956.

Arnold, Matthew. *The Complete Prose Works,* ed. R. H. Super. 11 vols. Ann Arbor: The University of Michigan Press, 1960-1977.

————. *The Letters of Matthew Arnold,* ed. Cecil Y. Lang. 6 vols. Charlottesville: University of Virginia Press, 1996-2001.

————. *The Poems of Matthew Arnold,* ed. Kenneth Allott, 2nd ed., Miriam Allott. New York: Longman, 1979.

Benjamin, Walter. *The Origin of German Tragic Drama,* trans. John Osborne. London: NLB, 1977.

Benson, A. C. *Edward Fitzgerald.* New York: Macmillan, 1905.

de Man, Paul. *Blindness and Insight: Essays on the Rhetoric of Contemporary Criticism.* 2nd ed. Minneapolis: University of Minnesota Press, 1983.

Ficino, Marsilio. *Commentary on Plato's Symposium on Love,* trans. Sears Jayne. Dallas, Tex.: Springs Publications, 1985.

Fitzgerald, Edward. *The Letters of Edward Fitzgerald,* ed. Albert McKinley Terhune and Annabelle Burdick Terhune. 4 vols. Princeton, N.J.: Princeton University Press, 1980.

————. *"The Rubaiyat of Omar Khayyam": A Critical Edition,* ed. Christopher Decker. Charlottesville: University Press of Virginia, 1997.

Jameson, Frederic. *The Political Unconscious: Narrative as Socially Symbolic Act.* Ithaca, N.Y.: Cornell University Press, 1981.

Keats, John. *The Poems of John Keats,* ed. Jack Stillinger. Cambridge, Mass.: Harvard University Press, 1978.

Pater, Walter. *Selected Writings of Walter Pater,* ed. Harold Bloom. New York: Signet, 1974.

Rossetti, Christina. *The Works of Christina Rossetti,* ed. Martin Corner. Ware, Hertfordshire: Wordsworth Editions, 1995.

Rossetti, Dante Gabriel. *Poems,* ed. Oswald Doughty. New York: Dutton, 1961.

Shelley, Percy Bysshe. *Shelley's Poetry and Prose,* ed. Donald H. Reiman and Sharon Powers. New York: W. W. Norton, 1977.

Swinburne, Algernon. *The Swinburne Letters,* ed. Cecil Y. Lang. 6 vols. New Haven, Conn.: Yale University Press, 1959-1962.

Tennyson, Alfred. *The Letters of Alfred Lord Tennyson,* ed. Cecil Y. Lang and Edgar F. Shannon, Jr. 3 vols. Cambridge, Mass.: Harvard University Press, 1981—.

———. *The Poems of Tennyson,* ed. Christopher Ricks. 3 vols. Berkeley: University of California Press, 1987.

FURTHER READING

Biographies

Martin, Robert Bernard. *With Friends Possessed: A Life of Edward FitzGerald.* London: Faber and Faber, 1985, 313 p.

> Comprehensive coverage of FitzGerald's life and his relationships with his literary friends.

Terhune, Alfred McKinley. *The Life of Edward FitzGerald: Translator of* The Rubáiyát of Omar Khayyám. New Haven, Conn.: Yale University Press, 1947, 373 p.

> Extensive coverage of FitzGerald's life, with special emphasis on his mastery of Persian and his translation of the *Rubáiyát.*

Criticism

Alexander, Doris. "FitzOmar: Live Eagle." In *Creating Literature out of Life,* pp. 45-84. University Park: Pennsylvania State University Press, 1996.

> Explores issues of originality within the translation of the *Rubáiyát.*

Arberry, A. J. Introduction to *FitzGerald's* Sálamán and Absál, pp. 3-50. Cambridge: Cambridge University Press, 1956.

> Provides background information on how FitzGerald learned Persian and decided to undertake the translation of Jāmī's poem *Sálamán and Absál.*

———. "Preliminary Essay." In *The Romance of* The Rubáiyát, pp. 13-39. London: George Allen & Unwin, 1959.

> Discusses FitzGerald's approach to translation as well as the publication history and early reception of the *Rubáiyát.*

Jewett, Iran B. Hassani. "Early Works." In *Edward FitzGerald,* pp. 40-55. Boston: Twayne, 1977.

> Brief discussion of the poetry and prose FitzGerald composed early in his writing career.

Woolford, John. "The Protean Precursor: Browning and Edward FitzGerald." *Victorian Literature and Culture* 24 (1996): 313-32.

> Refutes the common belief that FitzGerald's *Rubáiyát* inspired Robert Browning's "Rabbi ben Ezra."

Additional coverage of FitzGerald's life and career is contained in the following sources published by Thomson Gale: *British Writers,* **Vol. 4;** *Dictionary of Literary Biography,* **Vol. 32;** *Literary Resource Center;* *Nineteenth-Century Literature Criticism,* **Vols. 9, 153; and** *Reference Guide to English Literature,* **Ed. 2.**

Anne Sexton
1928-1974

(Born Anne Gray Harvey) American poet, short story writer, playwright, essayist, and author of children's books.

For further information on Sexton's writings, see *PC*, Vol. 2.

INTRODUCTION

Sexton has most often been identified with the "Confessional" school of poetry, a method of writing first identified in Robert Lowell's 1959 volume *Life Studies*. Much of Sexton's early poetry uses a first-person speaking voice relating personal experiences and memories, and this early "confessional" verse has been regarded by many critics to have been therapeutic for Sexton, who suffered from bouts of psychosis and suicidal depression throughout her adult life. Although her writing career lasted only about fifteen years, she published seven volumes of poetry during her lifetime (three more were published posthumously) and was awarded the Pulitzer Prize in 1967 for her 1966 collection *Live or Die*. Sexton is recognized for her willingness to treat previously taboo subjects involving the trials and triumphs of women, especially the anguish and confusion encountered in relationships between mothers and daughters. She also spoke frankly and boldly about sexuality and the female body, and wrote openly about the tenuous and fragile boundary between madness and sanity. In the several decades since her death in 1974, many critics have begun to view Sexton's writings—especially her later, more experimental and surreal work—as outside of the confessional mode, finding in them significant reflections on such subjects as religion, the need to live coupled with the desire for death, the feminine consciousness, and the search for self-understanding. In addition, scholars have begun to question the autobiographical nature of her poetry, debating the relationship between the author and her poetic personae.

BIOGRAPHICAL INFORMATION

The youngest of three sisters, Sexton was born on November 9, 1928, in Weston, Massachusetts, to Mary Gray Staples Harvey, a housewife, and Ralph Churchill Harvey, owner of a wool company. From the mid-1930s to the mid-1940s, Sexton attended public schools in Massachusetts, then entered a private prep school in Lowell, Massachusetts in 1945. While there Sexton began writing poetry, but stopped, according to biographers, after being accused of plagiarism by her mother. In 1947 Sexton began attending a finishing school in Boston; a year later she eloped with Alfred Muller Sexton II, whom she married in August 1948. Having already begun modeling school, by 1949 Sexton had completed training, and in 1951 began modeling in Boston. Two years later the couple's first daughter, Linda Gray Sexton, was born. The following year Sexton entered a mental institution after suffering a nervous breakdown and experiencing persistent depression. In 1955, after Sexton's release, her second daughter, Joyce Ladd Sexton, was born; however, the young mother again required psychiatric treatment, prompting the removal of her daughters from her care. Sexton first attempted suicide in November 1956; several later attempts followed.

In 1957 Sexton's psychiatrist and therapist, Dr. Martin Orne, encouraged her to write poetry as a form of therapy. Finding writing beneficial but having little knowledge of literature or composition, Sexton enrolled in John Holmes's poetry workshop in Boston. There she met fellow poet Maxine Kumin, beginning a lifelong friendship and professional alliance whereby each critiqued the other's work throughout the 1960s and into the 1970s. In 1958 Sexton attended Robert Lowell's graduate writing seminar at Boston University, along with Sylvia Plath and George Starbuck, and that same year published her first poem, "Eden Revisited," in the *Fiddlehead Review*. In 1960 she published her first collection, *To Bedlam and Part Way Back*, which received a National Book Award nomination, and she thereafter became increasingly active as a professional writer. In 1961 she was appointed a scholar at the newly established Radcliffe Institute, and in the mid-1960s began teaching writing at universities and high schools as well as at mental institutions. Her second volume, *All My Pretty Ones* (1962), also received a National Book Award nomination. A multitude of poetry awards followed, including numerous fellowships and grants, *Poetry* magazine's Levinson Prize (1962), the Poetry Society of America's Shelley Award (1967), and several honorary memberships and doctorates.

Throughout this time, though, her bouts with depression continued, made especially severe after the deaths of both her parents within months of each other in 1959. She was hospitalized again in the early 1960s, then reached a high point in her career in 1967, when she was awarded the Pulitzer Prize for her third collection, *Live or Die*. Within the next few years she completed her most popular volumes, *Love Poems* (1969) and *Transformations* (1971). Around this same time she began an affiliation with Boston University that eventually led to her appointment as full professor in 1973, an academic tribute especially significant considering the fact that Sexton had never received a college education. After another hospitalization, she divorced her husband of nearly twenty-five years in late 1973. A year later she published *The Death Notebooks* and completed the final editing of *The Awful Rowing toward God,* which was published posthumously in 1975. One of her final projects was making the preliminary selection of verses to be included in *45 Mercy Street* (1976). She committed suicide on October 4, 1974, dying of carbon monoxide poisoning in the garage of her home.

MAJOR WORKS

In form, Sexton's writings follow an overall movement from more formal, structured lyrics and intricate rhyme schemes early in her career to a freer, more open style much less reliant on revision in her later works. Her content, too, gradually shifted from the confessional to the surreal, as the poet/narrator moved from relying on personal experience to discover and accept herself to reinterpreting and retelling myths and religious accounts in order to understand herself, her relationship to God, and the meaning of life and death. Her "almost unnamable lust" for death permeates many of Sexton's writings, as do the correlative states of sanity and madness, and the emotional breakdowns involved within each. Other dominant themes include womanhood, in particular the mid-twentieth-century experience of the suburban housewife, and the strained relationships between parents and their children. Citing a mother who was "distant" and "shaming," at least one critic has proposed that this lack of sufficient love from her own mother caused Sexton to suffer tremendous remorse over not being able to be a mother to her own daughters. This complex and guilt-ridden relationship between mothers and daughters is represented in Sexton's first volume, *To Bedlam and Part Way Back,* which centers on Sexton's mental breakdown and her attempts at recovery. Set in traditional verse, the volume contains what is considered one of Sexton's best poems, "The Double Image," about the physical and mental conditions of the speaker and her cancer-ridden mother, and the speaker's anguish over losing her own daughters, who were sent to live with relatives when the narrator was considered dangerously suicidal. "The Double Image" is addressed to three-year-old Joyce and treats themes of absence and presence, and life and death, as

the speaker in the poem searches for the reasons "why I would rather / die than love."

Revealing the speaker's stance on confessionalism, the poem "To John, Who Begs Me Not to Enquire Further" is addressed to Boston poet John Holmes, Sexton's first poetry teacher, who discouraged Sexton from publishing her "clinical" poems about her experiences with psychiatric treatment, which he said would "haunt" her later and cause readers discomfort. "Said the Poet to the Analyst" and "You, Doctor Martin" consider themes of madness, while "The Division of Parts" returns to the mother-daughter motif, involving the dividing up of a mother's belongings after her death. Scholars also point out that Sexton struggled to ease her sense of her own personal evil through her poetry, a theme that surfaces in "Is It True?," in which the narrator asks a priest if she is evil. In this case, the speaker defines evil not in terms of deeds but as a state of being. Sexton utilized a less formal style in *All My Pretty Ones,* a volume centering on loss, the need for relief from suffering, and the desire for spiritual feeding. In "The Fortress," Sexton employed animal imagery in her depiction of a daughter in bed with her mother, portraying the security and comfort provided by the mother.

The themes of apprehension over sexual awakenings and the poet/narrator's fear of sexuality surface throughout Sexton's writings. "Little Girl, My String Bean, My Lovely Woman," from the Pulitzer Prize winning *Live or Die,* is addressed to her daughter Linda and talks about developing into womanhood. In the poem, the speaker, who compares the daughter to a garden, attempts to protect the daughter and prepare her for her budding sexuality. Turning once more to the subject of suicide, "Wanting to Die" involves what the personae calls the "passion" of suicide, the idea that the desire for death is erotic and life-giving. With "Live," the final poem in the volume, Sexton provided an affirmation of life, as the narrator celebrates her roles as wife and mother. The 1971 volume *Transformations* marked a move in Sexton's poetry toward free association, dream-like structures, and a change from personal poetry to a more "cultural" outlook. Evidencing the poet's sardonic wit and dark humor, *Transformations* contains the retellings of sixteen of *Grimms' Fairy Tales,* each with a subtle, dark twist. In these distortions of the best-known tales, including "Cinderella," "Red Riding Hood," and "Snow White and the Seven Dwarfs," sexual themes are exaggerated; for example, the father-daughter relationship in "Briar Rose" is incestuous, while the title character of "Rapunzel" is involved in a lesbian relationship. Happily-ever-after endings remain out of reach, as marriages are compared to nightmares and imprisonment, and result in madness or endless boredom.

After *Transformations* Sexton became increasingly bold in her poetry, and began focusing on her religious struggles—her need to make sense of the divinity of Jesus Christ and her search for the divine figure of God. In the experimental *The Death Notebooks,* which contains most of Sexton's religious poetry, the speaker communicates with Mary, Jesus, angels, and gods. One of the best-known poems from the collection, "Hurry up Please It's Time," is comprised of six sections and makes a strong public statement about Sexton's poetics, asking "What is death, I ask. / What is life, you ask." The final three volumes of Sexton's canon were published posthumously. The poems in *The Awful Rowing toward God,* the last volume that Sexton arranged and sent to the publisher (seven months before her death), were written within a few weeks. The entire collection is framed by two poems—"Rowing" and "The Rowing Endeth." Representing evil as a rat living inside a person, the opening poem depicts the narrator in a row boat searching for the island of God, hoping for freedom from the "rat" inside herself and to be embraced by God. In the closing poem the speaker has found the island of God. There, God and the speaker play a game of poker; God ends up with the winning hand. Sexton's last two collections, *45 Mercy Street* and *Words for Dr. Y: Uncollected Poems with Three Stories* (1978), were edited by her daughter Linda Gray Sexton.

CRITICAL RECEPTION

During Sexton's lifetime, the general critical consensus was that her early poetry was her best. After the publication of her first two collections—*To Bedlam and Part Way Back* and *All My Pretty Ones*—Sexton was reviewed extensively, her poetry was taught in schools, and she was widely referred to as a significant poet. By the end of the decade and into the early 1970s, however, there was a substantial decline in critical attention. This was due in part to her subject matter—her direct and straightforward treatment of "inappropriate" subjects such as menstruation and erotic pleasure; her emotionally charged verses about mothers and daughters; and her unguarded and blunt writings about mental instability. Though her 1969 publication *Love Poems* met with popular acclaim, many critics at the time decried its "bathos," and debated whether Sexton should be considered a serious poet at all.

Sexton's poetic status was redeemed for a time by the 1971 publication of the inventive and best-selling *Transformations,* which was well received by both critics and general readers. In the next few years, however, with the publication of *The Book of Folly* (1972), *The Death Notebooks,* and *The Awful Rowing toward God,* many critics again found fault with her work, pointing out her poor, "uncontrolled" technique as well as the unevenness and inconsistency of her entire body of work. Critics also expressed dismay over not being able to date

the works in her posthumously published volumes, and found her emphasis on religion distasteful. A number of scholars during the mid- to late 1970s, however, continued to analyze Sexton's writings as legitimate and serious work. Suzanne Juhasz, for example, discusses how Sexton's role as a "traditional," suburban wife and mother clashed with her creative urge to write. Detailing how 1960s suburban, middle-class women were not expected to make such private details of their lives public, Juhasz argues that Sexton gained power through her use of words. Jane McCabe (see Further Reading) contends that Sexton's poetry is important to feminist scholarship despite the fact that Sexton was not a feminist poet, and points out that "many of her experiences and feelings are the product of a society that oppresses women." Focusing on Sexton's treatment of mother-daughter relationships, Margaret Honton (see Further Reading) suggests that such poems as "The Double Image" and "The Division of Parts" reveal Sexton's attempts to resolve conflict with her mother and to create joyous relationships with her own daughters. The poems also depict, according to Honton, Sexton's acceptance of herself as a loving mother and daughter. Stephanie Demetrakopoulos also explores Sexton's portrayal of daughters, and how the speaker finds constancy in her relationship with them and calls them her "life-giving forces."

In the mid- to late 1980s critics increasingly sought to reevaluate Sexton's writings; the philosophical musings in her later poetry about religion, authority, and gender began to be considered at least as good, if not better, than her earlier works. Some critics also began to move away from looking at Sexton's poetry exclusively as autobiographical. Treating the themes of death and suicide in Sexton's writings, some critics have suggested that Sexton suffered a self-hatred that was tied to her ambivalent feelings about sexuality and gender. Others have examined her "fury" at human mortality as well as her supposed fear of death and her subsequent desire to "cheat" it. Diana Hume George studies the suicidal motif running through the "Dr. Y." poems in *Words for Dr. Y.,* suggesting that the speaker's death wish is tied to a feminine quest for power. Danny Wedding (see Further Reading), a doctor, examines Sexton's poetry in order to point out the many examples of distorted beliefs and ideas experienced by potential suicides. Other critical discussion in the decades surrounding the turn of the twenty-first century revolves around the sociocultural context of *Transformations* as it pertains to authority and patriarchal order. Carol Leventen (see Further Reading), for example, finds that the volume contains a hopeless and desolate vision of the role of women, calling the heroines "commodities" that are marketable for their physical and sexual value. Other critics have centered on issues such as the father-daughter motif in Sexton's poetry, calling Sexton the first artistic voice to describe a "normative" connection between fathers and daughters from a daughter's perspective. Looking at Sexton's religious search, Frances Bixler examines the poet's struggle to find a place somewhere between traditional Christianity and a new acceptance of her selfhood. Exploring the influence of Edna St. Vincent Millay on Sexton, Artemis Michailidou contends that Sexton's familiarity with Millay, who treated such "forbidden" subjects as the female body and gender stereotypes, aided Sexton in conceiving of her own woman-centered poetics.

PRINCIPAL WORKS

Poetry

To Bedlam and Part Way Back 1960

All My Pretty Ones 1962

*Selected Poems 1964

Live or Die 1966

†Poems [with Thomas Kinsella and Douglas Livingstone] 1968

Love Poems 1969

Transformations 1971

The Book of Folly 1972

The Death Notebooks 1974

The Awful Rowing toward God 1975

45 Mercy Street 1976

Words for Dr. Y.: Uncollected Poems With Three Stories (poetry and short stories) 1978

‡The Complete Poems 1981

Selected Poems of Anne Sexton 1988

Other Major Works

Eggs of Things [with Maxine Kumin] (children's book) 1963

More Eggs of Things [with Maxine Kumin] (children's book) 1964

45 Mercy Street (play) 1969

Joey and the Birthday Present [with Maxine Kumin] (children's book) 1971

The Wizard's Tears [with Maxine Kumin] (children's book) 1975

Anne Sexton: A Self-Portrait in Letters (letters) 1977

No Evil Star: Selected Essays, Interviews, and Prose (essays, interviews, and prose) 1985

*Contains poems from *To Bedlam and Part Way Back* and *All My Pretty Ones*.

†A selection of previously published poems.

‡Includes several previously uncollected poems written in the last year of Sexton's life.

CRITICISM

Suzanne Juhasz (essay date 1976)

SOURCE: Juhasz, Suzanne. "'The Excitable Gift': The Poetry of Anne Sexton." In *Anne Sexton: Telling the Tale*, edited by Steven E. Colburn, pp. 333-56. Ann Arbor: The University of Michigan Press, 1988.

[*In the following essay, originally published in 1976, Juhasz surveys the poetry Sexton published before her suicide in the fall of 1974, tracing her development from an inmate of a psychiatric hospital into a powerful poet whose words provide insight into her multiple roles.*]

This study of Anne Sexton's poetry was written before her death in October 1974. In it I describe her growing power through poetry, a triumph of life over death. Now it is apparent that the lure of death—always present, as her poems attest—grew too strong for her, despite the poetry. Yet her death does not negate either her art or the strength that she achieved through it. For the years in which she wrote, she held death at bay and with her poems sent a powerful awareness of life into the world. It was her tragedy, like that of others before her, to be both woman and poet. The struggle in this double-bind situation between such conflicting role demands is excruciating for all who will not choose between being "woman" or "poet." Anne Sexton's poetry is a testament to her courage and ability to be both for as long as she could.

"To Rage in Your Own Bowl"

Anne Sexton came to poetry through psychotherapy. She became a poet after having experienced the traditional woman's roles of wife, mother, housewife; *because* she had experienced them and needed a way, a form, a voice with which to deal with the fact of being a woman. "Until I was twenty-eight I had a kind of buried self who didn't know she could do anything but make white sauce and diaper babies," she remarked in 1968 to a *Paris Review* interviewer:

> All I wanted was a little piece of life, to be married, to have children. I thought the nightmares, the visions, the demons would go away if there was enough love to put them down. I was trying my damnedest to lead a conventional life, for that was how I was brought up, and it was what my husband wanted of me. But one can't build little white picket fences to keep nightmares out. The surface cracked when I was about twenty-eight. I had a psychotic break and tried to kill myself.[1]

After she began to write poems, her therapist encouraged her: "'Don't kill yourself,' he said. 'Your poems might mean something to someone else someday.' That gave me a feeling of purpose, a little cause, something to *do* with my life, no matter how rotten I was."[2]

Since Betty Friedan first analyzed "the problem that has no name,"[3] psychologists, sociologists, and others writing about women have described the kind of situation in which Sexton found herself and have provided extensive insight into the sources of the kind of madness that she experienced. In discussing the poetry that she created, it is essential to observe that her "confessionalism" grew out of the therapy situation, but that the therapy was occasioned by her womanhood itself, by the very real strains and conflicts that Sexton experienced while attempting to exist in her world as a woman.

The poems from *To Bedlam and Part Way Back* (1960)[4] to the volume appropriately titled *Live or Die* (1966)[5] closely follow the psychoanalytic model. They move in concern from the present or near past, from the trappings of madness (its hospitals, inmates, doctors, pills) to the more distant past in which the madness grew. It is a past not so much of events as relationships—relations with blood kin: mother, father, daughters. Endlessly exploring herself as she has been created by these interpersonal relationships, Sexton probes for the truth. The way back to sanity is through understanding, yet we may understand better with the unconscious than with the conscious mind. As artist, Sexton wills the memories with her conscious mind (sometimes, as in **"All My Pretty Ones," "Walking in Paris," "Some Foreign Letters,"** photographs or letters are carefully used as occasions to awaken memory), but the unconscious mind, it is hoped, will supply the images, the connections and associations that will give access to the truth. "The poetry is often more advanced, in terms of my unconscious, than I am," she tells the interviewer. "Poetry, after all, milks the unconscious. The unconscious is there to feed it little images, little symbols, the answers, the insights I know not of."[6] Thus in her poems she describes herself as patient: "And I am queen of this summer hotel / or the laughing bee on a stalk / of death" (**"You, Doctor Martin"**);[7] her mother: "That was the winter / that my mother died, / half mad on morphine, / blown up, at last, / like a pregnant pig. / I was her dreamy evil eye" (**"Flee on Your Donkey"**);[8] her daughter: ". . . I just pretended / you, small piglet, butterfly / girl with jelly bean cheeks" (**"The Double Image"**).[9]

The most characteristic form for these images is the simile or epithet-metaphor: "Words are like labels, / or coins, or better, like swarming bees," she writes in **"Said the Poet to the Analyst."**[10] The following litany to her dead mother is based upon her understanding (consistent with psychoanalytic theory) of the power of naming itself to define and to exorcise.

> Now it is Friday's noon
> and I would still curse
> you with my rhyming words

and bring you flapping back, old love,
old circus knitting, god-in-her-moon,
all fairest in my lang syne verse,
the gauzy bride among the children,
the fancy amid the absurd
and awkward, that horn for hounds
that skipper homeward, that museum
keeper of stiff starfish, that blaze
within the pilgrim woman,
a clown mender, a dove's
cheek among the stones,
my Lady of my first words,
this is the division of ways.

                              (**"The Division of Parts"**)[11]

First the naming, difficult enough; then, frequently, the definition expanded into a complex image: "I must always forget how one word is able to pick / out another, to manner another, until I have got / something I might have said" (**"Said the Poet to the Analyst"**). Thus Sexton "sees" her maternal guilt this way:

> . . . Ugly angels spoke to me. The blame,
> I heard them say, was mine. They tattled
> like green witches in my head, letting doom
> leak like a broken faucet;
> as if doom had flooded my belly and filled your bas-
>   sinet,
> an old debt I must assume.

                              (**"The Double Image"**)

"The Double Image," a long poem in eight sections from *To Bedlam and Part Way Back,* offers a good example of the method by which Anne Sexton in her early poetry analyzes the nature of her madness and her identity in terms of personal relationships: here, with her mother and her daughter. The poem begins in the present tense: mother and daughter stand by a window in November, watching the leaves fall. Yet this mother and child have been parted for three years because of the mother's madness and attempted suicide; the physical fact of their reunion is the result of a series of psychological facts, and events, which the poet, explaining to her daughter, explores by going back in time and memory. When the child, Joyce, asks where the yellow leaves go, her mother answers rather cryptically, that "today believed / in itself, or else it fell." She continues:

> Today, my small child, Joyce,
> love your self's self where it lives.
> There is no special God to refer to; or if there is,
> why did I let you grow
> in another place.

                              (part 1)

She then offers, in six poems, her memories to explain this advice.

Briefly, she describes her first suicide attempt (directly resulting from her guilt over the child's first serious illness) and the mental hospital. Then she focuses on the years when she was "part way back from Bedlam," living with her mother ("Too late, / too late, to live with your mother, the witches said") while her child lived elsewhere, occasionally visiting. The poem moves in anguish back and forth between the partial, inadequate relationship between the poet and her mother—

> I cannot forgive your suicide, my mother said.
> And she never could. She had my portrait
> done instead.
>
> (part 2)

> Only my mother grew ill.
> She turned from me, as if death were catching,
> as if death transferred,
> as if my dying had eaten inside of her.
> That August you were two, but I timed my days with
>   doubt.
> On the first of September she looked at me
> and said I gave her cancer.
> They carved her sweet hills out
> and still I couldn't answer.
>
> (part 3)

—and the partial, inadequate relationship between the poet and her daughter:

> Once I mailed you a picture of a rabbit
> and a postcard of Motif number one,
> as if it were normal
> to be a mother and be gone.
>
> (part 3)

> I could not get you back
> except for weekends. You came
> each time, clutching the picture of a rabbit
> that I had sent you. . . .
>
>   . . . . .
>
> The first visit you asked my name.
> . . . I will forget
> how we bumped away from each other like mari-
>   onettes
> on strings. It wasn't the same
> as love, letting weekends contain
> us.
>
> (part 7)

The fragmented nature of these relationships is poised against the poet's constant recognition of a profound underlying identity between herself and her mother, herself and her daughter: "Your smile is like your mother's, the artist said" (part 2).

> During the sea blizzards
> she had her
> own portrait painted.
> A cave of a mirror
> placed on the south wall;
> matching smile, matching contour.

> And you resembled me; unacquainted
> with my face, you wore it. But you were mine
> after all.
>
> (part 4)

The poet is caught between two images of herself that reflect her to herself, but each only partially; because as reflections they rely on her for their identity as much as she relies on them. And she has no sense of herself, of who she is, only guilt for the kind of daughter and mother she thinks she might be.

To talk about a condition of simultaneous separation and identity, the poem projects a series of "double images." The central double image is the pair of portraits, mother and daughter, in "the house that waits / still, on top of the sea," where "two portraits hang on opposite walls" (part 5). Yet mirrors, windows, and people themselves also reflect the idea, as the poem's words describe the portraits:

> In south light, her smile is held in place,
> her cheeks wilting like a dry
> orchid; my mocking mirror, my overthrown
> love, my first image. She eyes me from that face,
> that stony head of death
> I had outgrown.
>
>   . . . . .
>
> And this was the cave of the mirror,
> that double woman who stares
> at herself, as if she were petrified
> in time—two ladies sitting in umber chairs.
> You kissed your grandmother
> and she cried.
>
> (part 6)

Analyzing those years of the portraits in part 5, the poet is, I think, also describing the movement of her poem:

> . . . And I had to learn
> why I would rather
> die than love, how your innocence
> would hurt and how I gather
> guilt like a young intern
> his symptoms, his certain evidence.
>
> (part 5)

Part 7, the poem's final section, returns to the present tense of part 1: "Now you stay for good / . . . You call me *mother* and I remember my mother again, / somewhere in greater Boston, dying." It returns to mother and daughter at the window, looking out on the world, another double image. Yet the poem ends with a final memory, the mother's memory of her child as an infant, "all wrapped and moist / and strange at my heavy breast. / I needed you," in order that the poet may offer her understanding of herself to her daughter:

> I, who was never quite sure
> about being a girl, needed another

life, another image to remind me.
And this was my worst guilt; you could not cure
nor soothe it. I made you to find me.

(part 7)

The initial realization of her connection with her daughter had led the poet *into* madness: "as if doom had flooded my belly and filled your bassinet, / an old debt I must assume" (part 1); now an understanding of the same connection has led her out of madness. The difference, predictable in psychoanalytic terms, lies not in any severing of the connection, but in a dissolution of the guilt that arose from it. "I made you to find me," says the poet. And why not, because surely in some ways I am you and you are me, a girl child that I have made in my woman's body; and in other ways you are not me, I am not you, for I am mother, while you are child. We are a double image.

The ending and beginning of the poem focus upon the poet and her daughter, because this relationship, although dependent for its very being upon that other double image, the poet-daughter and *her* mother, can lead into life, while the other one cannot. This is not only because the poet's mother is literally dying, but because the guilt involved with that relationship is not gone. Whatever understanding has been achieved is partial and has come too late: "Too late to be forgiven now, the witches said" (part 2). The mother had accused her daughter of causing her death, and the poet could not answer, feeling the truth of the accusation, and feeling guilty for it.

The poem has demonstrated what the poet meant when in part 1 she advised loving oneself's self where it lives. True relationships between people, any kind of relationships, but especially those between people of blood ties, where a profound connection or identity exists, cannot occur unless each member of the pair is secure in her own identity. Granted that that identity may depend upon and even arise out of the relationship, it must yet be distinct: the person cannot *confuse* herself with the other person in the relationship. The double image can be both positive and negative, as it is in this poem: negative when it reflects beings who are creating their identities out of the reflections that they see, that in turn are creating identities out of the reflections that they see, that in turn, and on and on, into infinity; positive when each watcher sees another person who is like herself, who reflects herself, but who also reflects her own self!

If, as **"The Double Image"** and many of her early poems reveal, the cause of Sexton's madness and its accompanying desire for death has been her woman's situation, experience, identity, it is also true that the affirmation of life at which she arrives through the acts of her poems is founded in her womanhood. **"Live,"** the final poem in her third book, *Live or Die,* helps her to locate the source of and reason for life in woman's situation, experience, identity.

Today life opened inside me like an egg
and there inside
after considerable digging
I found the answer.
What a bargain!
There was the sun,
her yolk moving feverishly,
tumbling her prize—
and you realize that she does this daily!
I'd known she was a purifier
but I hadn't thought
she was solid,
hadn't known she was an answer.

("Live")

Life, of course, comes from inside herself—spiritually as well as physically. It is an egg, is life; and an egg is the sun, for the sun is an egg, for the sun is life; and it is not outside herself at all, for her to bask or not to bask in its (reflected) light. No, it is *inside* herself, and it is she who must deliver it, give it birth, make life happen. It is she who makes the world; it is an extension of her very body. "So I say *Live* / and turn my shadow three times round":

So I won't hang around in my hospital shift,
repeating The Black Mass and all of it.
I say *Live, Live* because of the sun,
the dream, the excitable gift.

Being a poet causes Anne Sexton to understand herself as possessor of "the excitable gift," because the act of poetry unites understanding with experience; its vision is insight. Though her poetry begins as therapy for her personal salvation, because it is a public act it reaches out to others. Yet it is always rooted in her personal self, her private life, as is the sun. It does not, like much of the "confessional" poetry of men, abstract or generalize upon its own experiences, either explicitly or implicitly; nevertheless, it communicates to others and offers its gift. In an early poem, **"For John, Who Begs Me Not to Enquire Further"** (*To Bedlam and Part Way Back*),[12] Sexton herself tries to explain how this gift works. Commenting upon her explorations of self, of "that narrow diary of my mind," she finds their purpose to have been, not beauty, but "a certain sense of order there." If she had tried "to give [him] something else, / something outside of myself," he would not then know "that the worst of anyone / can be, finally, / an accident of hope." Generalizing, in other words, destroys the very meaning sought.

I tapped my own head;
it was glass, an inverted bowl.
It is a small thing
to rage in your own bowl.
At first it was private.

Then it was more than myself;
it was you, or your house
or your kitchen.
And if you turn away
because there is no lesson here
I will hold my awkward bowl,
with all its cracked stars shining
like a complicated lie,
and fasten a new skin around it
as if I were dressing an orange
or a strange sun.
Not that it was beautiful,
but that I found some order there.
There ought to be something special
for someone
in this kind of hope.

("**For John, Who Begs Me Not to Enquire Further**")

"A Middle-Aged Witch, Me"

Love Poems (1969),[13] the volume that follows *Live or Die,* is a further extension of the decision for life into the living experience of love; it is almost a postscript to the previous volume. It is with the next book of poems, *Transformations* (1971),[14] that a major development, if not a transformation, does in fact begin to occur. Here Sexton shows where her journey from patient to poet has led her. It has led her to understanding the positive potential of herself as "middle-aged witch, me." Previous to this volume, she has equated madwoman and witch: "I have gone out, a possessed witch, / haunting the black air, braver at night" ("**Her Kind**," *To Bedlam and Part Way Back*). The refrain of "**Her Kind**" develops as follows: "A woman like that is not a woman, quite. / I have been her kind"; "A woman like that is misunderstood. / I have been her kind"; "A woman like that is not ashamed to die. / I have been her kind." The green witches of "**The Double Image**" who spoke inside Sexton's head of truth asked for death in payment for insight. Madness must lead to death, because the mad are "magic talking to itself, / noisy and alone" ("**You, Doctor Martin**"). "Talking" is a key word here, and equally so is "alone." Nobody listens; the language of the mad, like the world of women, is private. Nobody (the world) *cares* to hear, to know; for the world would not like what it learned. Yet if no one listens, the voice destroys itself with its truths. As has often been pointed out, the distance between fool or madman and poet is not great. Nor is the space between madwoman and woman poet, but it is less frequently traversed. Madwomen are doubly relegated to the private world, as mad and as women, while "poet" traditionally belongs to the male, the public world. The voice of the poet is a public voice; the poet's words affect other people: they may even cause changes, action. It is a voice of power. As Sexton's analyst had told her, poems can mean something to someone. For Sexton, as woman, the move from patient to poet has been a voyage from dependence and powerlessness to independence and power. By rooting her public voice in her

private experience, by creating a public persona, witch, out of her private self, witch, she is able to discuss the race in addition to herself. The witch is a wise-woman, storyteller, seer. A witch works magic: her magic is and has always been the magic of words, so that the word "magic" in the line from "**You, Doctor Martin**" is also a key word. Thus it is fitting that Sexton's poetic language itself, from *Transformations* on, embodies and expresses this development.

Her power as poet arises from the power, the magic of words: the witch/poet's spells make things happen; they plant "words in you like grass seed" ("**Iron Hans**").[15] In her early poetry, Sexton, as madwoman and potential suicide (only "part way back"), had to control her images, her metaphors and similes of association, by the conscious forms of meter, rhyme, and the sentence itself, which consistently supplied the links between images of insight. In *Transformations* Sexton begins to abandon a great deal of this "control," because, I think, she feels in control. Now bold figures of association cast their spell with little to mediate their effect.

In *Transformations* Sexton begins to extend her original themes. In later volumes, *The Book of Folly*[16] and *The Death Notebooks,*[17] she will make her own myths. Here, she is warming up on Grimms' scales. She retells *Grimms' Fairy Tales,* with "the speaker in this case / . . . a middle-aged witch, me." These tales do for the history of the race what the earlier poems did for Sexton's personal history: they attempt to create the truth by bridging the gap between the present of adult experience, the potential madness underlying the everyday, and the past of childhood, dream, and archetype. Like the earlier poetry, these poems move from present to past (the therapy situation), not from the traditional once-upon-a-time to the moral that encompasses the present and all future time. They begin with present-day examples of situations of which the tales are archetypes, and Dame Sexton feels no compunction against using herself as a present-day example.

> If you danced from midnight
> to six A.M. who would understand?
> . . . . .
>
> The night nurse
> with her eyes slit like Venetian blinds,
> she of the tubes and the plasma,
> listening to the heart monitor,
> the death cricket bleeping,
> she who calls you "we"
> and keeps vigil like a ballistic missile,
> would understand.
>
> ("**The Twelve Dancing Princesses**")

Many are the deceivers:
. . . . .

And I. I too.
Quite collected at cocktail parties,
meanwhile in my head
I'm undergoing open-heart surgery.
The heart, poor fellow,
pounding on his little tin drum
with a faint death beat.
The heart, that eyeless beetle,
enormous that Kafka beetle,
running panicked through his maze,
never stopping one foot after the other
one hour after the other
until he gags on an apple
and it's all over.

                    ("Red Riding Hood")

Here Sexton's characteristic figures of association are especially bold: the juxtaposition of seemingly incongruous material that, upon contact, produces sparks, shocks of definition, revelation—"her eyes slit like Venetian blinds"; "keeps vigil like a ballistic missile"; "The heart, that eyeless beetle, / enormous that Kafka beetle." The similes and epithet-metaphors embedded in the "fairy" part of the tales are particularly interesting, as they enact in microcosm the present to past movement of the poems: "tenor" belongs to the tale, the past, while "vehicle" belongs to the present, specifically modern situation—"[Rumpelstiltskin] tore himself in two. / Somewhat like a split broiler"; "The King looked like Munch's *Scream*"; "at the wedding the princesses averted their eyes / and sagged like old sweatshirts."

The tales that Dame Sexton chooses from Grimms' collection deal with her favorite themes: madness, death, and women. A cluster of the stories, "Snow White and the Seven Dwarfs." "The White Snake," "The Little Peasant," "Rapunzel," "Cinderella," "Red Riding Hood," "The Twelve Dancing Princesses," and "Briar Rose (Sleeping Beauty)," project without idealism the possible roles for women in the world. Young girls, heroines and princesses, begin in a state of mindless natural beauty, in an innocence and purity that is defined by its total physicality: "a daughter as lovely as a grape . . . / Poor grape with no one to pick. / Luscious and round and sleek" (**"Rumpelstiltskin"**); "The princess was as ripe as a tangerine. / Her breasts purred up and down like a cat" (**"Godfather Death"**):

No matter what life you lead
the virgin is a lovely number:
cheeks as fragile as cigarette paper,
arms and legs made of Limoges,
lips like Vin Du Rhône,
rolling her china-blue doll eyes
open and shut.
Open to say,
Good Day Mama,
and shut for the thrust
of the unicorn.

She is unsoiled.
She is as white as a bonefish.

                    ("Snow White and the Seven Dwarfs")

They move to the inevitable corruption of sexuality—"They lay together upon the yellowy threads [Rapunzel's hair], / swimming through them / like minnows through kelp / and they sang out benedictions like the Pope" (**"Rapunzel"**)—and thence to either meaninglessness or madness (or both).

Meanwhile Snow White held court,
rolling her china-blue doll eyes open and shut
and sometimes referring to her mirror
as women do.

                    ("Snow White and the Seven Dwarfs")

Briar Rose
was an insomniac . . .

            . . . . .

Each night I am nailed into place
and I forget who I am.
Daddy?
That's another kind of prison.
It's not the prince at all,
but my father
drunkenly bent over my bed,
circling the abyss like a shark,
my father thick upon me
like some sleeping jellyfish.

                    ("Briar Rose")

Like proper fairy tales, these abound with witches, for the witch has been traditionally the figure of the woman past middle age. Many of these women are embittered ex-princesses, like the wicked stepmother of **"Snow White,"** "a beauty in her own right, / though eaten, of course, by age," or embittered spinsters, like the thirteenth fairy of **"Briar Rose,"** "her fingers as long and thin as straws, / her eyes burnt by cigarettes, / her uterus an empty teacup." Primarily, their power is for evil, evil to aid in the corruption of innocence, corrupting the young into their own state of bitter age. Only Dame Sexton herself, because she is a poet, has broken the system and works for truth, if not goodness:

And then I knew that the voice
of the spirits had been let in—
as intense as an epileptic aura—
and that no longer would I sing
alone.

                    ("The White Snake")

There are no mothers and daughters in these tales, only daughters and lecherous fathers or evil stepmothers. Only once does Sexton attempt an analysis of a kind of mother-daughter relationship in the story of "Rapunzel," and here both the questions and the answers are fraught with ambiguity, as Sexton trods on dangerous ground in postulating any possible kind of salvation for women in the real world.

"**Rapunzel**" begins this way: "A woman / who loves a woman / is forever young." It is the tale of a witch, Mother Gothel, who had a magic garden, "more beautiful than Eve's." But this witch, unlike Eve, is a spinster. When a pregnant woman yearns for a magic root in her garden, the rampion, "a kind of harebell more potent than penicillin," the witch strikes a bargain, "typical enough in those times," with the woman's husband whom she catches in the garden: he promises his child to her. This is, of course, Rapunzel, "another name for the life-giving rampion." The witch vows that none but she will ever see or touch the beautiful girl and locks her in a high tower. Together, the pseudo-mother and daughter "play mother-me-do / all day." The witch sings:

> Give me your nether lips
> all puffy in their art
> and I will give you angel fire in return.
> We are two clouds
> glistening in the bottle glass.
> We are two birds
> washing in the same mirror.
> We were fair game
> but we have kept out of the cesspool.
> We are strong.
> We are the good ones.
> Do not discover us
> for we lie together all in green
> like pond weeds.
> Hold me, my young dear, hold me.

But the prince comes, as he always seems to do. Rapunzel is startled at this "beast . . . / with muscles on his arms / like a bag of snakes," by the "moss on his legs," and the "prickly plant" that "grows on his cheeks."

> Yet he dazzled her with his answers.
> Yet he dazzled her with his dancing stick.

When the so-called happy ending has occurred, Sexton pronounces upon it this way:

> They lived happily as you might expect
> proving that mother-me-do
> can be outgrown,
> just as the fish on Friday,
> just as a tricycle.
> The world, some say,
> is made up of couples.
> A rose must have a stem.

As for Mother Gothel, her heart shrinks to the size of a pin, never again to say "Hold me, my young dear, / hold me, / and only as she dreamt of the yellow hair / did moonlight sift into her mouth."

These tales are insistent upon the uncompromising reality of the real world, a place where neither childhood (tricycles), nor ideals (the fish on Friday), nor fantasy (dreaming of yellow hair) have any place or power. The love of Mother Gothel for her "daughter" seems to belong to all three; and although the plot of the poem, of the fairy tale, allows her no recourse, the language of the poem seems to be holding out for some other kind of validity: the bag of snakes and the dancing stick are posed against the two birds washing in the same mirror, the two clouds glistening in the bottle glass. The prince seems like a figurative as well as a literal comedown for Rapunzel, the "cesspool" out of which lesbian love with Mother Gothel had been keeping her. The other tales support this interpretation, with their portrayals of the fate of princesses. After having read all their happy endings (Cinderella and her prince, for example, living "they say" happily ever after, "like two dolls in a museum case / . . . never telling the same story twice, / never getting a middle-aged spread, / their darling smiles pasted on for eternity. / Regular Bobbsey Twins"), one might prefer the moonlight of Mother Gothel's dreams. Yet the questions remain: Were Rapunzel and Mother Gothel "the good ones?" Ought mother-me-do to be outgrown?

"For We Swallow Magic and We Deliver Anne"

The Book of Folly (1972) and *The Death Notebooks* (1974) are experimental, bold, frightening. The poet consorts with angels, Furies, Mary, Jesus, gods, and death in the writing of stories, poems, psalms. These works make it clear that she trusted her vision, wherever it might take her. The old themes are in no way gone, but their expression frequently occurs in a new dimension. It is difficult now to label this poetry "confessional," because the talking voice, immersing itself in memory and experience, is gone; the voice now chants or sings, and experience has been transformed into myth. Nevertheless, the poems still refuse to generalize, to abstract: the "awkward bowl" of Sexton's consciousness is more of a "strange sun" than ever: it is a dangerous and magical world of visionary truth-saying.

In her middle forties, Anne Sexton continued to be faithful to her own perceptions. Death became a major element in what she perceived: the death of age, the result of commitment to life. Two poems to her daughter Linda, at ages eleven and eighteen, about the coming of womanhood, document this change in tone. In **"Little Girl, My String Bean, My Lovely Woman"** (*Live or Die*), the poet says: "How can I say that I've known / just what you know and just where you are?"

> Oh, darling, let your body in,
> let it tie you in,
> in comfort.
> What I want to say, Linda,
> is that women are born twice.
> . . . . .

What I want to say, Linda,
is that there is nothing in your body that lies.
All that is new is telling the truth.
I'm here, that somebody else,
an old tree in the background.

In **"Mother and Daughter"** (*The Book of Folly*), the mother is at another stage in the process of physical connection and identification with her daughter, even as the daughter is at another stage, now a woman grown:

Linda, you are leaving
your old body now.
You've picked my pocket clean
and you've racked up all my
poker chips and left me empty

. . . . .

Question you about this
and you will see my death
drooling at these gray lips
while you, my burglar, will eat
fruit and pass the time of day.

"The Death Baby," a poem in six parts from *The Death Notebooks,* explores the nature of death in terms (now familiar) of woman's roles of daughter and mother. Death may be generalizable, and universal, since like birth it is an experience that all humans share; but one's own death is personal, private, peculiarly one's own. In this poem, Sexton is trying to know her death.

The poem is a process, perhaps of initiation: one knows death when one is ready, and when death is ready to be known. This process has six stages. In the first, the poet explores death in dreams; the "exploration" is not an analysis but a vision of dream death: her own death, as a baby, in the dreams of her older sister. The second death is by fantasy: the vision of a doll's death. The third is the lesson of death attempted, premature or false death: the vision, in the dream of the would-be suicide, is of an ice baby, an ice baby that rocks the dreamer and is rocked by the dreamer. The fourth is death by proxy: the vision is of the death of her mother, in which death becomes her mother's child, so that she can be neither her mother's daughter nor her mother's mother. The fifth is death averted: the vision of the attempt to kill death by friendship, a false vision. The sixth is death encountered in vision: death as a baby, to be rocked and to rock, where death is mother to its baby, baby to its mother, in an unending circle of mother and child. The poem is, of course, circular, its end in its beginning, but that is only to be expected in myths.

The poem begins:

I was an ice baby.
I turned to sky blue.
My tears became two glass beads.
My mouth stiffened into a dumb howl.

They say it was a dream
but I remember that hardening.

(1. **"Dreams"**)

Her older sister had dreamed, "nightly," of the death of the new baby: "'The baby turned to ice. / Somebody put her in the refrigerator / and she turned as hard as a Popsicle.'" But dreams are real experience, says the poem, and so the poet remembers "that hardening." Tears into glass beads, mouth stiffening into howl; and the refrigerator, too, the milk bottle hissing like a snake, caviar turning to lava, because "the rhythm of the refrigerator / had been disturbed" by the alien presence of a dying baby inside. (In yet another of her sister's dreams, the dogs think she is a bone, licking her apart, "loving" her until she is gone.) As always, it is the language of this poetry that effects its transformations. Yet it is difficult now to talk of metaphor or simile. "I was an ice baby"; "I turned to sky blue"; "The tomatoes vomited up their stomachs." Where is the comparison, either explicit or implicit? What is figurative here? Either nothing, or everything; but metaphor's transfer *from* literal *to* figurative is missing. This is, in fact, literal description of a visionary world, where any and all transformations into truth are possible. This is ritual, mantric language, with its significant repetitions and gnomic pronouncements: "I died seven times / in seven ways / letting death give me a sign, / letting death place his mark on my forehead" (3. **"Seven Times"**).

The Dy-dee doll of part 2 has only two lives. Once the child Anne "snapped / her head off / and let it float in the toilet"; another time she melted under the sun lamp, "trying to get warm."

She was a gloom,
her face embracing
her little bent arms.
She died in all her rubber wisdom.

The deaths of the doll are another form of experiencing death in imagination and thus without its finality. The doll dies in misery and knowledge, embracing herself.

From the doll's two deaths, Sexton moves to her own "seven": the premature or false deaths of attempted suicide. In these attempts, she was getting to know her death, asking for a sign, asking to be marked by death: "And death took root in that sleep," in the dream experience of an ice baby; "and I rocked it / and was rocked by it. / Oh Madonna, hold me." The baby is herself; the baby is death.

The most compelling of the poem's six visions are parts 4 and 6: two pietàs. The fourth, **"Madonna,"** I have called death by proxy; it describes her mother's death, and as any reader of Anne Sexton should know (as most women know), "A woman *is* her mother. / That's the main thing" (**"Housewife"**).[18] Sexton's mother died "unrocked," "thrashing like a fish on the hook": "her rocking horse was pain / with vomit steaming from her mouth." It was a death of horror, for mother and daughter alike. The daughter would help, wants to "place my head in her lap / or even take her in my arms somehow / and fondle her twisted gray hair"; she wants to be mothered, to mother. But death has replaced Anne as her mother's "baby": "Her belly was big with another child, / cancer's baby, big as a football."

What sort of response can be made to death? In part 5, **"Max,"** the poet and her friend Max make a pact "to beat death down with a stick. / To take over. / To build our death like carpenters." This entails talking turkey, shooting "words straight from the hip" when death comes; not being "polite." The pact, the talks, the conspiracy of the friends, is seen as a means, at first to avert and later to confront death. Yet it is a partial answer only, for in the moment of death one is alone.

The moment of death comes in the vision of part 6, **"Baby."** The description of the baby whom the poet rocks concentrates upon its eyes, which are made of glass, "as brittle as crystal." It is the ice baby of the refrigerator dreams, and the baby's sight reveals its knowledge: "Glass eye, ice eye, / primordial eye, / lava eye, / pin eye, / break eye, / how you stare back!" The death baby's gaze is like that of small children, because it knows exactly who she is: it has "worn my underwear," "read my newspaper." Poet and baby rock, locked in a death embrace:

> I rock. I rock.
> We plunge back and forth
> comforting each other.
> We are stone.
> We are carved, a pietà
> that swings and swings.
>
> . . . . .
>
> I rock. I rock.
> You are my stone child
> with still eyes like marbles.
> There is a death baby
> for each of us.
> We own him.
> His smell is our smell.
> Beware. Beware.
> There is a tenderness.
> There is a love
> for this dumb traveler
> waiting in his pink covers.

This is Sexton's winter's tale, a myth that does not praise the new life that must always grow from old life but rather seeks to reconcile the death that also must grow from life. The central actors, and images, of both myths are the same, because both myths are complementary, existing always simultaneously: mother and child,

child and mother—this is a woman's myth. One is born with one's death inside oneself, like an egg, or a baby. Through the process of living one transforms oneself into one's own death, through a process of hardening, stiffening, freezing. Each birth only hastens the process, so one grows from baby to child to daughter to mother: in the last act of birth, a mother gives birth to her own death, a death baby. The imagery of the poem underlines the nature of this process, beginning with its initial statement of truth: "I was an ice baby." "Ice," "I," "eyes," are all equated in the poem: death, identity, vision. Even as the ice baby of part 1 stiffens in that strange morgue, the refrigerator, so the poem's protagonist continues throughout the life of the poem, which follows the temporal course of her life, to stiffen, to grow towards death, until in the final pietà she and the death baby are carved stone, "a pietà / that swings and swings." They are a statue of themselves, their own tombstone. How can stone yet swing and swing? Because *rocking* is the primary act of the poem, an extraordinary pun on the word "rock" that can link stone and maternity. *Rocking*: turning into stone, mothering—I give birth to my own death. I am my mother's baby; I am my mother's death; I am my mother; I am my baby; I am my death. A cold vision, an icy vision, a crystal vision of truth, as Sexton looks into the glass beads of her own eye and finds herself, who is her death, reflected there. These reflections say that the mirroring process cannot go on ad infinitum, for glass turns to stone.

The poem ends this way:

> Someday,
> heavy with cancer or disaster,
> I will look up at Max
> and say: It is time.
> Hand me the death baby
> and there will be
> that final rocking.

There is no escaping death, but to know that one can say, "It is time. / Hand me the death baby" indicates that is the only possible way one might yet be powerful. To know and to ask.

Power. The word is everywhere in this essay; the sense of power comes through more and more strongly in the poetry of Anne Sexton. The power comes from making poems that "mean something to someone": from the power of magic, which has always been that of sending words to effect changes, to cause action. The power of the poet whose words are let loose upon the world. Yet the power in Sexton's words comes into them from her insight into herself; from her understanding of her identity in terms of both her own self and the others with whom she interacts, relates. Because she knew who she was, she could give out this knowledge. And the process was wonderfully reciprocal, circular; for she understood who she was with her poems; her words caused her to know who she was. She brought forth from herself the power of her vision, let loose upon the world with words: an egg, a "strange sun"—"the dream, the excitable gift."

Notes

1. Barbara Kevles, "The Art of Poetry: Anne Sexton," *Paris Review* 13 (1970-71): 160-91.

2. Kevles, 161.

3. Betty Friedan, *The Feminine Mystique* (New York: W. W. Norton, 1963), 11.

4. *To Bedlam and Part Way Back* (Boston: Houghton Mifflin, 1960).

5. *Live or Die* (Boston: Houghton Mifflin, 1966).

6. Kevles, 162.

7. *To Bedlam and Part Way Back,* 3.

8. *Live or Die,* 8.

9. *To Bedlam and Part Way Back,* 58.

10. *To Bedlam and Part Way Back,* 17.

11. *To Bedlam and Part Way Back,* 66.

12. *To Bedlam and Part Way Back,* 51-52.

13. *Love Poems* (Boston: Houghton Mifflin, 1969).

14. *Transformations* (Boston: Houghton Mifflin, 1971).

15. *Transformations,* 44.

16. *The Book of Folly* (Boston: Houghton Mifflin, 1972).

17. *The Death Notebooks* (Boston: Houghton Mifflin, 1974).

18. *All My Pretty Ones* (Boston: Houghton Mifflin, 1962), 48.

Diana Hume George (essay date 1986)

SOURCE: George, Diana Hume. "Death Is a Woman, Death Is a Man: Anne Sexton's Green Girls and the Leaves that Talk." *University of Hartford Studies in Literature* 18, no. 1 (1986): 31-44.

[*In the following essay, George discusses the theme of suicide in Sexton's "Letters to Dr. Y." sequence, focusing on how the speaker's death wish is tied to both the desire for power and her/his attitude toward mortality.*]

I infer that "Letters to Dr. Y." were of special significance to Anne Sexton, in part because they constitute the only finished work that Sexton permanently set aside

for posthumous publication.[1] My own conjectures about their significance for the poet arise in part from a 1968 *Paris Review* interview, in which Sexton speaks of her "ritualized visions" of God, Christ, and the saints:

> . . . I feel that I can touch them almost . . . that they are part of me. . . . It's reincarnation, speaking with another voice . . . or else with the Devil. If you want to know the truth, the leaves talk to me every June.

When the interviewer asks if Sexton tries to communicate her visions to other people, she answers, "I refuse to talk about it, which is why I'm having a hard time now."

The interviewer is tireless. She tries to elicit further response from Sexton on the nature of her visions, sacred or demonic. Finally, Sexton cuts her off: "I find this very difficult, and I'd just as soon leave it, if you please" (Kevles 184-85). Although the emphasis in this portion of the interview is on religious visions, Sexton has alluded to the "talking leaves" that form the core of the suicide poems in the Dr. Y. sequence, and she has spoken of them immediately following a reference to "the Devil." In the **"May 5, 1970"** Dr. Y. poem, the analyst asks her what the leaves say to her, and she answers, "I am not allowed to repeat it. There are rules about this." It is possible that Sexton was uncomfortable about publishing during her lifetime poems that would certainly break the rules imposed by her demonic voices. Although Sexton had in her earlier collections included poems to and about her doctors (such as the superb **"You, Dr. Martin"** and **"Said the Poet to the Analyst,"** in *To Bedlam and Part Way Back*), she had never so directly dealt with the therapeutic process in poetry. Even the most openly confessional poets refrain, it seems, from violating the therapeutic session. In the "Letters to Dr. Y." sequence, she does just that, and the result is remarkably, uncomfortably intimate. One unusual feature of these poems, then, is the concrete interpenetration of poetry and psychoanalytic method.

More important for my purposes here, the recurring theme of the speaker-patient's sessions with the analyst is suicide. In concert with her earlier poems on the subject, the Dr. Y sequence constitutes a body of poetry on suicide that is unique in modern American verse. Scattered throughout half a dozen collections, Sexton's earlier published poems on suicide are isolated, singly shaped attempts to convey the speaker's state of mind during suicidal depressions or suicidal highs. (**"The Death Baby"** sequence in *The Death Notebooks* is a partial exception, but it is not only, and not primarily, a suicide poem.) Although only three of the twenty-three poems in the "Letters to Dr. Y." sequence take suicide as their main subject, they represent the core of the speaker's "safe psychosis" throughout the series. Separated in time of composition by several years, and by position in the sequence by intervening poems, they form the nucleus of a case history that unfolds in ten years of "Letters." I will refer to the poems by date rather than title, since Sexton titles none of them.

"February 6, 1960" opens the sequence and sets the tone for the patient-poet's treatment by Dr. Y. Here Sexton speaks of the tiny internal voice that says, "Kill me." Between this suicide poem and the second one are ten poems that represent years of treatment. The intervening poems deal with poetry, word association, the speaker's mother's death, her relationship to Dr. Y., her religious quest. On **"June 6, 1967"** the voice resumes, this time as a grotesquely multiple chorus line: "What do the voices say?" Dr. Y. asks. The poem is her answer. Three years and six poems later, the series picks up the theme like a dropped stitch on **"May 5, 1970,"** with "What are the leaves saying?" Like *Live or Die,* the sequence ends with the decision to live, with the safe psychosis "broken;" the speaker is "happy today with the sheets of life," hung out on the line to dry with "all the oxygen in the world" in their windy lift and slap, just as she was happy with the new Dalmation puppies and the "excitable gift" of sun in *Live or Die*'s **"Live."** But the therapeutically successful shape of the "Letters" sequence—Sexton certainly intended a progress from sickness toward cure—is not my main subject here. I am concerned with the hard core of suicide poems at their conceptual center, through which, with references to others of her poems, I want to suggest two related hypotheses about Sexton that might have wide application: the connection of the death wish to a specifically feminine desire for power and control; and deeper still, an ironic relationship of the death wish to a protest against human mortality.

II

Green Girls and Santa Claus: Death Is a Woman, Death Is a Man

In the first Dr. Y. poem, the speaker begins by telling her doctor she needs his "Rescue Inc. voice" to keep her from "going underfoot" and "growing as stiff as a yardstick." The emotional situation she goes on to describe is indeed desperate; while the first stanza speaks to Dr. Y., the following ones make Dr. Y. privy to another private conversation, that between the patient and death:

> Death,
> I need your hot breath,
> my index finger in the flame,
> two cretins standing at my ears,
> listening for the cop car.

The speaker recognizes her "need," and conveys it in images that might make it familiar to a reader not personally acquainted with the desire to die. Who has

not played with an index finger in the flame? Who will not recognize that urge, in perfectly "normal" people, if not in oneself? Who has not known the fear of (and wish for) getting caught—if not at suicide, then at some slighter self-destruction?

> Death,
> I need a little cradle
> to carry me out . . .
> and no kiss
> on my kiss.

Sexton would later more fully explore the relationship between death and infancy in **"The Death Baby"** sequence of *The Death Notebooks.* In the **"March 14, 1964"** poem of the Dr. Y. sequence, she extends the connection between infancy and death in stanzas dealing with her mother's death from cancer. Her mother becomes deformed in her illness, and the speaker, bending over her bed, imagines her physical transformation as the "ugliness" of a new baby, "growing back to your first skull."

> A baby just lies there
> having come from its bath;
> lies there getting used to being outside the bath,
> lies there getting used to being outside of something,
> while you, death-child, lie fitfully
> waiting to go inside.

"No kiss on my kiss" may refer to the guilt and lovelessness that is likely to be the suicide's internalized legacy, even if she has been worthy and lovable in others' eyes. But perhaps "no kiss" is also of positive worth; the speaker may be weary of the kiss, the human touch that binds her to this world.

The final stanza of the first letter recalls Sexton's best translation of the language of the suicide in **"Wanting to Die"** (*Live or Die*). After acknowledging that she needs "my little addiction to you," she brings the force of that need to bear in a single, startling image:

> I need that tiny voice who,
> even as I rise from the sea,
> all woman, all there,
> says kill me, kill me.

Where does that voice come from? In later Dr. Y. poems, she will speak of other voices within, those of her "green girls," the homunculi in her soul. But here the voice is singular, and it says enough: a beautiful woman comes out of the sea, alive in every respect, risen from the source of all life. Probably she is smiling. Perhaps she is speaking to her children, her friends. The sun is shining. But behind her smile, the killer's voice speaks, just as much herself as this healthy creature rising from the waves. Here, as in **"Wanting to Die,"** her strategy suggests a reader or hearer who will not immediately comprehend, for whom this is foreign and frightening territory, and to whom she can only hope to translate. She is trying with considerable restraint to explain the suicide's passion, and the vehicle, as it often is for Sexton, is sexuality:

> To die whole,
> riddled with nothing
> but desire for it,
> is like breakfast
> after love.

In **"Wanting to Die,"** Sexton tried similarly to shock the reader into understanding, and to make unfailingly clear that the desire to die is erotically charged with life. In the earlier poem, the desire to die is an "unnameable lust," a "passion." Here the sexual allusions are more specific. Both poems attempt to make understandable the innocence of such a passion as well as its corruption, its purity as well as its infectedness. "Breakfast after love" suggests nurture and conversation following sexual release, perhaps the comfort of plumped pillows and folded coverlets. If this image conflicts grotesquely with a normal person's sense of what it must be like to die, so much the better. It is not, she tells us, what we would have it. It certainly is as awful, but we know that. The news, to readers anxious to divorce such urges from normality, is the sense of "wholeness" death promises. This conviction or desperate hope that the moment of death will coincide with a moment of wholeness is one Sexton returned to repeatedly to convey her predicament.

"June 6, 1967" begins with a question from the analyst: "What do the voices say? Dr. Y. asks." The poem consists of her answer, broken into five voices: leaves, rock, white clown, razor, whip. They are, she says, "as real as books." They tell her, while she is doing normal daily activities—this time eating soup, as last time rising from an ocean swim—that she is "on trial" every moment. The razor voice says, "Have you ever thought, my single one, / that your hands are thorns to be cut to the quick?" The razor's "language" is, appropriately, "a thin whine." While this is the only suicidal reference to razors in Sexton's poetry, the whip is a more familiar image: "You have seen my father whip me. / You have seen me stroke my father's whip" (**"The Death Baby,"** *The Death Notebooks*). Like many suicides, and especially women, Sexton both meant and did not mean every attempt. The shape of **"June 6, 1967"** suggests that not all of her suicidal voices are equally lethal. The whip is the fifth and final voice, emblem of father-daughter sexuality, of pain as pleasure, of psychic obliteration, but not quite of death. "I will mark you all over with little red fish. / You will be almost killed, a delight."

But the male voice is not always less lethal than the female. Voices number one and two illuminate a mystery rooted in paradox. Voice number one is the leaves: "I am forty young girls in green shells. / Come out of your house and come unto me . . ." The leaves are always very feminine girls who speak with sisterly seductiveness to the speaker. But voice number two, "the rock in front of your window" who tells her to "choke on me," is male, a "sword blade," a "Mr. Gobblegook."

Examined in concert with the last suicide poem in the Dr. Y. sequence, **"May 5, 1970,"** and several other poems in Sexton's canon, the voices of **"June 6, 1967"** present a clearly gendered imaging of death. Anne Sexton seems to have been well aware of this characteristic of her suicidal urges, and to have used it consciously in her poetry. In a 1964 letter to a friend who was also an analyst, Sexton reported on a particularly fruitful session with her own therapist, something she did not ordinarily do in letters: "When (to me) death takes you and puts you through the wringer, it's a man. But when you kill yourself, it's a woman." Suicide becomes a way of claiming power when she feels most powerless. "I guess I see it as a way of cheating death" (*Letters* [*Anne Sexton: A Self-Portrait in Letters*] 231). How this dismally ironic version of feminine power could make psychic sense becomes clearer in the **"May 5, 1970"** letter to Dr. Y.

"What do the leaves remind you of?" asks Dr. Y., and the speaker answers, "Green, Green!" In a poetic parallel for the technique of free association in analysis, the speaker answers at length when the analyst next asks, "What does green remind you of?" Our culture's collective connotations for green, and any reader's own personal associations, function as an unarticulated subtext: fertility, growth, grass, trees, perhaps money, jealousy. The speaker's list of associations includes both tonally negative and positive objects and feelings, but the negatives are overwhelming—green reminds her of a fisherman, for instance, but with "green fruit in his net." Thus no associations with benignly rich fertility here, and a surfeit of "slime pools" and "drunks vomiting." While "night baseball games" and "Lake Como" sneak into the list, the tally is still startlingly unbalanced. At the end of the list she says, "But those are painted colors. Only the leaves are human."

With this statement she introduces those associations most speakers would have articulated in the first place, images of fertility and life, but for her tainted always with death.

> They are girls. Green girls.
> Death and life is their daily work.
> Death seams up and down the leaf.
> I call the leaves my death girls.
> The death girls turn at the raggedy edge
> and swim another length down the veins
> to the raggedy heart.

English poetry has often associated fertility with mutability—"beauty that must die"—but this speaker turns the worm subtly. She calls the leaf voices "girls," not women, emphasizing their youth, and thus, one would think, their liveliness. But having connected them briefly to the obvious—fertility, life—she associates the rest of the description with a specifically feminine death. It is difficult to fear the death girls, as one is accustomed to fear and loathe standard images of death in western culture—the skeletal old man, the shrouded figure with scythe, even the sexually mature and seductive woman. Sexton means to make the death girls appealing, and she succeeds. "And these death girls sing to you? . . . And does it excite you?" Vibrating now with the charge of erotic excitement, the poem moves toward explanation of the "canker-suicide high," the "sisterhood" she feels with the green girls. Returning to the wish for wholeness, she explains that she needs to be "laid out at last / under them, as straight as a pea pod":

> To die whole. To die as soft and young as a leaf.
> To lie down whole in that green god's belly.

So it is again in search of wholeness, of purity, of innocence, that the speaker leans toward death. Mythologizing a moment of childhood, she answers the analyst's next question, which amounts to "and how long have you felt like this?"

> When I was five I played under pines.
> Pines that were stiff and sturdy.
> . . . . .
> Dark green.
> A different order.
> A different sign.
> I was safe there at five under that stiff crotch.

In the earlier associations to "green," the speaker remembered "the back lawn I danced on when I was eight." Now she chooses, as emblematic of the moment she first wished to die, the psychically redolent age of five, that "fifth me," the ritual age at which western and post-Freudian culture fix the first end of innocence. That the ages between birth and five are some of our most troubled and least stable is equally appropriate: the "fifth me" alludes to the massive transformations conflated in those first years. Five is still the age at which our society imagines innocence on the trembling verge of disintegration, the age at which we fix the apex of one kind of wholeness succumbing to the burden of a disillusionment of grand proportions.

The speaker notes that the pines under which she played at age five were "stiff and sturdy," just as she said she needed to be laid out under the green girls, "straight as a pea pod." In images laden with sexuality, she makes for herself a "stiff crotch" under the pines of her memory, and lays herself out dead there—dead, but whole. The "stiff crotch" is clearly both womb and phal-

lus, both feminine and masculine. Sexton's speaker first experiences the wish to die "whole" at the very moment at which she will otherwise be forced to relinquish that imagined wholeness. But even though the images suggest a perfect balance of feminine and masculine nurture, of magical union with both parents caught at the last possible moment, this is a primarily feminine and maternal dreamscape. The leaves are always female, always sisters or mothers or images of the self.

As I read it, the poem takes place in the domain of the "phallic mother." I am using the term "phallic" here in the Lacanian rather than the Freudian sense, as an attribute of power associated with the father, but which, unlike the penis, belongs to neither father nor mother—nor to any speaking being. The phallus symbolizes the unmediated power and protection always lacking in real people, but thought by all of us to exist in the parental imagos of imagination. The mother imago's phallus is veiled behind and before the father's, and her power, thus hidden, is literally boundless. As Jane Gallop writes in *The Daughter's Seduction*, the phallus is "the subject presumed to know, the object of transference, the Phallic mother, in command of the mysterious processes of life, death, meaning, and identity" (*Daughter's* 115). In exactly this sense, the speaker of Sexton's poem lies in a crotch of stiff pines of "a different order" and "a different sign," where she is protected by an entity "in command of the mysterious processes of life, death, meaning, and identity." However masculine in tenor, this is still a feminine death, presided over by the mother's priestesses, those green girls whose business is not only life, but the "death that seams up and down the leaf."

"May 5, 1970" is so intimately connected to **"Leaves That Talk"** (*45 Mercy Street*) that they read as parts of one poem. In **"Leaves That Talk,"** the same green girls call out their death wish to the speaker: "Anne, Anne, come to us." Concentrating again on their veins, she is beguiled by their "woman apron lives" and their "brown stick branches." The speaker is subject to the voices even while she goes about the mundane, sensible business of daily life. "They call, though I sit here / sensibly behind my window screen."

> They want me. They need me.
> I belong lying down under them,
> letting the green coffin fold and unfold
> above me as I go out.

In a remarkably analytic stanza, the speaker tells us as nearly as she can who the green girls are. "It has a body. / It has many bodies." She muses upon the possibility that the green girls are her female forbears: "the generation of women, down the line, / the genealogical line right to the *Mayflower*. . . ." Unsure she is right, she concludes: "whoever my green girls are—they *are*."

She knows it is vital to discover their identities. She knows equally well that they are veiled, may be veiled from her all her life, speaking to her from behind shrouds that obscure their faces.

But the dramatis personae of death for Sexton are not only or always female, even if always familial. In **"Leaves That Talk,"** she parades her pantheon of family ghosts, especially the male aspect of death represented by her grandfather, an infrequent but important visitor to her dream-thoughts. If the green girls sing to her over the common music of life like a "dream in a dream," it is in an equally dream-like state that she is "having a love affair / with grandfather," who "touches my neck and breast." This unnatural affair, this betrayal of the feminine conspiracy, causes the leaves to fall off, "clank, clank, / crashing down like stones, New England / stones, one by one . . ." A chorus of outraged pain issues from them: "There are one hundred thousand woman cries, / tree by tree. . . ."

No other such naked confrontation between male and female versions of death occurs in Sexton's poetry. It might seem that the male principle here, represented by the grandfather who tells her "Do not be afraid! It's only the leaves falling!" exerts a force of life in opposition to the feminine force of death, and in one respect, that may be true. Grandfather is, after all, making love to her, driving off and offending the green death women, causing the speaker to "scream out in my fear / that my green ladies are leaving, / my lovely obsessions, / and I need them." But for what is grandfather saving her from them? For life, for health? Perhaps. Just as likely, he saves her from the death women in order to claim her for himself. His incestuous love would weave her more tightly into the cyclonic neurosis of patriarchal romance, the pattern for which is woman as victimized daughter. My reading is that while grandfather temporarily represents a life force in opposition to the death the green girls offer, it is a fragmented and obliterated self he offers, a replication of herself as her grandmother, whereas, to her diseased imagination, the green girls call to her to be whole, to be herself. (When death puts you through the wringer, it's a man. When you do it yourself, it's a woman.)

In the **"May 30th"** poem of the **"Scorpio, Bad Spider, Die"** sequence in *Words for Dr. Y.,* Sexton identifies death with her father, indirectly but completely. The speaker addresses God: "Don't look now, God, we're all right. / All the suicides are eating Black Bean Soup." Her family is happy, even the dog. The poem ends with another plea:

> Please God, we're all right here. Please leave us alone.
> Don't send death in his fat red suit and his ho-ho
>   baritone.

Death as Santa Claus? In **"Santa"** (*The Book of Folly*), she remembers her dead father's Santa impersonations, telling him that the Santa Claus suit he bought before she was born is "dead," even though she can still hear him "all the time laughing that North Pole laugh." As a child, she once smelled liquor on him: "The year I ceased to believe in you / is the year you were drunk." Playing Santa was over for the rest of her own childhood, to be resumed for her own children. When the speaker was a child, "Mother would kiss you / for she was that tall." Years later, "We were conspirators, / secret actors, / and I kissed you / because I was tall enough." She has grown from daughter into wife, just as in **"May 30th"** she is her grandfather's lover. "Death in his fat red suit and ho-ho baritone" *is* her dear and dead father.

"For Mr. Death Who Stands With His Door Open" (*The Death Notebooks*) conflates nearly all of Sexton's personalized images of death as a familiar male. Contrasting time, here feminine, and death, masculine, she creates the dramatic conceit of a lifelong romance between herself and Mr. Death, faceless and yet many-faced. Mr. Death destroys time, "old gal of mine," who was once "all goggle-eyed, / wiggling her skirts, singing her torch song." As time grows short she remembers it young: "May I say how young she was back then, / playing piggley-witch and hoola-hoop." Evoking an oceanic myth of feminine nurture, as she does frequently from the *Death Notebooks* on, she remembers that when time was young, "the sea washed me daily in its delicate brine."

> Time was when I could hiccup and hold my breath
> and not in that instant meet Mr. Death.

But Mr. Death has been coming to her for many years as the poem opens. He is an actor with "many masks." Envisioning him first as "a kind of Valentino / with my father's bathtub gin in your flask," he is next a death camp manager who "held out the bait" for her suicide attempt. Now he is no longer the slim suitor, having aged as she has. "Your beer belly hangs out like Fatso. You are popping your buttons and expelling gas." Razzing him as one might a familiar old boy-friend, she asks, "How can I lie down with you, my comical beau / when you are so middle-aged and lower class." Yet she knows she must lie down with him, that he will "press me down in your envelope." Ironical and comical or not, the romance is still alive, as it must be until she is dead. So she will play the courtship with death to the hilt, as she has played life. She would have her final death slow:

> let it be pantomime, this last peep show,
> so that I may squat at the edge trying on
> my black necessary trousseau.

Knowing that at last she must marry this outrageous suitor, she savors the courtship for its comic and dramatic potential.

"**Mr. Death**" is a distant enough figure to merit being called by his surname, but his familiar faces rescue him from the purely abstract. This is the death one may flirt with, even patronize, at least until the wedding night. Not so the incarnation of death as the My Lai soldier in the 1969 untitled poem from the Dr. Y. sequence which begins with the speaker "dreaming the My Lai soldier again." The visitor at her door who first appears to be the Fuller Brush man "lowers me down with the other dead women and babies / saying, *It's my job. It's my job.*"

> I am lying in this belly of dead babies
> each one belching up the yellow gasses of death
> and their mothers tumble, eyeballs, knees, upon me,
> each for the last time, each authentically dead.
> The soldier stands on a stepladder above us
> pointing his red penis right at me and saying,
> Don't take this personally.

Here it is again: the contrary of suicide, in which she takes control, in which she has the power, is murder at the hands of a man, death by unpredictable, undeserved accident, death horribly out of her own control. And this death is accomplished by sexual assault, both here and in "**The Death Baby,**" where angry dogs devour an infant: "They loved me until I was gone." It is more than accidental that this mental condition is divided along gender lines. In a world where women are less powerful, where a My Lai soldier *can* victimize women and babies, where it is primarily men who murder women and children, Sexton's gendered imaging of death is not so much shocking—though it is that—as predictably shared knowledge, likely to be understood by a woman.

Unfortunately for this poet who spent the last decade of her life in search of an adequate god, death-as-a-man is ultimately God. However she may have sought his mercy in *The Awful Rowing toward God,* the deity in whom she believed was not one of love and forgiveness, but of judgment, bodily arbitrariness, abstract male principle. In "**Hurry up Please It's Time,**" (*The Death Notebooks*), the "power in the Lord" is a symbol of complete victimization for the penitent believer. "One noon as you walk out to the mailbox / He'll snatch you up—/ a woman beside the road like a red mitten." The only way Anne Sexton thought she could escape her legacy of powerlessness in a world presided over by this God was to kill herself before He could.

In *Women and Madness,* Chesler described the difficulty of suicide for women.

> Women are conditioned to experience *physicality*—be it violent, destructive or pleasurable—more in the presence of another, or at male hands, than alone or at their own female hands. Female suicide attempts are not so much realistic "calls for help" or hostile inconveniencing of others as they are the assigned baring of the powerless throat, signals of ritual readiness for self-sacrifice. Like female tears, female suicide attempts constitute an essential act of resignation and helplessness—which alone can command temporary relief or secondary rewards. Suicide *attempts* are the grand rites of 'femininity'—i.e., ideally women are supposed to 'lose' in order to 'win.' Women who *succeed* at suicide are, tragically, outwitting or rejecting their 'feminine' role, and at the only price possible: their death.

While Anne Sexton's personality and circumstances differed immeasurably from those of most of the victimized women in Chesler's study, she shared with most suicidal women a complexly ironic version of this uniquely feminine tragedy.

THE END OF FEAR AND THE FEAR OF DYING

While I think it is true that Anne Sexton's position as a woman contributed to both her illness and her death, I do not want to feminize away, or politicize into resolution, a situation so clearly and fundamentally beyond either gender or politics. Although the particular form of self-loathing she experienced was deeply and enduringly connected to her gender and her sexuality, the desire to die transcends sexual coinage. The tortuous web of psychic processes that ironically led her to perceive self-inflicted death as a way of claiming power as a woman against the overwhelmingly masculine adversary, death inflicted from outside the self, is only one component of her urge to die.

The central paradox of Sexton's suicide poems is the probability that the poems, and the act which ended them, were directed as much against mortality as against life. Sexton spoke of this only once in her letters, to Brian Sweeney in 1970: "You are so right about my fear of death. I think I have embraced it only because I feared it so" (*Letters* 368). And only once did she voice the thought undisguised in her poetry, in two slight lines from "**The Death King**" in *Words for Dr. Y.*:

> Death will be the end of fear
> and the fear of dying.

These two quotations crystallize the paradox that seems irreconcilable. Anne Sexton was a joyful poet who wrote witty fairy tales, who spoke with such authority about delight that we know her to have experienced it intensely, whose metaphors rose as often from limitless capacity to love and enjoy as from limitless capacity to suffer and to revel in suffering. How could one so open to life, so clearly in love with energy and vitality, choose to kill herself? What sense can it make to kill yourself because you fear death, or because you are angry at mortality?

Ernest Becker contends that if we were in constant touch with the truth of our mortality, we would be terrified every waking and sleeping moment. The terror of death is "all-consuming" to the human animal when he or she looks it full in the face. Repression of this fear "takes care of the complex symbol of death for most people" (620). But certainly there must be some people—and Anne Sexton was among them—who never do accomplish the great human task of primary repression of death, who never thicken their skins enough to block out the anguish of constant awareness. The greatest number of us expend considerable energy in order to avoid thinking about it except in fleeting flashes or in abstract terms. Writing this constitutes a safely abstract way for me to think about it, for instance.

But it is not only an awareness of the power of death that we must avoid. Most people are equally unable to experience life fully. We are collectively nostalgic about the wondrous sense of life commonly experienced in childhood, but that very sense of wonder would be impossible to sustain. We need to diminish it through repression if we are to function at all. Becker hypothesizes that by the time we leave childhood, we have successfully "repressed our vision of the primary miraculousness of creation:"

> . . . We change these heavily emotional perceptions precisely because we need to move about in the world with some kind of equanimity, some kind of strength and directness; we can't keep gaping with our heart in our mouth, greedily sucking up with our eyes everything great and powerful that strikes us. The great boon of repression is that it makes it possible to live decisively in an overwhelmingly miraculous and incomprehensible world. . . .
>
> (50)

It is just this kind of emotional equanimity that Anne Sexton seems never to have experienced, except in brief moments of her life. She was "gaping with her heart in her mouth" daily, sometimes hourly, absolutely filled with a sense of the "miraculous and incomprehensible." This is why she is so effective as a poet of childhood; her child speakers feel immediate and immanent and real because they are, because Anne Sexton never did repress the primary miraculousness of creation—nor the primary terror. In the course of normal development, the child represses both the consciousness of death and the surfeit of life, so that the human animal is characterized by the "two great fears" we believe other animals are protected from: the fear of life and the fear of death. Anne Sexton was, I think, protected from neither. As Erica Jong put it shortly after Sexton's death, Sexton simply had no skin (63).[2] For such a one, suicide might be a daily possibility. Life might always seem too much to live through, with no definite end in sight—even if, or especially if, that end were what one found most unthinkable in the face of the fierce daily miracle.

We can turn almost anywhere in Sexton's canon and find evidence of her anger against mortality, the fear of death that is sister to the desire. In **"The Fury of**

Sunrises"** (*The Death Notebooks*), the speaker travels literally from darkness to light, from night to day, in an anxious chant for life:

> After the death,
> after the black of black,
> this lightness—
> not to die, not to die—
> that God begot.

It is in large part *because* she so delights in life, is so consumed by its abundant beauty, that she mourns the necessity of death, and seeks it out of time. It is significantly the deaths of others, of "all her pretty ones," that are unbearable, and the sense of their loss suffuses almost every volume of Sexton's poetry. Her own death seems sometimes to be the penance she must pay for the fact of death in her universe. In a 1966 letter to Lois Ames, Sexton speaks of "the old need to die, and how it returns under any stress. An old command of my mother's" (*Letters* 298). Death is always her fault, and she is willing to pay with her life. But she would rather not. She would like everyone to live forever. **"Yellow,"** a 1972 poem published in *Words for Dr. Y.,* shares with **"The Fury of Sunrises"** the central image of unfolding light:

> there will be no poison anywhere, no plague
> in the sky and there will be a mother-broth
> for all of the people and we will
> never die, not one of us, we'll go on
> won't we?

"Won't we?" is childishly poignant, and also maturely ironic. She knows, of course, that we won't.

If the desire for immortality, if infinite sadness at the prospect of death, is finally what her death-wish is about, if it is a protest against our being what Becker calls "Gods with anuses" or "worms that think," then we can indeed fault her for childishness, whining, egomania. We can accuse Anne Sexton of an insufficient tolerance for the way things are, an inability gracefully to accept mortality. Certainly we can. But do we not, almost all of us, share this protest? Need someone to externalize it, to give voice to that part of us which feels this anguish? So that we can get on with the living that, however troubled it may be, is what we want to do? Forever?[3]

Notes

1. Linda Gray Sexton, editorial note for Anne Sexton, *Words for Dr. Y* (v). Unless otherwise noted, all Sexton citations are from *The Collected Poems.*

2. "Anne Sexton sometimes seemed like a woman without skin." Jong also writes that "she had no numbness at all," so that "all the little denials, all the stratagems of non-feeling by which most of us endure from minute to minute were unavailable to her."

3. My thanks to Richard Lehnert for the "opposition" that Blake said constitutes "true friendship."

Works Cited

Becker, Ernest. *The Denial of Death.* New York: The Free Press, 1973.

Chesler, Phyllis. *Women and Madness.* New York: Avon Books, 1973.

Gallop, Jane. *The Daughter's Seduction: Feminism and Psychoanalysis.* Ithaca: Cornell UP, 1982.

Jong, Erica. "Remembering Anne Sexton." *New York Times Book Review,* (October 27, 1974): 63.

Kevles, B. "Anne Sexton: The Art of Poetry." *The Paris Review* 13, (1971): 184-185.

Sexton, Anne. *The Collected Poems.* Boston: Houghton Mifflin, 1981.

———. *Words for Dr. Y.* Boston: Houghton Mifflin, 1976.

Sexton, Linda Gray and Lois Ames, eds. *Anne Sexton: A Self-Portrait in Letters.* Boston: Houghton Mifflin, 1977.

Diana Hume George (essay date 1986)

SOURCE: George, Diana Hume. "'How We Danced': Anne Sexton on Fathers and Daughters." In *Anne Sexton: Telling the Tale,* edited by Steven E. Colburn, pp. 411-36. Ann Arbor: University of Michigan Press, 1988.

[*In the following essay, originally published in 1986, George analyzes the father-daughter motif in Sexton's poetry.*]

"Love Grew Rings around Me": With Father in Bedlam

In ***To Bedlam and Part Way Back,*** Anne Sexton began composing the mythopoeic music of the father-daughter dance, which echoes now as a swan song for her poetic and personal lives. "We bent together like two lonely swans," she later wrote in **"How We Danced,"** a central poem in "The Death of the Fathers" sequence in ***The Book of Folly.*** The father-daughter motif is equalled in resonance and poignance in Sexton's canon only by the mother-daughter relationship, and for similar reasons: Sexton saw the nuclear family as the microcosmic analogue of the social and psychic structure of her culture. What began as a poetic journeying into the "narrow diary of my mind" became first "more than myself" in relation to people she knew and loved. "It was you, or your house / or your kitchen." But even very early, in **"For John, Who Begs Me Not to Enquire Further,"** "you" widens to include a fully peopled world: "your fear is anyone's fear. . . ."

Sexton's ablest critics have located the shift from personal to "transpersonal" or "cultural" in Sexton's work in her fourth volume, ***Transformations.***[1] While I agree that in ***Transformations*** such a shift is mythically embodied and newly garbed, there is within the "narrow diary" of even the early poems a structural outline for the psychic biography of a gender, and particularly for what Phyllis Chesler calls "woman's 'dependent' and 'incestuous' personality" in relation to her father[2]—a pattern long known to and exploited by psychoanalysis, to the degree that therapeutic method colludes with patriarchy. If Anne Sexton learned about her own incestuous dependencies from Freud and his proxies during the early stages of her life as a career mental patient, hers was still the first contemporary voice outside of the psychoanalytic world to describe the normative relationship between father and daughter from the daughter's perspective.[3] Sexton's early poetry both represents and dissects the subtle and pervasive psycho-social pattern that Phyllis Chesler would later discuss, and damn, in *Women and Madness,* and which now, in the wake of feminist inquiry, seems almost obvious: "romantic" love in the western world is "psychologically predicated on sexual union between Daughter and Father figures."

The "normal" woman in western society, whether or not she is a poet, and whether or not she is fully aware of the psychic dynamics, falls in love with her father, who delights her, despises her, seduces her, betrays her, and dies. The father who dies in 1959 in the poet's personal life undergoes a series of resurrections as man and imago—husband, doctor, lover, priest—and is finally reborn as the deity of *The Awful Rowing toward God.* Burial and resurrection of the fathers becomes a central theme in Sexton's poetry, as it is in the personal lives of her contemporaries and the collective life of her culture. In all of his incarnations in Sexton's poetry, the father finally fails himself and his daughter, for he is a god not sufficiently omnipotent, a man not sufficiently human, a male principle not sufficiently able to accommodate feminine powers and desires. But this ultimate failure is never judged harshly in Sexton's poetry, never evoked without the empathy that always accompanies insight; for the shortcomings of the father-god in a patriarchy are nearly definitive of the failures of the human enterprise, one in which all men and all women engage. This is not to say that Sexton's poetry lacks anger, or what Blake called "prophetic wrath": that is quite another matter. (In her personal life, Sexton seems to have saved her wrath for herself, a wrath "prophetic" only in the most mundane sense; that, too, is another matter.) In the world of Sexton's poetry, the men born into their myths are often as helpless and hapless as the women born into theirs; Sexton was inclined to portray the sad worthiness of all human effort, however doomed. Although she saw, reluctantly, the relentless "gender of things," her poetic eye was androgynously kind. (Too kind? Again, another matter.)

To Bedlam and Part Way Back lays the foundation for Sexton's version, or inversion, of Freud's *Totem and Taboo,* in which the father in the family evolves into the defiled and then worshipped God. Five poems in *Bedlam* establish the father figure as god, doctor, and cultural myth, as well as biological parent and great-grandparent. The collection opens with **"You, Doctor Martin,"** which immediately establishes the therapist as modern mediator between the religious and the familial. He is the confessor who is the "god of our block," the father of all the "large . . . foxy children" who inhabit Bedlam.

"You, Doctor Martin, walk / from breakfast to madness." The speaker, a patient in a mental institution, narrates both from within and outside of her own madness. Mad enough to be among the "moving dead," mad enough to be "queen of this summer hotel," mad enough to "make moccasins all morning," she is sane enough to look at the anatomy of her relationship to her confessor with insightful equanimity: "Of course, I love you." That calm awareness of psychic process (specifically, of the clinical phenomenon of transference) does not stop her from being "mad," nor does the madness inhibit her clear-sighted analytic knowledge. The speaker knows that the patient always "loves" the doctor, the sinner always loves the confessor, the daughter always loves the father. Speaking out of her own awareness of individual pain and comfort, the narrator is nevertheless detached enough to see exactly how that individual situation is an enactment of a paradigmatic drama, in which she plays her inevitable role of the crazy daughter in a scenario with the grown-up father-doctor whose very business is the eminently sane management of madness. He is the "god of our block, prince of all the foxes."

> . . . Your third eye
> moves among us and lights the separate boxes
>   where we sleep or cry.
>
>   What large children we are
> here. All over I grow most tall
> in the best ward. Your business is people,
>   you call at the madhouse, an oracular
>   eye in our nest. . . .
>
>   . . . You twist in the pull
> of the foxy children who fall
>
> like floods of life in frost.

Although the speaker talks of the doctor's third eye, she gazes from her own third eye, painfully and sanely aware of the psychic dynamics she and her fellow

inmates play out. She ironically and consciously regards the doctor as both god and father, herself as queen and daughter. His "third eye" is "oracular," prophetic and all-knowing, for it has, godlike, known all the separate sins of his patients. With his third eye he is able to "light" their separateness, illumine their pain, comfort merely by his presence. But he is also only human, a man attending to his "business": treating sick people. He is not, after all, one of them, for he only "calls at the madhouse" after his breakfast. With her own third eye, the speaker sees that they have all become his children, whom he can leave only by extricating himself from their desperate and clever grasps. The third eye is the doctor's blessing, his ability to see and to cope, but it is also his curse; perhaps the speaker-poet's own third eye is her blessing and curse as well, for when the father-god has gone, the patients become "magic talking to itself, / noisy and alone." When the magic of therapy departs, leaving only the magic of madness, the speaker turns her third eye toward what we might call "vision," toward the magic of the poem. The poem she writes is a hymn of praise to her doctor, the daughter-patient's version of Donne's "Hymn to God My God, in My Sickness." As Donne is Adam, Sexton's speaker is Eve, both paying tribute to their gods, both supplicants who ask: "Receive me, Lord."

"You, Doctor Martin," serves as frontispiece not only for the theme of madness, but for the further explorations of the father-daughter relationship in this first volume, one that ends with an extended discussion of the other and feminine source of the self—what Sexton will later call, in **"Old Dwarf Heart,"** the "mother, father, I'm made of." During the transference process of psychoanalysis, the therapist *becomes* in his person a condensation of all the images of the mind; although, ideally, he will "become" mother as well as father, his gender and the patriarchal nature of the process identify him most clearly with the gods and fathers, rather than the goddesses and mothers, of one's memory. The tightly condensed father-god figure of **"You, Doctor Martin"** fragments into his component parts in subsequent poems of *Bedlam,* becoming father, great-grandfather, Apollo, and, in a transcultural and quasi-mythic incarnation, a dead Arabian father buried with his daughter.

"MOTHER, FATHER, I'M MADE OF": *ALL MY PRETTY ONES* AND *LIVE OR DIE*

Sexton's second collection, **All My Pretty Ones,** takes place in an ever-present past, in the "deep museum" of entombed memory carved with words into a monument of the living dead. Here, perhaps more deliberately than in any other single volume of Sexton's poetry, the ambiguity of inheritance is the single strongest issue. The "frozen sea within us," Sexton knew, is always iced by consciousness, which keeps us from the depths of both pain and pleasure that arise from breaking the surface and plunging into the past that actually creates the present. The poems are not restricted to the speaker's personal losses, but range instead into poignant portraits of unknown people, unknown lives (**"Doors, Doors, Doors"**), lives that never were (**"The Abortion"**); and they reach from the sacred to the profane with the ease that will more and more character-ize Sexton's religious quest. The "mother, father, I'm made of" is the mother and father we are all made of, in which the concept of deity resides. So profoundly did Anne Sexton believe that family relationships are the foundation of all tragedy, all joy, that even God's plight is best understood through his son.

The second section of **All My Pretty Ones** is preceded by a Guardini epigraph: "I want no pallid humanitarian-ism—If Christ be not God, I want none of him; I will hack my way through existence alone." In this section, Sexton explores this other and related betrayal: that God is, after all, only the mortal father whose child inherits his weakness, which ends in her own death. The grandfather enters as mediator of this process in the final poem of the volume, **"Letter Written During a January Northeaster,"** in which the speaker is alone, awaiting a lover's letters that never come. The poem begins on a Monday, with snow falling upon "the small faces of the dead," in particular the mother and father. Divided into six days, the poem is an elaborate pretense: "I have invented a lie. / There is no other day but Monday." By this narrative device, the poet emphasizes the repetition enacted in time, the stasis underlying movement. The letters do not come.

> The mailman is an impostor.
> He is actually my grandfather.
> He floats far off in the storm
> with his nicotine mustache and a bagful of nickels.

Tenderly evoking the grandfather to whom Sexton dedicates the last section of poems in this volume, the speaker reveals the identity not only of the mailman, but of the letter, the word, as mediator between the present beloved (who is absent) and the past beloveds (who are dead). "Now he is gone / as you are gone." The grandfather, too, is dead; the lover is absent and in his absence as good as dead; and the mailman who should have brought the lovers together through the ef-ficacy of words has proved an imposter. But he, grandfather-mailman, "belongs to me like lost baggage." As the mailman recedes into the storm, so does the figure of that grandfather; unlike the mailman, and like the lover, he belongs to her in the same way that lost baggage still belongs to its owner. **"Letter"** establishes the virtual identifications of its imagined components: of one day with the next, of the present lost lover with the dead grandfather.

The identification of a woman's husband with her father remains implicit in the first two volumes, where it is hinted at, leapt beyond, or discussed at one remove through mythology, anthropology, or the buffer of an extra generation. In **Live or Die,** Sexton's third volume, that identification is made explicit for the first time. The speaker's father was "a born salesman" who sold wool, and a born talker "in love with maps," who "died on the road." Her husband also sells wool, also travels on the road:

> And when you drive off, my darling,
> Yes, sir! Yes, sir! It's one for my dame,
> your sample cases branded with my father's name,
> your itinerary open,
> its tolls ticking and greedy,
> its highways built up like new loves, raw and speedy.

This is a world where women stand and wait—"I sit at my desk / each night with no place to go"—while men explore and conquer, "greedy" for the open road and all it represents: freedom, independence, possession, the familiarly "raw and speedy" litany. The salesman father and husband of Sexton's real life symbolize a cultural axiom she would later explain in **Transformations,** where the fairy tale world is one of masculine and feminine principles meeting and conflicting. The man brings home "one for his dame," who sits and waits while he conquers a world in which the highway inflicted on the countryside is the equivalent of the penis entering the body of nature—always a woman's body. The "new loves" allude to the infidelity inherent not only literally in the salesman's life, but figuratively in the desertion of the wife or daughter for that new love, the road that is always open, offering adventure.

In **"Cripples and Other Stories,"** the father emerges as doctor once again, taking up where he left off in **Bedlam.** Responding to his laughter at a "silly rhyme" she wrote for him (*"Each time I give lectures / or gather in the grants / you send me off to boarding school / in training pants"*), she insists in sing-song rhyme that he and she both look at the facts:

> God damn it, father-doctor.
> I'm really thirty-six.
> I see dead rats in the toilet.
> I'm one of the lunatics.

The poem moves through childhood rituals that revolve around the speaker's mother and father. The child puts her hand through the wringer-washer. "My father took the crowbar / and broke that wringer's heart." Yet even if he was her champion here, he is usually indifferent, "fat on scotch" which "leaked from every orifice," or a "perfect man, / clean and rich and fat," intent only on making money and smoking cigars. The doctor is the father's surrogate, but unlike the father who "didn't know me," he responds on her behalf with tenderness instead of rage: "How strange that you're so tender!" At the end, she drops the "doctor" of the original address.

> Father, I'm thirty-six,
> yet I lie here in your crib.
> I'm getting born again, Adam.
> as you prod me with your rib.

The same process, that of rebirth through psychoanalytic therapy, of starting over and getting this time around a father who holds and kisses and is loving to her in her "fever," might be merely sentimental or silly if it were not for Sexton's choice of rhyme and meter. In carefully wrought tetrameter and trimeter lines, Sexton both exemplifies and parodies the process of therapy, through which the analysand becomes again a child responding to her parents. The process, and the poem, are thus tinged with a gentle, wry irony. Can it really work, this process? Phyllis Chesler asks the same question in *Women and Madness,* as part of her discussion of the infantilization of women in the therapeutic process:

> Can a technique based on transference, or on the resolution of an Oedipal conflict—i.e., on a romanticization of a rape-incest-procreative model of sexuality—wean women away from this very sexual model?[4]

The poet does not answer such polemical questions—that is not her role as she perceives it—but the tonal complexities of this "nursery rhyme" suggest her knowledge of the difficulties as well as the dynamics involved. Although I think we are meant to see the doctor's tenderness (he kisses and holds her in the poem) as properly humane rather than prurient in intent, there is something comically prurient in the very nature of the process as Sexton describes it: a grown woman first put in training pants by her doctor, then kept in a crib, and finally, in the regressive evolution of both the method and the poem, being reborn—all in the cadences of "This Little Piggy." And while I think Sexton's poem vindicates rather than damns the doctor's motivations, there is also no escaping the sexual overtones of the final line, in which the doctor, a new Adam, "prods" her with his "rib," corresponding neatly with Chesler's rape-incest-procreative description of psychoanalysis's *modus operandi.* This is particularly so since we are left with the image of a passive infant female being sexually assaulted (with whatever ostensibly benign motivation or effect) by an adult male doctor's prodding rib—or, in the illuminating vernacular, his hard cock.

It seems to me that Sexton neither endorses nor damns the method here, but merely subjects it to an interested and insightful scrutiny. The tone of the poem suggests that she is benefitting from this process of rebirth in which she reenacts a traumatic childhood "in your crib," and receives the love from the doctor that she was denied by his prototype, the father. The doctor may be able to bring to life the primal and potentially strong woman of the speaker's unconscious depths, and she accords him and his method this accession; but she is also suspicious, ironic, detached, a bit alarmed both at herself and at the method which seems to deny that she is "really thirty-six." Yet, thirty-six or not, if she sees "dead rats in the toilet," she needs help. And if her father is one of those dead rats, beyond either saving or damning her himself, then perhaps, she seems to say, she needs this second chance. She needs the mediation of the doctor as Father and Adam and God, in her effort to get the rats out of the toilet.

"WHAT VOYAGE THIS, LITTLE GIRL?": THE TRANSFORMATIONS OF DADDY

While the father of *Love Poems* is almost entirely subsumed by the lover's transmutation into the carpenter-god, he returns again in *Transformations* in differently transmuted form. The hearts of the passive princesses and daughters of *Transformations* are bonded as surely to the "mother, father, I'm made of," as are Sexton's early speakers. In **"Snow White," "Cinderella," "Red Riding Hood," "The Maiden without Hands," "The Twelve Dancing Princesses,"** and **"Briar Rose (Sleeping Beauty),"** fathers and mothers save or thwart or damn or damage or love or devour their mythic offspring in both literal and surrogate capacities. Most of the tales begin at home, with the heroes and heroines in domestic peril or at domestic peace; similarly, most of the tales end with either restoration or transformation of that domesticity. The lovers who marry the girls and women of most of the tales I mention are barely disguised fathers, protector figures who take their new wives home and live with them to dwell in infinitely protracted and infinitely patriarchal bliss. Because it most directly and sardonically addresses the subject, I will deal here with **"Briar Rose."**

In the Prologue, Sexton introduces us to a "little doll child":

> come here to Papa.
> Sit on my knee.
> I have kisses for the back of your neck.
> A penny for your thoughts, Princess.
> I will hunt them like an emerald.
> Come be my snooky
> and I will give you a root.

The tale Sexton has transformed here tells us only that the king dearly loved his child, and that because of this love and the fairy's curse, he overprotected her—a circumstance that, with or without a fairy's curse, is common enough to be normative in our culture. In her version of **"Briar Rose,"** Sexton plays out the effects of such smothering and overprotective love on the part of fathers for the "purity" and "safety" of their daughters—effects also sufficiently common to be normative. Briar Rose manages to get in trouble despite her father's obsessive restrictions on her activities; in due course, she pricks her finger on the spinning wheel and falls asleep. The prince who finally gets through the briars to wake her up gets a greeting not included in Grimm:

> He kissed Briar Rose
> and she woke up crying:
> Daddy! Daddy!

Since "Daddy" is the only man she has ever been permitted to know, the single source of love and safety, the prince is her daddy for life. The only hitch is that she has become an insomniac because of her fear of sleep—her long sleep was initiated, it is probably important to remember, by her father's omission of the proprieties; he did not propitiate the proper female deities by recognizing the thirteenth fairy. When Briar Rose sleeps, she returns to a kind of death-in-life. "You could lay her in a grave, . . . / and she'd never call back: Hello there!" Only the kiss can wake her when she gets this way, so the prince is forced to wake her always in a repetition of that initial awakening:

> But if you kissed her on the mouth
> her eyes would spring open
> and she'd call out: Daddy! Daddy!
> Presto!
> She's out of prison.

Permanently infantilized by her earlier relationship to an idolatrously loving father and a long and symbolic sleep in which no other men could come near her, she is never quite a woman, always a daughter, even to her husband.

In a rhetorical move uncharacteristic of the other "transformations" here, which have only prologues, Sexton appends an epilogue to the tale of Briar Rose. The identity of the speaker is ambiguous; because of an abrupt tone shift and a sudden change from third to first person, we cannot be sure if the "I" of the epilogue is Briar Rose or "Dame Sexton." The speaker tells us that "there was a theft," and "I was abandoned" and "forced backward." The closing of the poem also constitutes the end of the book:

> Each night I am nailed into place
> and I forget who I am.
> Daddy?
> That's another kind of prison.
> It's not the prince at all,
> but my father
> drunkenly bent over my bed,
> circling the abyss like a shark,
> my father thick upon me
> like some sleeping jellyfish.
> What voyage this, little girl?
> This coming out of prison?

> God help—
> this life after death?

The tone change is remarkably abrupt and complete. Throughout the tale Sexton has maintained that tongue-in-cheek tone so characteristic of *Transformations,* in which deadly serious matter is relieved by casual and sardonic wit. The seductive father of the prologue— "Come be my snooky / and I will give you a root"—is both doting daddy and dirty old man, and for him we are invited to feel an affectionately dismissive contempt. But the father of the prologue is a daylight daddy, a bringer of lollipops as well as that vaguely threatening "root." At only one moment does he appear truly sinister: "A penny for your thoughts, Princess. / I will hunt them like an emerald." But the father of the epilogue comes to the daughter at night, "circling the abyss like a shark." This is the flip side face of the daddy who bounces on the knee, just as this new perspective is the flip side of the daughter's irresistible seduction when she awakes: "Daddy!" If the body of the tale gives us the way in which the incestuous romance of father and daughter is carried *by the daughter* to her husband's bed, the epilogue is a sinister echo of the genesis of that behavior in the prologue. While Sexton, perhaps uncharacteristic of many contemporary women, is not afraid to acknowledge the daughter's part in the sexual drama of father and daughter, neither is she reticent to insist that the father share the blame— that, in fact, he be held responsible for its most exploitive and darkest form in the actual seduction or rape of daughters by their fathers.

We know from other sources that Anne Sexton was an insomniac and that her intensely ambivalent relationship to her father, Ralph Harvey, may have included such a "midnight visit," as she calls it elsewhere. In view of these circumstances and the internal evidence of the poem, I think it safe to say that the speaker of the final words in *Transformations* is a conflation of the mythical Briar Rose and the poet Anne Sexton. If the speaker of **"Mother and Jack and the Rain"** is also Sexton, we have both sides of a story Anne Sexton knew to be not only her own, but that of countless American women: fantasized seduction in which the daughter not only participates, but that she initiates in the close private recesses of her own bed and her own body, accompanied by actual seduction that becomes the source of lifelong trauma for the daughter. Of course the female child dreams of making love with her father, of bearing him a baby, of replacing her mother; and of course, when the father makes that dream come true, the daughter is betrayed. As Chesler says, in patriarchal society the father-daughter incest taboo is "*psychologically* obeyed by men and disobeyed by women." Although Chesler does not expand on this, I take her to mean something such as this: a female child, because of the stages of her psycho-social development, is nearly compelled to desire the father, while the male is not compelled to desire the daughter by that same process; rather, he will desire, and possibly find, the mother. But the *actual* disobedience of the taboo is usually initiated by the father, who is not only older, more powerful, and in a position of authority, but who is also—and this is probably crucial—a male member of a patriarchy. (The incidence of mother-son seduction is comparatively minor.) "What voyage this, little girl?" After the shark circles her in the dark, after the jellyfish is thick upon her, she will always awake crying, in more ways than one, "Daddy!"

"The Lost Signalman" and "The Train That Comes No More": The Death of the Fathers

Nothing for it but to put the father to death, and that is what Sexton does, mournfully and lovingly, in the sequence titled **"The Death of the Fathers"** in *The Book of Folly.* The death of the fathers marks the passage from innocence to experience. In **"Oysters,"** a simple seafood meal between father and daughter becomes her rite of passage into womanhood.

Through eating oysters for the first time—which despite or because of their source in the sea the speaker calls "father-food"—the speaker incorporates and conquers the sea in herself.

> Oysters we ate,
> sweet blue babies,
>   . . . . .
> It was a soft medicine
> that came from the sea into my mouth,
> moist and plump.
> I swallowed.

While the daughter makes her first attempts to get them down, her father laughs at her fear and drinks his martini, "clear as tears." This laughter, fatherly and benign, is tinged with friendly ridicule of her fear; but the clear tears of his martini reflect, perhaps, his own disguised sorrow at the ritual into which he knows he initiates his daughter. The challenge to her to eat something soft, moist, plump, and alien, which she must swallow in order to pass a test, hovers on the border between sensuality and sexuality; this might as easily be a description of fellatio as of eating oysters.

> Then I laughed and then we laughed
> and let me take note—
> there was a death,
> the death of childhood
> there at the Union Oyster House
> for I was fifteen
> and eating oysters
> and the child was defeated.
> The woman won.

The woman becomes she who devours and incorporates the sea-creature, the alien thing that is herself. It is particularly significant that the father, alone and without

the mother, escorts the speaker through this ritual while he drinks his martini, surely another father-food, surely another sexual signal. The laughter between them is canny; alone together, sans mother or siblings, father and daughter have their sweet and slightly wicked tête-a-tête. The unspoken understanding between them, one the poem itself articulates, is that the father has introduced his daughter not only to adulthood, but to the sexual ripeness of womanhood.

But this celebration of sexuality with the father, this triumph he shares with her, is also a defeat for him: **"Oysters"** marks one of his "deaths." By initiating her into womanhood, the father relinquishes his exclusive hold on her affections; and relinquishing the daughter-child status by which she has belonged only to him, she comes into her own. The event they celebrate together is his demise as the only lover in her life. Through this mediation from the sea, he hands her to her womanhood, and thereby to other men who will take his place.

In **"How We Danced,"** the dramatic situation is a family wedding. The speaker is nineteen, dancing with her father as man and woman rather than as father and daughter. They dance "like two birds on fire," and "we were dear, / very dear."

> Mother was a belle and danced with twenty men.
> You danced with me never saying a word.
> Instead the serpent spoke as you held me close.
> The serpent, that mocker, woke up and pressed against
>   me
> like a great god and we bent together
> like two lonely swans.

The mother in this Oedipal scenario is conveniently out of the way, dancing with other men as her husband and daughter perform a wedding dance that is both reflection and parody of the actual wedding. The serpent, the father's penis, speaks what he does not, disregards propriety and taboo, "mocking" both a cultural and a personal contract. His penis is like a god, because in the mythic world invoked here, incest is the paradigm, not the deviation. Together, irrevocably joined in their unspoken and by now implicitly mutual sin, father and daughter do not acknowledge what comes between them. Once again, something dies—this time, it is the swan-song of a fiction of sexless familial love, a demise that by the end of the poem compels the daughter's complicity. His "death" is his diminishment as "father," accompanied by his phoenixlike rebirth as the lover that he has always been, even if secretly, to his daughter. But the serpent is indeed a mocker, for the involuntary physical sign of his sexual desire constitutes a betrayal of his daughter *as daughter,* a betrayal of himself *as father.*

In **"Santa,"** the speaker remembers father dressing up as Santa Claus, another all-giving father, in the yearly Christmas scenario. Playing Santa is another in the series of lies that separates children from adults, the kindly lies that make mythology of family and sanity of familial madness. "But that is over." The daughter has replaced the mother, and now Father-Santa is dead.

> And you, you fade out of sight
> like a lost signalman
> wagging his lantern
> for the train that comes no more.

The father joins dead hands with the grandfather-mailman of **"Letter Written"** in *All My Pretty Ones.* The mailman with his "bagful of nickels" and the train signalman are both representatives of a life that is past, that passes even as it lives.

"The Death of the Fathers" marks a series of broken taboos through which the poet rejects, reclaims, is rejected by, reclaimed by, the fathers of her life. The deaths are plural because there are many small deaths before the large and literal one represented in the poet's life by Ralph Harvey's death in 1959; and the fathers are many because, as Sexton knew, her speaker claimed and rejected that paternal presence in many guises: father, grandfather, doctor, priest, God. I think Sexton also intended a double plurality of deaths and fathers to signify the culturally representative nature of her own biography; just as Ralph Harvey was not her only father, and just as he and his surrogates were to undergo many symbolic deaths in her life, there are many Annes among her readership, each with her own several fathers and multiple deaths.

"DIVORCING DADDY: DYBBUK! DYBBUK!": *45 MERCY STREET*

Sexton says her final published words on the father in **"Divorce, Thy Name Is Woman."** The speaker tries to break that archaic and infantile tie at last, by acknowledging the nature of the marriage bond with and the divorce from her husband.

> I am divorcing daddy—Dybbuk! Dybbuk!
> I have been doing it daily all my life
> since his sperm left him.

The speaker is all women who enact the paradigmatic relationship Sexton first explored in mythic terms in *To Bedlam and Part Way Back.* The dybbuk becomes a concretion of the mythic and the personal. The dybbuk, in medieval Jewish legend, may be either the spirit of a dead person who lives and speaks through a living human; or it may be a demon that possesses the living; here it is both. The spirit of the father is the spirit of the dear dead, whom the speaker always remembers as Macduff remembers his slain wife and children; but he is also the demon who possesses the living in order to dispossess her of herself. She addresses that paradox of the human condition: that we turn to the dead, to

memory, as individuals and as a culture, for our sense of identity and meaning; that we have no choice in this matter; that we piece together a sense of self out of the inheritance of family, enlarged into an inheritance of culture.

But at the same time that the legacy of the dead provides us with a raison d'être, and represents our own urge to propel ourselves into the future through the immortality of generations, it also represents the death-wish, the urge to annihilate oneself, to follow the dead to their stone graves. In a woman, the paradox is apparent in the relationship to the father who is succeeded by a reincarnation of himself in the husband. A woman may spend her life, in effect, divorcing and marrying her father. In this poem, Sexton constructs a kind of allegory for woman in western culture. The marriage of daughter to father is represented as literal.

> Later,
> when blood and eggs and breasts
> dropped onto me,
> Daddy and his whiskey breath
> made a long midnight visit
> in a dream that is not a dream
> and then called his lawyer quickly.
> Daddy divorcing me.

The "dream that is not a dream" is a psychic fact, a fact of mental life, something that "actually happens" in the netherland of unconscious primary process. The father seduces the daughter, then rejects her, disowning his own passion and hers. "I have been divorcing him ever since" in the interior world of psychic realities, where the Mother is her witness in the courtroom. The daughter keeps on divorcing him, "adding up the crimes / of how he came to me, / how he left me." Sexton's speaker takes on the voice of any woman working out her childhood love for her father, any woman still

> waiting, waiting for Daddy to come home
> and stuff me so full of our infected child
> that I turn invisible, but married,
> at last.

What Sexton speaks of here is as narrow as the room of each womb we come from, and as broad as our dedication to Classical culture. We are all implicated, fathers and daughters alike, all dwelling in a shadow world in which the realities we perceive are shadows of original forms—and of original desires. We stay in the cave willingly, perceiving reflected forms, because we cannot look upon those forms directly without becoming "invisible." Yet we seek that original form, the original desire, never quite content with its substitute.

While Sexton breaks this ultimate taboo, thereby acknowledging her self-effacement, her speaker also wants to affirm the divorce. The "solution" of the poem is a continual process of divorce, an unending courtroom scene, but one which always returns from courtroom to bedroom, where the woman is "opening and shutting the windows. Making the bed and pulling it apart." Before and after the divorce of man and wife is this continuous marriage to and divorce from the father, a permanent oscillation between two conflicting desires: to divorce and be done with; and to "marry, at last."

"THE ISLAND OF GOD": *THE DEATH NOTEBOOKS, THE AWFUL ROWING*

Although the father is entirely absent from *The Awful Rowing toward God* as a literal and familial presence, this entire collection has been accurately described by critics as a monument to Anne Sexton's need for a God who is the embodiment of paternal authority, absolutism, absolution; a God who will punish the "gnawing pestilential rat" inside of her, and then "take it with his two hands / and embrace it" (**"Rowing"**); a God who will finally guarantee her that immortality will be replication, eternal and writ large, of a perfected and idealized family circle in which she will at last win the love and acceptance and protection and approval denied her by her parents. This heavenly family will be presided over by a benevolent but exacting Papa who will drink mana instead of whiskey, punish her justly instead of capriciously, love her unconditionally instead of sporadically. Maxine Kumin calls this God of Sexton's deepest desires "a sure thing, an Old Testament avenger admonishing his Chosen People, an authoritarian yet forgiving Father decked out in sacrament and ceremony."[5] To Alicia Ostriker, the poet's attempt to "give imaginative birth to an adequate Godhead" becomes a "heroic failure," because the "decisive intelligence which dismantles religious myth is no match for the child-woman's ferocious need for cosmic love."[6] Estella Lauter finds that the "essential drama of her work in these years [1970-1974] lies in her repeated discoveries of the Father-God's inadequacy coupled with her inability to give Him up."[7]

Before I cluck too sympathetically or patronizingly at the pathetic end of Anne Sexton's quest for the Father, I must remind myself of two equally important facts, one about Anne Sexton, one about the culture of which she is both member and visionary spokesperson. First, and most humbling, is that Sexton's search for the traditional Father-God in dozens of poems that may be failures in the feminist sense—as Ostriker says, she "accepts humiliation on behalf of all beautiful women"—is an eloquent representation of an entire culture's search for that same God. The loving and admonishing Father for whom she searches is the Father for whom we have all searched, men and women alike. We have all sought his blessing, tried to conjure up his presence in times of crisis if not of ease. Even those of us who have rejected him outright in favor of no gods

at all—or of gods that offend our sensibilities less, or match our politics better, or seem to us truer, more imaginative—catch ourselves wishing, or fearing, that he might exist. Sexton's failing Father-God is, in short, our own; I cannot see how it could be otherwise in a patriarchy as old and enduring as ours. The idea of such a God is not original or rehabilitating or appealing, except to those instincts that are conservative, repetitive, and fearful. But to deny his vestigial hold on us is to pridefully declare that we are not, at whatever seemingly safe remove, influenced by the conservative, the repetitive, the fearful. Who has not asked, slightly desperate at the heart, "Is it true? Is it true?" Who has not been "in this country of black mud," longing for that God through whom one could be "born again / into something true?"

Second, and more important, the poet who needs to be beaten by God in that final poker game is the same one who dreams she can "piss in God's eye" (**"Hurry up Please It's Time,"** *The Death Notebooks*). She is, as Ostriker and Lauter explain, the poet who dismantles religious myth and reimagines Christianity in the most daring and original ways. She undertakes to rewrite Genesis, the Psalms, and, most radically, the Gospels. She is among the most original and radical of religious poets in our literary and spiritual heritage.

With this reservation in mind, I participate in regretting the imaginatively small and fraudulent God Sexton asked herself and her readers to settle for at the end of *The Awful Rowing toward God*. In *The Death Notebooks,* the God she searched out was still pluralistic, still appealingly heathen and varied. "Mrs. Sexton went out looking for the gods" in the first poem of *The Death Notebooks,* in lower case plural. Even *The Awful Rowing* finds God in the "chapel of eggs" with "the absurdities of the dinner table," sometimes "dressed up like a whore" or an old man or a child. He "lives in shit" and beans and butter and milk, in the poet's typewriter, in "the private holiness of my hands." It is, I think, primarily the final poem in the collection that so disturbs readers and critics.

In **"The Rowing Endeth,"** God has diminished back into the father of **"Oysters,"** who laughs as he drinks his martini and presides over a ritual of defeat as well as triumph for the speaker-poet. While **"Oysters"** may seem an oddly minor poem in thematic concerns compared to **"The Rowing Endeth"**—after all, one is about eating oysters for the first time and one is about rowing to the island of God for salvation—they are similar in situation, tone, even in language. Listen to the central scene in both: in **"Oysters"** the father is laughing at and with the daughter as she gags down her first oysters and he drinks his martini: "Then I laughed and then we laughed." We leave them laughing, celebrating "the death of childhood" and the speaker's rebirth into womanhood. In **"The Rowing Endeth,"** God wins the poker game, probably by cheating:

> He starts to laugh,
> the laughter rolling like a hoop out of His mouth
> and into mine,
> and such laughter that He doubles right over me
> laughing a Rejoice-Chorus at our two triumphs.

In both cases, the triumph for the daughter-poet—rebirth into womanhood, rebirth into salvation—is presided over by a Father-figure who has the edge over the speaker. He is bigger, older, wiser, male. He enjoys his power over her, and she enjoys it with him. In **"The Rowing Endeth,"** as in **"Oysters,"** the speaker is initiated into mysteries, made privy to secrets, included, endorsed, approved of, loved. Yet in both scenarios, there is no question of who enjoys the power. Reading both poems, I feel the edge of sexual humiliation through seduction, the kind felt by a girl who is told a dirty joke by an older man; she laughs, uncomfortably and too loud, half understanding the joke, half knowing that it is directed at her. Here, as in **"The Death Baby"** (*The Death Notebooks*), such "love" is both erotic and deathly, both the symbol of woman's self-assurance and of her self-annihilation. Her passionate responses enact both her wish to live and her wish to die. "You have seen my father whip me. / You have seen me stroke my father's whip."

Just such an unsavory seduction takes place in an untitled 1965 poem from the posthumously published sequence of poem-letters to her psychiatrist in **Words for Dr. Y.** An unnamed male the speaker called "Comfort" reads to the speaker during her childhood, from the Bible, "to prove I was sinful."

> *For in the night he was betrayed.*
> And then he let me give him a Judas-kiss,
> that red lock that held us in place,
> and then I gave him a drink from my cup
> and he whispered, "Rape, rape."
> And then I gave him my wrist
> and he sucked on the blood,
> hating himself for it,
> murmuring, "God will see. God will see."

In this extraordinarily ambiguous seduction, the girl-child appears to initiate the ritual of blood that is both sexual and religious. But the dynamics of power are unmistakably on the side of the older male, who ironically whispers "rape" when, if there is such a thing going on, we know very well who is the victim. While the male ostensibly worries that "God will see" what they are doing, it is clear that he is playing the part of God himself, "allowing" himself to be betrayed by this Judas-child. It might be illuminating to know the identity of this male in the poet's biography, and to find it, we need only turn to **All My Pretty Ones,** to the grandfather of the "bagful of nickels" in **"Letter Writ-** ten During a January Northeaster,"** to whom the final sequence of poems in that volume is dedicated: "For Comfort, who was actually my Grandfather."

This seduction scene between granddaughter and grandfather is repeated in reverse form in the posthumously published **"Leaves That Talk"** in **45 Mercy Street.**

> I dream it's the fourth of July
> and I'm having a love affair
> with grandfather (his real birthday)
>   . . . . .
> and in my dream
> grandfather touches my neck and breast
> and says, "Do not be afraid!
> It's only the leaves falling!"

Here the grandfather is the initiator of sexual contact, and the process he interferes with is the suicide's conversation with her voices, the "green girls"—leaves that call her to "come to us" and die. His role here as "comforter" is compromised by his seduction of his granddaughter; if his comfort were merely paternal, we could be glad of his saving presence, which calls her away from the voices that urge her to die. But the fact that he "touches her breast" lends this scene the sinister aura of the dirty old man, whose motivations in urging her away from the feminine-suicidal to the masculine-sacrificial are highly suspect.

Sexton's grandfather is a minor character in the family drama that unfolds in Sexton's poetry during the eighteen years and ten volumes of her writing career, overshadowed as he is by the poet's mother, father, daughters, and great-aunt, Nana. Yet it is he, finally, who most clearly connects the God of **The Awful Rowing** and the father-figures of the poet's personal life. Perhaps his title as "grand" father makes this connection appropriate, for what is a God in a patriarchy but a Grand Father? That he is also the person the child called "Comfort" is acutely apropos, for comfort is what she seeks from God. In **"Grandfather, Your Wound"** (*The Death Notebooks*), the speaker sits in a house on an "island" belonging to him.

> . . . you are a ceiling made of wood
> and the island you were the man of,
> is shaped like a squirrel and named thereof.
> On this island, Grandfather, made of your stuff

Sexton the writer stands "in your writing room" in this poem, surrounded by his belongings and mourning the absence of "Mr. Funnyman, Mr. Nativeman . . . Mr. Lectureman, Mr. Editor." Arthur Gray Staples was indeed a lecturer and writer, editor-in-chief of the *Lewiston Evening Journal* (one of Maine's largest newspapers) and author of several books of essays. Squirrel Island was the summer home of seven five-story houses described in **"Funnel"** (*All My Pretty Ones*). Staples's writing room, setting for **"Grandfather, Your Wound,"** was a spacious room with an ocean view.[8]

When Sexton moors her rowboat at the dock of the "island called God" at the end of *The Awful Rowing,* she is, I believe, mooring herself again at her beloved Squirrel Island. And "the flesh of The Island"—the flesh of God—is none other than her grandfather, that "ceiling made of wood" in **"Your Wound."** "I wouldn't mind if God were wooden," she writes in a peculiar and otherwise inexplicable line in **"Is It True?"**

> Oh wood, my father, my shelter,
> bless you

And in *The Death Notebooks,* to receive **"God's Backside,"** the "dark negative" turned against her, is cold, "like Grandfather's icehouse" (**"God's Backside"**). If we need any further indication that Grandfather is God, we find it in the closing of **"Your Wound,"** when dead "Comfort" comes back, resurrected with the same appositive/expletive construction that closes **"All My Pretty Ones"**:

> my God, Grandfather,
> you are here,
> you are laughing,
> you hold me and rock me
> and we watch the lighthouse come on,
> blinking its dry wings over us all,
> over my wound
> and yours.

The sun has gone down, but when he comes back to her, "it comes bright again." The unspecified "wound" of which he died is the flaw that she inherits, that she, too, will die of; but his presence, a resurrection from the dead, is the assurance that he lives to be her "comfort" once again—to tell her that she is sinful, to sin with her, to love her. He, perhaps alone among all her other familial gods, endorses her as a writer. (Mary Harvey, who once wanted to be a writer, inaugurated Anne's efforts with rejections and an accusation of plagiarism, while her father and husband, whose business was wool, were not able or likely to make her feel that such activity really qualified as "work.") The God "my typewriter believes in" (**"The Frenzy,"** *Awful Rowing*) is her grandfather as writer as well as father. Elsewhere in *Awful Rowing,* the typewriter is her "church," her "altar of keys." In her introduction to the *Complete Poems,* Maxine Kumin writes:

> An elderly, sympathetic priest she called on—"accosted" might be a better word—patiently explained that he could not make her a Catholic by fiat, nor could he administer the sacrament (the last rites) she longed for. But in his native wisdom he said a saving thing to her, said the magic and simple words that kept her

alive at least a year beyond her time and made *The Awful Rowing toward God* a possibility. "God is in your typewriter," he told her.[9]

"Your Wound" ends with the chillingly familiar scene of laughter between the daughter-poet and the father-God, but here the laughter seems genuinely mutual, truly benevolent. We may regret that in his metamorphosis from human grandfather to cosmic Grand Father, the male figure represented in this discussion by Arthur Gray Staples became such a sinister and fraudulent deity. It is difficult to "applaud" this "dearest dealer," as Sexton asks herself and us to do in **"The Rowing Endeth."** Doubling "right over me" in laughter, he is at least as much the circling shark and the "father thick upon me" like some "jelly-fish" of **"Briar Rose,"** as he is the benevolent "bagful of nickels" of **"Letter Written,"** holding and rocking her as the lighthouse flashes on to illuminate the darkness. Yet what we *can* applaud is that, as Kumin says, the search for the God in her typewriter kept her going, inspired by an old priest who may have been reminiscent of her grandfather—and who certainly offered her "comfort" through affirming her worth as a poet.

I find it poignant to discover that the "island of God" may have been the island of childhood where she summered, and where, as her editors remind us in the *Letters* [*Anne Sexton: A Self-Portrait in Letters*], "Anne's happy memories centered."[10] I also confess that I find it beautiful; I contemplate that simplicity, that perfect circle of sought-after comfort, one that brings the middle-aged poet back to the few ideal moments of a troubled and unhappy past. Perhaps anyone's idea of heaven is some such journey into the past. Did Anne Sexton know that the island of God was Squirrel Island? This most psychoanalytic, most autobiographical, most naked of all contemporary poets did not say that she knew this, either in the letters or explicitly in the poems. It seems a strange omission, from one who was so willing to be explicit. And although she was capable of the subtlest kinds of elusiveness, as all good poets are—"tell all the truth but tell it slant," as Dickinson put it—it was not this kind of subtlety she cultivated. Yet whether or not she knew, she left us a wake through the water as she rowed to the island of her God.

Notes

All Sexton citations are from Anne Sexton, *The Complete Poems* (Boston: Houghton Mifflin, 1981).

1. Critics who have identified this shift from personal to transpersonal, cultural, or mythic in Sexton's work include Alicia Ostriker and Estella Lauter; for full citations, see below.

2. Phyllis Chesler, *Women and Madness* (New York: Avon Books, 1972), 18.

3. Karen Horney was the first to re-envision the father-daughter relationship from within psychoanalysis. See *Feminine Psychology* (New York: W. W. Norton, 1967), Horney's collected essays on patriarchal psychoanalytic theory.

4. Chesler, 111.

5. Maxine Kumin, "How It Was: Maxine Kumin on Anne Sexton," in Anne Sexton, *The Complete Poems* (Boston: Houghton Mifflin, 1981), xxiii.

6. Alicia Ostriker, "That Story: The Changes of Anne Sexton," in *Writing Like a Woman* (Ann Arbor: University of Michigan Press, 1983) 78; "That Story" also appears in *American Poetry Review* 11, no. 4 (1982): 11-16.

7. Estella Lauter, "Anne Sexton's 'Radical Discontent with the Awful Order of Things,'" *Spring: An Annual of Archetypal Psychology and Jungian Thought* (1979): 82.

8. Editorial note, in *Anne Sexton: A Self-Portrait in Letters,* edited by Linda Gray Sexton and Lois Ames (Boston: Houghton Mifflin, 1977), 4.

9. Kumin, "How It Was," xxiii.

10. *Letters,* 4.

Frances Bixler (essay date 1988)

SOURCE: Bixler, Frances. "Journey into the Sun: The Religious Pilgrimage of Anne Sexton." In *Original Essays on the Poetry of Anne Sexton,* edited by Frances Bixler, pp. 203-37. Conway, Ark.: University of Central Arkansas Press, 1988.

[*In the following essay, Bixler examines the range of Sexton's religious poetry, suggesting that the poems reveal her search for God and for an understanding of her own identity.*]

> O yellow eye,
> let me be sick with your heat,
> let me be feverish and frowning.
> Now I am utterly given.
> I am your daughter, your sweet-meat,
> your priest, your mouth and your bird
> and I will tell them all stories of you
> until I am laid away forever,
> a thin gray banner.
>
>   **"The Sun"** (*LD* [*Live or Die*])

> The place I live in
> is kind of a maze
> and I keep seeking
> the exit or the home.
>
>   **"The Children"** (*AW* [*The Awful
>   Rowing toward God*])

This loneliness is just an exile from God.

> April 1, 1963, (*WY* [***Words for Dr. Y:
> Uncollected Poems With Three Stories***])

Anne Sexton's religious poetry presents different problems to different readers. For those who no longer accept the Christian God as a reality, her search seems dated and inexplicable.[1] Those who empathize with her need to make God a reality may yet feel at a loss to comprehend the twistings, contradictions, and confusions displayed by a large body of her work. Sexton's poetry is also a puzzlement for believers because of her frequent disregard for orthodox theology. Thus, no reader comes away from her religious poetry feeling fully at ease.

For this reason and because Sexton chose to concentrate so heavily on the theme of religious need, it seems important to attempt a critical analysis of Sexton's religious poems, with an eye to understanding her quest, as much as that is possible, and an ear to hearing variations in tonalities which add to or subtract from the meaning. My aim here is to suggest that by looking at a number of poems ranging over Sexton's entire canon and by taking into account the biographical facts of her life as we now have them, we can arrive at a definition of what Anne Sexton meant when she said she was "both saved and lost"; we can understand more clearly, if not fully, her need for contact with that which is Other—a need more universal than we sometimes admit; and we can also appreciate the struggle of one who was more doubter than believer, more "lost" than "saved."

Such a struggle has a long history in literature. Dante's famous journey, Augustine's *Confessions,* Bunyan's fictive depiction of the Christian life, the search for the Ideal among many of the British Romantics, C. S. Lewis's autobiography, *Surprised by Joy,* and even the fantasy world of J. R. R. Tolkien attempt the recounting of a journey into a world that is different from the natural order. However, Sandra Gilbert identifies the very different experience of the female poet when she attempts a similar journey:

> The female poet . . . writes in the hope of discovering or defining a self, a certainty, a tradition. Striving for self-knowledge, she experiments with different propositions about her own nature, never cool or comfortable enough to be (like her male counterparts) an ironic sociologist; always, instead, a desperate Galileo, a passionate empiricist who sees herself founding a new science rather than extending the techniques and discoveries of an old one.
>
>   (446)

Gilbert puts her finger on a number of the elements inherent in Sexton's journey. In her quest for God, Sexton was also discovering who she was, defining herself in terms of her relationship with God and especially, Jesus. Her need for establishing—with certainty—the Christian tradition or a new one of her own making is evident. And certainly, Sexton was never "cool or comfortable" about this matter. Her struggle was intense, deeply felt, and constant. In the end, she tried very hard to found a "new science."[2]

To understand the problem Sexton was trying to solve through her religious poetry, the reader must accept Sexton's description of her spiritual condition. She saw her gravest problem as being full of personal, internalized evil. It is this sense of being thoroughly poisoned that she attempts to assuage, to reason with, to kill, and especially to fight with words—those pieces of magic which did sometimes create order out of chaos, did assemble the fragments of the puzzle to make a whole. Sexton's religious poems comprise a great variety of forms and gain complexity with ironic layerings, straight-forward autobiography and confession, despair, prophecy, and celebration, poems that form a mass of imaginative, emotional, and poetic facts which don't always cohere logically, even after several readings. Looked at as a spiritual narrative, however, Sexton's religious poems do begin to speak to each other, and one gains new insights by considering all of her religious work as a unit, or perhaps more explicitly, as the record of a journey which has a specific goal, one fraught with enormous complications—complications the poet attempts to undo in an astounding variety of poetic endeavors.

Several poems shed light on the nature of Sexton's quest. The lightning changes in tone and voice of these selections suggest that Sexton was attempting to get at her subject through many avenues.[3] I have already cited three selections from her work. In **"The Sun"** Sexton identifies herself with fish who had the bad luck of coming up for sun and getting stuck on earth to rot and with flies that cannot bear the intense heat. They, too, die. My quotation completes the poem. The voice is that of supplication. I take the sun to be a pun on Son, meaning Christ. Thus, I interpret her petition as asking God for a trade-off. In essence, if you will not rot me with your heat or dry me out with your presence, I will do my best to tell what I know about you. Hence, she says, "I am your daughter," a statement affirming her sense of identity with God.[4] The second quotation, in a strikingly different voice, suggests the confusion that is constant on her journey, and the third is a single line published after her death but evidently written much earlier, indicating Sexton's analysis of her problem on one day of her life.

Three other poems provide insight into Sexton's religious quest. The first, **"Gods,"** begins with the sardonic statement, "Mrs. Sexton went out looking for the gods." The searcher looks in books, talks to a poet, prays in "all the churches of the world," goes to the Atlantic and Pacific oceans, goes to the "Buddha, the Brahma, the Pyramids. . . ." She finds no one. Sarcastically, the narrator concludes:

> Then she journeyed back to her own house
> and the gods of the world were shut in the lavatory.
> At last!
> she cried out,
> and locked the door.

> (*DN* [*The Death Notebooks*])

Readers of Sexton's poetry are familiar with this voice. It is that of the middle-aged witch in *Transformations* deliberately turning our fairy tales into nightmares, the voice that so often undercuts a serious poem with an ironic ending. This particular mixture of serious subject, deliberate mockery, and shocking images can leave the reader looking for a peg on which to hang meaning. However, I hear in this poem, in particular, a poignance masked by bravado. I also hear the deliberate attempt of the author to scoff at Mrs. Sexton's silly search—an attempt which doesn't quite come off. What does come through finally is the recognition that the search must be an inner one; and, of course, for Sexton this means a solid inquiry into the evil, imaged here by the lavatory, which pervades her life.

Radically different in tone and content is **"The Fury of Overshoes"** (*DN*). The speaker begins as the adult looking backward to childhood, asking the reader to remember all the indignities of childhood, but she concludes in the naive voice of the child herself:

> Oh thumb,
> I want a drink,
> it is dark,
> where are the big people,
> when will I get there,
> taking giant steps
> all day,
> each day
> and thinking
> nothing of it?

The child, sucking her thumb, speaks, nevertheless, in adult metaphor. The dark is her inability to understand herself and the god she is searching for. Big people are imaged constantly throughout Sexton's work as mothers and fathers, images which become archetypal representations of God. The steps the child is taking go nowhere, and the nothing she is thinking grows out of her ignorance.

A third selection, the short story "Dancing the Jig" (*BF* [*The Book of Folly*]), supplies yet another aspect of Sexton's search. In this story the main character finds herself dancing wildly to music. She cannot stop, no matter how much she wishes to do so; nor can she control her movements. She is embarrassed and most relieved when the music dies away. Sitting down, she contemplates a chair across the room and thinks how every time her wild desire leaps up in her she attempts to concentrate on something like the chair. Though I think that this story is also about the frenzy of insanity, it lends insight into Sexton's search for a stable, unchanging God. The final lines hint at the underlying meaning: "It [the chair] is fine. . . . It is a relief to dwell on it—a perfect object. So fixed. So always the same" (**BF** 65-71). These several works reveal the central elements in Sexton's spiritual quest: the need for identity, the hunger for security and certainty, the fear of passion, and the recognition that this journey, above all, is interior.

I

Two central religious problems preoccupied Sexton throughout her poetic career—what to do with Jesus Christ and how to assuage her personal sense of evil. In letters dated over a year apart Sexton admitted to her friend, Brian Sweeney, that she was grappling with her questions about faith and God and especially about the divinity of Christ. October 25, 1969, Sexton writes: "Perhaps I should worry about God—he's bigger than any of this. I'm glad you're straight with Him. I have yet to settle the matter. Oh, I really believe in God—it's Christ that boggles the mind" (*Letters* 346). A later letter, dated November 24, 1970, reiterates her thought: "Yes, it is time to think about Christ again. I keep putting it off. If he is the God/man, I would feel a hell of a lot better. If there is a God, Sweeney, how do you explain him swallowing all those people up in Pakistan? Of course there's a God, but what kind is he? Is he our Kind?" (*Letters* 368-69). Both comments reveal that Sexton has no trouble thinking about God as some distant First Cause. She is really not very interested in this kind of God however; her search is for a "husband" (i. e. "the one who carries you through," **"The God-Monger,"** *AW*). Thus, she constantly struggles with the need to believe in Christ, the God/man; yet her doubt just as constantly overrides her faith. Her reference to the terrible episode in Pakistan implies that God doesn't really work miracles. He's a fraud, a fake, someone totally unreliable.

Several poems reflect Sexton's vacillation regarding Christ's divinity. The first appears in one of her best-known poems, **"The Division of Parts"** (*TB* [*To Bedlam and Part Way Back*]). In a deadly serious autobiographical voice, Sexton recounts going through her mother's possessions, dividing them with her sisters, remembering her mother's agonizingly slow death from cancer, and the resultant division she feels. The poem is made up of four parts, all happening on Good Friday, the day Christ was crucified. In a sense, this division is a kind of crucifixion for Sexton. She is being separated by death from her mother, but this has only served to

bring her face to face with death. "I trip on your death and Jesus, *my stranger,* / floats up over / my Christian home, wearing his straight thorn tree. . . ." Sexton cannot get past the anguish of her mother's death and Christ's death; both seem too impossibly awful to accept as a part of life. She concludes:

> And Christ still waits. I have tried
> to exorcise the memory of each event
> and remain still, a mixed child,
> heavy with cloths of you.
> Sweet witch, you are my worried guide.
> Such dangerous angels walk through Lent.
> Their walls creak *Anne! Convert! Convert!*
> My desk moves. Its cave murmurs Boo
> and I am taken and beguiled.
> Or wrong. For all the way I've come
> I'll have to go again. Instead, I must convert
> to love. . . .
>
> (*TB*)

Sadly, Sexton realizes that her faith is really just a part of the "clutter of worship that you taught me, Mary Gray. . . ." In this poem she discards her religious heritage while acknowledging her human heritage.

A much later poem, **"The Falling Dolls,"** underlines Sexton's conviction that God, if there is a God, should be one who protects, preserves, heals, and feeds (*MS* [*45 Mercy Street*]). She tells of "Dolls, / by the thousands, / falling out of the sky." The implication is that these are people who have no one to help them, to protect them against the cruelties of life. Her rapid-fire questions at the end of the poem catch her anger:

> Why is there no mother?
> Why are all these dolls falling out of the sky?
> Was there a father?
> Or have the planets cut holes in their nets
> and let our childhood out,
> or are we the dolls themselves,
> born but never fed?

Here, as in so many of her poems, the use of mother and father is an archetypal image of God. Sexton, a mother herself, cannot comprehend a caring, loving God who does not feed his children.

Two more poems reflect the intensity of Sexton's sense of being left alone to work out her problems. She says hysterically:

> It makes me laugh
> to see a woman in this condition.
> It makes me laugh for America and New York City
> when your hands are cut off
> and no one answers the phone.
>
> **"The Fury of Abandonment"** (*DN*)

Typically, Sexton employs synecdoche to intensify her image. For her, "touch is all," yet she here images the woman as having her hands cut off; therefore, she has lost her ability to touch. Equally fatal is the unanswered telephone which Sexton consistently uses to represent the poet's connection to the imagination or to inspiration. With both these faculties out of order, the woman is in dire straits.

Again, using body imagery, Sexton talks about her inner pain:

> They hear how
> the artery of my soul has been severed
> and soul is spurting out upon them,
> bleeding on them,
> messing up their clothes,
> dirtying their shoes.
>
> **"The Big Heart"** (*AW*)

It is of this pain that she says, "I would sell my life to avoid / the pain that begins in the crib . . . for better or worse / as you marry life . . . (**"The Big Boots of Pain,"** *MS*).

Though Sexton's inability to believe in Christ's divinity caused her much frustration, her sense of being evil was her greatest source of anguish. A number of poems graphically illustrate my point. A short poem dated January 1, 1961, contains the lines, "None of them has / the sense of evil that I have . . . (*WY*). The people Sexton is talking about are her fellow poets, John Holmes, Maxine Kumin, and George Starbuck. Her assessment is probably accurate. Even Maxine Kumin, her sister poet, does not exhibit a similar obsession with evil. Sexton is more precise in **"Is It True?"**:

> When I tell the priest I am evil
> he asks for a definition of the word.
> Do you mean sin? he asks.
> Sin, hell! I reply.
> I've committed every one.
> What I mean is evil,
> (not meaning to be, you understand,
> just something I ate).
> Evil is maybe lying to God.
> Or better, lying to love.
>
> (*TB*)

I interpret these lines to mean that Sexton's sensitivity to pain and to her own willingness to inflict pain on others leads her to this much more general definition of evil. Sins are acts committed against God or other persons. Evil, however, is a state of being which the poet attempts to capture in the last two lines of the quotation.

"The Evil Seekers" explores the nature of being human, which according to Sexton must of necessity include knowing about evil:

> but one must learn about evil,
> learn what is subhuman,

> learn how the blood pops out like a scream,
> one must see the night
> before one can realize the day. . . .
>
> (*AW*)

Nevertheless, the poem ends with an assertion that humans must make a desperate attempt to "bury" evil. The irony embodied in the title thus comes full circle: though we as human beings "seek" evil, we must just as actively try to eliminate it.

Sadly, getting rid of evil is not an easy task for Sexton. The shocking images of **"After Auschwitz"** reinforce her underlying hatred of humanity's tendency toward mutual self-destruction. The poem begins

> Anger,
> as black as a hook,
> overtakes me.
> Each day,
> each Nazi
> took, at 8:00 A.M., a baby
> and sauteed him for breakfast
> in his frying pan.
>
> (*AW*)

Such hyperbole instantly pulls the reader into the horror of WW II and its terrible evil. Probably no Nazi ever fried a baby for breakfast; yet, the image captures the intent of the heart which guided Nazis to serve their country by killing six million Jews. It is the intent of the heart that Sexton cares about. She continues a few lines further to indicate the extent of humanity's degradation:

> Man is evil,
> I say aloud.
> Man is a flower
> that should be burnt,
> I say aloud.
> Man
> is a bird full of mud,
> I say aloud.

Both flowers and birds figure quite heavily in Sexton's imagery as good, beautiful things. Thus, man, though having the image of the good is nothing but evil in this poem. The voice of the poet here is that of the prophet, crying in the street. It is also one of public and personal confession. She speaks for herself, and she speaks for us all.

If these poems were the only ones concerned with human evil, one could overlook them as samples of the poet having a bad day. Sexton, however, employs numerous images which convey her meaning powerfully. **"The Fury of Flowers and Worms"** sets up in its title the polar extremes that often appear in Sexton's work. She wishes to be close to the flowers because they help her to be "close to the worms / who struggle blindly / moving deep into their slime, / moving deep into God's abdomen . . ." (*DN*). Lest one think that she is talking about real flowers and worms, another poem sets the matter straight:

> We are all earthworms,
> digging into our wrinkles.
> We live beneath the ground
> and if Christ should come in the form of a plow
> and dig a furrow and push us up into the day
> we earthworms would be blinded by the sudden light
> and writhe in our distress.
> As I write this sentence I too writhe.
>
> **"The Wall,"** (*AW*)

In spite of the obvious pain connected to being an earthworm, Sexton finds good in the fact that the worm is working its way to the light, an example of her "saved and lost" motif which I will explore in depth a bit later.[5]

In addition to the prominent worm imagery, Sexton wrote at least three important poems indicating that inner division provided much of her sense of dis-ease. Her name for this other self was **"Old Dwarf Heart"** (*APO* [*All My Pretty Ones*]). "When I lie down to love / old dwarf heart shakes her head," go the first two lines. This other self is ugly, old, fat, corrupt, full of worldly knowledge, and inseparable. The poem concludes with a parody of the childish prayer:

> Oh now I lay me down to love,
> how awkwardly her arms undo,
> how patiently I untangle her wrists
> like knots. Old ornament, old naked fist,
> even if I put on seventy coats I could not cover you
> . . .
> mother, father, I'm made of.

Here the implication is that the evil is passed down from generation to generation, with no possibility of escape. **"The Other"** (*BF*) carries on the same idea of inner division. This time, however, the image is that of "Mr. Doppelgänger. My brother. My spouse. / Mr. Doppel-gänger. My enemy. My lover." Sexton's ambivalence toward this double becomes obvious here. She both loves and hates this part of herself.[6] Finally, Sexton creates a second self in the form of Nana, the great aunt whom Sexton had turned to in her childhood for the nurturing that Mary Gray seemed unable to give. Unfortunately, when Sexton was thirteen Nana suddenly went insane and had to be institutionalized. **"The Hex"** (*BF*) is in part the recounting of a young girl's terror when her beloved aunt turned strange, but it is also an interpretation of that event. Nana's accusing voice saying, "You did it, You are the evil" steals the poet's joy of life. Consequently, Sexton names her the "Nana-hex." "Yes! I am still the criminal," Sexton admits. "Yes! Take me to the station house. / But book my double." Her double, though, is too intertwined with her, too much a part of her to be separated. The

consequence is **"The Civil War"** (*AW*) where God is nothing but pieces of a puzzle and the poet is torn in two by her struggle to "build a whole nation of God / in me—but united."

Most invidious of all is Sexton's image of evil as "the rat inside of me." The first poem of *The Awful Rowing toward God,* **"Rowing,"** includes this image. Indeed, it is the presence of the rat which motivates the rower to keep on rowing "though the oarlocks stick and are rusty / and the sea blinks and rolls / like a worried eyeball. . . ." So urgent is the narrator's need that she makes a prophecy:

> there will be a door
> and I will open it
> and I will get rid of the rat inside of me,
> the gnawing pestilential rat.
> God will take it with his two hands
> and embrace it.

The implication is that God's embrace will somehow make the rat an acceptable animal with which the poet can live. The retelling of the Genesis story in **"Rats Live On No Evil Star"** (*DN*) creates the myth whereby the rat's existence is explained. Here Adam and Eve appear on the scene and "God looked out through his tunnel / and was pleased." However, the business of the apple becomes the basis for Eve's giving birth to a most vile creature:

> with its bellyful of dirt
> its hair seven inches long.
> It had two eyes full of poison
> and routine pointed teeth.
> Thus Eve gave birth.
> In this unnatural act
> she gave birth to a rat.

Thus it is that Anne Sexton, poet, worm, "old dwarf heart," is also rat. One comes to this by being born.

No doubt the most unsettling images of evil are those having to do with excrement.[7] **"After Auschwitz"** (*AW*) contains the lines, "Man with his small pink toes . . . is not a temple / but an outhouse. . . ." **"Is It True?"** (*AW*) carries the image further:

> When I tell the priest I am full
> of bowel movement, right into the fingers,
> he shrugs. To him shit is good.
> To me, to my mother, it was poison
> and the poison was all of me
> in the nose, in the ears, in the lungs.

The poet continues employing the same images in **"The Sickness Unto Death"** (*AW*) when she says she could not "move nor eat bread" because she "was a house full of bowel movement. . . ." Other poems make oblique references to "this country of dirt" (**"The Fish That Walked,"** *AW*), and to the sun which "passes over filth" (**"Is It True?"** *AW*).

One further note needs to be added in regard to Sexton's spiritual condition. She often conceded that the evil she professed to hate so much was really a good.[8] Typically, nothing is ever simple for Sexton, and her ambivalence toward the dark side of the human self greatly complicated her life. For example, a poem I have already cited, **"Rats Live On No Evil Star"** (*DN*), is a palindrome. Sexton concludes this poem by saying that "all us cursed ones" end up on the "RAT'S STAR."[9] She is obviously making use of the reversibility of the words to turn meaning inside out. If one is a rat, one can depend on ending up on a star. The stability of the palindrome guarantees this. Sexton does a similar sleight-of-hand with the name Ms. Dog which she applies to herself in several late poems. Dog is God spelled backwards. I take this reversal to be a bit different in that a transformation is going on. The word is being turned around and so is different, yet related because all the letters are the same. Other indications that Sexton did not hate her evil as much as she said show up in her frequent use of Dalmatians—those black and white dogs. **"The Fallen Angels"** (*AW*) identifies the poet as "like them—both saved and lost." Furthermore, "they wiggle up life." The epigraph for **"Angels of the Love Affair"** (*BF*) reads, "Angels of the love affair, do you know that other, the dark one, that other me?" First lines of all six poems in this group begin with similar paradoxical questions:

1. Angel of fire and genitals, do you know slime . . . ?
2. Angel of clean sheets, do you know bedbugs . . . ?
3. Angel of flight and sleigh bells, do you know paralysis . . . ?
4. Angel of hope and calendars, do you know despair?
5. Angel of blizzards and blackouts, do you know raspberries . . . ?
6. Angel of beach houses and picnics, do you know solitaire?

The implication is that knowledge of evil is the source for much of Sexton's poetic energy. Indeed, she admits this quite plainly in a posthumously published poem dated December 4, 1967: "the old sense of evil remains, / evil that wife" (*WY*). Even more to the point is the poem **"Baby Picture"** (*DN*) in which Anne looks at her baby picture and thinks about who she was:

I open the dress
and I see a child bent on a toilet seat.
I crouch there, sitting dumbly
pushing the enemas out like ice cream,
letting the whole brown world
turn to sweets.

Having recognized excrement as one of Sexton's most powerful images for evil, the reader must also come to terms with the paradox of the good/evil which is represented by these lines and images. It is Sexton's double which "cries and cries and cries / until I put on

a painted mask / and leer at Jesus in His passion" (**"The Other,"** *BF*). Gilbert's thesis regarding women poets seems to be borne out in Sexton's turning inside out the consequences of evil and her evident disregard for orthodox theology, both as it relates to a definition of evil and as it relates to the nature of Jesus Christ. She does, indeed, seem to be creating "a new science."

II

Gilbert's metaphor built on Galileo and his courageous explorations into the unknown is a useful one to keep in mind when looking at Sexton's religious pilgrimage because she was equally courageous in exploring new foundations for religious faith. One direction she took was to employ the images and concepts of orthodoxy to create a new mythology; another was to renew the old Christian myth, adding dimensions peculiar to her own need.

Several stories and poems link together to form a new mythology—that of woman/poet/human who serves as redeemer. **"Making a Living"** (*DN*) stands as a clear statement underscoring Sexton's feeling that female sacrifice and death are a necessity. The poem is a retelling of the biblical story of Jonah and the Whale. Jonah finds himself inside the belly of the whale where he clearly understands that he must accept his own death. He diligently works his way toward total acceptance, including the "eating" of his past. Finally, Jonah is vomited up on shore and begins to tell his story to the world. The result is a conflation of the life stories of Jonah and Christ and the poet:

Then he [Jonah] told the news media
the strange details of his death
and they hammered him up in the marketplace
and sold him and sold him and sold him.
My death the same.

The suffering of all three persons is meant to be the same, and their mission is also similar. Jonah gave himself to being a prophet, warning people of coming doom. Christ gave himself to death in order to create life in others. The poet gives herself to writing poetry in order to write "books . . . that act upon us like a misfortune, that make us suffer like the death of someone we love more than ourselves . . ." (Epigraph for *APO* vii).

Sexton seems to have been able to explore this idea more fully in stories rather than in poetry, though a number of poems do hint broadly at her re-visioning of Christian orthodoxy. "The Bat" or "To Remember. To Remember" (*WY*) is told by a bat whose "reward" for life has been to be reincarnated the ninth time as a bat who can remember only flashes of scenes from his former eight lives. The scenes make no sense to the narrator, but they do carry meaning for the reader. The motif of crucifixion, which has been present in Sexton's poetry from the very beginning, appears central to this story. Among other scenes, the bat reports seeing himself listening to a man in the street below giving orders to the batman to nail "MISS NO-NAME" against the wall. The bat says, "The girl rises, as he calls up to her to do so and then it's Him, Him, Him *telling, commanding,* and we are the actors in His play" (98-99). The capital H gives away the identity of the director; it is God. As prompted, the bat-man nails the girl, spread-eagled to the wall and kills her with his hunting knife. She takes twenty-four hours to die. In the conclusion of the poem the bat-man calls this a scene of "damnation," but the reader is left to consider the fact that this story holds a strong clue to Sexton's self identity as poet and female.

A second story, "Vampire," (*WY*) contains a black Eucharist in which the woman is the provider of the wine. Again, the narrator is a male who purports to be a normal person, selling life insurance for a living. However, he is captured one day and given a drug which turns him into a human vampire. For his "daily bread," the narrator must go out, taking with him a fresh loaf of French bread, and find a young woman. When he locates his victim, he places his mouth on her navel and sucks blood from her. His description of the act is deeply sensuous, suggesting sexual union. He explains his need for this "transfusion" of life in cold, objective tones, apparently unable to feel guilt over stealing life from someone else so that he can live. The narrator justifies himself this way: "Food! Food! It is perfectly proper and absolutely necessary to have food. . . . I starve. I eat. Plain common sense. Blood and bread, blood and bread, but human blood only, woman blood only. It must be thus. It was ordained" (92). Mr. Ha-ha in **"The Ballet of the Buffoon,"** agrees with this pronouncement. He concludes his oration to the people by saying "Every man kills his wife. It's a matter of history" (*BF* 81). Sexton makes her plainest statement about her new mythology in **"The Author of the Jesus Papers Speaks"** (*BF*). She tells of having a dream that she was milking a cow and waiting for milk to come forth when, instead, the cow begins to give blood. The poet's reaction is to be ashamed. Following God's instructions, she goes to a well and pulls out a baby, giving birth in a sense as the Virgin Mary did. What follows is the kernel of Sexton's new religion:

> Then God spoke to me and said:
> Here. Take this gingerbread lady
> and put her in your oven.
> When the cow gives blood
> and the Christ is born
> we must all eat sacrifices.
> We must all eat beautiful women.

Having given up on believing in the efficacy of Christ's death and resurrection to "save" her, Sexton places

herself and other "beautiful women" in the position of bearing the burden of redemption for the human race. Diana Hume George suggests that these lines represent "the other 'sacrifice' of Christianity, corresponding to Christ's sacrifice on behalf of humanity in the person of his male body" (18). Certainly, the Christian church has demanded its pound of flesh from "beautiful women" who have chosen to step out of the boundaries prescribed for them by dogma and tradition. Sexton may also mean to imply in this poem that society asks women, especially female artists, to pay a high price for their calling. She asserts that these chosen ones must dig into their souls "and ask and ask and ask / until the kingdom, / however queer, / will come" (**"Hurry up Please It's Time"** (*DN*).

A discussion of Sexton's new mythology would not be complete without an examination of **"The Jesus Papers"** (*BF*). Alicia Ostriker sees the "radical vision of 'The Jesus Papers'" as a "systematic and structured . . . reinterpretation of Christian myth" . . . ("That Story" 13). Her comment is an apt one. Each of these poems debunks some aspect of Christ's life central to the Christian story. In **"Jesus Suckles"** the Christ child is at first warmly comfortable at Mary's breast, but the poem ends with the blunt, "No. No. / All Lies. / I am a truck. I run everything. / I own you." Jesus becomes the patriarchal male, determined to dominate and possess everything. Both **"Jesus Awake"** and **"Jesus Asleep"** mock Christ's celibacy, but the point of both of these poems is that the loss of touch and sexual union results in terrible pain for humanity. Christ's "celibate life" becomes a medal which is "pinned" on him but at great cost to those he supposedly came to serve. **"The Fury of Cocks"** (*DN*) serves as counterpoint for these poems where the final lines suggest:

> When they break away they are God.
> When they snore they are God.
> In the morning they butter the toast.
> They don't say much.
> They are still God.
> All the cocks of the world are God,
> blooming, blooming, blooming
> into the sweet blood of woman.

Sexual union, for Sexton, is an image of wholeness. Thus, Christ's refusal to participate in sex makes him small and mean. In **"Jesus Asleep"** the result of his refusal is that Mary, because she has had no touch from Christ, stays fixed forever on the crucifix with Christ.

An important part of the Gospels are the stories of the miracles Jesus did while on earth. Sexton retells several of these stories in **"The Jesus Papers"** giving them an ironic twist. **"Jesus Raises up the Harlot"** sets the scene where the harlot finds herself in fear for her life because she is being stoned to death. The biblical story places Jesus in the center of the controversy, suggesting to the religious men who were attempting to kill the woman that the one who was without sin should cast the first stone. Of course, none of them can since they probably had all helped to make an adulterous woman out of someone. Sexton's story, however, makes Christ the terrible rescuer. He keeps the harlot from being stoned, but he finds it necessary to "lance her twice on each breast" in order to remove her sickness. The milk flows out and the woman follows Jesus "like a puppy" for the rest of her days. Loss of milk in this context suggests that the woman had lost her god-like qualities and her individuality. She now is "cured," but she has no self. She has traded sickness for a kind of death-in-life.

In both **"Jesus Cooks"** and **"Jesus Summons Forth"** Sexton manages to make the miracles of feeding the five thousand and the raising of Lazarus from the dead look like a trick a magician or a con man would use. "Work on the sly / opening boxes of sardine cans," he tells the disciples. The people finally eat well "from invisible dishes." The figure of Lazarus is equally ridiculous. After strenuous efforts to put the body and bones back together, Jesus manages to get his soul dropped down into him only to have the narrator comment that Lazarus was grateful because "in heaven it had been no different. / In heaven there had been no change."

Sexton concludes **"The Jesus Papers"** with two companion poems—**"Jesus Dies"** and **"Jesus Unborn."** In the first poem Jesus is the speaker; his point of view is from the elevation of the cross. Every word he says identifies him as a man dying a cruel death but not a God taking on the sins of the world:

> I want heaven to descend and sit on My dinner plate
> and so do you.
> I want God to put His steaming arms around Me
> and so do you.
> Because we need.
> Because we are sore creatures.

In these lines Jesus is characterized as an empathetic, caring human being, suffering as all humanity suffers, and dying as we all must die. "This is a personal matter," he tells the crowd. Sexton refuses to recognize any global significance in this death.

"Jesus Unborn" is reminiscent of Yeats "The Second Coming." Mary lies in a kind of trance while a "strange being" hovers over her with "executioner's eyes." Mary is obviously one of the beautiful women who must be "eaten" in order for the world to go right. The poem continues in an apocalyptic tone: "All this will be remembered. / Now we will have a Christ." However, the ending of the poem suggests the violence of this act—a rape which ends Mary's own life, "shuts her lifetime up / into this dump-faced day." The birth of

Christ costs Mary her life—one life for one life. The sacrifice seems unjustifiable. So ends **"The Jesus Papers"** with Jesus a patriarchal male, a good person who refuses to touch anyone in need, a helpless human, a con man, a terrifying physician, and a thief of life similar to the vampire in the story I have already mentioned. Sexton's conclusion that under these circumstances "We must all eat beautiful women" seems somehow logical and fitting.

Though Sexton makes a valiant attempt to create a new myth, she appears unsure of herself and unsatisfied with its reality. **"The Passion of the Mad Rabbit"** (*MS*) suggests that her re-vision turned into a bad dream. In this poem the poet tells of undergoing a "removal" and allowing "a fool" to enter her. His name is Mr. Rabbit. The scene is "bad Friday" and Mr. Rabbit is crucified, taking three days to die. So far these images echo those of the stories and poems I have already cited. Easter comes and the bunny, Mr. Rabbit, is burned while he/she (by now the poet has identified herself with Mr. Rabbit) sings until her blood boils. Nevertheless, the last lines of the poem tell the ironic truth: "In place of the Lord, / I whispered, / a fool has risen." Humble, almost silent, awed by her own blasphemy, the poet admits her failure. It should be noted that most of the poems in which Sexton attempts to construct her new mythology are located in the collection she chose to title *The Book of Folly.* Her next collection takes on entirely new dimensions, employs new voices, and rarely reverts to sardonic irony.

III

The Death Notebooks and *The Awful Rowing toward God* comprise a new direction for Sexton's religious explorations. In them she returns to Christian myth, but adds her own dimensions to the story. The **"O Ye Tongues"** sequence (*DN*) is surely one of Sexton's finest achievements. Her appropriation of an apocalyptic voice, her deft handling of a new form, and her weaving together of narrative and lyric elements make these outstanding poems. Included in her achievements in these poems is the creation of a new character whose name is Christopher. I take him to be the sometimes mad religious poet, Christopher Smart, from whom Sexton obviously borrows the form for **"O Ye Tongues"**; but I also think Sexton is punning on the name and intends Christopher to stand for Christ as well. (Christopher comes from the Greek *Christophoros*—bearing Christ.) These ten psalms compress the story of Sexton's religious pilgrimage while they expand the reader's understanding of her quest.

The psalms begin with the powerful command "Let there be a God as large as a sunlamp to laugh his heat at you." This is the *let* of "Let there be light" spoken by God in Genesis—a statement of great strength and creative power. Immediately, in Genesis, there was light. We can assume that Sexton expects similar results from her commands. She continues creating a new heaven and a new earth in **"First Psalm"** where things fit together, where a "worm room" makes place for worms, where God does his part to make life good, and life contains laughter and fulfillment.

"Second Psalm" is a petition with the poet making trivial and important requests: "For I pray that John F. Kennedy will forgive me for stealing his free-from-the-Senate Manila envelope. . . . For I pray that God will digest me."

It is in **"Third Psalm"** that Christopher appears for the first time. Again each line begins with the powerful *let.* "Let Anne and Christopher kneel with a buzzard whose mouth will bite her toe so that she may offer it up." Together the two come to sacrifice, and this time the sacrificial gift is not a life but a big toe. The psalm continues with all the things that Anne and Christopher will do: "Praise the Lord. . . ." "Humble them-selves. . . ." "Serve. . . ." "Bless and rejoice."

"Fourth Psalm" creates the sharpest identity between Sexton and Christopher. It opens with the poignant line, "For I am an orphan with two death masks on the mantel and came from the grave of my mama's belly into the commerce of Boston." The poet's sense of loneliness gives way to joy, therefore, when she says:

> For Anne and Christopher were born in my head as I howled at the grave of the roses. . . .
>
> For Christopher, my imaginary brother, my twin hold-ing his baby cock like a minnow.
>
> For I became a *we* and this imaginary *we* became a kind company when the big balloons did not bend over us.
>
> . . . . .
>
> For I shat and Christopher smiled and said let the air be sweet with your soil.
>
> For I listened to Christopher unless the balloon came and changed my bandage.
>
> My crotch itched and hands oiled it.
>
> For I lay as single as death. Christopher lay beside me. He was living.
>
> For I lay as stiff as the paper roses and Christopher took a tin basin and bathed me.
>
> . . . . .
>
> For birth was a disease and Christopher and I invented the cure.

From being an orphan to being a twin who knows touch and love and acceptance, Sexton blossoms forth in new

life. She declares jubilantly, "For we swallow magic and we deliver Anne."

"Fifth Psalm" again employs the emphatic *let.*

> Let Christopher and Anne come forth with a pig as bold as an assistant professor. He who comes forth from soil and the subway makes poison sweet.

The psalm continues with all the things that Anne and Christopher will bring as they "come forth"—a mole, a daisy, an orange, a snail, a squid with poison to pour over the Lord, a rose, a daffodil, a spotted dog (Sexton's favorite Dalmatians), a cockroach "large enough to be Franz Kafka," a carp, a leopard, the Mediterranean, and a tree-frog. The succession of items includes many of the natural things we normally abhor as well as some of Sexton's favorite symbolic images such as the mole, the daisy and the orange embodying goodness.

"Sixth Psalm" and **"Seventh Psalm"** evolve slowly through the now-familiar succession of free-verse lines. "For" is the word introducing the lines in **"Sixth Psalm."** It is instructive in that the prior psalm employs the grand *let.* One needs to string together the succes-sive elements in this fashion: "Let . . . For. . . ." In this case, the opening lines read, "For America is a lady rocking on a porch in an unpainted house on an unused road but *Anne does not see it*" (my emphasis). This is the first implication that Anne is preparing for death. The psalm contains other hints that death is imminent: "Anne is locked in. . . . She has no one. She has Christopher." However, **"Seventh Psalm"** turns away from the heavy sound of death to rejoicing. Many lines begin "Rejoice. . . ." Others begin "Give praise. . . ."

"Eighth Psalm" continues in a celebration of joy. The reasons are given by the poet:

> No. No. The woman is cheerful, she smiles at her stomach.
> She has swallowed a bagful of oranges and she is well pleased.
>
> For she has come through the voyage fit and her room carries the little people.

Oranges, in Sexton's work, are always images of the sun, of light, and goodness. The poet is, thus, full of God. The voyage, which she explores in much greater depth in *The Awful Rowing,* appears to be over. The psalm continues to tell how dangerous has been the journey, how difficult. Christopher, however, has had a part. He has put her into a "neat package" which will hold together, a line implying that all the troubling inconsistencies of life have been made into a compre-hensive whole. The poem continues, suggesting that the poet is "nourished by darkness" and is "a hoarder," put-ting away "silks and wools and lips and small white eyes." The strange combination speaks of the various riches Sexton has found through her poetic endeavors. Finally, the penultimate moment arrives in stunning birth imagery:

> For she [Anne] is seeing the end of her confinement now and is waiting like a stone for the waters.
>
> For the baby crowns and there is a people-dawn in the world.
>
> For the baby lies in its water and blood and there is a people-cry in the world.
>
> For the baby suckles and there is a people made of milk for her to use. There are milk trees to hiss her on. There are milk beds in which to lie and dream of a warm room. There are milk fingers to fold and unfold. There are milk bottoms that are wet and caressed and put into their cotton.

I have no doubt that this baby is the same one of **"The Death Baby"** sequence. However, these lines indicate a birthing into something new, not just a "final rocking." The abundance of milk images confirm that the baby will find mothering and food enough for any need. The poem concludes:

> For the baby lives. The mother will die and when she does Christopher will go with her. Christopher who stabbed his kisses and cried up to make two out of one.

Sexton personalizes the Christian story to include this intensely personal sharing of an experience by two so closely intertwined that they cannot be separated, even by death.

"Ninth Psalm" is again a psalm of praise for the ordinary, mundane good things in life. **"Tenth Psalm"** returns, however, to the birth imagery of the **"Eighth"**: "For as the baby springs out like a starfish into her million light years Anne sees that she must climb her own mountain." Here, Sexton adds the dimension she insists upon so strongly in *The Awful Rowing*. She will help herself; she will "do her own wash," and the medium for this will be her words. In this poem the baby grows, becomes a woman, has a child, and walks "up and up" . . . "until she was old as the moon and its naggy voice." Journey's end finds Anne and Christopher working together:

> For Anne sat down with the blood of a hammer and built a tombstone for herself and Christopher sat beside her and was well pleased with their red shadow.
>
> For they hung up a picture of a rat and the rat smiled and held out his hand.
>
> For the rat was blessed on that mountain. He was given a white bath.

> *(DN)*

The prophecy of **"The Rowing"** comes true in these lines. The rat is transformed. Finally, Sexton says

> For God did not forsake them but put the blood angel to look after them until such time as they would enter their star.

The reference to the star, implies that Christopher too is a rat, waiting his time to be translated to this radiant world. Thus, Anne and Christopher share their suffering, their sacrificial living, and their reward. Together, they "hammer" out their salvation.

The Awful Rowing toward God is largely an expansion of **"O Ye Tongues."** Written between January 10 and January 30, 1973, just prior to the final settlement of Sexton's divorce, these poems seem flat and prosy after the intense power of the prior sequence. They do, however, add some valuable insight into the particular dimensions Sexton insisted upon in her personal mythology. Enclosed by two poems, **"Rowing"** and **"The Rowing Endeth,"** the collection carries the reader through the ups and downs of a search for God who is largely missing. Space will not permit me to follow the journey closely, but I would like to discuss briefly several poems which expand the meaning of the **"O Ye Tongues"** sequence.

"The Sickness Unto Death" appears in the very center of *The Awful Rowing,* suggesting that its placement marks a crucial turning point in Sexton's spiritual journey, which now is definitely a journey toward God. The title of the poem comes from a work by Kierkegaard which Sexton may have read. One of the epigraphs for this collection is also Kierkegaard's: "But above all do not make yourself important by doubting" (vi). In this poem Sexton suggests through images of dry seas and paralysis and an inability to eat or touch that God has left her completely. She cannot hold onto the usual things that comfort people such as Bibles, crucifixes or even her favorite flower, a yellow daisy. In despair she cries, "I who wanted to crawl toward God / could not move nor eat bread." Her solution is to "eat" herself, a phrase which appears many times in her poetry and usually means that she is trying to wash herself clean of the memories and sins of her past life. In doing so, she is eating a "beautiful woman"—herself. The result is that "Jesus stood over me looking down / and He laughed to find me gone, / and put His mouth to mine / and gave me His air." The Anne who is gone is the old, evil Anne; following the biblical and very orthodox paradox, she has lost her life in order to save it. Jesus "inspires" the new Anne; the image is an archetypal one from the Bible where the believer is breathed on by the Holy Spirit and so filled with new life. Evidence of a change comes when Sexton, calling Christ "my kindred, my brother," gives away her yellow daisy—that symbol of life which she cherishes. Several elements in this poem connect with the psalm sequence. There is the death/birth cycle, the brother, the necessary self-renewal of the poet, and the joy of new life.

Following this poem are several of Sexton's most joyous lyrics. **"Is It True?"** concludes with the poet imagining that all she longs for is, in fact, reality. One should not underestimate the power of the word "imagine" for Sexton; she is, after all, a poet of great image-making power. She has in the **"O Ye Tongues"** sequence created a new heaven and a new earth. It is not so hard to accept that what she "imagines" here is intensely true. **"Welcome Morning"** is a paean of praise for the joy she feels. **"What the Bird With the Human Head Knew"** suggests fulfillment. The poet has walked many days in a dry desert looking for God:

> Then, in the middle of the desert
> I found the well,
> it bubbled up and down like a litter of cats
> and there was water,
> and I drank,
> and there was water,
> and I drank.

The image of thirst has not appeared so often in prior poems; more often it has been of hunger. However, milk has figured very strongly as the ultimate food, so the water image works for both food and drink. Clearly, the poet finds the same satisfaction in this poem that she finds in the **"Eighth Psalm"** where milk flows everywhere.

Other poems suggest the same deeply felt satisfaction:

> And God is filling me,
> though there are times of doubt
> as hollow as the Grand Canyon,
> still God is filling me.
>
> ("The Big Heart")

"Frenzy," likens the poet's faith to a small wire and suggests that just such a fragile connection can carry faith to a person. **"Snow"** happily images everything covered with white: "The ground has on its clothes. / The trees poke out of sheets / and each branch wears the sock of God." Purity overlays all the filth and evil of the world. The poet joyfully concludes: "There is hope / There is hope everywhere. Today God gives milk / and I have the pail." Milk and snow, food and cleansing—again the images are reminiscent of **"Eighth"** and **"Tenth Psalm."**

"The Rowing Endeth" is a poem which has puzzled many, but a comparison of this poem with **"Tenth Psalm"** opens new avenues for understanding. Throughout this collection the overriding metaphor has been the image of the poet in her small wooden boat rowing against the waves toward her unknown and perhaps even unknowable destination. In this final poem, however, the suspense is over. "I'm mooring my rowboat / at the dock of the island called God," the poet asserts quietly. As in the psalm, she has "come

through the voyage fit. . . ." The poet then empties herself from her wooden rowboat onto "the flesh of The Island." The word flesh is biblical, referring to Christ: "I am the living bread that came down from heaven. If a man eats of this bread, he will live forever. This bread is my flesh, which I will give for the life of the world" (John 6:51). The emptying of herself, like the eating of herself in **"The Sickness . . . ,"** and like the "neat package" Christopher makes of her in **"Tenth Psalm,"** makes it possible for a birthing to occur.

Perhaps most perplexing and certainly amusingly irreverent is the image of God and Sexton playing poker. Some critics have seen this as Sexton's sardonic statement that life is a game of chance which can't be won because God cheats.[10] However, this game of chance is turned into a can't-lose situation by a special set of circumstances. A royal straight flush contains an ace. This is what the poet holds in her hand, and this is what enables her to say she wins. God also wins "because He holds five aces." In a normal deck of cards only four aces appear. It is possible to have two wild cards in a game of Poker which would explain the presence of a total of six aces. Perhaps this is what was in Sexton's mind. What is impossible to overlook are the clear statements that both God and Sexton win, and both share their mutual happiness. Just as Anne and Christopher share their death and together await their removal to their star, so God and Anne share their laughter imaged as union of man and woman, "the laughter rolling like a hoop out of His mouth / and into mine. . . ." Finally, though Anne has had to work very hard herself, she accepts the "win" of another as her "win." If we believe the **"Tenth Psalm,"** Christopher, her brother, has made this possible. He is the "wild card" God throws into the game.

IV

The religious poems of Anne Sexton form an integral part of her work. Equally important is their treatment as religious poems. Though Freudian and archetypal analyses lend valuable insight into the unconscious sources of Sexton's imagery, she deserves to be regarded as a fine religious poet in a long line from John Donne to the present. Such an analysis is always fraught with the danger that the critic sees what she wishes to see, or in Stanley Fish's terms, creates her own text. We all come to a poet's work with our own belief systems interacting with that of the poet. The fact that Sexton was working out her belief system makes her poetry more difficult to synthesize. She emphasized this herself in a letter to Rise and Steven Axelrod concerning *Live or Die*: "The poems stand for the moment they are written and make no promises to the future events and consciousness and raising of the unconscious as happens as one goes forward and does not look backward for an answer in an old poem"

(*Letters* 421). In a very good archetypal analysis of *The Awful Rowing,* Kathleen L. Nichols suggests that this is "precisely the problem, for in her [Sexton's] poetry the integrating process must also be attempted over and over again, establishing an exhausting cycle that finally can be stopped only by death" (no. 21). By placing various poems and stories side by side, by juxtaposing images from an entire canon, by attempting to recreate a narrative, by integrating what the poet has not integrated, I am, in some measure, doing violence to Sexton's work. Yet the loss is, in part, replaced by the gain in understanding which a single poem cannot give to the reader. Sexton is most especially a poet who employs clusters of images, recurrent themes, and telling details which only appear important when read in the context of her canon. In gathering up the significance of these details, one tends to simplify or to make systematic that which is anything but a system. Such is not my intent. Sexton was not able to create a "new science," nor was she completely comfortable with the old tradition. What Anne Sexton did was to courageously strike out where no woman poet has gone before, leaving us the record full of pain and joy, full of inconsistencies, of starts and stops, of defeats and victories.

Notes

1. Middlebrook sees her problem as that of being female (296). George feels Sexton's journey is a "return to the fathers" and a representation of that quest which is native to Western culture, one that she describes as deeply patriarchal ("How We Danced" in *Oedipus Anne,* 24-54).

2. Ostriker supports Gilbert in suggesting that "knowledge through women's mythmaking is achieved through personal, intuitive, and subjective means. It is never to be derived from prior authority and is always to be tested within the self" (*Stealing the Language* 235).

3. George's chapter in *Oedipus Anne,* "Sexton's Speakers: Many Kinds of *I,*" is an excellent exploration of the impact of voice upon meaning as well as the recognition of the wide range of voices Sexton is capable of employing. George also makes the point, with which I strongly concur, that though a poet chooses the pronoun *I,* she does not necessarily speak in an autobiographical voice. The very act of creating a poem means that the poet is *creating* a persona or a voice or a situation. Even when the content of a poem is markedly biographical, the tone, the choice of words, the form of the poem put distance between the author and her work. Thus, throughout this paper, though I will speak of Sexton as both author and actor in many of her poems, I readily recognize this important distinction George makes.

4. Other interpretations can be made of the sun image, but I base my interpretation on Sexton's use of the fish and the fly, two images which she consistently uses to represent good and evil through her work. Also, light or sun appears frequently as an archetypal image of God. See "Hurry up Please It's Time," (*DN,* 69); "The Fury of Sunrises," (*DN,* 50-51); "Fifth Psalm," images of light, sun, and oranges (*DN,* 87); "Is It True?"—"blaze of butter" (*AW*); "The Room of My Life," "lights keep poking at me," (*AW*); "The Wall," "blinded by the sudden light," (*AW*).

5. See "The Earthworm," (*MS,* 41).

6. Gilbert recognizes the tension between the public and the private woman also. She, in fact, thinks that it is a central problem for many female poets. The female poet, struggling to define herself in a male world, discovers that she has two selves—the one which everyone sees and knows and the other, darker self. "The female poet's second self, however, is associated with her secret name, her rebellious longings, her rage against imposed definitions, her creative passions, her anxiety, and—yes—her art. And it is this *Doppelgänger* of a second self which, generating the woman's uneasiness with male myths of femininity, gives energy as well as complexity to her struggle toward self-definition. For if the first self is public, rational, social, and therefore seems somehow 'natural,' this dark, other, second self is private, irrational, antisocial, and therefore—in the best romantic tradition—associated with the supernatural" (451).

7. Such imagery is not unique to Sexton, however. Dante (*The Inferno*) and Soltzhenitzen ("A Day in the Life of Ivan Denisovich") are two other writers who employ images of excrement to indicate utter depravity.

8. Ostriker suggests that "duplicity" in poetry is what gives it its energy, "when, in other words, the poet is driven by something forbidden to express but impossible to repress—is a means of creating high artistic excitement . . ." (*Stealing the Language* 41).

9. Middlebrook suggests that "star" in Sexton's mythology is the "place—the poetic symbol—where the language of private suffering grows radiant and magically ambiguous" (296).

10. Middlebrook suggests that Sexton loses because she cannot have an ace in her royal straight flush. However, Sexton says clearly that she wins. Thus, I cannot see how one could say that the "'wild card' signifies the privilege of Him over Her everywhere—the inscrutable possession of dominance" (310). The laughter at the end of the poem, the images of union suggested by the hoops flowing from one to the other, and the double win statements undercut such a reading.

Works Cited

George, Diana Hume. *Oedipus Anne: The Poetry of Anne Sexton*. Urbana: U of Illinois P, 1987.

Gilbert, Sandra M. "'My Name Is Darkness': The Poetry of Self-Definition." *Contemporary Literature*. 18 (1977): 443-57.

Middlebrook, Diane. "Poet of Weird Abundance." Rev. of *The Complete Poems: Anne Sexton. Parnassus: Poetry in Review*. 12-13 (1985): 293-315.

Nichols, Kathleen L. "The Hungry Beast Rowing Toward God: Anne Sexton's Later Religious Poetry." *Notes on Modern American Literature* 3 (Summer 1979), no. 21.

Ostriker, Alicia. *Stealing the Language: The Emergence of Women's Poetry in America*. Boston: Beacon Press, 1986.

————. "That Story: Anne Sexton and Her Transformations." *The American Poetry Review*. July-Aug. 1982: 11-16.

Sexton, Anne. *The Complete Poems*. Boston: Houghton Mifflin, 1981.

Sexton, Linda Gray and Lois Ames, eds. *Anne Sexton: A Self-Portrait in Letters*. Boston: Houghton Mifflin, 1977.

Stephanie Demetrakopoulos (essay date 1988)

SOURCE: Demetrakopoulos, Stephanie. "Goddess Manifestations as Stages in Feminine Metaphysics in the Poetry and Life of Anne Sexton." In *Sexton: Selected Criticism*, edited by Diana Hume George, pp. 117-44. Urbana: University of Illinois Press, 1988.

[*In the following essay, Demetrakopoulos compares the themes Sexton developed in her "daughter poems" with the Demeter-Kore myth, in which Persephone (also known as Kore), daughter of Demeter, is abducted by the god Hades.*]

Throughout her poetry Anne Sexton's urge toward suicide is apparent, particularly in her first book and again in her last two. But her mid-career poetry mutes this dark tone, presenting rather an affirmation of life that is rooted in matrilineal or goddess values. I will examine in this essay her poems about her daughters and how she finds stability and worth in her relationship to them. When her daughters grow up, her death urge reemerges in grotesquely gigantic forms as Sexton attempts to find herself within a cosmos that she perceives then as managed by an alienating, brutal masculine godhead.

Women can realize an extended and broadly based metaphysical connection through the growth and unfolding of their children, especially daughters. For Anne Sexton maternity was her most positive experience of cosmic patterns as we apprehend them through the body. Her loss of the mother role was apparently a loss of connection to the body of her family, which for her was a link to cosmic and spiritual reality.

Any woman living in our Judeo-Christian, Western culture becomes at times overwhelmed with masculine values, especially as embodied in the official religions. In these contexts we lose a sense of significance, of selfhood. Perhaps Sexton, Plath, and Woolf are in some way symbolic of a larger casualty: women who embrace masculine values without a sufficient sense of feminine roots to keep their balance.[1] At the end of this essay, I will look briefly at Sexton's demise in the face of masculine godhead.

But the bulk of my study will examine Sexton's naming of positive feminine values. Her lifework was a heroic struggle to claim and redeem things previously held not worthy of name. Her earliest reviewers say, for instance, that her "diction is not poetical"—and their examples are of such terms as *aprons* and other artifacts of women's culture. But she went on naming as she saw things. I see this essay as a furthering of her task of defining the significance of the feminine self, a bringing to collective consciousness of both strong, positive feminine values and some especially powerful feminine sources of despair.

The Demeter-Kore Archetype

I will refer often in this study to a myth that strongly underlies the development of feminine consciousness in women, the Demeter-Kore configuration, especially as it was institutionalized in the religious ceremonies of the Eleusinian Mysteries, the mother-daughter religion that the classicist C. Kerényi calls the archetype of feminine destiny.[2] In connecting Sexton's matrilineal experiences to these ancient patterns, I establish a depth of time, a universality for the roots of feminine being she expresses. The term *Demeter-Kore* can be roughly interpreted as meaning mother-daughter; it refers to Demeter and her daughter Persephone, who was stolen from her mother by the underworld god Hades. Since Demeter is the goddess of grain and presides over bountiful harvest, her grieving for the loss of her daughter brings winter and desolation to the earth so that Zeus forces Hades to release Persephone back to her mother for part of each year. This is the mythological account of the seasons. It is a rich myth, and its intricacy and many versions are brilliantly treated by Jean Bolen in *Goddesses in Everywoman*; Bolen also shows how it applies to women's psychology.[3]

C. G. Jung describes the archetype this way:

> Demeter and Kore, mother and daughter, extend the feminine consciousness both upwards and downwards. They add an "older and younger," "stronger and weaker," dimension to it and widen out the narrowly limited conscious mind bound in space and time, giving it intimations of a greater and more comprehensive personality which has a share in the eternal course of things . . . Every mother contains her daughter in herself and every daughter her mother, so that every woman extends backwards into her mother and forwards into her daughter. This participation and intermingling give rise to that peculiar uncertainty as regards *time*. . . . The conscious experience of these ties produces the feeling that her life is spread out over generations—the first step towards the immediate experience and conviction of being outside time, which brings with it a feeling of *immortality*. . . . This leads to a restoration . . . of the lives of her ancestors, who now, through the bridge of the momentary individual, pass down into the generations of the future. An experience of this kind gives the individual a place and a meaning in the life of the generations, so that all unnecessary obstacles are cleared out of the way of the life-stream that is to flow through her. At the same time the individual is rescued from her isolation and restored to wholeness. . . .
>
> It is immediately clear to the psychologist what cathartic and at the same time rejuvenating effects must flow from the Demeter cult into the feminine psyche, and what a lack of psychic hygiene characterizes our culture, which no longer knows the kind of wholesome experience afforded by Eleusinian emotions.[4]

Sexton's major images in developing her themes are typical of the Demeter-Kore archetype, which Neumann calls the fruit-mother to flower-child/maiden transition in the matriarchate.[5] Neumann has shown that "the woman, too has to 'kill the parents' by overthrowing the tyranny of the parental archetypes."[6] Only by killing the First Parents can a way be found out of the conflict into personal life. He traces the symbolic killing of the World Parents as the way to escape the biological and familial entrapment of the ego and individuality; he then examines the conscious coming to terms with those forces. The World Mother is a far more looming and sometimes sinister archetype for a woman than for a man. Sexton seldom writes of her father, but she is obsessed with her mother. The young woman's female ancestry, her personal experience of the matriarchy, can threaten and kill her individuation process. These older women can embody an oppressive, entrapping insistence on the insignificance of womanhood and its enslavement to patriarchy—for example, mothers with little sense of self project this feeling of worthlessness onto their daughters and at the same time try to bind those daughters to themselves as psychic handmaidens. The second deathblow to feminine individuation can also come through matriarchal alliances; this second face of psychic death is entrapment in the mother role itself. Sexton escapes both fixations in stasis. She seems to be moving outside and beyond the cyclicality of life that is almost solely dominated psychically and mythologically by such figures as Demeter. She becomes a Sophia, powerful with wisdom and transcendence over the natural world.

This transformation is worked out explicitly in *The Death Notebooks,* in which Sexton faces away from her family and begins to gaze into the metaphysical depths that she explores in her next book, *The Awful Rowing toward God.* The latter volume, significantly, contains no daughter poems; the poet loses touch with her matrilineal roots and her own feminine wisdom of the earth and relatedness as she moves toward the stifling yet spacelike, purely abstract spirituality of a male god. She embraces scatological images of herself that she remembers as a girl from her mother's disgust over the female body. Perhaps, like Plath, she wrote herself into the hands of death, but her experiments with consciousness and death are different from Plath's. *45 Mercy Street* reveals how Sexton's quest for God differs radically from Plath's.

As Sexton's development portrays, the Demeter role is not a simple one-step process; the role constantly reinitiates a woman into increasingly more complex psychic realms of consciousness, gradually leading her out of the earlier stages of mothering that entail immersion in the biological sphere into more spiritual tasks and higher consciousness, until Demeter becomes Sophia-Isis.[7] As a woman weans herself from mothering, she begins to act out more autonomous roles such as the Athena or Artemis who both move freely within, plumbing psychic depths, and also becomes more active in the social sphere, taking on more roles in the community. In her first book of poetry, Sexton writes her way out of Bedlam and out of the negative, pathological Kore role she has played vis-à-vis the devouring face of the matriarchate as embodied in her mother; she writes herself into the center of her young daughters' existence. In her next books, when the children are young, she enacts the role of Hestia, the goddess of the hearth, and Demeter, the mother and nursemaid. As she gains this foothold in reality, she grows steadier, more sure of her self-worth, and she continues to stand strong throughout her daughters' childhoods. As if to allay her own troubled development as a girl child, she participates in their more normal development and assimilates their growing consciousness into her own.

Finally, in her last books Sexton turns her back on the positive Demeter/Sophia/Isis plateau of feminine wisdom and maturity and becomes entangled psychically with patriarchal figures. She is in fact bedeviled with these figures, and her attention to them is a cause of the psychic distress that led to her suicide. But her earlier poetry portrays the power and profundity of her daughters as a ground of imagery for her metaphysics. This theme changes significantly as her daughters grow into different stages. Thus her chronological treatment of this theme presents the varieties of fulfillment and ambiguity women experience as both mother and daughter. The central spiritual strength in her life comes from the Demeter-Kore archetype as activated in her experience as mother.

ESCAPE FROM THE FIRST DEVOURING FACE OF THE MATRIARCHATE: FIXATION IN THE KORE

To Bedlam and Part Way Back (1960) is concerned much more with Sexton's relationship with her own mother than with her daughters; yet as she comes to terms with her role as a daughter, she moves more easily into her role as a mother. Part 7 of **"The Double Image"** explains how her sense of failure as a daughter checks her from fully embracing motherhood; she says to her daughter Joy, "You call me *mother* and I remember my mother again, / somewhere in greater Boston, dying." This turning back toward her own mother rather than toward her daughters reflects her initial inability to find her own place within the matrilineal generations. Yet she realizes that her daughters help her grope toward discovering herself:

> I didn't want a boy,
> only a girl, a small milky mouse
> of a girl, already loved, already loud in the house
> of herself. We named you Joy.
> I, who was never quite sure
> about being a girl, needed another
> life, another image to remind me.
> And this was my worst guilt; you could not cure
> nor soothe it. I made you to find me.

(*CP* [*The Complete Poems*], 41-42)[8]

Her dis-ease in her own identity as a woman makes her unable to relate easily and naturally with her daughter. Although these are her last words in this book to her daughter, in the same poem a permanent relationship is nevertheless finally solidified: "For the last time I unpack / your things. We touch from habit. / The first visit you asked my name. / Now you stay for good" (*CP*, 41).

Time itself and a determined, deliberate immersion in her own life assuage the guilt that tied her to her mother. Along with beginning anew with her own daughter is a catharsis, one she will carry of pain and grief, and an acknowledgment of loving memories of her mother, as she accepts the mother role as her own.

FIRST-STAGE DEMETER AS INITIAL ADULTHOOD

The arrangement of the sections of *All My Pretty Ones* (1962) reflects Sexton's adventures in the world of relatedness as opposed to the isolation of the insane in *Bedlam.* Her choice of **"The Fortress,"** the single poem for section 3, the heart of her five-section book, is especially significant. Her relationship with her daughter stands at the core of her new experiences in life. The centrality in her life of that nestlike bed she shares with Linda reminds me of the bed in which John Donne celebrates the amorcentricity of the universe, as his beloved and he provide the center around which all else revolves. The solidity of her relationship with the child is poignantly emphasized:

> I press down my index finger—
> half in jest, half in dread—
> on the brown mole
> under your left eye, inherited
> from my right cheek: a spot of danger
> where a bewitched worm ate its way through our soul
> in search of beauty. . . .

(*CP*, 66)

She looks in her daughter's face as in a mirror, her mole on the right cheek, reflected on the left side of Linda's face. The mole represents their shared soul and is in a way the transmission of original sin in the form of mutability. Muted anguish, too, resonates in the mother's knowledge that the child inherits from her a fallen life and all the pain that will grow out of that "spot of danger." The worm perhaps alludes to the apple of Eve, an apple passed on from mother to daughter in the form of their special beauty, which time will eat up.

The term *fortress* works two ways in this poem. First, the mother and daughter are in a fortress, taking refuge against the storm raging both outside and inside. Second, Anne recognizes that she is a fortress to the child, that her larger body gives the child a sense of protection, of comfort, that is (from the adult's perspective) all too fragile. Her child in bed with its mother experiences "the Feminine as the giver of shelter and protection."[9] Neumann remarks that this Great Mother is often represented as rounded and juglike, as a giver of fertility and riches, of abundance and stability; the poet evokes this cornucopian aspect of motherhood, describing the scene in vegetable and fruit terms (broccoli, beet-red, bittersweet, orange).

But the jarring complication that Sexton adds to this image contradicts the essence of the primordial Great Mother. Neumann says that such symbolic female forms are usually represented without mouths and often without eyes, as they are depersonalized, transpersonal forces.[10] Sexton insists that we be aware of her sense of hypocrisy in representing goodness and warmth and absolute safety to her child. She sees the falseness of all her daughter feels in the security of her mother as fortress: "Darling, life is not in my hands; / life with its terrible changes / will take you, bombs or glands. . . . I cannot promise very much. / I give you the images I know. . . . We laugh and we touch. / I promise you love. Time will not take away that" (*CP*, 67-68). And she does give her a special kind of love within the poem, a very personal love, by teaching the child to see with the poet's eye:

Lie still with me and watch.
A pheasant moves
by like a seal, pulled through the mulch
by his thick white collar. He's on show
like a clown. He drags a beige feather that he removed,
one time, from an old lady's hat.

(*CP*, 67-68)

The emphasis on seeing and saying denies the depersonalization of the mother. Sexton moves back and forth from the child's sense of her as mother to her sense of herself as mother. And the fortress of motherhood is a comfort to her, too. She wishes she could give forever in this inarticulate, warm, natural way. This sort of nurturing is a form of comfort to all women as they enact the maternal protectress.[11]

In *All My Pretty Ones,* then, Sexton establishes a concrete knowledge of her own motherhood and a comprehension of the love and need her daughter has for her. She does evoke the memory of her own mother once, musing on the time they trimmed the trees. But it is a memory of good connections, reminiscent of the figures of Demeter and Kore/Persephone—two women, mother and daughter, shaping nature's fertility. In **"The Fortress"** Sexton herself becomes a first-stage Demeter figure, giving her daughter the special fruits of her own experience.[12]

This poem is a complex view of the responsibilities and rewards of mothering a small child, so unquestioningly dependent on its mother. What is especially striking is that Sexton has so consciously come to terms with the ambivalence of what she must do. She must adopt the stable and serene persona that her daughter needs while grieving internally and unobtrusively that she must ultimately give that child over into the cruel hands of fortune.

Most important, the poem celebrates in an oblique way the coming of age of a woman as mother. It illustrates the first and simple level of being a mother, a level that requires an unconscious, instinctual kind of love for the small animal the child still is at that age. It is important to see that the invulnerable resource of strength this role provides for the child gives strength to the mother herself as she reenters life in this volume. She is too self-aware not to see the ambiguity and irony of this role, but these tensions are kept within so as to shelter the child even from this uneasiness in the mother. The Demeter role inevitably becomes more complex as the child develops; the love grows complicated, thorny, and fearful as the daughter reaches adolescence.

ACCEPTANCE OF SEXUALITY AND
CONSCIOUSNESS IN THE KORE/DAUGHTERS: THE
ASSIMILATION OF VENUS TO DEMETER-KORE

In *Live or Die* (1966) the center of the earlier *All My Pretty Ones,* the fortress of early motherhood—that safe and known role of nurturing young children—crumbles, its surety dissolved both by her daughters' growing awareness and by her own troubled and expanding consciousness. *Live or Die* deals with the cycle of falling apart, as the consolidated psyche, having rested on the plateau described in the center of *All My Pretty Ones,* begins to stir again, seeking new levels and new experiences for the next cycle of expanding awareness. This is a typical pattern, one that is not neurotic but part of growth:

> There is a meeting point between containment and liberation and we can find it in the rites of initiation [that] can make it possible for individuals, or whole groups of people to unite the opposing forces within themselves and achieve an equilibrium in their lives. . . . Initiation [growth] is, essentially, a process that begins with a rite of submission, followed by a period of containment, and then by a further rite of liberation.[13]

For a woman the rites of initiation often have to do with unfolding roles of motherhood as the child's developing self demands new responses. *Bedlam* is a rite of submission, an attempt to contain and understand the forces of matriarchy from which she issued. *All My Pretty Ones* explores a period of containment, of newly won maturity, but ends with a sense of breaking up that signals the beginning of a new cycle.

In *Live or Die* there is a sense of moral disease and confusion that is healed in and by her daughter poems much as **"The Fortress"** holds together *All My Pretty Ones.* The last one-third of the poems in *Live or Die* contains all four of her daughter poems; these appear as oases of balance and stability with the mother reaching out into life, relating and nurturing. The other poems are primarily regressive and suicidal (except for one, **"The Wedding Night,"** which, however, depicts a brutal deflowering). **"The Addict"** perhaps best distills a desire for the unconscious, painless euphoria of sedatives, an escape from the burgeoning of everyday reality. Her motherhood seems to pull her back into life, to face squarely its ongoing traumas.

One daughter poem, **"A Little Uncomplicated Hymn"** (dedicated to Joy), delineates the poet's guilt over earlier abdication of motherhood during her madness:

> In the naming of you I named
> all things you are . . .
> except the ditch
> where I left you once,
> like an old root that wouldn't take hold,
> that ditch where I left you
> while I sailed off in madness
>
>   . . . . .
>   you were mine
>   and I lent you out.
> I look for uncomplicated hymns
> but love has none.

(*CP*, 150-52)

She projects onto the daughter's activities a "need not to grow" that reflects the mother perhaps as much as the child:

> little fetus, little snail
> carrying a rage, a leftover rage
> I cannot undo.

The fetal, curling up imagery suggests her desire for the womblike Ouroboros, the unconscious, rather than ever new and expanding reality. This helpless passivity must be overcome; her daughter's and her own locked-in psyche cohere into a refusal to touch or be touched—a myopic vision of life expanded in **"Wanting to Die,"** in which she maintains that suicide is not a question of "why" but "how." How much of the pain over her daughter's refusal to grow is really her own pain? But **"A Little Uncomplicated Hymn"** ends in hope that her daughter will transcend, will "fly" above all the past, and shape her own life:

> After that you'll, quite simply, quite calmly
> make your own stones, your own floor plan,
> your own sound.
>
> (*CP,* 152)

The stone as self is a universal symbol of the strength and centrality of the ego. This hope for her children will blossom finally into hope for herself; and the psychic strength will carry over into her own life, buttressed by the maternal responsibilities she assumes and embraces.

In **"The Fortress"** and again in **"A Little Uncomplicated Hymn,"** Sexton names through animal imagery the lower-level consciousness at which she sees her children:

> Joy, I call you
> and yet your eyes just here
> with their shades half-drawn over the gunsights,
> over your gigantic knowledge,
> over the little blue fish who dart back and forth. . . .
>
> (*CP,* 151)

She imagines her daughter gazing at her: "Or will your eyes lie in wait, / little field mice nestling on their paws?" (**"Your Face on the Dog's Neck,"** *CP,* 154). The ego flickers out briefly at a world that it cannot yet understand; blessed still with an immersion in the fluid, easy world of childhood, like mice or fish, the children's minute identities gleam out briefly at the mother. In this image we see her understanding and compassion for their childish needs and dependencies. In a way, they are embodiments of the unconscious. Her tenderness and protectiveness will mother them forth to fuller identity, to help them be born into womanhood and adulthood. It seems that in facing this responsibility the poet can shoulder the burden of her own identity and

growth. Through their juxtaposition to the other poems at the end of *Live or Die* and through their treatment of ideas troubling the poet herself, the love poems to her daughters become love poems to womanhood and to her new self.

In seeking to understand her daughters' worlds and feminine roles, Sexton learns to understand her own. The poems that best treat the poet's fear of sexuality and the metaphysical consciousness embodied in fuller sexuality are, respectively, **"Little Girl, My String Bean, My Lovely Woman"** and **"Pain for a Daughter."** In **"Little Girl, My String Bean, My Lovely Woman,"** the Demeter-Kore relationship that provides the backdrop to **"The Fortress"** is again evoked through fruit and fertility allusions: "My daughter, at eleven / (almost twelve), is like a garden" (*CP,* 145). She sees her daughter under a "blueberry sky" and is reminded of "lemons as large as your desk-side globe," "market stalls of mushrooms," "garlic buds all engorged," "apples," and "yellow beans" (*CP,* 146). She describes the embryo of her daughter as fruit:

> if I could have seen through my magical transparent
>   belly,
> there would have been such ripening within:
> your embryo,
> the seed taking on its own,
>
>   . . . . .
> the becoming—
> while it becomes!
>
> (*CP,* 147)

In the Aristotelian world of becoming and process, she and her daughter take their place. The fruit imagery that symbolizes the daughter's relationship to the mother foreshadows the natural womanhood into which the daughter will soon move into her own plentitudinous, fulsome transition "from maiden-flower to fruit-mother." The daughter is the mother's harvest and will bear fruit herself someday. The mother herself welcomes her new role of an aging Demeter as her daughter replaces her; she will now play a new role to her daughter, a role of stability: "I'm here, that somebody else, / an old tree in the background" (*CP,* 148). She's an old but steady tree.[14] The tree reflects a strength and permanence in nature that underlies its seasonal cyclicality. An old tree is stronger and withstands storms better; Demeter is always alive for her daughters to lean on.

Through embracing and celebrating her daughter's growth into sexuality, Sexton acknowledges her own developing womanhood, her own desire for fuller sexual consummation vividly treated in her next volume, *Love Poems* (1969). She recognizes her own sexuality and fertility, her own personal yet transpersonal eros, bursting out in her daughter's body. As she tries to move her daughter peacefully, without fear, into a new awareness, into womanhood with assurance, we gain insight into her own dilemmas as a girl:

I hear
as in a dream
the conversation of the old wives
speaking of *womanhood.*
I remember that I heard nothing myself.
I was alone.
I waited like a target.

(*CP,* 146)

Considering her confusion about her own femininity and identity, her tenderness in this poem toward her daughter gains a lovely, almost heroic dimension. So many of her poems find her helpless, passive, facing mutilation; here, as she stands beside her daughter as mentor through the initiation rites, she perhaps mothers herself forth, too: "What I want to say, Linda, / is that women are born twice"; "What I want to say, Linda, / is that there is nothing in your body that lies" (*CP,* 147, 148). The poet herself is born again, too, into a new joy of motherhood, the giving of womanhood to daughters. There is no envy of the daughter's youth and beauty here, only joy and hope—an affirmation of the child's and poet's self in these puberty rites. The poet also celebrates her chthonic depths as an adult woman, noble and full in her ability to love, strong as an old tree, a force with which to be dealt.

The third to the last poem in *Live or Die,* "**Pain for a Daughter,**" takes the mother as mentor to the threshold of the world that the daughter must enter alone. She observes her daughter's affinity for power as symbolized in horses; the horse suggests the powers of male sexuality, which Neumann says correspond to "the negative [and] masculine death principle as experienced by the matriarchate."[15] As she completes a series of feminine initiation rites, Psyche cuts the wool off the golden rams without being destroyed by their masculine force. When the daughter scours the boil of the horse, she, too, is ministering to and controlling a force that is yet too large for her, that lashes back with demoniac powers, mutilating her finally (the horse crushes her foot) as an initiation into the world of sexuality. She is playing with a sexual (erotic) and masculine principle that is yet beyond her:

>   the swan-whipped thoroughbred
> that she tugs at and cajoles,
> thinking it will burn like a furnace
> under her small-hipped English seat.

(*CP,* 164)

In the midst of the experiment with power and sexuality, the daughter is sundered from her mother by pain—a force that makes us each aware of our ultimate aloneness. The mother is alone, too, unable to nurture or even assist at this time:

> She bites on a towel, sucked in breath,
> sucked in and arched against the pain,

her eyes glancing off me where
I stand at the door, eyes locked
on the ceiling, eyes of a stranger.

(*CP,* 164)

Eye imagery often signifies transcendence; here both mother and child are blind with fear and blind to each other. Or perhaps they see too much to be able to look at each other. This emphasis on seeing and blindness permeates the whole poem and begins each stanza, almost liturgically emphasizing the visionary aspects of the poem: "Blind with love," "Blind with loss," "Blind with pain," and "Blind with fear." This is, of course, an Oedipal kind of blindness.

The mother and daughter share an epiphany that features the force that will finally sunder them: death. And death is understood in terms of birth, its pain, its irrevocability. Through birth we experience our inevitable death in the most direct, inarticulate, and natural way. We are made aware that our identities are caught in a cycle that will destroy us. Most terrible, in this poem the mother sees the impinging consciousness of death, the birth of death, in the child she bore. This consciousness, says Neumann, is an initiation into adulthood that is perhaps exclusively woman's:

> To experience maidenhood, womanhood, and
> nascent motherhood in one, and in this transformation
> to plumb the depths of her own existence: this is
> given only to the woman.[16]

Neumann also says that for a woman the birth of the daughter is a birth of the new self. In this poem the mother is driven into cognizance of even darker levels of consciousness and the courage requisite to face them; but perhaps by recognizing her daughter's new identity and perceptions, she, too, acquires new aspects of self.

Certainly the last poem in this volume, entitled "**Live,**" answers finally the previous poem, "**The Addict,**" which is about death through sedation. The major theme of "**Live**" is that the poet accepts joyously her role in her family, celebrating even the fertility of the dog. The daughter poems clustered at the end of the book resonate in the resolution of "**Live**" and force us to see the daughters (as in *All My Pretty Ones*) as life-giving forces. They are life-giving in that they demand a parental response and adaptation—perhaps children have more to do with moving parents along the path of adulthood, from one stage to another, than we suspect. Sexton's daughter poems seem also to be the most powerful and affirmative of all her poems, issuing from a depth of self that is universal and archetypal. Thus in this volume of poetry, she has affirmed her daughters' entry into pubescence and the force of sexuality with which they must now contend; she has also lived through with one of them the dawn of consciousness and consciousness of death, this latter through the Demeter-Kore paradox of birth as death and death as birth.

THE SACRIFICE AND OUTGROWING OF THE DEMETER ROLE

Sexton's one daughter poem in **The Book of Folly** (1972) enacts the last phase of the maternal, which Harding says is both an "ordeal and deeper initiation" into selfhood. Harding discusses the "sacrifice of the son," which writers generally treat from the point of view of the (either male or female) child, "where the myth of his sacrifice refers to the need of each individual to sacrifice his own childishness and dependence."[17] Yet the mother, too, suffers a terrible ambivalence about weaning the child from her. There is the maternal in herself that craves fulfillment through the child; yet its dependency, softness, and clinging undermine her, and thus "in dark aspect she is fierce and terrible and will not tolerate the childish dependence of the child."[18] Harding points out that it is not truly maternal love that makes a mother hang on but rather her own selfness and selfishness; furthermore, society commends this self-indulgence, this possessiveness, as a virtue in the mother—the child is supposed to do the breaking away. Yet for her own psychological health, the mother also must break away.

This means a breaking out and away from a cyclical and generation-bound view of life into a transpersonal and far less sexually and relatedness-imbued role in life. And it means that, as far as her importance in the reproduction of her species is concerned, the woman must now accept that she is superfluous. Her death would be of negligible significance to the ongoing process of life itself. Death's chapped jaws draw nearer, perceptible now.

"Mother and Daughter" contains these ideas and more. Sexton experiences anger as well as a sense of poignancy about the now completely arrived womanhood of her daughter:

> Linda, you are leaving
> your old body now
>
> . . . . .
>
> I reach out toward it but
> my fingers turn to cankers
> and I am motherwarm and used,
> just as your childhood is used.
>
> . . . . .
>
> Linda, you are leaving
> your old body now.
> You've picked my pocket clean
> and you've racked up all my
> poker chips and left me empty.

> (*CP*, 305-6)

Besides this anger about being used up and left over, she also questions implicitly the sort of human beings young adults are. Linda's body at the peak of adolescence was "an old butterfly," the last and most beautiful stage of natural metamorphosis. Now Linda joins a heartless and militant army that mindlessly picks up the march of the species, carrying Homo sapiens forward, but where? She will now "pass by armies,"

> carrying keepsakes to the boys,
> carrying powders to the boys,
> carrying, my Linda, blood to
> the bloodletter.

> (*CP*, 306)

The male as bloodletter, a vampire that will prey on her daughter, recalls Plath's "Daddy"; but Sexton also labels as heartless, mechanistic, and mindless the young women who feed these armies. Linda's calisthenics become a "womanly leggy semaphore" that calls in the troops, soulless young men like the young Romans that lurk about for the crucifixion in **"Little Girl, My String Bean, My Lovely Woman."** But in that poem she had wished to protect her daughter and help prepare her for her entrance into sexuality. In **"Mother and Daughter"** there is a much darker maternal renunciation in her unflinching appraisal of her own daughter as a taker about to join an army of takers.

The Demeter-Kore relationship and matrilinearity underlie this poem as in her other daughter poems. The last lines reject the daughter in all her youthful callousness yet wryly and fondly comment on the daughter's place in the line of fertility and reproduction:

> Question you about this
> and you will see my death
> drooling at these gray lips
> while you, my burglar, will eat
> fruit and pass the time of day.

> (*CP*, 306-7)

Casual and unappreciative of her fertility, the daughter munches fruit, the emblem of reproduction. Yet in looking at her mother's death, Linda is unwittingly beholding the source of her own, for the poet with sinister irony bequeaths not only her own fertility and womanhood to Linda but also the cancer that strikes the women of her family:

> Now that you are eighteen
> I give you my booty, my spoils,
> my Mother & Co. and my ailments.
> Question you about this
> and you'll not know the answer—
> the muzzle at the mouth,
> the hopeful tent of oxygen,
> the tubes, the pathways,
> the war and the war's vomit.

> (*CP*, 306)

There is a suggestion that suicide ("muzzle at the mouth") and obsessions with the mother ("Mother & Co.") are perhaps hereditary; her daughter so certain, so filled with aplomb, will have her own psychic battles, too.

In this poem, then, we see the Demeter-Kore theme that first emerged in **"The Fortress"** with Sexton's own acceptance of herself as a young Demeter figure; the motif underlies **"My Little Girl, My String Bean, My Lovely Woman"** and **"Pain for a Daughter,"** which feature the mother older yet still a mentor; now the archetype is almost completely consummated with the mother symbolically dying as the daughter steps into the initial fertility rites of the Demeter role. The poem also completes the process and steps of active motherhood that I have been tracing chronologically in Sexton's canon.

Thus Sexton's daughter poems reveal to the reader the degree and quality of psychic consolidation with which she lives as she writes each group of poems. Both *Bedlam* and *All My Pretty Ones* reflect a positive, groping sensibility, and both illustrate the poet coming to terms with motherhood. *Live or Die,* the most complex of her books, embodies the fullest consolidation of her feminine life as she brings her daughters to puberty and comes to terms (for a time, at least) with her own sexuality through theirs. If these shifting roles of Demeter-Kore are a universal pattern of evolving consciousness for women, as M. Esther Harding insists, then the personal in Sexton's poems gains its particular force from its universality.

Love Poems and *The Book of Folly* are less successful, less effective as works of art, perhaps because they do not carry the poet into new stages of life and fuller identity. Yet they are a readying for a surge of fuller and more intense creativity. *Love Poems* seems about sexual exploration as much as a celebration of lovemaking. *The Book of Folly* moves her out of the world of process, beyond domination by the feminine principle; and the surreality of the poems represents new reachings and trials, the experiments of a mind no longer so entrapped by sex-determined roles. A new transformation is taking place, for the daughter poem in this volume gives us the most explicit statement I know on the process of a mother weaning *herself* from motherhood. Sexton's first volume released her from her mother; now she releases herself from being a mother. She has escaped two of the faces of death in the matriarchate. She has weaned *herself* from motherhood but must still come to terms with her daughter as an adult woman. This happens in *The Death Notebooks.* She and her daughter must *share* the Demeter role symbiotically as she and her mother did in **"The Fortress,"** pruning trees together.

Transformation of Demeter into Sophia

Like the two preceding volumes, *The Death Notebooks* (1974) portrays at first a scatological, sadomasochistic terror in the face of death but moves through these forces to a transcendent, calm embracing of life-in-death and death-in-life that has the same effect as the closing scene of a great tragedy. A reader who has read all of Sexton's poems experiences a purging of pity and fear, a catharsis.

This volume is an unflinching appraisal of the dark forces of life. Sexuality is at first seen in terms of death in this book, and the poet readies herself with a "black necessary trousseau" (**"For Mr. Death Who Stands With His Door Open,"** *CP,* 352). The book opens with a search for gods; then poem after poem dwells on the discovery of a dead baby.

But the persona/poet does finally encompass wisdom born of the sea and earth yet so transcendentally precious. Her last poem, **"Tenth Psalm"** (Ed. **"Ninth Psalm"** in *DN* [*The Death Notebooks*]), one of her best, is the only poem in this volume that treats her relationship with her daughters, and, as in her earlier volumes, her relationship with them is indicative of that to her own psyche, her own sense of balance and transformation. The biblical intonations are stirring and apocalyptic yet personal and intimate, gathering up and resolving her metaphysical questions, building to a fierce affirmation of life:

> For as the baby springs out like a starfish into her million light years Anne sees that she must climb her own mountain.

> For as she eats wisdom like the halves of a pear she puts one foot in front of the other. She climbs the dark wing.

> (*CP,* 411)

Neumann says of the highest level of the feminine principle: "The spiritual power of Sophia is living and saving; her overflowing heart is wisdom and food at once. The nourishing life that she communicates is a life of the spirit and transformation."[19] Sophia remains in touch with the earth; her wisdom never goes into abstract, unreal, immaterial regions like her counterpart in the masculine principle. To Sexton wisdom *is* fruit, thus spirit with nature conjoined. Yet her wisdom is transcendent as suggested by the ascent imagery. This imagery of food (pears as wisdom) as part of the poet's growth defines her voice as feminine in the way she gives of herself; as she gives, there is more for all, including herself:

> For as her child grows Anne grows and there is salt and cantaloupe and molasses for all.

> For as Anne walks, the music walks, and the family lies down in milk.

> (*CP,* 411)

These stanzas seem to acknowledge the growth of the mother's consciousness with her child's maturation. The imagery of milk picks up the image of the nurturing universe as a milk giver in the **"Eighth Psalm"** (ED. **"Seventh Psalm"** in *DN*) and again emphasizes, as Neumann explains, the spiritual transformation of the poet:

> Just as in the elementary phase the nourishing stream of the earth flows into the animal and the phallic power of the breast flows into the receiving child, so on the level of spiritual transformation the adult human being receives the "virgin's milk" of Sophia. This Sophia is also the "spirit and the bride" of the Apocalypse, of whom it is written: "And let him that is athirst come. And whosoever will, let him take the water of life freely."[20]

Her family, in other words, is transformed through immersion in her beatific vision. She again blesses her husband's fertility:

> For the husband sells his rain to God and God is well pleased with His family.

> (*CP,* 411)

Halfway through her last poem she delineates her relationship to her daughters and her sense of self in connection with them:

> For the child grows to a woman, her breasts coming up like the moon while Anne rubs the peace stone.

> For the child starts up her own mountain (not being locked in) and reaches the coastline of grapes.

> For Anne and her daughter master the mountain and again and again. Then the child finds a man who opens like the sea.

> For that daughter must build her own city and fill it with her own oranges, her own words.

> (*CP,* 412)

The poet's stone of peace is ground, rubbed down to a smooth inner ore of selfhood as the child grows. The grapes and oranges hark back to **"Little Girl, My String Bean,"** which defines her daughter as a *hortus conclusus* (an enclosed garden) that will bear its own fruits. Yet Sexton and her now fully adult daughter are shoulder to shoulder in the quest, the pilgrimage of life. Again, Neumann sheds light on the archetypal aspects of this mother-daughter unity: "The well-known reliefs, finally, show Kore full grown and almost identical with her virgin-mother Demeter. Virgin and mother stand to one another as flower and fruit, and essentially belong together in their transformation from one to the other. . . . In the pictures where the two appear together one cannot make out at first which is mother and which is daughter."[21] Oranges have been used by Sexton earlier in this volume as the roundness a woman swallows that swells out her womb. So the oranges are

children; the city, her daughter's home; and the man who opens like a sea, the beneficent and generous masculinity that Sexton desires for her daughter.

The poem ends affirmatively:

> For God was as large as a sunlamp and laughed his heat at us and therefore we did not cringe at the death hole.

> (*CP,* 413)

She and her brother/alter ego Christopher have washed clean a rat (born of Eve in an earlier poem) in the milk of the skies. The poem portrays a cleansing, cosmic vision far grander than **"Live"** of *Live or Die,* often considered the most positive poem in her canon.

This transformation, this pilgrimage, the quest through levels of consciousness, has been largely through female initiation rites. The link between sexual roles/knowledge and consciousness seems then to be borne out in Sexton's oeuvre. Her moon imagery in this last poem is important; after she leaves her daughter to her own "city," she tells us

> For Anne walked up and up and finally over the years until she was old as the moon and with its naggy voice.

> (*CP,* 412)

In discussing the necessity of the mother sacrificing her maternal urges as her children grow up, M. Esther Harding has said: "By facing her own emotion, love, fear, hate, whatever it may be, in stark reality, no longer camouflaged by the assumption of indulgence and maternal concern, she becomes once more one-in-herself, dependent only on the goddess, truly a Daughter of the Moon."[22] No longer resentful at all toward her daughter but rather assuming an adult woman-to-woman relationship with her, Sexton becomes her own wise old woman, her own mentor, proceeding on unflinchingly alone. She surveys the earth and all it contains from the height and scope of Sophia, a goddess of wisdom and love. No longer any part of cyclicality, though still in touch with nature, she faces death and transmutes it with her wisdom and her art.

Loss of Matrilineal Roots: The Devouring Masculine Principle

It is significant that Sexton's weakest volumes of poetry, *Love Poems* and *The Awful Rowing toward God,* are both attempts to make authentic connections with the male world. Father, lover, husband, fantasied son (**"Menstruation at Forty,"** *Live or Die*), and God—all are psychic vagaries that she tries to crystallize, to fix, that she may know them. But the most powerful and solid relationships in her life are those with the women in her family. Part of the fatality (and futility) in her search for God is her attaching all meaning in her life to contact with a male God. She seems to cast asunder all those matrilineal ties she so painfully forged earlier. Does she find herself adrift without her familiar foothold in the feminine principle to anchor her into life? Her central image of rowing suggests shipwreck and isolation.

Had she kept her sense of self as Demeter/Sophia—as the touchstone, the rudder—that identity may have guided her through the contradictory information about God with which we all struggle. She at times felt an alliance with other women even after her daughters left (see **"The Child Bearers,"** *45 Mercy Street*), but this tie obviously becomes a minor force in her life. The resurgence of her mother as devourer of Sexton's selfhood is curious. Did her conscious acceptance of patriarchal versions of God push the good Earth Mother (incorporated before into her sense of self as Demeter/Sophia) into a repressed demon that demands a sacrifice of the child, of her? In connection with this, the poem **"The Consecrating Mother,"** which ends *45 Mercy Street,* features a mother sea that calls Sexton to her depths.[23] The sea becomes for Sexton the same force that it is in Plath's *Ariel*—a soothing call to death. Unlike Plath, Sexton was a woman with intuitive, deep inner ties to the Mother Earth goddess of cyclical life and time, yet in her last years she strained to find a far away male God.

This desire for a father God must have been especially difficult for her, considering how isolated she apparently was from her father, whom she always speaks of as "on the road," as a salesman, drunk and faraway. No wonder she saw God as in a void, a helpless, ineffectual male who cannot reach her. She must be the active one, an unnatural state of being for a woman conditioned to passivity. *She* must row toward God.[24] Sexton comes from a tradition (New England Protestantism) espousing the nonrational Calvinistic God, a tradition that reinforces this sense of the faraway male. The rowboat becomes especially pitiful in view of the immense space between this inscrutable God and his depraved children. In Sexton's failure to find God, we find perhaps the confluence of a Calvinistic God and the removed father figure of the Industrial Revolution, a father figure who leaves the home and works at some inscrutable job all day, returning home a fearsome, unknown figure of authority.

In other words her sense of utter separateness from the whole male world clinches her inability to reach God. Instead of trying to redefine God in what Mary Daly calls an "ontological self-affirmation,"[25] instead of looking for God in a space and time she knew, she attempts to contact an inscrutable God whom she defines finally in Calvinistic terms. How much does this concept of God tie up with her father's absence in her childhood? There are special problems for the female artist in a

separation from her father. Concomitant to the absence of the father is the closure of the mother upon the sensibility of the child, who is no longer able to bifurcate the possible modes of human being and personality, no longer able to posit alternative ways of handling the world's response to her. Especially if the mother is a hostile, negative figure, the father takes on an alluring potential of sympathy and nurture, if only one could reach him.

Especially for the creative, artistic daughter, the father becomes a necessary possible mode of independence to fight the mother role that she has incorporated as her future. To write poetry as compulsively and in such quantity as Sexton did was a heroic act, considering how it must have horrified her incorporated mother. She even doubts the validity of this act in a way few men suffer—consider her poem **"The Hoarder"** in *The Book of Folly,* where she is afraid her poetry is only so much excrement.

Thus her father and God become emblems of potential comfort and belonging, but her background allows her to cast them only in terms of nothingness, great unknowns. As Daly points out, we must face nonbeing all the time to forge being. To this point in her life, Sexton's work reads like a series of fugues with the reassuring melody of Demeter and the emerging Sophia in the background as the one constant to stabilize her against the cacaphony of self-destruction and of loneliness that she allows finally to take over. She does not attempt to build the unknown out of the feminine roots of being that she has established. Nonbeing must be viewed from the boundaries of reality that give a solid foothold. Instead she tries to leap into the arms of an abstraction. She follows the masculine principle into its most dangerous phase, which Neumann calls its tendency to psychic withdrawal, separateness from body and earth.[26] Patricia Berry has discussed the depressive trends of Demeter as a regression into the realm of man that makes her neglect her connections with the divine; she becomes caught up in an endless cycle of meaningless, fruitless emotions, an empty repetition.[27] This seems to describe well the poems and tone of *Love Poems* and *The Awful Rowing toward God.* Perhaps Sexton neglected her own deepest particular and personal archetype in her sallies at God and lovers.

On the other hand, how much of Sexton's final opting for death was a refusal to transcend her Demeter persona by moving into a different and fuller aspect of womanhood? Are some individuals naturally more bound to their own sex in terms of identity? Certainly her move toward the masculine principle, as she understood it, proved disastrous. The current theories on the healthy arrival of androgynous personality to the mature person is belied by her canon. Her attempts to be genderless are exercises in passivity (**"Consorting**

With Angels," *Live or Die*). The search for God turns into a search for being that sees personal essence contained in the great other. Annihilation of *her* self is the logical conclusion.

In a negative way she demonstrates the journey toward consciousness that Neumann describes in *The History of Consciousness*. In *The Awful Rowing toward God*, God becomes the devouring Great Father in both her poetry and life. The early part of her canon reflects the slaying of the devouring Great Mother, the entrapment of the psyche by the biological sources of our being; at that time she could not seem to step forth into her own life as wife and mother. She ousts the negative force of the devouring Great Mother from her own being but is finally stymied and devoured by the World Father. Neumann discusses the devouring Great Father as that part of the psyche which accepts and incorporates without question the ideas of one's culture and traditions on both societal and ultimate reality. The last poem in *45 Mercy Street* features her mother as a calling, drowning sea that suggests a resurfacing of the devouring Great Mother even as the devouring Great Father triumphs. This convergence of the Bestial Royal Couple suggests an inverse royal couple, a hideous pair, a duality that brings together two poles of horror into a wholeness of nothingness. They are like the twins in Spenser's *Faerie Queene* who committed incest in the womb and gallop about as adults, ravishing innocent victims. This sister/brother-husband/wife appears again in Milton's Sin and Death, who also gobble their victims. This archetype seems to partake of the apocalyptic Antichrist, and together this pair commands Sexton to self-destruct rather than self-fulfill and consolidate as she would have under the influence of a healthy metaphysical archetype of the Royal Couple. Jung's essay on the stages of life treats as innate the psyche's movement in the second stage of life toward a sense of metaphysical androgyny. To accomplish this each person tries to assimilate contrasexual psychic modes of being. June Singer sees the Royal Couple as symbolic of the primordial Androgyne; she sees it as perhaps "the oldest archetype of which we have any experience": "It derives from, and is second only to, the archetype of the Absolute, which is beyond the possibility of human experience and must remain forever unknowable."[28] Sexton, on the other hand, appears to construct a Royal Couple that preys on her, two vampires that finally devour her.

THE IMPLICATIONS OF SEXTON'S QUEST

To summarize, Sexton's quest for higher and fuller consciousness begins with her first escaping the devouring Great Mother; she then moves into a Demeter role, incorporating only the positive aspects of the Great Mother. She attempts to move into the Venus or Juno archetype in her relationship to men but never seems to cope fully with that role, which perhaps requires an active, outgoing nature—somewhat antithetical to the more passive, protective, yet strong Demeter role with which she always appears more comfortable. In *The Death Notebooks* we see her ascension to a Sophia outlook, but all too briefly; she ends her canon and life with a fixation on connection with masculine archetypes. One can argue that this pattern is idiosyncratic to her, but the popularity of her poetry bespeaks the universal issues that she treats. Unafraid to face the deepest issues in her pilgrimage through life, bold enough to articulate her experience of the feminine, she speaks for many women.

Sexton's life demonstrates the richness and limitations of the Demeter archetype. (Perhaps more specifically, Sexton portrays the Demeter-Kore archetype with Sophia tendencies.) Men are not excluded from such a woman's life, but neither are they particularly necessary. It seems unlikely with what we know of her mother that Anne Sexton could have been enculturated toward the Demeter archetype. Are people naturally dominated more by one archetype than another? That is, are archetypes simply the naming of intrinsic integral tendencies of the personality? This, of course, flies in the face of the more popular theory that all gender behavior is conditioned, but is it not true that each woman relates to her own femininity/womanhood in a markedly characteristic fashion? Should we write off all possibility that modes of gender behavior are inborn? Sexton attempted other roles than the Demeter/Sophia, yet they seemed unnatural and finally even antithetical to her being.

With courage she has written of dim, inarticulate areas of feminine experience that many of us have felt afraid to acknowledge. Her voice is devastatingly authentic; she has made personal and lyrical many crucial experiences that before were shrouded in the language of treatises of feminine archetypes and depth psychology. She asserts feminine strength and its special ties and needs for matrilinearity. Her voice will make it more possible for modern woman to identify consciously with her own sex, instead of turning away to the alien models of patriarchy. She has written for the first time in an autobiographical mode of the bio-unity of three generations of mother and daughter.[29] She has written more graphically and movingly than any author hereto of how the child grows slowly beyond the vegetative principle of childhood, then bursts like a pupa into the full possession of a soul; she shows us the mother as a mentor, a Demeter figure that assists the child toward consciousness. She makes us see the mystical elements of motherhood. The mother is a Lady of our Plants that guides in the ascent toward the Sun of full being. We can even learn from Anne Sexton's failures; modern woman must forge her own deity. Most of all, women must learn to trust their own sense of reality, embrace it, articulate it, and celebrate it in a vision made flesh by language.

Notes

1. Waltraud Mitgutsch writes compellingly of this: "Unlike the explicit feminist of the sixties and seventies, Sexton and Gluck share a female self-consciousness rather than a feminist consciousness. Their poetry . . . explores the danger zones of women's departure from patriarchal concepts. . . . Self-hatred is as frequent as self-assertion and this frequency of self-loathing creates an atmosphere of disgust and suffering. . . . Although they challenge the patriarchal order their world view is still dichotomized into the male versus the female poles . . . the loss of orientation in the universe and in society that has become acute in most contemporary literature intensifies the problematics women writers are faced with. . . . For a woman self-definition in a predominantly male-oriented culture still means non-acceptance, refusal, negation, before any affirmative stance can be achieved" ("Women in Transition: The Poetry of Anne Sexton and Luise Gluck," *Arbeiten aus Anglistik und Amerikanistik* 9 [1984]: 131).

2. C. Kerényi, *Eleusis: Archetypal Image of Mother and Daughter,* trans. Ralph Manheim (New York: Schocken Books, 1977), xxxi.

3. Jean Shinoda Bolen, *Goddesses in Everywoman: A New Psychology of Women* (New York: Harper and Row, 1984). See also Nor Hall, *The Moon and the Virgin: Reflections on the Archetypal Feminine* (New York: Harper and Row, 1980).

4. Carl G. Jung and C. Kerényi, *Essays on a Science of Mythology: The Myth of the Divine Child and the Mysteries of Eleusis,* trans. R. F. C. Hull (New York: Bolligen Paperback, 1973), 162-63.

5. Erich Neumann, *The Great Mother: An Analysis of the Archetype,* trans. Ralph Manheim (New York: Princeton University Press, 1972), 307.

6. Erich Neumann, *The Origins and History of Consciousness,* trans. R. F. C. Hull (New York: Princeton University Press, 1954), 205.

7. Bolen says that this development of other goddess sides is what saves women with a primary Demeter identity from being stuck in depression when the children leave (*Goddesses,* 193).

8. All quotations of Sexton's poetry are from the standard edition, *The Complete Poems* [hereafter abbreviated *CP*], ed. Linda Gray Sexton (Boston: Houghton Mifflin Co., 1981).

9. Neumann, *The Great Mother,* 137.

10. Ibid., 96.

11. M. Esther Harding remarks on the maternal in woman "which craves for the contact with her infant." She further says that "a physical delight lurks in the relation to an infant, offspring of her own body, which is not far in its intensity and lure from the delight of an erotic contact, although different in its nature" (*Woman's Mysteries* [New York: Bantam Books, 1971], 36). It seems to me that this poem articulates an essential sacred space, a primordial mystery of motherhood, that all mothers feel in their physical relationship with small children. In *To the Lighthouse* Lily intuits this when she paints Mrs. Ramsey and her six-year-old son James as a purple triangle. Neumann has said that male mysteries take place in abstract spiritual space while "the primordial mysteries of the Feminine are connected more with the proximate realities of everyday life" (*The Great Mother,* 282). Significantly, my male students are generally surprised when they find out how much the women in the class identify with the mother in the poems; the men usually identify with the child.

12. As Diana Hume George remarks, "The mother-daughter poems in which she is a daughter are painfully ambivalent, but the ones in which she speaks as mother attempt to establish bodily integrity, wholeness, and dignity" (*Oedipus Anne: The Poetry of Anne Sexton* [Urbana: University of Illinois Press, 1987], 59). Diane Middlebrook offers incisive interpretations of Sexton's family background that explain her trouble with her own Kore identity: "The doctor's confidence in her intelligence conflicted with the family drama in which Sexton had been assigned the role of the dumb daughter. The sense of being rotten, purposeless, dumb was of course the issue in Sexton's therapy, where it was treated as a symptom" ("Becoming Anne Sexton," *Denver Quarterly* 18 [Winter 1984]: 27).

13. Joseph Henderson, "Ancient Myths and Modern Man," in *Man and His Symbols,* ed. Carl G. Jung (New York: Dell, 1964), 156.

14. I develop this image both in my *Listening to Our Bodies: The Rebirth of Feminine Wisdom* (Boston: Beacon Press, 1983), 131, and in a recent book coauthored with Karla Holloway, *New Dimensions of Spirituality: A Bi-Racial and Bi-Cultural Reading of the Novels of Toni Morrison* (Westport, Conn.: Greenwood Press, 1987). Morrison herself discusses old women as umbrella trees that protect the mothers and children.

15. Neumann, *Amor and Psyche,* 99.

16. Ibid., 64.

17. Harding, *Woman's Mysteries,* 266.

18. Ibid., 227.

19. Neumann, *The Great Mother,* 331.

20. Ibid., 329.

21. Ibid., 307.

22. Harding, *Woman's Mysteries,* 230.

23. It is important to note that Sexton did not arrange this book of poems; after Sexton's death her daughter arranged the remaining poems of her unpublished work, and it might have comforted the daughter as a survivor to think of her mother's death in this way. Although Sexton was not good with her children when they were young (see Middlebrook's analyses), she may have bonded with them more as they became older. Linda Wagner-Martin says: "Lost from even that maternal ancestry, searching as she honestly recounts, Sexton yet finds her strength in her kinship with her maturing daughters, and through them, with herself as woman. Her strength is, however, but fragile, tentative, a veil of bright motion, a daisy, which some eyes might consider ineffectual" ("45 Mercy Street and Other Vacant Houses," in *American Literature: The New England Heritage,* ed. James Nagel and Richard Astro [New York: Garland Publishing Co., 1981], 154, and *infra,* 227-47.).

24. For understanding the gentle, positive side of this God archetype, Diana Hume George's essay "Anne Sexton's Island God," in *Original Essays on the Poetry of Anne Sexton,* ed. Frances Bixler (Fayetteville: University of Arkansas Press, 1988), is definitive. She shows how Squirrel Island and Sexton's grandfather conflate into a comforting island of divinity, a kind of *omphalos*/navel that one reaches through the feminine sea.

25. Mary Daly, *Beyond God the Father: Toward a Philosophy of Women's Liberation* (Boston: Beacon Press, 1973), 32.

26. Neumann, *The Origins of History and Consciousness,* 187.

27. "The Rape of Demeter/Persephone and Neurosis," *Spring: An Annual of Archetypal Psychology and Jungian Thought* (1975): 191-93.

28. June Singer, *Androgyny* (New York: Anchor Press, 1976), 20.

29. At least two other sources treat this but more as a side issue: Margaret Mead's autobiography *Blackberry Winter* and Toni Morrison's novel *Sula.* But Sexton's is the first psychoanalytic-poetic rendition of this theme.

Caroline King Barnard Hall (essay date 1989)

SOURCE: Hall, Caroline King Barnard. "Last Volumes, Last Poems." In *Anne Sexton,* pp. 147-69. Boston: Twayne, 1989.

[*In the following essay, Hall offers a survey of Sexton's later volumes*—The Awful Rowing toward God, 45 Mercy Street, Words for Dr. Y., *and the* "Last Poems," *the final six poems in* The Complete Poems.]

The Awful Rowing toward God is the last volume of poetry that Anne Sexton planned, prepared, and submitted to the publisher. A consideration of the poems in this volume, then, is essential to a study of Sexton's work, even though most of the poems are interesting chiefly because they are there. By Sexton's own admission, the poetry in *The Awful Rowing toward God* is "raw" and "unworked" (*L* [*Anne Sexton: A Self-Portrait in Letters*], 390). By contrast, one remembers some of Sexton's comments about the composition of her earlier work: "I really prefer dramatic situations to anything else," she wrote while composing her first volume, *To Bedlam and Part Way Back.* "I prefer people in a situation . . . , and then, in the end, find the thought" (*L,* 61). "I am given to excess," she wrote in 1962; "I have found that I can control it best in a poem" (*L,* 144). Indeed, control of informed emotion is one of the great strengths of Sexton's poetry, for such control renders emotion even more powerful. Creation of a dramatic situation by which to realize theme is another strength of many of Sexton's best poems. Such strengths are largely absent from *The Awful Rowing toward God.*

Anne Sexton wrote the poems of this, her eighth volume, in January 1973 and submitted the volume to Houghton Mifflin in February 1974, seven months before her death. She had composed all the poems, as she revealed in a 1973 interview, "in two and a half weeks," the "poems coming five, six, seven or whatever . . . a day."[1] The volume was published in February 1975, four months after her death. Linda Gray Sexton and Lois Ames, editors of Sexton's *Letters,* provide further enlightening information about the composition of these poems:

> On the file folder of first drafts for *The Awful Rowing toward God* in the Boston University archive, [Anne] noted that "these poems were started 1/10th/73 and finished 1/30th/73 (with two days out for despair, and three days out in a mental hospital). I explain this so you will understand they are raw, unworked poems, all first drafts, written in a frenzy of despair and hope. To get out the *meaning* was the primary thing—while I had it, while the muse was with me. I apologize for the inadequate words. As I said in one of the poems, 'I fly like an eagle, but with the wings of a wren.' (1/31/73)"
>
> The published poems in *The Awful Rowing toward God* differ little from those early first drafts.
>
> (*L,* 390-91)

"Words" is the *Awful Rowing toward God* poem that the editors quote in this note. As other lines of the poem suggest, Sexton's creative instinct remained keen, yet the urge to express content had perhaps overcome the need to hone her craft: "Be careful of words, / even the miraculous ones. / . . . / . . . they can be both daisies and bruises. / . . . / . . . I am in love with words. / . . . / Yet often they fail me" (*AR* [*The Awful Rowing toward God*], 71). Sexton's observation that these *Awful Rowing toward God* poems were written in a "frenzy" becomes the title of another poem in the volume, a poem that also reveals both the poet's method and her approach. **"Frenzy"** opens with these lines: "I am, each day, / typing out the God / my typewriter believes in. / Very quick. Very intense" (*AR,* 76).

In these poems, Sexton is surely "typing out the God / [her] typewriter believes in." The editors of her *Letters* suggest that Sexton "had succeeded in creating her own private God—perhaps He would never leave her" (*L,* 390). Perhaps, indeed, her search for a God she could believe in was motivated in party by her need for constant love; however, the evidence of Sexton's finest religious poetry, largely collected in *The Death Notebooks,* reveals Sexton's search as profound and at least imaginatively fulfilling. **"The Godmonger"** begins with these words: "With all my questions, / all the nihilistic words in my head, / I went in search of an answer, / I went in search of the other world" (*AR,* 62). This is the search chronicled in *The Death Notebooks.* And although that search seems completed in that volume, it continues in *The Awful Rowing toward God.*

It is primarily an inner search that *The Awful Rowing toward God* verbalizes, an examination of both intellect and emotion. These poems take the form of intense musings about life, about death, and about the poet's relationship with her God. Here there are no fully realized dramatic situations, as in earlier poems; instead, these poems seem rather to be Sexton's own, undisguised thoughts and responses, recorded as they occurred. The hunger that threads through Sexton's earlier work is clearly evident here, still sharp and still unsated. "I am torn in two," writes Sexton in **"The Civil War,"** "but I will conquer myself. / . . . / I will pry out the broken / pieces of God in me. / . . . / I will put Him together again" (*AR,* 3). As she writes in **"The Children,"**

> the place I live in
> is a kind of maze
> and I keep seeking
> the exit or the home.
>
> . . . . .
>
> [to] find the real McCoy
> in the private holiness
> of my hands.
>
>   (*AR,* 6)

In these poems God is to be found within, in the poet's own hands, and the pain of unbelief is caused by the poet's own skepticism. "I have tried prayer," Sexton writes in **"The Poet of Ignorance,"** "but as I pray the crab grips harder / and the pain enlarges." In fact, she discovers, "the crab was my ignorance of God" (*AR,* 29). In this connection the defiant, secular Ms. Dog of **"Hurry up Please It's Time"** (*DN*[*The Death Notebooks*]) reappears here briefly, in **"Is It True?"** Still spiritually vacuous, the Ms. Dog of *The Awful Rowing toward God* is now labeled "evil":

> When I tell the priest I am evil
> he asks for a definition of the word.
>
> . . . . .
>
> Evil is maybe lying to God.
> Or better, lying to love.
>
> . . . . .
>
> Ms. Dog,
> Why is you evil?
> It climbed into me.
> It didn't mean to.
>
>   (*AR,* 49, 50)

Yet this manifestation of Ms. Dog seems a theological precursor to the Ms. Dog of **"Hurry up Please It's Time,"** since her dilemma is unresolved and her pain unrelieved:

> I have,
> for some time,
> called myself
> Ms. Dog.
> Why?
> Because I am almost animal
> and yet the animal I lost most—
> that animal is near to God,
> but lost from Him.
>
>   (*AR,* 55)

The search for God, then, must also assume another direction, still within the speaker's consciousness but moving away from pain and evil in an upward direction. Sexton may remain the witch, a familiar and thematically central guise throughout her poetry: "Yes," she writes in **"The Witch's Life,"** "It is the witch's life, / climbing the primordial climb" (*AR,* 12). But she must struggle toward God, either by crawling, as she does in **"The Sickness unto Death"** ("I . . . wanted to crawl toward God / . . . / [He] put his mouth to mine / and gave me his air" (*AR,* 41)) or by climbing. One must disregard danger, writes Sexton in **"Riding the Elevator into the Sky,"** "if you're climbing out of yourself. / If you're going to smash into the sky" (*AR,* 17). For this poem's celestial elevator may possibly reach God: "Floor six thousand: / the stars, / skeletons on fire, / . . . / And a key, / . . . / that opens something—/ . . . / up there" (*AR,* 18).

As in *The Death Notebooks,* "the exit" and "the home" that Sexton seeks (in **"The Children"** [*AR,* 6]) are finally the same place, the apocalyptic discovery of which must be both death and rebirth. "The stars," writes Sexton in **"The Earth Falls Down,"** "are pears / that no one can reach, / even for a wedding. / Perhaps for a death" (*AR,* 14). If evil and ignorance have separated her from the discovery of God, they can be shed in death, specifically, in **"The Wall,"** by dying "before it is time." "Take off the wall," Sexton writes in this poem, "the wall / that separates you from God." "In nature . . . / all is change, . . . / all disappear. Only to be reborn" (*AR,* 47, 46). The poem **"Welcome Morning"** recalls the sacramental breakfast imagery of **"The Fury of Sunrises"** (*DN*); here, "There is joy / in all: / . . . / for this is God, this laughter of the morning" (*AR,* 58, 59). And Sexton concludes **"Jesus, the Actor, Plays the Holy Ghost"** with this stanza:

> Oh, Mary,
> Gentle Mother,
> open the door and let me in.
>
> . . . . .
>
> I have been born many times, . . .
> but let me be born again
> into something true.
>
> (*AR,* 61)

This is the search Sexton records in *The Awful Rowing toward God,* the search for God, for understanding, and for figurative and perhaps actual rebirth. The quite successful framing and title poems of the volume establish and reinforce that thematic emphasis. Entitled **"Rowing"** and **"The Rowing Endeth,"** the volume's opening and closing poems might well be considered parts of a single poem, the first part introducing the search, and the second part affirming its conclusion.

"Rowing" offers a sort of biographical summary ("A story, a story!" [*AR,* 1]) in which Sexton, from birth to the present time, becomes a figurative boat-rower searching for an island called God. Although this island has always been there, the poet, even while compelled to row, has been ignorant of her destination: "God was there like an island I had not rowed to, / still ignorant of Him, my arms and legs worked, / and I grew, I grew" (*AR,* 1). In this poem, arrival at the destination is only promised, yet the poet anticipates her arrival as both release and fulfillment. "I know that that island will not be perfect, / . . . / but there will be a door / and I will open it" (*AR,* 2). In this place, "I will get rid of the rat inside of me" (remember the rat of the Irish palindrome and the *Death Notebooks* poem), "the gnawing pestilent rat. / God will take it with his two hands / and embrace it" (*AR,* 2).

As the speaker anticipates relief and perhaps even transfiguration, we must take note of another aspect of this journey and of this island. There is evidence here

of Anne's emotional and physical submission to the male Other who has defined her search throughout her poetic journey, and against whose dominating influence she has fought. As Diana Hume George observes,

> I find it poignant to discover that the "island of God" may have been the island of childhood where she summered, and where, as her editors remind us in the *Letters,* "Anne's happy memories centered." I also confess that I find it beautiful; I contemplate that simplicity, that perfect circle of sought-after comfort, one that brings the middle-aged poet back to the finest moments of a troubled and unhappy past. Perhaps anyone's idea of heaven is some such journey into the past.[2]

"The Rowing Endeth," as its title implies, describes that journey's end. Here, the speaker, blistered and salt-caked from her long journey, is "mooring my rowboat / at the dock of the island called God" (*AR,* 85). And this God, though he may be created out of Sexton's own need as the intervening poems suggest, is also a Christian God: "This dock is made in the shape of a fish" (*AR,* 85). The poem joyfully and successfully adopts a metaphor from the game of poker; God and Sexton are the players, and God, with five aces (one wild card) wins over the speaker's royal straight flush. Such an outcome, however, means that both God and Sexton are winners at this cosmic game; as Sexton commented in an interview conducted three and one-half months before her death, "Here he [God] is laughing: he is slumped over me laughing, and I'm laughing. He didn't beat me; we both won!"[3] The speaker has done her best to win; a royal straight flush is ordinarily an unbeatable combination. But God, with his wild card, has prevailed. And they laugh together,

> such laughter that He doubles right over me
> laughing a Rejoice-Chorus at our two triumphs.
> Then I laugh, the fishy dock laughs
> the sea laughs. The Island laughs.
> The Absurd laughs.
>
> Dearest dealer,
> I with my royal straight flush,
> love you so for your wild card,
> that untamable, eternal, gut-driven *ha-ha*
> and lucky love.
>
> (*AR,* 86)

For one of the epigraphs to this volume, Sexton offered this: "Sören Kierkegaard says, 'But above all do not make yourself important by doubting'" (*AR,* vi). In **"The Rowing Endeth,"** pain, evil, questioning, and doubt are joyfully abandoned in this "Rejoice-Chorus." Yet there is ambiguity in this outcome, since the speaker is, however joyfully, beaten by God. And God is the ultimate male Other who leans over her in a dominant (even sexually dominant) posture.

45 MERCY STREET: A STRANGE HEGIRA

45 Mercy Street, published by Houghton Mifflin in 1976, is the volume on which Anne Sexton was working at the time of her death. She had begun to compose the poems of this ninth volume while writing the poems of *The Death Notebooks* and *The Awful Rowing toward God*; according to Linda Gray Sexton and Lois Ames, "Between June of 1972 and October 1974, she had written three new books: *The Death Notebooks, The Awful Rowing toward God,* and *45 Mercy Street*" (*L*, 390). After submitting *The Awful Rowing toward God* in February 1974 for publication, then, Sexton turned to complete the planning for this new volume. By Sexton's own account, her new volume's working title was *The Life Notebooks*: "As of yesterday," she wrote in January 1973,

> I started a new book, entitled *The Life Notebooks* [later retitled *45 Mercy Street*], which indeed [it] could be called, because with the clear realization of death, one gets . . . less concerned with getting the house-cleaning done. . . . I ought to be able to write by now, and it seems to me at this point I ought to know how to live. That is, I ought to be able to dig a trench in my soul and find something there . . . this book will come out in the winter of 1974.
>
> (*L*, 392)

By February 1974, however, when Sexton submitted *The Awful Rowing toward God* for publication, she wrote to her agent that "another book [*45 Mercy Street*] slowly being filled, but I feel it must be quite delayed because part of it is too personal to publish for some time" (*L*, 403). In a June 1974 letter, Sexton wrote, "I actually have finished another book but am glad to have the time to reform the poems, rewrite and delete. I have it in mind to call it *45 Mercy Street,* . . . I absolutely cannot call it *The Life Notebooks* because I think I have yet to write that book" (*L*, 416). And a July 1974 letter refers to the "1976 (probably) publication" of *45 Mercy Street,* "which is a kind of jumble of a book but does deal with my divorce and a deep love affair that ended in disaster" (*L*, 419-20). Sexton committed suicide on 4 October 1974. Her daughter Linda Gray Sexton, whom Anne had appointed as her literary executor on Linda's twenty-first birthday in July 1974, finished preparing the volume and submitted it for publication.

In an editor's note, Linda Gray Sexton comments that "the manuscript [of *45 Mercy Street*] has been edited but changes are few."[4] The changes involve the arrangement of the poems ("the new arrangement allows the poems to build to a clear progression of thought and emotion," since Anne "had not yet arrived at a final arrangement"), the interpretation of some words ("I have struggled to decipher her handwriting"), and the deletion of an indeterminate number of poems ("omitted . . . because of their intensely personal content, and the pain their publication would bring to individuals still living") (*45M* [*45 Mercy Street*], vii-viii).

One can only guess at what direction *The Life Notebooks,* which remained unwritten, might have taken. Based on the evidence of the apocalyptic, life-in-death theme explored in *The Death Notebooks* and to a lesser extent in *The Awful Rowing toward God,* one might surmise that at one point, near the end of her life, Anne Sexton may have felt inclined to affirm and to explore in more elaborate detail the vision of such poems as **"The Furies," "Hurry up Please It's Time," "O Ye Tongues,"** and **"The Rowing Endeth."** Perhaps this is at least partly what Sexton meant by "know[ing] how to live" (*L*, 392). In any case, as Sexton herself observed, *45 Mercy Street* is not that book.

What *45 Mercy Street* is, perhaps surprisingly, is a volume that recalls and extends the poetry of Sexton's early confessional mode in combination with the free-associative dream-structures of her later work. Linda Gray Sexton points out that this volume "charts Anne Sexton's poetic growth and the events of her life from 1971 through 1974" (*45M*, vii). Presenting a variety of subjects and often a variety of modes, these poems show more evidence of care and revision than do the poems of the previous volume, and since Linda Gray Sexton assures us that "each line appears exactly as she wrote it" (*45M*, viii), we can assume that the care evident here is Anne Sexton's own. Only sometimes "raw" or "unworked . . . drafts," the poems of *45 Mercy Street* contribute positively to Anne Sexton's oeuvre and to our appreciation of it.

The volume is divided into four sections that do, as Linda Gray Sexton observes, "build to a clear progression of thought and emotion" (*45M*, vii). The first section is entitled "Beginning the Hegira"; a hegira is, as Linda Gray Sexton tells us she learned from Lois Ames, "a journey or trip especially when undertaken as a means of escaping from an undesirable or dangerous environment; or, as a means of arriving at a highly desirable destination" (*45M*, 1). Yet if, as that definition suggests, we look here for evidence of the abandoned *Life Notebooks,* we do so in vain. An undesirable environment appears rather to surround and preoccupy the speaker of this section's twelve poems, which deal with such subjects as the death or near-death of children, John F. Kennedy's assassination, and child abuse.

The first and title poem, **"45 Mercy Street,"** offers a dreamscape, "my real dream" (*45M*, 3) of the speaker's journey through memory in an unsuccessful search for mercy and redemption. Objectified by an address that the speaker cannot find, the speaker's elusive goal shifts through familiar materials (mother, grandmother, great-grandmother, Nana, married Anne); finally, the disillusioned speaker declares that "this is no dream / just my oily life" (*45M*, 5). The mood of the poem's conclusion is one of frustration and anger: "who wants to own the past / that went out on a dead ship / and left me only with paper?" (*45M*, 5). The speaker is indeed left with her poetry, but this seems like a consolation prize: "I pull the dream off / and slam into the cement wall /

of the clumsy calendar / I live in, / my life, / and its hauled up / notebooks" (*45M*, 6).

The volume's second poem, **"Talking to Sheep,"** offers a confessional manifesto such as we have not seen since the early volumes, but with a new, bitter twist. Like **"45 Mercy Street," "Talking to Sheep"** is largely retrospective both in its reference to subjects about which Sexton has written confessional poems (mother, father, great-aunt) and in the speaker's damning assessment of the way her confessions have been received and have demeaned her. "My life / has appeared unclothed in court, / detail by detail" (*45M*, 7), she begins. "I was shamed at the verdict / . . . / But nevertheless I went on / . . . / confessing, confessing" (*45M*, 7): Even now her confessional poems, "the latrine of my details," is an apparently unpleasant "compulsion," "my fate":

> Now,
> in my middle age,
> I'm well aware
> I keep making statues
> of my acts, carving them with my sleep—
> or if it is not my life I depict
> then someone's close enough to wear my nose—
>
> (*45M*, 7-8)

The fifth poem of this section, **"Food,"** recapitulates another familiar theme: the poet's unsated hunger. Here, again, the speaker's vocation seems to win last prize. The poem offers an extended image where the speaker experiences a series of rejections in her unsuccessful attempt to suckle like a baby: "I want mother's milk." "I need food / and you walk away reading the paper" (*45M*, 13). This is the rejection at the poem's center: "I am hungry and you give me / a dictionary to decipher" (*45M*, 13).

The volume's second section, called "Bestiary U.S.A.," has for its epigraph "(I look at the strangeness in them and the naturalness they cannot help, in order to find some virtue in the beast in me)" (*45M*, 25). This section comprises eighteen poems, each titled for a beast. As the epigraph suggests, each poem offers an extended metaphor that makes a thematic connection between certain traits held in common by the beast of the title and the human speaker. In **"Bat,"** for example, a complex relationship is established; the bat's skin's reminding the speaker of her own skin moves into an oblique reference to their common nocturnal witchery and resolves with a comment on the shared fate of the ugly, outcast bat-witch-speaker:

> I flew at night, too. . . .
>
> . . . . .
>
> If you had caught me with your flashlight
> you would have seen a pink corpse with wings,
>
> . . . . .

> That's why the dogs of your house sniff me.
> They know I'm something to be caught
> somewhere in the cemetery hanging upside down
> like a misshapen udder.
>
> (*45M*, 27)

These are well-constructed, carefully crafted poems. Yet the metaphorical realizations reveal a speaker who imagines herself as outcast, misunderstood, rejected, repulsive, barren, dead. In **"Hog,"** for instance, the speaker, waiting for death like the fat "brown bacon machine" (*45M*, 28), also experiences a "little death" each night. The **"Hornet"** threatens the speaker with its "red-hot needle," its "nest of knives" (*45M*, 31); the **"Snail"** is eaten; the **"Lobster"** is cooked. In **"Seal,"** the speaker-poet, like the seal, craves a new environment where she can fly: "Lord, let me see Jesus before it's all over, / crawling up some mountain, reckless and outrageous, / calling out poems / as he lets out his blood" (*45M*, 40). The **"Gull"** represents lost innocence for the speaker: "Oh Gull of my childhood, / . . . take me back, / . . . teach me to laugh / and cry again that way that was the good bargain / of youth" (*45M*, 45). Yet such a wish is futile. This poem repeats the theme, by now becoming quite familiar in this volume, of the speaker's surviving reluctantly in a dead world with only her art for company. In **"Gull,"** the sun is "a dead fruit / and all that flies today / is crooked and vain and has been cut from a book" (*45M*, 45).

The volume's third section, "The Divorce Papers," contains seventeen poems about divorce and about love. As Linda Gray Sexton and Lois Ames tell us, "In February of 1973 Anne asked Kayo for a divorce. . . . against the advice of her psychiatrist and many of her friends, she began legal proceedings. Kayo contested the divorce until its bitter end in November, convinced that Anne was acting precipitously" (*L*, 389). These poems reveal a speaker who is lost, confused, ambivalent, and troubled by her dreams. **"Where It Was Back Then"** recounts a dream of reconciliation: "Husband, / last night I dreamt / they cut off your hands and feet. / . . . / Now we are both incomplete." The speaker washes these hands and feet "in magical waters" and places "each one / where it belonged on you. / 'A miracle,' you said and we laughed / the laugh of the well-to-do" (*45M*, 49). The title (**"Back Then"**) suggests, however, that the possibility to achieve such wholeness is past. Indeed, **"Bayonet"** recalls a dream of violent aggression, in which the speaker considers possible uses for the bayonet she holds ("for the earth of your stomach," "to cut the daylight into you / and let out your buried heartland" (*45M*, 59). **"The Stand-Ins"** offers a dream of victimization and shunned salvation; in this dream, the speaker-victim (wearing a "Yellow Star") is cooked in an oven by a "killer" wearing a swastika, but at death ("when it is ready for serving") the speaker has a vision of Jesus on the cross, saying, "This is the start. / This is the end. / This is a light. / This is a start" (*45M*, 73). The speaker awakens, however, brusquely though tentatively rejecting the profound meaning of this dream: "Oh well, / it doesn't belong to me, / if a cigar can be a cigar / then a dream can be a dream. / Right? / Right?" (*45M*, 74).

Other poems of "The Divorce Papers" trace the speaker's ambivalence about this divorce, revealing conflicting emotion both within and between poems. Poems like **"The Wedlock," "Landscape Winter," "Despair," "Divorce,"** and **"Waking Alone"** show the speaker's perception of her failed marriage. Some of these poems achieve this result through images of coldness ("we lie / like two frozen paintings in a field of poppies" [*45M*, 51]); "Snow, . . . / my rock outside my word-window, / . . . / . . . soon, soon I'd better run out / while there is time" (*45M*, 52-53). Others (**"When the Glass of My Body Broke," "The Break Away"**), clearly developing a love-lost theme, are addressed to an unnamed lover, sometimes clearly Sexton's husband. (But we remember also the brief reference in Sexton's *Letters* to a "deep love affair that ended in disaster" [*L,* 420]). In **"Divorce"** and **"Waking Alone,"** guilt, fear, confusion, and love intermingle. In **"Divorce,"** for example, the speaker says that "I have killed our lives together, / . . . / I have killed all the good things, / but they are too stubborn for me." Memory revives love: "I loved you then, so wise from the shower, / and I loved you many other times / and I have been, for months, trying to drown it, / to push it under" (*45M*, 55). **"Waking Alone"** is a love poem framed with hate and fear:

> husband, husband,
> I lust for your smile,
>
> . . . . .
>
> and your chin, ever Nazi, ever stubborn
>
> . . . . .
>
> I love you the way the oboe plays.
> I love you the way skinny dipping makes a body feel.
> I love you the way a ripe artichoke tastes.
> Yet I fear you,
> as one in the desert fears the sun.
>
> (*45M*, 57)

Still other poems present a speaker who seeks death as a response to rejection or loss. In **"The Love Plant"** the speaker poisons herself. **"The Red Dance"** recalls the *Transformations* poem **"Snow White and the Seven Dwarfs"**; "but, oh my friends, in the end / you will dance the fire dance in iron shoes" *T* [*Transformations*], 5). Here, in the *45 Mercy Street* poem, the "girl"-protagonist, wearing a red dress, "danced and danced and danced. / It was a death dance" (*45M*, 79); at the poem's close, she drowns. **"Killing the Love"** reverses

the title and the thematic thrust of the *Love Poems* poem **"Loving the Killer."** In the earlier poem, the speaker loves her husband even though (or perhaps because) he is a killer of animals, and by extension of her. Here in the *45 Mercy Street* poem, the speaker herself is the killer; "alone with the dead," she kills all that she loves, including her husband ("I am the love killer" *45M*, 77). And she plans her own death as well: "When a life is over, / the one you were living for, / where do you go? / . . . / I'll dance in the city. / . . . / And there'll be no scream / from the lady in the red dress / . . . / as the cars go by" (*45M*, 78).

The fourth section of *45 Mercy Street*, "Eating the Leftovers," contains twelve quite good poems that continue and conclude the themes, so consistently pervading this volume, of loss and death. **"Divorce, Thy Name Is Woman"** extends the "Divorce Papers" theme, although here the speaker melds "Daddy" and husband together, divorcing them both. Also as in the "Divorce Papers" section, several poems of "Eating the Leftovers" imagine the speaker's death. **"The Consecrating Mother"** creates an extended image of the sea as a sacramental woman to be joined and, in a kind of love-death, "entered like kneeling your way into church, / descending into that ascension, / though she be slick as olive oil" (*45M*, 113); "at night when you enter her / you shine like a neon soprano" (*45M*, 114). In the short, concluding stanza, the speaker asserts: "I am that clumsy human / on the shore / loving you, coming, coming, / going, . . ." (*45M*, 114). If death is a kind of sexual inverse consecration in **"The Consecrating Mother,"** it offers clear escape for "Annie" from Daddy (and husband) in **"'Daddy' Warbucks."** And in **"Leaves That Talk,"** the leaves "[call] out their death wish: / 'Anne, Anne, Come to us.' / to die of course" (*45M*, 94).

Death in these poems is surely not conceptualized as a new beginning, except in occasional tentative or ironic ways. In **"The Big Boots of Pain,"** the speaker's whole painful life is projected as an accretion of teaspoonfuls of pain, building from "the pain that begins in the crib" (*45M*, 103) and becoming finally so overwhelming that "Somehow DECEASED keeps getting / stamped in red over the word HOPE" (*45M*, 104). "One learns not to blab about all this," says the speaker in a wry aside, "except to yourself or to the typewriter keys / who tell no one until they get brave / and crawl off onto the printed page" (*45M*, 104). This poem concludes with a humorous statement of limited hope, though diction and rhythm continue to project despair:

> Well,
> one gets out of bed
> and the planets don't always hiss
> or muck up the day, each day.
> As for the pain and its multiplying teaspoon,
> perhaps it is a medicine

that will cure the soul
of its greed for love
next Thursday.

(*45M,* 105)

Such typical Sexton humor, with its no-nonsense voice and its comic, absurd treatment of a very serious subject, also pervades **"The Passion of the Mad Rabbit."** This poem offers an absurd, comical, and intricate subversion of the crucifixion story; the speaker, "Mr. Rabbit," is crucified but doesn't die, and so is burned, singing, among his colored Easter eggs:

Fire lit, I tossed the eggs to them, *Hallelujah* I sang to
the eggs,

. . . . .

My blood came to a boil as I looked down the throat
of madness,
but singing yellow egg, blue egg, pink egg, red egg,
green egg,
Hallelujah, to each hard-boiled-colored egg.

In place of the Lord,
I whispered,
a fool has risen.

(*45M,* 91)

Finally, there is **"Cigarettes and Whiskey and Wild, Wild Women"** (where humor is implied, in the song from which this poem derives its title, in the line that follows the title: "They'll drive you crazy, they'll drive you insane"). This is the first poem of "Eating the Leftovers" and perhaps the thematically central poem of the volume. Here is its second and final stanza:

Now that I have written many words,
and let out so many loves, for so many,
and been altogether what I always was—
a woman of excess, of zeal and greed,
I find the effort useless.
Do I not look in the mirror,
these days,
and see a drunken rat avert her eyes?
Do I not feel the hunger so acutely
that I would rather die than look
into its face?
I kneel once more,
in case mercy should come
in the nick of time.

(*45M,* 89)

It is abundantly clear why Anne Sexton renamed this volume, reserving the title *The Life Notebooks* for a later date that never came. There is only scanty evidence in *45 Mercy Street* that Sexton "[knew] how to live," as she observed in an optimistic moment in early 1973, that she could "dig a trench in [her] soul and find something there" (*L,* 392). What she found there, if the poems of this volume can be said to offer sufficient evidence, was pain, loss, hunger, and emotional exhaus-

tion, from which no one or nothing could deliver her: not another human being, not God, and not her art. The poems do indeed "build to a clear progression of thought and emotion" (*45M,* vii), as Linda Gray Sexton observes, yet the final structure is hardly the one promised by "hegira," the title of the volume's opening section. These poems appear to document not a journey to escape a dangerous environment but a journey to catalogue the dangers. And if this journey succeeds in reaching a highly desirable destination, it is death with its obliteration of consciousness and pain that is desired, rather than the joyful rebirth prefigured in *The Death Notebooks.* This volume begins "the hegira" with **"45 Mercy Street,"** where mercy is an elusive dream. It ends, thematically, with the speaker "kneel[ing] once more, / in case mercy should come / in the nick of time." After reading this volume, one senses that the odds for that to happen are not very good.

Words for Dr. Y. and "Last Poems"

Words for Dr. Y., published posthumously in 1978, is the tenth and last volume of Anne Sexton's work to be published. It is also, as Linda Gray Sexton tells us in an editor's note, "the first collection of Anne Sexton's poetry from which her editorial guidance was totally absent."[5] Its contents are poems and stories that were found among her papers after her death, possibly including the "untitled binder of new poems" to which Linda Gray Sexton refers in the editor's note to *45 Mercy Street* (*45M,* vii). The poems of *Words for Dr. Y.* are arranged by order of composition and dated when possible; they span the years from 1960 to 1971. "Last Poems" is the concluding section of *The Complete Poems.* These six poems which Sexton wrote in the seven months before her death had been previously uncollected; they are dated as well, from March 24, 1974 to September 27, 1974. *Words for Dr. Y.* comprises four sections, chronologically ordered. Linda Gray Sexton tells us that the first section, "Letters to Dr. Y.," "written from 1960 to 1970, was originally a series of poems Anne wanted to include in her sixth volume, *The Book of Folly.* When friends and editors convinced her it did not belong there, she specifically reserved it for publication after her death. As far as I know, this is the only time she ever set work aside for such a purpose" (*WD* [***Words for Dr. Y.: Uncollected Poems with Three Stories***], v).

"Letters to Dr. Y." contains twenty-three poems, all untitled. Because they are untitled, and because they are chronologically arranged and dated, they take the form of journal entries presented as one long poem: records of meetings with the psychiatrist Dr. Y., responses to sessions, examinations of subjects discussed in or occasioned by therapy, notes addressed directly to Dr. Y., recollected dialogues with the doctor. These poems catalogue the peaks of a ten-year history of fears, desires, failures, psychoses, and triumphs.

The therapy itself is the theme of several poems; often it is represented, as well it might be, as a digging: "I begin again, Dr. Y., / this neverland journal, / full of my own sense of filth. / Why else keep a journal, if not / to examine your own filth?" **WD,** 8). Perceiving her task and her worth in this way, the speaker often becomes the child, being toilet-trained, trying to please her parent. As we have seen in many of Sexton's poems in *The Book of Folly* and elsewhere, the psychiatrist is the male Other who holds power over her and whom she tries to please. In another poem of this sequence, she writes: "But brown eyes where Father Inc. waits, / that little Freud shoveling dirt in the cellar, / that Mr. Man, Mr. Cellar Man, brown as / old blood" (**WD,** 16).

Several poems of this section record dialogues with Dr. Y. In one, in a refrain between stanzas, the doctor repeats, with the voice of the superego: *"And where is the order?"* (**WD,** 5-6). In another poem, Dr. Y. begins by asking *"What do the voices say?"* (**WD,** 20) The speaker answers, in the specific images of six stanzas, that her voices well up from her past and cover her present with paralysis and death. In another dialogue, the doctor asks questions based on statements and answers just offered by the speaker:

> *Have the leaves always talked? Even when you were young?*
> you ask.
>
> When I was five I played under pines.
> Pines that were stiff and sturdy.
> State of Maine pines . . .
>
> . . . . .
>
> *The leaves tell you to die?* you ask.
> Yes.
>
> (**WD,** 30)

Throughout this section of the volume, death is a persistent theme, heralded by the close of the first poem:

> Bravo, I cry,
> swallowing the pills,
> the do die pills.
> Listen ducky,
> death is as close to pleasure
> as a toothpick.
> To die whole,
> riddled with nothing
> but desire for it,
> is like breakfast
> after love.
>
> (**WD,** 4)

The reference to breakfast here recalls the sacramental morning imagery of **"The Fury of Sunrises"** (**DN**), suggesting again the familiar linkage of death with new life. In other poems of this "Letters to Dr. Y." sequence, death takes different forms: death calls for the speaker

in the surreal, nightmarish shape of a murderous **"My Lai soldier"** (**WD,** 27); it also appears as a man, a razor, a whip (**WD,** 20-21).

Other familiar themes appear here as well; one short entry states that "this loneliness is just an exile from God" (**WD,** 10), and in another, where the mocking speaker declares that "God is only mocked by believers!" God turns away: "And God was bored. / He turned on his side like an opium eater / and slept" (**WD,** 17-18). Here and elsewhere, God and Dr. Y. merge into a composite male-Other authority figure: "Your hand is the outrageous redeemer" (**WD,** 32), says the speaker to both of them. Evil and guilt appear here as well, as one might expect. The poet weaves evil into the practice of her craft: "None of them [John, Maxine, George] has / the sense of evil that I have, / evil that jaw breaker, / that word wife" (**WD,** 7). Here and in another poem, evil is given the name of "wife," indicating deep self-loathing in the very formation of this linguistic identification. Thus, in the other entry, although "I am no longer at war with sin,"

> the old sense of evil remains,
> evil that wife.
> Evil who leaves me here,
> most days,
> dead broke.
>
> . . . . .
>
> She is my other face. . . .
>
> (**WD,** 23)

Also among these entries, however, is interspersed affirmation and hope. One poem, free-associating on the pleasure of "the word warm," concludes: "In the beginning, / summer is a sense / of this earth, / or of yourself" (**WD,** 9). Another very short entry declares that "I begin to see. Today I am not all wood" (**WD,** 33). The closing poem of the sequence emphasizes this positive note, for it is a hymn to happiness:

> I am happy today with the sheets of life.
>
> . . . . .
>
> I hung out the bedsheets and watched them
> slap and lift like gulls.
> When they were dry I unfastened them
> and buried my head in them.
> All the oxygen of the world was in them.
>
> . . . . .
>
> So this is happiness,
> that journeyman.
>
> (**WD,** 34)

Clearly, Dr. Y. has helped the poet to know "that journeyman," for another poem in "Letters to Dr. Y." concludes with this couplet: "I am in a delight with you, Music Man. / Your name is Dr. Y. My name is Anne" (**WD,** 22).

The volume's second section, entitled "Poems 1971-1973," contains poems written between July and July of those years. Linda Gray Sexton comments cryptically in the editor's note that Sexton "had no chance to incorporate these [poems] into a book or place them with magazines" (**WD,** v). From their dates, we can ascertain that these nine poems were composed during the time that Sexton was writing the poems published in ***The Death Notebooks, The Awful Rowing toward God,*** and ***45 Mercy Street.*** Clearly, Sexton chose not to include these nine in any of those volumes, for reasons we cannot know. They are, in fact, "raw" and "un-worked" poems, much like those of ***The Awful Rowing toward God*** (*L,* 390), yet they are fiercer. There is the suggestion in them (**"To Like, To Love"**) of homosexual love, but we have seen that in earlier poems. There is in these poems an echo of the old, jaunty, angry voice (**"The Surgeon," "Buying the Whore"**). Some poems are Plath-like; some are prolix. Perhaps Sexton was saving these poems to rework for a later volume. Or perhaps she had simply discarded them.

The volume's third section is called "Scorpio, Bad Spider, Die: The Horoscope Poems (1971)." This series of poems, Linda Gray Sexton tells us, was one about which Anne Sexton was "quite uncertain about [the] final destination," even though they had been placed in Anne's "file [cabinet] beside ***45 Mercy Street*** and other poems intended for publication." Since these poems "never fit thematically into any book she worked on thereafter," Sexton may have been saving them for later publication. Or, "although written in the later years of her career, these poems often return to the stricter form, rhyme, and meter of her earlier work. Perhaps this return, coupled with the very personal content of these poems, made her initially uneasy about publishing them" (**WD,** v-vi).

The epigraph to these Scorpio poems is from Pushkin: "And reading my own life with loathing, I tremble and curse" (**WD,** 55). Anne Sexton was born on 9 November 1928 under the sign of Scorpio. The series opens with a letter from an astrologer: *"Dear Friend, / It may seem to you superstitious and childish to / consult the Forecast in your daily activities, but the / main object of reading your horoscope should be / self-training and knowledge of yourself and your / character traits"* (**WD,** 57). "Self-training and knowledge of yourself and your character traits" is the theme of the fifteen poems of the series, as the opening poem suggests: "Madame, I have a confusion, / will you take it away? / Madame, I have a sickness, / will you take it away? / Madame, I am the victim of an odor, / will you take it away? Take! For God's sake take! / Mend everything!" (**WD,** 57) The following fourteen poems follow similar form, each entitled with a date, and all but one opening with an italicized horoscope prediction (such as we might find in a newspaper). This structure is humorous in a typi-

cally Sexton, slant sort of way; the banality of the opening horoscope entry contrasts almost comically with the poem that follows.

Thematic unity here is achieved, loosely, by the shifting focus on "yourself and your character traits"; selection of subjects is various and wide-ranging. Since all, however, are subjects with which we are by now familiar, it is difficult to see which poems might have been so personal as to have made the poet "uneasy," at this point, "about publishing them." The theme suggested in the epigraph is evident here, although self-loathing seems strangely less evident here than in the poems of other volumes.

The poem **"February 17th"** can serve as an example:

> *Take nothing for granted.*
>
> Yes, I know.
> Wallace will be declared king.
> For his queen, Shirley Temple Black.
>
> . . . . .
>
> Yes, I know.
> Death sits with his key in my lock
> Not one day is taken for granted.
> Even nursery rhymes have put me in hock.
> *If I die before I wake.* Each night in bed.
> My husband sings *Baa Baa black sheep* and we pretend
> that all's certain and good, that the marriage won't end.
>
> (**WD,** 69)

Surely there is genuine humor here ameliorating the self-loathing. Sexton's special brand of dark laughter is evident, facing the absurd in a matter-of-fact voice, projecting the comical through rhythms and tone.

The fourth and last section of ***Words for Dr. Y.*** contains, as Linda Gray Sexton tells us, "three horror tales. Anne enjoyed writing these stories perhaps more than anything else she ever produced and was proud of the result" (**WD,** vi). Each of these stories has a first-person narrator (as we might expect from a poet who personifies speakers so clearly in her verse). And each can be read as a gloss to major themes of Sexton's poetry. "Ghost," the first of the three, is indeed a kind of horror story. Its speaker is Anne's great-aunt Anna, who figures so largely in Sexton's poetry, especially the early work. Here, "Nana," as Anne called her, haunts Anne from beyond the grave, claiming responsibility both for many of Anne's difficulties and for some of her successes. What Anne experiences as madness is a result of that haunting, as is her broken hip: "She had at the time been committing a major sin" (**WD,** 83). Anne's poetic gift results as well from this ghost's influence; "it is . . . unfortunate that she did not inherit my gift with the English language. But here I do interfere the most, for I put *my* words onto her page, and . . . she . . . calls it 'a gift from the muse.' Oh how sweet it is!" (*WD*, 85) Sexton's poems document extensively Sexton's love for and guilt over the death of this great-aunt. It is interesting that in this story Sexton fancifully (and seriously?) explores the possibility that their relationship has continued.

"Vampire," the second story, belongs more firmly in the horror-story genre. Its speaker is a male insurance agent turned vampire who, having been captured and imprisoned by unknown assailants, goes out each night carrying a loaf of bread and an address book. His goal is to find one of the "girls" listed in his book and eat his bread in her bedroom while sucking her blood from her navel: "that which held her to her mother to her mother to her mother—back into the eternal" (*WD*, 91). He loves these sojourns and is completely insensible of the fact that he is killing the girls: "Do I only dream that she cries out in joy? . . . She is very still, but that is proper" (*WD*, 91). One is reminded of Sylvia Plath's daddy-husband: "If I've killed one man, I've killed two—/ the vampire who said he was you / And drank my blood for a year."[6] One thinks also of Sexton's poem **"Loving the Killer"** (*LP* [*Love Poems*]), or her lines (peculiarly echoing Plath's "oo" rhyme in "Daddy"): "You do / drink me. The gulls kill fish" (**"Barefoot,"** *LP*). In Sexton's "Vampire," there is no angry retribution; the women-victims remain passive, dead. But somehow the anger vibrates around the edges of the story. In Plath's words at the conclusion of "Daddy," "There's a stake in your fat black heart / And the villagers never liked you. / They are dancing and stamping on you. / They always *knew* it was you. / Daddy, daddy, you bastard, I'm through."[7]

The third story, "The Bat," offers a surreal, nightmarish narrative. The narrator is a man who at first awaits his "verdict" in an atmosphere reminiscent of Kafka's *The Trial,* but with peculiar humor: called by his social security number to hear his verdict, the narrator exclaims, "Good God, . . . the same God-damned number even HERE!" (*WD*, 93) His verdict is reincarnation as a bat, with nine former human lives to remember. As he remembers fragments of these lives, however, an advertisement insistently interrupts, until he sees the entire "AD-a complete scenario" (*WD*, 97), which involves the narrator, now a man, rescuing a nameless girl from an attacker, trying to comfort her, and then following the attacker's instructions to, literally, crucify her against his closet wall. In this connection, one is reminded of similar imagery in many of Sexton's poems, where she, as speaker, is imaginatively crucified. One thinks also of her poem **"Bat"** (*45M*), where she likens herself to the ugly, "misshapen" creature who hangs upside down "in the cemetery," and where both, like witches, "[fly] at night" (*45M*, 27). In the complicated relationship established by this story

between various victims and victimizers, Sexton expresses frustration at the absurdity of existence, anger at her own perceived ugliness and at helpless victimization, and (as in "Vampire") rage against the male victimizer.

"Last Poems," the six final poems of Sexton's *Complete Poems,* written between 14 March 1974 and 27 September 1974, are principally about love and death, which may have been the two great themes coursing through Sexton's thoughts in the seven months before her suicide. The first poem, **"Admonition to a Special Person,"** offers a kind of valediction (to whom?) to "Watch out for power, . . . hate, . . . friends, . . . intellect, . . . games, . . . [and] love" (*CP* [*The Complete Poems*], 607):

> Watch out for love
> (unless it is true,
> and every part of you says yes including the toes)
>
> (*CP*, 607)

This poem sounds much like e. e. cummings's "dive for dreams":

> trust your heart
> if the seas catch fire
> (and live by love
> though the stars walk backward)[8]

The second poem, **"In Excelsis,"** is a love poem to "Barbara" (mentioned also in the epigraph to *45 Mercy Street* and in its poem **"There You Were"**). As in **"There You Were,"** Anne and Barbara stand on a beach in **"In Excelsis."** In this "Last Poem," Sexton imagistically links drowning (entering the sea) with sexual love, a linkage accomplished also in **"The Consecrating Mother"** (*45M*), as we have seen; it is interesting to note that in *45 Mercy Street,* **"The Consecrating Mother"** follows **"There You Were."** Several motifs may be at work simultaneously in this group of poems: the attractiveness of death, its possibility of offering new life, and (possibly homosexual) love. Yet this love-between-women theme is complex in itself; in another of Sexton's *45 Mercy Street* poems, **"The Red Dance,"** the speaker refers to herself as "Sappho." Such a reference, we should remember, suggests love of women (a feminist company of women) *and* of art; Sappho the poet leaped into the sea both to pay the price of art and to express despair at unrequited love.

"Uses," "As It Was Written," and **"Lessons in Hunger,"** the third, fourth, and fifth poems, explore the speaker's perception of victimization. In **"Uses,"** she echoes Plath's Jew imagery (not for the first time in these late poems) and cadences ("I, alone, came through, / starved but making it by eating / a body or two" [*CP*, 610]). **"As It Was Written"** suggests some of the more successful apocalyptic imagery of other, slightly earlier poems ("Earth, earth, / riding your merry-go-round / toward extinction" [*CP*, 611]) but ends with the speaker victimized "each night," with the moon "with its hungry red mouth" sucking, vampire-like, "at my scars" (*CP*, 612). **"Lessons in Hunger"** recalls and continues the familiar motif of unsated hunger. In a Kafkaesque scene vaguely reminiscent of the beginning of "The Bat," the speaker confronts a faceless, bodiless "blue blazer" (*CP*, 612), to be answered only in silence.

Sexton wrote the final poem, **"Love Letter Written in a Burning Building,"** one week before her death. The poem is addressed to "Dearest Foxxy"; the building of the title is a burning crate, and the crate is a coffin. Writes the speaker:

> I have on a mask in order to write my last words,
> and they are just for you, and I will place them
> in the icebox saved for vodka and tomatoes,
> and perhaps they will last.
>
> . . . . .
>
> If my toes weren't yielding to pitch
> I'd tell the whole story.

(CP, 613-14)

Seven days later, Anne Sexton removed her mask. And if she did not leave us with "the whole story," she left us with much that is valuable. Her poems will last.

Notes

1. Heyen and Poulin interview, *No Evil Star*, 143.

2. George, *Oedipus Anne*, 53.

3. "Interview With Gregory Fitzgerald," in *No Evil Star*, 192.

4. *45 Mercy Street*, ed. Linda Gray Sexton (Boston: Houghton Mifflin Co., 1976), vii; hereafter cited in the text as *45M*.

5. *Words for Dr. Y.*, ed. Linda Gray Sexton (Boston: Houghton Mifflin Co., 1978), v; hereafter cited in the text as *WD*.

6. Plath, "Daddy," [Sylvia Plath, "Daddy," in *Ariel* (New York: Harper & Row, 1966], 51.

7. Ibid., 51.

8. e. e. cummings, "dive for dreams," in *95 Poems* (New York: Harcourt, Brace & Co., 1958), 60.

Selected Bibliography

PRIMARY WORKS

NONFICTION

No Evil Star: Selected Essays, Interviews and Prose. Edited by Stephen E. Colburn. Ann Arbor: University of Michigan Press, 1985. This is a useful collection of essays, short stories, and interviews by Anne Sexton, most of which appeared originally in journals and are reprinted here. These are not listed elsewhere in this bibliography. Contents: Essays and Prose: "Classroom at Boston University," 3-5; "The Barfly Ought to Sing" (6-13); "Comment on 'Some Foreign Letters,'" 14-17; "The Last Believer," 18-22; "All God's Children Need Radios," 23-32; "The Freak Show," 33-38. Interviews (arranged chronologically): "With Harry Moore," 41-69; "With Patricia Marx," 70-82; "With Barbara Kevles," 83-111; "With Lois Ames," 119-29; "With William Heyen and Al Poulin," 130-57; "With Maxine Kumin, Elaine Showalter, and Carol Smith," 158-79; "With Gregory Fitzgerald," 180-206.

SECONDARY WORKS

BOOKS

George, Diana Hume. *Oedipus Anne: The Poetry of Anne Sexton.* Urbana: University of Illinois Press, 1987. An impressive study of Sexton as "a contemporary Oedipus," a "truth-seeker," connecting Sexton's work both with contemporary psychoanalysis and with feminism.

Linda Wagner-Martin (essay date 1989)

SOURCE: Wagner-Martin, Linda. "Anne Sexton, Poet." In *Critical Essays on Anne Sexton*, edited by Linda Wagner-Martin, pp. 1-18. Boston: G. K. Hall, 1989.

[*In the following essay, Wagner-Martin provides a summary of the critical response to Sexton's writings through the late 1980s.*]

> Poetry is special, is something else. As a poet . . . I want your real idea, unclothed from your feeling for the writer. . . . Poetry has saved my life and I respect it beyond both or any of us.[1]

In her 1958 letter to W. D. Snodgrass, Sexton expresses the theme that was to continue throughout the sixteen years that remained of her life: she had become a poet, and that identity was going to be the most important one in her existence. As Denise Levertov has so accurately pointed out, Sexton's poetry saved her as long as saving was possible.[2] It gave her productive years as a poet, and also as a woman—mother, wife, lover, friend. Through her art, Sexton was brought back into the mainstream of human response and human interaction. Without it, she was voiceless—worse, without a language, her knowledge and understandings frustrated in not having a means of expression. The wonder of Sexton's poetry is that it provided for her a magical language for communication, after an earlier lifetime of de facto isolation.[3]

One of the fascinations about poetry is that, in many ways, it is literally incomprehensible. Its spark-striking magic reaches beyond logic and reason, intellectual skills we like to pretend can be taught, into a fuller, more integral kind of reason, a reason that synthesizes and connects rather than separates into categories. The poet sees life—or some parts of it—whole. Better, the poet "sees" with multifaceted vision, and if his or her reach into language is commensurate, can find image and metaphor to express vision so comprehensive it can be frightening. As readers, caught in the surprising—sometimes astonishing—grip of a poet's accurate vision and language, we can only marvel at its existence. Literature is filled with praise to muses, white goddesses, other manifestations of inspiration: even the poet is not sure how certain visions come to the poem or, the more difficult part of the art, how those visions were caught and translated into language.

Anne Sexton, as poet, is very much in the mainstream of aeons of traditional poets and poetry. She wrote to give language to her visions, and much of the power of her art accrues from her honesty about those visions. Her first important long sequence poem, **"The Double Image,"** voices her personal confusion over what her scrutiny of herself within her family—daughter to both a mother and a father—meant. It is a paradigmatic expression of centuries of inherent conflict, divided loyalty, the ambivalence of pride and disdain, love and hate. As an expression of such ambivalence, **"The Double Image"** becomes every reader's poem. Almost immediately upon her becoming a poet, Sexton was tapping into archetypal conflicts—human concerns—that were meaningful to most human lives.

Sexton's ability to strike to the center of a complex problem in image stemmed in part from her lack of formal training in literature. Unlike the academically successful John Berryman, Adrienne Rich, Robert Lowell, Sylvia Plath, and John Holmes, Sexton did not compare her poems with "great" literature. She did not begin writing in 1957, at the suggestion of her therapist, under the shadow of essential texts and key literary figures, nor was she burdened with long years of adamant instruction in what were good subjects for poems (and what were not), or in the kinds of techniques poets used (or didn't attempt). Sexton knew she had a great deal to learn. What she probably didn't see as the advantage it was, was that she had comparatively little to unlearn.[4] She was free to use whatever subject, skill, form, technique she liked, and though she bounced ideas off countless other writers—endlessly, and demanded their best attention for her work—she made her own choices and, usually, went her own way.

A good example of Sexton's strange mixture of self-confidence and artistic dependence is her situation with the Boston poet John Holmes, one of her earliest teachers and mentors. As Diane Middlebrook retells the story, Sexton enrolled in a poetry workshop Holmes taught at the Boston Center for Adult Education. Regularly a faculty member at Tufts University, Holmes enjoyed teaching his nontraditional students in the workshop, and Sexton was keenly excited to find eighteen other people interested in what was fast becoming her art. During that first year of poetry workshops, Sexton worked "demonically," and as Maxine Kumin remembers, "She would willingly push a poem through twenty or more drafts. She had an unparalleled tenacity in those early days." As a result of Sexton's intense productivity, she soon had poems enough for a book, and approached Holmes about the possibility of publishing a collection. While he liked much of her poetry, he was hesitant to have her publish what he called her "clinical" poems, and replied in a letter, "Something about asserting the hospital and psychiatric experience seems to me very selfish. . . . It bothers me that you use poetry this way." His letter closed with the thought that her later life, and later poems, would grow away from her earlier psychic history, and that once she became "another person," her poems would "haunt and hurt" her.[5] In the face of this rejection of both her work and her self (for Holmes's implication was that what Sexton had been, and been through, was all a skin to be shed in the future, rather than some integral part of what she was becoming), Sexton wrote the fine poem **"For John, Who Begs Me Not to Enquire Further."** This defense of self and art, phrased cogently and in some ways impersonally, was the image of her understanding of herself as writer. The poem opens,

> Not that it was beautiful,
> but that, in the end, there was
> a certain sense of order there;
> something worth learning
> in that narrow diary of my mind.

Sexton was drawn to see the importance of her own vision, her own "sense of order," and so she became a poet. And in the same powerful poem, she explains her amazing capacity to translate visions into language. "I tapped my own head; / it was glass, an inverted bowl. / It is a small thing / to rage in your own bowl." So the poem as an internal process of knowing true emotion, experiencing it, coming to it through both feeling and language, changes:

> At first it was private.
> Then it was more than myself;
> it was you, or your house
> or your kitchen.

The joy as the poet sees herself becoming more than self through her expression is balanced with the risk to the poet of having that expression rejected:

> And if you turn away
> because there is no lesson here

I will hold my awkward bowl,
with all its cracked stars shining
like a complicated lie,
and fasten a new skin around it
as if I were dressing an orange
or a strange sun.

Even the poet's rejected expression has value. The poet will try again, assuming chameleonlike existences in the guise of new skins, and even if others cannot respond—regardless of how many new skins, new facades, new languages, as Holmes seemed to feel he could not respond to some of Sexton's poems—the poet continues:

Not that it was beautiful,
but that I found some order there.
There ought to be something special
for someone
in this kind of hope. . . .[6]

Anne Sexton wrote her way to a Pulitzer Prize (for *Live or Die* in 1966), to membership in the Royal Society of Literature in London, and to Crawshaw Professor of Literature at Colgate University—among other academic posts.[7] But she also, ironically, wrote her way into a kind of poetic notoriety, based on her outspoken comments, her dramatic readings, her alcoholism, her personal dependency; and into—and quickly out of—the critical establishment. A major irony of Sexton's career as poet is the speed with which she disappeared from the attention of both reviewers and academics. In the early 1960s, Sexton was talked about, reviewed, taught, published and reviewed widely in England, and called a "major" poet after only two collections had appeared. By the late 1960s, she was hardly reviewed any longer, and seldom taught. There were a number of reasons for the critical distaste for her work during the later 1960s and 1970s: she often wrote about nontraditional literary subjects (not only outré subjects like menstruation but equally threatening—that is, sentimental—topics like a mother's love for her daughters). She was often overly personal, which meant readers had to deal with the facts (or created facts) of both her femaleness and her mental instability, and there were few literary precedents for either. And she used such direct expression that there could be no pretending that she was saying anything other than she was. What alternate interpretations can there be for lines like "A woman *is* her mother," "Fat, white-bellied men, / wearing their genitals like old rags," "Since you ask, most days I cannot remember," or the powerful sequence included late in **"In Celebration of My Uterus"**:

Many women are singing together of this:
one is in a shoe factory cursing the machine,
one is at the aquarium tending a seal,
one is dull at the wheel of her Ford, . . .
one is dying but remembering a breakfast,
one is stretching on her mat in Thailand,
one is wiping the ass of her child. . . .

Initial reaction to Sexton's first book, the 1960 *To Bedlam and Part Way Back,* was enthusiastic, with most critics being struck by the vitality of voice and emotion. Neil Myers praises "how subtly rhetoric fits thought," admiring Sexton's themes and defending her work from any charge of sentimentality. Geoffrey Hartman contrasts Sexton with Denise Levertov and Jean Garrigue, who believe that the poem sets the poet on a voyage of discovery, and use it for exploration. Sexton's strength is that she *knows* the experiences she chooses to write about, and the experience as she presents it is "simple, moving, and universal." Hartman sees her themes as reflecting deep spiritual wounds, and makes comparisons with both Yeats and Lowell. Rather than finding her poems too personal, he considers them universal and truly moral. Hal Smith, who carefully delineates how much *can* be wrong with women's poetry, makes the point of defining Sexton as not a woman poet, but a poet: "from the first line of her book . . . we know that we are in the hands of a poet firmly in control, fully aware of the twin possibilities of shock and delight."[8]

Even James Dickey's review, which is often quoted to show negative response, is generally favorable. He acknowledges the power of Sexton's "harrowing" topics, though he thinks her treatment less successful than it might have been, largely because of her "poetic" language. His suggestion that her narratives might become important short stories echoes one of Hartman's comments. As fresh as her subject matter on the poetry scene in 1960 was Sexton's sense of narrative.[9]

Reviews of the 1962 *All My Pretty Ones* continued to mention similarities between Sexton's poetry and that of Robert Lowell and W. D. Snodgrass. May Swenson was impressed by Sexton's seemingly effortless diction, her ability to shape the forms of poems to match their import, and her use of humor and fantasy. Thom Gunn finds the book better than *Bedlam* (which he disliked for its self-dramatizing) because Sexton's poetry is more controlled. Gunn's concluding sentence, that Sexton is "at her best when she presents [experience] indirectly or from a distance," is representative of the opinion that her poems were too much like voice, that the experience was not transformed through the art but rather *became* the art in too real a presentation. In contrast to Gunn, Louise Bogan praised both Sexton's books because they showed the poet writing "from the center of feminine experience, with the direct and open feeling that women, always vulnerable, have been shy of expressing in recent years."[10] It is a rare direction—but for today's readers, a most crucial one—in the criticism, and one could wish that Bogan had written more, and more often, about Sexton's work. *All My Pretty Ones* was nominated for a National Book Award.

Sexton's first books were so well-received in England that in 1964 a volume called *Selected Poems* was published there as a Poetry Book Selection, and as it was reviewed, the critical gulf between the British poetry camps was revealed. Christopher Ricks, writing in the *New Statesman,* called the collection "a remarkable volume," marked by wit and cunning, the poems written with a skill that will outlast the current fascination with the confessional. C. B. Cox, writing in the *Spectator,* praised Sexton's remarkably flexible tone, so that her language can encompass swift changes in mood and content. He admires her "wry self-consciousness" and her tendency to deal with religious themes and images.

For Ian Hamilton, however, Sexton is overrated as a poet. He finds her work promising, but fears that she will become another cult figure of "neurotic breakdown, valued not for what she has written but for what her suffering seems to symptomatize." Hamilton prefers her first book, because by the second, he says, mannerisms have lost their freshness and seem habitual. He criticizes the "slick offhandedness" in Sexton's treatments of life's horrors—"prosy cleverness," "hardboiled whimsicality," "inert evocativeness" are other negating phrases.[11]

The important essay of A. R. Jones published in *Critical Quarterly* helped British readers to place Sexton's work in the tradition of dramatic monologue and pointed out the key distinction that writing that seemed autobiographical might well be fictional.[12] Jones's essay did a great deal to counter the almost frenetic tendency to describe much writing of the time as "confessional," and then to discount it as being too revelatory, too personal (and therefore undisciplined and formless, a definite aesthetic criticism at mid-century). Sexton's obvious connections to Robert Lowell, Snodgrass, Plath, Jarrell, Roethke, and others were soon to destroy the building current of admiration, but in 1964 and 1965 she still felt as if critics were according her serious readings.

Sexton's reputation in the United States peaked with the 1966 publication of *Live or Die,* the collection that used as an epigraph a quotation from Saul Bellow, in which he admonished Sexton to decide, to choose life or death, but to decide, and not poison everything in the process. Being awarded the Pulitzer Prize for Poetry for this collection meant that Sexton could dismiss detractors, if she had enough confidence to do so. Even in the most positive reviews, however, comparisons with Robert Lowell and Sylvia Plath (increasingly since the latter's suicide in 1963) were attempting to force Sexton into the confessional camp. Joel Conarroe's review in *Shenandoah* begins with that comparison, but concludes that Sexton's poetry of the interior voyage—handled as it is here with honesty and toughness—creates "a fierce, terrible, beautiful book, well deserving its Pulitzer award."[13]

Generally favorable criticism may have been influenced in part by Ralph Mills's serious attention to Sexton in his *Contemporary American Poetry.*[14] Richard Fein credited Sexton with broad thematic range and pointed out her humor as a saving quality; praise was the tone of reviews by Philip Legler, Thomas McDonnell, James Tulip writing in *Poetry Australia,* and even the difficult-to-please Hayden Carruth. Most of the critics of *Live or Die* seem reconciled to the fact that Sexton was a woman poet, and McDonnell speaks directly to the issue: "Anne Sexton is one of the few women writing poetry in the United States today of whom it is possible to say that her womanness is totally at one with her poems . . . if a woman alone, in the physiological sense, could have written a poem like **"Menstruation at Forty,"** then also a woman alone, in the fullest possible sense, could have written so exquisite a poem as **"Little Girl, My String Bean, My Lovely Woman."**[15] McDonnell also speaks to the deeply religious tone in many of Sexton's poems.

If *Live or Die* was a kind of apex for Sexton's reputation, then the 1969 *Love Poems* was the beginning of the descent. Most critics were harsh about the poet-persona's supposed affair—if it were true, they didn't like it; if it were not true (and why, after all, was a "confessional poet" writing untruths?), they objected on aesthetic grounds. Mona Van Duyn found the book full of macabre humor, as the back cover reported that Sexton was living with her husband and two daughters, after the reader had just been led through the poems about a devastating love affair. Van Duyn states, "*Love Poems* is not sentimental, not trivial, it is simply not believable. The poems have little to do with believable love, having none of love's privacy and therefore too frequently repelling the reader."[16] She compared Sexton's writing to that of Norman Mailer, in self-indulgence and self-absorption. Finally, after the highly critical review, Van Duyn concluded that Sexton writes consistently good poems, though the reader need select among them.

The tactic used by Joyce Carol Oates is to compare the later and what she sees as less scrupulously controlled poems with the strong early ones; whereas Daniel Hughes finds *Love Poems* stronger than the earlier books because it "depends less on shock tactics" and allows Sexton's lyric gift to show. For William Dickey, writing in the *Hudson Review,* it was another of Sexton's self-indulgent collections.

One can almost chart the impact on Sexton's work of negative reviews, and her search for a new kind of poem may have been prompted by the criticism of *Love Poems.* Sexton's poetry was the topic of keen attention from Richard Howard (*Alone with America*), who concentrated chiefly on her skillful craft, from M. L.

Rosenthal in *The New Poets,* from Robert Boyers in *Salmagundi,* and from Beverly Fields writing for *Poets in Progress,* edited by Edward Hungerford.[17] But the gist of much of this attention was either to place Sexton in the by now firmly established confessional group, or to continue to question her right to be in any serious poetry classification—and its net effect was demoralization. As she wrote to Tillie Olsen in 1966, "My work, at present, is [in] a dreadful slump . . . when one's poems are damned for being tragic and confessional constantly from both sides of the Atlantic—reviews are bad for us—we should be blinded before we read such public praise or damnation."[18]

She attended to writing her play, *Mercy Street,* and to living in New York while it was produced and ran, with Marian Seides in the leading role. She attempted prose, and wrote poems that were unlike anything she had tried before. The macabre versions of the Brothers Grimm fairy tales that were to comprise Sexton's 1972 book, *Transformations,* were as much a surprise to her as to her readers—but she liked them, and when Houghton Mifflin tried to discourage her from publishing them, she saw clearly that her choice was to go elsewhere, not to repress the poems. As she wrote to Paul Brooks in 1970, acknowledging that the poems were different for her,

> I look at my work in stages, and each new book is a kind of growth and reaching outward and as always backward. Perhaps the critics will be unhappy with this book and some of my readers maybe will not like it either. I feel I will gain new readers and critics who have always disliked my work and too true, the critics are not always kind to me may come around. . . . I would like my readers to see this side of me, and it is not in every case the lighter side. Some of the poems are grim. In fact I don't know how to typify them except to agree that I have made them very contemporary. It would further be a lie to say that they weren't about me, because they are just as much about me as my other poetry.[19]

Sexton's own assessment is prophetic, because most reviewers said nearly the same kinds of things about the long parodies of the tales. For Louis Martz, *Transformations* was a return to the fresh inventiveness of Sexton's early books, free of what he saw as the bathos of *Love Poems.* For William Pitt Root, the collection was a kind of wry extension of Sexton's usual voice, but the poems themselves were more explicit social criticism than readers expected from her. For Paul Zweig, however, Sexton's adaptations only spoil the stories, and her use of what he calls "mod" language distorts the value of the original tales. He calls *Transformations* a step toward "the death of story telling." Unlike the response of most critics, who even in her earlier work found strong narrative patterns and techniques, Zweig's criticism was typical of reviewers

who were determined not to like whatever Anne Sexton published. In contrast to this kind of hypercritical reaction, other poets such as Muriel Rukeyser praised most of what Sexton attempted, saying accurately about *Love Poems, Transformations,* and *The Book of Folly,* "The issue in most of Anne Sexton's poems has been survival, piece by piece of the body, step by step of poetic experience, and even more the life entire, sprung from our matrix of parental madness."[20]

As Rukeyser saw it, Sexton's concerns were age-old archetypal, particularly female, themes. In *Transformations,* the poet had been able to deal with a great many of the larger humanist and feminist issues, those that provided scaffolding for her own more specific narrative poems. The ethos of **"Cinderella,"** for example, lies at the heart of Sexton's countless laments about women trapped in the conventional, traditional female roles. As a result of, in effect, having challenged many social assumptions she had been reared to accept, Sexton's other late poems changed. As Arthur Oberg pointed out in his review of her 1972 *The Book of Folly,* she "shares Galway Kinnell's wish to move beyond the way, or ways, of the world, to a visionary humor that can reject the world's foolish fools for the unworldly wise fools to whose rank the poet has always made some claim. Although Anne Sexton has been intensely aware of herself as woman and a woman poet, there is a new militancy here that I have never detected in her previous work."[21]

What Oberg sees as passing beyond the petty to more essential concerns, Helen Vendler sees as a shift in voice, the first consistent expression of Sexton's lurking acerbic tone, definitely not little-girl "nice." As Vendler points out, "What is occurring in such writing is not so much the shattering of taboos as the expression of an extremity of nonparticipatory vision. . . . [A] satirist feels under no obligation to extend sympathy. Sexton feels a slashing glee in her perfect vignettes . . . , these fiendish cartoons." Whatever the description, Sexton's *Transformations* were clearly a surprise to critics who had already consigned her work to an unenviable predictability. As Charles Gullans had said in an earlier review, the materials of Sexton's poetry are so familiar to the reader that, even before reading, the reader's reaction is "painful, embarrassing, and irritating." Gullans goes on to deny that Sexton writes poems at all. She instead produces what he calls "documents of modern psychiatry," which should never have been published at all. Christopher Lehmann-Haupt builds on this attitude as he reviews *Transformations* positively, stressing that the negative responses to Sexton's art resulted from seeing her poetry as "personal yelps rather than universal cries." Lehmann-Haupt thinks readers will be able to read *Transformations* more intelligibly because "by using the artificial as the raw material of *Transformations* and working her way backwards to the immediacy of her personal vision, she draws her readers in more willingly, and thereby makes them more vulnerable to her sudden plunges into personal nightmare."[22]

Much criticism of Sexton's work was in a stock-taking period. Robert Phillips treats her "confessional" poetry as at least partly fictional (in *The Confessional Poets*), while Paul A. Lacey claims that Sexton's chief motivation is the making of ritual, and that her best poems are "built around rites of communion, prayer, and gift-giving (*The Inner War*). Karl Malkoff's sensible reading of Sexton is also helpful (in the *Crowell Handbook of Contemporary American Poetry*), as is criticism by J. D. McClatchy, who is later to edit the first collection of criticism on Sexton's work.[23]

The puzzlement that greeted **The Book of Folly** in 1972 seemed only to intensify with the publication of **The Death Notebooks** early in 1974. That collection was followed in October of 1974 by Sexton's suicide from carbon monoxide poisoning. A few months later, her collection **The Awful Rowing toward God**—which she had herself prepared for publication—appeared. Response to both collections was strongly influenced by the poet's death, and marked a turn in the tenor of all subsequent criticism. As Carol Duane pointed out in her survey of Sexton criticism, "If the recurrent critical problem of the 1960s was the persistent tendency to evaluate Sexton's poems as signs of process toward mental stability, toward an affirmative objectivity, then the corollary—to link her most recent work to her death—tended to dominate the criticism of the mid-1970s. Moreover, critics who had taken special delight in Sexton's careful crafting of her early poems were faced with a special challenge in these later volumes, which were frequently seen as evidencing poetic as well as psychic disintegration."[24] Although Steven Gould Axelrod said of these poems that Sexton was writing as well as she ever had, he too was bothered by her "jottings" and "notes," and Ben Howard, in *Poetry*, questions why the eloquence of Sexton's early work has disintegrated into such a "limited idiom."[25]

Muriel Rukeyser terms the late poems a second kind of poetry, growing out of the early confessions, enriched by their presence, but vastly different. Erica Jong also, writing a memoir of Sexton soon after her death, sees continuity within the work especially in terms of archetypal myth—not only feminine myth, but myths that expand the human consciousness. Such an approach has been fruitful for many recent critics, among them Diana Hume George whose 1986 book, *Oedipus Anne,* is the first book-length analysis of Sexton's work to appear. Such concerns have also motivated the criticism of Alicia Ostriker, Estella Lauter, Suzanne Juhasz, and Sarah Schuyler.[26]

It was at the point of her death, with the publication of two collections in 1974 and others to follow, quickly, posthumously (**45 Mercy Street,** 1976; *Anne Sexton: A Self-Portrait in Letters,* 1977; **Words for Dr. Y: Uncollected Poems with Three Stories,** 1978) that Sexton's work began receiving summary—rather, hasty—consideration. Because the poet grouped her poetry into categories, designing groups for one collection or another, Sexton's book publication was not necessarily the chronology of her poems individually. Knowing what poem had preceded another, what operating principles were at work, was therefore difficult. Only Maxine Kumin, who worked intimately with Sexton for the fifteen years that their households were connected by private telephone lines, had an accurate sense of the time of composition for Sexton's work. Even with this difficulty in dating, critics could see the immense differences between poems in the posthumously published books and most of the earlier work.

Troubled by what they saw as flaccidity, imprecision in craft, and the pervasive religious subject matter, most critics chose to emphasize disintegration of technique rather than trying to delineate important new directions. One exception to that tendency was William J. McGill's "Anne Sexton and God," an essay in which Sexton's intense desire for God is compared with the intensity in religious literature of all ages. For Sandra M. Gilbert, **The Death Notebooks** crystallized the meditative, haunting concern the poet expressed early for death and its transcendence. "If irony and shrewdness have always characterized Anne Sexton's work, the largeness of her metaphysical ambition is what is newly notable about **The Death Notebooks,**" contends Gilbert as she compares Sexton's poems with those of the eighteenth-century poet, Christopher Smart, absorbing a poetic tradition that gives her accrued meaning. For Robert Mazzocco, however, Sexton's themes seem arch, and her treatment inappropriate. He points to the poems titled "psalms", which he calls deliberately horrific (for what purpose)?, and questions Sexton's concept of her own readership. Where is the line between art and trickery? Kate Green points out that there is no excess of feeling, not excess in "the personal nature of the poems but in the images themselves, which seem, at times, to spill out of control."[27]

One of the most disparaging reviews of this group of books comes from Patricia Meyer Spacks, who finds **45 Mercy Street** a collection of poems "hardened into mannerism." Other comments in this review are that Sexton's poems are sentimental, "grotesquely uncontrolled," the work of a "victim of an era in which it has become easy to dramatize self-indulgence, stylish to invent unexpected imagery regardless of its relevance, fashionable to be a woman and as a woman to display one's misery."[28] Because Spacks is an influential critic, and a feminist, her view carried a great deal of significance, but it echoed the long line of critical opinion that was uneasy about Sexton's blend of the personal and the aesthetic. This trend in criticism of Sexton's late work continued, with Robert Pinsky calling **Words for Dr. Y** "mechanical" and its apparent "nakedness . . . another form of evasion." Pinsky described Sexton's poetic method as consistent throughout her work: "locating the emotion and lobbing the artillery of images at it persistently." He faulted her work too because it evinced no range or "intellectual scope."[29]

This is not a new kind of judgment, certainly. What did begin to occur in the usually troubled reviews of Sexton's late work was a different kind of assessment. Just as Sandra Gilbert came to see Sexton's mocking humor as appropriate in even her death poems and the obviously serious psalm-sequence ("poetry that anyone would flirt with almost any disasters to write"), so Rosemary Johnson points up the unpredictability of what she calls the "oil-and-water mix of the absolutely commonplace and the singular, of the quite literal curdled by the incredible" in Sexton's later work. Johnson also saw, accurately, that these poems contain a fuller realization of Sexton as female, as though after writing **Transformations** and seeing her themes in light of archetypal and sociological patterns, Sexton saw how being female was a crucial condition to her life as artist. In Johnson's words,

> Although Anne Sexton toys, for effect one feels, with notions of lack of gender, androgyny, hermaphroditicism, and the like, the obvious needs to be said: . . . the poet's perceptions and her sensibility are female, stem from her womanhood. . . . The description she dashes off to Erica Jong of herself as "The woman of the poems, the woman of the kitchen, the woman of the private (but published) hungers" fits. Indeed a lot of conflicting directions pull her apart. . . .[30]

From Nancy Yanes Hoffman as well came the recognition that Sexton had finally found both her audience and her voice, as she writes "of women growing older but not wiser" and of "choices made and choices lost." Hoffman then reads **The Awful Rowing toward God** as a metaphor for the woman who decides to go it alone, to cast off her dependency—"husband, lovers, psychiatrists, children, all of whom let her down. . . . She is depending upon the self, and that too, at the last, lets her down. . . . What Sexton was searching for was not only transformation of her self, but transcendence, both obsessions which arose out of the conviction of her own worthlessness. Her desire was to be joined to another in love. Each time that love was disappointed, she was left with her own insufficient resources—left, finally, rowing toward God, that ultimate transcendence of self which seemed to be the only love of which she could be certain because it was love imagined. But love imagined sustains only so long as the imagination works

and reality does not impinge too agonizingly."[31] Even Sexton's psychological state seemed to grow from the various difficulties women experienced as they matured.

Margaret Atwood, too, reviewing the Sexton letters, writes emphatically, "Anne Sexton was one of the most important American poets of her generation." For her, too, much of the mystery of the discrepancy between Sexton's letters—which are full of animation, enthusiasm, and life—and her poems, speaking consistently of death, lies in Sexton's position in the world as woman. In that, that difficulty to come to full voice, Atwood compares Sexton with Plath, both gifted writers caught in a labyrinth of frustrations and barricades to expression.[32]

Among the most insightful comments available on Sexton's writing and her personal reliance on her poetry are those of Maxine Kumin in her foreword ("How It Was, Maxine Kumin on Anne Sexton") to Sexton's 1981 **The Complete Poems.** In that essay Kumin pointed out how diametrically opposed the divided critical camps had been: "The intimate details divulged in Sexton's poetry enchanted or repelled with equal passion." Helpfully tracing key events in Sexton's life, including her two postpartum depressions that began her life of mental torment, Kumin points out that Sexton consistently relied on male authority figures. She even came to poetry—and stayed with it—because of the advice of, first, her male psychiatrist and, second, a Catholic priest. Kumin says, "I am convinced that poetry kept Anne alive for the eighteen years of her creative endeavors. When everything else soured; when a succession of therapists deserted her for whatever good, poor, or personal reasons; when intimates lost interest or could not fulfill all the roles they were asked to play; when a series of catastrophes and physical illnesses assaulted her, the making of poems remained her own constant. To use her own metaphor, 'out of used furniture she made a tree.'"

Kumin also spoke authoritatively in this preface about Sexton's later work, and since most critics were so bewildered about it, her remarks are useful. Kumin saw Sexton's turn to Jesus as an extension of her fascination with the fable as form, an interest she had initially found writing **Transformations.** When she applied that form to the Jesus figure, who still suffered knowingly in order to endure, the result was **"The Jesus Papers."** Kumin identifies Sexton's themes as being "Jesus, Mary, angels as good as the good fairy, and a personal, fatherly God to love and forgive her. . . . Always Sexton explored relentlessly the eternal themes that obsess her: love, loss, madness, the nature of the father-daughter compact, and death—the Death Baby we carry with us from the moment of birth."

Kumin describes Sexton's sense of freedom after **Transformations** was so well-received, her increased daring in her poetry and her consistent use of the parody name, Ms. Dog (*God* in reverse, with a feminist nod in *Ms.* to the women's movement). God was increasingly the subject of her poems, and she wrote even a quantity of imperfect poems as a way to try to reach what might be said about transcendent experiences. Kumin reminds readers of the humor, the joy, the affirmation Sexton brought to her work—for it was her work—and to trying to live so that her art would continue to provide meaning. As she concludes, "Women poets in particular owe a debt to Anne Sexton, who broke new ground, shattered taboos, and endured a barrage of attacks along the way because of the flamboyance of her subject matter, which, twenty years later, seems far less daring. . . . Today, the remonstrances seem almost quaint."[33]

Perhaps because of this excellent introduction, *The Complete Poems* of Anne Sexton was usually relatively well-reviewed—if it was reviewed at all. Unfortunately, its publication came during the same year that Sylvia Plath's long-awaited *Collected Poems* was issued, and the longer wait, the greater anticipation, brought the Plath volume into much greater prominence. When in the spring of 1982 Plath's collection won the Pulitzer Prize for Poetry, that award seemed the final quietus to the efforts by the Sexton estate to garner for Sexton what could just as rightfully have been hers. Among the most interesting reviews of the Sexton volume were James M. Rawley's assessment in the *National Review*. Calling *The Complete Poems* "an indispensable book" and Sexton "one of her generation's best poets," Rawley wonders why there had been such uproar about her work (was it objectionable, perhaps, for its sense of humor?). Part of his favorable review is a somewhat caustic assessment of her unhappy reception from critics: "The critics . . . blamed her for the facile melodrama of her lines, but said she had promise. Later, amid similar caviling, they would say she had failed to live up to her gifts. Meanwhile, prizes and praise rained on her, though prudery kept many from liking poems with titles like **'In Celebration of My Uterus'**. . . ."[34]

As if to illustrate Rawley's points, Alan Williamson's review of Sexton (paired with Plath's *Collected Poems*) finds little to redeem. After censuring Sexton for her untragic tone in what could have been tragic poems, Williamson asserts, "But it is much easier, at this point, to bury Sexton than to praise her." While he still admires her first two books, he sees only bad writing after that time ("What can explain so rapid a poetic decline in an initially serious and scrupulous writer?"). Williamson seems quick to jump to his answer—in part, "Mental instability and alcoholism"—though he does equate Sexton with a Dylan Thomas kind of syndrome. He saves his most vituperative comments for Maxine Kumin's introduction, where—he says—she "lashes out in all directions." Perhaps his tolerance was at low ebb,

though he clearly found Plath's poems admirable and convincing—and the similarities between Plath and Sexton are common knowledge. But this review shows the critical world at its most typical—finding reasons for disliking poetry because of its "quality," though giving no proof of qualitative criteria.[35]

Katha Pollitt's *Nation* review, though also praising Sexton's first three books and lamenting the quality of some of her later poems, places Sexton, her poems, and the reviewer's own response into credible context. For Pollitt, Sexton's importance as a *woman* poet is indisputable—subject matter, manner of expression, voice all had to contend with a male-dominated art world. Her *range* is also indisputable, and her willingness to make the attempt, rather than to play it safe. The same acknowledgment of Sexton's power, even if there are some mistakes, occurs in Diane Wood Middlebrook's somewhat later review (in *Parnassus*, 1985). For Middlebrook, however, the unevenness of Sexton's poems was an understandable result of her poetic method—that of "milking the unconscious." This tactic often produced a

> loosely-structured poetry dense with simile, freaked with improbable associations. In a poem addressed to James Wright, Sexton herself acknowledged she knew the effect offended certain tastes: "There is too much good and no one left over / to eat up all the weird abundance" (**"The Black Art"**). Weird: uncanny, magical, unconventional. While some of Sexton's most admired poems work, like little machines, on well-oiled armatures of rhythm or rhyme (such as **"All My Pretty Ones," "The Starry Night," "Wanting to Die"**), others equally powerful depend on manic or despairing or ecstatic cascades of association (**"The Furies," "O Ye Tongues"**) that flow like an open spigot. The gems, or closed forms, tend to be early; the looser style, later. In this collection, the reader can watch Sexton evolve her second style as a way of exploring a changing relation to her subject matter.

Middlebrook is, of course, the authorized Sexton biographer, so she brings a great deal of information and understanding to her reading of *The Complete Poems*. As she points out, "The witch-persona of Sexton's poetry is the voice Sexton invented to tell the story of her changing relationship to a severe, incurable, but apparently undiagnosable malady. . . . Sexton's *Complete Poems* yields most when read as if it contained a narrative: an account of a woman cursed with a desire to die. Why is she different from other women? Where did the curse come from? A story line with a beginning, middle, and end takes shape . . . as Sexton systematically exhausts a set of culturally acceptable explanations for the condition of her kind. These are, first, a psychiatric explanation; later, a sociological explanation; and finally a spiritual explanation."[36]

Luckily, published criticism on the oeuvre of Sexton's writing has begun to catch up with the large reading public that exists—more criticism has been published in the last three or four years, and is projected for the next several years, than appeared in the past ten. It seems important to recognize that the kind of stock-taking that needed to occur was directed at not only Sexton's place in the literary establishment, but at the place generally of poetry by women, and of so-called confessional poetry. For that reason, I have chosen to end this book with an important 1987 essay by British critic Laurence Lerner, assessing what confessional poetry—American confessional poetry as centered in the highly controversial poems of Anne Sexton—really is, and what its influence has been on the world of contemporary poetry. Sexton was, thoroughly and admittedly, an integral part of her culture. Complete with her mental instability and her worries about where she fit into the social structure, Sexton expressed much of the mid-century attitudes about women writers, women as professionals, women as independent beings. Critical reactions to her expressions were as typical as her writings were themselves.

This collection attempts, in some ways, to reflect Middlebrook's classifications of Sexton's work; essays included here deal with craft and text, particularly the essays written particularly for this book, which focus on single poems or groups of poems. They deal with psychiatric motivations, explanations, and the relationships between poet and poem, poet and culture, poet and self. Several also deal with sociology: Sexton as woman writer, as expressive writer, and as defensive writer; and they deal in more recent times with Sexton as spiritual writer. This may be the most difficult approach of all, because twentieth-century art of all kinds has been so thoroughly and antagonistically divorced from formal religion for much of its eighty-nine years.

One wonders, assessing the criticism of Sexton's work, if some more moderating tone, some more balanced perspective, might have saved the poet from the bitterness she evidently experienced as her career continued, and the savage criticism grew more and more frequent. One wishes Sexton could have seen the range of expert and wise readings collected here, because it seems clear—judging from her late poems—that part of her image of herself as failure was based on the critical reception her books received. Much of *The Awful Rowing toward God* reflects the poet's sensitivity to the response, just as much of her admitted fear of readings stems from her knowledge that many people who came to her readings were detractors rather than admirers. She wrote in **"The Play"**;

> I am the only actor.
> It is difficult for one woman
> to act out a whole play.
> The play is my life,
> my solo act. . . . The curtain falls.
> The audience rushes out. . . .

And, even more poignantly, in **"The Dead Heart,"** the poem in which the poet observes the small inert fact, she wrote:

> What it has cost me you can't imagine,
> shrinks, priests, lovers, children, husbands,
> friends and all the lot. . . .

Its demise occurred, however, as the last stanza recounts:

> How did it die?
> I called it EVIL.
> I said to it, your poems stink like vomit.
> I didn't stay to hear the last sentence.
> It died on the word EVIL.
> I did it with my tongue.
> The tongue, the Chinese say,
> is like a sharp knife:
> it kills
> without drawing blood.[37]

Once Sexton had put her whole identity into becoming a poet, surely the printed and verbal response to her art was of great importance to her, given her personal dependencies and the acculturation she had learned as an American woman at mid-century.

Notes

1. *Anne Sexton: A Self-Portrait in Letters,* ed. Linda Gray Sexton and Lois Ames (Boston: Houghton Mifflin, 1977), 42; dated "circa November 15, 1958."

2. Denise Levertov, "Anne Sexton: Light Up the Cave," *Ramparts* 13 (January 1975): 61-63.

3. Sexton's letters are filled with references to having no language, or to finding people with whom she has language (see Sexton and Ames, *Letters,* 244-46).

4. See Linda Wagner-Martin, *Sylvia Plath, A Biography* (New York: Simon & Schuster, 1987), for information about Plath's long process of self-discovery, and for some indication of Sexton's importance to Plath's late poems; see also Diane Wood Middlebrook, "'I Tapped My Own Head': The Apprenticeship of Anne Sexton" in *Coming to Light,* ed. Diane Wood Middlebrook and Marilyn Yalom (Ann Arbor: University of Michigan Press, 1985), 199.

5. Middlebrook, "I Tapped My Own Head," 195-213.

6. Anne Sexton, *The Complete Poems* (Boston: Houghton Mifflin, 1981), 34-35. Poems cited are also from this edition and will not be referenced.

7. Sexton's awards and various kinds of recognition are one mark of the distinctiveness of her writing, because I know of no other contemporary poet

who received this quantity of attention. She began writing poetry when she was twenty-eight and published during the first year in *Audience, Beloit Poetry Journal,* the *Hudson Review, Harper's,* and soon after that, in the *New Yorker, Accent, Epoch,* the *Yale Review, Antioch Review, Voices,* and other little magazines. As soon as she had put a collection together, Houghton Mifflin accepted it, and that company remained her publisher throughout her career. During the 1960s, she held the Robert Frost fellowship at Bread Loaf and was for two years a fellow at the Radcliffe (now Bunting) Institute. She won the *Audience* poetry prize, *Poetry*'s Levinson Prize, the traveling fellowship from the American Academy of Arts and Letters, the Congress for Cultural Freedom travel grant, a Ford Foundation grant for a year's residency with a professional theater, the Shelley Memorial Award, and in 1967 the Pulitzer Prize for Poetry. In 1969 she received a Guggenheim fellowship and honorary doctorates from Tufts University, Regis College, and Fairfield University. She held a teaching post at Boston University, and became a member of Phi Beta Kappa.

8. Neil Myers, "The Hungry Sheep Look Up," *Minnesota Review* 1 (October 1960): 99-104; Geoffrey Hartman, "Les Belles Dames Sans Merci," *Kenyon Review* 22 (Autumn 1960): 696-700; and Hal Smith, "Notes, Reviews and Speculations," *Epoch* 10 (Fall 1960): 253-55.

9. James Dickey, "Five First Books," *Poetry* 97 (February 1961): 316-20.

10. May Swenson, "Poetry of Three Women," *Nation,* 23 February 1963, 164-66; Thom Gunn, "Poems and Books of Poems," *Yale Review* 53 (October 1963): 140-41; Louise Bogan, "Verse," *New Yorker,* 27 April 1963, 175.

11. Christopher Ricks, "Beyond Gentility," *New Statesman* 68 (27 November 1964): 842; C. B. Cox, "New Beasts for Old," the *Spectator* 219 (28 July 1967): 106; see also John Fairfax in *Poetry Review* 55 (Winter 1964): 249-51; Ian Hamilton, "Poetry," *London Magazine* 4 (March 1965): 87-88.

12. A. R. Jones, "Necessity and Freedom," *Critical Quarterly* 7 (Spring 1965): 14-17, 24-30.

13. Joel O. Conarroe, "Review of *Live or Die,*" *Shenandoah* 18 (Summer 1967): 84-85.

14. Ralph J. Mills, Jr., *Contemporary American Poetry* (New York: Random House, 1965), 218-34.

15. Richard J. Fein, "The Demon of Anne Sexton," *English Record* 18 (October 1967): 16-21; Philip Legler, "O Yellow Eye," *Poetry* 110 (May 1967):
125-27; Thomas P. McDonnell, "Light in a Dark Journey," *America,* 13 May 1967, 729-31; James Tulip, "Three Women Poets," *Poetry Australia* 21 (December 1967): 37-39; Hayden Carruth, "In Spite of Artifice," *Hudson Review* 19 (Winter 1966-67): 698.

16. Mona Van Duyn, "Seven Women" *Poetry* 115 (March 1970): 430-32; Joyce Carol Oates, "The Rise and Fall of a Poet: *The Complete Poems* of Anne Sexton," *New York Times Book Review,* 18 October 1981, 3, 37; Daniel Hughes, "American Poetry 1969: From B to Z," *Massachusetts Review* 11 (Autumn 1970): 668-71; William Dickey, "A Place in the Country," *Hudson Review* 22 (Summer 1969): 347-52.

17. Richard Howard, "Anne Sexton: 'Some Tribal Female Who Is Known but Forbidden,'" *Alone with America: Essays on the Art of Poetry in the United States Since 1950* (New York: Atheneum, 1969), 442-50; M. L. Rosenthal, "Other Confessional Poets," *The New Poets: American and British Poetry Since World War II* (New York: Oxford University Press, 1967), 131-38; Robert Boyers, "*Live or Die*: The Achievement of Anne Sexton," *Salmagundi,* no. 2 (Spring 1967): 61-71; Beverly Fields, "The Poetry of Anne Sexton," *Poets in Progress,* ed. Edward Hungerford (Evanston, Ill.: Northwestern University Press, 1967), 251-85.

18. Sexton's *Letters,* 278.

19. Ibid., 362.

20. Louis L. Martz, "Review of *Transformations,*" the *Yale Review* 61 (1972): 414-16; William Pitt Root, "*Transformations,*" *Poetry* 123 (October 1973): 48-51; Paul Zweig, "Making and Unmaking," *Partisan Review* 40 (1973): 277-79; Muriel Rukeyser, "Glitter and Wounds, Several Wildernesses," *Parnassus* 2 (Fall/Winter 1973): 215-21.

21. Arthur Oberg, "The One Flea Which Is Laughing," *Shenandoah* 25 (Fall 1973)): 87-89.

22. Helen Vendler, "Malevolent Flippancy," *New Republic* 185 (11 November 1981): 33-36; Charles Gullans, "Poetry and Subject Matter: From Hart Crane to Turner Cassity," the *Southern Review* 7 (Spring 1970): 497-98; Christopher Lehmann-Haupt, "Grimms' Fairy Tales Retold," *New York Times,* 27 September 1971, 31.

23. Robert Phillips, "Anne Sexton: The Blooming Mouth and the Bleeding Rose," *The Confessional Poets* (Carbondale: Southern Illinois University Press, 1973), 73-91; Paul A. Lacey, "The Sacrament of Confession," in *The Inner War* (Philadelphia: Fortress Press, 1972), 8-31; Karl Malkoff, "Confessional Poetry" and "Anne Sex-

ton," *Crowell Handbook of Contemporary American Poetry* (New York: Thomas Y. Crowell, 1973); and J. D. McClatchy, "Anne Sexton: Somehow to Endure," *Centennial Review* 19 (Spring 1975): 1-36, and expanded in *Anne Sexton: The Artist and Her Critics* (Bloomington: Indiana University Press, 1978).

24. Carol Duane on Sexton in "Three Contemporary Women Poets: Marianne Moore, Anne Sexton, and Sylvia Plath"; Cindy Hoffman, Carol Duane, Katharen Soule, and Linda Wagner, in *American Women Writers,* ed. M. Thomas Inge, Jackson R. Bryer, Maurice Duke (Westport, Conn.: Greenwood Press, 1982), 392.

25. Steven Gould Axelrod, "Anne Sexton's Rowing Toward God," *Modern Poetry Studies* 6 (Autumn 1975): 187-89; Ben Howard, "Shattered Glass," *Poetry* 127 (February 1976): 286-92.

26. Muriel Rukeyser, "Glitter and Wounds, Several Wildernesses," *Parnassus* 2 (Fall-Winter 1973): 215-21; Erica Jong, "Remembering Anne Sexton," *New York Times Book Review,* 27 October 1974, 63; Diana Hume George, *Oedipus Anne, The Poetry of Anne Sexton* (Urbana: University of Illinois Press, 1986); Alicia Ostriker, "That Story: The Changes of Anne Sexton" in *Writing Like a Woman* (Ann Arbor: University of Michigan Press, 1983), 59-86; Estella Lauter, *Women as Mythmakers, Poetry and Visual Art by Twentieth-Century Women* (Bloomington: Indiana University Press, 1984); Suzanne Juhasz, "'The Excitable Gift': The Poetry of Anne Sexton" in *Naked and Fiery Forms: Modern American Poetry by Women, a New Tradition* (New York: Harper & Row, 1976), and "Seeking the Exit or the Home: Poetry and Salvation in the Career of Anne Sexton," in *Shakespeare's Sisters: Feminist Essays on Women Poets,* ed. Sandra M. Gilbert and Susan Gubar (Bloomington: Indiana University Press, 1979), 261-68; Sarah Schuyler, "Their Ambivalent Adventures with a Mother: Freud, Milton, Sexton," *Literature and Psychology* 32 (1986): 11-17.

27. William J. McGill, "Anne Sexton and God," *Commonweal,* 13 May 1977, 304-6; Sandra M. Gilbert, "Jubilate Anne," *Nation,* 14 September 1974, 214-16; Robert Mazzocco, "Matters of Life and Death," *New York Review of Books,* 3 April 1975, 22-23; Kate Green, "Inventory of Loss," *Moons and Lion Tailes* 2 (1976): 87-90.

28. Patricia Meyer Spacks, *"45 Mercy Street,"* *New York Times Book Review,* 30 May 1976, 6.

29. Robert Pinsky, "A Characteristic Figure," *New York Times Book Review,* 26 November 1976, 7.

30. Rosemary Johnson, "The Woman of Private (But Published) Hungers," *Parnassus* 8 (Fall / Winter 1979): 92-107.

31. Nancy Yanes Hoffman, "A Special Language," *Southwest Review* 64 (Summer 1979): 209-14.

32. Margaret Atwood, "Anne Sexton: A Self-Portrait in Letters," *New York Times Book Review,* 6 November 1977, 15.

33. Maxine Kumin, "Foreword" to Anne Sexton, *The Complete Poems* (Boston: Houghton Mifflin, 1981), xix-xxxv.

34. James M. Rawley, "Part Way Back," the *National Review* 33 (11 December 1981): 1491.

35. Alan Williamson, "Confession and Tragedy," *Poetry* 142 (June 1983): 170-78.

36. Katha Pollitt, "That Awful Rowing," the *Nation* 233 (21 November 1981): 533-37; Diane Wood Middlebrook, "Poet of Weird Abundance," *Parnassus* 12-13 (1985): 293-315.

37. "The Play" and "The Dead Heart," in Sexton, the *Complete Poems,* 440-1, 439-40.

Stephen Vinson (essay date 1992)

SOURCE: Vinson, Stephen. "'Wild Animals out in the Arena': Anne Sexton's Revisions for *All My Pretty Ones.*" In *Rossetti to Sexton: Six Women Poets at Texas,* edited by Dave Oliphant, pp. 191-221. Austin: Harry Ransom Humanities Research Center, The University of Texas at Austin, 1992.

[*In the following essay, Vinson uses Sexton's drafts of three poems in* All My Pretty Ones—*"The Fortress," "Letter Written on a Ferry While Crossing Long Island Sound," and "The Abortion"—to present a detailed study of her process of revision.*]

For Anne Sexton (1928-1974), the composition of her poetry proceeded from "a strong emotion," which was the content of her work and the easier step, to the revision process, which centered on shaping the poem and defining its parameters.[1] It was during the revision process that the poet would "fool around on the typewriter . . . hunting for (meaning)."[2] In revising her poems, Sexton made a conscious search for the correct form and, perhaps unconsciously, refocused her original vision in terms of an emerging theme. To describe this process, the poet utilized a circus analogy: form for her "was like letting a lot of wild animals out in the arena, but enclosing them in a cage, and you would let some extraordinary animals out if you had the right cage, and that cage would be form."[3] The power of Sexton's poetry derives from a tension between control and imagination, and the means for exploring the revision process that brought about this tension are to be found in the Anne Sexton Collection at the Harry Ransom Humanities Research Center [HRHRC].

The Sexton archives, which include the poet's working drafts for all her published books, are comprised of several types of unbound materials. Loosely arranged in manila folders with the name of the completed volume in which the poems first appeared, these materials are primarily unedited typescript drafts but also include typed pages with cursive notes, handwritten lines on the backs of envelopes, and note pads or lined notebook sheets. Many of these working drafts bear handwritten dates or contain comments Sexton made to herself concerning the evolution of the poems. The extensiveness of the collection suggests that the poet kept her many drafts intact with an eye to posterity. Certainly these materials make possible a step-by-step retracing of the poet's process of revision that led in the end to poems of an artistic power greater than the original strong emotions with which she began.

The two years between the autumns of 1959 and 1961 were a time of special productivity and growth for Anne Sexton. A large number of the poems for the poet's second volume, *All My Pretty Ones* (1962), which contains many of her most often anthologized pieces, were composed during this period.[4] Readers noted in this second collection an improvement in the poet's craft: May Swenson pointed out the book's "achievement not on the score of its subject matter, but because of its poetic mastery";[5] Thom Gunn observed that "the structure of her poems has become tighter and clearer."[6] The drafts for this volume also reveal that this was a time when Sexton revised over a period of months, in contrast, for example, to *The Awful Bowing toward God,* her last volume composed within a few weeks and published posthumously in 1975.[7]

In a 1968 interview with Sexton, Barbara Kevles asked the poet about her "technical development from book to book," and Sexton explained that she used "very tight form" in her first volume, *To Bedlam and Part Way Back* (1960), but that for *All My Pretty Ones* she "loosened up and in the last section didn't use any form at all."[8] These comments suggest Sexton's growth as a poet, but they are misleading in the sense that "form" encompasses much more than measured stanzas and end rhyme. Sexton stated in an interview with Priscilla Marx that she did not "care about the shape" of a poem on the page, but then she went on to contradict this assertion:

> About half my poems are in some kind of form. The poems that aren't in form have a shape, just the same, even if it isn't a vase or anything that simple, but they have a kind of shape, a body of their own.[9]

Sexton's second volume does in fact evince less reliance on form as a mechanical approach to writing poetry but it also reveals how form was the "cage" in which the poet controlled her thoughts and emotions. The circus analogy indicates as well that the proper "cage" would vary according to the particular poem which it "enclosed." As the work for *All My Pretty Ones* progressed, Sexton began to discover new "shapes" for her poems, which greatly improved their effectiveness. Her work in this regard was not in the nature of prescriptive arrangement of content to fit a preliminary rubric, but in a revision method that allowed form to evolve along with theme and tone in an organic, creative development.

The materials at the HRHRC for the thirty-one poems in *All My Pretty Ones* show that Sexton composed over five-hundred pages of typescript. Although handwritten drafts are also preserved among the Sexton Collection, they are rare and differ greatly from the typed drafts and resemble notes for poems more than poems themselves, being much more tentative, more set in content than in form. In order to understand how these drafts served an important function for the poet, I have selected for study two poems for which handwritten drafts exist along with typed drafts: **"The Fortress"** and **"Letter Written on a Ferry While Crossing Long Island Sound."** In addition, I will discuss the typed drafts of **"The Abortion"** for purposes of demonstrating that Sexton employed a similar revision process even when she began a poem at the typewriter rather than by hand.

At present, no variorium edition exists for the Anne Sexton canon. *The Complete Poems* (1981), edited by the poet's daughter, Linda Gray Sexton, contains all the poems published in Anne Sexton's lifetime and those which were published in two posthumous collections.[10] However, there are differences between some of the published poems and some of the completed typescripts, which is, for example, the case with **"The Fortress."** In order to facilitate reference to the manuscript material at the HRHRC, to the changes that take place during the revision process, and to the differences between the published version and the pre-publication drafts, it will be useful to quote **"The Fortress"** as it appears in *The Complete Poems*:

"The Fortress"

while taking a nap with Linda

Under the pink quilted covers
I hold the pulse that counts your blood.
I think the woods outdoors
are half asleep,
left over from summer
like a stack of books after a flood,
left over like those promises I never keep.

On the right, the scrub pine tree
waits like a fruit store
holding up bunches of tufted broccoli.

We watch the wind from our square bed.
I press down my index finger—
half in jest, half in dread—
on the brown mole
under your left eye, inherited
from my right cheek: a spot of danger
where a bewitched worm ate its way through our soul
in search of beauty. My child, since July
the leaves have been fed
secretly from a pool of beet-red dye.

And sometimes they are battle green
with trunks as wet as hunters' boots,
smacked hard by the wind, clean
as oilskins. No,
the wind's not off the ocean.
Yes, it cried in your room like a wolf
and your pony tail hurt you. That was a long time
   ago.
The wind rolled the tide like a dying
woman. She wouldn't sleep,
she rolled there all night, grunting and sighing.

Darling, life is not in my hands;
life with its terrible changes
will take you, bombs or glands,
your own child at
your breast, your own house on your own land.
Outside the bittersweet turns orange.
Before she died, my mother and I picked those fat
branches, finding orange nipples
on the gray wire strands.
We weeded the forest, curing trees like cripples.

Your feet thump-thump against my back
and you whisper to yourself. Child,
what are you wishing? What pact
are you making?
What mouse runs between your eyes? What ark
can I fill for you when the world goes wild?
The woods are underwater, their weeds are shaking
in the tide; birches like zebra fish
flash by in a pack.
Child, I cannot promise that you will get your wish.

I cannot promise very much.
I give you the images I know.
Lie still with me and watch.
A pheasant moves
by like a seal, pulled through the mulch
by his thick white collar. He's on show
like a clown. He drags a beige feather that he removed,
one time, from an old lady's hat.
We laugh and we touch.
I promise you love. Time will not take away that.[11]

The poem which became **"The Fortress,"** originally titled "Taking A Nap With Linda," represents one of several styles or types of poems to be found in *All My Pretty Ones* and also resembles many of the poems in Sexton's earlier volume, ***To Bedlam and Part Way Back***

(1960). Characterized by end rhyme, as well as carefully measured lines and stanzas, **"The Fortress"** can be grouped on the basis of these features with poems such as **"Unknown Girl in the Maternity Ward"** and **"The Double Image"** from the earlier volume and **"The Operation"** from *All My Pretty Ones*. Thematically, these poems center on relationships, especially those of immediate family, often tracing the legacies of generations. They are extremely visceral and intimate poems, with images drawn from the female anatomy, as well as from nature and the seasons of the year, including references to animals and to primary colors. The tone is sometimes that of a story meant to illustrate words of counsel. Such poems are characteristic of the early stages of Sexton's development and differ from those marked by a transitional movement to freer forms and other voices also found in *All My Pretty Ones*.

For **"The Fortress,"** thirty-seven pages of manuscripts are to be found in the HRHRC. These include two handwritten drafts, one of which is four pages written on loose leaves from a 4 × 6-inch notepad and the other of which is five pages numbered consecutively on loose-leaf notebook paper measuring 8½ × 11. An additional four pages of handwritten drafts include two pages resembling the 8½ × 11 sheets but containing fewer lines, these being perhaps revisions of the numbered pages. Two other pages in cursive consist of notes scribbled on the backs of other pages. The typewritten pages contain fifteen numbered drafts (page 15 dated "Oct 15th to Oct 30th 1961"), two pages of proofsheets for the finished poem, and two pages of worksheets for the final two stanzas. The back sides of the proofsheets bear printer's notes. Also included in the collection of drafts is a carbon of the page numbered "15." One of the typewritten versions of the poem seems to have been transcribed by the poet onto two typed pages from a handwritten version. The margins and the back sides of some of the typed pages and the margins of several of the 8½ × 11 pages contain trial rhymes and syllable counts. The thirteen pages of handwritten drafts are unusual because few handwritten drafts survive in the manila folders. It must be assumed that either Sexton did not do much of this kind of work or that she considered it too tentative to be worth saving. The handwritten drafts are messy, done in pencil, sometimes running off the page, but for the most part they are decipherable. These scribbled notes and lines were precursors to a more concentrated effort, by which the poet worked toward discovering the poem's form and even its theme.

Since Sexton normally composed on full-sized sheets, the smaller 4 × 6-inch sheets probably represent the earliest draft of **"The Fortress."** One may surmise that when this draft was written she was away from her desk, caught in the first moments of inspiration. Also, a comparison of this draft on smaller sheets with the one written on her usual 8½ × 11-inch paper reveals that only in the latter version did the poet begin to impose a structure on her work, which is consistent with her usual practice of shaping the poem structurally in the process of revision.

The draft written on the smaller notepad sheets begins:

> After Sunday dinner &
> a bottle of wine—
>   lion striped
> On the left, a ^ strang[led?]
> pinetree, its trunk
>   of iron
> hand crafted ^ its many limbs
> are as still as sculpture
> & [appear] at the edges
> stand gaudy bunches of
> fruit store broccoli—
> —I have just kissed your
> left ear—as soft as
>   you [?] whisper hair [?] is as
> c[?] [neck] ^ & your hair—
> straight & calm as mink—
> though the woods winds
> rustle the leaves
> green & yellow, each
> separate & wet from the
> October rain—shining
> like oilskin—

Compared with this draft, which fills the page and contains no marginal notes, the handwritten draft on the larger sheets evinces several important structural and thematic developments:

> After Sunday dinner and a bottle of wine—
>   lie here &
>   No let's not nap—[lets] ^ watch the rainy
> [tears out the window—] out the window—[see how
>   October]
>   On the left, the trunk of the pine tree
> is hand crafted & the [winter] cold rain hardly
> changes it at all, I think its built like
> shelves in a fruit store, full of bunches
> of broccoli—
>   I have just kissed your left ear,
> as soft as your secrets. Your hair, the color of
> honey, is as even & straight as mink. Your knees
> dig comfortably into my back.
>   lemon
>   There are so many colors, ^ [yellow], battle
> green, orange and color, all moving over
> black stems, all shiny as oilskin.

What Sexton has added from one draft to the other is a dramatic structure; she has made clear the setting and the occasion, a time after Sunday dinner when the mother and daughter lie down together to rest and to talk. The resting place is beside a window which provides a view of the scene outdoors, which establishes the multiple contrasts of mother/daughter, child/adult, and cold, hard outdoor scene/warm, soft indoor scene.

The poem is shaped into verse "paragraphs," but several features of the published poem—stanzas with rhyme and meter, a well-defined theme, and a consistent tone—have not been worked out yet, though the evolving structure will serve as the guide for all of these.

Before its final form became clear to Sexton, she worked through a number of drafts of the poem that remain in "paragraphs"—semantically grouped phrases without a consistent stress or syllable count per line—rather than in the poetic stanzas of the published work. Numerous handwritten notes in the margins of the later drafts indicate indecision about rhyme, meter, and stanza form, beginning with the handwritten draft on the larger 8½ × 11-inch sheets. In the upper left-hand corner of one draft page are letters suggesting a possible rhyme scheme: ABACABCDAD. In the margins of several pages are written trial words for the rhymes, for example: "cripple" "ripple," "July" "dry," and "proves" "you've." The notes written on the backs of several of the typewritten pages suggest that Sexton continued to work to establish a regular rhyme scheme for the poem. In fact, she succeeded in working the poem into a scheme that conformed to her original plan for rhymed ten-line stanzas, that is, her ABACAB-CDAD noted above. The published poem contains six ten-line stanzas rhyming according to this pattern. Many of the trial rhyme words appear in the published poem, but rhyme was only one of many structural problems which confronted the poet.

Following the handwritten drafts in the folder are fifteen pages of typewritten drafts, which are numbered successively. The result is an order of drafts which proceeds stanza-by-stanza, with the first five pages devoted to the first stanza of the poem. Sexton began by rearranging the contextual details to give the poem dramatic structure and a shape for the stanzas. Some details which are not to be found in the handwritten drafts were added later, but many of the details and much of the figurative language of the numbered typewritten drafts are already present in the handwritten drafts, such as "the pine tree . . . like a fruit store," "broccoli," and "oilskins."

By the fourth page of typed drafts, Sexton has nearly finished working out the first stanza. Her notes on this page show that she had become concerned with meter, having written after each line the letter for the rhyme pattern and a number indicating the syllable count. The number "10," also written in the margin, denoted ten-line stanzas. The fifth page is another worksheet closely resembling the version of page four, but typed in the margin of the sixth page, which contains the finished first stanza and work on the second stanza, are numbers which seem to conform to the number of stressed syllable counts or metrical feet for the first stanza rather than mere syllable counts.

Further analysis of other draft pages suggests that the poet's methods for revision follow a consistent process. After establishing her rhyme, meter, and stanza length for the first stanza, she set out to make the other stanzas conform to the pattern. Changes in the text of the poem were also designed to support this purpose: completion of the rhyme scheme; filling out of syllable counts; and fleshing out of stanzas. This procedure is illustrated by Sexton's marginal notes on the seventh page of typed drafts:

"Taking a Nap With Linda"

A-8	1.	Here, under the quilted covers
B-8	2.	I hold the pulse that means your blood
A-6	3.	I think the woods outdoors
C-4	4.	are half asleep,
A-6	5.	left over from summer
B-9	6.	like a stack of books after a flood;
C-12	7.	left over like the promises I never keep.
D-7	8.	On the right a scrub pine tree
A-5	9.	waits like a fruit store
D-11	10.	holding up bunches of tufted broccoli.

A-8	1.	We watch the wind from our square bed
B-8	2.	I press down my index finger
A-6	3.	half in jest, half in dread
C-4	4.	on the brown mole
B(12)A-9	5.	under your left eye, inherited
B-9	6.	from my right cheek. A spot of danger
C-12	7.	where a bewitched worm ate through our soul
D-7	8.	in search of beauty. [indecipherable word] roots.
A-5	9.	wind, you speak with dread
(10)D-11	10.	

Half in jest and half in dread
I press down my index finger
on the mole you inherited
from my left cheek
where a bewitched worm ate through our soul
in search of beauty. Both tall, both thin,
we have both been bred

where a bewitched worm ate through our soul in
    search of beauty. (Forgive the mark) my mark
you can never hide

Comparing this draft page with the handwritten draft written on loose-leaf notebook paper yields the following similarities of context:

(Handwritten draft)
    We discuss the wind, so many winds, different
        winds.

(Typed draft, pg. 7)
    We watch the wind from our square bed.

(Handwritten draft)
    Beneath your left eye I put my index finger
        on the mole
    you inherited from my right cheek

(Typed draft, pg. 7)
    I press down my index finger
    half in jest, half in dread
    on the brown mole
    under your left eye, inherited
    from my right cheek.

One way to describe Sexton's method here is to say that she "re-composed," using, for the most part, contextual material from previous drafts, but re-thinking and re-composing to fit her chosen structural pattern. The rearrangement or repositioning of details often elicited new creativity to complete or refine an image or further secure an appropriate change in tone. For example, Sexton's work on the second stanza of **"The Fortress"** brought the new image of "a bewitched worm" that "ate through our soul / in search of beauty," which added a sinister tone to the earlier "brown mole" image.

The fifth stanza, which was completed in only two typewritten drafts, reinforces the sinister tone of the second stanza. A slight but visceral change is made to stanza five when a sentence from the handwritten drafts—"Your knees dig comfortably into my back"— becomes, on typewritten draft page "13," "Your feet thump-thump against my back." Another section of stanza five adds yet another new element:

    The woods are underwater, their weeds are shaking
    in the tide; birches like zebra fish
    flash by in a pack.

The handwritten antecedents of these lines read:

    rocks like backs of fish—Fish—bark as rough as
    the backs of star fish—half asleep the gray sky
    is the only thing that's above water—the rest are
    sea plants

Like another creature from the handwritten drafts—"on the outside like a leopard coat"—the "zebra fish" evokes the imagery of the Dark Continent. Still another phrase in this stanza—"What mouse runs between your eyes"—achieves a transition between the worlds of the bedside scene and the outdoors scene. This "new" phrase was added, verbatim, from the handwritten drafts, just as the animal imagery, for the most part already in the handwritten drafts, accumulated around the image of the ancestral mole in order to establish fully the tone of fear and menace.

It is possible, at this juncture, to begin to speculate as to why Sexton preferred to work in the way that she did. We know that she liked to work at a poem until it was finished, if she could, as she told Patricia Marx: "Oh, it's a wonderful pleasure. It's a struggle, but there's great happiness in working. . . . And I'm pretty stubborn. I need to keep after it until I get it."[12] It cannot have been only ease or convenience which motivated Sexton to revise as she did—that is, establishing first her structure and then plugging in words already at hand from earlier drafts. As we have seen, it was not merely structure but tone and theme which evolved during the revision process for **"The Fortress."** It is difficult to imagine, from the evidence of these revision pages, that Sexton really knew beforehand the eventual shapes and meanings of her poems. She seems, rather, to have used the "raw materials" of earlier drafts composed in the heat of strong passions in a recursive way, finding along with the trial and error of her work on form what she wanted to say, as well as how she wanted to sound.

Viewed from the larger perspective, Sexton's methods resulted in her growing maturity as a craftsman, as is shown in the way in which her structures themselves became more sophisticated. In *All My Pretty Ones* we find poems like **"Letter Written on a Ferry While Crossing Long Island Sound"** that exhibit a structure quite different from the one noted in **"The Fortress."** Although Sexton maintained her familiar way of working, the drafts for this poem reveal that its revision involved distinct problems for the poet. **"Letter Written on a Ferry While Crossing Long Island Sound"** began with five pages of handwritten drafts composed suddenly during an event in Anne Sexton's life. In *The Complete Poems,* Maxine Kumin relates that the poem "began at the instant Anne sighted the nuns on an actual crossing."[13] Kumin also asserts that the poem underwent very little revision, "except for minor skirmishes required to affect the closure in each stanza," an assertion unsupported for the most part by the manuscript materials in the Sexton archive. With more foresight than she sometimes had when starting a poem, Sexton established the basic dramatic structure from the beginning: **"Letter Written on a Ferry While Crossing Long Island Sound"** resembles a personal letter, commencing with a greeting, "Dearest You," which was later revised to "Dearest." At another point in the text the greeting is repeated and, throughout, the words seem to be addressed to one particular person.[14] The early tone is confidential but evolves into philosophical musings which gather weight as the revision process continues. In order to observe how the poet transformed what must have been a letter to an unnamed person into a poetic and dramatic statement, it is necessary to reproduce in its entirety **"Letter Written on a Ferry While Crossing Long Island Sound"** as it appears in *The Complete Poems*:

> I am surprised to see
> that the ocean is still going on.

Now I am going back
and I have ripped my hand
from your hand as I said I would
and I have made it this far
as I said I would
and I am on the top deck now
holding my wallet, my cigarettes
and my car keys
at 2 o'clock on a Tuesday
in August of 1960.

Dearest,
although everything has happened,
nothing has happened.
The sea is very old.
The sea is the face of Mary,
without miracles or rage
or unusual hope,
grown rough and wrinkled
with incurable age.

Still,
I have eyes.
These are my eyes:
the orange letters that spell
ORIENT on the life preserver
that hangs by my knees;
the cement lifeboat that wears
its dirty canvas coat;
the faded sign that sits on its shelf
saying KEEP OFF.
Oh, all right, I say,
I'll save myself.

Over my right shoulder
I see four nuns
who sit like a bridge club,
their faces poked out
from under their habits,
as good as good babies who
have sunk into their carriages.
Without discrimination
the wind pulls the skirts
of their arms.
Almost undressed,
I see what remains:
that holy wrist,
that ankle,
that chain.

Oh God,
although I am very sad,
could you please
let these four nuns
loosen from their leather boots
and their wooden chairs
to rise out
over this greasy deck,
out over this iron rail,
nodding their pink heads to one side,
flying four abreast
in the old-fashioned side stroke;
each mouth open and round,
breathing together
as fish do,
singing without sound.

Dearest,
see how my dark girls sally forth,
over the passing lighthouse of Plum Gut,
its shell as rusty
as a camp dish,
as fragile as a pagoda
on a stone;
out over the little lighthouse
that warns me of drowning winds
that rub over its blind bottom
and its blue cover;
winds that will take the toes
and the ears of the rider
or the lover.

There go my dark girls,
their dresses puff
in the leeward air.
Oh, they are lighter than flying dogs
or the breath of dolphins;
each mouth opens gratefully,
wider than a milk cup.
My dark girls sing for this.
They are going up.
See them rise
on black wings, drinking
the sky, without smiles
or hands
or shoes.
They call back to us
from the gauzy edge of paradise,
good news, good news.[15]

Many of the important phrases and images of the published poem appear in the handwritten draft pages. On the first of five handwritten pages for the poem are found the following phrases: "ripped my hand from your hand as I said I would" (ll. 4-5), "four nuns sitting like a bridge club" (ll. 35-36), and "their faces poked out from under their habits as good as good babies who have sunk into their carriages" (ll. 37-40). Also present are descriptive details which Sexton included in the published poem: "I am on the top deck now" (l. 8), "the . . . letters that spell / ORIENT on the life preserver" (ll. 25-26), and "the cement lifeboat . . . saying KEEP OFF" (ll. 28-31). Elsewhere, poetic phrases abound among the five pages of scribbled draft, such as "I am . . . surprised to see that the ocean is still going on" (ll. 1-2), as well as vivid description: "this greasy deck" (l. 56), "their pink heads" (l. 58), "black wings" (l. 89).

The phrases in Sexton's handwritten drafts comprise three distinct sets of images, which she grouped together as she revised the poem. While she was assembling these phrases, or in some cases single words, Sexton discovered in them her emerging theme: the persona has taken a brave step toward independence by her willful act of separation; however, she stands hesitant, not entirely certain of her next step. The first image, that of the nuns, points both to the unconventionality and the correctness of feminine self-reliance. This image and its meaning are reinforced by the description of

the nuns' faces as those of babies unaccustomed, and perhaps unprepared, to confront life alone and independently. A second set of images relates to the ship, a locale of danger, unsure footing, and disorientation, but symbolic of journeys. A third set of images, intertwined with the first two, suggests emerging confidence in exploring new possibilities. Concerned with the ocean, the air, and stasis and change, this set of images shows the persona sensing the means for attaining freedom, metaphorically through flight but essentially in internal and personal terms. Ultimately the poet repositioned and concentrated this third set of images in the poem's sixth and seventh stanzas. Very little in the way of content was added in revision, but in order to "depersonalize" her theme and to make it more universal, Sexton made several major deletions of previously included references to the lover. It remained for her then to refine what was still only an initial effort at a poem, to fashion a dramatic structure from which her theme, borrowing from a phrase in the poem, "took wing."

Structurally, the published version of **"Letter Written on a Ferry While Crossing Long Island Sound"** is ninety-five lines arranged in seven or eight stanzas varying from nine to seventeen lines.[16] Visually, the poem has a tall look, with many short enjambed lines, and it lacks the "obvious" structure of **"The Fortress"** or **"The Abortion,"** which follow a close rhyme scheme and a regular pattern of stanzas of the same or close-to-the-same length. Only about a third of the poems in *All My Pretty Ones* are more structured and resemble **"The Fortress"** rather than **"Letter Written on a Ferry While Crossing Long Island Sound."** The greater number of less mechanically structured pieces is indicative of Sexton's growth as she moved toward freer, more ambitious poems in this volume. The "look" of the poem is in keeping with both the "letter" device and the theme of the ascendancy of the individual. Also, by eschewing a too regular pattern of rhyme and stanzas, Sexton maintains a confidential and musing tone.

The handwritten draft is not in stanzas, which appear in the first typewritten draft, and it is wordy and less focused than later stages of the text. The forming of the poem into stanzas was, to use a domestic analogy, like housecleaning. To achieve a "cleaner" look, nonessential or inappropriate language was discarded, in many instances what was too maudlin or personal. The first stanzas of **"Letter Written on a Ferry While Crossing Long Island Sound"** describe the poem's persona fleeing a relationship gone bad. Specifically, the poem seems to be addressed to a lover, but Sexton realized during revision that neither lover nor relationship was the real focus of what she wanted to say. Not present at later stages of the text are lines such as the following from the handwritten draft:

Oh, godamn, my heart, I'm
riding backwards
Oh, is it too sad to look at this?
Oh Dearest you—,
hear my eyes!
—I love you,!

Sexton chose from a surfeit of words what was useful in her thematic and dramatic context. She also refined her tone, creating a proper distance between woman and poet, poet and reader. Often, Sexton was able to create a tone which was "confessional" in the best sense of the term, eliciting empathy in her readers without mawkishness.

In keeping with the theme of feminine freedom which began to emerge as Sexton worked on the poem, she made other changes in revision which deemphasized the romantic focus of her letter. The letter device was useful, but the original "letter" had been subordinated by the nuns image that became her new focus, just as her theme of independence and raised consciousness had preempted the man who was the original subject of her thoughts. This man, and Sexton's feelings concerning her break-up with him, are very much the subject of several early drafts, such as the following:

> Dearest you,
> When I drove away, my mouth [was] clogged with
>   tears
> and your last touch curled against my cheek,
> remembering the high I ran toward death
> Dearest you,
> When I drove away from your face,
> my mouth was clogged with tears
> and your last touch cooled on my cheek,
> praying to the road
>
>   my heart splintering

The final form of the poem retains none of the tone here of helplessness and heartbreak; rather it suggests independence, even defiance: "and I have ripped my hand / from your hand as I said I would / and I have made it this far / as I said I would / and I am on the top deck now" (ll. 4-8). Notable here is the use of anaphora in the repeated "as. . . ." and "and," creating a chiding tone. The greeting, simply and sardonically "Dearest," was moved to the second stanza, its subject ever more forgotten as the writer gained courage and insight. The rhythm too was altered from four or five to two or three stresses per line, with the monosyllabic words and the placing of stressed syllables at the ends of lines reinforcing the poem's straightforward and assertive tone.

Beginning with the fourth stanza, Sexton shifted the emphasis of the poem from the account of her persona's estrangement from her lover to the nuns, who catch the eye of the persona: "Over my right shoulder / I see four nuns / who sit like a bridge club." This new focus has been presaged in the second stanza's description of the sea:

> The sea is very old.
> The sea is the face of Mary,
> without miracles or rage
> or unusual hope,
> grown rough and wrinkled
> with incurable age.

A note in cursive beside these lines on one draft shows that Sexton intended the image to suggest the life she was leaving and the person she would no longer be: "tired and monotonous."

As Sexton grouped her important images together she added transition words and created dramatic movement, usually as narration, but also as dynamisms of psychological and thematic tension suggested by careful juxtapositions of grouped imagery. Particularly in this poem, the poet in her descriptions of the nuns found a device which served almost as alter ego for the persona in her journey towards independence. Her musing account of the nuns transports them physically and spiritually to "paradise" itself. Completing the revery is the grouping of details from the ocean setting to achieve a quality of exotic places and miraculous events: "over the lighthouse . . . as fragile as a pagoda"; "There go my dark girls . . . Oh they are lighter than . . . the breath of dolphins."

This atmosphere in which the nuns rise up and become lighter than breath is in sharp contrast to their initial description in the fifth stanza where they are firmly planted on the deck of the prosaic ship. Now, in a bold but effortless transition, Sexton "releases" the nuns:

> Oh God,
> although I am very sad
> could you please
> let these four nuns
> loosen from their leather boots
> and their wooden chairs
> to rise out
> over this greasy deck,
> out over this iron rail
> nodding their pink heads to one side,
> flying four abreast
> in the old-fashioned side stroke;
> each mouth open and round,
> breathing together
> as fish do,
> singing without sound.

In grouping images of "leather boots," "wooden chairs," and "greasy deck," Sexton emphasizes the confinement and the "old-fashioned" plight of the women, riding on the sea but still cloistered in the thoughts and mores which have confined all women. In revising this stanza Sexton removed description which weakened the contrast between being held down and rising up. For example, the following lines are included in one version of the stanza: "each skirt stitched over their stockings / like a glossy fan / sallying forth / slapping their [*sic*] like an open fan." This description lends too much attention to the nuns' appearance without adding to the dramatic and thematic focus of the stanza, and so Sexton discarded what she probably considered redundant and perhaps even overly precious images of stockings and fans.

The diction of her emancipating words—"let . . . loosen," "rise out," "out over," "flying"—is dramatically effective in its capacity to free the persona's spirit. A note in the poet's handwriting on one of the draft pages explains her purpose in these lines: "I am not imploring God to set them loose, that is set them free. . . . I am asking that (they) be permitted to loosen themselves." Sexton seemed to favor (as she did in **"The Fortress"**) aquatic imagery to suggest freedom and whimsy. In the context of **"Letter Written on a Ferry While Crossing Long Island Sound"** this imagery seems particularly significant. Obviously, since the persona is on a ferry, sea imagery comes to mind, but Sexton imagines in her simile that the nuns are like fish which have breached the surface of the sea, not to return to it as flying fish might but to escape its confines permanently. Adding to this idea is the image of the nuns in their strange quartet, "singing without sound" as earthly "fish" or heavenly angels might do. A decision to delete a stanza from the worksheets further illustrates why Sexton's nuns could not return to the deck or, as fish, to the sea.

> Then,
> let the sea
> be greater than grass
> or a floating jam of cut lumber.
> Oh God, let the sea
> be greater than the eyes
> of all the terrible fish
> who wait for me.

Often using marine metaphors to suggest the innocent fascination with the sea, Sexton could be very ambivalent and express great fear of its real perils. This ambivalence works to good effect in **"Letter Written on a Ferry While Crossing Long Island Sound,"** maintaining the tension of the persona's difficult decision. Nevertheless, this stanza had to be deleted by the poet, for it implies a return to a weaker position held previously. Once the poet had called for the nuns' freedom, which is an advance, she could not go back to the fear of the terrible fish.

At times, words from the early drafts underwent transformation as parts of new images and description or seemed to be discarded temporarily, only to be reinserted in new places in the poem. Consider, for instance, these lines from the first page of handwritten drafts:

> splatted by the blue sea
> riding toward you over the blue stones
> of this blue sheet

The first typed draft contains the lines revised as part of the first stanza:

> splattered by the blue sun
> sitting on this same hard seat,
> riding toward you over the blue stones
> of this blue sheet

These lines survive through successive revisions until they almost disappear, then reappear as part of the sixth stanza: "running over the blind rocks / and their sweet blue cover. . . ." The published poem contains a further revision: "that rub over its blind bottom / and its blue cover" (ll. 74-75). This type of revision is typical of the way that Sexton found more sophisticated uses for the language of the first drafts, eliminating clichés ("blue sea"), replacing repetition with alliteration ("blue . . . blue" to "blind bottom / . . . blue"), eliminating sing-song rhyme ("seat / sheet"), and pragmatically moving a phrase to another stanza. The result is a poetic economy that saves invention for its most appropriate application and a subtlety that suggests rather than overstates.

The visual imagery of the sea as "blind bottom" and "blue cover" reinforces the metaphor of the sea as life unenlightened and unhappy. Escape from this undesirable state is achieved in passage through the air, Sexton's metaphor for movement upward and away from the persona's previous self-denying stasis. The image which captures this movement is one of "winds that will take the toes / and the ears of the rider / or the lover." Resembling the winds is the image of the nuns in the eighth and final stanza as almost invisible. Sexton's "dark girls" are "without smiles / or hands / or shoes." Invisibility does not suggest that the nuns are insignificant but rather it associates them with angels and heaven or with freedom. On one of the drafts, a handwritten note beside the poem's last line, which reads "bring it to life," is a critical comment that summarizes the thematic re-awakening of the poem's persona or, through the revisions the poet made after her first handwritten attempt, how Sexton made of her personal experience a poem which brings to life the good news of woman's emancipation.

"The Abortion" is one of Anne Sexton's poems that may have provoked the kind of criticism leveled at her by Rosemary Johnson, who wrote of Sexton in 1980 that "she indulges in self-revelation without stint, telling all in an exposé of her innermost workings that amounts to literary seppuku."[17] As shocking as the subject matter and language of this poem may have been to some readers, an analysis of the drafts for the poem reveals that Sexton approached its composition in the same way that she approached the writing of the other two poems considered here: concerned first with structure, she was receptive to new insights as the revision process proceeded. **"The Abortion"** is a poem almost as interesting for its shape on the page as for its theme:

> Somebody who should have been born
> is gone.
>
> Just as the earth puckered its mouth,
> each bud puffing out from its knot,
> I changed my shoes, and then drove south.
>
> Up past the Blue Mountains, where
> Pennsylvania humps on endlessly,
> wearing, like a crayoned cat, its green hair,
>
> its roads sunken in like a gray washboard;
> where, in truth, the ground cracks evilly,
> a dark socket from which the coal has poured,
>
> Somebody who should have been born
> is gone.
>
> the grass as bristly and stout as chives,
> and me wondering when the ground would break,
> and me wondering how anything fragile survives;
>
> up in Pennsylvania, I met a little man,
> not Rumpelstiltskin, at all, at all . . .
> he took the fullness that love began.
>
> Returning north, even the sky grew thin
> like a high window looking nowhere.
> The road was as flat as a sheet of tin.
>
> Somebody who should have been born
> is gone.
>
> Yes, woman, such logic will lead
> to loss without death. Or say what you meant,
> you coward . . . this baby that I bleed.[18]

The drafts for **"The Abortion"** do not include any handwritten pages, but the first typewritten pages give an early idea of what the important images and narrative of the poem would be. Sexton depended on her revision process for finding in the words and phrases which appeared in the first drafts the dramatic structure and evolving shape for the poem, and through multiple drafts she fixed on both a coherent theme and a final form for the poem. The HRHRC archival materials reveal that Sexton usually composed at the typewriter, and while the few handwritten drafts which exist for some poems offer an important clue to the poet's method of composition, the typed drafts do not alter the impression that her practice was the same whether composing by hand or at the typewriter.

"The Abortion" was composed in the summer months of 1960.[19] The working title of the poem was "Hollows," which appears on all but one of the titled drafts.

The word "hollow" appears in the text of the first and several subsequent drafts, and it is part of a stanza which underwent considerable revision before publication, when the word itself no longer appears in either the title or the text. The title change corresponds to a change—from oblique references to the "abortion" in the earlier drafts—to a new directness by the persona, an important shift in tone which is characterized by a line in the finished poem: "Say what you meant."

Sexton must have realized as she revised the poem that directness was the best way to eliminate ambiguity of feelings. But, with her economy of finding other uses for images, she did not discard all references to "hollows," but employed this type of physical description in other imagery that in its suggestiveness added to her theme. Thus the sense of the working title is still evident in the published poem: ". . . roads sunken in like a gray washboard . . . / a dark socket from which the coal has poured . . ." (ll. 9,11). Sexton wavered in her decision to change the title as the drafts progressed, with different titles appearing on different pages or with one title scratched through and another substituted. Her search for the proper title seemed to coincide with her search for the right tone and theme. She settled finally on a poem which moves from hesitation and uncertainty on a metaphorical level to catharsis and a reaffirmation of the realistic and literal. The poem juxtaposes realistic details—the "abortion" itself, geographic place names—with figurative language focused on natural phenomena as metaphors for her personal struggles—"each bud puffing out its knot," "I've been inside a mountain, a cave full of ghosts. . . ." At times during the revision process, Sexton seems to have strayed too far to the side of realism, not allowing the power of poetic suggestiveness to balance her sense of direct treatment. This point is illustrated by her revision of a stanza originally in eight lines and the most revised part of the poem which was later deleted. This stanza is found on the tentative final draft of page [1] and with other trial stanzas on eight subsequent draft pages, as well as on page [14]. In addition, this stanza is the sole subject of worksheets, which are the substance of pages [9], [12], and [13].

Two versions of the stanza, from page [12], illustrate its evolution:

> [Version One]
> Somebody who should have been born
> is gone. Somebody who wasn't anybody yet;
> that somebody who had a right was torn
> out of me . . . with my consent.
> Back from Pennsylvania, I tell the neighbors lies
> and you, with all your lust spent,
> are reasonable. Still, I avoid my children's eye.
>
> [Version Two]
> Somebody who should have been born

is gone. Somebody who wasn't anybody yet;
that somebody who had a right, was torn
out of me . . . with my consent.
Given away like a pint of blood I didn't need,
or, say it, you coward . . . this baby that I bleed.

The latter version contains the key phrases which survive in the published poem's last stanza. Recriminating remarks directed at the father of the unborn child, expressions of embarrassment concerning the neighbors, and even the telling guilt when she looks on her children—all were dropped in revision. She dramatized the situation by focusing the reader's attention on the event of the abortion rather than on her own anger, her denial, and her sense of guilt. Furthermore, the realism she achieves underscores the injustice done to a woman by a man, without her naming the man.

The working-out of the essential problem of tone for **"The Abortion"** was not a conscious act by Sexton as she revised, rather her conscious purpose was, as usual, to refine the structure. The drafts proceed by stanzas or by rearrangement of stanzas and other structural elements. The page [1] draft, for example, contains in the bottom margin penciled notations for a rhyme scheme and stressed syllable counts similar to those Sexton used for **"The Fortress."** The page [8] draft, which shows how she worked to organize the stanzas for **"The Abortion,"** appears to be an early version. This draft contains several lines and stanzas later deleted and reveals early word choices which Sexton later revised. The draft reads as follows:

"Hollows"

Just as the earth pursed its mouth,
1. each bud pushed out from its knot,
   I changed my shoes and then drove south . . .

*something that should have been born
is gone . . .*

Up past the Blue Mountains, where
2. Pennsylvania humps on endlessly,
   wearing, like a cat, its green hair . . .

*strange girl, strange girl, where
have you been . . .*

I've been inside a mountain, a cave
3. full of ghosts, where neon signs
   turn on and off like broadway . . .

*something that should have been born
is gone . . .*

In Pennsylvania, where King Coal is dead,
4. the mines empty, the hills all hollow,
   I visited a shabby town, a sad bed . . .

*strange girl, strange girl, where
have you been . . .*

Up in Pennsylvania, I met a little man,
5. not Rumplestiltskin at all, at all,
   he took the fullness that love began . . .

*something that should have been born
is gone . . .*

     I   I   ed   would
As ^ drove, you ^ wonder ^ when the ground ^ will
   break;
6. the road sinks in and out like a washboard
   and the bed is surgical for what you forsake . . .

*strange girl, strange girl, where
have you been
sh.. g*
How could I tell you how much sin
is possible?
strange girl, strange girl where
Somebody who should have been born
is gone. Somebody who wasn't anybody yet;
that somebody who had a right was torn
7. out of me . . . with my consent.
   Given away like a pint of blood I didn't need,
   this small gift, this impossible present
   to no one . . . or say what you meant,
   you coward, this baby that I bleed.

Like the drafts for the first stanzas of **"The Fortress"** and **"Letter Written on a Ferry While Crossing Long Island Sound"** this draft is the "template," which established the basic structure for **"The Abortion."** Comparing the page [8] draft with the published poem yields these similarities:

Published poem—twenty-seven lines
Page [8] draft—thirty-three lines
Published poem—seven stanzas with three refrains
Page [8] draft—seven stanzas with three refrains

Marked differences are also apparent from comparison of the two versions: the longer eight-line concluding stanza of the page [8] draft; major differences in stanzas three and four; changes in word choice in individual lines; and syntactical and narrative changes. Still, it was the working out of the poem's structure in this draft to fit Sexton's basic thoughts and language for the poem which solved most of her problems. It then remained for the poet to continue with more minor revisions in the nature of "fine tuning."

Often during this working-out of the final shapes of poems, Sexton altered or dropped certain "pet" phrases. As she matured as a poet, Sexton learned to temper some of the idiosyncrasies which she was tempted to incorporate in her poetry. For instance, we know of her fascination with the rhymes and stories of childhood, which is to be found in the diction of **"The Fortress"** ("a bewitched worm"; "cried . . . like a wolf") or in the inspiration for her book of re-interpreted fairy tales, ***Transformations.***[20] Sexton's revision of the refrain in

"The Abortion" shows how the poet at this stage of her development often would "catch herself" in a bad habit while in the process of revising. Her use of the traditional device of the refrain as a means of encapsulating details, of creating a sense of measure by repetition, is apparent in **"The Abortion"** with the repeated and *italicized* lines "Somebody who should have been born / is gone," followed by three tercets—a pattern repeated twice until the third refrain, which is followed by a single tercet. Not all of the drafts include the full number of six tercets before the final refrain. The drafts on pages [1], [4], and [6], for instance, include, in the position of the sixth tercet, an underlined couplet, as follows:

> *strange girl, strange girl,*
> *where have you been? . . .*

These lines are penciled out on the page [4] draft and are also scratched through but rewritten in the margin of the page [8] draft. The lines reappear in the full-length drafts, pages [10] and [11], but appear in no subsequent draft. Changing her mind several times before finally deleting these lines, Sexton may have done so because the lines echo a familiar nursery rhyme, an allusion inappropriate for the tone and the subject matter of the poem. Although she does retain the reference to Rumpelstiltskin, this is boding in tone, whereas the metrical allusion to a nursery rhyme like "Little Bo Peep" is ambivalent in this context. A close examination of other changes reveals that the early drafts have a sing-song quality which was gradually replaced by a more realistic sound—in keeping with other changes Sexton made in theme and tone.

For the ending of **"The Abortion,"** Sexton's problem was mainly one of narrative—how to get the "I" in the poem back to Boston. She worked this out tentatively in a page [19] draft revision, where the "I" is described as "returning North." The poet still considered the ending of the poem too abrupt and the eight lines too many, not consistent with the rest of the poem's tercets. The page [19] draft ends with this three-line stanza:

> Yes, Beezlebub, such logic will lead
> to loss without death. Or say what you meant,
> you coward . . . this baby that I bleed.[21]

Sexton nearly has her ending at this juncture; the eight-line stanza has been replaced with a tercet consistent with the other stanzas; the key phrase—"such logic will lead / to loss without death"—has been found, providing a necessary transition to the conclusion. But the reference to "Beezlebub" was not right, for "Beezlebub" was not to blame. In a change which once again found Sexton replacing metaphor with realistic words of strong semantic association, "Beezlebub" became

"woman." With this change the poet neatly concluded her thematic journey, replacing all metaphors for self with the one, realistic word, "woman."

This study has focused on three poems from Anne Sexton's volume, *All My Pretty Ones,* published at a time when the poet was perfecting her craft around a strong personal vision and a unique and exciting contemporary vocabulary, with accompanying images drawn from her personal experience and her fertile imagination. In her revisions, she worked first to find the right form, and as she did so, tone and theme emerged or were strengthened. As Sexton worked toward discovering original ways to structure her poems in *All My Pretty Ones,* she entered an important period in her growth as a poet. The structure of **"The Fortress"** is less sophisticated than that of **"Letter Written on a Ferry While Crossing Long Island Sound"** or **"The Abortion"** and is typical of a type of poem which is to be found in most of Sexton's volumes but with less frequency after *All My Pretty Ones.* Even as her structures became more sophisticated, however, Sexton continued to rely on her own particular method of revision. One crucial change in this process may have been her abandonment of the handwritten draft as a first stage in writing. The neatness and visual accuracy of the typed drafts may have made it easier for her to evaluate what was needed to improve the forms of her poems. As Sexton found new ways to approach structure, she also sought the effect of greater immediacy.

Anne Sexton was very much her own person as a writer—unique or idiosyncratic, a "quick study" or gifted. While the fashions of criticism fluctuate concerning her lasting contribution to poetry, Sexton's revision process in the poems of *All My Pretty Ones* demonstrates that her work was the product of a consistent and effective effort. The Sexton archive of handwritten and typed notes and drafts provides a valuable record of the poet's growing maturity as she discovered—in the process of revision—an extemporaneous and personal tone within poems more tightly crafted than might otherwise be apparent without this documentary evidence.

Notes

1. Anne Sexton, "Interview with William Packard (1970)," in *Anne Sexton: The Artist and Her Critics,* ed. J. D. McClatchy (Bloomington: Indiana University Press, 1978), p. 45.

2. Priscilla Marx, "Interview with Anne Sexton," *The Hudson Review* 18, no. 4 (Winter 1965-66): 562.

3. Ibid., p. 568.

4. Maxine Kumin, in her introduction to Sexton's *The Complete Poems* (see footnote 10 below), discusses the period of time in which the poems

for *All My Pretty Ones* were composed. The dates are also documented by Sexton's having mentioned her work on several of the poems in *Anne Sexton: A Self-Portrait in Letters,* ed. Linda Gray Sexton and Lois Ames (Boston: Houghton Mifflin Co., 1979), pp. 87-153. See the chapter entitled "All Her Pretty Ones October 1959-December 1962" where Sexton reveals that the summer months of 1960 and 1961 were especially productive for her. Further confirmation of these dates for the poems is found in Diane Wood Middlebrook, *Anne Sexton: A Biography* (Boston: Houghton Mifflin Co., 1991), chapters 6, 7, and 8.

5. *Anne Sexton: The Artist and Her Critics,* p. 122.

6. Ibid., p. 124.

7. Again, it is Maxine Kumin's comments in the introduction to *The Complete Poems* which confirm the dates of composition for *The Awful Rowing toward God.* In Kumin's words, the poems for the last volume published in Sexton's lifetime were composed "at white heat in January and February of 1973, and the poems were coming at the rate of two, three, even four a day . . ." (p. xxxi). For more on this last collection by Sexton, see the article . . . by Sexton's biographer, Diane Wood Middlebrook [*Rossetti to Sexton: Six Women Poets at Texas,* edited by Dave Oliphant, Austin, Tex.: Harry Ransom Humanities Research Center, The University of Texas at Austin, 1992], pp. 223-235, and p. 366 in the Middlebrook biography.

8. Barbara Kevles, "The Art of Poetry XV: Anne Sexton," *The Paris Review* 52 (Summer 1971): 172.

9. Marx, "Interview with Anne Sexton," p. 567.

10. Anne Sexton, *The Complete Poems,* ed. Linda Gray Sexton (Boston: Houghton Mifflin Co., 1981). This collection lists in the Table of Contents eight volumes of poems: *To Bedlam and Part Way Back* (1960); *All My Pretty Ones* (1962); *Live or Die* (1966); *Love Poems* (1969); *Transformations* (1971); *The Book of Folly* (1972); *The Death Notebooks* (1974); and *The Awful Rowing toward God* (1975). A separate section of posthumous publications lists *45 Mercy Street* and *Words For Dr. Y* published in 1976 and 1978, respectively. *The Complete Poems* also contains several previously uncollected poems written in the last year of Anne Sexton's life. Permission to quote from the drafts of Anne Sexton's poems and to reproduce the printed versions from *The Collected Poems* has been granted by Linda Gray Sexton, Executor of the Sexton Estate.

11. Ibid, pp. 66-68.

12. Marx, "Interview with Anne Sexton," p. 562.

13. *The Complete Poems,* p. xxvi.

14. According to the Middlebrook biography, "Letter Written on a Ferry While Crossing Long Island Sound" commemorates "the emotional dynamics between [James Wright and Sexton]," which resulted from their relationship during part of July-August 1960 while together at Montauk, Long Island (see pp. 133-34). For more on the Sexton-Wright relationship, see Middlebrook's article in . . . [*Rossetti to Sexton*], pp. 223-235.

15. *The Complete Poems,* pp. 81-84.

16. At least two published versions of the poem exist—in *The New Yorker* and in *The Collected Poems*—with differences in the number of lines and composition of stanzas and even a slight difference in the title. The original drafts may help to resolve which version is "correct."

17. Rosemary Johnson, "The Woman of Private (but Published) Hungers," *Parnassus* 8, no. 1 (1980): 92.

18. *The Complete Poems,* pp. 61-62.

19. One draft is dated June 2nd, 1960, and another is dated June 4, 1960, with the word "done" written in cursive. Both the author's notes and the order of drafts in the folders are unreliable for determining the exact date of completion, for there are numerous discrepancies. My ordering of the drafts as page [1], page [2], etc. is arbitrary but follows their order in the manila folders and facilitates a discussion of specific sheets.

20. Anne Sexton, *Transformations* (Boston: Houghton Mifflin, 1971).

21. The event which is the subject of this poem was Sexton's own abortion, which Middlebrook reports was performed in May 1960 (p. 121). The "Beezlebub" image appears only on two draft pages, [19] discussed here and the subsequent page [20]. Interestingly Sexton seems to have first wanted to blame the doctor who performed the abortion, the "Rumpelstiltskin" of the poem, or she may have blamed the man, who is implied on draft page [12]. Ultimately, Sexton blamed herself. Draft page [2], which shows how wrong she considered the act of abortion, contains the following stanza:

> Or worse, if I whine for a baby's life,
> I lie. Both woman and earth are breakers
> of laws, but only the woman can pity herself.
> I cry at my own coughing sore.
> When the child dies, the mother is dead.
> After such a small crime, who can be sure

that death itself is not the cure.
I cry *lost lost* at the red.

William Freedman (essay date summer 1993)

SOURCE: Freedman, William. "Sexton's 'The Legend of the One-Eyed Man.'" *Explicator* 51, no. 4 (summer 1993): 248-52.

[*In the following essay, Freedman contends that Sexton's "The Legend of the One-Eyed Man" is her "most extensive poetic meditation on the nature of her art."*]

As Diana Hume George has remarked, preparatory to her own analysis, Sexton's **"The Legend of the One-Eyed Man,"** is an "extraordinarily complex poem [that has been] almost entirely ignored by critics perhaps because of its obscurity and its problematic connection to Sexton's confessional poetry. . . ."[1] Indeed it has been ignored, and understandably, for it is among Sexton's most difficult poems, one that often shifts directions without warning and hints at origins and meanings just beyond our reach.

The poem is, as William H. Shurr observed, "a detailed meditation on the guilt which is central to [Sexton's poetic world]."[2] But George finds more. For her, **"Legend"** is one of the poet's "most analytic as well as prophetic works," "an intricately sketched outline of psychic and cultural malaise"; and a "psychosexual poem" that is at the same time a "heretical religious statement" providing "a revisionary [feminist] reading of Christianity."[3]

"The Legend of the One-Eyed Man" is all these things, but it is also at least one more: a frequently self-conscious poet's most extensive poetic meditation on the nature of her art. Unlike most of Sexton's typically expansive, at times excessively overt and transparent poetry, **"Legend"** is resistantly elliptical throughout. Nowhere is it more so than in two sections that neither George nor Shurr nor, to my knowledge, any other critic of the poem even refers to. I am speaking of the sixth and seventh paragraphs, where Sexton describes the contractual exchange between the purchaser of the cross and the carpenter and attempts to account for the transformation of its routine building and use into something unexpected. These sections, I think, constitute an intrusion into the poem that struggles to explain the fragmentary intrusiveness of the poem in general and the accidental intrusion, on rare occasions, of greatness into art.

Sexton (or the poem's speaker) presents herself, as she frequently does,[4] as a kind of prophet, the poetic seer who, blessed or cursed with a "deaf spot" that enables

her to "hear / the unsaid more clearly" ("Those Times . . ."), also sees what "you overlooked," or what was "forgotten / except by me." Where the speaker-as-creative-seer is centered, the poem-as-creation is at least a latent issue, an issue brought nearer the surface by the discussion of texts. The prophet questions not only the acuity of his forgetful readers, but the reliability of a prior text produced by "rival" visionaries: the New Testament, which "he" berates as "very small," "out-of-date as a prehistoric monster," "held together by pullies," and plagiaristically gouging its narrow space from the parental Judaic ground. In this environment of trenchant, imperceptive, and overrated seers, of reliable and unreliable visionaries and texts, the construction of the cross assumes a poetic identity suggestive of the nature of the writer's craft and art. The guilty speaker of the poem, the "man" who has raped his mother, is also the poet. He/she is the writer whose poetry often scathes the mother's character and role in the daughter's development: rapes her, in effect, or runs over her "mother's life like a truck" ("Those Times . . ."). In this context of creator and creation, the reduction of the crucifix and Crucifixion to a problem in carpentry and engineering becomes a slighting description of a certain kind of routinized, even commercialized, creativity.

The effort of these sections is to account for the surprising radiance that sometimes transforms such perfunctory work, the force that occasionally lifts the commonplace into the transcendent. It is to account, in other words, for the often mysterious workings of "the excitable gift" that made life worth holding onto, at least for a while (**"Live"**).

As Sexton characteristically conceived it, the role of poetry was the role that Kafka assigned to literature in a letter that Sexton used as the motto for her second volume. "[T]he books we need," Kafka wrote to Oskar Pollak, "are the kind that act upon us like a misfortune, that make us suffer like the death of someone we love more than ourselves, that make us feel as though we were on the verge of suicide, or lost in a forest remote from all human habitation." Poetry, in other words, is a kind of cross, which the poet loads upon our backs. "Its ugliness," she concedes, "is a matter of custom." Ugliness in poetry as Sexton wrote and thought of it was often essential to its mission as rude debunker of romantic myths and fatuous beliefs; essential, too, to shock readers out of the academic complacency into which the prevailing mode of poetry had lulled them.

"If there was a mistake made," if the hanging of a thief turns into the crucifixion of a god, if the ordinary confessional poem becomes, as this one had, or was becoming in her hands, something more,

then the Crucifix was constructed wrong . . .
not from the quality of the pine,

not from hanging a mirror,
not from dropping the studding or the drill
but from having an inspiration.

The lines are as baffling as they are surprising, and it is little wonder that critics have avoided them. But in the context of a metaphoric discussion of poetic creation they begin to yield. The "mistake" that alters the predictable dimensions of the standard product, producing the unique structure of this or other such extraordinary poems in Sexton's canon, can be accounted for not by the quality of the materials, that is, the language, not by its mirroring of visible reality, and not by a fortuitous mishandling of poetic devices or technique. Such transcendence comes "from having an inspiration." But even that will not suffice. For Judas, like the speaking poet, as she perceives herself, "was not a genius / or under the auspices of an inspiration."

There is a temptation in "confessional" poetry to attribute its special power to the personal intensity of its expression. The confessional poet, as Robert Phillips observes, "dispenses with a symbol or formula for an emotion and gives the naked emotion direct, personally rather than impersonally."[5] As her adoption of Kafka's letter seems to attest, Sexton often subscribed to the notion that the power of poetry is that of "the ax" that, as Kafka had it, breaks "the frozen sea within us." But in **"Legend,"** Sexton seems, at least temporarily, to step away from such an emotionalist perspective. "Do not think of the intense sensation / I have as I tell you this," she instructs the reader. "Honor and relish the facts!" "Judas had a mother / just as I had a mother." The exhortations seem to rise unsummoned from a depth. But their place in the poem, following the rejected explanation-by-inspiration, makes of these instructions a continuation of the exploration into the causes of exalting difference, the accidental conversion of ugliness into glory.

In the simplest, if somewhat vulgar, sense, the "facts" she speaks of are the personal similarities between herself and Judas: their shared status as the victimized child whose "mother had a dream," as a consequence of which "he was altogether managed by fate / and thus he raped her." Viewed in this way, Sexton's answer to the persistent question about the source of the artist's greatest power points us away from the intensity of her sensations as she speaks and toward the purported facts of her personal history, which define her and fortuitously, if only fitfully, assert themselves as art. It is not as subject (which they are routinely) but as the buried source of strange power, that they are the force that turns the craftsman, as though by mistake, into the one-eyed seer, the crippled poet of this and other poems that also transcend the materials of their construction.

But to read the poem in this way is, at the least, to limit it and surely to insist on simplistic correspondences that the poem does not demand. The alleged facts we are to honor and relish in this poem (more particularly, in this climactic segment of the poem) are those of a one-eyed, apparently incestuous, male speaker, whose similarity to the poem's author is by no means a decidably factual matter. The only "facts" in such a poem are those that are less in, than of, the poem. They are facts of transformation and evasive relation. What we honor and relish in this poem, and what we are invited to focus on exclusively, I believe, is the powerful and tantalizing interaction, first, between the speaker and Judas, then between the already prophetic, mythically reconstructed speaker and the poem's "confessional" author. What makes this poem different from the great body of Sexton's poetry, more ambitious perhaps and less exclusively personal, is the adoption of a persona who is at least as much "other" as "self" and one who becomes, through an analog that he insists on, a figure of historic, mythic, and prophetic dimensions. "It is clear now," wrote M. L. Rosenthal of Lowell's *Life Studies,*

> that the shock of the autobiographical sections of that book did not come altogether, as it seemed in 1959, from their self-exposing frankness and the humiliating things said by the poet about his family. . . . It came at least as much from the redirection of energy, through the free mastery of these "minutiae" for a particular purpose that now emerged, toward realizations so intense that at first reading they approached direct experience.[6]

Sexton is usually distinguished from Lowell and other more restrained and more encompassing "confessional" poets, and with some justice. **"The Legend of the One-Eyed Man"** marks an exception to Sexton's narrowing exceptionality and takes as its subject both its own self-transcendence and the mystery of poetic uniqueness more generally.

Notes

1. Diana Hume George, *Oedipus Anne* (Urbana: U of Illinois P, 1987) 17.

2. William H. Shurr, "Sexton's 'The Legend of the One-Eyed Man,'" *The Explicator* 39 (1981): 2.

3. George 17. "Sexton's theme," as George reads the poem, ". . . was the repression and sacrifice of the feminine that constitutes Christianity's other 'betrayal.'" "Because (Christianity represses the feminine and debars femininity from direct participation in godhead, it forgets this other forbidden crime, the rape of the mother. . . . We know, we 'remember,' that Judas had a 'father'; we 'forget' that he had a mother and that her sexual violation and sacrifice are among the conditions of this peculiar form of redemption that proceeds only in fulfilling the prophecy of betrayal and murder" (110;18).

4. See, for example, "Somewhere in Africa," "Consorting with Angels," "To Lose the Earth," and "In the Deep Museum."

5. Robert Phillips, *The Confessional Poets* (Carbondale and Edwardsville: Southern Illinois UP, 1973) 8.

6. M. L. Rosenthal, *The New Poets* (New York: Oxford UP, 1967) 31.

Jane Hedley (essay date winter 2000)

SOURCE: Hedley, Jane. "'I made you to find me': Sexton, Lowell, and the Gender of Poethood." *Raritan* 19, no. 3 (winter 2000): 87-114.

[*In the following essay, Hedley explores the confessional mode of writing practiced by Sexton and Robert Lowell, placing this method within the context of sociocultural attitudes of 1950s and 1960s middle-class America and noting how the issue of gender determined each writer's poetic stance and authority.*]

The last line of Anne Sexton's poem **"The Double Image"**—"I made you to find me"—is ostensibly a confession of maternal narcissism, but it could equally serve as a motto for Sexton's practice of the confessional mode. In the poems that created her reputation as a confessional poet she is almost always confessing *to* someone: she has an interlocutor within the poem itself. **"The Double Image"** is addressed to her three-year-old daughter, Joyce; more typically, however, the "you" she conjures up is adult and male, a father-doctor-mentor figure whose authority the poem's speaker both covets and is seeking to undermine. In such poems there is a difference not only of gender but also of status or power between the speaker and her "confessor"—a difference that is taken for granted by the society at large but that Sexton's poem highlights and destabilizes. More than any other device, it's this strategy of subversive apostrophe that gives *To Bedlam and Part Way Back,* her first published volume of poetry, its distinctive voice. In subsequent volumes Sexton found her way to an alternative persona whose effectiveness derives in a different way from the social power dynamic to which it calls attention: the persona of a "middle-aged witch," an outlaw storyteller who is mockingly inward with her own society's myths of gender. Both the middle-aged witch and the seductively vulnerable subject of her confessional poems are inescapably, transgressively female—and indeed Sexton's confessional persona was doubly transgressive when she first began to write poetry in the late 1950s.

For women poets who came of age in the fifties the decision to speak as a woman in poems was one that could not be taken lightly. Sexton's contemporary Adri-

enne Rich explains, with feminist hindsight, that in her first two published volumes she "tried very much not to identify myself as a female poet" because she "had been taught that poetry should be 'universal,' which meant, of course, nonfemale." The lesson Rich had learned was that a poet who called attention to her gender would be relegated to "minor" status and patronized by the critics. This had been the fate not only of Amy Lowell and Edna St. Vincent Millay but also of Emily Dickinson, epitomized for generations of students by John Crowe Ransom and R. P. Blackmur as "a little home-keeping person" who "wrote indefatigably, as some women cook or knit." Marianne Moore and Elizabeth Bishop resisted this stereotype by writing poems that kept their speakers' gender more or less out of play.

If "universal" meant nonfemale, it also meant transpersonal: the consensus of Eliot and Auden's generation was that poets should not traffic in merely personal experience. In his introduction to *A Change of World,* the volume that won Rich the Yale Younger Poets Prize in 1951, Auden noted approvingly that "the emotions which motivate [these poems] . . . are not peculiar to Miss Rich but are among the typical experiences of our time." What was riding on this criterion was poetic authority—the authority to speak to and for one's audience about matters of abiding human concern. The authority of poets—and of poetry as an institution—was predicated on their citation of generically human feelings and experiences: those of "a heart in unison with his time and country" is how Emerson had put it in one of his essays. And a woman's experiences and feelings did not count as generically human if they were those of a woman in any obvious way.

But how could poets keep from trafficking in personal experience, and how could they avoid "the gender of things," at a time when Americans were preoccupied as never before with family life and with a vision of the family that assigned men and women radically different tasks and roles? During the 1950s the middle-class family was the central focus of a peacetime renewal of democratic capitalism; in the political rhetoric of the Cold War period, the single-breadwinner household became the linchpin of a distinctively "American" way of life. The popular media reinforced that vision: according to Betty Friedan, the leading women's magazines in the 1950s ceased to give their middle-class readership any horizon of aspiration beyond the family and the home. But the roles of breadwinner-husband and homemaker-wife were vulnerable constructs, both economically and psychically: a high level of what we have subsequently learned to call "gender anxiety" was generated by the society's commitment to heterosexual monogamy and to an account of gender difference that justified the sharpest possible division of labor within the middle-class household. "Can This Marriage Be

Saved?"—a regular feature of *Ladies' Home Journal*— told a story that was always different in its particulars, but in structure and outcome always the same: the marriage in question, which had come to seem unworkable to both partners, always *could* be saved by a confessional process that brought each partner's disappointments and frustrations out in the open for a professional counselor to help them face together. These scenes from a marriage gave equal time to the *He says* and the *She says* for an exclusively female audience. Middle-class men subscribed in large numbers to *Playboy,* whose popularity during the fifties Barbara Ehrenreich attributes not to any real intention on the part of its readers of embracing a bachelor playboy lifestyle, but to a need for reassurance that their masculinity had not been sacrificed on the altar of middle-class marriage.

The surest way for a poet, male or female, to hold onto what Robert von Hallberg calls the "tone of the center" in poems with a domestic focus was to speak not from the gendered perspective of a husband or wife, but as a sympathetic onlooker of the marriages of others. That's the position from which John Hollander speaks in a 1958 poem von Hallberg cites as especially successful in this mode: "For Both of You, the Divorce Being Final." On behalf of the divorced couple's friends, Hollander laments not only that "your" marriage has ended but that, ironically, "our" very civility keeps us from responding to the breakup in a fully humane way. Alternatively, a dramatic monologue or persona poem could expose the fault lines in a domestic situation that was obviously not the poet's own: one of Rich's early poems takes on the perspective of a woman in her fifties, the childless wife of a distinguished Harvard professor, whose adult life has been so circumscribed as to leave her only partly able to fathom her own unhappiness. Like Hollander's, Rich's poem raises questions about marriage as a social institution—this time, by getting inside a marriage whose bargain has been scrupulously kept but has failed both partners in important ways.

When Robert Lowell began to write poems about marriage in the late 1950s he decided to move directly, by way of the *He says/She says,* onto the embattled terrain of middle-class domestic life. In doing this he put both his poetic authority and his masculinity at risk. In the first place, he committed himself to speaking not transpersonally but personally—to confessing, indeed, how badly he'd behaved as a husband. In the second place, "'To Speak of the Woe That Is in Marriage'" was a distaff prerogative: if not more authoritative on the subject of marriage, wives were at any rate well known to be more talkative than their husbands. That this was Lowell's assumption is confirmed by his choice of title for a poem in *Life Studies* (published in 1959) that ventriloquizes his second wife Lizzie: the allusion is to Chaucer's Wife of Bath, who embarks upon a garrulous

confessional monologue by assuring her audience of Canterbury pilgrims that "Experience, thogh noon auctoritee / Were in this world, is right ynough for me / To speke of wo that is in mariage." As Chaucer's Wife well knew, authority and experience—along with taciturnity and garrulity—have traditionally fought on opposite sides in the battle of the sexes. In *Life Studies* masculine authority and feminine experience, male taciturnity and female garrulity, are similarly pitted against each other on the social and psychic terrain of Cold War domesticity.

Like Sexton, Lowell is a poet who "made you to find me": he too used apostrophe strategically to put gender anxiety at his poems' disposal and enlist it as a poetic resource. But Lowell and Sexton had different motives for making an issue of gender in their poems, and different rhetorical options available to them for doing so. Discussions of confessional writing that treat Sexton as Lowell's protegee or fellow traveler in the confessional movement have neglected to notice this asymmetry, as well as to gauge its rhetorical impact.

* * *

During the fifties and well into the sixties, "it was difficult," remarks Judith McDaniel, "for a woman to escape the fact that poet was a masculine noun." Take, for example, the case of Denise Levertov, who had never been averse to writing poems from an unmistakably female subject-position. In 1967, after more than two decades and seven published volumes of poetry, Levertov published a manifesto entitled "The Poet in the World" that puts forth an activist vision of poethood in the high Emersonian tradition. The essay begins with an elaborate birth-allegory in which the poet is first a woman in labor, then a father looking on at the delivery of the child he has conceived, and finally a newborn—a man-child—who must enter the world and come to terms with it, in political as well as other ways. The purpose of this allegory, apparently, is to endow "the poet" with an androgynous creativity that transcends the limitations of conventional gender roles. It also functions, however, as McDaniel has astutely suggested, to negotiate access to generic masculinity for Levertov herself: "the female poet gives birth to a male child who becomes the poet-he, who then goes out into the world to experience it." The allegorical device betrays that although poets are sometimes women, poethood is not a gender-neutral status. And even though Levertov unabashedly claims that status for herself throughout the essay, the poet as she envisions him—a figure of mythic stature in modern dress who has "crossed in a day the great oceans his ancestors labored across in many months," who has looked up from reading of the death of Socrates while riding the New York subway to see "one man stab another and a third spring from his seat to assist the wounded one"—this Whitmanian figure of the poet is clearly a man among men.

Levertov shared with other women poets a "problem of voice" (McDaniel's phrase) which had more to do with institutional stereotypes than with any particular poet's willingness to speak as a woman in her poems. Adrienne Rich, for her part, had attempted to solve the problem by crafting a poetic stance that studiously avoided calling attention to her gender. Several of the poems in her first two published volumes, *A Change of World* (1951) and *The Diamond Cutters* (1955), are dramatic monologues whose speaker is a man; others have a generic protagonist who could be a woman but whose gender is given as masculine. In the Notes to her *Selected Poems* of 1975, Rich explains that in "The Tourist and the Town," written in 1953, she felt she could not afford to let "the tourist" be "she" even though, she confesses, "I never saw her as anything else." Poems that do have a female protagonist use the voice of a coolly omniscient observer to detect the irony or pathos of her situation on the reader's behalf. Looking back at "Aunt Jennifer's Tigers" twenty years later, Rich says she was startled by its obvious reference to her own predicament as a fledgling woman artist; at the time, she explains, "it was important to me that Aunt Jennifer was a person as distinct from myself as possible—distanced by the formalism of the poem, by its objective, observant tone." Also pervasive in Rich's first two published volumes is a transpersonal "we" that implicates the reader herself in a humanly generic dilemma or predicament:

> Is any light so proudly thrust
> From darkness on our lifted faces
> A sign of something we can trust,
> Or is it that in starry places
> We see the things we long to see
> In fiery iconography?

This is a stanza from "For the Conjunction of Two Planets," one of the poems Auden cites in his introduction to *A Change of World* as having successfully captured "the typical experiences of our time."

In "Storm Warnings," the first poem in the volume and another of Auden's favorites, Rich even managed to speak *in propria persona* from within a domestic setting without calling attention to her gender. As Auden recognized, the poem is allegorical: its New England country setting is specific, but also resonant with generalized historical foreboding. "Laying [her] book aside," the poem's speaker gets up and walks around the house "from window to closed window," closing shutters, drawing curtains, "set[ting] a match to candles sheathed in glass / Against the keyhole draught." These precautions against the coming storm are precisely detailed, but then subsumed by a "we"-statement that distills their significance at a higher level of abstraction:

> These are the things that we have learned to do
> Who live in troubled regions.

Arguably "these . . . things" belong to women's traditional domain of housekeeping, but no task is cited that strongly connotes women's work: the speaker does not interrupt the preparation of a meal, for instance, or look in on a sleeping child. Her attitude thus need not be written off as the timidity of the weaker sex, but can be taken instead for the prescience of a speaker who has divined—on behalf of "his" contemporaries—which way the wind is blowing.

And yet no matter what precautions she took, the achievement of Rich's early poems was bound to be refeminized—and by Auden himself, who assures us in his introduction to *A Change of World* that "the poems a reader will encounter in this book are neatly and modestly dressed, speak quietly but do not mumble, respect their elders . . . and do not tell fibs." Thus, ironically, the guardedness and self-detachment Rich had enjoined on herself as the price of "universality," and that made her sound middle-aged at twenty-one, were given a feminine inflection—found, indeed, to be ladylike—by the distinguished exponent of "the tone of the center" who had undertaken to sponsor her poetic debut.

In the late 1950s, in "Snapshots of a Daughter-in-Law," Rich did begin to write "directly about experiencing myself as a woman"; but "Snapshots" is far from having the naked intimacy of Lowell's or Sexton's confessional writing. Its speaker's stance is just as detached and objective as in "Aunt Jennifer's Tigers" or "The Tourist and the Town." Rich concedes that even though the poem felt like a breakthrough to her at the time, she "hadn't found the courage yet to do without authorities, or even to use the pronoun 'I.'" Actually there is some "I"-reference in the poem, but its function is to keep the one who has taken these "snapshots" in a position to speak as her female subjects' critic and judge:

> Two handsome women, gripped in argument,
> each proud, acute, subtle, I hear scream
> across the cut glass and majolica
> like Furies cornered from their prey:
> The argument *ad feminam*, all the old knives
> that have rusted in my back, I drive in yours,
> *ma semblable, ma soeur!*

The poem's speaker knows these women better than they know themselves. She may even be one of them; if so, she is divided against herself and has become the object of her own contempt. The rhetorical strategy is reminiscent of T. S. Eliot, not only because Rich has cited a line from Baudelaire that was used to similar effect in *The Waste Land,* but also because she has learned from Eliot how to savor the irony of a generic predicament that is also her own:

> "You all die at fifteen," said Diderot,
> and turn part legend, part convention.

Still, eyes inaccurately dream
behind closed windows blankening with steam.
Deliciously, all that we might have been,
all that we were—fire, tears,
wit, taste, martyred ambition—
stirs like the memory of refused adultery
the drained and flagging bosom of our middle years.

Claire Keyes has suggested that throughout the whole transitional volume that includes this poem "Rich [still] cannot reconcile *what* she is (a poet) with *who* she is (a woman)"; and sure enough, the poems in *Snapshots of a Daughter-in-Law* (1963) typically speak of women with a mixture of pity and contempt. "Readings of History," for example, plays off the women pictured in *Life* magazines from the war years, "so poor but honest," against those depicted in women's magazines of the fifties who frivolously "sail / to shop in Europe, ignorantly freed for you, an age ago." Rich was using autobiographical material more frankly in *Snapshots* than in the two earlier volumes, but always with rueful self-detachment, as when the speaker of "A Marriage in the Sixties" reminds her husband of their common vulnerability to inscrutable forces of change:

> The world breathes underneath our bed.
> Don't look. We're at each other's mercy too.

The only poem in the volume whose speaker casts her lot with the forces of change is one in which she uses a masculine persona to speak of her sense of having the wrong tools, as a poet, "for what I have to do":

> I'm naked, ignorant,
> a naked man fleeing across the roofs
> who could with a shade of difference
> be sitting in the lamplight
> against the cream wallpaper
> reading—not with indifference—
> about a naked man
> fleeing across the roofs.

The poet's "nakedness" comes of being ready to give up the formalism she had espoused in the title poem of *The Diamond Cutters* in favor of subjecting her poems more directly to the pressure of experience. And yet the courage (or is it recklessness?) that will enable her to do this is envisioned as a masculine prerogative.

Interestingly enough, "The Roofwalker" carries a dedication *"for Denise Levertov"*; Levertov had already published "From the Roof," a poem whose speaker is taking in the washing while she waits for her husband to join her in their new home. But the problem of voice Rich and Levertov shared in the fifties and sixties could not be solved by an individual poet working alone; only in the context of the women's movement, from a stance no longer detached and "objective" but politically engaged and adversarial, could a generic "I" that is female begin to be produced. Rich would not succeed

in making what she later described as "the mere, immense shift from male to female pronouns" until *The Dream of a Common Language* in 1978.

Anne Sexton, meanwhile, was venturing into women-only territory that both Rich and Levertov considered off limits. At a memorial service for Sexton following her suicide in 1974, Rich reminded other feminists that Sexton had written "poems alluding to abortion, masturbation, menopause, and the painful love of a powerless mother for her daughters, long before such themes became validated by a collective consciousness of women." Such themes were not just unmistakably, they were un*speak*ably female: these were the things that we had learned to do—and suffer—without expecting to read or to write about them. There were no dysfunctional families on Sunday night television, and the marriages in *Ladies' Home Journal* never had to be saved from incest or abortion or spousal abuse. But Sexton's transgressiveness involved not only her themes or subject matter; it also had to do with the positioning of her poems' aggressively female speakers. Whereas Rich and Levertov were both inclined to depict their poet-self as "not-a-woman" in some important sense, Sexton always led with her femaleness, as if unable or unwilling to do anything else.

Many of the poems in her first volume, published in 1960, call up a masculine interlocutor right at the outset—often in the title, as in **"You, Doctor Martin," "Said the Poet to the Analyst,"** and **"For John, Who Begs Me Not to Enquire Further"**—and oblige him to pay attention to what their female speaker has to say. He's obliged either by the terms of a specific professional relationship (he's her therapist or teacher) or simply by virtue of social arrangements that have placed women in a dependent status relative to men. Say he is the average middle-class man in the street, and she a woman who needs his assistance: if she accosts him on that basis, how can he refuse her? One of these early poems, set in a mental hospital, begins, "Wait Mister. Which way is home?"—a rhetorical question that is at once naive and sophisticated, simple and complex. Strikingly inappropriate as a request for information, it's easy to recognize as an appeal for help: sane or crazy, this woman knows how to get a passing stranger's attention by flaunting her helplessness. On another level her question is uncannily prescient: sane people do share a precious yet utterly commonplace knowledge which gives them the ability to walk out of this place that is nobody's home, but where she will have to stay. How come he knows the way home and she doesn't? If her interlocutor is a decent man with reasons of his own for coming to visit this "private institution on a hill," he will still be troubled by her question as he gets back into his Ford or his Buick and drives away.

Alicia Ostriker has trenchantly characterized the rhetorical strategy of Sexton's early poems as one which creates an "imperative of intimacy": "we feel," says Ostriker, "the hot breath of the poem upon us." Ostriker explains this propensity for turning poems into "personal transactions" as a particular instance of the "drive to connect" (Adrienne Rich's phrase) that Ostriker finds to be pervasive among women poets. But whether or not women share a drive to connect that is distinctive and gender-specific, Sexton's strategy was politically canny: one way for a woman to get the upper hand with a male interlocutor might be to personalize their transaction by playing the gender card. In a verbal encounter between a man and a woman the one who calls attention to their gender difference has turned that encounter into a personal transaction, whether the other likes it or not. Taking the initiative to do this might give the woman a chance to catch her interlocutor off-balance. It's a dangerous game for a woman to play, however—one reason, perhaps, why Sexton's poems are still unsettling to read.

"For John, Who Begs Me Not to Enquire Further" is an especially interesting case of this strategy because it is also a manifesto of sorts for confessional poetry. As such, it opens the second section of *To Bedlam and Part Way Back* with a frank admission that Sexton's poems will make their readers uncomfortable. She intends them to, but for a good cause. The unlovely things she has discovered by "tapp[ing] my own head"—the rage, the despair, the death wish—are dimensions of ourselves and our social reality also:

> At first it was private.
> then it was more than myself;
> it was you, or your house,
> or your kitchen.

As Sexton explains it here, confessional poetry is not only or even primarily a spilling of one's guts or a publicizing of one's private life; at its most powerful, it will have an uncanny transitivity:

> my kitchen, your kitchen,
> my face, your face.

Such poetry can do us good, and yet we fear the knowledge it offers us: the poem's title alludes to Schopenhauer's observation that the philosopher "must be like Sophocles' Oedipus" but that "most of us carry in our heart the Jocasta who begs Oedipus for God's sake not to inquire further." Oedipus had to learn the whole story of his relationship to Jocasta in order to lift the curse that was on his people; Sexton's claim is that her story is likewise one that an entire society needs to know. She has suffered on our behalf to gain the knowledge "that the worst of anyone / can be, finally, / an accident of hope."

This poem's "you" is not, however, just any and every reader of Sexton's poetry: its title specifies one reader in particular, as is by now well known. "John" was

John Holmes, Sexton's first poetry teacher, who according to Maxine Kumin she regarded as an "academic father" but who had spoken out in the strongest possible terms against the confessional direction of her work. Holmes, of all readers, was the one whose rejection would be hardest for Sexton to live with, because of the institutional authority his disapproval carried. His opposition may actually have helped her focus and clarify her poetic objectives, as Diane Middlebrook suggests; but it must also have frightened her. Without Holmes's poetry workshop she'd have been just a crazy housewife with no special claim on anyone's attention. And so, like Jacob wrestling with the angel, she could not let this interlocutor go without a blessing from him.

Sexton is rumored to have been discouraged from converting to Catholicism by an old priest who urged her instead to recognize that "God is in your typewriter." She'd had a version of the same advice from the psychiatrist who got her started writing poetry as a psychotherapeutic device. The sacrament of confession and the relation between analyst and analysand in psychotherapy are clearly analogous to the relationship **"For John"** sets up between its fledgling poet, who is female, and a male representative of the academic establishment. Like the psychoanalyst in Jacques Lacan's notorious formulation, John is "the one who is supposed to know"—in this case, how to become a published poet. Just as in therapy or in the confessional, his role is to hear her story and confer upon the occasion of her telling it the institutional authority his position carries. In this kind of interlocutory setup the one who *isn't* supposed to know does all the talking, seduced into self-revelation by the authority of her confessor and the power-knowledge imbalance between them. But by having John play Jocasta to her Oedipus, Sexton uses gender-reversal to call his authority into question even as she seeks his permission to tell a certain kind of story. What is driving her, I would argue, is not so much a desire for connection as a desire for recognition by a fellow-poet—recognition that, in validating her experience as normative, would also concede her the authority to tell him who he really is.

"For John" is just one example of Sexton's propensity throughout this first published volume for staging personal transactions that are politically loaded and complex. Most of the poems in *To Bedlam* call attention to a difference in status and authority between their female speaker and her male interlocutor, a difference they do not challenge directly, but contrive to unsettle in more insidious ways. The protagonist of **"The Exorcists,"** who will "solemnly swear / . . . / that I know you not," as she is about to have an (illegal) abortion at the hands of the doctor who was also, it seems, her partner in "summer loves"; the psychiatric patient in **"You, Doctor Martin"** who follows up a jaded acknowledgment that "Of course, I love you" with the observation that in the hospital dining room "There are no knives / for cutting your throat"; the crazy girl in **"Music Swims Back to Me"** who asks a passing stranger how to get home—these are all versions of a speaker whose attitude toward her interlocutor is disconcertingly ambiguous. Does she regard him as her potential savior, or as the one who got her into this fix? Does she think he can help her, or is she merely desperate for male attention? If she had a knife, whose throat would she use it on? These poems make such questions undecidable, and that's what gives them their political edge. "A woman like that is misunderstood," as Sexton liked to remind audiences at her poetry readings by opening with the early poem **"Her Kind."**

* * *

In the society whose illnesses both Sexton and Lowell unsparingly document, so much depends upon whether you are a man or a woman: the kind of education you will get, your relationship to money and property, your role within the family and in society at large. So much depends on whether you are a husband or a wife—marriage being of all social relationships the one most entirely predicated on gender difference. And if you are a man or a woman whose "business is words" (as the poet said to the analyst in one of Sexton's early poems), your marriage is a setting in which the relationship between language and power is liable to be especially complex. Adrienne Rich's early poem "An Unsaid Word" speaks to this, arguing that a wife has power she must not use to "call her man / From that estranged intensity / Where his mind forages alone." But whereas the attitude Rich assumes toward this "truth" is rueful, resigned, dispassionate, to Lowell and Sexton marriage presented itself as a more explosive setting in which to highlight the interrelationship of language, power, and gender.

Lowell broached the subject of marriage first in the persona poems of his second volume, *The Mills of the Kavanaughs,* which came out in 1951—the same year Rich was making her poetic debut with *A Change of World.* And whereas Rich had done her best *not* to sound like a woman in her poems, Lowell produced poem after poem for this volume in which he ventriloquizes a woman's voice. "It is immediately noticeable," remarks Lowell's biographer Ian Hamilton, "that the book is a clamor of distraught, near-hysterical first-person speech, and that almost always the speaker is a woman." These exercises in ventriloquism gained Lowell access to the domestic arena and to the political drama of domestic relationships. He would go on to do more trenchant confessional writing from the perspective of a son, husband, and father in *Life Studies,* but it was by speaking as a woman in the earlier volume that he could begin to move away from the public, prophetic stance of *Lord Weary's Castle* toward the personal,

confessional intimacy of "91 Revere Street," "Man and Wife," and "My Last Afternoon with Uncle Devereux Winslow."

In both Lowell's and Sexton's marriages the wife was the more talkative, vociferous partner, but it was the husband who had the upper hand in the most literal sense. Lowell broke his first wife's nose during a domestic quarrel; Sexton's husband often hit her, though it seemed to their daughter Linda that she goaded him into it for psychological reasons of her own. Such a husband knew himself to be verbally overmatched by his wife's powers of invective. The nonviolent way to hold his own in domestic disputes was to stay aloof and allow her to spend her fury verbally; so long as he would not be drawn into battle, her verbal advantage could gain her nothing. As Lowell makes clear in "91 Revere Street," the autobiographical prose piece that became part 2 of *Life Studies,* this is a strategy he learned at his mother's knee. The child depicted in "91 Revere Street" is the father not only of the man Robert Lowell, but of the poet as well.

" *'Weelawaugh, we-ee-eeelawaugh, weelawaugh,'* shrilled Mother's high voice. *'But-and, but-and, but-and!'* Father's low mumble would drone in answer." As a boy, Lowell confesses, he would "awake with rapture" night after night to "the rhythm of my parents' arguing." The man of the house invariably lost these arguments, and so his son grew up self-defensively hoarding speech. The way young Bobby "saved [him]self from emotional exhaustion" in the face of his mother's "prying questions" was by sullenly refusing to give her anything at all to pry into:

> "A penny for your thoughts, Schopenhauer," my mother would say.
>
> "I am thinking about pennies," I'd answer.
>
> "When *I* was a child I used to love telling Mamá everything I had done," Mother would say.
>
> "But you're not a child," I would answer.

Charlotte Lowell, as she is unsparingly depicted in "91 Revere Street," poses a clear and present danger to her son's masculinity. Having forced her "unmasterful" husband to leave the Navy, the only career for which he was temperamentally suited, she sends young Bobby to a girls' school whose "regime" is an extension of hers. Both at home and at school Bobby holds on grimly to the "outlaw" status of "boy," in spite of knowing that in either setting to be a boy "was to be small, denied, and weak." The memoir furnishes plenty of evidence that he is confused and ambivalent about his gender identity: he bullies other boys and earns the nickname Buffalo Bull on the soccer field, yet confesses to having asked Santa Claus for a field hockey stick and to "[wishing] I was an older girl."

So intriguingly does Lowell play out this personal scenario, and so tellingly does he draw upon it in the poems that come later in the *Life Studies* volume, that it is easy to miss the larger social picture his memoir has meanwhile sketched for us. The society depicted in "91 Revere Street" is one in which men's and women's roles and prerogatives are radically different, but these differences are unstable and volatile. All the women who figure in the memoir, with the exception of Charlotte Lowell, are anomalous in relation to the man-the-breadwinner, woman-the-housewife norm that nevertheless prevails unquestioned among them. "'Eric's mother and father are *both* called Dr. Burckhard,' my mother once said, and indeed there was something endearingly repellent about Mrs. Burckhard with her doctor's degree, her long, unstylish skirts, and her dramatic, dulling blond braids." Commander Billy Harkness's wife, whose husband calls her "Jimmy," is "an unpleasant rarity," "the only naval officer's wife we knew who was also a college graduate." Commander Billy goes in for "tireless, tasteless harangues" against a female member of the Lowells' own family, the poet Amy Lowell—she of the black cheroot, the "loud, bossy, unlady-like" free verse, the obscenely large fortune, and disinclination for marriage. What is "repellent" or "unpleasant" about these women is not only that they don't have what properly belongs to their station in life—stylish grooming, attractive figures—but that they do have what doesn't—a Ph.D., a college education, financial independence, or a taste for cigars. The one whose aberration is truly menacing, because of the position she is in to throw the next generation out of kilter, is the school principal aptly named Miss Manice, whose "pet theory was that 'women are simply not the equals of men'" but whose educational program for girls bred contempt, we are told, for "the male's two idols: career and earning power."

Feminist historians of the period between the world wars point out that middle- and upper-class women reaching adulthood during those years were considerably freer than their 1950s counterparts to envision adult lives that were not exclusively centered on home and family. The success of the suffrage movement was recent history; the New Woman of the twenties and thirties, as she is nostalgically remembered by Betty Friedan in *The Feminine Mystique,* was independent, ambitious to have a career and a life of her own, and "passionate[ly] involve[d] with the world." Clearly Lowell's nostalgia for the 1930s took a different form from Friedan's, a form more consistent not only with a masculinist outlook but also with a 1950s mindset. In "91 Revere Street" the most powerful female figures are the ones who yearn to be dominated by men but find themselves surrounded by males who are simply not up to the task:

I can hear Miss Manice browbeating my white and sheepish father, "How can we stand up to you? Where are our Archimedeses, our Wagners, our Admiral Simses?". . . .

[My mother] ran into my bedroom. She hugged me. She said, "Oh Bobby, it's such a comfort to have a man in the house." "I am not a man," I said, "I am a boy."

Lowell recalls this period between the wars as a "topsy-turvy era" from the Lowell family standpoint: "'people of the right sort' were no longer dominant in city elections." But a more conspicuous way in which people of the right sort are no longer dominant, though Lowell never says so explicitly, is that instead of having real wars to fight, the men are all fighting a losing battle against women for their masculinity and its prerogatives. Bobby's mother loves to phone the admiral and berate him for forcing her husband to spend his nights on the navy base; his father ridiculously hints at important military reasons for the admiral's arbitrary rules and "uncommunicative arrogance." Written all over this memoir is a conviction that personal identity is very much a function of gender, but that gender difference is unstable and that women are both individually and collectively to blame for this. "91 Revere Street" is a window on Lowell's childhood in the 1930s, but it is also a product of Lowell's obsession with his own masculinity as an adult in the 1950s.

The memoir's script for male-female and especially husband-wife relations strikingly prefigures his marriage to Elizabeth Hardwick, as depicted in the later section of the *Life Studies* volume that is itself subtitled "Life Studies." A speaker who is unmistakably Robert Lowell confesses, in "Man and Wife," to having married a woman he fell in love with because she shared his mother's gift for marital invective. As they "lie on Mother's bed," also the setting for the companion-poem that ventriloquizes Lizzie as a latter-day Wife of Bath, Lowell tenderly hearkens back twelve years to when

> you were in your twenties, and I . . .
> . . . . .
>
> outdrank the Rahvs in the heat
> of Greenwich Village, fainting at your feet—
> too boiled and shy
> and poker-faced to make a pass,
> while the shrill verve
> of your invective scorched the traditional South.

He continues to need her capacity for invective—it has saved him over and over from "the kingdom of the mad"—and he continues to be the silent, "poker-faced" partner in the relationship.

Specific references to their friends the Rahvs, to how long they have been together, to how many times he's been hospitalized, are in the poem to persuade us, as

Steven Axelrod points out, that we are gaining entrance "into its author's actual life and mode of consciousness": "the reader, as Lowell later explained, 'was to believe he was getting the *real* Robert Lowell.'" At the same time, however, these details are handled in such a way as to give this marriage the kind of exemplary status the poem's title implicitly claims for it. "Tamed by *Miltown*," this Man and Wife are denizens of "the tranquilized *Fifties*" and of "Boston's 'hardly passionate Marlborough Street'"—a classic address, though less fashionable now than it used to be. Their "gilded bedposts shine, / abandoned, almost Dionysian": the mythic resonance strengthens the Oedipal overtones of the *mise-en-scène* to suggest that their predicament is also classic in psychological terms. The wife delivers herself of an "*old-fashioned* tirade" (my italics) while her husband devises a love poem that extends the emotional reach of the traditional *aubade*: literarily also, there is subtle encouragement to recognize that where love and sexual intimacy between men and women are concerned, the more things change the more they remain the same.

Lowell uses apostrophe strategically part way through the poem to emphasize that the wife he is addressing is both absent and present, real and imaginary. She is there in bed with him, but has turned her back; she is "Oh my *Petite*, / clearest of all God's creatures, still all air and nerve"; but this characterization is a figment of his need and nostalgia rather than an overture toward present-tense dialogue between them:

> Now twelve years later, you turn your back.
> Sleepless, you hold
> your pillow to your hollows like a child,
> your old-fashioned tirade—
> loving, rapid, merciless—
> breaks like the Atlantic Ocean on my head.

Ironically, thus, his tenderness and gratitude are unavailable to mitigate her settled conviction, expressed in the monologue that immediately follows, of how "unjust" he is and of "the monotonous meanness of his lust."

Her monologue makes it even more obvious that in both poems Lowell was trying for a generic depiction of 1950s domesticity. Biographers tell us, for example, that it was not Lizzie but Delmore Schwartz's wife who went to bed each night with ten dollars and his car key tied to her thigh. The allusion to Chaucer's Wife of Bath confirms, moreover, that marital problems like the ones this diptych exposes are perennial and somehow typical of the human species. The poem's epigraph from Schopenhauer suggests this also: *It is the future generation that presses into being by means of these exuberant feelings and supersensible soap bubbles of ours.* From one generation to the next, both title and epigraph suggest, humankind reproduces itself through the loins of "hopped up husband[s]" whose wives have

no choice but to ride out their brutish randiness while angrily wondering "What makes him tick?" These suggestions are conveyed to us over Lizzie's head, as it were, by the way in which her "tirade" is set up and introduced.

"Man and Wife" and "'To Speak of the Woe That Is in Marriage'" had in earlier drafts been a single poem that gave both the husband's and the wife's perspective on their marriage. Separating that poem into companion monologues made it easier to depict the married couple at cross-purposes: perhaps their perspectives could be said to be in dialogue, but they themselves clearly are not. Separating the two poems also made room to frame the wife's monologue with a title and an epigraph that place her perspective in a particular way. Giving her a soliloquy of her own in which to deplore her husband's behavior is a gesture consistent with the unsparing self-irony that is the hallmark of Lowell's autobiographical persona in *Life Studies*; but it is an equivocal gesture, especially if the epigraph from Schopenhauer recalls "91 Revere Street" and young Bobby Lowell's successful evasion of his mother's curiosity as to what makes him tick.

Lowell's poems are not, for the most part, framed as encounters with particular interlocutors; they are addressed instead, as Lawrence Kramer points out, "to a featureless interlocutor who is never represented in the text." Kramer notes, however, that at strategic moments the poem's speaker *will* appeal to someone in particular: "Oh my *Petite*," he'll say, or "Grandpa, hold me, cherish me." These confessions of vulnerability or emotional neediness are rendered all the more poignant by the patent unavailability of the interlocutor who is thus apostrophized: "Grandpa" is long dead; "my *Petite*," "now twelve years later," turns her back to deliver a tirade that her husband perversely finds comforting. Such moments do not presage communication; instead they disclose the loneliness and isolation to which the poem's speaker is self-condemned by his poker-faced taciturnity. His predicament is reminiscent of the damned souls T. S. Eliot ventriloquizes in *The Waste Land*, "each in his prison / Thinking of the key": self-awareness only serves to exacerbate his sense of helplessness. In his need to be rescued and/or comforted he is still a little boy inside—a boy, moreover, whose gender identity is fragile and conflicted. His apostrophe to "Grandpa" amounts to a confession that his need to be held and cherished is still essentially the same as in the days of their yearly autumn trip to the family graveyard at Dunbarton, when he "cuddled like a paramour / in my Grandfather's bed." The reader is the "featureless interlocutor" to whom such confessions are addressed; it is we who have been put in a position to figure out what makes Robert Lowell tick.

. . . . .

For poet-critic Richard Tillinghast, a former student of Lowell's who explores his life and influence in a recent critical memoir, "the biggest question to be asked about Robert Lowell is how he managed to bring such an air of authority to his poems." Elizabeth Bishop grumbled, after reading *Life Studies* in manuscript, that he managed it by being a Massachusetts Lowell: "all you have to do is put down the names," she wrote to him enviously, "and . . . it seems significant, illustrative, American, etc." Brett Millier, Bishop's biographer, observes that Lowell's poetic authority "might have had as much to do with the privileges of gender as of family background"—to which Tillinghast irritably rejoins that his poems carried authority because he did in fact possess an acute sense of "the larger national mood." Whether he did or not, a crucial factor in his poems' "air of authority," as Tillinghast and others have noticed, was the way in which Lowell invoked a Freudian explanatory paradigm to lend depth, interpretability, and mythic resonance to his speaker's emotional predicament. And it was his pose of disinterestedness, a stance Lawrence Kramer has aptly characterized as one of "stylized dispassionate candor toward his own experience," that enabled him to invoke that explanatory paradigm so effectively. In large part, Lowell's authority accrues to him from our sense that he has not spared himself, that he has fully submitted his "case" for study, that it interests him just as much, and in the same way, as it interests us.

In this way, Lowell made himself heir apparent to T. S. Eliot. The speaker of "Life Studies" is a latter-day Tiresias, a man who knows too many secrets of the human heart for his own well-being and is sharing them with us at his own expense. But Lowell's version of this rhetorical posture is implicated more insistently than Eliot's in a characterological posture of beset masculinity. Gender is crucial to his poetic authority not only because "poet" is a masculine noun—the point Millier was presumably making—but also, paradoxically, because the self-intimacy Lowell dramatizes in these poems has effeminized him in an unsettling but interesting way. He achieves a kind of reverse androgyny that extends his poetic purview at the expense of his manhood by taking him onto emotional terrain that a "real man" stereotypically seeks to avoid—humiliations, experiences of dependency, feelings of tenderness or of ambivalence.

It is important to recognize, with Lawrence Kramer, that the confessional force of Lowell's poems lies "not . . . in their subject matter per se but in how and to whom they present it." That goes for Sexton's poems also: for both poets, gender is a key determinant not only of subject matter, but also of rhetorical posture or poetic stance. In their self-dramatization as confessional speakers both Lowell and Sexton were adepts of vulnerability. But a man's vulnerability differs from a woman's in its relationship to other attributes of personality and of self-presentation: emotional neediness, capacity for self-irony, need for approval. A male poet's access to and performance of his vulnerability is thus also in a different relationship to his poetic authority than is a woman poet's.

After Sexton had been in Lowell's poetry-writing class for a few months in 1958 she wrote to W. D. Snodgrass that she was "learning more than you could imagine from Lowell. I am learning what I am not . . . also a fear of writing as a woman writes." A few years later, she produced a poem that alludes directly to Lowell's marital diptych both in its title, **"Man and Wife,"** and its epigraph, *"To speke of wo that is in mariage."* But this poem shows that Sexton had learned less from Lowell than she imagined—less that could help her with her own rhetorical posture in her poems. In **"Man and Wife"** she seems to have been trying not to write as a woman writes, but instead to cultivate the tone of the center. The poem begins with a series of "we"-statements that epitomize the emotional sterility of a suburban marriage, then builds an extended simile that surreally anthropomorphizes a pair of city pigeons who "came to the suburbs / by mistake." Not until near the end of the poem, coming out the other side of this simile, does the poem's speaker address her husband directly, in an apostrophe that calls attention to their mutual helplessness to overcome their emotional estrangement from each other:

> Like them [the pigeons]
> we neither talk nor clear our throats,
> Oh Darling,
> we gasp in unison beside our window pane,
> drunk on the drunkard's dream.

In the same way as Lowell's "Oh my *Petite* . . . ," Sexton's apostrophe follows a description of the couple that highlights their physical proximity to heighten the pathos of their emotional estrangement: the pigeons "would pierce our heart," this wife finally tells her husband, "if they could only fly the distance."

Sexton's **"Man and Wife"** is not a very good poem for several reasons, but the one I want to highlight is that her use of apostrophe is banal and uninteresting here. As a term of endearment, "Oh Darling" does not bear the imprint of a particular couple's intimacy; nor does it take the poem's speaker to a new level of self-disclosure, as Lowell does by using "Oh my *Petite*" to call up a specific vignette from the past. In context, "Oh Darling" merely whines: it makes the poem's pathos all too easy, sounding a note that belongs to a stereotypically female range of emotional expression. When Rich used a version of this interlocutory strategy in "A Marriage in the Sixties," she handled it more wittily and with a more firmly crafted poetic line.

Thus whereas Lowell's confessional stance gave generic poethood a change of venue and a new lease on life, for Sexton generic poethood proved even more unworkable and uncongenial than it had proven to be for Rich. Sexton's best confessional poems, as we have seen, play the gender card right from the outset, in their first lines or even in their titles. Their speaker is aggressively, importunately female, and her speech acts have a relentless *ad hominem* urgency. It was in this speaker's complex, fraught relationship to a masculine figure of authority that Sexton found both the pretext and the resources for her most successful dramatization of self.

* * *

And yet the poem in which Sexton most openly confesses to having "made you to find me" is addressed not to a doctor or teacher or father-figure, but to her three-year-old daughter. This poem's ostensible purpose is to confess to little Joy that because her mother "would rather die than love," she has not been able to be with her daughter for the first three-plus years of the child's life. **"The Double Image"** tells the story of those years, spent partly in a mental hospital, partly living with her own mother (whom she uncannily resembles) and having companion portraits painted (the "double image" to which her title refers). The poet/mother finally puts her "worst guilt" into words in the poem's final lines, where she brings out a second meaning for her title by confessing that she brought her daughter into the world in the first place to assuage her own gender anxiety.

> I, who was never quite sure
> about being a girl, needed another
> life, another image to remind me.
> And this was my worst guilt, you could not cure
> nor soothe it. I made you to find me.

As in the poems Sexton addressed to male authority figures, but here in reverse, the power-knowledge imbalance between the poem's speaker and her interlocutor is conspicuous; and here again, her intentions with respect to this interlocutor are finally undecidable. As a mother, how could she possibly have felt it was okay to have this conversation with a three-year-old child?

According to Linda Gray Sexton, Anne Sexton did make a habit of asking her daughters to meet her need to be mothered at the expense of their own. But of course when a *poet* makes "you" to find "me" she has resorted to a rhetorical device that is perhaps as old as the lyric itself. Apostrophe is the device poets use to conjure up "an absent or imaginary person"; it is "always addressed," as Lawrence Kramer reminds us, "to someone who cannot listen to it." Jonathan Culler, Barbara Johnson, and Paul de Man have all suggested (thinking primarily of the Romantic lyric) that apostrophe is lyric poetry's foundational trope, insofar as it asserts a poet's

special prerogative to speak with the dead or to commune with extra-human powers and sources of being. Perhaps, then, the admission that "I made you to find me" is not so much a mother's as a poet's confession, exposing the logic whereby we conjure up an imagined interlocutor to find the poet in us. On this understanding of Sexton's rhetorical gesture and its motive, three-year-old Joy, like the sleeping child in Coleridge's "Frost at Midnight" or the beloved sister Wordsworth addresses in "Tintern Abbey," is the figment of a process of autobiographical reflection that is not really addressed to her, but is provoked and enabled by conjuring her up to speak with.

Closer to home, W. D. Snodgrass had movingly apostrophized a three-year-old child in his award-winning "Heart's Needle" sequence, published in 1959. Like **"The Double Image,"** the "Heart's Needle" sequence discloses the guilt as well as grief of a parent who cannot be with his daughter to help her grow up. "Though you are only three, / you are already growing / strange to me," the poet/father confesses to his daughter in "Heart's Needle 5": "You chatter about new playmates, sing strange songs." But Snodgrass's way of constructing his daughter as a poetic interlocutor is subtly different from Sexton's. His daughter figures vividly in the sequence, chattering or whining or singing, at one point suggesting that they pull a star out of the sky and cook it for dinner; clearly, however, she does not and cannot share his perspective on their relationship. The pathos of his predicament lies, indeed, in the distance or difference between the daughter he describes and the daughter he addresses. The poetic device of apostrophe enables him to say things, as if to another adult, that he could not possibly say to the child she really is. "I write you only the bitter poems / that you can't read," he confesses in the ninth poem of the sequence. In this way, her three-year-old innocence becomes a foil for his adult knowledge of loss and estrangement.

In **"The Double Image,"** by contrast, a parent is speaking who can't afford or can't manage to honor the difference between her daughter's level of awareness and her own. Her story takes its departure from a brief verbal exchange that could plausibly have taken place between them, on a rainy November day as they stand outside together "watching the yellow leaves go queer":

> You ask me where they go. I say today believed
> in itself, or else it fell.

Sexton has constructed the interlocutory relation between mother and daughter differently from Snodgrass: the three-year-old is more of a conversation partner for her mother here. Indeed, the child's language and perspective are so blended with her mother's that the mental conversation the mother is having with her daughter is hard to distinguish from the one that is actually occurring between them. What she would like to teach her daughter, she goes on to explain, is a lesson she herself failed to learn: "Today, my small child, Joyce, / love your self's self where it lives." Insofar as her failure to be there for her daughter has convinced her that "there is no special God to refer to," this is the best parental advice she can manage. But Sexton's allegory of the leaves, though it passes for a lesson at the level of a child's understanding in the importance of loving yourself or believing in yourself, is effectively a counsel of despair: leaves fall in the autumn whether they have believed in themselves or not. Implicitly, then, both the substance and the interpersonal dynamics of the mother-daughter exchange disclose a confessional imperative that is not only suicidal, but murderous. "I had to learn," says the mother, "why I would rather / die than love, how your innocence would hurt and how I gather / guilt like a young intern / . . . his certain evidence." The poem itself is evidence of her inability not only to protect but even to tolerate her daughter's innocence: her worst guilt is that she finds herself offering the child a poet's bitter wisdom in place of a mother's love.

"The Double Image" is the confession of a woman who, in becoming a poet, has transgressed against motherhood. The poem's interlocutory strategy puts being a poet and being a mother in tension and finally at odds with each other; it creates an unmistakable dissonance between these two roles and their prerogatives. Like the "middle-aged witch" of Sexton's fifth published volume, *Transformations* (1971), whose designated interlocutor is her teenage daughter Linda but also the child in each of us, the speaker/protagonist of "The Double Image" is a poet and an unconventional, outlaw mother, both at once. And like the mental patient in "You, Doctor Martin" and "Music Swims Back to Me" and the would-be poet of "Said the Poet to the Analyst" and "For John, Who Begs Me Not to Enquire Further," she writes as a woman writes: that is her strength and her weakness, both at once.

It is odd to find Sexton confessing in "The Double Image" that she was "never quite sure / about being a girl": how could she doubt what her interlocutors and equally her readers are never allowed to forget? But that, of course, is the paradox of female masquerade—and perhaps, as theorists of masquerade have urged us to recognize, of "femininity" as such. Three years later, in the 1963 poem "Consorting With Angels," she would declare herself "tired of the gender of things" and recount a dream she'd had of leaving it all behind:

> Last night I had a dream
> and I said to it . . .
> "You are the answer.
> You will outlive my husband and my father."

> In that dream there was a city made of chains
> where Joan was put to death in man's clothes
> and the nature of the angels went unexplained,
> no two made in the same species,
> one with a nose, one with an ear in its hand,
> one chewing a star and recording its orbit,
> each one like a poem obeying itself,
> performing God's functions,
> a people apart.

The transcendent beings Sexton here dreams of joining in heaven are *sui generis,* each "like a poem obeying itself." They have a hermetic self-sufficiency that is strikingly antithetical to her own poetic *modus vivendi*—her need for an interlocutor, her penchant for self-exposure and for courting societal judgment and censure. The interlocutor she envisions for herself in this poem is the dream itself of transcendent androgyny ("and I said to it . . . / 'You are the answer'"), which seems to offer salvation from the hall of mirrors in which she is caught.

* * *

For better or for worse, however, the confessional mode both Sexton and Lowell practiced was utterly steeped in the gender of things. With hindsight, the paradigms of male-female interaction their poems depict as immemorial and/or inevitable can be seen to have been produced by a particular set of economic pressures and ideological investments; from where we sit, what seems inevitable is that they could and would be displaced. But from the perspective of a white middle-class denizen of the fifties and early sixties, those paradigms were paramount: you could outlive your mother or father and divorce your wife or husband, but the family romance would continue to reassert itself in your life and in your poems. "The story of our lives becomes our lives," as Adrienne Rich observed in another context; her story changed in the 1970s, whereas theirs did not. The story they couldn't stop telling—*that* story," Sexton sarcastically calls it in *Transformations*—is a 1950s version of the suicide pact of Adam and Eve. The man and the woman need each other, they destroy one another, their marriage cannot be saved.

Joanna Gill (essay date fall 2003)

SOURCE: Gill, Joanna. "'My Sweeney, Mr. Eliot': Anne Sexton and the 'Impersonal Theory of Poetry.'" *Journal of Modern Literature* 27, nos. 1-2 (fall 2003): 36-56.

[*In the following essay, Gill examines the relationship between Sexton's "personal" poetry and T. S. Eliot's de-personalized writings, asserting that Sexton's "Hurry up Please It's Time" is a direct response to and reinterpretation of Eliot's* The Waste Land.]

The American poet Anne Sexton (1928-1974), although routinely categorized as a "confessional" poet—indeed as the "mother" or "High-Priestess"[1] of the mode—infrequently used the epithet, preferring the term "personal."[2] As she explains: "my poetry is very personal. I don't think I write public poems. I write very personal poems" and "I was writing personal poetry, often about the subject of madness."[3]

Sexton's appropriation of the adjective "personal" in preference to the more usual "confessional" sends a number of important messages. It signals her unease with the confessional mode as then defined, and her sense that the label is an inadequate descriptor of her own complex and sophisticated poetics. In identifying her work as "personal," Sexton stakes an ambitious claim to a particular position in wider contemporary debates about the nature and purpose of poetry. Specifically, she defines her writing in terms of its difference from—which is also, as we shall see, its relationship with—the poetry of impersonality championed by T. S. Eliot and still, arguably, dominant in American literature in the period when she was writing. Sexton's defiant defense of the "personal" and the private invokes and challenges Eliot's persistently influential dictum: his advocacy of the "process of depersonalization" and his admonition that there should be a complete separation between "the man who suffers and the mind which creates."[4] Her choice of adjective signals her willingness to engage with Eliot's writing, to examine the barriers which are thought to divide the two modes, and to explore areas of potential contiguity—the points at which the public and the private, the personal and the impersonal, may meet.[5]

In this [essay], I examine Sexton's sustained, and hitherto unrecognized, engagement with Eliot's writing, exploring the ways in which debates about the function of poetry are played out in her subtle revision of some of his work.[6] I consider a number of texts, including two unpublished Sexton manuscripts, and focus in particular on Sexton's long poem **"Hurry up Please It's Time."**[7] This complex and allusive piece borrows more than simply its title from Eliot's work, representing, I will argue, a sophisticated response to and reinterpretation of *The Waste Land.*[8] The commonality of interests which Sexton asserts in her self-reflexive revision of Eliot's metapoem is an indication that our understanding of the relationship between the "personal" and the "impersonal" and our assessment of Sexton's place in modern poetry require reappraisal.

"Tradition and the Individual Talent," the essay in which Eliot developed his theories about impersonality in poetry, was first published in *The Egoist* in 1919 and was reprinted in Eliot's collection *The Sacred Wood: Essays on Poetry and Criticism* the following year. The essay was greeted with some dissent at the time; the

Times Literary Supplement identified a contradiction at the heart of the piece whereby although scientific rather than artistic procedures are used, "certain perversities, instinctive rather than rational" are expressed.[9]

However, "Tradition" has come to be acknowledged as the "most celebrated" of Eliot's critical essays.[10] This is a reputation about which Eliot expressed some ambivalence. In his "Preface" to the 1964 edition of *The Use of Poetry and the Use of Criticism* he regrets the frequency with which the essay is anthologized and apologizes for its "juvenile" tone, although he explicitly refuses to "repudiate" it.[11] Certainly the essay has been hugely influential and is widely regarded as having paved the way for the rise of New Criticism, with its attempt at detached, objective appraisal of the literary text.[12]

Eliot's subject in "Tradition" is the "relation of the poem to its author" (p. 44). He rethinks Romantic notions of the necessary and direct relationship between individual artist, experience, and poem, arguing instead for the restoration of classical values (order, restraint, objectivity). As Charles Ferrall argues, his implicit target is "the romantic cult of personality."[13] Most importantly, Eliot insists on the importance to the artist of a sense of history, of the adoption of a long view of the place of the artist's work in an ever-mutating literary tradition. It is the poem and its contribution to this tradition which are to be evaluated, rather than the individual writer and his experience. Eliot argues for the mutual reliance of the poetry of the past and that of the present such that each defines the other and thereby the "*whole* existing order" (p. 41, Eliot's emphasis). For Eliot, this organic tradition is primary, and it is in obeisance to this that the individual artist must, in his much-quoted lines, "sacrifice" himself (p. 44).

As Maud Ellman indicates, "Tradition" presents "a series of paradoxes. Newness without novelty—imitation without repetition: any poet [. . .] must, moreover, be both conscious and unconscious, and though he must have 'emotions,' he must also know what it means to escape them."[14] Indeed, although Eliot's essay seems to proceed by examining and valorizing one side in a succession of binaries (past *v.* present, learning *v.* inspiration, impersonality *v.* personality, creative mind *v.* suffering man, tradition *v.* individual talent), the argument of the essay is fraught with complexity and ambiguity. Jewel Spears Brooker suggests that "the purpose of Eliot's essay [. . .] is to undermine binary logic."[15] Equally, as Maud Ellman, Kenneth Asher, and a number of other critics have indicated, "Eliot's classicism is [. . .] deeply implicated in the romanticism it so categorically rejects." Asher proceeds to argue that "Tradition" "justifies poetry on almost purely affective grounds, and the essay itself, read with sensitivity to the volcanic pressure behind it, strikes one as an emotionally charged piece on behalf of coolness and distance."[16]

The presence of T. S. Eliot and, in particular, of the argument of "Tradition and the Individual Talent" is implicit in contemporary attempts to delineate the confessional mode—a mode which, as I have suggested, induced some ambivalence in Sexton. Early studies of confessionalism by, for example, Robert Phillips, Michael Rosenthal, and Al Alvarez posit a strong and necessary relationship between speaker and poet, textual and "real" experience.[17] In so doing, they establish an opposition between confessionalism and the modern poetry which preceded it and which is Eliot's subject. In place of Eliot's "the more perfect the artist, the more completely separate in him will be the man who suffers and the mind which creates" (p. 44), we are introduced to a poetry in which "private humiliations, sufferings and psychological problems" are dominant, and in which "the literal Self [is placed] more and more at the center of the poem."[18] Whereas for Eliot "the poet has, not a 'personality' to express, but a particular medium, which is only a medium and not a personality" (p. 46), for Robert Phillips, the "direct expression of the self" and the "expression of personality" are essential.[19] Where Eliot insists that "poetry is not a turning loose of emotion, but an escape from emotion; it is not the expression of personality, but an escape from personality" (pp. 48-49), conventional views of confessionalism propose that its subject is incapable of escape. She is figured as the passive victim of her effervescent emotions, subject to inescapable compulsions, in thrall to her experience.[20]

Sexton's writing, I propose, resists the polarity suggested by such criticism. It refutes, or at least problematizes, the dichotomy between the new poetry and the old, the compulsive and the restrained. It interrogates the assumed distinction between poetry which is the expression of personality and poetry which is an escape from it, and refuses to be restricted to either pole. To paraphrase Eliot's "East Coker," Sexton's writing takes the "middle way," ranging across borders, effacing the boundaries between personal and impersonal, private and public, confession and invention. In this way, as Jewel Spears Brooker says of Eliot, Sexton too "undermine[s] binary logic."

Indeed, Sexton's poetry, while seeming to be "personal," while seeming to exemplify Eliot's despised "turning loose of emotion," may in fact be paradigmatic of the opposite tendency. Caroline Hall suggests of Sexton's work that:

> In its use of apparently biographical personae and speakers and in its themes of sexual love, oedipal hate, personal anguish, unbearable suffering, and emotional breakdown, this poetry represents not an escape from personality but an expression of it.[21]

However, it is arguable that the "apparently biographical personae and speakers" which Hall identifies, while seeming to "express personality" and "emotion" (to

paraphrase Eliot), may disguise, obliterate, or license an escape from it. The key word here is "apparently," for these personae—even the persona of "I" or "Anne"—are indeed only "apparently" biographical. In a supreme double bluff, they establish an unimpeachable impression of authenticity, frankness, and intimate revelation, while bearing no necessary relationship to the experience of the poet. We think that we see the real Anne Sexton, whereas all that we actually have in our sights is a substitute, or persona, of the kind that Eliot might approve. Although it seems that the "[wo]man who suffers" dominates Sexton's writing it is, arguably, the "mind which creates" that retains control.

Paul Lacey, too, situates confessional poetry in a dialectical relationship with the modernist aesthetic that preceded it:

> After a generation of criticism which insisted that the "I" of a poem was not to be identified with the writer, the *real* John Keats, T. S. Eliot, or W. B. Yeats, but was to be seen strictly as a persona in the poem, we have returned—in some of our most vital poetry—to first person utterances which are intended to be taken as autobiographical.[22]

Like Hall, Lacey inadvertently controverts his own argument. For if these personae are "intended to be taken as autobiographical" then it is possible that they are not "autobiographical" at all, that the "apparent" (Hall) or "intended" (Lacey) personal referentiality of the poems is a device or sleight of hand which misleads readers into believing that they have access or insight to the lived experience of a real author. In pretending to overturn conventional doctrines about the importance of impersonality in poetry, in faking a return to the heart of personal experience, Sexton's confessionalism steers us further away. It invokes a misplaced confidence in its own authenticity and expressiveness; it posits immediacy and presence while discreetly consolidating its own indeterminacy and distance.

In a great many respects, then, Sexton's relationship to Eliot's principles is more complex, fluid, and, at times, more positive than has hitherto been allowed. Notwithstanding the best efforts of critics and commentators to identify confessional speaker with poet, text with lived experience, Sexton insists repeatedly on the importance of distinguishing between the two. Her assertions that "to really get to the truth of something is the poem, not the poet" and "the poem counts for more than your life"[23] confirm Eliot's view that "honest criticism and sensitive appreciation is directed not upon the poet but upon the poetry" (p. 44) and that "a poem, in some sense, has its own life."[24]

Further, it is possible to read the abjection of many of the voices of Sexton's poetry as exemplifying Eliot's imperative: "the progress of an artist is a continual self-sacrifice, a continual extinction of personality" (p. 44). One could argue that throughout her work, Sexton responds to the challenge of Eliot's statement, displaying a multitude of voices in various states of decline, attenuation, and fragmentation.[25] Indeed there is a strong, albeit hitherto unrecognized, similarity between the process of self-effacement proposed by Eliot, and that which is evidenced in her own poetry. It is a misguided, indeed perverse, reading which would fail to notice the significance in Sexton's work of metaphors of violence, of images of writing as "blood letting," of subject as vulnerable prey.[26] The confessional poet, then, in accordance with the requirements of the poetics of impersonality, extinguishes or sacrifices herself again and again in her work. However, we arrive here at one of the paradoxes of Eliot's criticism. It is arguable that his 1919 rejection of the aesthetics of the personal is predicated on the understanding that the personality is a superficial object which masks the real source; that the creative artist should, instead of turning away from the "self," search even harder, dig deeper. As Tony Sharpe argues: "in his essay on 'The Metaphysical Poets' (1921), Eliot rebuked those who looked into their hearts and wrote for 'not looking deep enough': 'one must look into the cerebral cortex, the nervous system, and the digestive tracts.'"[27]

In furtherance of this dialogue, Sexton draws on Eliot's poetry repeatedly throughout her work. For example, her poem **"O Ye Tongues"** considers the same problem of origins as Eliot's "East Coker." It also, like his "Burnt Norton," debates the limitations and failures of language. Similarly Sexton's **"A Little Uncomplicated Hymn"** with its long examination and exemplification of its own failure to say what was intended—"a little uncomplicated hymn / is what I *wanted* to write" [my emphasis]—invokes a line from Eliot's "The Love Song of J. Alfred Prufrock": "It is impossible to say just what I mean!" Sexton's elegy for her tutor John Holmes (Holmes, himself, was violently opposed to "personal" elements in her writing) entitled **"Somewhere in Africa"** borrows, and feminizes, the idiom of Eliot's "The Dry Salvages." In her poem **"February 20th"** the figure of Eliot is invoked with pity ("Eliot remembers his long lost mother, / St. Louis and Sweeney") and with fear; his "tongue" is "like thunder." This poem, from Sexton's 1971 "Scorpio, Bad Spider, Die" sequence reads as a precursor to, or draft of, the longer process of engagement with Eliot's work exemplified in **"Hurry up Please It's Time"** and thus as a measure of Sexton's sustained interest in the relationship.

An earlier poem **"Sweeney"** (1969) explicitly and defiantly invokes Eliot's Sweeney poems. Its bravura opening lines read:

> My Sweeney, Mr. Eliot
> is that Australian who came

to the U.S.A. with one thought—
My books in the satchel, my name.

Sexton's poem provocatively pits personal experience (note the defiant "*My* Sweeney") against authority and impersonality (hence the mocking formality of "Mr. Eliot"). Her Sweeney, unlike Eliot's "apeneck" ("Sweeney Among the Nightingales") is a cosmopolitan figure, an educated creature of the mind (thus "books" and "satchel") rather than of the body.[28] Here, as in **"Hurry up Please It's Time"** and Eliot's *The Waste Land,* we have a juxtaposition of voices (those of the speaker and Sweeney), of places ("U.S.A.," "Zurich," "London"), and of the religious and secular ("a liturgy / of praise," "a big dollar man").

It is in **"Hurry up Please It's Time,"** however, that Sexton's contemplation and negotiation of Eliot's writing are most fully realized. The poem enters into a critical dialogue with Eliot's *The Waste Land,* making sophisticated and purposive use of multiple personae, self-reflexively contemplating questions about memory, language, and subjectivity, and juxtaposing private introspection and public display. It raises questions about spirituality and secularization, innocence and experience, male and female identity, and, ultimately, about life and death. The poem offers a sustained explication and defense of personal writing by addressing and refuting limited and limiting perceptions of confessionalism, and by confidently engaging with Eliot's influential thought and practice.

"Hurry up Please" was written in the winter of 1972 and was published in Sexton's 1974 volume *The Death Notebooks.* It is divided into six sections of varying lengths, against *The Waste Land*'s five, as though to claim the last word. It is impossible to overstate the importance of **"Hurry up Please"** to an understanding of Sexton's work. It functions as a manifesto of her poetics, it provides a résumé of many of the concerns of earlier poems, and it invokes and challenges the terms of the assumed dichotomy between Sexton's "personal" poetry and Eliot's impersonalism. Yet the poem has barely been considered by other Sexton critics, this notwithstanding Sexton's claim in a letter to Peter Davison, editor of *Atlantic Monthly,* that "it is major."[29] Critics, with the exception of Caroline Hall who offers a short reading, have paid scant attention to the poem. Diane middlebrook does not mention it in her *Biography.* It is discussed only briefly in Linda Wagner-Martin's and Diana Hume George's edited collections of criticism.[30] Sandra Gilbert dismisses the poem as symptomatic of "all those weaknesses familiar to Sexton's readers."[31] J. D. McClatchy decries it as "a sort of long hallucinatory diary entry," a comment which, surely, misreads the poem's complex structure and sophisticated allusiveness.[32]

Sexton's poem dramatizes an urgent—hence the title— quest, not just for an answer to the questions posed in the opening lines ("What is death, I ask. / What is life, you ask") but for an appropriate discourse in which to contemplate them. As in *The Waste Land,* the idiom changes repeatedly throughout the poem: from the simple and childlike (the appeal to the mother in section four, and the nursery rhyme rhythms and allusions throughout) to the learned and contemplative: "learning to talk is a complex business." The narration shifts tenses, moving from the present ("This is the rainy season") to the past ("Once upon a time we were all born") to anticipation of the future ("One noon as you walk out to the mailbox / He'll snatch you up"). The many different voices of the poem are shifting and elusive. They oscillate between the interrogatory and the declamatory, the defensive and the assertive, from the reverential refrain "Forgive us, Father, for we know not" to the irreverent aside: "I am God, la de dah." The voices are, in turn, violent ("Them angels gonna be cut down like wheat") and vulnerable ("I am sorrowful in November . . ."). They are repeatedly taxed by questions and doubts about language, about poetry and about the role (or meaning *in* life) of the poet.

The poem is allusive (*contra* Alvarez, who distinguishes between Eliot's modernism and confessionalism, or "Extremist poetry," on the grounds of the allusiveness of the former, and the introspection of the latter).[33] Sexton's poem refers to the Old and New Testaments of the Bible, to the Sibyls of classical mythology, and to Buddhist texts. Like Eliot's "The Hollow Men," her poem inserts incomplete fragments of prayer or Gospel, borrowing a line from the Book of Common Prayer ("Forgive us, Father, for we know not") which is, itself, a borrowing from the Gospels ("Father, forgive them; for they know not what they do" [Luke 23.34]). In both poems, these allusions are typographically set apart, as though to imply that they are spoken as an aside, or that we are in the presence of several simultaneous voices or levels of contemplation. That the quotations in both cases are incomplete suggests failure and confusion, and foreshadows the lack of resolution in the text as a whole. Sexton's poem juxtaposes the intense and mystical and the superficial and mocking, hence the refrain "La de dah" which mimics Eliot's "Weialala leia / Wallala leialala" and in so doing subverts its serious and incantatory potential. Indeed, Sexton's line parodies the presumptuous erudition of Eliot's phrase, mimicking its intonation and transforming it into a slang reference to snobbery.[34]

"Hurry up Please" combines the popular, the contemporary, the emphatically and purposefully American, as for example in section two: "Peanut butter is the American food / We all eat it, being patriotic," with the spiritual and transcendent. It posits that the American dream (the "Holy Grail" of domestic bliss) is in fact a nightmare, hence the lament: "Milk is the American drink. / Oh queen of sorrows." Sexton returns to this

theme later in the poem where references to "jello," "milk," "juice," and "peanut butter" again identify America with consumption and thus inevitably with expulsion—a process which is represented throughout the poem by scatological metaphors:

> Good morning life, we say when we wake,
> hail mary coffee toast
> and we Americans take juice,
> a liquid sun going down.

The shocking and sacrilegious juxtaposition of "mary" (we should note the demeaning lower case initial) and the American breakfast emphasizes the loss of faith characteristic of contemporary American society.[35] Here there are rituals for the feeding of the body, rituals which promise health and happiness, but no longer any rituals for the feeding of the soul. An early draft of Sexton's poem is entitled "Play it again, Sam," an idiomatic phrase which firmly locates her poem in an American bar, in contrast to Eliot's English public house setting ("Hurry up please, it's time" is a traditional closing-time call). Arguably, the defiant Americanisms of Sexton's poem may be read as a rhetorical riposte to the elision in Eliot's poem of his own American experience.

The first two lines of **"Hurry up Please"** foreground the dialogic or discursive nature of confessional poetry; the fact that, as Michel Foucault and Leigh Gilmore have argued, in order that the confession be realized, there must be an "I" and a "you," a speaker and a reader, a penitent and a confessor.[36] Sexton's lines also make explicit the ontological questions ("What is death, I ask. / What is life, you ask.") that remain merely implicit in Eliot's poem, and foreground the quest framework which underpins both texts. The insistence and juxtaposition of the opening antitheses ("death" and "life") invite us to anticipate a further one. We expect to find the verb "ask" completed with "answer" ("I ask. / [. . .] you answer") and we are disconcerted when we realize, particularly at such an early stage, that there may not be any answers. This introduces a primary uncertainty, one which persists throughout, and even motivates, the whole poem. It also dispels any confidence which we might have in the power of poetry, or language in general, to convey meaning. The speaker asks a question—of the reader, Eliot, a therapist, a spiritual advisor, God?—but is unable to command a response. The inability or refusal of the addressee to offer any answers signifies a general loss of faith in the power of religion, or of the secular religion of psychotherapy, neither of which can provide the satisfaction which they had once seemed to promise.

The implied dialogue with which **"Hurry up Please"** opens is made explicit at the end of the first section with the emergence of an "Interrogator." This may represent a religious or psychiatric confessor, hence the reference to "seven days," which connotes the weekly rite of confession to the priest or weekly therapeutic hour. The interrogator's role is to question "Anne":

INTERROGATOR:

> What can you say of your last seven days?

ANNE:

> They were tired.

INTERROGATOR:

> One day is enough to perfect a man.

ANNE:

> I watered and fed the plant.

This scripted exchange serves to unsettle our sense of the identity of the speaker of the poem (the "I" with which it opened) and of the relationship between "I" and "Anne" and the poet "Anne Sexton." The presence of these multiple characters also serves to confirm the dramatic or theatrical nature of confession, which may not be a "true" reflection of lived experience, but a staged spectacle.

As far as Sexton's appropriation of Eliot's poetic techniques is concerned, these seemingly abstruse lines are, like sections of *The Waste Land,* deeply allusive, and consequently profoundly resonant. The dialogue with the "Interrogator" permits Sexton both to make reassuring points about the therapeutic promise of confession ("one day *is* enough to perfect a man" [my emphasis]) and to exercise the voice of cynicism or doubt; the voice, indeed, of a Jonah. For Anne's response ("I watered and fed the plant") alludes to the Biblical parable wherein God proves his power to a doubting Jonah by creating and then destroying a great plant (Jonah 4.6-11). The Biblical allusion is important, too, because it reiterates the death wish of the poem's opening lines. Jonah in the Bible, like the poem's opening speaker, is tormented by his longing for death, complaining bitterly: "it is better for me to die than to live" (Jonah 4.3). Most importantly, in the context of Sexton's revision of Eliot's poem, the metaphor recalls and consolidates the Sibylline voice which heralds, and resonates throughout, both texts.

Indeed, the opening couplet of **"Hurry up Please It's Time"** is most significant in respect of its subtle allusion to the Sibyl of Cumae—the subject of Eliot's epigraph to *The Waste Land.* His epigraph refers to the mythological story of the Sibyl who, granted a wish by Apollo, asked for prolonged life, but neglected to ask for continued youthfulness. Eliot quotes Trimalchio—"a filthy-rich ex-slave and extravagant party host"[37]—and a witness to the Sibyl's plight: "For indeed I myself have

seen, with my own eyes, the Sibyl hanging in a bottle at Cumae, and when those boys would say to her: 'Sibyl, what do you want?' she replied, 'I want to die.'"[38] Sexton's speaker's insistent opening question, which evidences a preoccupation with death rather than an interest in life, places her firmly on the side of the Sibyl; she assumes her voice, her longing for death.[39] An earlier Sexton poem, **"Wanting to Die,"** pities those born with the suicidal desire within them and similarly pictures them, like the Sibyl, as the object of awed scrutiny by the innocent:

> Still-born, they don't always die,
> but dazzled, they can't forget a drug so sweet
> that even children would look on and smile.

The speaker in **"Hurry up Please,"** too, is caught between life and death. She is tormented by the scrutiny of her audience (the "executioners" and "interrogator" in Sexton's poem, the young boys in Eliot's epigraph). That she is displayed like an anatomical specimen in a glass bottle replicates the metaphor of the inverted glass bowl which is central to another Sexton poem, **"For John Who Begs Me Not to Enquire Further."** It also replicates Sylvia Plath's image of the "Bell Jar."[40] In each case, the glass jar signifies the control and public display of the female subject.

The confessional poet, like the Sibyl of Cumae, is caught and objectified by the gaze of her audience and resorts to what seems to be the only comprehensible language—the language of the body. Here, in **"Hurry up Please,"** the private self is put on public display:

> I give them both my buttocks,
> my two wheels rolling off toward Nirvana.
> They are as neat as a wallet,
> opening and closing on their coins,
> the quarters, the nickels,
> straight into the crapper.

The gesture mocks the self-exposure of confessional writing, developed subsequently in this poem, and elsewhere, in metaphors of sexual display and prostitution, and treats the corrupting business of poetry with contempt.[41] The dual meaning of "Nirvana" (a Buddhist state of peace, where individual existence ceases to signify, or the site of Hedonistic pleasure and individual gratification) conflates the spiritual and the vulgar (common, popular) promise of confessionalism.

Naked self-revelation (of the buttocks and their waste products; connoting a possible pun on *The Waste Land*) is commercialized and thus rendered sordid. The speaker in these lines is both childlike and sexually knowing. Most importantly, she is fully in command.[42] This confounds conventional readings of the distasteful lack of control of the confessional poet, as represented by Patricia Spacks's question: "how [. . .] can one properly respond to lines as grotesquely uncontrolled as these?"[43] and Eliot's insistence that: "poetry is not a turning loose of emotion" (p. 48). If, as Robert Phillips, for example, argues, confessional poetry is "purgative," then this is a purgation which is controlled (hence "neat"), productive or financially lucrative, and willingly entered into by the subject.[44]

The rhetoric here becomes defensive, as though anticipating criticism of such self display and testing the limits of confessional discourse. How far can the speaker go before the audience ("executioner"/Eliot?) tires of her? How "personal" can she be?

> Why shouldn't I pull down my pants
> and moon at the executioner
> as well as paste raisins on my breasts?
> Why shouldn't I pull down my pants
> and show my little cunny to Tom
> and Albert? They wee-wee funny.
> I wee-wee like a squaw.
> I have ink but no pen.

The metaphor of undressing invokes contemporary hostility against confessional self-revelation, or the "unbuttoned style of reminiscence," as Jonathan Raban has termed it.[45] "Tom" is, of course, Thomas Stearns Eliot, here addressed with more familiarity, and more contempt, than the apostrophe "Mr. Eliot" in Sexton's **"Sweeney."** "Albert" is an assimilation of Eliot's character of that name in section two of *The Waste Land.* In **"Hurry up Please,"** as in Eliot's poem, there is an implied imperative for women to be presentable, to attract and please men. As the second section of *The Waste Land* urges: "HURRY UP PLEASE ITS TIME / Now Albert's coming back, make yourself a bit smart." Yet this is an imperative which Sexton's speaker resists. The repetition of "Why shouldn't I" in lines nine and twelve indicates that the speaker is aware of her transgression, that she is testing the boundaries of what is acceptable, for women and specifically for writing women (hence "ink" and "pen").

The excremental imagery ("wee-wee") demonstrates, among other things, the speaker's own ambivalence about her writing—an ambivalence perhaps inculcated by others' repeated condemnation (a process similar to that by which, psychoanalytically speaking, the girl child is taught that her genitals are different and inferior). Notwithstanding the lack (absence, and also loss, in the Lacanian sense) of the penis, or power, the speaker still wishes, in a supreme effort of will and physical/writing energy, to make her mark. She wishes to retaliate against the regime which would leave her pen(is)-less: "still / I dream that I can piss in God's eye." The pettiness of the seemingly trivial, yet deeply symbolic, difference between the sexes is mocked in the subsequent lines: "I dream I'm a boy with a zipper. / It's so practical, la de dah."

The shifting, and thus foregrounding, of gender ("I dream I'm a boy") and, most importantly, the allusion in the lines quoted above to the "raisins" and the "breasts" invoke two figures from *The Waste Land.* First, Mr. Eugenides (Eliot's "Smyrna merchant / Unshaven, with a pocket full of currants") and thereafter, Tiresias, the "old man" with his/her "wrinkled female breasts" whose presence immediately succeeds Mr. Eugenides's in section three of Eliot's poem. Sexton uses a similar metaphor in her short story "All God's Children Need Radios," where the speaker anticipates her future identity as "An old hag, her breasts shrunken to the size of pearls."[46] In **"Hurry up Please,"** Sexton's speaker, like Tiresias, experiments with gender roles. She exploits archetypal metaphors for women's (personal) and men's (impersonal) writing; women's writing is equated with fertility and nurturance (the "orange") and men's with rationality and authority (the pun is on "ruler"). Yet the comparison also serves to draw attention to common areas of experience:

> I have swallowed an orange, being woman.
> You have swallowed a ruler, being a man.
> Yet waiting to die we are the same thing.

The phrase "waiting to die" recalls the plight, and the desperation, of the Sibyl in Eliot's epigraph who, as we have seen, "want[s] to die," and the Sibylline voice with which Sexton opens her poem, a voice which foretells that we are all, women and men, on a journey towards death. There is more contiguity between the sexes and perhaps by extension, between the kinds of writing produced by each, between the personal and the impersonal, than might be realized: "Skeezix, you are me. La de dah. / You grow a beard but our drool is identical." Here the polarized "you" and "me" of the opening lines of Sexton's poem are brought into proximity, unified, synthesized (hence the pronoun "our"). As Eliot comments in the notes to *The Waste Land*:

> Tiresias, although a mere spectator and not indeed a "character," is yet the most important personage in the poem, uniting all the rest [. . .] all the women are one woman, and the two sexes meet in Tiresias. What Tiresias *sees,* in fact, is the substance of the poem.
>
> (pp. 46-47)

The voice of Tiresias emerges again in section three of Sexton's **"Hurry up Please"**: "There's a sack over my head. / I can't see. I'm blind." Eliot's Tiresias, "though blind [. . .] / [. . .] *can* see" [my emphasis]. Sexton's tautology establishes that in her poem, unlike in Eliot's, the speaker is both literally and figuratively blind: she lacks the metaphorical insight which is Tiresias's consolation for his physical loss of vision. What Eliot's Tiresias "sees" is the comforting view of the sailors' safe return "home from sea" and the familiar domestic routine, with the typist laying out her tea. What Sexton's Tiresias fails to see is an antithetical reality, one where the "sea collapses," where the fishermen are determined and vicious.

In the second stanza of section two, Sexton's speaker adopts a further dramatic role; that of "Ms. Dog." Caroline Hall speculates that "Ms. Dog" is inspired by Eliot's waste land dog[47] and although this is one possible influence, we should also note that Sexton had likened herself to a dog (servile, inhuman) on a number of other occasions.[48] For example, in "All God's Children Need Radios," mentioned earlier, she asserts: "I am a dog" and "*Dog* stands for me" (pp. 27, 29). In the poem **"Is It True?"** she explains simply:

> I have,
> for some time,
> called myself,
> Ms. Dog.

Given Sexton's fondness for palindromes (notably, the metaphor of the "rats star" in the early poems **"With Mercy For the Greedy"** and **"An Obsessive Combination of Ontological Inscape, Trickery and Love"**),[49] the significance of "Dog" as a sinister inversion of "God" is worthy of note. The "Ms. Dog" persona has much in common with that developed by W. H. Auden, another profound, albeit usually unrecognized, influence on Sexton. Auden notoriously alluded to a "Miss God"—a persona whom he credited as the source of his poetic inspiration, or blamed for his own irrational behaviour, as occasion demanded.[50]

Immediately before writing **"Hurry up Please,"** Sexton had drafted two poems, both of which remain unpublished, in which the character "Dog God" appears. **"Dog-God Fights the Dollars"** and **"Dog-God's Wife Adopts a Monkey"** are of compelling interest in their evocation and examination of themes subsequently explored in **"Hurry up Please."**[51] The first, **"Dog-God Fights the Dollars"** (originally entitled "Commerce"), was written on October 4, 1972, some two months before **"Hurry up Please."** Similarities between its opening lines and the first two sections of the latter poem indicate that it may be a draft or aborted study:

> Dog-God was out fighting the dollars.
> He wanted to conquer them, the large
> green hearts, the sharp black knives
> and oh the numbers.

Thereafter, the original typescript contains a ten-line section which is crossed through in Sexton's hand. This makes clear the vicissitudes of the relationship between "Dog-God"—a metaphor for the confessional poet, encapsulating the mixture of disdain and reverence, contempt and adoration in which she is held—and audience:

> Dog-God was a bandit, he was a mugger,
> he was a friar praying to their faces,
> the ones, the fives, the fiftys [sic], the hundreds.

The abjection and self-loathing indicated by the designation of self as "Dog" surfaces in the final section of the poem, along with the dreadful admission that the speaker's work, the production and performance of confessional poetry, is done purely for financial gain: "Dollars / were his cure." Monetary recompense is product and evidence of the audience's attention and admiration or sympathy and is necessary to the speaker's sense of identity. If the attention ceases, so does the money, leading inevitably to the dissipation of the subject:

> The rain
> of bucks would not come and his life
> was vanishing.

Without an audience there can be no discourse, and the confession will remain incomplete, the penitent dissatisfied. Here, arguably, we have Eliot's "continual self-sacrifice," the "continual extinction of personality" (p. 44) played out for all to see.

The second of these unpublished typescripts, **"Dog-God's Wife Adopts a Monkey"** (dated October 8, 1972) is a disturbing and intense dream poem. Like **"Dog-God Fights the Dollars,"** it introduces and experiments with a number of themes, images and voices which re-emerge in **"Hurry up Please."** The poem opens with the overheard conversation of two women (a pastiche of the reported dialogue between "Lil" and her friend in section two of *The Waste Land*) discussing how to treat a visiting monkey. The monkey is, perhaps, a displaced metaphor for the visiting/ "demobilised" husband in Eliot's poem and a covert allusion to Eliot's "apeneck Sweeney":

> I couldn't really keep the monkey,
> the mother-in-law said, [. . .]
> The sister-in-law said, if he wouldn't
> stand there waiting for his bottom
> to be wiped, I'd take him.

The figure of the monkey serves to confirm the latent bestiality of the confessional subject. In **"Hurry up Please"** the speaker "blurting in the mike" is at once a "dog," a "turtle," and, in a punning metaphor ("turtle green / and monk black") a monkey. We should note that Sexton draws a parallel between the condition of the confessional poet and that of the monkey as performing animal, a source of amusement and entertainment because of its assimilation of ostensibly human traits. Both are cruelly trapped by their audience's demands for a spectacle. The connection is confirmed, and lamented, in the final lines of **"Dog-God's Wife Adopts a Monkey,"** which, incidentally, tacitly allude to the role of Tiresias the seer:

In this case, she resolved, you could
be a poet, a kind of seer, a kind
of monkey, and she woke up, trailing
her tail.

In respect of the origins of **"Hurry up Please,"** the dream poem **"Dog-God's Wife Adopts a Monkey"** suggests a source for the biological distinction between the sexes encapsulated in the former's "They wee-wee funny. / I wee-wee like a squaw." **"Dog-God's Wife"** is more explicit, and more transgressive. In a gesture which again implicitly draws on the figure of the man/woman Tiresias in Eliot's poem, Dog-God's wife appears to be both male and female. Speaking to the monkey, she declares:

> But I won't
> love you if you don't use the toilet
> like the rest of us and she pulled down
> her pants and showed him how. Then she
> took her own cock in her hand, her own
> visionary spout, and showed him how to go
> the other way.

To return to **"Hurry up Please It's Time,"** in section two of the poem, as in **"Dog-God Fights the Dollars,"** Ms. Dog shamelessly collects money with her body. She is pictured rolling in the dollars as a dog rolls in mud, making a living from the public display of the private self: "Ms. Dog is out fighting the dollars, / rolling in a field of bucks." The confessional poet, specifically the female confessional poet, is likened to a prostitute ("bucks" is a slang reference to men), and the poetic confession is perceived as a profanation of its supposedly sacred roots:

> You've got it made if
> you take the wafer,
> take some wine,
> take some bucks
> the green papery song of the office.

Sexton is explicit about the connection between money (the green paper) and poetry (in particular the performed poem, or "song"). Indeed, she confesses: "I wish I were the U.S. Mint, / turning it all out." The metaphor of "turning it out," particularly with its aural pun on "churning," indicates that confession is not, after all, some sacred calling or irrepressible release. It is a fabrication, a "made" or manufactured product of American consumer society.

"Ms. Dog" is at the heart of this chain of production and consumption, the one responsible for supporting the economy by means of her own physical labor or poetic performance:

> Who's that at the podium
> in black and white,
> blurting into the mike?
> Ms. Dog.

> Is she spilling her guts?
> You bet.

"Ms. Dog," like "Anne" in earlier sections, is represented in the third person and thereby emphatically dissociated from the original speaker. Indeed, the speaker is not certain who this performing subject is, hence: "Who's that at the podium?" This emphasizes the autonomy of the public persona. The performing/reading subject is to be understood as quite distinct from, even unrecognizable by, the writing subject (the "I"). This is, arguably, Eliot's complete separation of "the man who suffers and the mind which creates" (p. 45). Ms. Dog, here, is the suffering figure, the spectacular martyr "blurting" into the mike and "spilling" her guts.[52] The "I," in contrast, is deeply controlling and retains creative authority. Even the moments of apparent fragmentation and nonsense which frame Ms. Dog's appearance on the stage are paradoxically controlled and allusive. The song: "Toot, toot, tootsy don't cry. / Toot, toot, tootsy good-bye" implicitly draws on the "Goonight / Ta ta. Goonight. Goonight" refrain which closes section two of Eliot's *The Waste Land*.

Section three of **"Hurry up Please"** reverts to the urgent tone of the poem's title:

> Ms. Dog, how much time you got left?
> Ms. Dog, when you gonna feel that cold nose?
> You better get straight with the Maker
> cuz it's a coming, it's a coming!

The idiom is reminiscent of John Berryman's *Dream Songs*; the voices of "Ms. Dog" and the first-person speaker are, perhaps, to be compared with his "Henry" and "Mr. Bones."[53] The casual contractions ("gonna," "cuz") signify the haste and urgency with which the subject writes. The repetition of "gonna" in subsequent lines also draws on Eliot's "Fragment of an Agon" ("We're gona stay and we're gona go") which, like *The Waste Land* and **"Hurry up Please,"** foregrounds the contiguity between life and death. In the words of "Fragment," "Death is life and life is death."

The end which Sexton's speaker expects, and which—in a manner reminiscent of Eliot's "East Coker"—is anticipated in the poem's beginning, is figured in section three as a violent act of punishment. The speaker is to be judged and condemned both as a woman ("they're gonna stick your little doll's head" and "your clothes a gonna melt") and as a poet. As the speaker warns Ms. Dog:

> Hear that, Ms. Dog!
> You of the songs,
> you of the classroom,
> you of the pocketa-pocketa.[54]

In section four of **"Hurry up Please,"** however, Ms. Dog fights back, delighting in her nakedness (metaphorically, her poetry's public exposé of private concerns) and revelling in her performance:

Ms. Dog prefers to sunbathe nude.
Let the indifferent sky look on.
So what!

That Ms. Dog "prefers to sunbathe nude" (metaphorically, to strip herself bare in her writing) emphasizes that this is a choice. It is not an inadvertent compulsion that requires defense or apology, but a specific and effective strategy. Sexton celebrates her development and freedom as a woman writer. This section of **"Hurry up Please"** affirms the speaker's liberation from domestic routine and her new-found right to reveal all, to peel off her clothes, to make the once private and restricted public and shared:

because I've come a long way
from Brussels sprouts.
I've come a long way to peel off my clothes
and lay me down in the grass.

Similarly, section five acclaims the ability of the speaker, here metaphorically presented as "Middle-class lady," to construct something from every seemingly insignificant and personal event:

If someone hands you a glass of water
you start constructing a sailboat.
If someone hands you a candy wrapper,
you take it to the book binder.

The metaphor acknowledges the Freudian notion of sublimation, and celebrates the confessional poet's ability to transform apparent detritus into writing (in the terms of the poem **"An Obsessive Combination,"** mentioned earlier, to turn "RATS" into "STAR"). Subsequent stanzas of this section are introduced with the phrase "Once upon a time," which foregrounds the potential fictionality of the text. The use of the rhetoric of fiction permits the speaker to project her vision far into the future, and then speculatively to look back on events ("Once upon a time Ms. Dog was sixty-six. / She had white hair and wrinkles as deep as splinters") or to achieve the kind of separation between experience and text, actuality and representation, which Eliot advocates.[55] "Once upon a time" signifies the process by which we tell and read stories about our personal and collective pasts in order to divine their meaning. Indeed, the next stanza in this section emphasises the shift from the specific to the general, widening the perspective from a private, narcissistic moment to a shared condition: "Once upon a time we were all born, / popped out like jelly rolls."

Section five confronts this, the fundamental question for confessionalism: how can personal, individual experience be brought to bear? How can it be made meaningful in the public world? Conversely, it asks how ordinary, shared, communal life can continue in the presence of private suffering. Drawing, perhaps, on Eli-

ot's "Preludes" ("The winter evening settles down / With smell of steaks in passageways") Sexton comments:

Often there are wars
yet the shops stay open
and sausages are still fried.

The reproduction of the species ("People copulate / entering each other's blood") and the maintenance of routine, as previously evidenced in respect of the rituals of American domesticity, seem to function as a panacea or displacement activity. Thus the public is distracted from the terrifying vulnerability of the individual:

It doesn't matter if there are wars,
the business of life continues
unless you're the one that gets it.
Mama, they say as their intestines
leak out. Even without wars
life is dangerous.

The reference to copulation brings to mind the repeated words "birth, and copulation, and death" spoken by Eliot's Sweeney in "Fragment of an Agon." The image in Sexton's poem of the "intestines / leak[ing] out" on the battlefield suggests a relationship between that scene of violent attrition and the experience of the confessional speaker, who "spill[s] her guts" to the confessional audience (earlier, the "executioner"). Notwithstanding this personal and also political crisis, the poem insists that everyday life can and must continue.

Sexton's subject in **"Hurry up Please"** is, we find, still seeking an answer:

Ms. Dog stands on the shore
and the sea keeps rocking in
and she wants to talk to God.

Her position replicates that of Eliot's speaker in *The Waste Land*:

I sat upon the shore
Fishing, with the arid plain behind me
Shall I at least set my lands in order?

However, the increasing urgency of Ms. Dog's quest is signified by her "stand[ing] on the shore" while Eliot's speaker sits, and by her determination (she "wants") while Eliot's speaker exhibits only passive hesitancy ("shall I?").

The sixth and final section of Sexton's poem attempts to bring together the multiple strands of the earlier sections by means of a contemplation—or rather, an interrogation—of the single characteristic which unites them: their identity as language. Like Eliot in "East Coker" and "Burnt Norton," Sexton is concerned with the nature, origins, and capacity of language; concerned with the processes by which it constructs rather than reflects meaning. The section begins:

Learning to talk is a complex business.
My daughter's first word was *utta,*
meaning button.

The poem asks questions about language acquisition, problematizes the received relationship between thought and word, and experience and its expression, and raises the possibility that language precedes and dominates the speaker:

Before there are words
do you dream?
In utero
do you dream?
Who taught you to suck?
And how come?

Sexton's questions about language are, in part, questions about origins, and this returns the reader to the poem's opening questions: "What is death, I ask. / What is life, you ask." The specific connection is reinforced by the half-rhymes of "utta," "button," and "utero," which invoke the "buttocks" of section one, a noun that figures again in the next stanza of this final section as though to reinforce the syntactical and figurative connection. Paradoxically, and highly significantly, this quizzical expression of semantic anxiety is itself an exemplification of the way in which writing *can* succeed. The chain of signification ("utta," "button," "utero," "buttocks") and subsequent artful rhymes, associations, and oppositions ("help" / "hello," "crow" / "know," "beautiful" v. "ugly") emphasize contradiction by means of their own internal coherence.

Nevertheless, a profound sense of linguistic uncertainty lingers. The subject's plaintive cry seems incomprehensible:

Is the cry saying something?
Does it mean *help?*
Or hello?
The cry of a gull is beautiful
and the cry of a crow is ugly
but what I want to know
is whether they mean the same thing.

The insistent questions here exemplify the modern crisis of faith in the structure and power of language. What does come first: thought ("dream[s]") or "words?" Do two distinct cries uttered in different contexts "mean the same thing?" In essence, Sexton is questioning logocentrism, challenging the power of what Stan Smith calls the "originary statement," "In the beginning was the Word" (John. 1), and asking what, if anything, preceded "the Word."[56] Crucially, Sexton's poem illustrates the point Eliot makes in "East Coker" ("In my beginning is my end" and "In my end is my beginning") and "Little Gidding" ("What we call the beginning is often the end") about the indeterminacy, or interchangeability of ends and beginnings, about the circularity and ceaseless-

ness of experience. She imagines an "old man's *last* words: / More light! More light!" [my emphasis], words which are also potentially first words, generative utterances that summon life ("let there be light") as death approaches. This, or a similar, inversion of the creation myth appears in a number of Sexton's poems (for example, **"O Ye Tongues"**) as, indeed, in the Eliot poems I have mentioned. In both poets' work, it is used as a circular trope, as a way of refiguring the relationship between beginnings and endings and thus of forcing a re-evaluation, or even dismissal, of orthodox teleology.

As though to exemplify this, the ostensible conclusion of Sexton's poem takes the reader back to its own opening questions. It also newly foregrounds the dialogue with Eliot. Paradoxically, what Sexton's poem does—and I think that she is obliquely commenting here on what she finds in her model, *The Waste Land*—is refuse the conventional imperative or teleology that underpins the quest in each case. She side-steps the impossible task of finding resolute answers to the huge questions explicitly posed at the outset of her own poem ("What is death"? "What is life"?) and tacitly pursued in Eliot's. Instead, she celebrates the endless possibilities of uncertainty, embraces indeterminacy, abjures finite truth or definite answers in favor of a continuous process of faithful enquiry. Instead of seeking the answer (which is, of course, and dreadfully, the end) she advocates an attenuation of the enquiry, proposing "to worship the question itself." To know the answers, her poem implies, would be to usurp the authority of God. Better, it suggests, to reconcile oneself to living in a state of hopeful uncertainty, to not knowing, hence the refrain throughout the poem: "Forgive us, Father, for we know not," which becomes, from this perspective, a celebration rather than a lament. In a supreme metaphor for Sexton's larger poetics, it is the process of looking which is more important than any determinate solution or truth. And the place to engage in this process, to conduct this continuous "worship" of the question is by scrutiny of the greatest mystery, or miracle of creation, the self.

Here, again, Eliot's thought is tacitly invoked, and defiantly rebutted. For Sexton, such insight as one may hope to obtain can derive only from self-knowledge, from personal introspection, from private examination, from the exploration of "the body itself":

It is only known that they are here to worship,
to worship the terror of the rain,
the mud and all its people,
the body itself.

In the turn to the private self, to the body, as the source of enlightenment, we are redirected to the opening lines of the poem:

What is death, I ask.
What is life, you ask.
I give them both my buttocks.

In response to these abstract questions, the "buttocks"—as a metonym of the body, and a metaphor for self-examination—represent a valid source of understanding. More precisely, what Sexton's poem suggests is that the insights achieved by personal introspection (scrutiny of "the body itself" or, later, of "every corner of the brain") can be communicated, can be made meaningful, only by public display ("I give them both my buttocks"). For truth to be realized, personal experience must be shared. This confirms Michel Foucault's and Leigh Gilmore's theorization of how confessional discourse works, and it marks the point at which personal and impersonal poetics meet. As Gilmore explains: "in order to catalyze the dynamics of what we recognize as confession, the stage must be set with a penitent/teller, a listener and a tale."[57] **"Hurry up Please It's Time"** proffers terms of reconciliation with Eliot: defending and advocating the turn to the personal as a valid means of engaging with wider, abstract, "impersonal" questions. It demonstrates that "personal" poetry can work only in a public arena, that it is meaningless without exposure to, and judgment by, an "impersonal" auditor/confessor. Both sides exist in symbiosis.

As it reaches its conclusion, **"Hurry up Please It's Time"** diminishes typographically on the page, gradually losing the orchestra of images and voices that has reverberated throughout until only "Ms. Dog" remains. Sexton's poem closes with a final act of obeisance to T. S. Eliot. It proposes a "shantih shantih shantih," to quote from *The Waste Land,* to match Eliot's own. For Sexton's speaker, the "Peace which passeth understanding" (as Eliot glosses the phrase in his "Notes on *The Waste Land*") is precisely that: an acceptance of life beyond "understanding," a reconciliation with the possibility that the answers to the poem's own opening questions may never be found. This is also, confidently and defiantly, a peace with the self, a celebration of the insights to be obtained from private introspection:

Bring a flashlight, Ms. Dog,
and look in every corner of the brain
and ask and ask and ask
until the kingdom,
however queer,
will come.

Finally, as these closing lines avow, what ultimately unites Sexton's poetics, and Eliot's, is their shared anticipation of, and subjection to, a greater will; their hopeful expectation that notwithstanding their chosen paths, the kingdom of God, "however queer, / will come."

Notes

1. Unpublished Anne Sexton material is used with the permission of Linda Gray Sexton, for the estate of Anne Sexton, and with the permission of the Harry Ransom Humanities Research Center, The University of Texas at Austin (hereinafter HRHRC). The author gratefully acknowledges the support of the British Association for American Studies, whose award of a travel grant helped to finance the manuscript research on which this article is based.

2. Diana Hume George, *Oedipus Anne: The Poetry of Anne Sexton* (University of Illinois Press, 1987), p. 90; Robert Phillips, *The Confessional Poets* (Southern Illinois University Press, 1973), p. 6.

3. Harry Moore, Interview with Anne Sexton, *No Evil Star: Selected Essays, Interviews and Prose—Anne Sexton,* ed. Steven E. Colburn (University of Michigan Press, 1985), p. 50; Gregory Fitz Gerald, Interview with Anne Sexton, Colburn, p. 181.

4. T. S. Eliot, "Tradition and the Individual Talent," *The Sacred Wood: Essays on Poetry and Criticism* (Faber and Faber, 1997), pp. 44, 45. All subsequent quotations from this edition will be included parenthetically in the text.

5. A number of critics have argued recently for the presence in Eliot's work of deceptively "personal" elements, Steven K. Hoffman posits that Eliot is a "direct precursor of the confessionals" and proposes that "personality does have a place in Eliot's poetic." "Impersonal Personalism: The Making of a Confessional Poetic," *ELH* 45 (1978), p. 691. Similarly, Maud Ellman records—in terms which anticipate my argument about the slippages in Sexton's poetry—that "Eliot once told John Hayward that he had 'personal reasons' for asserting his impersonality, and this probably means that he was able to confess more freely if he disavowed these confessions as his own." *The Poetics of Impersonality: T. S. Eliot and Ezra Pound* (Harvester, 1987), p. 5.

6. Sexton studied Eliot's writing at Brandeis University in 1960 and mentions his *The Cocktail Party* as one of the few plays which she had seen before commencing work on her own play, *Tell Me Your Answer True.* See Diane Wood Middlebrook, *Anne Sexton: A Biography* (Virago, 1991), p. 127 and Anne Sexton, "Reactions of an Author in Residence." Unpublished manuscript. HRHRC.

7. Unless otherwise indicated the source used for Sexton's poems is *Anne Sexton: The Complete Poems* (Houghton Mifflin, 1981).

8. Quotations from T. S. Eliot's *The Waste Land,* and from his "Notes on *The Waste Land*," are taken from *The Waste Land and Other Poems* (Faber and Faber, 1940). The source of other Eliot poems is *T. S. Eliot: Collected Poems 1909-1962* (Faber and Faber, 1974).

9. Qtd. in Tony Sharpe, *T. S. Eliot: A Literary Life* (Macmillan, 1991), p. 66.

10. David Lodge, ed. *20th Century Literary Criticism: A Reader* (Longman, 1972), p. 70; Sharpe, p. 73.

11. *The Use of Poetry and the Use of Criticism: Studies in the Relation of Criticism to Poetry in England* (Faber and Faber, 1964), pp. 9, 10.

12. Lodge, p. 70; Frank Lentricchia, *Modernist Quartet* (Cambridge University Press, 1994), p. 256.

13. *Modernist Writing and Reactionary Politics* (Cambridge University Press, 2001), p. 102.

14. Ellman, p. 36.

15. Jewel Spears Brooker, *Mastery and Escape: T. S. Eliot and the Dialectic of Modernism* (University of Massachusetts Press, 1994), p. 220.

16. Kenneth Asher, *T. S. Eliot and Ideology* (Cambridge University Press, 1998), p. 163.

17. M. L. Rosenthal, *The New Poets: American and British Poetry Since World War Two* (Oxford University Press, 1967); Al Alvarez, "Beyond All This Fiddle," *Times Literary Supplement* (23 March 1967), pp. 229-32.

18. Rosenthal, pp. 26-27.

19. Phillips, pp. 8-9.

20. Eliot's notion of "meditative verse" similarly invokes this idea of compulsion and release. The writer of such poetry suffers under a non-specific, but nevertheless onerous and enervating "burden which he must bring to birth in order to obtain relief." See "The Three Voices of Poetry," *On Poetry and Poets* (Faber and Faber, 1957), p. 98.

21. *Anne Sexton* (G. K. Hall, 1989), p. 34.

22. Paul A. Lacey, "The Sacrament of Confession," *Critical Essays on Anne Sexton,* ed. Linda Wagner-Martin (G. K. Hall, 1989), p. 94.

23. Patricia Marx, Interview with Anne Sexton, Colburn, pp. 74, 75.

24. *The Sacred Wood,* p. xi.

25. "He Do the Police in Different Voices" was at one time Eliot's title for *The Waste Land.* See *The Waste Land: A Facsimile and Transcript of the Original Drafts including the Annotations of Ezra Pound,* ed. Valerie Eliot (Faber and Faber, 1971), p. 4.

26. Anne Sexton, Letter to Mrs. F. Peter Scigliano, 7 Feb. 1973, HRHRC.

27. Sharpe, p. 75. Frank Lentricchia reads the "continual self-sacrifice" section of Eliot's essay as being rooted in Eliot's own biography: Lloyds' Bank by day, jobbing writer/journalist at night, desperately trying to secure precious time for his own writing (p. 251).

28. By foregrounding Sweeney's Australian identity, Sexton playfully invokes the cultural fringe (the disparagement of Australian culture and identity) and thus implicitly challenges the kudos which Eliot is thought to represent. Her poem trumpets its Australian connections just as Eliot's discreetly, and with some disdain, buries its own. In his "Notes to *The Waste Land*" (explaining the reference to Mrs. Porter in line 199), Eliot delicately demurs: "I do not know the origin of the ballad from which these lines are taken: it was reported to me from Sydney, Australia." p. 46.

29. Letter, 28 Dec. 1972, HRHRC. Sexton's poem was rejected by the *Atlantic Monthly* and *Critical Quarterly.* In her submission letter to C. B. Cox (editor of the latter), Sexton wrote: "It is very different from my regular work and may not appeal to you with its many voices." Letter, 10 Jan. 1973, HRHRC.

30. *Anne Sexton: Selected Criticism,* ed. Diane Hume George (University of Illinois Press, 1988).

31. Sandra M. Gilbert, "On *The Death Notebooks,*" *Anne Sexton: The Artist and her Critics,* ed. J. D. McClatchy (Indiana University Press, 1978), p. 165.

32. J. D. McClatchy, "Anne Sexton: Somehow to Endure," McClatchy, p. 287.

33. Alvarez, p. 229.

34. *Brewer's Dictionary Of Phrase and Fable* (Cassell, 1990) has "la-di-da" as an adjective for affectation.

35. In "Dog-God's Wife Adopts a Monkey," discussed later, "madonna" is similarly written with a lower case initial.

36. See Michel Foucault, *The History of Sexuality, Volume One: An Introduction* (Peregrine, 1981) and Leigh Gilmore, *Autobiographics: A Feminist Theory of Women's Self-Representation* (Cornell University Press, 1994).

37. Claudia Roth Pierpont, "For Love and Money: An early version of Fitzgerald's Great American Novel is resurrected," *The New Yorker* (3 July 2000), p. 78. Pierpont examines the relationship between Eliot's use of the Trimalchio anecdote and F. Scott Fitzgerald's appropriation of the story in *The Great Gatsby* and of *Trimalchio* as a possible title. Fitzgerald sent a copy of his novel to Eliot, addressing it to the "'Greatest of Living Poets from his enthusiastic [sic] worshipper'" (p. 82).

38. *The Norton Anthology of Poetry* (4ᵗʰ edn.), ed. Margaret Ferguson et al (Norton, 1996), p. 1236, n. 9.

39. Sexton made extensive reference to the Sibyls and Sibylline leaves in poems (such as "May 5 1970") and interviews, explaining to Barbara Kevles that "the leaves talk to me every June." *The Paris Review Interviews: Women Writers at Work,* ed. George Plimpton (Random, 1998), p. 331. Sandra Gilbert and Susan Gubar use the story as a metaphor for the work of the woman artist, describing their own book as "an attempt at reconstructing the Sibyl's leaves, leaves which haunt us with the possibility that if we can piece together their fragments the parts will form a whole that tells the story of the career of a single woman artist." *The Madwoman in the Attic: The Woman Writer and the Nineteenth-Century Literary Imagination* (Yale University Press, 1984). p. 101.

40. Sylvia Plath, *The Bell Jar* (Faber and Faber, 1965).

41. As Freud suggests in "Character and Anal Erotism," "An invitation to a caress of the anal zone is still used today, as it was in ancient times, to express defiance or defiant scorn [. . .] an exposure of the buttocks represents a softening down of this spoken invitation into a gesture." *On Sexuality: Three Essays on the Theory of Sexuality and Other Works* (Pelican, 1977), p. 213.

42. Freud describes the relationship between faeces ("the gift"), money ("the connection between the complexes of interest in money and defecation [. . .] appear to be the most extensive of all") and relations of power ("its faeces are the infant's first gift, a part of his body which he will give up only on persuasion"). "Character and Anal Erotism," p. 213; "On Transformations of Instinct in Anal Erotism," *On Sexuality,* p. 299.

43. Patricia Meyer Spacks, "On *45 Mercy Street,*" McClatchy, p. 186.

44. Phillips, p. 16.

45. Jonathan Raban, ed. *Robert Lowell's Poems: A Selection* (Faber and Faber, 1974), p. 169.

46. Anne Sexton, "All God's Children Need Radios," Colburn, p. 28.

47. Hall, p. 137.

48. Ms. or Mrs. Dog is, of course, also a bitch. See Jacqueline Rose *The Haunting of Sylvia Plath* (Virago, 1991), p. 169 for a discussion of the application of the "bitch-goddess" epithet to Sylvia Plath.

49. Anne Sexton, *Selected Poems of Anne Sexton* (Houghton Mifflin, 1988).

50. Richard Davenport-Hines, *Auden* (Heinemann, 1995), pp. 215, 245. Auden was also fond of devising palindromes and, according to Charles Osborne, was particularly proud of "'T. Eliot, top bard, notes putrid tang emanating, is sad, I'd assign it a name: gnat dirt upset on drab pot toilet.'" *W. H. Auden: The Life of a Poet* (Eyre Methuen, 1980), p. 316.

51. Unpublished Manuscripts. HRHRC.

52. In a letter to a student, Sexton refers to herself as "'the me who is known for spilling her guts.'" See Alex Beam, "Anne Sexton's Awful Wish," *Double Take* (Summer 1999), p. 135.

53. John Berryman, *The Dream Songs* (Faber and Faber, 1990).

54. A metaphor, perhaps for the sound of the typewriter, and a pun on pocket book? That the sound recalls the retort of gun fire is probably no accident, given the recurrence of military metaphors for language in Sexton's work. The phrase is used in James Thurber's "The Secret Life of Walter Mitty." *The Thurber Carnival* (Penguin, 1965).

55. The analepsis recalls the opening lines from Eliot's "Burnt Norton": "Time present and time past / Are both perhaps present in time future / And time future contained in time past."

56. Stan Smith, *The Origins of Modernism: Eliot, Pound, Yeats and the Rhetorics of Renewal* (Harvester Wheatsheaf, 1994), p. 120.

57. Gilmore, p. 121.

Jo Gill (essay date spring 2004)

SOURCE: Gill, Jo. "Textual Confessions: Narcissism in Anne Sexton's Early Poetry." *Twentieth Century Literature* 50, no. 1 (spring 2004): 59-87.

[*In the following essay, Gill posits that although "authorial self-absorption verging on narcissism" is consistently associated with confessional poetry, Sexton's narcissistic tendencies should not be interpreted in this negative light. Instead, according to the critic, Sexton's self-reflexive tendencies can be understood as prefiguring the movement in postmodern poetry toward "sophisticated textual narcissism," in which the text, not the author, is described as narcissistic.*]

Confessional poetry, a mode that was prominent in the United States in the 1960s and early 70s, has, over time, come to be regarded as a regrettable, aberrant, and momentary spasm in the development of that nation's literature. It is habitually, if a little inaccurately, consigned to a specific and distant time and place: Robert Phillips, the author of the first and indeed only full-length account of the mode, situates it in "Post-Christian, post-Kennedy, post-Pill America" (xiii). Its chief impact is now understood as providing a foil against which to measure the sophistication and achievements of postconfessional writing—Language poetry, the New York school, and various other avant-garde and postmodern forms. As Alan Williamson suggests, "confessional poetry—almost from the moment that unfortunate term was coined—has been the whipping boy of half a dozen newer schools, New Surrealism, New Formalism, Language poetry" ("Stories" 51).

Marjorie Perloff defines the exciting "radical poetries" that dominate contemporary American poetry by distinguishing them from an earlier tradition of personal lyricism:

> The more radical poetries of the past few decades, whatever their particular differences, have come to reconceive the "opening of the field," not as an entrance into *authenticity* but, on the contrary, as a turn toward *artifice,* toward poetry as making or praxis rather than poetry as impassioned speech, as self-expression.
>
> ("Changing Face" 93)

Similarly, Michael Davidson characterizes the interests of current Language poetry by reference to its difference from the "expressive" poetry that preceded it:

> Language writing bases its analysis of authority not on the author's particular politics but in the verbal means by which any statement claims its status as truth. Moreover, by foregrounding the abstract features of the speech act rather than the authenticity of the expressive moment, the poet acknowledges the contingency of utterances in social interchange.
>
> (74)

Both Perloff and Davidson define postmodern poetry by reference to its other—confessional or self-expressive poetry. Yet paradoxically, as the argument below demonstrates, what fundamentally characterizes this other and thus gives definition to "radical poetries" is the same deeply embedded interest in "artifice," in "poetry as making or praxis," and in the "verbal means by which any statement claims its status as truth" as is thought to characterize postconfessional writing alone. "Authenticity," "artifice," "praxis," and "truth" are the crucial and contested terms here.

The implication that contemporary avant-garde poetry is "radical" while the confessional poetry that preceded it is reactionary and conservative itself merits scrutiny. In its own time confessional poetry was perceived to be a profoundly radical movement. It represented a startling departure from—and offered powerful and potentially fatal resistance to—the conventions of the high academic poetry that it succeeded, a literature that Irving Howe describes as "responsible and moderate. And tame" (qtd. in Gray 216). For A. Alvarez, one of the form's earliest champions and commentators, confessional or "extremist" (229) poetry had apocalyptic potential. Its function—indeed its responsibility—was to break the mould of what he termed "the accepted Academic-Modern style."

It is apparent from any survey of the criticism of confessional poetry that the mode is habitually and negatively associated with an authorial self-absorption verging on narcissism. Elizabeth Bruss, for example, refers to the "narcissistic indulgence of the confessional tradition" (18). Edward Lucie-Smith, writing in 1964 in *Critical Quarterly,* argues that in contemporary "personal" poetry "introversion seems to have triumphed over experiment. The poet gazes with obsessive narcissism at his own reflection in the mirror of art" (357). Alvarez, in his highly influential *Times Literary Supplement* essay "Beyond All This Fiddle," distinguishes Robert Lowell's *Life Studies* from the work of "vulgar" confessional poets, concluding in Lowell's defense that *Life Studies* "is left with something more sustaining than mere narcissism" (230). He also quotes, approvingly, Sylvia Plath's comment: "I think that personal experience shouldn't be a kind of shut box and a mirror-looking narcissistic experience. I believe it should be generally relevant to such things as Hiroshima and Dachau, and so on" (231).

Of the confessional poets of post-Second World War America, it has been said that none was "more consistently and uniformly confessional than Anne Sexton [. . .] her name has almost become identified with the genre" (Lerner 52). And it is Sexton, more than any of her peers, who has been pronounced guilty of narcissism. As Joyce Carol Oates explains: "Sexton has been criticized for the intensity of her preoccupations: always the self, the victimized, bullying, narcissistic self." Patricia Meyer Spacks condemns her "shrill narcissism" and "insistent mirroring" (188). Alan Williamson complains of the "later Sexton" that she has become "the uneasy narcissist, self-indulgent and sarcastic at once" ("Confession and Tragedy" 178), and Helen Vendler pointedly gives thanks for a rare volume in which the poet "turn[s] away from the morass of narcissism" (441). As Alicia Ostriker concludes, "Anne Sexton is the easiest poet in the world to condescend to. Critics get in line for the pleasure of filing her under N for Narcissist" ("That Story" 263).

It is the contention of this essay that narcissism, rather than exemplifying the difference between confessional and postconfessional forms of poetry, represents its potential convergence. By exploring the mythical and psychoanalytic roots of narcissism and examining recent readings of the term's place in contemporary literature and culture, it is possible to recuperate the adjective *narcissistic* and demonstrate its importance in apparently divergent poetic traditions. Narcissism is to be understood not as a limiting and inadvertent error peculiar to confessional poetry (and acute in the work of Anne Sexton) but as a sophisticated and productive strategy employed by confessional and avant-garde poetries alike in their negotiation of such shared preoccupations as language, subjectivity, representation, and referentiality.

What appears to be authorial self-absorption in Sexton's work may, then, be read and defended as a sophisticated *textual* narcissism of the kind delineated by Linda Hutcheon in *Narcissistic Narrative* and more typically identified with the "radical poetries" mentioned above. In Hutcheon's analysis, it is "the narrative text, and not the author, that is being described as narcissistic" (1). She concentrates on a writing that is textually rather than biographically "self-reflective, self-informing, self-reflexive, auto-referential, auto-representational" and that, above all, contemplates and interrogates its own "narrative and/or linguistic identity." Sexton's confessional poetry demands to be read in these terms. It foreshadows, in more fundamental ways than has been recognized, the markedly self-reflexive tendencies of more recent American poetry. This is not to assert that it represents a proto-postmodern rejection of authenticity, referentiality, or expression but rather to suggest that it is skeptical, knowing, and inquisitive about the status of these and about the processes by which they are established and understood.

Since Hutcheon's *Narcissistic Narrative* mainly concerns fiction, many of her examples and conclusions derive from a comparison of contemporary or postmodern novels with those of the dominant (that is, realist) tradition. Indeed, Hutcheon makes a point of distinguishing between poetry and fiction, arguing that, in this context, poetry is in advance of the novel: "Of all the literary genres, the novel is the one which has perhaps most resisted being 'rescued' from the myth of the instrumentality of language. Poetry escaped with the aid of the Symbolists, the New Critics, and others" (87). Further, she suggests that "whereas poetic language is now more or less accepted as autonomous and intransitive, fiction and narrative still suggest a transitive and referential use of words" (88). In both respects I would disagree with Hutcheon. Confession, unlike much other modern poetry, has not been entirely liberated from this "myth of the instrumentality of language." The language of the confessional text continues often to be read as "transitive and referential," as a truthful representation of the lived experience of the author. Confessional poetry, unlike other postmodern poetry, persists in being read as an expressive/realist mode, offering privileged and reliable insight into personal experience.

Yet Sexton's form of confession, like "narcissistic narrative," resists such readings. Her apparent self-absorption masks a knowing and theoretically astute textual engagement with the problematic processes of writing and representation. Her poetry is keenly aware—and indeed flaunts its awareness—that its truths are arbitrary and its authority disputable. Crucially, it is aware that its putative originality is displaced by a discursive and productive relationship between text and reader. Just as narcissistic narrative thematizes or mirrors its own processes of reception (Hutcheon, *Narcissistic* xvi), so too the confessional text takes as one of its subjects the complicity of its own audience in the generation of its meaning—in the "completion" of its truth (Foucault 66).

In *The Mirror and the Lamp*, M. H. Abrams distinguishes between expressive and mimetic theories of art. While conventionally, confessional poetry belongs to the expressive realm (it is the "internal made external" [22]), it is also, as I have suggested, possible and persuasive to read it as mimetic, as textually narcissistic, as mirroring its own aesthetic processes. Indeed, the image of the simultaneously luminous and reflective glass bowl that dominates Sexton's poem **"For John Who Begs Me Not to Enquire Further"** (hereafter **"For John"**) is important in encapsulating both of these possibilities—a point to which I will return. With this in mind, one might argue that Sexton's writing looks both inside and outside simultaneously and to that extent is always doubled, split, or fragmented in its perspective.

The early poems discussed here—**"An Obsessive Combination of Ontological Inscape, Trickery and Love"** (hereafter **"An Obsessive Combination"**) and **"The Double Image,"** both written in 1958, and **"For John,"** written in 1959, are narcissistic in the sense that they are intrigued by and reflect on how, exactly, their meanings are realized and shared.[1] They seek to reach and convey a better understanding not of the experience ostensibly at the source of each but of the way in which they themselves work as confession. Mirrors and other reflective surfaces (windows, glass bowls, portraits) are fundamental to this enquiry, either covertly—as in the case of **"An Obsessive Combination,"** where mirroring processes are "structuralized, internalized" (Hutcheon, *Narcissistic* 7)—or overtly—as in **"For John,"** where they are "explicitly thematized." The textual narcissism that we see here forms the foundation of Sexton's exploration of the dynamics of confession in later poems such as those in the "Letters to Dr. Y" sequence (1960-70), with their sophisticated analyses of their own linguistic processes, and in **"Talking to Sheep"** (1974), which displays an acute consciousness and condemnation of its own audience. Throughout, narcissism is presented as both strategy (reflection as process) and object (the reflection as material subject of enquiry) and, while generous in prolifer-ating meanings, is also always shown to be susceptible to error, to be potentially distorting and distorted.

The cultural origins of the concept of narcissism are to be found in the story of Echo and Narcissus from Ovid's *Metamorphoses*. Narcissus is a beautiful and proud youth, the object of many observers' unrequited desires—including those of the nymph Echo, who "can-not stay silent when another person speaks, but yet has not learned to speak first herself" (83). Narcissus spurns Echo's advances and in despair she retreats to the woods and caves, wasting away until only her voice remains. As punishment for his pride Narcissus is condemned to experience the same frustrated desire, and falls in love with his own reflected image in a pool. He is admon-ished: "the thing you are seeing does not exist: only turn aside and you will lose what you love" (85). Real-izing that, like Echo, he will never possess the object of his love, he too wastes away and dies, leaving in place of his body a circle of flowers.

The myth of Narcissus is important to Sexton's poetics in several respects. It offers a framework within which to develop themes of self-love and desire, it offers fruit-ful metaphors such as those of the mirror and the cave, and it lends the structural and linguistic potential of the echo. As James Goodwin has argued, in the context of the origins of autobiography,

> the figure of Narcissus represents complexes—or, in other words, structures of great intellectual and affec-tive force—that are indicative of the functions and consequences of self-knowledge at different stages in our cultural history.
>
> (69)

The story of Narcissus is also of profound significance in Sigmund Freud's account of human psychology and is instrumental to his recognition and definition of the superego. In "On Narcissism" Freud identifies a universal "primary and normal narcissism" (66)—an early and necessary stage of self-love that must be transcended, the other replacing the ego as love object, if the subject is to assume his or her proper place in relation to parents, to subsequent sex objects, and to the wider world.

In the context of Sexton's exploration and defense of narcissism, Freud's argument is influential because he asserts—in contradiction to the opinions of his predeces-sors and peers—that narcissism is common and "nor-mal," that there is contiguity between "healthy and neurotic subjects" (73). The belief that narcissism is a universal and shared condition dominates Sexton's poem **"For John."** It specifically informs the I/you dialogue that is sustained throughout and insists on the reciprocity of the subject's and implied reader's experi-ence. Freud's analysis is valuable too because it describes in psychoanalytic terms the tendency to turn inward, "away from the external world" (66) that, although apparently characteristic of confessionalism, is at issue in Sexton's poetry. It also traces the necessary route outward by which "our mental life [. . .] pass[es] beyond the limits of narcissism" and forms an attach-ment to objects (78). In addition, "On Narcissism" foregrounds the importance in psychological terms of observing and "being observed" (91). It recognizes—and this is crucial to an understanding of confessional writing and its reception—the compelling attraction of someone else's narcissism: "it seems very evident that another person's narcissism has a great attraction for those who have renounced part of their own narcissism and are in search of object-love" (82-83).

In Freud, then, we find what might be described as the first of several psychoanalytic defenses of narcissism—a defense that Jacques Lacan was later to take up.[2] For Lacan, narcissism—the gaze in the mirror—initiates the infant child's realization and confirmation of his or her identity. The mirror is vital to the two finally inextricable processes of finding and naming (or textualizing) the self. In Lacanian terms, it is by means of the mirror stage ("le stade du miroir" [2]) that the aspiring subject leaves the realm of the imaginary and gains access to the symbolic order of language—a journey that is invoked in Sexton's poem **"The Double Image,"** discussed later.

Richard Sennett and Christopher Lasch, writing about contemporary American culture in the 1970s—the period that had, contentiously, been labeled the "me decade" (Lasch 238)—study the growth and dominance of narcissistic "personality traits" in the "prevailing social conditions" (239). Sennett identifies a problem with the erosion of boundaries between public and private life, between external and internal worlds—a concern that is also voiced in Sexton's writing. He argues that "cultural forces [. . .] have produced this narcissistic self-absorption" (333) and insists that it is the "social environment" (12) that is at fault and must be changed. Lasch discusses narcissism—the extreme consequence and end of modern society's "logic of individualism" (xv)—in the context of changes in American domestic, cultural, and political life. Narcis-sism, he suggests, represents a reaction to and retreat from a general loss of faith in contemporary society, in the lessons of the past, and in the promise of the future (xvi-xvii). For Lasch, it is a limiting, impoverished (xviii) stance, one that exemplifies the individual's in-ability to "make connection with the world" (240).

For Sexton, however, as in Freud and Lacan, narcissism is broader, more complex, and finally more productive. Paradoxically, the self-disclosure in her work is made always with a view to its reader; while ostensibly focusing inward, it also looks outward and turns away from the self. Crucially, Sexton's poetry is predicated on restoring the "connection with the world" that Lasch sees as absent in narcissism (whereas Freud, as Jeffrey Berman explains, sees narcissism as precisely engendering a "relationship between the self and the object world" [10]) and on flamboyantly laying bare the processes by which this connection is established. This communicative impulse has tended to be lost in many readings of what narcissism signifies.

In Sexton's **"An Obsessive Combination," "The Double Image,"** and **"For John,"** the I can only be comprehended, the self only known, by placing itself in conjunction with an other. The I alone is not self-sufficient and cannot be expressed without a you. Thus all three poems are predicated on a persistent and sustaining dialogue. In this context, a narcissistic perspective denotes not a solipsistic devotion to the self but recognition that the self can only be perceived as part of a larger social context, as one among many. Narcissism here is an outward-looking gesture or process representing not stasis (Lasch's "diminishing expectations" [8]) but change, not silence (Plath's "shut box") but dialogue and communication—it engages the Echo at the heart of Ovid's tale.[3]

The seeds of this interest in the fertile and discursive possibilities of narcissism—understood as a purposive textual strategy rather than as a symptom of debilitating self-absorption—are apparent in one of Sexton's earliest and uncollected poems. **"An Obsessive Combination of Ontological Inscape, Trickery and Love"** was drafted in 1958 and first published in *Voices: A Journal of Poetry* in 1959. The poem is striking for the way in which it anticipates, and makes explicit, concerns that are developed subsequently in her writing. For example, we see here the roots of a sustained interest in the function and fallibility of language, expressed later in poems such as **"Is It True?"** and **"Hurry up Please It's Time"** (1972?) and throughout the posthumous volume *The Awful Rowing toward God* (1975). **"An Obsessive Combination,"** although described by Diane Wood Middlebrook as "an awkward little exercise" (124), is paradigmatic of Sexton's poetics in its determined and self-conscious exploration of its own linguistic and representational status.

"An Obsessive Combination" is narcissistic in the sense that in it "process [is] made visible" (Hutcheon, *Narcissistic* 6). It exemplifies what Hutcheon defines as a characteristically postmodern interest in "*how* art is created, not just in *what* is created" (8). Arguably, of course, such self-consciousness has a long literary history. For Hutcheon, however (and Sexton's writing, I would contend, sustains this reading), "the more modern textual self-preoccupation differs mostly in its explicitness, its intensity, and its own critical self-awareness,"

and this is a consequence of a post-Saussurian "change in the concept of language" (18).

To look first at the title of the poem, the adjective "obsessive" seems to lay itself open to typical accusations of confessional compulsion and self-absorption. However, it transpires that the obsession is not with the self but with writing, with the linguistic strategies by which meaning is generated and shared. "Ontological" shifts attention away from direct, lived, "raw" (to use Robert Lowell's term [qtd. in Hamilton 277]) experience to a more abstract, impersonal consideration of the condition of being. "Combination," too, has considerable resonance in the context of Sexton's poetics, signifying the combination or meeting of minds, the discursive relationship between speaker and reader required for the confession successfully to be created and disseminated.

Gerard Manley Hopkins's notion of "inscape" is the lodestone of the poem and plays a key role in disclosing Sexton's larger poetics. It is explained by *Webster's Third New International Dictionary* as

> Inward significant character or quality belonging uniquely to objects or events in nature and human experience esp. as perceived by the blended observation and introspection of the poet and in turn embodied in patterns of such specific poetic elements as imagery, rhythm, rhyme, assonance, sound symbolism, and allusion.

Clearly, "inscape" suggests the complex and seemingly contradictory process, subsequently explored in **"For John,"** by which looking out and in ("blend[ing] observation and introspection") become synonymous. It connotes the way in which meaning is realized—in the dual and seemingly contradictory sense of being made apparent ("embodied in patterns") and being received. Hopkins writes:

> *oftening, over-and-overing, aftering* of the inscape must take place in order to detach it to the mind and in this light poetry is speech which afters and oftens its inscape, speech couched in a repeating figure.
>
> (qtd. in Gardner xxiin2; Hopkins's emphasis)[4]

The inner essence is projected outward by the same kinds of linguistic and syntactical patterning, repetition, and palindromic construction as we see in Sexton's poem.

In one of the Crawshaw Lectures that Sexton delivered at Colgate University in 1972 she describes this projection: "one writes of oneself [. . .] in order to invite *in*" and "to find the way, *out* through experience" (Lecture 9, p. 1; my emphases). Thus **"An Obsessive Combination,"** like many later poems, takes as its subject the liminal space between I and you, speaker and reader, exposing and exploring the boundaries between self and object world. It traces the process by which the self and its metonyms (here imagination and ideas) manifest themselves in and connect with the exterior—and this is primarily, indeed unavoidably, through language.

"An Obsessive Combination" achieves its effects by the "generative [word] play" and "linguistic self-consciousness" identified by Hutcheon as characteristic of narcissistic narrative (*Narcissistic* 120, 118). Moreover, in its "performative" (Perloff, *Dance* 176) and "playful" (Hutcheon, *Politics* 34) aspects, the poem may be said to display some of the defining features of postmodernist writing. Hutcheon sees as typical of such texts linguistic features such as acrostics, anagrams, cryptograms, and puns (*Narcissistic* 119) that serve to "call the reader's attention to the fact that the text is made up of words, words which are delightfully fertile in creative suggestiveness" (101). The title of the poem is a near acrostic, containing the word *coital* (perhaps suggestive of self and other joining together).[5] The text itself features numerous puns, homonyms, and anagrams ("tiers," "tries," "rites," "right," "routes" [4]). It also incorporates the palindrome "RATS / . . . STAR," a supreme example of narcissistic wordplay, one that appears repeatedly in later poems: **"With Mercy for the Greedy"** (1960) concludes with a despairing and self-reflexive definition of poetry as "the tongue's wrangle, / the world's pottage, the rat's star" (63), and **"Hurry up Please It's Time"** features a sustained dialogue between the paired voices of "God" and "Ms. Dog" (384-95).

The opening lines of **"An Obsessive Combination"**— "Busy, with an idea for a code, I write / signals hurrying from left to right" (4)—confirm the self-reflexivity of the title. "Busy" suggests not only that the speaker is preoccupied ("obsessive"?) but also that this is important work (business). The fascination here is not with personal experience, but with thoughts, ideas, semantic and epistemological sequences—with an "idea for a code" in the first line and with "reasons" in line 4.

That the poem is "a code" and that writing "signals" confirm its interest in the hermeneutic process by which words emerge and are deciphered. The metaphor of the "code" indicates that the confessional text might obscure (as we will see in a moment, I use the verb advisedly) rather than, as is commonly thought, lay bare its secrets. The line break after "write" suggests, and the rest of the poem confirms, that the "signals" are autonomous; the poet writes, yet in what seems to be a distinct movement, it is the "signals" that hurry across the page. Language in this poem, as elsewhere in Sexton, pre-exists and dominates the subject, constructs rather than reflects experience. As Hutcheon argues: "in literature, words create worlds; they are not necessarily counters, however adequate, to any extraliterary reality. In that very fact lies their aesthetic validity and their ontological status" (*Narcissistic* 102-03).

"An Obsessive Combination" examines this complex and—as it transpires—amazing process:

> [. . .] I write
> signals hurrying from left to right,
> or right to left, by obscure routes,
> for my own reasons; taking a word like "writes"
> down tiers of tries until its secret rites
> make sense.

The image of the physical and orderly progression of language across the page ("left to right") offers a metaphor for the way the act of confession is, typically, thought to put things "right" in the therapeutic sense. However, as this poem demonstrates, it is not the simple act of release or the tapping of the wellspring of inner compulsion that makes things right but rather the textualization, the act of writing. Moreover, as the addendum in the next line ("or right to left") indicates, the act of confession may compound rather than resolve problems. It may not offer the "expressive-purgative release" that Alicia Ostriker (*Stealing* 126), for example, expects of the mode but may instead complicate, confuse, and ultimately make sinister.

The recourse to the "obscure routes" suggests that understanding may emerge from the dark (from the private, the unseemly, the sinister), which is thereby recuperated as a viable source for poetry. In this respect, the poem anticipates **"For John,"** where the inauspicious "narrow diary of my mind" (34) produces and refracts something of dazzling and broad significance ("something outside of myself"). It also paves the way for a number of later poems, including **"With Mercy for the Greedy"** and **"Hurry up Please It's Time,"** in which equally abject or occluded experience is "amazingly"—to speaker and reader alike—transformed into radiant meaning.

In **"An Obsessive Combination"** language, perception, and meaning are constantly in flux, multiplying ceaselessly:

> [. . .] taking a word like "writes"
> down tiers of tries until its secret rites
> make sense; or until, suddenly, RATS
> can amazingly and funnily become STAR
> and right to left that small star
> is mine, for my own liking, to stare
> its five lucky pins inside out [. . .]

Authorial responsibility is denied, hence the passivity of voice and the astonishment at these linguistic and ontological transformations. Certainly Sexton does not go as far as later Language poets in rupturing the bond between signifier and signified: "RATS" and "STAR," while locked in a palindromic relationship, do also connote distinct and opposing referents that are metaphorically suggestive within the context of the poem. However, she places this bond under critical scrutiny (the transposition of a letter or phoneme can drastically alter the signification of a word). Nothing, Sexton insists, can be made into something, and this by a seemingly random succession of semantic shifts.

The enthusiastic explanatory rhetoric of the second half of the poem, with its bright adverbs ("suddenly," "amazingly," and "funnily") and its gleeful aside ("for my own liking"), gives way, in the final clause, to a more skeptical and resigned tone:

> and right to left that small star
> is mine, for my own liking, to stare
> its five lucky pins inside out, to store
> forever kindly, as if it were a star
> I touched and a miracle I really wrote.

The tentative "as if" concedes that words—and the confessional text—may not deliver what is expected of them, that language may fail. The sudden shift at the end from the present tense to the conditional and qualified suggests that the epiphany that the poem seems to promise is a transient thing. **"An Obsessive Combination"** warns that "RATS" may become "STAR" not by a miracle but by semantic "trickery." Thus we are returned to the textuality of the confessional poem, to its status as "autonomous and intransitive object" (Hutcheon, *Narcissistic* 88). **"An Obsessive Combination,"** one of Sexton's earliest poems, is paradigmatic of much of her later writing in that it is unable or unwilling to proffer closure. It refuses the temptations of an easy and satisfying conclusion, finishing instead on an open-ended and conditional note ("as if it were"). In Hutcheon's terms—like many postmodern texts—it "admits its own provisionality" (*Poetics* 13).

Similar concerns inform **"The Double Image,"** a complex and profoundly artful poem that contemplates the relationships between three generations of women: the speaker, her dying mother, and her infant daughter. The defining motifs are the fluctuating mental and physical sickness of the speaker and her mother, the patterns of absence and presence that define the relationships, and the dual portraits (or double images) that the mother commissions of herself and the speaker and hangs "on opposite walls" (40). **"The Double Image"** may be read in terms of Lacan's understanding of narcissism—as an examination of the way in which we achieve subjectivity by perceiving and identifying ourselves in relation to others. For Lacan, as we have seen, the mirror (or the "mirror stage" [2]) is fundamental to this process. What is interesting in **"The Double Image,"** though, is that beneath the "transitive and referential" (Hutcheon, *Narcissistic* 88) surface of the poem—the narrative of loss and recovery that ostensibly inspires, shapes, and validates it—lies a compelling, effective examination of its own processes of production and reception.

"The Double Image" is not, then, only or primarily about the relationships and experiences it describes. It is about its own status as confession. It is a metapoem that flaunts its own mirroring processes (Hutcheon, *Narcissistic* 20) in order to draw attention to its constructed, contingent, and finally illusory nature. The poem's title gestures toward this doubleness and signals its larger achievement: its self-reflexive—and arguably postmodern—undermining of the mimetic strategies apparently at its thematic and structural core. For what the poem describes and finally exemplifies is a succession of doublings or reflections mimicking only each other (the dual portraits of the speaker and mother, the image of the speaker looking at her own painted image and drafting her own textual portrait). Speaker and reader alike are locked in the endless *mise en abyme* characteristic of postmodernism and typical of narcissistic narrative, a proliferation of images in infinite regress offering no necessary access to extratextual reality.

"The Double Image" is intensely catoptric. The arrangement of the poem's seven sections represents a near-perfect symmetry of action. In the first three sections we see the daughter and then the speaker leaving home, followed by the central (fourth) section, which denotes a liminal moment of uncertainty. The closing three sections complete the symmetry, first the speaker and then the daughter returning to the family home.

The multiple repetitions within the poem ("Too late, / too late" in section 2 [36], "as if," "as if," "as if" in section 3 [38]) echo, mimicking the proliferation of reflections that the poem describes. The emphatic if irregular end rhymes work in a similar way and reflect the claustrophobia of the situation with all three participants seemingly trapped in a hall of mirrors. There is a constant swaying, forward and backward movement within the poem—not only of action (the symmetrical pattern of departure and return mentioned above) but of attention—such that the reader, like the speaker, is forced to look from one mirrored image to another and then back again. In this way the text brings "to readers' attention their central and enabling role" in the production of meaning (Hutcheon, *Narcissistic* xii).

The poem emphasizes the symmetry of the double images and their implicit polarity. The paintings resemble each other—both women's smiles are described as being held "in place" (37, 40)—but they also invert each other: the speaker's portrait is illuminated by the "north light" (40) while the mother's is lit from the "south." (As Lacan points out, such inversion is characteristic of the mirror stage [2]). Sexton's speaker addresses both the mirror image of the mother and the reflection of the self, thus confirming the identity and inversion that unite them: "my mocking mirror, my overthrown / love, my first image" (40). That the mirror is "mocking" indicates that it offers an idealized image of what the speaker should be, reinforcing her inadequacy. We are reminded of the plight of the humiliated Echo in Ovid's tale and of Narcissus too, who perceives a "mocking mirror" and experiences the simultaneous enticement and rejection of his "first image."[6]

The closing stanza further elaborates the double image of the title. The speaker finally acknowledges to her daughter that "I needed you" (41), naming the bond between the "I" and "you" suggested in the opening lines. It is now the daughter, rather than the mother, who has bestowed (gender) identity on the speaker. The mother's failure is made good by the daughter:

> I, who was never quite sure
> about being a girl, needed another
> life, another image to remind me.

> (41-42)

The "image" is the daughter, produced by the speaker in order to confirm her own identity, just as the speaker's mother created first the speaker and then an image (portrait) of her in a vain attempt to cling to life. Hence the speaker's final admission: "And this was my worst guilt; you could not cure / nor soothe it. I made you to find me" (42). This is a compelling conclusion. However, the real interest lies in the confession not that the speaker made the daughter (biologically) but that she has constructed the daughter in the poem (textually). These final lines confirm the poem as textually narcissistic in Hutcheon's terms. For the ultimate referent of "double image" is the poem itself—the strategies it employs in its construction and its aestheticization of relationships, experience, subjectivity. The "worst guilt" pertains to the speaker's fabrication and manipulation of the mother/daughter relationship in order to construct this very poem and thereby to create or found (and emphatically not to reflect) her singular identity as poet: "to find me."

Narcissistic narrative, as we have seen, is a writing that is concerned with the role of the reader. Sexton's early poem **"For John"** is noteworthy for the way in which it exemplifies this concern, addressing in particular the discursive relationship between speaker and reader, penitent and confessor. There is a critical consensus about the importance of the poem as an expression of Sexton's poetics. Middlebrook describes **"For John"** as a "defense [. . .] of the whole genre of poetry that would soon be labeled 'confessional'" (100). Diana Hume George declares that "the autobiographical *I* becomes a spokesperson for the poetic and personal authenticity of the confessional stance" (101). Caroline King Barnard Hall argues that **"For John"** should be read as "a credo [. . .] for Sexton's entire oeuvre" (14). I agree that **"For John"** marks out Sexton's position as a poet and her conception of and aspirations for the confessional mode. However, I would argue that its

importance lies not in its defense of what confession reveals but in its exemplification of how it functions.

The images of the cracked mirror and glass bowl in **"For John,"** in addition to evoking Narcissus's pool, signify primary subjective narcissism ("the cracked mirror / or my own selfish death" [34]) and may be read as metaphors for the creative process (I, the poet, look to myself and show you a reflection of what I see) in all its multifaceted complexity. Moreover, in this particular poem, the reflective glass instigates the calling in of the reader and the exchange of responsibility between reader and writer in the act of perceiving and interpreting confessional meaning. The poem is predicated on the paradox that in order truthfully to tell us about telling the truth, the speaker must weave a "complicated lie" (35), which may itself be a lie—a *mise en abyme* of the kind that, as we've seen, characterizes narcissistic narrative. The poem's manipulation of successive shifting mirror images confirms the potential multiplicity and unreliability of self-representation. In place of a coherent subject, faithfully mirrored, we see only fleeting, oblique glimpses of a fragmentary reflection.

"For John" achieves its effects, in part, by anticipating—indeed parodying—orthodox expectations of its speaker's narcissism. It parades its insistent first-person voice, its emphatically domestic concerns ("the commonplaces" [34], the "kitchen" [35]), and its protagonist's prolonged self-scrutiny in the mirror. The poem resounds with images for the self, for self-admiration, idealization, and subjective pleasure. Lines end with terms of self-absorption ("mind," "mirror," "me," "myself," "private" [34]) that emphasize the narcissistic impulse at play. Yet the text's flamboyant narcissism is beguiling, masking the absence or dissipation of the self. Marjorie Perloff argues of postmodern poetry that "the Romantic or Modernist cult of personality has given way to what the new poets call 'the dispersal of the speaking subject,' the denial of the unitary, authoritative ego" (*Dance* x). However, I would contend that this fracturing or "dispersal of the speaking subject" is not unique to postmodern poetry and is carefully mapped in Sexton's poem. The fragmentation of the "unitary authoritarian ego" is represented in multiple and proliferating images of fracture and dissipation reminiscent of those in **"The Double Image"** and owing something to the characteristics of narcissism (a "fragmented" sense of self, and "identity diffusion" [Berman 25]) as perceived from certain psychoanalytic perspectives.

The self-assertion of the opening lines of **"For John"** is countermanded by a recognition of others ("you," "your," "something outside," "someone," "anyone" [34-35]). The characteristic confessional speaker does not emerge until line 5 and is swiftly counterbalanced by the "you"—the explicit (John) or implicit (the unspecified reader) addressee whose presence, although always latent in and instrumental to confession, is here unusually rendered visible within the text. The back and forth movement anticipates the exchanges between speaker, mother, and daughter in **"The Double Image"** (which appears immediately after **"For John"** in *To Bedlam and Part Way Back,* although it was written one year earlier). Further, the speaker and John/any reader share a mutually vengeful and predatory fate akin to that of Narcissus and Echo. Neither is able to satisfy his or her desire, both have reached the limits of identification, and neither can penetrate the boundary between self and other. This is the ever-present risk for confession: that it will not find an auditor and achieve realization.[7]

The poem addresses the critical hostility that seems to sustain many readings of confessional poetry. Its specific origins, arguably, lie in Sexton's response to a letter she had received from her mentor, the poet and teacher John Holmes, in which he expressed reservations about what he perceived to be the narrow narcissism of her work. Latent in the I/you exchange in the poem is a dialogue between Sexton (the implied author) and Holmes (the implied addressee). In identifying this letter as a possible source I do not, however, propose that it explains, or concede that it limits, the poem's potential meanings. (As Bonnie Costello argues of the overdetermination of sources in Marianne Moore's work: "This multiplicity of sources is quite different from the multiplicity of references" [6].) What I would contend is that Holmes's letter may be taken as a catalyst for the poem's self-conscious examination of larger confessional processes.

Scrutiny of the letter to Sexton, dated 8 February 1959, reveals the extent to which **"For John"** repudiates confessional poetry's detractors.[8] Her privileging of the "selfish death" may be read as a defiant challenge to Holmes's view that she should efface her "hospital and psychiatric experiences [which seem] to me very selfish." Holmes's letter accuses her of "forcing others to listen" and complains that, in her work, there is "nothing given the listeners, nothing that teaches them or helps them." He adjures her to "do something else, outside yourself." Sexton's speaker counters that she does teach something, that she offers a "lesson" (34) that is "worth learning." This is "something special" (35) and defiantly "something outside of myself."

"For John" insists that there is "sense" and "order" in even the most private and seemingly abject of experiences:

> Not that it was beautiful,
> but that, in the end, there was
> a certain sense of order there;
> something worth learning
> in that narrow diary of my mind,
> in the commonplaces of the asylum
>
> (34)

By opening the poem with the emphatic "Not," Sexton confronts from the outset the criticisms she anticipates and proceeds to refute them with her arguments in the subsequent two lines. The syntax of the first line refuses the chief motivation ascribed to Narcissus—that is, love of his own beauty. Sexton suggests that it is "not" the product (the "beautiful" object) that is worthy of attention but the process—the ordering, the reading, the making of "sense." The lesson that can be learned by scrutiny of the "narrow diary of my mind" and "the commonplaces of the asylum" is valuable because it is a lesson that can be shared. "Commonplaces" indicates the potential common ground that unites speaker and reader. Moreover, in its pun on commonplace book, it invokes the textualization, including that carried out in this very poem, by which the "lesson" will be delivered.

More generally, the opening lines of the poem foreground the hermeneutic processes of reading and evaluation by which meaning will be constructed. The opening line postulates a subject "it" that is never fully defined, remaining ambiguous throughout the poem in spite of the speaker's repeated efforts to identify and represent it. The reader's commitment and interpretative powers are first solicited and then held at bay by this persistent ontological uncertainty. He or she shares the speaker's uncertainty and (frustrated) desire for resolution. The poem thematizes this, inscribing within itself an interpretative place for the reader. In Hutcheon's terms, it is narcissistic in that "it encourages an active personal response to itself *and* encourages a space for that response within itself" (*Narcissistic* 141).

Fundamental to Sexton's representation in **"For John"** of how meaning is realized and dispersed are the metaphors of mirrors—first the "cracked mirror" (34) of line 7 and later the inverted glass bowl (line 18). The mirrors figure the text's own processes of contemplation and reflection. The poem concedes that narcissism is a frustrating and limiting practice, as the confessing subject's initial self-scrutiny in the mirror offers no reassurance: "my own selfish death / outstared me." She seeks in the mirror confirmation of her identity, yet is met with a disfigured reflection that is inverted; the living subject looks for signs of life and finds only evidence of death. We recall **"The Double Image"** and the distortion of the two women's images represented by the dual portraits. For Lacan, looking in the mirror is a progressive moment—a necessary step toward successful assumption of the "function as subject" (2)—but in this poem, there is no such progression. There is no pleasure in this literal and metaphorical introspection (nor, by extension, in the act of confession), and considerable psychic risk.

Here and subsequently, with the introduction of the metaphor of the glass bowl, the speaker gazes at the mirror expecting to see only her own self given back to her, but what she sees exceeds or "outstare[s]" her. In addition to her own face she sees reflected the larger context that surrounds or frames her; her context is thus perceived through and beyond the glass. Equally, when the reader contemplates the mirror (reads the poem), she thinks that she is looking at someone ("something") else. What she sees—alongside the putative object of her gaze—is herself in the process of observing. The shift is reified by the shift in line 11 from the address to an implied auditor to a specific addressee ("you" the reader). Thus in attending to this poem the reader recognizes her own participation in the discourse. As we saw with the indeterminate "it" of the poem's opening line, **"For John"** inscribes a place for the reader within the body of the text, rendering the public significance of what had once seemed merely private.

"For John" demonstrates that the narcissistic gesture becomes productive and meaningful only when it is shared. The "selfish" gaze must—if it is to mean anything "outside of myself"—be subject to dispersal and dissemination. The fragmentation of the cracked mirror is instrumental in bringing this shift to multiplicity about. The mirror in and of the text offers no clear image, no direct mimesis, but only multiple, scattered—though suggestive—shards. A similar process is figured in the lucky star in **"An Obsessive Combination"** that shines its "inside out." It is only by refraction that it externalizes its meaning. The language of Sexton's poetry, then, is multiplicitous, elusive; it functions less as a unifying mirror than as a prism, splitting and projecting fractured and elliptical images of its subject.

Consider the image in **"For John"** of the inverted glass bowl:

> I tapped my own head;
> it was glass, an inverted bowl.
> It is a small thing
> to rage in your own bowl.
>
> (34)

The inverted bowl, while sharing the mimetic properties of a mirror, is simultaneously transparent. It has the potential to contain and to reveal, to reflect and refract. The image signifies the potential entrapment and vulnerability of the subject (Sylvia Plath's *The Bell Jar* is an obvious palimpsest).[9] It discloses whatever lies within it and permits the observer to see all sides of the object, to gain a complete impression.[10] It also displays its own external properties, its hermetic identity. Revealing both its inside and its outside, it stands as a metaphor for the confessional poem and the larger narcissistic process by which the subject reaches a reconciliation with the object world. That the speaker "tapped" her "own head" confirms the potential contiguity of self and other and the fluidity of the boundaries between the private and the public. For "tapped" signifies both the process of

siphoning insights from inside the head and the act of beating out a pattern (a poem?) on the outside for the edification of others. The speaker may tap—make a sound—either to initiate a dialogue or cause an echo.[11] The image insinuates the indivisibility of subject and discourse, product and process.

The inverted bowl, like the earlier cracked mirror, gives back fragmented images (the awkward bowl's "cracked stars shining" [34] sustain the original disfigurement in and of the cracked mirror). As Jonathan Miller points out: "in contrast to a plain or flat surface, which faithfully reproduces the proportions of whatever it reflects, a curved surface systematically disfigures it" (43). As an image of the poem itself, the bowl suggests the confessional text's own distortions and unreliability. Sexton's mirrors are always imperfect, crazed, curved, oblique, or, as in **"The Double Image,"** set directly opposite another mirror so that all one sees is an endless, imprisoning cascade of reflections that allows no space for the growth and development of the subject. Self-reflection is not what it might seem, and gives back an image that is attenuated, fractured, separated, and dispersed.

Mimesis is to be treated warily; there is no such thing as direct, unproblematic reflection. The act of mirroring, we find, is fraught with error and uncertainty. It is both multiplicitous and duplicitous. We should note that Abrams's generally positive account of poetic mimesis is only able to refer to its subject in a sequence of synonyms that connote distortion and imprecision: "counterfeiting," "feigning" (11). Thus the representation of subjectivity or experience that confessional poetry (specifically **"For John"**) offers is to be understood as a copy of or approximation to the original, but not as identical with it. What confessional writing does is contemplate and expose the complexity of identity, the absence or elusiveness (even in this apparently self-expressive mode) of a unified, homogenous subject.[12]

Sexton's poem presents a fundamentally narcissistic moment—a moment of crisis in the subject's sense of self and her relation to the external world. This is laid bare for contemplation by both speaker and reader. It is the potential communality of experience here, the fact that narcissism forms "a place in the regular course of human sexual development" (Freud 65), that forms the heart of Sexton's argument and aesthetic defense. We all go through this process, and the poem reminds us of this, inviting us to revisit it:

> This is something I would never find
> in a lovelier place, my dear,
> although your fear is anyone's fear,
> like an invisible veil between us all . . .
> and sometimes in private,

my kitchen, your kitchen,
my face, your face.

(35)

The implicit I/you dialogue that has sustained the whole poem is here rendered more generally inclusive. "Anyone" invokes Everyman and registers the broadening of the speaker's attention from a specific reader (John) to a wider group; "us all" encapsulates both speaker and multiple readers. In the simultaneously transparent and reflective bowl, we look for self and find other, we look for other and find self. What we see is both "my kitchen" and "your kitchen," "my face" and "your face." Narcissism is revealed to be a public and discursive rather than private and hermetic gesture. The personal preoccupation ("my") gives way to public responsibility ("your"). The quiet, balanced, closing lines of the poem, with their symmetry and soft diminuendo, mimic the gentle sound of an echo tailing off:

and sometimes in private,
my kitchen, your kitchen,
my face, your face.

John Holmes's concluding message to Sexton in the letter that arguably inspired the poem specifically alludes to Ovid's tale. Holmes's anxiety about Sexton's writing is galvanized by his fear that Sexton's fate may repeat that of Narcissus: "You must liberate your gift, and let it create new life, not gaze always hypnotized on death and the wreck of nerves" (a comment that arguably provides a source for Sexton's line "my own selfish death / outstared me"). **"For John"** ultimately answers confessionalism's critics by expressly embracing the very process against which they warn. It not only explains, it shows. Sexton demonstrates that narcissism does not necessarily mean introspective stasis. As in Ovid's tale, where Narcissus's legacy is "a flower with a circle of white petals round a yellow centre" (87), Sexton's speaker's self-absorption is productive. It is transformed into "something outside of myself," something that at least "ought" to be "special / for someone."

It is illuminating to consider **"For John"** in relation to a prominent postconfessional poem that takes up the question of self-mirroring: John Ashbery's "Self-Portrait in a Convex Mirror." Ashbery's poem contemplates Parmigianino's painting of that name and, in particular, the resonance of the convex mirror that is both the source (the artist paints from his reflection in it) and product of the painting (the finished portrait is painted on a convex wooden form that replicates that of the mirror). Ashbery, too, acknowledges that such a self-portrait is distorted and distorting, indeed "that you could be fooled for a moment / Before you realize the reflection / Isn't yours" (194). In Ashbery's poem, as in

Sexton's, the convex mirror privileges surface over depth. For Ashbery "everything is surface. The surface is what's there" (190). In both poems the public display of the curved mirror emphasizes the outward-looking, social, discursive nature of what had previously been understood as a purely introspective narcissism. The imperative in each is not merely to gaze upon the self ("It is a small thing / to rage in your own bowl") but to share that which is found with the reader. Sexton wields her glass bowl so that its "cracked stars" shine forth, disseminating meaning. Ashbery's convex mirror similarly reaches outward. It is refracted in the "saw-toothed fragments" (191) of a puddle and finally reverberates more widely throughout "the city" in "the gibbous / Mirrored eye of an insect" (204) which, like Sexton's crazed mirror, functions as a prism.

As we saw in the opening lines of her poem, Sexton confronts the reader's reluctance to participate in the hermeneutic process that it reveals. Her defiant wielding of the bowl forces the reader to participate in the narcissistic process, prevents him or her from looking away, inscribes a place for the reader within the text as one part of the mirrored scene:

And if you turn away
because there is no lesson here
I will hold my awkward bowl,
with all its cracked stars shining
like a complicated lie,
and fasten a new skin around it
as if I were dressing an orange
or a strange sun.

(34-35)

Equally, Ashbery's poem reminds us that the self-portrait "is a metaphor / Made to include us, we are a part of it" (196-97). Both poems, then, may be read as a contemplation of the process by which art (Parmigianino's painting, Sexton's poem, Ashbery's self-portrait with a "pencil" [191]) enters into a productive and mutually sustaining relationship with its audience.

The surface of Parmigianino's self-portrait in Ashbery's poem glows with potential significations: it is a "silver blur" (192), its "cover burnishes," it has a "disguising radiance" (204). Sexton's bowl, too, radiates meaning. However, this is born not of authenticity but of artifice. Recognizing that alone it may not compel or retain the reader—indeed, that its very transparency or nakedness may repel him or her—the speaker takes steps to render her "lesson" more acceptable, dressing or disguising the bowl in luminous "orange" so that it shines like a "strange sun." As the poem's argument develops, what we see is emphatically not a pure, unmediated reflection of lived experience as might perhaps be expected of confessional poetry. Rather, it is a fabrication, an object masked or disguised, dressed with a "new skin."

In a genre apparently predicated on revelation, this metaconfession that the essence of confession lies in dressing up, rather than undressing, in disguise rather than nakedness, in deceit rather than honesty, is supremely telling.

Abrams, as we have seen, distinguishes between mimetic and expressive forms of art, between the mirror and the lamp. Perloff too posits a difference between postmodern and lyric forms of poetry based on a distinction between "artifice" and "authenticity." I would contend that Sexton's simultaneously reflective and luminous bowl refuses to choose between these aesthetics. The "glass bowl shining" both reflects and reveals. However, both functions are imperfect. The reflective surface is "awkward," "cracked," and "complicated," offering no clear mimesis. The sun, instead of merely figuring illumination and insight, is veiled and disguised; dressed in a "new skin," it cannot penetrate with directness or clarity but must carefully screen its message. In both cases, something ostensibly transparent or luminous is rendered translucent such that the confessional subject ostensibly being reflected or expressed is obscured by a crazed or veiled surface. However, with its self-consciously selected metaphors suggestive of the refraction and diffusion of light—of the prismatic splitting of its source into scattered elements—**"For John"** ensures that its meaning is shared. Something apparently singular, personal, and solipsistic is made multiple, social, discursive.

For self-reflexivity to be identified as characteristic of Ashbery's writing (and of the work of a number of other postmodern writers) it has been necessary to deny its presence in Sexton's work—to reduce confessionalism to this emergent poetry's other. (Such a will to classify is foreshadowed, perhaps, in Ashbery's suggestion in "Self-Portrait" that "If they are to become classics / They must decide which side they are on" [196]). Thus Harold Bloom declares that Ashbery "writes out of so profound a subjectivity as to make 'confessional' verse seem as self-defeating as that mode truly has been, from Coleridge (its inventor) down to Lowell and his disciples" (117-18). And Laurence Lieberman celebrates Ashbery's presentation of self as "swept clear of melodrama, the news-hawking debris of personality, all the detritus comprising the stock-in-trade of the confessional poets' school" (23). I would suggest, however, that the vehemence of these rejections of the confessional other reveals—while it attempts to deny—a profound commonality of poetic interests.

Marjorie Perloff sees as characteristic of modern (that is, pre-postmodernist) poetry the eventual realization of "some sort of epiphany, a moment of insight or vision with which the poem closes" (*Dance* 156-57). Yet, as we have seen in **"For John," "An Obsessive Combination,"** and the other poems mentioned here, this is not a characteristic of Sexton's work. Rather, her poetry features an arguably postmodernist tendency toward equivocation and indeterminacy, toward provisionality, uncertainty, and evasion. Sexton's reluctance to conclude her writing on a resounding, authoritative, and thus normative and reassuring note is a sign of refusal to concede to totalization and of a wish to keep multiple interpretive possibilities open. Hence the multifaceted bowl of **"For John"** and the many-pointed star of **"An Obsessive Combination"**: insight is always complex and diffuse. Sexton's poetry thus seeks the middle ground, the medial space between the outside and the inside, the public and the private, the mirror and the lamp (equally, between lies and truth, obfuscation and confession, artifice and authenticity). While exploiting the materiality of the mirror, Sexton's writing's primary interest is in the compelling intangibility of the reflection.

The received history of American poetry is the history of a movement from an impersonal, modernist aesthetic to a personal, lyrical, confessional narcissism and on to a cool, self-reflexive, linguistically sophisticated postmodernism. Sexton's poetry, I have suggested, transgresses received generic boundaries and problematizes this trajectory. By redefining our understanding of the apparent narcissism of her early work we can see that the profound self-reflexivity, the language play, and the undermining of processes of representation and revelation that are thought to characterize avant-garde and postmodernist poetic forms alone are, in fact, central to Sexton's poetics.

Notes

1. *Anne Sexton: The Complete Poems* is the source of all the poems I quote except "An Obsessive Combination," which is from *Selected Poems of Anne Sexton.*

2. Other important post-Freudian readings of narcissism include those of Otto Kernberg and Heinz Kohut, psychiatrists whose work, although offering entirely divergent perspectives on the condition, has dominated the understanding of narcissism in the United States since the 1970s. See Berman 20 ff.

3. Interestingly, as Juliet Mitchell points out, Freud does not mention the role of Echo in his interpretation of the Narcissus myth (30).

4. Middlebrook speculates that "An Obsessive Combination" was written during August 1958 (124). However, as it is apparent that Sexton studied Hopkins's poetry during her time as a student in Robert Lowell's writing class (September 1958 to 1959), it is arguable that her poem originates at least one month later. On Lowell and Hopkins, see Hamilton (78) and Lowell (167-70).

5. See Middlebrook 98-99 on Sexton's use of acrostics.

6. The mother's portrait is perceived as "a cave of a mirror" (38). Unrecognized by previous commentators on this poem, Sexton's linking of the mirror and the cave is profoundly significant, paralleling Echo's retreat to the caves in Ovid's story.

7. Heinz Kohut, a leading figure in the psychology of narcissism, notes the importance of empathy on the part of the observer/analyst to the resolution of primitive narcissism (Berman 31-32).

8. Manuscripts in the Anne Sexton collection at the Harry Ransom Humanities Research Center indicate that the poem was drafted on 12 February 1959.

9. Sexton's poem was probably critiqued in one of Robert Lowell's Boston University workshops in the spring of 1959. Plath audited the class alongside Sexton, George Starbuck, and others. She first joined the group on 24 February 1959 and in her journal entry for the next day uses the image of a bell jar (470). One month later (29 March 1959) the seeds of the plot of the novel are recorded in her journal. The bell jar motif had been used once before by Plath (in July 1952) to describe the ennui of summer vacations. Sexton's poem, with its image of the inverted glass bowl, may have prompted Plath to revisit the metaphor. Arguably, Sexton's use of the image in her sophisticated exploration of writing, gender, and subjectivity offered Plath exactly the figure she needed to represent Esther Greenwood's mixed sense of vulnerability and visibility.

10. As Jean-Jacques Rousseau explains in his *Confessions*: "I should like in some way to make my soul transparent to the reader's eye, and for that purpose I am trying to present it from all points of view, to show it in all lights" (169).

11. The influence of Henry James's *The Golden Bowl* is apparent here. Sexton annotated her copy of the book throughout, and there are many resemblances between the properties of his bowl and hers. In addition, the image of tapping is used to similar effect in both texts. In *The Golden Bowl,* Maggie has (metaphorically)

> sounded with a tap or two one of the rare porcelain plates. She had knocked, in short—though she could scarcely have said whether for admission or for what [. . .] and had waited to see what would happen. Something *had* happened: it was as if a sound, at her touch, after a little, had come back to her from within.

(328)

12. Christina Britzolakis makes a related point in connection with Plath's use of mirror metaphors in her journals: "ironically, these are almost invari-

ably linked with moments of specular mis- or non-recognition in which the subject is encountered as abject, resistant otherness" (16) and are seen as "the sign of a self-reflexivity which is alternately paralyzing and enabling" (17).

Unpublished manuscripts and letters are used with the permission of the Harry Ransom Humanities Research Center, University of Texas, Austin, and with the permission of Doris Holmes Eyges (for the letters of John Holmes) and Linda Gray Sexton (for material from the Anne Sexton archive). John Gery has offered incisive and stimulating comments on successive drafts of this essay, and his contribution is acknowledged with gratitude.

Works Cited

Abrams, M. H. *The Mirror and the Lamp: Romantic Theory and the Critical Tradition.* Oxford: Oxford UP, 1971.

Alvarez, A. "Beyond All This Fiddle." *Times Literary Supplement* 23 March 1967: 229-32.

Ashbery, John. *Selected Poems.* New York: Penguin, 1986.

Beach, Christopher, ed. *Artifice and Indeterminacy: An Anthology of New Poetics.* Tuscaloosa: U of Alabama P, 1998.

Berman, Jeffrey. *Narcissism and the Novel.* New York: New York UP, 1990.

Bloom, Harold. "John Ashbery: The Charity of the Hard Moments." *Contemporary Poetry in America: Essays and Interviews.* Ed. Robert Boyers. New York: Schocken, 1974. 110-38.

Britzolakis, Christina. *Sylvia Plath and the Theatre of Mourning.* Oxford: Clarendon, 1999.

Bruss, Elizabeth. *Autobiographical Acts: The Changing Situation of a Literary Genre.* Baltimore: Johns Hopkins UP, 1976.

Colburn, Steven E., ed. *Anne Sexton: Telling the Tale.* Ann Arbor: U of Michigan P, 1988.

Costello, Bonnie. *Marianne Moore: Imaginary Possessions.* Cambridge: Harvard UP, 1981.

Davidson, Michael. "'Skewed by Design': From Act to Speech Act in Language Writing." Beach 70-76.

Foucault, Michel. *The History of Sexuality, Volume 1: An Introduction.* Trans. Robert Hurley. Harmondsworth: Peregrine, 1984.

Freud, Sigmund. "On Narcissism." 1914. *On Metapsychology: The Theory of Psychoanalysis.* Trans. James Strachey. Ed. Angela Richards. Harmondsworth: Penguin, 1991. 61-97.

Gardner, W. H. Introduction. *Poems of Gerard Manley Hopkins.* Ed. W. H. Gardner and N. H. Mackenzie. 4th ed. London: Oxford UP, 1970. xiii-xxxviii.

George, Diana Hume. *Oedipus Anne: The Poetry of Anne Sexton.* Urbana: U of Illinois P, 1987.

Goodwin, James. "Narcissus and Autobiography." *Genre* 12 (Spring 1979): 69-92.

Gray, Richard. *American Poetry of the Twentieth Century.* Harlow: Longman, 1990.

Hall, Caroline King Barnard. *Anne Sexton.* Boston: Hall, 1989.

Hamilton, Ian. *Robert Lowell: A Biography.* London: Faber, 1983.

Holmes, John. Letter to Anne Sexton. 8 February 1959. Harry Ransom Humanities Research Center, University of Texas, Austin.

Hutcheon, Linda. *Narcissistic Narrative: The Metafictional Paradox.* New York: Methuen, 1984.

———. *A Poetics of Postmodernism.* New York: Routledge, 1988.

———. *The Politics of Postmodernism.* New York: Routledge, 1989.

James, Henry. *The Golden Bowl.* Harmondsworth: Penguin, 1987.

Jones, A. R. "Necessity and Freedom: The Poetry of Robert Lowell, Sylvia Plath, and Anne Sexton." *Critical Quarterly* 7.1 (Spring 1965): 11-30.

Lacan, Jacques. "The Mirror Stage as Formative of the Function of the I as Revealed in Psychoanalytic Experience." *Écrits: A Selection.* Trans. Alan Sheridan. London: Routledge, 1989. 1-7.

Lasch, Christopher. *The Culture of Narcissism: American Life in an Age of Diminishing Expectations.* 1979. London: Norton, 1991.

Lerner, Laurence. "What Is Confessional Poetry?" *Critical Quarterly* 29.2 (Summer 1987): 46-66.

Lieberman, Laurence. *Unassigned Frequencies: American Poetry in Review.* Urbana: U of Illinois P, 1977.

Lowell, Robert. *Collected Prose.* Ed. Robert Giroux. London: Faber, 1987.

Lucie-Smith, Edward. "A Murderous Art?" *Critical Quarterly* 6.4 (Winter 1964): 355-63.

McClatchy, J. D., ed. *Anne Sexton: The Artist and Her Critics.* Bloomington: Indiana UP, 1978.

McCorkle, James. *The Still Performance: Writing, Self, and Interconnection in Five Postmodern American Poets.* Charlottesville: UP of Virginia, 1989.

Middlebrook, Diane Wood. *Anne Sexton: A Biography.* London: Virago, 1991.

Miller, Jonathan. *On Reflection.* London: National Gallery, 1998.

Mitchell, Juliet. *Psychoanalysis and Feminism: A Radical Reassessment of Freudian Psychoanalysis.* Harmondsworth: Penguin, 1990.

Oates, Joyce Carol. "On *The Awful Rowing toward God.*" McClatchy 144.

Ostriker, Alicia. *Stealing the Language: The Emergence of Women's Poetry in America.* London: Women's, 1987.

———. "That Story: The Changes of Anne Sexton." Colburn 263-87.

Ovid. *Metamorphoses.* Trans. Mary M. Innes. Harmondsworth: Penguin, 1955.

Perloff, Marjorie. "The Changing Face of Common Intercourse: Talk Poetry, Talk Show, and the Scene of Writing." Beach 77-106.

———. *The Dance of the Intellect: Studies in the Poetry of the Pound Tradition.* Cambridge: Cambridge UP, 1985.

Phillips, Robert. *The Confessional Poets.* Carbondale: Southern Illinois UP, 1973.

Plath, Sylvia. *The Bell Jar.* London: Faber, 1965.

———. *The Journals of Sylvia Plath 1950-1962.* Ed. Karen V. Kukil. London: Faber, 2000.

Rousseau, Jean-Jacques. *The Confessions of Jean-Jacques Rousseau.* Trans. J. M. Cohen. Harmondsworth: Penguin, 1953.

Sennett, Richard. *The Fall of Public Man.* New York: Norton, 1974.

Sexton, Anne. *Anne Sexton: The Complete Poems.* Boston: Houghton, 1981.

———. *The Awful Rowing toward God.* Boston: Houghton, 1975.

———. Crawshaw Lectures. Typescript. Harry Ransom Humanities Research Center, University of Texas, Austin.

———. *Selected Poems of Anne Sexton.* Boston: Houghton, 1988.

———. *To Bedlam and Part Way Back.* Boston: Houghton, 1960.

Spacks, Patricia Meyer. "On *45 Mercy Street.*" McClatchy 186-89.

Vendler, Helen. "Malevolent Flippancy." Colburn 437-46.

Webster's Third New International Dictionary of the English Language, Unabridged. Springfield: Merriam-Webster, 1986.

Williamson, Alan. "Confession and Tragedy." *Poetry* 142 (June 1983): 170-78.

———. "Stories About the Self." *After Confession: Poetry as Autobiography.* Ed. Kate Sontag and David Graham. St. Paul: Graywolf, 2001. 51-70.

Artemis Michailidou (essay date 2004)

SOURCE: Michailidou, Artemis. "Gender, Body, and Feminine Performance: Edna St. Vincent Millay's Impact on Anne Sexton." *Feminist Review* 78, no. 1 (2004): 117-30.

[*In the following essay, Michailidou discusses Edna St. Vincent Millay's influence on Sexton, focusing on each writer's treatment of such themes as feminine physicality and gender politics, and on their respective approaches to public readings.*]

Edna Millay's literary reputation has always baffled scholars of American literature. Reviews written by her contemporaries praised the poet in the warmest possible terms; Millay was celebrated as an exceptionally talented writer, a gifted performer, a perfect example of the 1920s 'New Woman', a pioneering feminist. Her devoted readers could not get enough of her and the sales of her poetry volumes were impressive even during the Depression. In the 1940s, however, critical appreciations of Millay became far less generous, and shortly after her death in 1950 critics hardly read her or wrote about her. Millay's poetry, once hailed for its originality, was seen in the 1950s and 1960s as little more than immature articulation of the poet's personal (and, primarily, erotic) experiences. Millay had not grown artistically, had almost nothing in common with the high modernists and, worst of all, she relied too much on a sentimental aesthetic that was appealing only to middleclass women. The poet's five honorary doctorates were conveniently forgotten, and Millay was consistently presented as 'non-intellectual', 'simplistic', or 'unsophisticated'.

During the 1970s, there was a notable re-appearance of Millay in scholarly debates; critics like Jane Stanbrough and Frederick Eckman attempted to revive interest in her, arguing that, although she was best known as a love poet, she was by no means only that (see Stanbrough (1979) and Eckman (1976)). These critics' contribution played an instrumental role in the recuperation of Millay as a versatile writer but, on the whole, 1970s' appreciations of the poet tended to omit two crucial aspects that were inextricably linked with her

work. The first was her experimentation with modern forms of poetic composition; Millay was still viewed as a poet who deployed traditional literary genres and was not particularly interested in the literary developments of her time. The second was her radical feminist consciousness or, to be more accurate, the way this consciousness was presented. On the one hand, Millay was still credited with having written poetry representative of the 'New Woman', but the kind of poetry selected for scholarly discussion came all too often from her Greenwich Village, 'naughty girl' volumes. This consistent critical preference obscured almost entirely the poet's interest in the aging female body, and thus the poet's lifelong exploration of sexuality, femininity, and gender stereotypes could not be seen in its proper dimensions. Not surprisingly, during the 1980s Millay's status was only marginally better than that of the 1970s, despite attempts to expand the discussion concerning the poet's intellectual achievement by influential critics such as Debra Fried, William Drake and Jan Montefiore. Millay's place within the contexts of modernity, experimentation, and feminism was not to be seriously re-evaluated until the 1990s. The debate is still going on, and is far from complete or exhaustive. Suffice it to say here that, since 1990, there have been several new selections of Millay's poetry, two definitive biographies, videos commissioned by the Films for the Humanities and Sciences, as well as independent producers, newly launched websites, new editions of Millay's poetry recordings, interdisciplinary readings of her work, and even new versions of her books in Braille; hardly the treatment one would associate with a 'dated', 'minor' poet. The upsurge of interest in this complex woman indicates that Millay, as poet, feminist, and artistic influence, has been an important part of early twentieth-century American culture, and a part that needs to be examined if the diverse socio-cultural developments of the previous century are to be approached with perceptiveness and objectivity.

Nevertheless, despite the obvious change in Millay's critical treatment and the gradual recognition that she occupies a significant place within the context of twentieth century American poetry and, in particular, within the tradition of women's writing, it must be said that close comparative studies of Millay's impact on the next generation of American women poets have yet to appear. Although I can only agree with the great volume of scholarly work which argues for the full recognition of Millay's importance as a modern poet and feminist innovator, I am convinced that this importance will not be adequately established until Millay's influence on mid-century women poets is analyzed in greater depth. The purpose of this essay, therefore, is to fill some of the gaps in the Millay canon by showing how she impacted on one of the most controversial poets of this group—Anne Sexton. In particular, I will explore how the younger poet came to terms with her ambiguous feelings toward Millay, and how the latter's daring self-presentation as a woman writer and performer opened up the way for Sexton's notoriously theatrical poetic readings. Drawing attention to issues such as femininity, performativity, and the female body, I will argue that Sexton turned Millay's ideas into new themes for women's writing, and that the earlier poet's innovation within the above frameworks helped Sexton to conceptualize the need for a distinctively woman-oriented poetry.

In an anthology on modern American women writers first published in the early 1990s, Suzanne Juhasz argues that a full evaluation of Anne Sexton's artistic achievement is still pending, as are decisions about her place within the canon of American poetry. 'Sexton', Juhasz says, 'remains as controversial as she was during her lifetime. But she has persisted in affecting and influencing readers. [. . .] Sexton continues to provoke and engage her readers, and scholars are still trying to define the nature of her contribution and thereby assess its value.' (see Juhasz (1991), in Showalter *et al.,* 1993: 309-320). While an assessment of Sexton's poetry is beyond the scope of this study, an examination of her critical reception, particularly by her contemporaries, is necessary to establish the common ground she shares with Edna St. Vincent Millay.

Anne Sexton's poetry is part of a bigger movement toward autobiography that became fashionable in the early 1950s. As Richard Gray explains:

> Poetry became, once again, not a flight of personality but a dramatization, a reinvention of the personal. The first person, 'I', was restored to the centre of the poem. Recovering one of the major impulses [. . .] in the American tradition, poets began placing themselves equally at the centre of the poem. The poet's private self became both subject and speaker [. . .]. The poet addressed the reader directly, with an often unnerving intimacy, as if that reader were confessor, therapist, friend, or even lover.
>
> (Gray, 1998: 223)

This emphasis on the personal that Gray identifies as the main characteristic of the poetry of the 1950s dominates the work of Anne Sexton, and has been the subject of most of the poet's interviews. In an interview with Harry Moore (in Colburn, 1988: 50), for instance, Sexton declares that not only was poetry of an intimate experience her preferred mode of writing, but that intimacy was also her trademark and what made her particularly appealing to her readers: 'I write very personal poems but I hope that they will become the central theme to someone else's private life. [. . .] I can just do my own thing and that's the way I do it.' In a later interview, published posthumously, Sexton defended her stand even more forcefully: 'I can't worry about fashion and never could—from the very beginning, when they said "You can't write that way", to this very moment.' (in Colburn, 1988: 181).

Sexton's account of the critical objection that accompanied her intensely personal poems seems to contradict Gray's argument concerning the personal element in the poetry of the late 1950s and 1960s. An important parameter that explains the discrepancy in Sexton's critical reception is the foregrounding of femininity, or, to put it better, of feminine physicality in her work. Even those poems that ostensibly focus on neutral subjects, such as madness and mental disturbance, are written from a perspective that emphasizes the poet's femaleness, examining how these roles relate to the social structures that govern notions of feminine 'properness' and women's psychological fulfillment. Moreover, her body poems further accentuate the writer's strong interest in addressing (and identifying with) a female audience, thus continuing a tradition that goes back to Edna Millay's self-presentation as an original and daring woman poet. And although Sexton is perhaps more often associated with frustration, rather than celebration of her female nature, she wrote many poems that glorify womanhood in all its aspects; Gray, again, argues:

> [Sexton] was not only concerned with the pain of being daughter, wife, mother, lover. She also sang, as she put it, 'in celebration of the woman I am'. Long before it was fashionable to do so, she wrote in praise of her distinctive identity, not just as an American poet, but as an American female poet. [. . .] For her this [. . .] was, finally, a source of pride.
>
> (Gray, 1998: 229)

Unfortunately Gray does not mention that this articulation of female pride had been a central theme in Millay's poetry—published long before Sexton's—but his omission does not cancel the fact that much of the younger poet's most affirmative work in this respect sounds exactly like Millay's famous celebration of the potential of womanhood and the female artist in 'I too beneath your moon, almighty Sex': (see the earlier writer's: 'Such as I am, however, I have brought, / To what it is, this tower; it is my own; / Though it was reared To Beauty, it was wrought / From what I had to build with: honest bone / Is there, and anguish; pride; and burning thought') (Millay (1995)).

Nevertheless, Sexton's focus on womanhood meant that, like Millay, she was bound to be associated with a particularly limited set of themes—those pertaining to femininity and selfhood. It also meant that, despite the chronological gap, Sexton was exposing herself to the same kind of critical biases that had downgraded the poetry of her predecessor. And indeed, her critical reception mirrors that of Edna Millay in more than one respect. To begin with, as in the case of Millay, Sexton's contemporaries seemed to prefer her early work, which focused primarily on autobiography, mental instability, and female frustration, to the more abstract, philosophical meditations on gender, authority, and religion—subjects explored in collections such as *Transformations* (1971) or *The Awful Rowing toward God* (1975). Even though a great number of distinguished scholars have argued persuasively that Sexton's later work is of equal (if not higher) quality to her early writings, during her lifetime the majority of her critics insisted that Sexton's best poetry was to be found in *To Bedlam and Part Way Back* (1960), *All My Pretty Ones* (1962), and *Live Or Die* (1966). Joyce Carol Oates believes that the main reason behind the refusal of Sexton's critics to acknowledge the value of her late work was the fact that the poet attempted to enlarge her scope again through a perspective that foregrounded the self and the personal, a perspective that was essentially no different from that of her earlier work (see Oates (1983); Axelrod (1975), Shurr (1981), Ostriker (1982), and McGrath (1988)). In other words, the very element that had made Sexton's literary reputation—the directness and honesty with which she could talk about her private experiences regarding femininity, frustration, and mental disturbance—was eventually used against her in order to establish her 'failure' to grow as a poet and thus, the lesser value of her more philosophical, 'inauthentic' writings. Similar objections to Millay's later work and her alleged inability to attain artistic maturity are particularly relevant here, despite the fact that the earlier poet had also made a significant attempt to expand her poetic scope by turning to more abstract, philosophical writing (e.g. *Conversation at Midnight,* 1937) as a result of being too closely linked with the personal or 'private'.

Even when Sexton was praised, the terms of praise seemed to suggest a curious underestimation of the features that had given her poetry its distinctive texture. Thom Gunn, to name just one scholar, declared that the 'most encouraging' element of *All My Pretty Ones* was the fact that Sexton was 'getting rid of the faults of rhetoric and self-dramatization'—a comment that echoes the ambiguous praise the earlier poet often received. In his review of Millay's *Mine the Harvest*, for instance, John Ciardi is delighted to note the absence of the poet's 'save-the-world rhetoric'; 'the talent, nevertheless, remains self-dramatizing', he concludes, a statement that apparently requires no further clarifications to prove Millay's artistic inferiority (Gunn (1962); see also Ciardi (1954)).

The above examples suggest a clear link between Millay's and Sexton's critical reception, and it should come as no surprise that Robert Lowell's assessment of the younger poet's work directly and publicly connected the two women. Unfortunately, Lowell's view did neither poet a service; 'In the beginning', he wrote,

> [Sexton's] lines were overpoetic; she gave promise of becoming a fifties Edna Millay. Yet on her own, she developed a more sensitive, realistic idiom. Her gift was to grip, to give words to the drama of her personality. She did what few did, cut a figure. What went wrong? For a book or two, she grew more powerful. Then writing was too easy for her. She became meager and exaggerated.

> (Lowell (1974), in Colburn, 1991: 24)

Not only does Lowell manage to dismiss completely any opinions that might have argued for Millay's importance and talent but he also implies that Sexton did in fact become what he had predicted. Like Millay, Lowell seems to be saying, Sexton developed into a poet who relied too heavily on 'cutting a figure'; like Millay, she was particularly successful in articulating 'the drama of her personality'; like Millay, she was powerful 'for a book or two', but when her chief artistic resource—the emphasis on the self—was exhausted, Sexton lost her charm and became 'meager and exaggerated'. Although later criticism largely recovered Sexton (as it is currently recovering Millay), Lowell's evaluation was quite influential and set the 'standards' (in other words, unevenness and temporal appeal) by which Sexton's work could safely be undermined; interestingly enough, Helen Vendler's essay on Sexton also associates the, younger poet's artistic weaknesses with those of Millay (Vendler, 1995).

Such appreciations, however, made Sexton increasingly aware of the critical biases and double standards with which women's writing was being judged; the personal as such may have been esteemed, but the personal from a female perspective was apparently inferior. Not coincidentally, Lowell equated Sexton with Millay, a 'minor' female poet, not with a minor male. Sexton's later interviews demonstrate that she was much less reluctant to acknowledge publicly the influence of Millay on her work—a change that was probably triggered by the recognition that, like her, Millay was consistently misread and misrepresented in critical debates. Sexton's poetry, therefore, should be seen in the light of this influence, as well as in the light of her (semi)conscious recognition of it, and the oscillation between acceptance and denial that this influence produced. Although in-depth scholarly work on this area is yet to be carried out, a substantial amount of the younger poet's work reveals that Millay was never too far from her mind.

As can be expected, of course, initially Sexton felt anything but comfortable with the connection between herself and her predecessor. Beginning to write and publish poetry in the 1950s and early 1960s, that is to say, the decades in which Edna Millay's artistic reputation had indisputably reached its nadir, Anne Sexton was fully aware of the danger of being compared with Millay. Having internalized the New Critical mandate and its rejection of 'the Miss America of the 1920s', and having taken a writing seminar under the guidance of Robert Lowell, Sexton went so far as to express the fear that she might be 'a reincarnation of Edna St. Vincent Millay'. Despite the condescending, if not supercilious tone of that statement, however, it is obvious that Millay occupied an important place in Sexton's own poetic consciousness; when, in the late 1950s, the younger woman admitted that 'two years ago I had never heard of any poet but Edna St. Vincent', she clearly recognized that Millay's enormous success was something she would have to come to terms with (see Gilbert and Gubar (1996) and Middlebrook (1991)).

To argue that Sexton can indeed be seen as a reincarnation of Millay would be far-fetched; nevertheless, the two poets share much more than is commonly acknowledged, and the first important connection can be found in the significance that both poets attributed to their public performances and, indeed, in the consistency with which they projected various 'performance' personae onto their audiences. As far as Millay is concerned, the story has been told many times; from Edmund Wilson's observations regarding 'the intoxicating effect' Millay had on people, to Gilbert and Gubar's analysis of the theatricality of Millay's well-publicized fame, critics have found it difficult to discuss Millay's work independent of her public performances. Cheryl Walker, for instance, writes: '[Millay's] reading presence was notorious: clad in a long red velvet dress or diaphanous veils, she purposefully projected a sense of being the poet in the flesh, of the flesh; the poet whose flesh was somehow the very material of her material.' (Walker, 1991: 140; See also Gilbert and Gubar (1994)). Daniel Mark Epstein, Millay's most recent biographer, elaborates on this view, arguing that her readings were 'more electrifying than any that were ever heard before Dylan Thomas took to the hustings in the 1940s'. To use his own words:

> The 'graceful and floaty' negligees with their long trains were her charmed mantles, just as her theatrical stage-English was the melodeon of her magic on the platform. The Pulitzer Prize-winning poet Richard Eberhart heard her read in a red dress at Dartmouth in 1924. He was so captivated he 'followed her back to the Inn, lagging a hundred feet behind her. [. . .] I was not only enraptured but afraid of the greatness of poetry. I worshipped Millay as a possessor of immortality'.
>
> (Epstein, 2001: 118-119)

Adding that 'one could quote a hundred other witnesses echoing Eberhart', Epstein concludes with the conviction that Millay's gift was 'as much the genius of poetry as it was the stage technique of a stage actress' (Epstein, 2001: 118-119).

Sandra Gilbert and Susan Gubar, among others, have analyzed extensively Millay's performative powers, as well as the reasons behind the poet's determination to explore different theatrical expressions. They have

shown that Millay's stylized readings were almost as important as the writing itself in enabling the poet to destabilize fixed identities and gender roles. On stage, Millay tended to present herself either as a prototypical femme fatale, or as a medieval princess tired of chivalric romances. Employing the techniques of female 'masquerade' analyzed by theorists such as Joan Rivière and Simone de Beauvoir, Millay wrote 'as a being who impersonated "woman" in order to investigate both "female" costume and the very concept of "the feminine"' (Gilbert and Gubar, 1994: 65-73).

Millay's understanding of performance, masquerade, and impersonation aligns her work with concepts advocated by modern theorists of gender like Judith Butler. The latter has argued that 'what we take to be an essential essence of gender is manufactured through a sustained set of acts, posited through the gendered stylization of the body.' Gender becomes thus a performative entity that cannot be separated out 'from the political and cultural intersections in which it is invariably produced and maintained.' In addition, Butler insists that the 'regulatory practices that govern gender also govern culturally intelligible notions of identity', and is convinced that 'the "coherence" or "continuity" of "the person" are not logical or analytical features of personhood, but rather, socially constituted and maintained norms of intelligibility' (Butler, 1999: xv-23).

This theory is not only challenging as such but also very productive when applied to figures like Millay. By drawing attention to the element of artificiality behind gender and identity, Butler not only demonstrates the fluidity of social constructs but also implicitly argues that placing excessive significance on fixed identities and gender roles is not always the way to get reliable answers in literary analyses. Consequently, academic arguments that focus on Millay's alleged lack of personal maturity, intellectual autonomy, and temperamental instability, and approach these concepts from the perspective of an inflexible, idealized norm, begin to lose much of their weight. Moreover, by revealing and explaining the different faces that gender can adopt at a time, Butler illuminates both the multiple functions of Millay's poetry and the important cultural implications of the poet's diverse impersonations. Indeed, Millay's impersonations and her celebrated public readings displayed precisely this artificial construction of gender and the need to examine the constituents and purpose of this artifice through parody, play, mimicry, and performance. At the same time, her ability to shift between the various roles and faces of the mechanism of construction underlines the possibility of interrogating monolithic views of femininity and deconstructing accepted gender stereotypes.

According to Sexton's own admission that when she started to write poetry she was familiar only with

Millay, it would be reasonable to assume that she had also heard of the latter's celebrated public readings, and possibly of her ability to negotiate particularly high fees for these readings. Just as Millay was, in her time, the most well-paid poet-dramatist, Sexton eventually became one of 'the best paid poetry performers in America' (Epstein, 2001: 182). Moreover, Sexton's performances, her style of reciting, stage gestures, costume choice, and general rapport with the audience seem to have been modeled precisely on Millay's. The earlier poet, for instance, enjoyed chatting with the audience between poems; her program, however, would always follow a strict schedule, which would skillfully create the impression of spontaneity and improvization. Epstein cites the account of a journalist who had attended one of Millay's readings and had been surprised by the complete absence of 'artificial rhetoricism' and of 'posing' or 'affectation'. Epstein reminds us that 'this art [which] conceals art' was a crucial aspect of Millay's stage presence: 'the actress had learned to appear natural and spontaneous performing the same set pieces night after night' (Epstein, 2001: 185).

Similarly, Sexton would always begin with the poem **'Her Kind'** and would also interact with the audience. And, as it had happened with Millay, the younger poet's listeners found her public readings memorable, even when Sexton's stage manners were somewhat extravagant (or perhaps because her manners were often extravagant). Commenting on one such reading, Anthony Hecht said that '[Sexton] was sensational, and she was highly criticized for it in the press the next day. Nevertheless, she was the *only* poet the press paid any attention to. [. . .] She made the headlines.' (Hecht, in Middlebrook, 1991: 277-278).[1] Elaborating on Sexton's sensational public appearances, Middlebrook notes that the poet's readings 'were carefully rehearsed'. In response to an admirer who questioned her about her approach to performance, Sexton frankly replied that 'all the things you quote from the reading, my little introductory notes are [. . .] not in the least spontaneous with the exception of one or two sentences. I hate to admit that I am so studied, but there it is.' (Sexton, in Middlebrook, 1991: 319-320).[2] Middlebrook argues that, throughout her career, Sexton would give 'very upbeat' readings, with the audience applauding for a long time. She also refers to another statement made by the poet, which highlights Sexton's view of her performances: 'I could perform just before I die, I think, but it's a performance of the poems. I know the lines, it's a practiced emotion, one I've felt before.' And indeed, a day before her death, Sexton described to the students taking her poetry workshop at Boston University 'how she managed the button on the long red dress she wore for readings, which would open from both top and bottom as if by accident'. (Middlebrook, 1991: 391-395).[3]

This extended account of Sexton's public readings clearly reveals that, like Millay, Sexton saw an inextricable link between poetry and performance; she attempted to create in her readings an atmosphere equal to the one Millay's readings were famous for. The descriptions by Middlebrook and Hecht show that everything was there: the chatty, conversational approach toward the audience, the carefully rehearsed program, the excellent concealment of artificiality and rhetorical affectation, the extravagantly dramatic gestures, and even the red dress. These elements provide sufficient evidence of the fact that Sexton could not really negate Millay's influence on her own self-conception as both poet and performer, even when her more recent literary mentors were suggesting that this influence had to be sacrificed if Sexton wished to be considered 'major' rather than 'minor'. Far from leaving Millay behind and in spite of the fear of being associated too closely with the earlier poet, Sexton consciously tried to experiment with several features of the latter's artistic posturing, becoming, on stage, another unpredictable femme fatale figure. And although Millay's interest in performance and spectacle is best interpreted within the broader context of female poets exploring the relationship between femininity and dramatization, surveyor and surveyed, or real and artificial (her contemporaries Marianne Moore and Elinor Wylie provide two equally notable examples here), it seems that Millay's approach to linguistic and corporeal performativity influenced Sexton more than any other female poet. On the one hand, Millay's conscious and often provocative presentation of herself as both object and controller of desire struck a responsive nerve in Sexton's exhibitionist nature—something that Moore's self-restraint was clearly unable to have triggered. On the other, Millay's lifelong search to find a pattern that could accommodate both excess and discipline, in performance as well as art (manifested in poems such as 'I will put Chaos into fourteen lines / And keep him there / [. . .] till he with Order mingles and combines') was, for Sexton, a constant point of reference for her own need to strike a balance between exuberance and self-control. Finally, the exceptional harshness with which Millay was vilified, in later life and posthumously, for her histrionic gifts, gradually alerted Sexton to the fact that a similar fate was in store for her.

Moreover, Sexton's development as a poet suggests that Millay's influence extended to matters much more substantial than artistic posturing; as regards the issue of women's writing, for instance, not only did the younger poet's views shift from a position of reservation to one of recognition and acceptance that could accommodate the significance of writers like Millay but also this shift parallels a very similar change in Millay's own self-conception as a poet. The story of 'Renascence', the poem that made Millay famous overnight is well known; so is the initial mistaken assumption of Arthur Ficke and Witter Bynner, the two poets who declared that Millay could not have been the author of 'Renascence', because 'it takes a brawny male of forty-five to do that'. The interesting piece in the story, however, is Millay's reply, rather then the masculinist presuppositions of Ficke and Bynner:

> Gentlemen I must convince you of your error; my reputation is at stake. I simply will not be a 'brawny male'. Not that I have an aversion to brawny males; *au contraire, au contraire*. But I cling to my femininity! [. . .] Seriously: I thank you also for the compliment you have unwittingly given me. For tho I do not yet aspire to be forty-five and brawny, if my verse so represent me, I am more gratified than I can say.

> (Millay, in Macdougall, 1952: 18)

Suzanne Clark has a point when she argues that while, from a purely linguistic angle, Millay does indeed cling to her femininity, she articulates the desire 'to be in position of mastery with respect to poetry—that is, to be male.' The 'compliment' for which she thanks the two men 'is not that her verse represents her as forty-five and brawny of course; we must make the substitution of the omitted term and read: "For tho I do not yet aspire to be male."'[4] (Clark, 1991, in Dickie and Travisano, 1996: 154-155). Clark's equation between maleness and poetic mastery may appear less easy to accept today and it certainly requires further clarification; nevertheless, it is an equation Millay herself was likely to have taken for granted when she composed 'Renascence'. In addition, her letter shows that she rather enjoyed the mystery surrounding her gender and identity; her reputation may have been at stake, but Millay was simultaneously seeking the recognition of the 'masculine' literary tradition (of which 'Renascence', with its echoes of Coleridge and Marvell, among others, seemed to be a representative specimen). Emily Stipes-Watts, however, correctly observes that Millay soon realized the pitfalls of this stand and never again implied that she wished to be praised in such terms. Her poetry soon found its distinctively 'feminine' voice and the consistent identification of her largely female audience with her work demonstrates that she was perceived primarily as a poet writing for women (Stipes-Watts (1977)).

Even more straightforwardly than Millay, Sexton declared in 1962 that the highest accolade a woman poet could aspire to was that 'she writes like a man'. By 1969, however, the influence of Robert Lowell (partly responsible for this statement) had subsided, and Sexton was publicly acknowledged as an 'assertively emotional' female writer whose poetry 'presses intimately toward its audience'; this audience, furthermore, consisted largely of women readers. Sexton had realized that she could no longer maintain the distance between herself and her classification as a representa-

tive woman poet; neither did she wish to do so: 'As long as it can be said about a woman writer "she writes like a man" and that woman takes it as a compliment, we are in trouble', she asserted. (Sexton, in Middlebrook, 1991: 173) (See Ostriker (1982: 11) and Rees-Jones (1999)).

Middlebrook traces the shadow of Maxine Kumin behind this emergence of feminist awareness; however, an equally powerful influence seems to have been Tillie Olsen, with whom Sexton discovered that she could freely discuss and, indeed, voice her admiration of writers like Millay. Like Sexton, Olsen had been introduced to Millay's poetry when she was still at school, but, although she could understand Sexton's fear (in other words, that a close association with the earlier poet was no passport to literary prestige), she did not feel that she had to conceal her high regard for Millay and encouraged Sexton to share her views of 'the embodiment of the Jazz Age' with her. As Olsen remembers: 'Our love of Sara Teasdale or Edna St. Vincent Millay didn't shame us, with each other. We never needed to be guarded or to dissemble. Besides the deepest caring for each other's work, it was the love for and the talking about the writers—accepted or not—that were life to us that created the special bond between us (see Middlebrook (1994)).'

Olsen's account suggests that Sexton's poetic maturity entailed a growing recognition of the writers who had influenced her own work. While she remained anxious about the possibility of losing critical esteem, Sexton gradually began to realize that Millay's fall from grace was a complex cultural phenomenon, and only partially related to the limitations of her poetry. Olsen's description of Millay as a writer who was 'life' to herself and Sexton indicates that, despite Sexton's increasing awareness of other kinds of poetry that were in dialogue with her own writing (such as the confessional mode practised by W. D. Snodgrass, Robert Lowell, or Sylvia Plath), the earlier poet was never too far from her consciousness. In fact, it could be argued that Sexton's reluctance to discredit either Millay's writing or Millay's self-posturing was the result of her growing confidence as an original woman poet, which helped her to question the reasons behind the earlier poet's critical dismissal. And if, in the beginning, this questioning took place only in the company of Millay admirers, such as Olsen, when Sexton solidified her status as an important poet she felt no longer constrained to underplay the earlier writer's impact on her work. In an interview that appeared in *Boston Magazine* in 1968, Sexton openly admits to Millay's influence (See Anne Sexton's interview with Brigitte Weeks, in Colburn (1988: 112-118)). The role Millay played in shaping the younger woman's artistic development therefore needs to be examined in detail, from a perspective, however, that emphasizes not Sexton's initial discomfiture with

Millay, but Sexton's appropriation of the earlier poet's themes and writing strategies.

Femininity and the body are two of the themes most rigorously appropriated by Sexton, who was quite familiar with her predecessor's exceptional contribution within the above domains. Millay's attempts to transcend the dominant assumptions of her time regarding femininity and the female body are inextricably linked with the parameters just mentioned—her performance strategies (physical and linguistic), her gender, her immense popularity, and her fetishization as both woman poet and marketable cultural icon. However, the simultaneous presence of so many different contexts in literature may sometimes obscure the depth and dimensions of a poet's artistic achievement, and if Millay's critical treatment shows anything, it is precisely that. During her lifetime, Millay was struggling to overcome both the masculinist presuppositions of mid-century critics dealing with women's literature, and the personal denigration she was subjected to. Nina Miller's summary is particularly useful at this point: 'As a symbol of Free Love', she writes, '[Millay] had to balance male prerogative and conventional femininity, as well as control the meaning of her own universal desirability.' Miller also argues that the poet's 'almost literal equation' with the life of Greenwich Village and the defiant spirit of the 1920s 'locked her in to a tight set of possibilities, as well as a significant investment in her own image.' (Miller, 1999: 31-40). The poet's consistent efforts to construe various alternatives of femininity and different figurations of the female body clearly reflect her wish to break loose from this tight set of options. Millay's efforts represent both her intention to expand the scope of her work, and her attempt to negotiate a poetics that would not rely only on the artist's investment in her desirability or personal image—literal and symbolic alike. Her 'femininity' and 'body' poetry is better understood within a context that acknowledges both Millay's recognition of the limitations imposed upon her, and her attempt to bypass these limitations.

Sexton's attitude towards femininity, gender, and the body shows a strong Millay influence, and a close reading of the two poets uncovers some surprising similarities. Indeed, any approach to define Sexton's literary debt to Millay should primarily analyze the textual and conceptual connections between the two poets, and it is precisely this area of scholarship that can yield the most interesting results. Sexton's handling of femininity and the female body may be partly responsible for the status she attained as an original female poet, but this originality owes a great deal to Millay's earlier explorations of the same issues. Millay had furnished Sexton with a substantial body of work the younger poet felt she had

to respond to, and poems such as the latter's 'Self in 1958' provide perhaps the ideal starting point for comparison.

One of the first Sexton poems to interrogate the artificial construction of femininity, **'Self in 1958'** presents a speaker who describes herself as 'a plaster doll'; 'I have hair', she writes, 'black-angel-stuffing to comb, / nylon legs, luminous arms / and some advertised clothes.' Analyzing the split between her inner self and this artificial product that people 'think I am me', Sexton (1981a) concludes with this question:

> What is reality; To this synthetic doll; Who should smile, who should shift gears; Should spring the doors open in a wholesome disorder; And have no evidence of ruin or fears?[5]

The poem begins and ends with the vital question 'what is reality', a question that is beyond the speaker's comprehension. The woman's development from a 'plaster doll' to a 'synthetic' one cannot help her find any answers: the only versions of herself she is familiar with are artificial, and there is no actual difference in the move from the plaster to the synthetic. Both versions suggest the ease with which the speaker's identity is forged and molded by the requirements of those 'who think I am me', and both descriptions imply that the speaker is no longer able to make 'the real me' part of the equation.

In several respects, the above poem echoes 'The Plaid Dress' (*Huntsman, What Quarry?,* 1939), one of Millay's most overtly feminist poems, in which she criticizes the social structures that force her to perform, as it were, femininity in a fanciful dress that signifies for her only 'purple angers and red shames'. Like Sexton, Millay (1995: 348) draws attention to the split between appearance and reality, emphasizing the oppressive power of the former over the latter:

> Strong sun, that bleach; the curtains of my room, can you not render; colourless this dress I wear?; This violent plaid of purple angers and red shames, the yellow stripe; of thin but valid treacheries? [. . .]
>
> No more uncoloured than unmade; I fear, can be this garment that I may not doff;; Confession does not strip it off,; To send me homeward eased and bare.

The poem closes with the speaker entertaining her guests 'all through the formal, unoffending evening', playing with her 'clean, bright hair' and musing on the 'subtle gown', which is 'not seen, / but it is there'. This poem may initially appear more forceful than Sexton's **'Self in 1958'**, partly because Millay's speaker is clear about the distinction between the real and the socially constructed. The plaid dress, in other words, stands for the product that matches the woman's 'clean, bright hair', the artificial self she has to display 'all through the formal, unoffending evening'. The colorless dress she longs for, by contrast, represents the image she would like to project, the self that 'is not seen, but it is there'. Nevertheless, the speaker's awareness of the mechanisms of feminine construction does not alter the situation; 'confession', she explains, is not enough 'to send me homeward eased and bare'. The plaid dress will always replicate 'the thin but valid treachery' of feminine performance, the treachery of appearance over reality, and the speaker knows that this dress cannot be discarded. Walker succinctly observes that Millay writes about her inability 'to counter the force of endless replication'. 'One version of the body', she explains, 'calls up another, but none may be genuinely claimed as one's own.' (Walker (1992), in Freedman, 1998: 96). Along the same lines, Sexton shows that her shift from a plaster doll to a synthetic one represents precisely this process of meaningless replication, which society mistakenly perceives as the real 'me'.

For both Millay and Sexton, clothes are inextricably linked with feminine 'properness'; the two poets often sound alike in their attempts to mock the social rules that define this properness, and this affinity is sometimes evident in the focus of their poems. In **'Clothes'**, for instance, Sexton describes the garments she would like to wear before her death; the bra, she says, would have to be 'the padded black one that my lover demeaned / when I took it off', and the underpants will be white 'for it was my mother's dictum / that nice girls wore only white cotton'. And yet, Sexton concludes, 'If my mother had lived to see it / she would have put a WANTED sign up in the post office / for the black, the red, the blue I've worn (Sexton, 1981a: 381).' Implying that she had never been a 'nice girl' according to her mother's superficial standards, Sexton may also have had in mind Millay's 'The Shroud', a short poem that begins and ends with the words: 'Death, I say, my heart is bowed / Unto thine,—O mother! / This red gown will make a shroud / Good as any other!' At a first level, this poem seems fairly simple—the only thing that catches the reader's attention is the speaker's defiant declaration that the red gown will make a good shroud. The reference to the mother seems irrelevant, serving only metrical purposes. And yet, a second reading reveals that the presence of the mother is far from coincidental; despite her half-rebellious, half-playful tone, the speaker actually sounds as if she wishes to convince her mother of the legitimacy of her choice—a shroud not white, but red. With **'Clothes'**, written shortly before her death, Sexton returns to the older poet's themes—its relationship to Millay's poem is clearly intertextual, with the same idea about clothes to die in, and the presence of the mother. It is hard to understand why the two poets are so fascinated by this scenario, and it would not be sufficient to claim that their only purpose was to subvert the ideal of feminine

properness. In fact, both poets imply that the rules that govern this properness are not easy to transgress, and that even a woman approaching death often feels the need to go back to a maternal authority figure, in order to negotiate and seek approval for her 'feminine' (or 'non-feminine') choices. Neither **'Clothes'** nor 'The Shroud' is among each woman's best poems (after all, Millay and Sexton are often blamed for the same artistic fault, the unevenness and inconsistent quality of their work). But they do reflect the affinity in their poetic imaginations and give a good picture of the artistic focus through which they voiced their shared concerns.

Feminist critics generally hail Sexton for the ease with which she handled subjects such as the female body. Alicia Ostriker, for instance, argues that:

> Sexton's material is heavily female and biological. She gives us full helpings of her breasts, her uterus, her menstruation, her abortion. [. . .] Preoccupied with the flesh, she swings between experiencing it as sacred and fertile and experiencing it as filthy and defiled. [. . .] Sexton challenges our residual certainties that the life of the body should be private and not public, and that women especially should be seen and not heard, except among each other, talking about their messy anatomies.
>
> (Ostriker, 1982: 11)

A representative poem of this description is **'Consorting With Angels'** (from Sexton's collection *Live or Die* (1981a: 111-112)):

> I was tired of being a woman; tired of the spoons and the pots; tired of my mouth and my breasts; tired of the cosmetics and the silks; There were still men who sat at my table; circled around the bowl I offered up [. . .]; But I was tired of the gender of things.
>
> Last night I had a dream [. . .]; In that dream there was a city made of chains; where Joan was put to death in man's clothes; and the nature of the angels went unexplained; no two made in the same species; one with a nose, one with an ear in its hand; one chewing a star and recording its orbit; each one like a poem obeying itself; performing God's functions, a people apart.
>
> 'You are the answer'; I said, and entered; lying down on the gates of the city; Then the chains were fastened around me; and I lost my common gender and my final aspect; Adam was on the left of me; and Eve was on the right of me; both thoroughly inconsistent with the world of reason; We wove our arms together; And rode under the sun; I was not a woman anymore; not one thing or the other. [. . .]
>
> I've been opened and undressed; I have no arms or legs; I'm all one skin like a fish; I'm no more a woman; than Christ was a man.

The subject of the poem, that is to say, femininity, gender, and the body, is evident already at the outset: 'I was tired of being a woman / [. . .] tired of the gender of things', Sexton declares, echoing the directness and simplicity of Millay's famous sonnet: 'I, being born a woman and distressed / By all the needs and notions of my kind'. The development of Sexton's poem presents a speaker who questions gender constructions, gradually rejecting both the typical articles of feminine masquerade (cosmetics and silk), and the conventional appearance of the female body. The speaker's determination to liberate herself from 'the gender of things' climaxes in a rather disturbing imaginary mutilation of her own body, whose unique and unclassifiable nature brings her closer to the angels she saw in her dream ('the nature of angels went unexplained, / no two made in the same species / [. . .] each one like a poem obeying itself / [. . .] a people apart.') As Deryn Rees-Jones has noticed, the use of the angel is an appropriate medium for voicing suffering or anguish, simultaneously adding to Sexton's poetry an androgynous dimension 'which removes it from being a direct expression of her female self' (Rees-Jones, 1999: 286). The speaker's wish to reconcile the feminine and the masculine parts of her self is evident in her reference to Adam and Eve, whose presence on either side of her is 'thoroughly inconsistent with the world of reason'. The poem concludes with the speaker's celebration of the complete loss of her 'common gender and final aspect'; 'opened and undressed', she is 'all skin like a fish'.

'Consorting With Angels' is not, however, a masochistic fantasy, but a comment on the possible transcendence of gender and corporeal representation. The final image of the fish—a creature whose gender is not visibly identifiable—aptly accompanies the speaker's transforming journey with Adam and Eve, further reinforcing the impact of the desired transcendence. Sexton's vivid imagination has produced a poem that approaches gender and femininity from an undoubtedly original perspective. This originality, however, should not prevent us from acknowledging the dialogue with Millay's 'Desolation Dreamed Of' (*Wine from These Grapes*), as well as with her short story 'Powder, Rouge and Lip-stick'. Like Sexton, Millay utilizes the power of the dream and focuses on an ideal image of femininity free from artificial construction: 'Desolation dreamed of, though not accomplished, / Set my heart to rocking like a boat in a swell. / To every face I met, I said farewell. / Green rollers breaking white along a clean beach [. . .] when shall I reach that island? / Gladly, O painted nails and shaven arm-pits, would I see less of you! / Gladly, gladly would I be far from you for a long time, O noise and stench of man!'. Unlike Sexton, however, Millay concludes with a note of defeat, as her speaker is forced to admit that she is not proposing to leave behind any of her 'feminine' possessions (like, for instance, her painted nails): 'This feigning to be asleep while wide awake', she says, 'is all the loneliness / I shall ever achieve' (Millay, 1995: 297).

As is obvious, Millay's poem does not share the 'surreal, apocalyptic vision [and] biblical borrowing' of 'Consorting With Angels' (Rees-Jones, 1999). Neither does the earlier poem deny femaleness; at no point does its speaker declare that she is 'no more a woman'. 'Desolation Dreamed Of', as the title indicates, describes a wish that the speaker knows will never materialize; and yet, the word 'desolation', by virtue of its force, as well as its presence in the title, suggests that there is more than meets the eye—the images of 'painted nails' and 'shaven arm-pits' that follow directly afterwards demonstrate very clearly where the speaker's frustration lies in. To put it differently, it is once again the 'feminine' artifice that is under attack. Millay's imaginary haven island stands in direct analogy to Sexton's dream city, as both places are loaded with fantasies of escape and corporeal transcendence. Furthermore, through this moving exposition of the split between the outside image and inner self, Millay's poem manages to destabilize the shaky notion of an authentic femininity, and the earlier writer's water imagery and emphasis on cleanliness (white waves, clean beach, etc.) suggest the need for a kind of liberation and purification very similar to that attained by Sexton's speaker in her new, fish-like form. At the same time, the latter's androgynous, mutilated, and undressed body echoes Gwendolyn, the main character of Millay's 'Powder, Rouge and Lip-stick', who performs a symbolic mutilation of her elaborately feminine body when, after refusing to put on any make up, she reveals her 'rather boyish neck', 'pale mouth', and complete absence of eyebrows. Just as the nature of Sexton's angels 'went unexplained, / no two things in the same species, / one with a nose, one with an ear in its hand', Gwendolyn insists on diversity, questions her role as one of the female species and, ultimately, with no eyebrows and with 'awkward, purplish hands' makes a freakish appearance in front of her husband; when he declares that she looks 'like the very devil' she calmly responds that this is her 'natural self' (see also Woodard (1992) and Boyd [Edna St. Vincent Millay (1924)]).

It has already been said that second-wave feminist criticism was not particularly eager to recognize Millay's importance within the context of modern writing, mainly because the erratic quality of her artistic output made the poet a somewhat inferior candidate for academic study. Unfortunately, this marginalization of Millay within the academy, instead of arousing the suspicions of feminist critics, further undermined the poet's contribution to feminist and socially conscious literature, erasing almost her name from relative debates. It is true that, compared to 'Consorting With Angels', Millay's strategies of disrupting traditional gender stereotypes about femininity and the female body may initially appear less forceful and less subversive than those produced by mid-century women poets. The subtle, often stylized way with which Millay interrogates social constructions shares, at a first glance, little with Sexton's disturbing vision. At the same time, as Gilbert and Gubar argue, it was precisely this 'stylized dramatization of 'womanliness'' that shaped 'in a number of significant ways [. . .] the achievements of such mid-century artists as Sylvia Plath, Anne Sexton, Adrienne Rich, and Elizabeth Bishop',[6] (see Gilbert and Gubar, 1994: 74-75), and therefore the superficial stylistic differences should not take precedence over the crucial conceptual similarities.

It must also be remembered that Sexton often subscribes to Millay's perspective, rejecting surreal visions of physical transformation and gender transcendence. In **'The Poet of Ignorance'**, for instance, she writes: 'True, I have a body / and I cannot escape from it. / I would like to fly out of my head, / but that is out of the question. / It is written on the tablet of destiny / that I am stuck here in this human form.' The poem seems to be as much about religion and faith as it is about femininity and madness, but the conclusion, which emphasizes the poet's sense of hopelessness and distrust of dreams (cf.: 'who am I to believe in dreams?') (Sexton, 1981b), is certainly reminiscent of Millay's frustration in 'Desolation Dreamed Of'.

Sexton's familiarity with the body and its functions has been almost exhaustively analyzed by her critics; poems like **'In Celebration of My Uterus'** or **'Menstruation at Forty'** are perhaps the two critical favorites. Yet, few scholars have acknowledged that such poems owe a great deal to Millay's earlier attempts to bring the aging female body into the foreground, with poems such as 'Menses'. A notable exception is Jeannine Dobbs, who argued in the 1970s that Millay's bold thematology and outspokenness can be traced in the writings of Sylvia Plath, Maxine Kumin and Muriel Rukeyser. She furthermore insisted that Sexton's **'Menstruation at Forty'**, usually seen as 'a breakthrough in female honesty' and 'a rebelling against old taboos', should be read 'in the context of Millay's "Menses"' (Dobbs, 1979: 105). Nevertheless, with the possible exception of Gilbert and Gubar or Cheryl Walker—who has repeatedly written about Millay's 'impressive ability to externalize the language of the body' (Walker (1992), in Freedman, 1998: 93), the field of Millay's contribution to the radicalization of American women's poetry is still largely unexplored.

'Menses' provides indeed a representative example of the kind of influence Millay exercised on the following generation of American women writers, and it is definitely a poem that anticipates Sexton's **'Menstruation at Forty'**. Millay's poem is structurally more complex; the main speaking voice is that of a man trying to come to terms with his wife's irritability, caused by her monthly period. Throughout the poem, the man is sympathetic and understanding; however, when he describes his quarrel with his wife, he uses some particularly strong language:

> I felt it. Down my side; Innocent as oil I see the ugly venom slide; Poison enough to stiffen us both, and all our friends; But I am not pierced, so there the mischief ends.
>
> There is more to be said; I see it coiling; The impact will be pain; Yet coil; yet strike again. [. . .]
>
> You know how wild you can be. You are willing to be turned; To other matters; you would be grateful, even.
>
> (Millay (1995: 345-347))

The choice of a male speaker to open a poem about menstruation is certainly intriguing, and all the more so because it is difficult to decide whether this speaker assumes a competitive or a sympathetic attitude toward the woman. On the whole, he does try to sound sympathetic when he addresses his wife directly, but his private thoughts and the use of phrases such as 'ugly venom' or 'poison' suggest a more complex picture. What really gives us a hint about this man's attitude is the description of his wife's behavior as a 'mischief' that cannot 'pierce' him—an expression that sounds patronizing, to say the least, and relegates the woman to the position of an unruly child who needs to be properly disciplined. The poem develops around this idea of patronizing support, with the woman oscillating between acceptance and denial of the above pattern. She becomes more noticeable towards the end of the poem; after crying on her husband's breast 'for all the lovely things that are not and have been', she thanks him for his patience, concluding with the lines: 'I shall be better soon. Just Heaven consign and damn / To tedious Hell this body with its muddy feet in my mind!' Millay's conclusion suggests that, to a certain extent, the woman does see her behavior as a kind of mischief that needs to be corrected, and it is perhaps for this reason that 'Menses' attracted the attention of feminist critics relatively late. Walker, for instance, seems to be right in reading the poet's conclusion as 'a confession of helplessness, climaxing with a cry of anguish', but she does concede that 'Menses' should be 'recognized as a brave and original poem, perhaps the first to deal openly with pre-menstrual syndrome' (Walker, 1991: 155).

Even though Walker limits her discussion to the twentieth century, forgetting figures such as Anne Finch, whose poem 'The Spleen' (1713) also refers to PMS, her argument is by no means negligible. 'Menses' is indeed a poem that testifies to Millay's artistic versatility; the 'dated', 'sentimental' poet famous for her elegant lines and tightly crafted lyrics has written a three-page, free verse poem that perceptively depicts female psychology during menstruation and does not shrink from talking about the physical aspect of the situation either. Furthermore, the poet's perception mocks, as it were, Walker's implicit dismissal of Millay's 'confession of helplessness', for it is precisely the anguish and helplessness that make her female speaker credible. Millay should also be applauded for the skill with which she makes a point about the aging female body: the references to 'all the lovely things that are not and have been' alert the reader to the fact that s/he is not simply dealing with the quarrel of a couple in their twenties or thirties who had to cancel their weekend plans because of the woman's period. On the contrary, Millay's clever insertion of elements that emphasize irrevocable loss and suppressed bitterness throughout 'Menses' indicates that she is concerned primarily with the physical and psychological impact of the completion of the menstrual cycle. The speaker's condemnation of her body 'with its muddy feet in my mind' expresses both the wish to be liberated from all the features that remind her of the female body's unfulfilled potential (e.g. pregnancy?) and the fear that this wish will soon come true.

Sexton's **'Menstruation at Forty'** constitutes a direct parallel that simultaneously complements and questions Millay's point in 'Menses':

> I was thinking of a son; The womb is not a clock; nor a bell tolling; but in the eleventh month of its life; I feel the November; of the body as well as of the calendar; In two days it will be my birthday; and as always the earth is done with its harvest; This time I hunt for death; the night I lean toward; the night I want; Well then—; speak of it!; It was in the womb all along; I was thinking of a son . . . ; You! The never acquired; the never seeded or unfastened [. . .]; All this without you—; two days gone in blood. [. . .]
>
> Two days for your death; and two days until mine.
>
> Love! That red disease—; year after year, David, you make me wild!;
>
> (Sexton (1981a: 137-138))

Perhaps the first thing to notice here is the association of the womb with physical decay (also evident in Millay's poem). The speaker declares that her prime has passed; it is 'the November / of the body as well as of the calendar', and 'the earth is done with its harvest'. She attributes her pessimism and death wish to the specifics of female biology ('This time I hunt for death / [. . .] It was in the womb all along'), an element that reminds us of Millay's speaker, who seems to long for physical annihilation when she asks for her body to be consigned to hell and damned because it interferes with her mind. Similarly, in 'Menses' the speaker cries 'for all the lovely things that are not and have been', voicing thus a lament for her infertility that is repeatedly echoed by Sexton in her own poem (cf: 'All this without you / two days gone in blood / [. . .] two days for your death', etc.). Both speakers experience menstruation as a kind of death (although arguably this element is

stronger in Sexton's poem) and both associate it with temperamental instability. Millay, for instance, knows 'how wild' she can be, and Sexton declares that both 'the red disease' and a potential pregnancy 'would make her wild'. But in Sexton's poem there is no male voice (supportive or competitive), which indicates that her speaker has come to terms with the situation, and needs no mediator to interpret her feelings. In fact, **'Menstruation at Forty'** closes on a rather positive note, with Sexton accepting her infertility. Nevertheless, the textual affinities between the two poems are strong enough to show why Sexton's poem should be read in the context of Millay's 'Menses'—the former's speaker often seems like a younger version of the speaker in 'Menses', and the imagined dialogue with the 'never seeded' David both replaces the absence of the male voice, and responds directly to Millay's lament for 'the lovely things that are not and have been'.

It becomes obvious, therefore, that arguments like the following one by Deryn Rees-Jones, namely, that Sexton became 'notorious for breaking a variety of social taboos' (Rees-Jones, 1999: 286) should be read in the light of Millay's own pioneering efforts to renegotiate the legitimacy of intimate, female experiences as fit literary material. Jeannine Dobbs has a point when she reminds us that 'Millay, along with Amy Lowell, Genevieve Taggard, and May Sarton was among the first to write explicitly about formerly taboo subjects' (Dobbs, 1979: 92). Menstruation may remain Dobbs's primary focus, but more recent research has analyzed several other aspects of Millay's work that enhance her credentials within the above context. Abortion, for instance, is a further example of Millay's contribution to the disruption of social taboos; her short story 'Out of Reach of the Baby', a multi-layered text whose primary polemic is a clearly articulated argument for female independence and, ultimately, a justification for abortion, should be read in juxtaposition with the corresponding Sexton poem (**'The Abortion'**).[7] Although allowances must certainly be made in order to accommodate the technical differences (i.e. prose vs. poetry), Millay's influence on writers like Sexton offers a fresh, new interpretative perspective that simultaneously elevates the earlier poet to a more prominent position within the canon of American women's writing and places the work of her successors within a tradition that can provide a more complete appreciation of their achievements.

Anne Sexton arguably occupies a distinguished place among Millay's successors; the earlier poet's influence on her work may have been relatively overlooked, but it is definitely there. Millay was one of the first poets who brought female physicality into the foreground, not only from the perspective of the young and able-bodied but also from the perspective of the aging and the 'private'. She was a poet who repeatedly contested the concept of an 'authentic' femininity, drawing attention to the discrepancy between appearance and reality, and interrogating stereotypical models of 'proper' feminine behavior. The consistency with which Millay attempted to disrupt social taboos and remap the permissible thematology of women's poetry provoked a warm response in Sexton, who produced detailed, sensitive explorations of feminine artificiality, and cleverly reworked Millay's notion of linguistic and corporeal performance. Sexton's subversive way of destabilizing gender and reconstructing the female body not only testifies to the extent of the earlier poet's impact but also demonstrates that the younger woman was among Millay's most intelligent disciples. In spite of the fluctuations in scholarly opinion, Millay occupied a special place in Sexton's artistic consciousness, and the latter's decision to follow in Millay's steps, both with respect to preferred subject matter and artistic posturing explains, perhaps, why Sexton once wondered whether she was Millay's reincarnation.

Notes

1. Emphasis Hecht's; quoted by Middlebrook (1991: pp. 277-278). Hecht's comment regarding Sexton's impact is certainly not negligible, considering that Pablo Neruda and W. H. Auden were the two distinguished figures of that event.

2. Cited in Middlebrook (1991: 319-320). For a challenging reading of Sexton's 'feminine' poetic performances and of her self-packaging as a marketable cultural icon, see also Bronfen (1998).

3. For an interesting view of Sextons's use of the body, as well as of her understanding of performativity / poetic personae in relation to her teaching career, see also Salvio (1999).

4. The elements that Clark interprets as 'feminine' in the above excerpt are Millay's 'coquettish' use of language, and her 'girlish cleverness and wit'.

5. All poems quoted hereafter are reprinted by permission of Sterling Lord Literistic, Inc. Copyright by Anne Sexton.

6. Consider also Sandra M. Gilbert's argument in 'Female Female Impersonator: Millay and the Theatre of Personality', according to which 'a number of literary women—notably Plath and Sexton, along with such other poets as Rich and Levertov—have followed Millay's path of self-dramatization, narrating confessional histories of the self which use the fetishized private life of a woman to comment on the public state of the world'; cited in Thesing (1993: 293-312 (309)).

7. For an excellent reading of Millay's short story see Veatch-Pulley (1993).

References

Axelrod, S. G. (1975) 'Anne Sexton's *Rowing Toward God*' in L. Wagner-Martin (1989) editor, *Critical Essays on Anne Sexton,* Boston: Hall, 65-67, originally published *Modern Poetry Studies, no. 6.*

Boyd, N., [*Edna St. Vincent Millay* (1924)], *Distressing Dialogues,* New York: Harper, 111-122.

Bronfen, E. (1998) 'Performing hysteria: Anne Sexton's 'business' of writing suicide' in J. Simons and K. Fullbrook (1998) editors, *Writing: A Woman's Business: Women Writing and the Marketplace,* Manchester: Manchester University Press, 126-144.

Butler, J. (1999) *Gender Trouble: Feminism and the Subversion of Identity* 10th anniversary ed, London: Routledge, (originally published 1990).

Ciardi, J. (1954) 'Two nuns and a strolling player' (review of *Mine the Harvest*) in W. B. Thesing (1993) editor, *Critical Essays on Edna St. Vincent Millay,* New York: Hall, 95-96.

Clark, S. (1991) '*Jouissance* and the sentimental daughter: Edna St. Vincent Millay' in M. Dickie and T. Travisano (1996) editors, *Gendered Modernisms: American Women Poets and Their Readers,* Philadelphia: The University of Pennsylvania Press, 143-169, (154-155).

Colburn, S. (1988) editor, *No Evil Star: Essays, Interviews, and Prose: Anne Sexton,* Ann Arbor: The University of Michigan Press.

Dobbs, J. (1979) 'Edna St. Vincent Millay and the tradition of domestic poetry' *Journal of Women's Studies in Literature* Vol. 1: 89-106 (105).

Eckman, F. (1976) 'Edna St. Vincent Millay: notes toward a reappraisal' in L. Filler (1976) editor, *A Question of Quality: Popularity and Value in Modern Creative Writing,* Bowling Green: Bowling Green University Popular Press, 193-203.

Epstein, D. M. (2001) *What Lips My Lips Have Kissed: The Loves and Love Poems of Edna St. Vincent Millay,* New York: Holt.

Gilbert, S. and Gubar, S. (1994) *No Man's Land: The Place of the Woman Writer in the Twentieth Century* Vol. 3, New Haven: Yale University Press, 63-65.

Gilbert, S. and Gubar, S. (1996) editors, *The Norton Anthology of Literature by Women,* London: Norton, 1501-1502.

Gray, R. (1998) *American Poetry of the Twentieth Century,* London: Longman, (originally published 1990).

Gunn, T. (1962) 'Review of *All My Pretty Ones*' in J. D. McClatchy (1978) editor, *Anne Sexton: The Artist and Her Critics,* Bloomington: Indiana University Press, 124-126.

Juhasz, S. (1991) 'Anne Sexton' in E. Showalter, L. Baechler and A. Walton Litz (1993) editors, *Modern American Women Writers: Profiles of Their Lives and Works from the 1870s to the Present,* New York: Collier, (originally published New York: Charles Scribner's Sons, 1991).

Lowell, R. (1974) 'Anne Sexton' in S. Colburn (1991) editor, *Anne Sexton: Telling the Tale,* Ann Arbor: The University of Michigan Press.

Macdougall, A. R. (1952) editor, *Letters of Edna St. Vincent Millay,* New York: Grosset & Dunlap.

McGrath, L. (1988) 'Anne Sexton's poetic consciousness: death, god, and form' in F. Bixler (1988) editor, *Original Essays on the Poetry of Anne Sexton,* The University of Central Arkansas Press: Arkansas, 138-163.

Middlebrook, D. W. (1991) *Anne Sexton: A Biography,* London: Virago.

Middlebrook, D. W. (1994) 'Circle of women artists: Tillie Olsen and Anne Sexton at the Radcliffe Institute' in E. Hedges and S. Fisher-Fishkin (1994) editors, *Listening to Silences: New Essays in Feminist Criticism,* New York: Oxford University Press, 17-21.

Millay, E. (1995) in N. Millay Ellis (1995) editor, *Collected Poems,* Cutchogue, NY: Buccaneer, 688 (originally published New York: Harper, 1956).

Miller, N. (1999) *Making Love Modern: The Intimate Public Worlds of New York's Literary Women,* Oxford: Oxford University Press.

Oates, J. C. (1983) 'Anne Sexton: self-portrait in poetry and letters' in L. Wagner-Martin (1989) editor, *Critical Essays on Anne Sexton,* Boston: Hall, 52-65, originally published in Oates, J. C. (1983), *The Profane Art: Essays and Reviews,* New York: Dutton.

Ostriker, A. (1982) 'That story: Anne Sexton and her *Transformations' American Poetry Review* Vol. 11: 11-16.

Rees-Jones, D. (1999) 'Consorting with angels: Anne Sexton and the art of confession' *Women: A Cultural Review* Vol. 10, No. 3: 283-296.

Salvio, P. (1999) 'Teacher of 'weird abundance': portraits of the pedagogical tactics of Anne Sexton' *Cultural Studies* Vol. 13, No. 4: 639-660.

Sexton, A. (1981a) in L. G. Sexton (1981) editor, *The Complete Poems,* Boston: Houghton Mifflin, 155-156.

Sexton, A. (1981b) 'The poet of ignorance' in L. G. Sexton (1981) editor, *The Complete Poems,* Boston: Houghton Mifflin, 433-435.

Shurr, W. H. (1981) 'Anne Sexton's love poems: the genre and the differences' in L. Wagner-Martin (1989) editor, *Critical Essays on Anne Sexton,* Boston: Hall, 245-254, originally published in *Modern Poetry Studies,* vol. 10, no. 1.

Stanbrough, J. (1979) 'Edna St. Vincent Millay and the language of vulnerability' in S. Gilbert and S. Gubar (1979) editors, *Shakespeare's Sisters: Feminist Essays on Women Poets,* Bloomington: Indiana University Press, 183-199.

Stipes-Watts, E. (1977) *The Poetry of American Women from 1632 to 1945,* Austin: The University of Texas Press, 172.

Thesing, W. B. (1993) editor, *Critical Essays on Edna St. Vincent Millay,* New York: Hall.

Veatch-Pulley, J. (1993) 'Out of reach of the baby, the artist, and society: Millay's fiction and feminism' in W. B. Thesing (1993) editor, *Critical Essays on Edna St. Vincent Millay,* New York: Hall, 273-286.

Vendler, H. (1995) *The Music of What Happens: Poems, Poets, Critics,* Cambridge, MA: Harvard University Press, 300-309, (originally published 1988).

Walker, C. (1991) *Masks Outrageous and Austere: Culture, Psyche and Persona in Modern Women Poets,* Bloomington: Indiana University Press.

Walker, C. (1992) 'The female body as icon: Edna Millay wears a plaid dress' in D. P. Freedman (1998) editor, *Millay at 100: A Critical Reappraisal,* Carbondale: Southern Illinois University Press, 85-99, (96) (originally published 1995).

Woodard, D. (1992) 'I could do a woman better than that: masquerade in Millay's potboilers' in D. P. Freedman (1998) editor, *Millay at 100: A Critical Reappraisal,* Carbondale: Southern Illinois University Press, 145-162.

Philip McGowan (essay date 2004)

SOURCE: McGowan, Philip. "Sexton's *Transformations.*" In *Anne Sexton and Middle Generation Poetry: The Geography of Grief,* pp. 73-91. Westport, Conn.: Praeger, 2004.

[*In the following excerpt, McGowan analyzes six of Sexton's poems in* Transformations—*"Snow White and the Seven Dwarfs," "Rumpelstiltskin," "Cinderella," "Red Riding Hood," "Hansel and Gretel," and "Briar Rose"—showing her use of the transformative power of language "to produce new versions and voices that converse with the 'originals.'"*]

Anne Sexton does a deeper favor for me: she domesticates my terror, examines it and describes it, teaches it some tricks which will amuse me, then lets it gallop wild in my forest once more.

—Kurt Vonnegut Jr. from "Foreword" to
Transformations

Vonnegut's "Foreword" provides an enlightening prelude to Sexton's 1971 collection of revisited and revised readings of sixteen Grimm brothers' fairy tales. His above comment, following the assertion noted at the beginning of this study that an essential part of a poet's achievement is to extend language, sets in process trains of thought that run through the collection's own prefatory poem **"The Gold Key"** as well as the sixteen poems that follow. The personal of which and to which these poems speak is the reader's, Vonnegut's, our own personal worlds as reflected by the shared pool of folklore and fairy tales that had also so intrigued the Brothers Grimm in their two volumes of "Nursery and Household Tales" published in 1812 and 1814. Jacob and Wilhelm Grimm assembled and put into print over two hundred oral tales, collating in that endeavor a reservoir of children's stories, myths, and communal narratives simultaneously inflected by and influencing generations of Western storytelling. Vonnegut recognizes how the poetic gaze in this volume is one turned inward but, crucially, not toward the poet's own mental and emotional worlds. Sexton's role in *Transformations* is as a facilitator in the understanding of more general fears and apprehensions with which individuals can identify, distilled through the personalized terror of a fairy tale. Sexton herself noted how this collection was a break from the more typical landscapes of her previous poetry: "[t]here are two rather serious *Transformations* poems, the rest are—I didn't really mean them to be comic, I mean, I guess I did, but I mean I didn't really know what I was doing, I just did what I felt like, I was very *happy* writing those poems, I was having a good time, except for a few that gave me trouble" (*NES* [*No Evil Star: Selected Essays, Interviews, and Prose*], 154).[1] Comic asides, allusions to contemporary U.S. cultural and political life, and references to more global events are sprinkled throughout these pieces in a poetic blend of past and present, European and American, the humorous and the horrific. Quite what Sexton's motivations were for writing these poems is open to conjecture, but the result is a collection that, to varying degrees of success, alternates between registers of the fantastic and the mundane, the possible and the improbable, the poetic and the pragmatic.

It is unsurprising that this adventure meets with the disapproval of Vendler who reads these "fiendish cartoons" as a perfect example of what she refers to as "Sexton's childlike and vengeful mind."[2] Vendler continues that Sexton was able to locate in fairy tales a structure that she herself could not provide and that the tales "gave her infantile fantasy; they gave her a clean trajectory; they turned her away from the morass of narcissism. But most of all, they enabled her as a satirist."[3] If this is the highest acclaim that Vendler accords Sexton, it is couched in an archly critical tone that relegates Sexton to the bottom tier of American poetic achievement, devoid of personal ability, allusional insight, and educated sources of reference. Indeed, so much does Vendler wish to diminish Sexton's work that she notes "[f]airy tales and folk tales put forth a child's black-and-white ethics, with none of the complexity of the Gospels, and none of the worldliness of the Greeks."[4] Vendler's Sexton is a poet beset with one-dimensional, repetitious, and childish versions of existence, a "malicious"[5] writer of limited qualities and even weaker verse. While it is true that Sexton is outside of the pantheon of American poets that meets with Vendler's enthused acclamations, it is myopic at best to dismiss her work by way of Vendler's own one-dimensional, monadic view. Does Sexton have recourse, solely or otherwise, to black-and-white ethics? Are her verses quite so easily pigeonholed within the simplistic binaries that Vendler establishes? Moreover, as the previous chapters and the following chapter [of *Anne Sexton and Middle Generation Poetry: The Geography of Grief*] suggest, her interest in mystical and religious symbolism and imagery overturns Vendler's assertion that Sexton's poetic eye misses biblical reference or relevance. *Transformations,* while a detour through a somewhat removed poetic geography, retains key aspects of the Sexton poetic impulse that make these poems recognizably her own, that chart an ethics and an aesthetics that are far from black-and-white, and that merge across the seventeen poems to form a matrix of inference, reference, and commentary that situates this collection at the center of Sexton's obsessive poetic combinations. If satire is the aim of these poems, Vendler stops short of revealing the object of its intent: is it directed at contemporary America, linked by Sexton to her renditions of the fairy tales in each poem's introductory stanzas? Are they satires upon the fairy tales themselves and the sources from which they have sprung? Or are these satires upon the human imagination and its capacity for constructing terror out of domestic situations, gender relations, and familial circumstances? This chapter will provide possible avenues of inquiry for responding to these questions by looking at six of the poems, moving between the original tales and what, it can be argued, are Sexton's metatales, acknowledging once more her deployment of an oppositional structure which sets one language or literary register against another, the space between the two, then, the location where Sexton's poetic art finds a voice that speaks outside of language.

Before her transformations proper Sexton provides her own introductory piece, **"The Gold Key,"** in which her speaker addresses an audience of named individuals, none of whom are children. Two of the ages of these adults are given, twenty-two and fifty-six, Sexton hereby dislocating the world of the fairy tale as the province of children only. The speaker, herself "a middle-aged witch" (*T* [*Transformations*], 1), speculates at the beginning of each poem about the relevance of what will follow, postulating possible concurrences between the fairy tale and the contemporary world. In **"The Gold Key"** she presents a youth of sixteen who searches for answers before the rendition of sixteen poems; the concordance between the youth's age and the number of poems is not to be overlooked, nor is his discovery of a gold key that opens "this book of odd tales / which transform the Brothers Grimm" (*T*, 2). The discovered gold key, as with the poem of that name, is the device that opens this book of fairy tales, the cipher by which their poetic codes can be understood. The speaker proclaims that the youth is "each of us" (*T*, 2): corresponding exactly with the number of tales in the book, the youth is both fact and fiction, a personification of fairy tale fantasies and the embodiment of human realities. Fact and fiction, fairy tale and reality, then, are not discordant opposites; rather, they form an integrated whole, speaking of and to each other, the stories they relate indivisible from each other's spheres of influence and formation. Closing **"The Gold Key,"** the speaker highlights once more a familiar Sexton strategy, the role and possibility of language. Commenting on her use of the word "transform" in the poem's fifth to last line with regard to the sixteen versions of the Brothers Grimm that follow, she remarks, "Transform? / As if an enlarged paper clip / could be a piece of sculpture. / (And it could)" (*T*, 2). The ability of these poems to transform the tales of the Grimms can only be achieved in language, just as a paper clip can be a piece of sculpture if our language permits us to say that it is. Language is a transformative medium: it creates words in which meaning can be found, or diffused, or adapted; it attempts the translation of what exists beyond language into the containable units of communicable expression. Moreover, it allows humanity to define and redefine at will, sanctioning the interpretation of a paperclip as sculpture as readily as not, the transformation in its status from the functional to the aesthetic realized in language if not in practice. Recalling an earlier consideration that words are like labels, it is clear how such an interpretation holds relevance here: the transformations that these poems undertake are transformations of language, Sexton's changing of the linguistic labels to produce new versions and voices that converse with the "originals," themselves transformations into the written word from oral traditions. The dialectic that ensues questions (as Sexton's speaker questions) the term "transform," positioning possible meaning at all levels within the possibility of language.[6] That these tales speak of the fantasies and terrors and abominations that lurk in the unconscious provided Sexton with a stream of sources for her poems. Accepting that "[p]oetry, after all, milks the unconscious" (*NES*, 85), Sexton here plumbs the depths of a loosely defined communal unconscious for her wider poetic inquiries into the operations of aesthetics and language.

"Snow White and the Seven Dwarfs"

The first of the six poems that this chapter will consider is also the first in Sexton's choice, relating the story of Snow White, or Snowdrop as she is referred to in the Grimms' tale. Altering the age of the putative heroine from seven to thirteen,[7] Sexton makes further slight adjustments to the original, the length of time Snow White wanders in the hills and forests before coming to the house of the dwarfs and the punishment visited upon the evil stepmother of the two of them. Sexton previews her interpretation with a thirteen-line aside about virginity that both sexualizes and desexualizes this state of innocence. The artificial portrait of a virgin with "Limoges" porcelain limbs and "china-blue doll eyes" (*T*, 3) anticipates the gullible naïveté of Snow White who falls for the guiles of her disguised stepmother. By making Snow White thirteen, Sexton places her in early adolescence (as opposed to being the child she clearly is in the original tale) on the border between childhood and adulthood, a teenage fashion victim unwittingly stood at the center of a debate about female aesthetics. She is a "dumb bunny" (*T*, 8) in Sexton's rendition, protected by the dwarfs, themselves equally sexualized by Sexton. As with the tale, Snow White falls for each of the three temptations, apparently killed off by the third, thus rendered as futile as Mallarmé's effaced coin: "She lay as still as a gold piece" (*T*, 8). Unable to place such beauty, even in death, below the ground, the dwarfs construct a glass coffin for the display of this example of aesthetic if not intellectual perfection, although in the tale this occurs after the appropriate three days of mourning. Her resurrection from this "death" is as much the result of accident as it is of fortune. Having rejected the prince's offer to buy her, indeed the dwarfs "will not part with her for all the gold in the world" (*FT* [The Brothers Grimm, *Fairy Tales*], 197), they agree to let him take her out of pity. Once moved, she awakes and the tale concludes with their marriage that coincides with the death of the wicked stepmother. In the Grimm version the latter chokes with rage and dies; in Sexton, she has "red-hot iron shoes" put on her feet in which she dances until she dies, "a subterranean figure" (*T*, 9). The happy-ever-after ending of the tale is represented obliquely in Sexton's poem in which Snow White is featured as being prone to the vanity that had so plagued her stepmother's life.

Sexton's transformation of this tale is centered in a characterization of Snow White as a naïve, vain, stupid, and ultimately vindictive individual. Neither is the stepmother (ever the symbol in fairy tales of a malcontent maternity) redeemed, both her and her stepdaughter entrapped in cycles of repetitive behavior that condemn each of them to lives of indolent self-obsession. Sexton's poem also edits out the framing introduction of the tale in which Snowdrop's real mother wishes for and then gives birth to a child "as white as snow" with "hair as black as ebony" (*FT*, 189). The mother's desire that her daughter have cheeks "as rosy as blood" (*FT*, 189) is adjusted in Sexton's introductory stanza, where the virgin's lips are the red of "Vin Du Rhône" (*T*, 3). The sexualized taxonomy that Sexton institutes is a clear line of differentiation from that of the tale, lacing her poem with inferences left dormant in the original. The spur for the mother's wish is her pricking of her finger with a needle and her subsequent gazing upon three drops of blood on the snow; this symbolic piercing and resultant bleeding of the female is directly tied to a hope for a child. Whether the queen at this stage is pregnant or not is not told, but the fact that Snowdrop is an exact copy of the mother's wish conforms to fairy tale policy that the wishes of good people come true. The sexual product of the king and queen's marriage, Snowdrop bears the uncanny resemblance to the mother's fantasy of a child, a fantasy that stipulates aesthetics and not ethics in its dream of an ideal infant.

The poem's speaker's contempt for Snow White emanates from the thirteen-year-old's impossible stupidity and her exploitation of her feminine wiles to influence and control the men in her world, be they dwarfs or princes. The practical world of work that men, certainly the dwarfs, inhabit is wholly disassociated from that of women who are predisposed to vanity and viciousness. Even firsthand experience of this division does not impact upon Snow White who, if the end of the poem is any indication, is about to repeat the errors of her stepmother. By divesting her Snow White of any connection with her mother, Sexton locks her "dumb bunny" into a narrative economy that does not recognize the potentially traumatic loss of the mother with which to explain or help enlighten Snow White's relation with her stepmother. That Snow White is more like her vain stepmother than her sewing mother is a trace from the tale upon which Sexton elaborates. The nature/nurture argument appears to be settled in favor of the latter: although she corresponds in every detail to the mother's wishes, Snowdrop/Snow White acts according to her stepmother's example. The challenge to the stepmother's authority as the (second) wife of the king is figured wholly in a sexual tussle with the issue of his first marriage, a child who will subvert the attractiveness of both mother and stepmother. The stepmother's need to be the fairest of them all articulates her interpretation of her role as queen: the most powerful female is the most beautiful and hence is worthy of the king. The stepmother's malevolent jealousy regarding Snow White is an unconscious awareness of the latent incest taboo that Snow White's beauty will challenge when she matures into adulthood. The king, a wholly absented figure in both versions, is the unnamed suitor for whose attentions the stepmother and Snow White vie. He is displaced in Snow White's life by other male protectors: the dwarfs, who mine for silver and gold, and the

prince who acts impulsively upon seeing the "dead" Snow White. The king's absence maintains the overwriting of the incest narrative that is eventually eradicated by Snow White's marriage and the simultaneous death of the stepmother. The tale concludes in happiness with Snowdrop and the prince ruling for many years; the poem, alternatively, summarizes a darker history in which Snow White, by maintaining a feminine obsession with her looks by "referring to her mirror" (*T*, 9), becomes her stepmother after all. Sexton plots a transformation from a dubious morality tale to a narrative in which stepmother and stepdaughter are reflective parts of each other, trapped at the mirror stage, unable to function independently either of men or of each other.

"RUMPELSTILTSKIN"

Sexton's third poem in the series, **"Rumpelstiltskin"** not only establishes a literary conversation with the original Grimm tale but also with Sexton's own poem **"The Abortion,"** in which she avers to this fairy tale character who can spin gold from straw. As Chapter 2 [of *Anne Sexton and Middle Generation Poetry*] argued, Sexton's reference to Rumpelstiltskin, a denial that the abortionist could be named with this character's name, circulated within an economy of power regarding the ability or otherwise to name. The speaker's incapacity on that occasion to find the appropriate name for the abortionist resulted from the unspeakable trauma of the event and the continued mourning over the loss of the aborted child. The denouement of the tale of "Rumpelstiltskin" revolves around the same principle of naming: the miller's daughter, now queen, must locate the name of this horrific figure if she is to retain her firstborn child promised as the third reward for his services. As chance dictates, she succeeds in her quest for the name and Rumpelstiltskin's power is negated and he exits the court and the tale empty-handed. Introduced as "a very beautiful . . . very shrewd and clever" (*FT*, 159) individual, she believes she can hoodwink "the manikin" (*FT*, 161) with an empty promise and is only saved by a messenger who has happened upon Rumpelstiltskin's hut. Defeated by being the terror that can be named, Rumpelstiltskin's externalization throughout the tale is completed by its ending.

Sexton, on the contrary, turns this situation about somewhat, internalizing this figure from the start of her poem as "the enemy within," the sexualized "law of your members, / the kindred of blackness and impulse" (*T*, 17). Variously identified in this introductory section as "all decay" and speaking with "Truman's asexual voice" (*T*, 17), he is a doppelgänger entity, emanating from the unconscious, uncontrollable, a voice usually censored. That he speaks with the voice of the thirty-third president, Harry S. Truman (1884-1972), who held office between 1945 and 1952, who sanctioned the dropping of atomic bombs on Hiroshima and Nagasaki, and who initiated the United States' involvement in the Korean War, ensures that Sexton's humorous characterization carries dark undertones for the American population in a poem published one year before Truman's death. Her acerbic incorporation of Truman into this doppelgänger figure speaks of a latent possibility within the American character, a dark side to the acceptable public face of the nation. Locating such an insistently American political reference within a poetic rendition of a European fairy tale alters the angle of inquiry and intent, the remoteness of the possible horrors of such a fairy tale land brought within the realm of an American (sub)conscious. Indeed, Sexton continues lacing her version with American references, commenting how the miller's daughter may die and "never see Brooklyn" and how the dwarf figure reveals that he has been "exhibited on Bond Street" (*T,* 18). His freakishness and monstrous appearance, more familiar possibly to American freak show audiences, does not prevent him producing gold "as good as Fort Knox" (*T,* 20) from the rooms of straw. Central to Sexton's account of this character is his repeated lament that he will never be a father to which the miller's daughter is oblivious when it comes to her promise. Once married and the mother of a baby boy, Sexton's lacerating characterization of the leading ladies in these tales continues. The child is suckled with "her dumb lactation" (*T,* 20) and she weeps uncontrollably upon Rumpelstiltskin's return to claim the child. Her first attempts at guessing his name result in her offering two of the names of the three wise men as possibilities. Visited with the same luck as the queen of the Grimms' tale, she redeems her promise by providing the name that "Not even the census taker knows" (*T,* 21). Rumpelstiltskin's power is eliminated and Sexton's goblin splits himself in two, "one part soft as a woman, / one part a barbed hook, / one part papa, / one part Doppelgänger" (*T,* 22).

Sexton's queen succeeds, against her own intellectual abilities, by finding the name for what lurks in the unconscious. In **"The Abortion,"** what was retained in the unconscious could not be named: it spoke of a terror that could not be spoken and it sought a resolution that could in no way resolve its trauma. Here, Sexton shifts the focus, positing Rumpelstiltskin as the manifestation of the queen's unconscious. Lost to her father due to his boasting about her talents, she will either be killed or will be married to the king. Caught between these two possibilities, she weeps for a solution that arrives in the shape of a figure bemoaning its own fate never to be called "Papa" (*T,* 18, 19). He shares with her an awareness of this denial of a knowledge of the paternal and seeks to overturn this situation by providing the king with what he most wishes, gold. Once this task is accomplished, however, he necessarily disappears only to return upon the birth of a male child. The queen, in both tale and poem, overlooks his lack of material want and futilely offers

untold riches in exchange for her keeping of her promise. Her maternal instincts soften his demands allowing her time to discover the apparently unnameable. Despite not having an official appearance on census records, he is locatable within: neither wise man nor freak, he is the embodiment of the queen's alter ego that wishes to hold the power of the paternal in its hand. Sexton's poem sets up a dynamic between subject positions that relates to the one self, providing two points of view on the one subjective dilemma.[8] Having resolved her own position with regard to the paternal that had been in dispute from the moment of her father's initial boast, she is supplied with the name for that which threatens to deny her of her maternal role. The defeat of Rumpelstiltskin results in his complete disappearance and the concurrent resolution of the queen's identity both within the subject position of the maternal and under the wider dominion of the patriarchal.

"CINDERELLA"

Possibly the most famous of the Grimm brothers' tales, "Cinderella" (or "Ashputtel" as it was originally entitled in German) is the ultimate reversal of fortune story, the rags-to-riches impossibility come true. As with "Snow White," the heroine is afflicted by the loss of her mother and the hurried imposition of an inconsiderate stepmother. Once more the reader is entered into a realm of ineffectual males the central victim of which is a daughter grieving the loss of her mother. The cruelty of the original tale, in which Ashputtel's two stepsisters treat her as their maid and, at their mother's behest, amputate a big toe and a heel respectively so as to fit the golden slipper left behind by the anonymous lady, is not masked by Sexton. Indeed, she extends the horror to the pecking out of the stepsisters' eyes at Cinderella's wedding. She also provides an extensive introductory sequence of four stanzas that reiterate the central point of the tale: the sudden and possibly chance introduction of fate into people's lives that brings them material good fortune. The familiar story of the sweepstakes winner or the woman whose insurance claim comes through frames a rendition of the Ashputtel/ Cinderella story in which Sexton deploys race and racial readings to assign rank and position to the various characters. The stepsisters relegate Cinderella to "the sooty hearth" each night with the result that she walks around "looking like Al Jolson" (*T,* 54). Cinderella, in acting out the part of their maid, inevitably becomes "black" to their "white" positions as her superiors, even though the blackness of her face is as much a fictive covering as Jolson's was in his minstrel act. Her racially inflected disguise is paralleled by her later disguises at the king's three-day feast where she appears in a golden dress, unrecognized by her stepsisters who are thus doubly mislead. As with the tale, all is revealed when the slipper fits, though in Sexton's version, the young prince is industrious enough to coat the palace steps with wax so that he can snare one of the mysterious lady's shoes.

The barbarity of both tale and poem, highlighted by the self-mutilations of the vainglorious stepsisters, is raised to another level by Sexton's apparent throwaway racial inflection of Cinderella's subordinated position. For all intents and purposes an orphan following her mother's death (her father's role in the scenario is miniscule to the point of irrelevance), the daughter maintains devout observance of her mother's grave, planting a branch in it brought back by her father from one of his frequent trips away on her request. Indeed, as the Grimm fairy tale relates this part of the story, she "cried so much that it was watered with her tears; and there it grew and became a fine tree. Three times every day she went to it and cried; and soon a little bird came and built its nest upon the tree, and talked with her, and watched over her, and brought her whatever she wished for" (*FT,* 215). This bird, to whom Sexton's Cinderella calls out "Mama! Mama! My turtledove" (*T,* 55), grants her every wish, supplanting the grieving daughter's mourning with magical rewards. Unlike Snow White, whose idiocy is the key to her characterization by Sexton, Cinderella is pitied and, indeed, respected. Her transformation in the tale is manifold: from daughter to a virtual orphan, to a downtrodden and blackened character, and ultimately to the wife of the prince. Sexton's accenting of the racial dimension, particularly by way of reference to Al Jolson, is an intriguing addition to the tale. Jolson's pretend blackness was a chosen act, an application of make-up that, in depicting blackness, perpetuated the racial barrier that has divided America from the first days of slavery. Cinderella's placement as a substitute Al Jolson figure is a double denigration: not only is she relegated to the lowest social rank, she is read as a parallel to a "comedy" act that maintained the exclusion of blacks from American forms of entertainment. Indeed, following the example of **"Rumpelstiltskin,"** she becomes entered into an American system of racial representation that found its heyday in American carnivals and freakshows.[9] Her unmasking as both not black and as the anonymous lady is in part a transgressive act: Cinderella "passes" as white on the three nights of the ball, returning to her normal "black" social position each time. Her eventual victory in Sexton's rendition is marked by the blinding of the stepsisters whose racial readings of her resulted in their abusive treatment of her as a social (and racial) inferior. Moreover, their own blind desire to become the prince's bride leads them to acts of self-mutilation: unable to see Cinderella for the good sister that she is, and prepared to treat her as a slave, they ironically commit these ultimate acts of white cruelty upon themselves. For their troubles, the white dove, a suggested reincarnation of Cinderella's mother, pecks out their eyes forcing

blindness upon those who could not see the truth before them when they could see. As for Cinderella and her husband, Sexton consigns them to an oddly sterile future, "happily ever after, / like two dolls in a museum case / never bothered by diapers or dust" (*T,* 56). Restored to her true "white" position, Cinderella is then elevated to the highest social rank, yet the impetus of Sexton's interpretation legislates against the possibility of such a denouement; rather, she elects to suspend them in time, divorced from the possibilities of change, childbirth, and death. Cinderella's transformation is complete: from a daughter grieving over her mother's untimely death, she herself becomes immortalized, and the issue of death that had initially devastated her life is withheld "for eternity" (*T,* 57).

"RED RIDING HOOD"

Sexton's rewriting of the original tale "Little Red-Cap" departs only marginally from the traditional story of the little girl and her ill grandmother who, eaten whole by a wolf, are saved by a passing huntsman. While the basic narrative thread is followed in this the eleventh of Sexton's transformations, Sexton embellishes with a lengthy five-stanza prefatory comment on deception and the addition of a sexualized subnarrative to the main tale. In her introductory advice on those in society who are deceivers, the speaker of this poem singles out five examples, the last two of which refer to herself: first is the adulteress shopping in the supermarket before meeting her lover; second, the con women who succeed in swindling an old lady out of her savings hidden under her mattress; third, the "Tonight Show" comic who slashes his wrists in despair the morning after he has entertained the nation; fourth, the speaker herself, displaying a serene exterior at cocktail hour that conceals an inner turmoil, her heart "panicked" (*T,* 75) in its charge toward death; and lastly her own self once more partaking in the elaborate self-deception that she can escape her past by building and then moving into a new house. This is a rota of the commonplace, a series of snapshots of mostly routine events and circumstances in a set of standard American lives. As a contrast to the outlandish events of the tale to follow, it is a sobering palliative. "Where is the moral?" (*T,* 74) the speaker asks, a question that reflects two ways, one on the mundane deceptions of this everyday world, the second upon the tale of Red Riding Hood. Are these morality tales? Are the poems that comprise ***Transformations*** examples of moral and immoral behavior from which the reader is to draw a particular set of conclusions? If these are not morality tales, then what is their purpose?

If Sexton is domesticating a general or even a pervasive sense of terror, she achieves this effect via a distillation of the universal through selected American gauzes. Her introductory passages anticipate the narrative action of the revisited tale, applying an American gloss to these traditional European storylines. The urban and suburban monotony of American life with which she prefaces this particular tale asks fundamental questions about the moral order of the nation in which she lives and writes. Placed at the center of her five vignettes, whether arbitrarily or not, is the suicide of the stand-up comic, a man of national and televisual fame and renown. As the central deceiver in her gallery, he plays a key narrative role. Not only the last example before the speaker's turn to her own life's deceptions, and thus a possible associative link, the fifteen lines detailing the stand-up comic's suicide underline how this man's fraud is one based in language. The adulteress and the con women are fraudulent in love and in money respectively; this individual deceives with words, producing comedy and impersonations of the vice president for the public while in private he operates on a different linguistic register, the common pool of special language shared by suicides. Indeed, the act of suicide is here figured in terms of language, "the slash / as simple as opening a letter" (*T,* 74): the guiding impulse toward the intimacy of a moment that offers access to words still concealed is refigured in an act that will forever deny further access to language. Suicide is here the central and possibly the supreme human deceit, and is irrevocably tied to the act of writing: "both the writer and the suicide are deceived by forms of possibility, both want to have a power in the realms where power slips away and becomes impossible: in writing and dying."[10] The stand-up comic's power to "delay sleep for millions" (*T,* 74) the previous evening, one side of this individual's deceptive performance in life, conceals this movement toward the ultimate existential deceit.

As a digression from the main events of the tale, the five stanzas that situate the reader in a recognizably American set of urban and suburban geographies may initially appear excessive but through these Sexton questions the meaning and possibility of morality. In such worlds that circulate without apparent moral bearings, any criteria for assessing and judging personal choices are dissipated: "transgressive" behavior can no longer be defined as such within an amoral universe and it is within such a context Sexton revises the tale of "Little Red-Cap." The wolf's actions in plotting to eat the little girl are no more reprehensible than those of the adulteress, the con women, or the suicide. That said, Sexton's depiction of the wolf is colored by references to his possible sexual proclivities: referred to as "a kind of transvestite" (*T,* 76) when dressed as the grandmother, the wolf is then portrayed as being so fat that he "appeared to be in his ninth month" (*T,* 78) once he has eaten both grandmother and granddaughter. Whether a transvestite or a possible transsexual, the wolf is defeated by the "carnal knife" of the huntsman who cuts open the wolf in "a kind of caesarian section" (*T,* 78). As with the tale, both Red Riding Hood and her

grandmother are intact inside, and their release is figured as a (re)birth. However, they are reconceived as "two Jonahs" (*T,* 78) while inside the wolf: whether duplicates of the Old Testament prophet swallowed whole by a whale as he attempted to flee from God, or whether twinned symbols of mutual bad luck is open to debate. Certainly, the enterprise of visiting her grandmother and encountering the wolf on the way invites the inevitable ill fortune to fall on both Red Riding Hood and her grandmother. Their shared ignorance of the wolf's obvious intentions is coupled with their shared amnesia of being inside him, however brief their sojourn. As a pairing the grandmother and Red Riding Hood are well met, and Sexton's perception of the two as twins reborn due to the invasive surgical operations of the huntsman concludes the rewriting of this tale with a pseudomaternity scene that wholly lacks a maternal. Not only is Red Riding Hood's actual mother absent, the wolf's gender legislates against his conceiving of and giving birth to anyone. His false maternity, ended by the penetrating "carnal" knife, is replaced by another one of stones, the weight of which kill him. As the deceiver deceived, the wolf is in the end the tale's only victim, the grandmother and Red Riding Hood saved from the terror of their ordeal by their inability to remember. The Grimm brothers' tale, in contrast, adds a postscript in which both Red-Cap and her grandmother reveal how they have learned their lesson and are able to defeat the wiles of another wolf. Sexton, as shown in her depiction of Snow White, maintains these central female characters in ignorance, oblivious to the horror into which their folly lead them.

"HANSEL AND GRETEL"

The penultimate tale chosen to undergo the Sexton poetic transformation, "Hansel and Gretel" navigates the move from animals eating humans to humans, or at least supernatural beings such as witches eating humans, and Sexton's introductory note cannot overlook the cannibalistic motif that drives this story. Condensing the action of the original, Sexton's rewrite also elides the fact that this tale is another that circles the motivations of a heartless stepmother that override the anemic good intentions of the father of the children. In the original tale it is the stepmother who plots their demise in the forest due to the poverty-stricken situation of the family only foiled on the first occasion by the enterprising Hansel who drops pebbles that guide both him and his sister home. As with the tale, so the poem also narrates the second abandonment in the wood; this time the children have only bread to leave as a trail and this is eaten by birds. After three days in the tale, and twenty in Sexton's version, they discover "a little house built of bread and covered with cakes, [with] windows of clear sugar" (*FT,* 122). Given the poverty and hunger of the children, this incarnation is the ultimate temptation and they begin to eat pieces of the house until the witch that lives there invites them in and befriends them under false pretences. Having separated the two, she decides to fatten Hansel up for eating and is only disrupted in her plan by Gretel's turn to be ingenious: she feigns ignorance about what the witch means when she asks her how to climb into the oven, locking the "godless" (*FT*, 125) witch inside once she has demonstrated her requirement. The tale closes with the children's escape with pocketfuls of pearls and jewels that they bring back to their father, now somewhat miraculously widowed of their vindictive stepmother.

Sexton's version remains mostly true to the source, though it omits the final jubilant and treasure-laden reunion with the father. Running through her transformation is a religious line of reference, from the bread their mother gives them, described as being "like a page out of the Bible" (*T*, 102), to the witch's desire to eat Hansel "as in a feast / after a holy war" (*T*, 103), to the closing image of a latent memory of the horror of the witch's incineration, the smell of which is recalled when eating at suppertime and is an occasion that calls for wine and "fine white linen / like something religious" (*T*, 105). Religious superstition, particularly in America, regarding witches seeps into Sexton's translation of the tale into her idiomatic poetic, though to ambiguous effect. The bread, "like pages out of the Bible," unlike the pebbles, does not save them, and it is the witch that provides any overt religious contexts in the poem. The memory of her death is a trace that is reconfigured in Christ-like terms, the wine and white linen tokens of Christian ceremonies that mark his death and resurrection. The witch's death symbolizes Hansel and Gretel's triumph over their own deaths and, for that matter, celebrates the demise of their stepmother, a further example of a warped surrogate maternal figure eventually done down by faith and goodness.

"Hansel and Gretel" is arguably the most disturbing of the Grimm brothers' fairy tales as at its heart stand two near-infant children whose fate is at the mercy of two malevolent female figures, both of whom pretend to have their best welfare at heart. This twisting of the maternal into deformed versions of femininity has serious affects on the development of the children, particularly in relation to their use of language and sign systems. If, in Lacanian terms, our entry into language is precipitated by the separation from the maternal, Hansel and Gretel's entrance into the realm of signification is facilitated by the stepmother's selfish intention to see them die. The horror of their prospective abandonment, overheard by the children, motivates their development of a code that will lead them back to the former security of their home. The pebbles that Hansel collects and then secretly disperses provide the vital signifying route back home, forming a narrative of their trail into the forest. That they are unsuccessful the second time is on account of the stepmother's barring the door, closing off the children from this resource. The bread that they drop on this occasion will inevitably disappear, its salvational properties questioned both by Sexton's analogy to pages from the Bible and by the children's consequent discovery that they have no method of finding their way home. Abandoned and without a rescue narrative at their disposal, Hansel and Gretel are at the mercy of whatever forces lurk in the unknown forest. That they fall prey to a cannibalistic witch who lives in a house made of food is a circumstance befitting a tale in which they are disposed of due to a lack of food. The house promises succor but reveals itself a false paradise, its inhabitant an inversion of their stepmother. These two female characters figure as the polar extremes of the range of humanity, both of whose self-obsessed concerns negate concerns about the children's well-being. Their deaths release the children and their father from this malignant strain of femininity. Indeed, the death of the witch anticipates (and arguably coincides with) the stepmother's death, and Sexton figures it in remarkable imagery in which the witch "turned as red / as the Jap flag" (*T*, 105). Whether Sexton is lacing her account with post-World War II American antipathy toward the Japanese, or whether she could find no more appropriate description for this particular red that she imagines, is uncertain but is disconcerting, particularly due to the use of the shortened form "Jap" rather than Japanese. The characterization of the evil witch, at turns cannibal, at others deceptively kind, is here formed in conjunction with another (and, following Pearl Harbor, an alien and aggressive) nation.[11] Undoubtedly, the alien behavior of this female, tallied with that of the stepmother, provides the motivating factors in this story, a successful conclusion to which is reached only through the children's quick thinking and their awareness of the deceptive nature of language, that works both against them and ultimately in their favor.

"BRIAR ROSE (SLEEPING BEAUTY)"

If "Hansel and Gretel" jostles for first place as the most unsettling of the Grimm fairy tales, in the Sexton poetic lexicon of transformed fairy tales, **"Briar Rose,"** the last in the collection, is unrivaled as the most disconcerting of her sixteen revisions. Retelling the well-known tale of a beautiful princess bewitched into a century-long sleep, Sexton weaves an Oedipal narrative into the father-daughter relationship. Condensing the prehistory of Briar Rose's conception that appears at the opening of the Grimm brothers' tale, Sexton substitutes a twenty-four line introductory stanza in which she predicts both the cause and effect of Briar Rose's affliction. In the original tale, a king and queen, who live in a land of fairies, are unable to conceive until the queen, out of an act of kindness, returns a fish to its river and is thanked in turn soon after with the birth of a daughter that had been promised by the grateful fish. The king, who "could not cease looking on" (*FT,* 41) his daughter for joy, holds a feast to which twelve out of the thirteen fairies in the kingdom are invited. Out of spite the thirteenth fairy curses the child to die at the age of fifteen, a spell ameliorated by another fairy to a sleep of one hundred years. Sexton keeps to this outline, but previews the events of the rewritten tale with a warning concerning the arrested development of a girl-child due to her overtly physical relationship with her father. Such a transgression of the incest taboo can only result in dire consequences, the daughter "stuck in the time machine, / suddenly two years old sucking her thumb, / as inward as a snail, / learning to talk again" (*T,* 107). The girls' regression to a state of oral fixation that predates her entry into language results from the traumatic relation with the father who maintains her in a closeted world dependent upon his protection. The journey that this final transformation will take is one that is admittedly, in the speaker's opinion, "rank as honeysuckle" (*T,* 108), a dense, cloying and on occasion thorny manifestation: the briar roses that form a defensive barrier about the bewitched castle for one hundred years find their analogous double in the father's affection for his daughter.

Following the malevolent fairy's prophecy that Briar Rose shall die from a wound caused by a spindle, the king endeavors to banish all such instruments and contraptions from his kingdom, blind to the fact that one will either be created or will lurk nearby, awaiting the hour of its decisive intervention in his daughter's life. Sexton's reconstruction of his protective angst cloaks Briar Rose in an obsessive paternal watchfulness that wishes to sustain her life away from possible despoilation. The predicted death by the prick of a spindle results in the removal of all potential penetrative implements; even the males of court are symbolically sterilized, their tongues scoured "with Bab-o" (*T,* 109) to purify the air in which Briar Rose moves. The father's inability to control the conditions of either his daughter's life or of the thirteenth fairy's evil gift to the child is revealed twice over: by her pricking of her finger and by her release from her slumber one hundred years later by a prince. The century of sleep afflicts the whole court and palace, the buildings and inhabitants of which fall into a time warp enclosed by a thicket of briar roses and become things of legend. Venturing princes come to claim the daughter's hand or just to gaze upon her renowned beauty but die "wretchedly" (*FT,* 45) attempting to breach the thorn bushes. Sexton conceives of them as potential saviors "crucified" (*T,* 110) on the thorns until the arrival, after the requisite time, of a "Moses" (*T,* 110) prince for whom the briars part. His near-miraculous entrance, which in the tale is readily accounted for by the end of the spell, allows him unfettered access to the recumbent princess whom he awakens with a kiss. In the tale the whole court, including the king, is awakened; in Sexton, only Briar Rose is restored to life, calling out "Daddy! Daddy!" (*T,* 110) as she wakes.

The successful prince's ability to breach the rose briars to relieve the stricken Briar Rose is laden with sexual significance for Sexton. This protective wall of thorns and bushes, replicating the father's smothering love for his daughter while simultaneously sharing the princess's name, is finally breached by a prince who has both luck and time on his side. The parting of the branches of briar roses, symbolic of the breaking of both the thirteenth fairy's and the father's control, is a sexual incursion that penetrates both spell and princess. One hundred years on from her last words and last physical contact with anyone (or any male), it is unsurprising that Sexton's Oedipally-inflected revision has Briar Rose call out "Daddy! Daddy!" upon her awakening. The confirmation of her Oedipal subplot may be rather heavy-handed and obvious to the point of tedium, but the remainder of the poem's obliteration of the father is worthy of comment. His displacement by the prince instigates a substitution narrative in which the daughter's love for the father is transferred onto another surrogate male. The father's loss is a silenced narrative thread in Sexton's version, explained either by the length of time that Briar Rose has been asleep, or by her internalization of the lost father and the love she held for him. The prince's arrival is registered by Sexton as that of a sexual rival to the father and he is first recognized inevitably through her call for her father. Her subsequent and continued policy, initially comic, of hiding her intake of sleeping pills and draughts concocted by the chemist from her husband is an attempt to control when and for how long she sleeps: it is in long periods of sleep that she is returned to the traumatic world prior to her wounding, and these bouts of excessive sleep she must escape. Such sleep produces dreams in which she figures herself as the thirteenth fairy come to betray her; in such sleep she is "ninety" (*T,* 111) and nearing death; and it is here where she locates the lost father, internalized along with the ambiguous sexual connection that had existed between them.[12] Her guilt over the father's loss is realized through her self-recognition in the shape of the malignant thirteenth fairy, her doppelgänger that she must beware and whom the father had futilely attempted to defeat. The gift bestowed upon her by this fairy is that of death, which will separate her from the father and his love for her for eternity. His jealous guarding of her must also protect against the arrival of another male whom she may also love and with whom she may mate. Death, the thirteenth fairy's revenge for being excluded from the feast for the child's birth, is recognized in Briar Rose's penetration by both spindle and prince. Both oppose and subvert the law of the father and cancel his primacy in his daughter's affections. That Briar Rose in sleep dreams the thirteenth fairy in her place necessitates her betrayal of her father: in her unconscious she carries a guilt that her existence has caused the father's death and that it was in fact her and not the evil fairy that caused his loss.

The unresolved Oedipal conflict ensures Briar Rose's future as "an insomniac" (*T*, 110), entranced by the difficult legacy left her by her father that can never be escaped. She is the female subject regressed, the result of a recessed love that is unnameable within standard social conventions. Acknowledging that she has been deprived of her childhood, "There was a theft," and aware that she "was abandoned" (*T*, 112), Sexton's Briar Rose is denied the happily-ever-after ending of fairy tale: "Each night I am nailed into place / and I forget who I am" (*T*, 112). This version of a living crucifixion, recalling the earlier image of the vanquished princes upon the thorn bushes, speaks the living trauma in which Briar Rose is trapped. Lost to the father yet unable to be free of his claim, she lives entrapped by his memory and her own obsessional guilt concerning their relationship:

> Daddy?
> That's another kind of prison.
> It's not the prince at all,
> but my father
> drunkenly bent over my bed,
> circling the abyss like a shark,
> my father thick upon me
> like some sleeping jellyfish.
>
> (*T*, 112)

Her trace memories of her life before the coming true of the thirteenth fairy's prophecy recall the "prison" that the father's overly protective concern had created to shield his child from harm. His influence on her life then is superseded now by his perpetual return in her mind and by her regression to a pre-adult state of recognizing him as the sole object of her desires. The prince, previously a substitute father figure, has been overwritten by these deeper set emotions that contort and control Briar Rose's responses to her world. The gift of the thirteenth fairy, in whom she recognizes her own self, is ultimately not death but its living equivalent, a warped and abyssal condition that resists both understanding and explanation. Sexton's **"Briar Rose"** closes in irresolution and questioning:

> What voyage this, little girl?
> This coming out of prison?
> God help—
> this life after death?
>
> (*T*, 112)

Such a voyage is prophesied by Sexton's speaker in her prefatory comments, a voyage of regression, "rank"

with the father's imprint on his daughter's emotional and sexual life. Having awakened from the near equivalent of death, Briar Rose is suspended in the traumatic realm of a regression that cannot be spoken, the three questions with which the poem closes attempts to find the words to comprehend her condition. Caught between grief over the loss of her father and an unconscious memory trace of the illicit desire they shared, this Briar Rose attests to an intricate experience of mourning that simultaneously reconceives the lost father in the moments of sexual intercourse with her husband. As Abraham and Torok postulate, such incidents of incomplete mourning are not the result of "the affliction caused by the objectal loss itself, but rather from the feeling of an irreparable crime: the crime of having been overcome by desire . . . at the least appropriate moment, when it would behoove us to be grieved in despair."[13] Unable to remember who she herself is, Briar Rose is unable to extinguish the delayed mourning she carries inside with regard to her father's death. Her direct transference of affection onto the prince upon waking after her hundred years of sleep blocks any immediate attempt to mourn the dead father, her feelings for whom remain at best ambivalent and perpetually unresolved. His displacement by the prince at the moment of waking is only temporarily realized however; his centrality in the mental world of his daughter ensures that he is the one to whom her thoughts, desires, and her language turn.

DOMESTICATING TERROR

Sexton's audacity in rewriting sixteen of the Grimm brothers' fairy tales is matched by her ability, as Vonnegut elucidates in his foreword, to "domesticate" terror. The fears, traumas, and horrors that are subsumed deep in the unconscious are the poetic territories that she investigates in this collection of revisioned fairy tales. The service that she provides is many sided: for Vonnegut, she "examines" and "describes" such terrors and then releases them back into the individual mind where they roam with reinvigorated potential; further, she opposes the original with its redraft establishing a dialectic interrelation between the two; she counters prose with poetry, playing off one set of language tensions against another; and she domesticates these terrors for her American audience, prefacing them with guided advice and guarded warning about the narratives to follow. She explains her method of transformation as follows: "I take the fairy tale and transform it into a poem of my own, following the story line, exceeding the story line and adding my own pzazz [sic]. They are very wry and cruel and sadistic and funny."[14] The humor of these tales is a variable entity, sooner found in the earlier rather than the later poems, and couched in arch and on occasion vitriolic tones. Even within the six that have been the focus of this [essay's] attention, the humor is certainly in abeyance in relation to the cruelty on show. Snow White's idiocy, the miller and his daughter's vain ambitions, the sadism of Cinderella's stepsisters, Red Riding Hood's and her grandmother's docile ignorance, the barbarity of the mother and the witch in "Hansel and Gretel," and the traumatic experiences of Briar Rose all speak of a poetic universe riven with dark forces, inhuman impulses and forbidden desires. Whether ineffectual males or malicious females, obsessional fathers or malignant stepmothers, Sexton peoples this work with characters already imbued with the horror characteristics of fairy tale and adds to them further psychical or emotional dimensions that render them the victims or the villains of a deeply troubled worlds.

Her choice to end with the tales **"Hansel and Gretel"** and **"Briar Rose"** signals Sexton's unearthing of the poetic strategies and geographies of her earlier collections to which she will return in her next collection. Both tales circle the irresolvable question of language and how its signifying processes can encapsulate experiences so horrific and traumatic. The uncertain designation of the memory of the witch's death in **"Hansel and Gretel"** at that poem's close, to be observed "like something religious," does not answer the question of what holy or unholy force directs the action of that tale. Moreover, it excludes any memorial to the dead mother, a more horrific because more human example of feminine depravity. The reunion of the father with his son and daughter restores a triadic balance to their existence, a human trinity of survivors in the wake of poverty, cruelty, and near cannibalism. **"Briar Rose"** concludes the volume on the darkest possible note with a fear housed in nightmare and inexplicable memories. The final questions of that poem are a disturbing triumvirate of doubt, despair, and unbelief: the call on God to help what is unnameable ("God help—/ this life after death?") defeats this closing poem's and Briar Rose's efforts to say in words the full extent of the traumatic that circulates just beyond language's grasp.

Notes

1. Diane Wood Middlebrook also notes that, with *Transformations,* Sexton "had moved as far as possible from confessionalism." Diane Wood Middlebrook, *Anne Sexton: A Biography* (London: Virago, 1991) 338. Although she makes this point, it still does not prevent Middlebrook from returning to the biography of Sexton's life to elucidate possible meanings to these poems, overlooking Vonnegut's injunction that they speak either of a more generalized set of human perceptions or to a personal life removed from that of the poet. Indeed, an ambition for her poetry that Sexton expressed in interview with Harry Moore both summarizes the inherent problematics of confessionalism as a poetic or critical practice and

dovetails appositely with Vonnegut's comment: "I write very personal poems but I hope that they will become the central theme to someone else's private life" (*NES,* 50).

2. Helen Vendler, *The Music of What Happens: Poems, Poets, Critics* (Cambridge, Massachusetts and London: Harvard University Press, 1988) 303.

3. Ibid. 304.

4. Ibid. 303.

5. Ibid. 309.

6. Heidegger acknowledges that meaning exists only where language exists: "[n]o thing is where the word is lacking." For anything to exist within our comprehension, be it a paperclip or a sculpture, language itself must exist. Language is a prerequisite of our ability to know even though the totality of our existence can never be expressed in words: language allows the transmission of knowledge about our existence even as it circumscribes its own ability to say. Martin Heidegger, *On the Way to Language,* translated by Peter D. Hertz (New York and London: Harper & Row, Publishers, 1971) 62.

7. Snowdrop's age is a disconcerting factor in the original tale, a story that blurs any sense of the passing of time. Indeed, from the age of seven Snowdrop is written as a rival to the new queen. (Snowdrop's age is also of relevance given the number of the dwarfs that attend her, but the numeral significance of the tale is overwritten in Sexton.) The action of the rest of the tale occurs, it appears over a course of days, excepting the interlude in which Snowdrop lies in her glass coffin before being released from her "death" by the prince. Indeed, once she eats of the apple, the third temptation proffered by the stepmother, it is noted that "the little girl seemed quite dead" (*FT,* 195). With no suggestion given that Snowdrop's age or features change or develop during the course of her repose, nor is there any mention of the age of the prince, it is left to the flexible narrative license of fairy tale to account for a situation that both sexualizes and permits the marriage of minors.

8. I am reminded here of Deleuze's argument in *Cinema I,* where he indicates "[t]here is no subject which acts without another which watches it act, and which grasps it as acted, itself assuming the freedom of which it deprives the former. 'Thus two different egos [*moi*] one of which conscious of its freedom, sets itself up as an independent spectator of a scene which the other would play in a mechanical fashion. But this dividing-in-two never goes to the limit. It is rather an oscillation

of the person between two points of view on himself, a hither-and-thither of the spirit . . . ,' a being-with" (Gilles Deleuze, *Cinema I* [London: Athlone Press, 1997] 73-74).

9. For a fuller discussion of the reading of blackness and Otherness within American carnival forms see Philip McGowan, *American Carnival: Seeing and Reading American Culture* (Westport, Connecticut and London: Greenwood Press, 2001).

10. Simon Critchley, *Very Little . . . Almost Nothing: Death, Philosophy, Literature* (London and New York: Routledge, 1997) 72.

11. Intriguingly, the only words that Sexton provides for Gretel are two in German, "Ja, Fräulein" (*T*, 104): allies in the war, the "German" and the "Japanese" are here opposed, possibly reflective of the new international situation after the war; suspicion of the Japanese remains, while the Germans have become rehabilitated in American and Western eyes. This may be stretching a point, but latent traces of Sexton's political opinions, noted above in "Rumpelstiltskin" and its reference to President Truman, may possibly be detected in this poem.

12. As Judith Butler comments, summarizing Freud in "Mourning and Melancholia" in relation to such policies of internalization by sufferers from melancholic disorders, "[t]he melancholic refuses the loss of the object, and internalization becomes a strategy of magically resuscitating the lost object, not only because the loss is painful, but because the ambivalence felt toward the object requires that the object be retained until differences are settled." Judith Butler, *Gender Trouble: Feminism and the Subversion of Identity* (New York and London: Routledge, 1990, 1999) 78-79.

13. Nicolas Abraham and Maria Torok, *The Shell and the Kernel: Renewals of Psychoanalysis,* edited, translated and with an Introduction by Nicholas T. Rand (Chicago: University of Chicago Press, 1994) 110. Slightly further on in their analysis, Abraham and Torok continue, "[s]hould those ill from mourning consciously recall an orgasm (for which they secondarily blame themselves), its link to a desire for the dying or dead object is always severely censored. . . . [R]epression not only separates but has to preserve carefully, although in the unconscious, the wish the ego can only represent as an exquisite corpse lying somewhere inside it; the ego looks for this exquisite corpse continually in the hope of one day reviving it" (117-118).

14. Anne Sexton, quoted in Diane Wood Middlebrook, *Anne Sexton: A Biography* (London: Virago, 1991) 336-337.

Works Consulted

Abraham, Nicolas, and Maria Torok. *The Shell and the Kernel: Renewals of Psychoanalysis.* Edited, translated and with an Introduction by Nicholas T. Rand. Chicago: University of Chicago Press, 1994.

Butler, Judith. *Gender Trouble: Feminism and the Subversion of Identity.* New York and London: Routledge, 1990, 1999.

Critchley, Simon. *Very Little . . . Almost Nothing: Death, Philosophy, Literature.* London and New York: Routledge, 1997.

Deleuze, Gilles. *Cinema I.* London: Athlone Press, 1997.

Grimm, The Brothers. *Fairy Tales.* Translated by Edgar Taylor and Marian Edwardes with illustrations by Arthur Rackham. London: Everyman's Library, 1992.

Heidegger, Martin. *On the Way to Language.* Translated by Peter D. Hertz. New York and London: Harper & Row, Publishers, 1971.

McGowan, Philip. *American Carnival: Seeing and Reading American Culture.* Westport, Connecticut and London: Greenwood Press, 2001.

Middlebrook, Diane Wood. *Anne Sexton: A Biography.* London: Virago, 1991.

Sexton, Anne. *Transformations.* With a Foreword by Kurt Vonnegut Jr. Boston: Houghton Mifflin, 1971.

———. *No Evil Star: Selected Essays, Interviews, and Prose.* Edited by Steven E. Colburn. Ann Arbor: The University of Michigan Press, 1985.

Vendler, Helen. *The Music of What Happens: Poems, Poets, Critics.* Cambridge, Massachusetts and London: Harvard University Press, 1988.

Karen Alkalay-Gut (essay date fall 2005)

SOURCE: Alkalay-Gut, Karen. "The Dream Life of Ms. Dog: Anne Sexton's Revolutionary Use of Pop Culture." *College Literature* 32, no. 4 (fall 2005): 50-73.

[*In the following essay, Alkalay-Gut offers a detailed analysis of Sexton's references to popular culture, prevalent attitudes and ideas, and contemporary poetry in "Hurry up Please It's Time."*]

> Words in a poem, sounds in movement, rhythm in space, attempt to recapture personal meaning in personal time and space from out of the sights and sounds of a depersonalised, dehumanised world. They are bridgeheads into alien territory. They are acts of insurrection.
>
> (R. D. Laing)

It might be difficult to conceive of Anne Sexton as building "bridgeheads into alien territory." Indeed, despite her popularity she is often perceived as a kind of victim, and until very recently, much of the criticism of Sexton's poetry focused primarily upon her scandalous and disturbed life. This is particularly true in the decade following Diane Middlebrook's sensational biography (1991) which suggests that Sexton's work only leads back to a hallucinatory woman controlled by her madness and aberrations. But in the following pages I wish to argue that through the use of popular culture Anne Sexton attempts a revolution, a reconception of herself as well as the contemporary concepts of art and identity.

Because so many readers discuss the difficulty of separating Sexton's life from her work,[1] the devaluation of her life would in itself be a great obstacle to the understanding of her poetry. But just as it is difficult to imagine actually contextualizing her very personal voice in an additional or alternative framework to her biography, an alternative analysis seems irrelevant to her extraordinary poetry of the self. The usual paths into her poetry just don't seem to lead anywhere else than her self, and although we can identify the literary allusions, the psychoanalytic innuendoes, the feminist statements and the abject confessions, they fail to explain the attraction of her work. This is particularly true of her later poetry, which defies traditional methods of reading—not because the poems are impenetrable, but because they initially appear raw, associative, and replete with ostensible nonsense.

But nonsense is by nature comparative and relative, and depends upon an alternative rationale. Often Sexton's apparent *non sequiturs* can be discovered to be heard parts of dialogue, and Joanna Gill has recently discussed this as an intentional strategy in **"Hurry up Please, It's Time."** Gill argues that "the poem enters into a critical dialogue with Eliot's "The Waste Land," making sophisticated and purposive use of multiple personae, self-reflexively contemplating questions about memory, language, and subjectivity, and juxtaposing private introspection and public display." (2003, 41). This argument is strong and indicates that Sexton's work is not simply spun from the self, but that literary allusions and contexts are significant throughout her poetry.

> Sexton's poem refers to the Old and New Testaments of the Bible, to the Sibyls of classical mythology, and to Buddhist texts. Like Eliot's "The Hollow Men," her poem inserts incomplete fragments of prayer or Gospel, borrowing a line from the Book of Common Prayer ("Forgive us, Father, for we know not") which is, itself, a borrowing from the Gospels ("Father, forgive them; for they know not what they do" [Luke 23.34]). In both poems, these allusions are typographically set apart, as though to imply that they are spoken as an aside, or that we are in the presence of several simultaneous

voices or levels of contemplation. That the quotations in both cases are incomplete suggests failure and confusion, and foreshadows the lack of resolution in the text as a whole. Sexton's poem juxtaposes the intense and mystical and the superficial and mocking, hence the refrain "La de dah" which mimics Eliot's "Weialala leia / Wallala leialala" and in so doing subverts its serious and incantatory potential. Indeed, Sexton's line parodies the presumptuous erudition of Eliot's phrase, mimicking its intonation and transforming it into a slang reference to snobbery.

(Gill 2003, 43)

Gill's work is a powerful step forward in lending validity to Sexton's language, imagery, and purpose and countering the constant accusation concerning what David Trinidad calls "the blatant deterioration of her talent," echoing numerous other critics and poets. However, Gill's context remains a literary one, one to which Sexton can not be confined, and although Gill notes Sexton's references to "jello," "milk," "juice," and "peanut butter" and the subsequent identification of America "with consumption and thus inevitably with expulsion," there is a far greater and more significant context of popular culture within which Sexton places herself.

If, for example, we trace the snatches of pop culture that permeate this pivotal poem, **"Hurry up Please, It's Time,"**[2] the poem becomes part of a dialogue with contemporary social contexts. References to the comic film of Walter Mitty, suggestions of the comic strip Gasoline Alley, and verses from a quintessential pop song by Al Jolson (with significant hiatuses) create a larger social scaffolding, and the many literary and social allusions emerge as integral parts of developing dialogues. This substantive use of the popular arts obfuscates the distinctions between levels and degrees of culture, and favors instead the original, "mad" lateral thinking of the eccentric individual who is more driven by the need to comprehend contemporary existence and less by the need to be accommodated by and to transform a literary canon. In this way the exploration in the poem becomes far more intimate, unique, and genuine. This approach is aided by some of the concepts of R. D. Laing's existential explanation of schizophrenia and society in his popular classic, *The Politics of Experience* (1967), with the intention of a general, cultural quest out of a stratified and unsatisfying culture into unknown territory.[3]

The choice to use various elements of popular culture is critical. Although films are often employed by Sexton's contemporaries, they are usually references to "art films" such as films by Goddard in poetry by Adrienne Rich, or the classic film of *Dracula* at the conclusion of Sylvia Plath's "Daddy"[4] or even Sexton's own use of Carl Dreyer's *The Passion of Joan of Arc* in the final verse of **"Her Kind."** These references lend a patina of intellectual respectability to the image, whether the immediate reference is "caught" or not. In the earlier poem **"Her Kind,"** for instance, the allusion to Joan of Arc bestows upon the speaker a sainted identity even while it confirms a social definition of madness:

> I have ridden in your cart, driver,
> waving my nude arms at villages going by,
> learning the last bright routes, survivor,
> where your flames still bite my thigh
> and my ribs crack where your wheels wind.
> A woman like that is not ashamed to die.
> I have been her kind.

> (Sexton 1999, 15)

In Sexton's later poetry, however, the needs have changed. It is precisely the lack of respectability of film that is the issue in **"Hurry up,"** since it goes against the modernist cultural hierarchy. Popular films have rarely been considered acceptable points of reference in modern poetry. When Berryman jokingly quoted Eliot, "I seldom go to films . . . said the Honorable Possum." (1964, 60), he was not referring to Eliot's own echoes of *Tristan and Isolde* in "The Wasteland," but to a general poetic prejudice. Allusions to an ephemeral genre not only tie the alluding work to a transient source that will soon disappear, but also help to create the assumption that the alluding work is no "better" than the alluded work, for it possesses a similar transience.

Even if films can be granted, the use of comic strips in the seventies would have diminished the respectable patina of the poem. Stefan Economou recently noted, "Who apart from an academic rag-picker cherishes Pogo or Krazy Kat or Gasoline Alley, even while the movies of that era are still publicly revered on 100-best lists?" (n.d.). While contemporary cultural criticism may well find treasures in these strips, it is difficult to imagine a critic of the seventies taking seriously a poem with reference to these characters. But it is precisely the discrepancy between the prevailing culture and the proffered culture that is essential to the conflict in **"Hurry up,"** because it is indicative of more basic conflicts both within the society and within the individual.

In the poem, **"Hurry up Please It's Time,"** Sexton sets up two polarities, the normal life and the life of fantasy and imagination, and attempts to seek meaningful existence in their relationship. Skeezix, the foundling from the comic strip "Gasoline Alley" who grew up in real time with Sexton and millions of other readers of the 20th century, is the person against whom the speaker initially places herself. He is the "ear" of normality, and her repetition of the word "middle," living in Middle-sex, (l. 32) and middle-class (l. 218), emphasizes this need to be connected to and accepted by the norm.

The opening confirms this need to connect the eccentric behavior of the speaker with a normal world outside. The poem begins with a response to the Hemingway remark in *A Movable Feast* with which the entire collection, **The Death Notebooks,** begins: "Look, you con man, make a living out of your death" (Sexton 1999, 348). **"Hurry up"** opens with a dialogic analysis of this phrase: "What is death, I ask. / What is life, you ask" (l. 1-2). The rest of the poem addresses these issues—how to make a "living" out of death. "You," it will be determined twenty lines later, is Skeezix, who is set in opposition to the speaker, replying to the question of the speaker "What is Death?" with a suitably positive interrogatory-response, "What is Life?" This appears to be an encouragement to concentrate on the positive and realistic aspect of her inquiry. And indeed, the speaker immediately realizes the significance of this question, the distinction between "making a living" and actually living, and the necessity of understanding the importance of the question concerning the nature of life. This initial response becomes the basis for the exploration of the purpose of her existence. This search for an understanding of death and its reversal in the optimistic middle-class question is the entrance into the poem.

But there are also other dimensions, such as the repeated sound of "pocketa-pocketa," the neutral engine sound that the dreamer Walter Mitty hears as he drives, always transforming its rhythm into the changing musical score for his various fantasies. He is an astronaut, a pilot, a brain surgeon. The imaginariness of his existence, if not the specific fantasies, provides Sexton with a model for the conflict between what R. D. Laing calls ego and self,[5] social identity and personal identity. Laing's initial premise in *The Politics of Experience* is of contemporary identity as essentially schizophrenic,

> a split in our experience. We seem to live in two worlds,
> and many people are aware only of the "outer" rump.
> As long as we remember that the "inner" world is not
> some space "inside" the body or the mind, this way of
> talking can serve our purpose. (It was good enough for
> William Blake.) The "inner," then, is our personal idiom
> of experiencing our bodies, other people, the animate
> and inanimate world: imagination, dreams, phantasy,
> and beyond that to ever further reaches of experience.

> (Laing 1967, 18)

Labeled "anti-psychiatry" by his colleague David Cooper, Laing's basic theory is that the distinctions created between madness and sanity are essentially arbitrary social ones, determined by a society that finds certain behavior uncomfortable or threatening to itself, and promotes this split within the self which exists in everyone in varying degrees. In this context the discourse of madness can actually help to shed light upon the schizophrenia of modern experience. If it is possible to posit that it is the society that is mad, then the mad person may be just the one to find a sane alternative. This concept was extremely popular during the late sixties in discussions of individual and political madness and has many literary implications, but for a person certifiably insane, it must have been personally very liberating.

It is within the interrelationships between the outside world of popular culture and audience and the inner world of personal madness that the poem is attempting to maneuver. For this reason Skeezix, whose "father"—Walt Wallet—is the ideal combination of romantic American poet (Walt Whitman) and capitalistic metonymy, is a good "person" with whom to begin a dialogue. Skeezix not only seems to be a constant companion here casually referred to mid-dialogue, but also appears in an identical offhand yet intimate manner when he opens a short prose piece of Sexton's entitled "All God's Children Need Radios." The story, a series of diary entries from 1971, begins with an ambivalent address: "Thank you for the red roses. They were lovely. Listen, Skeezix, I know you didn't give them to me, but I like to pretend you did because, as you know, when you give me something my heart faints on the pillow" (1988, 23). While Skeezix might also refer to Sexton's husband, Kayo (whose real nickname is also cartoon-like), or a real or an imaginary lover, this popular and imaginary identity reinforces his role of what Alicia Ostriker terms a "courage-giving alter ego," a male muse (1986, 194). Skeezix provides an initial point of contact and contrast between her and the world.

Unlike the contemporary "fantasy" companion, such as James Stewart's giant rabbit Harvey in the 1950 film of that name, Skeezix is just an average orphan, yet "normality" itself is designated here as caricature[6] and two-dimensional. It is not surprising, therefore, that his usefulness as a partner for dialogue is limited and Skeezix retreats into the 3rd person and the wistful past (symbolic memories of his safeguarding the poet's hat while she is fishing) as the poem progresses. The speaker moves from desiring the comfortable funny-page "average" universe, from longing to fit into the "outside" vision of the world, to craving a more basic and exciting quest of imagination. And it is something of the awareness of Walter Mitty that allows it.

"'I was a nothing crouching in the closet,' Sexton told her therapist, Dr. Martin Orne, in 1961 and he replied, 'Never see "The Secret Life of Walter Mitty"?'" [sic] (Middlebrook, 1991, 401). Although it would take her over a decade to put this reference directly into her poetry, it was very good advice. The film adaptation of *The Secret Life of Walter Mitty* (1947) starring Danny Kaye varied greatly from its literary source. For Kaye's milquetoast protagonist actually becomes a far more heroic figure than Thurber's. Both protagonists have unrealistic fantasies of fame and success, but the moral of Thurber's story is that fantasizing makes Mitty unfit for the world.[7] Kaye's Mitty, on the other hand, actually has the opportunity to fulfill his wildest dreams, saving

beautiful and romantic heiress Virginia Mayo from jewel thieves and his country from evil Nazi spies. Mitty's liberation from the desperate need to make a living ultimately allows him to conceive and act upon creative moneymaking schemes, making him the superior man in all ways. Everything is reversed in this film: even the psychiatrist—who is supposed to help Mitty realize that his real romantic experiences have only been fantasies—is "really" a disguised Nazi spy played by Boris Karloff.[8] This is not only the kind of film Sexton must have seen as a teenager, but was most likely exposed to on television as an adult; and its parallel with her own madness as well as her experiences with psychiatrists, could not have failed to have significance to her.

The film of *The Secret Life of Walter Mitty* becomes significant in understanding **"Hurry up Please, Its Time"** and other poems from this period in a number of ways.[9] First, the "pocketa-pocketa" heard by Mitty and Sexton indicates the transformation of droning reality (and regular rhythm) into imaginative fantasy. (It is impossible to ignore the extent to which Sexton was under pressure by critics and friends to write a more controlled and regular verse. "Pocketa-pocketa" recalls this to some extent). Also, Danny Kaye's character does more than merely dream. In an incongruous but almost exact parallel of Sexton's later poems, Mitty discovers that his "real" life does not at all suit him. He has been defined and confined by his mother, fiancée and employer, and reduced to an almost nonfunctional figure. But it is his fantasies (constantly decried by these people who try to socialize him) that prepare him to cope with the extraordinary romance-spy situation; allow him an opportunity to conceive of a totally transformed life and most significantly to fulfill this conception.

There are three categories of existence in the film: 1) there is a "real world"—a stultifying middle-class existence. 2) There is also a fantasy world in which Mitty creates himself as hero. This world of imagination is considered by all to be detrimental to his ability to function in the "real world." 3) Finally there is a "real, real world" an integrated world in which Mitty's eccentricities and fantasies prove useful tools to transform the earlier, inadequate personal reality into a more significant and productive one. In fact through the openness of mind aided by his capacity for "fantasy," Mitty not only realizes that his psychiatrist *is* really out to get him, proving his paranoia real, but he is able to use that knowledge to stem the danger of fascism and nascent McCarthyism. Once Mitty understands that the "real, real world," the dialogue between his fantasy and reality, is the one which integrates all of his needs and allows all of his personalities to emerge, his ability to cope with—even control and change—his stultifying life, becomes apparent. He becomes the liberated and liberating hero he has always dreamed of being. This seems to be a lesson for the speaker of **"Hurry up"**—to follow through with the liberating dreams for her poetry despite the surrounding criticism, and this lesson is parallel with the development of the poem.

"Experience," notes R. D. Laing, "may be judged to be invalidly mad or to be validly mystical. The distinction is not easy . . ." (1967, 108). Like Walter Mitty, what Sexton sought was to transform the use of her madness from a sensationalist one that people sympathize and identify with, to a validly mystical one that can transform reality. The basic movement in the poem can be traced through the repetition of lines from prayer, moving from repeated apologies for her helplessness to an assertion of the usefulness of her madness in society, from echoing ritualistic pleas such as "Father, forgive me . . ." to envisioning the possibility of helping to bring transformation.[10] Rather than a divided self, with a total separation between the exhibitionist Ms. Dog, and the sorrowful Ann, there is an alliance. The bold Ms. Dog will be put in the service of the sincere quest for transformation.

> Bring a flashlight, Ms. Dog,
> and look in every corner of the brain
> and ask and ask and ask
> until the kingdom,
> however queer,
> will come.

> (Sexton 1999, 347-52)

If the last line of Sexton's poem recalls Ginsberg's 1956 poem, "America," "I'm putting my queer shoulder to the wheel," (1984: 146) it is because it also follows a similar development. The social misfit becomes the prophet. One of Laing's biographers, John Clay, recognizing the similarities of Laing and Sexton's vision, notes that Laing featured a poster of Breughel's "Fall of Icarus" in his consulting room. He adds that the figure of Icarus, in the painting and in Sexton's poem on the subject "symbolises the indifference of the ordinary world to the high-flier" (1996, 78). In their conclusions to their poems both Ginsberg and Sexton assert that it is their very aberrance, their very sense of being apart from and a part of society that can contribute something redemptive. The difference here is that while Ginsberg comes to accept himself as he is in "America," and approvingly finds that self a good and useful one in effecting change, Sexton's conclusion appears defiantly individual despite the disapprobation of the world. The "ego" who seeks approval will someday be the leader of the authentic self. Sexton's remarks to her psychiatrist reveal the lack of confidence in this direction, while confirming that this is, indeed, her direction.

"As a poet it may be better to be crazy than to be educated. But I doubt it" (Middlebrook, 1991, 126). The distinction made by Michel de Certeau between "strategies," a system created by an individual to function within a society of which one is a part, and "tactics," techniques of coping from within a social system in "the space of the other" (De Certeau 1984, 25) is relevant here. Sexton pledges to continue to search, but she remains alone, alienated, resolved. She is not putting her shoulder to the wheel, joining in on her own terms with society's struggle, but is seeing herself as the outsider who saves society, as the Joan of Arc of **"Her Kind,"** even at the expense of her own life.

With the general structure and direction of the poem in place we can return to the subject, which is as much poetry, poetic voices and goals, as "life." The setting, established early in the poem, is the arena of the presented self, the poetry reading:

> Who's that at the podium
> in black and white,
> blurting into the mike?
> Ms. Dog.
>
>   . . . . .
>
> The day is slipping away, why am I
> out here, what do they want?

> (Sexton 1999, 79-82, 86-87)

Sexton's brief essay, "The Freak Show" (1988), deals with this alienation outright, but her estrangement from her presented "poetry persona" and its association with her conception of her life as a solitary dramatic presentation appears most clearly in her posthumously collected poem, **"The Play."** The problem with the play, as she points out, is its monologic nature:

> The curtain falls.
> The audience rushes out.
> It was a bad performance.
> That's because I'm the only actor
> and there are few humans whose lives
> will make an interesting play.
> Don't you agree?

> (Sexton 1999, 440-41)

In both poems isolation and estrangement are presented clearly, and to deal with these complex inquiries into identity a dialogic structure is necessary, since identity is presented as something that can only be defined by others. If there is no other, there is no me.

In **"The Play,"** the audience is invited to become part of the dialogue if only to judge the failure of the performance, but in **"Hurry up,"** the dialogue emerges from discussions with others, with the reader, as well as with parts of the selves. Carrie Noland has pointed out the fact that poetry, like other literary discourses, is dialogic (1999, 41)[11] and for Sexton the need for an other in her poetry is desperate. Yet the dialogic nature of poetry is not usually observed because of the assumption of its lyrical and confessional character. When Sexton divides into two characters, Anne and "Ms. Dog," it is to engage in a dialogue with herself, to analyze the nature of these identities. As Estella Lauter has pointed out, Sexton's "later persona 'Ms. Dog' becomes a way of extending the parts of herself to and about whom she can speak. . . ." (Lauter 1984, 27). This is no more an artificial dialogue than a dialogue in a novel.

There are several characters and personae here. The first and most distracting for some is the willfully exhibitionistic child, who wants to show her "cunny" to little boys.

> Why shouldn't I pull down my pants
> and show my little cunny to Tom
> and Albert? They wee-wee funny.
> I wee-wee like a squaw.
>
> (Sexton 1999, 9-12)

One of the first reviews of this poem found the word and the childlike tone totally exasperating. Clearly, however, Sexton was trying out something that Theodore Roethke had attempted in his "Praise to the End," to revert to infancy, not only, as Steven E. Colburn argues, "to follow the associative leaps of the childhood imagination, with its intermingling of sensations, cognition, and fantasy" (n.d., 1), but also to prove to what extent the child-poet is mother to the woman. This "new boldness . . . a refusal to be shamed into silence" (Lauter 1984, 25) is as much a dramatization of a poetic goal as a return to infancy For the boys here need to see her "cunny," the intimacy in her poetry, not because of her exhibitionism, but because of her awareness of the limitations of their awareness of the relativity of their vision. It is "they" and not she who "wee-wee funny," but they have not been made aware of the "other." Although critics such as Ben Howard have said that the dominant voice of this volume is "that of the cute, defiant, and often naughty little girl . . ." (McClatchey 1978, 181), this tone masks defiance with an acceptable cuteness, and is not found in later stages of the poem. It appears to be regressive and exhibitionistic behavior, yet this childhood outburst develops into the basis of her poetics.

> I have swallowed an orange, being woman.
> You have swallowed a ruler, being man.
>
> (Sexton 1999, 23-24)

This "simplistic" definition of gender refers forward to the image of fruition in the myth of creation delineated in Sexton's **"Eighth Psalm"** (1999, 408), in which the goddess-woman of creation is "a magnitude . . . she is many," "well-pleased" because she has "swallowed a bagful of oranges" (93). The image of the male, on the other hand, is of penis-as-measuring-stick and as

instrument-of-absolute-power. This gender distinction is also the basis of her poetics. Unlike the "bag of green apples" swallowed by the fearful pregnant speaker in Plath's "Metaphors," Sexton's oranges are vaguely equated with fruition[12] and nurturing, providing no answers but only images. Therefore her conclusions will not be conclusive in any way, will not provide a standard measuring stick for others.

Because the nurturing child-woman cannot seek answers, yet answers are still needed, there are other aspects of the poet, such as the multi-faceted Ms. Dog, frequently linked by critics to "man's best friend" as well as Eliot's "foe to man" who digs up dangerous secrets.[13] There is also an obvious connection with Berryman's Mr. Bones, the alter ego who allows a freedom of exploration and expression forbidden to the "proper" individual. Ms. Dog appears in **"Is It True?"** from *The Awful Rowing toward God* (Sexton 1999, 452) as possessed: "Ms. Dog, / Why is you evil? / It climbed into me. / It didn't mean to." But this is a controlled and willed possession which includes both the animalian and the divine: "I have for some time, / called myself / Ms. Dog. / Why? / Because I am almost animal / and yet the animal I lost most—/ That animal is near to God, / but lost from Him" (448). Maxine Kumin confirms the biographical verity of this confession, noting Sexton's love of palindromes, (1999, xxx) and in "All God's Children Need Radios," her undisguised autobiographical narrator makes a complex association between herself and the dog,

> "Oh Lord," they said last night on TV, "the sea is so mighty and my dog is so small." I *heard* dog. You say, they said *boat* not *dog* and that further *dog* would have no meaning. But it does mean. The sea is mother-death and she is a mighty female, the one who wins, the one who sucks us all up. *Dog* stands for me and the new puppy, Daisy.
>
> (Kumin 1999, xxx)[14]

Ms. Dog is the existential poet-ego and for Sexton this poetry ego is extremely complex—despite the apparently intimate nature of her work, her unique role was spokeswoman for "the madwoman in the attic," the "middle-aged witch." The editors of her *Selected Poems* note: "She served as ritual witness to the inner lives of large numbers of troubled people" (1999, xx). This role was as confining as it was liberating. As Victoria Radin says in a review of Diane Middlebrook's biography, "Craziness was Sexton's public face" (1991, 46). And this face was reinforced by the approval of her readers. "Sexton's craziness was inextricably rubbered on to her poetic persona: it was her subject. Actually getting well—when in addition to the therapist there were relays of aides, relations, lovers, a heroic husband and even two small mothering daughters—must have seemed even more crazy" (47). That this was a manufactured persona, a role differing only in public acceptance from her previous "mad" self-conception as courtesan, is also clear. As Radin notes:

> it is hard to see that Sexton ever really got away from that pre-therapeutic notion that prostitution was all she could be good at. Her poetry sold things she should have reserved; delivered with rehearsed catches and breaks, they were the equivalent of her faked orgasm.
>
> (Radin 1991, 47)

Radin's discussion here shows the relationship between what has been called "confessional poetry" and the new celebrity culture after the popularization of television. Elaine Kendall notes that in this period: "publicists had learned that the more intimate a star's confession, the more widely his or her image could be disseminated" (1962, 38). In discussing the relationship between exposure and intimacy in the poetry of Berryman, for example, David Haven Blake points out the significance of the appearance of exposure: Blake's observation on Berryman, that "recognizing the relevance of fame to confessional poetry has serious implications to the ways in which we study and value this work" is, as he notes, significant in the works of his contemporaries (2001, 730).

Sexton too was very aware of this presentation of self. Middlebrook pointed out that Sexton always introduced her readings with the multi-pronouned, multi-perspectived, **"Her Kind."** "I have been her kind" introduces herself both as a witch and as the analyst of this witch, the difference in **"Hurry up"** is that she is trying to overcome the confinement of this mask, to begin a genuine exploration (1989, 449)[15].

Although early in **"Hurry up,"** she describes herself as a pond waiting for Novocain, Ms. Dog wishes for comfort, shelter and protection, yet continues to live the life of the Pobiz stripteaser, promoting her poems in readings that she perceives as a form of prostitution of integrity. It is a common division in Confessional poetry. Berryman and Plath write about it and Theodore Roethke's "Lost Son" also finds himself at this point at the beginning of his search into the self, his "schizophrenic experience," and complains:

> I have married my hands to perpetual agitation,
> I run, I run to the whistle of money.
>
> (Sexton 1999, 100-01)

But Sexton's is even more confusing a prostitution because it masquerades as "true confession," as "authentic" for effect, and in an alienated third person she describes this masquerade onstage:

> Is she spilling her guts?
> You bet.
> Otherwise they cough. . . .
>
> (Sexton 1999, 83-85)

The need to dig into the depths of the self has become something of an imperative, and the imperative has become of itself inauthentic. This inauthenticity is also understood to be true of the bold sexuality that was beginning to be perceived by reviewers as "too much," and the "straw that broke this camel's back."[16] The inauthenticity, furthermore, is understood by Ms. Dog to be linked to the mutual lack of communication, a function of preconceived demands by the audience for sensationalism and show.

> . . . what do they want?
> I am sorrowful in November . . .
> (no they don't want that,
> they want bee stings).
> Toot, toot, tootsy don't cry.
> Toot, toot, tootsy good-bye.
> If you don't get a letter then
> you'll know I'm in jail . . .
> Remember that, Skeezix,
> our first song?
>
> (Sexton 1999, 88-97)

Reverting to Al Jolson is not only an escape, a Berrymanlike blackface mask of joy and rhythm concealing sorrow, but also a reminder that an absence of communication is a sign of imprisonment, and that this truth (half-hidden) even appears in the most ubiquitous arts. The vague allusions to Berryman, who had earlier that year committed suicide, are also concerned with the isolation and alienation exhibited in his poetry. However the Al Jolson quote is incomplete.[17] The crucial line, the reassurance of reciprocity, felt in its absence, comes just after "goodbye": "Watch for the mail, I'll never fail." This situation in which honest interchange and support are deemed insignificant or intolerable by others is an important contribution to her isolation. Mikhail Ann Long, writing about the suicidal tendencies of Sexton, builds on the concept of David Richman that suicide "itself is a communication . . . a cry for help, an appeal to others. What has been largely overlooked . . . is the reciprocal, two-way nature of communication." Richman adds, "There also seems to be an imperviousness or non-reception to verbal messages from the suicidal person by the relatives" (Long 1993, 27). Long points out that in Sexton's *Live or Die*, of which **"Hurry up"** is a part, "the primary key to Sexton's mood is that the people around her remain inhuman, or at best non-human, throughout the poem . . ." (38-39). I prefer the term "complicity," a social agreement not to recognize certain subjects, to keep the inner and outer selves separate. "In the last months of my mother's life," says Linda Gray Sexton, "I chose to ignore her cry of loneliness. I refused to make her last days less painful . . ." (1994, 186).[18] This is what Laing calls "transpersonal invalidation," adding, "This is not unusual. People are doing such things to each other all the time" (1967, 31). The alternative to inauthentic communication, however, is total isolation, an even more frightening state. In Plath's "Daddy," isolation is freedom: "So daddy, I'm finally through. / The black telephone's off at the root, / The voices just can't worm through" (1981, 224). This assertion of freedom, however, is turned in Sexton's poem to a proof of punishment, as she steals and transforms Plath's state: "Them phones gonna be torn out at the root." Sexton's next, qualifying lines are: "There's power in the Lord, baby, and he's gonna turn off the moon" (1999, 144-45).

What appears as a victory over the other in Plath's "Daddy" is in **"Hurry up"** a terrible threat. And the result, total isolation, is also adapted from an image from Plath: "But they pulled me out of the sack, / And they stuck me together with glue," writes Plath, referring to the failure of her suicide attempt. And Sexton metaphorizes Plath's literal sack as a state of suicidal estrangement: "There's a sack over my head. / I can't see. I'm blind" (1999, 151-52).[19]

Throughout Sexton's poetry there are unsuccessful attempts to communicate with the other, and the failure throws the speaker back into a world in which there are no solutions. An early example is **"Music Swims Back to Me"** (1999, 6) in which the failure of the "Mister" to respond results in the closed framework of the poem—beginning with "Wait, Mister" and ending with "Mister?" Here it is a disconnected experience of isolation, but in **"Hurry up Please,"** the borders of complicity are understood as given. Complicity is assumed here not because the speaker has gone out of her mind and the others are needed for an anchor, but because she cannot perform, cannot present her audience with what she thinks they want, cannot really be what they need her to be. It is her very identity that is rejected.

Behind Ms. Dog is "Anne," weary and "sorrowful in November," knowing her role in the complicity, knowing her audience wants "bee stings"—powerful, compressed, painful and formal verse, "confessions" that no longer reflect her situation. Even the reader here is implicated as a victimizer, a kind of Plathian "Daddy." "And you too! Wants to stuff her in a cold shoe / and then amputate the foot" (Sexton 1999, 321-22). Plath opens her famous poem with an address to the father that strangely places the reader in the role as father:

· You do not do, you do not do
Any more, black shoe
In which I have lived like a foot

(Plath 1981, 222)

Plath's suicide (and her own potential demise) is clearly seen by Sexton as at least partly caused by external forces. The parallels between Sexton's alteration of Plath and a citation in *Politics of Experience* are surpris-

ing. "Men do not become what by nature they are meant to be, but what society makes them . . . generous feelings . . . are, as it were, shrunk up, seared, violently wrenched, and amputated to fit us for our intercourse with the world, something in the manner that beggars maim and mutilate their children to make them fit for the future situation in life" (qtd. in Laing 1967, 55-56).[20]

Expectations of the audience must have played a very large part in the new conception of the role of the woman poet, and examination of this subject is not only a personal matter but one basic to the woman poet. As Jane Hedley has recently noted: "Sexton's transgressiveness involved not only her themes or subject matter; it also had to do with the positioning of her poems' aggressively female speakers" (2000, 98). Sexton also seems to have been aware that Plath's demise was at least in part caused by the poetic limitations imposed by her audience during her life. Sexton's speaker here is clearly unwilling to live (and die) like Plath, apparently wanting not only the separation from the father/reader, but also a new integration, not to get rid of Ms. Dog, but to be able to use her to develop Anne.

This delineation of the separate selves, later to find a new integration is in fact the basis for the structure of this poem, a structure which may well be as organized as her earlier "workshop" poems were, but without a narrative or logical principle. The integration begins midway in the poem, as the images from the first half are completed in the second. The sack of the first half that covers her head and blinds her (Sexton 1999, 151-52) is escaped:

I am a fortunate lady.
I've gotten out of my pouch

(Sexton 1999, 211-12)

This integration is also reflected in the parallel images and their context. Morning rituals early in the poem sap her energy, so that even the toast is demanding.

I must butter the toast.
And give it jam too.
My kitchen is a heart.
I must feed it oxygen once in a while
and mother the mother.

(Sexton 1999, 112-16)

But from this imperative of nurturing she moves to the religious joy of being nurtured as the poem nears its conclusion and life begins again:

Once upon a time we were all born,
popped out like jelly rolls
forgetting our fishdom,
the pleasuring seas,
the country of comfort,

spanked into the oxygens of death,
Good morning life, we say when we wake,
hail mary coffee toast
and we Americans take juice,
a liquid sun going down.
Good morning life.
To wake up is to be born.

(Sexton 1999, 245-57)

The same activity that was seen as "mothering the mother" is now birthing the self. Oxygen fed to the world is now part of the birth/death image equated. From trying to fish, the imagery transforms the speaker to one fished.

Yet the entire construction is too pat, too much like a planned poem. At this point of integration the speaker turns, not to another, but to herself, if only to laugh at her poem and the formulaic structure it has followed:

Middle-class lady,
you make me smile.
You dig a hole
and come out with a sun burn.
If someone hands you a glass of water
you start constructing a sailboat.
If someone hands you a candy wrapper,
you take it to the book binder.
Pocketa-pocketa.

(Sexton 1999, 218-26)

The glib Ms. Dog, then, has only solved the problem poetically. And from the selling of packaged phrases the focus changes to learning primary language, to trying to approach the divine, to her baby's first word, "utter." Baby language in Roethke was a sign of deep regression into a pre-conscious state. In an interesting twist Sexton uses the most adult, maternal language possible to describe objectively her daughter's first word, "utter," the beginning of speech as a complete experience.

Learning to talk is a complex business.
My daughter's first word was utta,
meaning button.
Before there are words
do you dream?

(Sexton 1999, 285-89)

Sexton's language consciously and purposely broadens to include all the languages of the self.

The still-present need and the artificiality and the limitations of overcoming the complicity of isolation remain.

When the dog barks you let him in.
All we need is someone to let us in.
And one other thing:
to consider the lilies in the field.
Of course earth is a stranger, we pull at its
arms and still it won't speak.

(Sexton 1999, 331-36)

What has changed is the awareness that her quest has become valid and even possible, not in spite of her madness and her poetic prostitution, but because of it. And it is not a personal quest alone.[21] The references in this poem to works of other poets such as Roethke, Berryman and Plath indicate that by incorporating their quests her own quest becomes archetypal and she might learn to transcend their curtailment.[22] She will risk Prufrock's "overwhelming question," and will try to surpass the goals of "The Wasteland." Eliot's Sybil wishes only to die, and "The Wasteland" later is resolved only through acceptance, but Sexton's poem seeks to go beyond acceptance to resolution. She is resolved to transform the nature of life and her poetry, and the search itself becomes an attempt at integration of the self, successful or not. Although "living" is initially attached to Pobiz and "fighting dollars," it comes to address the quest to use her poetry to create life out of the desire for death.[23]

The need to get "straight with the Maker" is a need that is if not fulfilled, at least accepted in the course of the poem, and all who search, however awkwardly and misguidedly, are equally heroic. From the deep center of the poem which describes in Roethkean images the experience of negation of the self by others,

When mother left the room
and left me in the big black
and sent away my kitty
to be fried in the camps
and took away my blanket
to wash the me out of it
I lay in the soiled cold and prayed.
It was a little jail in which
I was never slapped with kisses.

I was the engine that couldn't.

(Sexton 1999, 168-77)

there is an unexplained movement toward the acceptance of all selves, a validation for all quests, a waking into the world after a schizophrenic experience that is unlike Roethke's recovery in "The Lost Son," "as my own tongue kissed my lips awake" (1966, 56) only in that it is consciously archetypal. It is this universality towards which the concluding images lead:

There is the hand of a small child
when you're crossing the street.
There is the old man's last words:
More light! More light!

(Sexton 1999, 336-39)

By evening out the cultural hierarchy, equating the mutual comfort of holding a child's hand with Goethe's dying hunger for "more light," the poem makes individual and disparate quests equally valuable, with only one kind of quest rendered unworthy. Returning to the image of exhibitionistic flaunting which begins the poem she comments on Goethe and the comfort of a child:

> Ms. Dog wouldn't give them her buttocks.
> She wouldn't moon at them.
> Just at the killers of the dream.

(Sexton 1999, 340-42)

The use of popular culture alongside contemporary poetry and philosophy, as well as the incorporation of different and dissenting voices, then, is quite central to the argument of **"Hurry up,"** as well as to many other works and performances by Sexton. This incorporation has been recently seen in a study of Sexton's teaching methods as well.[24] Alienation both within the individual and among members of society is ubiquitous and the crazy renegade woman poet is the most attuned to it, and therefore is most appropriate to lead the search for a solution. This is the validation of the dream, no matter how sloppy, crazy, and unpoetic it might be, and this is the recognition of its popular ubiquity.[25]

Liz Hankins has argued that this poem is concerned with a reaffirmation of the body, and states: "She transcends history, rationality, society, and assumes her own unique identity—she becomes through her body and its parts" (1987, 512). However, it should be clear that the body is not the end, but the means of communication. Showing her buttocks here or her nudity to the delivery boy is neither exhibitionism, nor confession nor revenge, but communication through the body. At the beginning of the poem the function of stripping is at first derisive mooning (What is death, I ask. / What is life, you ask. / I give them both my buttocks, / my two wheels rolling off toward Nirvana: (Sexton 1999, 1-4)

> Why shouldn't I pull down my pants
> and moon the executioner
> as well as paste raisins on my breasts?
> Why shouldn't I pull down my pants
> and show my little cunny to Tom
> and Albert? They wee-wee funny.
> I wee-wee like a squaw.

(Sexton 1999, 9-14)

Later it becomes an acknowledgment of a hidden difference that has to be acknowledged and incorporated. Naked, the speaker here can dare to seek what is hidden in the world. Naked also, the lack of a "ruler" is acknowledged and flaunted. This absence of a standard for measurement becomes the basis for the acknowledged rationale of the poem itself. "But more than that," Sexton's speaker concludes, "to worship the question itself" (344).

This resolution to stand naked before questions is certainly part of Sexton's final years. Paula Salvio's brilliant analysis of Sexton's pedagogical techniques in

her last workshop notes that Sexton assigned students to write an imagined interview with her, a question a week. The emphasis on the question left her consistently vulnerable, and necessitated the apparently open form of some of her later poems.

The conclusion of this poem is very similar to the way in which critics such as Lynette McGrath and William Shurr perceive Sexton's suicide. It is presented as a daring quest, a leap of faith. Shurr writes: "Should there be no light beyond, at least the adventurer has left behind a vision of sublime light" (1985, 353-54). Had Sexton not committed suicide, it would have been easier to perceive the argument of **"Hurry up Please It's Time"** in its positive direction. But as Laing reminds us:

> The experience of being the actual medium for a continual process of creation takes one past all depression or persecution or vain glory, past, even, chaos or emptiness, into the very mystery of that continual flip of nonbeing into being, and can be the occasion of that great liberation when one makes the transition from being afraid of nothing, to the realisation that there is nothing to fear. Nevertheless, it is very easy to lose one's way at any stage, and especially when one is nearest.

(Laing 1967, 38)

Despite the fact that she indeed did lose her way, in this poem at least Sexton appears very near. Her placing of **"Hurry up"** in *The Death Notebooks* after the poems concerning her anger and frustrations and before **"O Ye Tongues"** which alternate psalms of creation with psalms of explanation, makes it a pivotal one for the awareness in this book that the speaker is seeking to take control of existence, of creating a new world by proclamation. Despite her awareness that she was perceived by others as lacking "taste," and despite her internalization of this deep criticism, she was determined to find her own way. Her use of the popular culture surrounding her—as opposed to the elitist culture of modernism—was part of her attempted redefinition of culture, her act of insurrection.

Notes

1. See for example the discussion of Sexton by the Poetry Society of America in "Anne Sexton: The Life vs. the Work" (http://www.poetry society.org/journal/articles/sexton.html).

2. Since this article concentrates so closely on "Hurry up, Please, It's Time," quotations from this poem only will be referred to by line numbers. All other quotations from poetry are referenced by page number.

3. That Laing was already a household word in Sexton's lifetime is clear from the way he is

dismissed in Howard Moss's introduction to *The Poet's Story,* "Dr. Laing is shedding light on a problem Chekhov already understood . . ." (1973, xi).

4. The scene of the vampire impaled on a stake and the villagers' revenge was so popular in foreign classic vampire films it was parodied in Polanski's 1967 classic, *The Fearless Vampire Killers.*

5. For more academic discussions of this distinction, see the works of Ludwig Binswanger and Rollo May.

6. For the sense of ongoing identification readers still have with this comic strip, one need only read the fan letters at <http://gasalley.comics page.com/>.

7. Robert Secor has noted that Thurber's Mitty "is awakened from his dream by the mundane cares of ordinary life." (1987, 74)

8. I mention the actors and not the characters because of the key role they as stereotypes from other films play in Mitty's fantasy.

9. I will not here deal with another important element of the film. The psychiatrist in the film—who tries to convince Mitty by using his authority and other manipulations that Mitty has actually lost his ability to identify and control reality—is actually one of the villains in the film. Boris Karloff playing the psychiatrist is of course in actuality part of the Nazi spy ring, and his function is to keep Mitty from understanding that his actions in the past days have been real and significant ones. This transformation of the apparent trustworthy guide to reality into the miscreant and criminal must have made some impact on Sexton's evaluation of recent events with her own psychiatrist.

10. Morton has noted the progress in the use of this prayer, (1989, 110).

11. "If, as Bakhtin states, the 'dialogic orientation of discourse' is a phenomenon that is, of course, a property of any discourse, then poetry, too, must retain the trace of other types of contemporary discursive practice."

12. See George, who equates the Orange of "Psalm 8" with language, "especially the language of poetry that operates by the creation of metaphor and images—another gestation, another birthing" (1985, 370).

13. I disagree here with Carolyn King, who associates the name as "possibly a descendent of Eliot's Wasteland dog . . . whose activity underscores both the attempt to bury memory and the failure of faith in resurrection and thus in ultimacy of life" (1989, 137). Certainly in this poem, Ms. Dog doesn't seem to have that function.

14. The full noting in her diary of Nov. 19, 1971 is as follows:

> "Oh Lord," they said last night on TV, "the sea is so mighty and my dog is so small." I heard dog. You say, they said boat not dog and that further dog would have no meaning. But it does mean. The sea is mother-death and she is a mighty female, the one who wins, the one who sucks us all up. Dog stands for me and the new puppy, Daisy. . . . Me and my dog, my Dalmatian dog, against the world. . . . "My dog is so small" means that even the two of us will be stamped under. Further, dog is what's in the sky on winter mornings. Sun-dogs springing back and forth across the sky. But we dogs are small and the sun will burn us down and the sea has our number. Oh Lord, the sea is so mighty and my dog is so small, my dog whom I sail with into the west. The sea is mother, larger than Asia, both lowering their large breasts onto the coastline. Thus we ride on her praying for good moods and a smile in the heavens. She is mighty, oh Lord, but I wish my little puppy, Daisy, remain a child.
>
> "Too complicated, eh?"

15. Middlebrook's point is somewhat different, noting that the use of multiple pronouns "conveys the terms on which she wishes to be understood: not victim, but witness and witch."

16. As Louis Simpson called it, referring to "Menstruation at Forty" (qtd. in Kumin 1999, xix-xx).

17. The full chorus of the song written by G. Kahn, E. Erdman, D. Russo, and T. Fiorito and performed by Al Jolson in blackface is:

> "Toot, toot, Tootsie, don't cry,
> The choo choo train that takes me,
> Away from you, no words can tell how sad it makes me,
> Kiss me, Tootsie, and then,
> Do it over again.
> Watch for the mail, I'll never fail,
> If you don't get a letter then you'll know I'm in jail,
> Tut, tut, Tootsie, don't cry,
> Toot, toot, Tootsie, Goo' bye!"

18. The guilt of complicity marks Linda Sexton's autobiography. One example: "Daddy and I pretended nothing was happening: if we pretended maybe we could make it so" (1994, 111).

19. See Cam (1987).

20. E. Colby (ed.) *The Life of Thomas Holcroft,* continued by William Hazlitt (London: Constable & Co., 1925) Vol. 2, p. 82.

21. Estella Lauter has pointed out that "Sexton's quest is best understood . . . in terms of archetypal psychology, as an act of 'soul-making'—that is, the effort to find the connections between life and the fantasy images that are our 'privileged mode of access' to the soul and to those recurring worldwide figures who are tantamount to gods" (1984, 24).

22. One parallel, "When mother left the room / and left me in the big black / and sent away my kitty / to be fried in the camps" (Sexton 1999, 390) sounds like something of a summary of Roethke's "Praise to the End."

23. The pervasive influence of T. S. Eliot has been extensively noted by Caroline King, but one of the aspects of "The Wasteland" with which Sexton most identifies and which most influences her here is the division of aspects of the self into different and potentially regenerative personalities, and the need for a reintegration. Another influence here is Roethke's "I have married my hands to perpetual agitation / I run, I run to the whistle of money" (1966, 56).

24. Paula Salvio in studying Sexton's teaching methods comes to this conclusion: "By reading Sexton's teaching life through cultural texts that refuse to privilege high culture as the locus of political opposition, Sexton's pedagogic documents can be used to cue educators to develop more refined tastes for irony, parody, and the grotesque so that we might re-define the limited tastes that represent 'rationality' and emotional reliability in our classrooms" (1999, 660).

25. Not all readers are puzzled by this—Robert Boyers, for example, early noted: "There is something awesome, even sublime in a woman who is not afraid to sound crude or shrill so long as she is honest, who in her best work sounds honest" (1967, 71). Sexton also asked this:

> The cry of a gull is beautiful
> and the cry of a crow is ugly
> but what I want to know
> is whether they mean the same thing
>
> (Sexton 1999, 322-25)

Works Cited

Berryman, John. 1964. "Dream Song, 53." *77 Dream Songs.* New York: Farrar Straus & Giroux.

Blake, David Haven. 2001. "Public Dreams: Berryman, Celebrity, and the Culture of Confession." *American Literary History* 13.4: 716-36.

Boyers, Robert. 1967. "Live or Die: The Achievement of Anne Sexton." *Salmagundi* 2.1 (Spring): 41-71.

Cam, Heather. 1987. "'Daddy': Sylvia Plath's Debt to Anne Sexton." *American Literature* 59.3 (October): 429-32.

Clay, John. 1996. *R. D. Laing: A Divided Self.* London: Hodder and Stoughton.

Colburn, Steven E. n.d. "'As A Child's Heart Might': Childhood in Anne Sexton's Poetry." Unpublished.

Cooper David. 1967. *Psychiatry and Anti-psychiatry.* Tavistock Publications: London.

De Certeau, Michel. 1984. *The Practice of Everyday Life.* Berkeley: University of California Press.

Economou, Stefan. "Forgetting Peanuts." *Pop Matters.* <http://www.popmatters.com/comics/forgetting-peanuts/shtml>. Accessed 10 July 2005.

George, Diana Hume. 1985. "Is It True? Feeding, Feces, and Creativity in Anne Sexton's Poetry." *Soundings: An Interdisciplinary Journal* 68.3: 357-71.

Gill, Joanna. 2003. "'My Sweeney, Mr. Eliot': Anne Sexton and the 'Impersonal Theory of Poetry'." *Journal of Modern Literature* 27.1/2 (Fall): 36-57.

Ginsberg, Allen. 1984. *Collected Poems 1947-1980.* New York: Harper and Row.

Hankins, Liz Porter. 1987. "Summoning the Body: Anne Sexton's Body Poems." *Midwest Quarterly* 28.4 (Summer): 511-24.

Hedley, Jane. 2000. "'I Made You to Find Me': Sexton, Lowell, and the Gender of Poethood." *Raritan* 19.3 (Winter): 87-114.

Hoffman, Steven K. 1978. "Impersonal Personalism: The Making of a Confessional Poetic." *ELH* 45.4 (Winter): 687-709.

Kendall, Elaine. 1962. "Success (?) Secret of the Starmakers." *New York Times Magazine,* 30 September, 37-40.

King, Caroline. 1989. *Anne Sexton.* Boston: Twayne.

Kumin, Maxine. 1999. "How It Was," In *Anne Sexton: Complete Poems.* Boston: Mariner.

Laing, R. D. 1967. *The Politics of Experience and The Bird of Paradise.* Harmondsworth, Middlesex: Penguin Books.

Lauter, Estella. 1984. *Women as Mythmakers: Poetry and Visual Art by Twentieth Century Women.* Bloomington: Indiana.

Long, Mikhail Ann. 1993. "As if Day Had Rearranged Into Night: Suicidal Tendencies in the Poetry of Anne Sexton." *Literature and Psychology* 39. 1-2: 26-41.

McClatchey, J. D., ed. 1978. *Anne Sexton: The Artist and Her Critics.* Bloomington: Indiana University Press.

McGrath, Lynette. 1988. "Anne Sexton's Poetic Connections: Death, God, and Form." In *Original Essays on the Poetry of Anne Sexton,* ed. Francis Bixler. Conway: University of Central Arkansas Press.

Middlebrook, Diane Wood. 1989. "Poet of Weird Abundance." In *Telling The Tale,* ed. Steven Colburn. Ann Arbor: University of Michigan Press.

————. 1991. *Anne Sexton: A Biography.* Boston: Houghton-Mifflin.

Morton, Richard E. 1989. *Anne Sexton's Poetry of Redemption: The Chronology of a Pilgrimage.* Lewiston, New York: Mellen.

Moss, Howard. 1973. Introduction to *The Poet's Story.* New York: MacMillan.

Noland, Carrie. 1999. *Poetry at Stake: Lyric Aesthetics and the Challenge of Technology.* Princeton: Princeton University Press.

Ostriker, Alicia. 1986. *Stealing the Language: The Emergence of Women's Poetry in America.* Boston: Beacon.

Plath, Sylvia. 1981. *Collected Poems.* Boston: Perennial.

Radin, Victoria. 1991. "Ms Dog for Sale." *New Statesman & Society* 4: 46-47.

Richman, Joseph. 1971. "Family Determinants of Suicide Potential." In *Identifying Potential Suicide,* ed. Dorothy B. Anderson and Lenora J. McClean. New York: Behavioral Publications.

Roethke, Theodore. 1966. *Collected Poems.* New York: Doubleday.

Salvio, Paula. 1999. "Teacher of 'Weird Abundance': Portraits of the Pedagogical Tactics of Anne Sexton." *Cultural Studies* 13.4: 639-60.

Secor, Robert. 1987. "Walter Mitty and Lord Jim." *English Languages Notes* 25.1: 1974-77.

Secret Life of Walter Mitty, The. 1947. Directed by Norman Z. McLeod, Samuel Goldwyn Productions.

Sexton, Anne. 1988a. "All God's Children Need Radios." In *No Evil Star: Selected Essays, Interviews and Prose,* ed. Steven E. Colburn. Ann Arbor: The University of Michigan Press.

————. 1988b. "The Freak Show." In *No Evil Star: Selected Essays, Interviews and Prose,* ed. Steven E. Colburn. Ann Arbor: The University of Michigan Press.

————. 1999. *Complete Poems.* Boston: Mariner.

Sexton, Linda Gray. 1994. *Searching for Mercy Street: My Journey Back to My Mother, Anne Sexton.* New York: Little, Brown and Company.

Shurr, William. 1985. "Mysticism and Suicide: Anne Sexton's Last Poetry." *Soundings: An Interdisciplinary Journal* 68.3: 335-56.

Thurber, James. 1996. "The Secret Life of Walter Mitty." In *Writings and Drawings.* New York: Library of America.

Trinidad, David. "Anne Sexton: An Actress in Her Own Autobiographical Play." Crossroads: *Poetry Society of America Journal.* (Fall <http://www.poetrysociety.org/journal/articles/sexton.html>. Accessed 10 July 2005.

FURTHER READING

Criticism

Brown, Amy Benson. "'Much Madness Is Divinest Sense': The Biblical Revision of Anne Sexton and Sylvia Plath." In *Rewriting the Word: American Women Writers and the Bible,* pp. 67-125. Westport, Conn.: Greenwood Press, 1999.

> Examines the biblically informed poetry of Sexton and Plath, evaluating the poets' "biblical revisions" within the context of the confessional mode of writing.

Clark, Hilary. "Depression, Shame, and Reparation: The Case of Anne Sexton." In *Scenes of Shame: Psychoanalysis, Shame, and Writing,* edited by Joseph Adamson and Hilary Clark, pp. 189-206. Albany: State University of New York Press, 1999.

> Considers what role the writing of poetry played in Sexton's life—a life filled, according to the critic, with addictions, depression, irrational fears, and suicidal thoughts and attempts.

Gill, Jo. "Anne Sexton and Confessional Poetics." *Review of English Studies* n.s. 55, no. 220 (2004): 425-45.

> Uses remarks Sexton made in letters, during lectures, and in her poetry to dispute the critical claim that her writings unequivocally belong to the confessional mode. Gill also argues that Sexton challenged the limits of the confessional method and attempted to create her own poetics.

Hall, Caroline King Barnard. "*Transformations*: A Magic Mirror." In *Original Essays on the Poetry of Anne Sexton,* edited by Frances Bixler, pp. 107-29. Conway, Ark.: University of Central Arkansas Press, 1988.

> Considers Sexton's retelling of the Grimm Brothers' fairy tales, tracing her methodology, narration, themes, and use of language.

Honton, Margaret. "'The Double Image' and 'The Division of Parts': A Study of Mother-Daughter Relationships in the Poetry of Anne Sexton." In *Sexton: Selected Criticism,* edited by Diana Hume George, pp. 99-116. Urbana: University of Illinois Press, 1988.

> Exploration of Sexton's treatment of "daughterhood" and motherhood in her poetry.

Leventen, Carol. "*Transformations*'s Silencings." In *Critical Essays on Anne Sexton,* edited by Linda Wagner-Martin, pp. 136-49. Boston: G. K. Hall, 1989.

> Argues that, in the end, the fairy tale heroines Sexton created in *Transformations* "remain silent, passive, powerless victims frozen in—and fated to act out—the prescribed social roles in which her sources cast them."

McCabe, Jane. "'A Woman Who Writes': A Feminist Approach to the Early Poetry of Anne Sexton." In *Anne Sexton: The Artist and Her Critics,* edited by J. D. Mc-Clatchy, pp. 216-43. Bloomington: Indiana University Press, 1978.

Finds Sexton's poetry important to feminist scholarship despite her contention that Sexton was not a feminist poet.

Michailidou, Artemis. "Edna St. Vincent Millay and Anne Sexton: The Disruption of Domestic Bliss." *Journal of American Studies* 38, no. 1 (2004): 67-88.

Discusses the influence Millay's domestic writings had on Sexton, claiming that the way in which Millay treated subjects such as women's apprehension, self-exploration, and enforced domesticity helped Sexton to define and articulate her own ideas about womanhood.

Middlebrook, Diane Wood. Preface to *Anne Sexton: A Biography,* pp. xix-xxiii. Boston: Houghton Mifflin, 1991.

Brief overview of Sexton's publishing career.

———. "Circle of Women Artists: Tillie Olsen and Anne Sexton at the Radcliffe Institute." In *Listening to Silences: New Essays in Feminist Criticism,* edited by Elaine Hedges and Shelley Fisher Fishkin, pp. 17-22. New York: Oxford University Press, 1994.

Briefly summarizes Olsen's appointment during the early 1960s as a scholar at the Radcliffe Institute and her influence on fellow Radcliffe scholar Sexton.

Skorczewski, Dawn. "What Prison Is This? Literary Critics Cover Incest in Anne Sexton's 'Briar Rose.'" *Signs* 21, no. 2 (winter 1996): 309-42.

Argues that "Briar Rose" represents the dangers women face in a society that permits male-on-female sexual violence.

Wedding, Danny. "Cognitive Distortions in the Poetry of Anne Sexton." *Suicide & Life-Threatening Behavior* 30, no. 2 (summer 2000): 140-44.

Examines specific instances in Sexton's poetry that reveal the distortions in knowledge, beliefs, and ideas experienced by suicidal persons.

Additional coverage of Sexton's life and career is contained in the following sources published by Thomson Gale: *American Writers Supplement,* **Vol. 2;** *Concise Dictionary of American Literary Biography, 1941-1968;* *Contemporary Authors,* **Vols. 1-4R;** *Contemporary Authors—Obituary,* **Vols. 53-56;** *Contemporary Authors Bibliographical Series,* **Vol. 2;** *Contemporary Authors New Revision Series,* **Vols. 3, 36;** *Contemporary Literary Criticism,* **Vols. 2, 4, 6, 8, 10, 15, 53, 123;** *Contemporary Poets,* **Eds. 1, 2;** *Dictionary of Literary Biography,* **Vols. 5, 169;** *Discovering Authors; Discovering Authors, 3.0; Discovering Authors: British Edition; Discovering Authors: Canadian Edition; Discovering Authors Modules: Most-studied Authors* **and** *Poets; Encyclopedia of World Literature in the 20th Century,* **Ed. 3;** *Exploring Poetry; Feminism in Literature: A Gale Critical Companion,* **Ed. 1:6;** *Feminist Writers; Literature Resource Center; Major 20th-Century Writers,* **Eds. 1, 2;** *Major 21st-Century Writers,* **(ebook) 2005;** *Modern American Literature,* **Ed. 5;** *Modern American Women Writers; Poetry Criticism,* **Vol. 2;** *Poetry for Students,* **Vols. 4, 14;** *Poets: American and British; Reference Guide to American Literature,* **Ed. 4;** *Reference Guide to Holocaust Literature; Something about the Author,* **Vol. 10;** *Twayne's United States Authors;* **and** *World Literature Criticism,* **Vol. 5.**

How to Use This Index

The main references

> **Calvino, Italo**
> 1923-1985 .... CLC 5, 8, 11, 22, 33, 39,
> 73; SSC 3, 48

list all author entries in the following Thomson Gale Literary Criticism series:

AAL = *Asian American Literature*
BG = *The Beat Generation: A Gale Critical Companion*
BLC = *Black Literature Criticism*
BLCS = *Black Literature Criticism Supplement*
CLC = *Contemporary Literary Criticism*
CLR = *Children's Literature Review*
CMLC = *Classical and Medieval Literature Criticism*
DC = *Drama Criticism*
FL = *Feminism in Literature: A Gale Critical Companion*
GL = *Gothic Literature: A Gale Critical Companion*
HLC = *Hispanic Literature Criticism*
HLCS = *Hispanic Literature Criticism Supplement*
HR = *Harlem Renaissance: A Gale Critical Companion*
LC = *Literature Criticism from 1400 to 1800*
NCLC = *Nineteenth-Century Literature Criticism*
NNAL = *Native North American Literature*
PC = *Poetry Criticism*
SSC = *Short Story Criticism*
TCLC = *Twentieth-Century Literary Criticism*
WLC = *World Literature Criticism, 1500 to the Present*
WLCS = *World Literature Criticism Supplement*

The cross-references

> See also CA 85-88, 116; CANR 23, 61;
> DAM NOV; DLB 196; EW 13; MTCW 1, 2;
> RGSF 2; RGWL 2; SFW 4; SSFS 12

list all author entries in the following Thomson Gale biographical and literary sources:

AAYA = *Authors & Artists for Young Adults*
AFAW = *African American Writers*
AFW = *African Writers*
AITN = *Authors in the News*
AMW = *American Writers*
AMWR = *American Writers Retrospective Supplement*
AMWS = *American Writers Supplement*
ANW = *American Nature Writers*
AW = *Ancient Writers*
BEST = *Bestsellers*
BPFB = *Beacham's Encyclopedia of Popular Fiction: Biography and Resources*
BRW = *British Writers*
BRWS = *British Writers Supplement*
BW = *Black Writers*
BYA = *Beacham's Guide to Literature for Young Adults*
CA = *Contemporary Authors*
CAAS = *Contemporary Authors Autobiography Series*
CABS = *Contemporary Authors Bibliographical Series*
CAD = *Contemporary American Dramatists*
CANR = *Contemporary Authors New Revision Series*
CAP = *Contemporary Authors Permanent Series*
CBD = *Contemporary British Dramatists*
CCA = *Contemporary Canadian Authors*
CD = *Contemporary Dramatists*
CDALB = *Concise Dictionary of American Literary Biography*

CDALBS = *Concise Dictionary of American Literary Biography Supplement*

CDBLB = *Concise Dictionary of British Literary Biography*

CMW = *St. James Guide to Crime & Mystery Writers*

CN = *Contemporary Novelists*

CP = *Contemporary Poets*

CPW = *Contemporary Popular Writers*

CSW = *Contemporary Southern Writers*

CWD = *Contemporary Women Dramatists*

CWP = *Contemporary Women Poets*

CWRI = *St. James Guide to Children's Writers*

CWW = *Contemporary World Writers*

DA = *DISCovering Authors*

DA3 = *DISCovering Authors 3.0*

DAB = *DISCovering Authors: British Edition*

DAC = *DISCovering Authors: Canadian Edition*

DAM = *DISCovering Authors: Modules*

   DRAM: *Dramatists Module;* **MST:** *Most-studied Authors Module;*

   MULT: *Multicultural Authors Module;* **NOV:** *Novelists Module;*

   POET: *Poets Module;* **POP:** *Popular Fiction and Genre Authors Module*

DFS = *Drama for Students*

DLB = *Dictionary of Literary Biography*

DLBD = *Dictionary of Literary Biography Documentary Series*

DLBY = *Dictionary of Literary Biography Yearbook*

DNFS = *Literature of Developing Nations for Students*

EFS = *Epics for Students*

EXPN = *Exploring Novels*

EXPP = *Exploring Poetry*

EXPS = *Exploring Short Stories*

EW = *European Writers*

FANT = *St. James Guide to Fantasy Writers*

FW = *Feminist Writers*

GFL = *Guide to French Literature,* Beginnings to 1789, 1798 to the Present

GLL = *Gay and Lesbian Literature*

HGG = *St. James Guide to Horror, Ghost & Gothic Writers*

HW = *Hispanic Writers*

IDFW = *International Dictionary of Films and Filmmakers: Writers and Production Artists*

IDTP = *International Dictionary of Theatre: Playwrights*

LAIT = *Literature and Its Times*

LAW = *Latin American Writers*

JRDA = *Junior DISCovering Authors*

MAICYA = *Major Authors and Illustrators for Children and Young Adults*

MAICYAS = *Major Authors and Illustrators for Children and Young Adults Supplement*

MAWW = *Modern American Women Writers*

MJW = *Modern Japanese Writers*

MTCW = *Major 20th-Century Writers*

NCFS = *Nonfiction Classics for Students*

NFS = *Novels for Students*

PAB = *Poets: American and British*

PFS = *Poetry for Students*

RGAL = *Reference Guide to American Literature*

RGEL = *Reference Guide to English Literature*

RGSF = *Reference Guide to Short Fiction*

RGWL = *Reference Guide to World Literature*

RHW = *Twentieth-Century Romance and Historical Writers*

SAAS = *Something about the Author Autobiography Series*

SATA = *Something about the Author*

SFW = *St. James Guide to Science Fiction Writers*

SSFS = *Short Stories for Students*

TCWW = *Twentieth-Century Western Writers*

WLIT = *World Literature and Its Times*

WP = *World Poets*

YABC = *Yesterday's Authors of Books for Children*

YAW = *St. James Guide to Young Adult Writers*

Literary Criticism Series
Cumulative Author Index

20/1631
See Upward, Allen

A/C Cross
See Lawrence, T(homas) E(dward)

A. M.
See Megged, Aharon

Abasiyanik, Sait Faik 1906-1954
See Sait Faik
See also CA 231; CAAE 123

Abbey, Edward 1927-1989 .... **CLC 36, 59; TCLC 160**
See also AAYA 75; AMWS 13; ANW; CA 45-48; CAAS 128; CANR 2, 41, 131; DA3; DLB 256, 275; LATS 1:2; MTCW 2; MTFW 2005; TCWW 1, 2

Abbott, Edwin A. 1838-1926 .... **TCLC 139**
See also DLB 178

Abbott, Lee K(ittredge) 1947- .... **CLC 48**
See also CA 124; CANR 51, 101; DLB 130

Abe, Kobo 1924-1993 ...... **CLC 8, 22, 53, 81; SSC 61; TCLC 131**
See also CA 65-68; CAAS 140; CANR 24, 60; DAM NOV; DFS 14; DLB 182; EWL 3; MJW; MTCW 1, 2; MTFW 2005; NFS 22; RGWL 3; SFW 4

Abe Kobo
See Abe, Kobo

Abelard, Peter c. 1079-c. 1142 ..... **CMLC 11, 77**
See also DLB 115, 208

Abell, Kjeld 1901-1961 .... **CLC 15**
See also CA 191; CAAS 111; DLB 214; EWL 3

Abercrombie, Lascelles 1881-1938 .... **TCLC 141**
See also CAAE 112; DLB 19; RGEL 2

Abish, Walter 1931- .... **CLC 22; SSC 44**
See also CA 101; CANR 37, 114, 153; CN 3, 4, 5, 6; DLB 130, 227; MAL 5; RGHL

Abrahams, Peter (Henry) 1919- .... **CLC 4**
See also AFW; BW 1; CA 57-60; CANR 26, 125; CDWLB 3; CN 1, 2, 3, 4, 5, 6; DLB 117, 225; EWL 3; MTCW 1, 2; RGEL 2; WLIT 2

Abrams, M(eyer) H(oward) 1912- ... **CLC 24**
See also CA 57-60; CANR 13, 33; DLB 67

Abse, Dannie 1923- .... **CLC 7, 29; PC 41**
See also CA 53-56; 1; CANR 4, 46, 74, 124; CBD; CN 1, 2, 3; CP 1, 2, 3, 4, 5, 6, 7; DAB; DAM POET; DLB 27, 245; MTCW 2

Abutsu 1222(?)-1283 .... **CMLC 46**
See Abutsu-ni

Abutsu-ni
See Abutsu
See also DLB 203

Achebe, Albert Chinualumogu
See Achebe, Chinua

Achebe, Chinua 1930- .. **BLC 1; CLC 1, 3, 5, 7, 11, 26, 51, 75, 127, 152; WLC 1**
See also AAYA 15; AFW; BPFB 1; BRWC 2; BW 2, 3; CA 1-4R; CANR 6, 26, 47, 124; CDWLB 3; CLR 20; CN 1, 2, 3, 4, 5, 6, 7; CP 2, 3, 4, 5, 6, 7; CWRI 5; DA; DA3; DAB; DAC; DAM MST, MULT, NOV; DLB 117; DNFS 1; EWL 3; EXPN; EXPS; LAIT 2; LATS 1:2; MAICYA 1, 2; MTCW 1, 2; MTFW 2005; NFS 2; RGEL 2; RGSF 2; SATA 38, 40; SATA-Brief 38; SSFS 3, 13; TWA; WLIT 2; WWE 1

Acker, Kathy 1948-1997 .... **CLC 45, 111; TCLC 191**
See also AMWS 12; CA 122; CAAE 117; CAAS 162; CANR 55; CN 5, 6; MAL 5

Ackroyd, Peter 1949- .... **CLC 34, 52, 140**
See also BRWS 6; CA 127; CAAE 123; CANR 51, 74, 99, 132; CN 4, 5, 6, 7; DLB 155, 231; HGG; INT CA-127; MTCW 2; MTFW 2005; RHW; SATA 153; SUFW 2

Acorn, Milton 1923-1986 .... **CLC 15**
See also CA 103; CCA 1; CP 1, 2, 3, 4; DAC; DLB 53; INT CA-103

Adam de la Halle c. 1250-c. 1285 .... **CMLC 80**

Adamov, Arthur 1908-1970 .... **CLC 4, 25; TCLC 189**
See also CA 17-18; CAAS 25-28R; CAP 2; DAM DRAM; DLB 321; EWL 3; GFL 1789 to the Present; MTCW 1; RGWL 2, 3

Adams, Alice 1926-1999 .... **CLC 6, 13, 46; SSC 24**
See also CA 81-84; CAAS 179; CANR 26, 53, 75, 88, 136; CN 4, 5, 6; CSW; DLB 234; DLBY 1986; INT CANR-26; MTCW 1, 2; MTFW 2005; SSFS 14, 21

Adams, Andy 1859-1935 .... **TCLC 56**
See also TCWW 1, 2; YABC 1

Adams, (Henry) Brooks 1848-1927 .... **TCLC 80**
See also CA 193; CAAE 123

Adams, Douglas 1952-2001 .... **CLC 27, 60**
See also AAYA 4, 33; BEST 89:3; BYA 14; CA 106; CAAS 197; CANR 34, 64, 124; CPW; DA3; DAM POP; DLB 261; DLBY 1983; JRDA; MTCW 2; MTFW 2005; NFS 7; SATA 116; SATA-Obit 128; SFW 4

Adams, Francis 1862-1893 .... **NCLC 33**

Adams, Henry (Brooks) 1838-1918 .... **TCLC 4, 52**
See also AMW; CA 133; CAAE 104; CANR 77; DA; DAB; DAC; DAM MST; DLB 12, 47, 189, 284; EWL 3; MAL 5; MTCW 2; NCFS 1; RGAL 4; TUS

Adams, John 1735-1826 .... **NCLC 106**
See also DLB 31, 183

Adams, John Quincy 1767-1848 .. **NCLC 175**
See also DLB 37

Adams, Mary
See Phelps, Elizabeth Stuart

Adams, Richard (George) 1920- ... **CLC 4, 5, 18**
See also AAYA 16; AITN 1, 2; BPFB 1; BYA 5; CA 49-52; CANR 3, 35, 128; CLR 20, 121; CN 4, 5, 6, 7; DAM NOV; DLB 261; FANT; JRDA; LAIT 5; MAICYA 1, 2; MTCW 1, 2; NFS 11; SATA 7, 69; YAW

Adamson, Joy(-Friederike Victoria) 1910-1980 .... **CLC 17**
See also CA 69-72; CAAS 93-96; CANR 22; MTCW 1; SATA 11; SATA-Obit 22

Adcock, Fleur 1934- .... **CLC 41**
See also BRWS 12; CA 182; 25-28R, 182; 23; CANR 11, 34, 69, 101; CP 1, 2, 3, 4, 5, 6, 7; CWP; DLB 40; FW; WWE 1

Addams, Charles 1912-1988 .... **CLC 30**
See also CA 61-64; CAAS 126; CANR 12, 79

Addams, Charles Samuel
See Addams, Charles

Addams, (Laura) Jane 1860-1935 . **TCLC 76**
See also AMWS 1; CA 194; DLB 303; FW

Addison, Joseph 1672-1719 .... **LC 18**
See also BRW 3; CDBLB 1660-1789; DLB 101; RGEL 2; WLIT 3

Adler, Alfred (F.) 1870-1937 .... **TCLC 61**
See also CA 159; CAAE 119

Adler, C(arole) S(chwerdtfeger) 1932- .... **CLC 35**
See also AAYA 4, 41; CA 89-92; CANR 19, 40, 101; CLR 78; JRDA; MAICYA 1, 2; SAAS 15; SATA 26, 63, 102, 126; YAW

Adler, Renata 1938- .... **CLC 8, 31**
See also CA 49-52; CANR 95; CN 4, 5, 6; MTCW 1

Adorno, Theodor W(iesengrund) 1903-1969 .... **TCLC 111**
See also CA 89-92; CAAS 25-28R; CANR 89; DLB 242; EWL 3

Ady, Endre 1877-1919 .... **TCLC 11**
See also CAAE 107; CDWLB 4; DLB 215; EW 9; EWL 3

A.E. .... **TCLC 3, 10**
See Russell, George William
See also DLB 19

Aelfric c. 955-c. 1010 .... **CMLC 46**
See also DLB 146

Aeschines c. 390B.C.-c. 320B.C. .... **CMLC 47**
See also DLB 176

347

Aleshkovsky, Yuz .... **CLC 44**
   See Aleshkovsky, Joseph
   See also DLB 317
Alexander, Lloyd 1924-2007 .... **CLC 35**
   See also AAYA 1, 27; BPFB 1; BYA 5, 6,
   7, 9, 10, 11; CA 1-4R; CAAS 260; CANR
   1, 24, 38, 55, 113; CLR 1, 5, 48; CWRI
   5; DLB 52; FANT; JRDA; MAICYA 1, 2;
   MAICYAS 1; MTCW 1; SAAS 19; SATA
   3, 49, 81, 129, 135; SUFW; TUS; WYA;
   YAW
Alexander, Lloyd Chudley
   See Alexander, Lloyd
Alexander, Meena 1951- .... **CLC 121**
   See also CA 115; CANR 38, 70, 146; CP 5,
   6, 7; CWP; DLB 323; FW
Alexander, Samuel 1859-1938 .... **TCLC 77**
Alexeiev, Konstantin
   See Stanislavsky, Constantin
Alexeyev, Constantin Sergeivich
   See Stanislavsky, Constantin
Alexeyev, Konstantin Sergeyevich
   See Stanislavsky, Constantin
Alexie, Sherman 1966- .... **CLC 96, 154;**
   NNAL; PC 53
    See also AAYA 28; BYA 15; CA 138;
    CANR 65, 95, 133; CN 7; DA3; DAM
    MULT; DLB 175, 206, 278; LATS 1:2;
    MTCW 2; MTFW 2005; NFS 17; SSFS
    18
al-Farabi 870(?)-950 .... **CMLC 58**
   See also DLB 115
Alfau, Felipe 1902-1999 .... **CLC 66**
   See also CA 137
Alfieri, Vittorio 1749-1803 .... **NCLC 101**
   See also EW 4; RGWL 2, 3; WLIT 7
Alfonso X 1221-1284 .... **CMLC 78**
Alfred, Jean Gaston
   See Ponge, Francis
Alger, Horatio, Jr. 1832-1899 .... **NCLC 8, 83**
   See also CLR 87; DLB 42; LAIT 2; RGAL
   4; SATA 16; TUS
Al-Ghazali, Muhammad ibn Muhammad
   1058-1111 .... **CMLC 50**
   See also DLB 115
Algren, Nelson 1909-1981 ..... **CLC 4, 10, 33;**
   SSC 33
    See also AMWS 9; BPFB 1; CA 13-16R;
    CAAS 103; CANR 20, 61; CDALB 1941-
    1968; CN 1, 2; DLB 9; DLBY 1981,
    1982, 2000; EWL 3; MAL 5; MTCW 1,
    2; MTFW 2005; RGAL 4; RGSF 2
al-Hamadhani 967-1007 .... **CMLC 93**
   See also WLIT 6
al-Hariri, al-Qasim ibn 'Ali Abu
   Muhammad al-Basri
   1054-1122 .... **CMLC 63**
   See also RGWL 3
Ali, Ahmed 1908-1998 .... **CLC 69**
   See also CA 25-28R; CANR 15, 34; CN 1,
   2, 3, 4, 5; DLB 323; EWL 3
Ali, Tariq 1943- .... **CLC 173**
   See also CA 25-28R; CANR 10, 99, 161
Alighieri, Dante
   See Dante
   See also WLIT 7
al-Kindi, Abu Yusuf Ya'qub ibn Ishaq c.
   801-c. 873 .... **CMLC 80**
Allan, John B.
   See Westlake, Donald E.
Allan, Sidney
   See Hartmann, Sadakichi
Allan, Sydney
   See Hartmann, Sadakichi

Allard, Janet .... **CLC 59**
Allen, Edward 1948- .... **CLC 59**
Allen, Fred 1894-1956 .... **TCLC 87**
Allen, Paula Gunn 1939- .... **CLC 84, 202;**
   NNAL
    See also AMWS 4; CA 143; CAAE 112;
    CANR 63, 130; CWP; DA3; DAM
    MULT; DLB 175; FW; MTCW 2; MTFW
    2005; RGAL 4; TCWW 2
Allen, Roland
   See Ayckbourn, Alan
Allen, Sarah A.
   See Hopkins, Pauline Elizabeth
Allen, Sidney H.
   See Hartmann, Sadakichi
Allen, Woody 1935- .... **CLC 16, 52, 195**
   See also AAYA 10, 51; AMWS 15; CA 33-
   36R; CANR 27, 38, 63, 128; DAM POP;
   DLB 44; MTCW 1; SSFS 21
Allende, Isabel 1942- ... **CLC 39, 57, 97, 170;**
   HLC 1; SSC 65; WLCS
    See also AAYA 18, 70; CA 130; CAAE 125;
    CANR 51, 74, 129, 165; CDWLB 3; CLR
    99; CWW 2; DA3; DAM MULT, NOV;
    DLB 145; DNFS 1; EWL 3; FL 1:5; FW;
    HW 1, 2; INT CA-130; LAIT 5; LAWS
    1; LMFS 2; MTCW 1, 2; MTFW 2005;
    NCFS 1; NFS 6, 18; RGSF 2; RGWL 3;
    SATA 163; SSFS 11, 16; WLIT 1
Alleyn, Ellen
   See Rossetti, Christina
Alleyne, Carla D. .... **CLC 65**
Allingham, Margery (Louise)
   1904-1966 .... **CLC 19**
    See also CA 5-8R; CAAS 25-28R; CANR
    4, 58; CMW 4; DLB 77; MSW; MTCW
    1, 2
Allingham, William 1824-1889 ...... **NCLC 25**
   See also DLB 35; RGEL 2
Allison, Dorothy E. 1949- .... **CLC 78, 153**
   See also AAYA 53; CA 140; CANR 66, 107;
   CN 7; CSW; DA3; FW; MTCW 2; MTFW
   2005; NFS 11; RGAL 4
Alloula, Malek .... **CLC 65**
Allston, Washington 1779-1843 .... **NCLC 2**
   See also DLB 1, 235
Almedingen, E. M. .... **CLC 12**
   See Almedingen, Martha Edith von
   See also SATA 3
Almedingen, Martha Edith von 1898-1971
   See Almedingen, E. M.
   See also CA 1-4R; CANR 1
Almodovar, Pedro 1949(?)- .... **CLC 114, 229;**
   HLCS 1
    See also CA 133; CANR 72, 151; HW 2
Almqvist, Carl Jonas Love
   1793-1866 .... **NCLC 42**
al-Mutanabbi, Ahmad ibn al-Husayn Abu
   al-Tayyib al-Jufi al-Kindi
   915-965 .... **CMLC 66**
   See Mutanabbi, Al-
   See also RGWL 3
Alonso, Damaso 1898-1990 .... **CLC 14**
   See also CA 131; CAAE 110; CAAS 130;
   CANR 72; DLB 108; EWL 3; HW 1, 2
Alov
   See Gogol, Nikolai (Vasilyevich)
al'Sadaawi, Nawal
   See El Saadawi, Nawal
   See also FW
al-Shaykh, Hanan 1945- .... **CLC 218**
   See Shaykh, al- Hanan
   See also CA 135; CANR 111; WLIT 6
Al Siddik
   See Rolfe, Frederick (William Serafino
   Austin Lewis Mary)
   See also GLL 1; RGEL 2
Alta 1942- .... **CLC 19**
   See also CA 57-60

Alter, Robert B. 1935- .... **CLC 34**
   See also CA 49-52; CANR 1, 47, 100, 160
Alter, Robert Bernard
   See Alter, Robert B.
Alther, Lisa 1944- .... **CLC 7, 41**
   See also BPFB 1; CA 65-68; 30; CANR 12,
   30, 51; CN 4, 5, 6, 7; CSW; GLL 2;
   MTCW 1
Althusser, L.
   See Althusser, Louis
Althusser, Louis 1918-1990 .... **CLC 106**
   See also CA 131; CAAS 132; CANR 102;
   DLB 242
Altman, Robert 1925-2006 .... **CLC 16, 116,**
   242
    See also CA 73-76; CAAS 254; CANR 43
Alurista .... **HLCS 1; PC 34**
   See Urista (Heredia), Alberto (Baltazar)
   See also CA 45-48R; DLB 82; LLW
Alvarez, A. 1929- .... **CLC 5, 13**
   See also CA 1-4R; CANR 3, 33, 63, 101,
   134; CN 3, 4, 5, 6; CP 1, 2, 3, 4, 5, 6, 7;
   DLB 14, 40; MTFW 2005
Alvarez, Alejandro Rodriguez 1903-1965
   See Casona, Alejandro
   See also CA 131; CAAS 93-96; HW 1
Alvarez, Julia 1950- .... **CLC 93; HLCS 1**
   See also AAYA 25; AMWS 7; CA 147;
   CANR 69, 101, 133, 166; DA3; DLB 282;
   LATS 1:2; LLW; MTCW 2; MTFW 2005;
   NFS 5, 9; SATA 129; WLIT 1
Alvaro, Corrado 1896-1956 .... **TCLC 60**
   See also CA 163; DLB 264; EWL 3
Amado, Jorge 1912-2001 ... **CLC 13, 40, 106,**
   232; HLC 1
    See also CA 77-80; CAAS 201; CANR 35,
    74, 135; CWW 2; DAM MULT, NOV;
    DLB 113, 307; EWL 3; HW 2; LAW;
    LAWS 1; MTCW 1, 2; MTFW 2005;
    RGWL 2, 3; TWA; WLIT 1
Ambler, Eric 1909-1998 .... **CLC 4, 6, 9**
   See also BRWS 4; CA 9-12R; CAAS 171;
   CANR 7, 38, 74; CMW 4; CN 1, 2, 3, 4,
   5, 6; DLB 77; MSW; MTCW 1, 2; TEA
Ambrose, Stephen E. 1936-2002 ..... **CLC 145**
   See also AAYA 44; CA 1-4R; CAAS 209;
   CANR 3, 43, 57, 83, 105; MTFW 2005;
   NCFS 2; SATA 40, 138
Amichai, Yehuda 1924-2000 .. **CLC 9, 22, 57,**
   116; PC 38
    See also CA 85-88; CAAS 189; CANR 46,
    60, 99, 132; CWW 2; EWL 3; MTCW 1,
    2; MTFW 2005; PFS 24; RGHL; WLIT 6
Amichai, Yehudah
   See Amichai, Yehuda
Amiel, Henri Frederic 1821-1881 .... **NCLC 4**
   See also DLB 217
Amis, Kingsley 1922-1995 . **CLC 1, 2, 3, 5, 8,**
   13, 40, 44, 129
    See also AITN 2; BPFB 1; BRWS 2; CA
    9-12R; CAAS 150; CANR 8, 28, 54; CD-
    BLB 1945-1960; CN 1, 2, 3, 4, 5, 6; CP
    1, 2, 3, 4; DA; DA3; DAB; DAC; DAM
    MST, NOV; DLB 15, 27, 100, 139, 326;
    DLBY 1996; EWL 3; HGG; INT
    CANR-8; MTCW 1, 2; MTFW 2005;
    RGEL 2; RGSF 2; SFW 4
Amis, Martin 1949- ... **CLC 4, 9, 38, 62, 101,**
   213
    See also BEST 90:3; BRWS 4; CA 65-68;
    CANR 8, 27, 54, 73, 95, 132, 166; CN 5,
    6, 7; DA3; DLB 14, 194; EWL 3; INT
    CANR-27; MTCW 2; MTFW 2005
Amis, Martin Louis
   See Amis, Martin
Ammianus Marcellinus c. 330-c.
   395 .... **CMLC 60**
   See also AW 2; DLB 211

Ammons, A.R. 1926-2001 .. **CLC 2, 3, 5, 8, 9, 25, 57, 108; PC 16**
See also AITN 1; AMWS 7; CA 9-12R; CAAS 193; CANR 6, 36, 51, 73, 107, 156; CP 1, 2, 3, 4, 5, 6, 7; CSW; DAM POET; DLB 5, 165; EWL 3; MAL 5; MTCW 1, 2; PFS 19; RGAL 4; TCLE 1:1

Ammons, Archie Randolph
See Ammons, A.R.

Amo, Tauraatua i
See Adams, Henry (Brooks)

Amory, Thomas 1691(?)-1788 .... **LC 48**
See also DLB 39

Anand, Mulk Raj 1905-2004 ..... **CLC 23, 93, 237**
See also CA 65-68; CAAS 231; CANR 32, 64; CN 1, 2, 3, 4, 5, 6, 7; DAM NOV; DLB 323; EWL 3; MTCW 1, 2; MTFW 2005; RGSF 2

Anatol
See Schnitzler, Arthur

Anaximander c. 611B.C.-c. 546B.C. .... **CMLC 22**

Anaya, Rudolfo A. 1937- .... **CLC 23, 148; HLC 1**
See also AAYA 20; BYA 13; CA 45-48; 4; CANR 1, 32, 51, 124; CN 4, 5, 6, 7; DAM MULT, NOV; DLB 82, 206, 278; HW 1; LAIT 4; LLW; MAL 5; MTCW 1, 2; MTFW 2005; NFS 12; RGAL 4; RGSF 2; TCWW 2; WLIT 1

Andersen, Hans Christian 1805-1875 .... **NCLC 7, 79; SSC 6, 56; WLC 1**
See also AAYA 57; CLR 6, 113; DA; DA3; DAB; DAC; DAM MST, POP; EW 6; MAICYA 1, 2; RGSF 2; RGWL 2, 3; SATA 100; TWA; WCH; YABC 1

Anderson, C. Farley
See Mencken, H(enry) L(ouis); Nathan, George Jean

Anderson, Jessica (Margaret) Queale 1916- .... **CLC 37**
See also CA 9-12R; CANR 4, 62; CN 4, 5, 6, 7; DLB 325

Anderson, Jon (Victor) 1940- .... **CLC 9**
See also CA 25-28R; CANR 20; CP 1, 3, 4, 5; DAM POET

Anderson, Lindsay (Gordon) 1923-1994 .... **CLC 20**
See also CA 128; CAAE 125; CAAS 146; CANR 77

Anderson, Maxwell 1888-1959 .... **TCLC 2, 144**
See also CA 152; CAAE 105; DAM DRAM; DFS 16, 20; DLB 7, 228; MAL 5; MTCW 2; MTFW 2005; RGAL 4

Anderson, Poul 1926-2001 .... **CLC 15**
See also AAYA 5, 34; BPFB 1; BYA 6, 8, 9; CA 181; 1-4R, 181; 2; CAAS 199; CANR 2, 15, 34, 64, 110; CLR 58; DLB 8; FANT; INT CANR-15; MTCW 1, 2; MTFW 2005; SATA 90; SATA-Brief 39; SATA-Essay 106; SCFW 1, 2; SFW 4; SUFW 1, 2

Anderson, Robert (Woodruff) 1917- .... **CLC 23**
See also AITN 1; CA 21-24R; CANR 32; CD 6; DAM DRAM; DLB 7; LAIT 5

Anderson, Roberta Joan
See Mitchell, Joni

Anderson, Sherwood 1876-1941 ... **SSC 1, 46, 91; TCLC 1, 10, 24, 123; WLC 1**
See also AAYA 30; AMW; AMWC 2; BPFB 1; CA 121; CAAE 104; CANR 61; CDALB 1917-1929; DA; DA3; DAB; DAC; DAM MST, NOV; DLB 4, 9, 86; DLBD 1; EWL 3; EXPS; GLL 2; MAL 5; MTCW 1, 2; MTFW 2005; NFS 4; RGAL 4; RGSF 2; SSFS 4, 10, 11; TUS

Anderson, Wes 1969- .... **CLC 227**
See also CA 214

Andier, Pierre
See Desnos, Robert

Andouard
See Giraudoux, Jean(-Hippolyte)

Andrade, Carlos Drummond de ..... **CLC 18**
See Drummond de Andrade, Carlos
See also EWL 3; RGWL 2, 3

Andrade, Mario de .... **TCLC 43**
See de Andrade, Mario
See also DLB 307; EWL 3; LAW; RGWL 2, 3; WLIT 1

Andreae, Johann V(alentin) 1586-1654 .... **LC 32**
See also DLB 164

Andreas Capellanus fl. c. 1185- .... **CMLC 45**
See also DLB 208

Andreas-Salome, Lou 1861-1937 ... **TCLC 56**
See also CA 178; DLB 66

Andreev, Leonid
See Andreyev, Leonid (Nikolaevich)
See also DLB 295; EWL 3

Andress, Lesley
See Sanders, Lawrence

Andrewes, Lancelot 1555-1626 .... **LC 5**
See also DLB 151, 172

Andrews, Cicily Fairfield
See West, Rebecca

Andrews, Elton V.
See Pohl, Frederik

Andrews, Peter
See Soderbergh, Steven

Andreyev, Leonid (Nikolaevich) 1871-1919 .... **TCLC 3**
See Andreev, Leonid
See also CA 185; CAAE 104

Andric, Ivo 1892-1975 .... **CLC 8; SSC 36; TCLC 135**
See also CA 81-84; CAAS 57-60; CANR 43, 60; CDWLB 4; DLB 147, 329; EW 11; EWL 3; MTCW 1; RGSF 2; RGWL 2, 3

Androvar
See Prado (Calvo), Pedro

Angela of Foligno 1248(?)-1309 .... **CMLC 76**

Angelique, Pierre
See Bataille, Georges

Angell, Roger 1920- .... **CLC 26**
See also CA 57-60; CANR 13, 44, 70, 144; DLB 171, 185

Angelou, Maya 1928- ... **BLC 1; CLC 12, 35, 64, 77, 155; PC 32; WLCS**
See also AAYA 7, 20; AMWS 4; BPFB 1; BW 2, 3; BYA 2; CA 65-68; CANR 19, 42, 65, 111, 133; CDALBS; CLR 53; CP 4, 5, 6, 7; CPW; CWP; DA; DA3; DAB; DAC; DAM MST, MULT, POET, POP; DLB 38; EWL 3; EXPN; EXPP; FL 1:5; LAIT 4; MAICYA 2; MAICYAS 1; MAL 5; MBL; MTCW 1, 2; MTFW 2005; NCFS 2; NFS 2; PFS 2, 3; RGAL 4; SATA 49, 136; TCLE 1:1; WYA; YAW

Angouleme, Marguerite d'
See de Navarre, Marguerite

Anna Comnena 1083-1153 .... **CMLC 25**

Annensky, Innokentii Fedorovich
See Annensky, Innokenty (Fyodorovich)
See also DLB 295

Annensky, Innokenty (Fyodorovich) 1856-1909 .... **TCLC 14**
See also CA 155; CAAE 110; EWL 3

Annunzio, Gabriele d'
See D'Annunzio, Gabriele

Anodos
See Coleridge, Mary E(lizabeth)

Anon, Charles Robert
See Pessoa, Fernando (Antonio Nogueira)

Anouilh, Jean 1910-1987 ..... **CLC 1, 3, 8, 13, 40, 50; DC 8, 21**
See also AAYA 67; CA 17-20R; CAAS 123; CANR 32; DAM DRAM; DFS 9, 10, 19; DLB 321; EW 13; EWL 3; GFL 1789 to the Present; MTCW 1, 2; MTFW 2005; RGWL 2, 3; TWA

Anselm of Canterbury 1033(?)-1109 .... **CMLC 67**
See also DLB 115

Anthony, Florence
See Ai

Anthony, John
See Ciardi, John (Anthony)

Anthony, Peter
See Shaffer, Anthony; Shaffer, Peter

Anthony, Piers 1934- .... **CLC 35**
See also AAYA 11, 48; BYA 7; CA 200; 200; CANR 28, 56, 73, 102, 133; CLR 118; CPW; DAM POP; DLB 8; FANT; MAICYA 2; MAICYAS 1; MTCW 1, 2; MTFW 2005; SAAS 22; SATA 84, 129; SATA-Essay 129; SFW 4; SUFW 1, 2; YAW

Anthony, Susan B(rownell) 1820-1906 .... **TCLC 84**
See also CA 211; FW

Antiphon c. 480B.C.-c. 411B.C. .... **CMLC 55**

Antoine, Marc
See Proust, (Valentin-Louis-George-Eugene) Marcel

Antoninus, Brother
See Everson, William (Oliver)
See also CP 1

Antonioni, Michelangelo 1912-2007 .... **CLC 20, 144**
See also CA 73-76; CANR 45, 77

Antschel, Paul 1920-1970
See Celan, Paul
See also CA 85-88; CANR 33, 61; MTCW 1; PFS 21

Anwar, Chairil 1922-1949 .... **TCLC 22**
See Chairil Anwar
See also CA 219; CAAE 121; RGWL 3

Anzaldua, Gloria (Evanjelina) 1942-2004 .... **CLC 200; HLCS 1**
See also CA 175; CAAS 227; CSW; CWP; DLB 122; FW; LLW; RGAL 4; SATA-Obit 154

Apess, William 1798-1839(?) .... **NCLC 73; NNAL**
See also DAM MULT; DLB 175, 243

Apollinaire, Guillaume 1880-1918 .... **PC 7; TCLC 3, 8, 51**
See Kostrowitzki, Wilhelm Apollinaris de
See also CA 152; DAM POET; DLB 258, 321; EW 9; EWL 3; GFL 1789 to the Present; MTCW 2; PFS 24; RGWL 2, 3; TWA; WP

Apollonius of Rhodes
See Apollonius Rhodius
See also AW 1; RGWL 2, 3

Apollonius Rhodius c. 300B.C.-c. 220B.C. .... **CMLC 28**
See Apollonius of Rhodes
See also DLB 176

Appelfeld, Aharon 1932- ... **CLC 23, 47; SSC 42**
See also CA 133; CAAE 112; CANR 86, 160; CWW 2; DLB 299; EWL 3; RGHL; RGSF 2; WLIT 6

Appelfeld, Aron
See Appelfeld, Aharon

Apple, Max (Isaac) 1941- .... **CLC 9, 33; SSC 50**
See also AMWS 17; CA 81-84; CANR 19, 54; DLB 130

Appleman, Philip (Dean) 1926- .... **CLC 51**
See also CA 13-16R; 18; CANR 6, 29, 56

Appleton, Lawrence
See Lovecraft, H. P.

Apteryx
See Eliot, T(homas) S(tearns)

Apuleius, (Lucius Madaurensis) c. 125-c. 164 .... **CMLC 1, 84**
See also AW 2; CDWLB 1; DLB 211; RGWL 2, 3; SUFW; WLIT 8

Aquin, Hubert 1929-1977 .... **CLC 15**
See also CA 105; DLB 53; EWL 3

Aquinas, Thomas 1224(?)-1274 ..... **CMLC 33**
See also DLB 115; EW 1; TWA

Aragon, Louis 1897-1982 .... **CLC 3, 22; TCLC 123**
See also CA 69-72; CAAS 108; CANR 28, 71; DAM NOV, POET; DLB 72, 258; EW 11; EWL 3; GFL 1789 to the Present; GLL 2; LMFS 2; MTCW 1, 2; RGWL 2, 3

Arany, Janos 1817-1882 .... **NCLC 34**

Aranyos, Kakay 1847-1910
See Mikszath, Kalman

Aratus of Soli c. 315B.C.-c. 240B.C. .... **CMLC 64**
See also DLB 176

Arbuthnot, John 1667-1735 .... **LC 1**
See also DLB 101

Archer, Herbert Winslow
See Mencken, H(enry) L(ouis)

Archer, Jeffrey 1940- .... **CLC 28**
See also AAYA 16; BEST 89:3; BPFB 1; CA 77-80; CANR 22, 52, 95, 136; CPW; DA3; DAM POP; INT CANR-22; MTFW 2005

Archer, Jeffrey Howard
See Archer, Jeffrey

Archer, Jules 1915- .... **CLC 12**
See also CA 9-12R; CANR 6, 69; SAAS 5; SATA 4, 85

Archer, Lee
See Ellison, Harlan

Archilochus c. 7th cent. B.C.- .... **CMLC 44**
See also DLB 176

Arden, John 1930- .... **CLC 6, 13, 15**
See also BRWS 2; CA 13-16R; 4; CANR 31, 65, 67, 124; CBD; CD 5, 6; DAM DRAM; DFS 9; DLB 13, 245; EWL 3; MTCW 1

Arenas, Reinaldo 1943-1990 .. **CLC 41; HLC 1; TCLC 191**
See also CA 128; CAAE 124; CAAS 133; CANR 73, 106; DAM MULT; DLB 145; EWL 3; GLL 2; HW 1; LAW; LAWS 1; MTCW 2; MTFW 2005; RGSF 2; RGWL 3; WLIT 1

Arendt, Hannah 1906-1975 .... **CLC 66, 98; TCLC 193**
See also CA 17-20R; CAAS 61-64; CANR 26, 60; DLB 242; MTCW 1, 2

Aretino, Pietro 1492-1556 .... **LC 12**
See also RGWL 2, 3

Arghezi, Tudor .... **CLC 80**
See Theodorescu, Ion N.
See also CA 167; CDWLB 4; DLB 220; EWL 3

Arguedas, Jose Maria 1911-1969 .... **CLC 10, 18; HLCS 1; TCLC 147**
See also CA 89-92; CANR 73; DLB 113; EWL 3; HW 1; LAW; RGWL 2, 3; WLIT 1

Argueta, Manlio 1936- .... **CLC 31**
See also CA 131; CANR 73; CWW 2; DLB 145; EWL 3; HW 1; RGWL 3

Arias, Ron 1941- .... **HLC 1**
See also CA 131; CANR 81, 136; DAM MULT; DLB 82; HW 1, 2; MTCW 2; MTFW 2005

Ariosto, Lodovico
See Ariosto, Ludovico
See also WLIT 7

Ariosto, Ludovico 1474-1533 ... **LC 6, 87; PC 42**
See Ariosto, Lodovico
See also EW 2; RGWL 2, 3

Aristides
See Epstein, Joseph

Aristophanes 450B.C.-385B.C. .... **CMLC 4, 51; DC 2; WLCS**
See also AW 1; CDWLB 1; DA; DA3; DAB; DAC; DAM DRAM, MST; DFS 10; DLB 176; LMFS 1; RGWL 2, 3; TWA; WLIT 8

Aristotle 384B.C.-322B.C. .... **CMLC 31; WLCS**
See also AW 1; CDWLB 1; DA; DA3; DAB; DAC; DAM MST; DLB 176; RGWL 2, 3; TWA; WLIT 8

Arlt, Roberto (Godofredo Christophersen) 1900-1942 .... **HLC 1; TCLC 29**
See also CA 131; CAAE 123; CANR 67; DAM MULT; DLB 305; EWL 3; HW 1, 2; IDTP; LAW

Armah, Ayi Kwei 1939- . **BLC 1; CLC 5, 33, 136**
See also AFW; BRWS 10; BW 1; CA 61-64; CANR 21, 64; CDWLB 3; CN 1, 2, 3, 4, 5, 6, 7; DAM MULT, POET; DLB 117; EWL 3; MTCW 1; WLIT 2

Armatrading, Joan 1950- .... **CLC 17**
See also CA 186; CAAE 114

Armin, Robert 1568(?)-1615(?) .... **LC 120**

Armitage, Frank
See Carpenter, John (Howard)

Armstrong, Jeannette (C.) 1948- .... **NNAL**
See also CA 149; CCA 1; CN 6, 7; DAC; DLB 334; SATA 102

Arnette, Robert
See Silverberg, Robert

Arnim, Achim von (Ludwig Joachim von Arnim) 1781-1831 .. **NCLC 5, 159; SSC 29**
See also DLB 90

Arnim, Bettina von 1785-1859 ...... **NCLC 38, 123**
See also DLB 90; RGWL 2, 3

Arnold, Matthew 1822-1888 ..... **NCLC 6, 29, 89, 126; PC 5; WLC 1**
See also BRW 5; CDBLB 1832-1890; DA; DAB; DAC; DAM MST, POET; DLB 32, 57; EXPP; PAB; PFS 2; TEA; WP

Arnold, Thomas 1795-1842 .... **NCLC 18**
See also DLB 55

Arnow, Harriette (Louisa) Simpson 1908-1986 .... **CLC 2, 7, 18**
See also BPFB 1; CA 9-12R; CAAS 118; CANR 14; CN 2, 3, 4; DLB 6; FW; MTCW 1, 2; RHW; SATA 42; SATA-Obit 47

Arouet, Francois-Marie
See Voltaire

Arp, Hans
See Arp, Jean

Arp, Jean 1887-1966 .... **CLC 5; TCLC 115**
See also CA 81-84; CAAS 25-28R; CANR 42, 77; EW 10

Arrabal
See Arrabal, Fernando

Arrabal (Teran), Fernando
See Arrabal, Fernando
See also CWW 2

Arrabal, Fernando 1932- ... **CLC 2, 9, 18, 58**
See Arrabal (Teran), Fernando
See also CA 9-12R; CANR 15; DLB 321; EWL 3; LMFS 2

Arreola, Juan Jose 1918-2001 .... **CLC 147; HLC 1; SSC 38**
See also CA 131; CAAE 113; CAAS 200; CANR 81; CWW 2; DAM MULT; DLB 113; DNFS 2; EWL 3; HW 1, 2; LAW; RGSF 2

Arrian c. 89(?)-c. 155(?) .... **CMLC 43**
See also DLB 176

Arrick, Fran .... **CLC 30**
See Gaberman, Judie Angell
See also BYA 6

Arrley, Richmond
See Delany, Samuel R., Jr.

Artaud, Antonin (Marie Joseph) 1896-1948 .... **DC 14; TCLC 3, 36**
See also CA 149; CAAE 104; DA3; DAM DRAM; DFS 22; DLB 258, 321; EW 11; EWL 3; GFL 1789 to the Present; MTCW 2; MTFW 2005; RGWL 2, 3

Arthur, Ruth M(abel) 1905-1979 ..... **CLC 12**
See also CA 9-12R; CAAS 85-88; CANR 4; CWRI 5; SATA 7, 26

Artsybashev, Mikhail (Petrovich) 1878-1927 .... **TCLC 31**
See also CA 170; DLB 295

Arundel, Honor (Morfydd) 1919-1973 .... **CLC 17**
See also CA 21-22; CAAS 41-44R; CAP 2; CLR 35; CWRI 5; SATA 4; SATA-Obit 24

Arzner, Dorothy 1900-1979 .... **CLC 98**

Asch, Sholem 1880-1957 .... **TCLC 3**
See also CAAE 105; DLB 333; EWL 3; GLL 2; RGHL

Ascham, Roger 1516(?)-1568 .... **LC 101**
See also DLB 236

Ash, Shalom
See Asch, Sholem

Ashbery, John 1927- ... **CLC 2, 3, 4, 6, 9, 13, 15, 25, 41, 77, 125, 221; PC 26**
See Berry, Jonas
See also AMWS 3; CA 5-8R; CANR 9, 37, 66, 102, 132; CP 1, 2, 3, 4, 5, 6, 7; DA3; DAM POET; DLB 5, 165; DLBY 1981; EWL 3; INT CANR-9; MAL 5; MTCW 1, 2; MTFW 2005; PAB; PFS 11; RGAL 4; TCLE 1:1; WP

Ashbery, John Lawrence
See Ashbery, John

Ashdown, Clifford
See Freeman, R(ichard) Austin

Ashe, Gordon
See Creasey, John

Ashton-Warner, Sylvia (Constance) 1908-1984 .... **CLC 19**
See also CA 69-72; CAAS 112; CANR 29; CN 1, 2, 3; MTCW 1, 2

Asimov, Isaac 1920-1992 ..... **CLC 1, 3, 9, 19, 26, 76, 92**
See also AAYA 13; BEST 90:2; BPFB 1; BYA 4, 6, 7, 9; CA 1-4R; CAAS 137; CANR 2, 19, 36, 60, 125; CLR 12, 79; CMW 4; CN 1, 2, 3, 4, 5; CPW; DA3; DAM POP; DLB 8; DLBY 1992; INT CANR-19; JRDA; LAIT 5; LMFS 2; MAICYA 1, 2; MAL 5; MTCW 1, 2; MTFW 2005; RGAL 4; SATA 1, 26, 74; SCFW 1, 2; SFW 4; SSFS 17; TUS; YAW

Askew, Anne 1521(?)-1546 .... **LC 81**
See also DLB 136

Assis, Joaquim Maria Machado de
See Machado de Assis, Joaquim Maria

Astell, Mary 1666-1731 .... **LC 68**
See also DLB 252, 336; FW

Astley, Thea (Beatrice May) 1925-2004 .... **CLC 41**
See also CA 65-68; CAAS 229; CANR 11, 43, 78; CN 1, 2, 3, 4, 5, 6, 7; DLB 289; EWL 3

Astley, William 1855-1911
See Warung, Price

Aston, James
See White, T(erence) H(anbury)

Asturias, Miguel Angel 1899-1974 .... **CLC 3, 8, 13; HLC 1; TCLC 184**
See also CA 25-28; CAAS 49-52; CANR 32; CAP 2; CDWLB 3; DA3; DAM MULT, NOV; DLB 113, 290, 329; EWL 3; HW 1; LAW; LMFS 2; MTCW 1, 2; RGWL 2, 3; WLIT 1

Atares, Carlos Saura
See Saura (Atares), Carlos

Athanasius c. 295-c. 373 .... **CMLC 48**

Atheling, William
See Pound, Ezra (Weston Loomis)

Atheling, William, Jr.
See Blish, James (Benjamin)

Atherton, Gertrude (Franklin Horn)
1857-1948 .... **TCLC 2**
See also CA 155; CAAE 104; DLB 9, 78, 186; HGG; RGAL 4; SUFW 1; TCWW 1, 2

Atherton, Lucius
See Masters, Edgar Lee

Atkins, Jack
See Harris, Mark

Atkinson, Kate 1951- .... **CLC 99**
See also CA 166; CANR 101, 153; DLB 267

Attaway, William (Alexander)
1911-1986 .... **BLC 1; CLC 92**
See also BW 2, 3; CA 143; CANR 82; DAM MULT; DLB 76; MAL 5

Atticus
See Fleming, Ian; Wilson, (Thomas) Woodrow

Atwood, Margaret 1939- . **CLC 2, 3, 4, 8, 13, 15, 25, 44, 84, 135, 232, 239; PC 8; SSC 2, 46; WLC 1**
See also AAYA 12, 47; AMWS 13; BEST 89:2; BPFB 1; CA 49-52; CANR 3, 24, 33, 59, 95, 133; CN 2, 3, 4, 5, 6, 7; CP 1, 2, 3, 4, 5, 6, 7; CPW; CWP; DA; DA3; DAB; DAC; DAM MST, NOV, POET; DLB 53, 251, 326; EWL 3; EXPN; FL 1:5; FW; GL 2; INT CANR-24; LAIT 5; MTCW 1, 2; MTFW 2005; NFS 4, 12, 13, 14, 19; PFS 7; RGSF 2; SATA 50, 170; SSFS 3, 13; TCLE 1:1; TWA; WWE 1; YAW

Atwood, Margaret Eleanor
See Atwood, Margaret

Aubigny, Pierre d'
See Mencken, H(enry) L(ouis)

Aubin, Penelope 1685-1731(?) .... **LC 9**
See also DLB 39

Auchincloss, Louis 1917- ..... **CLC 4, 6, 9, 18, 45; SSC 22**
See also AMWS 4; CA 1-4R; CANR 6, 29, 55, 87, 130; CN 1, 2, 3, 4, 5, 6, 7; DAM NOV; DLB 2, 244; DLBY 1980; EWL 3; INT CANR-29; MAL 5; MTCW 1; RGAL 4

Auchincloss, Louis Stanton
See Auchincloss, Louis

Auden, W(ystan) H(ugh) 1907-1973 . **CLC 1, 2, 3, 4, 6, 9, 11, 14, 43, 123; PC 1; WLC 1**
See also AAYA 18; AMWS 2; BRW 7; BRWR 1; CA 9-12R; CAAS 45-48; CANR 5, 61, 105; CDBLB 1914-1945; CP 1, 2; DA; DA3; DAB; DAC; DAM DRAM, MST, POET; DLB 10, 20; EWL 3; EXPP; MAL 5; MTCW 1, 2; MTFW 2005; PAB; PFS 1, 3, 4, 10; TUS; WP

Audiberti, Jacques 1899-1965 .... **CLC 38**
See also CA 252; CAAS 25-28R; DAM DRAM; DLB 321; EWL 3

Audubon, John James 1785-1851 . **NCLC 47**
See also AAYA 76; AMWS 16; ANW; DLB 248

Auel, Jean M(arie) 1936- .... **CLC 31, 107**
See also AAYA 7, 51; BEST 90:4; BPFB 1; CA 103; CANR 21, 64, 115; CPW; DA3; DAM POP; INT CANR-21; NFS 11; RHW; SATA 91

Auerbach, Berthold 1812-1882 .... **NCLC 171**
See also DLB 133

Auerbach, Erich 1892-1957 .... **TCLC 43**
See also CA 155; CAAE 118; EWL 3

Augier, Emile 1820-1889 .... **NCLC 31**
See also DLB 192; GFL 1789 to the Present

August, John
See De Voto, Bernard (Augustine)

Augustine, St. 354-430 .... **CMLC 6, 95; WLCS**
See also DA; DA3; DAB; DAC; DAM MST; DLB 115; EW 1; RGWL 2, 3; WLIT 8

Aunt Belinda
See Braddon, Mary Elizabeth

Aunt Weedy
See Alcott, Louisa May

Aurelius
See Bourne, Randolph S(illiman)

Aurelius, Marcus 121-180 .... **CMLC 45**
See Marcus Aurelius
See also RGWL 2, 3

Aurobindo, Sri
See Ghose, Aurabinda

Aurobindo Ghose
See Ghose, Aurabinda

Ausonius, Decimus Magnus c. 310-c. 394 .... **CMLC 88**
See also RGWL 2, 3

Austen, Jane 1775-1817 ...... **NCLC 1, 13, 19, 33, 51, 81, 95, 119, 150; WLC 1**
See also AAYA 19; BRW 4; BRWC 1; BRWR 2; BYA 3; CDBLB 1789-1832; DA; DA3; DAB; DAC; DAM MST, NOV; DLB 116; EXPN; FL 1:2; GL 2; LAIT 2; LATS 1:1; LMFS 1; NFS 1, 14, 18, 20, 21; TEA; WLIT 3; WYAS 1

Auster, Paul 1947- .... **CLC 47, 131, 227**
See also AMWS 12; CA 69-72; CANR 23, 52, 75, 129, 165; CMW 4; CN 5, 6, 7; DA3; DLB 227; MAL 5; MTCW 2; MTFW 2005; SUFW 2; TCLE 1:1

Austin, Frank
See Faust, Frederick (Schiller)

Austin, Mary (Hunter) 1868-1934 . **SSC 104; TCLC 25**
See also ANW; CA 178; CAAE 109; DLB 9, 78, 206, 221, 275; FW; TCWW 1, 2

Averroes 1126-1198 .... **CMLC 7**
See also DLB 115

Avicenna 980-1037 .... **CMLC 16**
See also DLB 115

Avison, Margaret 1918-2007 .... **CLC 2, 4, 97**
See also CA 17-20R; CANR 134; CP 1, 2, 3, 4, 5, 6, 7; DAC; DAM POET; DLB 53; MTCW 1

Avison, Margaret Kirkland
See Avison, Margaret

Avison, Margaret Kirkland
See Avison, Margaret

Axton, David
See Koontz, Dean R.

Ayckbourn, Alan 1939- ...... **CLC 5, 8, 18, 33, 74; DC 13**
See also BRWS 5; CA 21-24R; CANR 31, 59, 118; CBD; CD 5, 6; DAB; DAM DRAM; DFS 7; DLB 13, 245; EWL 3; MTCW 1, 2; MTFW 2005

Aydy, Catherine
See Tennant, Emma

Ayme, Marcel (Andre) 1902-1967 ... **CLC 11; SSC 41**
See also CA 89-92; CANR 67, 137; CLR 25; DLB 72; EW 12; EWL 3; GFL 1789 to the Present; RGSF 2; RGWL 2, 3; SATA 91

Ayrton, Michael 1921-1975 .... **CLC 7**
See also CA 5-8R; CAAS 61-64; CANR 9, 21

Aytmatov, Chingiz
See Aitmatov, Chingiz (Torekulovich)
See also EWL 3

Azorin .... **CLC 11**
See Martinez Ruiz, Jose
See also DLB 322; EW 9; EWL 3

Azuela, Mariano 1873-1952 .. **HLC 1; TCLC 3, 145**
See also CA 131; CAAE 104; CANR 81; DAM MULT; EWL 3; HW 1, 2; LAW; MTCW 1, 2; MTFW 2005

Ba, Mariama 1929-1981 .... **BLCS**
See also AFW; BW 2; CA 141; CANR 87; DNFS 2; WLIT 2

Baastad, Babbis Friis
See Friis-Baastad, Babbis Ellinor

Bab
See Gilbert, W(illiam) S(chwenck)

Babbis, Eleanor
See Friis-Baastad, Babbis Ellinor

Babel, Isaac
See Babel, Isaak (Emmanuilovich)
See also EW 11; SSFS 10

Babel, Isaak (Emmanuilovich)
1894-1941(?) . **SSC 16, 78; TCLC 2, 13, 171**
See Babel, Isaac
See also CA 155; CAAE 104; CANR 113; DLB 272; EWL 3; MTCW 2; MTFW 2005; RGSF 2; RGWL 2, 3; TWA

Babits, Mihaly 1883-1941 .... **TCLC 14**
See also CAAE 114; CDWLB 4; DLB 215; EWL 3

Babur 1483-1530 .... **LC 18**

Babylas 1898-1962
See Ghelderode, Michel de

Baca, Jimmy Santiago 1952- . **HLC 1; PC 41**
See also CA 131; CANR 81, 90, 146; CP 6, 7; DAM MULT; DLB 122; HW 1, 2; LLW; MAL 5

Baca, Jose Santiago
See Baca, Jimmy Santiago

Bacchelli, Riccardo 1891-1985 .... **CLC 19**
See also CA 29-32R; CAAS 117; DLB 264; EWL 3

Bach, Richard 1936- .... **CLC 14**
See also AITN 1; BEST 89:2; BPFB 1; BYA 5; CA 9-12R; CANR 18, 93, 151; CPW; DAM NOV, POP; FANT; MTCW 1; SATA 13

Bach, Richard David
See Bach, Richard

Bache, Benjamin Franklin
1769-1798 .... **LC 74**
See also DLB 43

Bachelard, Gaston 1884-1962 ...... **TCLC 128**
See also CA 97-100; CAAS 89-92; DLB 296; GFL 1789 to the Present

Bachman, Richard
See King, Stephen

Bachmann, Ingeborg 1926-1973 ..... **CLC 69; TCLC 192**
See also CA 93-96; CAAS 45-48; CANR 69; DLB 85; EWL 3; RGHL; RGWL 2, 3

Bacon, Francis 1561-1626 ..... **LC 18, 32, 131**
See also BRW 1; CDBLB Before 1660; DLB 151, 236, 252; RGEL 2; TEA

Bacon, Roger 1214(?)-1294 .... **CMLC 14**
See also DLB 115

Barker, Patricia
  See Barker, Pat
Barlach, Ernst (Heinrich)
  1870-1938 .... **TCLC 84**
  See also CA 178; DLB 56, 118; EWL 3
Barlow, Joel 1754-1812 .... **NCLC 23**
  See also AMWS 2; DLB 37; RGAL 4
Barnard, Mary (Ethel) 1909- .... **CLC 48**
  See also CA 21-22; CAP 2; CP 1
Barnes, Djuna 1892-1982 .... **CLC 3, 4, 8, 11,
  29, 127; SSC 3**
  See Steptoe, Lydia
  See also AMWS 3; CA 9-12R; CAAS 107;
  CAD; CANR 16, 55; CN 1, 2, 3; CWD;
  DLB 4, 9, 45; EWL 3; GLL 1; MAL 5;
  MTCW 1, 2; MTFW 2005; RGAL 4;
  TCLE 1:1; TUS
Barnes, Jim 1933- .... **NNAL**
  See also CA 175; 108, 175; 28; DLB 175
Barnes, Julian 1946- .... **CLC 42, 141**
  See also BRWS 4; CA 102; CANR 19, 54,
  115, 137; CN 4, 5, 6, 7; DAB; DLB 194;
  DLBY 1993; EWL 3; MTCW 2; MTFW
  2005; SSFS 24
Barnes, Julian Patrick
  See Barnes, Julian
Barnes, Peter 1931-2004 .... **CLC 5, 56**
  See also CA 65-68; 12; CAAS 230; CANR
  33, 34, 64, 113; CBD; CD 5, 6; DFS 6;
  DLB 13, 233; MTCW 1
Barnes, William 1801-1886 .... **NCLC 75**
  See also DLB 32
Baroja, Pio 1872-1956 .... **HLC 1; TCLC 8**
  See also CA 247; CAAE 104; EW 9
Baroja y Nessi, Pio
  See Baroja, Pio
Baron, David
  See Pinter, Harold
Baron Corvo
  See Rolfe, Frederick (William Serafino
  Austin Lewis Mary)
Barondess, Sue K(aufman)
  1926-1977 .... **CLC 8**
  See Kaufman, Sue
  See also CA 1-4R; CAAS 69-72; CANR 1
Baron de Teive
  See Pessoa, Fernando (Antonio Nogueira)
Baroness Von S.
  See Zangwill, Israel
Barres, (Auguste-)Maurice
  1862-1923 .... **TCLC 47**
  See also CA 164; DLB 123; GFL 1789 to
  the Present
Barreto, Afonso Henrique de Lima
  See Lima Barreto, Afonso Henrique de
Barrett, Andrea 1954- .... **CLC 150**
  See also CA 156; CANR 92; CN 7; DLB
  335; SSFS 24
Barrett, Michele .... **CLC 65**
Barrett, (Roger) Syd 1946-2006 .... **CLC 35**
Barrett, William (Christopher)
  1913-1992 .... **CLC 27**
  See also CA 13-16R; CAAS 139; CANR
  11, 67; INT CANR-11
Barrett Browning, Elizabeth
  1806-1861 ...... **NCLC 1, 16, 61, 66, 170;
  PC 6, 62; WLC 1**
  See also AAYA 63; BRW 4; CDBLB 1832-
  1890; DA; DA3; DAB; DAC; DAM MST,
  POET; DLB 32, 199; EXPP; FL 1:2; PAB;
  PFS 2, 16, 23; TEA; WLIT 4; WP
Barrie, J(ames) M(atthew)
  1860-1937 .... **TCLC 2, 164**
  See also BRWS 3; BYA 4, 5; CA 136;
  CAAE 104; CANR 77; CDBLB 1890-
  1914; CLR 16; CWRI 5; DA3; DAB;

DAM DRAM; DFS 7; DLB 10, 141, 156;
  EWL 3; FANT; MAICYA 1, 2; MTCW 2;
  MTFW 2005; SATA 100; SUFW; WCH;
  WLIT 4; YABC 1
Barrington, Michael
  See Moorcock, Michael
Barrol, Grady
  See Bograd, Larry
Barry, Mike
  See Malzberg, Barry N(athaniel)
Barry, Philip 1896-1949 .... **TCLC 11**
  See also CA 199; CAAE 109; DFS 9; DLB
  7, 228; MAL 5; RGAL 4
Bart, Andre Schwarz
  See Schwarz-Bart, Andre
Barth, John (Simmons) 1930- ... **CLC 1, 2, 3,
  5, 7, 9, 10, 14, 27, 51, 89, 214; SSC 10,
  89**
  See also AITN 1, 2; AMW; BPFB 1; CA
  1-4R; CABS 1; CANR 5, 23, 49, 64, 113;
  CN 1, 2, 3, 4, 5, 6, 7; DAM NOV; DLB
  2, 227; EWL 3; FANT; MAL 5; RGAL
  1; RGAL 4; RGSF 2; RHW; SSFS 6; TUS
Barthelme, Donald 1931-1989 ... **CLC 1, 2, 3,
  5, 6, 8, 13, 23, 46, 59, 115; SSC 2, 55**
  See also AMWS 4; BPFB 1; CA 21-24R;
  CAAS 129; CANR 20, 58; CN 1, 2, 3, 4;
  DA3; DAM NOV; DLB 2, 234; DLBY
  1980, 1989; EWL 3; FANT; LMFS 2;
  MAL 5; MTCW 1, 2; MTFW 2005;
  RGAL 4; RGSF 2; SATA 7; SATA-Obit
  62; SSFS 17
Barthelme, Frederick 1943- ...... **CLC 36, 117**
  See also AMWS 11; CA 122; CAAE 114;
  CANR 77; CN 4, 5, 6, 7; CSW; DLB 244;
  DLBY 1985; EWL 3; INT CA-122
Barthes, Roland (Gerard)
  1915-1980 .... **CLC 24, 83; TCLC 135**
  See also CA 130; CAAS 97-100; CANR
  66; DLB 296; EW 13; EWL 3; GFL 1789
  to the Present; MTCW 1, 2; TWA
Bartram, William 1739-1823 .... **NCLC 145**
  See also ANW; DLB 37
Barzun, Jacques (Martin) 1907- ..... **CLC 51,
  145**
  See also CA 61-64; CANR 22, 95
Bashevis, Isaac
  See Singer, Isaac Bashevis
Bashevis, Yitskhok
  See Singer, Isaac Bashevis
Bashkirtseff, Marie 1859-1884 .... **NCLC 27**
Basho, Matsuo
  See Matsuo Basho
  See also RGWL 2, 3; WP
Basil of Caesaria c. 330-379 .... **CMLC 35**
Basket, Raney
  See Edgerton, Clyde (Carlyle)
Bass, Kingsley B., Jr.
  See Bullins, Ed
Bass, Rick 1958- .... **CLC 79, 143; SSC 60**
  See also AMWS 16; ANW; CA 126; CANR
  53, 93, 145; CSW; DLB 212, 275
Bassani, Giorgio 1916-2000 .... **CLC 9**
  See also CA 65-68; CAAS 190; CANR 33;
  CWW 2; DLB 128, 177, 299; EWL 3;
  MTCW 1; RGHL; RGWL 2, 3
Bastian, Ann .... **CLC 70**
Bastos, Augusto Roa
  See Roa Bastos, Augusto
Bataille, Georges 1897-1962 .... **CLC 29;
  TCLC 155**
  See also CA 101; CAAS 89-92; EWL 3
Bates, H(erbert) E(rnest)
  1905-1974 .... **CLC 46; SSC 10**
  See also CA 93-96; CAAS 45-48; CANR
  34; CN 1; DA3; DAB; DAM POP; DLB
  162, 191; EWL 3; EXPS; MTCW 1, 2;
  RGSF 2; SSFS 7

Bauchart
  See Camus, Albert
Baudelaire, Charles 1821-1867 . **NCLC 6, 29,
  55, 155; PC 1; SSC 18; WLC 1**
  See also DA; DA3; DAB; DAC; DAM
  MST, POET; DLB 217; EW 7; GFL 1789
  to the Present; LMFS 2; PFS 21; RGWL
  2, 3; TWA
Baudouin, Marcel
  See Peguy, Charles (Pierre)
Baudouin, Pierre
  See Peguy, Charles (Pierre)
Baudrillard, Jean 1929-2007 .... **CLC 60**
  See also CA 252; CAAS 258; DLB 296
Baum, L(yman) Frank 1856-1919 .. **TCLC 7,
  132**
  See also AAYA 46; BYA 16; CA 133;
  CAAE 108; CLR 15, 107; CWRI 5; DLB
  22; FANT; JRDA; MAICYA 1, 2; MTCW
  1, 2; NFS 13; RGAL 4; SATA 18, 100;
  WCH
Baum, Louis F.
  See Baum, L(yman) Frank
Baumbach, Jonathan 1933- .... **CLC 6, 23**
  See also CA 13-16R; 5; CANR 12, 66, 140;
  CN 3, 4, 5, 6, 7; DLBY 1980; INT CANR-
  12; MTCW 1
Bausch, Richard 1945- .... **CLC 51**
  See also AMWS 7; CA 101; 14; CANR 43,
  61, 87, 164; CN 7; CSW; DLB 130; MAL
  5
Bausch, Richard Carl
  See Bausch, Richard
Baxter, Charles 1947- .... **CLC 45, 78**
  See also AMWS 17; CA 57-60; CANR 40,
  64, 104, 133; CPW; DAM POP; DLB
  130; MAL 5; MTCW 2; MTFW 2005;
  TCLE 1:1
Baxter, George Owen
  See Faust, Frederick (Schiller)
Baxter, James K(eir) 1926-1972 .... **CLC 14**
  See also CA 77-80; CP 1; EWL 3
Baxter, John
  See Hunt, E. Howard
Bayer, Sylvia
  See Glassco, John
Bayle, Pierre 1647-1706 .... **LC 126**
  See also DLB 268, 313; GFL Beginnings to
  1789
Baynton, Barbara 1857-1929 .... **TCLC 57**
  See also DLB 230; RGSF 2
Beagle, Peter S. 1939- .... **CLC 7, 104**
  See also AAYA 47; BPFB 1; BYA 9, 10,
  16; CA 9-12R; CANR 4, 51, 73, 110;
  DA3; DLBY 1980; FANT; INT CANR-4;
  MTCW 2; MTFW 2005; SATA 60, 130;
  SUFW 1, 2; YAW
Beagle, Peter Soyer
  See Beagle, Peter S.
Bean, Normal
  See Burroughs, Edgar Rice
Beard, Charles A(ustin)
  1874-1948 .... **TCLC 15**
  See also CA 189; CAAE 115; DLB 17;
  SATA 18
Beardsley, Aubrey 1872-1898 .... **NCLC 6**
Beattie, Ann 1947- ..... **CLC 8, 13, 18, 40, 63,
  146; SSC 11**
  See also AMWS 5; BEST 90:2; BPFB 1;
  CA 81-84; CANR 53, 73, 128; CN 4, 5,
  6, 7; CPW; DA3; DAM NOV, POP; DLB
  218, 278; DLBY 1982; EWL 3; MAL 5;
  MTCW 1, 2; MTFW 2005; RGAL 4;
  RGSF 2; SSFS 9; TUS
Beattie, James 1735-1803 .... **NCLC 25**
  See also DLB 109

Beauchamp, Kathleen Mansfield 1888-1923
See Mansfield, Katherine
See also CA 134; CAAE 104; DA; DA3;
DAC; DAM MST; MTCW 2; TEA

Beaumarchais, Pierre-Augustin Caron de
1732-1799 .... **DC 4; LC 61**
See also DAM DRAM; DFS 14, 16; DLB
313; EW 4; GFL Beginnings to 1789;
RGWL 2, 3

Beaumont, Francis 1584(?)-1616 .. **DC 6; LC 33**
See also BRW 2; CDBLB Before 1660;
DLB 58; TEA

Beauvoir, Simone de 1908-1986 .... **CLC 1, 2, 4, 8, 14, 31, 44, 50, 71, 124; SSC 35; WLC 1**
See also BPFB 1; CA 9-12R; CAAS 118;
CANR 28, 61; DA; DA3; DAB; DAC;
DAM MST, NOV; DLB 72; DLBY 1986;
EW 12; EWL 3; FL 1:5; FW; GFL 1789
to the Present; LMFS 2; MTCW 1, 2;
MTFW 2005; RGSF 2; RGWL 2, 3; TWA

Beauvoir, Simone Lucie Ernestine Marie Bertrand de
See Beauvoir, Simone de

Becker, Carl (Lotus) 1873-1945 ..... **TCLC 63**
See also CA 157; DLB 17

Becker, Jurek 1937-1997 .... **CLC 7, 19**
See also CA 85-88; CAAS 157; CANR 60,
117; CWW 2; DLB 75, 299; EWL 3;
RGHL

Becker, Walter 1950- .... **CLC 26**

Becket, Thomas a 1118(?)-1170 ...... **CMLC 83**

Beckett, Samuel 1906-1989 ... **CLC 1, 2, 3, 4, 6, 9, 10, 11, 14, 18, 29, 57, 59, 83; DC 22; SSC 16, 74; TCLC 145; WLC 1**
See also BRWC 2; BRWR 1; BRWS 1; CA
5-8R; CAAS 130; CANR 33, 61; CBD;
CDBLB 1945-1960; CN 1, 2, 3, 4; CP 1,
2, 3, 4; DA; DA3; DAB; DAC; DAM
DRAM, MST, NOV; DFS 2, 7, 18; DLB
13, 15, 233, 319, 321, 329; DLBY 1990;
EWL 3; GFL 1789 to the Present; LATS
1:2; LMFS 2; MTCW 1, 2; MTFW 2005;
RGSF 2; RGWL 2, 3; SSFS 15; TEA;
WLIT 4

Beckford, William 1760-1844 .... **NCLC 16**
See also BRW 3; DLB 39, 213; GL 2; HGG;
LMFS 1; SUFW

Beckham, Barry (Earl) 1944- .... **BLC 1**
See also BW 1; CA 29-32R; CANR 26, 62;
CN 1, 2, 3, 4, 5, 6; DAM MULT; DLB 33

Beckman, Gunnel 1910- .... **CLC 26**
See also CA 33-36R; CANR 15, 114; CLR
25; MAICYA 1, 2; SAAS 9; SATA 6

Becque, Henri 1837-1899 .... **DC 21; NCLC 3**
See also DLB 192; GFL 1789 to the Present

Becquer, Gustavo Adolfo
1836-1870 .... **HLCS 1; NCLC 106**
See also DAM MULT

Beddoes, Thomas Lovell 1803-1849 .. **DC 15; NCLC 3, 154**
See also BRWS 11; DLB 96

Bede c. 673-735 .... **CMLC 20**
See also DLB 146; TEA

Bedford, Denton R. 1907-(?) .... **NNAL**

Bedford, Donald F.
See Fearing, Kenneth (Flexner)

Beecher, Catharine Esther
1800-1878 .... **NCLC 30**
See also DLB 1, 243

Beecher, John 1904-1980 .... **CLC 6**
See also AITN 1; CA 5-8R; CAAS 105;
CANR 8; CP 1, 2, 3

Beer, Johann 1655-1700 .... **LC 5**
See also DLB 168

Beer, Patricia 1924- .... **CLC 58**
See also CA 61-64; CAAS 183; CANR 13,
46; CP 1, 2, 3, 4, 5, 6; CWP; DLB 40;
FW

Beerbohm, Max
See Beerbohm, (Henry) Max(imilian)

Beerbohm, (Henry) Max(imilian)
1872-1956 .... **TCLC 1, 24**
See also BRWS 2; CA 154; CAAE 104;
CANR 79; DLB 34, 100; FANT; MTCW
2

Beer-Hofmann, Richard
1866-1945 .... **TCLC 60**
See also CA 160; DLB 81

Beg, Shemus
See Stephens, James

Begiebing, Robert J(ohn) 1946- .... **CLC 70**
See also CA 122; CANR 40, 88

Begley, Louis 1933- .... **CLC 197**
See also CA 140; CANR 98; DLB 299;
RGHL; TCLE 1:1

Behan, Brendan (Francis)
1923-1964 .... **CLC 1, 8, 11, 15, 79**
See also BRWS 2; CA 73-76; CANR 33,
121; CBD; CDBLB 1945-1960; DAM
DRAM; DFS 7; DLB 13, 233; EWL 3;
MTCW 1, 2

Behn, Aphra 1640(?)-1689 .. **DC 4; LC 1, 30, 42, 135; PC 13; WLC 1**
See also BRWS 3; DA; DA3; DAB; DAC;
DAM DRAM, MST, NOV, POET; DFS
16, 24; DLB 39, 80, 131; FW; TEA;
WLIT 3

Behrman, S(amuel) N(athaniel)
1893-1973 .... **CLC 40**
See also CA 13-16; CAAS 45-48; CAD;
CAP 1; DLB 7, 44; IDFW 3; MAL 5;
RGAL 4

Bekederemo, J. P. Clark
See Clark Bekederemo, J.P.
See also CD 6

Belasco, David 1853-1931 .... **TCLC 3**
See also CA 168; CAAE 104; DLB 7; MAL
5; RGAL 4

Belcheva, Elisaveta Lyubomirova
1893-1991 .... **CLC 10**
See Bagryana, Elisaveta

Beldone, Phil "Cheech"
See Ellison, Harlan

Beleno
See Azuela, Mariano

Belinski, Vissarion Grigoryevich
1811-1848 .... **NCLC 5**
See also DLB 198

Belitt, Ben 1911- .... **CLC 22**
See also CA 13-16R; 4; CANR 7, 77; CP 1,
2, 3, 4, 5, 6; DLB 5

Belknap, Jeremy 1744-1798 .... **LC 115**
See also DLB 30, 37

Bell, Gertrude (Margaret Lowthian)
1868-1926 .... **TCLC 67**
See also CA 167; CANR 110; DLB 174

Bell, J. Freeman
See Zangwill, Israel

Bell, James Madison 1826-1902 .... **BLC 1; TCLC 43**
See also BW 1; CA 124; CAAE 122; DAM
MULT; DLB 50

Bell, Madison Smartt 1957- ..... **CLC 41, 102, 223**
See also AMWS 10; BPFB 1; CA 183; 111,
183; CANR 28, 54, 73, 134; CN 5, 6, 7;
CSW; DLB 218, 278; MTCW 2; MTFW
2005

Bell, Marvin (Hartley) 1937- ...... **CLC 8, 31; PC 79**
See also CA 21-24R; 14; CANR 59, 102;
CP 1, 2, 3, 4, 5, 6, 7; DAM POET; DLB
5; MAL 5; MTCW 1; PFS 25

Bell, W. L. D.
See Mencken, H(enry) L(ouis)

Bellamy, Atwood C.
See Mencken, H(enry) L(ouis)

Bellamy, Edward 1850-1898 ..... **NCLC 4, 86, 147**
See also DLB 12; NFS 15; RGAL 4; SFW 4

Belli, Gioconda 1948- .... **HLCS 1**
See also CA 152; CANR 143; CWW 2;
DLB 290; EWL 3; RGWL 3

Bellin, Edward J.
See Kuttner, Henry

Bello, Andres 1781-1865 .... **NCLC 131**
See also LAW

Belloc, (Joseph) Hilaire (Pierre Sebastien Rene Swanton) 1870-1953 .... **PC 24; TCLC 7, 18**
See also CA 152; CAAE 106; CLR 102;
CWRI 5; DAM POET; DLB 19, 100, 141,
174; EWL 3; MTCW 2; MTFW 2005;
SATA 112; WCH; YABC 1

Belloc, Joseph Peter Rene Hilaire
See Belloc, (Joseph) Hilaire (Pierre Sebastien Rene Swanton)

Belloc, Joseph Pierre Hilaire
See Belloc, (Joseph) Hilaire (Pierre Sebastien Rene Swanton)

Belloc, M. A.
See Lowndes, Marie Adelaide (Belloc)

Belloc-Lowndes, Mrs.
See Lowndes, Marie Adelaide (Belloc)

Bellow, Saul 1915-2005 ...... **CLC 1, 2, 3, 6, 8, 10, 13, 15, 25, 33, 34, 63, 79, 190, 200; SSC 14, 101; WLC 1**
See also AITN 2; AMW; AMWC 2; AMWR
2; BEST 89:3; BPFB 1; CA 5-8R; CAAS
238; CABS 1; CANR 29, 53, 95, 132;
CDALB 1941-1968; CN 1, 2, 3, 4, 5, 6,
7; DA; DA3; DAB; DAC; DAM MST,
NOV, POP; DLB 2, 28, 299, 329; DLBD
3; DLBY 1982; EWL 3; MAL 5; MTCW
1, 2; MTFW 2005; NFS 4, 14; RGAL 4;
RGHL; RGSF 2; SSFS 12, 22; TUS

Belser, Reimond Karel Maria de 1929-
See Ruyslinck, Ward
See also CA 152

Bely, Andrey .... **PC 11; TCLC 7**
See Bugayev, Boris Nikolayevich
See also DLB 295; EW 9; EWL 3

Belyi, Andrei
See Bugayev, Boris Nikolayevich
See also RGWL 2, 3

Bembo, Pietro 1470-1547 .... **LC 79**
See also RGWL 2, 3

Benary, Margot
See Benary-Isbert, Margot

Benary-Isbert, Margot 1889-1979 .... **CLC 12**
See also CA 5-8R; CAAS 89-92; CANR 4,
72; CLR 12; MAICYA 1, 2; SATA 2;
SATA-Obit 21

Benavente (y Martinez), Jacinto
1866-1954 .... **DC 26; HLCS 1; TCLC 3**
See also CA 131; CAAE 106; CANR 81;
DAM DRAM, MULT; DLB 329; EWL 3;
GLL 2; HW 1, 2; MTCW 1, 2

Benchley, Peter 1940-2006 .... **CLC 4, 8**
See also AAYA 14; AITN 2; BPFB 1; CA
17-20R; CAAS 248; CANR 12, 35, 66,
115; CPW; DAM NOV, POP; HGG;
MTCW 1, 2; MTFW 2005; SATA 3, 89,
164

Benchley, Peter Bradford
See Benchley, Peter

Benchley, Robert (Charles)
1889-1945 .... **TCLC 1, 55**
See also CA 153; CAAE 105; DLB 11;
MAL 5; RGAL 4

Berryman, John 1914-1972 ... **CLC 1, 2, 3, 4, 6, 8, 10, 13, 25, 62; PC 64**
See also AMW; CA 13-16; CAAS 33-36R; CABS 2; CANR 35; CAP 1; CDALB 1941-1968; CP 1; DAM POET; DLB 48; EWL 3; MAL 5; MTCW 1, 2; MTFW 2005; PAB; RGAL 4; WP

Bertolucci, Bernardo 1940- ...... **CLC 16, 157**
See also CA 106; CANR 125

Berton, Pierre (Francis de Marigny) 1920-2004 .... **CLC 104**
See also CA 1-4R; CAAS 233; CANR 2, 56, 144; CPW; DLB 68; SATA 99; SATA-Obit 158

Bertrand, Aloysius 1807-1841 .... **NCLC 31**
See Bertrand, Louis oAloysiusc

Bertrand, Louis oAloysiusc
See Bertrand, Aloysius
See also DLB 217

Bertran de Born c. 1140-1215 .... **CMLC 5**

Besant, Annie (Wood) 1847-1933 ..... **TCLC 9**
See also CA 185; CAAE 105

Bessie, Alvah 1904-1985 .... **CLC 23**
See also CA 5-8R; CAAS 116; CANR 2, 80; DLB 26

Bestuzhev, Aleksandr Aleksandrovich 1797-1837 .... **NCLC 131**
See also DLB 198

Bethlen, T. D.
See Silverberg, Robert

Beti, Mongo .... **BLC 1; CLC 27**
See Biyidi, Alexandre
See also AFW; CANR 79; DAM MULT; EWL 3; WLIT 2

Betjeman, John 1906-1984 ...... **CLC 2, 6, 10, 34, 43; PC 75**
See also BRW 7; CA 9-12R; CAAS 112; CANR 33, 56; CDBLB 1945-1960; CP 1, 2, 3; DA3; DAB; DAM MST, POET; DLB 20; DLBY 1984; EWL 3; MTCW 1, 2

Bettelheim, Bruno 1903-1990 .... **CLC 79; TCLC 143**
See also CA 81-84; CAAS 131; CANR 23, 61; DA3; MTCW 1, 2; RGHL

Betti, Ugo 1892-1953 .... **TCLC 5**
See also CA 155; CAAE 104; EWL 3; RGWL 2, 3

Betts, Doris (Waugh) 1932- ..... **CLC 3, 6, 28; SSC 45**
See also CA 13-16R; CANR 9, 66, 77; CN 6, 7; CSW; DLB 218; DLBY 1982; INT CANR-9; RGAL 4

Bevan, Alistair
See Roberts, Keith (John Kingston)

Bey, Pilaff
See Douglas, (George) Norman

Bialik, Chaim Nachman 1873-1934 .... **TCLC 25**
See Bialik, Hayyim Nahman
See also CA 170; EWL 3

Bialik, Hayyim Nahman
See Bialik, Chaim Nachman
See also WLIT 6

Bickerstaff, Isaac
See Swift, Jonathan

Bidart, Frank 1939- .... **CLC 33**
See also AMWS 15; CA 140; CANR 106; CP 5, 6, 7; PFS 26

Bienek, Horst 1930- .... **CLC 7, 11**
See also CA 73-76; DLB 75

Bierce, Ambrose (Gwinett) 1842-1914(?) ..... **SSC 9, 72; TCLC 1, 7, 44; WLC 1**
See also AAYA 55; AMW; BYA 11; CA 139; CAAE 104; CANR 78; CDALB 1865-1917; DA; DA3; DAC; DAM MST;

DLB 11, 12, 23, 71, 74, 186; EWL 3; EXPS; HGG; LAIT 2; MAL 5; RGAL 4; RGSF 2; SSFS 9; SUFW 1

Biggers, Earl Derr 1884-1933 .... **TCLC 65**
See also CA 153; CAAE 108; DLB 306

Billiken, Bud
See Motley, Willard (Francis)

Billings, Josh
See Shaw, Henry Wheeler

Billington, (Lady) Rachel (Mary) 1942- .... **CLC 43**
See also AITN 2; CA 33-36R; CANR 44; CN 4, 5, 6, 7

Binchy, Maeve 1940- .... **CLC 153**
See also BEST 90:1; BPFB 1; CA 134; CAAE 127; CANR 50, 96, 134; CN 5, 6, 7; CPW; DA3; DAM POP; DLB 319; INT CA-134; MTCW 2; MTFW 2005; RHW

Binyon, T(imothy) J(ohn) 1936-2004 .... **CLC 34**
See also CA 111; CAAS 232; CANR 28, 140

Bion 335B.C.-245B.C. .... **CMLC 39**

Bioy Casares, Adolfo 1914-1999 ... **CLC 4, 8, 13, 88; HLC 1; SSC 17, 102**
See Casares, Adolfo Bioy; Miranda, Javier; Sacastru, Martin
See also CA 29-32R; CAAS 177; CANR 19, 43, 66; CWW 2; DAM MULT; DLB 113; EWL 3; HW 1, 2; LAW; MTCW 1, 2; MTFW 2005

Birch, Allison .... **CLC 65**

Bird, Cordwainer
See Ellison, Harlan

Bird, Robert Montgomery 1806-1854 .... **NCLC 1**
See also DLB 202; RGAL 4

Birkerts, Sven 1951- .... **CLC 116**
See also CA 176; 133, 176; 29; CAAE 128; CANR 151; INT CA-133

Birney, (Alfred) Earle 1904-1995 .. **CLC 1, 4, 6, 11; PC 52**
See also CA 1-4R; CANR 5, 20; CN 1, 2, 3, 4; CP 1, 2, 3, 4, 5, 6; DAC; DAM MST, POET; DLB 88; MTCW 1; PFS 8; RGEL 2

Biruni, al 973-1048(?) .... **CMLC 28**

Bishop, Elizabeth 1911-1979 ..... **CLC 1, 4, 9, 13, 15, 32; PC 3, 34; TCLC 121**
See also AMWR 2; AMWS 1; CA 5-8R; CAAS 89-92; CABS 2; CANR 26, 61, 108; CDALB 1968-1988; CP 1, 2, 3; DA; DA3; DAC; DAM MST, POET; DLB 5, 169; EWL 3; GLL 2; MAL 5; MBL; MTCW 1, 2; PAB; PFS 6, 12; RGAL 4; SATA-Obit 24; TUS; WP

Bishop, John 1935- .... **CLC 10**
See also CA 105

Bishop, John Peale 1892-1944 ..... **TCLC 103**
See also CA 155; CAAE 107; DLB 4, 9, 45; MAL 5; RGAL 4

Bissett, Bill 1939- .... **CLC 18; PC 14**
See also CA 69-72; 19; CANR 15; CCA 1; CP 1, 2, 3, 4, 5, 6, 7; DLB 53; MTCW 1

Bissoondath, Neil 1955- .... **CLC 120**
See also CA 136; CANR 123, 165; CN 6, 7; DAC

Bissoondath, Neil Devindra
See Bissoondath, Neil

Bitov, Andrei (Georgievich) 1937- ... **CLC 57**
See also CA 142; DLB 302

Biyidi, Alexandre 1932-
See Beti, Mongo
See also BW 1, 3; CA 124; CAAE 114; CANR 81; DA3; MTCW 1, 2

Bjarme, Brynjolf
See Ibsen, Henrik (Johan)

Bjoernson, Bjoernstjerne (Martinius) 1832-1910 .... **TCLC 7, 37**
See also CAAE 104

Black, Benjamin
See Banville, John

Black, Robert
See Holdstock, Robert

Blackburn, Paul 1926-1971 .... **CLC 9, 43**
See also BG 1:2; CA 81-84; CAAS 33-36R; CANR 34; CP 1; DLB 16; DLBY 1981

Black Elk 1863-1950 .... **NNAL; TCLC 33**
See also CA 144; DAM MULT; MTCW 2; MTFW 2005; WP

Black Hawk 1767-1838 .... **NNAL**

Black Hobart
See Sanders, (James) Ed(ward)

Blacklin, Malcolm
See Chambers, Aidan

Blackmore, R(ichard) D(oddridge) 1825-1900 .... **TCLC 27**
See also CAAE 120; DLB 18; RGEL 2

Blackmur, R(ichard) P(almer) 1904-1965 .... **CLC 2, 24**
See also AMWS 2; CA 11-12; CAAS 25-28R; CANR 71; CAP 1; DLB 63; EWL 3; MAL 5

Black Tarantula
See Acker, Kathy

Blackwood, Algernon (Henry) 1869-1951 .... **TCLC 5**
See also CA 150; CAAE 105; DLB 153, 156, 178; HGG; SUFW 1

Blackwood, Caroline (Maureen) 1931-1996 .... **CLC 6, 9, 100**
See also BRWS 9; CA 85-88; CAAS 151; CANR 32, 61, 65; CN 3, 4, 5, 6; DLB 14, 207; HGG; MTCW 1

Blade, Alexander
See Hamilton, Edmond; Silverberg, Robert

Blaga, Lucian 1895-1961 .... **CLC 75**
See also CA 157; DLB 220; EWL 3

Blair, Eric (Arthur) 1903-1950 .... **TCLC 123**
See Orwell, George
See also CA 132; CAAE 104; DA; DA3; DAB; DAC; DAM MST, NOV; MTCW 1, 2; MTFW 2005; SATA 29

Blair, Hugh 1718-1800 .... **NCLC 75**

Blais, Marie-Claire 1939- .... **CLC 2, 4, 6, 13, 22**
See also CA 21-24R; 4; CANR 38, 75, 93; CWW 2; DAC; DAM MST; DLB 53; EWL 3; FW; MTCW 1, 2; MTFW 2005; TWA

Blaise, Clark 1940- .... **CLC 29**
See also AITN 2; CA 231; 53-56, 231; 3; CANR 5, 66, 106; CN 4, 5, 6, 7; DLB 53; RGSF 2

Blake, Fairley
See De Voto, Bernard (Augustine)

Blake, Nicholas
See Day Lewis, C(ecil)
See also DLB 77; MSW

Blake, Sterling
See Benford, Gregory

Blake, William 1757-1827 . **NCLC 13, 37, 57, 127, 173; PC 12, 63; WLC 1**
See also AAYA 47; BRW 3; BRWR 1; CD-BLB 1789-1832; CLR 52; DA; DA3; DAB; DAC; DAM MST, POET; DLB 93, 163; EXPP; LATS 1:1; LMFS 1; MAI-CYA 1, 2; PAB; PFS 2, 12, 24; SATA 30; TEA; WCH; WLIT 3; WP

Blanchot, Maurice 1907-2003 .... **CLC 135**
See also CA 144; CAAE 117; CAAS 213; CANR 138; DLB 72, 296; EWL 3

Borowski, Tadeusz 1922-1951 .... **SSC 48;**
TCLC 9
See also CA 154; CAAE 106; CDWLB 4;
DLB 215; EWL 3; RGHL; RGSF 2;
RGWL 3; SSFS 13

Borrow, George (Henry)
1803-1881 .... **NCLC 9**
See also BRWS 12; DLB 21, 55, 166

Bosch (Gavino), Juan 1909-2001 ..... **HLCS 1**
See also CA 151; CAAS 204; DAM MST,
MULT; DLB 145; HW 1, 2

Bosman, Herman Charles
1905-1951 .... **TCLC 49**
See Malan, Herman
See also CA 160; DLB 225; RGSF 2

Bosschere, Jean de 1878(?)-1953 ... **TCLC 19**
See also CA 186; CAAE 115

Boswell, James 1740-1795 ... **LC 4, 50; WLC**
1
See also BRW 3; CDBLB 1660-1789; DA;
DAB; DAC; DAM MST; DLB 104, 142;
TEA; WLIT 3

Bottomley, Gordon 1874-1948 ..... **TCLC 107**
See also CA 192; CAAE 120; DLB 10

Bottoms, David 1949- .... **CLC 53**
See also CA 105; CANR 22; CSW; DLB
120; DLBY 1983

Boucicault, Dion 1820-1890 .... **NCLC 41**

Boucolon, Maryse
See Conde, Maryse

Bourdieu, Pierre 1930-2002 .... **CLC 198**
See also CA 130; CAAS 204

Bourget, Paul (Charles Joseph)
1852-1935 .... **TCLC 12**
See also CA 196; CAAE 107; DLB 123;
GFL 1789 to the Present

Bourjaily, Vance (Nye) 1922- .... **CLC 8, 62**
See also CA 1-4R; 1; CANR 2, 72; CN 1,
2, 3, 4, 5, 6, 7; DLB 2, 143; MAL 5

Bourne, Randolph S(illiman)
1886-1918 .... **TCLC 16**
See also AMW; CA 155; CAAE 117; DLB
63; MAL 5

Bova, Ben 1932- .... **CLC 45**
See also AAYA 16; CA 5-8R; 18; CANR
11, 56, 94, 111, 157; CLR 3, 96; DLBY
1981; INT CANR-11; MAICYA 1, 2;
MTCW 1; SATA 6, 68, 133; SFW 4

Bova, Benjamin William
See Bova, Ben

Bowen, Elizabeth (Dorothea Cole)
1899-1973 . **CLC 1, 3, 6, 11, 15, 22, 118;**
SSC 3, 28, 66; TCLC 148
See also BRWS 2; CA 17-18; CAAS 41-
44R; CANR 35, 105; CAP 2; CDBLB
1945-1960; CN 1; DA3; DAM NOV;
DLB 15, 162; EWL 3; EXPS; FW; HGG;
MTCW 1, 2; MTFW 2005; NFS 13;
RGSF 2; SSFS 5, 22; SUFW 1; TEA;
WLIT 4

Bowering, George 1935- .... **CLC 15, 47**
See also CA 21-24R; 16; CANR 10; CN 7;
CP 1, 2, 3, 4, 5, 6, 7; DLB 53

Bowering, Marilyn R(uthe) 1949- .... **CLC 32**
See also CA 101; CANR 49; CP 4, 5, 6, 7;
CWP; DLB 334

Bowers, Edgar 1924-2000 .... **CLC 9**
See also CA 5-8R; CAAS 188; CANR 24;
CP 1, 2, 3, 4, 5, 6, 7; CSW; DLB 5

Bowers, Mrs. J. Milton 1842-1914
See Bierce, Ambrose (Gwinett)

Bowie, David .... **CLC 17**
See Jones, David Robert

Bowles, Jane (Sydney) 1917-1973 ..... **CLC 3,**
68
See Bowles, Jane Auer
See also CA 19-20; CAAS 41-44R; CAP 2;
CN 1; MAL 5

Bowles, Jane Auer
See Bowles, Jane (Sydney)
See also EWL 3

Bowles, Paul 1910-1999 ..... **CLC 1, 2, 19, 53;**
SSC 3, 98
See also AMWS 4; CA 1-4R; 1; CAAS 186;
CANR 1, 19, 50, 75; CN 1, 2, 3, 4, 5, 6;
DA3; DLB 5, 6, 218; EWL 3; MAL 5;
MTCW 1, 2; MTFW 2005; RGAL 4;
SSFS 17

Bowles, William Lisle 1762-1850 . **NCLC 103**
See also DLB 93

Box, Edgar
See Vidal, Gore
See also GLL 1

Boyd, James 1888-1944 .... **TCLC 115**
See also CA 186; DLB 9; DLBD 16; RGAL
4; RHW

Boyd, Nancy
See Millay, Edna St. Vincent
See also GLL 1

Boyd, Thomas (Alexander)
1898-1935 .... **TCLC 111**
See also CA 183; CAAE 111; DLB 9;
DLBD 16, 316

Boyd, William (Andrew Murray)
1952- .... **CLC 28, 53, 70**
See also CA 120; CAAE 114; CANR 51,
71, 131; CN 4, 5, 6, 7; DLB 231

Boyesen, Hjalmar Hjorth
1848-1895 .... **NCLC 135**
See also DLB 12, 71; DLBD 13; RGAL 4

Boyle, Kay 1902-1992 .... **CLC 1, 5, 19, 58,**
121; SSC 5, 102
See also CA 13-16R; 1; CAAS 140; CANR
29, 61, 110; CN 1, 2, 3, 4, 5; CP 1, 2, 3,
4, 5; DLB 4, 9, 48, 86; DLBY 1993; EWL
3; MAL 5; MTCW 1, 2; MTFW 2005;
RGAL 4; RGSF 2; SSFS 10, 13, 14

Boyle, Mark
See Kienzle, William X.

Boyle, Patrick 1905-1982 .... **CLC 19**
See also CA 127

Boyle, T. C.
See Boyle, T. Coraghessan
See also AMWS 8

Boyle, T. Coraghessan 1948- ..... **CLC 36, 55,**
90; SSC 16
See Boyle, T. C.
See also AAYA 47; BEST 90:4; BPFB 1;
CA 120; CANR 44, 76, 89, 132; CN 6, 7;
CPW; DA3; DAM POP; DLB 218, 278;
DLBY 1986; EWL 3; MAL 5; MTCW 2;
MTFW 2005; SSFS 13, 19

Boz
See Dickens, Charles (John Huffam)

Brackenridge, Hugh Henry
1748-1816 .... **NCLC 7**
See also DLB 11, 37; RGAL 4

Bradbury, Edward P.
See Moorcock, Michael
See also MTCW 2

Bradbury, Malcolm (Stanley)
1932-2000 .... **CLC 32, 61**
See also CA 1-4R; CANR 1, 33, 91, 98,
137; CN 1, 2, 3, 4, 5, 6, 7; CP 1; DA3;
DAM NOV; DLB 14, 207; EWL 3;
MTCW 1, 2; MTFW 2005

Bradbury, Ray 1920- ... **CLC 1, 3, 10, 15, 42,**
98, 235; SSC 29, 53; WLC 1
See also AAYA 15; AITN 1, 2; AMWS 4;
BPFB 1; BYA 4, 5, 11; CA 1-4R; CANR
2, 30, 75, 125; CDALB 1968-1988; CN
1, 2, 3, 4, 5, 6, 7; CPW; DA; DA3; DAB;
DAC; DAM MST, NOV, POP; DLB 2, 8;
EXPN; EXPS; HGG; LAIT 3, 5; LATS
1:2; LMFS 2; MAL 5; MTCW 1, 2;
MTFW 2005; NFS 1, 22; RGAL 4; RGSF
2; SATA 11, 64, 123; SCFW 1, 2; SFW 4;
SSFS 1, 20; SUFW 1, 2; TUS; YAW

Braddon, Mary Elizabeth
1837-1915 .... **TCLC 111**
See also BRWS 8; CA 179; CAAE 108;
CMW 4; DLB 18, 70, 156; HGG

Bradfield, Scott 1955- .... **SSC 65**
See also CA 147; CANR 90; HGG; SUFW
2

Bradfield, Scott Michael
See Bradfield, Scott

Bradford, Gamaliel 1863-1932 .... **TCLC 36**
See also CA 160; DLB 17

Bradford, William 1590-1657 .... **LC 64**
See also DLB 24, 30; RGAL 4

Bradley, David, Jr. 1950- ... **BLC 1; CLC 23,**
118
See also BW 1, 3; CA 104; CANR 26, 81;
CN 4, 5, 6, 7; DAM MULT; DLB 33

Bradley, David Henry, Jr.
See Bradley, David, Jr.

Bradley, John Ed 1958- .... **CLC 55**
See also CA 139; CANR 99; CN 6, 7; CSW

Bradley, John Edmund, Jr.
See Bradley, John Ed

Bradley, Marion Zimmer
1930-1999 .... **CLC 30**
See Chapman, Lee; Dexter, John; Gardner,
Miriam; Ives, Morgan; Rivers, Elfrida
See also AAYA 40; BPFB 1; CA 57-60; 10;
CAAS 185; CANR 7, 31, 51, 75, 107;
CPW; DA3; DAM POP; DLB 8; FANT;
FW; MTCW 1, 2; MTFW 2005; SATA 90,
139; SATA-Obit 116; SFW 4; SUFW 2;
YAW

Bradshaw, John 1933- .... **CLC 70**
See also CA 138; CANR 61

Bradstreet, Anne 1612(?)-1672 .... **LC 4, 30,**
130; PC 10
See also AMWS 1; CDALB 1640-1865;
DA; DA3; DAC; DAM MST, POET; DLB
24; EXPP; FW; PFS 6; RGAL 4; TUS;
WP

Brady, Joan 1939- .... **CLC 86**
See also CA 141

Bragg, Melvyn 1939- .... **CLC 10**
See also BEST 89:3; CA 57-60; CANR 10,
48, 89, 158; CN 1, 2, 3, 4, 5, 6, 7; DLB
14, 271; RHW

Brahe, Tycho 1546-1601 .... **LC 45**
See also DLB 300

Braine, John (Gerard) 1922-1986 . **CLC 1, 3,**
41
See also CA 1-4R; CAAS 120; CANR 1,
33; CDBLB 1945-1960; CN 1, 2, 3, 4;
DLB 15; DLBY 1986; EWL 3; MTCW 1

Braithwaite, William Stanley (Beaumont)
1878-1962 .... **BLC 1; HR 1:2; PC 52**
See also BW 1; CA 125; DAM MULT; DLB
50, 54; MAL 5

Bramah, Ernest 1868-1942 .... **TCLC 72**
See also CA 156; CMW 4; DLB 70; FANT

Brammer, Billy Lee
See Brammer, William

Brammer, William 1929-1978 .... **CLC 31**
See also CA 235; CAAS 77-80

Brancati, Vitaliano 1907-1954 .... **TCLC 12**
See also CAAE 109; DLB 264; EWL 3

Brancato, Robin F(idler) 1936- .... **CLC 35**
See also AAYA 9, 68; BYA 6; CA 69-72;
CANR 11, 45; CLR 32; JRDA; MAICYA
2; MAICYAS 1; SAAS 9; SATA 97;
WYA; YAW

Brand, Dionne 1953- .... **CLC 192**
See also BW 2; CA 143; CANR 143; CWP;
DLB 334

Brand, Max
See Faust, Frederick (Schiller)
See also BPFB 1; TCWW 1, 2

Brooks, Gwendolyn 1917-2000 .... **BLC 1; CLC 1, 2, 4, 5, 15, 49, 125; PC 7; WLC 1**
See also AAYA 20; AFAW 1, 2; AITN 1; AMWS 3; BW 2, 3; CA 1-4R; CAAS 190; CANR 1, 27, 52, 75, 132; CDALB 1941-1968; CLR 27; CP 1, 2, 3, 4, 5, 6, 7; CWP; DA; DA3; DAC; DAM MST, MULT, POET; DLB 5, 76, 165; EWL 3; EXPP; FL 1:5; MAL 5; MBL; MTCW 1, 2; MTFW 2005; PFS 1, 2, 4, 6; RGAL 4; SATA 6; SATA-Obit 123; TUS; WP

Brooks, Mel 1926-
See Kaminsky, Melvin
See also CA 65-68; CANR 16; DFS 21

Brooks, Peter (Preston) 1938- .... **CLC 34**
See also CA 45-48; CANR 1, 107

Brooks, Van Wyck 1886-1963 .... **CLC 29**
See also AMW; CA 1-4R; CANR 6; DLB 45, 63, 103; MAL 5; TUS

Brophy, Brigid (Antonia) 1929-1995 .... **CLC 6, 11, 29, 105**
See also CA 5-8R; 4; CAAS 149; CANR 25, 53; CBD; CN 1, 2, 3, 4, 5, 6; CWD; DA3; DLB 14, 271; EWL 3; MTCW 1, 2

Brosman, Catharine Savage 1934- ..... **CLC 9**
See also CA 61-64; CANR 21, 46, 149

Brossard, Nicole 1943- .... **CLC 115, 169**
See also CA 122; 16; CANR 140; CCA 1; CWP; CWW 2; DLB 53; EWL 3; FW; GLL 2; RGWL 3

Brother Antoninus
See Everson, William (Oliver)

Brothers Grimm
See Grimm, Jacob Ludwig Karl; Grimm, Wilhelm Karl

The Brothers Quay
See Quay, Stephen; Quay, Timothy

Broughton, T(homas) Alan 1936- ..... **CLC 19**
See also CA 45-48; CANR 2, 23, 48, 111

Broumas, Olga 1949- .... **CLC 10, 73**
See also CA 85-88; CANR 20, 69, 110; CP 5, 6, 7; CWP; GLL 2

Broun, Heywood 1888-1939 .... **TCLC 104**
See also DLB 29, 171

Brown, Alan 1950- .... **CLC 99**
See also CA 156

Brown, Charles Brockden
1771-1810 .... **NCLC 22, 74, 122**
See also AMWS 1; CDALB 1640-1865; DLB 37, 59, 73; FW; GL 2; HGG; LMFS 1; RGAL 4; TUS

Brown, Christy 1932-1981 .... **CLC 63**
See also BYA 13; CA 105; CAAS 104; CANR 72; DLB 14

Brown, Claude 1937-2002 ... **BLC 1; CLC 30**
See also AAYA 7; BW 1, 3; CA 73-76; CAAS 205; CANR 81; DAM MULT

Brown, Dan 1964- .... **CLC 209**
See also AAYA 55; CA 217; MTFW 2005

Brown, Dee 1908-2002 .... **CLC 18, 47**
See also AAYA 30; CA 13-16R; 6; CAAS 212; CANR 11, 45, 60, 150; CPW; CSW; DA3; DAM POP; DLBY 1980; LAIT 2; MTCW 1, 2; MTFW 2005; NCFS 5; SATA 5, 110; SATA-Obit 141; TCWW 1, 2

Brown, Dee Alexander
See Brown, Dee

Brown, George
See Wertmueller, Lina

Brown, George Douglas
1869-1902 .... **TCLC 28**
See Douglas, George
See also CA 162

Brown, George Mackay 1921-1996 ... **CLC 5, 48, 100**
See also BRWS 6; CA 21-24R; 6; CAAS 151; CANR 12, 37, 67; CN 1, 2, 3, 4, 5, 6; CP 1, 2, 3, 4, 5, 6; DLB 14, 27, 139, 271; MTCW 1; RGSF 2; SATA 35

Brown, James Wlllie
See Komunyakaa, Yusef

Brown, James Wlllie, Jr.
See Komunyakaa, Yusef

Brown, Larry 1951-2004 .... **CLC 73**
See also CA 134; CAAE 130; CAAS 233; CANR 117, 145; CSW; DLB 234; INT CA-134

Brown, Moses
See Barrett, William (Christopher)

Brown, Rita Mae 1944- .... **CLC 18, 43, 79**
See also BPFB 1; CA 45-48; CANR 2, 11, 35, 62, 95, 138; CN 5, 6, 7; CPW; CSW; DA3; DAM NOV, POP; FW; INT CANR-11; MAL 5; MTCW 1, 2; MTFW 2005; NFS 9; RGAL 4; TUS

Brown, Roderick (Langmere) Haig-
See Haig-Brown, Roderick (Langmere)

Brown, Rosellen 1939- .... **CLC 32, 170**
See also CA 77-80; 10; CANR 14, 44, 98; CN 6, 7

Brown, Sterling Allen 1901-1989 ...... **BLC 1; CLC 1, 23, 59; HR 1:2; PC 55**
See also AFAW 1, 2; BW 1, 3; CA 85-88; CAAS 127; CANR 26; CP 3, 4; DA3; DAM MULT, POET; DLB 48, 51, 63; MAL 5; MTCW 1, 2; MTFW 2005; RGAL 4; WP

Brown, Will
See Ainsworth, William Harrison

Brown, William Hill 1765-1793 .... **LC 93**
See also DLB 37

Brown, William Larry
See Brown, Larry

Brown, William Wells 1815-1884 ...... **BLC 1; DC 1; NCLC 2, 89**
See also DAM MULT; DLB 3, 50, 183, 248; RGAL 4

Browne, Clyde Jackson
See Browne, Jackson

Browne, Jackson 1948(?)- .... **CLC 21**
See also CA 120

Browne, Sir Thomas 1605-1682 .... **LC 111**
See also BRW 2; DLB 151

Browning, Robert 1812-1889 . **NCLC 19, 79; PC 2, 61; WLCS**
See also BRW 4; BRWC 2; BRWR 2; CDBLB 1832-1890; CLR 97; DA; DA3; DAB; DAC; DAM MST, POET; DLB 32, 163; EXPP; LATS 1:1; PAB; PFS 1, 15; RGEL 2; TEA; WLIT 4; WP; YABC 1

Browning, Tod 1882-1962 .... **CLC 16**
See also CA 141; CAAS 117

Brownmiller, Susan 1935- .... **CLC 159**
See also CA 103; CANR 35, 75, 137; DAM NOV; FW; MTCW 1, 2; MTFW 2005

Brownson, Orestes Augustus
1803-1876 .... **NCLC 50**
See also DLB 1, 59, 73, 243

Bruccoli, Matthew J(oseph) 1931- ... **CLC 34**
See also CA 9-12R; CANR 7, 87; DLB 103

Bruce, Lenny .... **CLC 21**
See Schneider, Leonard Alfred

Bruchac, Joseph 1942- .... **NNAL**
See also AAYA 19; CA 256; 33-36R, 256; CANR 13, 47, 75, 94, 137, 161; CLR 46; CWRI 5; DAM MULT; JRDA; MAICYA 2; MAICYAS 1; MTCW 2; MTFW 2005; SATA 42, 89, 131, 176; SATA-Essay 176

Bruin, John
See Brutus, Dennis

Brulard, Henri
See Stendhal

Brulls, Christian
See Simenon, Georges (Jacques Christian)

Brunetto Latini c. 1220-1294 .... **CMLC 73**

Brunner, John (Kilian Houston)
1934-1995 .... **CLC 8, 10**
See also CA 1-4R; 8; CAAS 149; CANR 2, 37; CPW; DAM POP; DLB 261; MTCW 1, 2; SCFW 1, 2; SFW 4

Bruno, Giordano 1548-1600 .... **LC 27**
See also RGWL 2, 3

Brutus, Dennis 1924- ... **BLC 1; CLC 43; PC 24**
See also AFW; BW 2, 3; CA 49-52; 14; CANR 2, 27, 42, 81; CDWLB 3; CP 1, 2, 3, 4, 5, 6, 7; DAM MULT, POET; DLB 117, 225; EWL 3

Bryan, C(ourtlandt) D(ixon) B(arnes)
1936- .... **CLC 29**
See also CA 73-76; CANR 13, 68; DLB 185; INT CANR-13

Bryan, Michael
See Moore, Brian
See also CCA 1

Bryan, William Jennings
1860-1925 .... **TCLC 99**
See also DLB 303

Bryant, William Cullen 1794-1878 . **NCLC 6, 46; PC 20**
See also AMWS 1; CDALB 1640-1865; DA; DAB; DAC; DAM MST, POET; DLB 3, 43, 59, 189, 250; EXPP; PAB; RGAL 4; TUS

Bryusov, Valery Yakovlevich
1873-1924 .... **TCLC 10**
See also CA 155; CAAE 107; EWL 3; SFW 4

Buchan, John 1875-1940 .... **TCLC 41**
See also CA 145; CAAE 108; CMW 4; DAB; DAM POP; DLB 34, 70, 156; HGG; MSW; MTCW 2; RGEL 2; RHW; YABC 2

Buchanan, George 1506-1582 .... **LC 4**
See also DLB 132

Buchanan, Robert 1841-1901 .... **TCLC 107**
See also CA 179; DLB 18, 35

Buchheim, Lothar-Guenther
1918-2007 .... **CLC 6**
See also CA 85-88; CAAS 257

Buchner, (Karl) Georg
1813-1837 .... **NCLC 26, 146**
See also CDWLB 2; DLB 133; EW 6; RGSF 2; RGWL 2, 3; TWA

Buchwald, Art 1925-2007 .... **CLC 33**
See also AITN 1; CA 5-8R; CAAS 256; CANR 21, 67, 107; MTCW 1, 2; SATA 10

Buchwald, Arthur
See Buchwald, Art

Buck, Pearl S(ydenstricker)
1892-1973 .... **CLC 7, 11, 18, 127**
See also AAYA 42; AITN 1; AMWS 2; BPFB 1; CA 1-4R; CAAS 41-44R; CANR 1, 34; CDALBS; CN 1; DA; DA3; DAB; DAC; DAM MST, NOV; DLB 9, 102, 329; EWL 3; LAIT 3; MAL 5; MTCW 1, 2; MTFW 2005; NFS 25; RGAL 4; RHW; SATA 1, 25; TUS

Buckler, Ernest 1908-1984 .... **CLC 13**
See also CA 11-12; CAAS 114; CAP 1; CCA 1; CN 1, 2, 3; DAC; DAM MST; DLB 68; SATA 47

Buckley, Christopher 1952- .... **CLC 165**
See also CA 139; CANR 119

Buckley, Christopher Taylor
See Buckley, Christopher

Buckley, Vincent (Thomas)
1925-1988 .... **CLC 57**
See also CA 101; CP 1, 2, 3, 4; DLB 289

Byatt, Antonia Susan Drabble
See Byatt, A.S.
Byatt, A.S. 1936- .... **CLC 19, 65, 136, 223; SSC 91**
See also BPFB 1; BRWC 2; BRWS 4; CA 13-16R; CANR 13, 33, 50, 75, 96, 133; CN 1, 2, 3, 4, 5, 6; DA3; DAM NOV, POP; DLB 14, 194, 319, 326; EWL 3; MTCW 1, 2; MTFW 2005; RGSF 2; RHW; TEA
Byrd, William II 1674-1744 .... **LC 112**
See also DLB 24, 140; RGAL 4
Byrne, David 1952- .... **CLC 26**
See also CA 127
Byrne, John Keyes 1926-
See Leonard, Hugh
See also CA 102; CANR 78, 140; INT CA-102
Byron, George Gordon (Noel)
1788-1824 ..... **DC 24; NCLC 2, 12, 109, 149; PC 16; WLC 1**
See also AAYA 64; BRW 4; BRWC 2; CD-BLB 1789-1832; DA; DA3; DAB; DAC; DAM MST, POET; DLB 96, 110; EXPP; LMFS 1; PAB; PFS 1, 14; RGEL 2; TEA; WLIT 3; WP
Byron, Robert 1905-1941 .... **TCLC 67**
See also CA 160; DLB 195
C. 3. 3.
See Wilde, Oscar (Fingal O'Flahertie Wills)
Caballero, Fernan 1796-1877 .... **NCLC 10**
Cabell, Branch
See Cabell, James Branch
Cabell, James Branch 1879-1958 .... **TCLC 6**
See also CA 152; CAAE 105; DLB 9, 78; FANT; MAL 5; MTCW 2; RGAL 4; SUFW 1
Cabeza de Vaca, Alvar Nunez
1490-1557(?) .... **LC 61**
Cable, George Washington
1844-1925 .... **SSC 4; TCLC 4**
See also CA 155; CAAE 104; DLB 12, 74; DLBD 13; RGAL 4; TUS
Cabral de Melo Neto, Joao
1920-1999 .... **CLC 76**
See Melo Neto, Joao Cabral de
See also CA 151; DAM MULT; DLB 307; LAW; LAWS 1
Cabrera Infante, G. 1929-2005 ... **CLC 5, 25, 45, 120; HLC 1; SSC 39**
See also CA 85-88; CAAS 236; CANR 29, 65, 110; CDWLB 3; CWW 2; DA3; DAM MULT; DLB 113; EWL 3; HW 1, 2; LAW; LAWS 1; MTCW 1, 2; MTFW 2005; RGSF 2; WLIT 1
Cabrera Infante, Guillermo
See Cabrera Infante, G.
Cade, Toni
See Bambara, Toni Cade
Cadmus and Harmonia
See Buchan, John
Caedmon fl. 658-680 .... **CMLC 7**
See also DLB 146
Caeiro, Alberto
See Pessoa, Fernando (Antonio Nogueira)
Caesar, Julius .... **CMLC 47**
See Julius Caesar
See also AW 1; RGWL 2, 3; WLIT 8
Cage, John (Milton), (Jr.)
1912-1992 .... **CLC 41; PC 58**
See also CA 13-16R; CAAS 169; CANR 9, 78; DLB 193; INT CANR-9; TCLE 1:1
Cahan, Abraham 1860-1951 .... **TCLC 71**
See also CA 154; CAAE 108; DLB 9, 25, 28; MAL 5; RGAL 4
Cain, G.
See Cabrera Infante, G.
Cain, Guillermo
See Cabrera Infante, G.

Cain, James M(allahan) 1892-1977 .. **CLC 3, 11, 28**
See also AITN 1; BPFB 1; CA 17-20R; CAAS 73-76; CANR 8, 34, 61; CMW 1; CN 1, 2; DLB 226; EWL 3; MAL 5; MSW; MTCW 1; RGAL 4
Caine, Hall 1853-1931 .... **TCLC 97**
See also RHW
Caine, Mark
See Raphael, Frederic (Michael)
Calasso, Roberto 1941- .... **CLC 81**
See also CA 143; CANR 89
Calderon de la Barca, Pedro
1600-1681 . **DC 3; HLCS 1; LC 23, 136**
See also DFS 23; EW 2; RGWL 2, 3; TWA
Caldwell, Erskine 1903-1987 ... **CLC 1, 8, 14, 50, 60; SSC 19; TCLC 117**
See also AITN 1; AMW; BPFB 1; CA 1-4R; 1; CAAS 121; CANR 2, 33; CN 1, 2, 3, 4; DA3; DAM NOV; DLB 9, 86; EWL 3; MAL 5; MTCW 1, 2; MTFW 2005; RGAL 4; RGSF 2; TUS
Caldwell, (Janet Miriam) Taylor (Holland)
1900-1985 .... **CLC 2, 28, 39**
See also BPFB 1; CA 5-8R; CAAS 116; CANR 5; DA3; DAM NOV, POP; DLBD 17; MTCW 2; RHW
Calhoun, John Caldwell
1782-1850 .... **NCLC 15**
See also DLB 3, 248
Calisher, Hortense 1911- ..... **CLC 2, 4, 8, 38, 134; SSC 15**
See also CA 1-4R; CANR 1, 22, 117; CN 1, 2, 3, 4, 5, 6, 7; DA3; DAM NOV; DLB 2, 218; INT CANR-22; MAL 5; MTCW 1, 2; MTFW 2005; RGAL 4; RGSF 2
Callaghan, Morley Edward
1903-1990 ..... **CLC 3, 14, 41, 65; TCLC 145**
See also CA 9-12R; CAAS 132; CANR 33, 73; CN 1, 2, 3, 4; DAC; DAM MST; DLB 68; EWL 3; MTCW 1, 2; MTFW 2005; RGEL 2; RGSF 2; SSFS 19
Callimachus c. 305B.C.-c.
240B.C. .... **CMLC 18**
See also AW 1; DLB 176; RGWL 2, 3
Calvin, Jean
See Calvin, John
See also DLB 327; GFL Beginnings to 1789
Calvin, John 1509-1564 .... **LC 37**
See Calvin, Jean
Calvino, Italo 1923-1985 .... **CLC 5, 8, 11, 22, 33, 39, 73; SSC 3, 48; TCLC 183**
See also AAYA 58; CA 85-88; CAAS 116; CANR 23, 61, 132; DAM NOV; DLB 196; EW 13; EWL 3; MTCW 1, 2; MTFW 2005; RGHL; RGSF 2; RGWL 2, 3; SFW 4; SSFS 12; WLIT 7
Camara Laye
See Laye, Camara
See also EWL 3
Camden, William 1551-1623 .... **LC 77**
See also DLB 172
Cameron, Carey 1952- .... **CLC 59**
See also CA 135
Cameron, Peter 1959- .... **CLC 44**
See also AMWS 12; CA 125; CANR 50, 117; DLB 234; GLL 2
Camoens, Luis Vaz de 1524(?)-1580
See Camoes, Luis de
See also EW 2
Camoes, Luis de 1524(?)-1580 . **HLCS 1; LC 62; PC 31**
See Camoens, Luis Vaz de
See also DLB 287; RGWL 2, 3
Campana, Dino 1885-1932 .... **TCLC 20**
See also CA 246; CAAE 117; DLB 114; EWL 3

Campanella, Tommaso 1568-1639 .... **LC 32**
See also RGWL 2, 3
Campbell, John W(ood, Jr.)
1910-1971 .... **CLC 32**
See also CA 21-22; CAAS 29-32R; CANR 34; CAP 2; DLB 8; MTCW 1; SCFW 1, 2; SFW 4
Campbell, Joseph 1904-1987 .... **CLC 69; TCLC 140**
See also AAYA 3, 66; BEST 89:2; CA 1-4R; CAAS 124; CANR 3, 28, 61, 107; DA3; MTCW 1, 2
Campbell, Maria 1940- .... **CLC 85; NNAL**
See also CA 102; CANR 54; CCA 1; DAC
Campbell, (John) Ramsey 1946- ..... **CLC 42; SSC 19**
See also AAYA 51; CA 228; 57-60, 228; CANR 7, 102; DLB 261; HGG; INT CANR-7; SUFW 1, 2
Campbell, (Ignatius) Roy (Dunnachie)
1901-1957 .... **TCLC 5**
See also AFW; CA 155; CAAE 104; DLB 20, 225; EWL 3; MTCW 2; RGEL 2
Campbell, Thomas 1777-1844 .... **NCLC 19**
See also DLB 93, 144; RGEL 2
Campbell, Wilfred .... **TCLC 9**
See Campbell, William
Campbell, William 1858(?)-1918
See Campbell, Wilfred
See also CAAE 106; DLB 92
Campbell, William Edward March
1893-1954
See March, William
See also CAAE 108
Campion, Jane 1954- .... **CLC 95, 229**
See also AAYA 33; CA 138; CANR 87
Campion, Thomas 1567-1620 .... **LC 78**
See also CDBLB Before 1660; DAM POET; DLB 58, 172; RGEL 2
Camus, Albert 1913-1960 ...... **CLC 1, 2, 4, 9, 11, 14, 32, 63, 69, 124; DC 2; SSC 9, 76; WLC 1**
See also AAYA 36; AFW; BPFB 1; CA 89-92; CANR 131; DA; DA3; DAB; DAC; DAM DRAM, MST, NOV; DLB 72, 321, 329; EW 13; EWL 3; EXPN; EXPS; GFL 1789 to the Present; LATS 1:2; LMFS 2; MTCW 1, 2; MTFW 2005; NFS 6, 16; RGHL; RGSF 2; RGWL 2, 3; SSFS 4; TWA
Canby, Vincent 1924-2000 .... **CLC 13**
See also CA 81-84; CAAS 191
Cancale
See Desnos, Robert
Canetti, Elias 1905-1994 .. **CLC 3, 14, 25, 75, 86; TCLC 157**
See also CA 21-24R; CAAS 146; CANR 23, 61, 79; CDWLB 2; CWW 2; DA3; DLB 85, 124, 329; EW 12; EWL 3; MTCW 1, 2; MTFW 2005; RGWL 2, 3; TWA
Canfield, Dorothea F.
See Fisher, Dorothy (Frances) Canfield
Canfield, Dorothea Frances
See Fisher, Dorothy (Frances) Canfield
Canfield, Dorothy
See Fisher, Dorothy (Frances) Canfield
Canin, Ethan 1960- .... **CLC 55; SSC 70**
See also CA 135; CAAE 131; DLB 335; MAL 5
Cankar, Ivan 1876-1918 .... **TCLC 105**
See also CDWLB 4; DLB 147; EWL 3
Cannon, Curt
See Hunter, Evan
Cao, Lan 1961- .... **CLC 109**
See also CA 165
Cape, Judith
See Page, P(atricia) K(athleen)
See also CCA 1

Cassiodorus, Flavius Magnus c. 490(?)-c.
583(?) .... **CMLC 43**
Cassirer, Ernst 1874-1945 .... **TCLC 61**
See also CA 157
Cassity, (Allen) Turner 1929- .... **CLC 6, 42**
See also CA 223; 17-20R, 223; 8; CANR
11; CSW; DLB 105
Castaneda, Carlos (Cesar Aranha)
1931(?)-1998 .... **CLC 12, 119**
See also CA 25-28R; CANR 32, 66, 105;
DNFS 1; HW 1; MTCW 1
Castedo, Elena 1937- .... **CLC 65**
See also CA 132
Castedo-Ellerman, Elena
See Castedo, Elena
Castellanos, Rosario 1925-1974 .... **CLC 66;
HLC 1; SSC 39, 68**
See also CA 131; CAAS 53-56; CANR 58;
CDWLB 3; DAM MULT; DLB 113, 290;
EWL 3; FW; HW 1; LAW; MTCW 2;
MTFW 2005; RGSF 2; RGWL 2, 3
Castelvetro, Lodovico 1505-1571 .... **LC 12**
Castiglione, Baldassare 1478-1529 ...... **LC 12**
See Castiglione, Baldesar
See also LMFS 1; RGWL 2, 3
Castiglione, Baldesar
See Castiglione, Baldassare
See also EW 2; WLIT 7
Castillo, Ana 1953- .... **CLC 151**
See also AAYA 42; CA 131; CANR 51, 86,
128; CWP; DLB 122, 227; DNFS 2; FW;
HW 1; LLW; PFS 21
Castle, Robert
See Hamilton, Edmond
Castro (Ruz), Fidel 1926(?)- .... **HLC 1**
See also CA 129; CAAE 110; CANR 81;
DAM MULT; HW 2
Castro, Guillen de 1569-1631 .... **LC 19**
Castro, Rosalia de 1837-1885 ... **NCLC 3, 78;
PC 41**
See also DAM MULT
Cather, Willa (Sibert) 1873-1947 . **SSC 2, 50;
TCLC 1, 11, 31, 99, 132, 152; WLC 1**
See also AAYA 24; AMW; AMWC 1;
AMWR 1; BPFB 1; CA 128; CAAE 104;
CDALB 1865-1917; CLR 98; DA; DA3;
DAB; DAC; DAM MST, NOV; DLB 9,
54, 78, 256; DLBD 1; EWL 3; EXPN;
EXPS; FL 1:5; LAIT 3; LATS 1:1; MAL
5; MBL; MTCW 1, 2; MTFW 2005; NFS
2, 19; RGAL 4; RGSF 2; RHW; SATA
30; SSFS 2, 7, 16; TCWW 1, 2; TUS
Catherine II
See Catherine the Great
See also DLB 150
Catherine the Great 1729-1796 .... **LC 69**
See Catherine II
Cato, Marcus Porcius
234B.C.-149B.C. .... **CMLC 21**
See Cato the Elder
Cato, Marcus Porcius, the Elder
See Cato, Marcus Porcius
Cato the Elder
See Cato, Marcus Porcius
See also DLB 211
Catton, (Charles) Bruce 1899-1978 . **CLC 35**
See also AITN 1; CA 5-8R; CAAS 81-84;
CANR 7, 74; DLB 17; MTCW 2; MTFW
2005; SATA 2; SATA-Obit 24
Catullus c. 84B.C.-54B.C. .... **CMLC 18**
See also AW 2; CDWLB 1; DLB 211;
RGWL 2, 3; WLIT 8
Cauldwell, Frank
See King, Francis (Henry)
Caunitz, William J. 1933-1996 .... **CLC 34**
See also BEST 89:3; CA 130; CAAE 125;
CAAS 152; CANR 73; INT CA-130

Causley, Charles (Stanley)
1917-2003 .... **CLC 7**
See also CA 9-12R; CAAS 223; CANR 5,
35, 94; CLR 30; CP 1, 2, 3, 4, 5; CWRI
5; DLB 27; MTCW 1; SATA 3, 66; SATA-
Obit 149
Caute, (John) David 1936- .... **CLC 29**
See also CA 1-4R; 4; CANR 1, 33, 64, 120;
CBD; CD 5, 6; CN 1, 2, 3, 4, 5, 6, 7;
DAM NOV; DLB 14, 231
Cavafy, C(onstantine) P(eter) .... **PC 36;
TCLC 2, 7**
See Kavafis, Konstantinos Petrou
See also CA 148; DA3; DAM POET; EW
8; EWL 3; MTCW 2; PFS 19; RGWL 2,
3; WP
Cavalcanti, Guido c. 1250-c.
1300 .... **CMLC 54**
See also RGWL 2, 3; WLIT 7
Cavallo, Evelyn
See Spark, Muriel
Cavanna, Betty .... **CLC 12**
See Harrison, Elizabeth (Allen) Cavanna
See also JRDA; MAICYA 1; SAAS 4;
SATA 1, 30
Cavendish, Margaret Lucas
1623-1673 .... **LC 30, 132**
See also DLB 131, 252, 281; RGEL 2
Caxton, William 1421(?)-1491(?) .... **LC 17**
See also DLB 170
Cayer, D. M.
See Duffy, Maureen (Patricia)
Cayrol, Jean 1911-2005 .... **CLC 11**
See also CA 89-92; CAAS 236; DLB 83;
EWL 3
Cela (y Trulock), Camilo Jose
See Cela, Camilo Jose
See also CWW 2
Cela, Camilo Jose 1916-2002 .... **CLC 4, 13,
59, 122; HLC 1; SSC 71**
See Cela (y Trulock), Camilo Jose
See also BEST 90:2; CA 21-24R; 10; CAAS
206; CANR 21, 32, 76, 139; DAM MULT;
DLB 322; DLBY 1989; EW 13; EWL 3;
HW 1; MTCW 1, 2; MTFW 2005; RGSF
2; RGWL 2, 3
Celan, Paul .... **CLC 10, 19, 53, 82; PC 10**
See Antschel, Paul
See also CDWLB 2; DLB 69; EWL 3;
RGHL; RGWL 2, 3
Celine, Louis-Ferdinand .. **CLC 1, 3, 4, 7, 9,
15, 47, 124**
See Destouches, Louis-Ferdinand
See also DLB 72; EW 11; EWL 3; GFL
1789 to the Present; RGWL 2, 3
Cellini, Benvenuto 1500-1571 .... **LC 7**
See also WLIT 7
Cendrars, Blaise .... **CLC 18, 106**
See Sauser-Hall, Frederic
See also DLB 258; EWL 3; GFL 1789 to
the Present; RGWL 2, 3; WP
Centlivre, Susanna 1669(?)-1723 .... **DC 25;
LC 65**
See also DLB 84; RGEL 2
Cernuda (y Bidon), Luis
1902-1963 .... **CLC 54; PC 62**
See also CA 131; CAAS 89-92; DAM
POET; DLB 134; EWL 3; GLL 1; HW 1;
RGWL 2, 3
Cervantes, Lorna Dee 1954- ..... **HLCS 1; PC
35**
See also CA 131; CANR 80; CP 7; CWP;
DLB 82; EXPP; HW 1; LLW
Cervantes (Saavedra), Miguel de
1547-1616 .... **HLCS; LC 6, 23, 93; SSC
12; WLC 1**
See also AAYA 56; BYA 1, 14; DA; DAB;
DAC; DAM MST, NOV; EW 2; LAIT 1;
LATS 1:1; LMFS 1; NFS 8; RGSF 2;
RGWL 2, 3; TWA

Cesaire, Aime 1913- ..... **BLC 1; CLC 19, 32,
112; DC 22; PC 25**
See also BW 2, 3; CA 65-68; CANR 24,
43, 81; CWW 2; DA3; DAM MULT,
POET; DLB 321; EWL 3; GFL 1789 to
the Present; MTCW 1, 2; MTFW 2005;
WP
Chabon, Michael 1963- ... **CLC 55, 149; SSC
59**
See also AAYA 45; AMWS 11; CA 139;
CANR 57, 96, 127, 138; DLB 278; MAL
5; MTFW 2005; NFS 25; SATA 145
Chabrol, Claude 1930- .... **CLC 16**
See also CA 110
Chairil Anwar
See Anwar, Chairil
See also EWL 3
Challans, Mary 1905-1983
See Renault, Mary
See also CA 81-84; CAAS 111; CANR 74;
DA3; MTCW 2; MTFW 2005; SATA 23;
SATA-Obit 36; TEA
Challis, George
See Faust, Frederick (Schiller)
Chambers, Aidan 1934- .... **CLC 35**
See also AAYA 27; CA 25-28R; CANR 12,
31, 58, 116; JRDA; MAICYA 1, 2; SAAS
12; SATA 1, 69, 108, 171; WYA; YAW
Chambers, James 1948-
See Cliff, Jimmy
See also CAAE 124
Chambers, Jessie
See Lawrence, D(avid) H(erbert Richards)
See also GLL 1
Chambers, Robert W(illiam)
1865-1933 .... **SSC 92; TCLC 41**
See also CA 165; DLB 202; HGG; SATA
107; SUFW 1
Chambers, (David) Whittaker
1901-1961 .... **TCLC 129**
See also CAAS 89-92; DLB 303
Chamisso, Adelbert von
1781-1838 .... **NCLC 82**
See also DLB 90; RGWL 2, 3; SUFW 1
Chance, James T.
See Carpenter, John (Howard)
Chance, John T.
See Carpenter, John (Howard)
Chandler, Raymond (Thornton)
1888-1959 .... **SSC 23; TCLC 1, 7, 179**
See also AAYA 25; AMWC 2; AMWS 4;
BPFB 1; CA 129; CAAE 104; CANR 60,
107; CDALB 1929-1941; CMW 4; DA3;
DLB 226, 253; DLBD 6; EWL 3; MAL
5; MSW; MTCW 1, 2; MTFW 2005; NFS
17; RGAL 4; TUS
Chang, Diana 1934- .... **AAL**
See also CA 228; CWP; DLB 312; EXPP
Chang, Eileen 1921-1995 .... **AAL; SSC 28;
TCLC 184**
See Chang Ai-Ling; Zhang Ailing
See also CA 166
Chang, Jung 1952- .... **CLC 71**
See also CA 142
Chang Ai-Ling
See Chang, Eileen
See also EWL 3
Channing, William Ellery
1780-1842 .... **NCLC 17**
See also DLB 1, 59, 235; RGAL 4
Chao, Patricia 1955- .... **CLC 119**
See also CA 163; CANR 155
Chaplin, Charles Spencer
1889-1977 .... **CLC 16**
See Chaplin, Charlie
See also CA 81-84; CAAS 73-76
Chaplin, Charlie
See Chaplin, Charles Spencer
See also AAYA 61; DLB 44

Chopin, Kate .... **SSC 8, 68; TCLC 127; WLCS**
See Chopin, Katherine
See also AAYA 33; AMWR 2; AMWS 1; BYA 11, 15; CDALB 1865-1917; DA; DAB; DLB 12, 78; EXPN; EXPS; FL 1:3; FW; LAIT 3; MAL 5; MBL; NFS 3; RGAL 4; RGSF 2; SSFS 2, 13, 17; TUS

Chopin, Katherine 1851-1904
See Chopin, Kate
See also CA 122; CAAE 104; DA3; DAC; DAM MST, NOV

Chretien de Troyes c. 12th cent. - . **CMLC 10**
See also DLB 208; EW 1; RGWL 2, 3; TWA

Christie
See Ichikawa, Kon

Christie, Agatha (Mary Clarissa)
1890-1976 .. **CLC 1, 6, 8, 12, 39, 48, 110**
See also AAYA 9; AITN 1, 2; BPFB 1; BRWS 2; CA 17-20R; CAAS 61-64; CANR 10, 37, 108; CBD; CDBLB 1914-1945; CMW 4; CN 1, 2; CPW; CWD; DA3; DAB; DAC; DAM NOV; DFS 2; DLB 13, 77, 245; MSW; MTCW 1, 2; MTFW 2005; NFS 8; RGEL 2; RHW; SATA 36; TEA; YAW

Christie, Philippa .... **CLC 21**
See Pearce, Philippa
See also BYA 5; CANR 109; CLR 9; DLB 161; MAICYA 1; SATA 1, 67, 129

Christine de Pisan
See Christine de Pizan
See also FW

Christine de Pizan 1365(?)-1431(?) ...... **LC 9, 130; PC 68**
See Christine de Pisan; de Pizan, Christine
See also DLB 208; FL 1:1; RGWL 2, 3

Chuang-Tzu c. 369B.C.-c.
286B.C. .... **CMLC 57**

Chubb, Elmer
See Masters, Edgar Lee

Chulkov, Mikhail Dmitrievich
1743-1792 .... **LC 2**
See also DLB 150

Churchill, Caryl 1938- .... **CLC 31, 55, 157; DC 5**
See Churchill, Chick
See also BRWS 4; CA 102; CANR 22, 46, 108; CBD; CD 6; CWD; DFS 12, 16; DLB 13, 310; EWL 3; FW; MTCW 1; RGEL 2

Churchill, Charles 1731-1764 .... **LC 3**
See also DLB 109; RGEL 2

Churchill, Chick
See Churchill, Caryl
See also CD 5

Churchill, Sir Winston (Leonard Spencer)
1874-1965 .... **TCLC 113**
See also BRW 6; CA 97-100; CDBLB 1890-1914; DA3; DLB 100, 329; DLBD 16; LAIT 4; MTCW 1, 2

Chute, Carolyn 1947- .... **CLC 39**
See also CA 123; CANR 135; CN 7

Ciardi, John (Anthony) 1916-1986 . **CLC 10, 40, 44, 129; PC 69**
See also CA 5-8R; 2; CAAS 118; CANR 5, 33; CLR 19; CP 1, 2, 3, 4; CWRI 5; DAM POET; DLB 5; DLBY 1986; INT CANR-5; MAICYA 1, 2; MAL 5; MTCW 1, 2; MTFW 2005; RGAL 4; SAAS 26; SATA 1, 65; SATA-Obit 46

Cibber, Colley 1671-1757 .... **LC 66**
See also DLB 84; RGEL 2

Cicero, Marcus Tullius
106B.C.-43B.C. .... **CMLC 3, 81**
See also AW 1; CDWLB 1; DLB 211; RGWL 2, 3; WLIT 8

Cimino, Michael 1943- .... **CLC 16**
See also CA 105

Cioran, E(mil) M. 1911-1995 .... **CLC 64**
See also CA 25-28R; CAAS 149; CANR 91; DLB 220; EWL 3

Cisneros, Sandra 1954- .... **CLC 69, 118, 193; HLC 1; PC 52; SSC 32, 72**
See also AAYA 9, 53; AMWS 7; CA 131; CANR 64, 118; CLR 123; CN 7; CWP; DA3; DAM MULT; DLB 122, 152; EWL 3; EXPN; FL 1:5; FW; HW 1, 2; LAIT 5; LATS 1:2; LLW; MAICYA 2; MAL 5; MTCW 2; MTFW 2005; NFS 2; PFS 19; RGAL 4; RGSF 2; SSFS 3, 13; WLIT 1; YAW

Cixous, Helene 1937- .... **CLC 92**
See also CA 126; CANR 55, 123; CWW 2; DLB 83, 242; EWL 3; FL 1:5; FW; GLL 2; MTCW 1, 2; MTFW 2005; TWA

Clair, Rene .... **CLC 20**
See Chomette, Rene Lucien

Clampitt, Amy 1920-1994 .... **CLC 32; PC 19**
See also AMWS 9; CA 110; CAAS 146; CANR 29, 79; CP 4, 5; DLB 105; MAL 5

Clancy, Thomas L., Jr. 1947-
See Clancy, Tom
See also CA 131; CAAE 125; CANR 62, 105; DA3; INT CA-131; MTCW 1, 2; MTFW 2005

Clancy, Tom .... **CLC 45, 112**
See Clancy, Thomas L., Jr.
See also AAYA 9, 51; BEST 89:1, 90:1; BPFB 1; BYA 10, 11; CANR 132; CMW 4; CPW; DAM NOV, POP; DLB 227

Clare, John 1793-1864 .. **NCLC 9, 86; PC 23**
See also BRWS 11; DAB; DAM POET; DLB 55, 96; RGEL 2

Clarin
See Alas (y Urena), Leopoldo (Enrique Garcia)

Clark, Al C.
See Goines, Donald

Clark, Brian (Robert)
See Clark, (Robert) Brian
See also CD 6

Clark, (Robert) Brian 1932- .... **CLC 29**
See Clark, Brian (Robert)
See also CA 41-44R; CANR 67; CBD; CD 5

Clark, Curt
See Westlake, Donald E.

Clark, Eleanor 1913-1996 .... **CLC 5, 19**
See also CA 9-12R; CAAS 151; CANR 41; CN 1, 2, 3, 4, 5, 6; DLB 6

Clark, J. P.
See Clark Bekederemo, J.P.
See also CDWLB 3; DLB 117

Clark, John Pepper
See Clark Bekederemo, J.P.
See also AFW; CD 5; CP 1, 2, 3, 4, 5, 6, 7; RGEL 2

Clark, Kenneth (Mackenzie)
1903-1983 .... **TCLC 147**
See also CA 93-96; CAAS 109; CANR 36; MTCW 1, 2; MTFW 2005

Clark, M. R.
See Clark, Mavis Thorpe

Clark, Mavis Thorpe 1909-1999 ...... **CLC 12**
See also CA 57-60; CANR 8, 37, 107; CLR 30; CWRI 5; MAICYA 1, 2; SAAS 5; SATA 8, 74

Clark, Walter Van Tilburg
1909-1971 .... **CLC 28**
See also CA 9-12R; CAAS 33-36R; CANR 63, 113; CN 1; DLB 9, 206; LAIT 2; MAL 5; RGAL 4; SATA 8; TCWW 1, 2

Clark Bekederemo, J.P. 1935- . **BLC 1; CLC 38; DC 5**
See Bekederemo, J. P. Clark; Clark, J. P.; Clark, John Pepper
See also BW 1; CA 65-68; CANR 16, 72; DAM DRAM, MULT; DFS 13; EWL 3; MTCW 2; MTFW 2005

Clarke, Arthur C. 1917- .... **CLC 1, 4, 13, 18, 35, 136; SSC 3**
See also AAYA 4, 33; BPFB 1; BYA 13; CA 1-4R; CANR 2, 28, 55, 74, 130; CLR 119; CN 1, 2, 3, 4, 5, 6, 7; CPW; DA3; DAM POP; DLB 261; JRDA; LAIT 5; MAICYA 1, 2; MTCW 1, 2; MTFW 2005; SATA 13, 70, 115; SCFW 1, 2; SFW 4; SSFS 4, 18; TCLE 1:1; YAW

Clarke, Austin 1896-1974 .... **CLC 6, 9**
See also CA 29-32; CAAS 49-52; CAP 2; CP 1; DAM POET; DLB 10, 20; EWL 3; RGEL 2

Clarke, Austin C. 1934- . **BLC 1; CLC 8, 53; SSC 45**
See also BW 1; CA 25-28R; 16; CANR 14, 32, 68, 140; CN 1, 2, 3, 4, 5, 6, 7; DAC; DAM MULT; DLB 53, 125; DNFS 2; MTCW 2; MTFW 2005; RGSF 2

Clarke, Gillian 1937- .... **CLC 61**
See also CA 106; CP 3, 4, 5, 6, 7; CWP; DLB 40

Clarke, Marcus (Andrew Hislop)
1846-1881 .... **NCLC 19; SSC 94**
See also DLB 230; RGEL 2; RGSF 2

Clarke, Shirley 1925-1997 .... **CLC 16**
See also CA 189

Clash, The
See Headon, (Nicky) Topper; Jones, Mick; Simonon, Paul; Strummer, Joe

Claudel, Paul (Louis Charles Marie)
1868-1955 .... **TCLC 2, 10**
See also CA 165; CAAE 104; DLB 192, 258, 321; EW 8; EWL 3; GFL 1789 to the Present; RGWL 2, 3; TWA

Claudian 370(?)-404(?) .... **CMLC 46**
See also RGWL 2, 3

Claudius, Matthias 1740-1815 .... **NCLC 75**
See also DLB 97

Clavell, James 1925-1994 .... **CLC 6, 25, 87**
See also BPFB 1; CA 25-28R; CAAS 146; CANR 26, 48; CN 5; CPW; DA3; DAM NOV, POP; MTCW 1, 2; MTFW 2005; NFS 10; RHW

Clayman, Gregory .... **CLC 65**

Cleaver, (Leroy) Eldridge
1935-1998 .... **BLC 1; CLC 30, 119**
See also BW 1, 3; CA 21-24R; CAAS 167; CANR 16, 75; DA3; DAM MULT; MTCW 2; YAW

Cleese, John (Marwood) 1939- .... **CLC 21**
See Monty Python
See also CA 116; CAAE 112; CANR 35; MTCW 1

Cleishbotham, Jebediah
See Scott, Sir Walter

Cleland, John 1710-1789 .... **LC 2, 48**
See also DLB 39; RGEL 2

Clemens, Samuel Langhorne 1835-1910
See Twain, Mark
See also CA 135; CAAE 104; CDALB 1865-1917; DA; DA3; DAB; DAC; DAM MST, NOV; DLB 12, 23, 64, 74, 186, 189; JRDA; LMFS 1; MAICYA 1, 2; NCFS 4; NFS 20; SATA 100; YABC 2

Clement of Alexandria
150(?)-215(?) .... **CMLC 41**

Cleophil
See Congreve, William

Clerihew, E.
See Bentley, E(dmund) C(lerihew)

Clerk, N. W.
See Lewis, C.S.

Cleveland, John 1613-1658 .... **LC 106**
See also DLB 126; RGEL 2

Cliff, Jimmy .... **CLC 21**
See Chambers, James
See also CA 193

Cliff, Michelle 1946- .... **BLCS; CLC 120**
See also BW 2; CA 116; CANR 39, 72; CD-WLB 3; DLB 157; FW; GLL 2

Clifford, Lady Anne 1590-1676 .... **LC 76**
See also DLB 151

Clifton, Lucille 1936- ... **BLC 1; CLC 19, 66, 162; PC 17**
See also AFAW 2; BW 2, 3; CA 49-52; CANR 2, 24, 42, 76, 97, 138; CLR 5; CP 2, 3, 4, 5, 6, 7; CSW; CWP; CWRI 5; DA3; DAM MULT, POET; DLB 5, 41; EXPP; MAICYA 1, 2; MTCW 1, 2; MTFW 2005; PFS 1, 14; SATA 20, 69, 128; WP

Clinton, Dirk
See Silverberg, Robert

Clough, Arthur Hugh 1819-1861 .. **NCLC 27, 163**
See also BRW 5; DLB 32; RGEL 2

Clutha, Janet Paterson Frame 1924-2004
See Frame, Janet
See also CA 1-4R; CAAS 224; CANR 2, 36, 76, 135; MTCW 1, 2; SATA 119

Clyne, Terence
See Blatty, William Peter

Cobalt, Martin
See Mayne, William (James Carter)

Cobb, Irvin S(hrewsbury) 1876-1944 .... **TCLC 77**
See also CA 175; DLB 11, 25, 86

Cobbett, William 1763-1835 .... **NCLC 49**
See also DLB 43, 107, 158; RGEL 2

Coburn, D(onald) L(ee) 1938- .... **CLC 10**
See also CA 89-92; DFS 23

Cocteau, Jean 1889-1963 ... **CLC 1, 8, 15, 16, 43; DC 17; TCLC 119; WLC 2**
See also AAYA 74; CA 25-28; CANR 40; CAP 2; DA; DA3; DAB; DAC; DAM DRAM, MST, NOV; DFS 24; DLB 65, 258, 321; EW 10; EWL 3; GFL 1789 to the Present; MTCW 1, 2; RGWL 2, 3; TWA

Cocteau, Jean Maurice Eugene Clement
See Cocteau, Jean

Codrescu, Andrei 1946- .... **CLC 46, 121**
See also CA 33-36R; 19; CANR 13, 34, 53, 76, 125; CN 7; DA3; DAM POET; MAL 5; MTCW 2; MTFW 2005

Coe, Max
See Bourne, Randolph S(illiman)

Coe, Tucker
See Westlake, Donald E.

Coen, Ethan 1958- .... **CLC 108**
See also AAYA 54; CA 126; CANR 85

Coen, Joel 1955- .... **CLC 108**
See also AAYA 54; CA 126; CANR 119

The Coen Brothers
See Coen, Ethan; Coen, Joel

Coetzee, J.M. 1940- ...... **CLC 23, 33, 66, 117, 161, 162**
See also AAYA 37; AFW; BRWS 6; CA 77-80; CANR 41, 54, 74, 114, 133; CN 4, 5, 6, 7; DA3; DAM NOV; DLB 225, 326, 329; EWL 3; LMFS 2; MTCW 1, 2; MTFW 2005; NFS 21; WLIT 2; WWE 1

Coetzee, John Maxwell
See Coetzee, J.M.

Coffey, Brian
See Koontz, Dean R.

Coffin, Robert P(eter) Tristram 1892-1955 .... **TCLC 95**
See also CA 169; CAAE 123; DLB 45

Cohan, George M. 1878-1942 .... **TCLC 60**
See also CA 157; DLB 249; RGAL 4

Cohan, George Michael
See Cohan, George M.

Cohen, Arthur A(llen) 1928-1986 ...... **CLC 7, 31**
See also CA 1-4R; CAAS 120; CANR 1, 17, 42; DLB 28; RGHL

Cohen, Leonard 1934- .... **CLC 3, 38**
See also CA 21-24R; CANR 14, 69; CN 1, 2, 3, 4, 5, 6; CP 1, 2, 3, 4, 5, 6, 7; DAC; DAM MST; DLB 53; EWL 3; MTCW 1

Cohen, Leonard Norman
See Cohen, Leonard

Cohen, Matt(hew) 1942-1999 .... **CLC 19**
See also CA 61-64; 18; CAAS 187; CANR 40; CN 1, 2, 3, 4, 5, 6; DAC; DLB 53

Cohen-Solal, Annie 1948- .... **CLC 50**
See also CA 239

Colegate, Isabel 1931- .... **CLC 36**
See also CA 17-20R; CANR 8, 22, 74; CN 4, 5, 6, 7; DLB 14, 231; INT CANR-22; MTCW 1

Coleman, Emmett
See Reed, Ishmael

Coleridge, Hartley 1796-1849 .... **NCLC 90**
See also DLB 96

Coleridge, M. E.
See Coleridge, Mary E(lizabeth)

Coleridge, Mary E(lizabeth) 1861-1907 .... **TCLC 73**
See also CA 166; CAAE 116; DLB 19, 98

Coleridge, Samuel Taylor 1772-1834 .... **NCLC 9, 54, 99, 111, 177; PC 11, 39, 67; WLC 2**
See also AAYA 66; BRW 4; BRWR 2; BYA 4; CDBLB 1789-1832; DA; DA3; DAB; DAC; DAM MST, POET; DLB 93, 107; EXPP; LATS 1:1; LMFS 1; PAB; PFS 4, 5; RGEL 2; TEA; WLIT 3; WP

Coleridge, Sara 1802-1852 .... **NCLC 31**
See also DLB 199

Coles, Don 1928- .... **CLC 46**
See also CA 115; CANR 38; CP 5, 6, 7

Coles, Robert (Martin) 1929- .... **CLC 108**
See also CA 45-48; CANR 3, 32, 66, 70, 135; INT CANR-32; SATA 23

Colette, (Sidonie-Gabrielle) 1873-1954 .. **SSC 10, 93; TCLC 1, 5, 16**
See Willy, Colette
See also CA 131; CAAE 104; DA3; DAM NOV; DLB 65; EW 9; EWL 3; GFL 1789 to the Present; MTCW 1, 2; MTFW 2005; RGWL 2, 3; TWA

Collett, (Jacobine) Camilla (Wergeland) 1813-1895 .... **NCLC 22**

Collier, Christopher 1930- .... **CLC 30**
See also AAYA 13; BYA 2; CA 33-36R; CANR 13, 33, 102; JRDA; MAICYA 1, 2; SATA 16, 70; WYA; YAW 1

Collier, James Lincoln 1928- .... **CLC 30**
See also AAYA 13; BYA 2; CA 9-12R; CANR 4, 33, 60, 102; CLR 3; DAM POP; JRDA; MAICYA 1, 2; SAAS 21; SATA 8, 70, 166; WYA; YAW 1

Collier, Jeremy 1650-1726 .... **LC 6**
See also DLB 336

Collier, John 1901-1980 . **SSC 19; TCLC 127**
See also CA 65-68; CAAS 97-100; CANR 10; CN 1, 2; DLB 77, 255; FANT; SUFW 1

Collier, Mary 1690-1762 .... **LC 86**
See also DLB 95

Collingwood, R(obin) G(eorge) 1889(?)-1943 .... **TCLC 67**
See also CA 155; CAAE 117; DLB 262

Collins, Billy 1941- .... **PC 68**
See also AAYA 64; CA 151; CANR 92; CP 7; MTFW 2005; PFS 18

Collins, Hunt
See Hunter, Evan

Collins, Linda 1931- .... **CLC 44**
See also CA 125

Collins, Tom
See Furphy, Joseph
See also RGEL 2

Collins, (William) Wilkie 1824-1889 .... **NCLC 1, 18, 93; SSC 93**
See also BRWS 6; CDBLB 1832-1890; CMW 4; DLB 18, 70, 159; GL 2; MSW; RGEL 2; RGSF 2; SUFW 1; WLIT 4

Collins, William 1721-1759 ...... **LC 4, 40; PC 72**
See also BRW 3; DAM POET; DLB 109; RGEL 2

Collodi, Carlo .... **NCLC 54**
See Lorenzini, Carlo
See also CLR 5, 120; WCH; WLIT 7

Colman, George
See Glassco, John

Colman, George, the Elder 1732-1794 .... **LC 98**
See also RGEL 2

Colonna, Vittoria 1492-1547 .... **LC 71**
See also RGWL 2, 3

Colt, Winchester Remington
See Hubbard, L. Ron

Colter, Cyrus J. 1910-2002 .... **CLC 58**
See also BW 1; CA 65-68; CAAS 205; CANR 10, 66; CN 2, 3, 4, 5, 6; DLB 33

Colton, James
See Hansen, Joseph
See also GLL 1

Colum, Padraic 1881-1972 .... **CLC 28**
See also BYA 4; CA 73-76; CAAS 33-36R; CANR 35; CLR 36; CP 1; CWRI 5; DLB 19; MAICYA 1, 2; MTCW 1; RGEL 2; SATA 15; WCH

Colvin, James
See Moorcock, Michael

Colwin, Laurie (E.) 1944-1992 .... **CLC 5, 13, 23, 84**
See also CA 89-92; CAAS 139; CANR 20, 46; DLB 218; DLBY 1980; MTCW 1

Comfort, Alex(ander) 1920-2000 .... **CLC 7**
See also CA 1-4R; CAAS 190; CANR 1, 45; CN 1, 2, 3, 4; CP 1, 2, 3, 4, 5, 6, 7; DAM POP; MTCW 2

Comfort, Montgomery
See Campbell, (John) Ramsey

Compton-Burnett, I(vy) 1892(?)-1969 .... **CLC 1, 3, 10, 15, 34; TCLC 180**
See also BRW 7; CA 1-4R; CAAS 25-28R; CANR 4; DAM NOV; DLB 36; EWL 3; MTCW 1, 2; RGEL 2

Comstock, Anthony 1844-1915 ...... **TCLC 13**
See also CA 169; CAAE 110

Comte, Auguste 1798-1857 .... **NCLC 54**

Conan Doyle, Arthur
See Doyle, Sir Arthur Conan
See also BPFB 1; BYA 4, 5, 11

Conde (Abellan), Carmen 1901-1996 .... **HLCS 1**
See also CA 177; CWW 2; DLB 108; EWL 3; HW 2

Conde, Maryse 1937- ..... **BLCS; CLC 52, 92**
See also BW 2, 3; CA 190; 110, 190; CANR 30, 53, 76; CWW 2; DAM MULT; EWL 3; MTCW 2; MTFW 2005

Condillac, Etienne Bonnot de 1714-1780 .... **LC 26**
See also DLB 313

Condon, Richard 1915-1996 ...... **CLC 4, 6, 8, 10, 45, 100**
See also BEST 90:3; BPFB 1; CA 1-4R; 1; CAAS 151; CANR 2, 23, 164; CMW 4; CN 1, 2, 3, 4, 5, 6; DAM NOV; INT CANR-23; MAL 5; MTCW 1, 2

Condon, Richard Thomas
See Condon, Richard

Cruz, Victor Hernandez 1949- ... **HLC 1; PC 37**
See also BW 2; CA 65-68; 17; CANR 14, 32, 74, 132; CP 1, 2, 3, 4, 5, 6, 7; DAM MULT, POET; DLB 41; DNFS 1; EXPP; HW 1, 2; LLW; MTCW 2; MTFW 2005; PFS 16; WP

Cryer, Gretchen (Kiger) 1935- .... **CLC 21**
See also CA 123; CAAE 114

Csath, Geza .... **TCLC 13**
See Brenner, Jozef
See also CAAE 111

Cudlip, David R(ockwell) 1933- .... **CLC 34**
See also CA 177

Cullen, Countee 1903-1946 . **BLC 1; HR 1:2; PC 20; TCLC 4, 37; WLCS**
See also AFAW 2; AMWS 4; BW 1; CA 124; CAAE 108; CDALB 1917-1929; DA; DA3; DAC; DAM MST, MULT, POET; DLB 4, 48, 51; EWL 3; EXPP; LMFS 2; MAL 5; MTCW 1, 2; MTFW 2005; PFS 3; RGAL 4; SATA 18; WP

Culleton, Beatrice 1949- .... **NNAL**
See also CA 120; CANR 83; DAC

Cum, R.
See Crumb, R.

Cumberland, Richard
1732-1811 .... **NCLC 167**
See also DLB 89; RGEL 2

Cummings, Bruce F(rederick) 1889-1919
See Barbellion, W. N. P.
See also CA 123

Cummings, E(dward) E(stlin)
1894-1962 .. **CLC 1, 3, 8, 12, 15, 68; PC 5; TCLC 137; WLC 2**
See also AAYA 41; AMW; CA 73-76; CANR 31; CDALB 1929-1941; DA; DA3; DAB; DAC; DAM MST, POET; DLB 4, 48; EWL 3; EXPP; MAL 5; MTCW 1, 2; MTFW 2005; PAB; PFS 1, 3, 12, 13, 19; RGAL 4; TUS; WP

Cummins, Maria Susanna
1827-1866 .... **NCLC 139**
See also DLB 42; YABC 1

Cunha, Euclides (Rodrigues Pimenta) da
1866-1909 .... **TCLC 24**
See also CA 219; CAAE 123; DLB 307; LAW; WLIT 1

Cunningham, E. V.
See Fast, Howard

Cunningham, J(ames) V(incent)
1911-1985 .... **CLC 3, 31**
See also CA 1-4R; CAAS 115; CANR 1, 72; CP 1, 2, 3, 4; DLB 5

Cunningham, Julia (Woolfolk)
1916- .... **CLC 12**
See also CA 9-12R; CANR 4, 19, 36; CWRI 5; JRDA; MAICYA 1, 2; SAAS 2; SATA 1, 26, 132

Cunningham, Michael 1952- .... **CLC 34**
See also AMWS 15; CA 136; CANR 96, 160; CN 7; DLB 292; GLL 2; MTFW 2005; NFS 23

Cunninghame Graham, R. B.
See Cunninghame Graham, Robert (Gallnigad) Bontine

Cunninghame Graham, Robert (Gallnigad) Bontine 1852-1936 .... **TCLC 19**
See Graham, R(obert) B(ontine) Cunninghame
See also CA 184; CAAE 119

Curnow, (Thomas) Allen (Monro)
1911-2001 .... **PC 48**
See also CA 69-72; CAAS 202; CANR 48, 99; CP 1, 2, 3, 4, 5, 6, 7; EWL 3; RGEL 2

Currie, Ellen 19(?)- .... **CLC 44**

Curtin, Philip
See Lowndes, Marie Adelaide (Belloc)

Curtin, Phillip
See Lowndes, Marie Adelaide (Belloc)

Curtis, Price
See Ellison, Harlan

Cusanus, Nicolaus 1401-1464 .... **LC 80**
See Nicholas of Cusa

Cutrate, Joe
See Spiegelman, Art

Cynewulf c. 770- .... **CMLC 23**
See also DLB 146; RGEL 2

Cyrano de Bergerac, Savinien de
1619-1655 .... **LC 65**
See also DLB 268; GFL Beginnings to 1789; RGWL 2, 3

Cyril of Alexandria c. 375-c. 430 . **CMLC 59**

Czaczkes, Shmuel Yosef Halevi
See Agnon, S(hmuel) Y(osef Halevi)

Dabrowska, Maria (Szumska)
1889-1965 .... **CLC 15**
See also CA 106; CDWLB 4; DLB 215; EWL 3

Dabydeen, David 1955- .... **CLC 34**
See also BW 1; CA 125; CANR 56, 92; CN 6, 7; CP 5, 6, 7

Dacey, Philip 1939- .... **CLC 51**
See also CA 231; 37-40R, 231; 17; CANR 14, 32, 64; CP 4, 5, 6, 7; DLB 105

Dacre, Charlotte c. 1772-1825(?) . **NCLC 151**

Dafydd ap Gwilym c. 1320-c. 1380 ..... **PC 56**

Dagerman, Stig (Halvard)
1923-1954 .... **TCLC 17**
See also CA 155; CAAE 117; DLB 259; EWL 3

D'Aguiar, Fred 1960- .... **CLC 145**
See also CA 148; CANR 83, 101; CN 7; CP 5, 6, 7; DLB 157; EWL 3

Dahl, Roald 1916-1990 ...... **CLC 1, 6, 18, 79; TCLC 173**
See also AAYA 15; BPFB 1; BRWS 4; BYA 5; CA 1-4R; CAAS 133; CANR 6, 32, 37, 62; CLR 1, 7, 41, 111; CN 1, 2, 3, 4; CPW; DA3; DAB; DAC; DAM MST, NOV, POP; DLB 139, 255; HGG; JRDA; MAICYA 1, 2; MTCW 1, 2; MTFW 2005; RGSF 2; SATA 1, 26, 73; SATA-Obit 65; SSFS 4; TEA; YAW

Dahlberg, Edward 1900-1977 .. **CLC 1, 7, 14**
See also CA 9-12R; CAAS 69-72; CANR 31, 62; CN 1, 2; DLB 48; MAL 5; MTCW 1; RGAL 4

Daitch, Susan 1954- .... **CLC 103**
See also CA 161

Dale, Colin .... **TCLC 18**
See Lawrence, T(homas) E(dward)

Dale, George E.
See Asimov, Isaac

d'Alembert, Jean Le Rond
1717-1783 .... **LC 126**

Dalton, Roque 1935-1975(?) ..... **HLCS 1; PC 36**
See also CA 176; DLB 283; HW 1

Daly, Elizabeth 1878-1967 .... **CLC 52**
See also CA 23-24; CAAS 25-28R; CANR 60; CAP 2; CMW 4

Daly, Mary 1928- .... **CLC 173**
See also CA 25-28R; CANR 30, 62, 166; FW; GLL 1; MTCW 1

Daly, Maureen 1921-2006 .... **CLC 17**
See also AAYA 5, 58; BYA 6; CAAS 253; CANR 37, 83, 108; CLR 96; JRDA; MAICYA 1, 2; SAAS 1; SATA 2, 129; SATA-Obit 176; WYA; YAW

Damas, Leon-Gontran 1912-1978 .... **CLC 84**
See also BW 1; CA 125; CAAS 73-76; EWL 3

Dana, Richard Henry Sr.
1787-1879 .... **NCLC 53**

Daniel, Samuel 1562(?)-1619 .... **LC 24**
See also DLB 62; RGEL 2

Daniels, Brett
See Adler, Renata

Dannay, Frederic 1905-1982 .... **CLC 11**
See Queen, Ellery
See also CA 1-4R; CAAS 107; CANR 1, 39; CMW 4; DAM POP; DLB 137; MTCW 1

D'Annunzio, Gabriele 1863-1938 ... **TCLC 6, 40**
See also CA 155; CAAE 104; EW 8; EWL 3; RGWL 2, 3; TWA; WLIT 7

Danois, N. le
See Gourmont, Remy(-Marie-Charles) de

Dante 1265-1321 .... **CMLC 3, 18, 39, 70; PC 21; WLCS**
See Alighieri, Dante
See also DA; DA3; DAB; DAC; DAM MST, POET; EFS 1; EW 1; LAIT 1; RGWL 2, 3; TWA; WP

d'Antibes, Germain
See Simenon, Georges (Jacques Christian)

Danticat, Edwidge 1969- . **CLC 94, 139, 228; SSC 100**
See also AAYA 29; CA 192; 152, 192; CANR 73, 129; CN 7; DNFS 1; EXPS; LATS 1:2; MTCW 2; MTFW 2005; SSFS 1, 25; YAW

Danvers, Dennis 1947- .... **CLC 70**

Danziger, Paula 1944-2004 .... **CLC 21**
See also AAYA 4, 36; BYA 6, 7, 14; CA 115; CAAE 112; CAAS 229; CANR 37, 132; CLR 20; JRDA; MAICYA 1, 2; MTFW 2005; SATA 36, 63, 102, 149; SATA-Brief 30; SATA-Obit 155; WYA; YAW

Da Ponte, Lorenzo 1749-1838 .... **NCLC 50**

d'Aragona, Tullia 1510(?)-1556 .... **LC 121**

Dario, Ruben 1867-1916 .... **HLC 1; PC 15; TCLC 4**
See also CA 131; CANR 81; DAM MULT; DLB 290; EWL 3; HW 1, 2; LAW; MTCW 1, 2; MTFW 2005; RGWL 2, 3

Darley, George 1795-1846 .... **NCLC 2**
See also DLB 96; RGEL 2

Darrow, Clarence (Seward)
1857-1938 .... **TCLC 81**
See also CA 164; DLB 303

Darwin, Charles 1809-1882 .... **NCLC 57**
See also BRWS 7; DLB 57, 166; LATS 1:1; RGEL 2; TEA; WLIT 4

Darwin, Erasmus 1731-1802 .... **NCLC 106**
See also DLB 93; RGEL 2

Daryush, Elizabeth 1887-1977 ...... **CLC 6, 19**
See also CA 49-52; CANR 3, 81; DLB 20

Das, Kamala 1934- .... **CLC 191; PC 43**
See also CA 101; CANR 27, 59; CP 1, 2, 3, 4, 5, 6, 7; CWP; DLB 323; FW

Dasgupta, Surendranath
1887-1952 .... **TCLC 81**
See also CA 157

Dashwood, Edmee Elizabeth Monica de la Pasture 1890-1943
See Delafield, E. M.
See also CA 154; CAAE 119

da Silva, Antonio Jose
1705-1739 .... **NCLC 114**

Daudet, (Louis Marie) Alphonse
1840-1897 .... **NCLC 1**
See also DLB 123; GFL 1789 to the Present; RGSF 2

Daudet, Alphonse Marie Leon
1867-1942 .... **SSC 94**
See also CA 217

d'Aulnoy, Marie-Catherine c.
1650-1705 .... **LC 100**

Daumal, Rene 1908-1944 .... **TCLC 14**
See also CA 247; CAAE 114; EWL 3

Davenant, William 1606-1668 .... **LC 13**
See also DLB 58, 126; RGEL 2

De La Salle, Innocent
 See Hartmann, Sadakichi
de Laureamont, Comte
 See Lautreamont
Delbanco, Nicholas 1942- ..... **CLC 6, 13, 167**
 See also CA 189; 17-20R, 189; 2; CANR
 29, 55, 116, 150; CN 7; DLB 6, 234
Delbanco, Nicholas Franklin
 See Delbanco, Nicholas
del Castillo, Michel 1933- .... **CLC 38**
 See also CA 109; CANR 77
Deledda, Grazia (Cosima)
 1875(?)-1936 .... **TCLC 23**
 See also CA 205; CAAE 123; DLB 264,
 329; EWL 3; RGWL 2, 3; WLIT 7
Deleuze, Gilles 1925-1995 .... **TCLC 116**
 See also DLB 296
Delgado, Abelardo (Lalo) B(arrientos)
 1930-2004 .... **HLC 1**
 See also CA 131; 15; CAAS 230; CANR
 90; DAM MST, MULT; DLB 82; HW 1,
 2
Delibes, Miguel .... **CLC 8, 18**
 See Delibes Setien, Miguel
 See also DLB 322; EWL 3
Delibes Setien, Miguel 1920-
 See Delibes, Miguel
 See also CA 45-48; CANR 1, 32; CWW 2;
 HW 1; MTCW 1
DeLillo, Don 1936- ..... **CLC 8, 10, 13, 27, 39,**
 54, 76, 143, 210, 213
 See also AMWC 2; AMWS 6; BEST 89:1;
 BPFB 1; CA 81-84; CANR 21, 76, 92,
 133; CN 3, 4, 5, 6, 7; CPW; DA3; DAM
 NOV, POP; DLB 6, 173; EWL 3; MAL 5;
 MTCW 1, 2; MTFW 2005; RGAL 4; TUS
de Lisser, H. G.
 See De Lisser, H(erbert) G(eorge)
 See also DLB 117
De Lisser, H(erbert) G(eorge)
 1878-1944 .... **TCLC 12**
 See de Lisser, H. G.
 See also BW 2; CA 152; CAAE 109
Deloire, Pierre
 See Peguy, Charles (Pierre)
Deloney, Thomas 1543(?)-1600 .... **LC 41; PC**
 79
 See also DLB 167; RGEL 2
Deloria, Ella (Cara) 1889-1971(?) ..... **NNAL**
 See also CA 152; DAM MULT; DLB 175
Deloria, Vine, Jr. 1933-2005 .... **CLC 21, 122;**
 NNAL
 See also CA 53-56; CAAS 245; CANR 5,
 20, 48, 98; DAM MULT; DLB 175;
 MTCW 1; SATA 21; SATA-Obit 171
Deloria, Vine Victor, Jr.
 See Deloria, Vine, Jr.
del Valle-Inclan, Ramon (Maria)
 See Valle-Inclan, Ramon (Maria) del
 See also DLB 322
Del Vecchio, John M(ichael) 1947- .. **CLC 29**
 See also CA 110; DLBD 9
de Man, Paul (Adolph Michel)
 1919-1983 .... **CLC 55**
 See also CA 128; CAAS 111; CANR 61;
 DLB 67; MTCW 1, 2
DeMarinis, Rick 1934- .... **CLC 54**
 See also CA 184; 57-60, 184; 24; CANR 9,
 25, 50, 160; DLB 218; TCWW 2
de Maupassant, (Henri Rene Albert) Guy
 See Maupassant, (Henri Rene Albert) Guy
 de
Dembry, R. Emmet
 See Murfree, Mary Noailles
Demby, William 1922- .... **BLC 1; CLC 53**
 See also BW 1, 3; CA 81-84; CANR 81;
 DAM MULT; DLB 33
de Menton, Francisco
 See Chin, Frank (Chew, Jr.)

Demetrius of Phalerum c.
 307B.C.- .... **CMLC 34**
Demijohn, Thom
 See Disch, Thomas M.
De Mille, James 1833-1880 .... **NCLC 123**
 See also DLB 99, 251
Deming, Richard 1915-1983
 See Queen, Ellery
 See also CA 9-12R; CANR 3, 94; SATA 24
Democritus c. 460B.C.-c. 370B.C. . **CMLC 47**
de Montaigne, Michel (Eyquem)
 See Montaigne, Michel (Eyquem) de
de Montherlant, Henry (Milon)
 See Montherlant, Henry (Milon) de
Demosthenes 384B.C.-322B.C. ...... **CMLC 13**
 See also AW 1; DLB 176; RGWL 2, 3;
 WLIT 8
de Musset, (Louis Charles) Alfred
 See Musset, Alfred de
de Natale, Francine
 See Malzberg, Barry N(athaniel)
de Navarre, Marguerite 1492-1549 ... **LC 61;**
 SSC 85
 See Marguerite d'Angouleme; Marguerite
 de Navarre
 See also DLB 327
Denby, Edwin (Orr) 1903-1983 .... **CLC 48**
 See also CA 138; CAAS 110; CP 1
de Nerval, Gerard
 See Nerval, Gerard de
Denham, John 1615-1669 .... **LC 73**
 See also DLB 58, 126; RGEL 2
Denis, Julio
 See Cortazar, Julio
Denmark, Harrison
 See Zelazny, Roger
Dennis, John 1658-1734 .... **LC 11**
 See also DLB 101; RGEL 2
Dennis, Nigel (Forbes) 1912-1989 ...... **CLC 8**
 See also CA 25-28R; CAAS 129; CN 1, 2,
 3, 4; DLB 13, 15, 233; EWL 3; MTCW 1
Dent, Lester 1904-1959 .... **TCLC 72**
 See also CA 161; CAAE 112; CMW 4;
 DLB 306; SFW 4
De Palma, Brian 1940- .... **CLC 20**
 See also CA 109
De Palma, Brian Russell
 See De Palma, Brian
de Pizan, Christine
 See Christine de Pizan
 See also FL 1:1
De Quincey, Thomas 1785-1859 ..... **NCLC 4,**
 87
 See also BRW 4; CDBLB 1789-1832; DLB
 110, 144; RGEL 2
Deren, Eleanora 1908(?)-1961
 See Deren, Maya
 See also CA 192; CAAS 111
Deren, Maya .... **CLC 16, 102**
 See Deren, Eleanora
Derleth, August (William)
 1909-1971 .... **CLC 31**
 See also BPFB 1; BYA 9, 10; CA 1-4R;
 CAAS 29-32R; CANR 4; CMW 4; CN 1;
 DLB 9; DLBD 17; HGG; SATA 5; SUFW
 1
Der Nister 1884-1950 .... **TCLC 56**
 See Nister, Der
de Routisie, Albert
 See Aragon, Louis
Derrida, Jacques 1930-2004 ...... **CLC 24, 87,**
 225
 See also CA 127; CAAE 124; CAAS 232;
 CANR 76, 98, 133; DLB 242; EWL 3;
 LMFS 2; MTCW 2; TWA
Derry Down Derry
 See Lear, Edward

Dersonnes, Jacques
 See Simenon, Georges (Jacques Christian)
Der Stricker c. 1190-c. 1250 .... **CMLC 75**
 See also DLB 138
Desai, Anita 1937- .... **CLC 19, 37, 97, 175**
 See also BRWS 5; CA 81-84; CANR 33,
 53, 95, 133; CN 1, 2, 3, 4, 5, 6, 7; CWRI
 5; DA3; DAB; DAM NOV; DLB 271,
 323; DNFS 2; EWL 3; FW; MTCW 1, 2;
 MTFW 2005; SATA 63, 126
Desai, Kiran 1971- .... **CLC 119**
 See also BYA 16; CA 171; CANR 127
de Saint-Luc, Jean
 See Glassco, John
de Saint Roman, Arnaud
 See Aragon, Louis
Desbordes-Valmore, Marceline
 1786-1859 .... **NCLC 97**
 See also DLB 217
Descartes, Rene 1596-1650 .... **LC 20, 35**
 See also DLB 268; EW 3; GFL Beginnings
 to 1789
Deschamps, Eustache 1340(?)-1404 .. **LC 103**
 See also DLB 208
De Sica, Vittorio 1901(?)-1974 .... **CLC 20**
 See also CAAS 117
Desnos, Robert 1900-1945 .... **TCLC 22**
 See also CA 151; CAAE 121; CANR 107;
 DLB 258; EWL 3; LMFS 2
Destouches, Louis-Ferdinand
 1894-1961 .... **CLC 9, 15**
 See Celine, Louis-Ferdinand
 See also CA 85-88; CANR 28; MTCW 1
de Tolignac, Gaston
 See Griffith, D(avid Lewelyn) W(ark)
Deutsch, Babette 1895-1982 .... **CLC 18**
 See also BYA 3; CA 1-4R; CAAS 108;
 CANR 4, 79; CP 1, 2, 3; DLB 45; SATA
 1; SATA-Obit 33
Devenant, William 1606-1649 .... **LC 13**
Devkota, Laxmiprasad 1909-1959 . **TCLC 23**
 See also CAAE 123
De Voto, Bernard (Augustine)
 1897-1955 .... **TCLC 29**
 See also CA 160; CAAE 113; DLB 9, 256;
 MAL 5; TCWW 1, 2
De Vries, Peter 1910-1993 ..... **CLC 1, 2, 3, 7,**
 10, 28, 46
 See also CA 17-20R; CAAS 142; CANR
 41; CN 1, 2, 3, 4, 5; DAM NOV; DLB 6;
 DLBY 1982; MAL 5; MTCW 1, 2;
 MTFW 2005
Dewey, John 1859-1952 .... **TCLC 95**
 See also CA 170; CAAE 114; CANR 144;
 DLB 246, 270; RGAL 4
Dexter, John
 See Bradley, Marion Zimmer
 See also GLL 1
Dexter, Martin
 See Faust, Frederick (Schiller)
Dexter, Pete 1943- .... **CLC 34, 55**
 See also BEST 89:2; CA 131; CAAE 127;
 CANR 129; CPW; DAM POP; INT CA-
 131; MAL 5; MTCW 1; MTFW 2005
Diamano, Silmang
 See Senghor, Leopold Sedar
Diamant, Anita 1951- .... **CLC 239**
 See also CA 145; CANR 126
Diamond, Neil 1941- .... **CLC 30**
 See also CA 108
Diaz del Castillo, Bernal c.
 1496-1584 .... **HLCS 1; LC 31**
 See also DLB 318; LAW
di Bassetto, Corno
 See Shaw, George Bernard

Donovan, John 1928-1992 .... CLC 35
    See also AAYA 20; CA 97-100; CAAS 137;
    CLR 3; MAICYA 1, 2; SATA 72; SATA-
    Brief 29; YAW
Don Roberto
    See Cunninghame Graham, Robert
    (Gallnigad) Bontine
Doolittle, Hilda 1886-1961 . CLC 3, 8, 14, 31,
    34, 73; PC 5; WLC 3
    See H. D.
    See also AAYA 66; AMWS 1; CA 97-100;
    CANR 35, 131; DA; DAC; DAM MST,
    POET; DLB 4, 45; EWL 3; FW; GLL 1;
    LMFS 2; MAL 5; MBL; MTCW 1, 2;
    MTFW 2005; PFS 6; RGAL 4
Doppo, Kunikida .... TCLC 99
    See Kunikida Doppo
Dorfman, Ariel 1942- .... CLC 48, 77, 189;
    HLC 1
    See also CA 130; CAAE 124; CANR 67,
    70, 135; CWW 2; DAM MULT; DFS 4;
    EWL 3; HW 1, 2; INT CA-130; WLIT 1
Dorn, Edward (Merton)
    1929-1999 .... CLC 10, 18
    See also CA 93-96; CAAS 187; CANR 42,
    79; CP 1, 2, 3, 4, 5, 6, 7; DLB 5; INT
    CA-93-96; WP
Dor-Ner, Zvi .... CLC 70
Dorris, Michael 1945-1997 .... CLC 109;
    NNAL
    See also AAYA 20; BEST 90:1; BYA 12;
    CA 102; CAAS 157; CANR 19, 46, 75;
    CLR 58; DA3; DAM MULT, NOV; DLB
    175; LAIT 5; MTCW 2; MTFW 2005;
    NFS 3; RGAL 4; SATA 75; SATA-Obit
    94; TCWW 2; YAW
Dorris, Michael A.
    See Dorris, Michael
Dorsan, Luc
    See Simenon, Georges (Jacques Christian)
Dorsange, Jean
    See Simenon, Georges (Jacques Christian)
Dorset
    See Sackville, Thomas
Dos Passos, John (Roderigo)
    1896-1970 ... CLC 1, 4, 8, 11, 15, 25, 34,
    82; WLC 2
    See also AMW; BPFB 1; CA 1-4R; CAAS
    29-32R; CANR 3; CDALB 1929-1941;
    DA; DA3; DAB; DAC; DAM MST, NOV;
    DLB 4, 9, 274, 316; DLBD 1, 15; DLBY
    1996; EWL 3; MAL 5; MTCW 1, 2;
    MTFW 2005; NFS 14; RGAL 4; TUS
Dossage, Jean
    See Simenon, Georges (Jacques Christian)
Dostoevsky, Fedor Mikhailovich
    1821-1881 .. NCLC 2, 7, 21, 33, 43, 119,
    167; SSC 2, 33, 44; WLC 2
    See Dostoevsky, Fyodor
    See also AAYA 40; DA; DA3; DAB; DAC;
    DAM MST, NOV; EXPN; NFS 3,
    8; RGSF 2; RGWL 2, 3; SSFS 8; TWA
Dostoevsky, Fyodor
    See Dostoevsky, Fedor Mikhailovich
    See also DLB 238; LATS 1:1; LMFS 1, 2
Doty, M. R.
    See Doty, Mark
Doty, Mark 1953(?)- .... CLC 176; PC 53
    See also AMWS 11; CA 183; 161, 183;
    CANR 110; CP 7
Doty, Mark A.
    See Doty, Mark
Doty, Mark Alan
    See Doty, Mark
Doughty, Charles M(ontagu)
    1843-1926 .... TCLC 27
    See also CA 178; CAAE 115; DLB 19, 57,
    174

Douglas, Ellen .... CLC 73
    See Haxton, Josephine Ayres; Williamson,
    Ellen Douglas
    See also CN 5, 6, 7; CSW; DLB 292
Douglas, Gavin 1475(?)-1522 .... LC 20
    See also DLB 132; RGEL 2
Douglas, George
    See Brown, George Douglas
    See also RGEL 2
Douglas, Keith (Castellain)
    1920-1944 .... TCLC 40
    See also BRW 7; CA 160; DLB 27; EWL
    3; PAB; RGEL 2
Douglas, Leonard
    See Bradbury, Ray
Douglas, Michael
    See Crichton, Michael
Douglas, (George) Norman
    1868-1952 .... TCLC 68
    See also BRW 6; CA 157; CAAE 119; DLB
    34, 195; RGEL 2
Douglas, William
    See Brown, George Douglas
Douglass, Frederick 1817(?)-1895 ..... BLC 1;
    NCLC 7, 55, 141; WLC 2
    See also AAYA 48; AFAW 1, 2; AMWC 1;
    AMWS 3; CDALB 1640-1865; DA; DA3;
    DAC; DAM MST, MULT; DLB 1, 43, 50,
    79, 243; FW; LAIT 2; NCFS 2; RGAL 4;
    SATA 29
Dourado, (Waldomiro Freitas) Autran
    1926- .... CLC 23, 60
    See also CA 25-28R, 179; CANR 34, 81;
    DLB 145, 307; HW 2
Dourado, Waldomiro Freitas Autran
    See Dourado, (Waldomiro Freitas) Autran
Dove, Rita 1952- .. BLCS; CLC 50, 81; PC 6
    See also AAYA 46; AMWS 4; BW 2; CA
    109; 19; CANR 27, 42, 68, 76, 97, 132;
    CDALBS; CP 5, 6, 7; CSW; CWP; DA3;
    DAM MULT, POET; DLB 120; EWL 3;
    EXPP; MAL 5; MTCW 2; MTFW 2005;
    PFS 1, 15; RGAL 4
Dove, Rita Frances
    See Dove, Rita
Doveglion
    See Villa, Jose Garcia
Dowell, Coleman 1925-1985 .... CLC 60
    See also CA 25-28R; CAAS 117; CANR
    10; DLB 130; GLL 2
Downing, Major Jack
    See Smith, Seba
Dowson, Ernest (Christopher)
    1867-1900 .... TCLC 4
    See also CA 150; CAAE 105; DLB 19, 135;
    RGEL 2
Doyle, A. Conan
    See Doyle, Sir Arthur Conan
Doyle, Sir Arthur Conan
    1859-1930 ..... SSC 12, 83, 95; TCLC 7;
    WLC 2
    See Conan Doyle, Arthur
    See also AAYA 14; BRWS 2; CA 122;
    CAAE 104; CANR 131; CDBLB 1890-
    1914; CLR 106; CMW 4; DA; DA3;
    DAB; DAC; DAM MST, NOV; DLB 18,
    70, 156, 178; EXPS; HGG; LAIT 2;
    MSW; MTCW 1, 2; MTFW 2005; RGEL
    2; RGSF 2; RHW; SATA 24; SCFW 1, 2;
    SFW 4; SSFS 2; TEA; WCH; WLIT 4;
    WYA; YAW
Doyle, Conan
    See Doyle, Sir Arthur Conan
Doyle, John
    See Graves, Robert
Doyle, Roddy 1958- .... CLC 81, 178
    See also AAYA 14; BRWS 5; CA 143;
    CANR 73, 128; CN 6, 7; DA3; DLB 194,
    326; MTCW 2; MTFW 2005

Doyle, Sir A. Conan
    See Doyle, Sir Arthur Conan
Dr. A
    See Asimov, Isaac; Silverstein, Alvin; Sil-
    verstein, Virginia B(arbara Opshelor)
Drabble, Margaret 1939- ...... CLC 2, 3, 5, 8,
    10, 22, 53, 129
    See also BRWS 4; CA 13-16R; CANR 18,
    35, 63, 112, 131; CDBLB 1960 to Present;
    CN 1, 2, 3, 4, 5, 6, 7; CPW; DA3; DAB;
    DAC; DAM MST, NOV, POP; DLB 14,
    155, 231; EWL 3; FW; MTCW 1, 2;
    MTFW 2005; RGEL 2; SATA 48; TEA
Drakulic, Slavenka 1949- .... CLC 173
    See also CA 144; CANR 92
Drakulic-Ilic, Slavenka
    See Drakulic, Slavenka
Drapier, M. B.
    See Swift, Jonathan
Drayham, James
    See Mencken, H(enry) L(ouis)
Drayton, Michael 1563-1631 .... LC 8
    See also DAM POET; DLB 121; RGEL 2
Dreadstone, Carl
    See Campbell, (John) Ramsey
Dreiser, Theodore 1871-1945 .... SSC 30;
    TCLC 10, 18, 35, 83; WLC 2
    See also AMW; AMWC 2; AMWR 2; BYA
    15, 16; CA 132; CAAE 106; CDALB
    1865-1917; DA; DA3; DAC; DAM MST,
    NOV; DLB 9, 12, 102, 137; DLBD 1;
    EWL 3; LAIT 2; LMFS 2; MAL 5;
    MTCW 1, 2; MTFW 2005; NFS 8, 17;
    RGAL 4; TUS
Dreiser, Theodore Herman Albert
    See Dreiser, Theodore
Drexler, Rosalyn 1926- .... CLC 2, 6
    See also CA 81-84; CAD; CANR 68, 124;
    CD 5, 6; CWD; MAL 5
Dreyer, Carl Theodor 1889-1968 ...... CLC 16
    See also CAAS 116
Drieu la Rochelle, Pierre
    1893-1945 .... TCLC 21
    See also CA 250; CAAE 117; DLB 72;
    EWL 3; GFL 1789 to the Present
Drieu la Rochelle, Pierre-Eugene 1893-1945
    See Drieu la Rochelle, Pierre
Drinkwater, John 1882-1937 .... TCLC 57
    See also CA 149; CAAE 109; DLB 10, 19,
    149; RGEL 2
Drop Shot
    See Cable, George Washington
Droste-Hulshoff, Annette Freiin von
    1797-1848 .... NCLC 3, 133
    See also CDWLB 2; DLB 133; RGSF 2;
    RGWL 2, 3
Drummond, Walter
    See Silverberg, Robert
Drummond, William Henry
    1854-1907 .... TCLC 25
    See also CA 160; DLB 92
Drummond de Andrade, Carlos
    1902-1987 .... CLC 18; TCLC 139
    See Andrade, Carlos Drummond de
    See also CA 132; CAAS 123; DLB 307;
    LAW
Drummond of Hawthornden, William
    1585-1649 .... LC 83
    See also DLB 121, 213; RGEL 2
Drury, Allen (Stuart) 1918-1998 .... CLC 37
    See also CA 57-60; CAAS 170; CANR 18,
    52; CN 1, 2, 3, 4, 5, 6; INT CANR-18
Druse, Eleanor
    See King, Stephen

Dryden, John 1631-1700 ..... **DC 3; LC 3, 21, 115; PC 25; WLC 2**
See also BRW 2; CDBLB 1660-1789; DA; DAB; DAC; DAM DRAM, MST, POET, DLB 80, 101, 131; EXPP; IDTP; LMFS 1; RGEL 2; TEA; WLIT 3

du Bellay, Joachim 1524-1560 .... **LC 92**
See also DLB 327; GFL Beginnings to 1789; RGWL 2, 3

Duberman, Martin 1930- .... **CLC 8**
See also CA 1-4R; CAD; CANR 2, 63, 137; CD 5, 6

Dubie, Norman (Evans) 1945- .... **CLC 36**
See also CA 69-72; CANR 12, 115; CP 3, 4, 5, 6, 7; DLB 120; PFS 12

Du Bois, W(illiam) E(dward) B(urghardt) 1868-1963 ..... **BLC 1; CLC 1, 2, 13, 64, 96; HR 1:2; TCLC 169; WLC 2**
See also AAYA 40; AFAW 1, 2; AMWC 1; AMWS 2; BW 1, 3; CA 85-88; CANR 34, 82, 132; CDALB 1865-1917; DA; DA3; DAC; DAM MST, MULT, NOV; DLB 47, 50, 91, 246, 284; EWL 3; EXPP; LAIT 2; LMFS 2; MAL 5; MTCW 1, 2; MTFW 2005; NCFS 1; PFS 13; RGAL 4; SATA 42

Dubus, Andre 1936-1999 ..... **CLC 13, 36, 97; SSC 15**
See also AMWS 7; CA 21-24R; CAAS 177; CANR 17; CN 5, 6; CSW; DLB 130; INT CANR-17; RGAL 4; SSFS 10; TCLE 1:1

Duca Minimo
See D'Annunzio, Gabriele

Ducharme, Rejean 1941- .... **CLC 74**
See also CAAS 165; DLB 60

du Chatelet, Emilie 1706-1749 .... **LC 96**
See Chatelet, Gabrielle-Emilie Du

Duchen, Claire .... **CLC 65**

Duclos, Charles Pinot- 1704-1772 .... **LC 1**
See also GFL Beginnings to 1789

Ducornet, Erica 1943-
See Ducornet, Rikki
See also CA 37-40R; CANR 14, 34, 54, 82; SATA 7

Ducornet, Rikki .... **CLC 232**
See Ducornet, Erica

Dudek, Louis 1918-2001 .... **CLC 11, 19**
See also CA 45-48; 14; CAAS 215; CANR 1; CP 1, 2, 3, 4, 5, 6, 7; DLB 88

Duerrenmatt, Friedrich 1921-1990 ... **CLC 1, 4, 8, 11, 15, 43, 102**
See Durrenmatt, Friedrich
See also CA 17-20R; CANR 33; CMW 4; DAM DRAM; DLB 69, 124; MTCW 1, 2

Duffy, Bruce 1953(?)- .... **CLC 50**
See also CA 172

Duffy, Maureen (Patricia) 1933- ...... **CLC 37**
See also CA 25-28R; CANR 33, 68; CBD; CN 1, 2, 3, 4, 5, 6, 7; CP 5, 6, 7; CWD; CWP; DFS 15; DLB 14, 310; FW; MTCW 1

Du Fu
See Tu Fu
See also RGWL 2, 3

Dugan, Alan 1923-2003 .... **CLC 2, 6**
See also CA 81-84; CAAS 220; CANR 119; CP 1, 2, 3, 4, 5, 6, 7; DLB 5; MAL 5; PFS 10

du Gard, Roger Martin
See Martin du Gard, Roger

Duhamel, Georges 1884-1966 .... **CLC 8**
See also CA 81-84; CAAS 25-28R; CANR 35; DLB 65; EWL 3; GFL 1789 to the Present; MTCW 1

Dujardin, Edouard (Emile Louis) 1861-1949 .... **TCLC 13**
See also CAAE 109; DLB 123

Duke, Raoul
See Thompson, Hunter S.

Dulles, John Foster 1888-1959 .... **TCLC 72**
See also CA 149; CAAE 115

Dumas, Alexandre (pere) 1802-1870 .... **NCLC 11, 71; WLC 2**
See also AAYA 22; BYA 3; DA; DA3; DAB; DAC; DAM MST, NOV; DLB 119, 192; EW 6; GFL 1789 to the Present; LAIT 1, 2; NFS 14, 19; RGWL 2, 3; SATA 18; TWA; WCH

Dumas, Alexandre (fils) 1824-1895 ...... **DC 1; NCLC 9**
See also DLB 192; GFL 1789 to the Present; RGWL 2, 3

Dumas, Claudine
See Malzberg, Barry N(athaniel)

Dumas, Henry L. 1934-1968 .... **CLC 6, 62**
See also BW 1; CA 85-88; DLB 41; RGAL 4

du Maurier, Daphne 1907-1989 .. **CLC 6, 11, 59; SSC 18**
See also AAYA 37; BPFB 1; BRWS 3; CA 5-8R; CAAS 128; CANR 6, 55; CMW 4; CN 1, 2, 3, 4; CPW; DA3; DAB; DAC; DAM MST, POP; DLB 191; GL 2; HGG; LAIT 3; MSW; MTCW 1, 2; NFS 12; RGEL 2; RGSF 2; RHW; SATA 27; SATA-Obit 60; SSFS 14, 16; TEA

Du Maurier, George 1834-1896 ..... **NCLC 86**
See also DLB 153, 178; RGEL 2

Dunbar, Paul Laurence 1872-1906 ... **BLC 1; PC 5; SSC 8; TCLC 2, 12; WLC 2**
See also AAYA 75; AFAW 1, 2; AMWS 2; BW 1, 3; CA 124; CAAE 104; CANR 79; CDALB 1865-1917; DA; DA3; DAC; DAM MST, MULT, POET; DLB 50, 54, 78; EXPP; MAL 5; RGAL 4; SATA 34

Dunbar, William 1460(?)-1520(?) .... **LC 20; PC 67**
See also BRWS 8; DLB 132, 146; RGEL 2

Dunbar-Nelson, Alice .... **HR 1:2**
See Nelson, Alice Ruth Moore Dunbar

Duncan, Dora Angela
See Duncan, Isadora

Duncan, Isadora 1877(?)-1927 .... **TCLC 68**
See also CA 149; CAAE 118

Duncan, Lois 1934- .... **CLC 26**
See also AAYA 4, 34; BYA 6, 8; CA 1-4R; CANR 2, 23, 36, 111; CLR 29; JRDA; MAICYA 1, 2; MAICYAS 1; MTFW 2005; SAAS 2; SATA 1, 36, 75, 133, 141; SATA-Essay 141; WYA; YAW

Duncan, Robert 1919-1988 ... **CLC 1, 2, 4, 7, 15, 41, 55; PC 2, 75**
See also BG 1:2; CA 9-12R; CAAS 124; CANR 28, 62; CP 1, 2, 3, 4; DAM POET; DLB 5, 16, 193; EWL 3; MAL 5; MTCW 1, 2; MTFW 2005; PFS 13; RGAL 4; WP

Duncan, Sara Jeannette 1861-1922 .... **TCLC 60**
See also CA 157; DLB 92

Dunlap, William 1766-1839 .... **NCLC 2**
See also DLB 30, 37, 59; RGAL 4

Dunn, Douglas (Eaglesham) 1942- .... **CLC 6, 40**
See also BRWS 10; CA 45-48; CANR 2, 33, 126; CP 1, 2, 3, 4, 5, 6, 7; DLB 40; MTCW 1

Dunn, Katherine 1945- .... **CLC 71**
See also CA 33-36R; CANR 72; HGG; MTCW 2; MTFW 2005

Dunn, Stephen 1939- .... **CLC 36, 206**
See also AMWS 11; CA 33-36R; CANR 12, 48, 53, 105; CP 3, 4, 5, 6, 7; DLB 105; PFS 21

Dunn, Stephen Elliott
See Dunn, Stephen

Dunne, Finley Peter 1867-1936 ...... **TCLC 28**
See also CA 178; CAAE 108; DLB 11, 23; RGAL 4

Dunne, John Gregory 1932-2003 ..... **CLC 28**
See also CA 25-28R; CAAS 222; CANR 14, 50; CN 5, 6, 7; DLBY 1980

Dunsany, Lord .... **TCLC 2, 59**
See Dunsany, Edward John Moreton Drax Plunkett
See also DLB 77, 153, 156, 255; FANT; IDTP; RGEL 2; SFW 4; SUFW 1

Dunsany, Edward John Moreton Drax Plunkett 1878-1957
See Dunsany, Lord
See also CA 148; CAAE 104; DLB 10; MTCW 2

Duns Scotus, John 1266(?)-1308 ... **CMLC 59**
See also DLB 115

du Perry, Jean
See Simenon, Georges (Jacques Christian)

Durang, Christopher 1949- .... **CLC 27, 38**
See also CA 105; CAD; CANR 50, 76, 130; CD 5, 6; MTCW 2; MTFW 2005

Durang, Christopher Ferdinand
See Durang, Christopher

Duras, Claire de 1777-1832 .... **NCLC 154**

Duras, Marguerite 1914-1996 . **CLC 3, 6, 11, 20, 34, 40, 68, 100; SSC 40**
See also BPFB 1; CA 25-28R; CAAS 151; CANR 50; CWW 2; DFS 21; DLB 83, 321; EWL 3; FL 1:5; GFL 1789 to the Present; IDFW 4; MTCW 1, 2; RGWL 2, 3; TWA

Durban, (Rosa) Pam 1947- .... **CLC 39**
See also CA 123; CANR 98; CSW

Durcan, Paul 1944- .... **CLC 43, 70**
See also CA 134; CANR 123; CP 1, 5, 6, 7; DAM POET; EWL 3

d'Urfe, Honore
See Urfe, Honore d'

Durfey, Thomas 1653-1723 .... **LC 94**
See also DLB 80; RGEL 2

Durkheim, Emile 1858-1917 .... **TCLC 55**
See also CA 249

Durrell, Lawrence (George) 1912-1990 ..... **CLC 1, 4, 6, 8, 13, 27, 41**
See also BPFB 1; BRWS 1; CA 9-12R; CAAS 132; CANR 40, 77; CDBLB 1945-1960; CN 1, 2, 3, 4; CP 1, 2, 3, 4, 5; DAM NOV; DLB 15, 27, 204; DLBY 1990; EWL 3; MTCW 1, 2; RGEL 2; SFW 4; TEA

Durrenmatt, Friedrich
See Duerrenmatt, Friedrich
See also CDWLB 2; EW 13; EWL 3; RGHL; RGWL 2, 3

Dutt, Michael Madhusudan 1824-1873 .... **NCLC 118**

Dutt, Toru 1856-1877 .... **NCLC 29**
See also DLB 240

Dwight, Timothy 1752-1817 .... **NCLC 13**
See also DLB 37; RGAL 4

Dworkin, Andrea 1946-2005 ..... **CLC 43, 123**
See also CA 77-80; 21; CAAS 238; CANR 16, 39, 76, 96; FL 1:5; FW; GLL 1; INT CANR-16; MTCW 1, 2; MTFW 2005

Dwyer, Deanna
See Koontz, Dean R.

Dwyer, K. R.
See Koontz, Dean R.

Dybek, Stuart 1942- .... **CLC 114; SSC 55**
See also CA 97-100; CANR 39; DLB 130; SSFS 23

Dye, Richard
See De Voto, Bernard (Augustine)

Dyer, Geoff 1958- .... **CLC 149**
See also CA 125; CANR 88

Dyer, George 1755-1841 .... **NCLC 129**
See also DLB 93

Dylan, Bob 1941- .... **CLC 3, 4, 6, 12, 77; PC 37**
See also CA 41-44R; CANR 108; CP 1, 2, 3, 4, 5, 6, 7; DLB 16

Dyson, John 1943- .... **CLC 70**
See also CA 144

Dzyubin, Eduard Georgievich 1895-1934
See Bagritsky, Eduard
See also CA 170

E. V. L.
See Lucas, E(dward) V(errall)

Eagleton, Terence (Francis) 1943- .. **CLC 63, 132**
See also CA 57-60; CANR 7, 23, 68, 115; DLB 242; LMFS 2; MTCW 1, 2; MTFW 2005

Eagleton, Terry
See Eagleton, Terence (Francis)

Early, Jack
See Scoppettone, Sandra
See also GLL 1

East, Michael
See West, Morris L(anglo)

Eastaway, Edward
See Thomas, (Philip) Edward

Eastlake, William (Derry)
1917-1997 .... **CLC 8**
See also CA 5-8R; 1; CAAS 158; CANR 5, 63; CN 1, 2, 3, 4, 5, 6; DLB 6, 206; INT CANR-5; MAL 5; TCWW 1, 2

Eastman, Charles A(lexander)
1858-1939 .... **NNAL; TCLC 55**
See also CA 179; CANR 91; DAM MULT; DLB 175; YABC 1

Eaton, Edith Maude 1865-1914 .... **AAL**
See Far, Sui Sin
See also CA 154; DLB 221, 312; FW

Eaton, (Lillie) Winnifred 1875-1954 .... **AAL**
See also CA 217; DLB 221, 312; RGAL 4

Eberhart, Richard 1904-2005 ...... **CLC 3, 11, 19, 56; PC 76**
See also AMW; CA 1-4R; CAAS 240; CANR 2, 125; CDALB 1941-1968; CP 1, 2, 3, 4, 5, 6, 7; DAM POET; DLB 48; MAL 5; MTCW 1; RGAL 4

Eberhart, Richard Ghormley
See Eberhart, Richard

Eberstadt, Fernanda 1960- .... **CLC 39**
See also CA 136; CANR 69, 128

Echegaray (y Eizaguirre), Jose (Maria Waldo) 1832-1916 .... **HLCS 1; TCLC 4**
See also CAAE 104; CANR 32; DLB 329; EWL 3; HW 1; MTCW 1

Echeverria, (Jose) Esteban (Antonino)
1805-1851 .... **NCLC 18**
See also LAW

Echo
See Proust, (Valentin-Louis-George-Eugene) Marcel

Eckert, Allan W. 1931- .... **CLC 17**
See also AAYA 18; BYA 2; CA 13-16R; CANR 14, 45; INT CANR-14; MAICYA 2; MAICYAS 1; SAAS 21; SATA 29, 91; SATA-Brief 27

Eckhart, Meister 1260(?)-1327(?) .. **CMLC 9, 80**
See also DLB 115; LMFS 1

Eckmar, F. R.
See de Hartog, Jan

Eco, Umberto 1932- .... **CLC 28, 60, 142**
See also BEST 90:1; BPFB 1; CA 77-80; CANR 12, 33, 55, 110, 131; CPW; CWW 2; DA3; DAM NOV, POP; DLB 196, 242; EWL 3; MSW; MTCW 1, 2; MTFW 2005; NFS 22; RGWL 3; WLIT 7

Eddison, E(ric) R(ucker)
1882-1945 .... **TCLC 15**
See also CA 156; CAAE 109; DLB 255; FANT; SFW 4; SUFW 1

Eddy, Mary (Ann Morse) Baker
1821-1910 .... **TCLC 71**
See also CA 174; CAAE 113

Edel, (Joseph) Leon 1907-1997 .. **CLC 29, 34**
See also CA 1-4R; CAAS 161; CANR 1, 22, 112; DLB 103; INT CANR-22

Eden, Emily 1797-1869 .... **NCLC 10**

Edgar, David 1948- .... **CLC 42**
See also CA 57-60; CANR 12, 61, 112; CBD; CD 5, 6; DAM DRAM; DFS 15; DLB 13, 233; MTCW 1

Edgerton, Clyde (Carlyle) 1944- ...... **CLC 39**
See also AAYA 17; CA 134; CAAE 118; CANR 64, 125; CN 7; CSW; DLB 278; INT CA-134; TCLE 1:1; YAW

Edgeworth, Maria 1768-1849 ... **NCLC 1, 51, 158; SSC 86**
See also BRWS 3; DLB 116, 159, 163; FL 1:3; FW; RGEL 2; SATA 21; TEA; WLIT 3

Edmonds, Paul
See Kuttner, Henry

Edmonds, Walter D(umaux)
1903-1998 .... **CLC 35**
See also BYA 2; CA 5-8R; CANR 2; CWRI 5; DLB 9; LAIT 1; MAICYA 1, 2; MAL 5; RHW; SAAS 4; SATA 1, 27; SATA-Obit 99

Edmondson, Wallace
See Ellison, Harlan

Edson, Margaret 1961- ...... **CLC 199; DC 24**
See also CA 190; DFS 13; DLB 266

Edson, Russell 1935- .... **CLC 13**
See also CA 33-36R; CANR 115; CP 2, 3, 4, 5, 6, 7; DLB 244; WP

Edwards, Bronwen Elizabeth
See Rose, Wendy

Edwards, G(erald) B(asil)
1899-1976 .... **CLC 25**
See also CA 201; CAAS 110

Edwards, Gus 1939- .... **CLC 43**
See also CA 108; INT CA-108

Edwards, Jonathan 1703-1758 .... **LC 7, 54**
See also AMW; DA; DAC; DAM MST; DLB 24, 270; RGAL 4; TUS

Edwards, Sarah Pierpont 1710-1758 .. **LC 87**
See also DLB 200

Efron, Marina Ivanovna Tsvetaeva
See Tsvetaeva (Efron), Marina (Ivanovna)

Egeria fl. 4th cent. - .... **CMLC 70**

Eggers, Dave 1970- .... **CLC 241**
See also AAYA 56; CA 198; CANR 138; MTFW 2005

Egoyan, Atom 1960- .... **CLC 151**
See also AAYA 63; CA 157; CANR 151

Ehle, John (Marsden, Jr.) 1925- ...... **CLC 27**
See also CA 9-12R; CSW

Ehrenbourg, Ilya (Grigoryevich)
See Ehrenburg, Ilya (Grigoryevich)

Ehrenburg, Ilya (Grigoryevich)
1891-1967 .... **CLC 18, 34, 62**
See Erenburg, Il'ia Grigor'evich
See also CA 102; CAAS 25-28R; EWL 3

Ehrenburg, Ilyo (Grigoryevich)
See Ehrenburg, Ilya (Grigoryevich)

Ehrenreich, Barbara 1941- .... **CLC 110**
See also BEST 90:4; CA 73-76; CANR 16, 37, 62, 117; DLB 246; FW; MTCW 1, 2; MTFW 2005

Eich, Gunter
See Eich, Gunter
See also RGWL 2, 3

Eich, Gunter 1907-1972 .... **CLC 15**
See Eich, Gunter
See also CA 111; CAAS 93-96; DLB 69, 124; EWL 3

Eichendorff, Joseph 1788-1857 .... **NCLC 8**
See also DLB 90; RGWL 2, 3

Eigner, Larry .... **CLC 9**
See Eigner, Laurence (Joel)
See also CA 23; CP 1, 2, 3, 4, 5, 6; DLB 5; WP

Eigner, Laurence (Joel) 1927-1996
See Eigner, Larry
See also CA 9-12R; CAAS 151; CANR 6, 84; CP 7; DLB 193

Eilhart von Oberge c. 1140-c.
1195 .... **CMLC 67**
See also DLB 148

Einhard c. 770-840 .... **CMLC 50**
See also DLB 148

Einstein, Albert 1879-1955 .... **TCLC 65**
See also CA 133; CAAE 121; MTCW 1, 2

Eiseley, Loren
See Eiseley, Loren Corey
See also DLB 275

Eiseley, Loren Corey 1907-1977 .... **CLC 7**
See Eiseley, Loren
See also AAYA 5; ANW; CA 1-4R; CAAS 73-76; CANR 6; DLBD 17

Eisenstadt, Jill 1963- .... **CLC 50**
See also CA 140

Eisenstein, Sergei (Mikhailovich)
1898-1948 .... **TCLC 57**
See also CA 149; CAAE 114

Eisner, Simon
See Kornbluth, C(yril) M.

Eisner, Will 1917-2005 .... **CLC 237**
See also AAYA 52; CA 108; CAAS 235; CANR 114, 140; MTFW 2005; SATA 31, 165

Eisner, William Erwin
See Eisner, Will

Ekeloef, (Bengt) Gunnar
1907-1968 .... **CLC 27; PC 23**
See Ekelof, (Bengt) Gunnar
See also CA 123; CAAS 25-28R; DAM POET

Ekelof, (Bengt) Gunnar 1907-1968
See Ekeloef, (Bengt) Gunnar
See also DLB 259; EW 12; EWL 3

Ekelund, Vilhelm 1880-1949 .... **TCLC 75**
See also CA 189; EWL 3

Ekwensi, C. O. D.
See Ekwensi, Cyprian (Odiatu Duaka)

Ekwensi, Cyprian (Odiatu Duaka)
1921- .... **BLC 1; CLC 4**
See also AFW; BW 2, 3; CA 29-32R; CANR 18, 42, 74, 125; CDWLB 3; CN 1, 2, 3, 4, 5, 6; CWRI 5; DAM MULT; DLB 117; EWL 3; MTCW 1, 2; RGEL 2; SATA 66; WLIT 2

Elaine .... **TCLC 18**
See Leverson, Ada Esther

El Crummo
See Crumb, R.

Elder, Lonne III 1931-1996 ..... **BLC 1; DC 8**
See also BW 1, 3; CA 81-84; CAAS 152; CAD; CANR 25; DAM MULT; DLB 7, 38, 44; MAL 5

Eleanor of Aquitaine 1122-1204 ... **CMLC 39**

Elia
See Lamb, Charles

Eliade, Mircea 1907-1986 .... **CLC 19**
See also CA 65-68; CAAS 119; CANR 30, 62; CDWLB 4; DLB 220; EWL 3; MTCW 1; RGWL 3; SFW 4

Eliot, A. D.
See Jewett, (Theodora) Sarah Orne

Eliot, Alice
See Jewett, (Theodora) Sarah Orne

Eliot, Dan
See Silverberg, Robert

FL 1:5; LAIT 5; LATS 1:2; MAL 5; MTCW 1, 2; MTFW 2005; NFS 5; PFS 14; RGAL 4; SATA 94, 141; SSFS 14, 22; TCWW 2

Erenburg, Ilya (Grigoryevich)
See Ehrenburg, Ilya (Grigoryevich)

Erickson, Stephen Michael
See Erickson, Steve

Erickson, Steve 1950- .... **CLC 64**
See also CA 129; CANR 60, 68, 136; MTFW 2005; SFW 4; SUFW 2

Erickson, Walter
See Fast, Howard

Ericson, Walter
See Fast, Howard

Eriksson, Buntel
See Bergman, Ingmar

Eriugena, John Scottus c.
810-877 .... **CMLC 65**
See also DLB 115

Ernaux, Annie 1940- .... **CLC 88, 184**
See also CA 147; CANR 93; MTFW 2005; NCFS 3, 5

Erskine, John 1879-1951 .... **TCLC 84**
See also CA 159; CAAE 112; DLB 9, 102; FANT

Erwin, Will
See Eisner, Will

Eschenbach, Wolfram von
See von Eschenbach, Wolfram
See also RGWL 3

Eseki, Bruno
See Mphahlele, Ezekiel

Esenin, S.A.
See Esenin, Sergei
See also EWL 3

Esenin, Sergei 1895-1925 .... **TCLC 4**
See Esenin, S.A.
See also CAAE 104; RGWL 2, 3

Esenin, Sergei Aleksandrovich
See Esenin, Sergei

Eshleman, Clayton 1935- .... **CLC 7**
See also CA 212; 33-36R, 212; 6; CANR 93; CP 1, 2, 3, 4, 5, 6, 7; DLB 5

Espada, Martin 1957- .... **PC 74**
See also CA 159; CANR 80; CP 7; EXPP; LLW; MAL 5; PFS 13, 16

Espriella, Don Manuel Alvarez
See Southey, Robert

Espriu, Salvador 1913-1985 .... **CLC 9**
See also CA 154; CAAS 115; DLB 134; EWL 3

Espronceda, Jose de 1808-1842 ..... **NCLC 39**

Esquivel, Laura 1950(?)- ... **CLC 141; HLCS 1**
See also AAYA 29; CA 143; CANR 68, 113, 161; DA3; DNFS 2; LAIT 3; LMFS 2; MTCW 2; MTFW 2005; NFS 5; WLIT 1

Esse, James
See Stephens, James

Esterbrook, Tom
See Hubbard, L. Ron

Estleman, Loren D. 1952- .... **CLC 48**
See also AAYA 27; CA 85-88; CANR 27, 74, 139; CMW 4; CPW; DA3; DAM NOV, POP; DLB 226; INT CANR-27; MTCW 1, 2; MTFW 2005; TCWW 1, 2

Etherege, Sir George 1636-1692 . **DC 23; LC 78**
See also BRW 2; DAM DRAM; DLB 80; PAB; RGEL 2

Euclid 306B.C.-283B.C. .... **CMLC 25**

Eugenides, Jeffrey 1960(?)- .... **CLC 81, 212**
See also AAYA 51; CA 144; CANR 120; MTFW 2005; NFS 24

Euripides c. 484B.C.-406B.C. .... **CMLC 23, 51; DC 4; WLCS**
See also AW 1; CDWLB 1; DA; DA3; DAB; DAC; DAM DRAM, MST; DFS 1, 4, 6; DLB 176; LAIT 1; LMFS 1; RGWL 2, 3; WLIT 8

Evan, Evin
See Faust, Frederick (Schiller)

Evans, Caradoc 1878-1945 ... **SSC 43; TCLC 85**
See also DLB 162

Evans, Evan
See Faust, Frederick (Schiller)

Evans, Marian
See Eliot, George

Evans, Mary Ann
See Eliot, George
See also NFS 20

Evarts, Esther
See Benson, Sally

Everett, Percival
See Everett, Percival L.
See also CSW

Everett, Percival L. 1956- .... **CLC 57**
See Everett, Percival
See also BW 2; CA 129; CANR 94, 134; CN 7; MTFW 2005

Everson, R(onald) G(ilmour)
1903-1992 .... **CLC 27**
See also CA 17-20R; CP 1, 2, 3, 4; DLB 88

Everson, William (Oliver)
1912-1994 .... **CLC 1, 5, 14**
See Antoninus, Brother
See also BG 1:2; CA 9-12R; CAAS 145; CANR 20; CP 2, 3, 4, 5; DLB 5, 16, 212; MTCW 1

Evtushenko, Evgenii Aleksandrovich
See Yevtushenko, Yevgeny (Alexandrovich)
See also CWW 2; RGWL 2, 3

Ewart, Gavin (Buchanan)
1916-1995 .... **CLC 13, 46**
See also BRWS 7; CA 89-92; CAAS 150; CANR 17, 46; CP 1, 2, 3, 4, 5, 6; DLB 40; MTCW 1

Ewers, Hanns Heinz 1871-1943 ..... **TCLC 12**
See also CA 149; CAAE 109

Ewing, Frederick R.
See Sturgeon, Theodore (Hamilton)

Exley, Frederick (Earl) 1929-1992 .... **CLC 6, 11**
See also AITN 2; BPFB 1; CA 81-84; CAAS 138; CANR 117; DLB 143; DLBY 1981

Eynhardt, Guillermo
See Quiroga, Horacio (Sylvestre)

Ezekiel, Nissim (Moses) 1924-2004 .. **CLC 61**
See also CA 61-64; CAAS 223; CP 1, 2, 3, 4, 5, 6, 7; DLB 323; EWL 3

Ezekiel, Tish O'Dowd 1943- .... **CLC 34**
See also CA 129

Fadeev, Aleksandr Aleksandrovich
See Bulgya, Alexander Alexandrovich
See also DLB 272

Fadeev, Alexandr Alexandrovich
See Bulgya, Alexander Alexandrovich
See also EWL 3

Fadeyev, A.
See Bulgya, Alexander Alexandrovich

Fadeyev, Alexander .... **TCLC 53**
See Bulgya, Alexander Alexandrovich

Fagen, Donald 1948- .... **CLC 26**

Fainzil'berg, Il'ia Arnol'dovich
See Fainzilberg, Ilya Arnoldovich

Fainzilberg, Ilya Arnoldovich
1897-1937 .... **TCLC 21**
See Il'f, Il'ia
See also CA 165; CAAE 120; EWL 3

Fair, Ronald L. 1932- .... **CLC 18**
See also BW 1; CA 69-72; CANR 25; DLB 33

Fairbairn, Roger
See Carr, John Dickson

Fairbairns, Zoe (Ann) 1948- .... **CLC 32**
See also CA 103; CANR 21, 85; CN 4, 5, 6, 7

Fairfield, Flora
See Alcott, Louisa May

Fairman, Paul W. 1916-1977
See Queen, Ellery
See also CAAS 114; SFW 4

Falco, Gian
See Papini, Giovanni

Falconer, James
See Kirkup, James

Falconer, Kenneth
See Kornbluth, C(yril) M.

Falkland, Samuel
See Heijermans, Herman

Fallaci, Oriana 1930-2006 .... **CLC 11, 110**
See also CA 77-80; CAAS 253; CANR 15, 58, 134; FW; MTCW 1

Faludi, Susan 1959- .... **CLC 140**
See also CA 138; CANR 126; FW; MTCW 2; MTFW 2005; NCFS 3

Faludy, George 1913- .... **CLC 42**
See also CA 21-24R

Faludy, Gyoergy
See Faludy, George

Fanon, Frantz 1925-1961 ... **BLC 2; CLC 74; TCLC 188**
See also BW 1; CA 116; CAAS 89-92; DAM MULT; DLB 296; LMFS 2; WLIT 2

Fanshawe, Ann 1625-1680 .... **LC 11**

Fante, John (Thomas) 1911-1983 .... **CLC 60; SSC 65**
See also AMWS 11; CA 69-72; CAAS 109; CANR 23, 104; DLB 130; DLBY 1983

Far, Sui Sin .... **SSC 62**
See Eaton, Edith Maude
See also SSFS 4

Farah, Nuruddin 1945- ...... **BLC 2; CLC 53, 137**
See also AFW; BW 2, 3; CA 106; CANR 81, 148; CDWLB 3; CN 4, 5, 6, 7; DAM MULT; DLB 125; EWL 3; WLIT 2

Fargue, Leon-Paul 1876(?)-1947 .... **TCLC 11**
See also CAAE 109; CANR 107; DLB 258; EWL 3

Farigoule, Louis
See Romains, Jules

Farina, Richard 1936(?)-1966 .... **CLC 9**
See also CA 81-84; CAAS 25-28R

Farley, Walter (Lorimer)
1915-1989 .... **CLC 17**
See also AAYA 58; BYA 14; CA 17-20R; CANR 8, 29, 84; DLB 22; JRDA; MAICYA 1, 2; SATA 2, 43, 132; YAW

Farquhar, George 1677-1707 .... **LC 21**
See also BRW 2; DAM DRAM; DLB 84; RGEL 2

Farrell, J(ames) G(ordon)
1935-1979 .... **CLC 6**
See also CA 73-76; CAAS 89-92; CANR 36; CN 1, 2; DLB 14, 271, 326; MTCW 1; RGEL 2; RHW; WLIT 4

Farrell, James T(homas) 1904-1979 . **CLC 1, 4, 8, 11, 66; SSC 28**
See also AMW; BPFB 1; CA 5-8R; CAAS 89-92; CANR 9, 61; CN 1, 2; DLB 4, 9, 86; DLBD 2; EWL 3; MAL 5; MTCW 1, 2; MTFW 2005; RGAL 4

Farrell, Warren (Thomas) 1943- ...... **CLC 70**
See also CA 146; CANR 120

Farren, Richard J.
See Betjeman, John

Farren, Richard M.
See Betjeman, John

Fassbinder, Rainer Werner
1946-1982 .... **CLC 20**
See also CA 93-96; CAAS 106; CANR 31

Fast, Howard 1914-2003 .... **CLC 23, 131**
See also AAYA 16; BPFB 1; CA 181; 1-4R,
181; 18; CAAS 214; CANR 1, 33, 54, 75,
98, 140; CMW 4; CN 1, 2, 3, 4, 5, 6, 7;
CPW; DAM NOV; DLB 9; INT CANR-
33; LATS 1:1; MAL 5; MTCW 2; MTFW
2005; RHW; SATA 7; SATA-Essay 107;
TCWW 1, 2; YAW

Faulcon, Robert
See Holdstock, Robert

Faulkner, William (Cuthbert)
1897-1962 .... **CLC 1, 3, 6, 8, 9, 11, 14,
18, 28, 52, 68; SSC 1, 35, 42, 92, 97;
TCLC 141; WLC 2**
See also AAYA 7; AMW; AMWR 1; BPFB
1; BYA 5, 15; CA 81-84; CANR 33;
CDALB 1929-1941; DA; DA3; DAB;
DAC; DAM MST, NOV; DLB 9, 11, 44,
102, 316, 330; DLBD 2; DLBY 1986,
1997; EWL 3; EXPN; EXPS; GL 2; LAIT
2; LATS 1:1; LMFS 2; MAL 5; MTCW
1, 2; MTFW 2005; NFS 4, 8, 13, 24;
RGAL 4; RGSF 2; SSFS 2, 5, 6, 12; TUS

Fauset, Jessie Redmon
1882(?)-1961 .. **BLC 2; CLC 19, 54; HR
1:2**
See also AFAW 2; BW 1; CA 109; CANR
83; DAM MULT; DLB 51; FW; LMFS 2;
MAL 5; MBL

Faust, Frederick (Schiller)
1892-1944 .... **TCLC 49**
See Brand, Max; Dawson, Peter; Frederick,
John
See also CA 152; CAAE 108; CANR 143;
DAM POP; DLB 256; TUS

Faust, Irvin 1924- .... **CLC 8**
See also CA 33-36R; CANR 28, 67; CN 1,
2, 3, 4, 5, 6, 7; DLB 2, 28, 218, 278;
DLBY 1980

Fawkes, Guy
See Benchley, Robert (Charles)

Fearing, Kenneth (Flexner)
1902-1961 .... **CLC 51**
See also CA 93-96; CANR 59; CMW 4;
DLB 9; MAL 5; RGAL 4

Fecamps, Elise
See Creasey, John

Federman, Raymond 1928- .... **CLC 6, 47**
See also CA 208; 17-20R, 208; 8; CANR
10, 43, 83, 108; CN 3, 4, 5, 6; DLBY
1980

Federspiel, J.F. 1931-2007 .... **CLC 42**
See also CA 146; CAAS 257

Federspiel, Juerg F.
See Federspiel, J.F.

Federspiel, Jurg F.
See Federspiel, J.F.

Feiffer, Jules 1929- .... **CLC 2, 8, 64**
See also AAYA 3, 62; CA 17-20R; CAD;
CANR 30, 59, 129, 161; CD 5, 6; DAM
DRAM; DLB 7, 44; INT CANR-30;
MTCW 1; SATA 8, 61, 111, 157

Feiffer, Jules Ralph
See Feiffer, Jules

Feige, Hermann Albert Otto Maximilian
See Traven, B.

Feinberg, David B. 1956-1994 .... **CLC 59**
See also CA 135; CAAS 147

Feinstein, Elaine 1930- .... **CLC 36**
See also CA 69-72; 1; CANR 31, 68, 121,
162; CN 3, 4, 5, 6, 7; CP 2, 3, 4, 5, 6, 7;
CWP; DLB 14, 40; MTCW 1

Feke, Gilbert David .... **CLC 65**

Feldman, Irving (Mordecai) 1928- ..... **CLC 7**
See also CA 1-4R; CANR 1; CP 1, 2, 3, 4,
5, 6, 7; DLB 169; TCLE 1:1

Felix-Tchicaya, Gerald
See Tchicaya, Gerald Felix

Fellini, Federico 1920-1993 .... **CLC 16, 85**
See also CA 65-68; CAAS 143; CANR 33

Felltham, Owen 1602(?)-1668 .... **LC 92**
See also DLB 126, 151

Felsen, Henry Gregor 1916-1995 ..... **CLC 17**
See also CA 1-4R; CAAS 180; CANR 1;
SAAS 2; SATA 1

Felski, Rita .... **CLC 65**

**Fenelon, Francois de Pons de Salignac de la
Mothe-** 1651-1715 .... **LC 134**
See also DLB 268; EW 3; GFL Beginnings
to 1789

Fenno, Jack
See Calisher, Hortense

Fenollosa, Ernest (Francisco)
1853-1908 .... **TCLC 91**

Fenton, James 1949- .... **CLC 32, 209**
See also CA 102; CANR 108, 160; CP 2, 3,
4, 5, 6, 7; DLB 40; PFS 11

Fenton, James Martin
See Fenton, James

Ferber, Edna 1887-1968 .... **CLC 18, 93**
See also AITN 1; CA 5-8R; CAAS 25-28R;
CANR 68, 105; DLB 9, 28, 86, 266; MAL
5; MTCW 1, 2; MTFW 2005; RGAL 4;
RHW; SATA 7; TCWW 1, 2

Ferdowsi, Abu'l Qasem
940-1020(?) .... **CMLC 43**
See Firdawsi, Abu al-Qasim
See also RGWL 2, 3

Ferguson, Helen
See Kavan, Anna

Ferguson, Niall 1964- .... **CLC 134**
See also CA 190; CANR 154

Ferguson, Samuel 1810-1886 .... **NCLC 33**
See also DLB 32; RGEL 2

Fergusson, Robert 1750-1774 .... **LC 29**
See also DLB 109; RGEL 2

Ferling, Lawrence
See Ferlinghetti, Lawrence

Ferlinghetti, Lawrence 1919(?)- .... **CLC 2, 6,
10, 27, 111; PC 1**
See also AAYA 74; BG 1:2; CA 5-8R; CAD;
CANR 3, 41, 73, 125; CDALB 1941-
1968; CP 1, 2, 3, 4, 5, 6, 7; DA3; DAM
POET; DLB 5, 16; MAL 5; MTCW 1, 2;
MTFW 2005; RGAL 4; WP

Ferlinghetti, Lawrence Monsanto
See Ferlinghetti, Lawrence

Fern, Fanny
See Parton, Sara Payson Willis

Fernandez, Vicente Garcia Huidobro
See Huidobro Fernandez, Vicente Garcia

Fernandez-Armesto, Felipe .... **CLC 70**
See Fernandez-Armesto, Felipe Fermin
Ricardo
See also CANR 153

Fernandez-Armesto, Felipe Fermin Ricardo
1950-
See Fernandez-Armesto, Felipe
See also CA 142; CANR 93

Fernandez de Lizardi, Jose Joaquin
See Lizardi, Jose Joaquin Fernandez de

Ferre, Rosario 1938- ...... **CLC 139; HLCS 1;
SSC 36**
See also CA 131; CANR 55, 81, 134; CWW
2; DLB 145; EWL 3; HW 1, 2; LAWS 1;
MTCW 2; MTFW 2005; WLIT 1

Ferrer, Gabriel (Francisco Victor) Miro
See Miro (Ferrer), Gabriel (Francisco
Victor)

Ferrier, Susan (Edmonstone)
1782-1854 .... **NCLC 8**
See also DLB 116; RGEL 2

Ferrigno, Robert 1948(?)- .... **CLC 65**
See also CA 140; CANR 125, 161

Ferron, Jacques 1921-1985 .... **CLC 94**
See also CA 129; CAAE 117; CCA 1; DAC;
DLB 60; EWL 3

Feuchtwanger, Lion 1884-1958 .... **TCLC 3**
See also CA 187; CAAE 104; DLB 66;
EWL 3; RGHL

Feuerbach, Ludwig 1804-1872 ..... **NCLC 139**
See also DLB 133

Feuillet, Octave 1821-1890 .... **NCLC 45**
See also DLB 192

Feydeau, Georges (Leon Jules Marie)
1862-1921 .... **TCLC 22**
See also CA 152; CAAE 113; CANR 84;
DAM DRAM; DLB 192; EWL 3; GFL
1789 to the Present; RGWL 2, 3

Fichte, Johann Gottlieb
1762-1814 .... **NCLC 62**
See also DLB 90

Ficino, Marsilio 1433-1499 .... **LC 12**
See also LMFS 1

Fiedeler, Hans
See Doeblin, Alfred

Fiedler, Leslie A(aron) 1917-2003 ..... **CLC 4,
13, 24**
See also AMWS 13; CA 9-12R; CAAS 212;
CANR 7, 63; CN 1, 2, 3, 4, 5, 6; DLB
28, 67; EWL 3; MAL 5; MTCW 1, 2;
RGAL 4; TUS

Field, Andrew 1938- .... **CLC 44**
See also CA 97-100; CANR 25

Field, Eugene 1850-1895 .... **NCLC 3**
See also DLB 23, 42, 140; DLBD 13; MAI-
CYA 1, 2; RGAL 4; SATA 16

Field, Gans T.
See Wellman, Manly Wade

Field, Michael 1915-1971 .... **TCLC 43**
See also CAAS 29-32R

Fielding, Helen 1958- .... **CLC 146, 217**
See also AAYA 65; CA 172; CANR 127;
DLB 231; MTFW 2005

Fielding, Henry 1707-1754 .... **LC 1, 46, 85;
WLC 2**
See also BRW 3; BRWR 1; CDBLB 1660-
1789; DA; DA3; DAB; DAC; DAM
DRAM, MST, NOV; DLB 39, 84, 101;
NFS 18; RGEL 2; TEA; WLIT 3

Fielding, Sarah 1710-1768 .... **LC 1, 44**
See also DLB 39; RGEL 2; TEA

Fields, W. C. 1880-1946 .... **TCLC 80**
See also DLB 44

Fierstein, Harvey (Forbes) 1954- ..... **CLC 33**
See also CA 129; CAAE 123; CAD; CD 5,
6; CPW; DA3; DAM DRAM, POP; DFS
6; DLB 266; GLL; MAL 5

Figes, Eva 1932- .... **CLC 31**
See also CA 53-56; CANR 4, 44, 83; CN 2,
3, 4, 5, 6, 7; DLB 14, 271; FW; RGHL

Filippo, Eduardo de
See de Filippo, Eduardo

Finch, Anne 1661-1720 ..... **LC 3, 137; PC 21**
See also BRWS 9; DLB 95

Finch, Robert (Duer Claydon)
1900-1995 .... **CLC 18**
See also CA 57-60; CANR 9, 24, 49; CP 1,
2, 3, 4, 5, 6; DLB 88

Findley, Timothy (Irving Frederick)
1930-2002 .... **CLC 27, 102**
See also CA 25-28R; CAAS 206; CANR
12, 42, 69, 109; CCA 1; CN 4, 5, 6, 7;
DAC; DAM MST; DLB 53; FANT; RHW

Fink, William
See Mencken, H(enry) L(ouis)
Firbank, Louis 1942-
See Reed, Lou
See also CAAE 117
Firbank, (Arthur Annesley) Ronald
1886-1926 .... **TCLC 1**
See also BRWS 2; CA 177; CAAE 104;
DLB 36; EWL 3; RGEL 2
Firdawsi, Abu al-Qasim
See Ferdowsi, Abu'l Qasem
See also WLIT 6
Fish, Stanley
See Fish, Stanley Eugene
Fish, Stanley E.
See Fish, Stanley Eugene
Fish, Stanley Eugene 1938- .... **CLC 142**
See also CA 132; CAAE 112; CANR 90;
DLB 67
Fisher, Dorothy (Frances) Canfield
1879-1958 .... **TCLC 87**
See also CA 136; CAAE 114; CANR 80;
CLR 71; CWRI 5; DLB 9, 102, 284;
MAICYA 1, 2; MAL 5; YABC 1
Fisher, M(ary) F(rances) K(ennedy)
1908-1992 .... **CLC 76, 87**
See also AMWS 17; CA 77-80; CAAS 138;
CANR 44; MTCW 2
Fisher, Roy 1930- .... **CLC 25**
See also CA 81-84; 10; CANR 16; CP 1, 2,
3, 4, 5, 6, 7; DLB 40
Fisher, Rudolph 1897-1934 . **BLC 2; HR 1:2;**
SSC 25; TCLC 11
See also BW 1, 3; CA 124; CAAE 107;
CANR 80; DAM MULT; DLB 51, 102
Fisher, Vardis (Alvero) 1895-1968 .... **CLC 7;**
TCLC 140
See also CA 5-8R; CAAS 25-28R; CANR
68; DLB 9, 206; MAL 5; RGAL 4;
TCWW 1, 2
Fiske, Tarleton
See Bloch, Robert (Albert)
Fitch, Clarke
See Sinclair, Upton
Fitch, John IV
See Cormier, Robert
Fitzgerald, Captain Hugh
See Baum, L(yman) Frank
FitzGerald, Edward 1809-1883 ...... **NCLC 9,**
153; PC 79
See also BRW 4; DLB 32; RGEL 2
Fitzgerald, F(rancis) Scott (Key)
1896-1940 ... **SSC 6, 31, 75; TCLC 1, 6,**
14, 28, 55, 157; WLC 2
See also AAYA 24; AITN 1; AMW; AMWC
2; AMWR 1; BPFB 1; CA 123; CAAE
110; CDALB 1917-1929; DA; DA3;
DAB; DAC; DAM MST, NOV; DLB 4,
9, 86, 219, 273; DLBD 1, 15, 16; DLBY
1981, 1996; EWL 3; EXPN; EXPS; LAIT
3; MAL 5; MTCW 1, 2; MTFW 2005;
NFS 2, 19, 20; RGAL 4; RGSF 2; SSFS
4, 15, 21, 25; TUS
Fitzgerald, Penelope 1916-2000 . **CLC 19, 51,**
61, 143
See also BRWS 5; CA 85-88; 10; CAAS
190; CANR 56, 86, 131; CN 3, 4, 5, 6, 7;
DLB 14, 194, 326; EWL 3; MTCW 2;
MTFW 2005
Fitzgerald, Robert (Stuart)
1910-1985 .... **CLC 39**
See also CA 1-4R; CAAS 114; CANR 1;
CP 1, 2, 3, 4; DLBY 1980; MAL 5
FitzGerald, Robert D(avid)
1902-1987 .... **CLC 19**
See also CA 17-20R; CP 1, 2, 3, 4; DLB
260; RGEL 2

Fitzgerald, Zelda (Sayre)
1900-1948 .... **TCLC 52**
See also AMWS 9; CA 126; CAAE 117;
DLBY 1984
Flanagan, Thomas (James Bonner)
1923-2002 .... **CLC 25, 52**
See also CA 108; CAAS 206; CANR 55;
CN 3, 4, 5, 6, 7; DLBY 1980; INT CA-
108; MTCW 1; RHW; TCLE 1:1
Flaubert, Gustave 1821-1880 .... **NCLC 2, 10,**
19, 62, 66, 135, 179, 185; SSC 11, 60;
WLC 2
See also DA; DA3; DAB; DAC; DAM
MST, NOV; DLB 119, 301; EW 7; EXPS;
GFL 1789 to the Present; LAIT 2; LMFS
1; NFS 14; RGSF 2; RGWL 2, 3; SSFS
6; TWA
Flavius Josephus
See Josephus, Flavius
Flecker, Herman Elroy
See Flecker, (Herman) James Elroy
Flecker, (Herman) James Elroy
1884-1915 .... **TCLC 43**
See also CA 150; CAAE 109; DLB 10, 19;
RGEL 2
Fleming, Ian 1908-1964 ... **CLC 3, 30; TCLC**
193
See also AAYA 26; BPFB 1; CA 5-8R;
CANR 59; CDBLB 1945-1960; CMW 4;
CPW; DA3; DAM POP; DLB 87, 201;
MSW; MTCW 1, 2; MTFW 2005; RGEL
2; SATA 9; TEA; YAW
Fleming, Ian Lancaster
See Fleming, Ian
Fleming, Thomas 1927- .... **CLC 37**
See also CA 5-8R; CANR 10, 102, 155;
INT CANR-10; SATA 8
Fleming, Thomas James
See Fleming, Thomas
Fletcher, John 1579-1625 .... **DC 6; LC 33**
See also BRW 2; CDBLB Before 1660;
DLB 58; RGEL 2; TEA
Fletcher, John Gould 1886-1950 .... **TCLC 35**
See also CA 167; CAAE 107; DLB 4, 45;
LMFS 2; MAL 5; RGAL 4
Fleur, Paul
See Pohl, Frederik
Flieg, Helmut
See Heym, Stefan
Flooglebuckle, Al
See Spiegelman, Art
Flora, Fletcher 1914-1969
See Queen, Ellery
See also CA 1-4R; CANR 3, 85
Flying Officer X
See Bates, H(erbert) E(rnest)
Fo, Dario 1926- .... **CLC 32, 109, 227; DC 10**
See also CA 128; CAAE 116; CANR 68,
114, 134, 164; CWW 2; DA3; DAM
DRAM; DFS 23; DLB 330; DLBY 1997;
EWL 3; MTCW 1, 2; MTFW 2005; WLIT
7
Foden, Giles 1967- .... **CLC 231**
See also CA 240; DLB 267; NFS 15
Fogarty, Jonathan Titulescu Esq.
See Farrell, James T(homas)
Follett, Ken 1949- .... **CLC 18**
See also AAYA 6, 50; BEST 89:4; BPFB 1;
CA 81-84; CANR 13, 33, 54, 102, 156;
CMW 4; CPW; DA3; DAM NOV, POP;
DLB 87; DLBY 1981; INT CANR-33;
MTCW 1
Follett, Kenneth Martin
See Follett, Ken
Fondane, Benjamin 1898-1944 ..... **TCLC 159**
Fontane, Theodor 1819-1898 . **NCLC 26, 163**
See also CDWLB 2; DLB 129; EW 6;
RGWL 2, 3; TWA

Fonte, Moderata 1555-1592 .... **LC 118**
Fontenelle, Bernard Le Bovier de
1657-1757 .... **LC 140**
See also DLB 268, 313; GFL Beginnings to
1789
Fontenot, Chester .... **CLC 65**
Fonvizin, Denis Ivanovich
1744(?)-1792 .... **LC 81**
See also DLB 150; RGWL 2, 3
Foote, Horton 1916- .... **CLC 51, 91**
See also CA 73-76; CAD; CANR 34, 51,
110; CD 5, 6; CSW; DA3; DAM DRAM;
DFS 20; DLB 26, 266; EWL 3; INT
CANR-34; MTFW 2005
Foote, Mary Hallock 1847-1938 .. **TCLC 108**
See also DLB 186, 188, 202, 221; TCWW
2
Foote, Samuel 1721-1777 .... **LC 106**
See also DLB 89; RGEL 2
Foote, Shelby 1916-2005 .... **CLC 75, 224**
See also AAYA 40; CA 5-8R; CAAS 240;
CANR 3, 45, 74, 131; CN 1, 2, 3, 4, 5, 6,
7; CPW; CSW; DA3; DAM NOV, POP;
DLB 2, 17; MAL 5; MTCW 2; MTFW
2005; RHW
Forbes, Cosmo
See Lewton, Val
Forbes, Esther 1891-1967 .... **CLC 12**
See also AAYA 17; BYA 2; CA 13-14;
CAAS 25-28R; CAP 1; CLR 27; DLB 22;
JRDA; MAICYA 1, 2; RHW; SATA 2,
100; YAW
Forche, Carolyn 1950- .. **CLC 25, 83, 86; PC**
10
See also CA 117; CAAE 109; CANR 50,
74, 138; CP 4, 5, 6, 7; CWP; DA3; DAM
POET; DLB 5, 193; INT CA-117; MAL
5; MTCW 2; MTFW 2005; PFS 18;
RGAL 4
Forche, Carolyn Louise
See Forche, Carolyn
Ford, Elbur
See Hibbert, Eleanor Alice Burford
Ford, Ford Madox 1873-1939 ... **TCLC 1, 15,**
39, 57, 172
See Chaucer, Daniel
See also BRW 6; CA 132; CAAE 104;
CANR 74; CDBLB 1914-1945; DA3;
DAM NOV; DLB 34, 98, 162; EWL 3;
MTCW 1, 2; RGEL 2; TEA
Ford, Henry 1863-1947 .... **TCLC 73**
See also CA 148; CAAE 115
Ford, Jack
See Ford, John
Ford, John 1586-1639 .... **DC 8; LC 68**
See also BRW 2; CDBLB Before 1660;
DA3; DAM DRAM; DFS 7; DLB 58;
IDTP; RGEL 2
Ford, John 1895-1973 .... **CLC 16**
See also AAYA 75; CA 187; CAAS 45-48
Ford, Richard 1944- .... **CLC 46, 99, 205**
See also AMWS 5; CA 69-72; CANR 11,
47, 86, 128, 164; CN 5, 6, 7; CSW; DLB
227; EWL 3; MAL 5; MTCW 2; MTFW
2005; NFS 25; RGAL 4; RGSF 2
Ford, Webster
See Masters, Edgar Lee
Foreman, Richard 1937- .... **CLC 50**
See also CA 65-68; CAD; CANR 32, 63,
143; CD 5, 6
Forester, C(ecil) S(cott) 1899-1966 . **CLC 35;**
TCLC 152
See also CA 73-76; CAAS 25-28R; CANR
83; DLB 191; RGEL 2; RHW; SATA 13
Forez
See Mauriac, Francois (Charles)
Forman, James
See Forman, James D.

Forman, James D. 1932- .... **CLC 21**
See also AAYA 17; CA 9-12R; CANR 4, 19, 42; JRDA; MAICYA 1, 2; SATA 8, 70; YAW

Forman, James Douglas
See Forman, James D.

Forman, Milos 1932- .... **CLC 164**
See also AAYA 63; CA 109

Fornes, Maria Irene 1930- .... **CLC 39, 61, 187; DC 10; HLCS 1**
See also CA 25-28R; CAD; CANR 28, 81; CD 5, 6; CWD; DLB 7; HW 1, 2; INT CANR-28; LLW; MAL 5; MTCW 1; RGAL 4

Forrest, Leon (Richard)
1937-1997 .... **BLCS; CLC 4**
See also AFAW 2; BW 2; CA 89-92; 7; CAAS 162; CANR 25, 52, 87; CN 4, 5, 6; DLB 33

Forster, E(dward) M(organ)
1879-1970 ...... **CLC 1, 2, 3, 4, 9, 10, 13, 15, 22, 45, 77; SSC 27, 96; TCLC 125; WLC 2**
See also AAYA 2, 37; BRW 6; BRWR 2; BYA 12; CA 13-14; CAAS 25-28R; CANR 45; CAP 1; CDBLB 1914-1945; DA; DA3; DAB; DAC; DAM MST, NOV; DLB 34, 98, 162, 178, 195; DLBD 10; EWL 3; EXPN; LAIT 3; LMFS 1; MTCW 1, 2; MTFW 2005; NCFS 1; NFS 3, 10, 11; RGEL 2; RGSF 2; SATA 57; SUFW 1; TEA; WLIT 4

Forster, John 1812-1876 .... **NCLC 11**
See also DLB 144, 184

Forster, Margaret 1938- .... **CLC 149**
See also CA 133; CANR 62, 115; CN 4, 5, 6, 7; DLB 155, 271

Forsyth, Frederick 1938- .... **CLC 2, 5, 36**
See also BEST 89:4; CA 85-88; CANR 38, 62, 115, 137; CMW 4; CN 3, 4, 5, 6, 7; CPW; DAM NOV, POP; DLB 87; MTCW 1, 2; MTFW 2005

Forten, Charlotte L. 1837-1914 .... **BLC 2; TCLC 16**
See Grimke, Charlotte L(ottie) Forten
See also DLB 50, 239

Fortinbras
See Grieg, (Johan) Nordahl (Brun)

Foscolo, Ugo 1778-1827 .... **NCLC 8, 97**
See also EW 5; WLIT 7

Fosse, Bob 1927-1987
See Fosse, Robert L.
See also CAAE 110; CAAS 123

Fosse, Robert L. .... **CLC 20**
See Fosse, Bob

Foster, Hannah Webster
1758-1840 .... **NCLC 99**
See also DLB 37, 200; RGAL 4

Foster, Stephen Collins
1826-1864 .... **NCLC 26**
See also RGAL 4

Foucault, Michel 1926-1984 . **CLC 31, 34, 69**
See also CA 105; CAAS 113; CANR 34; DLB 242; EW 13; EWL 3; GFL 1789 to the Present; GLL 1; LMFS 2; MTCW 1, 2; TWA

Fouque, Friedrich (Heinrich Karl) de la Motte 1777-1843 .... **NCLC 2**
See also DLB 90; RGWL 2, 3; SUFW 1

Fourier, Charles 1772-1837 .... **NCLC 51**

Fournier, Henri-Alban 1886-1914
See Alain-Fournier
See also CA 179; CAAE 104

Fournier, Pierre 1916-1997 .... **CLC 11**
See Gascar, Pierre
See also CA 89-92; CANR 16, 40

Fowles, John 1926-2005 .... **CLC 1, 2, 3, 4, 6, 9, 10, 15, 33, 87; SSC 33**
See also BPFB 1; BRWS 1; CA 5-8R; CAAS 245; CANR 25, 71, 103; CDBLB 1960 to Present; CN 1, 2, 3, 4, 5, 6, 7; DA3; DAB; DAC; DAM MST; DLB 14, 139, 207; EWL 3; HGG; MTCW 1, 2; MTFW 2005; NFS 21; RGEL 2; RHW; SATA 22; SATA-Obit 171; TEA; WLIT 4

Fowles, John Robert
See Fowles, John

Fox, Paula 1923- .... **CLC 2, 8, 121**
See also AAYA 3, 37; BYA 3, 8; CA 73-76; CANR 20, 36, 62, 105; CLR 1, 44, 96; DLB 52; JRDA; MAICYA 1, 2; MTCW 1; NFS 12; SATA 17, 60, 120, 167; WYA; YAW

Fox, William Price (Jr.) 1926- .... **CLC 22**
See also CA 17-20R; 19; CANR 11, 142; CSW; DLB 2; DLBY 1981

Foxe, John 1517(?)-1587 .... **LC 14**
See also DLB 132

Frame, Janet .. **CLC 2, 3, 6, 22, 66, 96, 237; SSC 29**
See Clutha, Janet Paterson Frame
See also CN 1, 2, 3, 4, 5, 6, 7; CP 2, 3, 4; CWP; EWL 3; RGEL 2; RGSF 2; TWA

France, Anatole .... **TCLC 9**
See Thibault, Jacques Anatole Francois
See also DLB 123, 330; EWL 3; GFL 1789 to the Present; RGWL 2, 3; SUFW 1

Francis, Claude .... **CLC 50**
See also CA 192

Francis, Dick
See Francis, Richard Stanley
See also CN 2, 3, 4, 5, 6

Francis, Richard Stanley 1920- ... **CLC 2, 22, 42, 102**
See Francis, Dick
See also AAYA 5, 21; BEST 89:3; BPFB 1; CA 5-8R; CANR 9, 42, 68, 100, 141; CD-BLB 1960 to Present; CMW 4; CN 7; DA3; DAM POP; DLB 87; INT CANR-9; MSW; MTCW 1, 2; MTFW 2005

Francis, Robert (Churchill)
1901-1987 .... **CLC 15; PC 34**
See also AMWS 9; CA 1-4R; CAAS 123; CANR 1; CP 1, 2, 3, 4; EXPP; PFS 12; TCLE 1:1

Francis, Lord Jeffrey
See Jeffrey, Francis
See also DLB 107

Frank, Anne(lies Marie)
1929-1945 .... **TCLC 17; WLC 2**
See also AAYA 12; BYA 1; CA 133; CAAE 113; CANR 68; CLR 101; DA; DA3; DAB; DAC; DAM MST; LAIT 4; MAICYA 2; MAICYAS 1; MTCW 1, 2; MTFW 2005; NCFS 2; RGHL; SATA 87; SATA-Brief 42; WYA; YAW

Frank, Bruno 1887-1945 .... **TCLC 81**
See also CA 189; DLB 118; EWL 3

Frank, Elizabeth 1945- .... **CLC 39**
See also CA 126; CAAE 121; CANR 78, 150; INT CA-126

Frankl, Viktor E(mil) 1905-1997 ...... **CLC 93**
See also CA 65-68; CAAS 161; RGHL

Franklin, Benjamin
See Hasek, Jaroslav (Matej Frantisek)

Franklin, Benjamin 1706-1790 .. **LC 25, 134; WLCS**
See also AMW; CDALB 1640-1865; DA; DA3; DAB; DAC; DAM MST; DLB 24, 43, 73, 183; LAIT 1; RGAL 4; TUS

Franklin, (Stella Maria Sarah) Miles (Lampe) 1879-1954 .... **TCLC 7**
See also CA 164; CAAE 104; DLB 230; FW; MTCW 2; RGEL 2; TWA

Franzen, Jonathan 1959- .... **CLC 202**
See also AAYA 65; CA 129; CANR 105, 166

Fraser, Antonia 1932- .... **CLC 32, 107**
See also AAYA 57; CA 85-88; CANR 44, 65, 119, 164; CMW; DLB 276; MTCW 1, 2; MTFW 2005; SATA-Brief 32

Fraser, George MacDonald 1925- ...... **CLC 7**
See also AAYA 48; CA 180; 45-48, 180; CANR 2, 48, 74; MTCW 2; RHW

Fraser, Sylvia 1935- .... **CLC 64**
See also CA 45-48; CANR 1, 16, 60; CCA 1

Frayn, Michael 1933- .... **CLC 3, 7, 31, 47, 176; DC 27**
See also AAYA 69; BRWC 2; BRWS 7; CA 5-8R; CANR 30, 69, 114, 133, 166; CBD; CD 5, 6; CN 1, 2, 3, 4, 5, 6, 7; DAM DRAM, NOV; DFS 22; DLB 13, 14, 194, 245; FANT; MTCW 1, 2; MTFW 2005; SFW 4

Fraze, Candida (Merrill) 1945- .... **CLC 50**
See also CA 126

Frazer, Andrew
See Marlowe, Stephen

Frazer, J(ames) G(eorge)
1854-1941 .... **TCLC 32**
See also BRWS 3; CAAE 118; NCFS 5

Frazer, Robert Caine
See Creasey, John

Frazer, Sir James George
See Frazer, J(ames) G(eorge)

Frazier, Charles 1950- .... **CLC 109, 224**
See also AAYA 34; CA 161; CANR 126; CSW; DLB 292; MTFW 2005; NFS 25

Frazier, Ian 1951- .... **CLC 46**
See also CA 130; CANR 54, 93

Frederic, Harold 1856-1898 ... **NCLC 10, 175**
See also AMW; DLB 12, 23; DLBD 13; MAL 5; NFS 22; RGAL 4

Frederick, John
See Faust, Frederick (Schiller)
See also TCWW 2

Frederick the Great 1712-1786 .... **LC 14**

Fredro, Aleksander 1793-1876 .... **NCLC 8**

Freeling, Nicolas 1927-2003 .... **CLC 38**
See also CA 49-52; 12; CAAS 218; CANR 1, 17, 50, 84; CMW 4; CN 1, 2, 3, 4, 5, 6; DLB 87

Freeman, Douglas Southall
1886-1953 .... **TCLC 11**
See also CA 195; CAAE 109; DLB 17; DLBD 17

Freeman, Judith 1946- .... **CLC 55**
See also CA 148; CANR 120; DLB 256

Freeman, Mary E(leanor) Wilkins
1852-1930 .... **SSC 1, 47; TCLC 9**
See also CA 177; CAAE 106; DLB 12, 78, 221; EXPS; FW; HGG; MBL; RGAL 4; RGSF 2; SSFS 4, 8; SUFW 1; TUS

Freeman, R(ichard) Austin
1862-1943 .... **TCLC 21**
See also CAAE 113; CANR 84; CMW 4; DLB 70

French, Albert 1943- .... **CLC 86**
See also BW 3; CA 167

French, Antonia
See Kureishi, Hanif

French, Marilyn 1929- .. **CLC 10, 18, 60, 177**
See also BPFB 1; CA 69-72; CANR 3, 31, 134, 163; CN 5, 6, 7; CPW; DAM DRAM, NOV, POP; FL 1:5; FW; INT CANR-31; MTCW 1, 2; MTFW 2005

French, Paul
See Asimov, Isaac

Freneau, Philip Morin 1752-1832 .. **NCLC 1, 111**
See also AMWS 2; DLB 37, 43; RGAL 4

Freud, Sigmund 1856-1939 .... **TCLC 52**
See also CA 133; CAAE 115; CANR 69;
DLB 296; EW 8; EWL 3; LATS 1:1;
MTCW 1, 2; MTFW 2005; NCFS 3; TWA

Freytag, Gustav 1816-1895 .... **NCLC 109**
See also DLB 129

Friedan, Betty 1921-2006 .... **CLC 74**
See also CA 65-68; CAAS 248; CANR 18,
45, 74; DLB 246; FW; MTCW 1, 2;
MTFW 2005; NCFS 5

Friedan, Betty Naomi
See Friedan, Betty

Friedlander, Saul 1932- .... **CLC 90**
See also CA 130; CAAE 117; CANR 72;
RGHL

Friedman, B(ernard) H(arper)
1926- .... **CLC 7**
See also CA 1-4R; CANR 3, 48

Friedman, Bruce Jay 1930- ...... **CLC 3, 5, 56**
See also CA 9-12R; CAD; CANR 25, 52,
101; CD 5, 6; CN 1, 2, 3, 4, 5, 6, 7; DLB
2, 28, 244; INT CANR-25; MAL 5; SSFS
18

Friel, Brian 1929- .... **CLC 5, 42, 59, 115; DC
8; SSC 76**
See also BRWS 5; CA 21-24R; CANR 33,
69, 131; CBD; CD 5, 6; DFS 11; DLB
13, 319; EWL 3; MTCW 1; RGEL 2; TEA

Friis-Baastad, Babbis Ellinor
1921-1970 .... **CLC 12**
See also CA 17-20R; CAAS 134; SATA 7

Frisch, Max 1911-1991 ...... **CLC 3, 9, 14, 18,
32, 44; TCLC 121**
See also CA 85-88; CAAS 134; CANR 32,
74; CDWLB 2; DAM DRAM, NOV; DLB
69, 124; EW 13; EWL 3; MTCW 1, 2;
MTFW 2005; RGHL; RGWL 2, 3

Fromentin, Eugene (Samuel Auguste)
1820-1876 .... **NCLC 10, 125**
See also DLB 123; GFL 1789 to the Present

Frost, Frederick
See Faust, Frederick (Schiller)

Frost, Robert 1874-1963 . **CLC 1, 3, 4, 9, 10,
13, 15, 26, 34, 44; PC 1, 39, 71; WLC 2**
See also AAYA 21; AMW; AMWR 1; CA
89-92; CANR 33; CDALB 1917-1929;
CLR 67; DA; DA3; DAB; DAC; DAM
MST, POET; DLB 54, 284; DLBD 7;
EWL 3; EXPP; MAL 5; MTCW 1, 2;
MTFW 2005; PAB; PFS 1, 2, 3, 4, 5, 6,
7, 10, 13; RGAL 4; SATA 14; TUS; WP;
WYA

Frost, Robert Lee
See Frost, Robert

Froude, James Anthony
1818-1894 .... **NCLC 43**
See also DLB 18, 57, 144

Froy, Herald
See Waterhouse, Keith (Spencer)

Fry, Christopher 1907-2005 ... **CLC 2, 10, 14**
See also BRWS 3; CA 17-20R; 23; CAAS
240; CANR 9, 30, 74, 132; CBD; CD 5,
6; CP 1, 2, 3, 4, 5, 6, 7; DAM DRAM;
DLB 13; EWL 3; MTCW 1, 2; MTFW
2005; RGEL 2; SATA 66; TEA

Frye, (Herman) Northrop
1912-1991 .... **CLC 24, 70; TCLC 165**
See also CA 5-8R; CAAS 133; CANR 8,
37; DLB 67, 68, 246; EWL 3; MTCW 1,
2; MTFW 2005; RGAL 4; TWA

Fuchs, Daniel 1909-1993 .... **CLC 8, 22**
See also CA 81-84; 5; CAAS 142; CANR
40; CN 1, 2, 3, 4, 5; DLB 9, 26, 28;
DLBY 1993; MAL 5

Fuchs, Daniel 1934- .... **CLC 34**
See also CA 37-40R; CANR 14, 48

Fuentes, Carlos 1928- .. **CLC 3, 8, 10, 13, 22,
41, 60, 113; HLC 1; SSC 24; WLC 2**
See also AAYA 4, 45; AITN 2; BPFB 1;
CA 69-72; CANR 10, 32, 68, 104, 138;
CDWLB 3; CWW 2; DA; DA3; DAB;
DAC; DAM MST, MULT, NOV; DLB
113; DNFS 2; EWL 3; HW 1, 2; LAIT 3;
LATS 1:2; LAW; LAWS 1; LMFS 2;
MTCW 1, 2; MTFW 2005; NFS 8; RGSF
2; RGWL 2, 3; TWA; WLIT 1

Fuentes, Gregorio Lopez y
See Lopez y Fuentes, Gregorio

Fuertes, Gloria 1918-1998 .... **PC 27**
See also CA 178, 180; DLB 108; HW 2;
SATA 115

Fugard, (Harold) Athol 1932- . **CLC 5, 9, 14,
25, 40, 80, 211; DC 3**
See also AAYA 17; AFW; CA 85-88; CANR
32, 54, 118; CD 5, 6; DAM DRAM; DFS
3, 6, 10, 24; DLB 225; DNFS 1, 2; EWL
3; LATS 1:2; MTCW 1; MTFW 2005;
RGEL 2; WLIT 2

Fugard, Sheila 1932- .... **CLC 48**
See also CA 125

Fujiwara no Teika 1162-1241 .... **CMLC 73**
See also DLB 203

Fukuyama, Francis 1952- .... **CLC 131**
See also CA 140; CANR 72, 125

Fuller, Charles (H.), (Jr.) 1939- .... **BLC 2;
CLC 25; DC 1**
See also BW 2; CA 112; CAAE 108; CAD;
CANR 87; CD 5, 6; DAM DRAM,
MULT; DFS 8; DLB 38, 266; EWL 3;
INT CA-112; MAL 5; MTCW 1

Fuller, Henry Blake 1857-1929 .... **TCLC 103**
See also CA 177; CAAE 108; DLB 12;
RGAL 4

Fuller, John (Leopold) 1937- .... **CLC 62**
See also CA 21-24R; CANR 9, 44; CP 1, 2,
3, 4, 5, 6, 7; DLB 40

Fuller, Margaret
See Ossoli, Sarah Margaret (Fuller)
See also AMWS 2; DLB 183, 223, 239; FL
1:3

Fuller, Roy (Broadbent) 1912-1991 ... **CLC 4,
28**
See also BRWS 7; CA 5-8R; 10; CAAS
135; CANR 53, 83; CN 1, 2, 3, 4, 5; CP
1, 2, 3, 4, 5; CWRI 5; DLB 15, 20; EWL
3; RGEL 2; SATA 87

Fuller, Sarah Margaret
See Ossoli, Sarah Margaret (Fuller)

Fuller, Sarah Margaret
See Ossoli, Sarah Margaret (Fuller)
See also DLB 1, 59, 73

Fuller, Thomas 1608-1661 .... **LC 111**
See also DLB 151

Fulton, Alice 1952- .... **CLC 52**
See also CA 116; CANR 57, 88; CP 5, 6, 7;
CWP; DLB 193; PFS 25

Furphy, Joseph 1843-1912 .... **TCLC 25**
See Collins, Tom
See also CA 163; DLB 230; EWL 3; RGEL
2

Fuson, Robert H(enderson) 1927- .... **CLC 70**
See also CA 89-92; CANR 103

Fussell, Paul 1924- .... **CLC 74**
See also BEST 90:1; CA 17-20R; CANR 8,
21, 35, 69, 135; INT CANR-21; MTCW
1, 2; MTFW 2005

Futabatei, Shimei 1864-1909 .... **TCLC 44**
See Futabatei Shimei
See also CA 162; MJW

Futabatei Shimei
See Futabatei, Shimei
See also DLB 180; EWL 3

Futrelle, Jacques 1875-1912 .... **TCLC 19**
See also CA 155; CAAE 113; CMW 4

Gaboriau, Emile 1835-1873 .... **NCLC 14**
See also CMW 4; MSW

Gadda, Carlo Emilio 1893-1973 ...... **CLC 11;
TCLC 144**
See also CA 89-92; DLB 177; EWL 3;
WLIT 7

Gaddis, William 1922-1998 ... **CLC 1, 3, 6, 8,
10, 19, 43, 86**
See also AMWS 4; BPFB 1; CA 17-20R;
CAAS 172; CANR 21, 48, 148; CN 1, 2,
3, 4, 5, 6; DLB 2, 278; EWL 3; MAL 5;
MTCW 1, 2; MTFW 2005; RGAL 4

Gage, Walter
See Inge, William (Motter)

Gaiman, Neil 1960- .... **CLC 195**
See also AAYA 19, 42; CA 133; CANR 81,
129; CLR 109; DLB 261; HGG; MTFW
2005; SATA 85, 146; SFW 4; SUFW 2

Gaiman, Neil Richard
See Gaiman, Neil

Gaines, Ernest J. 1933- .. **BLC 2; CLC 3, 11,
18, 86, 181; SSC 68**
See also AAYA 18; AFAW 1, 2; AITN 1;
BPFB 1; BW 2, 3; BYA 6; CA 9-12R;
CANR 6, 24, 42, 75, 126; CDALB 1968-
1988; CLR 62; CN 1, 2, 3, 4, 5, 6, 7;
CSW; DA3; DAM MULT; DLB 2, 33,
152; DLBY 1980; EWL 3; EXPN; LAIT
5; LATS 1:2; MAL 5; MTCW 1, 2;
MTFW 2005; NFS 5, 7, 16; RGAL 4;
RGSF 2; RHW; SATA 86; SSFS 5; YAW

Gaitskill, Mary 1954- .... **CLC 69**
See also CA 128; CANR 61, 152; DLB 244;
TCLE 1:1

Gaitskill, Mary Lawrence
See Gaitskill, Mary

Gaius Suetonius Tranquillus
See Suetonius

Galdos, Benito Perez
See Perez Galdos, Benito
See also EW 7

Gale, Zona 1874-1938 .... **TCLC 7**
See also CA 153; CAAE 105; CANR 84;
DAM DRAM; DFS 17; DLB 9, 78, 228;
RGAL 4

Galeano, Eduardo 1940- ... **CLC 72; HLCS 1**
See also CA 29-32R; CANR 13, 32, 100,
163; HW 1

Galeano, Eduardo Hughes
See Galeano, Eduardo

Galiano, Juan Valera y Alcala
See Valera y Alcala-Galiano, Juan

Galilei, Galileo 1564-1642 .... **LC 45**

Gallagher, Tess 1943- .... **CLC 18, 63; PC 9**
See also CA 106; CP 3, 4, 5, 6, 7; CWP;
DAM POET; DLB 120, 212, 244; PFS 16

Gallant, Mavis 1922- ..... **CLC 7, 18, 38, 172;
SSC 5, 78**
See also CA 69-72; CANR 29, 69, 117;
CCA 1; CN 1, 2, 3, 4, 5, 6, 7; DAC; DAM
MST; DLB 53; EWL 3; MTCW 1, 2;
MTFW 2005; RGEL 2; RGSF 2

Gallant, Roy A(rthur) 1924- .... **CLC 17**
See also CA 5-8R; CANR 4, 29, 54, 117;
CLR 30; MAICYA 1, 2; SATA 4, 68, 110

Gallico, Paul (William) 1897-1976 ..... **CLC 2**
See also AITN 1; CA 5-8R; CAAS 69-72;
CANR 23; CN 1, 2; DLB 9, 171; FANT;
MAICYA 1, 2; SATA 13

Gallo, Max Louis 1932- .... **CLC 95**
See also CA 85-88

Gallois, Lucien
See Desnos, Robert

Gallup, Ralph
See Whitemore, Hugh (John)

Gellhorn, Martha (Ellis)
1908-1998 .... **CLC 14, 60**
See also CA 77-80; CAAS 164; CANR 44; CN 1, 2, 3, 4, 5, 6 7; DLBY 1982, 1998

Genet, Jean 1910-1986 .. **CLC 1, 2, 5, 10, 14, 44, 46; DC 25; TCLC 128**
See also CA 13-16R; CANR 18; DA3; DAM DRAM; DFS 10; DLB 72, 321; DLBY 1986; EW 13; EWL 3; GFL 1789 to the Present; GLL 1; LMFS 2; MTCW 1, 2; MTFW 2005; RGWL 2, 3; TWA

Genlis, Stephanie-Felicite Ducrest
1746-1830 .... **NCLC 166**
See also DLB 313

Gent, Peter 1942- .... **CLC 29**
See also AITN 1; CA 89-92; DLBY 1982

Gentile, Giovanni 1875-1944 .... **TCLC 96**
See also CAAE 119

Geoffrey of Monmouth c.
1100-1155 .... **CMLC 44**
See also DLB 146; TEA

George, Jean
See George, Jean Craighead

George, Jean Craighead 1919- .... **CLC 35**
See also AAYA 8, 69; BYA 2, 4; CA 5-8R; CANR 25; CLR 1; 80; DLB 52; JRDA; MAICYA 1, 2; SATA 2, 68, 124, 170; WYA; YAW

George, Stefan (Anton) 1868-1933 . **TCLC 2, 14**
See also CA 193; CAAE 104; EW 8; EWL 3

Georges, Georges Martin
See Simenon, Georges (Jacques Christian)

Gerald of Wales c. 1146-c. 1223 ... **CMLC 60**

Gerhardi, William Alexander
See Gerhardie, William Alexander

Gerhardie, William Alexander
1895-1977 .... **CLC 5**
See also CA 25-28R; CAAS 73-76; CANR 18; CN 1, 2; DLB 36; RGEL 2

Gerson, Jean 1363-1429 .... **LC 77**
See also DLB 208

Gersonides 1288-1344 .... **CMLC 49**
See also DLB 115

Gerstler, Amy 1956- .... **CLC 70**
See also CA 146; CANR 99

Gertler, T. .... **CLC 34**
See also CA 121; CAAE 116

Gertsen, Aleksandr Ivanovich
See Herzen, Aleksandr Ivanovich

Ghalib .... **NCLC 39, 78**
See Ghalib, Asadullah Khan

Ghalib, Asadullah Khan 1797-1869
See Ghalib
See also DAM POET; RGWL 2, 3

Ghelderode, Michel de 1898-1962 ..... **CLC 6, 11; DC 15; TCLC 187**
See also CA 85-88; CANR 40, 77; DAM DRAM; DLB 321; EW 11; EWL 3; TWA

Ghiselin, Brewster 1903-2001 .... **CLC 23**
See also CA 13-16R; 10; CANR 13; CP 1, 2, 3, 4, 5, 6, 7

Ghose, Aurabinda 1872-1950 .... **TCLC 63**
See Ghose, Aurobindo
See also CA 163

Ghose, Aurobindo
See Ghose, Aurabinda
See also EWL 3

Ghose, Zulfikar 1935- .... **CLC 42, 200**
See also CA 65-68; CANR 67; CN 1, 2, 3, 4, 5, 6, 7; CP 1, 2, 3, 4, 5, 6, 7; DLB 323; EWL 3

Ghosh, Amitav 1956- .... **CLC 44, 153**
See also CA 147; CANR 80, 158; CN 6, 7; DLB 323; WWE 1

Giacosa, Giuseppe 1847-1906 .... **TCLC 7**
See also CAAE 104

Gibb, Lee
See Waterhouse, Keith (Spencer)

Gibbon, Edward 1737-1794 .... **LC 97**
See also BRW 3; DLB 104, 336; RGEL 2

Gibbon, Lewis Grassic .... **TCLC 4**
See Mitchell, James Leslie
See also RGEL 2

Gibbons, Kaye 1960- .... **CLC 50, 88, 145**
See also AAYA 34; AMWS 10; CA 151; CANR 75, 127; CN 7; CSW; DA3; DAM POP; DLB 292; MTCW 2; MTFW 2005; NFS 3; RGAL 4; SATA 117

Gibran, Kahlil 1883-1931 . **PC 9; TCLC 1, 9**
See also CA 150; CAAE 104; DA3; DAM POET, POP; EWL 3; MTCW 2; WLIT 6

Gibran, Khalil
See Gibran, Kahlil

Gibson, Mel 1956- .... **CLC 215**

Gibson, William 1914- .... **CLC 23**
See also CA 9-12R; CAD; CANR 9, 42, 75, 125; CD 5, 6; DA; DAB; DAC; DAM DRAM, MST; DFS 2; DLB 7; LAIT 2; MAL 5; MTCW 2; MTFW 2005; SATA 66; YAW

Gibson, William 1948- .... **CLC 39, 63, 186, 192; SSC 52**
See also AAYA 12, 59; AMWS 16; BPFB 2; CA 133; CAAE 126; CANR 52, 90, 106; CN 6, 7; CPW; DA3; DAM POP; DLB 251; MTCW 2; MTFW 2005; SCFW 2; SFW 4

Gibson, William Ford
See Gibson, William

Gide, Andre (Paul Guillaume)
1869-1951 ...... **SSC 13; TCLC 5, 12, 36, 177; WLC 3**
See also CA 124; CAAE 104; DA; DA3; DAB; DAC; DAM MST, NOV; DLB 65, 321, 330; EW 8; EWL 3; GFL 1789 to the Present; MTCW 1, 2; MTFW 2005; NFS 21; RGSF 2; RGWL 2, 3; TWA

Gifford, Barry (Colby) 1946- .... **CLC 34**
See also CA 65-68; CANR 9, 30, 40, 90

Gilbert, Frank
See De Voto, Bernard (Augustine)

Gilbert, W(illiam) S(chwenck)
1836-1911 .... **TCLC 3**
See also CA 173; CAAE 104; DAM DRAM, POET; RGEL 2; SATA 36

Gilbert of Poitiers c. 1085-1154 .... **CMLC 85**

Gilbreth, Frank B(unker), Jr.
1911-2001 .... **CLC 17**
See also CA 9-12R; SATA 2

Gilchrist, Ellen (Louise) 1935- .. **CLC 34, 48, 143; SSC 14, 63**
See also BPFB 2; CA 116; CAAE 113; CANR 41, 61, 104; CN 4, 5, 6, 7; CPW; CSW; DAM POP; DLB 130; EWL 3; EXPS; MTCW 1, 2; MTFW 2005; RGAL 4; RGSF 2; SSFS 9

Giles, Molly 1942- .... **CLC 39**
See also CA 126; CANR 98

Gill, Eric .... **TCLC 85**
See Gill, (Arthur) Eric (Rowton Peter Joseph)

Gill, (Arthur) Eric (Rowton Peter Joseph)
1882-1940
See Gill, Eric
See also CAAE 120; DLB 98

Gill, Patrick
See Creasey, John

Gillette, Douglas .... **CLC 70**

Gilliam, Terry 1940- .... **CLC 21, 141**
See Monty Python
See also AAYA 19, 59; CA 113; CAAE 108; CANR 35; INT CA-113

Gilliam, Terry Vance
See Gilliam, Terry

Gillian, Jerry
See Gilliam, Terry

Gilliatt, Penelope (Ann Douglass)
1932-1993 .... **CLC 2, 10, 13, 53**
See also AITN 2; CA 13-16R; CAAS 141; CANR 49; CN 1, 2, 3, 4, 5; DLB 14

Gilligan, Carol 1936- .... **CLC 208**
See also CA 142; CANR 121; FW

Gilman, Charlotte (Anna) Perkins (Stetson)
1860-1935 ...... **SSC 13, 62; TCLC 9, 37, 117**
See also AAYA 75; AMWS 11; BYA 11; CA 150; CAAE 106; DLB 221; EXPS; FL 1:5; FW; HGG; LAIT 2; MBL; MTCW 2; MTFW 2005; RGAL 4; RGSF 2; SFW 4; SSFS 1, 18

Gilmour, David 1946- .... **CLC 35**

Gilpin, William 1724-1804 .... **NCLC 30**

Gilray, J. D.
See Mencken, H(enry) L(ouis)

Gilroy, Frank D(aniel) 1925- .... **CLC 2**
See also CA 81-84; CAD; CANR 32, 64, 86; CD 5, 6; DFS 17; DLB 7

Gilstrap, John 1957(?)- .... **CLC 99**
See also AAYA 67; CA 160; CANR 101

Ginsberg, Allen 1926-1997 .... **CLC 1, 2, 3, 4, 6, 13, 36, 69, 109; PC 4, 47; TCLC 120; WLC 3**
See also AAYA 33; AITN 1; AMWC 1; AMWS 2; BG 1:2; CA 1-4R; CAAS 157; CANR 2, 41, 63, 95; CDALB 1941-1968; CP 1, 2, 3, 4, 5, 6; DA; DA3; DAB; DAC; DAM MST, POET; DLB 5, 16, 169, 237; EWL 3; GLL 1; LMFS 2; MAL 5; MTCW 1, 2; MTFW 2005; PAB; PFS 5; RGAL 4; TUS; WP

Ginzburg, Eugenia .... **CLC 59**
See Ginzburg, Evgeniia

Ginzburg, Evgeniia 1904-1977
See Ginzburg, Eugenia
See also DLB 302

Ginzburg, Natalia 1916-1991 .... **CLC 5, 11, 54, 70; SSC 65; TCLC 156**
See also CA 85-88; CAAS 135; CANR 33; DFS 14; DLB 177; EW 13; EWL 3; MTCW 1, 2; MTFW 2005; RGHL; RGWL 2, 3

Giono, Jean 1895-1970 .... **CLC 4, 11; TCLC 124**
See also CA 45-48; CAAS 29-32R; CANR 2, 35; DLB 72, 321; EWL 3; GFL 1789 to the Present; MTCW 1; RGWL 2, 3

Giovanni, Nikki 1943- ...... **BLC 2; CLC 2, 4, 19, 64, 117; PC 19; WLCS**
See also AAYA 22; AITN 1; BW 2, 3; CA 29-32R; 6; CANR 18, 41, 60, 91, 130; CDALBS; CLR 6, 73; CP 2, 3, 4, 5, 6, 7; CSW; CWP; CWRI 5; DA; DA3; DAB; DAC; DAM MST, MULT, POET; DLB 5, 41; EWL 3; EXPP; INT CANR-18; MAICYA 1, 2; MAL 5; MTCW 1, 2; MTFW 2005; PFS 17; RGAL 4; SATA 24, 107; TUS; YAW

Giovene, Andrea 1904-1998 .... **CLC 7**
See also CA 85-88

Gippius, Zinaida (Nikolaevna) 1869-1945
See Hippius, Zinaida (Nikolaevna)
See also CA 212; CAAE 106

Giraudoux, Jean(-Hippolyte)
1882-1944 .... **TCLC 2, 7**
See also CA 196; CAAE 104; DAM DRAM; DLB 65, 321; EW 9; EWL 3; GFL 1789 to the Present; RGWL 2, 3; TWA

Gironella, Jose Maria (Pous)
1917-2003 .... **CLC 11**
See also CA 101; CAAS 212; EWL 3; RGWL 2, 3

Gordimer, Nadine 1923- ...... **CLC 3, 5, 7, 10, 18, 33, 51, 70, 123, 160, 161; SSC 17, 80; WLCS**
See also AAYA 39; AFW; BRWS 2; CA 5-8R; CANR 3, 28, 56, 88, 131; CN 1, 2, 3, 4, 5, 6, 7; DA; DA3; DAB; DAC; DAM MST, NOV; DLB 225, 326, 330; EWL 3; EXPS; INT CANR-28; LATS 1:2; MTCW 1, 2; MTFW 2005; NFS 4; RGEL 2; RGSF 2; SSFS 2, 14, 19; TWA; WLIT 2; YAW

Gordon, Adam Lindsay
1833-1870 .... **NCLC 21**
See also DLB 230

Gordon, Caroline 1895-1981 . **CLC 6, 13, 29, 83; SSC 15**
See also AMW; CA 11-12; CAAS 103; CANR 36; CAP 1; CN 1, 2; DLB 4, 9, 102; DLBD 17; DLBY 1981; EWL 3; MAL 5; MTCW 1, 2; MTFW 2005; RGAL 4; RGSF 2

Gordon, Charles William 1860-1937
See Connor, Ralph
See also CAAE 109

Gordon, Mary 1949- .. **CLC 13, 22, 128, 216; SSC 59**
See also AMWS 4; BPFB 2; CA 102; CANR 44, 92, 154; CN 4, 5, 6, 7; DLB 6; DLBY 1981; FW; INT CA-102; MAL 5; MTCW 1

Gordon, Mary Catherine
See Gordon, Mary

Gordon, N. J.
See Bosman, Herman Charles

Gordon, Sol 1923- .... **CLC 26**
See also CA 53-56; CANR 4; SATA 11

Gordone, Charles 1925-1995 .. **CLC 1, 4; DC 8**
See also BW 1, 3; CA 180; 93-96, 180; CAAS 150; CAD; CANR 55; DAM DRAM; DLB 7; INT CA-93-96; MTCW 1

Gore, Catherine 1800-1861 .... **NCLC 65**
See also DLB 116; RGEL 2

Gorenko, Anna Andreevna
See Akhmatova, Anna

Gorky, Maxim .... **SSC 28; TCLC 8; WLC 3**
See Peshkov, Alexei Maximovich
See also DAB; DFS 9; DLB 295; EW 8; EWL 3; TWA

Goryan, Sirak
See Saroyan, William

Gosse, Edmund (William)
1849-1928 .... **TCLC 28**
See also CAAE 117; DLB 57, 144, 184; RGEL 2

Gotlieb, Phyllis (Fay Bloom) 1926- .. **CLC 18**
See also CA 13-16R; CANR 7, 135; CN 7; CP 1, 2, 3, 4; DLB 88, 251; SFW 4

Gottesman, S. D.
See Kornbluth, C(yril) M.; Pohl, Frederik

Gottfried von Strassburg fl. c.
1170-1215 .... **CMLC 10**
See also CDWLB 2; DLB 138; EW 1; RGWL 2, 3

Gotthelf, Jeremias 1797-1854 .... **NCLC 117**
See also DLB 133; RGWL 2, 3

Gottschalk, Laura Riding
See Jackson, Laura (Riding)

Gould, Lois 1932(?)-2002 .... **CLC 4, 10**
See also CA 77-80; CAAS 208; CANR 29; MTCW 1

Gould, Stephen Jay 1941-2002 .... **CLC 163**
See also AAYA 26; BEST 90:2; CA 77-80; CAAS 205; CANR 10, 27, 56, 75, 125; CPW; INT CANR-27; MTCW 1, 2; MTFW 2005

Gourmont, Remy(-Marie-Charles) de
1858-1915 .... **TCLC 17**
See also CA 150; CAAE 109; GFL 1789 to the Present; MTCW 2

Gournay, Marie le Jars de
See de Gournay, Marie le Jars

Govier, Katherine 1948- .... **CLC 51**
See also CA 101; CANR 18, 40, 128; CCA 1

Gower, John c. 1330-1408 .... **LC 76; PC 59**
See also BRW 1; DLB 146; RGEL 2

Goyen, (Charles) William
1915-1983 .... **CLC 5, 8, 14, 40**
See also AITN 2; CA 5-8R; CAAS 110; CANR 6, 71; CN 1, 2, 3; DLB 2, 218; DLBY 1983; EWL 3; INT CANR-6; MAL 5

Goytisolo, Juan 1931- .... **CLC 5, 10, 23, 133; HLC 1**
See also CA 85-88; CANR 32, 61, 131; CWW 2; DAM MULT; DLB 322; EWL 3; GLL 2; HW 1, 2; MTCW 1, 2; MTFW 2005

Gozzano, Guido 1883-1916 .... **PC 10**
See also CA 154; DLB 114; EWL 3

Gozzi, (Conte) Carlo 1720-1806 .... **NCLC 23**

Grabbe, Christian Dietrich
1801-1836 .... **NCLC 2**
See also DLB 133; RGWL 2, 3

Grace, Patricia Frances 1937- .... **CLC 56**
See also CA 176; CANR 118; CN 4, 5, 6, 7; EWL 3; RGSF 2

Gracian y Morales, Baltasar
1601-1658 .... **LC 15**

Gracq, Julien .... **CLC 11, 48**
See Poirier, Louis
See also CWW 2; DLB 83; GFL 1789 to the Present

Grade, Chaim 1910-1982 .... **CLC 10**
See also CA 93-96; CAAS 107; DLB 333; EWL 3; RGHL

Grade, Khayim
See Grade, Chaim

Graduate of Oxford, A
See Ruskin, John

Grafton, Garth
See Duncan, Sara Jeannette

Grafton, Sue 1940- .... **CLC 163**
See also AAYA 11, 49; BEST 90:3; CA 108; CANR 31, 55, 111, 134; CMW 4; CPW; CSW; DA3; DAM POP; DLB 226; FW; MSW; MTFW 2005

Graham, John
See Phillips, David Graham

Graham, Jorie 1950- .... **CLC 48, 118; PC 59**
See also AAYA 67; CA 111; CANR 63, 118; CP 4, 5, 6, 7; CWP; DLB 120; EWL 3; MTFW 2005; PFS 10, 17; TCLE 1:1

Graham, R(obert) B(ontine) Cunninghame
See Cunninghame Graham, Robert (Gallnigad) Bontine
See also DLB 98, 135, 174; RGEL 2; RGSF 2

Graham, Robert
See Haldeman, Joe

Graham, Tom
See Lewis, (Harry) Sinclair

Graham, W(illiam) S(ydney)
1918-1986 .... **CLC 29**
See also BRWS 7; CA 73-76; CAAS 118; CP 1, 2, 3, 4; DLB 20; RGEL 2

Graham, Winston (Mawdsley)
1910-2003 .... **CLC 23**
See also CA 49-52; CAAS 218; CANR 2, 22, 45, 66; CMW 4; CN 1, 2, 3, 4, 5, 6, 7; DLB 77; RHW

Grahame, Kenneth 1859-1932 ...... **TCLC 64, 136**
See also BYA 5; CA 136; CAAE 108; CANR 80; CLR 5; CWRI 5; DA3; DAB; DLB 34, 141, 178; FANT; MAICYA 1, 2; MTCW 2; NFS 20; RGEL 2; SATA 100; TEA; WCH; YABC 1

Granger, Darius John
See Marlowe, Stephen

Granin, Daniil 1918- .... **CLC 59**
See also DLB 302

Granovsky, Timofei Nikolaevich
1813-1855 .... **NCLC 75**
See also DLB 198

Grant, Skeeter
See Spiegelman, Art

Granville-Barker, Harley
1877-1946 .... **TCLC 2**
See Barker, Harley Granville
See also CA 204; CAAE 104; DAM DRAM; RGEL 2

Granzotto, Gianni
See Granzotto, Giovanni Battista

Granzotto, Giovanni Battista
1914-1985 .... **CLC 70**
See also CA 166

Grasemann, Ruth Barbara
See Rendell, Ruth

Grass, Guenter
See Grass, Gunter
See also CWW 2; DLB 330; RGHL

Grass, Gunter 1927- .. **CLC 1, 2, 4, 6, 11, 15, 22, 32, 49, 88, 207; WLC 3**
See Grass, Guenter
See also BPFB 2; CA 13-16R; CANR 20, 75, 93, 133; CDWLB 2; DA; DA3; DAB; DAC; DAM MST, NOV; DLB 75, 124; EW 13; EWL 3; MTCW 1, 2; MTFW 2005; RGWL 2, 3; TWA

Grass, Gunter Wilhelm
See Grass, Gunter

Gratton, Thomas
See Hulme, T(homas) E(rnest)

Grau, Shirley Ann 1929- .... **CLC 4, 9, 146; SSC 15**
See also CA 89-92; CANR 22, 69; CN 1, 2, 3, 4, 5, 6, 7; CSW; DLB 2, 218; INT CA-89-92; CANR-22; MTCW 1

Gravel, Fern
See Hall, James Norman

Graver, Elizabeth 1964- .... **CLC 70**
See also CA 135; CANR 71, 129

Graves, Richard Perceval
1895-1985 .... **CLC 44**
See also CA 65-68; CANR 9, 26, 51

Graves, Robert 1895-1985 ... **CLC 1, 2, 6, 11, 39, 44, 45; PC 6**
See also BPFB 2; BRW 7; BYA 4; CA 5-8R; CAAS 117; CANR 5, 36; CDBLB 1914-1945; CN 1, 2, 3; CP 1, 2, 3, 4; DA3; DAB; DAC; DAM MST, POET; DLB 20, 100, 191; DLBD 18; DLBY 1985; EWL 3; LATS 1:1; MTCW 1, 2; MTFW 2005; NCFS 2; NFS 21; RGEL 2; RHW; SATA 45; TEA

Graves, Valerie
See Bradley, Marion Zimmer

Gray, Alasdair 1934- .... **CLC 41**
See also BRWS 9; CA 126; CANR 47, 69, 106, 140; CN 4, 5, 6, 7; DLB 194, 261, 319; HGG; INT CA-126; MTCW 1, 2; MTFW 2005; RGSF 2; SUFW 2

Gray, Amlin 1946- .... **CLC 29**
See also CA 138

Gray, Francine du Plessix 1930- ..... **CLC 22, 153**
See also BEST 90:3; CA 61-64; 2; CANR 11, 33, 75, 81; DAM NOV; INT CANR-11; MTCW 1, 2; MTFW 2005

Grove, Frederick Philip .... **TCLC 4**
See Greve, Felix Paul (Berthold Friedrich)
See also DLB 92; RGEL 2; TCWW 1, 2
Grubb
See Crumb, R.
Grumbach, Doris 1918- .... **CLC 13, 22, 64**
See also CA 5-8R; 2; CANR 9, 42, 70, 127;
CN 6, 7; INT CANR-9; MTCW 2; MTFW
2005
Grundtvig, Nikolai Frederik Severin
1783-1872 .... **NCLC 1, 158**
See also DLB 300
Grunge
See Crumb, R.
Grunwald, Lisa 1959- .... **CLC 44**
See also CA 120; CANR 148
Gryphius, Andreas 1616-1664 .... **LC 89**
See also CDWLB 2; DLB 164; RGWL 2, 3
Guare, John 1938- .... **CLC 8, 14, 29, 67; DC 20**
See also CA 73-76; CAD; CANR 21, 69,
118; CD 5, 6; DAM DRAM; DFS 8, 13;
DLB 7, 249; EWL 3; MAL 5; MTCW 1,
2; RGAL 4
Guarini, Battista 1537-1612 .... **LC 102**
Gubar, Susan (David) 1944- .... **CLC 145**
See also CA 108; CANR 45, 70, 139; FW;
MTCW 1; RGAL 4
Gudjonsson, Halldor Kiljan 1902-1998
See Halldor Laxness
See also CA 103; CAAS 164
Guenter, Erich
See Eich, Gunter
Guest, Barbara 1920-2006 ... **CLC 34; PC 55**
See also BG 1:2; CA 25-28R; CAAS 248;
CANR 11, 44, 84; CP 1, 2, 3, 4, 5, 6, 7;
CWP; DLB 5, 193
Guest, Edgar A(lbert) 1881-1959 ... **TCLC 95**
See also CA 168; CAAE 112
Guest, Judith 1936- .... **CLC 8, 30**
See also AAYA 7, 66; CA 77-80; CANR
15, 75, 138; DA3; DAM NOV, POP;
EXPN; INT CANR-15; LAIT 5; MTCW
1, 2; MTFW 2005; NFS 1
Guevara, Che .... **CLC 87; HLC 1**
See Guevara (Serna), Ernesto
Guevara (Serna), Ernesto
1928-1967 .... **CLC 87; HLC 1**
See Guevara, Che
See also CA 127; CAAS 111; CANR 56;
DAM MULT; HW 1
Guicciardini, Francesco 1483-1540 ..... **LC 49**
Guido delle Colonne c. 1215-c.
1290 .... **CMLC 90**
Guild, Nicholas M. 1944- .... **CLC 33**
See also CA 93-96
Guillemin, Jacques
See Sartre, Jean-Paul
Guillen, Jorge 1893-1984 . **CLC 11; HLCS 1; PC 35**
See also CA 89-92; CAAS 112; DAM
MULT, POET; DLB 108; EWL 3; HW 1;
RGWL 2, 3
Guillen, Nicolas (Cristobal)
1902-1989 .... **BLC 2; CLC 48, 79; HLC 1; PC 23**
See also BW 2; CA 125; CAAE 116; CAAS
129; CANR 84; DAM MST, MULT,
POET; DLB 283; EWL 3; HW 1; LAW;
RGWL 2, 3; WP
Guillen y Alvarez, Jorge
See Guillen, Jorge
Guillevic, (Eugene) 1907-1997 .... **CLC 33**
See also CA 93-96; CWW 2
Guillois
See Desnos, Robert
Guillois, Valentin
See Desnos, Robert

Guimaraes Rosa, Joao 1908-1967 .... **HLCS 2**
See Rosa, Joao Guimaraes
See also CA 175; LAW; RGSF 2; RGWL 2,
3
Guiney, Louise Imogen
1861-1920 .... **TCLC 41**
See also CA 160; DLB 54; RGAL 4
Guinizelli, Guido c. 1230-1276 ...... **CMLC 49**
See Guinizzelli, Guido
Guinizzelli, Guido
See Guinizelli, Guido
See also WLIT 7
Guiraldes, Ricardo (Guillermo)
1886-1927 .... **TCLC 39**
See also CA 131; EWL 3; HW 1; LAW;
MTCW 1
Gumilev, Nikolai (Stepanovich)
1886-1921 .... **TCLC 60**
See Gumilyov, Nikolay Stepanovich
See also CA 165; DLB 295
Gumilyov, Nikolay Stepanovich
See Gumilev, Nikolai (Stepanovich)
See also EWL 3
Gump, P. Q.
See Card, Orson Scott
Gunesekera, Romesh 1954- .... **CLC 91**
See also BRWS 10; CA 159; CANR 140;
CN 6, 7; DLB 267, 323
Gunn, Bill .... **CLC 5**
See Gunn, William Harrison
See also DLB 38
Gunn, Thom(son William)
1929-2004 . **CLC 3, 6, 18, 32, 81; PC 26**
See also BRWS 4; CA 17-20R; CAAS 227;
CANR 9, 33, 116; CDBLB 1960 to
Present; CP 1, 2, 3, 4, 5, 6, 7; DAM
POET; DLB 27; INT CANR-33; MTCW
1; PFS 9; RGEL 2
Gunn, William Harrison 1934(?)-1989
See Gunn, Bill
See also AITN 1; BW 1, 3; CA 13-16R;
CAAS 128; CANR 12, 25, 76
Gunn Allen, Paula
See Allen, Paula Gunn
Gunnars, Kristjana 1948- .... **CLC 69**
See also CA 113; CCA 1; CP 6, 7; CWP;
DLB 60
Gunter, Erich
See Eich, Gunter
Gurdjieff, G(eorgei) I(vanovich)
1877(?)-1949 .... **TCLC 71**
See also CA 157
Gurganus, Allan 1947- .... **CLC 70**
See also BEST 90:1; CA 135; CANR 114;
CN 6, 7; CPW; CSW; DAM POP; GLL 1
Gurney, A. R.
See Gurney, A(lbert) R(amsdell), Jr.
See also DLB 266
Gurney, A(lbert) R(amsdell), Jr.
1930- .... **CLC 32, 50, 54**
See Gurney, A. R.
See also AMWS 5; CA 77-80; CAD; CANR
32, 64, 121; CD 5, 6; DAM DRAM; EWL
3
Gurney, Ivor (Bertie) 1890-1937 ... **TCLC 33**
See also BRW 6; CA 167; DLBY 2002;
PAB; RGEL 2
Gurney, Peter
See Gurney, A(lbert) R(amsdell), Jr.
Guro, Elena (Genrikhovna)
1877-1913 .... **TCLC 56**
See also DLB 295
Gustafson, James M(oody) 1925- ... **CLC 100**
See also CA 25-28R; CANR 37
Gustafson, Ralph (Barker)
1909-1995 .... **CLC 36**
See also CA 21-24R; CANR 8, 45, 84; CP
1, 2, 3, 4, 5, 6; DLB 88; RGEL 2

Gut, Gom
See Simenon, Georges (Jacques Christian)
Guterson, David 1956- .... **CLC 91**
See also CA 132; CANR 73, 126; CN 7;
DLB 292; MTCW 2; MTFW 2005; NFS
13
Guthrie, A(lfred) B(ertram), Jr.
1901-1991 .... **CLC 23**
See also CA 57-60; CAAS 134; CANR 24;
CN 1, 2, 3; DLB 6, 212; MAL 5; SATA
62; SATA-Obit 67; TCWW 1, 2
Guthrie, Isobel
See Grieve, C(hristopher) M(urray)
Guthrie, Woodrow Wilson 1912-1967
See Guthrie, Woody
See also CA 113; CAAS 93-96
Guthrie, Woody .... **CLC 35**
See Guthrie, Woodrow Wilson
See also DLB 303; LAIT 3
Gutierrez Najera, Manuel
1859-1895 .... **HLCS 2; NCLC 133**
See also DLB 290; LAW
Guy, Rosa (Cuthbert) 1925- .... **CLC 26**
See also AAYA 4, 37; BW 2; CA 17-20R;
CANR 14, 34, 83; CLR 13; DLB 33;
DNFS 1; JRDA; MAICYA 1, 2; SATA 14,
62, 122; YAW
Gwendolyn
See Bennett, (Enoch) Arnold
H. D. .... **CLC 3, 8, 14, 31, 34, 73; PC 5**
See Doolittle, Hilda
See also FL 1:5
H. de V.
See Buchan, John
Haavikko, Paavo Juhani 1931- .. **CLC 18, 34**
See also CA 106; CWW 2; EWL 3
Habbema, Koos
See Heijermans, Herman
Habermas, Juergen 1929- .... **CLC 104**
See also CA 109; CANR 85, 162; DLB 242
Habermas, Jurgen
See Habermas, Juergen
Hacker, Marilyn 1942- ...... **CLC 5, 9, 23, 72, 91; PC 47**
See also CA 77-80; CANR 68, 129; CP 3,
4, 5, 6, 7; CWP; DAM POET; DLB 120,
282; FW; GLL 2; MAL 5; PFS 19
Hadewijch of Antwerp fl. 1250- ... **CMLC 61**
See also RGWL 3
Hadrian 76-138 .... **CMLC 52**
Haeckel, Ernst Heinrich (Philipp August)
1834-1919 .... **TCLC 83**
See also CA 157
Hafiz c. 1326-1389(?) .... **CMLC 34**
See also RGWL 2, 3; WLIT 6
Hagedorn, Jessica T(arahata)
1949- .... **CLC 185**
See also CA 139; CANR 69; CWP; DLB
312; RGAL 4
Haggard, H(enry) Rider
1856-1925 .... **TCLC 11**
See also BRWS 3; BYA 4, 5; CA 148;
CAAE 108; CANR 112; DLB 70, 156,
174, 178; FANT; LMFS 1; MTCW 2;
RGEL 2; RHW; SATA 16; SCFW 1, 2;
SFW 4; SUFW 1; WLIT 4
Hagiosy, L.
See Larbaud, Valery (Nicolas)
Hagiwara, Sakutaro 1886-1942 .... **PC 18; TCLC 60**
See Hagiwara Sakutaro
See also CA 154; RGWL 3
Hagiwara Sakutaro
See Hagiwara, Sakutaro
See also EWL 3
Haig, Fenil
See Ford, Ford Madox

Haig-Brown, Roderick (Langmere)
1908-1976 .... **CLC 21**
See also CA 5-8R; CAAS 69-72; CANR 4, 38, 83; CLR 31; CWRI 5; DLB 88; MAI-CYA 1, 2; SATA 12; TCWW 2

Haight, Rip
See Carpenter, John (Howard)

Haij, Vera
See Jansson, Tove (Marika)

Hailey, Arthur 1920-2004 .... **CLC 5**
See also AITN 2; BEST 90:3; BPFB 2; CA 1-4R; CAAS 233; CANR 2, 36, 75; CCA 1; CN 1, 2, 3, 4, 5, 6, 7; CPW; DAM NOV, POP; DLB 88; DLBY 1982; MTCW 1, 2; MTFW 2005

Hailey, Elizabeth Forsythe 1938- ..... **CLC 40**
See also CA 188; 93-96, 188; 1; CANR 15, 48; INT CANR-15

Haines, John (Meade) 1924- .... **CLC 58**
See also AMWS 12; CA 17-20R; CANR 13, 34; CP 1, 2, 3, 4, 5; CSW; DLB 5, 212; TCLE 1:1

Ha Jin 1956- .... **CLC 109**
See Jin, Xuefei
See also CA 152; CANR 91, 130; DLB 244, 292; MTFW 2005; NFS 25; SSFS 17

Hakluyt, Richard 1552-1616 .... **LC 31**
See also DLB 136; RGEL 2

Haldeman, Joe 1943- .... **CLC 61**
See Graham, Robert
See also AAYA 38; CA 179; 53-56, 179; 25; CANR 6, 70, 72, 130; DLB 8; INT CANR-6; SCFW 2; SFW 4

Haldeman, Joe William
See Haldeman, Joe

Hale, Janet Campbell 1947- .... **NNAL**
See also CA 49-52; CANR 45, 75; DAM MULT; DLB 175; MTCW 2; MTFW 2005

Hale, Sarah Josepha (Buell)
1788-1879 .... **NCLC 75**
See also DLB 1, 42, 73, 243

Halevy, Elie 1870-1937 .... **TCLC 104**

Haley, Alex(ander Murray Palmer)
1921-1992 .... **BLC 2; CLC 8, 12, 76; TCLC 147**
See also AAYA 26; BPFB 2; BW 2, 3; CA 77-80; CAAS 136; CANR 61; CDALBS; CPW; CSW; DA; DA3; DAB; DAC; DAM MST, MULT, POP; DLB 38; LAIT 5; MTCW 1, 2; NFS 9

Haliburton, Thomas Chandler
1796-1865 .... **NCLC 15, 149**
See also DLB 11, 99; RGEL 2; RGSF 2

Hall, Donald 1928- ... **CLC 1, 13, 37, 59, 151, 240; PC 70**
See also AAYA 63; CA 5-8R; 7; CANR 2, 44, 64, 106, 133; CP 1, 2, 3, 4, 5, 6, 7; DAM POET; DLB 5; MAL 5; MTCW 2; MTFW 2005; RGAL 4; SATA 23, 97

Hall, Donald Andrew, Jr.
See Hall, Donald

Hall, Frederic Sauser
See Sauser-Hall, Frederic

Hall, James
See Kuttner, Henry

Hall, James Norman 1887-1951 ..... **TCLC 23**
See also CA 173; CAAE 123; LAIT 1; RHW 1; SATA 21

Hall, Joseph 1574-1656 .... **LC 91**
See also DLB 121, 151; RGEL 2

Hall, Marguerite Radclyffe
See Hall, Radclyffe

Hall, Radclyffe 1880-1943 .... **TCLC 12**
See also BRWS 6; CA 150; CAAE 110; CANR 83; DLB 191; MTCW 2; MTFW 2005; RGEL 2; RHW

Hall, Rodney 1935- .... **CLC 51**
See also CA 109; CANR 69; CN 6, 7; CP 1, 2, 3, 4, 5, 6, 7; DLB 289

Hallam, Arthur Henry
1811-1833 .... **NCLC 110**
See also DLB 32

Halldor Laxness .... **CLC 25**
See Gudjonsson, Halldor Kiljan
See also DLB 293; EW 12; EWL 3; RGWL 2, 3

Halleck, Fitz-Greene 1790-1867 .... **NCLC 47**
See also DLB 3, 250; RGAL 4

Halliday, Michael
See Creasey, John

Halpern, Daniel 1945- .... **CLC 14**
See also CA 33-36R; CANR 93; CP 3, 4, 5, 6, 7

Hamburger, Michael 1924-2007 ... **CLC 5, 14**
See also CA 196; 5-8R, 196; 4; CANR 2, 47; CP 1, 2, 3, 4, 5, 6, 7; DLB 27

Hamburger, Michael Peter Leopold
See Hamburger, Michael

Hamill, Pete 1935- .... **CLC 10**
See also CA 25-28R; CANR 18, 71, 127

Hamilton, Alexander
1755(?)-1804 .... **NCLC 49**
See also DLB 37

Hamilton, Clive
See Lewis, C.S.

Hamilton, Edmond 1904-1977 .... **CLC 1**
See also CA 1-4R; CANR 3, 84; DLB 8; SATA 118; SFW 4

Hamilton, Elizabeth 1758-1816 ... **NCLC 153**
See also DLB 116, 158

Hamilton, Eugene (Jacob) Lee
See Lee-Hamilton, Eugene (Jacob)

Hamilton, Franklin
See Silverberg, Robert

Hamilton, Gail
See Corcoran, Barbara (Asenath)

Hamilton, (Robert) Ian 1938-2001 . **CLC 191**
See also CA 106; CAAS 203; CANR 41, 67; CP 1, 2, 3, 4, 5, 6, 7; DLB 40, 155

Hamilton, Jane 1957- .... **CLC 179**
See also CA 147; CANR 85, 128; CN 7; MTFW 2005

Hamilton, Mollie
See Kaye, M.M.

Hamilton, (Anthony Walter) Patrick
1904-1962 .... **CLC 51**
See also CA 176; CAAS 113; DLB 10, 191

Hamilton, Virginia 1936-2002 .... **CLC 26**
See also AAYA 2, 21; BW 2, 3; BYA 1, 2, 8; CA 25-28R; CAAS 206; CANR 20, 37, 73, 126; CLR 1, 11, 40; DAM MULT; DLB 33, 52; DLBY 2001; INT CANR-20; JRDA; LAIT 5; MAICYA 1, 2; MAI-CYAS 1; MTCW 1, 2; MTFW 2005; SATA 4, 56, 79, 123; SATA-Obit 132; WYA; YAW

Hammett, (Samuel) Dashiell
1894-1961 ..... **CLC 3, 5, 10, 19, 47; SSC 17; TCLC 187**
See also AAYA 59; AITN 1; AMWS 4; BPFB 2; CA 81-84; CANR 42; CDALB 1929-1941; CMW 4; DA3; DLB 226, 280; DLBD 6; DLBY 1996; EWL 3; LAIT 3; MAL 5; MSW; MTCW 1, 2; MTFW 2005; NFS 21; RGAL 4; RGSF 2; TUS

Hammon, Jupiter 1720(?)-1800(?) .... **BLC 2; NCLC 5; PC 16**
See also DAM MULT, POET; DLB 31, 50

Hammond, Keith
See Kuttner, Henry

Hamner, Earl (Henry), Jr. 1923- ...... **CLC 12**
See also AITN 2; CA 73-76; DLB 6

Hampton, Christopher 1946- .... **CLC 4**
See also CA 25-28R; CD 5, 6; DLB 13; MTCW 1

Hampton, Christopher James
See Hampton, Christopher

Hamsun, Knut .... **TCLC 2, 14, 49, 151**
See Pedersen, Knut
See also DLB 297, 330; EW 8; EWL 3; RGWL 2, 3

Handke, Peter 1942- .... **CLC 5, 8, 10, 15, 38, 134; DC 17**
See also CA 77-80; CANR 33, 75, 104, 133; CWW 2; DAM DRAM, NOV; DLB 85, 124; EWL 3; MTCW 1, 2; MTFW 2005; TWA

Handy, W(illiam) C(hristopher)
1873-1958 .... **TCLC 97**
See also BW 3; CA 167; CAAE 121

Hanley, James 1901-1985 ..... **CLC 3, 5, 8, 13**
See also CA 73-76; CAAS 117; CANR 36; CBD; CN 1, 2, 3; DLB 191; EWL 3; MTCW 1; RGEL 2

Hannah, Barry 1942- .. **CLC 23, 38, 90; SSC 94**
See also BPFB 2; CA 110; CAAE 108; CANR 43, 68, 113; CN 4, 5, 6, 7; CSW; DLB 6, 234; INT CA-110; MTCW 1; RGSF 2

Hannon, Ezra
See Hunter, Evan

Hansberry, Lorraine (Vivian)
1930-1965 .. **BLC 2; CLC 17, 62; DC 2; TCLC 192**
See also AAYA 25; AFAW 1, 2; AMWS 4; BW 1, 3; CA 109; CAAS 25-28R; CABS 3; CAD; CANR 58; CDALB 1941-1968; CWD; DA; DA3; DAB; DAC; DAM DRAM, MST, MULT; DFS 2; DLB 7, 38; EWL 3; FL 1:6; FW; LAIT 4; MAL 5; MTCW 1, 2; MTFW 2005; RGAL 4; TUS

Hansen, Joseph 1923-2004 .... **CLC 38**
See Brock, Rose; Colton, James
See also BPFB 2; CA 29-32R; 17; CAAS 233; CANR 16, 44, 66, 125; CMW 4; DLB 226; GLL 1; INT CANR-16

Hansen, Karen V. 1955- .... **CLC 65**
See also CA 149; CANR 102

Hansen, Martin A(lfred)
1909-1955 .... **TCLC 32**
See also CA 167; DLB 214; EWL 3

Hanson, Kenneth O(stlin) 1922- .... **CLC 13**
See also CA 53-56; CANR 7; CP 1, 2, 3, 4, 5

Hardwick, Elizabeth 1916- .... **CLC 13**
See also AMWS 3; CA 5-8R; CANR 3, 32, 70, 100, 139; CN 4, 5, 6; CSW; DA3; DAM NOV; DLB 6; MBL; MTCW 1, 2; MTFW 2005; TCLE 1:1

Hardy, Thomas 1840-1928 .... **PC 8; SSC 2, 60; TCLC 4, 10, 18, 32, 48, 53, 72, 143, 153; WLC 3**
See also AAYA 69; BRW 6; BRWC 1, 2; BRWR 1; CA 123; CAAE 104; CDBLB 1890-1914; DA; DA3; DAB; DAC; DAM MST, NOV, POET; DLB 18, 19, 135, 284; EWL 3; EXPN; EXPP; LAIT 2; MTCW 1, 2; MTFW 2005; NFS 3, 11, 15, 19; PFS 3, 4, 18; RGEL 2; RGSF 2; TEA; WLIT 4

Hare, David 1947- . **CLC 29, 58, 136; DC 26**
See also BRWS 4; CA 97-100; CANR 39, 91; CBD; CD 5, 6; DFS 4, 7, 16; DLB 13, 310; MTCW 1; TEA

Harewood, John
See Van Druten, John (William)

Harford, Henry
See Hudson, W(illiam) H(enry)

Hargrave, Leonie
See Disch, Thomas M.

Hariri, Al- al-Qasim ibn 'Ali Abu Muhammad al-Basri
See al-Hariri, al-Qasim ibn 'Ali Abu Muhammad al-Basri

Harjo, Joy 1951- ..... **CLC 83; NNAL; PC 27**
See also AMWS 12; CA 114; CANR 35, 67, 91, 129; CP 6, 7; CWP; DAM MULT; DLB 120, 175; EWL 3; MTCW 2; MTFW 2005; PFS 15; RGAL 4

Harlan, Louis R(udolph) 1922- .... **CLC 34**
See also CA 21-24R; CANR 25, 55, 80

Harling, Robert 1951(?)- .... **CLC 53**
See also CA 147

Harmon, William (Ruth) 1938- .... **CLC 38**
See also CA 33-36R; CANR 14, 32, 35; SATA 65

Harper, F. E. W.
See Harper, Frances Ellen Watkins

Harper, Frances E. W.
See Harper, Frances Ellen Watkins

Harper, Frances E. Watkins
See Harper, Frances Ellen Watkins

Harper, Frances Ellen
See Harper, Frances Ellen Watkins

Harper, Frances Ellen Watkins
1825-1911 ..... **BLC 2; PC 21; TCLC 14**
See also AFAW 1, 2; BW 1, 3; CA 125; CAAE 111; CANR 79; DAM MULT, POET; DLB 50, 221; MBL; RGAL 4

Harper, Michael S(teven) 1938- ... **CLC 7, 22**
See also AFAW 2; BW 1; CA 224; 33-36R, 224; CANR 24, 108; CP 2, 3, 4, 5, 6, 7; DLB 41; RGAL 4; TCLE 1:1

Harper, Mrs. F. E. W.
See Harper, Frances Ellen Watkins

Harpur, Charles 1813-1868 .... **NCLC 114**
See also DLB 230; RGEL 2

Harris, Christie
See Harris, Christie (Lucy) Irwin

Harris, Christie (Lucy) Irwin
1907-2002 .... **CLC 12**
See also CA 5-8R; CANR 6, 83; CLR 47; DLB 88; JRDA; MAICYA 1, 2; SAAS 10; SATA 6, 74; SATA-Essay 116

Harris, Frank 1856-1931 .... **TCLC 24**
See also CA 150; CAAE 109; CANR 80; DLB 156, 197; RGEL 2

Harris, George Washington
1814-1869 .... **NCLC 23, 165**
See also DLB 3, 11, 248; RGAL 4

Harris, Joel Chandler 1848-1908 ..... **SSC 19, 103; TCLC 2**
See also CA 137; CAAE 104; CANR 80; CLR 49; DLB 11, 23, 42, 78, 91; LAIT 2; MAICYA 1, 2; RGSF 2; SATA 100; WCH; YABC 1

Harris, John (Wyndham Parkes Lucas) Beynon 1903-1969
See Wyndham, John
See also CA 102; CAAS 89-92; CANR 84; SATA 118; SFW 4

Harris, MacDonald .... **CLC 9**
See Heiney, Donald (William)

Harris, Mark 1922-2007 .... **CLC 19**
See also CA 5-8R; 3; CAAS 260; CANR 2, 55, 83; CN 1, 2, 3, 4, 5, 6, 7; DLB 2; DLBY 1980

Harris, Norman .... **CLC 65**

Harris, (Theodore) Wilson 1921- .... **CLC 25, 159**
See also BRWS 5; BW 2, 3; CA 65-68; 16; CANR 11, 27, 69, 114; CDWLB 3; CN 1, 2, 3, 4, 5, 6, 7; CP 1, 2, 3, 4, 5, 6, 7; DLB 117; EWL 3; MTCW 1; RGEL 2

Harrison, Barbara Grizzuti
1934-2002 .... **CLC 144**
See also CA 77-80; CAAS 205; CANR 15, 48; INT CANR-15

Harrison, Elizabeth (Allen) Cavanna
1909-2001
See Cavanna, Betty
See also CA 9-12R; CAAS 200; CANR 6, 27, 85, 104, 121; MAICYA 2; SATA 142; YAW

Harrison, Harry (Max) 1925- .... **CLC 42**
See also CA 1-4R; CANR 5, 21, 84; DLB 8; SATA 4; SCFW 2; SFW 4

Harrison, James
See Harrison, Jim

Harrison, James Thomas
See Harrison, Jim

Harrison, Jim 1937- .... **CLC 6, 14, 33, 66, 143; SSC 19**
See also AMWS 8; CA 13-16R; CANR 8, 51, 79, 142; CN 5, 6; CP 1, 2, 3, 4, 5, 6; DLBY 1982; INT CANR-8; RGAL 4; TCWW 2; TUS

Harrison, Kathryn 1961- .... **CLC 70, 151**
See also CA 144; CANR 68, 122

Harrison, Tony 1937- .... **CLC 43, 129**
See also BRWS 5; CA 65-68; CANR 44, 98; CBD; CD 5, 6; CP 2, 3, 4, 5, 6, 7; DLB 40, 245; MTCW 1; RGEL 2

Harriss, Will(ard Irvin) 1922- .... **CLC 34**
See also CA 111

Hart, Ellis
See Ellison, Harlan

Hart, Josephine 1942(?)- .... **CLC 70**
See also CA 138; CANR 70, 149; CPW; DAM POP

Hart, Moss 1904-1961 .... **CLC 66**
See also CA 109; CAAS 89-92; CANR 84; DAM DRAM; DFS 1; DLB 7, 266; RGAL 4

Harte, (Francis) Bret(t)
1836(?)-1902 ... **SSC 8, 59; TCLC 1, 25; WLC 3**
See also AMWS 2; CA 140; CAAE 104; CANR 80; CDALB 1865-1917; DA; DA3; DAC; DAM MST; DLB 12, 64, 74, 79, 186; EXPS; LAIT 2; RGAL 4; RGSF 2; SATA 26; SSFS 3; TUS

Hartley, L(eslie) P(oles) 1895-1972 ... **CLC 2, 22**
See also BRWS 7; CA 45-48; CAAS 37-40R; CANR 33; CN 1; DLB 15, 139; EWL 3; HGG; MTCW 1, 2; MTFW 2005; RGEL 2; RGSF 2; SUFW 1

Hartman, Geoffrey H. 1929- .... **CLC 27**
See also CA 125; CAAE 117; CANR 79; DLB 67

Hartmann, Sadakichi 1869-1944 ... **TCLC 73**
See also CA 157; DLB 54

Hartmann von Aue c. 1170-c. 1210 .... **CMLC 15**
See also CDWLB 2; DLB 138; RGWL 2, 3

Hartog, Jan de
See de Hartog, Jan

Haruf, Kent 1943- .... **CLC 34**
See also AAYA 44; CA 149; CANR 91, 131

Harvey, Caroline
See Trollope, Joanna

Harvey, Gabriel 1550(?)-1631 .... **LC 88**
See also DLB 167, 213, 281

Harwood, Ronald 1934- .... **CLC 32**
See also CA 1-4R; CANR 4, 55, 150; CBD; CD 5, 6; DAM DRAM, MST; DLB 13

Hasegawa Tatsunosuke
See Futabatei, Shimei

Hasek, Jaroslav (Matej Frantisek)
1883-1923 .... **SSC 69; TCLC 4**
See also CA 129; CAAE 104; CDWLB 4; DLB 215; EW 9; EWL 3; MTCW 1, 2; RGSF 2; RGWL 2, 3

Hass, Robert 1941- ... **CLC 18, 39, 99; PC 16**
See also AMWS 6; CA 111; CANR 30, 50, 71; CP 3, 4, 5, 6, 7; DLB 105, 206; EWL 3; MAL 5; MTFW 2005; RGAL 4; SATA 94; TCLE 1:1

Hastings, Hudson
See Kuttner, Henry

Hastings, Selina .... **CLC 44**
See also CA 257

Hastings, Selina Shirley
See Hastings, Selina

Hathorne, John 1641-1717 .... **LC 38**

Hatteras, Amelia
See Mencken, H(enry) L(ouis)

Hatteras, Owen .... **TCLC 18**
See Mencken, H(enry) L(ouis); Nathan, George Jean

Hauff, Wilhelm 1802-1827 .... **NCLC 185**
See also DLB 90; SUFW 1

Hauptmann, Gerhart (Johann Robert)
1862-1946 .... **SSC 37; TCLC 4**
See also CA 153; CAAE 104; CDWLB 2; DAM DRAM; DLB 66, 118, 330; EW 8; EWL 3; RGSF 2; RGWL 2, 3; TWA

Havel, Vaclav 1936- ..... **CLC 25, 58, 65, 123; DC 6**
See also CA 104; CANR 36, 63, 124; CD-WLB 4; CWW 2; DA3; DAM DRAM; DFS 10; DLB 232; EWL 3; LMFS 2; MTCW 1, 2; MTFW 2005; RGWL 3

Haviaras, Stratis .... **CLC 33**
See Chaviaras, Strates

Hawes, Stephen 1475(?)-1529(?) .... **LC 17**
See also DLB 132; RGEL 2

Hawkes, John 1925-1998 .. **CLC 1, 2, 3, 4, 7, 9, 14, 15, 27, 49**
See also BPFB 2; CA 1-4R; CAAS 167; CANR 2, 47, 64; CN 1, 2, 3, 4, 5, 6; DLB 2, 7, 227; DLBY 1980, 1998; EWL 3; MAL 5; MTCW 1, 2; MTFW 2005; RGAL 4

Hawking, S. W.
See Hawking, Stephen W.

Hawking, Stephen W. 1942- ..... **CLC 63, 105**
See also AAYA 13; BEST 89:1; CA 129; CAAE 126; CANR 48, 115; CPW; DA3; MTCW 2; MTFW 2005

Hawkins, Anthony Hope
See Hope, Anthony

Hawthorne, Julian 1846-1934 .... **TCLC 25**
See also CA 165; HGG

Hawthorne, Nathaniel 1804-1864 ... **NCLC 2, 10, 17, 23, 39, 79, 95, 158, 171; SSC 3, 29, 39, 89; WLC 3**
See also AAYA 18; AMW; AMWC 1; AMWR 1; BPFB 2; BYA 3; CDALB 1640-1865; CLR 103; DA; DA3; DAB; DAC; DAM MST, NOV; DLB 1, 74, 183, 223, 269; EXPN; EXPS; GL 2; HGG; LAIT 1; NFS 1, 20; RGAL 4; RGSF 2; SSFS 1, 7, 11, 15; SUFW 1; TUS; WCH; YABC 2

Hawthorne, Sophia Peabody
1809-1871 .... **NCLC 150**
See also DLB 183, 239

Haxton, Josephine Ayres 1921-
See Douglas, Ellen
See also CA 115; CANR 41, 83

Hayaseca y Eizaguirre, Jorge
See Echegaray (y Eizaguirre), Jose (Maria Waldo)

Hayashi, Fumiko 1904-1951 .... **TCLC 27**
See Hayashi Fumiko
See also CA 161

Hayashi Fumiko
See Hayashi, Fumiko
See also DLB 180; EWL 3

Haycraft, Anna 1932-2005
See Ellis, Alice Thomas
See also CA 122; CAAS 237; CANR 90, 141; MTCW 2; MTFW 2005

Hayden, Robert E(arl) 1913-1980 ..... **BLC 2; CLC 5, 9, 14, 37; PC 6**
See also AFAW 1, 2; AMWS 2; BW 1, 3; CA 69-72; CAAS 97-100; CABS 2; CANR 24, 75, 82; CDALB 1941-1968; CP 1, 2, 3; DA; DAC; DAM MST, MULT,

POET; DLB 5, 76; EWL 3; EXPP; MAL
5; MTCW 1, 2; PFS 1; RGAL 4; SATA
19; SATA-Obit 26; WP

Haydon, Benjamin Robert
1786-1846 .... **NCLC 146**
See also DLB 110

Hayek, F(riedrich) A(ugust von)
1899-1992 .... **TCLC 109**
See also CA 93-96; CAAS 137; CANR 20;
MTCW 1, 2

Hayford, J(oseph) E(phraim) Casely
See Casely-Hayford, J(oseph) E(phraim)

Hayman, Ronald 1932- .... **CLC 44**
See also CA 25-28R; CANR 18, 50, 88; CD
5, 6; DLB 155

Hayne, Paul Hamilton 1830-1886 . **NCLC 94**
See also DLB 3, 64, 79, 248; RGAL 4

Hays, Mary 1760-1843 .... **NCLC 114**
See also DLB 142, 158; RGEL 2

Haywood, Eliza (Fowler)
1693(?)-1756 .... **LC 1, 44**
See also BRWS 12; DLB 39; RGEL 2

Hazlitt, William 1778-1830 ...... **NCLC 29, 82**
See also BRW 4; DLB 110, 158; RGEL 2;
TEA

Hazzard, Shirley 1931- .... **CLC 18, 218**
See also CA 9-12R; CANR 4, 70, 127; CN
1, 2, 3, 4, 5, 6, 7; DLB 289; DLBY 1982;
MTCW 1

Head, Bessie 1937-1986 ...... **BLC 2; CLC 25,
67; SSC 52**
See also AFW; BW 2, 3; CA 29-32R; CAAS
119; CANR 25, 82; CDWLB 3; CN 1, 2,
3, 4; DA3; DAM MULT; DLB 117, 225;
EWL 3; EXPS; FL 1:6; FW; MTCW 1, 2;
MTFW 2005; RGSF 2; SSFS 5, 13; WLIT
2; WWE 1

Headon, (Nicky) Topper 1956(?)- ..... **CLC 30**

Heaney, Seamus 1939- . **CLC 5, 7, 14, 25, 37,
74, 91, 171, 225; PC 18; WLCS**
See also AAYA 61; BRWR 1; BRWS 2; CA
85-88; CANR 25, 48, 75, 91, 128; CD-
BLB 1960 to Present; CP 1, 2, 3, 4, 5, 6,
7; DA3; DAB; DAM POET; DLB 40,
330; DLBY 1995; EWL 3; EXPP; MTCW
1, 2; MTFW 2005; PAB; PFS 2, 5, 8, 17;
RGEL 2; TEA; WLIT 4

Hearn, (Patricio) Lafcadio (Tessima Carlos)
1850-1904 .... **TCLC 9**
See also CA 166; CAAE 105; DLB 12, 78,
189; HGG; MAL 5; RGAL 4

Hearne, Samuel 1745-1792 .... **LC 95**
See also DLB 99

Hearne, Vicki 1946-2001 .... **CLC 56**
See also CA 139; CAAS 201

Hearon, Shelby 1931- .... **CLC 63**
See also AITN 2; AMWS 8; CA 25-28R;
11; CANR 18, 48, 103, 146; CSW

Heat-Moon, William Least .... **CLC 29**
See Trogdon, William (Lewis)
See also AAYA 9

Hebbel, Friedrich 1813-1863 . **DC 21; NCLC
43**
See also CDWLB 2; DAM DRAM; DLB
129; EW 6; RGWL 2, 3

Hebert, Anne 1916-2000 .... **CLC 4, 13, 29**
See also CA 85-88; CAAS 187; CANR 69,
126; CCA 1; CWP; CWW 2; DA3; DAC;
DAM MST, POET; DLB 68; EWL 3; GFL
1789 to the Present; MTCW 1, 2; MTFW
2005; PFS 20

Hecht, Anthony (Evan) 1923-2004 .... **CLC 8,
13, 19; PC 70**
See also AMWS 10; CA 9-12R; CAAS 232;
CANR 6, 108; CP 1, 2, 3, 4, 5, 6, 7; DAM
POET; DLB 5, 169; EWL 3; PFS 6; WP

Hecht, Ben 1894-1964 ..... **CLC 8; TCLC 101**
See also CA 85-88; DFS 9; DLB 7, 9, 25,
26, 28, 86; FANT; IDFW 3, 4; RGAL 4

Hedayat, Sadeq 1903-1951 .... **TCLC 21**
See also CAAE 120; CANR 34; RGSF 2

Hegel, Georg Wilhelm Friedrich
1770-1831 .... **NCLC 46, 151**
See also DLB 90; TWA

Heidegger, Martin 1889-1976 .... **CLC 24**
See also CA 81-84; CAAS 65-68; CANR
34; DLB 296; MTCW 1, 2; MTFW 2005

Heidenstam, (Carl Gustaf) Verner von
1859-1940 .... **TCLC 5**
See also CAAE 104; DLB 330

Heidi Louise
See Erdrich, Louise

Heifner, Jack 1946- .... **CLC 11**
See also CA 105; CANR 47

Heijermans, Herman 1864-1924 .... **TCLC 24**
See also CAAE 123; EWL 3

Heilbrun, Carolyn G(old)
1926-2003 .... **CLC 25, 173**
See Cross, Amanda
See also CA 45-48; CAAS 220; CANR 1,
28, 58, 94; FW

Hein, Christoph 1944- .... **CLC 154**
See also CA 158; CANR 108; CDWLB 2;
CWW 2; DLB 124

Heine, Heinrich 1797-1856 .... **NCLC 4, 54,
147; PC 25**
See also CDWLB 2; DLB 90; EW 5; RGWL
2, 3; TWA

Heinemann, Larry 1944- .... **CLC 50**
See also CA 110; 21; CANR 31, 81, 156;
DLBD 9; INT CANR-31

Heinemann, Larry Curtiss
See Heinemann, Larry

Heiney, Donald (William) 1921-1993
See Harris, MacDonald
See also CA 1-4R; CAAS 142; CANR 3,
58; FANT

Heinlein, Robert A. 1907-1988 .. **CLC 1, 3, 8,
14, 26, 55; SSC 55**
See also AAYA 17; BPFB 2; BYA 4, 13;
CA 1-4R; CAAS 125; CANR 1, 20, 53;
CLR 75; CN 1, 2, 3, 4; CPW; DA3; DAM
POP; DLB 8; EXPS; JRDA; LAIT 5;
LMFS 2; MAICYA 1, 2; MTCW 1, 2;
MTFW 2005; RGAL 4; SATA 9, 69;
SATA-Obit 56; SCFW 1, 2; SFW 4; SSFS
7; YAW

Helforth, John
See Doolittle, Hilda

Heliodorus fl. 3rd cent. - .... **CMLC 52**
See also WLIT 8

Hellenhofferu, Vojtech Kapristian z
See Hasek, Jaroslav (Matej Frantisek)

Heller, Joseph 1923-1999 . **CLC 1, 3, 5, 8, 11,
36, 63; TCLC 131, 151; WLC 3**
See also AAYA 24; AITN 1; AMWS 4;
BPFB 2; BYA 1; CA 5-8R; CAAS 187;
CABS 1; CANR 8, 42, 66, 126; CN 1, 2,
3, 4, 5, 6; CPW; DA; DA3; DAB; DAC;
DAM MST, NOV, POP; DLB 2, 28, 227;
DLBY 1980, 2002; EWL 3; EXPN; INT
CANR-8; LAIT 4; MAL 5; MTCW 1, 2;
MTFW 2005; NFS 1; RGAL 4; TUS;
YAW

Hellman, Lillian 1906-1984 . **CLC 2, 4, 8, 14,
18, 34, 44, 52; DC 1; TCLC 119**
See also AAYA 47; AITN 1, 2; AMWS 1;
CA 13-16R; CAAS 112; CAD; CANR 33;
CWD; DA3; DAM DRAM; DFS 1, 3, 14;
DLB 7, 228; DLBY 1984; EWL 3; FL 1:6;
FW; LAIT 3; MAL 5; MBL; MTCW 1, 2;
MTFW 2005; RGAL 4; TUS

Helprin, Mark 1947- .... **CLC 7, 10, 22, 32**
See also CA 81-84; CANR 47, 64, 124;
CDALBS; CN 7; CPW; DA3; DAM NOV,
POP; DLB 335; DLBY 1985; FANT;
MAL 5; MTCW 1, 2; MTFW 2005; SSFS
25; SUFW 2

Helvetius, Claude-Adrien 1715-1771 .. **LC 26**
See also DLB 313

Helyar, Jane Penelope Josephine 1933-
See Poole, Josephine
See also CA 21-24R; CANR 10, 26; CWRI
5; SATA 82, 138; SATA-Essay 138

Hemans, Felicia 1793-1835 ...... **NCLC 29, 71**
See also DLB 96; RGEL 2

Hemingway, Ernest (Miller)
1899-1961 .... **CLC 1, 3, 6, 8, 10, 13, 19,
30, 34, 39, 41, 44, 50, 61, 80; SSC 1, 25,
36, 40, 63; TCLC 115; WLC 3**
See also AAYA 19; AMW; AMWC 1;
AMWR 1; BPFB 2; BYA 2, 3, 13, 15; CA
77-80; CANR 34; CDALB 1917-1929;
DA; DA3; DAB; DAC; DAM MST, NOV;
DLB 4, 9, 102, 210, 308, 316, 330; DLBD
1, 15, 16; DLBY 1981, 1987, 1996, 1998;
EWL 3; EXPN; EXPS; LAIT 3, 4; LATS
1:1; MAL 5; MTCW 1, 2; MTFW 2005;
NFS 1, 5, 6, 14; RGAL 4; RGSF 2; SSFS
17; TUS; WYA

Hempel, Amy 1951- .... **CLC 39**
See also CA 137; CAAE 118; CANR 70,
166; DA3; DLB 218; EXPS; MTCW 2;
MTFW 2005; SSFS 2

Henderson, F. C.
See Mencken, H(enry) L(ouis)

Henderson, Sylvia
See Ashton-Warner, Sylvia (Constance)

Henderson, Zenna (Chlarson)
1917-1983 .... **SSC 29**
See also CA 1-4R; CAAS 133; CANR 1,
84; DLB 8; SATA 5; SFW 4

Henkin, Joshua .... **CLC 119**
See also CA 161

Henley, Beth .... **CLC 23; DC 6, 14**
See Henley, Elizabeth Becker
See also AAYA 70; CABS 3; CAD; CD 5,
6; CSW; CWD; DFS 2, 21; DLBY 1986;
FW

Henley, Elizabeth Becker 1952-
See Henley, Beth
See also CA 107; CANR 32, 73, 140; DA3;
DAM DRAM, MST; MTCW 1, 2; MTFW
2005

Henley, William Ernest 1849-1903 .. **TCLC 8**
See also CA 234; CAAE 105; DLB 19;
RGEL 2

Hennissart, Martha 1929-
See Lathen, Emma
See also CA 85-88; CANR 64

Henry VIII 1491-1547 .... **LC 10**
See also DLB 132

Henry, O. . **SSC 5, 49; TCLC 1, 19; WLC 3**
See Porter, William Sydney
See also AAYA 41; AMWS 2; EXPS; MAL
5; RGAL 4; RGSF 2; SSFS 2, 18; TCWW
1, 2

Henry, Patrick 1736-1799 .... **LC 25**
See also LAIT 1

Henryson, Robert 1430(?)-1506(?) ..... **LC 20,
110; PC 65**
See also BRWS 7; DLB 146; RGEL 2

Henschke, Alfred
See Klabund

Henson, Lance 1944- .... **NNAL**
See also CA 146; DLB 175

Hentoff, Nat(han Irving) 1925- .... **CLC 26**
See also AAYA 4, 42; BYA 6; CA 1-4R;
CANR 5, 25, 77, 114; CLR 1, 52; INT
CANR-25; JRDA; MAICYA 1, 2; SATA
42, 69, 133; SATA-Brief 27; WYA; YAW

Heppenstall, (John) Rayner
1911-1981 .... **CLC 10**
See also CA 1-4R; CAAS 103; CANR 29;
CN 1, 2; CP 1, 2, 3; EWL 3

Heraclitus c. 540B.C.-c. 450B.C. ... **CMLC 22**
See also DLB 176

Herbert, Frank 1920-1986 ... **CLC 12, 23, 35, 44, 85**
See also AAYA 21; BPFB 2; BYA 4, 14; CA 53-56; CAAS 118; CANR 5, 43; CDALBS; CPW; DAM POP; DLB 8; INT CANR-5; LAIT 5; MTCW 1, 2; MTFW 2005; NFS 17; SATA 9, 37; SATA-Obit 47; SCFW 1, 2; SFW 4; YAW

Herbert, George 1593-1633 . **LC 24, 121; PC 4**
See also BRW 2; BRWR 2; CDBLB Before 1660; DAB; DAM POET; DLB 126; EXPP; PFS 25; RGEL 2; TEA; WP

Herbert, Zbigniew 1924-1998 ..... **CLC 9, 43; PC 50; TCLC 168**
See also CA 89-92; CAAS 169; CANR 36, 74; CDWLB 4; CWW 2; DAM POET; DLB 232; EWL 3; MTCW 1; PFS 22

Herbst, Josephine (Frey) 1897-1969 .... **CLC 34**
See also CA 5-8R; CAAS 25-28R; DLB 9

Herder, Johann Gottfried von 1744-1803 .... **NCLC 8, 186**
See also DLB 97; EW 4; TWA

Heredia, Jose Maria 1803-1839 .... **HLCS 2**
See also LAW

Hergesheimer, Joseph 1880-1954 ... **TCLC 11**
See also CA 194; CAAE 109; DLB 102, 9; RGAL 4

Herlihy, James Leo 1927-1993 .... **CLC 6**
See also CA 1-4R; CAAS 143; CAD; CANR 2; CN 1, 2, 3, 4, 5

Herman, William
See Bierce, Ambrose (Gwinett)

Hermogenes fl. c. 175- .... **CMLC 6**

Hernandez, Jose 1834-1886 .... **NCLC 17**
See also LAW; RGWL 2, 3; WLIT 1

Herodotus c. 484B.C.-c. 420B.C. .. **CMLC 17**
See also AW 1; CDWLB 1; DLB 176; RGWL 2, 3; TWA; WLIT 8

Herr, Michael 1940(?)- .... **CLC 231**
See also CA 89-92; CANR 68, 142; DLB 185; MTCW 1

Herrick, Robert 1591-1674 .... **LC 13; PC 9**
See also BRW 2; BRWC 2; DA; DAB; DAC; DAM MST, POP; DLB 126; EXPP; PFS 13; RGAL 4; RGEL 2; TEA; WP

Herring, Guilles
See Somerville, Edith Oenone

Herriot, James 1916-1995 .... **CLC 12**
See Wight, James Alfred
See also AAYA 1, 54; BPFB 2; CAAS 148; CANR 40; CLR 80; CPW; DAM POP; LAIT 3; MAICYA 2; MAICYAS 1; MTCW 2; SATA 86, 135; TEA; YAW

Herris, Violet
See Hunt, Violet

Herrmann, Dorothy 1941- .... **CLC 44**
See also CA 107

Herrmann, Taffy
See Herrmann, Dorothy

Hersey, John 1914-1993 .. **CLC 1, 2, 7, 9, 40, 81, 97**
See also AAYA 29; BPFB 2; CA 17-20R; CAAS 140; CANR 33; CDALBS; CN 1, 2, 3, 4, 5; CPW; DAM POP; DLB 6, 185, 278, 299; MAL 5; MTCW 1, 2; MTFW 2005; RGHL; SATA 25; SATA-Obit 76; TUS

Herzen, Aleksandr Ivanovich 1812-1870 .... **NCLC 10, 61**
See Herzen, Alexander

Herzen, Alexander
See Herzen, Aleksandr Ivanovich
See also DLB 277

Herzl, Theodor 1860-1904 .... **TCLC 36**
See also CA 168

Herzog, Werner 1942- .... **CLC 16, 236**
See also CA 89-92

Hesiod c. 8th cent. B.C.- .... **CMLC 5**
See also AW 1; DLB 176; RGWL 2, 3; WLIT 8

Hesse, Hermann 1877-1962 ... **CLC 1, 2, 3, 6, 11, 17, 25, 69; SSC 9, 49; TCLC 148; WLC 3**
See also AAYA 43; BPFB 2; CA 17-18; CAP 2; CDWLB 2; DA; DAB; DAC; DAM MST, NOV; DLB 66, 330; EW 9; EWL 3; EXPN; LAIT 1; MTCW 1, 2; MTFW 2005; NFS 6, 15, 24; RGWL 2, 3; SATA 50; TWA

Hewes, Cady
See De Voto, Bernard (Augustine)

Heyen, William 1940- .... **CLC 13, 18**
See also CA 220; 33-36R, 220; 9; CANR 98; CP 3, 4, 5, 6, 7; DLB 5; RGHL

Heyerdahl, Thor 1914-2002 .... **CLC 26**
See also CA 5-8R; CAAS 207; CANR 5, 22, 66, 73; LAIT 4; MTCW 1, 2; MTFW 2005; SATA 2, 52

Heym, Georg (Theodor Franz Arthur) 1887-1912 .... **TCLC 9**
See also CA 181; CAAE 106

Heym, Stefan 1913-2001 .... **CLC 41**
See also CA 9-12R; CAAS 203; CANR 4; CWW 2; DLB 69; EWL 3

Heyse, Paul (Johann Ludwig von) 1830-1914 .... **TCLC 8**
See also CA 209; CAAE 104; DLB 129, 330

Heyward, (Edwin) DuBose 1885-1940 .... **HR 1:2; TCLC 59**
See also CA 157; CAAE 108; DLB 7, 9, 45, 249; MAL 5; SATA 21

Heywood, John 1497(?)-1580(?) .... **LC 65**
See also DLB 136; RGEL 2

Heywood, Thomas 1573(?)-1641 .... **LC 111**
See also DAM DRAM; DLB 62; LMFS 1; RGEL 2; TEA

Hiaasen, Carl 1953- .... **CLC 238**
See also CA 105; CANR 22, 45, 65, 113, 133; CMW 4; CPW; CSW; DA3; DLB 292; MTCW 2; MTFW 2005

Hibbert, Eleanor Alice Burford 1906-1993 .... **CLC 7**
See Holt, Victoria
See also BEST 90:4; CA 17-20R; CAAS 140; CANR 9, 28, 59; CMW 4; CPW; DAM POP; MTCW 2; MTFW 2005; RHW; SATA 2; SATA-Obit 74

Hichens, Robert (Smythe) 1864-1950 .... **TCLC 64**
See also CA 162; DLB 153; HGG; RHW; SUFW

Higgins, Aidan 1927- .... **SSC 68**
See also CA 9-12R; CANR 70, 115, 148; CN 1, 2, 3, 4, 5, 6, 7; DLB 14

Higgins, George V(incent) 1939-1999 .... **CLC 4, 7, 10, 18**
See also BPFB 2; CA 77-80; 5; CAAS 186; CANR 17, 51, 89, 96; CMW 4; CN 2, 3, 4, 5, 6; DLB 2; DLBY 1981, 1998; INT CANR-17; MSW; MTCW 1

Higginson, Thomas Wentworth 1823-1911 .... **TCLC 36**
See also CA 162; DLB 1, 64, 243

Higgonet, Margaret .... **CLC 65**

Highet, Helen
See MacInnes, Helen (Clark)

Highsmith, Patricia 1921-1995 ...... **CLC 2, 4, 14, 42, 102**
See Morgan, Claire
See also AAYA 48; BRWS 5; CA 1-4R; CAAS 147; CANR 1, 20, 48, 62, 108; CMW 4; CN 1, 2, 3, 4, 5; CPW; DA3; DAM NOV, POP; DLB 306; MSW; MTCW 1, 2; MTFW 2005; SSFS 25

Highwater, Jamake (Mamake) 1942(?)-2001 .... **CLC 12**
See also AAYA 7, 69; BPFB 2; BYA 4; CA 65-68; 7; CAAS 199; CANR 10, 34, 84; CLR 17; CWRI 5; DLB 52; DLBY 1985; JRDA; MAICYA 1, 2; SATA 32, 69; SATA-Brief 30

Highway, Tomson 1951- ...... **CLC 92; NNAL**
See also CA 151; CANR 75; CCA 1; CD 5, 6; CN 7; DAC; DAM MULT; DFS 2; DLB 334; MTCW 2

Hijuelos, Oscar 1951- .... **CLC 65; HLC 1**
See also AAYA 25; AMWS 8; BEST 90:1; CA 123; CANR 50, 75, 125; CPW; DA3; DAM MULT, POP; DLB 145; HW 1, 2; LLW; MAL 5; MTCW 2; MTFW 2005; NFS 17; RGAL 4; WLIT 1

Hikmet, Nazim 1902-1963 .... **CLC 40**
See Nizami of Ganja
See also CA 141; CAAS 93-96; EWL 3; WLIT 6

Hildegard von Bingen 1098-1179 . **CMLC 20**
See also DLB 148

Hildesheimer, Wolfgang 1916-1991 .. **CLC 49**
See also CA 101; CAAS 135; DLB 69, 124; EWL 3; RGHL

Hill, Geoffrey (William) 1932- ...... **CLC 5, 8, 18, 45**
See also BRWS 5; CA 81-84; CANR 21, 89; CDBLB 1960 to Present; CP 1, 2, 3, 4, 5, 6, 7; DAM POET; DLB 40; EWL 3; MTCW 1; RGEL 2; RGHL

Hill, George Roy 1921-2002 .... **CLC 26**
See also CA 122; CAAE 110; CAAS 213

Hill, John
See Koontz, Dean R.

Hill, Susan 1942- .... **CLC 4, 113**
See also CA 33-36R; CANR 29, 69, 129; CN 2, 3, 4, 5, 6, 7; DAB; DAM MST, NOV; DLB 14, 139; HGG; MTCW 1; RHW

Hill, Susan Elizabeth
See Hill, Susan

Hillard, Asa G. III .... **CLC 70**

Hillerman, Tony 1925- .... **CLC 62, 170**
See also AAYA 40; BEST 89:1; BPFB 2; CA 29-32R; CANR 21, 42, 65, 97, 134; CMW 4; CPW; DA3; DAM POP; DLB 206, 306; MAL 5; MSW; MTCW 2; MTFW 2005; RGAL 4; SATA 6; TCWW 2; YAW

Hillesum, Etty 1914-1943 .... **TCLC 49**
See also CA 137; RGHL

Hilliard, Noel (Harvey) 1929-1996 ... **CLC 15**
See also CA 9-12R; CANR 7, 69; CN 1, 2, 3, 4, 5, 6

Hillis, Rick 1956- .... **CLC 66**
See also CA 134

Hilton, James 1900-1954 .... **TCLC 21**
See also AAYA 76; CA 169; CAAE 108; DLB 34, 77; FANT; SATA 34

Hilton, Walter (?)-1396 .... **CMLC 58**
See also DLB 146; RGEL 2

Himes, Chester (Bomar) 1909-1984 .. **BLC 2; CLC 2, 4, 7, 18, 58, 108; TCLC 139**
See also AFAW 2; AMWS 16; BPFB 2; BW 2; CA 25-28R; CAAS 114; CANR 22, 89; CMW 4; CN 1, 2, 3; DAM MULT; DLB 2, 76, 143, 226; EWL 3; MAL 5; MSW; MTCW 1, 2; MTFW 2005; RGAL 4

Himmelfarb, Gertrude 1922- .... **CLC 202**
See also CA 49-52; CANR 28, 66, 102, 166

Hinde, Thomas .... **CLC 6, 11**
See Chitty, Thomas Willes
See also CN 1, 2, 3, 4, 5, 6; EWL 3

Hine, (William) Daryl 1936- .... **CLC 15**
See also CA 1-4R; 15; CANR 1, 20; CP 1, 2, 3, 4, 5, 6, 7; DLB 60

DAM DRAM, MST, MULT, POET; DFS 6, 18; DLB 4, 7, 48, 51, 86, 228, 315; EWL 3; EXPP; EXPS; JRDA; LAIT 3; LMFS 2; MAICYA 1, 2; MAL 5; MTCW 1, 2; MTFW 2005; NFS 21; PAB; PFS 1, 3, 6, 10, 15; RGAL 4; RGSF 2; SATA 4, 33; SSFS 4, 7; TUS; WCH; WP; YAW

Hughes, Richard (Arthur Warren)
1900-1976 .... **CLC 1, 11**
See also CA 5-8R; CAAS 65-68; CANR 4; CN 1, 2; DAM NOV; DLB 15, 161; EWL 3; MTCW 1; RGEL 2; SATA 8; SATA-Obit 25

Hughes, Ted 1930-1998 . **CLC 2, 4, 9, 14, 37, 119; PC 7**
See Hughes, Edward James
See also BRWC 2; BRWR 2; BRWS 1; CA 1-4R; CAAS 171; CANR 1, 33, 66, 108; CLR 3; CP 1, 2, 3, 4, 5, 6; DAB; DAC; DLB 40, 161; EWL 3; EXPP; MAICYA 1, 2; MTCW 1, 2; MTFW 2005; PAB; PFS 4, 19; RGEL 2; SATA 49; SATA-Brief 27; SATA-Obit 107; TEA; YAW

Hugo, Richard
See Huch, Ricarda (Octavia)

Hugo, Richard F(ranklin)
1923-1982 .... **CLC 6, 18, 32; PC 68**
See also AMWS 6; CA 49-52; CAAS 108; CANR 3; CP 1, 2, 3; DAM POET; DLB 5, 206; EWL 3; MAL 5; PFS 17; RGAL 4

Hugo, Victor (Marie) 1802-1885 .... **NCLC 3, 10, 21, 161; PC 17; WLC 3**
See also AAYA 28; DA; DA3; DAB; DAC; DAM DRAM, MST, NOV, POET; DLB 119, 192, 217; EFS 2; EW 6; EXPN; GFL 1789 to the Present; LAIT 1, 2; NFS 5, 20; RGWL 2, 3; SATA 47; TWA

Huidobro, Vicente
See Huidobro Fernandez, Vicente Garcia
See also DLB 283; EWL 3; LAW

Huidobro Fernandez, Vicente Garcia
1893-1948 .... **TCLC 31**
See Huidobro, Vicente
See also CA 131; HW 1

Hulme, Keri 1947- .... **CLC 39, 130**
See also CA 125; CANR 69; CN 4, 5, 6, 7; CP 6, 7; CWP; DLB 326; EWL 3; FW; INT CA-125; NFS 24

Hulme, T(homas) E(rnest)
1883-1917 .... **TCLC 21**
See also BRWS 6; CA 203; CAAE 117; DLB 19

Humboldt, Alexander von
1769-1859 .... **NCLC 170**
See also DLB 90

Humboldt, Wilhelm von
1767-1835 .... **NCLC 134**
See also DLB 90

Hume, David 1711-1776 .... **LC 7, 56**
See also BRWS 3; DLB 104, 252, 336; LMFS 1; TEA

Humphrey, William 1924-1997 .... **CLC 45**
See also AMWS 9; CA 77-80; CAAS 160; CANR 68; CN 1, 2, 3, 4, 5, 6; CSW; DLB 6, 212, 234, 278; TCWW 1, 2

Humphreys, Emyr Owen 1919- .... **CLC 47**
See also CA 5-8R; CANR 3, 24; CN 1, 2, 3, 4, 5, 6, 7; DLB 15

Humphreys, Josephine 1945- ..... **CLC 34, 57**
See also CA 127; CAAE 121; CANR 97; CSW; DLB 292; INT CA-127

Huneker, James Gibbons
1860-1921 .... **TCLC 65**
See also CA 193; DLB 71; RGAL 4

Hungerford, Hesba Fay
See Brinsmead, H(esba) F(ay)

Hungerford, Pixie
See Brinsmead, H(esba) F(ay)

Hunt, E. Howard 1918-2007 .... **CLC 3**
See also AITN 1; CA 45-48; CAAS 256; CANR 2, 47, 103, 160; CMW 4

Hunt, Everette Howard, Jr.
See Hunt, E. Howard

Hunt, Francesca
See Holland, Isabelle (Christian)

Hunt, Howard
See Hunt, E. Howard

Hunt, Kyle
See Creasey, John

Hunt, (James Henry) Leigh
1784-1859 .... **NCLC 1, 70; PC 73**
See also DAM POET; DLB 96, 110, 144; RGEL 2; TEA

Hunt, Marsha 1946- .... **CLC 70**
See also BW 2, 3; CA 143; CANR 79

Hunt, Violet 1866(?)-1942 .... **TCLC 53**
See also CA 184; DLB 162, 197

Hunter, E. Waldo
See Sturgeon, Theodore (Hamilton)

Hunter, Evan 1926-2005 .... **CLC 11, 31**
See McBain, Ed
See also AAYA 39; BPFB 2; CA 5-8R; CAAS 241; CANR 5, 38, 62, 97, 149; CMW 4; CN 1, 2, 3, 4, 5, 6, 7; CPW; DAM POP; DLB 306; DLBY 1982; INT CANR-5; MSW; MTCW 1; SATA 25; SATA-Obit 167; SFW 4

Hunter, Kristin
See Lattany, Kristin (Elaine Eggleston) Hunter
See also CN 1, 2, 3, 4, 5, 6

Hunter, Mary
See Austin, Mary (Hunter)

Hunter, Mollie 1922- .... **CLC 21**
See McIlwraith, Maureen Mollie Hunter
See also AAYA 13, 71; BYA 6; CANR 37, 78; CLR 25; DLB 161; JRDA; MAICYA 1, 2; SAAS 7; SATA 54, 106, 139; SATA-Essay 139; WYA; YAW

Hunter, Robert (?)-1734 .... **LC 7**

Hurston, Zora Neale 1891-1960 .... **BLC 2; CLC 7, 30, 61; DC 12; HR 1:2; SSC 4, 80; TCLC 121, 131; WLCS**
See also AAYA 15, 71; AFAW 1, 2; AMWS 6; BW 1, 3; BYA 12; CA 85-88; CANR 61; CDALBS; DA; DA3; DAC; DAM MST, MULT, NOV; DFS 6; DLB 51, 86; EWL 3; EXPN; EXPS; FL 1:6; FW; LAIT 3; LATS 1:1; LMFS 2; MAL 5; MBL; MTCW 1, 2; MTFW 2005; NFS 3; RGAL 4; RGSF 2; SSFS 1, 6, 11, 19, 21; TUS; YAW

Husserl, E. G.
See Husserl, Edmund (Gustav Albrecht)

Husserl, Edmund (Gustav Albrecht)
1859-1938 .... **TCLC 100**
See also CA 133; CAAE 116; DLB 296

Huston, John (Marcellus)
1906-1987 .... **CLC 20**
See also CA 73-76; CAAS 123; CANR 34; DLB 26

Hustvedt, Siri 1955- .... **CLC 76**
See also CA 137; CANR 149

Hutten, Ulrich von 1488-1523 .... **LC 16**
See also DLB 179

Huxley, Aldous (Leonard)
1894-1963 .... **CLC 1, 3, 4, 5, 8, 11, 18, 35, 79; SSC 39; WLC 3**
See also AAYA 11; BPFB 2; BRW 7; CA 85-88; CANR 44, 99; CDBLB 1914-1945; DA; DA3; DAB; DAC; DAM MST, NOV, DLB 36, 100, 162, 195, 255; EWL 3; EXPN; LAIT 5; LMFS 2; MTCW 1, 2; MTFW 2005; NFS 6; RGEL 2; SATA 63; SCFW 1, 2; SFW 4; TEA; YAW

Huxley, T(homas) H(enry)
1825-1895 .... **NCLC 67**
See also DLB 57; TEA

Huygens, Constantijn 1596-1687 ...... **LC 114**
See also RGWL 2, 3

Huysmans, Joris-Karl 1848-1907 ... **TCLC 7, 69**
See also CA 165; CAAE 104; DLB 123; EW 7; GFL 1789 to the Present; LMFS 2; RGWL 2, 3

Hwang, David Henry 1957- .... **CLC 55, 196; DC 4, 23**
See also CA 132; CAAE 127; CAD; CANR 76, 124; CD 5, 6; DA3; DAM DRAM; DFS 11, 18; DLB 212, 228, 312; INT CA-132; MAL 5; MTCW 2; MTFW 2005; RGAL 4

Hyde, Anthony 1946- .... **CLC 42**
See Chase, Nicholas
See also CA 136; CCA 1

Hyde, Margaret O(ldroyd) 1917- ..... **CLC 21**
See also CA 1-4R; CANR 1, 36, 137; CLR 23; JRDA; MAICYA 1, 2; SAAS 8; SATA 1, 42, 76, 139

Hynes, James 1956(?)- .... **CLC 65**
See also CA 164; CANR 105

Hypatia c. 370-415 .... **CMLC 35**

Ian, Janis 1951- .... **CLC 21**
See also CA 187; CAAE 105

Ibanez, Vicente Blasco
See Blasco Ibanez, Vicente
See also DLB 322

Ibarbourou, Juana de
1895(?)-1979 .... **HLCS 2**
See also DLB 290; HW 1; LAW

Ibarguengoitia, Jorge 1928-1983 ..... **CLC 37; TCLC 148**
See also CA 124; CAAS 113; EWL 3; HW 1

Ibn Battuta, Abu Abdalla
1304-1368(?) .... **CMLC 57**
See also WLIT 2

Ibn Hazm 994-1064 .... **CMLC 64**

Ibn Zaydun 1003-1070 .... **CMLC 89**

Ibsen, Henrik (Johan) 1828-1906 .... **DC 2; TCLC 2, 8, 16, 37, 52; WLC 3**
See also AAYA 46; CA 141; CAAE 104; DA; DA3; DAB; DAC; DAM DRAM, MST; DFS 1, 6, 8, 10, 11, 15, 16; EW 7; LAIT 2; LATS 1:1; MTFW 2005; RGWL 2, 3

Ibuse, Masuji 1898-1993 .... **CLC 22**
See Ibuse Masuji
See also CA 127; CAAS 141; MJW; RGWL 3

Ibuse Masuji
See Ibuse, Masuji
See also CWW 2; DLB 180; EWL 3

Ichikawa, Kon 1915- .... **CLC 20**
See also CA 121

Ichiyo, Higuchi 1872-1896 .... **NCLC 49**
See also MJW

Idle, Eric 1943- .... **CLC 21**
See Monty Python
See also CA 116; CANR 35, 91, 148

Idris, Yusuf 1927-1991 .... **SSC 74**
See also AFW; EWL 3; RGSF 2, 3; RGWL 3; WLIT 2

Ignatieff, Michael 1947- .... **CLC 236**
See also CA 144; CANR 88, 156; CN 6, 7; DLB 267

Ignatieff, Michael Grant
See Ignatieff, Michael

Ignatow, David 1914-1997 .... **CLC 4, 7, 14, 40; PC 34**
See also CA 9-12R; 3; CAAS 162; CANR 31, 57, 96; CP 1, 2, 3, 4, 5, 6; DLB 5; EWL 3; MAL 5

Ignotus
See Strachey, (Giles) Lytton
Ihimaera, Witi (Tame) 1944- .... **CLC 46**
See also CA 77-80; CANR 130; CN 2, 3, 4, 5, 6, 7; RGSF 2; SATA 148
Il'f, Il'ia
See Fainzilberg, Ilya Arnoldovich
See also DLB 272
Ilf, Ilya
See Fainzilberg, Ilya Arnoldovich
Illyes, Gyula 1902-1983 .... **PC 16**
See also CA 114; CAAS 109; CDWLB 4; DLB 215; EWL 3; RGWL 2, 3
Imalayen, Fatima-Zohra
See Djebar, Assia
Immermann, Karl (Lebrecht)
1796-1840 .... **NCLC 4, 49**
See also DLB 133
Ince, Thomas H. 1882-1924 .... **TCLC 89**
See also IDFW 3, 4
Inchbald, Elizabeth 1753-1821 ...... **NCLC 62**
See also DLB 39, 89; RGEL 2
Inclan, Ramon (Maria) del Valle
See Valle-Inclan, Ramon (Maria) del
Infante, G(uillermo) Cabrera
See Cabrera Infante, G.
Ingalls, Rachel 1940- .... **CLC 42**
See also CA 127; CAAE 123; CANR 154
Ingalls, Rachel Holmes
See Ingalls, Rachel
Ingamells, Reginald Charles
See Ingamells, Rex
Ingamells, Rex 1913-1955 .... **TCLC 35**
See also CA 167; DLB 260
Inge, William (Motter) 1913-1973 ..... **CLC 1, 8, 19**
See also CA 9-12R; CAD; CDALB 1941-1968; DA3; DAM DRAM; DFS 1, 3, 5, 8; DLB 7, 249; EWL 3; MAL 5; MTCW 1, 2; MTFW 2005; RGAL 4; TUS
Ingelow, Jean 1820-1897 .... **NCLC 39, 107**
See also DLB 35, 163; FANT; SATA 33
Ingram, Willis J.
See Harris, Mark
Innaurato, Albert (F.) 1948(?)- ... **CLC 21, 60**
See also CA 122; CAAE 115; CAD; CANR 78; CD 5, 6; INT CA-122
Innes, Michael
See Stewart, J(ohn) I(nnes) M(ackintosh)
See also DLB 276; MSW
Innis, Harold Adams 1894-1952 .... **TCLC 77**
See also CA 181; DLB 88
Insluis, Alanus de
See Alain de Lille
Iola
See Wells-Barnett, Ida B(ell)
Ionesco, Eugene 1912-1994 ... **CLC 1, 4, 6, 9, 11, 15, 41, 86; DC 12; WLC 3**
See also CA 9-12R; CAAS 144; CANR 55, 132; CWW 2; DA; DA3; DAB; DAC; DAM DRAM, MST; DFS 4, 9; DLB 321; EW 13; EWL 3; GFL 1789 to the Present; LMFS 2; MTCW 1, 2; MTFW 2005; RGWL 2, 3; SATA 7; SATA-Obit 79; TWA
Iqbal, Muhammad 1877-1938 .... **TCLC 28**
See also CA 215; EWL 3
Ireland, Patrick
See O'Doherty, Brian
Irenaeus St. 130- .... **CMLC 42**
Irigaray, Luce 1930- .... **CLC 164**
See also CA 154; CANR 121; FW
Iron, Ralph
See Schreiner, Olive (Emilie Albertina)
Irving, John 1942- . **CLC 13, 23, 38, 112, 175**
See also AAYA 8, 62; AMWS 6; BEST 89:3; BPFB 2; CA 25-28R; CANR 28, 73, 112, 133; CN 3, 4, 5, 6, 7; CPW; DA3;

DAM NOV, POP; DLB 6, 278; DLBY 1982; EWL 3; MAL 5; MTCW 1, 2; MTFW 2005; NFS 12, 14; RGAL 4; TUS
Irving, John Winslow
See Irving, John
Irving, Washington 1783-1859 . **NCLC 2, 19, 95; SSC 2, 37, 104; WLC 3**
See also AAYA 56; AMW; CDALB 1640-1865; CLR 97; DA; DA3; DAB; DAC; DAM MST; DLB 3, 11, 30, 59, 73, 74, 183, 186, 250, 254; EXPS; GL 2; LAIT 1; RGAL 4; RGSF 2; SSFS 1, 8, 16; SUFW 1; TUS; WCH; YABC 2
Irwin, P. K.
See Page, P(atricia) K(athleen)
Isaacs, Jorge Ricardo 1837-1895 ... **NCLC 70**
See also LAW
Isaacs, Susan 1943- .... **CLC 32**
See also BEST 89:1; BPFB 2; CA 89-92; CANR 20, 41, 65, 112, 134, 165; CPW; DA3; DAM POP; INT CANR-20; MTCW 1, 2; MTFW 2005
Isherwood, Christopher 1904-1986 ... **CLC 1, 9, 11, 14, 44; SSC 56**
See also AMWS 14; BRW 7; CA 13-16R; CAAS 117; CANR 35, 97, 133; CN 1, 2, 3; DA3; DAM DRAM, NOV; DLB 15, 195; DLBY 1986; EWL 3; IDTP; MTCW 1, 2; MTFW 2005; RGAL 4; RGEL 2; TUS; WLIT 4
Ishiguro, Kazuo 1954- . **CLC 27, 56, 59, 110, 119**
See also AAYA 58; BEST 90:2; BPFB 2; BRWS 4; CA 120; CANR 49, 95, 133; CN 5, 6, 7; DA3; DAM NOV; DLB 194, 326; EWL 3; MTCW 1, 2; MTFW 2005; NFS 13; WLIT 4; WWE 1
Ishikawa, Hakuhin
See Ishikawa, Takuboku
Ishikawa, Takuboku 1886(?)-1912 ..... **PC 10; TCLC 15**
See Ishikawa Takuboku
See also CA 153; CAAE 113; DAM POET
Iskander, Fazil (Abdulovich) 1929- .. **CLC 47**
See Iskander, Fazil' Abdulevich
See also CA 102; EWL 3
Iskander, Fazil' Abdulevich
See Iskander, Fazil (Abdulovich)
See also DLB 302
Isler, Alan (David) 1934- .... **CLC 91**
See also CA 156; CANR 105
Ivan IV 1530-1584 .... **LC 17**
Ivanov, V.I.
See Ivanov, Vyacheslav
Ivanov, Vyacheslav 1866-1949 .... **TCLC 33**
See also CAAE 122; EWL 3
Ivanov, Vyacheslav Ivanovich
See Ivanov, Vyacheslav
Ivask, Ivar Vidrik 1927-1992 .... **CLC 14**
See also CA 37-40R; CAAS 139; CANR 24
Ives, Morgan
See Bradley, Marion Zimmer
See also GLL 1
Izumi Shikibu c. 973-c. 1034 .... **CMLC 33**
J. R. S.
See Gogarty, Oliver St. John
Jabran, Kahlil
See Gibran, Kahlil
Jabran, Khalil
See Gibran, Kahlil
Jackson, Daniel
See Wingrove, David
Jackson, Helen Hunt 1830-1885 .... **NCLC 90**
See also DLB 42, 47, 186, 189; RGAL 4
Jackson, Jesse 1908-1983 .... **CLC 12**
See also BW 1; CA 25-28R; CAAS 109; CANR 27; CLR 28; CWRI 5; MAICYA 1, 2; SATA 2, 29; SATA-Obit 48

Jackson, Laura (Riding) 1901-1991 .... **PC 44**
See Riding, Laura
See also CA 65-68; CAAS 135; CANR 28, 89; DLB 48
Jackson, Sam
See Trumbo, Dalton
Jackson, Sara
See Wingrove, David
Jackson, Shirley 1919-1965 . **CLC 11, 60, 87; SSC 9, 39; TCLC 187; WLC 3**
See also AAYA 9; AMWS 9; BPFB 2; CA 1-4R; CAAS 25-28R; CANR 4, 52; CDALB 1941-1968; DA; DA3; DAC; DAM MST; DLB 6, 234; EXPS; HGG; LAIT 4; MAL 5; MTCW 2; MTFW 2005; RGAL 4; RGSF 2; SATA 2; SSFS 1; SUFW 1, 2
Jacob, (Cyprien-)Max 1876-1944 .... **TCLC 6**
See also CA 193; CAAE 104; DLB 258; EWL 3; GFL 1789 to the Present; GLL 2; RGWL 2, 3
Jacobs, Harriet A(nn)
1813(?)-1897 .... **NCLC 67, 162**
See also AFAW 1, 2; DLB 239; FL 1:3; FW; LAIT 2; RGAL 4
Jacobs, Jim 1942- .... **CLC 12**
See also CA 97-100; INT CA-97-100
Jacobs, W(illiam) W(ymark)
1863-1943 .... **SSC 73; TCLC 22**
See also CA 167; CAAE 121; DLB 135; EXPS; HGG; RGEL 2; RGSF 2; SSFS 2; SUFW 1
Jacobsen, Jens Peter 1847-1885 .... **NCLC 34**
Jacobsen, Josephine (Winder)
1908-2003 .... **CLC 48, 102; PC 62**
See also CA 33-36R; 18; CAAS 218; CANR 23, 48; CCA 1; CP 2, 3, 4, 5, 6, 7; DLB 244; PFS 23; TCLE 1:1
Jacobson, Dan 1929- ...... **CLC 4, 14; SSC 91**
See also AFW; CA 1-4R; CANR 2, 25, 66; CN 1, 2, 3, 4, 5, 6, 7; DLB 14, 207, 225, 319; EWL 3; MTCW 1; RGSF 2
Jacopone da Todi 1236-1306 .... **CMLC 95**
Jacqueline
See Carpentier (y Valmont), Alejo
Jacques de Vitry c. 1160-1240 ...... **CMLC 63**
See also DLB 208
Jagger, Michael Philip
See Jagger, Mick
Jagger, Mick 1943- .... **CLC 17**
See also CA 239
Jahiz, al- c. 780-c. 869 .... **CMLC 25**
See also DLB 311
Jakes, John 1932- .... **CLC 29**
See also AAYA 32; BEST 89:4; BPFB 2; CA 214; 57-60, 214; CANR 10, 43, 66, 111, 142; CPW; CSW; DA3; DAM NOV, POP; DLB 278; DLBY 1983; FANT; INT CANR-10; MTCW 1, 2; MTFW 2005; RHW; SATA 62; SFW 4; TCWW 1, 2
James I 1394-1437 .... **LC 20**
See also RGEL 2
James, Andrew
See Kirkup, James
James, C(yril) L(ionel) R(obert)
1901-1989 .... **BLCS; CLC 33**
See also BW 2; CA 125; CAAE 117; CAAS 128; CANR 62; CN 1, 2, 3, 4; DLB 125; MTCW 1
James, Daniel (Lewis) 1911-1988
See Santiago, Danny
See also CA 174; CAAS 125
James, Dynely
See Mayne, William (James Carter)
James, Henry Sr. 1811-1882 .... **NCLC 53**
James, Henry 1843-1916 .... **SSC 8, 32, 47; TCLC 2, 11, 24, 40, 47, 64, 171; WLC 3**
See also AMW; AMWC 1; AMWR 1; BPFB 2; BRW 6; CA 132; CAAE 104; CDALB 1865-1917; DA; DA3; DAB; DAC; DAM

Johnson, Helene 1907-1995 .... **HR 1:3**
    See also CA 181; DLB 51; WP

Johnson, J. R.
    See James, C(yril) L(ionel) R(obert)

Johnson, James Weldon 1871-1938 .. **BLC 2;**
    HR 1:3; PC 24; TCLC 3, 19, 175
    See also AAYA 73; AFAW 1, 2; BW 1, 3;
    CA 125; CAAE 104; CANR 82; CDALB
    1917-1929; CLR 32; DA3; DAM MULT,
    POET; DLB 51; EWL 3; EXPP; LMFS 2;
    MAL 5; MTCW 1, 2; MTFW 2005; NFS
    22; PFS 1; RGAL 4; SATA 31; TUS

Johnson, Joyce 1935- .... **CLC 58**
    See also BG 1:3; CA 129; CAAE 125;
    CANR 102

Johnson, Judith (Emlyn) 1936- .... **CLC 7, 15**
    See Sherwin, Judith Johnson
    See also CA 25-28R, 153; CANR 34; CP 6,
    7

Johnson, Lionel (Pigot)
    1867-1902 .... **TCLC 19**
    See also CA 209; CAAE 117; DLB 19;
    RGEL 2

Johnson, Marguerite Annie
    See Angelou, Maya

Johnson, Mel
    See Malzberg, Barry N(athaniel)

Johnson, Pamela Hansford
    1912-1981 .... **CLC 1, 7, 27**
    See also CA 1-4R; CAAS 104; CANR 2,
    28; CN 1, 2, 3; DLB 15; MTCW 1, 2;
    MTFW 2005; RGEL 2

Johnson, Paul 1928- .... **CLC 147**
    See also BEST 89:4; CA 17-20R; CANR
    34, 62, 100, 155

Johnson, Paul Bede
    See Johnson, Paul

Johnson, Robert .... **CLC 70**

Johnson, Robert 1911(?)-1938 .... **TCLC 69**
    See also BW 3; CA 174

Johnson, Samuel 1709-1784 . **LC 15, 52, 128;**
    WLC 3
    See also BRW 3; BRWR 1; CDBLB 1660-
    1789; DA; DAB; DAC; DAM MST; DLB
    39, 95, 104, 142, 213; LMFS 1; RGEL 2;
    TEA

Johnson, Uwe 1934-1984 .. **CLC 5, 10, 15, 40**
    See also CA 1-4R; CAAS 112; CANR 1,
    39; CDWLB 2; DLB 75; EWL 3; MTCW
    1; RGWL 2, 3

Johnston, Basil H. 1929- .... **NNAL**
    See also CA 69-72; CANR 11, 28, 66;
    DAC; DAM MULT; DLB 60

Johnston, George (Benson) 1913- .... **CLC 51**
    See also CA 1-4R; CANR 5, 20; CP 1, 2, 3,
    4, 5, 6, 7; DLB 88

Johnston, Jennifer (Prudence)
    1930- .... **CLC 7, 150, 228**
    See also CA 85-88; CANR 92; CN 4, 5, 6,
    7; DLB 14

Joinville, Jean de 1224(?)-1317 ..... **CMLC 38**

Jolley, Elizabeth 1923-2007 ..... **CLC 46; SSC**
    19
    See also CA 127; 13; CAAS 257; CANR
    59; CN 4, 5, 6, 7; DLB 325; EWL 3;
    RGSF 2

Jolley, Monica Elizabeth
    See Jolley, Elizabeth

Jones, Arthur Llewellyn 1863-1947
    See Machen, Arthur
    See also CA 179; CAAE 104; HGG

Jones, D(ouglas) G(ordon) 1929- ..... **CLC 10**
    See also CA 29-32R; CANR 13, 90; CP 1,
    2, 3, 4, 5, 6, 7; DLB 53

Jones, David (Michael) 1895-1974 .... **CLC 2,**
    4, 7, 13, 42
    See also BRW 6; BRWS 7; CA 9-12R;
    CAAS 53-56; CANR 28; CDBLB 1945-
    1960; CP 1, 2; DLB 20, 100; EWL 3;
    MTCW 1; PAB; RGEL 2

Jones, David Robert 1947-
    See Bowie, David
    See also CA 103; CANR 104

Jones, Diana Wynne 1934- .... **CLC 26**
    See also AAYA 12; BYA 6, 7, 9, 11, 13, 16;
    CA 49-52; CANR 4, 26, 56, 120; CLR
    23, 120; DLB 161; FANT; JRDA; MAI-
    CYA 1, 2; MTFW 2005; SAAS 7; SATA
    9, 70, 108, 160; SFW 4; SUFW 2; YAW

Jones, Edward P. 1950- .... **CLC 76, 223**
    See also AAYA 71; BW 2, 3; CA 142;
    CANR 79, 134; CSW; MTFW 2005

Jones, Gayl 1949- ...... **BLC 2; CLC 6, 9, 131**
    See also AFAW 1, 2; BW 2, 3; CA 77-80;
    CANR 27, 66, 122; CN 4, 5, 6, 7; CSW;
    DA3; DAM MULT; DLB 33, 278; MAL
    5; MTCW 1, 2; MTFW 2005; RGAL 4

Jones, James 1921-1977 ...... **CLC 1, 3, 10, 39**
    See also AITN 1, 2; AMWS 11; BPFB 2;
    CA 1-4R; CAAS 69-72; CANR 6; CN 1,
    2; DLB 2, 143; DLBD 17; DLBY 1998;
    EWL 3; MAL 5; MTCW 1; RGAL 4

Jones, John J.
    See Lovecraft, H. P.

Jones, LeRoi .... **CLC 1, 2, 3, 5, 10, 14**
    See Baraka, Amiri
    See also CN 1, 2; CP 1, 2, 3; MTCW 2

Jones, Louis B. 1953- .... **CLC 65**
    See also CA 141; CANR 73

Jones, Madison 1925- .... **CLC 4**
    See also CA 13-16R; 11; CANR 7, 54, 83,
    158; CN 1, 2, 3, 4, 5, 6, 7; CSW; DLB
    152

Jones, Madison Percy, Jr.
    See Jones, Madison

Jones, Mervyn 1922- .... **CLC 10, 52**
    See also CA 45-48; 5; CANR 1, 91; CN 1,
    2, 3, 4, 5, 6, 7; MTCW 1

Jones, Mick 1956(?)- .... **CLC 30**

Jones, Nettie (Pearl) 1941- .... **CLC 34**
    See also BW 2; CA 137; 20; CANR 88

Jones, Peter 1802-1856 .... **NNAL**

Jones, Preston 1936-1979 .... **CLC 10**
    See also CA 73-76; CAAS 89-92; DLB 7

Jones, Robert F(rancis) 1934-2003 .... **CLC 7**
    See also CA 49-52; CANR 2, 61, 118

Jones, Rod 1953- .... **CLC 50**
    See also CA 128

Jones, Terence Graham Parry
    1942- .... **CLC 21**
    See Jones, Terry; Monty Python
    See also CA 116; CAAE 112; CANR 35,
    93; INT CA-116; SATA 127

Jones, Terry
    See Jones, Terence Graham Parry
    See also SATA 67; SATA-Brief 51

Jones, Thom (Douglas) 1945(?)- ..... **CLC 81;**
    SSC 56
    See also CA 157; CANR 88; DLB 244;
    SSFS 23

Jong, Erica 1942- .... **CLC 4, 6, 8, 18, 83**
    See also AITN 1; AMWS 5; BEST 90:2;
    BPFB 2; CA 73-76; CANR 26, 52, 75,
    132, 166; CN 3, 4, 5, 6, 7; CP 2, 3, 4, 5,
    6, 7; CPW; DA3; DAM NOV, POP; DLB
    2, 5, 28, 152; FW; INT CANR-26; MAL
    5; MTCW 1, 2; MTFW 2005

Jonson, Ben(jamin) 1572(?)-1637 . **DC 4; LC**
    6, 33, 110; PC 17; WLC 3
    See also BRW 1; BRWC 1; BRWR 1; CD-
    BLB Before 1660; DA; DAB; DAC;
    DAM DRAM, MST, POET; DFS 4, 10;
    DLB 62, 121; LMFS 1; PFS 23; RGEL 2;
    TEA; WLIT 3

Jordan, June 1936-2002 .. **BLCS; CLC 5, 11,**
    23, 114, 230; PC 38
    See also AAYA 2, 66; AFAW 1, 2; BW 2,
    3; CA 33-36R; CAAS 206; CANR 25, 70,
    114, 154; CLR 10; CP 3, 4, 5, 6, 7; CWP;

DAM MULT, POET; DLB 38; GLL 2;
LAIT 5; MAICYA 1, 2; MTCW 1; SATA
4, 136; YAW

Jordan, June Meyer
    See Jordan, June

Jordan, Neil 1950- .... **CLC 110**
    See also CA 130; CAAE 124; CANR 54,
    154; CN 4, 5, 6, 7; GLL 2; INT CA-130

Jordan, Neil Patrick
    See Jordan, Neil

Jordan, Pat(rick M.) 1941- .... **CLC 37**
    See also CA 33-36R; CANR 121

Jorgensen, Ivar
    See Ellison, Harlan

Jorgenson, Ivar
    See Silverberg, Robert

Joseph, George Ghevarughese .... **CLC 70**

Josephson, Mary
    See O'Doherty, Brian

Josephus, Flavius c. 37-100 ..... **CMLC 13, 93**
    See also AW 2; DLB 176; WLIT 8

Josiah Allen's Wife
    See Holley, Marietta

Josipovici, Gabriel (David) 1940- ...... **CLC 6,**
    43, 153
    See also CA 224; 37-40R, 224; 8; CANR
    47, 84; CN 3, 4, 5, 6, 7; DLB 14, 319

Joubert, Joseph 1754-1824 .... **NCLC 9**

Jouve, Pierre Jean 1887-1976 .... **CLC 47**
    See also CA 252; CAAS 65-68; DLB 258;
    EWL 3

Jovine, Francesco 1902-1950 .... **TCLC 79**
    See also DLB 264; EWL 3

Joyce, James (Augustine Aloysius)
    1882-1941 .... **DC 16; PC 22; SSC 3, 26,**
    44, 64; TCLC 3, 8, 16, 35, 52, 159;
    WLC 3
    See also AAYA 42; BRW 7; BRWC 1;
    BRWR 1; BYA 11, 13; CA 126; CAAE
    104; CDBLB 1914-1945; DA; DA3;
    DAB; DAC; DAM MST, NOV, POET;
    DLB 10, 19, 36, 162, 247; EWL 3; EXPN;
    EXPS; LAIT 3; LMFS 1, 2; MTCW 1, 2;
    MTFW 2005; NFS 7; RGSF 2; SSFS 1,
    19; TEA; WLIT 4

Jozsef, Attila 1905-1937 .... **TCLC 22**
    See also CA 230; CAAE 116; CDWLB 4;
    DLB 215; EWL 3

Juana Ines de la Cruz, Sor
    1651(?)-1695 ... **HLCS 1; LC 5, 136; PC**
    24
    See also DLB 305; FW; LAW; RGWL 2, 3;
    WLIT 1

Juana Inez de La Cruz, Sor
    See Juana Ines de la Cruz, Sor

Juan Manuel, Don 1282-1348 .... **CMLC 88**

Judd, Cyril
    See Kornbluth, C(yril) M.; Pohl, Frederik

Juenger, Ernst 1895-1998 .... **CLC 125**
    See Junger, Ernst
    See also CA 101; CAAS 167; CANR 21,
    47, 106; DLB 56

Julian of Norwich 1342(?)-1416(?) . **LC 6, 52**
    See also BRWS 12; DLB 146; LMFS 1

Julius Caesar 100B.C.-44B.C.
    See Caesar, Julius
    See also CDWLB 1; DLB 211

Junger, Ernst
    See Juenger, Ernst
    See also CDWLB 2; EWL 3; RGWL 2, 3

Junger, Sebastian 1962- .... **CLC 109**
    See also AAYA 28; CA 165; CANR 130;
    MTFW 2005

Juniper, Alex
    See Hospital, Janette Turner

Junius
    See Luxemburg, Rosa

Keillor, Garrison 1942- ..... **CLC 40, 115, 222**
See also AAYA 2, 62; AMWS 16; BEST 89:3; BPFB 2; CA 117; CAAE 111; CANR 36, 59, 124; CPW; DA3; DAM POP; DLBY 1987; EWL 3; MTCW 1, 2; MTFW 2005; SATA 58; TUS

Keith, Carlos
See Lewton, Val

Keith, Michael
See Hubbard, L. Ron

Keller, Gottfried 1819-1890 .... **NCLC 2; SSC 26**
See also CDWLB 2; DLB 129; EW; RGSF 2; RGWL 2, 3

Keller, Nora Okja 1965- .... **CLC 109**
See also CA 187

Kellerman, Jonathan 1949- .... **CLC 44**
See also AAYA 35; BEST 90:1; CA 106; CANR 29, 51, 150; CMW 4; CPW; DA3; DAM POP; INT CANR-29

Kelley, William Melvin 1937- .... **CLC 22**
See also BW 1; CA 77-80; CANR 27, 83; CN 1, 2, 3, 4, 5, 6, 7; DLB 33; EWL 3

Kellogg, Marjorie 1922-2005 .... **CLC 2**
See also CA 81-84; CAAS 246

Kellow, Kathleen
See Hibbert, Eleanor Alice Burford

Kelly, Lauren
See Oates, Joyce Carol

Kelly, M(ilton) T(errence) 1947- ...... **CLC 55**
See also CA 97-100; 22; CANR 19, 43, 84; CN 6

Kelly, Robert 1935- .... **SSC 50**
See also CA 17-20R; 19; CANR 47; CP 1, 2, 3, 4, 5, 6, 7; DLB 5, 130, 165

Kelman, James 1946- .... **CLC 58, 86**
See also BRWS 5; CA 148; CANR 85, 130; CN 5, 6, 7; DLB 194, 319, 326; RGSF 2; WLIT 4

Kemal, Yasar
See Kemal, Yashar
See also CWW 2; EWL 3; WLIT 6

Kemal, Yashar 1923(?)- .... **CLC 14, 29**
See also CA 89-92; CANR 44

Kemble, Fanny 1809-1893 .... **NCLC 18**
See also DLB 32

Kemelman, Harry 1908-1996 .... **CLC 2**
See also AITN 1; BPFB 2; CA 9-12R; CAAS 155; CANR 6, 71; CMW 4; DLB 28

Kempe, Margery 1373(?)-1440(?) ... **LC 6, 56**
See also BRWS 12; DLB 146; FL 1:1; RGEL 2

Kempis, Thomas a 1380-1471 .... **LC 11**

Kendall, Henry 1839-1882 .... **NCLC 12**
See also DLB 230

Keneally, Thomas 1935- .... **CLC 5, 8, 10, 14, 19, 27, 43, 117**
See also BRWS 4; CA 85-88; CANR 10, 50, 74, 130, 165; CN 1, 2, 3, 4, 5, 6, 7; CPW; DA3; DAM NOV; DLB 289, 299, 326; EWL 3; MTCW 1, 2; MTFW 2005; NFS 17; RGEL 2; RGHL; RHW

Keneally, Thomas Michael
See Keneally, Thomas

Kennedy, A(lison) L(ouise) 1965- ... **CLC 188**
See also CA 213; 168, 213; CANR 108; CD 5, 6; CN 6, 7; DLB 271; RGSF 2

Kennedy, Adrienne (Lita) 1931- .... **BLC 2; CLC 66; DC 5**
See also AFAW 2; BW 2, 3; CA 103; 20; CABS 3; CAD; CANR 26, 53, 82; CD 5, 6; DAM MULT; DFS 9; DLB 38; FW; MAL 5

Kennedy, John Pendleton
1795-1870 .... **NCLC 2**
See also DLB 3, 248, 254; RGAL 4

Kennedy, Joseph Charles 1929-
See Kennedy, X. J.
See also CA 201; 1-4R, 201; CANR 4, 30, 40; CWRI 5; MAICYA 2; MAICYAS 1; SATA 14, 86, 130; SATA-Essay 130

Kennedy, William 1928- .. **CLC 6, 28, 34, 53, 239**
See also AAYA 1, 73; AMWS 7; BPFB 2; CA 85-88; CANR 14, 31, 76, 134; CN 4, 5, 6, 7; DA3; DAM NOV; DLB 143; DLBY 1985; EWL 3; INT CANR-31; MAL 5; MTCW 1, 2; MTFW 2005; SATA 57

Kennedy, X. J. .... **CLC 8, 42**
See Kennedy, Joseph Charles
See also AMWS 15; CA 9; CLR 27; CP 1, 2, 3, 4, 5, 6, 7; DLB 5; SAAS 22

Kenny, Maurice (Francis) 1929- ..... **CLC 87; NNAL**
See also CA 144; 22; CANR 143; DAM MULT; DLB 175

Kent, Kelvin
See Kuttner, Henry

Kenton, Maxwell
See Southern, Terry

Kenyon, Jane 1947-1995 .... **PC 57**
See also AAYA 63; AMWS 7; CA 118; CAAS 148; CANR 44, 69; CP 6, 7; CWP; DLB 120; PFS 9, 17; RGAL 4

Kenyon, Robert O.
See Kuttner, Henry

Kepler, Johannes 1571-1630 .... **LC 45**

Ker, Jill
See Conway, Jill K(er)

Kerkow, H. C.
See Lewton, Val

Kerouac, Jack 1922-1969 ...... **CLC 1, 2, 3, 5, 14, 29, 61; TCLC 117; WLC 3**
See Kerouac, Jean-Louis Lebris de
See also AAYA 25; AMWC 1; AMWS 3; BG 3; BPFB 2; CDALB 1941-1968; CP 1; CPW; DLB 2, 16, 237; DLBD 3; DLBY 1995; EWL 3; GLL 1; LATS 1:2; LMFS 2; MAL 5; NFS 8; RGAL 4; TUS; WP

Kerouac, Jean-Louis Lebris de 1922-1969
See Kerouac, Jack
See also AITN 1; CA 5-8R; CAAS 25-28R; CANR 26, 54, 95; DA; DA3; DAB; DAC; DAM MST, NOV, POET, POP; MTCW 1, 2; MTFW 2005

Kerr, (Bridget) Jean (Collins)
1923(?)-2003 .... **CLC 22**
See also CA 5-8R; CAAS 212; CANR 7; INT CANR-7

Kerr, M. E. .... **CLC 12, 35**
See Meaker, Marijane
See also AAYA 2, 23; BYA 1, 7, 8; CLR 29; SAAS 1; WYA

Kerr, Robert .... **CLC 55**

Kerrigan, (Thomas) Anthony 1918- .. **CLC 4, 6**
See also CA 49-52; 11; CANR 4

Kerry, Lois
See Duncan, Lois

Kesey, Ken 1935-2001 .... **CLC 1, 3, 6, 11, 46, 64, 184; WLC 3**
See also AAYA 25; BG 1:3; BPFB 2; CA 1-4R; CAAS 204; CANR 22, 38, 66, 124; CDALB 1968-1988; CN 1, 2, 3, 4, 5, 6, 7; CPW; DA; DA3; DAB; DAC; DAM MST, NOV, POP; DLB 2, 16, 206; EWL 3; EXPN; LAIT 4; MAL 5; MTCW 1, 2; MTFW 2005; NFS 2; RGAL 4; SATA 66; SATA-Obit 131; TUS; YAW

Kesselring, Joseph (Otto)
1902-1967 .... **CLC 45**
See also CA 150; DAM DRAM, MST; DFS 20

Kessler, Jascha (Frederick) 1929- ...... **CLC 4**
See also CA 17-20R; CANR 8, 48, 111; CP 1

Kettelkamp, Larry (Dale) 1933- .... **CLC 12**
See also CA 29-32R; CANR 16; SAAS 3; SATA 2

Key, Ellen (Karolina Sofia)
1849-1926 .... **TCLC 65**
See also DLB 259

Keyber, Conny
See Fielding, Henry

Keyes, Daniel 1927- .... **CLC 80**
See also AAYA 23; BYA 11; CA 181; 17-20R, 181; CANR 10, 26, 54, 74; DA; DA3; DAC; DAM MST, NOV; EXPN; LAIT 4; MTCW 2; MTFW 2005; NFS 2; SATA 37; SFW 4

Keynes, John Maynard
1883-1946 .... **TCLC 64**
See also CA 162, 163; CAAE 114; DLBD 10; MTCW 2; MTFW 2005

Khanshendel, Chiron
See Rose, Wendy

Khayyam, Omar 1048-1131 ... **CMLC 11; PC 8**
See Omar Khayyam
See also DA3; DAM POET; WLIT 6

Kherdian, David 1931- .... **CLC 6, 9**
See also AAYA 42; CA 192; 21-24R, 192; 2; CANR 39, 78; CLR 24; JRDA; LAIT 3; MAICYA 1, 2; SATA 16, 74; SATA-Essay 125

Khlebnikov, Velimir .... **TCLC 20**
See Khlebnikov, Viktor Vladimirovich
See also DLB 295; EW 10; EWL 3; RGWL 2, 3

Khlebnikov, Viktor Vladimirovich 1885-1922
See Khlebnikov, Velimir
See also CA 217; CAAE 117

Khodasevich, V.F.
See Khodasevich, Vladislav

Khodasevich, Vladislav
1886-1939 .... **TCLC 15**
See also CAAE 115; DLB 317; EWL 3

Khodasevich, Vladislav Felitsianovich
See Khodasevich, Vladislav

Kielland, Alexander Lange
1849-1906 .... **TCLC 5**
See also CAAE 104

Kiely, Benedict 1919-2007 . **CLC 23, 43; SSC 58**
See also CA 1-4R; CAAS 257; CANR 2, 84; CN 1, 2, 3, 4, 5, 6, 7; DLB 15, 319; TCLE 1:1

Kienzle, William X. 1928-2001 .... **CLC 25**
See also CA 93-96; 1; CAAS 203; CANR 9, 31, 59, 111; CMW 4; DA3; DAM POP; INT CANR-31; MSW; MTCW 1, 2; MTFW 2005

Kierkegaard, Soren 1813-1855 ..... **NCLC 34, 78, 125**
See also DLB 300; EW 6; LMFS 2; RGWL 3; TWA

Kieslowski, Krzysztof 1941-1996 .... **CLC 120**
See also CA 147; CAAS 151

Killens, John Oliver 1916-1987 .... **CLC 10**
See also BW 2; CA 77-80; 2; CAAS 123; CANR 26; CN 1, 2, 3, 4; DLB 33; EWL 3

Killigrew, Anne 1660-1685 .... **LC 4, 73**
See also DLB 131

Killigrew, Thomas 1612-1683 .... **LC 57**
See also DLB 58; RGEL 2

Kim
See Simenon, Georges (Jacques Christian)

Kock, Charles Paul de 1794-1871 . NCLC 16

Koda Rohan
See Koda Shigeyuki

Koda Rohan
See Koda Shigeyuki
See also DLB 180

Koda Shigeyuki 1867-1947 .... TCLC 22
See Koda Rohan
See also CA 183; CAAE 121

Koestler, Arthur 1905-1983 ... CLC 1, 3, 6, 8,
15, 33
See also BRWS 1; CA 1-4R; CAAS 109;
CANR 1, 33; CDBLB 1945-1960; CN 1,
2, 3; DLBY 1983; EWL 3; MTCW 1, 2;
MTFW 2005; NFS 19; RGEL 2

Kogawa, Joy Nozomi 1935- ...... CLC 78, 129
See also AAYA 47; CA 101; CANR 19, 62,
126; CN 6, 7; CP 1; CWP; DAC; DAM
MST, MULT; DLB 334; FW; MTCW 2;
MTFW 2005; NFS 3; SATA 99

Kohout, Pavel 1928- .... CLC 13
See also CA 45-48; CANR 3

Koizumi, Yakumo
See Hearn, (Patricio) Lafcadio (Tessima
Carlos)

Kolmar, Gertrud 1894-1943 .... TCLC 40
See also CA 167; EWL 3; RGHL

Komunyakaa, Yusef 1947- .. BLCS; CLC 86,
94, 207; PC 51
See also AFAW 2; AMWS 13; CA 147;
CANR 83, 164; CP 6, 7; CSW; DLB 120;
EWL 3; PFS 5, 20; RGAL 4

Konrad, George
See Konrad, Gyorgy

Konrad, Gyorgy 1933- .... CLC 4, 10, 73
See also CA 85-88; CANR 97; CDWLB 4;
CWW 2; DLB 232; EWL 3

Konwicki, Tadeusz 1926- .... CLC 8, 28, 54,
117
See also CA 101; 9; CANR 39, 59; CWW
2; DLB 232; EWL 3; IDFW 3; MTCW 1

Koontz, Dean R. 1945- .... CLC 78, 206
See also AAYA 9, 31; BEST 89:3, 90:2; CA
108; CANR 19, 36, 52, 95, 138; CMW 4;
CPW; DA3; DAM NOV, POP; DLB 292;
HGG; MTCW 1; MTFW 2005; SATA 92,
165; SFW 4; SUFW 2; YAW

Koontz, Dean Ray
See Koontz, Dean R.

Kopernik, Mikolaj
See Copernicus, Nicolaus

Kopit, Arthur (Lee) 1937- ...... CLC 1, 18, 33
See also AITN 1; CA 81-84; CABS 3;
CAD; CD 5, 6; DAM DRAM; DFS 7, 14,
24; DLB 7; MAL 5; MTCW 1; RGAL 4

Kopitar, Jernej (Bartholomaus)
1780-1844 .... NCLC 117

Kops, Bernard 1926- .... CLC 4
See also CA 5-8R; CANR 84, 159; CBD;
CN 1, 2, 3, 4, 5, 6, 7; CP 1, 2, 3, 4, 5, 6,
7; DLB 13; RGHL

Kornbluth, C(yril) M. 1923-1958 .... TCLC 8
See also CA 160; CAAE 105; DLB 8;
SCFW 1, 2; SFW 4

Korolenko, V.G.
See Korolenko, Vladimir G.

Korolenko, Vladimir
See Korolenko, Vladimir G.

Korolenko, Vladimir G.
1853-1921 .... TCLC 22
See also CAAE 121; DLB 277

Korolenko, Vladimir Galaktionovich
See Korolenko, Vladimir G.

Korzybski, Alfred (Habdank Skarbek)
1879-1950 .... TCLC 61
See also CA 160; CAAE 123

Kosinski, Jerzy 1933-1991 ..... CLC 1, 2, 3, 6,
10, 15, 53, 70
See also AMWS 7; BPFB 2; CA 17-20R;
CAAS 134; CANR 9, 46; CN 1, 2, 3, 4;
DA3; DAM NOV; DLB 2, 299; DLBY
1982; EWL 3; HGG; MAL 5; MTCW 1,
2; MTFW 2005; NFS 12; RGAL 4;
RGHL; TUS

Kostelanetz, Richard (Cory) 1940- .. CLC 28
See also CA 13-16R; 8; CANR 38, 77; CN
4, 5, 6; CP 2, 3, 4, 5, 6, 7

Kostrowitzki, Wilhelm Apollinaris de
1880-1918
See Apollinaire, Guillaume
See also CAAE 104

Kotlowitz, Robert 1924- .... CLC 4
See also CA 33-36R; CANR 36

Kotzebue, August (Friedrich Ferdinand) von
1761-1819 .... NCLC 25
See also DLB 94

Kotzwinkle, William 1938- ..... CLC 5, 14, 35
See also BPFB 2; CA 45-48; CANR 3, 44,
84, 129; CLR 6; CN 7; DLB 173; FANT;
MAICYA 1, 2; SATA 24, 70, 146; SFW
4; SUFW 2; YAW

Kowna, Stancy
See Szymborska, Wislawa

Kozol, Jonathan 1936- .... CLC 17
See also AAYA 46; CA 61-64; CANR 16,
45, 96; MTFW 2005

Kozoll, Michael 1940(?)- .... CLC 35

Kramer, Kathryn 19(?)- .... CLC 34

Kramer, Larry 1935- .... CLC 42; DC 8
See also CA 126; CAAE 124; CANR 60,
132; DAM POP; DLB 249; GLL 1

Krasicki, Ignacy 1735-1801 .... NCLC 8

Krasinski, Zygmunt 1812-1859 .... NCLC 4
See also RGWL 2, 3

Kraus, Karl 1874-1936 .... TCLC 5
See also CA 216; CAAE 104; DLB 118;
EWL 3

Kreve (Mickevicius), Vincas
1882-1954 .... TCLC 27
See also CA 170; DLB 220; EWL 3

Kristeva, Julia 1941- .... CLC 77, 140
See also CA 154; CANR 99; DLB 242;
EWL 3; FW; LMFS 2

Kristofferson, Kris 1936- .... CLC 26
See also CA 104

Krizanc, John 1956- .... CLC 57
See also CA 187

Krleza, Miroslav 1893-1981 .... CLC 8, 114
See also CA 97-100; CAAS 105; CANR
50; CDWLB 4; DLB 147; EW 11; RGWL
2, 3

Kroetsch, Robert (Paul) 1927- .... CLC 5, 23,
57, 132
See also CA 17-20R; CANR 8, 38; CCA 1;
CN 2, 3, 4, 5, 6, 7; CP 6, 7; DAC; DAM
POET; DLB 53; MTCW 1

Kroetz, Franz
See Kroetz, Franz Xaver

Kroetz, Franz Xaver 1946- .... CLC 41
See also CA 130; CANR 142; CWW 2;
EWL 3

Kroker, Arthur (W.) 1945- .... CLC 77
See also CA 161

Kroniuk, Lisa
See Berton, Pierre (Francis de Marigny)

Kropotkin, Peter (Aleksieevich)
1842-1921 .... TCLC 36
See Kropotkin, Petr Alekseevich
See also CA 219; CAAE 119

Kropotkin, Petr Alekseevich
See Kropotkin, Peter (Aleksieevich)
See also DLB 277

Krotkov, Yuri 1917-1981 .... CLC 19
See also CA 102

Krumb
See Crumb, R.

Krumgold, Joseph (Quincy)
1908-1980 .... CLC 12
See also BYA 1, 2; CA 9-12R; CAAS 101;
CANR 7; MAICYA 1, 2; SATA 1, 48;
SATA-Obit 23; YAW

Krumwitz
See Crumb, R.

Krutch, Joseph Wood 1893-1970 ..... CLC 24
See also ANW; CA 1-4R; CAAS 25-28R;
CANR 4; DLB 63, 206, 275

Krutzch, Gus
See Eliot, T(homas) S(tearns)

Krylov, Ivan Andreevich
1768(?)-1844 .... NCLC 1
See also DLB 150

Kubin, Alfred (Leopold Isidor)
1877-1959 .... TCLC 23
See also CA 149; CAAE 112; CANR 104;
DLB 81

Kubrick, Stanley 1928-1999 .... CLC 16;
TCLC 112
See also AAYA 30; CA 81-84; CAAS 177;
CANR 33; DLB 26

Kumin, Maxine 1925- .... CLC 5, 13, 28, 164;
PC 15
See also AITN 2; AMWS 4; ANW; CA
1-4R; 8; CANR 1, 21, 69, 115, 140; CP 2,
3, 4, 5, 6, 7; CWP; DA3; DAM POET;
DLB 5; EWL 3; EXPP; MTCW 1, 2;
MTFW 2005; PAB; PFS 18; SATA 12

Kundera, Milan 1929- . CLC 4, 9, 19, 32, 68,
115, 135, 234; SSC 24
See also AAYA 2, 62; BPFB 2; CA 85-88;
CANR 19, 52, 74, 144; CDWLB 4; CWW
2; DA3; DAM NOV; DLB 232; EW 13;
EWL 3; MTCW 1, 2; MTFW 2005; NFS
18; RGSF 2; RGWL 3; SSFS 10

Kunene, Mazisi 1930-2006 .... CLC 85
See also BW 1, 3; CA 125; CAAS 252;
CANR 81; CP 1, 6, 7; DLB 117

Kunene, Mazisi Raymond
See Kunene, Mazisi

Kunene, Mazisi Raymond Fakazi Mngoni
See Kunene, Mazisi

Kung, Hans .... CLC 130
See Kung, Hans

Kung, Hans 1928-
See Kung, Hans
See also CA 53-56; CANR 66, 134; MTCW
1, 2; MTFW 2005

Kunikida Doppo 1869(?)-1908
See Doppo, Kunikida
See also DLB 180; EWL 3

Kunitz, Stanley 1905-2006 ..... CLC 6, 11, 14,
148; PC 19
See also AMWS 3; CA 41-44R; CAAS 250;
CANR 26, 57, 98; CP 1, 2, 3, 4, 5, 6, 7;
DA3; DLB 48; INT CANR-26; MAL 5;
MTCW 1, 2; MTFW 2005; PFS 11;
RGAL 4

Kunitz, Stanley Jasspon
See Kunitz, Stanley

Kunze, Reiner 1933- .... CLC 10
See also CA 93-96; CWW 2; DLB 75; EWL
3

Kuprin, Aleksander Ivanovich
1870-1938 .... TCLC 5
See Kuprin, Aleksandr Ivanovich; Kuprin,
Alexandr Ivanovich
See also CA 182; CAAE 104

Kuprin, Aleksandr Ivanovich
See Kuprin, Aleksander Ivanovich
See also DLB 295

Kuprin, Alexandr Ivanovich
See Kuprin, Aleksander Ivanovich
See also EWL 3

Lardner, Ring W., Jr.
See Lardner, Ring(gold) W(ilmer)

Lardner, Ring(gold) W(ilmer)
1885-1933 .... **SSC 32; TCLC 2, 14**
See Lardner, Ring
See also AMW; CA 131; CAAE 104;
MTCW 1, 2; MTFW 2005; TUS

Laredo, Betty
See Codrescu, Andrei

Larkin, Maia
See Wojciechowska, Maia (Teresa)

Larkin, Philip (Arthur) 1922-1985 ... **CLC 3,
5, 8, 9, 13, 18, 33, 39, 64; PC 21**
See also BRWS 1; CA 5-8R; CAAS 117;
CANR 24, 62; CDBLB 1960 to Present;
CP 1, 2, 3, 4; DA3; DAB; DAM MST,
POET; DLB 27; EWL 3; MTCW 1, 2;
MTFW 2005; PFS 3, 4, 12; RGEL 2

La Roche, Sophie von
1730-1807 .... **NCLC 121**
See also DLB 94

La Rochefoucauld, Francois
1613-1680 .... **LC 108**

**Larra (y Sanchez de Castro), Mariano Jose
de** 1809-1837 .... **NCLC 17, 130**

Larsen, Eric 1941- .... **CLC 55**
See also CA 132

Larsen, Nella 1893(?)-1963 .... **BLC 2; CLC
37; HR 1:3**
See also AFAW 1, 2; BW 1; CA 125; CANR
83; DAM MULT; DLB 51; FW; LATS
1:1; LMFS 2

Larson, Charles R(aymond) 1938- ... **CLC 31**
See also CA 53-56; CANR 4, 121

Larson, Jonathan 1960-1996 .... **CLC 99**
See also AAYA 28; CA 156; DFS 23;
MTFW 2005

La Sale, Antoine de c. 1386-1460(?) . **LC 104**
See also DLB 208

Las Casas, Bartolome de
1474-1566 .... **HLCS; LC 31**
See Casas, Bartolome de las
See also DLB 318; LAW

Lasch, Christopher 1932-1994 .... **CLC 102**
See also CA 73-76; CAAS 144; CANR 25,
118; DLB 246; MTCW 1, 2; MTFW 2005

Lasker-Schueler, Else 1869-1945 ... **TCLC 57**
See Lasker-Schuler, Else
See also CA 183; DLB 66, 124

Lasker-Schuler, Else
See Lasker-Schueler, Else
See also EWL 3

Laski, Harold J(oseph) 1893-1950 . **TCLC 79**
See also CA 188

Latham, Jean Lee 1902-1995 .... **CLC 12**
See also AITN 1; BYA 1; CA 5-8R; CANR
7, 84; CLR 50; MAICYA 1, 2; SATA 2,
68; YAW

Latham, Mavis
See Clark, Mavis Thorpe

Lathen, Emma .... **CLC 2**
See Hennissart, Martha; Latsis, Mary J(ane)
See also BPFB 2; CMW 4; DLB 306

Lathrop, Francis
See Leiber, Fritz (Reuter, Jr.)

Latsis, Mary J(ane) 1927-1997
See Lathen, Emma
See also CA 85-88; CAAS 162; CMW 4

Lattany, Kristin
See Lattany, Kristin (Elaine Eggleston)
Hunter

Lattany, Kristin (Elaine Eggleston) Hunter
1931- .... **CLC 35**
See Hunter, Kristin
See also AITN 1; BW 1; BYA 3; CA 13-
16R; CANR 13, 108; CLR 3; CN 7; DLB
33; INT CANR-13; MAICYA 1, 2; SAAS
10; SATA 12, 132; YAW

Lattimore, Richmond (Alexander)
1906-1984 .... **CLC 3**
See also CA 1-4R; CAAS 112; CANR 1;
CP 1, 2, 3; MAL 5

Laughlin, James 1914-1997 .... **CLC 49**
See also CA 21-24R; 22; CAAS 162; CANR
9, 47; CP 1, 2, 3, 4, 5, 6; DLB 48; DLBY
1996, 1997

Laurence, Margaret 1926-1987 ..... **CLC 3, 6,
13, 50, 62; SSC 7**
See also BYA 13; CA 5-8R; CAAS 121;
CANR 33; CN 1, 2, 3, 4; DAC; DAM
MST; DLB 53; EWL 3; FW; MTCW 1, 2;
MTFW 2005; NFS 11; RGEL 2; RGSF 2;
SATA-Obit 50; TCWW 2

Laurent, Antoine 1952- .... **CLC 50**

Lauscher, Hermann
See Hesse, Hermann

Lautreamont 1846-1870 .. **NCLC 12; SSC 14**
See Lautreamont, Isidore Lucien Ducasse
See also GFL 1789 to the Present; RGWL
2, 3

Lautreamont, Isidore Lucien Ducasse
See Lautreamont
See also DLB 217

Lavater, Johann Kaspar
1741-1801 .... **NCLC 142**
See also DLB 97

Laverty, Donald
See Blish, James (Benjamin)

Lavin, Mary 1912-1996 . **CLC 4, 18, 99; SSC
4, 67**
See also CA 9-12R; CAAS 151; CANR 33;
CN 1, 2, 3, 4, 5, 6; DLB 15, 319; FW;
MTCW 1; RGEL 2; RGSF 2; SSFS 23

Lavond, Paul Dennis
See Kornbluth, C(yril) M.; Pohl, Frederik

Lawes, Henry 1596-1662 .... **LC 113**
See also DLB 126

Lawler, Ray
See Lawler, Raymond Evenor
See also DLB 289

Lawler, Raymond Evenor 1922- .... **CLC 58**
See Lawler, Ray
See also CA 103; CD 5, 6; RGEL 2

Lawrence, D(avid) H(erbert Richards)
1885-1930 .... **PC 54; SSC 4, 19, 73;
TCLC 2, 9, 16, 33, 48, 61, 93; WLC 3**
See Chambers, Jessie
See also BPFB 2; BRW 7; BRWR 2; CA
121; CAAE 104; CANR 131; CDBLB
1914-1945; DA; DA3; DAB; DAC; DAM
MST, NOV, POET; DLB 10, 19, 36, 98,
162, 195; EWL 3; EXPP; EXPS; LAIT 2,
3; MTCW 1, 2; MTFW 2005; NFS 18;
PFS 6; RGEL 2; RGSF 2; SSFS 2, 6;
TEA; WLIT 4; WP

Lawrence, T(homas) E(dward)
1888-1935 .... **TCLC 18**
See Dale, Colin
See also BRWS 2; CA 167; CAAE 115;
DLB 195

Lawrence of Arabia
See Lawrence, T(homas) E(dward)

Lawson, Henry (Archibald Hertzberg)
1867-1922 .... **SSC 18; TCLC 27**
See also CA 181; CAAE 120; DLB 230;
RGEL 2; RGSF 2

Lawton, Dennis
See Faust, Frederick (Schiller)

Layamon fl. c. 1200- .... **CMLC 10**
See also DLB 146; RGEL 2

Laye, Camara 1928-1980 ..... **BLC 2; CLC 4,
38**
See Camara Laye
See also AFW; BW 1; CA 85-88; CAAS
97-100; CANR 25; DAM MULT; MTCW
1, 2; WLIT 2

Layton, Irving 1912-2006 ..... **CLC 2, 15, 164**
See also CA 1-4R; CAAS 247; CANR 2,
33, 43, 66, 129; CP 1, 2, 3, 4, 5, 6, 7;
DAC; DAM MST, POET; DLB 88; EWL
3; MTCW 1, 2; PFS 12; RGEL 2

Layton, Irving Peter
See Layton, Irving

Lazarus, Emma 1849-1887 ...... **NCLC 8, 109**

Lazarus, Felix
See Cable, George Washington

Lazarus, Henry
See Slavitt, David R.

Lea, Joan
See Neufeld, John (Arthur)

Leacock, Stephen (Butler)
1869-1944 .... **SSC 39; TCLC 2**
See also CA 141; CAAE 104; CANR 80;
DAC; DAM MST; DLB 92; EWL 3;
MTCW 2; MTFW 2005; RGEL 2; RGSF
2

Lead, Jane Ward 1623-1704 .... **LC 72**
See also DLB 131

Leapor, Mary 1722-1746 .... **LC 80**
See also DLB 109

Lear, Edward 1812-1888 ..... **NCLC 3; PC 65**
See also AAYA 48; BRW 5; CLR 1, 75;
DLB 32, 163, 166; MAICYA 1, 2; RGEL
2; SATA 18, 100; WCH; WP

Lear, Norman (Milton) 1922- .... **CLC 12**
See also CA 73-76

Leautaud, Paul 1872-1956 .... **TCLC 83**
See also CA 203; DLB 65; GFL 1789 to the
Present

Leavis, F(rank) R(aymond)
1895-1978 .... **CLC 24**
See also BRW 7; CA 21-24R; CAAS 77-
80; CANR 44; DLB 242; EWL 3; MTCW
1, 2; RGEL 2

Leavitt, David 1961- .... **CLC 34**
See also CA 122; CAAE 116; CANR 50,
62, 101, 134; CPW; DA3; DAM POP;
DLB 130; GLL 1; INT CA-122; MAL 5;
MTCW 2; MTFW 2005

Leblanc, Maurice (Marie Emile)
1864-1941 .... **TCLC 49**
See also CAAE 110; CMW 4

Lebowitz, Fran(ces Ann) 1951(?)- ... **CLC 11,
36**
See also CA 81-84; CANR 14, 60, 70; INT
CANR-14; MTCW 1

Lebrecht, Peter
See Tieck, (Johann) Ludwig

le Carre, John 1931- .... **CLC 9, 15**
See also AAYA 42; BEST 89:4; BPFB 2;
BRWS 2; CA 5-8R; CANR 13, 33, 59,
107, 132; CDBLB 1960 to Present; CMW
4; CN 1, 2, 3, 4, 5, 6, 7; CPW; DA3;
DAM POP; DLB 87; EWL 3; MSW;
MTCW 1, 2; MTFW 2005; RGEL 2; TEA

Le Clezio, J. M.G. 1940- .... **CLC 31, 155**
See also CA 128; CAAE 116; CANR 147;
CWW 2; DLB 83; EWL 3; GFL 1789 to
the Present; RGSF 2

Le Clezio, Jean Marie Gustave
See Le Clezio, J. M.G.

Leconte de Lisle, Charles-Marie-Rene
1818-1894 .... **NCLC 29**
See also DLB 217; EW 6; GFL 1789 to the
Present

Le Coq, Monsieur
See Simenon, Georges (Jacques Christian)

Leduc, Violette 1907-1972 .... **CLC 22**
See also CA 13-14; CAAS 33-36R; CANR
69; CAP 1; EWL 3; GFL 1789 to the
Present; GLL 1

Ledwidge, Francis 1887(?)-1917 .... **TCLC 23**
See also CA 203; CAAE 123; DLB 20

Leskov, Nikolai Semenovich
See Leskov, Nikolai (Semyonovich)
See also DLB 238

Lesser, Milton
See Marlowe, Stephen

Lessing, Doris 1919- .. **CLC 1, 2, 3, 6, 10, 15, 22, 40, 94, 170; SSC 6, 61; WLCS**
See also AAYA 57; AFW; BRWS 1; CA 9-12R; 14; CANR 33, 54, 76, 122; CBD; CD 5, 6; CDBLB 1960 to Present; CN 1, 2, 3, 4, 5, 6, 7; CWD; DA; DA3; DAB; DAC; DAM MST, NOV; DFS 20; DLB 15, 139; DLBY 1985; EWL 3; EXPS; FL 1:6; FW; LAIT 4; MTCW 1, 2; MTFW 2005; RGEL 2; RGSF 2; SFW 4; SSFS 1, 12, 20; TEA; WLIT 2, 4

Lessing, Doris May
See Lessing, Doris

Lessing, Gotthold Ephraim 1729-1781 ...... **DC 26; LC 8, 124**
See also CDWLB 2; DLB 97; EW 4; RGWL 2, 3

Lester, Richard 1932- .... **CLC 20**

Levenson, Jay .... **CLC 70**

Lever, Charles (James) 1806-1872 .... **NCLC 23**
See also DLB 21; RGEL 2

Leverson, Ada Esther 1862(?)-1933(?) .... **TCLC 18**
See Elaine
See also CA 202; CAAE 117; DLB 153; RGEL 2

Levertov, Denise 1923-1997 .. **CLC 1, 2, 3, 5, 8, 15, 28, 66; PC 11**
See also AMWS 3; CA 178; 1-4R, 178; 19; CAAS 163; CANR 3, 29, 50, 108; CDALBS; CP 1, 2, 3, 4, 5, 6; CWP; DAM POET; DLB 5, 165; EWL 3; EXPP; FW; INT CANR-29; MAL 5; MTCW 1, 2; PAB; PFS 7, 17; RGAL 4; RGHL; TUS; WP

Levi, Carlo 1902-1975 .... **TCLC 125**
See also CA 65-68; CAAS 53-56; CANR 10; EWL 3; RGWL 2, 3

Levi, Jonathan .... **CLC 76**
See also CA 197

Levi, Peter (Chad Tigar) 1931-2000 .... **CLC 41**
See also CA 5-8R; CAAS 187; CANR 34, 80; CP 1, 2, 3, 4, 5, 6, 7; DLB 40

Levi, Primo 1919-1987 ...... **CLC 37, 50; SSC 12; TCLC 109**
See also CA 13-16R; CAAS 122; CANR 12, 33, 61, 70, 132; DLB 177, 299; EWL 3; MTCW 1, 2; MTFW 2005; RGHL; RGWL 2, 3; WLIT 7

Levin, Ira 1929- .... **CLC 3, 6**
See also CA 21-24R; CANR 17, 44, 74, 139; CMW 4; CN 1, 2, 3, 4, 5, 6, 7; CPW; DA3; DAM POP; HGG; MTCW 1, 2; MTFW 2005; SATA 66; SFW 4

Levin, Meyer 1905-1981 .... **CLC 7**
See also AITN 1; CA 9-12R; CAAS 104; CANR 15; CN 1, 2, 3; DAM POP; DLB 9, 28; DLBY 1981; MAL 5; RGHL; SATA 21; SATA-Obit 27

Levine, Albert Norman
See Levine, Norman
See also CN 7

Levine, Norman 1923-2005 .... **CLC 54**
See Levine, Albert Norman
See also CA 73-76; 23; CAAS 240; CANR 14, 70; CN 1, 2, 3, 4, 5, 6; CP 1; DLB 88

Levine, Norman Albert
See Levine, Norman

Levine, Philip 1928- .. **CLC 2, 4, 5, 9, 14, 33, 118; PC 22**
See also AMWS 5; CA 9-12R; CANR 9, 37, 52, 116, 156; CP 1, 2, 3, 4, 5, 6, 7; DAM POET; DLB 5; EWL 3; MAL 5; PFS 8

Levinson, Deirdre 1931- .... **CLC 49**
See also CA 73-76; CANR 70

Levi-Strauss, Claude 1908- .... **CLC 38**
See also CA 1-4R; CANR 6, 32, 57; DLB 242; EWL 3; GFL 1789 to the Present; MTCW 1, 2; TWA

Levitin, Sonia (Wolff) 1934- .... **CLC 17**
See also AAYA 13, 48; CA 29-32R; CANR 14, 32, 79; CLR 53; JRDA; MAICYA 1, 2; SAAS 2; SATA 4, 68, 119, 131; SATA-Essay 131; YAW

Levon, O. U.
See Kesey, Ken

Levy, Amy 1861-1889 .... **NCLC 59**
See also DLB 156, 240

Lewes, George Henry 1817-1878 ... **NCLC 25**
See also DLB 55, 144

Lewis, Alun 1915-1944 .... **SSC 40; TCLC 3**
See also BRW 7; CA 188; CAAE 104; DLB 20, 162; PAB; RGEL 2

Lewis, C. Day
See Day Lewis, C(ecil)
See also CN 1

Lewis, Cecil Day
See Day Lewis, C(ecil)

Lewis, Clive Staples
See Lewis, C.S.

Lewis, C.S. 1898-1963 ... **CLC 1, 3, 6, 14, 27, 124; WLC 4**
See also AAYA 3, 39; BPFB 2; BRWS 3; BYA 15, 16; CA 81-84; CANR 33, 71, 132; CDBLB 1945-1960; CLR 3, 27, 109; CWRI 5; DA; DA3; DAB; DAC; DAM MST, NOV, POP; DLB 15, 100, 160, 255; EWL 3; FANT; JRDA; LMFS 2; MAICYA 1, 2; MTCW 1, 2; MTFW 2005; NFS 24; RGEL 2; SATA 13, 100; SCFW 1, 2; SFW 4; SUFW 1; TEA; WCH; WYA; YAW

Lewis, Janet 1899-1998 .... **CLC 41**
See Winters, Janet Lewis
See also CA 9-12R; CAAS 172; CANR 29, 63; CAP 1; CN 1, 2, 3, 4, 5, 6; DLBY 1987; RHW; TCWW 2

Lewis, Matthew Gregory 1775-1818 .... **NCLC 11, 62**
See also DLB 39, 158, 178; GL 3; HGG; LMFS 1; RGEL 2; SUFW

Lewis, (Harry) Sinclair 1885-1951 . **TCLC 4, 13, 23, 39; WLC 4**
See also AMW; AMWC 1; BPFB 2; CA 133; CAAE 104; CANR 132; CDALB 1917-1929; DA; DA3; DAB; DAC; DAM MST, NOV; DLB 9, 102, 284, 331; DLBD 1; EWL 3; LAIT 3; MAL 5; MTCW 1, 2; MTFW 2005; NFS 15, 19, 22; RGAL 4; TUS

Lewis, (Percy) Wyndham 1884(?)-1957 .. **SSC 34; TCLC 2, 9, 104**
See also BRW 7; CA 157; CAAE 104; DLB 15; EWL 3; FANT; MTCW 2; MTFW 2005; RGEL 2

Lewisohn, Ludwig 1883-1955 .... **TCLC 19**
See also CA 203; CAAE 107; DLB 4, 9, 28, 102; MAL 5

Lewton, Val 1904-1951 .... **TCLC 76**
See also CA 199; IDFW 3, 4

Leyner, Mark 1956- .... **CLC 92**
See also CA 110; CANR 28, 53; DA3; DLB 292; MTCW 2; MTFW 2005

Lezama Lima, Jose 1910-1976 .... **CLC 4, 10, 101; HLCS 2**
See also CA 77-80; CANR 71; DAM MULT; DLB 113, 283; EWL 3; HW 1, 2; LAW; RGWL 2, 3

L'Heureux, John (Clarke) 1934- ...... **CLC 52**
See also CA 13-16R; CANR 23, 45, 88; CP 1, 2, 3, 4; DLB 244

Li Ch'ing-chao 1081(?)-1141(?) .... **CMLC 71**

Liddell, C. H.
See Kuttner, Henry

Lie, Jonas (Lauritz Idemil) 1833-1908(?) .... **TCLC 5**
See also CAAE 115

Lieber, Joel 1937-1971 .... **CLC 6**
See also CA 73-76; CAAS 29-32R

Lieber, Stanley Martin
See Lee, Stan

Lieberman, Laurence (James) 1935- .... **CLC 4, 36**
See also CA 17-20R; CANR 8, 36, 89; CP 1, 2, 3, 4, 5, 6, 7

Lieh Tzu fl. 7th cent. B.C.-5th cent. B.C. .... **CMLC 27**

Lieksman, Anders
See Haavikko, Paavo Juhani

Lifton, Robert Jay 1926- .... **CLC 67**
See also CA 17-20R; CANR 27, 78, 161; INT CANR-27; SATA 66

Lightfoot, Gordon 1938- .... **CLC 26**
See also CA 242; CAAE 109

Lightfoot, Gordon Meredith
See Lightfoot, Gordon

Lightman, Alan P(aige) 1948- .... **CLC 81**
See also CA 141; CANR 63, 105, 138; MTFW 2005

Ligotti, Thomas (Robert) 1953- ...... **CLC 44; SSC 16**
See also CA 123; CANR 49, 135; HGG; SUFW 2

Li Ho 791-817 .... **PC 13**

Li Ju-chen c. 1763-c. 1830 .... **NCLC 137**

Lilar, Francoise
See Mallet-Joris, Francoise

Liliencron, Detlev
See Liliencron, Detlev von

Liliencron, Detlev von 1844-1909 .. **TCLC 18**
See also CAAE 117

Liliencron, Friedrich Adolf Axel Detlev von
See Liliencron, Detlev von

Liliencron, Friedrich Detlev von
See Liliencron, Detlev von

Lille, Alain de
See Alain de Lille

Lillo, George 1691-1739 .... **LC 131**
See also DLB 84; RGEL 2

Lilly, William 1602-1681 .... **LC 27**

Lima, Jose Lezama
See Lezama Lima, Jose

Lima Barreto, Afonso Henrique de 1881-1922 .... **TCLC 23**
See Lima Barreto, Afonso Henriques de
See also CA 181; CAAE 117; LAW

Lima Barreto, Afonso Henriques de
See Lima Barreto, Afonso Henrique de
See also DLB 307

Limonov, Eduard
See Limonov, Edward
See also DLB 317

Limonov, Edward 1944- .... **CLC 67**
See Limonov, Eduard
See also CA 137

Lin, Frank
See Atherton, Gertrude (Franklin Horn)

Lin, Yutang 1895-1976 .... **TCLC 149**
See also CA 45-48; CAAS 65-68; CANR 2; RGAL 4

Lincoln, Abraham 1809-1865 .... **NCLC 18**
See also LAIT 2

Lind, Jakov 1927-2007 ... **CLC 1, 2, 4, 27, 82**
See Landwirth, Heinz
See also CA 4; CAAS 257; DLB 299; EWL 3; RGHL

Lord Houghton
See Milnes, Richard Monckton
Lord Jeffrey
See Jeffrey, Francis
Loreaux, Nichol .... **CLC 65**
Lorenzini, Carlo 1826-1890
See Collodi, Carlo
See also MAICYA 1, 2; SATA 29, 100
Lorenzo, Heberto Padilla
See Padilla (Lorenzo), Heberto
Loris
See Hofmannsthal, Hugo von
Loti, Pierre .... **TCLC 11**
See Viaud, (Louis Marie) Julien
See also DLB 123; GFL 1789 to the Present
Lou, Henri
See Andreas-Salome, Lou
Louie, David Wong 1954- .... **CLC 70**
See also CA 139; CANR 120
Louis, Adrian C. .... **NNAL**
See also CA 223
Louis, Father M.
See Merton, Thomas (James)
Louise, Heidi
See Erdrich, Louise
Lovecraft, H. P. 1890-1937 .... **SSC 3, 52;**
TCLC 4, 22
See also AAYA 14; BPFB 2; CA 133;
CAAE 104; CANR 106; DA3; DAM
POP; HGG; MTCW 1, 2; MTFW 2005;
RGAL 4; SCFW 1, 2; SFW 4; SUFW
Lovecraft, Howard Phillips
See Lovecraft, H. P.
Lovelace, Earl 1935- .... **CLC 51**
See also BW 2; CA 77-80; CANR 41, 72,
114; CD 5, 6; CDWLB 3; CN 1, 2, 3, 4,
5, 6, 7; DLB 125; EWL 3; MTCW 1
Lovelace, Richard 1618-1657 . **LC 24; PC 69**
See also BRW 2; DLB 131; EXPP; PAB;
RGEL 2
Lowe, Pardee 1904- .... **AAL**
Lowell, Amy 1874-1925 ... **PC 13; TCLC 1, 8**
See also AAYA 57; AMW; CA 151; CAAE
104; DAM POET; DLB 54, 140; EWL 3;
EXPP; LMFS 2; MAL 5; MBL; MTCW
2; MTFW 2005; RGAL 4; TUS
Lowell, James Russell 1819-1891 ... **NCLC 2,**
90
See also AMWS 1; CDALB 1640-1865;
DLB 1, 11, 64, 79, 189, 235; RGAL 4
Lowell, Robert (Traill Spence, Jr.)
1917-1977 .... **CLC 1, 2, 3, 4, 5, 8, 9, 11,**
15, 37, 124; PC 3; WLC 4
See also AMW; AMWC 2; AMWR 2; CA
9-12R; CAAS 73-76; CABS 2; CAD;
CANR 26, 60; CDALBS; CP 1, 2; DA;
DA3; DAB; DAC; DAM MST, NOV;
DLB 5, 169; EWL 3; MAL 5; MTCW 1,
2; MTFW 2005; PAB; PFS 6, 7; RGAL 4;
WP
Lowenthal, Michael 1969- .... **CLC 119**
See also CA 150; CANR 115, 164
Lowenthal, Michael Francis
See Lowenthal, Michael
Lowndes, Marie Adelaide (Belloc)
1868-1947 .... **TCLC 12**
See also CAAE 107; CMW 4; DLB 70;
RHW
Lowry, (Clarence) Malcolm
1909-1957 .... **SSC 31; TCLC 6, 40**
See also BPFB 2; BRWS 3; CA 131; CAAE
105; CANR 62, 105; CDBLB 1945-1960;
DLB 15; EWL 3; MTCW 1, 2; MTFW
2005; RGEL 2
Lowry, Mina Gertrude 1882-1966
See Loy, Mina
See also CA 113
Lowry, Sam
See Soderbergh, Steven

Loxsmith, John
See Brunner, John (Kilian Houston)
Loy, Mina .... **CLC 28; PC 16**
See Lowry, Mina Gertrude
See also DAM POET; DLB 4, 54; PFS 20
Loyson-Bridet
See Schwob, Marcel (Mayer Andre)
Lucan 39-65 .... **CMLC 33**
See also AW 2; DLB 211; EFS; RGWL 2,
3
Lucas, Craig 1951- .... **CLC 64**
See also CA 137; CAD; CANR 71, 109,
142; CD 5, 6; GLL 2; MTFW 2005
Lucas, E(dward) V(errall)
1868-1938 .... **TCLC 73**
See also CA 176; DLB 98, 149, 153; SATA
20
Lucas, George 1944- .... **CLC 16**
See also AAYA 1, 23; CA 77-80; CANR
30; SATA 56
Lucas, Hans
See Godard, Jean-Luc
Lucas, Victoria
See Plath, Sylvia
Lucian c. 125-c. 180 .... **CMLC 32**
See also AW 2; DLB 176; RGWL 2, 3
Lucilius c. 180B.C.-102B.C. .... **CMLC 82**
See also DLB 211
Lucretius c. 94B.C.-c. 49B.C. .... **CMLC 48**
See also AW 2; CDWLB 1; DLB 211; EFS
2; RGWL 2, 3; WLIT 8
Ludlam, Charles 1943-1987 .... **CLC 46, 50**
See also CA 85-88; CAAS 122; CAD;
CANR 72, 86; DLB 266
Ludlum, Robert 1927-2001 .... **CLC 22, 43**
See also AAYA 10, 59; BEST 89:1, 90:3;
BPFB 2; CA 33-36R; CAAS 195; CANR
25, 41, 68, 105, 131; CMW 4; CPW;
DA3; DAM NOV, POP; DLBY 1982;
MSW; MTCW 1, 2; MTFW 2005
Ludwig, Ken 1950- .... **CLC 60**
See also CA 195; CAD; CD 6
Ludwig, Otto 1813-1865 .... **NCLC 4**
See also DLB 129
Lugones, Leopoldo 1874-1938 .... **HLCS 2;**
TCLC 15
See also CA 131; CAAE 116; CANR 104;
DLB 283; EWL 3; HW 1; LAW
Lu Hsun .... **SSC 20; TCLC 3**
See Shu-Jen, Chou
See also EWL 3
Lukacs, George .... **CLC 24**
See Lukacs, Gyorgy (Szegeny von)
Lukacs, Gyorgy (Szegeny von) 1885-1971
See Lukacs, George
See also CA 101; CAAS 29-32R; CANR
62; CDWLB 4; DLB 215, 242; EW 10;
EWL 3; MTCW 1, 2
Luke, Peter (Ambrose Cyprian)
1919-1995 .... **CLC 38**
See also CA 81-84; CAAS 147; CANR 72;
CBD; CD 5, 6; DLB 13
Lunar, Dennis
See Mungo, Raymond
Lurie, Alison 1926- ..... **CLC 4, 5, 18, 39, 175**
See also BPFB 2; CA 1-4R; CANR 2, 17,
50, 88; CN 1, 2, 3, 4, 5, 6, 7; DLB 2;
MAL 5; MTCW 1; NFS 24; SATA 46,
112; TCLE 1:1
Lustig, Arnost 1926- .... **CLC 56**
See also AAYA 3; CA 69-72; CANR 47,
102; CWW 2; DLB 232, 299; EWL 3;
RGHL; SATA 56
Luther, Martin 1483-1546 .... **LC 9, 37**
See also CDWLB 2; DLB 179; EW 2;
RGWL 2, 3
Luxemburg, Rosa 1870(?)-1919 ..... **TCLC 63**
See also CAAE 118

Luzi, Mario (Egidio Vincenzo)
1914-2005 .... **CLC 13**
See also CA 61-64; CAAS 236; CANR 9,
70; CWW 2; DLB 128; EWL 3
L'vov, Arkady .... **CLC 59**
Lydgate, John c. 1370-1450(?) .... **LC 81**
See also BRW 1; DLB 146; RGEL 2
Lyly, John 1554(?)-1606 .... **DC 7; LC 41**
See also BRW 1; DAM DRAM; DLB 62,
167; RGEL 2
L'Ymagier
See Gourmont, Remy(-Marie-Charles) de
Lynch, B. Suarez
See Borges, Jorge Luis
Lynch, David 1946- .... **CLC 66, 162**
See also AAYA 55; CA 129; CAAE 124;
CANR 111
Lynch, David Keith
See Lynch, David
Lynch, James
See Andreyev, Leonid (Nikolaevich)
Lyndsay, Sir David 1485-1555 .... **LC 20**
See also RGEL 2
Lynn, Kenneth S(chuyler)
1923-2001 .... **CLC 50**
See also CA 1-4R; CAAS 196; CANR 3,
27, 65
Lynx
See West, Rebecca
Lyons, Marcus
See Blish, James (Benjamin)
Lyotard, Jean-Francois
1924-1998 .... **TCLC 103**
See also DLB 242; EWL 3
Lyre, Pinchbeck
See Sassoon, Siegfried (Lorraine)
Lytle, Andrew (Nelson) 1902-1995 ... **CLC 22**
See also CA 9-12R; CAAS 150; CANR 70;
CN 1, 2, 3, 4, 5, 6; CSW; DLB 6; DLBY
1995; RGAL 4; RHW
Lyttelton, George 1709-1773 .... **LC 10**
See also RGEL 2
Lytton of Knebworth, Baron
See Bulwer-Lytton, Edward (George Earle
Lytton)
Maas, Peter 1929-2001 .... **CLC 29**
See also CA 93-96; CAAS 201; INT CA-
93-96; MTCW 2; MTFW 2005
Mac A'Ghobhainn, Iain
See Smith, Iain Crichton
Macaulay, Catherine 1731-1791 .... **LC 64**
See also DLB 104, 336
Macaulay, (Emilie) Rose
1881(?)-1958 .... **TCLC 7, 44**
See also CAAE 104; DLB 36; EWL 3;
RGEL 2; RHW
Macaulay, Thomas Babington
1800-1859 .... **NCLC 42**
See also BRW 4; CDBLB 1832-1890; DLB
32, 55; RGEL 2
MacBeth, George (Mann)
1932-1992 .... **CLC 2, 5, 9**
See also CA 25-28R; CAAS 136; CANR
61, 66; CP 1, 2, 3, 4, 5; DLB 40; MTCW
1; PFS 8; SATA 4; SATA-Obit 70
MacCaig, Norman (Alexander)
1910-1996 .... **CLC 36**
See also BRWS 6; CA 9-12R; CANR 3, 34;
CP 1, 2, 3, 4, 5, 6; DAB; DAM POET;
DLB 27; EWL 3; RGEL 2
MacCarthy, Sir (Charles Otto) Desmond
1877-1952 .... **TCLC 36**
See also CA 167
MacDiarmid, Hugh .... **CLC 2, 4, 11, 19, 63;**
PC 9
See Grieve, C(hristopher) M(urray)
See also BRWS 12; CDBLB 1945-1960;
CP 1, 2; DLB 20; EWL 3; RGEL 2

Mason, Lee W.
See Malzberg, Barry N(athaniel)

Mason, Nick 1945- .... **CLC 35**

Mason, Tally
See Derleth, August (William)

Mass, Anna .... **CLC 59**

Mass, William
See Gibson, William

Massinger, Philip 1583-1640 .... **LC 70**
See also BRWS 11; DLB 58; RGEL 2

Master Lao
See Lao Tzu

Masters, Edgar Lee 1868-1950 ...... **PC 1, 36;**
TCLC 2, 25; WLCS
See also AMWS 1; CA 133; CAAE 104;
CDALB 1865-1917; DA; DAC; DAM
MST, POET; DLB 54; EWL 3; EXPP;
MAL 5; MTCW 1, 2; MTFW 2005;
RGAL 4; TUS; WP

Masters, Hilary 1928- .... **CLC 48**
See also CA 217; 25-28R, 217; CANR 13,
47, 97; CN 6, 7; DLB 244

Mastrosimone, William 1947- .... **CLC 36**
See also CA 186; CAD; CD 5, 6

Mathe, Albert
See Camus, Albert

Mather, Cotton 1663-1728 .... **LC 38**
See also AMWS 2; CDALB 1640-1865;
DLB 24, 30, 140; RGAL 4; TUS

Mather, Increase 1639-1723 .... **LC 38**
See also DLB 24

Mathers, Marshall
See Eminem

Mathers, Marshall Bruce
See Eminem

Matheson, Richard (Burton) 1926- .. **CLC 37**
See also AAYA 31; CA 97-100; CANR 88,
99; DLB 8, 44; HGG; INT CA-97-100;
SCFW 1, 2; SFW 4; SUFW 2

Mathews, Harry 1930- .... **CLC 6, 52**
See also CA 21-24R; 6; CANR 18, 40, 98,
160; CN 5, 6, 7

Mathews, John Joseph 1894-1979 .. **CLC 84;**
NNAL
See also CA 19-20; CAAS 142; CANR 45;
CAP 2; DAM MULT; DLB 175; TCWW
1, 2

Mathias, Roland 1915-2007 .... **CLC 45**
See also CA 97-100; CANR 19, 41; CP 1,
2, 3, 4, 5, 6, 7; DLB 27

Mathias, Roland Glyn
See Mathias, Roland

Matsuo Basho 1644(?)-1694 ...... **LC 62; PC 3**
See Basho, Matsuo
See also DAM POET; PFS 2, 7, 18

Mattheson, Rodney
See Creasey, John

Matthews, (James) Brander
1852-1929 .... **TCLC 95**
See also CA 181; DLB 71, 78; DLBD 13

Matthews, Greg 1949- .... **CLC 45**
See also CA 135

Matthews, William (Procter III)
1942-1997 .... **CLC 40**
See also AMWS 9; CA 29-32R; 18; CAAS
162; CANR 12, 57; CP 2, 3, 4, 5, 6; DLB
5

Matthias, John (Edward) 1941- .... **CLC 9**
See also CA 33-36R; CANR 56; CP 4, 5, 6,
7

Matthiessen, F(rancis) O(tto)
1902-1950 .... **TCLC 100**
See also CA 185; DLB 63; MAL 5

Matthiessen, Peter 1927- ... **CLC 5, 7, 11, 32,**
64
See also AAYA 6, 40; AMWS 5; ANW;
BEST 90:4; BPFB 2; CA 9-12R; CANR
21, 50, 73, 100, 138; CN 1, 2, 3, 4, 5, 6,
7; DA3; DAM NOV; DLB 6, 173, 275;
MAL 5; MTCW 1, 2; MTFW 2005; SATA
27

Maturin, Charles Robert
1780(?)-1824 .... **NCLC 6, 169**
See also BRWS 8; DLB 178; GL 3; HGG;
LMFS 1; RGEL 2; SUFW

Matute (Ausejo), Ana Maria 1925- .. **CLC 11**
See also CA 89-92; CANR 129; CWW 2;
DLB 322; EWL 3; MTCW 1; RGSF 2

Maugham, W. S.
See Maugham, W(illiam) Somerset

Maugham, W(illiam) Somerset
1874-1965 .. **CLC 1, 11, 15, 67, 93; SSC**
8, 94; WLC 4
See also AAYA 55; BPFB 2; BRW 6; CA
5-8R; CAAS 25-28R; CANR 40, 127;
CDBLB 1914-1945; CMW 4; DA; DA3;
DAB; DAC; DAM DRAM, MST, NOV;
DFS 22; DLB 10, 36, 77, 100, 162, 195;
EWL 3; LAIT 3; MTCW 1, 2; MTFW
2005; NFS 23; RGEL 2; RGSF 2; SATA
54; SSFS 17

Maugham, William Somerset
See Maugham, W(illiam) Somerset

Maupassant, (Henri Rene Albert) Guy de
1850-1893 . **NCLC 1, 42, 83; SSC 1, 64;**
WLC 4
See also BYA 14; DA; DA3; DAB; DAC;
DAM MST; DLB 123; EW 7; EXPS; GFL
1789 to the Present; LAIT 2; LMFS 1;
RGSF 2; RGWL 2, 3; SSFS 4, 21; SUFW;
TWA

Maupin, Armistead 1944- .... **CLC 95**
See also CA 130; CAAE 125; CANR 58,
101; CPW; DA3; DAM POP; DLB 278;
GLL 1; INT CA-130; MTCW 2; MTFW
2005

Maupin, Armistead Jones, Jr.
See Maupin, Armistead

Maurhut, Richard
See Traven, B.

Mauriac, Claude 1914-1996 .... **CLC 9**
See also CA 89-92; CANR 152; CWW 2;
DLB 83; EWL 3; GFL 1789 to the Present

Mauriac, Francois (Charles)
1885-1970 .... **CLC 4, 9, 56; SSC 24**
See also CA 25-28; CAP 2; DLB 65, 331;
EW 10; EWL 3; GFL 1789 to the Present;
MTCW 1, 2; MTFW 2005; RGWL 2, 3;
TWA

Mavor, Osborne Henry 1888-1951
See Bridie, James
See also CAAE 104

Maxwell, Glyn 1962- .... **CLC 238**
See also CA 154; CANR 88; CP 6, 7; PFS
23

Maxwell, William (Keepers, Jr.)
1908-2000 .... **CLC 19**
See also AMWS 8; CA 93-96; CAAS 189;
CANR 54, 95; CN 1, 2, 3, 4, 5, 6, 7; DLB
218, 278; DLBY 1980; INT CA-93-96;
MAL 5; SATA-Obit 128

May, Elaine 1932- .... **CLC 16**
See also CA 142; CAAE 124; CAD; CWD;
DLB 44

Mayakovski, Vladimir (Vladimirovich)
1893-1930 .... **TCLC 4, 18**
See Maiakovskii, Vladimir; Mayakovsky,
Vladimir
See also CA 158; CAAE 104; EWL 3;
MTCW 2; MTFW 2005; SFW 4; TWA

Mayakovsky, Vladimir
See Mayakovski, Vladimir (Vladimirovich)
See also EW 11; WP

Mayhew, Henry 1812-1887 .... **NCLC 31**
See also DLB 18, 55, 190

Mayle, Peter 1939(?)- .... **CLC 89**
See also CA 139; CANR 64, 109

Maynard, Joyce 1953- .... **CLC 23**
See also CA 129; CAAE 111; CANR 64

Mayne, William (James Carter)
1928- .... **CLC 12**
See also AAYA 20; CA 9-12R; CANR 37,
80, 100; CLR 25, 123; FANT; JRDA;
MAICYA 1, 2; MAICYAS 1; SAAS 11;
SATA 6, 68, 122; SUFW 2; YAW

Mayo, Jim
See L'Amour, Louis

Maysles, Albert 1926- .... **CLC 16**
See also CA 29-32R

Maysles, David 1932-1987 .... **CLC 16**
See also CA 191

Mazer, Norma Fox 1931- .... **CLC 26**
See also AAYA 5, 36; BYA 1, 8; CA 69-72;
CANR 12, 32, 66, 129; CLR 23; JRDA;
MAICYA 1, 2; SAAS 1; SATA 24, 67,
105, 168; WYA; YAW

Mazzini, Guiseppe 1805-1872 .... **NCLC 34**

McAlmon, Robert (Menzies)
1895-1956 .... **TCLC 97**
See also CA 168; CAAE 107; DLB 4, 45;
DLBD 15; GLL 1

McAuley, James Phillip 1917-1976 .. **CLC 45**
See also CA 97-100; CP 1, 2; DLB 260;
RGEL 2

McBain, Ed
See Hunter, Evan
See also MSW

McBrien, William (Augustine)
1930- .... **CLC 44**
See also CA 107; CANR 90

McCabe, Patrick 1955- .... **CLC 133**
See also BRWS 9; CA 130; CANR 50, 90;
CN 6, 7; DLB 194

McCaffrey, Anne 1926- .... **CLC 17**
See also AAYA 6, 34; AITN 2; BEST 89:2;
BPFB 2; BYA 5; CA 227; 25-28R, 227;
CANR 15, 35, 55, 96; CLR 49; CPW;
DA3; DAM NOV, POP; DLB 8; JRDA;
MAICYA 1, 2; MTCW 1, 2; MTFW 2005;
SAAS 11; SATA 8, 70, 116, 152; SATA-
Essay 152; SFW 4; SUFW 2; WYA; YAW

McCaffrey, Anne Inez
See McCaffrey, Anne

McCall, Nathan 1955(?)- .... **CLC 86**
See also AAYA 59; BW 3; CA 146; CANR
88

McCann, Arthur
See Campbell, John W(ood, Jr.)

McCann, Edson
See Pohl, Frederik

McCarthy, Charles, Jr.
See McCarthy, Cormac

McCarthy, Cormac 1933- .... **CLC 4, 57, 101,**
204
See also AAYA 41; AMWS 8; BPFB 2; CA
13-16R; CANR 10, 42, 69, 101, 161; CN
6, 7; CPW; CSW; DA3; DAM POP; DLB
6, 143, 256; EWL 3; LATS 1:2; MAL 5;
MTCW 2; MTFW 2005; TCLE 1:2;
TCWW 2

McCarthy, Mary (Therese)
1912-1989 .. **CLC 1, 3, 5, 14, 24, 39, 59;**
SSC 24
See also AMW; BPFB 2; CA 5-8R; CAAS
129; CANR 16, 50, 64; CN 1, 2, 3, 4;
DA3; DLB 2; DLBY 1981; EWL 3; FW;
INT CANR-16; MAL 5; MBL; MTCW 1,
2; MTFW 2005; RGAL 4; TUS

McCartney, James Paul
See McCartney, Paul

McCartney, Paul 1942- .... **CLC 12, 35**
See also CA 146; CANR 111

Medoff, Mark (Howard) 1940- .... **CLC 6, 23**
See also AITN 1; CA 53-56; CAD; CANR 5; CD 5, 6; DAM DRAM; DFS 4; DLB 7; INT CANR-5

Medvedev, P. N.
See Bakhtin, Mikhail Mikhailovich

Meged, Aharon
See Megged, Aharon

Meged, Aron
See Megged, Aharon

Megged, Aharon 1920- .... **CLC 9**
See also CA 49-52; 13; CANR 1, 140; EWL 3; RGHL

Mehta, Deepa 1950- .... **CLC 208**

Mehta, Gita 1943- .... **CLC 179**
See also CA 225; CN 7; DNFS 2

Mehta, Ved 1934- .... **CLC 37**
See also CA 212; 1-4R, 212; CANR 2, 23, 69; DLB 323; MTCW 1; MTFW 2005

Melanchthon, Philipp 1497-1560 .... **LC 90**
See also DLB 179

Melanter
See Blackmore, R(ichard) D(oddridge)

Meleager c. 140B.C.-c. 70B.C. ...... **CMLC 53**

Melies, Georges 1861-1938 .... **TCLC 81**

Melikow, Loris
See Hofmannsthal, Hugo von

Melmoth, Sebastian
See Wilde, Oscar (Fingal O'Flahertie Wills)

Melo Neto, Joao Cabral de
See Cabral de Melo Neto, Joao
See also CWW 2; EWL 3

Meltzer, Milton 1915- .... **CLC 26**
See also AAYA 8, 45; BYA 2, 6; CA 13-16R; CANR 38, 92, 107; CLR 13; DLB 61; JRDA; MAICYA 1, 2; SAAS 1; SATA 1, 50, 80, 128; SATA-Essay 124; WYA; YAW

Melville, Herman 1819-1891 ..... **NCLC 3, 12, 29, 45, 49, 91, 93, 123, 157, 181; SSC 1, 17, 46, 95; WLC 4**
See also AAYA 25; AMW; AMWR 1; CDALB 1640-1865; DA; DA3; DAB; DAC; DAM MST, NOV; DLB 3, 74, 250, 254; EXPN; EXPS; GL 3; LAIT 1, 2; NFS 7, 9; RGAL 4; RGSF 2; SATA 59; SSFS 3; TUS

Members, Mark
See Powell, Anthony

Membreno, Alejandro .... **CLC 59**

Menand, Louis 1952- .... **CLC 208**
See also CA 200

Menander c. 342B.C.-c. 293B.C. .... **CMLC 9, 51; DC 3**
See also AW 1; CDWLB 1; DAM DRAM; DLB 176; LMFS 1; RGWL 2, 3

Menchu, Rigoberta 1959- .. **CLC 160; HLCS 2**
See also CA 175; CANR 135; DNFS 1; WLIT 1

Mencken, H(enry) L(ouis) 1880-1956 .... **TCLC 13**
See also AMW; CA 125; CAAE 105; CDALB 1917-1929; DLB 11, 29, 63, 137, 222; EWL 3; MAL 5; MTCW 1, 2; MTFW 2005; NCFS 4; RGAL 4; TUS

Mendelsohn, Jane 1965- .... **CLC 99**
See also CA 154; CANR 94

Mendoza, Inigo Lopez de
See Santillana, Inigo Lopez de Mendoza, Marques de

Menton, Francisco de
See Chin, Frank (Chew, Jr.)

Mercer, David 1928-1980 .... **CLC 5**
See also CA 9-12R; CAAS 102; CANR 23; CBD; DAM DRAM; DLB 13, 310; MTCW 1; RGEL 2

Merchant, Paul
See Ellison, Harlan

Meredith, George 1828-1909 .. **PC 60; TCLC 17, 43**
See also CA 153; CAAE 117; CANR 80; CDBLB 1832-1890; DAM POET; DLB 18, 35, 57, 159; RGEL 2; TEA

Meredith, William 1919-2007 ...... **CLC 4, 13, 22, 55; PC 28**
See also CA 9-12R; 14; CAAS 260; CANR 6, 40, 129; CP 1, 2, 3, 4, 5, 6, 7; DAM POET; DLB 5; MAL 5

Meredith, William Morris
See Meredith, William

Merezhkovsky, Dmitrii Sergeevich
See Merezhkovsky, Dmitry Sergeyevich
See also DLB 295

Merezhkovsky, Dmitry Sergeevich
See Merezhkovsky, Dmitry Sergeyevich
See also EWL 3

Merezhkovsky, Dmitry Sergeyevich 1865-1941 .... **TCLC 29**
See Merezhkovsky, Dmitrii Sergeevich; Merezhkovsky, Dmitry Sergeevich
See also CA 169

Merimee, Prosper 1803-1870 ... **NCLC 6, 65; SSC 7, 77**
See also DLB 119, 192; EW 6; EXPS; GFL 1789 to the Present; RGSF 2; RGWL 2, 3; SSFS 8; SUFW

Merkin, Daphne 1954- .... **CLC 44**
See also CA 123

Merleau-Ponty, Maurice 1908-1961 .... **TCLC 156**
See also CA 114; CAAS 89-92; DLB 296; GFL 1789 to the Present

Merlin, Arthur
See Blish, James (Benjamin)

Mernissi, Fatima 1940- .... **CLC 171**
See also CA 152; FW

Merrill, James 1926-1995 ...... **CLC 2, 3, 6, 8, 13, 18, 34, 91; PC 28; TCLC 173**
See also AMWS 3; CA 13-16R; CAAS 147; CANR 10, 49, 63, 108; CP 1, 2, 3, 4; DA3; DAM POET; DLB 5, 165; DLBY 1985; EWL 3; INT CANR-10; MAL 5; MTCW 1, 2; MTFW 2005; PAB; PFS 23; RGAL 4

Merrill, James Ingram
See Merrill, James

Merriman, Alex
See Silverberg, Robert

Merriman, Brian 1747-1805 .... **NCLC 70**

Merritt, E. B.
See Waddington, Miriam

Merton, Thomas (James) 1915-1968 . **CLC 1, 3, 11, 34, 83; PC 10**
See also AAYA 61; AMWS 8; CA 5-8R; CAAS 25-28R; CANR 22, 53, 111, 131; DA3; DLB 48; DLBY 1981; MAL 5; MTCW 1, 2; MTFW 2005

Merwin, W.S. 1927- ..... **CLC 1, 2, 3, 5, 8, 13, 18, 45, 88; PC 45**
See also AMWS 3; CA 13-16R; CANR 15, 51, 112, 140; CP 1, 2, 3, 4, 5, 6, 7; DA3; DAM POET; DLB 5, 169; EWL 3; INT CANR-15; MAL 5; MTCW 1, 2; MTFW 2005; PAB; PFS 5, 15; RGAL 4

Metastasio, Pietro 1698-1782 .... **LC 115**
See also RGWL 2, 3

Metcalf, John 1938- .... **CLC 37; SSC 43**
See also CA 113; CN 4, 5, 6, 7; DLB 60; RGSF 2; TWA

Metcalf, Suzanne
See Baum, L(yman) Frank

Mew, Charlotte (Mary) 1870-1928 .. **TCLC 8**
See also CA 189; CAAE 105; DLB 19, 135; RGEL 2

Mewshaw, Michael 1943- .... **CLC 9**
See also CA 53-56; CANR 7, 47, 147; DLBY 1980

Meyer, Conrad Ferdinand 1825-1898 .... **NCLC 81; SSC 30**
See also DLB 129; EW; RGWL 2, 3

Meyer, Gustav 1868-1932
See Meyrink, Gustav
See also CA 190; CAAE 117

Meyer, June
See Jordan, June

Meyer, Lynn
See Slavitt, David R.

Meyers, Jeffrey 1939- .... **CLC 39**
See also CA 186; 73-76, 186; CANR 54, 102, 159; DLB 111

Meynell, Alice (Christina Gertrude Thompson) 1847-1922 .... **TCLC 6**
See also CA 177; CAAE 104; DLB 19, 98; RGEL 2

Meyrink, Gustav .... **TCLC 21**
See Meyer, Gustav
See also DLB 81; EWL 3

Michaels, Leonard 1933-2003 ..... **CLC 6, 25; SSC 16**
See also AMWS 16; CA 61-64; CAAS 216; CANR 21, 62, 119; CN 3, 45, 6, 7; DLB 130; MTCW 1; TCLE 1:2

Michaux, Henri 1899-1984 .... **CLC 8, 19**
See also CA 85-88; CAAS 114; DLB 258; EWL 3; GFL 1789 to the Present; RGWL 2, 3

Micheaux, Oscar (Devereaux) 1884-1951 .... **TCLC 76**
See also BW 3; CA 174; DLB 50; TCWW 2

Michelangelo 1475-1564 .... **LC 12**
See also AAYA 43

Michelet, Jules 1798-1874 .... **NCLC 31**
See also EW 5; GFL 1789 to the Present

Michels, Robert 1876-1936 .... **TCLC 88**
See also CA 212

Michener, James A. 1907(?)-1997 . **CLC 1, 5, 11, 29, 60, 109**
See also AAYA 27; AITN 1; BEST 90:1; BPFB 2; CA 5-8R; CAAS 161; CANR 21, 45, 68; CN 1, 2, 3, 4, 5, 6; CPW; DA3; DAM NOV, POP; DLB 6; MAL 5; MTCW 1, 2; MTFW 2005; RHW; TCWW 1, 2

Mickiewicz, Adam 1798-1855 . **NCLC 3, 101; PC 38**
See also EW 5; RGWL 2, 3

Middleton, (John) Christopher 1926- .... **CLC 13**
See also CA 13-16R; CANR 29, 54, 117; CP 1, 2, 3, 4, 5, 6, 7; DLB 40

Middleton, Richard (Barham) 1882-1911 .... **TCLC 56**
See also CA 187; DLB 156; HGG

Middleton, Stanley 1919- .... **CLC 7, 38**
See also CA 25-28R; 23; CANR 21, 46, 81, 157; CN 1, 2, 3, 4, 5, 6, 7; DLB 14, 326

Middleton, Thomas 1580-1627 ...... **DC 5; LC 33, 123**
See also BRW 2; DAM DRAM, MST; DFS 18, 22; DLB 58; RGEL 2

Mieville, China 1972(?)- .... **CLC 235**
See also AAYA 52; CA 196; CANR 138; MTFW 2005

Migueis, Jose Rodrigues 1901-1980 . **CLC 10**
See also DLB 287

Mikszath, Kalman 1847-1910 .... **TCLC 31**
See also CA 170

Miles, Jack .... **CLC 100**
See also CA 200

Miles, John Russiano
See Miles, Jack

Mohr, Nicholasa 1938- .... **CLC 12; HLC 2**
See also AAYA 8, 46; CA 49-52; CANR 1, 32, 64; CLR 22; DAM MULT; DLB 145; HW 1, 2; JRDA; LAIT 5; LLW; MAICYA 2; MAICYAS 1; RGAL 4; SAAS 8; SATA 8, 97; SATA-Essay 113; WYA; YAW

Moi, Toril 1953- .... **CLC 172**
See also CA 154; CANR 102; FW

Mojtabai, A(nn) G(race) 1938- ..... **CLC 5, 9, 15, 29**
See also CA 85-88; CANR 88

Moliere 1622-1673 ..... **DC 13; LC 10, 28, 64, 125, 127; WLC 4**
See also DA; DA3; DAB; DAC; DAM DRAM, MST; DFS 13, 18, 20; DLB 268; EW 3; GFL Beginnings to 1789; LATS 1:1; RGWL 2, 3; TWA

Molin, Charles
See Mayne, William (James Carter)

Molnar, Ferenc 1878-1952 .... **TCLC 20**
See also CA 153; CAAE 109; CANR 83; CDWLB 4; DAM DRAM; DLB 215; EWL 3; RGWL 2, 3

Momaday, N. Scott 1934- ...... **CLC 2, 19, 85, 95, 160; NNAL; PC 25; WLCS**
See also AAYA 11, 64; AMWS 4; ANW; BPFB 2; BYA 12; CA 25-28R; CANR 14, 34, 68, 134; CDALBS; CN 2, 3, 4, 5, 6, 7; CPW; DA; DA3; DAB; DAC; DAM MST, MULT, NOV, POP; DLB 143, 175, 256; EWL 3; EXPP; INT CANR-14; LAIT 4; LATS 1:2; MAL 5; MTCW 1, 2; MTFW 2005; NFS 10; PFS 2, 11; RGAL 4; SATA 48; SATA-Brief 30; TCWW 1, 2; WP; YAW

Monette, Paul 1945-1995 .... **CLC 82**
See also AMWS 10; CA 139; CAAS 147; CN 6; GLL 1

Monroe, Harriet 1860-1936 .... **TCLC 12**
See also CA 204; CAAE 109; DLB 54, 91

Monroe, Lyle
See Heinlein, Robert A.

Montagu, Elizabeth 1720-1800 .... **NCLC 7, 117**
See also FW

Montagu, Mary (Pierrepont) Wortley
1689-1762 .... **LC 9, 57; PC 16**
See also DLB 95, 101; FL 1:1; RGEL 2

Montagu, W. H.
See Coleridge, Samuel Taylor

Montague, John (Patrick) 1929- ..... **CLC 13, 46**
See also CA 9-12R; CANR 9, 69, 121; CP 1, 2, 3, 4, 5, 6, 7; DLB 40; EWL 3; MTCW 1; PFS 12; RGEL 2; TCLE 1:2

Montaigne, Michel (Eyquem) de
1533-1592 .... **LC 8, 105; WLC 4**
See also DA; DAB; DAC; DAM MST; DLB 327; EW 2; GFL Beginnings to 1789; LMFS 1; RGWL 2, 3; TWA

Montale, Eugenio 1896-1981 ... **CLC 7, 9, 18; PC 13**
See also CA 17-20R; CAAS 104; CANR 30; DLB 114, 331; EW 11; EWL 3; MTCW 1; PFS 22; RGWL 2, 3; TWA; WLIT 7

Montesquieu, Charles-Louis de Secondat
1689-1755 .... **LC 7, 69**
See also DLB 314; EW 3; GFL Beginnings to 1789; TWA

Montessori, Maria 1870-1952 ...... **TCLC 103**
See also CA 147; CAAE 115

Montgomery, (Robert) Bruce 1921(?)-1978
See Crispin, Edmund
See also CA 179; CAAS 104; CMW 4

Montgomery, L(ucy) M(aud)
1874-1942 .... **TCLC 51, 140**
See also AAYA 12; BYA 1; CA 137; CAAE 108; CLR 8, 91; DA3; DAC; DAM MST; DLB 92; DLBD 14; JRDA; MAICYA 1, 2; MTCW 2; MTFW 2005; RGEL 2; SATA 100; TWA; WCH; WYA; YABC 1

Montgomery, Marion, Jr. 1925- .... **CLC 7**
See also AITN 1; CA 1-4R; CANR 3, 48, 162; CSW; DLB 6

Montgomery, Marion H. 1925-
See Montgomery, Marion, Jr.

Montgomery, Max
See Davenport, Guy (Mattison, Jr.)

Montherlant, Henry (Milon) de
1896-1972 .... **CLC 8, 19**
See also CA 85-88; CAAS 37-40R; DAM DRAM; DLB 72, 321; EW 11; EWL 3; GFL 1789 to the Present; MTCW 1

Monty Python
See Chapman, Graham; Cleese, John (Marwood); Gilliam, Terry; Idle, Eric; Jones, Terence Graham Parry; Palin, Michael (Edward)
See also AAYA 7

Moodie, Susanna (Strickland)
1803-1885 .... **NCLC 14, 113**
See also DLB 99

Moody, Hiram 1961-
See Moody, Rick
See also CA 138; CANR 64, 112; MTFW 2005

Moody, Minerva
See Alcott, Louisa May

Moody, Rick .... **CLC 147**
See Moody, Hiram

Moody, William Vaughan
1869-1910 .... **TCLC 105**
See also CA 178; CAAE 110; DLB 7, 54; MAL 5; RGAL 4

Mooney, Edward 1951-
See Mooney, Ted
See also CA 130

Mooney, Ted .... **CLC 25**
See Mooney, Edward

Moorcock, Michael 1939- ...... **CLC 5, 27, 58, 236**
See Bradbury, Edward P.
See also AAYA 26; CA 45-48; 5; CANR 2, 17, 38, 64, 122; CN 5, 6, 7; DLB 14, 231, 261, 319; FANT; MTCW 1, 2; MTFW 2005; SATA 93, 166; SCFW 1, 2; SFW 4; SUFW 1, 2

Moorcock, Michael John
See Moorcock, Michael

Moore, Alan 1953- .... **CLC 230**
See also AAYA 51; CA 204; CANR 138; DLB 261; MTFW 2005; SFW 4

Moore, Brian 1921-1999 ... **CLC 1, 3, 5, 7, 8, 19, 32, 90**
See Bryan, Michael
See also BRWS 9; CA 1-4R; CAAS 174; CANR 1, 25, 42, 63; CCA 1; CN 1, 2, 3, 4, 5, 6; DAB; DAC; DAM MST; DLB 251; EWL 3; FANT; MTCW 1, 2; MTFW 2005; RGEL 2

Moore, Edward
See Muir, Edwin
See also RGEL 2

Moore, G. E. 1873-1958 .... **TCLC 89**
See also DLB 262

Moore, George Augustus
1852-1933 .... **SSC 19; TCLC 7**
See also BRW 6; CA 177; CAAE 104; DLB 10, 18, 57, 135; EWL 3; RGEL 2; RGSF 2

Moore, Lorrie .... **CLC 39, 45, 68**
See Moore, Marie Lorena
See also AMWS 10; CN 5, 6, 7; DLB 234; SSFS 19

Moore, Marianne (Craig)
1887-1972 .... **CLC 1, 2, 4, 8, 10, 13, 19, 47; PC 4, 49; WLCS**
See also AMW; CA 1-4R; CAAS 33-36R; CANR 3, 61; CDALB 1929-1941; CP 1; DA; DA3; DAB; DAC; DAM MST, POET; DLB 45; DLBD 7; EWL 3; EXPP; FL 1:6; MAL 5; MBL; MTCW 1, 2; MTFW 2005; PAB; PFS 14, 17; RGAL 4; SATA 20; TUS; WP

Moore, Marie Lorena 1957- .... **CLC 165**
See Moore, Lorrie
See also CA 116; CANR 39, 83, 139; DLB 234; MTFW 2005

Moore, Michael 1954- .... **CLC 218**
See also AAYA 53; CA 166; CANR 150

Moore, Thomas 1779-1852 ..... **NCLC 6, 110**
See also DLB 96, 144; RGEL 2

Moorhouse, Frank 1938- .... **SSC 40**
See also CA 118; CANR 92; CN 3, 4, 5, 6, 7; DLB 289; RGSF 2

Mora, Pat 1942- .... **HLC 2**
See also AMWS 13; CA 129; CANR 57, 81, 112; CLR 58; DAM MULT; DLB 209; HW 1, 2; LLW; MAICYA 2; MTFW 2005; SATA 92, 134

Moraga, Cherrie 1952- ...... **CLC 126; DC 22**
See also CA 131; CANR 66, 154; DAM MULT; DLB 82, 249; FW; GLL 1; HW 1, 2; LLW

Morand, Paul 1888-1976 .... **CLC 41; SSC 22**
See also CA 184; CAAS 69-72; DLB 65; EWL 3

Morante, Elsa 1918-1985 .... **CLC 8, 47**
See also CA 85-88; CAAS 117; CANR 35; DLB 177; EWL 3; MTCW 1, 2; MTFW 2005; RGHL; RGWL 2, 3; WLIT 7

Moravia, Alberto .... **CLC 2, 7, 11, 27, 46; SSC 26**
See Pincherle, Alberto
See also DLB 177; EW 12; EWL 3; MTCW 2; RGSF 2; RGWL 2, 3; WLIT 7

More, Hannah 1745-1833 ...... **NCLC 27, 141**
See also DLB 107, 109, 116, 158; RGEL 2

More, Henry 1614-1687 .... **LC 9**
See also DLB 126, 252

More, Sir Thomas 1478(?)-1535 ... **LC 10, 32, 140**
See also BRWC 1; BRWS 7; DLB 136, 281; LMFS 1; RGEL 2; TEA

Moreas, Jean .... **TCLC 18**
See Papadiamantopoulos, Johannes
See also GFL 1789 to the Present

Moreton, Andrew Esq.
See Defoe, Daniel

Morgan, Berry 1919-2002 .... **CLC 6**
See also CA 49-52; CAAS 208; DLB 6

Morgan, Claire
See Highsmith, Patricia
See also GLL 1

Morgan, Edwin (George) 1920- .... **CLC 31**
See also BRWS 9; CA 5-8R; CANR 3, 43, 90; CP 1, 2, 3, 4, 5, 6, 7; DLB 27

Morgan, (George) Frederick
1922-2004 .... **CLC 23**
See also CA 17-20R; CAAS 224; CANR 21, 144; CP 2, 3, 4, 5, 6, 7

Morgan, Harriet
See Mencken, H(enry) L(ouis)

Morgan, Jane
See Cooper, James Fenimore

Morgan, Janet 1945- .... **CLC 39**
See also CA 65-68

Morgan, Lady 1776(?)-1859 .... **NCLC 29**
See also DLB 116, 158; RGEL 2

Morgan, Robin (Evonne) 1941- .... **CLC 2**
See also CA 69-72; CANR 29, 68; FW; GLL 2; MTCW 1; SATA 80

NOV; DLB 53; EWL 3; MTCW 1, 2; MTFW 2005; RGEL 2; RGSF 2; SATA 29; SSFS 5, 13, 19; TCLE 1:2; WWE 1

Munro, H(ector) H(ugh) 1870-1916
See Saki
See also AAYA 56; CA 130; CAAE 104; CANR 104; CDBLB 1890-1914; DA; DA3; DAB; DAC; DAM MST, NOV; DLB 34, 162; EXPS; MTCW 1, 2; MTFW 2005; RGEL 2; SSFS 15

Murakami, Haruki 1949- .... **CLC 150**
See Murakami Haruki
See also CA 165; CANR 102, 146; MJW; RGWL 3; SFW 4; SSFS 23

Murakami Haruki
See Murakami, Haruki
See also CWW 2; DLB 182; EWL 3

Murasaki, Lady
See Murasaki Shikibu

Murasaki Shikibu 978(?)-1026(?) .. **CMLC 1, 79**
See also EFS 2; LATS 1:1; RGWL 2, 3

Murdoch, Iris 1919-1999 .. **CLC 1, 2, 3, 4, 6, 8, 11, 15, 22, 31, 51; TCLC 171**
See also BRWS 1; CA 13-16R; CAAS 179; CANR 8, 43, 68, 103, 142; CBD; CDBLB 1960 to Present; CN 1, 2, 3, 4, 5, 6; CWD; DA3; DAB; DAC; DAM MST, NOV; DLB 14, 194, 233, 326; EWL 3; INT CANR-8; MTCW 1, 2; MTFW 2005; NFS 18; RGEL 2; TCLE 1:2; TEA; WLIT 4

Murfree, Mary Noailles 1850-1922 .. **SSC 22; TCLC 135**
See also CA 176; CAAE 122; DLB 12, 74; RGAL 4

Murglie
See Murnau, F.W.

Murnau, Friedrich Wilhelm
See Murnau, F.W.

Murnau, F.W. 1888-1931 .... **TCLC 53**
See also CAAE 112

Murphy, Richard 1927- .... **CLC 41**
See also BRWS 5; CA 29-32R; CP 1, 2, 3, 4, 5, 6, 7; DLB 40; EWL 3

Murphy, Sylvia 1937- .... **CLC 34**
See also CA 121

Murphy, Thomas (Bernard) 1935- ... **CLC 51**
See Murphy, Tom
See also CA 101

Murphy, Tom
See Murphy, Thomas (Bernard)
See also DLB 310

Murray, Albert 1916- .... **CLC 73**
See also BW 2; CA 49-52; CANR 26, 52, 78, 160; CN 7; CSW; DLB 38; MTFW 2005

Murray, Albert L.
See Murray, Albert

Murray, James Augustus Henry 1837-1915 .... **TCLC 117**

Murray, Judith Sargent 1751-1820 .... **NCLC 63**
See also DLB 37, 200

Murray, Les(lie Allan) 1938- .... **CLC 40**
See also BRWS 7; CA 21-24R; CANR 11, 27, 56, 103; CP 1, 2, 3, 4, 5, 6, 7; DAM POET; DLB 289; DLBY 2001; EWL 3; RGEL 2

Murry, J. Middleton
See Murry, John Middleton

Murry, John Middleton 1889-1957 .... **TCLC 16**
See also CA 217; CAAE 118; DLB 149

Musgrave, Susan 1951- .... **CLC 13, 54**
See also CA 69-72; CANR 45, 84; CCA 1; CP 2, 3, 4, 5, 6, 7; CWP

Musil, Robert (Edler von) 1880-1942 .... **SSC 18; TCLC 12, 68**
See also CAAE 109; CANR 55, 84; CDWLB 2; DLB 81, 124; EW 9; EWL 3; MTCW 2; RGSF 2; RGWL 2, 3

Muske, Carol .... **CLC 90**
See Muske-Dukes, Carol (Anne)

Muske-Dukes, Carol (Anne) 1945-
See Muske, Carol
See also CA 203; 65-68, 203; CANR 32, 70; CWP; PFS 24

Musset, Alfred de 1810-1857 . **DC 27; NCLC 7, 150**
See also DLB 192, 217; EW 6; GFL 1789 to the Present; RGWL 2, 3; TWA

Musset, Louis Charles Alfred de
See Musset, Alfred de

Mussolini, Benito (Amilcare Andrea) 1883-1945 .... **TCLC 96**
See also CAAE 116

Mutanabbi, Al-
See al-Mutanabbi, Ahmad ibn al-Husayn Abu al-Tayyib al-Jufi al-Kindi
See also WLIT 6

My Brother's Brother
See Chekhov, Anton (Pavlovich)

Myers, L(eopold) H(amilton) 1881-1944 .... **TCLC 59**
See also CA 157; DLB 15; EWL 3; RGEL 2

Myers, Walter Dean 1937- .. **BLC 3; CLC 35**
See Myers, Walter M.
See also AAYA 4, 23; BW 2; BYA 6, 8, 11; CA 33-36R; CANR 20, 42, 67, 108; CLR 4, 16, 35, 110; DAM MST, NOV; DLB 33; INT CANR-20; JRDA; LAIT 5; MAICYA 1, 2; MAICYAS 1; MTCW 2; MTFW 2005; SAAS 2; SATA 41, 71, 109, 157; SATA-Brief 27; WYA; YAW

Myers, Walter M.
See Myers, Walter Dean

Myles, Symon
See Follett, Ken

Nabokov, Vladimir (Vladimirovich) 1899-1977 .... **CLC 1, 2, 3, 6, 8, 11, 15, 23, 44, 46, 64; SSC 11, 86; TCLC 108, 189; WLC 4**
See also AAYA 45; AMW; AMWC 1; AMWR 1; BPFB 2; CA 5-8R; CAAS 69-72; CANR 20, 102; CDALB 1941-1968; CN 1, 2; CP 2; DA; DA3; DAB; DAC; DAM MST, NOV; DLB 2, 244, 278, 317; DLBD 3; DLBY 1980, 1991; EWL 3; EXPS; LATS 1:2; MAL 5; MTCW 1, 2; MTFW 2005; NCFS 4; NFS 9; RGAL 4; RGSF 2; SSFS 6, 15; TUS

Naevius c. 265B.C.-201B.C. .... **CMLC 37**
See also DLB 211

Nagai, Kafu .... **TCLC 51**
See Nagai, Sokichi
See also DLB 180

Nagai, Sokichi 1879-1959
See Nagai, Kafu
See also CAAE 117

Nagy, Laszlo 1925-1978 .... **CLC 7**
See also CA 129; CAAS 112

Naidu, Sarojini 1879-1949 .... **TCLC 80**
See also EWL 3; RGEL 2

Naipaul, Shiva 1945-1985 .... **CLC 32, 39; TCLC 153**
See also CA 112; CAAE 110; CAAS 116; CANR 33; CN 2, 3; DA3; DAM NOV; DLB 157; DLBY 1985; EWL 3; MTCW 1, 2; MTFW 2005

Naipaul, V.S. 1932- .. **CLC 4, 7, 9, 13, 18, 37, 105, 199; SSC 38**
See also BPFB 2; BRWS 1; CA 1-4R; CANR 1, 33, 51, 91, 126; CDBLB 1960 to Present; CDWLB 3; CN 1, 2, 3, 4, 5, 6, 7; DA3; DAB; DAC; DAM MST,

NOV; DLB 125, 204, 207, 326, 331; DLBY 1985, 2001; EWL 3; LATS 1:2; MTCW 1, 2; MTFW 2005; RGEL 2; RGSF 2; TWA; WLIT 4; WWE 1

Nakos, Lilika 1903(?)-1989 .... **CLC 29**

Napoleon
See Yamamoto, Hisaye

Narayan, R.K. 1906-2001 ...... **CLC 7, 28, 47, 121, 211; SSC 25**
See also BPFB 2; CA 81-84; CAAS 196; CANR 33, 61, 112; CN 1, 2, 3, 4, 5, 6, 7; DA3; DAM NOV; DLB 323; DNFS 1; EWL 3; MTCW 1, 2; MTFW 2005; RGEL 2; RGSF 2; SATA 62; SSFS 5; WWE 1

Nash, (Frediric) Ogden 1902-1971 . **CLC 23; PC 21; TCLC 109**
See also CA 13-14; CAAS 29-32R; CANR 34, 61; CAP 1; CP 1; DAM POET; DLB 11; MAICYA 1, 2; MAL 5; MTCW 1, 2; RGAL 4; SATA 2, 46; WP

Nashe, Thomas 1567-1601(?) .... **LC 41, 89**
See also DLB 167; RGEL 2

Nathan, Daniel
See Dannay, Frederic

Nathan, George Jean 1882-1958 .... **TCLC 18**
See Hatteras, Owen
See also CA 169; CAAE 114; DLB 137; MAL 5

Natsume, Kinnosuke
See Natsume, Soseki

Natsume, Soseki 1867-1916 .... **TCLC 2, 10**
See Natsume Soseki; Soseki
See also CA 195; CAAE 104; RGWL 2, 3; TWA

Natsume Soseki
See Natsume, Soseki
See also DLB 180; EWL 3

Natti, (Mary) Lee 1919-
See Kingman, Lee
See also CA 5-8R; CANR 2

Navarre, Marguerite de
See de Navarre, Marguerite

Naylor, Gloria 1950- ..... **BLC 3; CLC 28, 52, 156; WLCS**
See also AAYA 6, 39; AFAW 1, 2; AMWS 8; BW 2, 3; CA 107; CANR 27, 51, 74, 130; CN 4, 5, 6, 7; CPW; DA; DA3; DAC; DAM MST, MULT, NOV, POP; DLB 173; EWL 3; FW; MAL 5; MTCW 1, 2; MTFW 2005; NFS 4, 7; RGAL 4; TCLE 1:2; TUS

Neal, John 1793-1876 .... **NCLC 161**
See also DLB 1, 59, 243; FW; RGAL 4

Neff, Debra .... **CLC 59**

Neihardt, John Gneisenau 1881-1973 .... **CLC 32**
See also CA 13-14; CANR 65; CAP 1; DLB 9, 54, 256; LAIT 2; TCWW 1, 2

Nekrasov, Nikolai Alekseevich 1821-1878 .... **NCLC 11**
See also DLB 277

Nelligan, Emile 1879-1941 .... **TCLC 14**
See also CA 204; CAAE 114; DLB 92; EWL 3

Nelson, Willie 1933- .... **CLC 17**
See also CA 107; CANR 114

Nemerov, Howard 1920-1991 .... **CLC 2, 6, 9, 36; PC 24; TCLC 124**
See also AMW; CA 1-4R; CAAS 134; CABS 2; CANR 1, 27, 53; CN 1, 2, 3; CP 1, 2, 3, 4, 5; DAM POET; DLB 5, 6; DLBY 1983; EWL 3; INT CANR-27; MAL 5; MTCW 1, 2; MTFW 2005; PFS 10, 14; RGAL 4

Nepos, Cornelius c. 99B.C.-c. 24B.C. .... **CMLC 89**
See also DLB 211

Owen, Wilfred (Edward Salter)
  1893-1918 ... **PC 19; TCLC 5, 27; WLC 4**
  See also BRW 6; CA 141; CAAE 104; CD-BLB 1914-1945; DA; DAB; DAC; DAM MST, POET; DLB 20; EWL 3; EXPP; MTCW 2; MTFW 2005; PFS 10; RGEL 2; WLIT 4

Owens, Louis (Dean) 1948-2002 .... **NNAL**
  See also CA 179; 137, 179; 24; CAAS 207; CANR 71

Owens, Rochelle 1936- .... **CLC 8**
  See also CA 17-20R; 2; CAD; CANR 39; CD 5, 6; CP 1, 2, 3, 4, 5, 6, 7; CWD; CWP

Oz, Amos 1939- ...... **CLC 5, 8, 11, 27, 33, 54; SSC 66**
  See also CA 53-56; CANR 27, 47, 65, 113, 138; CWW 2; DAM NOV; EWL 3; MTCW 1, 2; MTFW 2005; RGHL; RGSF 2; RGWL 3; WLIT 6

Ozick, Cynthia 1928- .... **CLC 3, 7, 28, 62, 155; SSC 15, 60**
  See also AMWS 5; BEST 90:1; CA 17-20R; CANR 23, 58, 116, 160; CN 3, 4, 5, 6, 7; CPW; DA3; DAM NOV, POP; DLB 28, 152, 299; DLBY 1982; EWL 3; EXPS; INT CANR-23; MAL 5; MTCW 1, 2; MTFW 2005; RGAL 4; RGHL; RGSF 2; SSFS 3, 12, 22

Ozu, Yasujiro 1903-1963 .... **CLC 16**
  See also CA 112

Pabst, G. W. 1885-1967 .... **TCLC 127**

Pacheco, C.
  See Pessoa, Fernando (Antonio Nogueira)

Pacheco, Jose Emilio 1939- .... **HLC 2**
  See also CA 131; CAAE 111; CANR 65; CWW 2; DAM MULT; DLB 290; EWL 3; HW 1, 2; RGSF 2

Pa Chin .... **CLC 18**
  See Jin, Ba
  See also EWL 3

Pack, Robert 1929- .... **CLC 13**
  See also CA 1-4R; CANR 3, 44, 82; CP 1, 2, 3, 4, 5, 6, 7; DLB 5; SATA 118

Padgett, Lewis
  See Kuttner, Henry

Padilla (Lorenzo), Heberto
  1932-2000 .... **CLC 38**
  See also AITN 1; CA 131; CAAE 123; CAAS 189; CWW 2; EWL 3; HW 1

Page, James Patrick 1944-
  See Page, Jimmy
  See also CA 204

Page, Jimmy 1944- .... **CLC 12**
  See Page, James Patrick

Page, Louise 1955- .... **CLC 40**
  See also CA 140; CANR 76; CBD; CD 5, 6; CWD; DLB 233

Page, P(atricia) K(athleen) 1916- ...... **CLC 7, 18; PC 12**
  See Cape, Judith
  See also CA 53-56; CANR 4, 22, 65; CP 1, 2, 3, 4, 5, 6, 7; DAC; DAM MST; DLB 68; MTCW 1; RGEL 2

Page, Stanton
  See Fuller, Henry Blake

Page, Stanton
  See Fuller, Henry Blake

Page, Thomas Nelson 1853-1922 .... **SSC 23**
  See also CA 177; CAAE 118; DLB 12, 78; DLBD 13; RGAL 4

Pagels, Elaine
  See Pagels, Elaine Hiesey

Pagels, Elaine Hiesey 1943- .... **CLC 104**
  See also CA 45-48; CANR 2, 24, 51, 151; FW; NCFS 4

Paget, Violet 1856-1935
  See Lee, Vernon
  See also CA 166; CAAE 104; GLL 1; HGG

Paget-Lowe, Henry
  See Lovecraft, H. P.

Paglia, Camille 1947- .... **CLC 68**
  See also CA 140; CANR 72, 139; CPW; FW; GLL 2; MTCW 2; MTFW 2005

Paige, Richard
  See Koontz, Dean R.

Paine, Thomas 1737-1809 .... **NCLC 62**
  See also AMWS 1; CDALB 1640-1865; DLB 31, 43, 73, 158; LAIT 1; RGAL 4; RGEL 2; TUS

Pakenham, Antonia
  See Fraser, Antonia

Palamas, Costis
  See Palamas, Kostes

Palamas, Kostes 1859-1943 .... **TCLC 5**
  See Palamas, Kostis
  See also CA 190; CAAE 105; RGWL 2, 3

Palamas, Kostis
  See Palamas, Kostes
  See also EWL 3

Palazzeschi, Aldo 1885-1974 .... **CLC 11**
  See also CA 89-92; CAAS 53-56; DLB 114, 264; EWL 3

Pales Matos, Luis 1898-1959 .... **HLCS 2**
  See Pales Matos, Luis
  See also DLB 290; HW 1; LAW

Paley, Grace 1922-2007 ... **CLC 4, 6, 37, 140; SSC 8**
  See also AMWS 6; CA 25-28R; CANR 13, 46, 74, 118; CN 2, 3, 4, 5, 6, 7; CPW; DA3; DAM POP; DLB 28, 218; EWL 3; EXPS; FW; INT CANR-13; MAL 5; MBL; MTCW 1, 2; MTFW 2005; RGAL 4; RGSF 2; SSFS 3, 20

Palin, Michael (Edward) 1943- .... **CLC 21**
  See Monty Python
  See also CA 107; CANR 35, 109; SATA 67

Palliser, Charles 1947- .... **CLC 65**
  See also CA 136; CANR 76; CN 5, 6, 7

Palma, Ricardo 1833-1919 .... **TCLC 29**
  See also CA 168; LAW

Pamuk, Orhan 1952- .... **CLC 185**
  See also CA 142; CANR 75, 127; CWW 2; WLIT 6

Pancake, Breece Dexter 1952-1979
  See Pancake, Breece D'J
  See also CA 123; CAAS 109

Pancake, Breece D'J .... **CLC 29; SSC 61**
  See Pancake, Breece Dexter
  See also DLB 130

Panchenko, Nikolai .... **CLC 59**

Pankhurst, Emmeline (Goulden)
  1858-1928 .... **TCLC 100**
  See also CAAE 116; FW

Panko, Rudy
  See Gogol, Nikolai (Vasilyevich)

Papadiamantis, Alexandros
  1851-1911 .... **TCLC 29**
  See also CA 168; EWL 3

Papadiamantopoulos, Johannes 1856-1910
  See Moreas, Jean
  See also CA 242; CAAE 117

Papini, Giovanni 1881-1956 .... **TCLC 22**
  See also CA 180; CAAE 121; DLB 264

Paracelsus 1493-1541 .... **LC 14**
  See also DLB 179

Parasol, Peter
  See Stevens, Wallace

Pardo Bazan, Emilia 1851-1921 .... **SSC 30; TCLC 189**
  See also EWL 3; FW; RGSF 2; RGWL 2, 3

Pareto, Vilfredo 1848-1923 .... **TCLC 69**
  See also CA 175

Paretsky, Sara 1947- .... **CLC 135**
  See also AAYA 30; BEST 90:3; CA 129; CAAE 125; CANR 59, 95; CMW 4; CPW; DA3; DAM POP; DLB 306; INT CA-129; MSW; RGAL 4

Parfenie, Maria
  See Codrescu, Andrei

Parini, Jay (Lee) 1948- .... **CLC 54, 133**
  See also CA 229; 97-100, 229; 16; CANR 32, 87

Park, Jordan
  See Kornbluth, C(yril) M.; Pohl, Frederik

Park, Robert E(zra) 1864-1944 ..... **TCLC 73**
  See also CA 165; CAAE 122

Parker, Bert
  See Ellison, Harlan

Parker, Dorothy (Rothschild)
  1893-1967 . **CLC 15, 68; PC 28; SSC 2, 101; TCLC 143**
  See also AMWS 9; CA 19-20; CAAS 25-28R; CAP 2; DA3; DAM POET; DLB 11, 45, 86; EXPP; FW; MAL 5; MBL; MTCW 1, 2; MTFW 2005; PFS 18; RGAL 4; RGSF 2; TUS

Parker, Robert B. 1932- .... **CLC 27**
  See also AAYA 28; BEST 89:4; BPFB 3; CA 49-52; CANR 1, 26, 52, 89, 128, 165; CMW 4; CPW; DAM NOV, POP; DLB 306; INT CANR-26; MSW; MTCW 1; MTFW 2005

Parker, Robert Brown
  See Parker, Robert B.

Parker, Theodore 1810-1860 .... **NCLC 186**
  See also DLB 1, 235

Parkin, Frank 1940- .... **CLC 43**
  See also CA 147

Parkman, Francis, Jr. 1823-1893 .. **NCLC 12**
  See also AMWS 2; DLB 1, 30, 183, 186, 235; RGAL 4

Parks, Gordon 1912-2006 .... **BLC 3; CLC 1, 16**
  See also AAYA 36; AITN 2; BW 2, 3; CA 41-44R; CAAS 249; CANR 26, 66, 145; DA3; DAM MULT; DLB 33; MTCW 2; MTFW 2005; SATA 8, 108; SATA-Obit 175

Parks, Suzan-Lori 1964(?)- .... **DC 23**
  See also AAYA 55; CA 201; CAD; CD 5, 6; CWD; DFS 22; RGAL 4

Parks, Tim(othy Harold) 1954- ...... **CLC 147**
  See also CA 131; CAAE 126; CANR 77, 144; CN 7; DLB 231; INT CA-131

Parmenides c. 515B.C.-c. 450B.C. .... **CMLC 22**
  See also DLB 176

Parnell, Thomas 1679-1718 .... **LC 3**
  See also DLB 95; RGEL 2

Parr, Catherine c. 1513(?)-1548 .... **LC 86**
  See also DLB 136

Parra, Nicanor 1914- ... **CLC 2, 102; HLC 2; PC 39**
  See also CA 85-88; CANR 32; CWW 2; DAM MULT; DLB 283; EWL 3; HW 1; LAW; MTCW 1

Parra Sanojo, Ana Teresa de la
  1890-1936 .... **HLCS 2**
  See de la Parra, (Ana) Teresa (Sonojo)
  See also LAW

Parrish, Mary Frances
  See Fisher, M(ary) F(rances) K(ennedy)

Parshchikov, Aleksei 1954- .... **CLC 59**
  See Parshchikov, Aleksei Maksimovich

Parshchikov, Aleksei Maksimovich
  See Parshchikov, Aleksei
  See also DLB 285

Parson, Professor
  See Coleridge, Samuel Taylor

Parson Lot
  See Kingsley, Charles

Parton, Sara Payson Willis
1811-1872 .... **NCLC 86**
See also DLB 43, 74, 239

Partridge, Anthony
See Oppenheim, E(dward) Phillips

Pascal, Blaise 1623-1662 .... **LC 35**
See also DLB 268; EW 3; GFL Beginnings
to 1789; RGWL 2, 3; TWA

Pascoli, Giovanni 1855-1912 .... **TCLC 45**
See also CA 170; EW 7; EWL 3

Pasolini, Pier Paolo 1922-1975 .. **CLC 20, 37,
106; PC 17**
See also CA 93-96; CAAS 61-64; CANR
63; DLB 128, 177; EWL 3; MTCW 1;
RGWL 2, 3

Pasquini
See Silone, Ignazio

Pastan, Linda (Olenik) 1932- .... **CLC 27**
See also CA 61-64; CANR 18, 40, 61, 113;
CP 3, 4, 5, 6, 7; CSW; CWP; DAM
POET; DLB 5; PFS 8, 25

Pasternak, Boris 1890-1960 ... **CLC 7, 10, 18,
63; PC 6; SSC 31; TCLC 188; WLC 4**
See also BPFB 3; CA 127; CAAS 116; DA;
DA3; DAB; DAC; DAM MST, NOV,
POET; DLB 302, 331; EW 10; MTCW 1,
2; MTFW 2005; RGSF 2; RGWL 2, 3;
TWA; WP

Patchen, Kenneth 1911-1972 .... **CLC 1, 2, 18**
See also BG 1:3; CA 1-4R; CAAS 33-36R;
CANR 3, 35; CN 1; CP 1; DAM POET;
DLB 16, 48; EWL 3; MAL 5; MTCW 1;
RGAL 4

Pater, Walter (Horatio) 1839-1894 . **NCLC 7,
90, 159**
See also BRW 5; CDBLB 1832-1890; DLB
57, 156; RGEL 2; TEA

Paterson, A(ndrew) B(arton)
1864-1941 .... **TCLC 32**
See also CA 155; DLB 230; RGEL 2; SATA
97

Paterson, Banjo
See Paterson, A(ndrew) B(arton)

Paterson, Katherine 1932- .... **CLC 12, 30**
See also AAYA 1, 31; BYA 1, 2, 7; CA 21-
24R; CANR 28, 59, 111; CLR 7, 50;
CWRI 5; DLB 52; JRDA; LAIT 4; MAI-
CYA 1, 2; MAICYAS 1; MTCW 1; SATA
13, 53, 92, 133; WYA; YAW

Paterson, Katherine Womeldorf
See Paterson, Katherine

Patmore, Coventry Kersey Dighton
1823-1896 .... **NCLC 9; PC 59**
See also DLB 35, 98; RGEL 2; TEA

Paton, Alan 1903-1988 ..... **CLC 4, 10, 25, 55,
106; TCLC 165; WLC 4**
See also AAYA 26; AFW; BPFB 3; BRWS
2; BYA 1; CA 13-16; CAAS 125; CANR
22; CAP 1; CN 1, 2, 3, 4; DA; DA3;
DAB; DAC; DAM MST, NOV; DLB 225;
DLBD 17; EWL 3; EXPN; LAIT 4;
MTCW 1, 2; MTFW 2005; NFS 3, 12;
RGEL 2; SATA 11; SATA-Obit 56; TWA;
WLIT 2; WWE 1

Paton Walsh, Gillian
See Paton Walsh, Jill
See also AAYA 47; BYA 1, 8

Paton Walsh, Jill 1937- .... **CLC 35**
See Paton Walsh, Gillian; Walsh, Jill Paton
See also AAYA 11; CANR 38, 83, 158; CLR
2, 65; DLB 161; JRDA; MAICYA 1, 2;
SAAS 3; SATA 4, 72, 109; YAW

Patsauq, Markoosie 1942- .... **NNAL**
See also CA 101; CLR 23; CWRI 5; DAM
MULT

Patterson, (Horace) Orlando (Lloyd)
1940- .... **BLCS**
See also BW 1; CA 65-68; CANR 27, 84;
CN 1, 2, 3, 4, 5, 6

Patton, George S(mith), Jr.
1885-1945 .... **TCLC 79**
See also CA 189

Paulding, James Kirke 1778-1860 ... **NCLC 2**
See also DLB 3, 59, 74, 250; RGAL 4

Paulin, Thomas Neilson
See Paulin, Tom

Paulin, Tom 1949- .... **CLC 37, 177**
See also CA 128; CAAE 123; CANR 98;
CP 3, 4, 5, 6, 7; DLB 40

Pausanias c. 1st cent. - .... **CMLC 36**

Paustovsky, Konstantin (Georgievich)
1892-1968 .... **CLC 40**
See also CA 93-96; CAAS 25-28R; DLB
272; EWL 3

Pavese, Cesare 1908-1950 .... **PC 13; SSC 19;
TCLC 3**
See also CA 169; CAAE 104; DLB 128,
177; EW 12; EWL 3; PFS 20; RGSF 2;
RGWL 2, 3; TWA; WLIT 7

Pavic, Milorad 1929- .... **CLC 60**
See also CA 136; CDWLB 4; CWW 2; DLB
181; EWL 3; RGWL 3

Pavlov, Ivan Petrovich 1849-1936 . **TCLC 91**
See also CA 180; CAAE 118

Pavlova, Karolina Karlovna
1807-1893 .... **NCLC 138**
See also DLB 205

Payne, Alan
See Jakes, John

Payne, Rachel Ann
See Jakes, John

Paz, Gil
See Lugones, Leopoldo

Paz, Octavio 1914-1998 . **CLC 3, 4, 6, 10, 19,
51, 65, 119; HLC 2; PC 1, 48; WLC 4**
See also AAYA 50; CA 73-76; CAAS 165;
CANR 32, 65, 104; CWW 2; DA; DA3;
DAB; DAC; DAM MST, MULT, POET;
DLB 290, 331; DLBY 1990, 1998; DNFS
1; EWL 3; HW 1, 2; LAW; LAWS 1;
MTCW 1, 2; MTFW 2005; PFS 18;
RGWL 2, 3; SSFS 13; TWA; WLIT 1

p'Bitek, Okot 1931-1982 .... **BLC 3; CLC 96;
TCLC 149**
See also AFW; BW 2, 3; CA 124; CAAS
107; CANR 82; CP 1, 2, 3; DAM MULT;
DLB 125; EWL 3; MTCW 1, 2; MTFW
2005; RGEL 2; WLIT 2

Peabody, Elizabeth Palmer
1804-1894 .... **NCLC 169**
See also DLB 1, 223

Peacham, Henry 1578-1644(?) .... **LC 119**
See also DLB 151

Peacock, Molly 1947- .... **CLC 60**
See also CA 103; 21; CANR 52, 84; CP 5,
6, 7; CWP; DLB 120, 282

Peacock, Thomas Love
1785-1866 .... **NCLC 22**
See also BRW 4; DLB 96, 116; RGEL 2;
RGSF 2

Peake, Mervyn 1911-1968 .... **CLC 7, 54**
See also CA 5-8R; CAAS 25-28R; CANR
3; DLB 15, 160, 255; FANT; MTCW 1;
RGEL 2; SATA 23; SFW 4

Pearce, Philippa 1920-2006
See Christie, Philippa
See also CA 5-8R; CAAS 255; CANR 4,
109; CWRI 5; FANT; MAICYA 2; SATA-
Obit 179

Pearl, Eric
See Elman, Richard (Martin)

Pearson, T. R. 1956- .... **CLC 39**
See also CA 130; CAAE 120; CANR 97,
147; CSW; INT CA-130

Pearson, Thomas Reid
See Pearson, T. R.

Peck, Dale 1967- .... **CLC 81**
See also CA 146; CANR 72, 127; GLL 2

Peck, John (Frederick) 1941- .... **CLC 3**
See also CA 49-52; CANR 3, 100; CP 4, 5,
6, 7

Peck, Richard 1934- .... **CLC 21**
See also AAYA 1, 24; BYA 1, 6, 8, 11; CA
85-88; CANR 19, 38, 129; CLR 15; INT
CANR-19; JRDA; MAICYA 1, 2; SAAS
2; SATA 18, 55, 97, 110, 158; SATA-
Essay 110; WYA; YAW

Peck, Richard Wayne
See Peck, Richard

Peck, Robert Newton 1928- .... **CLC 17**
See also AAYA 3, 43; BYA 1, 6; CA 182;
81-84, 182; CANR 31, 63, 127; CLR 45;
DA; DAC; DAM MST; JRDA; LAIT 3;
MAICYA 1, 2; SAAS 1; SATA 21, 62,
111, 156; SATA-Essay 108; WYA; YAW

Peckinpah, David Samuel
See Peckinpah, Sam

Peckinpah, Sam 1925-1984 .... **CLC 20**
See also CA 109; CAAS 114; CANR 82

Pedersen, Knut 1859-1952
See Hamsun, Knut
See also CA 119; CAAE 104; CANR 63;
MTCW 1, 2

Peele, George 1556-1596 .... **DC 27; LC 115**
See also BRW 1; DLB 62, 167; RGEL 2

Peeslake, Gaffer
See Durrell, Lawrence (George)

Peguy, Charles (Pierre)
1873-1914 .... **TCLC 10**
See also CA 193; CAAE 107; DLB 258;
EWL 3; GFL 1789 to the Present

Peirce, Charles Sanders
1839-1914 .... **TCLC 81**
See also CA 194; DLB 270

Pelecanos, George P. 1957- .... **CLC 236**
See also CA 138; CANR 122, 165; DLB
306

Pelevin, Victor 1962- .... **CLC 238**
See Pelevin, Viktor Olegovich
See also CA 154; CANR 88, 159

Pelevin, Viktor Olegovich
See Pelevin, Victor
See also DLB 285

Pellicer, Carlos 1897(?)-1977 .... **HLCS 2**
See also CA 153; CAAS 69-72; DLB 290;
EWL 3; HW 1

Pena, Ramon del Valle y
See Valle-Inclan, Ramon (Maria) del

Pendennis, Arthur Esquir
See Thackeray, William Makepeace

Penn, Arthur
See Matthews, (James) Brander

Penn, William 1644-1718 .... **LC 25**
See also DLB 24

PEPECE
See Prado (Calvo), Pedro

Pepys, Samuel 1633-1703 ... **LC 11, 58; WLC
4**
See also BRW 2; CDBLB 1660-1789; DA;
DA3; DAB; DAC; DAM MST; DLB 101,
213; NCFS 4; RGEL 2; TEA; WLIT 3

Percy, Thomas 1729-1811 .... **NCLC 95**
See also DLB 104

Percy, Walker 1916-1990 .... **CLC 2, 3, 6, 8,
14, 18, 47, 65**
See also AMWS 3; BPFB 3; CA 1-4R;
CAAS 131; CANR 1, 23, 64; CN 1, 2, 3,
4; CPW; CSW; DA3; DAM NOV, POP;
DLB 2; DLBY 1980, 1990; EWL 3; MAL
5; MTCW 1, 2; MTFW 2005; RGAL 4;
TUS

Percy, William Alexander
1885-1942 .... **TCLC 84**
See also CA 163; MTCW 2

Perec, Georges 1936-1982 .... **CLC 56, 116**
See also CA 141; DLB 83, 299; EWL 3;
GFL 1789 to the Present; RGHL; RGWL
3

Pereda (y Sanchez de Porrua), Jose Maria de 1833-1906 .... **TCLC 16**
See also CAAE 117

Pereda y Porrua, Jose Maria de
See Pereda (y Sanchez de Porrua), Jose
Maria de

Peregoy, George Weems
See Mencken, H(enry) L(ouis)

Perelman, S(idney) J(oseph)
1904-1979 .. **CLC 3, 5, 9, 15, 23, 44, 49;
SSC 32**
See also AITN 1, 2; BPFB 3; CA 73-76;
CAAS 89-92; CANR 18; DAM DRAM;
DLB 11, 44; MTCW 1, 2; MTFW 2005;
RGAL 4

Peret, Benjamin 1899-1959 .... **PC 33; TCLC
20**
See also CA 186; CAAE 117; GFL 1789 to
the Present

Peretz, Isaac Leib
See Peretz, Isaac Loeb
See also CA 201; DLB 333

Peretz, Isaac Loeb 1851(?)-1915 ...... **SSC 26;
TCLC 16**
See Peretz, Isaac Leib
See also CAAE 109

Peretz, Yitzkhok Leibush
See Peretz, Isaac Loeb

Perez Galdos, Benito 1843-1920 ..... **HLCS 2;
TCLC 27**
See Galdos, Benito Perez
See also CA 153; CAAE 125; EWL 3; HW
1; RGWL 2, 3

Peri Rossi, Cristina 1941- .. **CLC 156; HLCS
2**
See also CA 131; CANR 59, 81; CWW 2;
DLB 145, 290; EWL 3; HW 1, 2

Perlata
See Peret, Benjamin

Perloff, Marjorie G(abrielle)
1931- .... **CLC 137**
See also CA 57-60; CANR 7, 22, 49, 104

Perrault, Charles 1628-1703 .... **LC 2, 56**
See also BYA 4; CLR 79; DLB 268; GFL
Beginnings to 1789; MAICYA 1, 2;
RGWL 2, 3; SATA 25; WCH

Perry, Anne 1938- .... **CLC 126**
See also CA 101; CANR 22, 50, 84, 150;
CMW 4; CN 6, 7; CPW; DLB 276

Perry, Brighton
See Sherwood, Robert E(mmet)

Perse, St.-John
See Leger, (Marie-Rene Auguste) Alexis
Saint-Leger

Perse, Saint-John
See Leger, (Marie-Rene Auguste) Alexis
Saint-Leger
See also DLB 258, 331; RGWL 3

Persius 34-62 .... **CMLC 74**
See also AW 2; DLB 211; RGWL 2, 3

Perutz, Leo(pold) 1882-1957 .... **TCLC 60**
See also CA 147; DLB 81

Peseenz, Tulio F.
See Lopez y Fuentes, Gregorio

Pesetsky, Bette 1932- .... **CLC 28**
See also CA 133; DLB 130

Peshkov, Alexei Maximovich 1868-1936
See Gorky, Maxim
See also CA 141; CAAE 105; CANR 83;
DA; DAC; DAM DRAM, MST, NOV;
MTCW 2; MTFW 2005

Pessoa, Fernando (Antonio Nogueira)
1888-1935 ..... **HLC 2; PC 20; TCLC 27**
See also CA 183; CAAE 125; DAM MULT;
DLB 287; EW 10; EWL 3; RGWL 2, 3;
WP

Peterkin, Julia Mood 1880-1961 ...... **CLC 31**
See also CA 102; DLB 9

Peters, Joan K(aren) 1945- .... **CLC 39**
See also CA 158; CANR 109

Peters, Robert L(ouis) 1924- .... **CLC 7**
See also CA 13-16R; 8; CP 1, 5, 6, 7; DLB
105

Petofi, Sandor 1823-1849 .... **NCLC 21**
See also RGWL 2, 3

Petrakis, Harry Mark 1923- .... **CLC 3**
See also CA 9-12R; CANR 4, 30, 85, 155;
CN 1, 2, 3, 4, 5, 6, 7

Petrarch 1304-1374 .... **CMLC 20; PC 8**
See also DA3; DAM POET; EW 2; LMFS
1; RGWL 2, 3; WLIT 7

Petronius c. 20-66 .... **CMLC 34**
See also AW 2; CDWLB 1; DLB 211;
RGWL 2, 3; WLIT 8

Petrov, Evgeny .... **TCLC 21**
See Kataev, Evgeny Petrovich

Petry, Ann (Lane) 1908-1997 .. **CLC 1, 7, 18;
TCLC 112**
See also AFAW 1, 2; BPFB 3; BW 1, 3;
BYA 2; CA 5-8R; 6; CAAS 157; CANR
4, 46; CLR 12; CN 1, 2, 3, 4, 5, 6; DLB
76; EWL 3; JRDA; LAIT 1; MAICYA 1,
2; MAICYAS 1; MTCW 1; RGAL 4;
SATA 5; SATA-Obit 94; TUS

Petursson, Halligrimur 1614-1674 .... **LC 8**

Peychinovich
See Vazov, Ivan (Minchov)

Phaedrus c. 15B.C.-c. 50 .... **CMLC 25**
See also DLB 211

Phelps (Ward), Elizabeth Stuart
See Phelps, Elizabeth Stuart
See also FW

Phelps, Elizabeth Stuart
1844-1911 .... **TCLC 113**
See Phelps (Ward), Elizabeth Stuart
See also CA 242; DLB 74

Philips, Katherine 1632-1664 . **LC 30; PC 40**
See also DLB 131; RGEL 2

Philipson, Ilene J. 1950- .... **CLC 65**
See also CA 219

Philipson, Morris H. 1926- .... **CLC 53**
See also CA 1-4R; CANR 4

Phillips, Caryl 1958- ..... **BLCS; CLC 96, 224**
See also BRWS 5; BW 2; CA 141; CANR
63, 104, 140; CBD; CD 5; CN 5, 6, 7;
DA3; DAM MULT; DLB 157; EWL 3;
MTCW 2; MTFW 2005; WLIT 4; WWE
1

Phillips, David Graham
1867-1911 .... **TCLC 44**
See also CA 176; CAAE 108; DLB 9, 12,
303; RGAL 4

Phillips, Jack
See Sandburg, Carl (August)

Phillips, Jayne Anne 1952- .... **CLC 15, 33,
139; SSC 16**
See also AAYA 57; BPFB 3; CA 101;
CANR 24, 50, 96; CN 4, 5, 6, 7; CSW;
DLBY 1980; INT CANR-24; MTCW 1,
2; MTFW 2005; RGAL 4; RGSF 2; SSFS
4

Phillips, Richard
See Dick, Philip K.

Phillips, Robert (Schaeffer) 1938- .... **CLC 28**
See also CA 17-20R; 13; CANR 8; DLB
105

Phillips, Ward
See Lovecraft, H. P.

Philostratus, Flavius c. 179-c.
244 .... **CMLC 62**

Piccolo, Lucio 1901-1969 .... **CLC 13**
See also CA 97-100; DLB 114; EWL 3

Pickthall, Marjorie L(owry) C(hristie)
1883-1922 .... **TCLC 21**
See also CAAE 107; DLB 92

Pico della Mirandola, Giovanni
1463-1494 .... **LC 15**
See also LMFS 1

Piercy, Marge 1936- ... **CLC 3, 6, 14, 18, 27,
62, 128; PC 29**
See also BPFB 3; CA 187; 21-24R, 187; 1;
CANR 13, 43, 66, 111; CN 3, 4, 5, 6, 7;
CP 1, 2, 3, 4, 5, 6, 7; CWP; DLB 120,
227; EXPP; FW; MAL 5; MTCW 1, 2;
MTFW 2005; PFS 9, 22; SFW 4

Piers, Robert
See Anthony, Piers

Pieyre de Mandiargues, Andre 1909-1991
See Mandiargues, Andre Pieyre de
See also CA 103; CAAS 136; CANR 22,
82; EWL 3; GFL 1789 to the Present

Pilnyak, Boris 1894-1938 . **SSC 48; TCLC 23**
See Vogau, Boris Andreyevich
See also EWL 3

Pinchback, Eugene
See Toomer, Jean

Pincherle, Alberto 1907-1990 ...... **CLC 11, 18**
See Moravia, Alberto
See also CA 25-28R; CAAS 132; CANR
33, 63, 142; DAM NOV; MTCW 1;
MTFW 2005

Pinckney, Darryl 1953- .... **CLC 76**
See also BW 2, 3; CA 143; CANR 79

Pindar 518(?)B.C.-438(?)B.C. .... **CMLC 12;
PC 19**
See also AW 1; CDWLB 1; DLB 176;
RGWL 2

Pineda, Cecile 1942- .... **CLC 39**
See also CA 118; DLB 209

Pinero, Arthur Wing 1855-1934 .... **TCLC 32**
See also CA 153; CAAE 110; DAM DRAM;
DLB 10; RGEL 2

Pinero, Miguel (Antonio Gomez)
1946-1988 .... **CLC 4, 55**
See also CA 61-64; CAAS 125; CAD;
CANR 29, 90; DLB 266; HW 1; LLW

Pinget, Robert 1919-1997 .... **CLC 7, 13, 37**
See also CA 85-88; CAAS 160; CWW 2;
DLB 83; EWL 3; GFL 1789 to the Present

Pink Floyd
See Barrett, (Roger) Syd; Gilmour, David;
Mason, Nick; Waters, Roger; Wright, Rick

Pinkney, Edward 1802-1828 .... **NCLC 31**
See also DLB 248

Pinkwater, D. Manus
See Pinkwater, Daniel Manus

Pinkwater, Daniel
See Pinkwater, Daniel Manus

Pinkwater, Daniel M.
See Pinkwater, Daniel Manus

Pinkwater, Daniel Manus 1941- .... **CLC 35**
See also AAYA 1, 46; BYA 9; CA 29-32R;
CANR 12, 38, 89, 143; CLR 4; CSW;
FANT; JRDA; MAICYA 1, 2; SAAS 3;
SATA 8, 46, 76, 114, 158; SFW 4; YAW

Pinkwater, Manus
See Pinkwater, Daniel Manus

Pinsky, Robert 1940- .... **CLC 9, 19, 38, 94,
121, 216; PC 27**
See also AMWS 6; CA 29-32R; 4; CANR
58, 97, 138; CP 3, 4, 5, 6, 7; DA3; DAM
POET; DLBY 1982, 1998; MAL 5;
MTCW 2; MTFW 2005; PFS 18; RGAL
4; TCLE 1:2

Pinta, Harold
See Pinter, Harold

Rae, Ben
See Griffiths, Trevor
Raeburn, John (Hay) 1941- .... **CLC 34**
See also CA 57-60
Ragni, Gerome 1942-1991 .... **CLC 17**
See also CA 105; CAAS 134
Rahv, Philip .... **CLC 24**
See Greenberg, Ivan
See also DLB 137; MAL 5
Raimund, Ferdinand Jakob
1790-1836 .... **NCLC 69**
See also DLB 90
Raine, Craig (Anthony) 1944- .. **CLC 32, 103**
See also BRWS 13; CA 108; CANR 29, 51,
103; CP 3, 4, 5, 6, 7; DLB 40; PFS 7
Raine, Kathleen (Jessie) 1908-2003 .. **CLC 7,
45**
See also CA 85-88; CAAS 218; CANR 46,
109; CP 1, 2, 3, 4, 5, 6, 7; DLB 20; EWL
3; MTCW 1; RGEL 2
Rainis, Janis 1865-1929 .... **TCLC 29**
See also CA 170; CDWLB 4; DLB 220;
EWL 3
Rakosi, Carl .... **CLC 47**
See Rawley, Callman
See also CA 5; CAAS 228; CP 1, 2, 3, 4, 5,
6, 7; DLB 193
Ralegh, Sir Walter
See Raleigh, Sir Walter
See also BRW 1; RGEL 2; WP
Raleigh, Richard
See Lovecraft, H. P.
Raleigh, Sir Walter 1554(?)-1618 .... **LC 31,
39; PC 31**
See Ralegh, Sir Walter
See also CDBLB Before 1660; DLB 172;
EXPP; PFS 14; TEA
Rallentando, H. P.
See Sayers, Dorothy L(eigh)
Ramal, Walter
See de la Mare, Walter (John)
Ramana Maharshi 1879-1950 .... **TCLC 84**
Ramoacn y Cajal, Santiago
1852-1934 .... **TCLC 93**
Ramon, Juan
See Jimenez (Mantecon), Juan Ramon
Ramos, Graciliano 1892-1953 .... **TCLC 32**
See also CA 167; DLB 307; EWL 3; HW 2;
LAW; WLIT 1
Rampersad, Arnold 1941- .... **CLC 44**
See also BW 2, 3; CA 133; CAAE 127;
CANR 81; DLB 111; INT CA-133
Rampling, Anne
See Rice, Anne
See also GLL 2
Ramsay, Allan 1686(?)-1758 .... **LC 29**
See also DLB 95; RGEL 2
Ramsay, Jay
See Campbell, (John) Ramsey
Ramuz, Charles-Ferdinand
1878-1947 .... **TCLC 33**
See also CA 165; EWL 3
Rand, Ayn 1905-1982 ...... **CLC 3, 30, 44, 79;
WLC 5**
See also AAYA 10; AMWS 4; BPFB 3;
BYA 12; CA 13-16R; CAAS 105; CANR
27, 73; CDALBS; CN 1, 2, 3; CPW; DA;
DA3; DAC; DAM MST, NOV, POP; DLB
227, 279; MTCW 1, 2; MTFW 2005; NFS
10, 16; RGAL 4; SFW 4; TUS; YAW
Randall, Dudley (Felker) 1914-2000 . **BLC 3;
CLC 1, 135**
See also BW 1, 3; CA 25-28R; CAAS 189;
CANR 23, 82; CP 1, 2, 3, 4, 5; DAM
MULT; DLB 41; PFS 5
Randall, Robert
See Silverberg, Robert
Ranger, Ken
See Creasey, John

Rank, Otto 1884-1939 .... **TCLC 115**
Ransom, John Crowe 1888-1974 .. **CLC 2, 4,
5, 11, 24; PC 61**
See also AMW; CA 5-8R; CAAS 49-52;
CANR 6, 34; CDALBS; CP 1, 2; DA3;
DAM POET; DLB 45, 63; EWL 3; EXPP;
MAL 5; MTCW 1, 2; MTFW 2005;
RGAL 4; TUS
Rao, Raja 1908-2006 .... **CLC 25, 56; SSC 99**
See also CA 73-76; CAAS 252; CANR 51;
CN 1, 2, 3, 4, 5, 6; DAM NOV; DLB 323;
EWL 3; MTCW 1, 2; MTFW 2005; RGEL
2; RGSF 2
Raphael, Frederic (Michael) 1931- ... **CLC 2,
14**
See also CA 1-4R; CANR 1, 86; CN 1, 2,
3, 4, 5, 6, 7; DLB 14, 319; TCLE 1:2
Raphael, Lev 1954- .... **CLC 232**
See also CA 134; CANR 72, 145; GLL 1
Ratcliffe, James P.
See Mencken, H(enry) L(ouis)
Rathbone, Julian 1935- .... **CLC 41**
See also CA 101; CANR 34, 73, 152
Rattigan, Terence (Mervyn)
1911-1977 .... **CLC 7; DC 18**
See also BRWS 7; CA 85-88; CAAS 73-76;
CBD; CDBLB 1945-1960; DAM DRAM;
DFS 8; DLB 13; IDFW 3, 4; MTCW 1,
2; MTFW 2005; RGEL 2
Ratushinskaya, Irina 1954- .... **CLC 54**
See also CA 129; CANR 68; CWW 2
Raven, Simon (Arthur Noel)
1927-2001 .... **CLC 14**
See also CA 81-84; CAAS 197; CANR 86;
CN 1, 2, 3, 4, 5, 6; DLB 271
Ravenna, Michael
See Welty, Eudora
Rawley, Callman 1903-2004
See Rakosi, Carl
See also CA 21-24R; CAAS 228; CANR
12, 32, 91
Rawlings, Marjorie Kinnan
1896-1953 .... **TCLC 4**
See also AAYA 20; AMWS 10; ANW;
BPFB 3; BYA 3; CA 137; CAAE 104;
CANR 74; CLR 63; DLB 9, 22, 102;
DLBD 17; JRDA; MAICYA 1, 2; MAL 5;
MTCW 2; MTFW 2005; RGAL 4; SATA
100; WCH; YABC 1; YAW
Ray, Satyajit 1921-1992 .... **CLC 16, 76**
See also CA 114; CAAS 137; DAM MULT
Read, Herbert Edward 1893-1968 ..... **CLC 4**
See also BRW 6; CA 85-88; CAAS 25-28R;
DLB 20, 149; EWL 3; PAB; RGEL 2
Read, Piers Paul 1941- .... **CLC 4, 10, 25**
See also CA 21-24R; CANR 38, 86, 150;
CN 2, 3, 4, 5, 6, 7; DLB 14; SATA 21
Reade, Charles 1814-1884 .... **NCLC 2, 74**
See also DLB 21; RGEL 2
Reade, Hamish
See Gray, Simon (James Holliday)
Reading, Peter 1946- .... **CLC 47**
See also BRWS 8; CA 103; CANR 46, 96;
CP 5, 6, 7; DLB 40
Reaney, James 1926- .... **CLC 13**
See also CA 41-44R; 15; CANR 42; CD 5,
6; CP 1, 2, 3, 4, 5, 6, 7; DAC; DAM MST;
DLB 68; RGEL 2; SATA 43
Rebreanu, Liviu 1885-1944 .... **TCLC 28**
See also CA 165; DLB 220; EWL 3
Rechy, John 1934- ..... **CLC 1, 7, 14, 18, 107;
HLC 2**
See also CA 195; 5-8R, 195; 4; CANR 6,
32, 64, 152; CN 1, 2, 3, 4, 5, 6, 7; DAM
MULT; DLB 122, 278; DLBY 1982; HW
1, 2; INT CANR-6; LLW; MAL 5; RGAL
4
Rechy, John Francisco
See Rechy, John

Redcam, Tom 1870-1933 .... **TCLC 25**
Reddin, Keith 1956- .... **CLC 67**
See also CAD; CD 6
Redgrove, Peter (William)
1932-2003 .... **CLC 6, 41**
See also BRWS 6; CA 1-4R; CAAS 217;
CANR 3, 39, 77; CP 1, 2, 3, 4, 5, 6, 7;
DLB 40; TCLE 1:2
Redmon, Anne .... **CLC 22**
See Nightingale, Anne Redmon
See also DLBY 1986
Reed, Eliot
See Ambler, Eric
Reed, Ishmael 1938- ..... **BLC 3; CLC 2, 3, 5,
6, 13, 32, 60, 174; PC 68**
See also AFAW 1, 2; AMWS 10; BPFB 3;
BW 2, 3; CA 21-24R; CANR 25, 48, 74,
128; CN 1, 2, 3, 4, 5, 6, 7; CP 1, 2, 3, 4,
5, 6, 7; CSW; DA3; DAM MULT; DLB
2, 5, 33, 169, 227; DLBD 8; EWL 3;
LMFS 2; MAL 5; MSW; MTCW 1, 2;
MTFW 2005; PFS 6; RGAL 4; TCWW 2
Reed, John (Silas) 1887-1920 .... **TCLC 9**
See also CA 195; CAAE 106; MAL 5; TUS
Reed, Lou .... **CLC 21**
See Firbank, Louis
Reese, Lizette Woodworth
1856-1935 .... **PC 29; TCLC 181**
See also CA 180; DLB 54
Reeve, Clara 1729-1807 .... **NCLC 19**
See also DLB 39; RGEL 2
Reich, Wilhelm 1897-1957 .... **TCLC 57**
See also CA 199
Reid, Christopher (John) 1949- .... **CLC 33**
See also CA 140; CANR 89; CP 4, 5, 6, 7;
DLB 40; EWL 3
Reid, Desmond
See Moorcock, Michael
Reid Banks, Lynne 1929-
See Banks, Lynne Reid
See also AAYA 49; CA 1-4R; CANR 6, 22,
38, 87; CLR 24; CN 1, 2, 3, 7; JRDA;
MAICYA 1, 2; SATA 22, 75, 111, 165;
YAW
Reilly, William K.
See Creasey, John
Reiner, Max
See Caldwell, (Janet Miriam) Taylor
(Holland)
Reis, Ricardo
See Pessoa, Fernando (Antonio Nogueira)
Reizenstein, Elmer Leopold
See Rice, Elmer (Leopold)
See also EWL 3
Remarque, Erich Maria 1898-1970 . **CLC 21**
See also AAYA 27; BPFB 3; CA 77-80;
CAAS 29-32R; CDWLB 2; DA; DA3;
DAB; DAC; DAM MST, NOV; DLB 56;
EWL 3; EXPN; LAIT 3; MTCW 1, 2;
MTFW 2005; NFS 4; RGHL; RGWL 2, 3
Remington, Frederic S(ackrider)
1861-1909 .... **TCLC 89**
See also CA 169; CAAE 108; DLB 12, 186,
188; SATA 41; TCWW 2
Remizov, A.
See Remizov, Aleksei (Mikhailovich)
Remizov, A. M.
See Remizov, Aleksei (Mikhailovich)
Remizov, Aleksei (Mikhailovich)
1877-1957 .... **TCLC 27**
See Remizov, Alexey Mikhaylovich
See also CA 133; CAAE 125; DLB 295
Remizov, Alexey Mikhaylovich
See Remizov, Aleksei (Mikhailovich)
See also EWL 3
Renan, Joseph Ernest 1823-1892 . **NCLC 26,
145**
See also GFL 1789 to the Present

Renard, Jules(-Pierre) 1864-1910 .. **TCLC 17**
See also CA 202; CAAE 117; GFL 1789 to the Present

Renart, Jean fl. 13th cent. - .... **CMLC 83**

Renault, Mary .... **CLC 3, 11, 17**
See Challans, Mary
See also BPFB 3; BYA 2; CN 1, 2, 3; DLBY 1983; EWL 3; GLL 1; LAIT 1; RGEL 2; RHW

Rendell, Ruth 1930- .... **CLC 28, 48**
See Vine, Barbara
See also BPFB 3; BRWS 9; CA 109; CANR 32, 52, 74, 127, 162; CN 5, 6, 7; CPW; DAM POP; DLB 87, 276; INT CANR-32; MSW; MTCW 1, 2; MTFW 2005

Rendell, Ruth Barbara
See Rendell, Ruth

Renoir, Jean 1894-1979 .... **CLC 20**
See also CA 129; CAAS 85-88

Rensie, Willis
See Eisner, Will

Resnais, Alain 1922- .... **CLC 16**

Revard, Carter 1931- .... **NNAL**
See also CA 144; CANR 81, 153; PFS 5

Reverdy, Pierre 1889-1960 .... **CLC 53**
See also CA 97-100; CAAS 89-92; DLB 258; EWL 3; GFL 1789 to the Present

Rexroth, Kenneth 1905-1982 .... **CLC 1, 2, 6, 11, 22, 49, 112; PC 20**
See also BG 1:3; CA 5-8R; CAAS 107; CANR 14, 34, 63; CDALB 1941-1968; CP 1, 2, 3; DAM POET; DLB 16, 48, 165, 212; DLBY 1982; EWL 3; INT CANR-14; MAL 5; MTCW 1, 2; MTFW 2005; RGAL 4

Reyes, Alfonso 1889-1959 .... **HLCS 2; TCLC 33**
See also CA 131; EWL 3; HW 1; LAW

Reyes y Basoalto, Ricardo Eliecer Neftali
See Neruda, Pablo

Reymont, Wladyslaw (Stanislaw) 1868(?)-1925 .... **TCLC 5**
See also CAAE 104; DLB 332; EWL 3

Reynolds, John Hamilton 1794-1852 .... **NCLC 146**
See also DLB 96

Reynolds, Jonathan 1942- .... **CLC 6, 38**
See also CA 65-68; CANR 28

Reynolds, Joshua 1723-1792 .... **LC 15**
See also DLB 104

Reynolds, Michael S(hane) 1937-2000 .... **CLC 44**
See also CA 65-68; CAAS 189; CANR 9, 89, 97

Reznikoff, Charles 1894-1976 .... **CLC 9**
See also AMWS 14; CA 33-36; CAAS 61-64; CAP 2; CP 1, 2; DLB 28, 45; RGHL; WP

Rezzori, Gregor von
See Rezzori d'Arezzo, Gregor von

Rezzori d'Arezzo, Gregor von 1914-1998 .... **CLC 25**
See also CA 136; CAAE 122; CAAS 167

Rhine, Richard
See Silverstein, Alvin; Silverstein, Virginia B(arbara Opshelor)

Rhodes, Eugene Manlove 1869-1934 .... **TCLC 53**
See also CA 198; DLB 256; TCWW 1, 2

R'hoone, Lord
See Balzac, Honore de

Rhys, Jean 1890-1979 .... **CLC 2, 4, 6, 14, 19, 51, 124; SSC 21, 76**
See also BRWS 2; CA 25-28R; CAAS 85-88; CANR 35, 62; CDBLB 1945-1960; CDWLB 3; CN 1, 2; DA3; DAM NOV;

DLB 36, 117, 162; DNFS 2; EWL 3; LATS 1:1; MTCW 1, 2; MTFW 2005; NFS 19; RGEL 2; RGSF 2; RHW; TEA; WWE 1

Ribeiro, Darcy 1922-1997 .... **CLC 34**
See also CA 33-36R; CAAS 156; EWL 3

Ribeiro, Joao Ubaldo (Osorio Pimentel) 1941- .... **CLC 10, 67**
See also CA 81-84; CWW 2; EWL 3

Ribman, Ronald (Burt) 1932- .... **CLC 7**
See also CA 21-24R; CAD; CANR 46, 80; CD 5, 6

Ricci, Nino (Pio) 1959- .... **CLC 70**
See also CA 137; CANR 130; CCA 1

Rice, Anne 1941- .... **CLC 41, 128**
See Rampling, Anne
See also AAYA 9, 53; AMWS 7; BEST 89:2; BPFB 3; CA 65-68; CANR 12, 36, 53, 74, 100, 133; CN 6, 7; CPW; CSW; DA3; DAM POP; DLB 292; GL 3; GLL 2; HGG; MTCW 2; MTFW 2005; SUFW 2; YAW

Rice, Elmer (Leopold) 1892-1967 ...... **CLC 7, 49**
See Reizenstein, Elmer Leopold
See also CA 21-22; CAAS 25-28R; CAP 2; DAM DRAM; DFS 12; DLB 4, 7; IDTP; MAL 5; MTCW 1, 2; RGAL 4

Rice, Tim(othy Miles Bindon) 1944- .... **CLC 21**
See also CA 103; CANR 46; DFS 7

Rich, Adrienne 1929- ..... **CLC 3, 6, 7, 11, 18, 36, 73, 76, 125; PC 5**
See also AAYA 69; AMWR 2; AMWS 1; CA 9-12R; CANR 20, 53, 74, 128; CDALBS; CP 1, 2, 3, 4, 5, 6, 7; CSW; CWP; DA3; DAM POET; DLB 5, 67; EWL 3; EXPP; FL 1:6; FW; MAL 5; MBL; MTCW 1, 2; MTFW 2005; PAB; PFS 15; RGAL 4; RGHL; WP

Rich, Barbara
See Graves, Robert

Rich, Robert
See Trumbo, Dalton

Richard, Keith .... **CLC 17**
See Richards, Keith

Richards, David Adams 1950- .... **CLC 59**
See also CA 93-96; CANR 60, 110, 156; CN 7; DAC; DLB 53; TCLE 1:2

Richards, I(vor) A(rmstrong) 1893-1979 .... **CLC 14, 24**
See also BRWS 2; CA 41-44R; CAAS 89-92; CANR 34, 74; CP 1, 2; DLB 27; EWL 3; MTCW 2; RGEL 2

Richards, Keith 1943-
See Richard, Keith
See also CA 107; CANR 77

Richardson, Anne
See Roiphe, Anne

Richardson, Dorothy Miller 1873-1957 .... **TCLC 3**
See also BRWS 13; CA 192; CAAE 104; DLB 36; EWL 3; FW; RGEL 2

Richardson (Robertson), Ethel Florence Lindesay 1870-1946
See Richardson, Henry Handel
See also CA 190; CAAE 105; DLB 230; RHW

Richardson, Henry Handel .... **TCLC 4**
See Richardson (Robertson), Ethel Florence Lindesay
See also DLB 197; EWL 3; RGEL 2; RGSF 2

Richardson, John 1796-1852 .... **NCLC 55**
See also CCA 1; DAC; DLB 99

Richardson, Samuel 1689-1761 ...... **LC 1, 44, 138; WLC 5**
See also BRW 3; CDBLB 1660-1789; DA; DAB; DAC; DAM MST, NOV; DLB 39; RGEL 2; TEA; WLIT 3

Richardson, Willis 1889-1977 .... **HR 1:3**
See also BW 1; CA 124; DLB 51; SATA 60

Richler, Mordecai 1931-2001 .... **CLC 3, 5, 9, 13, 18, 46, 70, 185**
See also AITN 1; CA 65-68; CAAS 201; CANR 31, 62, 111; CCA 1; CLR 17; CN 1, 2, 3, 4, 5, 7; CWRI 5; DAC; DAM MST, NOV; DLB 53; EWL 3; MAICYA 1, 2; MTCW 1, 2; MTFW 2005; RGEL 2; RGHL; SATA 44, 98; SATA-Brief 27; TWA

Richter, Conrad (Michael) 1890-1968 .... **CLC 30**
See also AAYA 21; BYA 2; CA 5-8R; CAAS 25-28R; CANR 23; DLB 9, 212; LAIT 1; MAL 5; MTCW 1, 2; MTFW 2005; RGAL 4; SATA 3; TCWW 1, 2; TUS; YAW

Ricostranza, Tom
See Ellis, Trey

Riddell, Charlotte 1832-1906 .... **TCLC 40**
See Riddell, Mrs. J. H.
See also CA 165; DLB 156

Riddell, Mrs. J. H.
See Riddell, Charlotte
See also HGG; SUFW

Ridge, John Rollin 1827-1867 ...... **NCLC 82; NNAL**
See also CA 144; DAM MULT; DLB 175

Ridgeway, Jason
See Marlowe, Stephen

Ridgway, Keith 1965- .... **CLC 119**
See also CA 172; CANR 144

Riding, Laura .... **CLC 3, 7**
See Jackson, Laura (Riding)
See also CP 1, 2, 3, 4, 5; RGAL 4

Riefenstahl, Berta Helene Amalia 1902-2003
See Riefenstahl, Leni
See also CA 108; CAAS 220

Riefenstahl, Leni .... **CLC 16, 190**
See Riefenstahl, Berta Helene Amalia

Riffe, Ernest
See Bergman, Ingmar

Riffe, Ernest Ingmar
See Bergman, Ingmar

Riggs, (Rolla) Lynn 1899-1954 .... **NNAL; TCLC 56**
See also CA 144; DAM MULT; DLB 175

Riis, Jacob A(ugust) 1849-1914 ..... **TCLC 80**
See also CA 168; CAAE 113; DLB 23

Riley, James Whitcomb 1849-1916 .... **PC 48; TCLC 51**
See also CA 137; CAAE 118; DAM POET; MAICYA 1, 2; RGAL 4; SATA 17

Riley, Tex
See Creasey, John

Rilke, Rainer Maria 1875-1926 .... **PC 2; TCLC 1, 6, 19**
See also CA 132; CAAE 104; CANR 62, 99; CDWLB 2; DA3; DAM POET; DLB 81; EW 9; EWL 3; MTCW 1, 2; MTFW 2005; PFS 19; RGWL 2, 3; TWA; WP

Rimbaud, (Jean Nicolas) Arthur 1854-1891 ... **NCLC 4, 35, 82; PC 3, 57; WLC 5**
See also DA; DA3; DAB; DAC; DAM MST, POET; DLB 217; EW 7; GFL 1789 to the Present; LMFS 2; RGWL 2, 3; TWA; WP

Rinehart, Mary Roberts 1876-1958 .... **TCLC 52**
See also BPFB 3; CA 166; CAAE 108; RGAL 4; RHW

Ringmaster, The
See Mencken, H(enry) L(ouis)

Ringwood, Gwen(dolyn Margaret) Pharis 1910-1984 .... **CLC 48**
See also CA 148; CAAS 112; DLB 88

Rio, Michel 1945(?)- .... **CLC 43**
See also CA 201
Rios, Alberto 1952- .... **PC 57**
See also AAYA 66; AMWS 4; CA 113;
CANR 34, 79, 137; CP 6, 7; DLB 122;
HW 2; MTFW 2005; PFS 11
Ritsos, Giannes
See Ritsos, Yannis
Ritsos, Yannis 1909-1990 .... **CLC 6, 13, 31**
See also CA 77-80; CAAS 133; CANR 39,
61; EW 12; EWL 3; MTCW 1; RGWL 2,
3
Ritter, Erika 1948(?)- .... **CLC 52**
See also CD 5, 6; CWD
Rivera, Jose Eustasio 1889-1928 ... **TCLC 35**
See also CA 162; EWL 3; HW 1, 2; LAW
Rivera, Tomas 1935-1984 .... **HLCS 2**
See also CA 49-52; CANR 32; DLB 82;
HW 1; LLW; RGAL 4; SSFS 15; TCWW
2; WLIT 1
Rivers, Conrad Kent 1933-1968 .... **CLC 1**
See also BW 1; CA 85-88; DLB 41
Rivers, Elfrida
See Bradley, Marion Zimmer
See also GLL 1
Riverside, John
See Heinlein, Robert A.
Rizal, Jose 1861-1896 .... **NCLC 27**
Roa Bastos, Augusto 1917-2005 ...... **CLC 45;**
HLC 2
See also CA 131; CAAS 238; CWW 2;
DAM MULT; DLB 113; EWL 3; HW 1;
LAW; RGSF 2; WLIT 1
Roa Bastos, Augusto Jose Antonio
See Roa Bastos, Augusto
Robbe-Grillet, Alain 1922- .... **CLC 1, 2, 4, 6,**
8, 10, 14, 43, 128
See also BPFB 3; CA 9-12R; CANR 33,
65, 115; CWW 2; DLB 83; EW 13; EWL
3; GFL 1789 to the Present; IDFW 3, 4;
MTCW 1, 2; MTFW 2005; RGWL 2, 3;
SSFS 15
Robbins, Harold 1916-1997 .... **CLC 5**
See also BPFB 3; CA 73-76; CAAS 162;
CANR 26, 54, 112, 156; DA3; DAM
NOV; MTCW 1, 2
Robbins, Thomas Eugene 1936-
See Robbins, Tom
See also CA 81-84; CANR 29, 59, 95, 139;
CN 7; CPW; CSW; DA3; DAM NOV;
POP; MTCW 1, 2; MTFW 2005
Robbins, Tom .... **CLC 9, 32, 64**
See Robbins, Thomas Eugene
See also AAYA 32; AMWS 10; BEST 90:3;
BPFB 3; CN 3, 4, 5, 6, 7; DLBY 1980
Robbins, Trina 1938- .... **CLC 21**
See also AAYA 61; CA 128; CANR 152
Robert de Boron fl. 12th cent. - .... **CMLC 94**
Roberts, Charles G(eorge) D(ouglas)
1860-1943 .... **SSC 91; TCLC 8**
See also CA 188; CAAE 105; CLR 33;
CWRI 5; DLB 92; RGEL 2; RGSF 2;
SATA 88; SATA-Brief 29
Roberts, Elizabeth Madox
1886-1941 .... **TCLC 68**
See also CA 166; CAAE 111; CLR 100;
CWRI 5; DLB 9, 54, 102; RGAL 4;
RHW; SATA 33; SATA-Brief 27; TCWW
2; WCH
Roberts, Kate 1891-1985 .... **CLC 15**
See also CA 107; CAAS 116; DLB 319
Roberts, Keith (John Kingston)
1935-2000 .... **CLC 14**
See also BRWS 10; CA 25-28R; CANR 46;
DLB 261; SFW 4
Roberts, Kenneth (Lewis)
1885-1957 .... **TCLC 23**
See also CA 199; CAAE 109; DLB 9; MAL
5; RGAL 4; RHW

Roberts, Michele 1949- .... **CLC 48, 178**
See also CA 115; CANR 58, 120, 164; CN
6, 7; DLB 231; FW
Roberts, Michele Brigitte
See Roberts, Michele
Robertson, Ellis
See Ellison, Harlan; Silverberg, Robert
Robertson, Thomas William
1829-1871 .... **NCLC 35**
See Robertson, Tom
See also DAM DRAM
Robertson, Tom
See Robertson, Thomas William
See also RGEL 2
Robeson, Kenneth
See Dent, Lester
Robinson, Edwin Arlington
1869-1935 .... **PC 1, 35; TCLC 5, 101**
See also AAYA 72; AMW; CA 133; CAAE
104; CDALB 1865-1917; DA; DAC;
DAM MST, POET; DLB 54; EWL 3;
EXPP; MAL 5; MTCW 1, 2; MTFW
2005; PAB; PFS 4; RGAL 4; WP
Robinson, Henry Crabb
1775-1867 .... **NCLC 15**
See also DLB 107
Robinson, Jill 1936- .... **CLC 10**
See also CA 102; CANR 120; INT CA-102
Robinson, Kim Stanley 1952- .... **CLC 34**
See also AAYA 26; CA 126; CANR 113,
139; CN 6, 7; MTFW 2005; SATA 109;
SCFW 4; SFW 4
Robinson, Lloyd
See Silverberg, Robert
Robinson, Marilynne 1944- ...... **CLC 25, 180**
See also AAYA 69; CA 116; CANR 80, 140;
CN 4, 5, 6, 7; DLB 206; MTFW 2005;
NFS 24
Robinson, Mary 1758-1800 .... **NCLC 142**
See also BRWS 13; DLB 158; FW
Robinson, Smokey .... **CLC 21**
See Robinson, William, Jr.
Robinson, William, Jr. 1940-
See Robinson, Smokey
See also CAAE 116
Robison, Mary 1949- .... **CLC 42, 98**
See also CA 116; CAAE 113; CANR 87;
CN 4, 5, 6, 7; DLB 130; INT CA-116;
RGSF 2
Roches, Catherine des 1542-1587 ...... **LC 117**
See also DLB 327
Rochester
See Wilmot, John
See also RGEL 2
Rod, Edouard 1857-1910 .... **TCLC 52**
Roddenberry, Eugene Wesley 1921-1991
See Roddenberry, Gene
See also CA 110; CAAS 135; CANR 37;
SATA 45; SATA-Obit 69
Roddenberry, Gene .... **CLC 17**
See Roddenberry, Eugene Wesley
See also AAYA 5; SATA-Obit 69
Rodgers, Mary 1931- .... **CLC 12**
See also BYA 5; CA 49-52; CANR 8, 55,
90; CLR 20; CWRI 5; INT CANR-8;
JRDA; MAICYA 1, 2; SATA 8, 130
Rodgers, W(illiam) R(obert)
1909-1969 .... **CLC 7**
See also CA 85-88; DLB 20; RGEL 2
Rodman, Eric
See Silverberg, Robert
Rodman, Howard 1920(?)-1985 .... **CLC 65**
See also CAAS 118
Rodman, Maia
See Wojciechowska, Maia (Teresa)
Rodo, Jose Enrique 1871(?)-1917 .... **HLCS 2**
See also CA 178; EWL 3; HW 2; LAW
Rodolph, Utto
See Ouologuem, Yambo

Rodriguez, Claudio 1934-1999 .... **CLC 10**
See also CA 188; DLB 134
Rodriguez, Richard 1944- .... **CLC 155; HLC**
2
See also AMWS 14; CA 110; CANR 66,
116; DAM MULT; DLB 82, 256; HW 1,
2; LAIT 5; LLW; MTFW 2005; NCFS 3;
WLIT 1
Roelvaag, O(le) E(dvart) 1876-1931
See Rolvaag, O(le) E(dvart)
See also AAYA 75; CA 171; CAAE 117
Roethke, Theodore (Huebner)
1908-1963 .... **CLC 1, 3, 8, 11, 19, 46,**
101; PC 15
See also AMW; CA 81-84; CABS 2;
CDALB 1941-1968; DA3; DAM POET;
DLB 5, 206; EWL 3; EXPP; MAL 5;
MTCW 1, 2; PAB; PFS 3; RGAL 4; WP
Rogers, Carl R(ansom)
1902-1987 .... **TCLC 125**
See also CA 1-4R; CAAS 121; CANR 1,
18; MTCW 1
Rogers, Samuel 1763-1855 .... **NCLC 69**
See also DLB 93; RGEL 2
Rogers, Thomas 1927-2007 .... **CLC 57**
See also CA 89-92; CAAS 259; CANR 163;
INT CA-89-92
Rogers, Thomas Hunton
See Rogers, Thomas
Rogers, Will(iam Penn Adair)
1879-1935 .... **NNAL; TCLC 8, 71**
See also CA 144; CAAE 105; DA3; DAM
MULT; DLB 11; MTCW 2
Rogin, Gilbert 1929- .... **CLC 18**
See also CA 65-68; CANR 15
Rohan, Koda
See Koda Shigeyuki
Rohlfs, Anna Katharine Green
See Green, Anna Katharine
Rohmer, Eric .... **CLC 16**
See Scherer, Jean-Marie Maurice
Rohmer, Sax .... **TCLC 28**
See Ward, Arthur Henry Sarsfield
See also DLB 70; MSW; SUFW
Roiphe, Anne 1935- .... **CLC 3, 9**
See also CA 89-92; CANR 45, 73, 138;
DLBY 1980; INT CA-89-92
Roiphe, Anne Richardson
See Roiphe, Anne
Rojas, Fernando de 1475-1541 ... **HLCS 1, 2;**
LC 23
See also DLB 286; RGWL 2, 3
Rojas, Gonzalo 1917- .... **HLCS 2**
See also CA 178; HW 2; LAWS 1
Roland (de la Platiere), Marie-Jeanne
1754-1793 .... **LC 98**
See also DLB 314
Rolfe, Frederick (William Serafino Austin
Lewis Mary) 1860-1913 .... **TCLC 12**
See Al Siddik
See also CA 210; CAAE 107; DLB 34, 156;
RGEL 2
Rolland, Romain 1866-1944 .... **TCLC 23**
See also CA 197; CAAE 118; DLB 65, 284,
332; EWL 3; GFL 1789 to the Present;
RGWL 2, 3
Rolle, Richard c. 1300-c. 1349 ...... **CMLC 21**
See also DLB 146; LMFS 1; RGEL 2
Rolvaag, O(le) E(dvart) .... **TCLC 17**
See Roelvaag, O(le) E(dvart)
See also DLB 9, 212; MAL 5; NFS 5;
RGAL 4
Romain Arnaud, Saint
See Aragon, Louis
Romains, Jules 1885-1972 .... **CLC 7**
See also CA 85-88; CANR 34; DLB 65,
321; EWL 3; GFL 1789 to the Present;
MTCW 1

Runeberg, Johan 1804-1877 .... **NCLC 41**

Runyon, (Alfred) Damon
1884(?)-1946 .... **TCLC 10**
See also CA 165; CAAE 107; DLB 11, 86, 171; MAL 5; MTCW 2; RGAL 4

Rush, Norman 1933- .... **CLC 44**
See also CA 126; CAAE 121; CANR 130; INT CA-126

Rushdie, Salman 1947- .... **CLC 23, 31, 55, 100, 191; SSC 83; WLCS**
See also AAYA 65; BEST 89:3; BPFB 3; BRWS 4; CA 111; CAAE 108; CANR 33, 56, 108, 133; CN 4, 5, 6, 7; CPW 1; DA3; DAB; DAC; DAM MST, NOV, POP; DLB 194, 323, 326; EWL 3; FANT; INT CA-111; LATS 1:2; LMFS 2; MTCW 1, 2; MTFW 2005; NFS 22, 23; RGEL 2; RGSF 2; TEA; WLIT 4

Rushforth, Peter 1945-2005 .... **CLC 19**
See also CA 101; CAAS 243

Rushforth, Peter Scott
See Rushforth, Peter

Ruskin, John 1819-1900 .... **TCLC 63**
See also BRW 5; BYA 5; CA 129; CAAE 114; CDBLB 1832-1890; DLB 55, 163, 190; RGEL 2; SATA 24; TEA; WCH

Russ, Joanna 1937- .... **CLC 15**
See also BPFB 3; CA 25-28; CANR 11, 31, 65; CN 4, 5, 6, 7; DLB 8; FW; GLL 1; MTCW 1; SCFW 1, 2; SFW 4

Russ, Richard Patrick
See O'Brian, Patrick

Russell, George William 1867-1935
See A.E.; Baker, Jean H.
See also BRWS 8; CA 153; CAAE 104; CDBLB 1890-1914; DAM POET; EWL 3; RGEL 2

Russell, Jeffrey Burton 1934- .... **CLC 70**
See also CA 25-28R; CANR 11, 28, 52

Russell, (Henry) Ken(neth Alfred)
1927- .... **CLC 16**
See also CA 105

Russell, William Martin 1947-
See Russell, Willy
See also CA 164; CANR 107

Russell, Willy .... **CLC 60**
See Russell, William Martin
See also CBD; CD 5, 6; DLB 233

Russo, Richard 1949- .... **CLC 181**
See also AMWS 12; CA 133; CAAE 127; CANR 87, 114; NFS 25

Rutherford, Mark .... **TCLC 25**
See White, William Hale
See also DLB 18; RGEL 2

Ruysbroeck, Jan van 1293-1381 ... **CMLC 85**

Ruyslinck, Ward .... **CLC 14**
See Belser, Reimond Karel Maria de

Ryan, Cornelius (John) 1920-1974 ..... **CLC 7**
See also CA 69-72; CAAS 53-56; CANR 38

Ryan, Michael 1946- .... **CLC 65**
See also CA 49-52; CANR 109; DLBY 1982

Ryan, Tim
See Dent, Lester

Rybakov, Anatoli (Naumovich)
1911-1998 .... **CLC 23, 53**
See Rybakov, Anatolii (Naumovich)
See also CA 135; CAAE 126; CAAS 172; SATA 79; SATA-Obit 108

Rybakov, Anatolii (Naumovich)
See Rybakov, Anatoli (Naumovich)
See also DLB 302; RGHL

Ryder, Jonathan
See Ludlum, Robert

Ryga, George 1932-1987 .... **CLC 14**
See also CA 101; CAAS 124; CANR 43, 90; CCA 1; DAC; DAM MST; DLB 60

Rymer, Thomas 1643(?)-1713 .... **LC 132**
See also DLB 101, 336

S. H.
See Hartmann, Sadakichi

S. S.
See Sassoon, Siegfried (Lorraine)

Sa'adawi, al- Nawal
See El Saadawi, Nawal
See also AFW; EWL 3

Saadawi, Nawal El
See El Saadawi, Nawal
See also WLIT 2

Saba, Umberto 1883-1957 .... **TCLC 33**
See also CA 144; CANR 79; DLB 114; EWL 3; RGWL 2, 3

Sabatini, Rafael 1875-1950 .... **TCLC 47**
See also BPFB 3; CA 162; RHW

Sabato, Ernesto 1911- ... **CLC 10, 23; HLC 2**
See also CA 97-100; CANR 32, 65; CD-WLB 3; CWW 2; DAM MULT; DLB 145; EWL 3; HW 1, 2; LAW; MTCW 1, 2; MTFW 2005

Sa-Carneiro, Mario de 1890-1916 . **TCLC 83**
See also DLB 287; EWL 3

Sacastru, Martin
See Bioy Casares, Adolfo
See also CWW 2

Sacher-Masoch, Leopold von
1836(?)-1895 .... **NCLC 31**

Sachs, Hans 1494-1576 .... **LC 95**
See also CDWLB 2; DLB 179; RGWL 2, 3

Sachs, Marilyn 1927- .... **CLC 35**
See also AAYA 2; BYA 6; CA 17-20R; CANR 13, 47, 150; CLR 2; JRDA; MAI-CYA 1, 2; SAAS 2; SATA 3, 68, 164; SATA-Essay 110; WYA; YAW

Sachs, Marilyn Stickle
See Sachs, Marilyn

Sachs, Nelly 1891-1970 .. **CLC 14, 98; PC 78**
See also CA 17-18; CAAS 25-28R; CANR 87; CAP 2; DLB 332; EWL 3; MTCW 2; MTFW 2005; PFS 20; RGHL; RGWL 2, 3

Sackler, Howard (Oliver)
1929-1982 .... **CLC 14**
See also CA 61-64; CAAS 108; CAD; CANR 30; DFS 15; DLB 7

Sacks, Oliver 1933- .... **CLC 67, 202**
See also CA 53-56; CANR 28, 50, 76, 146; CPW; DA3; INT CANR-28; MTCW 1, 2; MTFW 2005

Sacks, Oliver Wolf
See Sacks, Oliver

Sackville, Thomas 1536-1608 .... **LC 98**
See also DAM DRAM; DLB 62, 132; RGEL 2

Sadakichi
See Hartmann, Sadakichi

Sa'dawi, Nawal al-
See El Saadawi, Nawal
See also CWW 2

Sade, Donatien Alphonse Francois
1740-1814 .... **NCLC 3, 47**
See also DLB 314; EW 4; GFL Beginnings to 1789; RGWL 2, 3

Sade, Marquis de
See Sade, Donatien Alphonse Francois

Sadoff, Ira 1945- .... **CLC 9**
See also CA 53-56; CANR 5, 21, 109; DLB 120

Saetone
See Camus, Albert

Safire, William 1929- .... **CLC 10**
See also CA 17-20R; CANR 31, 54, 91, 148

Sagan, Carl 1934-1996 .... **CLC 30, 112**
See also AAYA 2, 62; CA 25-28R; CAAS 155; CANR 11, 36, 74; CPW; DA3; MTCW 1, 2; MTFW 2005; SATA 58; SATA-Obit 94

Sagan, Francoise .... **CLC 3, 6, 9, 17, 36**
See Quoirez, Francoise
See also CWW 2; DLB 83; EWL 3; GFL 1789 to the Present; MTCW 2

Sahgal, Nayantara (Pandit) 1927- .... **CLC 41**
See also CA 9-12R; CANR 11, 88; CN 1, 2, 3, 4, 5, 6, 7; DLB 323

Said, Edward W. 1935-2003 .... **CLC 123**
See also CA 21-24R; CAAS 220; CANR 45, 74, 107, 131; DLB 67; MTCW 2; MTFW 2005

Saikaku, Ihara 1642-1693 .... **LC 141**
See also RGWL 3

Saikaku Ihara
See Saikaku, Ihara

Saint, H(arry) F. 1941- .... **CLC 50**
See also CA 127

St. Aubin de Teran, Lisa 1953-
See Teran, Lisa St. Aubin de
See also CA 126; CAAE 118; CN 6, 7; INT CA-126

Saint Birgitta of Sweden c.
1303-1373 .... **CMLC 24**

Sainte-Beuve, Charles Augustin
1804-1869 .... **NCLC 5**
See also DLB 217; EW 6; GFL 1789 to the Present

Saint-Exupery, Antoine de
1900-1944 .... **TCLC 2, 56, 169; WLC**
See also AAYA 63; BPFB 3; BYA 3; CA 132; CAAE 108; CLR 10; DA3; DAM NOV; DLB 72; EW 12; EWL 3; GFL 1789 to the Present; LAIT 3; MAICYA 1, 2; MTCW 1, 2; MTFW 2005; RGWL 2, 3; SATA 20; TWA

Saint-Exupery, Antoine Jean Baptiste Marie Roger de
See Saint-Exupery, Antoine de

St. John, David
See Hunt, E. Howard

St. John, J. Hector
See Crevecoeur, Michel Guillaume Jean de

Saint-John Perse
See Leger, (Marie-Rene Auguste) Alexis Saint-Leger
See also EW 10; EWL 3; GFL 1789 to the Present; RGWL 2

Saintsbury, George (Edward Bateman)
1845-1933 .... **TCLC 31**
See also CA 160; DLB 57, 149

Sait Faik .... **TCLC 23**
See Abasiyanik, Sait Faik

Saki .... **SSC 12; TCLC 3; WLC 5**
See Munro, H(ector) H(ugh)
See also BRWS 6; BYA 11; LAIT 2; RGEL 2; SSFS 1; SUFW

Sala, George Augustus 1828-1895 . **NCLC 46**

Saladin 1138-1193 .... **CMLC 38**

Salama, Hannu 1936- .... **CLC 18**
See also CA 244; EWL 3

Salamanca, J(ack) R(ichard) 1922- .. **CLC 4, 15**
See also CA 193; 25-28R, 193

Salas, Floyd Francis 1931- .... **HLC 2**
See also CA 119; 27; CANR 44, 75, 93; DAM MULT; DLB 82; HW 1, 2; MTCW 2; MTFW 2005

Sale, J. Kirkpatrick
See Sale, Kirkpatrick

Sale, John Kirkpatrick
See Sale, Kirkpatrick

Sale, Kirkpatrick 1937- .... **CLC 68**
See also CA 13-16R; CANR 10, 147

Salinas, Luis Omar 1937- ... **CLC 90; HLC 2**
See also AMWS 13; CA 131; CANR 81, 153; DAM MULT; DLB 82; HW 1, 2

Salinas (y Serrano), Pedro
1891(?)-1951 .... **TCLC 17**
See also CAAE 117; DLB 134; EWL 3

NOV; DLB 6, 28, 52, 278, 332, 333; DLBY 1991; EWL 3; EXPS; HGG; JRDA; LAIT 3; MAICYA 1, 2; MAL 5; MTCW 1, 2; MTFW 2005; RGAL 4; RGHL; RGSF 2; SATA 3, 27; SATA-Obit 68; SSFS 2, 12, 16; TUS; TWA

Singer, Israel Joshua 1893-1944 .... **TCLC 33**
See Zinger, Yisroel-Yehoyshue
See also CA 169; DLB 333; EWL 3

Singh, Khushwant 1915- .... **CLC 11**
See also CA 9-12R; 9; CANR 6, 84; CN 1, 2, 3, 4, 5, 6, 7; DLB 323; EWL 3; RGEL 2

Singleton, Ann
See Benedict, Ruth

Singleton, John 1968(?)- .... **CLC 156**
See also AAYA 50; BW 2, 3; CA 138; CANR 67, 82; DAM MULT

Siniavskii, Andrei
See Sinyavsky, Andrei (Donatevich)
See also CWW 2

Sinjohn, John
See Galsworthy, John

Sinyavsky, Andrei (Donatevich)
1925-1997 .... **CLC 8**
See Siniavskii, Andrei; Sinyavsky, Andrey Donatovich; Tertz, Abram
See also CA 85-88; CAAS 159

Sinyavsky, Andrey Donatovich
See Sinyavsky, Andrei (Donatevich)
See also EWL 3

Sirin, V.
See Nabokov, Vladimir (Vladimirovich)

Sissman, L(ouis) E(dward)
1928-1976 .... **CLC 9, 18**
See also CA 21-24R; CAAS 65-68; CANR 13; CP 2; DLB 5

Sisson, C(harles) H(ubert)
1914-2003 .... **CLC 8**
See also BRWS 11; CA 1-4R; 3; CAAS 220; CANR 3, 48, 84; CP 1, 2, 3, 4, 5, 6, 7; DLB 27

Sitting Bull 1831(?)-1890 .... **NNAL**
See also DA3; DAM MULT

Sitwell, Dame Edith 1887-1964 ..... **CLC 2, 9, 67; PC 3**
See also BRW 7; CA 9-12R; CANR 35; CDBLB 1945-1960; DAM POET; DLB 20; EWL 3; MTCW 1, 2; MTFW 2005; RGEL 2; TEA

Siwaarmill, H. P.
See Sharp, William

Sjoewall, Maj 1935- .... **CLC 7**
See Sjowall, Maj
See also CA 65-68; CANR 73

Sjowall, Maj
See Sjoewall, Maj
See also BPFB 3; CMW 4; MSW

Skelton, John 1460(?)-1529 ..... **LC 71; PC 25**
See also BRW 1; DLB 136; RGEL 2

Skelton, Robin 1925-1997 .... **CLC 13**
See Zuk, Georges
See also AITN 2; CA 5-8R; 5; CAAS 160; CANR 28, 89; CCA 1; CP 1, 2, 3, 4, 5, 6; DLB 27, 53

Skolimowski, Jerzy 1938- .... **CLC 20**
See also CA 128

Skram, Amalie (Bertha)
1847-1905 .... **TCLC 25**
See also CA 165

Skvorecky, Josef 1924- . **CLC 15, 39, 69, 152**
See also CA 61-64; 1; CANR 10, 34, 63, 108; CDWLB 4; CWW 2; DA3; DAC; DAM NOV; DLB 232; EWL 3; MTCW 1, 2; MTFW 2005

Slade, Bernard 1930- .... **CLC 11, 46**
See Newbound, Bernard Slade
See also CA 9; CCA 1; CD 6; DLB 53

Slaughter, Carolyn 1946- .... **CLC 56**
See also CA 85-88; CANR 85; CN 5, 6, 7

Slaughter, Frank G(ill) 1908-2001 ... **CLC 29**
See also AITN 2; CA 5-8R; CAAS 197; CANR 5, 85; INT CANR-5; RHW

Slavitt, David R. 1935- .... **CLC 5, 14**
See also CA 21-24R; 3; CANR 41, 83, 166; CN 1, 2, 3, 4, 5, 6, 7; DLB 5, 6

Slavitt, David Rytman
See Slavitt, David R.

Slesinger, Tess 1905-1945 .... **TCLC 10**
See also CA 199; CAAE 107; DLB 102

Slessor, Kenneth 1901-1971 .... **CLC 14**
See also CA 102; CAAS 89-92; DLB 260; RGEL 2

Slowacki, Juliusz 1809-1849 .... **NCLC 15**
See also RGWL 3

Smart, Christopher 1722-1771 .... **LC 3, 134; PC 13**
See also DAM POET; DLB 109; RGEL 2

Smart, Elizabeth 1913-1986 .... **CLC 54**
See also CA 81-84; CAAS 118; CN 4; DLB 88

Smiley, Jane 1949- ...... **CLC 53, 76, 144, 236**
See also AAYA 66; AMWS 6; BPFB 3; CA 104; CANR 30, 50, 74, 96, 158; CN 6, 7; CPW 1; DA3; DAM POP; DLB 227, 234; EWL 3; INT CANR-30; MAL 5; MTFW 2005; SSFS 19

Smiley, Jane Graves
See Smiley, Jane

Smith, A(rthur) J(ames) M(arshall)
1902-1980 .... **CLC 15**
See also CA 1-4R; CAAS 102; CANR 4; CP 1, 2, 3; DAC; DLB 88; RGEL 2

Smith, Adam 1723(?)-1790 .... **LC 36**
See also DLB 104, 252, 336; RGEL 2

Smith, Alexander 1829-1867 .... **NCLC 59**
See also DLB 32, 55

Smith, Anna Deavere 1950- ...... **CLC 86, 241**
See also CA 133; CANR 103; CD 5, 6; DFS 2, 22

Smith, Betty (Wehner) 1904-1972 .... **CLC 19**
See also AAYA 72; BPFB 3; BYA 3; CA 5-8R; CAAS 33-36R; DLBY 1982; LAIT 3; RGAL 4; SATA 6

Smith, Charlotte (Turner)
1749-1806 .... **NCLC 23, 115**
See also DLB 39, 109; RGEL 2; TEA

Smith, Clark Ashton 1893-1961 .... **CLC 43**
See also AAYA 76; CA 143; CANR 81; FANT; HGG; MTCW 2; SCFW 1, 2; SFW 4; SUFW

Smith, Dave .... **CLC 22, 42**
See Smith, David (Jeddie)
See also CA 7; CP 3, 4, 5, 6, 7; DLB 5

Smith, David (Jeddie) 1942-
See Smith, Dave
See also CA 49-52; CANR 1, 59, 120; CSW; DAM POET

Smith, Iain Crichton 1928-1998 .... **CLC 64**
See also BRWS 9; CA 21-24R; CAAS 171; CN 1, 2, 3, 4, 5, 6; CP 1, 2, 3, 4, 5, 6; DLB 40, 139, 319; RGSF 2

Smith, John 1580(?)-1631 .... **LC 9**
See also DLB 24, 30; TUS

Smith, Johnston
See Crane, Stephen (Townley)

Smith, Joseph, Jr. 1805-1844 .... **NCLC 53**

Smith, Kevin 1970- .... **CLC 223**
See also AAYA 37; CA 166; CANR 131

Smith, Lee 1944- .... **CLC 25, 73**
See also CA 119; CAAE 114; CANR 46, 118; CN 7; CSW; DLB 143; DLBY 1983; EWL 3; INT CA-119; RGAL 4

Smith, Martin
See Smith, Martin Cruz

Smith, Martin Cruz 1942- .. **CLC 25; NNAL**
See also BEST 89:4; BPFB 3; CA 85-88; CANR 6, 23, 43, 65, 119; CMW 4; CPW; DAM MULT, POP; HGG; INT CANR-23; MTCW 2; MTFW 2005; RGAL 4

Smith, Patti 1946- .... **CLC 12**
See also CA 93-96; CANR 63

Smith, Pauline (Urmson)
1882-1959 .... **TCLC 25**
See also DLB 225; EWL 3

Smith, Rosamond
See Oates, Joyce Carol

Smith, Seba 1792-1868 .... **NCLC 187**
See also DLB 1, 11, 243

Smith, Sheila Kaye
See Kaye-Smith, Sheila

Smith, Stevie 1902-1971 .... **CLC 3, 8, 25, 44; PC 12**
See also BRWS 2; CA 17-18; CAAS 29-32R; CANR 35; CAP 2; CP 1; DAM POET; DLB 20; EWL 3; MTCW 1, 2; PAB; PFS 3; RGEL 2; TEA

Smith, Wilbur 1933- .... **CLC 33**
See also CA 13-16R; CANR 7, 46, 66, 134; CPW; MTCW 1, 2; MTFW 2005

Smith, William Jay 1918- .... **CLC 6**
See also AMWS 13; CA 5-8R; CANR 44, 106; CP 1, 2, 3, 4, 5, 6, 7; CSW; CWRI 5; DLB 5; MAICYA 1, 2; SAAS 22; SATA 2, 68, 154; SATA-Essay 154; TCLE 1:2

Smith, Woodrow Wilson
See Kuttner, Henry

Smith, Zadie 1975- .... **CLC 158**
See also AAYA 50; CA 193; MTFW 2005

Smolenskin, Peretz 1842-1885 .... **NCLC 30**

Smollett, Tobias (George) 1721-1771 ... **LC 2, 46**
See also BRW 3; CDBLB 1660-1789; DLB 39, 104; RGEL 2; TEA

Snodgrass, W.D. 1926- .... **CLC 2, 6, 10, 18, 68; PC 74**
See also AMWS 6; CA 1-4R; CANR 6, 36, 65, 85; CP 1, 2, 3, 4, 5, 6, 7; DAM POET; DLB 5; MAL 5; MTCW 1, 2; MTFW 2005; RGAL 4; TCLE 1:2

Snorri Sturluson 1179-1241 .... **CMLC 56**
See also RGWL 2, 3

Snow, C(harles) P(ercy) 1905-1980 ... **CLC 1, 4, 6, 9, 13, 19**
See also BRW 7; CA 5-8R; CAAS 101; CANR 28; CDBLB 1945-1960; CN 1, 2; DAM NOV; DLB 15, 77; DLBD 17; EWL 3; MTCW 1, 2; MTFW 2005; RGEL 2; TEA

Snow, Frances Compton
See Adams, Henry (Brooks)

Snyder, Gary 1930- . **CLC 1, 2, 5, 9, 32, 120; PC 21**
See also AAYA 72; AMWS 8; ANW; BG 1:3; CA 17-20R; CANR 30, 60, 125; CP 1, 2, 3, 4, 5, 6, 7; DA3; DAM POET; DLB 5, 16, 165, 212, 237, 275; EWL 3; MAL 5; MTCW 2; MTFW 2005; PFS 9, 19; RGAL 4; WP

Snyder, Zilpha Keatley 1927- .... **CLC 17**
See also AAYA 15; BYA 1; CA 252; 9-12R, 252; CANR 38; CLR 31, 121; JRDA; MAICYA 1, 2; SAAS 2; SATA 1, 28, 75, 110, 163; SATA-Essay 112, 163; YAW

Soares, Bernardo
See Pessoa, Fernando (Antonio Nogueira)

Sobh, A.
See Shamlu, Ahmad

Sobh, Alef
See Shamlu, Ahmad

Sobol, Joshua 1939- .... **CLC 60**
See Sobol, Yehoshua
See also CA 200; RGHL

Sobol, Yehoshua 1939-
See Sobol, Joshua
See also CWW 2

Socrates 470B.C.-399B.C. .... CMLC 27

Soderberg, Hjalmar 1869-1941 ...... TCLC 39
See also DLB 259; EWL 3; RGSF 2

Soderbergh, Steven 1963- .... CLC 154
See also AAYA 43; CA 243

Soderbergh, Steven Andrew
See Soderbergh, Steven

Sodergran, Edith (Irene) 1892-1923
See Soedergran, Edith (Irene)
See also CA 202; DLB 259; EW 11; EWL 3; RGWL 2, 3

Soedergran, Edith (Irene)
1892-1923 .... TCLC 31
See Sodergran, Edith (Irene)

Softly, Edgar
See Lovecraft, H. P.

Softly, Edward
See Lovecraft, H. P.

Sokolov, Alexander V(sevolodovich) 1943-
See Sokolov, Sasha
See also CA 73-76

Sokolov, Raymond 1941- .... CLC 7
See also CA 85-88

Sokolov, Sasha .... CLC 59
See Sokolov, Alexander V(sevolodovich)
See also CWW 2; DLB 285; EWL 3; RGWL 2, 3

Solo, Jay
See Ellison, Harlan

Sologub, Fyodor .... TCLC 9
See Teternikov, Fyodor Kuzmich
See also EWL 3

Solomons, Ikey Esquir
See Thackeray, William Makepeace

Solomos, Dionysios 1798-1857 .... NCLC 15

Solwoska, Mara
See French, Marilyn

Solzhenitsyn, Aleksandr I. 1918- .. CLC 1, 2, 4, 7, 9, 10, 18, 26, 34, 78, 134, 235; SSC 32; WLC 5
See Solzhenitsyn, Aleksandr Isayevich
See also AAYA 49; AITN 1; BPFB 3; CA 69-72; CANR 40, 65, 116; DA; DA3; DAB; DAC; DAM MST, NOV; DLB 302, 332; EW 13; EXPS; LAIT 4; MTCW 1, 2; MTFW 2005; NFS 6; RGSF 2; RGWL 2, 3; SSFS 9; TWA

Solzhenitsyn, Aleksandr Isayevich
See Solzhenitsyn, Aleksandr I.
See also CWW 2; EWL 3

Somers, Jane
See Lessing, Doris

Somerville, Edith Oenone
1858-1949 .... SSC 56; TCLC 51
See also CA 196; DLB 135; RGEL 2; RGSF 2

Somerville & Ross
See Martin, Violet Florence; Somerville, Edith Oenone

Sommer, Scott 1951- .... CLC 25
See also CA 106

Sommers, Christina Hoff 1950- ...... CLC 197
See also CA 153; CANR 95

Sondheim, Stephen (Joshua) 1930- . CLC 30, 39, 147; DC 22
See also AAYA 11, 66; CA 103; CANR 47, 67, 125; DAM DRAM; LAIT 4

Sone, Monica 1919- .... AAL
See also DLB 312

Song, Cathy 1955- .... AAL; PC 21
See also CA 154; CANR 118; CWP; DLB 169, 312; EXPP; FW; PFS 5

Sontag, Susan 1933-2004 ... CLC 1, 2, 10, 13, 31, 105, 195
See also AMWS 3; CA 17-20R; CAAS 234; CANR 25, 51, 74, 97; CN 1, 2, 3, 4, 5, 6, 7; CPW; DA3; DAM POP; DLB 2, 67; EWL 3; MAL 5; MBL; MTCW 1, 2; MTFW 2005; RGAL 4; RHW; SSFS 10

Sophocles 496(?)B.C.-406(?)B.C. .... CMLC 2, 47, 51, 86; DC 1; WLCS
See also AW 1; CDWLB 1; DA; DA3; DAB; DAC; DAM DRAM, MST; DFS 1, 4, 8, 24; DLB 176; LAIT 1; LATS 1:1; LMFS 1; RGWL 2, 3; TWA; WLIT 8

Sordello 1189-1269 .... CMLC 15

Sorel, Georges 1847-1922 .... TCLC 91
See also CA 188; CAAE 118

Sorel, Julia
See Drexler, Rosalyn

Sorokin, Vladimir .... CLC 59
See Sorokin, Vladimir Georgievich
See also CA 258

Sorokin, Vladimir Georgievich
See Sorokin, Vladimir
See also DLB 285

Sorrentino, Gilbert 1929-2006 .... CLC 3, 7, 14, 22, 40
See also CA 77-80; CAAS 250; CANR 14, 33, 115, 157; CN 3, 4, 5, 6, 7; CP 1, 2, 3, 4, 5, 6, 7; DLB 5, 173; DLBY 1980; INT CANR-14

Soseki
See Natsume, Soseki
See also MJW

Soto, Gary 1952- ... CLC 32, 80; HLC 2; PC 28
See also AAYA 10, 37; BYA 11; CA 125; CAAE 119; CANR 50, 74, 107, 157; CLR 38; CP 4, 5, 6, 7; DAM MULT; DLB 82; EWL 3; EXPP; HW 1, 2; INT CA-125; JRDA; LLW; MAICYA 1; MAICYAS 1; MAL 5; MTCW 2; MTFW 2005; PFS 7; RGAL 4; SATA 80, 120, 174; WYA; YAW

Soupault, Philippe 1897-1990 .... CLC 68
See also CA 147; CAAE 116; CAAS 131; EWL 3; GFL 1789 to the Present; LMFS 2

Souster, (Holmes) Raymond 1921- .... CLC 5, 14
See also CA 13-16R; 14; CANR 13, 29, 53; CP 1, 2, 3, 4, 5, 6, 7; DA3; DAC; DAM POET; DLB 88; RGEL 2; SATA 63

Southern, Terry 1924(?)-1995 .... CLC 7
See also AMWS 11; BPFB 3; CA 1-4R; CAAS 150; CANR 1, 55, 107; CN 1, 2, 3, 4, 5, 6; DLB 2; IDFW 3, 4

Southerne, Thomas 1660-1746 .... LC 99
See also DLB 80; RGEL 2

Southey, Robert 1774-1843 .... NCLC 8, 97
See also BRW 4; DLB 93, 107, 142; RGEL 2; SATA 54

Southwell, Robert 1561(?)-1595 .... LC 108
See also DLB 167; RGEL 2; TEA

Southworth, Emma Dorothy Eliza Nevitte
1819-1899 .... NCLC 26
See also DLB 239

Souza, Ernest
See Scott, Evelyn

Soyinka, Wole 1934- .. BLC 3; CLC 3, 5, 14, 36, 44, 179; DC 2; WLC 5
See also AFW; BW 2, 3; CA 13-16R; CANR 27, 39, 82, 136; CD 5, 6; CDWLB 3; CN 6, 7; CP 1, 2, 3, 4, 5, 6 ,7; DA; DA3; DAB; DAC; DAM DRAM, MST, MULT; DFS 10; DLB 125, 332; EWL 3; MTCW 1, 2; MTFW 2005; RGEL 2; TWA; WLIT 2; WWE 1

Spackman, W(illiam) M(ode)
1905-1990 .... CLC 46
See also CA 81-84; CAAS 132

Spacks, Barry (Bernard) 1931- .... CLC 14
See also CA 154; CANR 33, 109; CP 3, 4, 5, 6, 7; DLB 105

Spanidou, Irini 1946- .... CLC 44
See also CA 185

Spark, Muriel 1918-2006 .... CLC 2, 3, 5, 8, 13, 18, 40, 94, 242; PC 72; SSC 10
See also BRWS 1; CA 5-8R; CAAS 251; CANR 12, 36, 76, 89, 131; CDBLB 1945-1960; CN 1, 2, 3, 4, 5, 6, 7; CP 1, 2, 3, 4, 5, 6, 7; DA3; DAB; DAC; DAM MST, NOV; DLB 15, 139; EWL 3; FW; INT CANR-12; LAIT 4; MTCW 1, 2; MTFW 2005; NFS 22; RGEL 2; TEA; WLIT 4; YAW

Spark, Muriel Sarah
See Spark, Muriel

Spaulding, Douglas
See Bradbury, Ray

Spaulding, Leonard
See Bradbury, Ray

Speght, Rachel 1597-c. 1630 .... LC 97
See also DLB 126

Spence, J. A. D.
See Eliot, T(homas) S(tearns)

Spencer, Anne 1882-1975 ...... HR 1:3; PC 77
See also BW 2; CA 161; DLB 51, 54

Spencer, Elizabeth 1921- .... CLC 22; SSC 57
See also CA 13-16R; CANR 32, 65, 87; CN 1, 2, 3, 4, 5, 6, 7; CSW; DLB 6, 218; EWL 3; MTCW 1; RGAL 4; SATA 14

Spencer, Leonard G.
See Silverberg, Robert

Spencer, Scott 1945- .... CLC 30
See also CA 113; CANR 51, 148; DLBY 1986

Spender, Stephen 1909-1995 ..... CLC 1, 2, 5, 10, 41, 91; PC 71
See also BRWS 2; CA 9-12R; CAAS 149; CANR 31, 54; CDBLB 1945-1960; CP 1, 2, 3, 4, 5, 6; DA3; DAM POET; DLB 20; EWL 3; MTCW 1, 2; MTFW 2005; PAB; PFS 23; RGEL 2; TEA

Spengler, Oswald (Arnold Gottfried)
1880-1936 .... TCLC 25
See also CA 189; CAAE 118

Spenser, Edmund 1552(?)-1599 ...... LC 5, 39, 117; PC 8, 42; WLC 5
See also AAYA 60; BRW 1; CDBLB Before 1660; DA; DA3; DAB; DAC; DAM MST, POET; DLB 167; EFS 2; EXPP; PAB; RGEL 2; TEA; WLIT 3; WP

Spicer, Jack 1925-1965 .... CLC 8, 18, 72
See also BG 1:3; CA 85-88; DAM POET; DLB 5, 16, 193; GLL 1; WP

Spiegelman, Art 1948- .... CLC 76, 178
See also AAYA 10, 46; CA 125; CANR 41, 55, 74, 124; DLB 299; MTCW 2; MTFW 2005; RGHL; SATA 109, 158; YAW

Spielberg, Peter 1929- .... CLC 6
See also CA 5-8R; CANR 4, 48; DLBY 1981

Spielberg, Steven 1947- .... CLC 20, 188
See also AAYA 8, 24; CA 77-80; CANR 32; SATA 32

Spillane, Frank Morrison
See Spillane, Mickey
See also BPFB 3; CMW 4; DLB 226; MSW

Spillane, Mickey 1918-2006 .. CLC 3, 13, 241
See Spillane, Frank Morrison
See also CA 25-28R; CAAS 252; CANR 28, 63, 125; DA3; MTCW 1, 2; MTFW 2005; SATA 66; SATA-Obit 176

Spinoza, Benedictus de 1632-1677 .. LC 9, 58

Spinrad, Norman (Richard) 1940- ... CLC 46
See also BPFB 3; CA 233; 37-40R, 233; 19; CANR 20, 91; DLB 8; INT CANR-20; SFW 4

Spitteler, Carl 1845-1924 .... **TCLC 12**
See also CAAE 109; DLB 129, 332; EWL 3

Spitteler, Karl Friedrich Georg
See Spitteler, Carl

Spivack, Kathleen (Romola Drucker)
1938- .... **CLC 6**
See also CA 49-52

Spivak, Gayatri Chakravorty
1942- .... **CLC 233**
See also CA 154; CAAE 110; CANR 91; FW; LMFS 2

Spofford, Harriet (Elizabeth) Prescott
1835-1921 .... **SSC 87**
See also CA 201; DLB 74, 221

Spoto, Donald 1941- .... **CLC 39**
See also CA 65-68; CANR 11, 57, 93

Springsteen, Bruce 1949- .... **CLC 17**
See also CA 111

Springsteen, Bruce F.
See Springsteen, Bruce

Spurling, Hilary 1940- .... **CLC 34**
See also CA 104; CANR 25, 52, 94, 157

Spurling, Susan Hilary
See Spurling, Hilary

Spyker, John Howland
See Elman, Richard (Martin)

Squared, A.
See Abbott, Edwin A.

Squires, (James) Radcliffe
1917-1993 .... **CLC 51**
See also CA 1-4R; CAAS 140; CANR 6, 21; CP 1, 2, 3, 4, 5

Srivastava, Dhanpat Rai 1880(?)-1936
See Premchand
See also CA 197; CAAE 118

Stacy, Donald
See Pohl, Frederik

Stael
See Stael-Holstein, Anne Louise Germaine Necker
See also EW 5; RGWL 2, 3

Stael, Germaine de
See Stael-Holstein, Anne Louise Germaine Necker
See also DLB 119, 192; FL 1:3; FW; GFL 1789 to the Present; TWA

Stael-Holstein, Anne Louise Germaine Necker 1766-1817 .... **NCLC 3, 91**
See Stael; Stael, Germaine de

Stafford, Jean 1915-1979 .. **CLC 4, 7, 19, 68; SSC 26, 86**
See also CA 1-4R; CAAS 85-88; CANR 3, 65; CN 1, 2; DLB 2, 173; MAL 5; MTCW 1, 2; MTFW 2005; RGAL 4; RGSF 2; SATA-Obit 22; SSFS 21; TCWW 1, 2; TUS

Stafford, William (Edgar)
1914-1993 .... **CLC 4, 7, 29; PC 71**
See also AMWS 11; CA 5-8R; 3; CAAS 142; CANR 5, 22; CP 1, 2, 3, 4, 5; DAM POET; DLB 5, 206; EXPP; INT CANR-22; MAL 5; PFS 2, 8, 16; RGAL 4; WP

Stagnelius, Eric Johan 1793-1823 . **NCLC 61**

Staines, Trevor
See Brunner, John (Kilian Houston)

Stairs, Gordon
See Austin, Mary (Hunter)

Stalin, Joseph 1879-1953 .... **TCLC 92**

Stampa, Gaspara c. 1524-1554 .. **LC 114; PC 43**
See also RGWL 2, 3; WLIT 7

Stampflinger, K. A.
See Benjamin, Walter

Stancykowna
See Szymborska, Wislawa

Standing Bear, Luther
1868(?)-1939(?) .... **NNAL**
See also CA 144; CAAE 113; DAM MULT

Stanislavsky, Constantin
1863(?)-1938 .... **TCLC 167**
See also CAAE 118

Stanislavsky, Konstantin
See Stanislavsky, Constantin

Stanislavsky, Konstantin Sergeievich
See Stanislavsky, Constantin

Stanislavsky, Konstantin Sergeivich
See Stanislavsky, Constantin

Stanislavsky, Konstantin Sergeyevich
See Stanislavsky, Constantin

Stannard, Martin 1947- .... **CLC 44**
See also CA 142; DLB 155

Stanton, Elizabeth Cady
1815-1902 .... **TCLC 73**
See also CA 171; DLB 79; FL 1:3; FW

Stanton, Maura 1946- .... **CLC 9**
See also CA 89-92; CANR 15, 123; DLB 120

Stanton, Schuyler
See Baum, L(yman) Frank

Stapledon, (William) Olaf
1886-1950 .... **TCLC 22**
See also CA 162; CAAE 111; DLB 15, 255; SCFW 1, 2; SFW 4

Starbuck, George (Edwin)
1931-1996 .... **CLC 53**
See also CA 21-24R; CAAS 153; CANR 23; CP 1, 2, 3, 4, 5, 6; DAM POET

Stark, Richard
See Westlake, Donald E.

Statius c. 45-c. 96 .... **CMLC 91**
See also AW 2; DLB 211

Staunton, Schuyler
See Baum, L(yman) Frank

Stead, Christina (Ellen) 1902-1983 ... **CLC 2, 5, 8, 32, 80**
See also BRWS 4; CA 13-16R; CAAS 109; CANR 33, 40; CN 1, 2, 3; DLB 260; EWL 3; FW; MTCW 1, 2; MTFW 2005; RGEL 2; RGSF 2; WWE 1

Stead, William Thomas
1849-1912 .... **TCLC 48**
See also BRWS 13; CA 167

Stebnitsky, M.
See Leskov, Nikolai (Semyonovich)

Steele, Richard 1672-1729 .... **LC 18**
See also BRW 3; CDBLB 1660-1789; DLB 84, 101; RGEL 2; WLIT 3

Steele, Timothy (Reid) 1948- .... **CLC 45**
See also CA 93-96; CANR 16, 50, 92; CP 5, 6, 7; DLB 120, 282

Steffens, (Joseph) Lincoln
1866-1936 .... **TCLC 20**
See also CA 198; CAAE 117; DLB 303; MAL 5

Stegner, Wallace (Earle) 1909-1993 .. **CLC 9, 49, 81; SSC 27**
See also AITN 1; AMWS 4; ANW; BEST 90:3; BPFB 3; CA 1-4R; 9; CAAS 141; CANR 1, 21, 46; CN 1, 2, 3, 4, 5; DAM NOV; DLB 9, 206, 275; DLBY 1993; EWL 3; MAL 5; MTCW 1, 2; MTFW 2005; RGAL 4; TCWW 1, 2; TUS

Stein, Gertrude 1874-1946 .... **DC 19; PC 18; SSC 42; TCLC 1, 6, 28, 48; WLC 5**
See also AAYA 64; AMW; AMWC 2; CA 132; CAAE 104; CANR 108; CDALB 1917-1929; DA; DA3; DAB; DAC; DAM MST, NOV, POET; DLB 4, 54, 86, 228; DLBD 15; EWL 3; EXPS; FL 1:6; GLL 1; MAL 5; MBL; MTCW 1, 2; MTFW 2005; NCFS 4; RGAL 4; RGSF 2; SSFS 5; TUS; WP

Steinbeck, John (Ernst) 1902-1968 ... **CLC 1, 5, 9, 13, 21, 34, 45, 75, 124; SSC 11, 37, 77; TCLC 135; WLC 5**
See also AAYA 12; AMW; BPFB 3; BYA 2, 3, 13; CA 1-4R; CAAS 25-28R; CANR 1, 35; CDALB 1929-1941; DA; DA3; DAB;
DAC; DAM DRAM, MST, NOV; DLB 7, 9, 212, 275, 309, 332; DLBD 2; EWL 3; EXPS; LAIT 3; MAL 5; MTCW 1, 2; MTFW 2005; NFS 1, 5, 7, 17, 19; RGAL 4; RGSF 2; RHW; SATA 9; SSFS 3, 6, 22; TCWW 1, 2; TUS; WYA; YAW

Steinem, Gloria 1934- .... **CLC 63**
See also CA 53-56; CANR 28, 51, 139; DLB 246; FL 1:1; FW; MTCW 1, 2; MTFW 2005

Steiner, George 1929- .... **CLC 24, 221**
See also CA 73-76; CANR 31, 67, 108; DAM NOV; DLB 67, 299; EWL 3; MTCW 1, 2; MTFW 2005; RGHL; SATA 62

Steiner, K. Leslie
See Delany, Samuel R., Jr.

Steiner, Rudolf 1861-1925 .... **TCLC 13**
See also CAAE 107

Stendhal 1783-1842 .... **NCLC 23, 46, 178; SSC 27; WLC 5**
See also DA; DA3; DAB; DAC; DAM MST, NOV; DLB 119; EW 5; GFL 1789 to the Present; RGWL 2, 3; TWA

Stephen, Adeline Virginia
See Woolf, (Adeline) Virginia

Stephen, Sir Leslie 1832-1904 .... **TCLC 23**
See also BRW 5; CAAE 123; DLB 57, 144, 190

Stephen, Sir Leslie
See Stephen, Sir Leslie

Stephen, Virginia
See Woolf, (Adeline) Virginia

Stephens, James 1882(?)-1950 .... **SSC 50; TCLC 4**
See also CA 192; CAAE 104; DLB 19, 153, 162; EWL 3; FANT; RGEL 2; SUFW

Stephens, Reed
See Donaldson, Stephen R(eeder)

Stephenson, Neal 1959- .... **CLC 220**
See also AAYA 38; CA 122; CANR 88, 138; CN 7; MTFW 2005; SFW 4

Steptoe, Lydia
See Barnes, Djuna
See also GLL 1

Sterchi, Beat 1949- .... **CLC 65**
See also CA 203

Sterling, Brett
See Bradbury, Ray; Hamilton, Edmond

Sterling, Bruce 1954- .... **CLC 72**
See also CA 119; CANR 44, 135; CN 7; MTFW 2005; SCFW 2; SFW 4

Sterling, George 1869-1926 .... **TCLC 20**
See also CA 165; CAAE 117; DLB 54

Stern, Gerald 1925- .... **CLC 40, 100**
See also AMWS 9; CA 81-84; CANR 28, 94; CP 3, 4, 5, 6, 7; DLB 105; PFS 26; RGAL 4

Stern, Richard (Gustave) 1928- ... **CLC 4, 39**
See also CA 1-4R; CANR 1, 25, 52, 120; CN 1, 2, 3, 4, 5, 6, 7; DLB 218; DLBY 1987; INT CANR-25

Sternberg, Josef von 1894-1969 .... **CLC 20**
See also CA 81-84

Sterne, Laurence 1713-1768 .... **LC 2, 48; WLC 5**
See also BRW 3; BRWC 1; CDBLB 1660-1789; DA; DAB; DAC; DAM MST, NOV; DLB 39; RGEL 2; TEA

Sternheim, (William Adolf) Carl
1878-1942 .... **TCLC 8**
See also CA 193; CAAE 105; DLB 56, 118; EWL 3; IDTP; RGWL 2, 3

Stevens, Margaret Dean
See Aldrich, Bess Streeter

Stevens, Mark 1951- .... **CLC 34**
See also CA 122

Stevens, Wallace 1879-1955 . **PC 6; TCLC 3, 12, 45; WLC 5**
See also AMW; AMWR 1; CA 124; CAAE 104; CDALB 1929-1941; DA; DA3; DAB; DAC; DAM MST, POET; DLB 54; EWL 3; EXPP; MAL 5; MTCW 1, 2; PAB; PFS 13, 16; RGAL 4; TUS; WP

Stevenson, Anne (Katharine) 1933- .. **CLC 7, 33**
See also BRWS 6; CA 17-20R; 9; CANR 9, 33, 123; CP 3, 4, 5, 6, 7; CWP; DLB 40; MTCW 1; RHW

Stevenson, Robert Louis (Balfour) 1850-1894 ...... **NCLC 5, 14, 63; SSC 11, 51; WLC 5**
See also AAYA 24; BPFB 3; BRW 5; BRWC 1; BRWR 1; BYA 1, 2, 4, 13; CD-BLB 1890-1914; CLR 10, 11, 107; DA; DA3; DAB; DAC; DAM MST, NOV; DLB 18, 57, 141, 156, 174; DLBD 13; GL 3; HGG; JRDA; LAIT 1, 3; MAICYA 1, 2; NFS 11, 20; RGEL 2; RGSF 2; SATA 100; SUFW; TEA; WCH; WLIT 4; WYA; YABC 2; YAW

Stewart, J(ohn) I(nnes) M(ackintosh) 1906-1994 .... **CLC 7, 14, 32**
See Innes, Michael
See also CA 85-88; 3; CAAS 147; CANR 47; CMW 4; CN 1, 2, 3, 4, 5; MTCW 1, 2

Stewart, Mary (Florence Elinor) 1916- .... **CLC 7, 35, 117**
See also AAYA 29, 73; BPFB 3; CA 1-4R; CANR 1, 59, 130; CMW 4; CPW; DAB; FANT; RHW; SATA 12; YAW

Stewart, Mary Rainbow
See Stewart, Mary (Florence Elinor)

Stifle, June
See Campbell, Maria

Stifter, Adalbert 1805-1868 .. **NCLC 41; SSC 28**
See also CDWLB 2; DLB 133; RGSF 2; RGWL 2, 3

Still, James 1906-2001 .... **CLC 49**
See also CA 65-68; 17; CAAS 195; CANR 10, 26; CSW; DLB 9; DLBY 01; SATA 29; SATA-Obit 127

Sting 1951-
See Sumner, Gordon Matthew
See also CA 167

Stirling, Arthur
See Sinclair, Upton

Stitt, Milan 1941- .... **CLC 29**
See also CA 69-72

Stockton, Francis Richard 1834-1902
See Stockton, Frank R.
See also AAYA 68; CA 137; CAAE 108; MAICYA 1, 2; SATA 44; SFW 4

Stockton, Frank R. .... **TCLC 47**
See Stockton, Francis Richard
See also BYA 4, 13; DLB 42, 74; DLBD 13; EXPS; SATA-Brief 32; SSFS 3; SUFW; WCH

Stoddard, Charles
See Kuttner, Henry

Stoker, Abraham 1847-1912
See Stoker, Bram
See also CA 150; CAAE 105; DA; DA3; DAC; DAM MST, NOV; HGG; MTFW 2005; SATA 29

Stoker, Bram . **SSC 62; TCLC 8, 144; WLC 6**
See Stoker, Abraham
See also AAYA 23; BPFB 3; BRWS 3; BYA 5; CDBLB 1890-1914; DAB; DLB 304; GL 3; LATS 1:1; NFS 18; RGEL 2; SUFW; TEA; WLIT 4

Stolz, Mary 1920-2006 .... **CLC 12**
See also AAYA 8, 73; AITN 1; CA 5-8R; CAAS 255; CANR 13, 41, 112; JRDA; MAICYA 1, 2; SAAS 3; SATA 10, 71, 133; SATA-Obit 180; YAW

Stolz, Mary Slattery
See Stolz, Mary

Stone, Irving 1903-1989 .... **CLC 7**
See also AITN 1; BPFB 3; CA 1-4R; 3; CAAS 129; CANR 1, 23; CN 1, 2, 3, 4; CPW; DA3; DAM POP; INT CANR-23; MTCW 1, 2; MTFW 2005; RHW; SATA 3; SATA-Obit 64

Stone, Oliver 1946- .... **CLC 73**
See also AAYA 15, 64; CA 110; CANR 55, 125

Stone, Oliver William
See Stone, Oliver

Stone, Robert 1937- .... **CLC 5, 23, 42, 175**
See also AMWS 5; BPFB 3; CA 85-88; CANR 23, 66, 95; CN 4, 5, 6, 7; DLB 152; EWL 3; INT CANR-23; MAL 5; MTCW 1; MTFW 2005

Stone, Ruth 1915- .... **PC 53**
See also CA 45-48; CANR 2, 91; CP 5, 6, 7; CSW; DLB 105; PFS 19

Stone, Zachary
See Follett, Ken

Stoppard, Tom 1937- ... **CLC 1, 3, 4, 5, 8, 15, 29, 34, 63, 91; DC 6; WLC 6**
See also AAYA 63; BRWC 1; BRWR 2; BRWS 1; CA 81-84; CANR 39, 67, 125; CBD; CD 5, 6; CDBLB 1960 to Present; DA; DA3; DAB; DAC; DAM DRAM, MST; DFS 2, 5, 8, 11, 13, 16; DLB 13, 233; DLBY 1985; EWL 3; LATS 1:2; MTCW 1, 2; MTFW 2005; RGEL 2; TEA; WLIT 4

Storey, David (Malcolm) 1933- . **CLC 2, 4, 5, 8**
See also BRWS 1; CA 81-84; CANR 36; CBD; CD 5, 6; CN 1, 2, 3, 4, 5, 6; DAM DRAM; DLB 13, 14, 207, 245, 326; EWL 3; MTCW 1; RGEL 2

Storm, Hyemeyohsts 1935- ... **CLC 3; NNAL**
See also CA 81-84; CANR 45; DAM MULT

Storm, (Hans) Theodor (Woldsen) 1817-1888 .... **NCLC 1; SSC 27**
See also CDWLB 2; DLB 129; EW; RGSF 2; RGWL 2, 3

Storni, Alfonsina 1892-1938 . **HLC 2; PC 33; TCLC 5**
See also CA 131; CAAE 104; DAM MULT; DLB 283; HW 1; LAW

Stoughton, William 1631-1701 .... **LC 38**
See also DLB 24

Stout, Rex (Todhunter) 1886-1975 ..... **CLC 3**
See also AITN 2; BPFB 3; CA 61-64; CANR 71; CMW 4; CN 2; DLB 306; MSW; RGAL 4

Stow, (Julian) Randolph 1935- ... **CLC 23, 48**
See also CA 13-16R; CANR 33; CN 1, 2, 3, 4, 5, 6, 7; CP 1, 2, 3, 4; DLB 260; MTCW 1; RGEL 2

Stowe, Harriet (Elizabeth) Beecher 1811-1896 ..... **NCLC 3, 50, 133; WLC 6**
See also AAYA 53; AMWS 1; CDALB 1865-1917; DA; DA3; DAB; DAC; DAM MST, NOV; DLB 1, 12, 42, 74, 189, 239, 243; EXPN; FL 1:3; JRDA; LAIT 2; MAICYA 1, 2; NFS 6; RGAL 4; TUS; YABC 1

Strabo c. 64B.C.-c. 25 .... **CMLC 37**
See also DLB 176

Strachey, (Giles) Lytton 1880-1932 .... **TCLC 12**
See also BRWS 2; CA 178; CAAE 110; DLB 149; DLBD 10; EWL 3; MTCW 2; NCFS 4

Stramm, August 1874-1915 .... **PC 50**
See also CA 195; EWL 3

Strand, Mark 1934- .. **CLC 6, 18, 41, 71; PC 63**
See also AMWS 4; CA 21-24R; CANR 40, 65, 100; CP 1, 2, 3, 4, 5, 6, 7; DAM POET; DLB 5; EWL 3; MAL 5; PAB; PFS 9, 18; RGAL 4; SATA 41; TCLE 1:2

Stratton-Porter, Gene(va Grace) 1863-1924
See Porter, Gene(va Grace) Stratton
See also ANW; CA 137; CLR 87; DLB 221; DLBD 14; MAICYA 1, 2; SATA 15

Straub, Peter 1943- .... **CLC 28, 107**
See also BEST 89:1; BPFB 3; CA 85-88; CANR 28, 65, 109; CPW; DAM POP; DLBY 1984; HGG; MTCW 1, 2; MTFW 2005; SUFW 2

Straub, Peter Francis
See Straub, Peter

Strauss, Botho 1944- .... **CLC 22**
See also CA 157; CWW 2; DLB 124

Strauss, Leo 1899-1973 .... **TCLC 141**
See also CA 101; CAAS 45-48; CANR 122

Streatfeild, (Mary) Noel 1897(?)-1986 .... **CLC 21**
See also CA 81-84; CAAS 120; CANR 31; CLR 17, 83; CWRI 5; DLB 160; MAICYA 1, 2; SATA 20; SATA-Obit 48

Stribling, T(homas) S(igismund) 1881-1965 .... **CLC 23**
See also CA 189; CAAS 107; CMW 4; DLB 9; RGAL 4

Strindberg, (Johan) August 1849-1912 ... **DC 18; TCLC 1, 8, 21, 47; WLC 6**
See also CA 135; CAAE 104; DA; DA3; DAB; DAC; DAM DRAM, MST; DFS 4, 9; DLB 259; EW 7; EWL 3; IDTP; LMFS 2; MTCW 2; MTFW 2005; RGWL 2, 3; TWA

Stringer, Arthur 1874-1950 .... **TCLC 37**
See also CA 161; DLB 92

Stringer, David
See Roberts, Keith (John Kingston)

Stroheim, Erich von 1885-1957 ..... **TCLC 71**

Strugatskii, Arkadii (Natanovich) 1925-1991 .... **CLC 27**
See Strugatsky, Arkadii Natanovich
See also CA 106; CAAS 135; SFW 4

Strugatskii, Boris (Natanovich) 1933- .... **CLC 27**
See Strugatsky, Boris (Natanovich)
See also CA 106; SFW 4

Strugatsky, Arkadii Natanovich
See Strugatskii, Arkadii (Natanovich)
See also DLB 302

Strugatsky, Boris (Natanovich)
See Strugatskii, Boris (Natanovich)
See also DLB 302

Strummer, Joe 1952-2002 .... **CLC 30**

Strunk, William, Jr. 1869-1946 ...... **TCLC 92**
See also CA 164; CAAE 118; NCFS 5

Stryk, Lucien 1924- .... **PC 27**
See also CA 13-16R; CANR 10, 28, 55, 110; CP 1, 2, 3, 4, 5, 6, 7

Stuart, Don A.
See Campbell, John W(ood, Jr.)

Stuart, Ian
See MacLean, Alistair (Stuart)

Stuart, Jesse (Hilton) 1906-1984 ... **CLC 1, 8, 11, 14, 34; SSC 31**
See also CA 5-8R; CAAS 112; CANR 31; CN 1, 2, 3; DLB 9, 48, 102; DLBY 1984; SATA 2; SATA-Obit 36

Stubblefield, Sally
See Trumbo, Dalton

Sturgeon, Theodore (Hamilton)
    1918-1985 .... **CLC 22, 39**
    See Queen, Ellery
    See also AAYA 51; BPFB 3; BYA 9, 10;
    CA 81-84; CAAS 116; CANR 32, 103;
    DLB 8; DLBY 1985; HGG; MTCW 1, 2;
    MTFW 2005; SCFW; SFW 4; SUFW
Sturges, Preston 1898-1959 .... **TCLC 48**
    See also CA 149; CAAE 114; DLB 26
Styron, William 1925-2006 .. **CLC 1, 3, 5, 11,**
    15, 60, 232; SSC 25
    See also AMW; AMWC 2; BEST 90:4;
    BPFB 3; CA 5-8R; CAAS 255; CANR 6,
    33, 74, 126; CDALB 1968-1988; CN 1,
    2, 3, 4, 5, 6, 7; CPW; CSW; DA3; DAM
    NOV, POP; DLB 2, 143, 299; DLBY
    1980; EWL 3; INT CANR-6; LAIT 2;
    MAL 5; MTCW 1, 2; MTFW 2005; NCFS
    1; NFS 22; RGAL 4; RGHL; RHW; TUS
Styron, William Clark
    See Styron, William
Su, Chien 1884-1918
    See Su Man-shu
    See also CAAE 123
Suarez Lynch, B.
    See Bioy Casares, Adolfo; Borges, Jorge
    Luis
Suassuna, Ariano Vilar 1927- .... **HLCS 1**
    See also CA 178; DLB 307; HW 2; LAW
Suckert, Kurt Erich
    See Malaparte, Curzio
Suckling, Sir John 1609-1642 . **LC 75; PC 30**
    See also BRW 2; DAM POET; DLB 58,
    126; EXPP; PAB; RGEL 2
Suckow, Ruth 1892-1960 .... **SSC 18**
    See also CA 193; CAAS 113; DLB 9, 102;
    RGAL 4; TCWW 2
Sudermann, Hermann 1857-1928 .. **TCLC 15**
    See also CA 201; CAAE 107; DLB 118
Sue, Eugene 1804-1857 .... **NCLC 1**
    See also DLB 119
Sueskind, Patrick 1949- .... **CLC 44, 182**
    See Suskind, Patrick
Suetonius c. 70-c. 130 .... **CMLC 60**
    See also AW 2; DLB 211; RGWL 2, 3;
    WLIT 8
Sukenick, Ronald 1932-2004 ..... **CLC 3, 4, 6,**
    48
    See also CA 209; 25-28R, 209; 8; CAAS
    229; CANR 32, 89; CN 3, 4, 5, 6, 7; DLB
    173; DLBY 1981
Suknaski, Andrew 1942- .... **CLC 19**
    See also CA 101; CP 3, 4, 5, 6, 7; DLB 53
Sullivan, Vernon
    See Vian, Boris
Sully Prudhomme, Rene-Francois-Armand
    1839-1907 .... **TCLC 31**
    See Prudhomme, Rene Francois Armand
    See also DLB 332; GFL 1789 to the Present
Su Man-shu .... **TCLC 24**
    See Su, Chien
    See also EWL 3
Sumarokov, Aleksandr Petrovich
    1717-1777 .... **LC 104**
    See also DLB 150
Summerforest, Ivy B.
    See Kirkup, James
Summers, Andrew James
    See Summers, Andy
Summers, Andy 1942- .... **CLC 26**
    See also CA 255
Summers, Hollis (Spurgeon, Jr.)
    1916- .... **CLC 10**
    See also CA 5-8R; CANR 3; CN 1, 2, 3;
    CP 1, 2, 3, 4; DLB 6; TCLE 1:2
Summers, (Alphonsus Joseph-Mary
    Augustus) Montague
    1880-1948 .... **TCLC 16**
    See also CA 163; CAAE 118

Sumner, Gordon Matthew .... **CLC 26**
    See Police, The; Sting
Sun Tzu c. 400B.C.-c. 320B.C. ...... **CMLC 56**
Surrey, Henry Howard 1517-1574 ... **LC 121;**
    PC 59
    See also BRW 1; RGEL 2
Surtees, Robert Smith 1805-1864 .. **NCLC 14**
    See also DLB 21; RGEL 2
Susann, Jacqueline 1921-1974 .... **CLC 3**
    See also AITN 2; BPFB 3; CA 65-68;
    CAAS 53-56; MTCW 1, 2
Su Shi
    See Su Shih
    See also RGWL 2, 3
Su Shih 1036-1101 .... **CMLC 15**
    See Su Shi
Suskind, Patrick .... **CLC 182**
    See Sueskind, Patrick
    See also BPFB 3; CA 145; CWW 2
Suso, Heinrich c. 1295-1366 .... **CMLC 87**
Sutcliff, Rosemary 1920-1992 .... **CLC 26**
    See also AAYA 10; BYA 1, 4; CA 5-8R;
    CAAS 139; CANR 37; CLR 1, 37; CPW;
    DAB; DAC; DAM MST, POP; JRDA;
    LATS 1:1; MAICYA 1, 2; MAICYAS 1;
    RHW; SATA 6, 44, 78; SATA-Obit 73;
    WYA; YAW
Sutro, Alfred 1863-1933 .... **TCLC 6**
    See also CA 185; CAAE 105; DLB 10;
    RGEL 2
Sutton, Henry
    See Slavitt, David R.
Suzuki, D. T.
    See Suzuki, Daisetz Teitaro
Suzuki, Daisetz T.
    See Suzuki, Daisetz Teitaro
Suzuki, Daisetz Teitaro
    1870-1966 .... **TCLC 109**
    See also CA 121; CAAS 111; MTCW 1, 2;
    MTFW 2005
Suzuki, Teitaro
    See Suzuki, Daisetz Teitaro
Svevo, Italo .... **SSC 25; TCLC 2, 35**
    See Schmitz, Aron Hector
    See also DLB 264; EW 8; EWL 3; RGWL
    2, 3; WLIT 7
Swados, Elizabeth 1951- .... **CLC 12**
    See also CA 97-100; CANR 49, 163; INT
    CA-97-100
Swados, Elizabeth A.
    See Swados, Elizabeth
Swados, Harvey 1920-1972 .... **CLC 5**
    See also CA 5-8R; CAAS 37-40R; CANR
    6; CN 1; DLB 2, 335; MAL 5
Swados, Liz
    See Swados, Elizabeth
Swan, Gladys 1934- .... **CLC 69**
    See also CA 101; CANR 17, 39; TCLE 1:2
Swanson, Logan
    See Matheson, Richard (Burton)
Swarthout, Glendon (Fred)
    1918-1992 .... **CLC 35**
    See also AAYA 55; CA 1-4R; CAAS 139;
    CANR 1, 47; CN 1, 2, 3, 4, 5; LAIT 5;
    SATA 26; TCWW 1, 2; YAW
Swedenborg, Emanuel 1688-1772 ..... **LC 105**
Sweet, Sarah C.
    See Jewett, (Theodora) Sarah Orne
Swenson, May 1919-1989 ...... **CLC 4, 14, 61,**
    106; PC 14
    See also AMWS 4; CA 5-8R; CAAS 130;
    CANR 36, 61, 131; CP 1, 2, 3, 4; DA;
    DAB; DAC; DAM MST, POET; DLB 5;
    EXPP; GLL 2; MAL 5; MTCW 1, 2;
    MTFW 2005; PFS 16; SATA 15; WP
Swift, Augustus
    See Lovecraft, H. P.

Swift, Graham 1949- .... **CLC 41, 88, 233**
    See also BRWC 2; BRWS 5; CA 122;
    CAAE 117; CANR 46, 71, 128; CN 4, 5,
    6, 7; DLB 194, 326; MTCW 2; MTFW
    2005; NFS 18; RGSF 2
Swift, Jonathan 1667-1745 ..... **LC 1, 42, 101;**
    PC 9; WLC 6
    See also AAYA 41; BRW 3; BRWC 1;
    BRWR 1; BYA 5, 14; CDBLB 1660-1789;
    CLR 53; DA; DA3; DAB; DAC; DAM
    MST, NOV, POET; DLB 39, 95, 101;
    EXPN; LAIT 1; NFS 6; RGEL 2; SATA
    19; TEA; WCH; WLIT 3
Swinburne, Algernon Charles
    1837-1909 ... **PC 24; TCLC 8, 36; WLC**
    6
    See also BRW 5; CA 140; CAAE 105; CD-
    BLB 1832-1890; DA; DA3; DAB; DAC;
    DAM MST, POET; DLB 35, 57; PAB;
    RGEL 2; TEA
Swinfen, Ann .... **CLC 34**
    See also CA 202
Swinnerton, Frank (Arthur)
    1884-1982 .... **CLC 31**
    See also CA 202; CAAS 108; CN 1, 2, 3;
    DLB 34
Swinnerton, Frank Arthur
    1884-1982 .... **CLC 31**
    See also CAAS 108; DLB 34
Swithen, John
    See King, Stephen
Sylvia
    See Ashton-Warner, Sylvia (Constance)
Symmes, Robert Edward
    See Duncan, Robert
Symonds, John Addington
    1840-1893 .... **NCLC 34**
    See also DLB 57, 144
Symons, Arthur 1865-1945 .... **TCLC 11**
    See also CA 189; CAAE 107; DLB 19, 57,
    149; RGEL 2
Symons, Julian (Gustave)
    1912-1994 .... **CLC 2, 14, 32**
    See also CA 49-52; 3; CAAS 147; CANR
    3, 33, 59; CMW 4; CN 1, 2, 3, 4, 5; CP 1,
    3, 4; DLB 87, 155; DLBY 1992; MSW;
    MTCW 1
Synge, (Edmund) J(ohn) M(illington)
    1871-1909 .... **DC 2; TCLC 6, 37**
    See also BRW 6; BRWR 1; CA 141; CAAE
    104; CDBLB 1890-1914; DAM DRAM;
    DFS 18; DLB 10, 19; EWL 3; RGEL 2;
    TEA; WLIT 4
Syruc, J.
    See Milosz, Czeslaw
Szirtes, George 1948- .... **CLC 46; PC 51**
    See also CA 109; CANR 27, 61, 117; CP 4,
    5, 6, 7
Szymborska, Wislawa 1923- ... **CLC 99, 190;**
    PC 44
    See also AAYA 76; CA 154; CANR 91, 133;
    CDWLB 4; CWP; CWW 2; DA3; DLB
    232, 332; DLBY 1996; EWL 3; MTCW
    2; MTFW 2005; PFS 15; RGHL; RGWL
    3
T. O., Nik
    See Annensky, Innokenty (Fyodorovich)
Tabori, George 1914-2007 .... **CLC 19**
    See also CA 49-52; CANR 4, 69; CBD; CD
    5, 6; DLB 245; RGHL
Tacitus c. 55-c. 117 .... **CMLC 56**
    See also AW 2; CDWLB 1; DLB 211;
    RGWL 2, 3; WLIT 8
Tagore, Rabindranath 1861-1941 .... **PC 8;**
    SSC 48; TCLC 3, 53
    See also CA 120; CAAE 104; DA3; DAM
    DRAM, POET; DLB 323, 332; EWL 3;
    MTCW 1, 2; MTFW 2005; PFS 18; RGEL
    2; RGSF 2; RGWL 2, 3; TWA

Taine, Hippolyte Adolphe
1828-1893 .... **NCLC 15**
See also EW 7; GFL 1789 to the Present

Talayesva, Don C. 1890-(?) .... **NNAL**

Talese, Gay 1932- .... **CLC 37, 232**
See also AITN 1; AMWS 17; CA 1-4R;
CANR 9, 58, 137; DLB 185; INT
CANR-9; MTCW 1, 2; MTFW 2005

Tallent, Elizabeth 1954- .... **CLC 45**
See also CA 117; CANR 72; DLB 130

Tallmountain, Mary 1918-1997 .... **NNAL**
See also CA 146; CAAS 161; DLB 193

Tally, Ted 1952- .... **CLC 42**
See also CA 124; CAAE 120; CAD; CANR
125; CD 5, 6; INT CA-124

Talvik, Heiti 1904-1947 .... **TCLC 87**
See also EWL 3

Tamayo y Baus, Manuel
1829-1898 .... **NCLC 1**

Tammsaare, A(nton) H(ansen)
1878-1940 .... **TCLC 27**
See also CA 164; CDWLB 4; DLB 220;
EWL 3

Tam'si, Tchicaya U
See Tchicaya, Gerald Felix

Tan, Amy 1952- ...... **AAL; CLC 59, 120, 151**
See also AAYA 9, 48; AMWS 10; BEST
89:3; BPFB 3; CA 136; CANR 54, 105,
132; CDALBS; CN 6, 7; CPW 1; DA3;
DAM MULT, NOV, POP; DLB 173, 312;
EXPN; FL 1:6; FW; LAIT 3, 5; MAL 5;
MTCW 1, 2; MTFW 2005; NFS 1, 13, 16;
RGAL 4; SATA 75; SSFS 9; YAW

Tandem, Carl Felix
See Spitteler, Carl

Tandem, Felix
See Spitteler, Carl

Tanizaki, Jun'ichiro 1886-1965 ... **CLC 8, 14,
28; SSC 21**
See Tanizaki Jun'ichiro
See also CA 93-96; CAAS 25-28R; MJW;
MTCW 2; MTFW 2005; RGSF 2; RGWL
2

Tanizaki Jun'ichiro
See Tanizaki, Jun'ichiro
See also DLB 180; EWL 3

Tannen, Deborah 1945- .... **CLC 206**
See also CA 118; CANR 95

Tannen, Deborah Frances
See Tannen, Deborah

Tanner, William
See Amis, Kingsley

Tante, Dilly
See Kunitz, Stanley

Tao Lao
See Storni, Alfonsina

Tapahonso, Luci 1953- .... **NNAL; PC 65**
See also CA 145; CANR 72, 127; DLB 175

Tarantino, Quentin (Jerome)
1963- .... **CLC 125, 230**
See also AAYA 58; CA 171; CANR 125

Tarassoff, Lev
See Troyat, Henri

Tarbell, Ida M(inerva) 1857-1944 . **TCLC 40**
See also CA 181; CAAE 122; DLB 47

**Tardieu d'Esclavelles,
Louise-Florence-Petronille**
See Epinay, Louise d'

Tarkington, (Newton) Booth
1869-1946 .... **TCLC 9**
See also BPFB 3; BYA 3; CA 143; CAAE
110; CWRI 5; DLB 9, 102; MAL 5;
MTCW 2; RGAL 4; SATA 17

Tarkovskii, Andrei Arsen'evich
See Tarkovsky, Andrei (Arsenyevich)

Tarkovsky, Andrei (Arsenyevich)
1932-1986 .... **CLC 75**
See also CA 127

Tartt, Donna 1964(?)- .... **CLC 76**
See also AAYA 56; CA 142; CANR 135;
MTFW 2005

Tasso, Torquato 1544-1595 .... **LC 5, 94**
See also EFS 2; EW 2; RGWL 2, 3; WLIT
7

Tate, (John Orley) Allen 1899-1979 .. **CLC 2,
4, 6, 9, 11, 14, 24; PC 50**
See also AMW; CA 5-8R; CAAS 85-88;
CANR 32, 108; CN 1, 2; CP 1, 2; DLB 4,
45, 63; DLBD 17; EWL 3; MAL 5;
MTCW 1, 2; MTFW 2005; RGAL 4;
RHW

Tate, Ellalice
See Hibbert, Eleanor Alice Burford

Tate, James (Vincent) 1943- ..... **CLC 2, 6, 25**
See also CA 21-24R; CANR 29, 57, 114;
CP 1, 2, 3, 4, 5, 6, 7; DLB 5, 169; EWL
3; PFS 10, 15; RGAL 4; WP

Tate, Nahum 1652(?)-1715 .... **LC 109**
See also DLB 80; RGEL 2

Tauler, Johannes c. 1300-1361 ...... **CMLC 37**
See also DLB 179; LMFS 1

Tavel, Ronald 1940- .... **CLC 6**
See also CA 21-24R; CAD; CANR 33; CD
5, 6

Taviani, Paolo 1931- .... **CLC 70**
See also CA 153

Taylor, Bayard 1825-1878 .... **NCLC 89**
See also DLB 3, 189, 250, 254; RGAL 4

Taylor, C(ecil) P(hilip) 1929-1981 .... **CLC 27**
See also CA 25-28R; CAAS 105; CANR
47; CBD

Taylor, Edward 1642(?)-1729 . **LC 11; PC 63**
See also AMW; DA; DAB; DAC; DAM
MST, POET; DLB 24; EXPP; RGAL 4;
TUS

Taylor, Eleanor Ross 1920- .... **CLC 5**
See also CA 81-84; CANR 70

Taylor, Elizabeth 1912-1975 .... **CLC 2, 4, 29;
SSC 100**
See also CA 13-16R; CANR 9, 70; CN 1,
2; DLB 139; MTCW 1; RGEL 2; SATA
13

Taylor, Frederick Winslow
1856-1915 .... **TCLC 76**
See also CA 188

Taylor, Henry (Splawn) 1942- .... **CLC 44**
See also CA 33-36R; 7; CANR 31; CP 6, 7;
DLB 5; PFS 10

Taylor, Kamala 1924-2004
See Markandaya, Kamala
See also CA 77-80; CAAS 227; MTFW
2005; NFS 13

Taylor, Mildred D. 1943- .... **CLC 21**
See also AAYA 10, 47; BW 1; BYA 3, 8;
CA 85-88; CANR 25, 115, 136; CLR 9,
59, 90; CSW; DLB 52; JRDA; LAIT 3;
MAICYA 1, 2; MTFW 2005; SAAS 5;
SATA 135; WYA; YAW

Taylor, Peter (Hillsman) 1917-1994 .. **CLC 1,
4, 18, 37, 44, 50, 71; SSC 10, 84**
See also AMWS 5; BPFB 3; CA 13-16R;
CAAS 147; CANR 9, 50; CN 1, 2, 3, 4,
5; CSW; DLB 218, 278; DLBY 1981,
1994; EWL 3; EXPS; INT CANR-9;
MAL 5; MTCW 1, 2; MTFW 2005; RGSF
2; SSFS 9; TUS

Taylor, Robert Lewis 1912-1998 .... **CLC 14**
See also CA 1-4R; CAAS 170; CANR 3,
64; CN 1, 2; SATA 10; TCWW 1, 2

Tchekhov, Anton
See Chekhov, Anton (Pavlovich)

Tchicaya, Gerald Felix 1931-1988 .. **CLC 101**
See Tchicaya U Tam'si
See also CA 129; CAAS 125; CANR 81

Tchicaya U Tam'si
See Tchicaya, Gerald Felix
See also EWL 3

Teasdale, Sara 1884-1933 .... **PC 31; TCLC 4**
See also CA 163; CAAE 104; DLB 45;
GLL 1; PFS 14; RGAL 4; SATA 32; TUS

Tecumseh 1768-1813 .... **NNAL**
See also DAM MULT

Tegner, Esaias 1782-1846 .... **NCLC 2**

Teilhard de Chardin, (Marie Joseph) Pierre
1881-1955 .... **TCLC 9**
See also CA 210; CAAE 105; GFL 1789 to
the Present

Temple, Ann
See Mortimer, Penelope (Ruth)

Tennant, Emma 1937- .... **CLC 13, 52**
See also BRWS 9; CA 65-68; 9; CANR 10,
38, 59, 88; CN 3, 4, 5, 6, 7; DLB 14;
EWL 3; SFW 4

Tenneshaw, S. M.
See Silverberg, Robert

Tenney, Tabitha Gilman
1762-1837 .... **NCLC 122**
See also DLB 37, 200

Tennyson, Alfred 1809-1892 ... **NCLC 30, 65,
115; PC 6; WLC 6**
See also AAYA 50; BRW 4; CDBLB 1832-
1890; DA; DA3; DAB; DAC; DAM MST,
POET; DLB 32; EXPP; PAB; PFS 1, 2, 4,
11, 15, 19; RGEL 2; TEA; WLIT 4; WP

Teran, Lisa St. Aubin de .... **CLC 36**
See St. Aubin de Teran, Lisa

Terence c. 184B.C.-c. 159B.C. ...... **CMLC 14;
DC 7**
See also AW 1; CDWLB 1; DLB 211;
RGWL 2, 3; TWA; WLIT 8

Teresa de Jesus, St. 1515-1582 .... **LC 18**

Teresa of Avila, St.
See Teresa de Jesus, St.

Terkel, Louis .... **CLC 38**
See Terkel, Studs
See also AAYA 32; AITN 1; MTCW 2; TUS

Terkel, Studs 1912-
See Terkel, Louis
See also CA 57-60; CANR 18, 45, 67, 132;
DA3; MTCW 1, 2; MTFW 2005

Terry, C. V.
See Slaughter, Frank G(ill)

Terry, Megan 1932- .... **CLC 19; DC 13**
See also CA 77-80; CABS 3; CAD; CANR
43; CD 5, 6; CWD; DFS 18; DLB 7, 249;
GLL 2

Tertullian c. 155-c. 245 .... **CMLC 29**

Tertz, Abram
See Sinyavsky, Andrei (Donatevich)
See also RGSF 2

Tesich, Steve 1943(?)-1996 .... **CLC 40, 69**
See also CA 105; CAAS 152; CAD; DLBY
1983

Tesla, Nikola 1856-1943 .... **TCLC 88**

Teternikov, Fyodor Kuzmich 1863-1927
See Sologub, Fyodor
See also CAAE 104

Tevis, Walter 1928-1984 .... **CLC 42**
See also CA 113; SFW 4

Tey, Josephine .... **TCLC 14**
See Mackintosh, Elizabeth
See also DLB 77; MSW

Thackeray, William Makepeace
1811-1863 ...... **NCLC 5, 14, 22, 43, 169;
WLC 6**
See also BRW 5; BRWC 2; CDBLB 1832-
1890; DA; DA3; DAB; DAC; DAM MST,
NOV; DLB 21, 55, 159, 163; NFS 13;
RGEL 2; SATA 23; TEA; WLIT 3

Thakura, Ravindranatha
See Tagore, Rabindranath

Thames, C. H.
See Marlowe, Stephen

Tharoor, Shashi 1956- .... **CLC 70**
See also CA 141; CANR 91; CN 6, 7

Trimball, W. H.
See Mencken, H(enry) L(ouis)

Tristan
See Gomez de la Serna, Ramon

Tristram
See Housman, A(lfred) E(dward)

Trogdon, William (Lewis) 1939-
See Heat-Moon, William Least
See also AAYA 66; CA 119; CAAE 115; CANR 47, 89; CPW; INT CA-119

Trollope, Anthony 1815-1882 .... NCLC 6, 33, 101; SSC 28; WLC 6
See also BRW 5; CDBLB 1832-1890; DA; DA3; DAB; DAC; DAM MST, NOV; DLB 21, 57, 159; RGEL 2; RGSF 2; SATA 22

Trollope, Frances 1779-1863 .... NCLC 30
See also DLB 21, 166

Trollope, Joanna 1943- .... CLC 186
See also CA 101; CANR 58, 95, 149; CN 7; CPW; DLB 207; RHW

Trotsky, Leon 1879-1940 .... TCLC 22
See also CA 167; CAAE 118

Trotter (Cockburn), Catharine 1679-1749 .... LC 8
See also DLB 84, 252

Trotter, Wilfred 1872-1939 .... TCLC 97

Trout, Kilgore
See Farmer, Philip Jose

Trow, George William Swift
See Trow, George W.S.

Trow, George W.S. 1943-2006 .... CLC 52
See also CA 126; CAAS 255; CANR 91

Troyat, Henri 1911-2007 .... CLC 23
See also CA 45-48; CAAS 258; CANR 2, 33, 67, 117; GFL 1789 to the Present; MTCW 1

Trudeau, Garry B. .... CLC 12
See Trudeau, G.B.
See also AAYA 10; AITN 2

Trudeau, G.B. 1948-
See Trudeau, Garry B.
See also AAYA 60; CA 81-84; CANR 31; SATA 35, 168

Truffaut, Francois 1932-1984 ... CLC 20, 101
See also CA 81-84; CAAS 113; CANR 34

Trumbo, Dalton 1905-1976 .... CLC 19
See also CA 21-24R; CAAS 69-72; CANR 10; CN 1, 2; DLB 26; IDFW 3, 4; YAW

Trumbull, John 1750-1831 .... NCLC 30
See also DLB 31; RGAL 4

Trundlett, Helen B.
See Eliot, T(homas) S(tearns)

Truth, Sojourner 1797(?)-1883 ...... NCLC 94
See also DLB 239; FW; LAIT 2

Tryon, Thomas 1926-1991 .... CLC 3, 11
See also AITN 1; BPFB 3; CA 29-32R; CAAS 135; CANR 32, 77; CPW; DA3; DAM POP; HGG; MTCW 1

Tryon, Tom
See Tryon, Thomas

Ts'ao Hsueh-ch'in 1715(?)-1763 .... LC 1

Tsurayuki Ed. fl. 10th cent. - .... PC 73

Tsushima, Shuji 1909-1948
See Dazai Osamu
See also CAAE 107

Tsvetaeva (Efron), Marina (Ivanovna) 1892-1941 .... PC 14; TCLC 7, 35
See also CA 128; CAAE 104; CANR 73; DLB 295; EW 11; MTCW 1, 2; RGWL 2, 3

Tuck, Lily 1938- .... CLC 70
See also AAYA 74; CA 139; CANR 90

Tu Fu 712-770 .... PC 9
See Du Fu
See also DAM MULT; TWA; WP

Tunis, John R(oberts) 1889-1975 ..... CLC 12
See also BYA 1; CA 61-64; CANR 62; DLB 22, 171; JRDA; MAICYA 1, 2; SATA 37; SATA-Brief 30; YAW

Tuohy, Frank .... CLC 37
See Tuohy, John Francis
See also CN 1, 2, 3, 4, 5, 6, 7; DLB 14, 139

Tuohy, John Francis 1925-
See Tuohy, Frank
See also CA 5-8R; CAAS 178; CANR 3, 47

Turco, Lewis (Putnam) 1934- ..... CLC 11, 63
See also CA 13-16R; 22; CANR 24, 51; CP 1, 2, 3, 4, 5, 6, 7; DLBY 1984; TCLE 1:2

Turgenev, Ivan (Sergeevich) 1818-1883 ..... DC 7; NCLC 21, 37, 122; SSC 7, 57; WLC 6
See also AAYA 58; DA; DAB; DAC; DAM MST, NOV; DFS 6; DLB 238, 284; EW 6; LATS 1:1; NFS 16; RGSF 2; RGWL 2, 3; TWA

Turgot, Anne-Robert-Jacques 1727-1781 .... LC 26
See also DLB 314

Turner, Frederick 1943- .... CLC 48
See also CA 227; 73-76, 227; 10; CANR 12, 30, 56; DLB 40, 282

Turton, James
See Crace, Jim

Tutu, Desmond M(pilo) 1931- .. BLC 3; CLC 80
See also BW 1, 3; CA 125; CANR 67, 81; DAM MULT

Tutuola, Amos 1920-1997 ..... BLC 3; CLC 5, 14, 29; TCLC 188
See also AAYA 76; AFW; BW 2, 3; CA 9-12R; CAAS 159; CANR 27, 66; CD-WLB 3; CN 1, 2, 3, 4, 5, 6; DA3; DAM MULT; DLB 125; DNFS 2; EWL 3; MTCW 1, 2; MTFW 2005; RGEL 2; WLIT 2

Twain, Mark .... SSC 6, 26, 34, 87; TCLC 6, 12, 19, 36, 48, 59, 161, 185; WLC 6
See Clemens, Samuel Langhorne
See also AAYA 20; AMW; AMWC 1; BPFB 3; BYA 2, 3, 11, 14; CLR 58, 60, 66; DLB 11; EXPN; EXPS; FANT; LAIT 2; MAL 5; NCFS 4; NFS 1, 6; RGAL 4; RGSF 2; SFW 4; SSFS 1, 7, 16, 21; SUFW; TUS; WCH; WYA; YAW

Tyler, Anne 1941- . CLC 7, 11, 18, 28, 44, 59, 103, 205
See also AAYA 18, 60; AMWS 4; BEST 89:1; BPFB 3; BYA 12; CA 9-12R; CANR 11, 33, 53, 109, 132; CDALBS; CN 1, 2, 3, 4, 5, 6, 7; CPW; CSW; DAM NOV, POP; DLB 6, 143; DLBY 1982; EWL 3; EXPN; LATS 1:2; MAL 5; MBL; MTCW 1, 2; MTFW 2005; NFS 2, 7, 10; RGAL 4; SATA 7, 90, 173; SSFS 17; TCLE 1:2; TUS; YAW

Tyler, Royall 1757-1826 .... NCLC 3
See also DLB 37; RGAL 4

Tynan, Katharine 1861-1931 .... TCLC 3
See also CA 167; CAAE 104; DLB 153, 240; FW

Tyndale, William c. 1484-1536 .... LC 103
See also DLB 132

Tyutchev, Fyodor 1803-1873 .... NCLC 34

Tzara, Tristan 1896-1963 .... CLC 47; PC 27; TCLC 168
See also CA 153; CAAS 89-92; DAM POET; EWL 3; MTCW 2

Uchida, Yoshiko 1921-1992 .... AAL
See also AAYA 16; BYA 2, 3; CA 13-16R; CAAS 139; CANR 6, 22, 47, 61; CDALBS; CLR 6, 56; CWRI 5; DLB 312; JRDA; MAICYA 1, 2; MTCW 1, 2; MTFW 2005; SAAS 1; SATA 1, 53; SATA-Obit 72

Udall, Nicholas 1504-1556 .... LC 84
See also DLB 62; RGEL 2

Ueda Akinari 1734-1809 .... NCLC 131

Uhry, Alfred 1936- .... CLC 55
See also CA 133; CAAE 127; CAD; CANR 112; CD 5, 6; CSW; DA3; DAM DRAM, POP; DFS 11, 15; INT CA-133; MTFW 2005

Ulf, Haerved
See Strindberg, (Johan) August

Ulf, Harved
See Strindberg, (Johan) August

Ulibarri, Sabine R(eyes) 1919-2003 .... CLC 83; HLCS 2
See also CA 131; CAAS 214; CANR 81; DAM MULT; DLB 82; HW 1, 2; RGSF 2

Unamuno (y Jugo), Miguel de 1864-1936 .. HLC 2; SSC 11, 69; TCLC 2, 9, 148
See also CA 131; CAAE 104; CANR 81; DAM MULT, NOV; DLB 108, 322; EW 8; EWL 3; HW 1, 2; MTCW 1, 2; MTFW 2005; RGSF 2; RGWL 2, 3; SSFS 20; TWA

Uncle Shelby
See Silverstein, Shel

Undercliffe, Errol
See Campbell, (John) Ramsey

Underwood, Miles
See Glassco, John

Undset, Sigrid 1882-1949 .. TCLC 3; WLC 6
See also CA 129; CAAE 104; DA; DA3; DAB; DAC; DAM MST, NOV; EW 9; EWL 3; FW; MTCW 1, 2; MTFW 2005; RGWL 2, 3

Ungaretti, Giuseppe 1888-1970 ... CLC 7, 11, 15; PC 57
See also CA 19-20; CAAS 25-28R; CAP 2; DLB 114; EW 10; EWL 3; PFS 20; RGWL 2, 3; WLIT 7

Unger, Douglas 1952- .... CLC 34
See also CA 130; CANR 94, 155

Unsworth, Barry (Forster) 1930- .... CLC 76, 127
See also BRWS 7; CA 25-28R; CANR 30, 54, 125; CN 6, 7; DLB 194, 326

Updike, John 1932- . CLC 1, 2, 3, 5, 7, 9, 13, 15, 23, 34, 43, 70, 139, 214; SSC 13, 27, 103; WLC 6
See also AAYA 36; AMW; AMWC 1; AMWR 1; BPFB 3; BYA 12; CA 1-4R; CABS 1; CANR 4, 33, 51, 94, 133; CDALB 1968-1988; CN 1, 2, 3, 4, 5, 6, 7; CP 1, 2, 3, 4, 5, 6, 7; CPW 1; DA; DA3; DAB; DAC; DAM MST, NOV, POET, POP; DLB 2, 5, 143, 218, 227; DLBD 3; DLBY 1980, 1982, 1997; EWL 3; EXPP; HGG; MAL 5; MTCW 1, 2; MTFW 2005; NFS 12, 24; RGAL 4; RGSF 2; SSFS 3, 19; TUS

Updike, John Hoyer
See Updike, John

Upshaw, Margaret Mitchell
See Mitchell, Margaret (Munnerlyn)

Upton, Mark
See Sanders, Lawrence

Upward, Allen 1863-1926 .... TCLC 85
See also CA 187; CAAE 117; DLB 36

Urdang, Constance (Henriette) 1922-1996 .... CLC 47
See also CA 21-24R; CANR 9, 24; CP 1, 2, 3, 4, 5, 6; CWP

Urfe, Honore d' 1567(?)-1625 .... LC 132
See also DLB 268; GFL Beginnings to 1789; RGWL 2, 3

Uriel, Henry
See Faust, Frederick (Schiller)

Uris, Leon 1924-2003 .... **CLC 7, 32**
See also AITN 1, 2; BEST 89:2; BPFB 3;
CA 1-4R; CAAS 217; CANR 1, 40, 65,
123; CN 1, 2, 3, 4, 5, 6; CPW 1; DA3;
DAM NOV, POP; MTCW 1, 2; MTFW
2005; RGHL; SATA 49; SATA-Obit 146

Urista (Heredia), Alberto (Baltazar)
1947- .... **HLCS 1**
See Alurista
See also CA 182; CANR 2, 32; HW 1

Urmuz
See Codrescu, Andrei

Urquhart, Guy
See McAlmon, Robert (Menzies)

Urquhart, Jane 1949- .... **CLC 90, 242**
See also CA 113; CANR 32, 68, 116, 157;
CCA 1; DAC; DLB 334

Usigli, Rodolfo 1905-1979 .... **HLCS 1**
See also CA 131; DLB 305; EWL 3; HW 1;
LAW

Usk, Thomas (?)-1388 .... **CMLC 76**
See also DLB 146

Ustinov, Peter (Alexander)
1921-2004 .... **CLC 1**
See also AITN 1; CA 13-16R; CAAS 225;
CANR 25, 51; CBD; CD 5, 6; DLB 13;
MTCW 2

U Tam'si, Gerald Felix Tchicaya
See Tchicaya, Gerald Felix

U Tam'si, Tchicaya
See Tchicaya, Gerald Felix

Vachss, Andrew 1942- .... **CLC 106**
See also CA 214; 118, 214; CANR 44, 95,
153; CMW 4

Vachss, Andrew H.
See Vachss, Andrew

Vachss, Andrew Henry
See Vachss, Andrew

Vaculik, Ludvik 1926- .... **CLC 7**
See also CA 53-56; CANR 72; CWW 2;
DLB 232; EWL 3

Vaihinger, Hans 1852-1933 .... **TCLC 71**
See also CA 166; CAAE 116

Valdez, Luis (Miguel) 1940- ..... **CLC 84; DC
10; HLC 2**
See also CA 101; CAD; CANR 32, 81; CD
5, 6; DAM MULT; DFS 5; DLB 122;
EWL 3; HW 1; LAIT 4; LLW

Valenzuela, Luisa 1938- .... **CLC 31, 104;
HLCS 2; SSC 14, 82**
See also CA 101; CANR 32, 65, 123; CD-
WLB 3; CWW 2; DAM MULT; DLB 113;
EWL 3; FW; HW 1, 2; LAW; RGSF 2;
RGWL 3

Valera y Alcala-Galiano, Juan
1824-1905 .... **TCLC 10**
See also CAAE 106

Valerius Maximus fl. 20- .... **CMLC 64**
See also DLB 211

Valery, (Ambroise) Paul (Toussaint Jules)
1871-1945 .... **PC 9; TCLC 4, 15**
See also CA 122; CAAE 104; DA3; DAM
POET; DLB 258; EW 8; EWL 3; GFL
1789 to the Present; MTCW 1, 2; MTFW
2005; RGWL 2, 3; TWA

Valle-Inclan, Ramon (Maria) del
1866-1936 .... **HLC 2; TCLC 5**
See del Valle-Inclan, Ramon (Maria)
See also CA 153; CAAE 106; CANR 80;
DAM MULT; DLB 134; EW 8; EWL 3;
HW 2; RGSF 2; RGWL 2, 3

Vallejo, Antonio Buero
See Buero Vallejo, Antonio

Vallejo, Cesar (Abraham)
1892-1938 .... **HLC 2; TCLC 3, 56**
See also CA 153; CAAE 105; DAM MULT;
DLB 290; EWL 3; HW 1; LAW; PFS 26;
RGWL 2, 3

Valles, Jules 1832-1885 .... **NCLC 71**
See also DLB 123; GFL 1789 to the Present

Vallette, Marguerite Eymery
1860-1953 .... **TCLC 67**
See Rachilde
See also CA 182; DLB 123, 192

Valle Y Pena, Ramon del
See Valle-Inclan, Ramon (Maria) del

Van Ash, Cay 1918-1994 .... **CLC 34**
See also CA 220

Vanbrugh, Sir John 1664-1726 .... **LC 21**
See also BRW 2; DAM DRAM; DLB 80;
IDTP; RGEL 2

Van Campen, Karl
See Campbell, John W(ood, Jr.)

Vance, Gerald
See Silverberg, Robert

Vance, Jack 1916-
See Queen, Ellery; Vance, John Holbrook
See also CA 29-32R; CANR 17, 65, 154;
CMW 4; MTCW 1

Vance, John Holbrook .... **CLC 35**
See Vance, Jack
See also DLB 8; FANT; SCFW 1, 2; SFW
4; SUFW 1, 2

**Van Den Bogarde, Derek Jules Gaspard
Ulric Niven** 1921-1999 .... **CLC 14**
See Bogarde, Dirk
See also CA 77-80; CAAS 179

Vandenburgh, Jane .... **CLC 59**
See also CA 168

Vanderhaeghe, Guy 1951- .... **CLC 41**
See also BPFB 3; CA 113; CANR 72, 145;
CN 7; DLB 334

van der Post, Laurens (Jan)
1906-1996 .... **CLC 5**
See also AFW; CA 5-8R; CAAS 155;
CANR 35; CN 1, 2, 3, 4, 5, 6; DLB 204;
RGEL 2

van de Wetering, Janwillem 1931- ... **CLC 47**
See also CA 49-52; CANR 4, 62, 90; CMW
4

Van Dine, S. S. .... **TCLC 23**
See Wright, Willard Huntington
See also DLB 306; MSW

Van Doren, Carl (Clinton)
1885-1950 .... **TCLC 18**
See also CA 168; CAAE 111

Van Doren, Mark 1894-1972 .... **CLC 6, 10**
See also CA 1-4R; CAAS 37-40R; CANR
3; CN 1; CP 1; DLB 45, 284, 335; MAL
5; MTCW 1, 2; RGAL 4

Van Druten, John (William)
1901-1957 .... **TCLC 2**
See also CA 161; CAAE 104; DLB 10;
MAL 5; RGAL 4

Van Duyn, Mona 1921-2004 .... **CLC 3, 7, 63,
116**
See also CA 9-12R; CAAS 234; CANR 7,
38, 60, 116; CP 1, 2, 3, 4, 5, 6, 7; CWP;
DAM POET; DLB 5; MAL 5; MTFW
2005; PFS 20

Van Dyne, Edith
See Baum, L(yman) Frank

van Itallie, Jean-Claude 1936- .... **CLC 3**
See also CA 45-48; 2; CAD; CANR 1, 48;
CD 5, 6; DLB 7

Van Loot, Cornelius Obenchain
See Roberts, Kenneth (Lewis)

van Ostaijen, Paul 1896-1928 .... **TCLC 33**
See also CA 163

Van Peebles, Melvin 1932- .... **CLC 2, 20**
See also BW 2, 3; CA 85-88; CANR 27,
67, 82; DAM MULT

van Schendel, Arthur(-Francois-Emile)
1874-1946 .... **TCLC 56**
See also EWL 3

Vansittart, Peter 1920- .... **CLC 42**
See also CA 1-4R; CANR 3, 49, 90; CN 4,
5, 6, 7; RHW

Van Vechten, Carl 1880-1964 ... **CLC 33; HR
1:3**
See also AMWS 2; CA 183; CAAS 89-92;
DLB 4, 9, 51; RGAL 4

van Vogt, A(lfred) E(lton) 1912-2000 . **CLC 1**
See also BPFB 3; BYA 13, 14; CA 21-24R;
CAAS 190; CANR 28; DLB 8, 251;
SATA 14; SATA-Obit 124; SCFW 1, 2;
SFW 4

Vara, Madeleine
See Jackson, Laura (Riding)

Varda, Agnes 1928- .... **CLC 16**
See also CA 122; CAAE 116

Vargas Llosa, Jorge Mario Pedro
See Vargas Llosa, Mario

Vargas Llosa, Mario 1936- .. **CLC 3, 6, 9, 10,
15, 31, 42, 85, 181; HLC 2**
See Llosa, Jorge Mario Pedro Vargas
See also BPFB 3; CA 73-76; CANR 18, 32,
42, 67, 116, 140; CDWLB 3; CWW 2;
DA; DA3; DAB; DAC; DAM MST,
MULT, NOV; DLB 145; DNFS 2; EWL
3; HW 1, 2; LAIT 5; LATS 1:2; LAW;
LAWS 1; MTCW 1, 2; MTFW 2005;
RGWL 2; SSFS 14; TWA; WLIT 1

Varnhagen von Ense, Rahel
1771-1833 .... **NCLC 130**
See also DLB 90

Vasari, Giorgio 1511-1574 .... **LC 114**

Vasilikos, Vasiles
See Vassilikos, Vassilis

Vasiliu, George
See Bacovia, George

Vasiliu, Gheorghe
See Bacovia, George
See also CA 189; CAAE 123

Vassa, Gustavus
See Equiano, Olaudah

Vassilikos, Vassilis 1933- .... **CLC 4, 8**
See also CA 81-84; CANR 75, 149; EWL 3

Vaughan, Henry 1621-1695 .... **LC 27**
See also BRW 2; DLB 131; PAB; RGEL 2

Vaughn, Stephanie .... **CLC 62**

Vazov, Ivan (Minchov) 1850-1921 . **TCLC 25**
See also CA 167; CAAE 121; CDWLB 4;
DLB 147

Veblen, Thorstein B(unde)
1857-1929 .... **TCLC 31**
See also AMWS 1; CA 165; CAAE 115;
DLB 246; MAL 5

Vega, Lope de 1562-1635 ... **HLCS 2; LC 23,
119**
See also EW 2; RGWL 2, 3

Veldeke, Heinrich von c. 1145-c.
1190 .... **CMLC 85**

Vendler, Helen (Hennessy) 1933- ... **CLC 138**
See also CA 41-44R; CANR 25, 72, 136;
MTCW 1, 2; MTFW 2005

Venison, Alfred
See Pound, Ezra (Weston Loomis)

Ventsel, Elena Sergeevna 1907-2002
See Grekova, I.
See also CA 154

Verdi, Marie de
See Mencken, H(enry) L(ouis)

Verdu, Matilde
See Cela, Camilo Jose

Verga, Giovanni (Carmelo)
1840-1922 .... **SSC 21, 87; TCLC 3**
See also CA 123; CAAE 104; CANR 101;
EW 7; EWL 3; RGSF 2; RGWL 2, 3;
WLIT 7

Warren, Robert Penn 1905-1989 .. **CLC 1, 4, 6, 8, 10, 13, 18, 39, 53, 59; PC 37; SSC 4, 58; WLC 6**
See also AITN 1; AMW; AMWC 2; BPFB 3; BYA 1; CA 13-16R; CAAS 129; CANR 10, 47; CDALB 1968-1988; CN 1, 2, 3, 4; CP 1, 2, 3, 4; DA; DA3; DAB; DAC; DAM MST, NOV, POET; DLB 2, 48, 152, 320; DLBY 1980, 1989; EWL 3; INT CANR-10; MAL 5; MTCW 1, 2; MTFW 2005; NFS 13; RGAL 4; RGSF 2; RHW; SATA 46; SATA-Obit 63; SSFS 8; TUS

Warrigal, Jack
See Furphy, Joseph

Warshofsky, Isaac
See Singer, Isaac Bashevis

Warton, Joseph 1722-1800 ... **LC 128; NCLC 118**
See also DLB 104, 109; RGEL 2

Warton, Thomas 1728-1790 .... **LC 15, 82**
See also DAM POET; DLB 104, 109, 336; RGEL 2

Waruk, Kona
See Harris, (Theodore) Wilson

Warung, Price .... **TCLC 45**
See Astley, William
See also DLB 230; RGEL 2

Warwick, Jarvis
See Garner, Hugh
See also CCA 1

Washington, Alex
See Harris, Mark

Washington, Booker T(aliaferro)
1856-1915 .... **BLC 3; TCLC 10**
See also BW 1; CA 125; CAAE 114; DA3; DAM MULT; LAIT 2; RGAL 4; SATA 28

Washington, George 1732-1799 .... **LC 25**
See also DLB 31

Wassermann, (Karl) Jakob
1873-1934 .... **TCLC 6**
See also CA 163; CAAE 104; DLB 66; EWL 3

Wasserstein, Wendy 1950-2006 . **CLC 32, 59, 90, 183; DC 4**
See also AAYA 73; AMWS 15; CA 129; CAAE 121; CAAS 247; CABS 3; CAD; CANR 53, 75, 128; CD 5, 6; CWD; DA3; DAM DRAM; DFS 5, 17; DLB 228; EWL 3; FW; INT CA-129; MAL 5; MTCW 2; MTFW 2005; SATA 94; SATA-Obit 174

Waterhouse, Keith (Spencer) 1929- . **CLC 47**
See also BRWS 13; CA 5-8R; CANR 38, 67, 109; CBD; CD 6; CN 1, 2, 3, 4, 5, 6, 7; DLB 13, 15; MTCW 1; MTFW 2005

Waters, Frank (Joseph) 1902-1995 .. **CLC 88**
See also CA 5-8R; 13; CAAS 149; CANR 3, 18, 63, 121; DLB 212; DLBY 1986; RGAL 4; TCWW 1, 2

Waters, Mary C. .... **CLC 70**

Waters, Roger 1944- .... **CLC 35**

Watkins, Frances Ellen
See Harper, Frances Ellen Watkins

Watkins, Gerrold
See Malzberg, Barry N(athaniel)

Watkins, Gloria Jean
See hooks, bell

Watkins, Paul 1964- .... **CLC 55**
See also CA 132; CANR 62, 98

Watkins, Vernon Phillips
1906-1967 .... **CLC 43**
See also CA 9-10; CAAS 25-28R; CAP 1; DLB 20; EWL 3; RGEL 2

Watson, Irving S.
See Mencken, H(enry) L(ouis)

Watson, John H.
See Farmer, Philip Jose

Watson, Richard F.
See Silverberg, Robert

Watts, Ephraim
See Horne, Richard Henry Hengist

Watts, Isaac 1674-1748 .... **LC 98**
See also DLB 95; RGEL 2; SATA 52

Waugh, Auberon (Alexander)
1939-2001 .... **CLC 7**
See also CA 45-48; CAAS 192; CANR 6, 22, 92; CN 1, 2, 3; DLB 14, 194

Waugh, Evelyn (Arthur St. John)
1903-1966 .. **CLC 1, 3, 8, 13, 19, 27, 44, 107; SSC 41; WLC 6**
See also BPFB 3; BRW 7; CA 85-88; CAAS 25-28R; CANR 22; CDBLB 1914-1945; DA; DA3; DAB; DAC; DAM MST, NOV, POP; DLB 15, 162, 195; EWL 3; MTCW 1, 2; MTFW 2005; NFS 13, 17; RGEL 2; RGSF 2; TEA; WLIT 4

Waugh, Harriet 1944- .... **CLC 6**
See also CA 85-88; CANR 22

Ways, C. R.
See Blount, Roy (Alton), Jr.

Waystaff, Simon
See Swift, Jonathan

Webb, Beatrice (Martha Potter)
1858-1943 .... **TCLC 22**
See also CA 162; CAAE 117; DLB 190; FW

Webb, Charles (Richard) 1939- .... **CLC 7**
See also CA 25-28R; CANR 114

Webb, Frank J. .... **NCLC 143**
See also DLB 50

Webb, James, Jr.
See Webb, James

Webb, James 1946- .... **CLC 22**
See also CA 81-84; CANR 156

Webb, James H.
See Webb, James

Webb, James Henry
See Webb, James

Webb, Mary Gladys (Meredith)
1881-1927 .... **TCLC 24**
See also CA 182; CAAS 123; DLB 34; FW; RGEL 2

Webb, Mrs. Sidney
See Webb, Beatrice (Martha Potter)

Webb, Phyllis 1927- .... **CLC 18**
See also CA 104; CANR 23; CCA 1; CP 1, 2, 3, 4, 5, 6, 7; CWP; DLB 53

Webb, Sidney (James) 1859-1947 .. **TCLC 22**
See also CA 163; CAAE 117; DLB 190

Webber, Andrew Lloyd .... **CLC 21**
See Lloyd Webber, Andrew
See also DFS 7

Weber, Lenora Mattingly
1895-1971 .... **CLC 12**
See also CA 19-20; CAAS 29-32R; CAP 1; SATA 2; SATA-Obit 26

Weber, Max 1864-1920 .... **TCLC 69**
See also CA 189; CAAE 109; DLB 296

Webster, John 1580(?)-1634(?) ...... **DC 2; LC 33, 84, 124; WLC 6**
See also BRW 2; CDBLB Before 1660; DA; DAB; DAC; DAM DRAM, MST; DFS 17, 19; DLB 58; IDTP; RGEL 2; WLIT 3

Webster, Noah 1758-1843 .... **NCLC 30**
See also DLB 1, 37, 42, 43, 73, 243

Wedekind, Benjamin Franklin
See Wedekind, Frank

Wedekind, Frank 1864-1918 .... **TCLC 7**
See also CA 153; CAAE 104; CANR 121, 122; CDWLB 2; DAM DRAM; DLB 118; EW 8; EWL 3; LMFS 2; RGWL 2, 3

Wehr, Demaris .... **CLC 65**

Weidman, Jerome 1913-1998 .... **CLC 7**
See also AITN 2; CA 1-4R; CAAS 171; CAD; CANR 1; CD 1, 2, 3, 4, 5; DLB 28

Weil, Simone (Adolphine)
1909-1943 .... **TCLC 23**
See also CA 159; CAAE 117; EW 12; EWL 3; FW; GFL 1789 to the Present; MTCW 2

Weininger, Otto 1880-1903 .... **TCLC 84**

Weinstein, Nathan
See West, Nathanael

Weinstein, Nathan von Wallenstein
See West, Nathanael

Weir, Peter (Lindsay) 1944- .... **CLC 20**
See also CA 123; CAAE 113

Weiss, Peter (Ulrich) 1916-1982 .. **CLC 3, 15, 51; TCLC 152**
See also CA 45-48; CAAS 106; CANR 3; DAM DRAM; DFS 3; DLB 69, 124; EWL 3; RGHL; RGWL 2, 3

Weiss, Theodore (Russell)
1916-2003 .... **CLC 3, 8, 14**
See also CA 189; 9-12R, 189; 2; CAAS 216; CANR 46, 94; CP 1, 2, 3, 4, 5, 6, 7; DLB 5; TCLE 1:2

Welch, (Maurice) Denton
1915-1948 .... **TCLC 22**
See also BRWS 8, 9; CA 148; CAAE 121; RGEL 2

Welch, James (Phillip) 1940-2003 ..... **CLC 6, 14, 52; NNAL; PC 62**
See also CA 85-88; CAAS 219; CANR 42, 66, 107; CN 5, 6, 7; CP 2, 3, 4, 5, 6, 7; CPW; DAM MULT, POP; DLB 175, 256; LATS 1:1; NFS 23; RGAL 4; TCWW 1, 2

Weldon, Fay 1931- . **CLC 6, 9, 11, 19, 36, 59, 122**
See also BRWS 4; CA 21-24R; CANR 16, 46, 63, 97, 137; CDBLB 1960 to Present; CN 3, 4, 5, 6, 7; CPW; DAM POP; DLB 14, 194, 319; EWL 3; FW; HGG; INT CANR-16; MTCW 1, 2; MTFW 2005; RGEL 2; RGSF 2

Wellek, Rene 1903-1995 .... **CLC 28**
See also CA 5-8R; 7; CAAS 150; CANR 8; DLB 63; EWL 3; INT CANR-8

Weller, Michael 1942- .... **CLC 10, 53**
See also CA 85-88; CAD; CD 5, 6

Weller, Paul 1958- .... **CLC 26**

Wellershoff, Dieter 1925- .... **CLC 46**
See also CA 89-92; CANR 16, 37

Welles, (George) Orson 1915-1985 .. **CLC 20, 80**
See also AAYA 40; CA 93-96; CAAS 117

Wellman, John McDowell 1945-
See Wellman, Mac
See also CA 166; CD 5

Wellman, Mac .... **CLC 65**
See Wellman, John McDowell; Wellman, John McDowell
See also CAD; CD 6; RGAL 4

Wellman, Manly Wade 1903-1986 ... **CLC 49**
See also CA 1-4R; CAAS 118; CANR 6, 16, 44; FANT; SATA 6; SATA-Obit 47; SFW 4; SUFW

Wells, Carolyn 1869(?)-1942 .... **TCLC 35**
See also CA 185; CAAE 113; CMW 4; DLB 11

Wells, H(erbert) G(eorge) 1866-1946 . **SSC 6, 70; TCLC 6, 12, 19, 133; WLC 6**
See also AAYA 18; BPFB 3; BRW 6; CA 121; CAAE 110; CDBLB 1914-1945; CLR 64; DA; DA3; DAB; DAC; DAM MST, NOV; DLB 34, 70, 156, 178; EWL 3; EXPS; HGG; LAIT 3; LMFS 2; MTCW 1, 2; MTFW 2005; NFS 17, 20; RGEL 2; RGSF 2; SATA 20; SCFW 1, 2; SFW 4; SSFS 3; SUFW; TEA; WCH; WLIT 4; YAW

Whitehead, E(dward) A(nthony)
1933- .... **CLC 5**
See Whitehead, Ted
See also CA 65-68; CANR 58, 118; CBD;
CD 5; DLB 310

Whitehead, Ted
See Whitehead, E(dward) A(nthony)
See also CD 6

Whiteman, Roberta J. Hill 1947- ...... **NNAL**
See also CA 146

Whitemore, Hugh (John) 1936- .... **CLC 37**
See also CA 132; CANR 77; CBD; CD 5,
6; INT CA-132

Whitman, Sarah Helen (Power)
1803-1878 .... **NCLC 19**
See also DLB 1, 243

Whitman, Walt(er) 1819-1892 .. **NCLC 4, 31,
81; PC 3; WLC 6**
See also AAYA 42; AMW; AMWR 1;
CDALB 1640-1865; DA; DA3; DAB;
DAC; DAM MST, POET; DLB 3, 64,
224, 250; EXPP; LAIT 2; LMFS 1; PAB;
PFS 2, 3, 13, 22; RGAL 4; SATA 20;
TUS; WP; WYAS 1

Whitney, Isabella fl. 1565-fl. 1575 ..... **LC 130**
See also DLB 136

Whitney, Phyllis A(yame) 1903- .... **CLC 42**
See also AAYA 36; AITN 2; BEST 90:3;
CA 1-4R; CANR 3, 25, 38, 60; CLR 59;
CMW 4; CPW; DA3; DAM POP; JRDA;
MAICYA 1, 2; MTCW 2; RHW; SATA 1,
30; YAW

Whittemore, (Edward) Reed, Jr.
1919- .... **CLC 4**
See also CA 219; 9-12R, 219; 8; CANR 4,
119; CP 1, 2, 3, 4, 5, 6, 7; DLB 5; MAL
5

Whittier, John Greenleaf
1807-1892 .... **NCLC 8, 59**
See also AMWS 1; DLB 1, 243; RGAL 4

Whittlebot, Hernia
See Coward, Noel (Peirce)

Wicker, Thomas Grey 1926-
See Wicker, Tom
See also CA 65-68; CANR 21, 46, 141

Wicker, Tom .... **CLC 7**
See Wicker, Thomas Grey

Wideman, John Edgar 1941- ... **BLC 3; CLC
5, 34, 36, 67, 122; SSC 62**
See also AFAW 1, 2; AMWS 10; BPFB 4;
BW 2, 3; CA 85-88; CANR 14, 42, 67,
109, 140; CN 4, 5, 6, 7; DAM MULT;
DLB 33, 143; MAL 5; MTCW 2; MTFW
2005; RGAL 4; RGSF 2; SSFS 6, 12, 24;
TCLE 1:2

Wiebe, Rudy 1934- .... **CLC 6, 11, 14, 138**
See also CA 37-40R; CANR 42, 67, 123;
CN 1, 2, 3, 4, 5, 6, 7; DAC; DAM MST;
DLB 60; RHW; SATA 156

Wiebe, Rudy Henry
See Wiebe, Rudy

Wieland, Christoph Martin
1733-1813 .... **NCLC 17, 177**
See also DLB 97; EW 4; LMFS 1; RGWL
2, 3

Wiene, Robert 1881-1938 .... **TCLC 56**

Wieners, John 1934- .... **CLC 7**
See also BG 1:3; CA 13-16R; CP 1, 2, 3, 4,
5, 6, 7; DLB 16; WP

Wiesel, Elie 1928- ...... **CLC 3, 5, 11, 37, 165;
WLCS**
See also AAYA 7, 54; AITN 1; CA 5-8R; 4;
CANR 8, 40, 65, 125; CDALBS; CWW
2; DA; DA3; DAB; DAC; DAM MST,
NOV; DLB 83, 299; DLBY 1987; EWL
3; INT CANR-8; LAIT 4; MTCW 1, 2;
MTFW 2005; NCFS 4; NFS 4; RGHL;
RGWL 3; SATA 56; YAW

Wiesel, Eliezer
See Wiesel, Elie

Wiggins, Marianne 1947- .... **CLC 57**
See also AAYA 70; BEST 89:3; CA 130;
CANR 60, 139; CN 7; DLB 335

Wigglesworth, Michael 1631-1705 .... **LC 106**
See also DLB 24; RGAL 4

Wiggs, Susan .... **CLC 70**
See also CA 201

Wight, James Alfred 1916-1995
See Herriot, James
See also CA 77-80; SATA 55; SATA-Brief
44

Wilbur, Richard 1921- .. **CLC 3, 6, 9, 14, 53,
110; PC 51**
See also AAYA 72; AMWS 3; CA 1-4R;
CABS 2; CANR 2, 29, 76, 93, 139;
CDALBS; CP 1, 2, 3, 4, 5, 6, 7; DA;
DAB; DAC; DAM MST, POET; DLB 5,
169; EWL 3; EXPP; INT CANR-29;
MAL 5; MTCW 1, 2; MTFW 2005; PAB;
PFS 11, 12, 16; RGAL 4; SATA 9, 108;
WP

Wilbur, Richard Purdy
See Wilbur, Richard

Wild, Peter 1940- .... **CLC 14**
See also CA 37-40R; CP 1, 2, 3, 4, 5, 6, 7;
DLB 5

Wilde, Oscar (Fingal O'Flahertie Wills)
1854(?)-1900 .... **DC 17; SSC 11, 77;
TCLC 1, 8, 23, 41, 175; WLC 6**
See also AAYA 49; BRW 5; BRWC 1, 2;
BRWR 2; BYA 15; CA 119; CAAE 104;
CANR 112; CDBLB 1890-1914; CLR
114; DA; DA3; DAB; DAC; DAM
DRAM, MST, NOV; DFS 4, 8, 9, 21;
DLB 10, 19, 34, 57, 141, 156, 190; EXPS;
FANT; GL 3; LATS 1:1; NFS 20; RGEL
2; RGSF 2; SATA 24; SSFS 7; SUFW;
TEA; WCH; WLIT 4

Wilder, Billy .... **CLC 20**
See Wilder, Samuel
See also AAYA 66; DLB 26

Wilder, Samuel 1906-2002
See Wilder, Billy
See also CA 89-92; CAAS 205

Wilder, Stephen
See Marlowe, Stephen

Wilder, Thornton (Niven)
1897-1975 .. **CLC 1, 5, 6, 10, 15, 35, 82;
DC 1, 24; WLC 6**
See also AAYA 29; AITN 2; AMW; CA 13-
16R; CAAS 61-64; CAD; CANR 40, 132;
CDALBS; CN 1, 2; DA; DA3; DAB;
DAC; DAM DRAM, MST, NOV; DFS 1,
4, 16; DLB 4, 7, 9, 228; DLBY 1997;
EWL 3; LAIT 3; MAL 5; MTCW 1, 2;
MTFW 2005; NFS 24; RGAL 4; RHW;
WYAS 1

Wilding, Michael 1942- ...... **CLC 73; SSC 50**
See also CA 104; CANR 24, 49, 106; CN
4, 5, 6, 7; DLB 325; RGSF 2

Wiley, Richard 1944- .... **CLC 44**
See also CA 129; CAAE 121; CANR 71

Wilhelm, Kate .... **CLC 7**
See Wilhelm, Katie
See also AAYA 20; BYA 16; CA 5; DLB 8;
INT CANR-17; SCFW 2

Wilhelm, Katie 1928-
See Wilhelm, Kate
See also CA 37-40R; CANR 17, 36, 60, 94;
MTCW 1; SFW 4

Wilkins, Mary
See Freeman, Mary E(leanor) Wilkins

Willard, Nancy 1936- .... **CLC 7, 37**
See also BYA 5; CA 89-92; CANR 10, 39,
68, 107, 152; CLR 5; CP 2, 3, 4, 5; CWP;
CWRI 5; DLB 5, 52; FANT; MAICYA 1,
2; MTCW 1; SATA 37, 71, 127; SATA-
Brief 30; SUFW 2; TCLE 1:2

William of Malmesbury c. 1090B.C.-c.
1140B.C. .... **CMLC 57**

William of Moerbeke c. 1215-c.
1286 .... **CMLC 91**

William of Ockham 1290-1349 ..... **CMLC 32**

Williams, Ben Ames 1889-1953 ..... **TCLC 89**
See also CA 183; DLB 102

Williams, Charles
See Collier, James Lincoln

Williams, Charles (Walter Stansby)
1886-1945 .... **TCLC 1, 11**
See also BRWS 9; CA 163; CAAE 104;
DLB 100, 153, 255; FANT; RGEL 2;
SUFW 1

Williams, C.K. 1936- .... **CLC 33, 56, 148**
See also CA 37-40R; 26; CANR 57, 106;
CP 1, 2, 3, 4, 5, 6, 7; DAM POET; DLB
5; MAL 5

Williams, Ella Gwendolen Rees
See Rhys, Jean

Williams, (George) Emlyn
1905-1987 .... **CLC 15**
See also CA 104; CAAS 123; CANR 36;
DAM DRAM; DLB 10, 77; IDTP; MTCW
1

Williams, Hank 1923-1953 .... **TCLC 81**
See Williams, Hiram King

Williams, Helen Maria
1761-1827 .... **NCLC 135**
See also DLB 158

Williams, Hiram Hank
See Williams, Hank

Williams, Hiram King
See Williams, Hank
See also CA 188

Williams, Hugo (Mordaunt) 1942- ... **CLC 42**
See also CA 17-20R; CANR 45, 119; CP 1,
2, 3, 4, 5, 6, 7; DLB 40

Williams, J. Walker
See Wodehouse, P(elham) G(renville)

Williams, John A(lfred) 1925- . **BLC 3; CLC
5, 13**
See also AFAW 2; BW 2, 3; CA 195; 53-
56; 195; 3; CANR 6, 26, 51, 118; CN 1,
2, 3, 4, 5, 6, 7; CSW; DAM MULT; DLB
2, 33; EWL 3; INT CANR-6; MAL 5;
RGAL 4; SFW 4

Williams, Jonathan (Chamberlain)
1929- .... **CLC 13**
See also CA 9-12R; 12; CANR 8, 108; CP
1, 2, 3, 4, 5, 6, 7; DLB 5

Williams, Joy 1944- .... **CLC 31**
See also CA 41-44R; CANR 22, 48, 97;
DLB 335; SSFS 25

Williams, Norman 1952- .... **CLC 39**
See also CA 118

Williams, Roger 1603(?)-1683 .... **LC 129**
See also DLB 24

Williams, Sherley Anne 1944-1999 ... **BLC 3;
CLC 89**
See also AFAW 2; BW 2, 3; CA 73-76;
CAAS 185; CANR 25, 82; DAM MULT,
POET; DLB 41; INT CANR-25; SATA
78; SATA-Obit 116

Williams, Shirley
See Williams, Sherley Anne

Williams, Tennessee 1911-1983 . **CLC 1, 2, 5,
7, 8, 11, 15, 19, 30, 39, 45, 71, 111; DC
4; SSC 81; WLC 6**
See also AAYA 31; AITN 1, 2; AMW;
AMWC 1; CA 5-8R; CAAS 108; CABS
3; CAD; CANR 31, 132; CDALB 1941-
1968; CN 1, 2, 3; DA; DA3; DAB; DAC;
DAM DRAM, MST; DFS 17; DLB 7;
DLBD 4; DLBY 1983; EWL 3; GLL 1;
LAIT 4; LATS 1:2; MAL 5; MTCW 1, 2;
MTFW 2005; RGAL 4; TUS

PC Cumulative Nationality Index

Nationality Index

1

ISBN-13:978-0-7876-9876-8
ISBN-10:0-7876-9876-8

9 780787 698768

90008